Beginning ASP.NET 3.5 in VB 2008

From Novice to Professional, Second Edition

■ ■ ■

Matthew MacDonald

Apress®

Beginning ASP.NET 3.5 in VB 2008: From Novice to Professional, Second Edition

ISBN-13 (pbk): 978-1-59059-892-4

ISBN-10 (pbk): 1-59059-892-X

Printed and bound in the United States of America 9 8 7 6 5 4 3 2 1

Lead Editor: Jonathan Hassell
Technical Reviewer: Andy Olsen
Editorial Board: Steve Anglin, Ewan Buckingham, Tony Campbell, Gary Cornell, Jonathan Gennick, Jason Gilmore, Kevin Goff, Jonathan Hassell, Matthew Moodie, Joseph Ottinger, Jeffrey Pepper, Ben Renow-Clarke, Dominic Shakeshaft, Matt Wade, Tom Welsh
Project Manager | Production Editor: Laura Esterman
Copy Editor: Liz Welch
Associate Production Director: Kari Brooks-Copony
Compositor: Susan Glinert-Stevens
Proofreaders: Linda Seifert, Elizabeth Berry
Indexer: John Collin
Artist: April Milne
Cover Designer: Kurt Krames
Manufacturing Director: Tom Debolski

Distributed to the book trade worldwide by Springer-Verlag New York, Inc., 233 Spring Street, 6th Floor, New York, NY 10013. Phone 1-800-SPRINGER, fax 201-348-4505, e-mail orders-ny@springer-sbm.com, or visit http://www.springeronline.com.

For information on translations, please contact Apress directly at 2855 Telegraph Avenue, Suite 600, Berkeley, CA 94705. Phone 510-549-5930, fax 510-549-5939, e-mail info@apress.com, or visit http://www.apress.com.

The source code for this book is available to readers at www.apress.com.

For my wonderful family,
Faria and Maya

Contents at a Glance

PART 4 ■■■ Working with Data

PART 5 ■■■ Website Security

PART 6 ■■■ Advanced ASP.NET

Contents

PART 2 Developing ASP.NET Applications

PART 5 ■■■ Website Security

About the Author

MATTHEW MACDONALD is an author, educator, and Microsoft MVP. He's a regular contributor to programming journals and the author of more than a dozen books about .NET programming, including *Pro ASP.NET 3.5 in C# 2008* (Apress, 2007), *Pro WPF: Windows Presentation Foundation in .NET 3.0* (Apress, 2007), and *Pro .NET 2.0 Windows Forms and Custom Controls in VB 2005* (Apress, 2006). He lives in Toronto with his wife and daughter.

About the Technical Reviewer

ANDY OLSEN is a freelance developer and consultant based in the UK. Andy has been working with .NET since Beta 1 days and has coauthored and reviewed several books for Apress, covering C#, Visual Basic, ASP.NET, and other topics. Andy is a keen football and rugby fan and enjoys running and skiing (badly). Andy lives by the seaside in Swansea with his wife Jayne and children Emily and Thomas, who have just discovered the thrills of surfing and look much cooler than he ever will!

Acknowledgments

No author could complete a book without a small army of helpful individuals. I'm deeply indebted to the whole Apress team, including Laura Esterman, who helped everything move swiftly and smoothly; Liz Welch, who performed the copy edit; Andy Olsen, who performed a thorough technical review; and many other individuals who worked behind the scenes indexing pages, drawing figures, and proofreading the final copy. I also owe a special thanks to Gary Cornell, who always offers invaluable advice about projects and the publishing world.

I'd also like to thank those who were involved with previous editions of this book. This includes Emma Acker and Jane Brownlow at Osborne McGraw-Hill and previous tech reviewers Ronald Landers, Gavin Smyth, Tim Verycruysse, and Julian Skinner. I also owe a hearty thanks to all the readers who caught errors and took the time to report problems and ask good questions, including Rick Falck, who submitted detailed comments for virtually every chapter. Keep sending in the feedback—it helps make better books!

Finally, I'd never write *any* book without the support of my wife and these special individuals: Nora, Razia, Paul, and Hamid. Thanks, everyone!

Introduction

ASP.NET is Microsoft's platform for developing web applications. Using ASP.NET, you can create e-commerce shops, data-driven portal sites, and just about anything else you can find on the Internet. Best of all, you don't need to paste together a jumble of HTML and script code in order to program the Web. Instead, you can create full-scale web applications using nothing but code and a design tool such as Visual Studio 2008.

The cost of all this innovation is the learning curve. To master ASP.NET, you need to learn how to use an advanced design tool (Visual Studio), a toolkit of objects (the .NET Framework), and an object-oriented programming language (such as Visual Basic 2008). Taken together, these topics provide more than enough to overwhelm any first-time web developer.

Beginning ASP.NET 3.5 in VB 2008 assumes you want to master ASP.NET, starting from the basics. Using this book, you'll build your knowledge until you understand the concepts, techniques, and best practices for writing sophisticated web applications. The journey is long, but it's also satisfying. At the end of the day, you'll find that ASP.NET allows you to tackle challenges that are simply out of reach on many other platforms.

About This Book

This book explores ASP.NET, which is a core part of Microsoft's .NET Framework. The .NET Framework is not a single application—it's actually a collection of technologies bundled into one marketing term. The .NET Framework includes languages such as C# 2008 and VB 2008, an engine for hosting programmable web pages and web services (ASP.NET), a model for interacting with databases (ADO.NET), and a class library stocked with tools for everything from reading files to validating a password. To master ASP.NET, you need to learn about each of these ingredients.

This book covers all these topics from the ground up. As a result, you'll find yourself learning many techniques that will interest any .NET developer, even those who create Windows applications. For example, you'll learn about component-based programming, you'll discover structured error handling, and you'll see how to access files, XML, and relational databases. You'll also learn the key topics you need for web programming, such as state management, web controls, and caching. By the end of this book, you'll be ready to create your own rich web applications and make them available over the Internet.

■Note This book has a single goal: to be as relentlessly practical as possible. I take special care not to leave you hanging in the places where other ASP.NET books abandon their readers. For example, when encountering a new technology, you'll learn not only how it works but also why (and when) you should use it. I also highlight common questions and best practices with tip boxes and sidebars at every step of the way. Finally, if a topic is covered in this book, it's covered *right*. This means you won't learn how to perform a task without learning about potential drawbacks and the problems you might run into—and how you can safeguard yourself with real-world code.

Who Should Read This Book

This book is aimed at anyone who wants to create dynamic websites with ASP.NET. Ideally, you'll have experience with a previous version of a programming language such as Visual Basic 6 or Java. If not, you should be familiar with basic programming concepts (loops, conditional structures, arrays, and so on), whether you've learned them in C, Pascal, Turing, or a completely different programming language. This is the only requirement for reading this book.

Understanding HTML and XHTML (the markup languages used to write web pages) will help you, but it's not required. ASP.NET works at a higher level, allowing you to deal with full-featured web controls instead of raw web page markup. However, you'll get a quick overview of XHTML fundamentals in Chapter 4, and you'll learn about CSS, the Cascading Style Sheet standard, in Chapter 13.

This book will also appeal to programmers who have some experience with Visual Basic and .NET but haven't worked with ASP.NET in the past. However, if you've used a previous version of ASP.NET, you'll probably be more interested in a faster-paced book such as *Pro ASP.NET 3.5 in VB 2008* (Apress, 2007) instead.

■Note This book begins with the fundamentals: VB syntax, the basics of object-oriented programming, and the philosophy of the .NET Framework. If you haven't worked with VB before, you can spend a little more time with the syntax review in Chapter 2 to pick up everything you need to know. If you aren't familiar with the ideas of object-oriented programming, Chapter 3 fills in the blanks with a quick, but comprehensive, review of the subject. The rest of the book builds on this foundation, from ASP.NET basics to advanced examples that show the techniques you'll use in real-world web applications.

What You Need to Use This Book

The main prerequisite for this book is a computer with Visual Studio 2008. You can use the scaled-down Visual Studio Web Developer 2008 Express Edition (available at `http://msdn.microsoft.com/vstudio/express`) with a few minor limitations. Most significantly, you can't use Visual Studio Web Developer to create separate components, a technique discussed in Chapter 23. However, you can get around this limitation by using *two* express editions—Visual Studio Web Developer Express Edition to create your websites and Visual Basic 2008

Express Edition to create your components. Even if you don't use this trick, you'll still be able to run all the sample code for this book.

To develop ASP.NET web pages, you need Windows XP, Windows Vista, Windows Server 2003, or Windows Server 2008. To *use* an ASP.NET web page (in other words, to surf to it over the Internet), you simply need a web browser. ASP.NET fully supports Internet Explorer, Firefox, Opera, Safari, Netscape, and any other browser that respects the HTML standard on virtually any operating system. There are a few features that won't work with extremely old browsers (such as the ASP.NET AJAX techniques you'll learn about in Chapter 25), and you'll consider these limitations when they crop up. You'll also notice that this book features a variety of screen captures—some taken in Windows XP and others in Windows Vista. This should make perfect sense. After all, your choice of operating system (and the operating system of the people who are browsing your website) won't change how your web pages work.

If you plan to host websites on your computer, you'll also need to use IIS (Internet Information Services), the web hosting software that's part of the Windows operating system. You might also use IIS if you want to test deployment strategies. You'll learn how to use and configure IIS in Chapter 9.

Finally, this book includes several examples that use SQL Server. You can use any version of SQL Server to try these examples, including SQL Server 2005 Express Edition, which is included with some versions of Visual Studio (and freely downloadable at `http://msdn.microsoft.com/sql/express`). If you use other relational database engines, the same concepts will apply; you will just need to modify the example code.

Code Samples

To master ASP.NET, you need to experiment with it. One of the best ways to learn ASP.NET is to try the code samples for this book, examine them, and dive in with your own modifications. To obtain the sample code, surf to `http://www.prosetech.com` or the publisher's website at `http://www.apress.com`. You'll also find some links to additional resources and any updates or errata that affect the book.

Note Previous editions of this book tackled *web services*, a feature that allows you to create code routines that can be called by other applications over the Internet. Web services are more interesting when considering rich client development (because they allow you to give web features to ordinary desktop applications), and they're in the process of being replaced by a new technology known as WCF (Windows Communication Foundation). For those reasons, web services aren't covered in this book. However, if you want to branch out and explore the web service world, you can download the web service chapters from the previous edition of this book from the book's download page. The information in these chapters still applies to ASP.NET 3.5, because the web service feature hasn't changed.

Chapter Overview

This book is divided into six parts. Unless you've already had experience with the .NET Framework, the most productive way to read this book is in order from start to finish. Chapters later in the book sometimes incorporate features that were introduced earlier in order to create more well-rounded and realistic examples. On the other hand, if you're already familiar with the .NET platform, VB, and object-oriented programming, you'll make short work of the first part of this book.

Part 1: Introducing .NET

You could start coding an ASP.NET application right away by following the examples in the second part of this book. But to really master ASP.NET, you need to understand a few fundamental concepts about the .NET Framework.

Chapter 1 sorts through the Microsoft jargon and explains what the .NET Framework really does and why you need it. Chapter 2 introduces you to VB 2008 with a comprehensive language tour. Finally, Chapter 3 explains the basics of modern object-oriented programming.

Part 2: Developing ASP.NET Applications

The second part of this book delves into the heart of ASP.NET programming and introduces its new event-based model. In Chapter 4, you'll take a look around the Visual Studio design environment and learn a few fundamentals about web forms, events, and XHTML. In Chapters 5 and 6, you learn how to program a web page's user interface through a layer of objects called *server controls*.

Next, you'll explore a few more essentials of ASP.NET programming. Chapter 7 describes different strategies for state management. Chapter 8 presents different techniques for handling errors. Finally, Chapter 9 walks you through the steps for deploying your application to a web server. Taken together, these chapters contain all the core concepts you need to design web pages and create a basic ASP.NET website.

Part 3: Building Better Web Forms

The third part of this book explores several topics that can help you transform ordinary web pages into polished web applications. In Chapter 10 you'll learn to use the validation controls to catch invalid data before the user submits it. In Chapter 11 you'll move on to consider some of ASP.NET's more exotic controls, such as the Calendar and Wizard. In Chapter 12, you'll learn how to build your own reusable blocks of web page user interface and draw custom graphics on the fly. Finally, Chapter 13 shows how you can standardize the appearance of an entire website with themes and master pages, and Chapter 14 shows you how to add navigation to a website.

Part 4: Working with Data

Almost all software needs to work with data, and web applications are no exception. In Chapter 15, you begin exploring the world of data by considering ADO.NET—Microsoft's .NET-powered technology for interacting with relational databases. Chapters 16 and 17 explain how to use data binding and the advanced ASP.NET data controls to create web pages that integrate attractive, customizable data displays with automatic support for paging, sorting, and editing.

Chapter 18 moves out of the database world and considers how to interact with files. Chapter 19 broadens the picture even further and describes how ASP.NET applications can use the XML support that's built into the .NET Framework.

Part 5: Website Security

Every public website needs to deal with security—making sure that sensitive data cannot be accessed by the wrong users. In Chapter 20, you'll start out learning how ASP.NET provides different authentication systems for dealing with users. You can write your own custom logic to verify user names and passwords, or you can use existing Windows account information. In Chapter 21, you'll learn about the membership model, which extends the authentication system with prebuilt security controls and handy objects that automate common tasks. If you want, you can even get ASP.NET to create and manage a database with user information automatically. Finally, Chapter 21 deals with another add-on—the profiles model that lets you store information for each user automatically, without writing any database code.

Part 6: Advanced ASP.NET

This part includes the advanced topics you can use to take your web applications that extra step. Chapter 23 covers how you can create reusable components for ASP.NET applications. Chapter 24 demonstrates how careful use of caching can boost the performance of almost any web application. Finally Chapter 25 introduces ASP.NET AJAX, one of the hottest new topics in web development. Using ASP.NET AJAX, you can build web pages that feel more responsive and add rich features that are usually limited to desktop applications, like text autocompletion and drag-and-drop.

Feedback

This book has the ambitious goal of being the best tutorial and reference for ASP.NET. Toward that end, your comments and suggestions are extremely helpful. You can send complaints, adulation, and everything in between directly to `apress@prosetech.com`. I can't solve your ASP.NET problems or critique your code, but I do benefit from information about what this book did right and wrong (and what it may have done in an utterly confusing way). You can also send comments about the website support for this book.

PART 1

Introducing .NET

CHAPTER 1

The .NET Framework

Microsoft has a time-honored reputation for creating innovative technologies and wrapping them in buzzwords that confuse everyone. The .NET Framework is the latest example—it's been described as a feeble Java clone, a meaningless marketing term, and an attempt to take over the Internet with proprietary technology. But none of these descriptions is truly accurate.

.NET is actually a cluster of technologies—some revolutionary, some not—that are designed to help developers build a variety of different types of applications. Developers can use the .NET Framework to build rich Windows applications, long-running services, and even command-line tools. Of course, if you're reading this book you're most interested in using .NET to craft web applications. You'll use a specific subset of the .NET Framework called ASP.NET, and you'll work with one of .NET's core languages: Visual Basic.

In this chapter, you'll examine the technologies that underlie .NET. First, you'll take a quick look at the history of web development and learn why the .NET Framework was created. Next, you'll get a high-level overview of the different parts of .NET and see how ASP.NET 3.5 fits into the picture.

The Evolution of Web Development

The Internet began in the late 1960s as an experiment. Its goal was to create a truly resilient information network—one that could withstand the loss of several computers without preventing the others from communicating. Driven by potential disaster scenarios (such as nuclear attack), the U.S. Department of Defense provided the initial funding.

The early Internet was mostly limited to educational institutions and defense contractors. It flourished as a tool for academic collaboration, allowing researchers across the globe to share information. In the early 1990s, modems were created that could work over existing phone lines, and the Internet began to open up to commercial users. In 1993, the first HTML browser was created, and the Internet revolution began.

HTML and HTML Forms

It would be difficult to describe early websites as web *applications.* Instead, the first generation of websites often looked more like brochures, consisting mostly of fixed HTML pages that needed to be updated by hand.

A basic HTML page is a little like a word-processing document—it contains formatted content that can be displayed on your computer, but it doesn't actually *do* anything. The following example shows HTML at its simplest, with a document that contains a heading and single line of text:

```
<html>
    <head>
        <title>Sample Web Page</title>
    </head>
    <body>
        <h1>Sample Web Page Heading</h1>
        <p>This is a sample web page.</p>
    </body>
</html>
```

An HTML document has two types of content: the text and the elements (or tags) that tell the browser how to format it. The elements are easily recognizable, because they are designated with angled brackets (< >). HTML defines elements for different levels of headings, paragraphs, hyperlinks, italic and bold formatting, horizontal lines, and so on. For example, `<h1>Some Text</h1>` uses the <h1> element. This element tells the browser to display *Some Text* in the Heading 1 style, which uses a large, bold font. Similarly, `<p>This is a sample web page.</p>` creates a paragraph with one line of text. The <head> element groups the header information together, including the title that appears in the browser window, while the <body> element groups together the actual document content that's displayed in the browser window.

Figure 1-1 shows this simple HTML page in a browser. Right now, this is just a fixed file (named sample_web_page_heading.htm) that contains HTML content. It has no interactivity, doesn't require a web server, and certainly can't be considered a web application.

Figure 1-1. *Ordinary HTML: the "brochure" site*

■ **Tip** You don't need to master HTML to program ASP.NET web pages, although it's often useful. For a quick introduction to HTML, refer to one of the excellent HTML tutorials on the Internet, such as `www.w3schools.com/html`. You'll also get a mini-introduction in Chapter 4.

HTML 2.0 introduced the first seed of web programming with a technology called *HTML forms*. HTML forms expand HTML so that it includes not only formatting tags but also tags for graphical widgets, or *controls*. These controls include common ingredients such as drop-down lists, text boxes, and buttons. Here's a sample web page created with HTML form controls:

```
<html>
    <head>
        <title>Sample Web Page</title>
    </head>
    <body>
        <form>
            <input type="checkbox" />
             This is choice #1<br />
            <input type="checkbox" />
             This is choice #2<br /><br />
            <input type="submit" value="Submit" />
        </form>
    </body>
</html>
```

In an HTML form, all controls are placed between the <form> and </form> tags. The preceding example includes two check boxes (represented by the <input type="checkbox" /> element) and a button (represented by the <input type="submit" /> element). The <br /> element adds a line break in between lines. In a browser, this page looks like Figure 1-2.

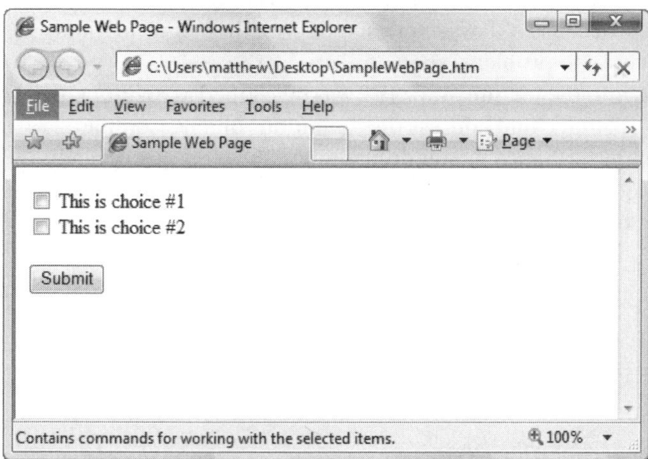

Figure 1-2. *An HTML form*

HTML forms allow web application developers to design standard input pages. When the user clicks the Submit button on the page shown in Figure 1-2, all the data in the input controls (in this case, the two check boxes) is patched together into one long string of text and sent to the web server. On the server side, a custom application receives and processes the data.

Amazingly enough, the controls that were created for HTML forms more than ten years ago are still the basic foundation that you'll use to build dynamic ASP.NET pages! The difference is the type of application that runs on the server side. In the past, when the user clicked a button on a form page, the information might have been e-mailed to a set account or sent to an application on the server that used the challenging Common Gateway Interface (GCI) standard. Today, you'll work with the much more capable and elegant ASP.NET platform.

Server-Side Programming

To understand why ASP.NET was created, it helps to understand the problems of early web development technologies. With the original CGI standard, for example, the web server must launch a completely separate instance of the application for each web request. If the website is popular, the web server struggles under the weight of hundreds of separate copies of the application, eventually becoming a victim of its own success. Furthermore, technologies such as CGI provide a bare-bones programming environment. If you want higher-level features, like the ability to authenticate users, store personalized information, or display records you've retrieved from a database, you need to write pages of code from scratch. Building a web application this way is tedious and error-prone.

To counter these problems, Microsoft created higher-level development platforms, such as ASP and ASP.NET. Both of these technologies allow developers to program dynamic web pages without worrying about the low-level implementation details. For that reason, both platforms have been incredibly successful.

The original ASP platform garnered a huge audience of nearly one million developers, becoming far more popular than even Microsoft anticipated. It wasn't long before it was being wedged into all sorts of unusual places, including mission-critical business applications and highly trafficked e-commerce sites. Because ASP wasn't designed with these uses in mind, performance, security, and configuration problems soon appeared.

That's where ASP.NET comes into the picture. ASP.NET was developed as an industrial-strength web application framework that could address the limitations of ASP. Compared to classic ASP, ASP.NET offers better performance, better design tools, and a rich set of ready-made features. ASP.NET was wildly popular from the moment it was released—in fact, it was put to work in dozens of large-scale commercial websites while still in beta form.

Note Despite having similar underpinnings, ASP and ASP.NET are radically different. ASP is a script-based programming language that requires a thorough understanding of HTML and a good deal of painful coding. ASP.NET, on the other hand, is an object-oriented programming model that lets you put together a web page as easily as you would build a Windows application. The sidebar "The Many Faces of ASP.NET," which appears later in this chapter, describes a bit more about the different versions of ASP.NET.

Client-Side Programming

At the same time that server-side web development was moving through an alphabet soup of technologies, a new type of programming was gaining popularity. Developers began to experiment with the different ways they could enhance web pages by embedding miniature applets built with JavaScript, ActiveX, Java, and Flash into web pages. These client-side technologies don't involve any server processing. Instead, the complete application is downloaded to the client browser, which executes it locally.

The greatest problem with client-side technologies is that they aren't supported equally by all browsers and operating systems. One of the reasons that web development is so popular in the first place is because web applications don't require setup CDs, downloads, and other tedious (and error-prone) deployment steps. Instead, a web application can be used on any computer that has Internet access. But when developers use client-side technologies, they encounter a few familiar headaches. Suddenly, cross-browser compatibility becomes a problem. Developers are forced to test their websites with different operating systems and browsers, and they might even need to distribute browser updates to their clients. In other words, the client-side model sacrifices some of the most important benefits of web development.

For that reason, ASP.NET is designed as a server-side technology. All ASP.NET code executes on the server. When the code is finished executing, the user receives an ordinary HTML page, which can be viewed in any browser. Figure 1-3 shows the difference between the server-side and the client-side model.

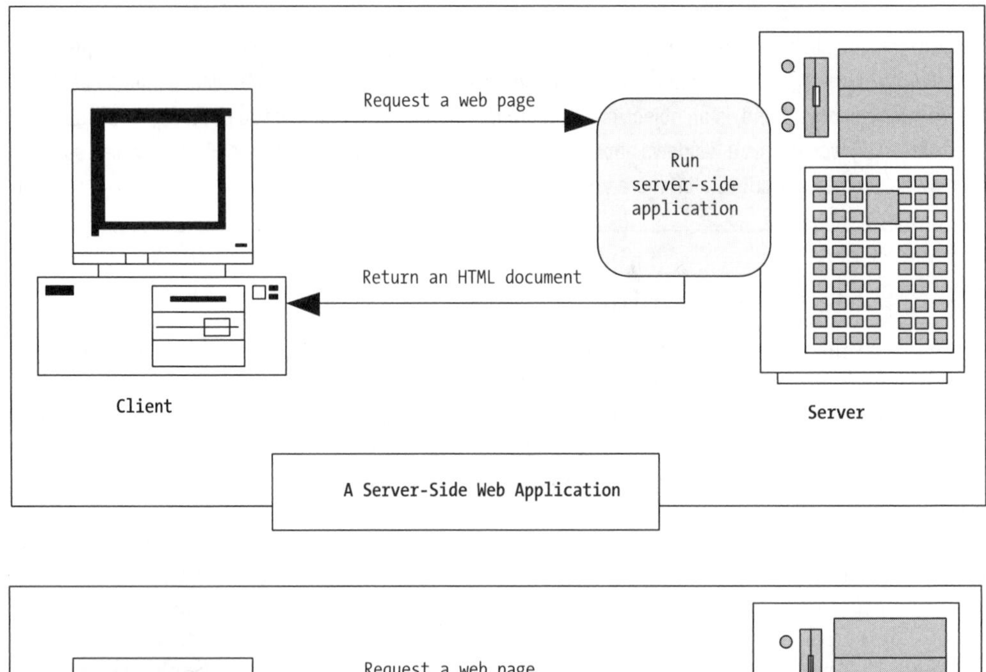

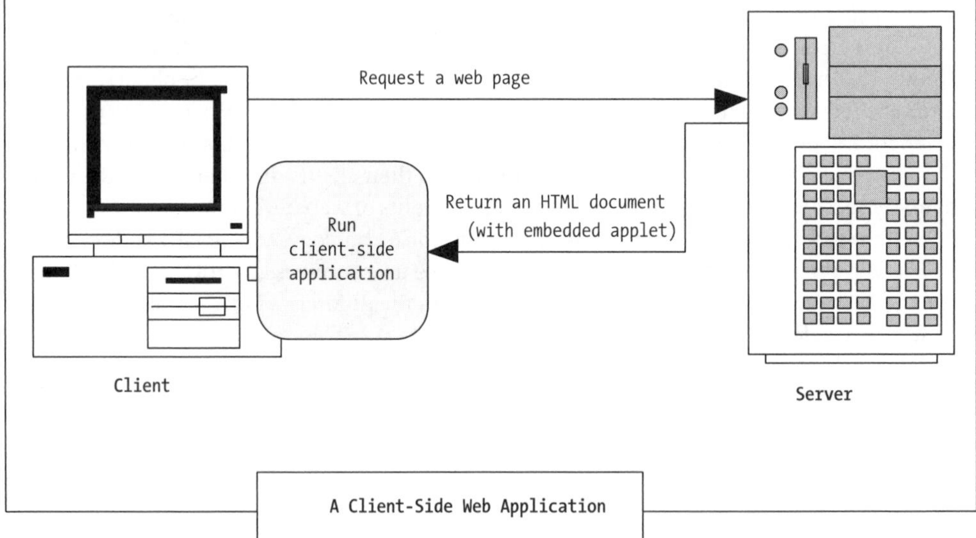

Figure 1-3. *Server-side and client-side web applications*

These are some other reasons for avoiding client-side programming:

Isolation: Client-side code can't access server-side resources. For example, a client-side application has no easy way to read a file or interact with a database on the server (at least not without running into problems with security and browser compatibility).

Security: End users can view client-side code. And once malicious users understand how an application works, they can often tamper with it.

Thin clients: As the Internet continues to evolve, web-enabled devices such as mobile phones, palmtop computers, and PDAs (personal digital assistants) are appearing. These devices can communicate with web servers, but they don't support all the features of a traditional browser. Thin clients can use server-based web applications, but they won't support client-side features such as JavaScript.

However, client-side programming isn't truly dead. In many cases, ASP.NET allows you to combine the best of client-side programming with server-side programming. For example, the best ASP.NET controls can intelligently detect the features of the client browser. If the browser supports JavaScript, these controls will return a web page that incorporates JavaScript for a richer, more responsive user interface. And in Chapter 25, you'll learn how you can super-charge ordinary ASP.NET pages with Ajax features, which use even more client-side JavaScript. However, no matter what the capabilities of the browser, *your* code is always executed on the server. The client-side frills are just the icing on the cake.

The .NET Framework

As you've already learned, the .NET Framework is really a cluster of several technologies. These include the following:

The .NET languages: These include Visual Basic, C#, JScript .NET (a server-side version of JavaScript), J# (a Java clone), and C++.

The Common Language Runtime (CLR): This is the engine that executes all .NET programs and provides automatic services for these applications, such as security checking, memory management, and optimization.

The .NET Framework class library: The class library collects thousands of pieces of prebuilt functionality that you can "snap in" to your applications. These features are sometimes organized into technology sets, such as ADO.NET (the technology for creating database applications) and Windows Forms (the technology for creating desktop user interfaces).

ASP.NET: This is the engine that hosts the web applications you create with .NET, and supports almost any feature from the .NET class library. ASP.NET also includes a set of web-specific services, like secure authentication and data storage.

Visual Studio: This optional development tool contains a rich set of productivity and debugging features. The Visual Studio setup DVD includes the complete .NET Framework, so you won't need to download it separately.

Sometimes the division between these components isn't clear. For example, the term *ASP.NET* is sometimes used in a narrow sense to refer to the portion of the .NET class library used to design web pages. On the other hand, ASP.NET also refers to the whole topic of .NET web applications, which includes .NET languages and many fundamental pieces of the class library that aren't web-specific. (That's generally the way we use the term in this book. Our exhaustive examination of ASP.NET includes .NET basics, the VB language, and topics that any .NET developer could use, such as component-based programming and database access.)

Figure 1-4 shows the .NET class library and CLR—the two fundamental parts of .NET.

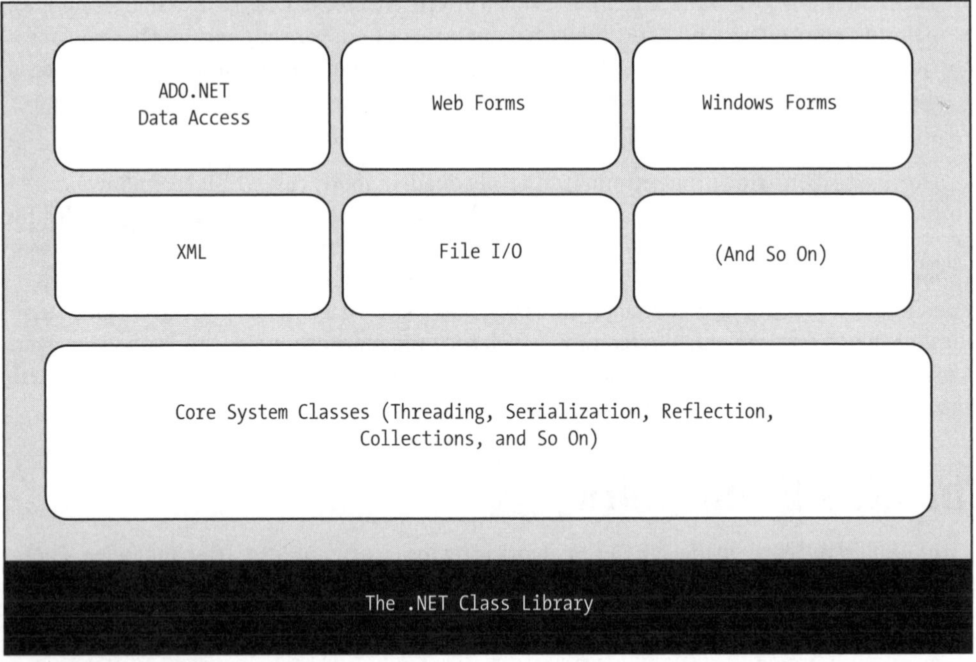

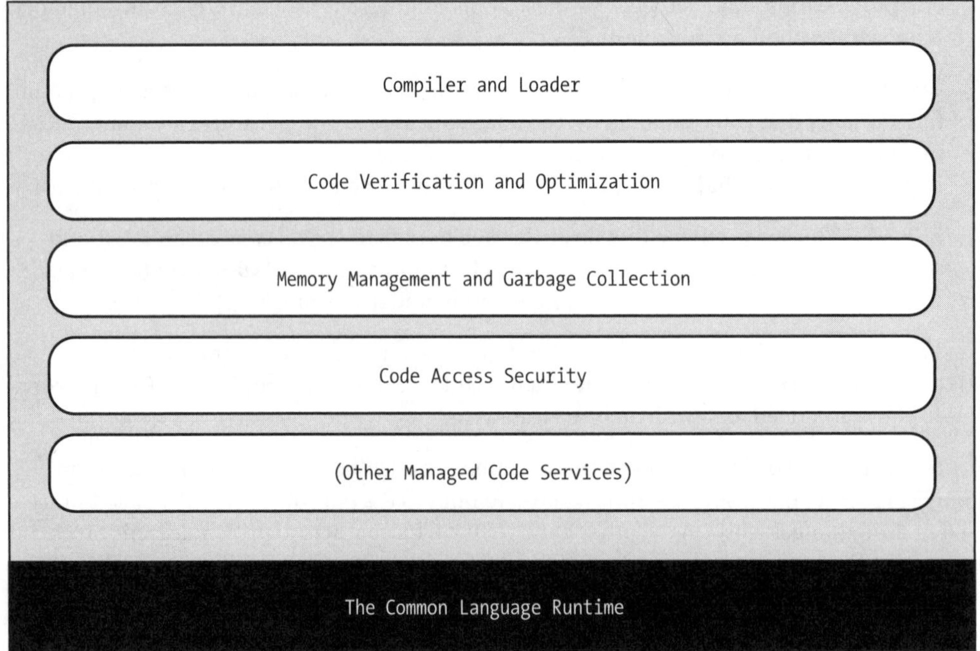

Figure 1-4. *The .NET Framework*

In the remainder of this chapter, you'll take a quick look at the different ingredients that make up the .NET Framework.

THE MANY FACES OF ASP.NET

With ASP.NET 3.5, Microsoft aims to continue its success by refining and enhancing ASP.NET. The good news is that Microsoft hasn't removed features, replaced functionality, or reversed direction. Instead, almost all the changes add higher-level features that can make your programming more productive.

All in all, there have been four major releases of ASP.NET:

- *ASP.NET 1.0:* This first release created the core ASP.NET platform and introduced a wide range of essential features.
- *ASP.NET 1.1:* This second release added performance tune-ups and bug fixes, but no new features.
- *ASP.NET 2.0:* This third release piled on a huge set of new features, all of which were built on top of the existing ASP.NET plumbing. The overall emphasis was to supply developers with prebuilt goodies that they could use without writing much (if any) code. Some of the new features included built-in support for website navigation, a theming feature for standardizing web page design, and an easier way to pull information out of a database.
- *ASP.NET 3.5:* This fourth release keeps the same basic engine as ASP.NET 2.0, but adds a few frills and two more dramatic changes. The most significant enhancement is the ASP.NET AJAX toolkit, which gives web developers better tools for creating highly responsive web pages that incorporate rich effects usually seen in desktop applications (such as drag-and-drop and autocomplete). The other innovation is support for LINQ, a set of language enhancements included with .NET 3.5 that allows you to search in-memory data in the same way that you query a database.

If you're wondering what happened to ASP.NET 3.0—well, it doesn't exist! Somewhat confusingly, Microsoft used the .NET 3.0 name to release a set of new technologies, including Windows Presentation Foundation (WPF), a platform for building slick Windows applications; Windows Workflow Foundation (WF), a platform for modeling application logic using flowchart-style diagrams; and Windows Communication Foundation (WCF), a platform for designing services that can be called from other computers. However, .NET 3.0 did not include an updated version of ASP.NET.

VB, C#, and the .NET Languages

This book uses VB 2008, the object-oriented and modernized successor to the traditional Visual Basic language. Somewhat schizophrenically, Microsoft renamed VB twice, calling it VB .NET when .NET 1.0 hit the scene and dropping the .NET part of the name when .NET 2.0 was released. These name changes can't hide that the .NET versions of VB are dramatically different from the language that classic VB 6 developers know. In fact, the .NET version of Visual Basic is really a redesigned language that improves on traditional VB 6 and breaks compatibility with existing VB 6 applications. Migrating to .NET is a stretch and a process of discovery for the most seasoned classic VB developer.

Interestingly, VB and C# are actually quite similar. Though the syntax is different, both VB and C# use the .NET class library and are supported by the CLR. In fact, almost any block of C# code can be translated, line by line, into an equivalent block of VB code (and vice versa). An occasional language difference pops up (for example, VB supports a language feature called *optional parameters*, while C# doesn't), but for the most part, a developer who has learned one .NET language can move quickly and efficiently to another.

In short, both VB and C# are elegant, modern languages that are ideal for creating the next generation of web applications.

Note .NET 1.0 introduced completely new languages. However, the changes in subsequent versions of .NET have been more subtle. Although the version of VB and C# in .NET 3.5 adds a few new features, most parts of these languages remain unchanged. In Chapter 2 and Chapter 3, you'll sort through the syntax of VB and learn the basics of object-oriented programming.

Intermediate Language

All the .NET languages are compiled into another lower-level language before the code is executed. This lower-level language is the Common Intermediate Language (CIL, or just IL). The CLR, the engine of .NET, uses only IL code. Because all .NET languages are designed based on IL, they all have profound similarities. This is the reason that the VB and C# languages provide essentially the same features and performance. In fact, the languages are so compatible that a web page written with C# can use a VB component in the same way it uses a C# component, and vice versa.

The .NET Framework formalizes this compatibility with something called the Common Language Specification (CLS). Essentially, the CLS is a contract that, if respected, guarantees that a component written in one .NET language can be used in all the others. One part of the CLS is the common type system (CTS), which defines the rules for data types such as strings, numbers, and arrays that are shared in all .NET languages. The CLS also defines object-oriented ingredients such as classes, methods, events, and quite a bit more. For the most part, .NET developers don't need to think about how the CLS works, even though they rely on it every day.

Figure 1-5 shows how the .NET languages are compiled to IL. Every EXE or DLL file that you build with a .NET language contains IL code. This is the file you deploy to other computers. In the case of a web application, you deploy your compiled code to a live web server.

The CLR runs only IL code, which means it has no idea which .NET language you originally used. Notice, however, that the CLR actually performs another compilation step—it takes the IL code and transforms it to native machine language code that's appropriate for the current platform. This step occurs when the application is launched, just before the code is actually executed. In an ASP.NET application, these machine-specific files are cached while the web application is running so they can be reused, ensuring optimum performance.

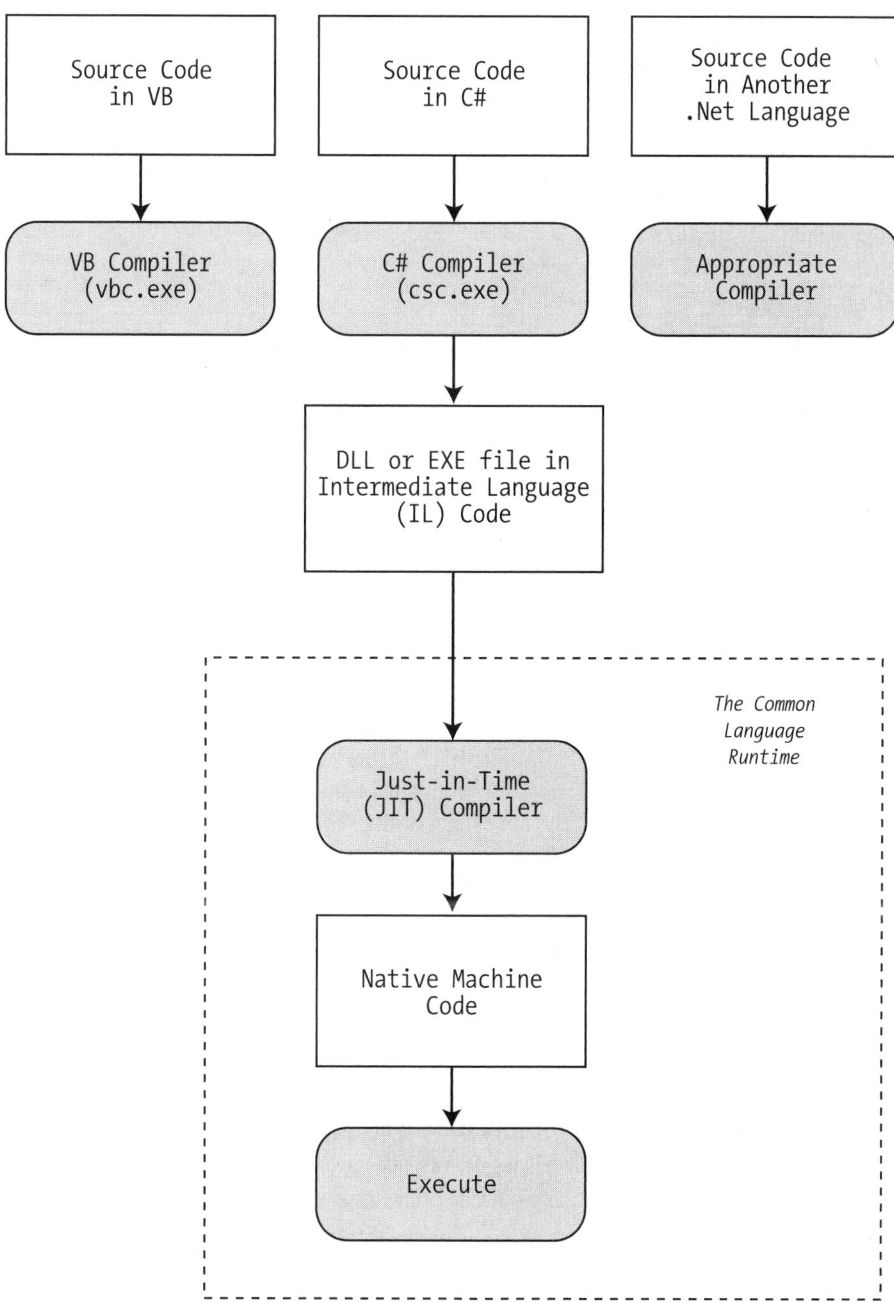

Figure 1-5. *Language compilation in .NET*

■ **Note** You might wonder why .NET compilers don't compile straight to machine code. The reason is that the machine code depends on several factors, including the CPU. For example, if you create machine code for a computer with an Intel processor, the compiler may be able to use Hyper-Threading to produce enhanced code. This machine-specific version isn't suitable for deployment to other computers, because no guarantee exists that they're using the same processor.

Other .NET Languages

VB and C# aren't the only choices for ASP.NET development. Developers can also use J# (a language with Java-like syntax). You can even use a .NET language provided by a third-party developer, such as a .NET version of Eiffel or even COBOL. This increasing range of language choices is possible thanks to the CLS and CTS, which define basic requirements and standards that allow other companies to write languages that can be compiled to IL.

Although you can use any .NET language to create an ASP.NET web application, some of them do not provide the same level of design support in Visual Studio, and virtually all ASP.NET developers use VB and C#. For more information about third-party .NET languages, check out the website `www.dotnetlanguages.net`.

The Common Language Runtime

The CLR is the engine that supports all the .NET languages. Many modern languages use runtimes. In VB 6, the runtime logic is contained in a DLL file named msvbvm60.dll. In C++, many applications link to a file named mscrt40.dll to gain common functionality. These runtimes may provide libraries used by the language, or they may have the additional responsibility of executing the code (as with Java).

Runtimes are nothing new, but the CLR is Microsoft's most ambitious runtime to date. Not only does the CLR execute code, it also provides a whole set of related services such as code verification, optimization, and object management.

■ **Note** The CLR is the reason that some developers have accused .NET of being a Java clone. The claim is fairly silly. It's true that .NET is quite similar to Java in key respects (both use a special managed environment and provide features through a rich class library), but it's also true that every programming language "steals" from and improves on previous programming languages. This includes Java, which adopted parts of the C/C++ language and syntax when it was created. Of course, in many other aspects .NET differs just as radically from Java as it does from VBScript.

All .NET code runs inside the CLR. This is true whether you're running a Windows application or a web service. For example, when a client requests an ASP.NET web page, the ASP.NET service runs inside the CLR environment, executes your code, and creates a final HTML page to send to the client.

The implications of the CLR are wide-ranging:

Deep language integration: VB and C#, like all .NET languages, compile to IL. In other words, the CLR makes no distinction between different languages—in fact, it has no way of knowing what language was used to create an executable. This is far more than mere language compatibility; it's language *integration*.

Side-by-side execution: The CLR also has the ability to load more than one version of a component at a time. In other words, you can update a component many times, and the correct version will be loaded and used for each application. As a side effect, multiple versions of the .NET Framework can be installed, meaning that you're able to upgrade to new versions of ASP.NET without replacing the current version or needing to rewrite your applications.

Fewer errors: Whole categories of errors are impossible with the CLR. For example, the CLR prevents many memory mistakes that are possible with lower-level languages such as C++.

Along with these truly revolutionary benefits, the CLR has some potential drawbacks. Here are three issues that are often raised by new developers but aren't always answered:

Performance: A typical ASP.NET application is much faster than a comparable ASP application, because ASP.NET code is compiled to machine code before it's executed. However, processor-crunching algorithms still can't match the blinding speed of well-written C++ code, because the CLR imposes some additional overhead. Generally, this is a factor only in a few performance-critical high-workload applications (such as real-time games). With high-volume web applications, the potential bottlenecks are rarely processor-related but are usually tied to the speed of an external resource such as a database or the web server's file system. With ASP.NET caching and some well-written database code, you can ensure excellent performance for any web application.

Code transparency: IL is much easier to disassemble, meaning that if you distribute a compiled application or component, other programmers may have an easier time determining how your code works. This isn't much of an issue for ASP.NET applications, which aren't distributed but are hosted on a secure web server.

Questionable cross-platform support: No one is entirely sure whether .NET will ever be adopted for use on other operating systems and platforms. Ambitious projects such as Mono (a free implementation of .NET on Linux, Unix, and Windows) are currently underway (see `www.mono-project.com`). However, .NET will probably never have the wide reach of a language such as Java because it incorporates too many different platform-specific and operating system–specific technologies and features.

■ **Tip** Although implementations of .NET are available for other platforms, they aren't supported by Microsoft, and they provide only a subset of the total range of features. The general consensus is that these implementations aren't ideal for mission-critical business systems.

The .NET Class Library

The .NET class library is a giant repository of classes that provide prefabricated functionality for everything from reading an XML file to sending an e-mail message. If you've had any exposure to Java, you may already be familiar with the idea of a class library. However, the .NET class library is more ambitious and comprehensive than just about any other programming framework. Any .NET language can use the .NET class library's features by interacting with the right objects. This helps encourage consistency among different .NET languages and removes the need to install numerous components on your computer or web server.

Some parts of the class library include features you'll never need to use in web applications (such as the classes used to create desktop applications with the Windows interface). Other parts of the class library are targeted directly at web development. Still more classes can be used in various programming scenarios and aren't specific to web or Windows development. These include the base set of classes that define common variable types and the classes for data access, to name just a few. You'll explore the .NET Framework throughout this book.

You can think of the class library as a well-stocked programmer's toolkit. Microsoft's philosophy is that it will provide the tedious infrastructure so that application developers need only to write business-specific code. For example, the .NET Framework deals with thorny issues like database transactions and concurrency, making sure that hundreds or thousands of simultaneous users can request the same web page at once. You just add the logic needed for your specific application.

Visual Studio

The last part of .NET is the Visual Studio development tool, which provides a rich environment where you can rapidly create advanced applications. Although in theory you could create an ASP.NET application without Visual Studio (for example, by writing all the source code in a text editor and compiling it with .NET's command-line compilers), this task would be tedious, painful, and prone to error. For that reason, all professional ASP.NET developers use a design tool like Visual Studio.

Some of the features of Visual Studio include the following:

Page design: You can create an attractive page with drag-and-drop ease using Visual Studio's integrated web form designer. You don't need to understand HTML.

Automatic error detection: You could save hours of work when Visual Studio detects and reports an error before you run your application. Potential problems are underlined, just like the "spell-as-you-go" feature found in many word processors.

Debugging tools: Visual Studio retains its legendary debugging tools, which allow you to watch your code in action and track the contents of variables. And you can test web applications just as easily as any other application type, because Visual Studio has a built-in web server that works just for debugging.

IntelliSense: Visual Studio provides statement completion for recognized objects and automatically lists information such as function parameters in helpful tooltips.

You don't need to use Visual Studio to create web applications. In fact, you might be tempted to use the freely downloadable .NET Framework and a simple text editor to create ASP.NET web pages and web services. However, in doing so you'll multiply your work, and you'll have a much harder time debugging, organizing, and maintaining your code. Chapter 4 introduces the latest version of Visual Studio.

Visual Studio is available in several editions. The Standard Edition has all the features you need to build any type of application (Windows or web). The Professional Edition and the Team Edition increase the cost and pile on more tools and frills (which aren't discussed in this book). For example, they incorporate features for managing source code that's edited by multiple people on a development team and running automated tests.

The scaled-down Visual Web Developer Express Edition is a completely free version of Visual Studio that's surprising capable, but it has a few significant limitations. Visual Web Developer Express Edition gives you full support for developing web applications, but it doesn't support any other type of application. This means you can't use it to develop separate components for use in your applications or to develop Windows applications. However, rest assured that Visual Web Developer Express Edition is still a bona fide version of Visual Studio, with a similar set of features and development interface.

The Last Word

This chapter presented a high-level overview that gave you your first taste of ASP.NET and the .NET Framework. You also looked at how web development has evolved, from the basic HTML forms standard to the latest changes in .NET 3.5.

In the next chapter, you'll get a comprehensive overview of the VB language.

CHAPTER 2

The Visual Basic Language

Before you can create an ASP.NET application, you need to choose a .NET language in which to program it. If you're an ASP or VB developer, the natural choice is VB 2008. If you're a long-time Java programmer or old-hand C coder, C# will suit you best.

This chapter presents an overview of the VB 2008 language. You'll learn about the data types you can use, the operations you can perform, and the code you'll need to define functions, loops, and conditional logic. This chapter assumes you've programmed before and you're already familiar with most of these concepts—you just need to see how they're implemented in VB 2008.

If you've programmed with a pre-.NET version of Visual Basic, you might find that the most beneficial way to use this chapter is to browse through it without reading every section. This approach will give you a general overview of the VB 2008 language. You can then return to this chapter later as a reference when needed. But remember, though you can program an ASP.NET application without mastering all the language details, this deep knowledge is often what separates the casual programmer from the legendary programming guru.

Note The examples in this chapter show individual lines and code snippets. You won't actually be able to use these code snippets in an application until you've learned about objects and .NET types. But don't despair—the next chapter builds on this information, fills in the gaps, and presents an ASP.NET example for you to try.

The .NET Languages

The .NET Framework ships with three core languages that are commonly used for building ASP.NET applications: VB, C#, and J#. These languages are, to a large degree, functionally equivalent. Microsoft has worked hard to eliminate language conflicts in the .NET Framework. These battles slow down adoption, distract from the core framework features, and make it difficult for the developer community to solve problems together and share solutions. According to Microsoft, choosing to program in VB instead of C# is just a lifestyle choice and won't affect the performance, interoperability, feature set, or development time of your applications. Surprisingly, this ambitious claim is essentially true.

.NET also allows other third-party developers to release languages that are just as feature rich as C# or VB. These languages (which include Eiffel, Pascal, Python, and even COBOL) "snap in" to the .NET Framework effortlessly. In fact, if you want to install another .NET language, all you need to do is copy the compiler to your computer and add a line to register it in the computer's machine.config file. Typically, a setup program would perform these steps for you automatically. Once installed, the new compiler can transform your code creations into a sequence of Intermediate Language (IL) instructions, just like the VB and C# compilers do with VB and C# code.

IL is the only language that the Common Language Runtime (CLR) recognizes. When you create the code for an ASP.NET web form, it's changed into IL using the C# compiler (csc.exe), the VB compiler (vbc.exe), or the J# compiler (vjc.exe). Although you can perform the compilation manually, you're more likely to let ASP.NET handle it automatically when a web page is requested.

The Evolution of Visual Basic

Before .NET appeared, traditional ASP development was restricted to the VBScript programming language, which was first developed as a basic scripting language for writing macros and other simple code that would be used by another application. VBScript was never intended for sophisticated, interactive web applications, hence expert programmers had to strain the language to its limit to create first-rate ASP pages. To get around many limitations in VBScript, advanced pages needed to rely on separate components written in other languages, which generally had to be installed and configured separately on the web server. In the end, even though VBScript was intended to be easier to use than ordinary Visual Basic, writing industrial-strength ASP pages actually became much more complicated because of the additional effort needed to circumvent VBScript's limitations.

Just replacing VBScript with any full-fledged version of Visual Basic would have been a significant advantage for web developers. However, .NET completely skipped over this stage in evolution and introduced a complete language redesign. This language, first called VB .NET and now named VB 2008, answers years of feature requests and complaints and extends the VB language into new territory.

Some of the changes include the following:

- *Structured error handling*: The end of the aggravating "On Error Goto" message has finally arrived. VB 2008 uses .NET's standard—clean, concise, structured exception handling. You'll see it in Chapter 8.

- *Language refinements*: Every aspect of the VB language has been tweaked and refined for .NET. You can now overload functions, declare and assign variables on the same line, and use shortened assignment syntax.

- *Strong typing*: Visual Basic 6 performed some automatic variable conversions that could cause unusual bugs. VB 2008 allows you to rein in your program and prevent possible errors with strict type checking.

- *True object-oriented programming*: Inheritance, interfaces, polymorphism, constructors, shared members, and abstract classes . . . the list goes on, and VB 2008 integrates them all into the language.

These are only some of the changes, but they're enough to show you that VB 2008 is separated from VBScript by two major evolutionary leaps. All of these features are available in other .NET languages such as C#, but Visual Basic and VBScript developers will have to adjust the most.

■Note From this point on, all references to VB in this book are referring to Visual Basic 2008, the latest version of the VB language for the .NET platform.

Variables and Data Types

As with all programming languages, you keep track of data in VB using *variables*. Variables can store numbers, text, dates, and times, and they can even point to full-fledged objects.

When you declare a variable, you give it a name, and you specify the type of data it will store. To declare a local variable, you use the Dim statement, as shown here:

```
' Declare an integer variable named ErrorCode.
Dim ErrorCode As Integer

' Declare a string variable named MyName.
Dim MyName As String
```

■Note This example shows one other ingredient in VB programming: *comments*. Comments are descriptive text that is ignored by the compiler. VB comments always start with an apostrophe (') and continue for the entire line.

Every .NET language uses the same variable data types. Different languages may provide slightly different names (for example, a VB Integer is the same as a C# int), but the CLR makes no distinction—in fact, they are just two different names for the same base data type. This design allows for deep language integration. Because languages share the same core data types, you can easily use objects written in one .NET language in an application written in another .NET language. No data type conversions are required.

■Note The reason all .NET languages have the same data types is because they all adhere to the common type system (CTS), a Microsoft-designed ECMA standard that sets out the ground rules that all .NET languages must follow when dealing with data.

To create this common data type system, Microsoft needed to iron out many of the inconsistencies that existed between VBScript, VB 6, C++, and other languages. The solution was to create a set of basic data types, which are provided in the .NET class library. Table 2-1 lists the most important core data types.

Table 2-1. *Common Data Types*

.NET Type Name	VB Name	C# Name	Contains
Byte	Byte	byte	An integer from 0 to 255.
Int16	Short	short	An integer from –32,768 to 32,767.
Int32	Integer	int	An integer from –2,147,483,648 to 2,147,483,647.
Int64	Long	long	An integer from about –9.2e18 to 9.2e18.
Single	Single	float	A single-precision floating point number from approximately –3.4e38 to 3.4e38 (for big numbers) or –1.5e-45 to 1.5e-45 (for small fractional numbers).
Double	Double	double	A double-precision floating point number from approximately –1.8e308 to 1.8e308 (for big numbers) or –5.0e-324 to 5.0e-324 (for small fractional numbers).
Decimal	Decimal	decimal	A 128-bit fixed-point fractional number that supports up to 28 significant digits.
Char	Char	char	A single 16-bit Unicode character.
String	String	string	A variable-length series of Unicode characters.
Boolean	Boolean	bool	A True or False value.
DateTime	Date	*	Represents any date and time from 12:00:00 AM, January 1 of the year 1 in the Gregorian calendar, to 11:59:59 PM, December 31 of the year 9999. Time values can resolve values to 100 nanosecond increments. Internally, this data type is stored as a 64-bit integer.
TimeSpan	*	*	Represents a period of time, as in ten seconds or three days. The smallest possible interval is 1 *tick* (100 nanoseconds).
Object	Object	object	The ultimate base class of all .NET types. Can contain any data type or object.

* *If the language does not provide an alias for a given type, you can just use the .NET type name.*

You can also declare a variable by using the type name from the .NET class library. This approach produces identical variables. It's also a requirement when the data type doesn't have an alias built into the language. For example, you can rewrite the earlier example that used VB data type names with this code snippet that uses the class library names:

```
Dim ErrorCode As System.Int32
Dim MyName As System.String
```

This code snippet uses fully qualified type names that indicate that the Int32 type and the String type are found in the System namespace (along with all the most fundamental types). In Chapter 3, you'll learn about types and namespaces in more detail.

WHAT'S IN A NAME? NOT THE DATA TYPE!

You'll notice that the preceding examples don't use variable prefixes. Many longtime programmers are in the habit of adding a few characters to the start of a variable name to indicate its data type. In .NET, this practice is discouraged, because data types can be used in a much more flexible range of ways without any problem, and most variables hold references to full objects anyway. In this book, variable prefixes aren't used, except for web controls, where it helps to distinguish among lists, text boxes, buttons, and other common user interface elements. In your own programs, you should follow a consistent (typically company-wide) standard that may or may not adopt a system of variable prefixes.

Assignment and Initializers

Once you've declared your variable, you can freely assign values to them, as long as these values have the correct data type. Here's the code that shows this two-step process:

```
' Declare variables.
Dim ErrorCode As Integer
Dim MyName As String


' Assign values.
ErrorCode = 10
MyName = "Matthew"
```

You can also assign a value to a variable in the same line that you declare it. This example compresses four lines of code into two:

```
Dim ErrorCode As Integer = 10
Dim MyName As String = "Matthew"
```

Visual Basic is kind enough to let you use simple data types without initializing them. Numbers are automatically initialized to 0 and strings are initialized to an empty string (""). That means the following code will succeed in VB:

```
Dim Number As Integer   ' Number now contains 0.
Number = Number + 1     ' Number now contains 1.
```

There's one additional option when declaring a variable. If you're declaring and initializing a variable in a single statement, and if the VB compiler can infer the correct data type based on the value you're using, you don't need to specify the data type. Here's an example:

```
Dim StringVariable1 As String = "This is a string"
Dim StringVariable2 = "This is also a string"
```

Both StringVariable1 and StringVariable2 are created as strings, even though the second code statement doesn't indicate the string data type. That's because the Visual Basic compiler is able to determine that you're using a string to initialize StringVariable2, and so no other type makes sense. Both lines of code compile to the same low-level instructions—there's no performance difference. Type inference is just a shortcut that lets you save a few keystrokes.

Type inference is perfectly legitimate, but it can lead to accidents. For example, consider this code:

```
Dim MysteryVariable1 = 10
Dim MysteryVariable2 = 10.1
```

The values 10 and 10.1 can be stored using a range of different numeric data types, so it's not immediately obvious what the compiler will choose. In this case, MysteryVariable1 is created as an integer (because it doesn't include a fractional portion), and MysteryVariable2 is created as a double (because it does). If you want to use something else, you'll need to be a bit clearer and specify your data types explicitly.

Arrays

Arrays allow you to store a series of values that have the same data type. Each individual value in the array is accessed using one or more index numbers. It's often convenient to picture arrays as lists of data (if the array has one dimension) or grids of data (if the array has two dimensions). Typically, arrays are laid out contiguously in memory.

All arrays start at a fixed lower bound of 0. This rule has no exceptions. When you create an array in C#, you specify the number of elements. Because counting starts at 0, the highest index is actually one fewer than the number of elements. (In other words, if you have three elements, the highest index is 2.) When you create an array in VB, you simply specify the upper bound:

```
' Create an array with four strings (from index 0 to index 3).
Dim StringArray(3) As String

' Create a 2 x 4 grid array (with a total of eight integers).
Dim IntArray(1, 3) As Integer
```

You can also fill an array with data at the same time that you create it. In this case, you don't need to explicitly specify the number of elements, because .NET can determine it automatically:

```
' Create an array with four strings, one for each number from 1 to 4.
Dim StringArray() As String = {"1", "2", "3", "4"}
```

The same technique works for multidimensional arrays, except that two sets of curly brackets are required:

```
' Create a 4 x 2 array (a grid with four rows and two columns).
Dim IntArray(,) As Integer = {{1, 2}, {3, 4}, {5, 6}, {7, 8}}
```

Figure 2-1 shows what this array looks like in memory.

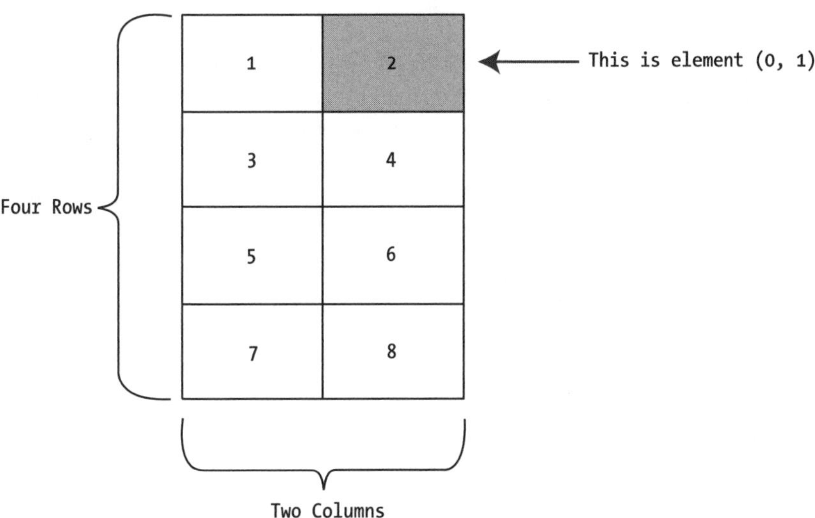

Figure 2-1. *A sample two-dimensional array of integers*

To access an element in an array, you specify the corresponding index number in parentheses. Array indices are always zero-based. That means that MyArray(0) accesses the first value in a one-dimensional array, MyArray(1) accesses the second value, and so on.

```
' Access the value in row 0 (first row), column 1 (second column).
Dim Element As Integer
Element = IntArray(0, 1)      ' Element is now set to 2.
```

One nice feature that VB offers is array redimensioning. In VB, all arrays start with an initial size, and any array can be resized. To resize an array, you use the ReDim keyword.

```
Dim MyArray(10, 10) As Integer
ReDim MyArray(20, 20)
```

In this example, all the contents in the array will be erased when it's resized. To preserve the contents, you can use the optional Preserve keyword when redimensioning the array. However, if you're using a multidimensional array you'll only be able to change the last dimension when using the Preserve keyword or a runtime error will occur.

```
Dim MyArray(10, 10) As Integer
ReDim Preserve MyArray(10, 20)    ' Allowed, and the contents will remain.
ReDim Preserve MyArray(20, 20)    ' Not allowed. A runtime error will occur.
```

Redimensioning arrays isn't terribly efficient, especially if your array is very large. That's because it often involves allocating new memory and copying all your values to that new memory. It's best to use arrays when you know in advance how many items you want to store, and you won't need to redimension the array often (if at all). If you need to store a varying number of elements, you're better off with a collection class, like the ArrayList that's described next.

The ArrayList

In many cases, it's easier to dodge counting issues and use a full-fledged collection rather than an array. Collections are generally better suited to modern object-oriented programming and are used extensively in ASP.NET. The .NET class library provides many types of collection classes, including sorted lists, key-indexed lists (dictionaries), and queues.

One of the simplest collection classes that .NET provides is the ArrayList, which always allows dynamic resizing. Here's a snippet of VB code that uses an ArrayList:

```
' Create an ArrayList object. It's a collection, not an array,
' so the syntax is slightly different.
Dim DynamicList As New ArrayList()

' Add several strings to the list.
' The ArrayList is not strongly typed, so you can add any data type
' although it's simplest if you store just one type of object
' in any given collection.
DynamicList.Add("one")
DynamicList.Add("two")
DynamicList.Add("three")

' Retrieve the first string. Notice that the object must be converted to a
' string, because there's no way for .NET to be certain what it is.
Dim Item As String = CType(DynamicList(0), String)
```

You'll learn more about the ArrayList and other, more powerful collections in Chapter 3. You'll examine the CType() function, which is used to perform the conversion in the preceding example, later in this chapter (in the "Type Conversions" section).

Enumerations

An enumeration is a group of related constants, each of which is given a descriptive name. Each value in an enumeration corresponds to a preset integer. In your code, however, you can refer to an enumerated value by name, which makes your code clearer and helps prevent errors. For example, it's much more straightforward to set the border of a label to the enumerated value BorderStyle.Dashed rather than the obscure numeric constant 3. In this case, Dashed is a value in the BorderStyle enumeration, and it represents the number 3.

■ **Note** Just to keep life interesting, the word *enumeration* actually has more than one meaning. As described in this section, enumerations are sets of constant values. However, programmers often talk about the process of *enumerating*, which means to loop, or *iterate*, over a collection. For example, it's common to talk about enumerating over all the characters of a string (which means looping through the string and examining each character in a separate pass).

Here's an example of an enumeration that defines different types of users:

```
' Define an enumeration called UserType with three possible values.
Enum UserType
    Admin
    Guest
    Invalid
End Enum
```

Now you can use the UserType enumeration as a special data type that is restricted to one of three possible values. You assign or compare the enumerated value using the dot notation shown in the following example:

```
' Create a new value and set it equal to the UserType.Admin constant.
Dim NewUserType As UserType
NewUserType = UserType.Admin
```

Internally, enumerations are maintained as numbers. In the preceding example, 0 is automatically assigned to Admin, 1 to Guest, and 2 to Invalid. You can set a number directly in an enumeration variable, although this can lead to an undetected error if you use a number that doesn't correspond to one of the defined values.

In some scenarios, you might want to control what numbers are used for various values in an enumeration. This technique is typically used when the number has some specific meaning or corresponds to some other piece of information. For example, the following code defines an enumeration that represents the error code returned by a legacy component:

```
Enum ErrorCode
    NoResponse = 166
    TooBusy = 167
    Pass = 0
End Enum
```

Now you can use the ErrorCode enumeration with a function that returns an integer representing an error condition, as shown here:

```
Dim Err As ErrorCode
Err = DoSomething()

If Err = ErrorCode.Pass
    ' Operation succeeded.
End If
```

Clearly, enumerations create more readable code. They also simplify coding, because once you type in the enumeration type name (ErrorCode) and add the dot (.), Visual Studio will pop up a list of possible values using IntelliSense.

■ **Tip** Enumerations are used widely in .NET. You won't need to create your own enumerations to use in ASP.NET applications, unless you're designing your own components. However, the concept of enumerated values is extremely important, because the .NET class library uses it extensively. For example, you set colors, border styles, alignment, and various other web control styles using enumerations provided in the .NET class library.

Variable Operations

You can use all the standard types of variable operations in VB. When working with numbers, you can use various math symbols, as listed in Table 2-2.

Table 2-2. *Arithmetic Operations*

Operator	Description	Example	Result
+	Addition	1 + 1	2
-	Subtraction (and to indicate negative numbers)	5 - 2	3
*	Multiplication	2 * 5	10
/	Division	5 / 2	2.5
Mod	Gets the remainder left after integer division	7 Mod 3	1

VB follows the conventional order of operations, performing exponentiation first, followed by multiplication and division and then addition and subtraction. You can also control order by grouping subexpressions with parentheses.

```
Dim Number As Integer

Number = 4 + 2 * 3
' Number will be 10.

Number = (4 + 2) * 3
' Number will be 18.
```

When dealing with strings, you can use the concatenation operator (&), which joins together two strings.

```
' Join two strings together. Could also use the + operator.
MyName = FirstName & " " & LastName
```

The addition operator (+) can also be used to join strings, but it's generally clearer and safer to use the concatenation operator. The concatenation operator (&) automatically attempts to convert both variables in the expression to the string data type, if they are not already strings.

In addition, VB also provides special shorthand assignment operators. Here are a few examples:

```
' Add 10 to MyValue (the same as MyValue = MyValue + 10).
MyValue += 10

' Multiply MyValue by 3 (the same as MyValue = MyValue * 3).
MyValue *= 3

' Divide MyValue by 12 (the same as MyValue = MyValue / 12).
MyValue /= 12
```

LINE TERMINATION

Sometimes, code statements are too long to efficiently fit on a single line. In Visual Basic, you can break a code statement over multiple lines by adding a space followed by the line-continuation character (an underscore) to the end of the line. Here's an example:

```
' A long line of code.
MyValue = MyValue1 + MyValue2 + MyValue3

' A code statement split over several lines in VB.
MyValue = MyValue1 + MyValue2 + _
          MyValue3
```

Advanced Math

In the past, every language has had its own set of keywords for common math operations such as rounding and trigonometry. In .NET languages, many of these keywords remain. However, you can also use a centralized System.Math class that's part of the .NET Framework. This has the pleasant side effect of ensuring that the code you use to perform mathematical operations can easily be translated into equivalent statements in any .NET language with minimal fuss.

To use the math operations, you invoke the methods of the Math class. These methods are *shared*, which means they are always available and ready to use. (The next chapter explores the difference between shared and instance members in more detail.)

The following code snippet shows some sample calculations that you can perform with the Math class:

```
Dim MyValue As Double
MyValue = Math.Sqrt(81)              ' MyValue = 9.0
MyValue = Math.Round(42.889, 2)      ' MyValue = 42.89
MyValue = Math.Abs(-10)              ' MyValue = 10.0
MyValue = Math.Log(24.212)           ' MyValue = 3.18.. (and so on)
MyValue = Math.PI                    ' MyValue = 3.14.. (and so on)
```

The features of the Math class are too numerous to list here in their entirety. The preceding examples show some common numeric operations. For more information about the trigonometric and logarithmic functions that are available, refer to the Visual Studio Help and look up the Math class in the index.

Type Conversions

Converting information from one data type to another is a fairly common programming task. For example, you might retrieve text input for a user that contains the number you want to use for a calculation. Or, you might need to take a calculated value and transform it into text you can display in a web page.

The Visual Basic rules for type conversion are slightly less strict than some other languages, such as C#. For example, VB will automatically allow the (potentially risky) conversions shown here:

```
Dim BigValue As Integer = 100
Dim SmallValue As Short
Dim MyText As String = "100"

' Convert your 32-bit BigValue number into a 16-bit number.
SmallValue = BigValue

' Convert your MyText into a number.
BigValue = MyText
```

The problem with code like this is that it isn't guaranteed to work correctly at runtime. Conversions are of two types: widening and narrowing. *Widening* conversions always succeed. For example, you can always convert a number into a string, or a 16-bit integer into a 32-bit integer.

On the other hand, *narrowing* conversions may or may not succeed, depending on the data. If you're converting a 32-bit integer to a 16-bit integer, you could encounter a runtime error if the 32-bit number is larger than the maximum value that can be stored in the 16-bit data type. Similarly, some strings can't be converted to numbers. A failed narrowing conversion will lead to an unexpected runtime error.

It's possible to tighten up Visual Basic's type conversion habits by adding an Option Strict instruction to the beginning of your code files.

```
Option Strict On
```

In this case, VB will not allow automatic or *implicit* data type conversions if they could cause an error or lose data. Instead, you'll need to explicitly indicate that you want to perform a conversion.

To perform an *explicit* data type conversion in VB, you can use the CType() function. This function takes two arguments. The first specifies the variable you want to convert, and the second specifies the data type you're converting it to. Here's how you could rewrite the earlier example with explicit conversions:

```
Dim BigValue As Integer = 100
Dim SmallValue As Short
Dim MyText As String = "100"

' Explicitly convert your 32-bit number into a 16-bit number.
SmallValue = CType(BigValue, Short)

' Explicitly convert your string into a number.
BigValue = CType(MyText, Integer)
```

Just like implicit conversions, explicit conversions can still fail and produce a runtime error. The difference is that when you add the CType() function, you clearly indicate that you are aware a conversion is taking place. At the same time you use CType(), you should add code that validates your data before you attempt to convert it, or catches any errors using the error-handling techniques described in Chapter 8.

■ **Tip** You can tell Visual Studio to use Option Strict for an entire project. However, the way you configure this depends on the type of project. For a Windows application or a class library component you need to select Project ➤ [ProjectName] Properties from the menu, choose the Compile tab, and set the Option Strict box to On. In a web application, you need to edit the web.config file configuration file (which you'll learn about in Chapter 5). Just find the <compilation> element and add the `strict="true"` attribute.

You can also use the classic Visual Basic keywords such as Val(), CStr(), CInt(), CBool(), and so on to perform data type conversions with the standard data types. However, the CType() function is a nice generic solution that works for all scenarios. The examples in this book almost always use explicit conversion with the CType() function. A few exceptions apply. For example, Visual Basic's built-in Val() function is more convenient than CType() in some scenarios because it just returns a zero if it fails to convert a string to a number.

```
Dim TextString As String = "Hello"

Dim Number As Integer
Number = Val(TextString)
' Number is now 0, because TextString contains no numeric information.
```

You'll also find that you can use object methods to perform some conversions a little more elegantly. The next section demonstrates this approach.

Object-Based Manipulation

.NET is object-oriented to the core. In fact, even ordinary numeric variables like the ones you've seen earlier are really full-fledged objects in disguise. This means that common data types have the built-in smarts to handle basic operations. For example, all strings are actually complete string objects, with useful methods and properties (such as a Length property that counts the number of characters in the string). Thanks to this design, you can manipulate strings, dates, and numbers in the same way in C# and in VB. This wouldn't be true if developers used special keywords that were built into the C# or VB language.

As an example, every type in the .NET class library includes a ToString() method. The default implementation of this method returns the class name. In simple variables, a more useful result is returned: the string representation of the given variable. The following code snippet demonstrates how to use the ToString() method with an integer:

```
Dim MyString As String
Dim MyInteger As Integer = 100
' Convert a number to a string. MyString will have the contents "100".
MyString = MyInteger.ToString()
```

To understand this example, you need to remember that all integer variables are based on the Int32 type in the .NET class library. The ToString() method is built in to the Int32 type, so it's available when you use an integer in any language. (You'll learn more about types in Chapter 3.)

The next few sections explore the object-oriented underpinnings of the .NET data types in more detail.

The String Type

One of the best examples of how class members can replace built-in functions is found with strings. In the past, every language has defined its own specialized functions for string manipulation. In .NET, however, you use the methods of the String type, which ensures consistency between all .NET languages.

The following code snippet shows several ways to manipulate a string using the methods in the String type:

```
Dim MyString As String = "This is a test string       "
MyString = MyString.Trim()                  ' = "This is a test string"
MyString = MyString.Substring(0, 4)         ' = "This"
MyString = MyString.ToUpper()               ' = "THIS"
MyString = MyString.Replace("IS", "AT")     ' = "THAT"
Dim Length As Integer = MyString.Length     ' = 4
```

The first few statements use built-in methods of the String type, such as Trim(), Substring(), ToUpper(), and Replace(). Each of these methods generates a new string object, which replaces the current contents of the MyString variable. The final statement uses the built-in Length property of the String type, which returns an integer that represents the number of characters in the string.

■ **Tip** A method is just a function or procedure that's hardwired into an object. A property is similar to a variable—it's a way to access a piece of data that's associated with an object. You'll learn more about methods and properties in the next chapter.

Note that the Substring() method requires a starting offset and a character length. Strings use zero-based counting. This means that the first character is in position 0, the second character is in position 1, and so on. You'll find this standard of zero-based counting throughout the .NET Framework for the sake of consistency. You've already seen it at work with arrays.

You can even use the string methods in succession in a single (rather ugly) line:

```
MyString = MyString.Trim().SubString(0, 4).ToUpper().Replace("IS", "AT")
```

Or, to make life more interesting, you can use the string methods on string literals just as easily as string variables:

```
MyString = "hello".ToUpper()     ' Sets MyString to "HELLO"
```

Table 2-3 lists some useful members of the String class.

Table 2-3. *Useful String Members**

Member	Description
Length	Returns the number of characters in the string (as an integer).
ToUpper() and ToLower()	Returns a copy of the string with all the characters changed to uppercase or lowercase characters.
Trim(), TrimEnd(), and TrimStart()	Removes spaces or some other characters from either (or both) ends of a string.
PadLeft() and PadRight()	Adds the specified character to the appropriate side of a string, as many times as necessary to make the total length of the string equal to the number you specify. For example, "Hi".PadLeft(5, '@') returns the string "@@@Hi".
Insert()	Puts another string inside a string at a specified (zero-based) index position. For example, Insert(1, "pre") adds the string *pre* after the first character of the current string.
Remove()	Removes a specified number of characters from a specified position. For example, Remove(0, 1) removes the first character.
Replace()	Replaces a specified substring with another string. For example, Replace("a", "b") changes all *a* characters in a string into *b* characters.
Substring()	Retrieves a portion of a string of the specified length at the specified location (as a new string). For example, Substring(0, 2) retrieves the first two characters.
StartsWith() and EndsWith()	Determines whether a string starts or ends with a specified substring. For example, StartsWith("pre") will return either True or False, depending on whether the string begins with the letters *pre* in lowercase.
IndexOf() and LastIndexOf()	Finds the zero-based position of a substring in a string. This returns only the first match and can start at the end or beginning. You can also use overloaded versions of these methods that accept a parameter that specifies the position to start the search.
Split()	Divides a string into an array of substrings delimited by a specific substring. For example, with Split(".") you could chop a paragraph into an array of sentence strings.
Join()	Fuses an array of strings into a new string. You can also specify a separator that will be inserted between each element.

* *Technically, strings are never modified. All the string methods that appear to change a string actually return a copy of the string that has the changes.*

The DateTime and TimeSpan Types

The DateTime and TimeSpan data types also have built-in methods and properties. These class members allow you to perform three useful tasks:

- Extract a part of a DateTime (for example, just the year) or convert a TimeSpan to a specific representation (such as the total number of days or total number of minutes).
- Easily perform date and time calculations.
- Determine the current date and time and other information (such as the day of the week or whether the date occurs in a leap year).

For example, the following block of code creates a DateTime object, sets it to the current date and time, and adds a number of days. It then creates a string that indicates the year that the new date falls in (for example, 2008).

```
Dim MyDate As DateTime = DateTime.Now
MyDate = MyDate.AddDays(100)
Dim DateString As String = MyDate.Year.ToString()
```

The next example shows how you can use a TimeSpan object to find the total number of minutes between two DateTime objects.

```
Dim MyDate1 As Date = DateTime.Now
Dim MyDate2 As Date = DateTime.Now.AddHours(3000)

Dim Difference As TimeSpan
Difference = MyDate2.Subtract(MyDate1)

Dim NumberOfMinutes As Double
NumberOfMinutes = Difference.TotalMinutes
```

The DateTime and TimeSpan classes also support the + and – arithmetic operators, which do the same work as the built-in methods. That means you can rewrite the example shown previously like this:

```
Dim MyDate1 As DateTime = DateTime.Now
Dim Interval As TimeSpan = TimeSpan.FromHours(3000)
Dim MyDate2 As DateTime = MyDate1 + Interval

' Subtracting one DateTime object from another produces a TimeSpan.
Dim Difference As TimeSpan
Difference = MyDate2 - MyDate1
```

These examples give you an idea of the flexibility .NET provides for manipulating date and time data. Tables 2-4 and 2-5 list some of the more useful built-in features of the DateTime and TimeSpan types.

Table 2-4. *Useful DateTime Members*

Member	Description
Now	Gets the current date and time. You can also use the UtcNow property to take the current computer's time zone into account. UtcNow gets the time as a *coordinated universal time* (UTC). Assuming your computer is correctly configured, this corresponds to the current time in the Western European (UTC+0) time zone.
Today	Gets the current date and leaves time set to 00:00:00.
Year, Date, Month, Day, Hour, Minute,	Returns one part of the DateTime object as an Second, and Millisecond integer. For example, Month will return 12 for any day in December.

Table 2-4. *Useful DateTime Members*

Member	Description
DayOfWeek	Returns an enumerated value that indicates the day of the week for this DateTime, using the DayOfWeek enumeration. For example, if the date falls on Sunday, this will return DayOfWeek.Sunday.
Add()	Adds a TimeSpan to a DateTime and returns the result as a new DateTime.
Subtract()	Subtracts a TimeSpan or DateTime from another DateTime. Returns a TimeSpan that represents the difference.
AddYears(), AddMonths(), AddDays(), AddHours(), AddMinutes(), AddSeconds(), AddMilliseconds()	Accepts an integer that represents a number of years, months, and so on, and returns a new DateTime. You can use a negative integer to perform a date subtraction.
DaysInMonth()	Returns the number of days in the specified month in the specified year.
IsLeapYear()	Returns True or False depending on whether the specified year is a leap year.
ToString()	Returns a string representation of the current DateTime object. You can also use an overloaded version of this method that allows you to specify a parameter with a format string.

■ **Note** Methods like Add() and Subtract() don't *change* a DateTime object. Instead, they return a new DateTime or TimeSpan object.

Table 2-5. *Useful TimeSpan Members*

Member	Description
Days, Hours, Minutes, Seconds, Milliseconds	Returns one component of the current TimeSpan. For example, the Hours property can return an integer from –23 to 23.
TotalDays, TotalHours, TotalMinutes, TotalSeconds, TotalMilliseconds	Returns the total value of the current TimeSpan, as a number of days, hours, minutes, and so on. The value is returned as a double, which may include a fractional value. For example, the TotalDays property might return a number like 234.342.
Add() and Subtract()	Combines TimeSpan objects together.
FromDays(), FromHours(), FromMinutes(), FromSeconds(), FromMilliseconds()	Allows you to quickly create a new TimeSpan. For example, you can use TimeSpan.FromHours(24) to create a TimeSpan object exactly 24 hours long.
ToString()	Returns a string representation of the current TimeSpan object. You can also use an overloaded version of this method that allows you to specify a parameter with a format string.

The Array Type

Arrays also behave like objects in the new world of .NET. All arrays in .NET are actually instances of the Array type, which provides its own built-in features. For example, if you want to find out the size of a one-dimensional array, you can use the Length property or the GetLength() method, both of which return the total number of elements in an array:

```
Dim MyArray() As Integer = {1, 2, 3, 4, 5}
Dim NumberOfElements As Integer

NumberOfElements = MyArray.Length       ' NumberOfElements = 5
```

You can also use the GetUpperBound() method to find the highest index number in an array. The following code snippet shows this technique in action:

```
Dim MyArray() As Integer = {1, 2, 3, 4, 5}
Dim Bound As Integer

' Zero represents the first dimension of an array.
Bound = MyArray.GetUpperBound(0)         ' Bound = 4
```

On a one-dimensional array, GetUpperBound() always returns a number that's one less than the length. That's because the first index number is 0, and the last index number is always one less than the total number of items. However, in a two-dimensional array, you can find the highest index number for a specific dimension in that array. For example, the following code snippet uses GetUpperBound() to find the total number of rows and the total number of columns in a two-dimensional array:

```
' Create a 4 x 2 array (a grid with four rows and two columns).
Dim IntArray(,) As Integer = {{1, 2}, {3, 4}, {5, 6}, {7, 8}}

Dim Rows, Columns As Integer
Rows = IntArray.GetUpperBound(0)          ' Rows = 4
Columns = IntArray.GetUpperBound(1)     ' Columns = 2
```

Having these values—the array length and indexes—is handy when looping through the contents of an array, as you'll see later in this chapter, in the "Loops" section.

Arrays also provide a few other useful methods, which allow you to sort them, reverse them, and search them for a specified element. Table 2-6 lists some useful members of the System.Array type.

Table 2-6. *Useful Array Members*

Member	Description
Length	Returns an integer that represents the total number of elements in all dimensions of an array. For example, a 3×3 array has a length of 9.
GetLowerBound() and GetUpperBound()	Determines the index position of the last element in an array. As with just about everything in .NET, you start counting at zero (which represents the first dimension).

Table 2-6. *Useful Array Members*

Member	Description
Clear()	Resets part or all of an array's contents. Depending on the index values that you supply. The elements revert to their initial empty values (such as 0 for numbers, and an empty string for strings).
IndexOf() and LastIndexOf()	Searches a one-dimensional array for a specified value and returns the index number. You cannot use this with multidimensional arrays.
Sort()	Sorts a one-dimensional array made up of comparable data such as strings or numbers.
Reverse()	Reverses a one-dimensional array so that its elements are backward, from last to first.

Conditional Logic

In many ways, conditional logic—deciding which action to take based on user input, external conditions, or other information—is the heart of programming.

All conditional logic starts with a *condition*: a simple expression that can be evaluated to True or False. Your code can then make a decision to execute different logic depending on the outcome of the condition. To build a condition, you can use any combination of literal values or variables along with *logical operators*. Table 2-7 lists the basic logical operators.

Table 2-7. *Logical Operators*

Operator	Description
=	Equal to.
<>	Not equal to.
<	Less than.
>	Greater than.
<=	Less than or equal to.
>=	Greater than or equal to.
And	Logical and (evaluates to True only if both expressions are True).
AndAlso	Similar to And, but it doesn't evaluate the second expression if the first one is False. This is a useful approach if evaluating the second option would be time consuming or could cause an error if the first condition is False.
Or	Logical or (evaluates to True if either expression is True).
OrElse	Similar to Or, but it doesn't evaluate the second expression if the first one is True. This is a useful approach if evaluating the second option would be time-consuming or could cause an error if the first condition is True.

You can use the comparison operators (<, >, <=, >=) with numeric types and with strings. A string is deemed to be "less than" another string if it occurs earlier in an alphabetic sort. Thus "apple" is less than "attach."

The If . . . End If Block

The If block is the powerhouse of conditional logic, able to evaluate any combination of conditions and deal with multiple and different pieces of data. Here's an example with an If block that features two conditions:

```
If MyNumber > 10 Then
    ' Do something.
ElseIf MyString = "hello" Then
    ' Do something.
Else
    ' Do something.
End If
```

Keep in mind that the If block matches one condition at most. For example, if MyNumber is greater than 10, the first condition will be met. That means the code in the first conditional block will run and no other conditions will be evaluated. Whether MyString contains the text *hello* becomes irrelevant, because that condition will not be evaluated.

An If block can have any number of conditions. If you test only a single condition, you don't need to include any other ElseIf or Else blocks.

The Select Case Block

VB also provides a Select Case block that you can use to evaluate a single variable or expression for multiple possible values. The Select Case statement supports the String, Char, Date, and Boolean data types, as well as virtually every simple numeric data type.

In the following code, each case examines the MyNumber variable and tests whether it's equal to a specific integer.

```
Select Case MyNumber
    Case 1
        ' Do something if MyNumber = 1.
    Case 2
        ' Do something if MyNumber = 2.
    Case Else
        ' Do something if MyNumber is anything else.
End Select
```

If desired, you can handle multiple cases with one segment of code by including a list of comma-separated values in the Case statement.

```
Select Case MyNumber
    Case 1, 2
        ' Do something if MyNumber = 1 Or MyNumber = 2.
    Case Else
        ' Do something if MyNumber is anything else.
End Select
```

Unlike the If block, Select Case is limited to evaluating a single piece of information at a time. However, it provides a leaner, clearer syntax than the If block for situations where you need to test a single variable against a limited set of possible values.

Loops

Loops allow you to repeat a segment of code multiple times. VB has three basic types of loops. You choose the type of loop based on the type of task you need to perform. Your choices are as follows:

- You can loop a set number of times with a For . . . Next loop.
- You can loop through all the items in a collection of data using a For Each loop.
- You can loop until a certain condition is met, using a Do . . . Loop.

The For . . . Next and For Each loops are ideal for chewing through sets of data that have known, fixed sizes. The Do . . . Loop block is a more flexible construct that allows you to continue processing until a complex condition is met. Do . . . Loop is often used with repetitive tasks or calculations that don't have a set number of iterations.

The For . . . Next Block

The For block is a basic ingredient in many programs. It allows you to repeat a block of code a set number of times, using a built-in counter. To create a For loop, you need to specify a starting value, an ending value, and (optionally) the amount to increment with each pass. Here's one example:

```
Dim i As Integer
For i = 1 To 10 Step 1
    ' This code executes 10 times.
    Debug.Write(i & " ")
Next
```

In this example, the counter you're using is a variable named i. The loop begins at 1 and ends at 10. The Step 1 clause specifies that i will be increased by 1 after every loop iteration. You can omit this part of the code, because 1 is the default increment. Once i reaches 10 the final pass is made through the loop, with i set to 10.

Because the counter variable is generally used in your For block but nowhere else, it's customary to define it as part of the For statement, as shown here:

```
For i As Integer = 1 To 10
    ' This code executes 10 times.
    Debug.Write(i & " ")
Next
```

If you run this code using a tool such as Visual Studio, it will write the following numbers in the Debug window:

```
1 2 3 4 5 6 7 8 9 10
```

It often makes sense to set the counter variable based on the number of items you're processing. For example, you can use a For loop to step through the elements in an array by checking the size of the array before you begin. Here's the code you would use:

```
Dim StringArray() As String = {"one", "two", "three"}
For i As Integer = 0 To StringArray.GetUpperBound(0)
    Debug.Write(StringArray(i) & " ")
Next
```

This code produces the following output:

```
one two three
```

BLOCK-LEVEL SCOPE

If you define a variable inside some sort of block structure (such as a loop or a conditional block), the variable is automatically released when your code exits the block. That means you will no longer be able to access it. The following code demonstrates this behavior:

```
Dim TempVariableA As Integer
For i As Integer = 1 To 10
    Dim TempVariableB As Integer
    TempVariableA = 1
    TempVariableB = 1
Next
' You cannot access TempVariableB here.
' However, you can still access TempVariableA.
```

This change won't affect many programs. It's really designed to catch a few more accidental errors. If you do need to access a variable inside and outside of some type of block structure, just define the variable *before* the block starts.

The For Each Block

VB also provides a For Each block that allows you to loop through the items in a set of data. With a For Each block, you don't need to create an explicit counter variable. Instead, you create a variable that represents the type of data for which you're looking. Your code will then loop until you've had a chance to process each piece of data in the set.

The For Each block is particularly useful for traversing the data in collections and arrays. For example, the next code segment loops through the items in an array using For Each. This code has the same effect as the code in the previous example but is a little simpler:

```
Dim StringArray() As String = {"one", "two", "three"}
For Each Element As String In StringArray
    ' This code loops three times, with the Element variable set to
    ' "one", then "two", and then "three".
    Debug.Write(Element & " ")
Next
```

In this case, the For Each loop examines each item in the array and tries to access it as a string. Thus, the For Each loop defines a string variable named Element. If you used a different data type as the loop variable, you'd receive an error.

The For Each block has one key limitation: it's read-only. For example, if you wanted to loop through an array and change the values in that array at the same time, For Each code wouldn't work. Here's an example of some flawed code:

```
Dim IntArray() As Integer = {1,2,3}
For Each Num As Integer In IntArray
    Num += 1
Next
' IntArray is still unchanged at this point.
```

In this case, you would need to fall back on a basic For block with a counter.

The Do . . . Loop Block

Finally, VB supports a Do . . . Loop block that tests a specific condition before or after each pass through the loop. When this condition evaluates to False, the loop is exited. Or, depending on the way you've written the loop, you can flip this behavior so the loop runs until the test condition evaluates to True—there's really no difference. Either way, the test condition allows you to create freeform looping code that continues until a specific condition is met.

To build a condition for a loop, you use the While or Until keyword. These two keywords are opposites. *While* means "as long as this is true," and *Until* means "as long as this is not true."

Here's an example that loops ten times. At the end of each pass, the code evaluates whether the counter (i) has exceeded a set value:

```
Dim i As Integer = 0
Do
    i += 1
    ' This code executes 10 times.
Loop While i < 10
```

You can also place the condition at the beginning of the loop. In the following example, the condition is tested at the start of each pass through the loop:

```
Dim i As Integer = 0
Do While i < 10
    i += 1
    ' This code executes 10 times.
Loop
```

Both of these examples are equivalent, unless the condition you're testing is False to start. In that case, the second example (with the condition at the beginning) will skip the code entirely. On the other hand, the first example (with the condition at the end) will always execute the code at least once.

■ **Tip** Sometimes you need to skip to the next iteration of a loop in a hurry. In VB, you can use the Continue Do statement to skip the rest of the current pass, evaluate the condition, and (if it returns True) start the next pass. You can perform the same feat with a For block using the Continue For statement. Finally, you can use the Exit Do and Exit For statements to jump straight out of a loop.

Methods

Methods are the most basic building block you can use to organize your code. Essentially, a method is a named grouping of one or more lines of code. Ideally, each method will perform a distinct, logical task. By breaking your code down into methods, you not only simplify your life, but you also make it easier to organize your code into classes and step into the world of object-oriented programming.

■ **Note** In pre-.NET versions of Visual Basic (such as VB 6), functions and subroutines are usually described as *procedures*. In object-oriented speak, the term *method* is equivalent to procedure. Method is the standard term in .NET, and it's what you'll see in this book.

Visual Basic distinguishes between two types of methods: subroutines and functions. The only difference between the two is that functions return a value, while subroutines do not. For example, a function named GetStartTime() might return a DateTime object that represents the time an application was first started. To return a value from a function and exit it immediately, you use the Return keyword.

Subroutines are declared with the Sub keyword, and functions are declared with the Function keyword. Here's an example of each one:

```
' This method doesn't return any information.
Private Sub MySub()
    ' Code goes here.
End Sub
```

```
' This method returns an integer.
Private Function MyFunc() As Integer
    ' As an example, return the number 10.
    Return 10
End Function
```

You'll notice that both of these methods are preceded with the accessibility keyword Private. This indicates that these procedures won't be accessible to code in a different class or module. The next chapter considers classes and accessibility in more detail.

Calling a method is straightforward—you simply enter the name of the method, followed by parentheses. If you call a function, you have the option of using the data it returns, or just ignoring it.

```
' This call is allowed.
MySub()

' This call is allowed.
MyFunc()

' This call is allowed.
Dim MyNumber As Integer
MyNumber = MyFunc()

' This call isn't allowed.
' MySub does not return any information.
MyNumber = MySub()
```

Parameters

Methods can also accept information through parameters. By .NET convention, parameter names always begin with a lowercase letter in any language.

Here's how you might create a function that accepts two parameters and returns their sum:

```
Private Function AddNumbers(number1 As Integer, number2 As Integer) _
  As Integer
    Return number1 + number2
End Sub
```

■ Note When you create a method in Visual Studio, it automatically adds the ByVal keyword before each parameter. This parameter isn't required (and it won't affect any of the examples you'll see in this chapter). However, you'll learn what it means and how it works in Chapter 3.

When calling a method, you specify any required parameters in parentheses or use an empty set of parentheses if no parameters are required.

```
' Call a subroutine with no parameters.
MySub()

' Call a subroutine with two Integer parameters.
MySub2(10, 20)

' Call a function with two Integer parameters and an Integer return value.
Dim ReturnValue As Integer = AddNumbers(10, 10)
```

Method Overloading

VB supports method *overloading*, which allows you to create more than one method with the same name, but with a different set of parameters. When you call the method, the CLR automatically chooses the correct version by examining the parameters you supply.

This technique allows you to collect different versions of several methods together. For example, you might allow a database search that returns an array of Product objects representing records in the database. Rather than create three functions with different names depending on the criteria, such as GetAllProducts(), GetProductsInCategory(), GetActiveProducts(), you could create three versions of the GetProducts() method. Each method would have the same name but a different *signature*, meaning it would require different parameters. Additionally, you need to add the Overloads keyword before the word Function (or Sub) for each of the three methods. This is a safety feature built into VB—it prevents you from inadvertently defining more than one method with the same name.

This example provides two overloaded versions for the GetProductPrice() method:

```
Private Overloads Function GetProductPrice(id As Integer) As Decimal
    ' Code here.
End Function

Private Overloads Function GetProductPrice(name As String) As Decimal
    ' Code here.
End Function

' And so on...
```

Now you can look up product prices based on the unique product ID or the full product name, depending on whether you supply an integer or string argument:

```
Dim Price As Decimal

' Get price by product ID (the first version).
Price = GetProductPrice(1001)

' Get price by product name (the second version).
Price = GetProductPrice("DVD Player")
```

You cannot overload a method with versions that have the same signature—that is, the same number of parameters and parameter data types—because the CLR will not be able to distinguish them from each other. When you call an overloaded method, the version that matches the parameter list you supply is used. If no version matches, an error occurs.

Note .NET uses overloaded methods in most of its classes. This approach allows you to use a flexible range of parameters while centralizing functionality under common names. Even the methods you've seen so far (such as the string methods for padding or replacing text) have multiple versions that provide similar features with various options.

Delegates

Delegates allow you to create a variable that "points" to a method. You can use this variable at any time to invoke the method. Delegates help you write flexible code that can be reused in many situations. They're also the basis for events, an important .NET concept that you'll consider in the next chapter.

The first step when using a delegate is to define its *signature*. The signature is a combination of several pieces of information about a method: its return type, the number of parameters it has, and the data type of each parameter.

A delegate variable can point only to a method that matches its specific signature. In other words, the method must have the same return type, the same number of parameters, and the same data type for each parameter as the delegate. For example, if you have a method that accepts a single string parameter and another method that accepts two string parameters, you'll need to use a separate delegate type for each method.

To consider how this works in practice, assume your program has the following function:

```
Private Function TranslateEnglishToFrench(English As String) As String
    ' Code goes here.
End Function
```

This function accepts a single string argument and returns a string. With those two details in mind, you can define a delegate type that matches this signature. Here's how you would do it:

```
Private Delegate Function StringFunction(inputText As String) As String
```

Notice that the name you choose for the parameters and the name of the delegate don't matter. The only requirement is that the data types for the return value and parameters match exactly.

Once you've defined a type of delegate, you can create and assign a delegate variable at any time. Using the StringFunction delegate type, you could create a delegate variable like this:

```
Dim FunctionReference As StringFunction
```

Once you have a delegate variable, the fun begins. Using your delegate variable, you can point to any method that has the matching signature. In this example, the StringFunction delegate type requires one string parameter and returns a string. Thus, you can use the FunctionReference variable to store a reference to the TranslateEnglishToFrench() function you saw earlier. To actually store the reference to the TranslateEnglishToFrench() function, you use the AddressOf operator. Here's how to do it:

```
FunctionReference = AddressOf TranslateEnglishToFrench
```

Now that you have a delegate variable that references a function, you can invoke the function *through* the delegate. To do this, just use the delegate variable as though it were the function name.

```
Dim FrenchString As String
FrenchString = FunctionReference("Hello")
```

In the previous code example, the method that the FunctionReference delegate points to will be invoked with the parameter value "Hello," and the return value will be stored in the FrenchString variable.

The following code shows all these steps—creating a delegate variable, assigning a method, and calling the method—from start to finish.

```
' Create a delegate variable.
Dim FunctionReference As StringFunction

' Store a reference to a matching method in the delegate.
FunctionReference = AddressOf TranslateEnglishToFrench

' Run the method that FunctionReference points to.
' In this case, it will be TranslateEnglishToFrench().
Dim FrenchString As String
FrenchString = FunctionReference("Hello")
```

The value of delegates is in the extra layer of flexibility they add. It's not apparent in this example, because the same piece of code creates the delegate variable and uses it. However, in a more complex application one piece of code would create the delegate variable, and another piece of code would use it. The benefit in this scenario is that the second piece of code doesn't need to know where the delegate points. Instead, it's flexible enough to use any method that has the right signature. In the previous example, imagine a translation library that could translate between English and a variety of different languages, depending on whether the delegate it uses points to TranslateEnglishToFrench(), TranslateEnglishToSpanish(), TranslateEnglishToGerman(), and so on.

DELEGATES ARE THE BASIS OF EVENTS

Wouldn't it be nice to have a delegate that could refer to more than one function at once and invoke them both? This would allow the client application to have multiple "listeners" and notify the listeners all at once when something happens.

In fact, delegates do have this functionality, but you're more likely to see it in use with .NET events. Events, which are described in the next chapter, are based on delegates but work at a slightly higher level. In a typical ASP.NET application, you'll use events extensively, but you'll probably never work directly with delegates.

The Last Word

It's impossible to do justice to an entire language in a single chapter. However, if you've programmed before, you'll find that this chapter provides all the information you need to get started with the VB 2008 language. As you work through the full ASP.NET examples in the following chapters, you can refer to this chapter to clear up any language issues.

In the next chapter, you'll learn about more important language concepts and the object-oriented nature of .NET.

CHAPTER 3

Types, Objects, and Namespaces

.NET is thoroughly object oriented. Not only does .NET allow you to use objects, it demands it. Almost every ingredient you'll need to use to create a web application is, on some level, really a kind of object.

So how much do you need to know about object-oriented programming to write web pages in .NET? It depends on whether you want to follow existing examples and cut and paste code samples or have a deeper understanding of the way .NET works and gain more control. This book assumes that if you're willing to pick up a thousand-page book, then you're the type of programmer who excels by understanding how and why things work the way they do. It also assumes you're interested in some of the advanced ASP.NET programming tasks that *will* require class-based design, such as creating your own database component (see Chapter 23).

This chapter explains objects from the point of view of the .NET Framework. It doesn't rehash the typical object-oriented theory, because countless excellent programming books cover the subject. Instead, you'll see the types of objects .NET allows, how they're constructed, and how they fit into the larger framework of namespaces and assemblies.

The Basics of Classes

As a developer you've probably already created classes or at least heard about them. *Classes* are the code definitions for objects. The nice thing about a class is that you can use it to create as many objects as you need. For example, you might have a class that represents an XML file, which can be used to read some data. If you want to access multiple XML files at once, you can create several instances of your class, as shown in Figure 3-1. These instances are called *objects*.

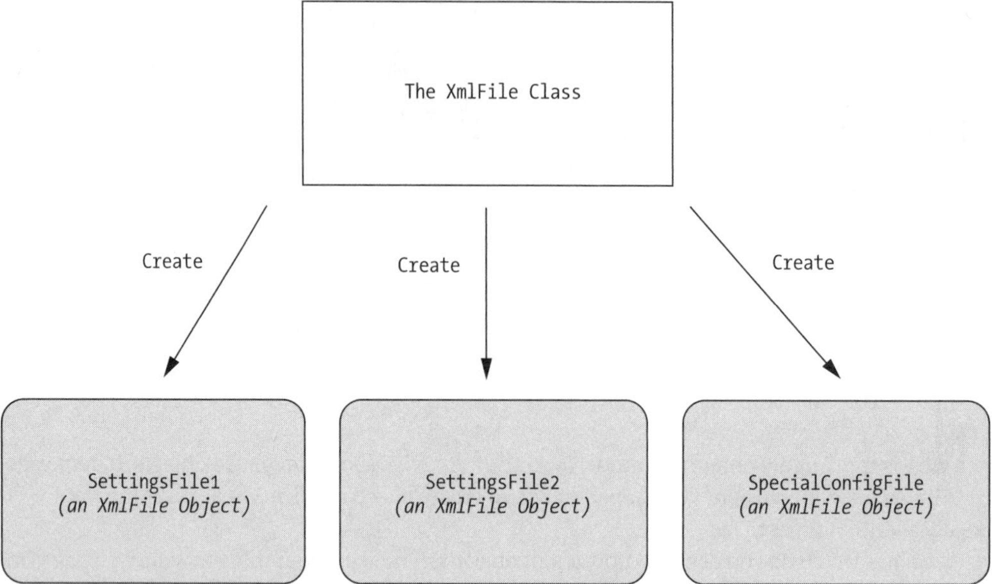

Figure 3-1. *Classes are used to create objects.*

Classes interact with each other with the help of three key ingredients:

- *Properties*: Properties allow you to access an object's data. Some properties may be read-only, so they cannot be modified, while others can be changed. For example, the previous chapter demonstrated how you can use the read-only Length property of a string object to find out how many characters are in a string.
- *Methods*: Methods allow you to perform an action on an object. Unlike properties, methods are used for actions that perform a distinct task or may change the object's state significantly. For example, to open a connection to a database, you might call the Open() method of a Connection object.
- *Events*: Events provide notification that something has happened. If you've ever programmed an ordinary desktop application in Visual Basic, you know how controls can fire events to trigger your code. For example, if a user clicks a button, the Button object fires a Click event, which your code can react to. ASP.NET controls also provide events.

Classes contain their own code and internal set of private data. Classes behave like *black boxes*, which means that when you use an object, you shouldn't waste any time wondering how it works internally or what low-level information it's using. Instead, you need to worry only about the public interface of a class, which is the set of properties, methods, and events available for you to use. Together, these elements are called class *members*.

In ASP.NET, you'll create your own custom classes to represent individual web pages. In addition, you'll create custom classes if you design separate components. For the most part, however, you'll be using prebuilt classes from the .NET class library, rather than programming your own.

Shared and Instance Members

One of the tricks about .NET classes is that you really use them in two ways. You can use some class members without creating an object first. These are called *shared* members, and they're accessed by class name. For example, you can use the shared property DateTime.Now to retrieve a DateTime object that represents the current date and time. You don't need to create a DateTime object first.

On the other hand, the majority of the DateTime members require a valid instance. For example, you can't use the AddDays() method or the Hour property without a valid object. These *instance* members have no meaning without a live object and some valid data to draw on.

The following code snippet uses shared and instance members:

```
' Get the current date using a shared property.
' Note that you use the type name DateTime.
Dim myDate As DateTime = DateTime.Now

' Use an instance method to add a day.
' Note that you need to use the object name myDate.
myDate = myDate.AddDays(1)

' The following code makes no sense.
' It tries to use the instance method AddDays() with the class name DateTime!
myDate = DateTime.AddDays(1)
```

Both properties and methods can be designated as shared. Shared properties and methods are a major part of the .NET Framework, and you will use them frequently in this book. Some classes may consist entirely of shared members (such as the Math class shown in the previous chapter), and some may use only instance members. Other classes, such as DateTime, provide a combination of the two.

The next example, which introduces a basic class, will use only instance members. This is the most common design and a good starting point.

A Simple Class

To create a class, you must define it in a class block:

```
Public Class MyClass
    ' Class code goes here.
End Class
```

You can define as many classes as you need in the same file. However, good coding practices suggest that in most cases you use a single file for each class.

Classes exist in many forms. They may represent an actual thing in the real world (as they do in most programming textbooks), they may represent some programming abstraction (such as a rectangle or color structure), or they may just be a convenient way to group related functionality (like with the Math class). Deciding what a class should represent and breaking down your code into a group of interrelated classes are part of the art of object-oriented programming.

Building a Basic Class

In the next example, you'll see how to construct a .NET class piece by piece. This class will represent a product from the catalog of an e-commerce company. The Product class will store product data, and it will include the built-in functionality needed to generate a block of HTML that displays the product on a web page. When this class is complete, you'll be able to put it to work with a sample ASP.NET test page.

Once you've defined the basic skeleton for your class, the next step is to add some basic data members. This example defines three member variables that store information about the product—namely, its name, price, and a URL that points to an image file:

```
Public Class Product
    Private name As String
    Private price As Decimal
    Private imageUrl As String
End Class
```

A local variable exists only until the current method ends. On the other hand, a *member variable* (or *field*) is declared as part of a class. It's available to all the methods in the class; it's created when the object is created; and it lives as long as the containing object lives.

When you declare a member variable, you set its *accessibility*. The accessibility determines whether other parts of your code will be able to read and alter this variable. For example, if ClassA contains a private variable, the code in ClassB will not be able to read or modify it. Only the code in ClassA will have that ability. On the other hand, if ClassA has a public variable, any other object in your application is free to read and alter the information it contains. Local variables don't support any accessibility keywords, because they can never be made available to any code outside of the current method. Generally, in a simple ASP.NET application, most of your member variables will be private because the majority of your code will be self-contained in a single web page class. As you start creating separate components to reuse functionality, however, accessibility becomes much more important. Table 3-1 explains the access levels you can use.

Table 3-1. *Accessibility Keywords*

Keyword	Accessibility
Public	Can be accessed by any class
Private	Can be accessed only by members inside the current class
Friend	Can be accessed by members in any of the classes in the current assembly (the compiled code file)
Protected	Can be accessed by methods in the current class or in any class that inherits from this class
Protected Friend	Can be accessed by members in the current application (as with Friend) *and* by the members in any class that inherits from this class (as with Protected).

The accessibility keywords don't just apply to member variables. They also apply to methods, properties, and events, all of which will be explored in this chapter.

■ **Tip** By convention, all the public pieces of your class (the class name, public events, properties and methods, and so on) should use *Pascal case*. This means the name starts with an initial capital. (The function name DoSomething() is one example of Pascal case.) On the other hand, private member variables can use any case you want. Usually, private members will adopt *camel case*. This means the name starts with an initial lowercase letter. (The variable name myInformation is one example of camel case.)

Creating an Object

When creating an object, you need to specify the New keyword. For example, the following code snippet creates a Product object (that is, an instance of the Product class) and then stores a reference to the object in the saleProduct variable:

```
Dim saleProduct As New Product()

' Optionally you could do this in two steps:
' Dim saleProduct As Product
' saleProduct = new Product()
```

If you omit the New keyword, you'll declare the variable, but you won't create the object. Here's an example:

```
Dim saleProduct As Product
```

In this case, your saleProduct variable doesn't point to any object at all. (Technically, it's Nothing, which is the VB keyword that represents a null reference.) If you try to use the saleProduct variable, you'll receive the common "null reference" error, because no object exists for you to use. When you're finished using an object, you can release it by removing all references to the object. In the previous code snippet, there is only one variable that points to the Product object—the saleProduct variable. Here's how you release the saleProduct reference:

```
saleProduct = Nothing
```

In .NET, you almost never need to use this code. That's because objects are automatically released when the appropriate variable goes out of scope. For example, if you declare the saleProduct variable inside a method, the object is released once the method ends.

■ **Tip** Just because an object is released doesn't mean the memory it uses is immediately reclaimed. The CLR uses a background task (called the *garbage collection service*) that periodically scans for released objects and reclaims the memory they hold.

In some cases, you will want to declare an object variable without actually creating an object. For example, you might want to call a function that generates an object for you, and then use the object that's returned from the function.

In order to do this, declare your variable without using the New keyword, and then assign the object to your variable. Here's an example:

```
' Declare but don't create the product.
Dim saleProduct As Product

' Call a function that accepts a numeric product ID parameter,
' and returns a Product object.
' Assign the Product object to the saleProduct variable.
saleProduct = FetchProduct(23)
```

Once you understand the concept, you can compress this code into one statement:

```
Dim saleProduct As Product = FetchProduct(23)
```

In these cases, when you aren't actually creating an object, you shouldn't use the New keyword.

Adding Properties

The simple Product class is essentially useless because your code cannot manipulate it. All its information is private and unreachable. Other classes won't be able to set or read this information.

To overcome this limitation, you could make the member variables public. Unfortunately, that approach could lead to problems because it would give other objects free access to change everything, even allowing them to apply invalid or inconsistent data. Instead, you need to add a "control panel" through which your code can manipulate Product objects in a safe way. You can do this by adding *property accessors.*

Accessors usually have two parts. The Get accessor allows your code to retrieve data from the object. The Set accessor allows your code to set the object's data. In some cases, you might omit one of these parts, such as when you want to create a property that can be examined but not modified.

Accessors are similar to any other type of method in that you can write as much code as you need. For example, your Set accessor could raise an error to alert the client code of invalid data and prevent the change from being applied. Or your Set accessor could change multiple private variables at once, thereby making sure the object's internal state remains consistent. In the Product class example, this sophistication isn't required. Instead, the property accessors just provide straightforward access to the private variables. For example, the Name property simply gets or sets the value of the _name private member variable.

Here's a revised version of the Product class that renames its private member variables (giving them an underscore at the beginning of the name) and adds three public properties to provide access to them:

```
Public Class Product
    Private _name As String
    Private _price As Decimal
    Private _imageUrl As String

    Public Property Name() As String
        Get
            Return _name
        End Get
        Set(ByVal value As String)
            _name = value
        End Set
    End Property

    Public Property Price() As Decimal
        Get
            Return _price
        End Get
        Set(ByVal value As Decimal)
            _price = value
        End Set
    End Property

    Public Property ImageUrl() As String
        Get
            Return _imageUrl
        End Get
        Set(ByVal value As String)
            _imageUrl = value
        End Set
    End Property
End Class
```

Property accessors, like any other public piece of a class, should start with an initial capital. Usually, the private variable will have a similar name, but prefixed with an underscore (as in the previous code example), or the m_ prefix (which means "member variable"). Although it's technically possible, it's not recommended to use the same name for a property as for a private variable, because it's too easy to make a mistake and refer to one when you want the other.

The client can now create and configure an instance of the class by using its properties and the familiar dot syntax. For example, if the object variable is named saleProduct, you can set the product name using the saleProduct.Name property. Here's an example:

```
Dim saleProduct As New Product()
saleProduct.Name = "Kitchen Garbage"
saleProduct.Price = 49.99D
saleProduct.ImageUrl = "http://mysite/garbage.png"
```

■ **Note** Visual Basic treats all literal decimal values (hard-coded numbers such as 49.99) as the Double data type. In the preceding code, this doesn't cause a problem because Visual Basic is able to seamlessly convert a Double into a Decimal, which is the required data type for the Product.Price property. However, if you've switched on Option Strict, this implicit conversion isn't allowed, so you need to replace 49.99 with 49.99D. The *D* character at the end of any number tells Visual Basic to interpret the number as a Decimal data type straight off.

Usually, property accessors come in pairs—that is, every property has both a Get and a Set accessor. But this isn't always the case. You can create properties that can be read but not set (which are called read-only properties), and properties that can be set but not retrieved (called write-only). All you need to do is include either the ReadOnly or the WriteOnly keyword in the property declaration, and then leave out whichever part of the property you don't need. Here's an example:

```
Public ReadOnly Property Price() As Decimal
    Get
        Return _price
    End Get
End Property
```

This technique is particularly handy if you want to create properties that don't correspond directly to a private member variable. For example, you might want to use properties that represent calculated values, or properties that are based on other properties.

Adding a Method

The current Product class consists entirely of data, which is exposed by a small set of properties. This type of class is often useful in an application. For example, you might use it to send information about a product from one function to another. However, it's more common to add functionality to your classes along with the data. This functionality takes the form of *methods*.

Methods are simply procedures or functions that are built into your class. When you call a method on an object, the method does something useful, such as return some calculated data. In this example, we'll add a GetHtml() method to the Product class. This method will return a string representing a formatted block of HTML based on the current data in the Product object. This HTML includes a heading with the product name, the product price, and an <img> element that shows the associated product picture. (You'll explore HTML more closely in Chapter 4.)

```
Public Class Product
    ' (Variables and properties omitted for clarity.)

    Public Function GetHtml() As String
        Dim htmlString As String
        htmlString = "<h1>" & Name & "</h1><br />"
        htmlString &= "<h3>Costs: " & Price.ToString() & "</h3><br />"
        htmlString &= "<img src='" & ImageUrl & "' />"
        Return htmlString
```

```
    End Function
End Class
```

All the GetHtml() method does is read the private data and format it in some attractive way. You can take this block of HTML and place it on a web page to represent the product. This really targets the class as a user interface class rather than as a pure data class or "business object."

Adding a Constructor

Currently, the Product class has a problem. Ideally, classes should ensure that instances are always in a valid state. However, unless you explicitly set all the appropriate properties, the Product object won't correspond to a valid product. This could cause an error if you try to use a method that relies on some of the data that hasn't been supplied. To solve this problem, you need to equip your class with one or more *constructors.*

A constructor is a method that automatically runs when an instance is created. In VB, the constructor is always a method with the name New().

The next code example shows a new version of the Product class. It adds a constructor that requires the product price and name as arguments.

```
Public Class Product
    ' (Additional class code omitted for clarity.)

    Public Sub New(ByVal name As String, ByVal price As Decimal)
        _name = name
        _price = price
    End Sub
End Class
```

Here's an example of the code you need to create an object based on the new Product class, using its constructor:

```
Dim saleProduct As New Product("Kitchen Garbage", 49.99D)
```

The preceding code is much leaner than the code that was required to create and initialize an instance of the previous Product class. With the help of the constructor, you can create a Product object and configure it with the basic data it needs in a single line.

If you don't create a constructor, .NET supplies a default public constructor that does nothing. If you create at least one constructor, .NET will not supply a default constructor. Thus, in the preceding example, the Product class has exactly one constructor, which is the one that is explicitly defined in code. To create a Product object, you *must* use this constructor. This restriction prevents a client from creating an object without specifying the bare minimum amount of data that's required:

```
' This will not be allowed, because there is
' no zero-argument constructor.
Dim saleProduct As New Product()
```

■ **Note** In order to create an instance of a class, you need to use a constructor. The preceding code fails because it attempts to use a zero-argument constructor, which doesn't exist in the Product class.

Most of the classes you use will have constructors that require parameters. As with ordinary methods, constructors can be overloaded with multiple versions, each providing a different set of parameters. When creating an object, you can choose the constructor that suits you best based on the information that you have available. The .NET Framework classes use overloaded constructors extensively.

Adding an Event

Classes can also use events to notify your code. To define an event in VB, you use the Event keyword, followed by the name of the event, and a list of parameters that the event will use. As with properties and methods, events can be declared with different accessibilities, although public events are the default. Usually, this is what you want, because you'll use the events to allow one object to notify another object that's an instance of a different class. Once you've defined your event, you can fire it anytime using the RaiseEvent statement.

As an illustration, the Product class example has been enhanced with a PriceChanged event that occurs whenever the Price property is modified through the property accessor. This event won't fire if code inside the class changes the underlying private name variable without going through the property accessor.

```
Public Class Product
    ' (Additional class code omitted for clarity.)

    ' Define the event.
    Public Event PriceChanged()

    Public Property Price() As Decimal
        Get
            Return _price
        End Get
        Set(value As Decimal)
            _price = value

            ' Fire the event to all listeners.
            RaiseEvent PriceChanged()
        End Set
    End Property
End Class
```

ASP.NET uses an *event-driven* programming model, so you'll soon become used to writing code that reacts to events. But unless you're creating your own components, you won't need to fire your own custom events. For an example where custom events are useful, refer to Chapter 12, which discusses how you can add an event to a user control you've created.

Handling an Event

It's quite possible that you'll create dozens of ASP.NET applications without once defining a custom event. However, you'll be hard-pressed to write a single ASP.NET web page without *handling* an event. To handle an event, you first create a method called an *event handler*. The event handler contains the code that should be executed when the event occurs. Then, you connect the event handler to the event.

To handle the PriceChanged event, you need to create an event handler. Usually, this event handler will be placed in another class, one that needs to respond to the change. The event handler needs to have the same signature as the event it's handling. In the Product example, the PriceChanged event has no parameters, so the event handler would look like the simple subroutine shown here:

```
Private Sub ChangeDetected()
    ' This code executes in response to the PriceChanged event.
End Sub
```

The next step is to hook up the event handler to the event. There are two ways to connect an event handler. The first option is to connect an event handler at runtime using the AddHandler statement. Here's an example:

```
Dim saleProduct As New Product("Kitchen Garbage", 49.99D)

' This connects the saleProduct.PriceChanged event to an event handling
' method called ChangeDetected.
AddHandler saleProduct.PriceChanged, AddressOf ChangeDetected

' Now the event will occur in response to this code:
saleProduct.Price = saleProduct.Price * 2
```

This code attaches an event handler to a method named ChangeDetected. This method is in the same class as the event hookup code shown here, and for that reason you don't need to specify the object name when you attach the event handler. If you want to connect an event to a different object, you'd need to use the dot syntax when referring the event handler method, as in myObject.ChangeDetected.

You'll notice that this code is quite similar to the delegate example in the previous chapter. In fact, events use delegates behind the scenes to keep track of the event handlers they need to notify.

■ Tip You can also detach an event handler using the RemoveHandler statement.

Declarative Event Handling

Instead of connecting events at runtime using code statements (as described in the previous section), you can connect them *declaratively*. This approach is often more convenient because it requires less code.

The first step is to declare the event-firing object at the class level. Here's an example that takes this step with the saleProduct variable:

```
Public Class EventTester

    Private saleProduct As New Product("Kitchen Garbage", 49.99D)

    Private Sub ChangeDetected()
        ' This code executes in response to the PriceChanged event.
    End Sub

    ...
End Class
```

By declaring saleProduct at the class level (rather than inside a method), you make it available for declarative event handling. Note that it isn't necessary to use the New keyword to create the object immediately, as this example does. Instead, you could create the object somewhere else in your code, as long as it's *defined* at the class level.

Once you have this basic design, the next step is to hook up your event handler. In this case, you won't use the AddHandler statement. Instead, you'll use the WithEvents keyword and the Handles clause.

The WithEvents keyword is added to the declaration of the object that raises the event, like so:

```
Private WithEvents saleProduct As New Product("Kitchen Garbage", 49.99D)
```

The Handles clause is added to the end the declaration for your event handler. It specifies the event you want to handle:

```
Private Sub ChangeDetected() Handles saleProduct.PriceChanged
```

Here's the complete code:

```
Public Class EventTester

    Private WithEvents saleProduct As New Product("Kitchen Garbage", 49.99D)

    Private Sub ChangeDetected() Handles saleProduct.PriceChanged
        ' This code executes in response to the PriceChanged event.
    End Sub

    ...
End Class
```

The difference between the declarative and the programmatic approaches to event handling is just skin deep. When you use WithEvents and Handles, the VB compiler will generate the necessary AddHandler statements to link up your event handler automatically. This approach is often more convenient than the programmatic approach, but it doesn't give you quite the same flexibility. For example, you won't have the ability to attach and detach event handlers while your program is running, which is useful in some specialized scenarios.

Visual Studio uses declarative event handling, so you'll see this technique in the web form examples in the next few chapters. However, it's worth noting that you don't need to add the WithEvents and Handles keywords yourself. Instead, Visual Studio adds the necessary code to connect all the event handlers you create.

■ **Note** In traditional Visual Basic programming, events were connected to event handlers based on the method name. In .NET, this clumsy system is abandoned. Your event handler can have any name you want, and it can even be used to handle more than one event, provided they pass the same type of information in their parameters.

Testing the Product Class

To learn a little more about how the Product class works, it helps to create a simple web page. This web page will create a Product object, get its HTML representation, and then display it in the web page. To try this example, you'll need to use the three files that are provided with the online samples in the Chapter03 directory:

- *Product.vb*: This file contains the code for the Product class. It's in the App_Code subdirectory, which allows ASP.NET to compile it automatically.
- *Garbage.jpg*: This is the image that the Product class will use.
- *Default.aspx*: This file contains the web page code that uses the Product class.

The easiest way to test this example is to use Visual Studio, because it includes an integrated web server. Without Visual Studio, you would need to create a virtual directory for this application using IIS, which is much more awkward.

Here are the steps you need to perform the test:

1. Start Visual Studio.
2. Select File ➤ Open ➤ Web Site from the menu.
3. In the Open Web Site dialog box, browse to the Chapter03 directory, select it, and click Open. This loads your project into Visual Studio.
4. Choose Debug ➤ Start Without Debugging to launch the website. Visual Studio will open a new window with your default browser and navigate to the Default.aspx page.

When the Default.aspx page executes, it creates a new Product object, configures it, and uses the GetHtml() method. The HTML is written to the web page using the Response.Write() method. Here's the code:

```
<%@ Page Language='VB' %>
<script runat='server'>
    Protected Sub Page_Load(ByVal sender As Object, ByVal e As EventArgs)
        Dim saleProduct As New Product("Kitchen Garbage", 49.99D)
        saleProduct.ImageUrl = "garbage.jpg"
        Response.Write(saleProduct.GetHtml())
    End Sub
</script>

<html>
    <head>
        <title>Product Test</title>
    </head>
    <body></body>
</html>
```

The <script> block holds a subroutine named Page_Load. This subroutine is triggered when the page is first created. Once this code is finished, the HTML is sent to the client. Figure 3-2 shows the web page you'll see.

Figure 3-2. *Output generated by a Product object*

Interestingly, the GetHtml() method is similar to how an ASP.NET web control works, but on a much cruder level. To use an ASP.NET control, you create an object (explicitly or implicitly) and configure some properties. Then ASP.NET automatically creates a web page by examining all these objects and requesting their associated HTML (by calling a hidden GetHtml() method or by doing something conceptually similar).[1] It then sends the completed page to the user. The end result is that you work with objects, instead of dealing directly with raw HTML code.

When using a web control, you see only the public interface made up of properties, methods, and events. However, understanding how class code actually works will help you master advanced development.

Now that you've seen the basics of classes and a demonstration of how you can use a class, it's time to introduce a little more theory about .NET objects and revisit the basic data types introduced in the previous chapter.

Value Types and Reference Types

In Chapter 2, you learned how simple data types such as dates and integers are actually objects created from the class library. This allows some impressive tricks, such as built-in string handling and date calculation. However, simple data types differ from more complex objects in one important way. Simple data types are *value types,* while classes are *reference types.*

This means a variable for a simple data type contains the actual information you put in it (such as the number 7). On the other hand, object variables actually store a reference that points to a location in memory where the full object is stored. In most cases, .NET masks you from this underlying reality, and in many programming tasks you won't notice the difference. However, in three cases you will notice that object variables act a little differently than ordinary data types: in assignment operations, in equality testing, and when passing parameters.

Assignment Operations

When you assign a simple data variable to another simple data variable, the contents of the variable are copied:

```
integerA = integerB    ' integerA now has a copy of the contents of integerB.
                       ' There are two duplicate integers in memory.
```

Reference types work a little differently. Reference types tend to deal with larger amounts of data. Copying the entire contents of a reference type object could slow down an application, particularly if you are performing multiple assignments. For that reason, when you assign a reference type you copy the reference that *points* to the object, not the full object content:

```
' Create a new Product object.
Dim productVariable1 As New Product()

' Declare a second variable.
Dim productVariable2 As Product
productVariable2 = productVariable1

' productVariable1 and productVariable2 now both point to the same thing.
' There is one object and two ways to access it.
```

1. Actually, the ASP.NET engine calls a method named Render() in every web control.

The consequences of this behavior are far ranging. This example modifies the Product object using productVariable2:

```
productVariable2.Price = 25.99D
```

You'll find that productVariable1.Price is set to 25.99. Of course, this only makes sense because productVariable1 and productVariable2 are two variables that point to the same in-memory object.

If you really do want to copy an object (not a reference), you need to create a new object, and then initialize its information to match the first object. Some objects provide a Clone() method that allows you to easily copy the object. One example is the DataSet, which is used to store information from a database.

Equality Testing

A similar distinction between reference types and value types appears when you compare two variables. When you compare value types (such as integers), you're comparing the contents:

```
If integerA = integerB Then
    ' This is true as long as the integers have the same content.
End If
```

When you compare reference type variables, you're actually testing whether they're the same instance. In other words, you're testing whether the references are pointing to the same object in memory, not if their contents match. VB emphasizes this difference by forcing you to use the Is keyword to compare reference types. Using the equals (=) sign will generate a compile-time error.

```
If productVariable1 Is productVariable2 Then
    ' This is True if both productVariable1 and productVariable2
    ' point to the same thing.
    ' This is False if they are separate objects, even if they have
    ' identical content.
End If
```

Passing Parameters by Reference and by Value

You can use two types of method parameters. The standard type is *pass-by-value*. When you use pass-by-value parameters, the method receives a copy of the parameter data. That means that if the method modifies the parameter, this change won't affect the calling code. By default, all parameters are pass-by-value. (Visual Studio also inserts the ByVal keyword automatically to make that fact explicit.)

The second type of parameter is *pass-by-reference*. With pass-by-reference, the method accesses the parameter value directly. If a method changes the value of a pass-by-reference parameter, the original object is also modified.

To get a better understanding of the difference, consider the following code, which shows a method that uses a parameter named number. This code uses the ByVal keyword to indicate that number should be passed by value:

```
Private Sub ProcessNumber(ByVal number As Integer)
    number *= 2
End Sub
```

Here's how you can call ProcessNumber():

```
Dim num As Integer = 10
ProcessNumber(num)          ' When this call completes, Num will still be 10.
```

Here's what happens. When this code calls ProcessNumber() it passes a copy of the num variable. This copy is multiplied by two. However, the variable in the calling code isn't affected at all.

This behavior changes when you use the ByRef keyword, as shown here:

```
Private Sub ProcessNumber(ByRef number As Integer)
    number *= 2
End Sub
```

Now when the method modifies this parameter (multiplying it by 2), the calling code is also affected:

```
Dim num As Integer = 10
ProcessNumber(num)          ' Once this call completes, Num will be 20.
```

The difference between ByVal and ByRef is straightforward when you're using value types, such as integers. However, if you use reference types, such as a Product object or an array, you won't see this behavior. The reason is because the entire object isn't passed in the parameter. Instead, it's just the *reference* that's transmitted. This is much more efficient for large objects (it saves having to copy a large block of memory), but it doesn't always lead to the behavior you expect.

To understand the difference, consider this method:

```
Private Sub ProcessProduct(ByVal prod As Product)
    prod.Price *= 2
End Sub
```

This code accepts a Product object and increases the price by a factor of 2. Because the Product object is passed by value, you might reasonably expect that the ProcessProduct() method receives a copy of the Product object. However, this isn't the case. Instead, the ProcessProduct() method gets a copy of the *reference*. However, this new reference still points to the same in-memory Product object. That means that the change shown in this example will affect the calling code.

Reviewing .NET Types

So far, the discussion has focused on simple data types and classes. The .NET class library is actually composed of *types*, which is a catchall term that includes several object-like relatives:

Classes: This is the most common type in .NET Framework. Strings and arrays are two examples of .NET classes, although you can easily create your own.

Structures: Structures, like classes, can include fields, properties, methods, and events. Unlike classes, they are value types, which alters the way they behave with assignment and comparison operations. Structures also lack some of the more advanced class features (such as inheritance) and are generally simpler and smaller. Integers, dates, and characters are all structures.

Enumerations: An enumeration defines a set of integer constants with descriptive names. Enumerations were introduced in the previous chapter.

Delegates: A delegate is a method pointer that allows you to invoke a method indirectly. Delegates are the foundation for .NET event handling and were introduced in the previous chapter.

Interfaces: They define contracts to which a class must adhere. Interfaces are an advanced technique of object-oriented programming, and they're useful when standardizing how objects interact. Interfaces aren't discussed in this book.

WOULD THE REAL REFERENCE TYPES PLEASE STAND UP?

Occasionally, a class can override its behavior to act more like a value type. For example, the String type is a full-featured class, not a simple value type. (This is required to make strings efficient, because they can contain a variable amount of data.) However, the String type overrides its equality and assignment operations so that these operations work like those of a simple value type. This makes the String type work in the way that programmers intuitively expect. Arrays, on the other hand, are reference types through and through. If you assign one array variable to another, you copy the reference, not the array (although the Array class also provides a Clone() method that returns a duplicate array to allow true copying).

Table 3-2 sets the record straight and explains a few common types.

Table 3-2. *Common Reference and Value Types*

Data Type	Nature	Behavior
Int32, Decimal, Single, Double, and all other basic numeric types	Value Type	Equality and assignment operations work with the variable contents, not a reference.
DateTime, TimeSpan	Value Type	Equality and assignment operations work with the variable contents, not a reference.
Char, Byte, and Boolean	Value Type	Equality and assignment operations work with the variable contents, not a reference.
String	Reference Type	Equality and assignment operations appear to work with the variable contents, not a reference.
Array	Reference Type	Equality and assignment operations work with the reference, not the contents.

Understanding Namespaces and Assemblies

Whether you realize it at first, every piece of code in .NET exists inside a .NET type (typically a class). In turn, every type exists inside a namespace. Figure 3-3 shows this arrangement for your own code and the DateTime class. Keep in mind that this is an extreme simplification—the System namespace alone is stocked with several hundred classes. This diagram is designed only to show you the layers of organization.

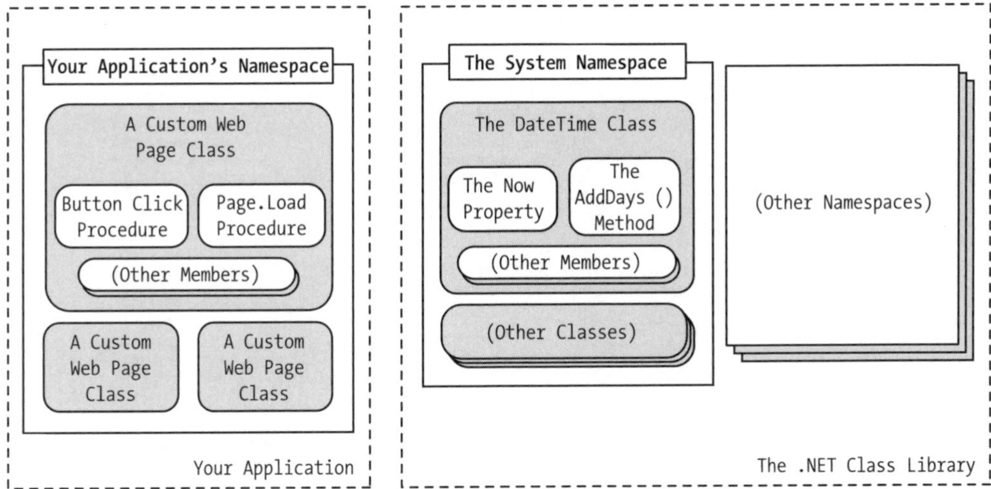

Figure 3-3. *A look at two namespaces*

Namespaces can organize all the different types in the class library. Without namespaces, these types would all be grouped into a single long and messy list. This sort of organization is practical for a small set of information, but it would be impractical for the thousands of types included with .NET.

Many of the chapters in this book introduce new .NET classes and namespaces. For example, in the chapters on web controls, you'll learn how to use the objects in the System.Web.UI namespace. In the chapters about web services, you'll study the types in the System.Web.Services namespace. For databases, you'll turn to the System.Data namespace. In fact, you've already learned a little about one namespace: the basic System namespace that contains all the simple data types explained in the previous chapter.

To continue your exploration after you've finished the book, you'll need to turn to the Visual Studio Help reference, which painstakingly documents the properties, methods, and events of every class in every namespace (see Figure 3-4). If you have Visual Studio installed, you can view the Visual Studio Help by selecting Start ➤ Programs ➤ Microsoft Visual Studio 2008 ➤ Microsoft Visual Studio 2008 Documentation (the exact path depends on the version of Visual Studio you've installed). You can find class reference information on the Contents tab, grouped by namespace, under the .NET Development ➤ .NET Framework SDK ➤ .NET Framework ➤ .NET Framework Class Library node.

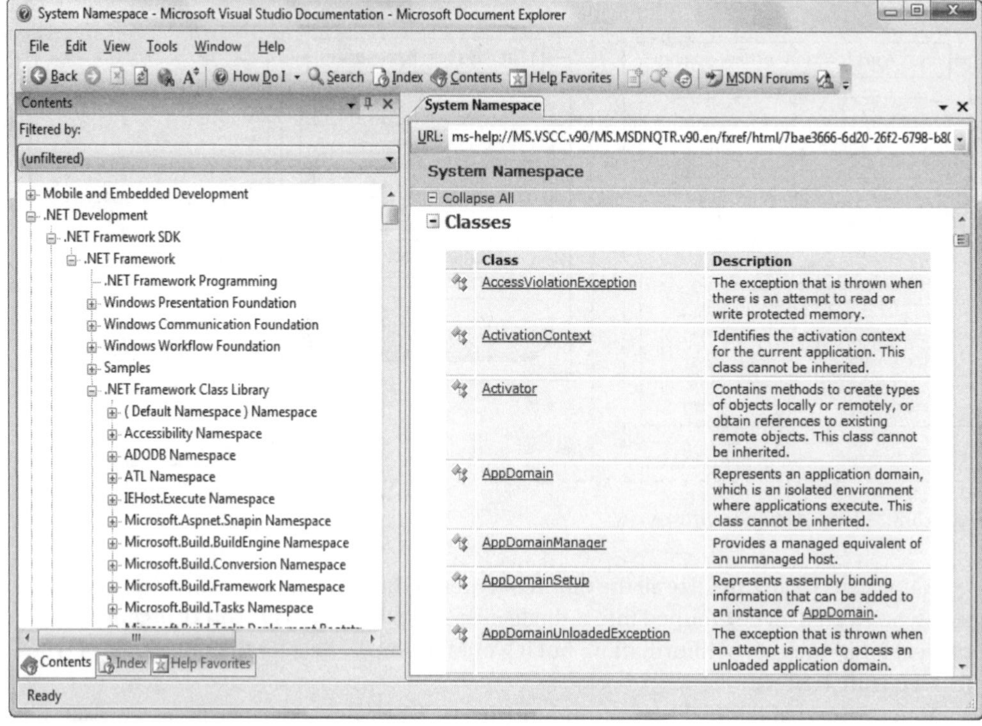

Figure 3-4. *The Class Library reference in the Visual Studio Help*

Using Namespaces

Often when you write ASP.NET code, you'll just use the namespace that Visual Studio creates automatically. If, however, you want to organize your code into multiple namespaces, you can define the namespace using a simple block structure, as shown here:

```
Namespace MyCompany

    Namespace MyApp

        Public Class Product
            ' Code goes here.
        End Class

    End Namespace

End Namespace
```

In the preceding example, the Product class is in the namespace MyCompany.MyApp. Code inside this namespace can access the Product class by name. Code outside it needs to use the fully qualified name, as in MyCompany.MyApp.Product. This ensures that you can use the components from various third-party developers without worrying about a name collision. If those developers follow the recommended naming standards, their classes will always be in a namespace that uses the name of their company and software product. The fully qualified name of a class will then almost certainly be unique.

Namespaces don't take an accessibility keyword and can be nested as many layers deep as you need. Nesting is purely cosmetic—for instance, in the previous example, no special relationship exists between the MyCompany namespace and the MyApp namespace. In fact, you could create the namespace MyCompany.MyApp using this syntax without using nesting:

```
Namespace MyCompany.MyApp

    Public Class Product
        ' Code goes here.
    End Class

End Namespace
```

You can declare the same namespace in various code files. In fact, more than one project can even use the same namespace. Namespaces are really nothing more than convenient, logical containers that help you organize your classes.

Importing Namespaces

Having to type long, fully qualified names is certain to tire your fingers and create overly verbose code. To simplify matters, it's standard practice to import the namespaces you want to use. When you import a namespace, you don't need to type the fully qualified type names. Instead, you can use the types in that namespace as though they were defined locally.

To import a namespace, you use the Imports statement. These statements must appear as the first lines in your code file, outside of any namespaces or classes (and after any Option statements, such as Option Strict):

```
Imports MyCompany.MyApp
```

Consider the situation without importing a namespace:

```
Dim salesProduct As New MyCompany.MyApp.Product()
```

It's much more manageable when you import the MyCompany.MyApp namespace. Once you do, you can use this shortened syntax instead:

```
Dim salesProduct As New Product()
```

Importing namespaces is really just a convenience. It has no effect on the performance of your application. In fact, whether you use namespace imports, the compiled IL code will look the same. That's because the language compiler will translate your relative class references into fully qualified class names when it generates an EXE or a DLL file.

Assemblies

You might wonder what gives you the ability to use the class library namespaces in a .NET program. Are they hardwired directly into the language? The truth is that all .NET classes are contained in *assemblies*. Assemblies are the physical files that contain compiled code. Typically, assembly files have the extension .exe if they are stand-alone applications, or .dll if they're reusable components.

■ **Tip** The .dll extension is also used for code that needs to be executed (or *hosted*) by another type of program. When your web application is compiled, it's turned into a DLL file, because your code doesn't represent a stand-alone application. Instead, the ASP.NET engine executes it when a web request is received.

A strict relationship doesn't exist between assemblies and namespaces. An assembly can contain multiple namespaces. Conversely, more than one assembly file can contain classes in the same namespace. Technically, namespaces are a *logical* way to group classes. Assemblies, however, are a *physical* package for distributing code.

The .NET classes are actually contained in a number of assemblies. For example, the basic types in the System namespace come from the mscorlib.dll assembly. Many ASP.NET types are found in the System.Web.dll assembly. In addition, you might want to use other, third-party assemblies. Often, assemblies and namespaces have the same names. For example, you'll find the namespace System.Web in the assembly file System.Web.dll. However, this is a convenience, not a requirement.

When compiling an application, you need to tell the language compiler what assemblies the application uses. By default, a wide range of .NET assemblies is automatically made available to ASP.NET applications. If you need to use additional assemblies, you need to define them in a configuration file for your website. Visual Studio makes this process seamless, letting you add assembly references to the configuration file using the Website ➤ Add Reference command. You'll use the Add Reference command in Chapter 23.

Advanced Class Programming

Part of the art of object-oriented programming is determining object relations. For example, you could create a Product object that contains a ProductFamily object or a Car object that contains four Wheel objects. To create this sort of object relationship, all you need to do is define the appropriate variable or properties in the class. This type of relationship is called *containment* (or *aggregation*).

For example, the following code shows a ProductCatalog class, which holds an array of Product objects:

```
Public Class ProductCatalog
    Private _products() As Product

    ' (Other class code goes here.)
End Class
```

In ASP.NET programming, you'll find special classes called *collections* that have no purpose other than to group various objects. Some collections also allow you to sort and retrieve objects using a unique name. In the previous chapter, you saw an example with the ArrayList from the System.Collections namespace, which provides a dynamically resizable array. Here's how you might use the ArrayList to modify the ProductCatalog class:

```
Public Class ProductCatalog
    Private _products As New ArrayList()

    ' (Other class code goes here.)
End Class
```

This approach has benefits and disadvantages. It makes it easier to add and remove items from the list, but it also removes a useful level of error checking, because the ArrayList supports any type of object. You'll learn more about this issue later in this chapter (in the "Generics" section).

In addition, classes can have a different type of relationship known as *inheritance*.

Inheritance

Inheritance is a form of code reuse. It allows one class to acquire and extend the functionality of another class. For example, you could create a class called TaxableProduct that inherits (or *derives*) from Product. The TaxableProduct class would gain all the same fields, methods, properties, and events of the Product class. You could then add additional members that relate to taxation:

```
Public Class TaxableProduct
    Inherits Product

    Private _taxRate As Decimal = 1.15D

    Public ReadOnly Property TotalPrice() As Decimal
        Get
            ' The code can access the Price property because it's
            ' a public member of base Product class.
            Return (Price * _taxRate)
            ' The code cannot access the private _price variable, however,
            ' because it's a private member of the base class.
        End Get
    End Property

End Class
```

This technique is often less useful than you might expect. In an ordinary application, most classes use containment and other relationships instead of inheritance, which can complicate life needlessly without delivering many benefits. Dan Appleman, a renowned .NET programmer, once described inheritance as "the coolest feature you'll almost never use."

However, you'll see inheritance at work in ASP.NET in at least one place. Inheritance allows you to create a custom class that inherits the features of a class in the .NET class library. For example, when you create a custom web form, you actually inherit from a basic Page class to gain the standard set of features. Similarly, when you create a custom web service, you inherit from the WebService class. You'll see this type of inheritance throughout this book.

There are many more subtleties of class-based programming with inheritance. For example, you can override parts of a base class, prevent classes from being inherited, or create a class that must be used for inheritance and can't be directly created. However, these topics aren't covered in this book, and they aren't required to build ASP.NET applications. For more information about these language features, consult a more detailed book that covers the Visual Basic language, like Andrew Troelsen's *Pro VB 9.0 and the .NET 3.5 Framework,* Third Edition (Apress, 2007).

Shared Members

The beginning of this chapter introduced the idea of shared properties and methods, which can be used without a live object. Shared members are often used to provide helper functionality (such as conversion routines, validation tests, or miscellaneous pieces of information) that you'll want to access without being forced to create an object. The .NET class library uses shared members heavily (as with the System.Math class explored in the previous chapter).

Shared members have a wide variety of possible uses. Sometimes they provide basic conversions and utility functions that support a class. To create a shared property or method, you just need to use the Shared keyword right after the accessibility keyword.

The following example shows a TaxableProduct class that contains a shared TaxRate property and private variable. This means there is one copy of the tax rate information, and it applies to all TaxableProduct objects.

```
Public Class TaxableProduct
    Inherits Product

    ' (Other class code omitted for clarity.)

    Private Shared _taxRate As Decimal = 1.15D

    ' TaxRate is shared, which means that you can call
    ' TaxableProduct.TaxRate, even without an object.
    Public Shared Property TaxRate() As Decimal
        Get
            Return _taxRate
        End Get
        Set(value As Decimal)
            _taxRate = value
        End Set
    End Property

End Class
```

You can now get or set the tax rate information directly from the class, without needing to create an object first:

```
' Change the TaxRate. This will affect all TotalPrice calculations for any
' TaxableProduct object.
TaxableProduct.TaxRate = 1.24D
```

Shared data isn't tied to the lifetime of an object. In fact, it's available throughout the life of the entire application. This means shared members are the closest thing .NET programmers have to global data.

A shared member can't access an instance member. To access a nonshared member, it needs an actual instance of your object.

Casting Objects

Object variables can be converted with the same syntax that's used for simple data types. This process is called *casting*. When you perform casting, you don't actually change anything about an object—in fact, it remains the exact same blob of binary data floating somewhere in memory. What you change is the variable that points to the object—in other words, the way your code "sees" the object. This is important, because the way your code sees an object determines what you can do with that object.

An object variable can be cast into one of three things: itself, an interface that it supports, or a base class from which it inherits. You can't cast an object variable into a string or an integer. Instead, you need to call a conversion method, if it's available, such as ToString() or Parse().

As you've already seen, the TaxableProduct class derives from Product. That means you cast a TaxableProduct reference to a Product reference, as shown here:

```
' Create a TaxableProduct.
Dim theTaxableProduct() As TaxableProduct
theTaxableProduct = New TaxableProduct()

' Cast the TaxableProduct reference to a Product reference.
Dim theProduct As Product
theProduct = theTaxableProduct
```

You don't lose any information when you perform this casting. There is still just one object in memory (with two variables pointing to it), and this object really *is* a TaxableProduct. However, when you use the variable theProduct to access your TaxableProduct object, you'll be limited to the properties and methods that are defined in the Product class. That means code like this won't work:

```
' This code generates a compile-time error.
Dim TotalPrice As Decimal = theProduct.TotalPrice
```

Even though theProduct actually holds a reference that points to a TaxableProduct, and even though the TaxableProduct has a TotalPrice property, you can't access it through theProduct. That's because theProduct treats the object it refers to as an ordinary Product.

You can also cast in the reverse direction—for example, cast a Product reference to a TaxableProduct reference. The trick here is that this only works if the object that's in memory really is a TaxableProduct. This code is correct:

```
Dim theProduct As New TaxableProduct()

Dim theTaxableProduct() As TaxableProduct
theTaxableProduct = CType(theProduct, TaxableProduct)
```

But this code generates a runtime error when the last line is executed:

```
Dim theProduct As New Product()

Dim theTaxableProduct() As TaxableProduct
theTaxableProduct = CType(theProduct, TaxableProduct)
```

Note When casting an object from a base class to a derived class, as in this example, you must use the CType() function that you learned about in Chapter 2. This is a safeguard designed to highlight the fact that casting is taking place. It's required because this casting operation might fail.

Incidentally, you can check if you have the right type of object before you attempt to cast with the help of the TypeOf keyword:

```
Dim theTaxableProduct As TaxableProduct

If TypeOf theProduct Is TaxableProduct Then
    ' It's safe to cast the reference.
    theTaxableProduct = CType(theProduct, TaxableProduct)
End If
```

Note One of the reasons casting is used is to facilitate more reusable code. For example, you might design an application that uses the Product object. That application is actually able to handle an instance of any Product-derived class. Your application doesn't need to distinguish between all the different derived classes (TaxableProduct, NonTaxableProduct, PromoProduct, and so on); it can work seamlessly with all of them.

At this point, it might seem that being able to convert objects is a fairly specialized technique that will be required only when you're using inheritance. This isn't always true. Object conversions are also required when you use some particularly flexible classes.

One example is the ArrayList class introduced in the previous chapter. The ArrayList is designed in such a way that it can store any type of object. To have this ability, it treats all objects in the same way—as instances of the root System.Object class. (All classes in .NET inherit from System.Object at some point, even if this relationship isn't explicitly defined in the class code.) The end result is that when you retrieve an object from an ArrayList collection, you need to cast it from a System.Object to its real type, as shown here:

```
' Create the ArrayList.
Dim products As New ArrayList()

' Add several Product objects.
products.Add(product1)
products.Add(product2)
products.Add(product3)

' Retrieve the first item, with casting.
Dim retrievedProduct As Product = CType(products(0), Product)

' This works.
Response.Write(retrievedProduct.GetHtml())

' Retrieve the first item, as an object. This doesn't require casting,
' but you won't be able to use any of the Product methods or properties.
Dim retrievedObject As Object = products(0)

' This generates an error. There is no Object.GetHtml() method.
Response.Write(retrievedObject.GetHtml())
```

As you can see, if you don't perform the casting, you won't be able to use the methods and properties of the object you retrieve. You'll find many cases like this in .NET code, where your code is handed one of several possible object types and it's up to you to cast the object to the correct type in order to use its full functionality.

Note Occasionally, you might run into a custom method that "converts" an object to another data type. For example, you can use the ToString() method in many objects to get a string that's based on that object. However, this process isn't really a conversion—instead, you're generating a *representation* of your object. This representation probably doesn't preserve all the data of your original object, and usually the conversion is one-way only.

Partial Classes

Partial classes give you the ability to split a single class into more than one source code (.vb) file. For example, if the Product class becomes particularly long and intricate, you might decide to break it into two pieces, as shown here:

```
' This part is stored in file Product1.vb.
Public Partial Class Product
    Private _name As String
    Private _price As Decimal
    Private _imageUrl As String

    Public Property Name() As String
        Get
            Return _name
        End Get
        Set(ByVal value As String)
            _name = value
        End Set
    End Property

    Public Property Price() As Decimal
        Get
            Return _price
        End Get
        Set(ByVal value As Decimal)
            _price = value
        End Set
    End Property

    Public Property ImageUrl() As String
        Get
            Return _imageUrl
        End Get
        Set(ByVal value As String)
            _imageUrl = value
        End Set
    End Property

    Public Sub New(ByVal name As String, ByVal price As Decimal)
        _name = name
        _price = price
    End Sub
End Class

' This part is stored in file Product2.vb.
Public Partial Class Product
    Public Function GetHtml() As String
        Dim htmlString As String
        htmlString = "<h1>" & _name & "</h1><br />"
        htmlString &= "<h3>Costs: " & _price.ToString() & "</h3><br />"
        htmlString &= "<img src='" & _imageUrl & "' />"
        Return htmlString
```

```
    End Function
End Class
```

A partial class behaves the same as a normal class. This means every method, property, and variable you've defined in the class is available everywhere, no matter which source file contains it. When you compile the application, the compiler tracks down each piece of the Product class and assembles it into a complete unit. It doesn't matter what you name the source code files, so long as you keep the class name consistent.

Partial classes don't offer much in the way of solving programming problems, but they can be useful if you have extremely large, unwieldy classes. The real purpose of partial classes in .NET is to hide automatically generated designer code by placing it in a separate file from your code. Visual Studio uses this technique when you create web pages for a web application and forms for a Windows application.

■ **Tip** Technically, you only need to use the Partial keyword on *one* of the class declarations. As long as the compiler finds one partial definition, it assumes all the others are partial as well.

Generics

Generics are a more subtle and powerful feature than partial classes. Generics allow you to create classes that are parameterized by type. In other words, you create a class template that supports any type. When you instantiate that class, you specify the type you want to use, and from that point on, your object is "locked in" to the type you chose.

To understand how this works, it's easiest to consider some of the .NET classes that support generics. In the previous chapter (and earlier in this chapter), you saw how the ArrayList class allows you to create a dynamically sized collection that expands as you add items and shrinks as you remove them. The ArrayList has one weakness, however—it supports any type of object. This makes it extremely flexible, but it also means you can inadvertently run into an error. For example, imagine you use an ArrayList to track a catalog of products. You intend to use the ArrayList to store Product objects, but there's nothing to stop a piece of misbehaving code from inserting strings, integers, or any arbitrary object in the ArrayList. Here's an example:

```
' Create the ArrayList.
Dim products As New ArrayList()

' Add several Product objects.
products.Add(product1)
products.Add(product2)
products.Add(product3)

' Notice how you can still add other types to the ArrayList.
products.Add("This string doesn't belong here.")
```

The solution is a new List collection class. Like the ArrayList, the List class is flexible enough to store different objects in different scenarios. But because it uses generics, you must lock it into a specific type whenever you instantiate a List object. To do this, you specify the class you want to use in parentheses, preceded by the word "Of." So if you want to create a collection of products, you need this code statement:

```
' Create the List for storing Product objects.
Dim products As New List(Of Product)()
```

Now you can add only Product objects to the collection:

```
' Add several Product objects.
products.Add(product1)
products.Add(product2)
products.Add(product3)

' This line fails. In fact, it won't even compile.
products.Add("This string can't be inserted.")
```

You can find the List class, and many more collections that use generics, in the System.Collections.Generic namespace. (The original ArrayList resides in the System.Collections namespace.)

■ **Note** Now that you've seen the advantage of the List class, you might wonder why .NET includes the ArrayList at all. In truth, the ArrayList is still useful if you really do need to store different types of objects in one place (which isn't terribly common). However, the real answer is that generics weren't implemented in .NET until version 2.0, so many existing classes don't use them because of backward compatibility.

You can also create your own classes that are parameterized by type, such as the List collection. Creating classes that use generics is beyond the scope of this book, but you can find a solid overview in the Visual Studio Help. Look for the "generics [Visual Basic]" index entry.

The Last Word

At its simplest, object-oriented programming is the idea that your code should be organized into separate classes. If followed carefully, this approach leads to code that's easier to alter, enhance, debug, and reuse. Now that you know the basics of object-oriented programming, you can take a tour of the premier ASP.NET development tool: Visual Studio.

■ **Note** In the previous two chapters, you learned the essentials about VB and object-oriented programming. The VB language continues to evolve, and there are many more advanced language features that you haven't seen in these two chapters. If you want to continue your exploration of VB and become a language guru, you can visit Microsoft's VB Developer Center online at `http://msdn2.microsoft.com/en-us/vbasic`, or you can refer to a more in-depth book about VB, such as the excellent and very in-depth *Pro VB 2008 and the .NET 3.5 Framework* (Apress, 2007).

PART 2

Developing ASP.NET Applications

CHAPTER 4

■ ■ ■

Visual Studio

In the ancient days of web programming, developers created web pages with simple text editors such as Notepad. Other choices were available, but each suffered from its own quirks and limitations. The standard was a gloves-off approach of raw HTML with blocks of code inserted wherever necessary.

Visual Studio changes all that. First, it's extensible and can even work in tandem with other straight HTML editors such as Microsoft Expression Web or Adobe Dreamweaver. In other words, you can do the heavy-duty coding with Visual Studio, but use another web design tool to make everything look pretty. Second, Visual Studio includes indispensable time-saving features. For example, it gives you the ability to drag and drop web pages into existence and troubleshoot misbehaving code. Visual Studio even includes a built-in test web server, which allows you to create and test a complete ASP.NET website without worrying about web server settings.

In this chapter, you'll learn how to create a web application using Visual Studio. Along the way, you'll take a look at the anatomy of an ASP.NET web form, and review the essentials of XHTML. You'll also learn how IntelliSense can dramatically reduce the number of errors you'll make, and how to use Visual Studio's legendary single-step debugger to look under the hood and "watch" your program in action. By the end of this chapter, you'll be well acquainted with the most important tool in any ASP.NET developer's toolkit (Visual Studio) and you'll understand the basic principles of web development with ASP.NET.

The Promise of Visual Studio

All .NET applications are built from plain-text source files. VB code is stored in .vb files and C# code is stored in .cs files, regardless of whether this code is designed for a stand-alone Windows application or the Web. Despite this fact, you'll rarely find VB or C# developers creating Windows applications by hand in a text editor. The process is not only tiring, but it also opens the door to a host of possible errors that a design tool could catch easily. The same is true for ASP.NET programmers. Although you can write your web page classes and code your web page controls by hand, you'll spend hours developing and testing your code. Instead, it makes sense to use one of the many editions of Visual Studio.

Visual Studio is an indispensable tool for developers on any platform. It provides several impressive benefits:

Integrated error checking: Visual Studio can detect a wide range of problems, such as data type conversion errors, missing namespaces or classes, and undefined variables. As you type, errors are detected, underlined, and added to an error list for quick reference.

The web form designer: To create a web page in Visual Studio, you simply drag ASP.NET controls to the appropriate location and configure their properties. Visual Studio does the heavy lifting and automatically creates the actual web page markup.

An integrated web server: To host an ASP.NET web application, you need web server software such as IIS (Internet Information Services), which waits for browser requests and serves the appropriate pages. Setting up your web server isn't difficult, but it is inconvenient. Thanks to the integrated development web server in Visual Studio, you can run a website directly from the design environment. (Of course, you'll still need to deploy your application to a real web server when it's finished, as you'll see in Chapter 9.)

Developer productivity enhancements: Visual Studio makes coding quick and efficient, with a collapsible code display, automatic statement completion, and color-coded syntax. You can even create sophisticated macro programs that automate repetitive tasks.

Fine-grained debugging: Visual Studio's integrated debugger allows you to watch code execution, pause your program at any point, and inspect the contents of any variable. These debugging tools can save endless headaches when writing complex code routines.

Complete extensibility: You can use macros, change project templates, and even add your own custom add-ins to Visual Studio. And even if you don't intend to use these features yourself, you might still want to use handy third-party utilities that depend on them.

■ **Note** Almost all the tips and techniques you learn in this chapter will work equally well with the Standard Edition, Professional Edition, and Team Edition of Visual Studio 2008 as well as Visual Web Developer 2008 Express Edition.

Creating Websites

You start Visual Studio by selecting Start ➤ Programs ➤ Microsoft Visual Studio 2008 ➤ Microsoft Visual Studio 2008. When Visual Studio first loads, it shows the Start Page (Figure 4-1).

The Start Page includes a list of recently opened projects. You can click a link in this list to quickly resume your work where you last left off. The Start Page also includes links to online developer content from Microsoft's MSDN website. Although you're free to ignore this content, you might find an interesting article, a handy code example, or a nifty add-on that you'll want to try out. (If your surfing habits are a bit more traditional, you can find the same content online. A good starting point is the ASP.NET Developer Center at `http://msdn.microsoft.com/asp.net`.)

To do anything practical with Visual Studio, you need to create a web application. The following sections show you how.

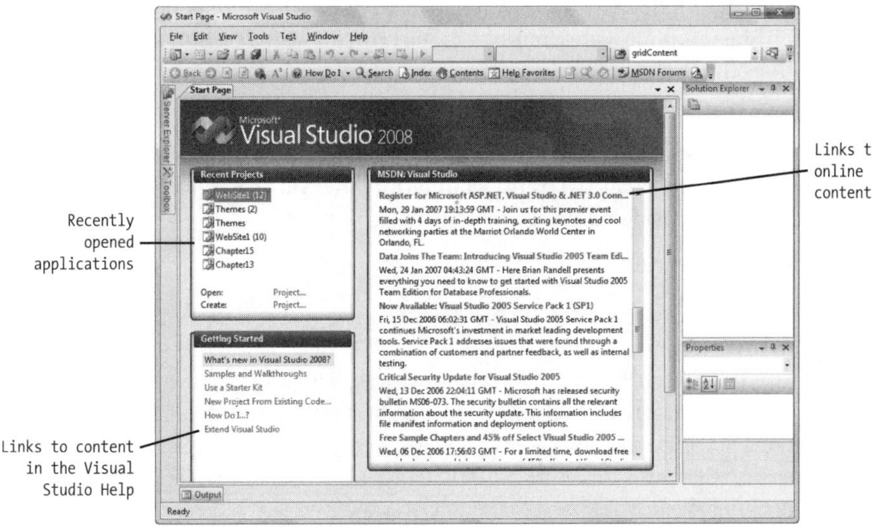

Figure 4-1. *The Visual Studio Start Page*

Creating a New Web Application

To create your first Visual Studio application, follow these steps:

1. Select File ➤ New ➤ Web Site from the Visual Studio menu. The New Web Site dialog box (shown in Figure 4-2) will appear.

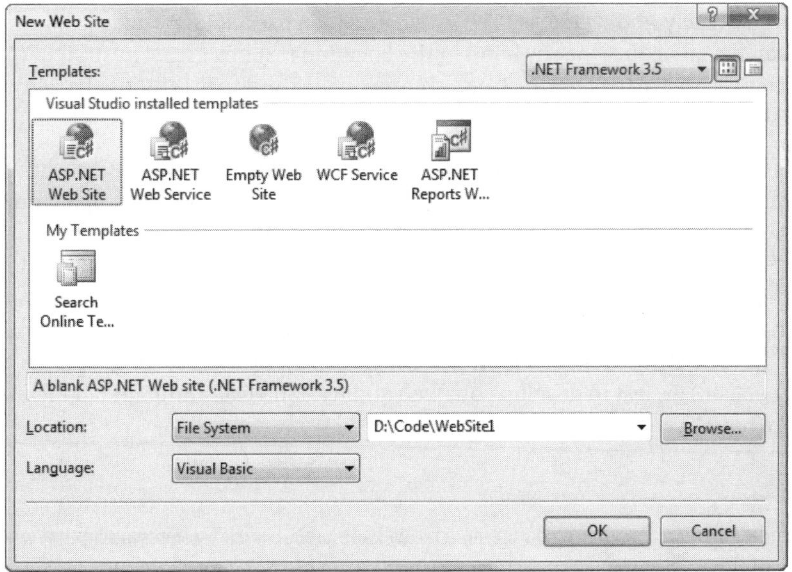

Figure 4-2. *The New Web Site dialog box*

2. Choose the type of application. To build an ordinary ASP.NET application, select the ASP.NET Web Site template. Other templates start you off with additional files or configuration settings that help you build a more specialized type of website.

3. Choose the version of .NET that you want to use. Usually, you'll pick .NET Framework 3.5 from the list in the top-right corner of the New Web Site dialog box. However, you can also use Visual Studio to create web applications for older versions of .NET, as described in the "Mutlitargeting" sidebar.

MULTITARGETING

Visual Studio 2008 supports *multitargeting*, which means you can build web applications that are intended for .NET 2.0, .NET 3.0, or .NET 3.5. You pick the version you want to use in the top-right corner of the New Web Site dialog box. Changing this option changes the configuration of your website.

Interestingly enough, all three versions of .NET share exactly the same ASP.NET engine, which hasn't changed since .NET 2.0. The difference is the extra features that are piled on. In a .NET 3.0 application, you can use the new WCF (Windows Communication Foundation) features to build services. In a .NET 3.5 application, you can use a few new ASP.NET controls and the ASP.NET AJAX toolkit (which is discussed in Chapter 25). In this book, we assume you're using the latest and greatest version of .NET. However, most of the features that you'll learn about work in exactly the same way with .NET 2.0 or .NET 3.0 as they do with .NET 3.5.

Incidentally, you can also change the version of .NET that you're using after you've created your website. To pull this off, choose Website ➤ Start Options from the menu. Then, choose the Build group of settings and make a different selection in the Target Framework list.

4. Choose a location for the website. The location specifies where the website files will be stored. Typically, you'll choose File System and then use a folder on the local computer. You can type in a directory by hand in the Location text box and skip straight to step 6. Alternatively, you can click the Browse button, which shows the Choose Location dialog box (see Figure 4-3) that's discussed in step 5.

5. Using the Choose Location dialog box, browse to the directory where you want to place the website. Often, you'll want to create a new directory for your web application. To do this, select the directory where you want to place the subdirectory, and click the Create New Folder icon (found just above the top-right corner of the directory tree). Either way, once you've selected your directory, click Open. The Choose Location dialog box also has options (represented by the buttons on the left) for creating a web application on an IIS virtual directory or a remote web server. You can ignore these options for now. In general, it's easiest to develop your web application locally and upload the files once they're perfect.

■ **Tip** Remember, the location where you create your website probably isn't where you'll put it when you deploy it. Don't worry about this wrinkle—in Chapter 9 you'll learn how to take your development website and put it on a live web server so it can be accessible to others over a network or the Internet.

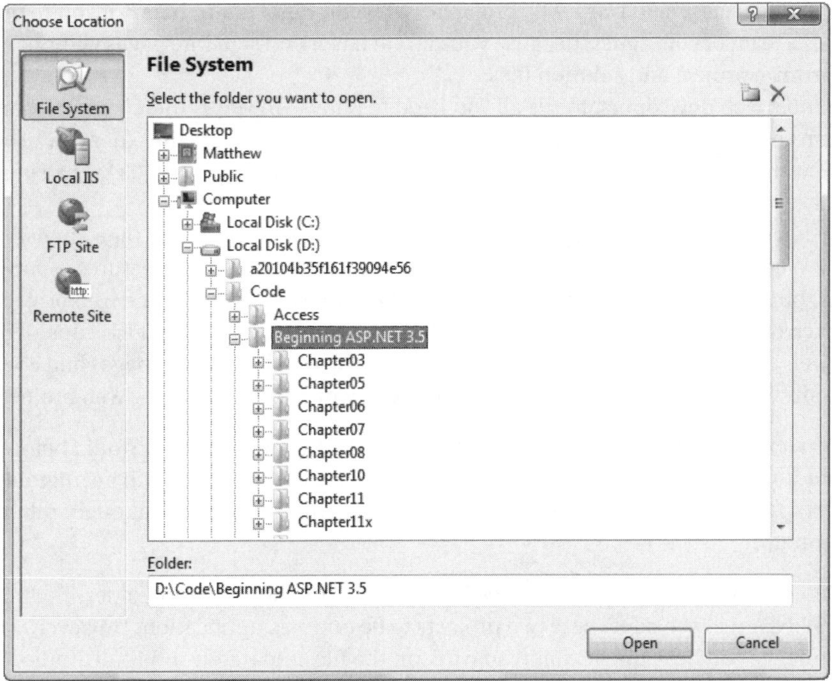

Figure 4-3. *The Choose Location dialog box*

6. Click OK to create the website. At this point, Visual Studio generates a new website with just three files. This website includes a blank web page named Default.aspx, which is its home page and starting point, and a file named Default.aspx.cs, which holds the code for that web page. The third file is a configuration file named web.config, which you'll explore in Chapter 5. You'll also get a subfolder named App_Data, which you can use to store data files that your application uses.

Now you have a plain vanilla new website, and you're ready to begin designing your first web page. But before you go ahead, you might want to know a bit more about how Visual Studio keeps track of your website files using projects (optionally) and solutions. The next two sections have all the details.

Websites and Web Projects

Ordinarily, Visual Studio uses project files to store information about the applications you create. Web applications are a little unusual because Visual Studio doesn't necessarily create project files for them. In fact, if you followed the steps in the previous section, you created a new website with no project file.

This system, which is called *projectless development*, is different from the way Visual Studio works with other types of applications, such as stand-alone components and Windows programs. It's designed to keep your website directory clean and uncluttered, and thereby simplify the deployment of your web application. This way, when it's finally time to upload your website to a live web server, you can copy the entire folder without worrying about excluding files that are only used for development purposes. Projectless development is also handy if you're programming with a team of colleagues, because you can each work on separate pages without needing to synchronize project and solution files.

For most web developers, this is all you need to know. However, there's actually another option: project-based development, or *web projects*. Web projects are the older way of creating ASP.NET web applications, and they're still supported in Visual Studio 2008 for use in specific scenarios.

You can create a web project by choosing File ➤ New ➤ Project, and then choosing the ASP.NET Web Application template. Web projects support all the same features as projectless websites, but they use an extra project file (with the extension .vbproj). The web project file keeps track of the web pages, configuration files, and other resources that are considered part of your web application. It's stored in the same directory as all your web pages and code files.

Essentially, there are just a few reasons why you would consider using web projects:

- You have an old web project that was created in a version of Visual Studio before Visual Studio 2005. When you open this project in Visual Studio 2008, it will be migrated as a web project automatically to avoid strange compatibility quirks that might otherwise crop up.

- You want to place two (or more) web projects in the same website folder. Technically, ASP.NET will consider these two projects to be one web application. However, with web projects, you have the flexibility to work on the files separately in Visual Studio. You simply add the files that you want to group together to your project.

- You have a really huge website that has lots of resources files (for example, thousands of images). Even though these files are a part of your website, you might not want them to appear in the Solution Explorer window in Visual Studio because they can slow down the development environment. If you use web projects, you can easily get around this issue—just don't add these resource files to your project.

- You are using the MSBuild utility to create an automated deployment process. The MSBuild utility uses project files. For example, a large company might devise a build strategy that automatically signs compiled web application files and deploys them to a production web server. MSBuild isn't discussed in this book, but you can find more information by looking up the "MSBuild" entry (with that capitalization) in the index of the Visual Studio Help.

All the examples that are shown in this book use the projectless website model. However, you're free to create web projects if you fit into one of the scenarios I just described. You still write the same code to power your web pages. It's really just a matter of taste.

The Hidden Solution Files

As you've learned, Visual Studio allows you to create ASP.NET applications without project files. However, you might be surprised to learn that Visual Studio still creates one type of resource file, called a *solution* file. Solutions are a similar concept to projects—the difference is that a single solution can hold one or more projects. Whenever you're working in Visual Studio, you're working with a solution. Often, that solution contains a single projectless website, but in more advanced scenarios it might actually hold additional projects, such as a web application and a component that you're using with your website.

At this point, you're probably wondering where Visual Studio places solution files. It depends, but in a typical projectless web application, Visual Studio quietly tucks the solution files away into the user-specific document directory. In Windows Vista, you'll find it in a directory that's named in this form:

```
c:\Users\[UserName]\Documents\Visual Studio 2008\Projects\[WebsiteFolderName]
```

In earlier versions of Windows, the directory is named in this form:

```
c:\Documents and Settings\[UserName]\My Documents\Visual Studio 2008\
Projects\[WebsiteFolderName]
```

Either way, this system can get a bit confusing, because the rest of your website files will be placed in a completely different directory.

Each solution has two solution files, with the file extensions .sln and .suo. In the previous section, a new website was created named SampleSite. Behind the scenes, Visual Studio generates the following solution files for SampleSite:

```
SampleSite.sln
SampleSite.suo
```

When you open a previously created website, Visual Studio locates the matching solution file automatically, and uses the settings in that solution.

The solution files store some Visual Studio–specific details that aren't directly related to ASP.NET, such as debugging and view settings. For example, Visual Studio tracks the files that are currently open so it can reopen them when you resume your website development.

The solution files aren't essential. In fact, if you move your website to another computer (or just place them in another location on your computer), Visual Studio won't be able to locate the original solution files, and you'll lose the information they store. You'll can also run into trouble if you create two websites with the same name in different locations, in which case the newer solution files may overwrite the older ones. However, because the information in the solution files isn't really all that important, losing it isn't a serious problem. The overall benefits of a projectless system are usually worth the trade-off.

Usually, you can forget about solutions altogether, and let Visual Studio manage them seamlessly. But in some cases, you might want to keep a closer eye on your solution files so you can use them later. For example, you might want to use a solution file to open up a combination of projects that you're working on at the same time. You'll see this technique in action in Chapter 23, when you develop your own components.

The Solution Explorer

To take a high-level look at your website, you can use the Solution Explorer—the window at the top-right corner of the design environment that lists all the files in your web application directory (see Figure 4-4).

The Solution Explorer reflects *everything* that's in the application directory of a projectless website. No files are hidden. This means if you add a plain HTML file, a graphic, or a subdirectory in Windows Explorer, the next time you fire up Visual Studio you'll see the new contents in the Solution Explorer. If you add these same ingredients while Visual Studio is open, you won't see them right away. Instead, you'll need to refresh the display. To do so, right-click the website folder in the Solution Explorer (which appears just under the Solution item at the top of the tree) and choose Refresh Folder.

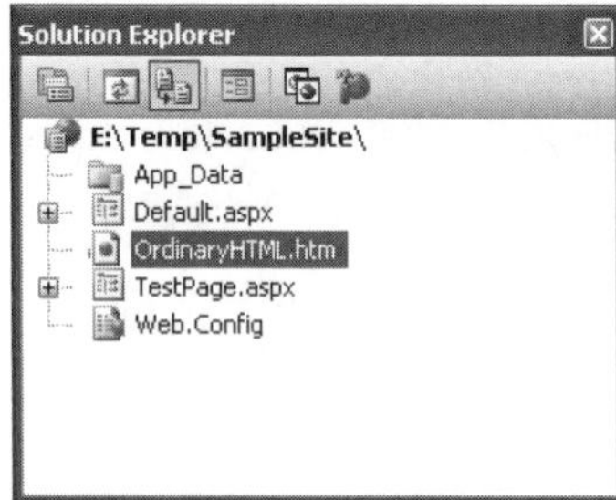

Figure 4-4. *The Solution Explorer*

Of course, the whole point of the Solution Explorer is to save you from resorting to using Windows Explorer. Instead, it allows you to perform a variety of file management tasks within Visual Studio. You can rename, delete, or copy files by simply right-clicking the item and choosing the appropriate command.

Adding Web Forms

As you build your website, you'll need to add new web pages and other items. To add these ingredients, choose Website ➤ Add New Item from the Visual Studio menu. When you do, the Add New Item dialog box will appear.

You can add various types of files to your web application, including resources you want to use (such as bitmaps), ordinary HTML files, code files with class definitions, style sheets, data files, configuration files, and much more. Visual Studio even provides basic designers that allow you to edit most of these types of files directly in the IDE. However, the most common ingredients that you'll add to any website are *web forms*—ASP.NET web pages that are fueled with VB code. Your website begins with one (named Default.aspx), but you're sure to need many more before your application is complete.

To add a web form, choose Web Form in the Add New Item dialog box. You'll see two new options at the bottom of the Add New Item dialog box (as shown in Figure 4-5).

The Place Code in a Separate File option allows you to choose the coding model for your web page. If you clear this check box, Visual Studio will create a single-file web page. You must then place all the VB code for the file in the same file that holds the HTML markup. If you select the Place Code in a Separate File option, Visual Studio will create two distinct files for the web page, one with the markup and the other for your VB code. This is the more structured approach that you'll use in this book. The key advantage of splitting the web page into separate files is that it's more manageable when you need to work with complex pages. However, both approaches give you the same performance and functionality.

You'll also see another option named Select Master Page, which allows you to create a page that uses the layout you've standardized in a separate file. For now, disregard this setting. You'll learn how to create master pages in Chapter 13.

Once you've chosen the coding model and typed in a suitable name for your web page, click Add to create it. If you've chosen to use the Place Code in Separate File check box (which is recommended), your project will end up with two files for each web page. One file includes the web page markup (and has the file extension .aspx). The other file stores the source code for the page (and uses the same file name, with the file extension .aspx.vb). To make the relationship clear, the Solution Explorer displays the code file underneath the .aspx file (see Figure 4-6).

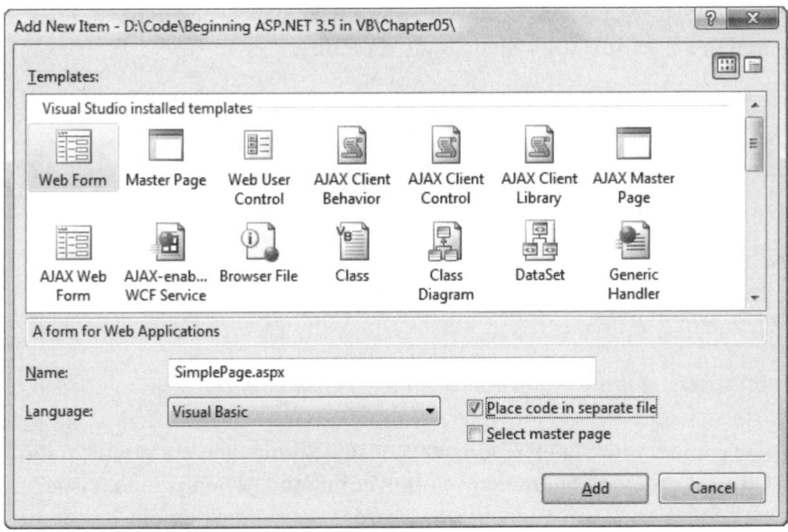

Figure 4-5. *Adding an ASP.NET web form*

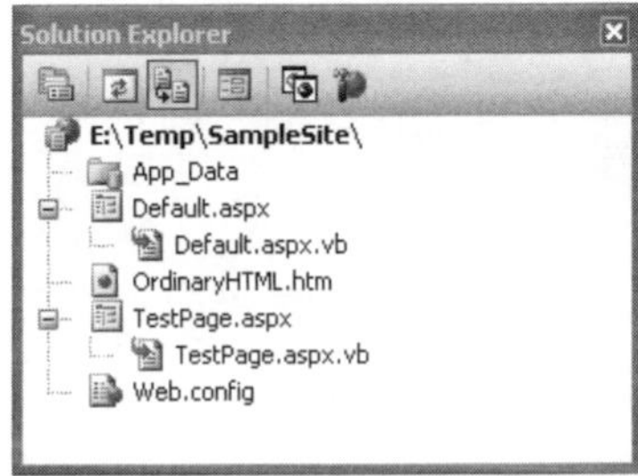

Figure 4-6. *A code file for a web page*

You can also add files that already exist by selecting Website ➤ Add Existing Item. You can use this technique to copy files from one website to another. Visual Studio leaves the original file alone and simply creates a copy in your web application directory. However, don't use this approach with a web page that has been created in an older version of Visual Studio. Instead, refer to the following section to convert your old application and bring it into Visual Studio 2008.

Migrating a Website from a Previous Version of Visual Studio

If you have an existing ASP.NET web application created with an earlier version of Visual Studio, you can migrate it to the ASP.NET world with ease.

If you created a projectless website with Visual Studio 2005, you use the File ➤ Open ➤ Web Site command, just as you would with a website created in Visual Studio 2008. The first time you open a Visual Studio 2005 website, you'll be asked if you want to adjust it to use ASP.NET 3.5 (see Figure 4-7). If you choose Yes, Visual Studio makes a few simple changes to the web.config configuration file, so that the application can use .NET 3.5. If you choose No, your website will stay as it is, and it will continue targeting ASP.NET 2.0. (You can modify this detail at any time by choosing Website ➤ Start Options.) Either way, you won't be asked again the next time you open the website, because your preference will be recorded in the hidden solution file that's stored in a user-specific Visual Studio directory.

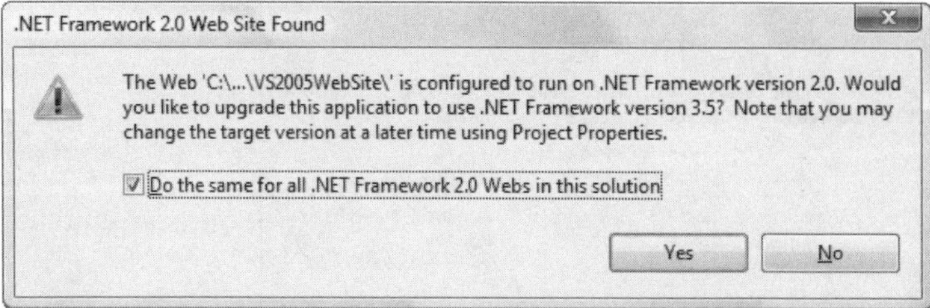

Figure 4-7. *Opening a projectless website that was created with Visual Studio 2005*

If you created a web project with Visual Studio 2005, Visual Studio 2003, or Visual Studio .NET, you need to use the File ➤ Open ➤ Project/Solution command. When you do, Visual Studio begins the Conversion Wizard. The Conversion Wizard is exceedingly simple. It prompts you to choose whether to create a backup and, if so, where it should be placed (see Figure 4-8). If this is your only copy of the application, a backup is a good idea in case some aspects of your application can't be converted successfully. Otherwise, you can skip this option.

Figure 4-8. *Importing a web project that was created with an older version of Visual Studio*

When you click Finish, Visual Studio performs an *in-place conversion*, which means it overwrites your web page files with the new versions. Any errors and warnings are added to a conversion log, which you can display when the conversion is complete.

Designing a Web Page

Now that you understand the basic organization of Visual Studio, you can begin designing a simple web page. To start, in the Solution Explorer, double-click the web page you want to design. (Start with Default.aspx if you haven't added any additional pages.)

Visual Studio gives you three ways to look at an .aspx page:

Design view: Here you'll see a graphical representation of what your page looks like.

Source view: Here you'll see the underlying markup, with the HTML for the page and the ASP.NET control tags.

Split view: This combined view allows you to see both the design view and source view at once, stacked one on top of the other. This is the view that most ASP.NET developers prefer, provided they have enough screen space.

You can switch between these three views freely by clicking the Design, Split, and Source buttons at the bottom of the designer window.

You'll spend some time in the source view a bit later in this chapter, when you dig into the web page markup. But first, it's easiest to start with the friendlier design view, and start adding content to your page.

■ **Tip** If you have a widescreen monitor, you'll probably prefer to have the split view use two side-by-side regions (rather than a top and bottom region). Fortunately, it's easy to configure Visual Studio to do so. Just select Tools ➤ Options, and then head to the HTML Designer ➤ General section in the tree of settings. Finally, select the Split Views Vertically option and click OK.

Adding Web Controls

To add an ASP.NET web control, drag the control you want from the Toolbox on the left and drop it onto your web page. Technically speaking, you can drop your controls onto a design view window or onto a source view window. However, it's usually easiest to position the control in the right place when you use design view. If you drop controls carelessly into the source view, they might not end up in the <form> section, which means they won't work in your page.

The controls in the Toolbox are grouped in numerous categories based on their functions, but you'll find basic ingredients such as buttons, labels, and text boxes in the Standard tab.

■ **Tip** By default, the Toolbox is enabled to automatically hide itself when your mouse moves away from it, somewhat like the AutoHide feature for the Windows taskbar. This behavior is often exasperating, so you may want to click the pushpin in the top-right corner of the Toolbox to make it stop in its fully expanded position.

In a web form, controls are positioned line by line, like in a word processor document. To add a control, you need to drag and drop it to an appropriate place. To organize several controls in design view, you'll probably need to add spaces and hard returns (just hit Enter) to position elements the way you want them. Figure 4-9 shows an example with a TextBox, a Label, and a Button control.

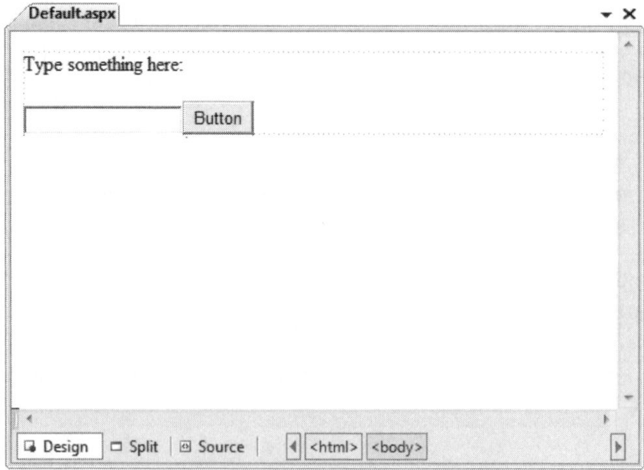

Figure 4-9. *The design view for a page*

You'll find that some controls can't be resized. Instead, they grow or shrink to fit the amount of content in them. For example, the size of a Label control depends on how much text you enter in it. On the other hand, you can adjust the size of a Button or a TextBox control by clicking and dragging in the design environment.

As you add web controls to the design surface, Visual Studio automatically adds the corresponding control tags to your .aspx file. To look at the markup it's generated, you can click the Source button to switch to source view (or click the Split button to see both at once). Figure 4-10 shows what you might see in the source view for the page displayed in Figure 4-9.

Using the source view, you can manually add attributes or rearrange controls. In fact, Visual Studio even provides IntelliSense features that automatically complete opening tags and alert you if you use an invalid tag. Whether you use the design or source view is entirely up to you—Visual Studio keeps them both synchronized.

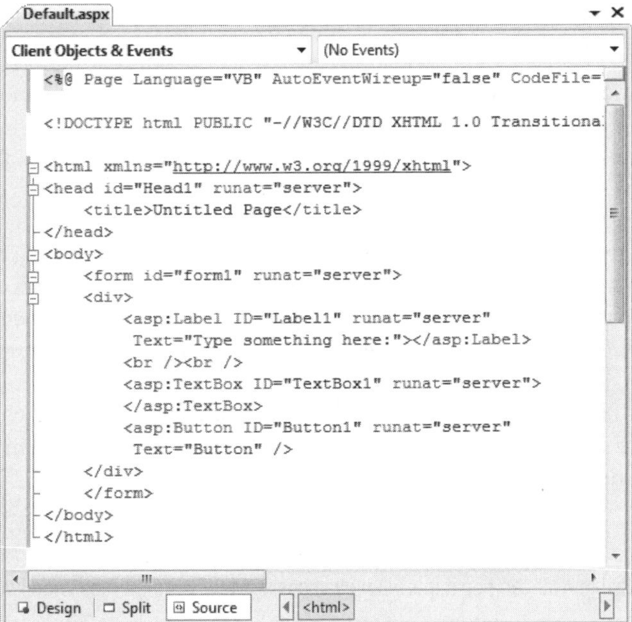

Figure 4-10. *The source view for a page*

THE MISSING GRID LAYOUT FEATURE

If you've used previous versions of Visual Studio, you may remember a feature called *grid layout*, which allowed you to position elements with absolute coordinates by dragging them where you wanted them. Although this model seems convenient, it really isn't suited to most web pages because controls can't adjust their positioning when the web page content changes (or when text is resized based on user preferences). This leads to inflexible layouts (such as controls that overwrite each other).

That said, Visual Studio 2008 has a back door way to use grid layout. All you need to do is to switch to source view and add a style attribute that uses CSS to specify absolute positioning. This attribute will already exist in any pages you've created with a previous version of Visual Studio .NET in grid layout mode.

Here's an example:

```
<asp:Button ID="cmd" style="POSITION: absolute; left: 100px; top: 50px;"
 runat="server" Text="Floating Button" ... />
```

Once you've made this change, you're free to drag the button around the window at will. Of course, you shouldn't go this route just because it seems closer to the Windows model. Most great web pages use absolute positioning rarely, if at all, because it's just too awkward and inflexible.

If you do decide to use absolute positioning, the best idea is to apply it to a container, such as the <div> element. The <div> element represents a box that is invisible by default but can optionally have borders, a background fill, and other formatting. Using absolute positioning, you can then place your <div> container precisely, but let the content inside use normal flow layout. This greatly simplifies the amount of layout you need to do. For example, if you want to create a sidebar with a list of links, it's much easier to position the sidebar using absolute positioning than to try and place each link in the right place individually.

The Properties Window

Once you've added a web control to a web page, you'll probably want to tweak it a bit. For example, you might want to change the text in the button, the color of a label, and so on. Although you can make all your changes by editing the source markup by hand, Visual Studio provides an easier option. Just under the Solution Explorer, in the bottom-right corner of the Visual Studio window, you'll see the Properties window, which shows you the properties of the currently selected web control—and lets you tweak them.

To configure a control in design view you must first select it on the page (either click it once in the design view or click somewhere inside the tag for that control in the source view). You'll know the right control is selected when you see its name appear in the drop-down list at the top of the Properties window. Alternatively, you can select your control by picking its name from the Properties window list.

Once you've selected the control you want you can modify any of its properties. Good ones to try include Text (the content of the control), ID (the name you use to interact with the control in your code), and ForeColor (the color used for the control's text).

■ Note If the Properties window isn't visible, you can pop it into view by choosing View ➤ Properties Window.

Every time you make a selection in the Properties window, Visual Studio adjusts the web page markup accordingly. Visual Studio even provides special "choosers" that allow you to select extended properties. For example, if you select a color property (such as ForeColor or BackColor) in the Properties window, a button with three dots (...) will appear next to the property, as shown in Figure 4-11.

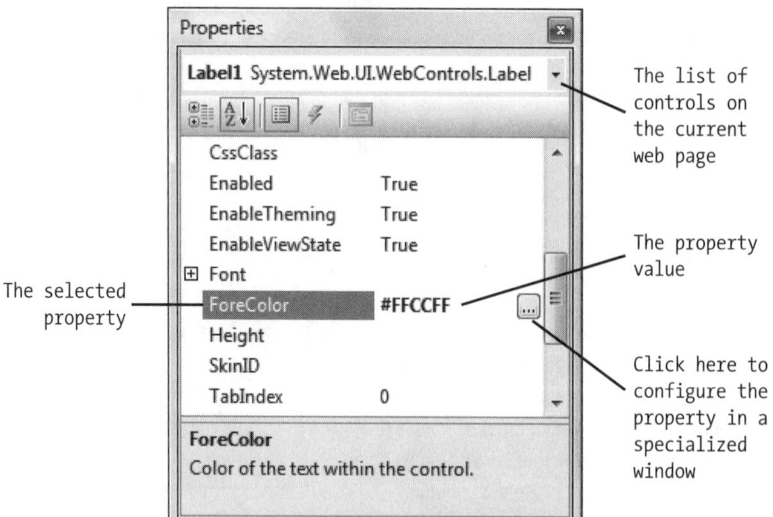

Figure 4-11. *The ForeColor property in the Properties window*

If you click this button, Visual Studio will show a dialog box where you can pick a custom color (Figure 4-12). Once you make your selection and click OK, Visual Studio will insert the HTML color code into the Properties window and update your web page markup.

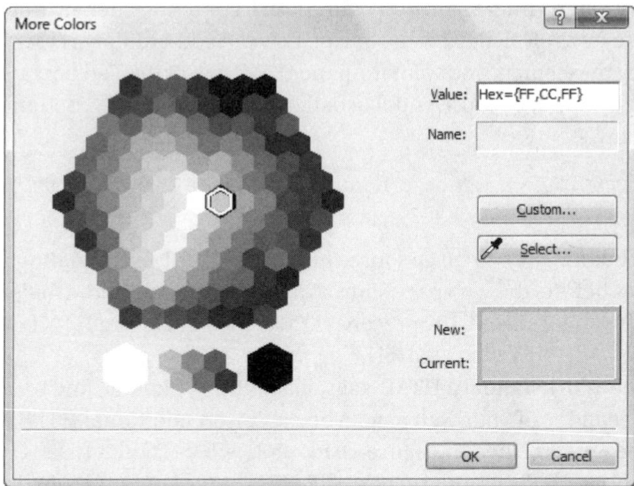

Figure 4-12. *Choosing a color value*

You'll see a similar feature when configuring fonts. First, select the appropriate control on the design surface (or in the list at the top of the Properties window). Next, expand the Font property in the properties window and select the Name subproperty. A drop-down arrow will appear next to the property. Click this to choose from a list of all the fonts that are installed on your computer. (Don't go too crazy here. If you choose a font that isn't installed on the computer of the person who is visiting your web page, the browser will revert to a standard font. Chapter 6 has more about font choosing.)

Along with web controls, you can also select ordinary HTML tags in the Properties window. However, there's a lot less you can do with them. Ordinary HTML tags aren't live programming objects, so they don't have nifty features that you can control. And ordinary HTML tags don't offer many options for formatting. If you want to change the appearance of a tag, your best choice is to create a *style* for your control. If you're a web guru, you can do this by hand. If not, you can use Visual Studio's style building features, which you'll learn about in Chapter 13.

Finally, you can select one object in the Properties window that needs some explanation—the DOCUMENT object, which represents the web page itself. Using this object, you can set various options for the entire page, including the title that will be displayed in the browser, linked style sheets, and support for other features that are discussed later in this book (such as tracing and session state).

The Anatomy of a Web Form

So far, you've spent most of your time working with the web page in design view. There's nothing wrong with that—after all, it makes it easy to quickly assemble a basic web page without requiring any HTML knowledge.

However, it probably won't be long before you dip into the source view. Some types of changes are easier to make when you are working directly with your markup. Finding the control you want on the design surface, selecting it, and editing the properties one at a time in the Properties window can be tedious.

The source view is often helpful when you want to add plain HTML content—after all, not everything in your web page needs to be a full-fledged web control. You can add ordinary HTML elements using design view (just drag the element you want from the HTML tab of the Toolbox), but it's often easier to type them in by hand, because you'll usually need to use a combination of elements to get the result you want.

The Web Form Markup

If you haven't written HTML pages before, the web page source might look a little intimidating. And if you have written HTML pages before, the web page source might look a little odd. That's because the source for an ASP.NET web form isn't 100 percent HTML. Instead, it's an HTML document with an extra ingredient—ASP.NET web controls.

Every ASP.NET web form includes the standard HTML tags, like <html>, <head>, and <body>, which delineate the basic sections of your web page. You can insert additional HTML tags, like paragraphs of text (use the <p> tag), headings (use <h1>, <h2>, <h3>), tables (use <table>), and so on. Along with standard HTML, you can add ASP.NET-only elements to your web pages. For example, <asp:Button> represents a clickable button that triggers a task on the web server. When you add an ASP.NET web control, you create an object that you can interact with in your web page code, which is tremendously useful.

Here's a look at the web page shown in Figure 4-7. The details that are not part of ordinary HTML are highlighted, and the lines are numbered for easy reference:

```
<%@ Page Language="VB" AutoEventWireup="False"
    CodeFile="Default.aspx.vb" Inherits="_Default" %>

<!DOCTYPE html PUBLIC "-//W3C//DTD XHTML 1.0 Transitional//EN"
"http://www.w3.org/TR/xhtml1/DTD/xhtml1-transitional.dtd">

<html xmlns="http://www.w3.org/1999/xhtml">
  <head runat="server">
    <title>Untitled Page</title>
  </head>
  <body>
    <form ID="form1" runat="server">
      <div>
        <asp:Label ID="Label1" runat="server"
         Text="Type something here:" />
        <asp:TextBox ID="TextBox1" runat="server" />
        <br />
        <asp:Button ID="Button1" runat="server" Text="Button" />
      </div>
    </form>
  </body>
</html>
```

Obviously, the ASP.NET-specific details (the highlighted bits) don't mean anything to a web browser because they aren't valid HTML. This isn't a problem, because the web browser never sees these details. Instead, the ASP.NET engine creates an HTML "snapshot" of your page after all your code has finished processing on the server. At this point, details like the <asp:Button> are replaced with HTML tags that have the same appearance. The ASP.NET engine sends this HTML snapshot to the browser.

This summary is just a quick introduction to the ASP.NET web control model. You'll learn much more about web controls and how web forms work behind the scenes in the following two chapters. But before you go any further, it's important to consider a few essential details about ASP.NET web forms. In the following sections, you'll learn about the page directive (lines 1 and 2 in the previous code sample) and the doctype (lines 3 and 4). You'll then take a quick detour to review some of the essential rules of XHTML, the markup language used to create modern web pages.

The Page Directive

The Default.aspx page, like all ASP.NET web forms, consists of three sections. The first section is the *page directive*:

```
<%@ Page Language="VB" AutoEventWireup="False"
    CodeFile="Default.aspx.vb" Inherits="_Default" %>
```

The page directive gives ASP.NET basic information about how to compile the page. It indicates the language you're using for your code and the way you connect your event handlers. If you're using the code-behind approach (which is recommended), the page directive also indicates where the code file is located and the name of your custom page class. You won't need to modify the page directive by hand, because Visual Studio maintains it for you.

Note The page directive is for ASP.NET's eyes only. The page directive doesn't appear in the HTML that's sent to the browser—instead, ASP.NET strips it out.

The Doctype

In an ordinary, non-ASP.NET web page, the *doctype* occupies the very first line. In an ASP.NET web form, the doctype gets second place, and appears just underneath the page directive.

The doctype indicates the type of markup (for example, HTML or XHTML) that you're using to create your web page. Technically, the doctype is optional, but Visual Studio adds it automatically. This is important, because depending on the type of markup you're using there may be certain tricks that aren't allowed. For example, strict XHTML doesn't let you use HTML formatting features that are considered obsolete and have been replaced by CSS.

The doctype is also important because it influences how a browser interprets your web page. For example, if you don't include a doctype on your web page, Internet Explorer (IE) switches itself into a legacy mode known as *quirks mode*. While IE is in quirks mode, certain formatting details are processed in inconsistent, nonstandard ways, simply because this is historically the way IE behaved. Later versions of IE don't attempt to change this behavior, even though it's faulty, because some websites may depend on it. However, you can specify a more standardized rendering that more closely matches the behavior of other browsers (like Firefox) by adding a doctype.

■ **Tip** If you have a web page that looks dramatically different in Internet Explorer than it does in Firefox, the culprit may be a missing or invalid doctype. Common idiosyncrasies that appear in web pages that don't have doctypes include varying text sizes and varying margin space between elements.

There are a small set of allowable doctypes that you can use. By default, newly created web pages in Visual Studio use the following doctype:

```
<!DOCTYPE html PUBLIC "-//W3C//DTD XHTML 1.0 Transitional//EN"
 "http://www.w3.org/TR/xhtml1/DTD/xhtml1-transitional.dtd">
```

This indicates that the web page uses *XHTML 1.0 transitional.* The word transitional refers to the fact that this version of XHTML is designed to be a stepping stone between the old-fashioned HTML world and the ultra-strict XHTML world. XHTML transitional enforces all the structural rules of XHTML but allows some HTML formatting features that have been replaced by Cascading Style Sheets (CSS) and are considered obsolete.

If you don't need to use these details, you can step up to XHTML strict using this doctype:

```
<!DOCTYPE html PUBLIC "-//W3C//DTD XHTML 1.0 Strict//EN"
 "http://www.w3.org/TR/xhtml1/DTD/xhtml1-strict.dtd">
```

These are the two most common doctypes in use today.

XHTML VS. HTML

XHTML is a *reformulation* of HTML that tightens up its rules. Although XHTML looks quite similar to HTML (and is identical in many cases), it doesn't tolerate the same looseness as HTML. For example, HTML tolerates missing information and many minor mistakes. Unfortunately, this creates a problem with web browser support, because different browsers may react differently to these minor glitches. XHTML doesn't allow the same sloppiness, so the final result is more consistent in different browsers.

The *X* at the beginning of XHTML stands for XML, because XHTML is technically a flavor of XML and plays by its rules. (XML is an all-purpose standard for storing information in a flexible way that's not tied to any particular application, operating system, or programming environment. Although you may not know much about XML right now, you'll take a detailed look at it in Chapter 19.)

There is a deeply buried configuration setting that allows you to change the way ASP.NET works so that it uses HTML instead of XHTML. But developers rarely use this option unless they have issues with old web documents (for example, they want to take legacy HTML pages and transform them to ASP.NET web forms in the fastest way possible). If you're developing a new website, there's no reason not to use XHTML. (And avoiding XHTML can cause problems if you try to use ASP.NET's new AJAX toolkit, which is described in Chapter 25.) But if you really must know how to get back to the past, search the Visual Studio Help for the xhtmlConformance configuration setting.

■ **Note** Throughout this book, you'll find many references to HTML. However, this is just a convenient shorthand that includes HTML and XHTML. The web page examples that you'll see in this book use valid XHTML.

There are still a few more doctypes that you can use. If you're working with an existing website that's based on the somewhat out-of-date HTML standard, this is the doctype you need:

```
<!DOCTYPE HTML PUBLIC "-//W3C//DTD HTML 4.01//EN"
 "http://www.w3.org/TR/html4/strict.dtd">
```

And if you want to use the slightly tweaked XHTML 1.1 standard (rather than XHTML 1.0), you need the following doctype:

```
<!DOCTYPE html PUBLIC "-//W3C//DTD XHTML 1.1//EN"
 "http://www.w3.org/TR/xhtml11/DTD/xhtml11.dtd">
```

XHTML 1.1 is mostly identical to XHTML 1.0 but streamlines a few more details and removes a few more legacy details. It doesn't provide a transitional option.

■ **Note** There are a few more doctypes that you can use to create *frames* pages, which allow you to split a browser window into multiple panes, each of which shows a separate page. Frames pages are discouraged in modern day web development, because they don't work well with different window sizes and aren't always indexed correctly by search engines. You can see a more complete list of allowed doctypes, which includes the doctype for a frames page, at `www.w3.org/QA/2002/04/Web-Quality`.

Remember, the ASP.NET server controls will work equally well with any doctype. It's up to you to choose the level of standards compliance and backward compatibility you want in your web pages. If you're still in doubt, it's best to start out with XHTML 1.0 transitional, as it eliminates the quirks in different browser versions without removing all the legacy features. If you're ready to make a clean break with HTML, even if it means a bit more pain, consider switching to XHTML 1.0 strict or XHTML 1.1 (which is always strict) instead.

■ **Note** In this book, the web page markup listings omit the doctype (because it's just one more detail chewing up extra pages). If you download the sample code, you'll find that most pages use the XHTML 1.1 doctype.

The Essentials of XHTML

Part of the goal of ASP.NET is to allow you to build rich web pages without forcing you to slog through the tedious details of XHTML (or HTML). ASP.NET delivers on this promise in many ways—for example, in many situations you can get the result you want using a single slick web control rather than writing a page full of XHTML markup.

However, ASP.NET doesn't isolate you from XHTML altogether. In fact, a typical ASP.NET web page mingles ASP.NET web controls with ordinary XHTML content. When that page is processed by the web server, the ASP.NET web controls are converted to XHTML markup (a process known as *rendering*) and inserted into the page. The final result is a standard XHTML document that's sent back to the browser.

This design gives you the best of both worlds—you can mix ordinary XHTML markup for the parts of your page that don't change, and use handy ASP.NET web controls for the parts that need to be interactive (such as buttons, lists, text boxes, and so on) or the parts that you need to update with new information (for example, a block of dynamic text). This design also suggests that ASP.NET developers should have a solid understanding of XHTML basics before they begin coding web forms. The following sections provide a brief overview that introduces you to the XHTML standard (or refreshes your memory, if you've learned it before). If you already know all you want to know about XHTML, feel free to skip ahead to the next section, "Writing Code."

■ **Note** The full XHTML standard is fairly straightforward, but it's a bit beyond the scope of this book. If you want to learn all the details, you can surf to `www.w3schools.com/xhtml` for a concise online tutorial.

Elements

The most important concept in the XHTML (and HTML) standard is the idea of *elements*. Elements are containers that contain bits of your web page content. For example, if you want to add a paragraph of text to a web page, you stuff it inside a paragraph element. A typical web page is actually composed of dozens (or hundreds) of elements. Taken together, these elements define the structure of the web page. They're also the starting point for formatting the web page. For example, headings usually look different than ordinary paragraphs, and tables look different than bulleted lists.

The XHTML language defines a small set of elements that you can use—in fact, there are fewer than you probably expect. XHTML also defines the syntax for using these elements. A typical element consists of three pieces: a start tag, some content, and an end tag. Here's an example:

```
<p>This is a sentence in a paragraph.</p>
```

This example uses the paragraph element. The element starts with the <p> start tag, ends with the </p> end tag, and contains some text inside. Tags are easy to recognize, because they're always enclosed in angled brackets. And here's a combination that adds a heading to a web page followed by a paragraph:

```
<h1>A Heading</h1>
<p>This is a sentence in a paragraph.</p>
```

Browsers have built-in rules about how to process and display different elements. When a browser digests this markup, it always places the heading in a large, bold font, and adds a line break and some extra space underneath it, before starting the paragraph. Of course, there are ways to modify these formatting rules using the CSS standard, which you'll consider in Chapter 13.

Many XHTML elements can contain other elements. For example, you can use the <b> element inside the <p> element to apply bold formatting to a portion of a paragraph:

```
<p>This is a <b>sentence</b> in a paragraph.</p>
```

The <h1> and <p> elements usually hold content inside. As a result, they're split into a start tag and an end tag. For example, a heading begins with <h1> and ends with </h1>. However, some elements don't need any content, and can be declared using a special empty tag syntax that fuses the start and end tag together. For example, the <br> element represents a line break. Rather than writing
</br>, you can simply use <br />, as shown here:

```
<p>This is line one.<br />
This is line two.<br />
This is line three.</p>
```

Other elements that can be used in this fashion include <img> (for showing an image), <hr> (for creating a horizontal rule, or line), and most ASP.NET controls.

■ **Note** Line breaks are important because XHTML collapses whitespace. That means you can add a series of spaces, tabs, and hard returns in your element content, and the browser will simply render a single space character. If you really *do* want line breaks, you need to use separate elements (for example, more than one <p> paragraph) or line breaks. If you want extra spaces, you need to add the HTML character entity   instead (which stands for nonbreaking space). The browser converts this code into a single space character.

Table 4-1 lists some the most commonly used XHTML elements. The Type column distinguishes between two types of XHTML—those that typically hold content or other nested elements (containers), and those that can be used on their own with the empty tag syntax you just considered (standalone).

Table 4-1. *Basic XHTML Elements*

Tag	Name	Type	Description
<b>, <i>, <u>	Bold, Italic, Underline	Container	These elements are used to apply basic formatting, and make text bold, italic, or underlined. Some web designers prefer to use <strong> instead of <b> and <emphasis> instead of <i>. Although these elements have the same standard rendering (bold and italic, respectively), they make more sense if you plan to use styles to change the formatting sometime in the future.
<p>	Paragraph	Container	The paragraph groups a block of free-flowing text together. The browser automatically adds a bit of space between paragraphs and other elements (like headings) or between subsequent paragraphs.

Table 4-1. *Basic XHTML Elements (Continued)*

Tag	Name	Type	Description
<h1>, <h2>, <h3>, <h4>, <h5>, <h6>	Heading	Container	These elements are headings, which give text bold formatting and a large font size. The lower the number, the larger the text, so <h1> is for the largest heading. The <h5> heading is normal text size, and <h6> is actually a bit smaller than ordinary text.
<img>	Image	Standalone	The image element shows an external image file (specified by the src attribute) in a web page.
 	Line Break	Standalone	This element adds a single line break, with no extra space.
<hr>	Horizontal Line	Standalone	This element adds a horizontal line (which gets the full width of the containing element). You can use the horizontal line to separate different content regions.
<a>	Anchor	Container	The anchor element wraps a piece of text, and turns it into a link. You set the link target using the href attribute.
<ul>, <li>	Unordered List, List Item	Container	These elements allow you to build bulleted lists. The <ul> element defines the list, while the <li> element defines an item in the list (you nest the actual content for that item inside).
<ol>, <li>	Ordered List, List Item	Container	These elements allow you to build numbered lists. The <ol> element defines the list, while the <li> element defines an item in the list (you nest the actual content for that item inside).
<table>, <tr>, <td>	Table	Container	The <table> element allows you to create a multicolumn, multirow table. Each row is represented by a <tr> element inside the <table>. Each cell in a row is represented by a <td> element inside a <tr>. You place the actual content for the cell in the individual <td> elements.
<div>	Division	Container	This element is an all-purpose container for other elements. It's used to separate different regions on the page, so you can format them or position them separately. For example, you can use a <div> to create a shaded box around a group of elements.
<span>	Span	Container	This element is an all-purpose container for bits of text content inside other elements (like headings or paragraphs). It's most commonly used to format those bits of text. For example, you can use a <span> to change the color of a few words in a sentence.

Table 4-1. *Basic XHTML Elements (Continued)*

Tag	Name	Type	Description
<form>	Form	Container	This element is used to hold all the controls on a web page. Controls are HTML elements that can send information back to the web server when the page is submitted. For example, text boxes submit their text, list boxes submit the currently selected item in the list, and so on.

Attributes

Every XHTML document fuses together two types of information: the document content, and information about how that content should be presented. You control the presentation of your content in just three ways: by using the right elements, by arranging these elements to get the right structure, and by adding attributes to your elements.

Attributes are individual pieces of information that you attach to an element, inside the start tag. Attributes have many uses—for example, they allow you to explicitly attach a style to an element so that it gets the right formatting. Some elements require attributes. The most obvious example is the <img> element, which allows you to pull the content from an image file and place it in your web page.

The <img> tag requires two pieces of information—the image URL (the source), and the alternate text that describes the picture (which is used for accessibility purposes, as with screen reading software). These two pieces of information are specified using two attributes, named *src* and *alt*:

```
<img src="happy.gif" alt="Happy Face" />
```

The <a> anchor element is an example of an element that uses attributes and takes content. The content inside the <a> element is the blue, underline text of the hyperlink. The href attribute defines the destination that the browser will navigate to when the link is clicked.

```
<p>
Click <a href="http://www.prosetech.com">here</a> to visit my website.
</p>
```

You'll use attributes extensively with ASP.NET control tags. With ASP.NET controls, every attribute maps to a property of the control class.

Formatting

Along with the <b> tag for bold, XHTML also supports <i> for italics and <u> for underlining. However, this is about as far its formatting goes.

XHTML elements are intended to indicate the *structure* of a document, not its formatting. Although you can adjust colors, fonts, and some formatting characteristics using XHTML elements, a better approach is to define formatting using a CSS style sheet. For example, a style sheet can tell the browser to use specific formatting for every <h1> element in a page. You can even apply the styles in a style sheet to all the pages in your website.

■ **Tip** In the downloadable samples, you'll find that many of the web pages use a style sheet named Styles.css. This style sheet applies the Verdana font to all elements of the web page.

In an ASP.NET web page, there are two ways you can use CSS. You can use it directly to format elements. Chapter 13 outlines the basics of this approach. Or, you can configure the properties of the ASP.NET controls you're using, and they'll generate the styles they need automatically. This is the way you'll use formatting for the first half of this book.

A Complete Web Page

You now know enough to put together a complete XHTML page.

Every XHTML document starts out with this basic structure (right after the doctype):

```
<html xmlns="http://www.w3.org/1999/xhtml">
  <head runat="server">
    <title>Untitled Page</title>
  </head>
  <body>

  </body>
</html>
```

When you create a new web form in Visual Studio, this is the structure you start with. Here's what you get:

- XHTML documents start with the <html> tag and end with the </html> tag. This <html> element contains the complete content of the web page.
- Inside the <html> element, the web page is divided into two portions. The first portion is the <head> element, which stores some information about the web page. You'll use this to store the title of your web page, which will appear in the title bar in your web browser. (You can also add other details here like search keywords, although these are mostly ignored by web browsers these days.) When you generate a web page in Visual Studio, the <head> section has a runat="server" attribute. This gives you the ability to manipulate it in your code (a topic you'll explore in the next chapter).
- The second portion is the <body> element, which contains the actual page content that appears in the web browser window.

In an ASP.NET web page, there's at least one more element. Inside the <body> element is a <form> element. The <form> element is required because it defines a portion of the page that can send information back to the web server. This becomes important when you start adding text boxes, lists, and other controls. As long as they're in a form, information like the current text in the text box and the current selection in the list will be sent to the web server using a process known as a postback. Fortunately, you don't need to worry about this detail yet—just place all your web page content inside the <form> element.

Most of the time, when you're working with a page you'll focus on the markup inside the <form> tag, because that's the actual page content. When you create a new web page in Visual Studio, there's one more detail—the <div> element inside the <form> element:

```
<html xmlns="http://www.w3.org/1999/xhtml">
  <head runat="server">
    <title>Untitled Page</title>
  </head>
  <body>
    <form ID="form1" runat="server">
      <div>
      </div>
    </form>
  </body>
</html>
```

Strictly speaking, the <div> element is optional—it's just a container. You can think of it as an invisible box that has no built-in appearance or formatting. However, it's useful to use a <div> tag to group portions of your page that you want to format in a similar way (for example, with the same font, background color, or border). That way, you can apply style settings to the <div> tag, and they'll cascade down into every tag it contains. You can also create a real box on your page by giving the <div> a border. You'll learn more about formatting and the <div> element in Chapter 13.

■ Note The <div> element is also useful because you can place text directly inside it, without needing a container element (such as a paragraph). On the other hand, adding text directly inside the <form> element violates the rules of XHTML.

Now you're ready to pop the rest of your content in the <div> tag. If you add the Label and TextBox web controls, you'll end up with the same markup you created using the designer earlier in this chapter—but now you'll understand its markup underpinnings.

Writing Code

Many of Visual Studio's most welcome enhancements appear when you start to write the code that supports your user interface. To start coding, you need to switch to the code-behind view. To switch back and forth, you can use two View Code or View Designer buttons, which appear just above the Solution Explorer window. Another approach that works just as well is to double-click either the .aspx page in the Solution Explorer (to get to the designer) or the .aspx.vb page (to get to the code view). The "code" in question is the code, not the HTML markup in the .aspx file.

The Code-Behind Class

When you switch to code view, you'll see the page class for your web page. For example, if you've created a web page named SimplePage.aspx, you'll see a code-behind class that looks like this:

```
Partial Class SimplePage
    Inherits System.Web.UI.Page

End Class
```

You may notice that your code files are surprisingly bare. In particular, they don't have any Imports statements. (As you learned in Chapter 3, Imports statements allow you to access classes in a specific namespace without writing a long, fully qualified name. For example, you can replace the qualified name System.Web.UI.Page with just Page if you import the System.Web.UI namespace.)

As you begin coding with ASP.NET, you'll find that a great many ASP.NET classes are available for you to use, without requiring fully qualified names. That's because many commonly used namespaces *are* imported. However, they're imported automatically based on the settings in a computer-wide configuration file that you'll learn about in Chapter 5. For the most part, this is a worthwhile convenience. But as you'll see throughout this book, you'll still need to import additional namespaces to get access to more specialized features, such as the classes for reading and writing files and the classes for connecting to SQL Server.

Inside your page class you can place methods, which will respond to control events. For example, you can add a method with code that reacts when the user clicks a button. The following section explains how you can create an event handler.

Adding Event Handlers

Most of the code in an ASP.NET web page is placed inside event handlers that react to web control events. Using Visual Studio, you have three easy ways to add an event handler to your code:

Type it in manually: In this case, you add the subroutine directly to the page class. You must specify the appropriate parameters. You'll also need to add the Handles keyword at the end to specifically connect the event handler to the appropriate event.

Double-click a control in Design view: In this case, Visual Studio will create an event handler for that control's default event, if it doesn't already exist. For example, if you double-click a Button control, it will create an event handler for the Button.Click event. If you double-click a TextBox control, you'll get an event handler for the TextBox.TextChanged event. If you double-click the surface of the page, you'll get an event handler for the Page.Load event.

Choose the event from the Properties window: Just select the control, and click the lightning bolt in the Properties window. You'll see a list of all the events provided by that control. Double-click next to the event you want to handle, and Visual Studio will automatically generate the event handler in your page class. Alternatively, if you've already created the event handler method, just select the event in the Properties window, and click the drop-down arrow at the right. You'll see a list that includes all the methods in your class that match the signature this event requires. You can then choose a method from the list to connect it. Figure 4-13 shows an example where the Button.Click event is connected to the Button1_Click method in the page class.

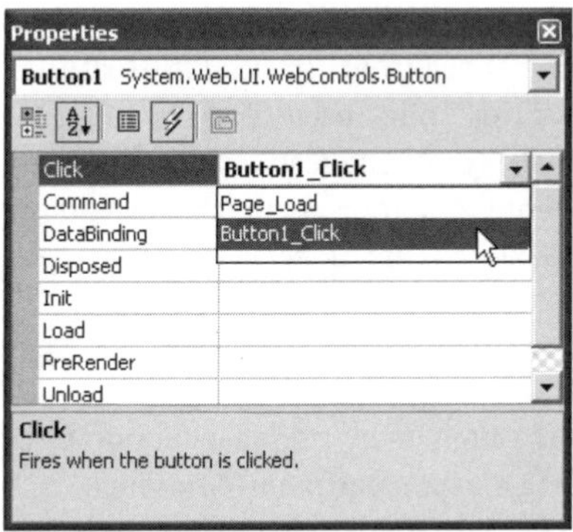

Figure 4-13. *Creating or attaching an event handler*

No matter which approach you use, the event handler looks (and functions) the same.

For example, when you double-click a Button control, Visual Studio creates an event handler like this:

```
Protected Sub Button1_Click(ByVal sender As Object, ByVal e As EventArgs) _
  Handles Button1.Click
    ' Your code for reacting to the button click goes here.
End Sub
```

The important part is the Handles clause at the end. This tells ASP.NET to wire up the Click event from the Button1 control to this event handler. (If you want to disconnect your event handler, just remove this part of the code.)

Inside your event handler method, you can interact with any of the control objects on your web page using their IDs. For example, if you've created a TextBox control named TextBox1, you can set the text using the following line of code:

```
Protected Sub Button1_Click(ByVal sender As Object, ByVal e As EventArgs) _
  Handles Button1.Click
    TextBox1.Text = "Here is some sample text."
End Sub
```

This is a simple event handler that reacts when Button1 is clicked and updates the text in TextBox1.

Note You might wonder why your code file includes the event handlers, but it doesn't actually *declare* the controls that you use (like the Button1 and TextBox1 objects in the previous example). The reason is that ASP.NET generates the declarations for these controls automatically. You'll never see these declarations, but you can assume they're a part of your class. That's also why every page class you create is defined with the Partial keyword. This allows ASP.NET to merge your code with the portion it generates automatically. The end result is that you can easily access all the controls on your page by name, but you don't need to bother with extra code to create and initialize these objects.

You'll learn much more about how the ASP.NET web form model works in the next two chapters. But for the rest of the chapter, it's time to take a small break and consider the features that Visual Studio provides to make your life easier when writing code and testing a web page. First you'll tackle IntelliSense, which prompts you with valuable code suggestions (and catches mistakes) as you type. Next, you'll look at Visual Studio's debugging tools, which allow you to dissect the most complex code routines to find out what's really taking place.

IntelliSense and Outlining

Visual Studio provides a number of automatic time-savers through its IntelliSense technology. They are similar to features such as automatic spell checking and formatting in Microsoft Office applications. This chapter introduces most of these features, but you'll need many hours of programming before you'll become familiar with all of Visual Studio's time-savers. We don't have enough space to describe advanced tricks such as the intelligent search-and-replace features and Visual Studio's programmable macros. These features could occupy an entire book of their own!

Outlining

Outlining allows Visual Studio to "collapse" a method, class, structure, namespace, or region to a single line. It allows you to see the code that interests you while hiding unimportant code. To collapse a portion of code, click the minus (–) symbol next to the first line. To expand it, click the box again, which will now have a plus (+) symbol (see Figure 4-14).

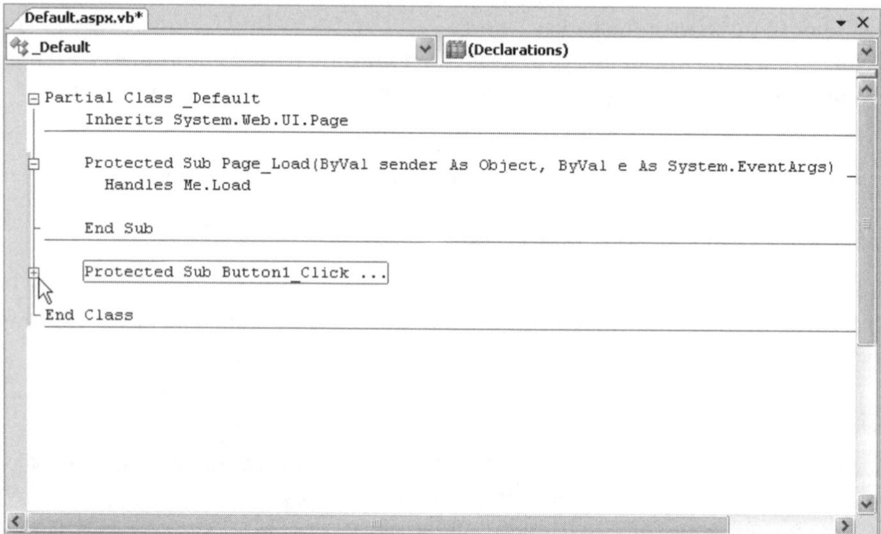

Figure 4-14. *Collapsing code*

You can hide every method at once by right-clicking anywhere in the code window and choosing Outlining ➤ Collapse to Definitions.

Member List

Visual Studio makes it easy for you to interact with controls and classes. When you type a class or object name, it pops up a list of available properties and methods (see Figure 4-15). It uses a similar trick to provide a list of data types when you define a variable or to provide a list of valid values when you assign a value to an enumeration.

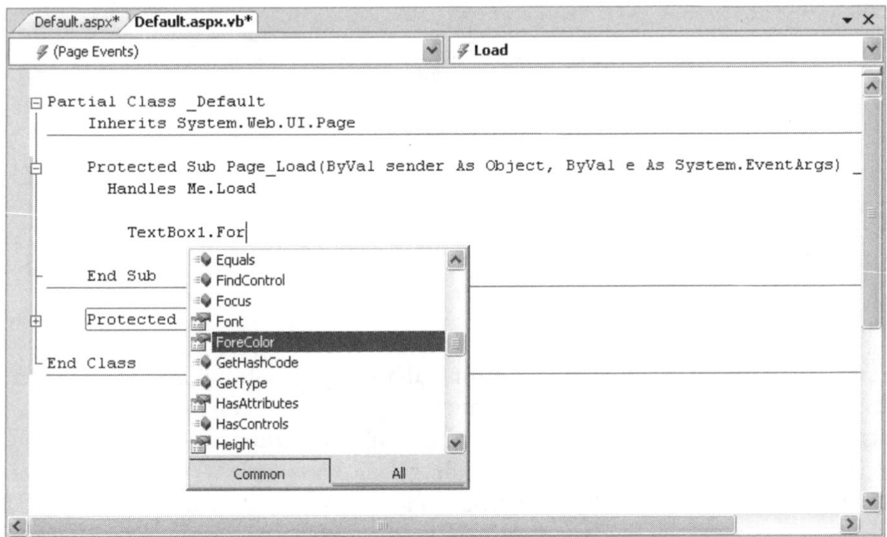

Figure 4-15. *IntelliSense at work*

Tip Forgotten the names of the controls in your web page? You can get IntelliSense to help you. Just type the Me keyword followed by the dot operator (.). Visual Studio will pop up a list with all the methods and properties of the current form class, including the control variables.

Visual Studio also provides a list of parameters and their data types when you call a method or invoke a constructor. This information is presented in a tooltip below the code and appears as you type. Because the .NET class library uses method overloading a lot, these methods may have multiple versions. When they do, Visual Studio indicates the number of versions and allows you to see the method definitions for each one by clicking the small up and down arrows in the tooltip. Each time you click the arrow, the tooltip displays a different version of the overloaded method (see Figure 4-16).

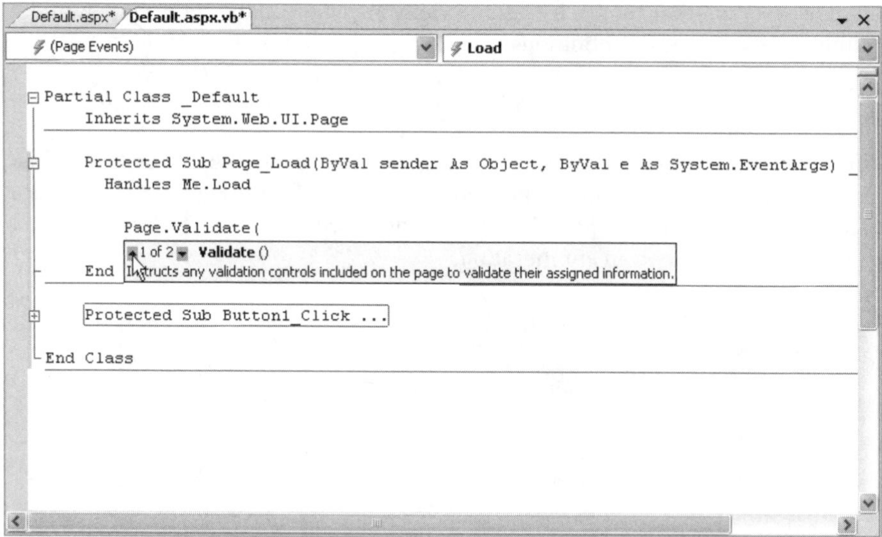

Figure 4-16. *IntelliSense with overloaded methods*

Error Underlining

One of the code editor's most useful features is error underlining. Visual Studio is able to detect a variety of error conditions, such as undefined variables, properties, or methods; invalid data type conversions; and missing code elements. Rather than stopping you to alert you that a problem exists, the Visual Studio editor underlines the offending code. You can hover your mouse over an underlined error to see a brief tooltip description of the problem (see Figure 4-17).

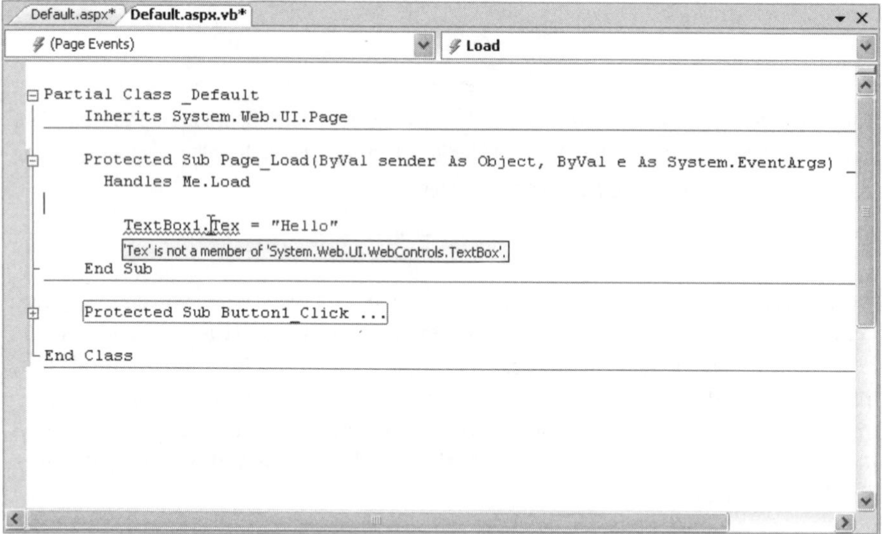

Figure 4-17. *Highlighting errors at design time*

If you try to run a web page that contains an error, Visual Studio will ask you whether it should continue. At this point, you'll almost always decide to cancel the operation and fix the problems Visual Studio has discovered. (If you choose to continue, you'll actually wind up using the last compiled version of your application, because Visual Studio can't build an application that has errors.)

Whenever you attempt to build an application that has errors, Visual Studio will display the Error List window with a list of all the problems it detected, as shown in Figure 4-18. You can then jump quickly to a problem by double-clicking it in the list.

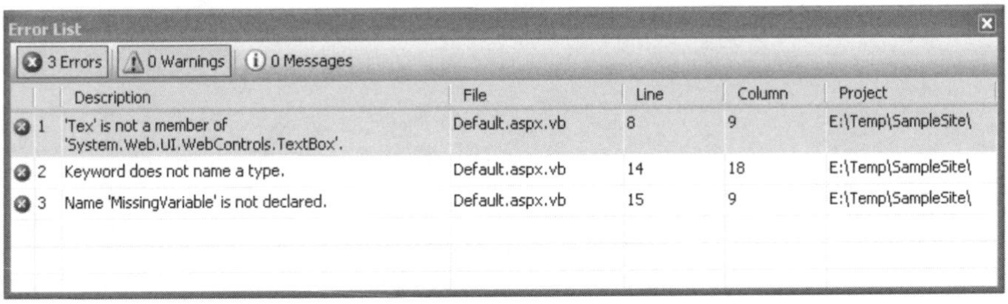

Error List

3 Errors | 0 Warnings | 0 Messages

	Description	File	Line	Column	Project
1	'Tex' is not a member of 'System.Web.UI.WebControls.TextBox'.	Default.aspx.vb	8	9	E:\Temp\SampleSite\
2	Keyword does not name a type.	Default.aspx.vb	14	18	E:\Temp\SampleSite\
3	Name 'MissingVariable' is not declared.	Default.aspx.vb	15	9	E:\Temp\SampleSite\

Figure 4-18. *The Error List window*

You can also configure the level of error checking Visual Studio performs for markup in your .aspx files. Usually, you'll want to set the level of validation to match the doctype that you're using. Unfortunately, Visual Studio doesn't take this step automatically. Instead, it's up to you to choose the level of validation you want from the drop-down list in the HTML Source Editing toolbar. (If the HTML Source Editing toolbar is not currently displayed, right-click the toolbar strip and choose HTML Source Editing.) The most common validation choices are HTML 4.01, XHTML 1.0 Transitional, and XHTML 1.1. For example, if you choose XHTML 1.0 Transitional or XHTML 1.1, you'll receive a warning in the Error List if your web page includes syntax that's not legal in XHTML, like incorrect capitalization, an obsolete formatting attribute, or an element that's not properly closed. You'll still be able to run your web page, but you'll know that your page isn't completely consistent with the XHTML standard.

AutoCorrect

Not only does IntelliSense help you code and catch mistakes you make, but it can also suggest corrections with a feature called AutoCorrect.

To see AutoCorrect in action, enter this line of code inside an event handler:

```
Dim fs As New FileStream("newfile.txt", FileMode.Create)
```

This line creates an instance of the FileStream class, which resides in the System.IO namespace. However, if you haven't imported the System.IO namespace, you'll run into a compile-time error and the line will be underlined in blue. Unfortunately, the error simply indicates that no known class named FileStream exists—it doesn't indicate whether the problem is a misspelling or a missing import, and it doesn't tell you which namespace has the class you need. However, AutoCorrect can help.

To see AutoCorrect in action, hover over the error. A red exclamation mark icon will appear that, when clicked, shows a window with the suggested correction (see Figure 4-19).

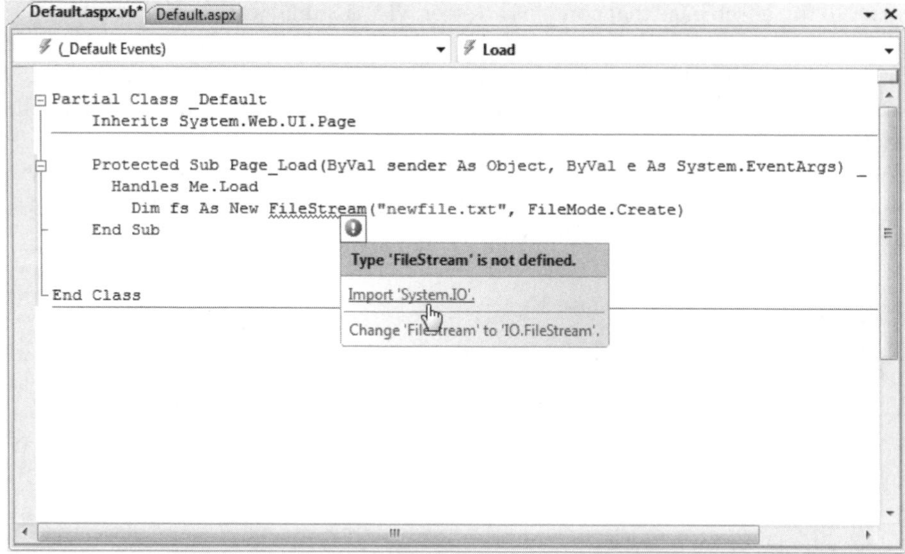

Figure 4-19. *Fixing an error with AutoCorrect*

Other problems that AutoCorrect can resolve include automatic data type conversion (if you have Option Strict switched on), misspelled keywords, and missing lines in a block structure.

Auto Format and Color

Visual Studio also provides some cosmetic conveniences. It automatically colors your code, making comments green, keywords blue, and normal code black. The result is much more readable code. You can even configure the colors Visual Studio uses by selecting Tools ➤ Options and then choosing the Environment ➤ Fonts and Colors section.

In addition, Visual Studio is configured by default to automatically format your code. This means you can type your code lines freely without worrying about tabs and positioning. Visual Studio automatically applies the "correct" indenting. Fortunately, if you have a different preference (for example, you want five spaces instead of four spaces of indenting, or you want to use tabs instead of spaces), you can configure this behavior. Just select Tools ➤ Options, and find the Text Editor ➤ Basic group of settings.

Visual Studio Debugging

Once you've created an application, you can compile and run it by choosing Debug ➤ Start Debugging from the menu or by clicking the Start Debugging button on the toolbar (which looks like a DVD-style play button). Visual Studio launches your default web browser and requests the page that's currently selected in the Solution Explorer. This is a handy trick—if you're in the middle of coding SalesPage1.aspx, you'll see SalesPage1.aspx appear in the browser, not the Default.aspx home page.

The first time you launch a web application, Visual Studio will ask you whether you want to configure your web application to allow debugging by adjusting its configuration file.

(Figure 4-20 shows the message you'll see.) Choose "Modify the Web.config file to enable debugging." and click OK.

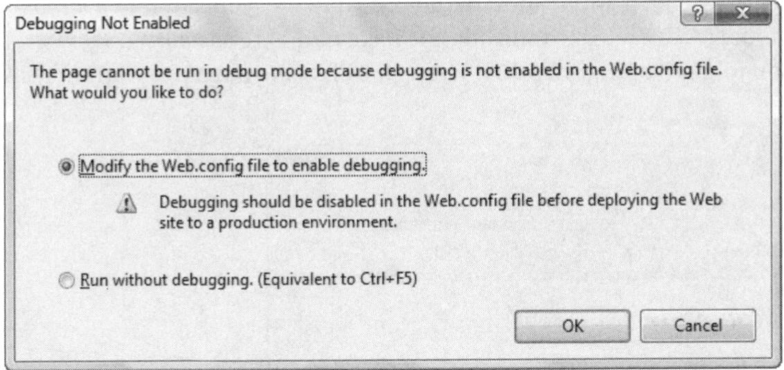

Figure 4-20. *Enabling debugging*

Visual Studio may also warn you that script debugging is disabled, depending on your browser preferences. Script debugging is a useful tool that works with Visual Studio to help you debug pages that use ASP.NET AJAX (a feature you'll consider in Chapter 25). However, there's no reason to turn script debugging on unless you're writing client-side JavaScript code in your web pages. (By default, script debugging is disabled in Internet Explorer so that you don't get error messages when you run someone else's problematic JavaScript code when visiting a website.) It's a good idea to choose the "Don't show this dialog again" to make sure Visual Studio doesn't repeat the same warning every time you run your web application.

■ **Tip** Regardless of what you choose in Visual Studio, you can change the script debugging setting at any time through Internet Explorer. Just choose Tools ➤ Internet Options from the Internet Explorer menu, pick the Advanced tab, and look for the "Disable Script Debugging" setting under the Browsing group.

The Visual Studio Web Server

When you run a web application, Visual Studio starts its integrated web server. Behind the scenes, ASP.NET compiles the code for your web application, runs your web page, and then returns the final HTML to the browser. The first time you run a web page, you'll see a new icon appear in the system tray at the bottom-right corner of the taskbar. This icon is Visual Studio's test web server, which runs in the background hosting your website. The test server only runs while Visual Studio is running, and it only accepts requests from your computer (so other users can't connect to it over a network).

When you run a web page, you'll notice that the URL in the browser includes a port number. For example, if you run a web application in a folder named OnlineBank, you might see a URL like `http://localhost:4235/OnlineBank/Default.aspx`. This URL indicates that the web server is running on your computer (localhost), so its requests aren't being sent over the Internet. It also indicates that all requests are being transmitted to port number 4235. That way, the requests won't conflict with any other applications that might be running on your computer and listening for requests. Every time Visual Studio starts the integrated web server, it randomly chooses an available port.

Visual Studio's built-in web server also allows you to retrieve a listing of all the files in your website. This means if you create a web application named SampleSite, you can request it in the form `http://localhost:port/SampleSite` (omitting the page name) to see a list of all the files in your web application folder (see Figure 4-21). Then, just click the page you want to test.

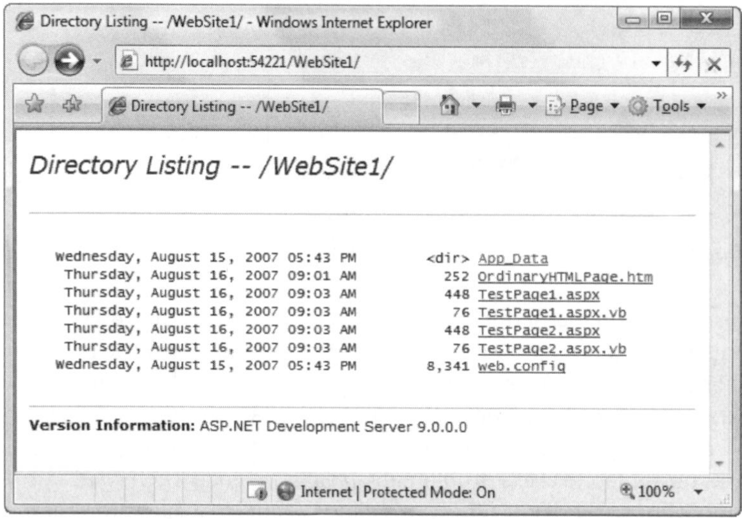

Figure 4-21. *Choosing from a list of pages*

This trick won't work if you have a Default.aspx page. If you do, any requests that don't indicate the page you want are automatically redirected to this page.

Single-Step Debugging

Single-step debugging allows you to test your assumptions about how your code works and see what's really happening under the hood of your application. It's incredibly easy to use. Just follow these steps:

1. Find a location in your code where you want to pause execution. (You can use any executable line of code but not a variable declaration, comment, or blank line.) Click in the margin next to the line of code, and a red breakpoint will appear (see Figure 4-22).

2. Now start your program as you would ordinarily (by pressing the F5 key or using the Start button on the toolbar). When the program reaches your breakpoint, execution will pause, and you'll be switched to the Visual Studio code window. The breakpoint statement won't be executed yet.

3. At this point, you have several options. You can execute the current line by pressing F8. The following line in your code will be highlighted with a yellow arrow, indicating that this is the next line that will be executed. You can continue like this through your program, running one line at a time by pressing F8 and following the code's path of execution.

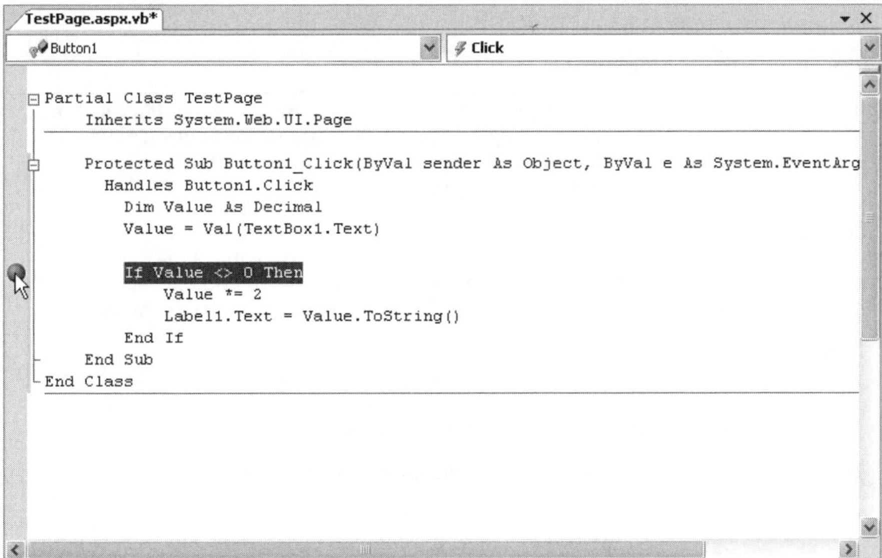

Figure 4-22. *Setting a breakpoint*

4. Whenever the code is in break mode, you can hover over variables to see their current contents (see Figure 4-23). This allows you to verify that variables contain the values you expect.

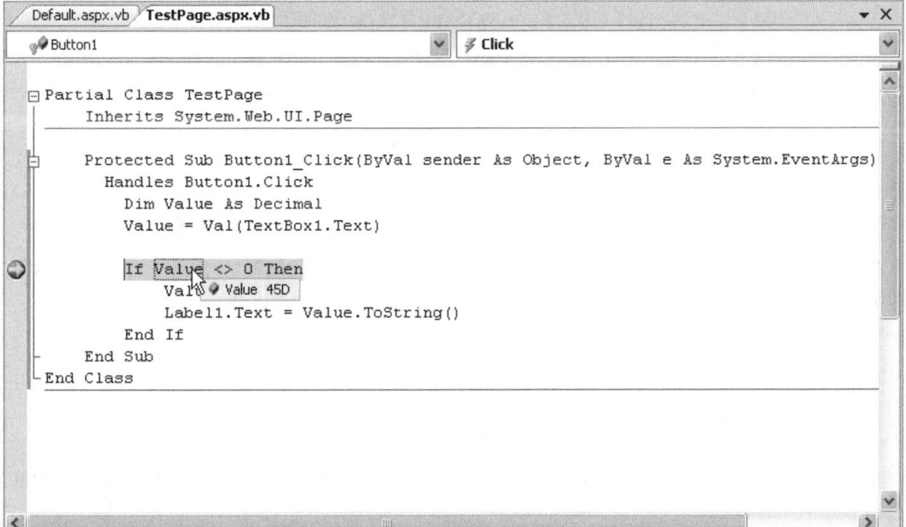

Figure 4-23. *Viewing variable contents in break mode*

5. You can also use any of the commands listed in Table 4-2 while in break mode. These commands are available from the context menu by right-clicking the code window or by using the associated hot key.

Table 4-2. *Commands Available in Break Mode*

Command (Hot Key)	Description
Step Into (F8)	Executes the currently highlighted line and then pauses. If the currently highlighted line calls a method, execution will pause at the first executable line inside the method (which is why this feature is called stepping *into*).
Step Over (Shift+F8)	The same as Step Into, except it runs methods as though they are a single line. If you select Step Over while a method call is highlighted, the entire method will be executed. Execution will pause at the next executable statement in the current method.
Step Out (Ctrl+Shift+F8)	Executes all the code in the current procedure and then pauses at the statement that immediately follows the one that called this method or function. In other words, this allows you to step "out" of the current procedure in one large jump.
Continue (F5)	Resumes the program and continues to run it normally, without pausing until another breakpoint is reached.
Run to Cursor	Allows you to run all the code up to a specific line (where your cursor is currently positioned). You can use this technique to skip a time-consuming loop.
Set Next Statement	Allows you to change the path of execution of your program while debugging. This command causes your program to mark the current line (where your cursor is positioned) as the current line for execution. When you resume execution, this line will be executed, and the program will continue from that point. Although this technique is convenient for jumping over large loops and simulating certain conditions, it's easy to cause confusion and runtime errors by using it recklessly.
Show Next Statement	Brings you to the line of code where Visual Studio is currently halted. (This is the line of code that will be executed next when you continue.) This line is marked by a yellow arrow. The Show Next Statement command is useful if you lose your place while editing.

You can switch your program into break mode at any point by clicking the Pause button in the toolbar or selecting Debug ➤ Break All. This might not stop your code where you expect, however, so you'll need to rummage around to get your bearings.

■ **Tip** As you're just starting out with ASP.NET, you won't have a lot of code to debug. However, be sure to return to this section as you try out more detailed examples in the following chapters. Visual Studio's debugging tools are an invaluable way to get a close-up look at how code operates.

When debugging a large website, you might place breakpoints in different places in your code and in multiple web pages. To get an at-a-glance look at all the breakpoints in your web application, choose Debug ➤ Windows ➤ Breakpoints. You'll see a list of all your breakpoints, as shown in Figure 4-24.

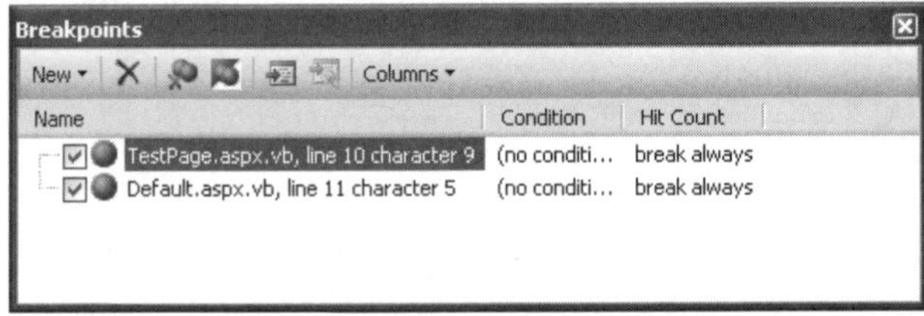

Figure 4-24. *The Breakpoints window*

You can jump to the location in code where a breakpoint is placed by double-clicking it in the list. You can also remove a breakpoint (select it and press Delete) or temporarily disable a breakpoint (by removing the check mark next to it). This allows you to keep a breakpoint to use in testing later, without leaving it active.

ADVANCED BREAKPOINTS

Visual Studio allows you to customize breakpoints so they occur only if certain conditions are true. To customize a breakpoint, right-click it in the Breakpoints window. A pop-up menu will appear with several options for making the breakpoint conditional:

- Click Location to see the exact code file and line where this breakpoint is positioned.
- Click Condition to set an expression. You can choose to break when this expression is true or when it has changed since the last time the breakpoint was hit.
- Click Hit Count to create a breakpoint that pauses only after a breakpoint has been hit a certain number of times (for example, at least 20) or a specific multiple of times (for example, every fifth time).
- Click Filter to restrict the breakpoint to specific processes or threads. (This technique is rarely useful in ASP.NET web page code.)
- Click When Hit to choose another action that Visual Studio should take when the breakpoint is reached, such as running a macro or printing a debug message. If you choose to take one of these actions, you can also specify whether the breakpoint should force Visual Studio into break mode, or whether your code should continue executing.

Breakpoints are automatically saved with the Visual Studio solution files, although they aren't used when you compile the application in release mode.

Variable Watches

In some cases, you might want to track the status of a variable without switching into break mode repeatedly. In this case, it's more useful to use the Autos, Locals, and Watch windows, which allow you to track variables across an entire application. Table 4-3 describes these windows.

Table 4-3. *Variable Watch Windows*

Window	Description
Autos	Automatically displays variables that Visual Studio determines are important for the current code statement. For example, this might include variables that are accessed or changed in the previous line.
Locals	Automatically displays all the variables that are in scope in the current method. This offers a quick summary of important variables.
Watch	Displays variables you have added. Watches are saved with your project, so you can continue tracking a variable later. To add a watch, right-click a variable in your code, and select Add Watch; alternatively, double-click the last row in the Watch window, and type in the variable name.

Each row in the Autos, Locals, and Watch windows provides information about the type or class of the variable and its current value. If the variable holds an object instance, you can expand the variable and see its members and properties. For example, in the Locals window you'll see the variable Me (see Figure 4-25), which is a reference to the current object inside of which your code is executing (in this case, the web page). If you click the plus (+) sign next to the word Me, a full list will appear that describes many page properties (and some system values).

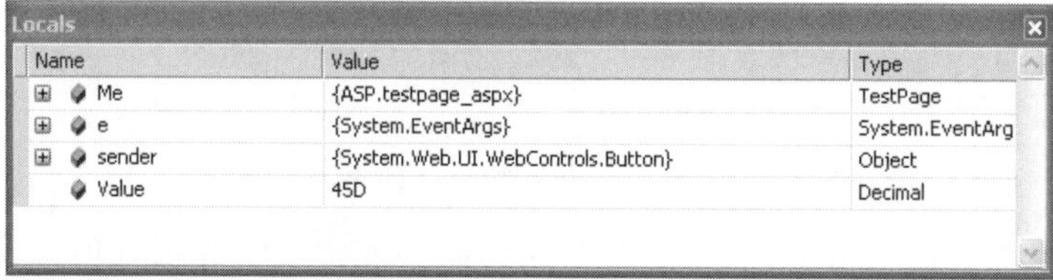

Figure 4-25. *Viewing the current page object in the Locals window*

If you are missing one of the Watch windows, you can show it manually by selecting it from the Debug ➤ Windows submenu.

■ **Tip** The Autos, Locals, and Watch windows allow you to change simple variables while your program is in break mode. Just double-click the current value in the Value column, and type in a new value. This allows you to simulate scenarios that are difficult or time-consuming to re-create manually and allows you to test specific error conditions.

The Last Word

In this chapter, you took a quick look at Visual Studio 2008. First, you saw how to create a new web application using the clean projectless website model. Next, you considered how to design basic web pages, complete with controls and code. Finally, you saw how to use Visual Studio's rich set of debugging features to get into the brain of your web page code and track down elusive problems.

In the next chapter, you'll start building simple web applications with Visual Studio, and get your first full look at the ASP.NET web page model.

CHAPTER 5

■ ■ ■

Web Form Fundamentals

In this chapter, you'll learn some of the core topics that every ASP.NET developer must master. You'll begin by taking a closer look at the ASP.NET application model, and considering what files and folders belong in a web application. Next, you'll take a closer look at server controls, the basic building block of any web form. You'll study a simple currency converter page that demonstrates how to convert ordinary HTML into a dynamic ASP.NET-powered web page. You'll then explore the web page model, and pick up the skills you need to create controls on the fly, navigate from one page to another, and handle special characters in HTML. Finally, you'll consider the ASP.NET configuration model.

The Anatomy of an ASP.NET Application

It's sometimes difficult to define exactly what a web application is. Unlike a traditional desktop program (which users start by running a stand-alone EXE file), ASP.NET applications are almost always divided into multiple web pages. This division means a user can enter an ASP.NET application at several different points or follow a link from the application to another part of the website or another web server. So, does it make sense to consider a website as an application?

In ASP.NET, the answer is yes. Every ASP.NET application shares a common set of resources and configuration settings. Web pages from other ASP.NET applications don't share these resources, even if they're on the same web server. Technically speaking, every ASP.NET application is executed inside a separate *application domain*. Application domains are isolated areas in memory, and they ensure that even if one web application causes a fatal error, it's unlikely to affect any other application that is currently running on the same computer. Similarly, application domains restrict a web page in one application from accessing the in-memory information of another application. Each web application is maintained separately and has its own set of cached, application, and session data.

The standard definition of an ASP.NET application describes it as a combination of files, pages, handlers, modules, and executable code that can be invoked from a virtual directory (and, optionally, its subdirectories) on a web server. In other words, the virtual directory is the basic grouping structure that delimits an application. Figure 5-1 shows a web server that hosts four separate web applications.

Note A *virtual directory* is a directory that's exposed to the public on a web server. As you'll discover in Chapter 9, you deploy your perfected ASP.NET web application by copying it to a virtual directory.

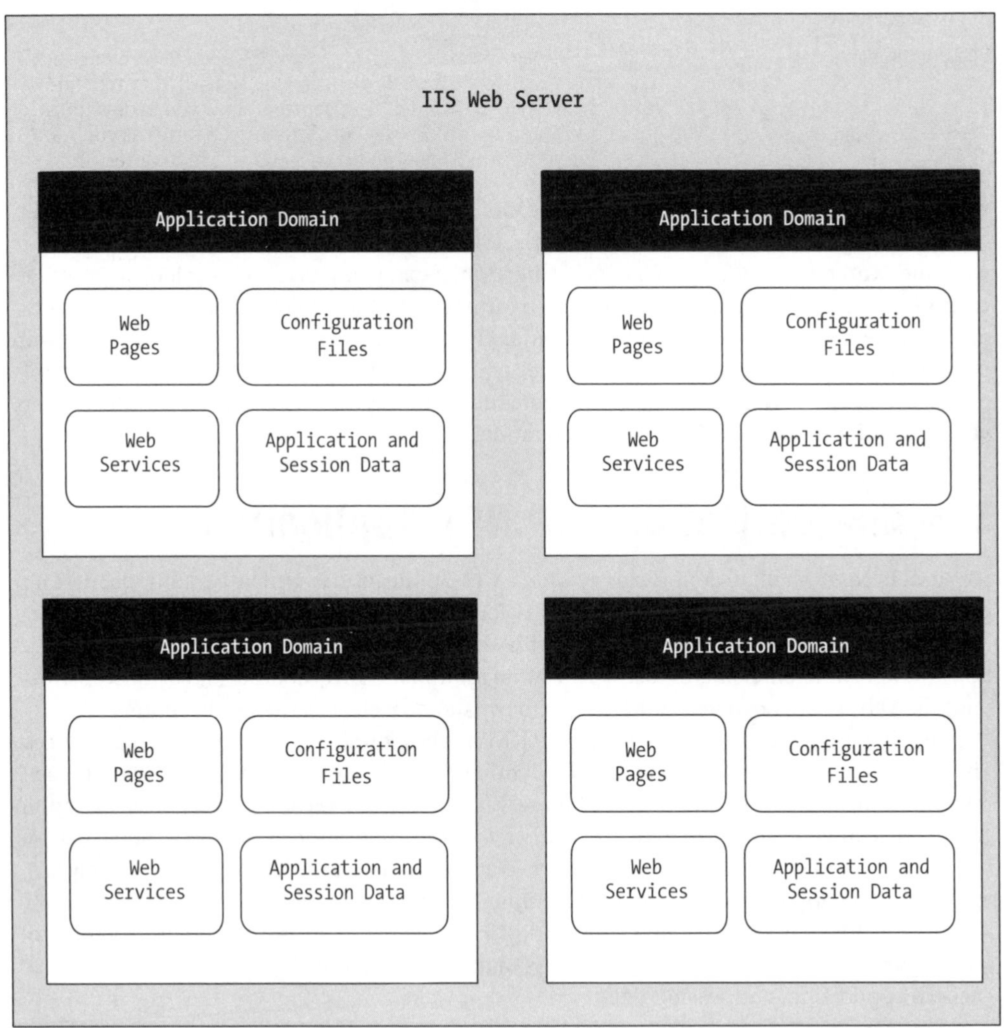

Figure 5-1. *ASP.NET applications*

ASP.NET File Types

ASP.NET applications can include many types of files. Table 5-1 introduces the essential ingredients.

Table 5-1. *ASP.NET File Types*

File Name	Description
Ends with .aspx	These are ASP.NET web pages (the .NET equivalent of the .asp file in an ASP application). They contain the user interface and, optionally, the underlying application code. Users request or navigate directly to one of these pages to start your web application.
Ends with .ascx	These are ASP.NET user controls. User controls are similar to web pages, except that the user can't access these files directly. Instead, they must be hosted inside an ASP.NET web page. User controls allow you to develop a small piece of user interface and reuse it in as many web forms as you want without repetitive code. You'll learn about user controls in Chapter 12.
Ends with .asmx	These are ASP.NET web services—collections of methods that can be called over the Internet. Web services work differently than web pages, but they still share the same application resources, configuration settings, and memory. You'll see an example that uses a web service in Chapter 25.
web.config	This is the XML-based configuration file for your ASP.NET application. It includes settings for customizing security, state management, memory management, and much more. You'll get an introduction to the web.config file in this chapter, and you'll explore its settings throughout this book.
Global.asax	This is the global application file. You can use this file to define global variables (variables that can be accessed from any web page in the web application) and react to global events (such as when a web application first starts). You'll learn about it in Chapter 7.
Ends with .vb	These are code-behind files that contain VB code. They allow you to separate the application logic from the user interface of a web page. We'll introduce the code-behind model in this chapter and use it extensively in this book.

In addition, your web application can contain other resources that aren't special ASP.NET files. For example, your virtual directory can hold image files, HTML files, or CSS files. These resources might be used in one of your ASP.NET web pages, or they might be used independently. A website could even combine static HTML pages with dynamic ASP.NET pages.

Most of the file types in Table 5-1 are optional. You can create a legitimate ASP.NET application with a single .aspx web page file.

ASP.NET Application Directories

Every web application should have a well-planned directory structure. For example, you'll probably want to store images in a separate folder from where you store your web pages. Or you might want to put public ASP.NET pages in one folder and restricted ones in another so you can apply different security settings based on the directory. (See Chapter 20 for more about how to create authorization rules like this.)

Along with the directories you create, ASP.NET also uses a few specialized subdirectories, which it recognizes by name (see Table 5-2). Keep in mind that you won't see all these directories in a typical application. Visual Studio will prompt you to create them as needed.

Table 5-2. *ASP.NET Directories*

Directory	Description
Bin	Contains all the compiled .NET components (DLLs) that the ASP.NET web application uses. For example, if you develop a custom component for accessing a database (see Chapter 23), you'll place the component here. ASP.NET will automatically detect the assembly, and any page in the web application will be able to use it. This seamless deployment model is far easier than working with traditional COM components, which must be registered before they can be used (and often reregistered when they change).
App_Code	Contains source code files that are dynamically compiled for use in your application. You can use this directory in a similar way as the Bin directory; the only difference is that you place source code files here instead of compiled assemblies.
App_GlobalResources	Stores global resources that are accessible to every page in the web application. This directory is used in localization scenarios, when you need to have a website in more than one language. Localization isn't covered in this book, although you can refer to *Pro ASP.NET 3.5 in VB* (Apress, 2007) for more information.
App_LocalResources	Serves the same purpose as App_GlobalResources, except these resources are accessible to a specific page only.
App_WebReferences	Stores references to web services that the web application uses. For more information about web services, you can download a three-chapter introduction from the previous edition of this book, in PDF form, at `www.prosetech.com`.
App_Data	Stores data, including SQL Server 2005 Express Edition database files and XML files. Of course, you're free to store data files in other directories.
App_Themes	Stores the themes that are used by your web application. You'll learn about themes in Chapter 13.

Introducing Server Controls

ASP.NET introduces a remarkable new model for creating web pages. In old-style web development, programmers had to master the quirks and details of HTML before they could design a dynamic web page. Pages had to be carefully tailored to a specific task, and the only way to generate additional content was to generate raw HTML tags.

ASP.NET solves this problem with a higher-level model of *server controls*. These controls are created and configured as objects. They run on the web server and they automatically provide their own HTML output. Even better, server controls behave like their Windows counterparts by maintaining state and raising events that you can react to in code.

In the previous chapter, you built an exceedingly simple web page that incorporated a few controls you dragged in from the Visual Studio Toolbox. But before you create a more complex page, it's worth taking a step back to look at the big picture. ASP.NET actually provides *two* sets of server-side controls that you can incorporate into your web forms. These two different types of controls play subtly different roles:

HTML server controls: These are server-based equivalents for standard HTML elements. These controls are ideal if you're a seasoned web programmer who prefers to work with familiar HTML tags (at least at first). They are also useful when migrating ordinary HTML pages or ASP pages to ASP.NET, because they require the fewest changes.

Web controls: These are similar to the HTML server controls, but they provide a richer object model with a variety of properties for style and formatting details. They also provide more events and more closely resemble the controls used for Windows development. Web controls also feature some user interface elements that have no direct HTML equivalent, such as the GridView, Calendar, and validation controls.

You'll learn about web controls in the next chapter. In this chapter, you'll take a detailed look at HTML server controls.

■ **Note** Even if you plan to use web controls exclusively, it's worth reading through this section to master the basics of HTML controls. Along the way, you'll get an introduction to a few ASP.NET essentials that apply to all kinds of server controls, including view state, postbacks, and event handling.

HTML Server Controls

HTML server controls provide an object interface for standard HTML elements. They provide three key features:

They generate their own interface: You set properties in code, and the underlying HTML tag is created automatically when the page is rendered and sent to the client.

They retain their state: Because the Web is stateless, ordinary web pages need to do a lot of work to store information between requests. HTML server controls handle this task automatically. For example, if the user selects an item in a list box, that item remains selected the next time the page is generated. Or, if your code changes the text in a button, the new text sticks the next time the page is posted back to the web server.

They fire server-side events: For example, buttons fire an event when clicked, text boxes fire an event when the text they contain is modified, and so on. Your code can respond to these events, just like ordinary controls in a Windows application. In ASP code, everything is grouped into one block that executes from start to finish. With event-based programming, you can easily respond to individual user actions and create more structured code. If a given event doesn't occur, the event-handler code won't be executed.

HTML server controls are ideal when you're performing a quick translation to add server-side code to an existing HTML page. That's the task you'll tackle in the next section, with a simple one-page web application.

Converting an HTML Page to an ASP.NET Page

Figure 5-2 shows a currency converter web page. It allows the user to convert a number of U.S. dollars to the equivalent amount of euros—or at least it would, if it had the code it needed to do the job. Right now, it's just a plain, inert HTML page. Nothing happens when the button is clicked.

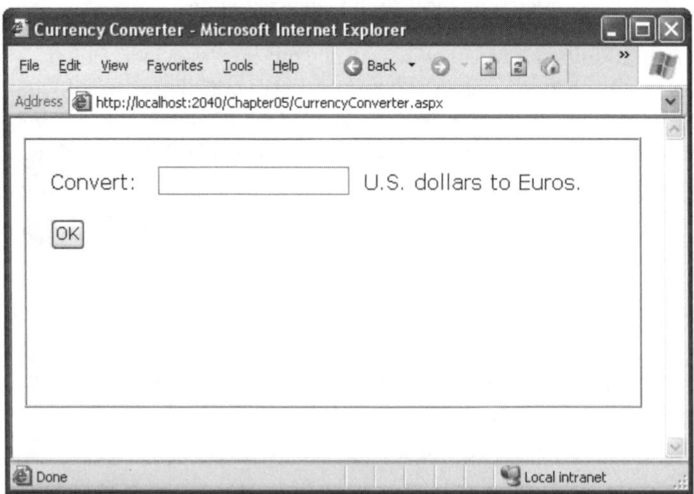

Figure 5-2. *A simple currency converter*

The following listing shows the markup for this page. To make it as clear as possible, this listing omits the style attribute of the <div> element used for the border. This page has two <input> elements: one for the text box and one for the submit button. These elements are enclosed in a <form> tag, so they can submit information to the server when the button is clicked. The rest of the page consists of static text. The   character entity is used to add an extra space to separate the controls. A doctype at the top of the page declares that it's written according to the strict markup rules of XHTML 1.1.

```
<!DOCTYPE html PUBLIC "-//W3C//DTD XHTML 1.1//EN"
 "http://www.w3.org/TR/xhtml11/DTD/xhtml11.dtd">

<html xmlns="http://www.w3.org/1999/xhtml">
  <head>
    <title>Currency Converter</title>
  </head>
  <body>
    <form method="post">
      <div>
        Convert: 
        <input type="text" />
         U.S. dollars to Euros.
        <br /><br />
        <input type="submit" value="OK" />
      </div>
    </form>
```

```
  </body>
</html>
```

Note In HTML all input controls are represented with the <input> element. You set the type attribute to indicate the type of control you want. The <input type="text"> tag is a text box, while <input type="submit"> creates a submit button for sending the web page back to the web server. This is quite a bit different than the web controls you'll see in Chapter 6, which use a different element for each type of control.

As it stands, this page looks nice but provides no functionality. It consists entirely of the user interface (HTML elements) and contains no code. It's an ordinary HTML page—not a web form.

The easiest way to convert the currency converter to ASP.NET is to start by generating a new web form in Visual Studio. To do this, select Website ➤ Add New Item. In the Add New Item dialog box, choose Web Form, type a name for the new page (such as CurrencyConverter.aspx), make sure the Place Code in Separate File option is checked, and click Add to create the page.

In the new web form, delete everything that's currently in the .aspx file, except the *page directive*. The page directive gives ASP.NET basic information about how to compile the page. It indicates the language you're using for your code and the way you connect your event handlers. If you're using the code-behind approach, which is recommended, the page directive also indicates where the code file is located and the name of your custom page class.

Finally, copy all the content from the original HTML page, and paste it into the new page, right after the page directive. Here's the resulting web form, with the page directive (in bold) followed by the HTML content that's copied from the original page:

```
<%@ Page Language="VB" AutoEventWireup="false"
    CodeFile="CurrencyConverter.aspx.vb" Inherits="CurrencyConverter" %>

<!DOCTYPE html PUBLIC "-//W3C//DTD XHTML 1.1//EN"
 "http://www.w3.org/TR/xhtml11/DTD/xhtml11.dtd">
<html xmlns="http://www.w3.org/1999/xhtml">
  <head>
    <title>Currency Converter</title>
  </head>
  <body>
    <form method="post">
      <div>
        Convert:  
        <input type="text" />
          U.S. dollars to Euros.
        <br /><br />
        <input type="submit" value="OK" />
      </div>
    </form>
 </body>
</html>
```

Now you need to add the attribute runat="server" to each tag that you want to transform into a server control. You should also add an ID attribute to each control that you need to interact with in code. The ID attribute assigns the unique name that you'll use to refer to the control in code.

In the currency converter application, it makes sense to change the input text box and the submit button into HTML server controls. In addition, the <form> element must be processed as a server control to allow ASP.NET to access the controls it contains. Here's the complete, correctly modified page:

```
<%@ Page Language="VB" AutoEventWireup="false"
    CodeFile="CurrencyConverter.aspx.vb" Inherits="CurrencyConverter" %>

<!DOCTYPE html PUBLIC "-//W3C//DTD XHTML 1.1//EN"
 "http://www.w3.org/TR/xhtml11/DTD/xhtml11.dtd">
<html xmlns="http://www.w3.org/1999/xhtml">
  <head>
    <title>Currency Converter</title>
  </head>
  <body>
    <form runat="server">
      <div>
        Convert:  
        <input type="text" ID="US" runat="server" />
          U.S. dollars to Euros.
        <br /><br />
        <input type="submit" value="OK" ID="Convert" runat="server" />
      </div>
    </form>
  </body>
</html>
```

■ **Note** ASP.NET controls are always placed inside the <form> tag of the page. The <form> tag is a part of the standard for HTML forms, and it allows the browser to send information to the web server.

The web page still won't do anything when you run it, because you haven't written any code. However, now that you've converted the static HTML elements to HTML server controls, you're ready to work with them.

View State

To try this page, launch it in Visual Studio by pressing F5. Remember, the first time you run your web application you'll be prompted to let Visual Studio modify your web.config file to allow debugging. Click OK to accept its recommendation and launch your web page in the browser. Then, select View ➤ Source in your browser to look at the HTML that ASP.NET sent your way.

The first thing you'll notice is that the HTML that was sent to the browser is slightly different from the information in the .aspx file. First, the runat="server" attributes are stripped out (because they have no meaning to the client browser, which can't interpret them). Second, and more important, an additional hidden field has been added to the form. Here's what you'll see (in a slightly simplified form):

```
<!DOCTYPE html PUBLIC "-//W3C//DTD XHTML 1.1//EN"
 "http://www.w3.org/TR/xhtml11/DTD/xhtml11.dtd">
<html xmlns="http://www.w3.org/1999/xhtml">
  <head>
    <title>Currency Converter</title>
  </head>
  <body>
    <form ID="form1" name="form1" method="post" action="CurrencyConverter.aspx">
      <div>
        <input type="hidden" ID="__VIEWSTATE" name="__VIEWSTATE"
         value="dDw3NDg2NTI5MDg7Oz4=" />
      </div>
      <div>
        Convert:  
        <input type="text" ID="US" name="US" />
          U.S. dollars to Euros.
        <br /><br />
        <input type="submit" value="OK" ID="Convert" name="Convert" />
      </div>
    </form>
  </body>
</html>
```

This hidden field stores information, in a compressed format, about the state of every control in the page. It allows you to manipulate control properties in code and have the changes automatically persisted across multiple trips from the browser to the web server. This is a key part of the web forms programming model. Thanks to view state, you can often forget about the stateless nature of the Internet and treat your page like a continuously running application.

Even though the currency converter program doesn't yet include any code, you'll already notice one change. If you enter information in the text box and click the submit button to post the page, the refreshed page will still contain the value you entered in the text box. (In the original example that uses ordinary HTML elements, the value will be cleared every time the page is submitted.) This change occurs because ASP.NET controls automatically retain their state.

The HTML Control Classes

Before you can continue any further with the currency converter, you need to know about the control objects you've created. All the HTML server controls are defined in the System.Web.UI.HtmlControls namespace. Each kind of control has a separate class. Table 5-3 describes the basic HTML server controls and shows you the related HTML element.

Table 5-3. *The HTML Server Control Classes*

Class Name	HTML Element	Description
HtmlForm	<form>	Wraps all the controls on a web page. All ASP.NET server controls must be placed inside an HtmlForm control so that they can send their data to the server when the page is submitted. You don't need to add the <form> section—instead, Visual Studio will add it to your web page automatically. However, you *do* need to ensure that every other control you add is placed inside the <form> section.
HtmlAnchor	<a>	A hyperlink that the user clicks to jump to another page.
HtmlImage	<img>	A link that points to an image, which will be inserted into the web page at the current location.
HtmlTable, HtmlTableRow, and HtmlTableCell	<table>, <tr>, <th>, and <td>	A table that displays multiple rows and columns of static text.
HtmlInputButton, HtmlInputSubmit, and HtmlInputReset	<input type="button">, <input type="submit">, and <input type="reset">	A button that the user clicks to perform an action (HtmlInputButton), submit the page (HtmlInputSubmit), or clear all the user-supplied values in all the controls (HtmlInputReset).
HtmlButton	<button>	A button that the user clicks to perform an action. This is not supported by all browsers, so HtmlInputButton is usually used instead. The key difference is that the HtmlButton is a container element. As a result, you can insert just about anything inside it, including text and pictures. The HtmlInputButton, on the other hand, is strictly text-only.
HtmlInputCheckBox	<input type="checkbox">	A check box that the user can check or clear. Doesn't include any text of its own.
HtmlInputRadioButton	<input type="radio">	A radio button that can be selected in a group. Doesn't include any text of its own.

Table 5-3. *The HTML Server Control Classes*

Class Name	HTML Element	Description
HtmlInputText and HtmlInputPassword	<input type="text"> and <input type="password">	A single-line text box where the user can enter information. Can also be displayed as a password field (which displays bullets instead of characters to hide the user input).
HtmlTextArea	<textarea>	A large text box where the user can type multiple lines of text.
HtmlInputImage	<input type="image">	Similar to the <img> tag, but inserts a "clickable" image that submits the page. Using server-side code, you can determine exactly where the user clicked in the image—a technique you'll consider later in this chapter.
HtmlInputFile	<input type="file">	A Browse button and text box that can be used to upload a file to your web server, as described in Chapter 18.
HtmlInputHidden	<input type="hidden">	Contains text information that will be sent to the server when the page is posted back but won't be visible in the browser.
HtmlSelect	<select>	A drop-down or regular list box where the user can select an item.
HtmlHead and HtmlTitle	<head> and <title>	Represents the header information for the page, which includes information about the page that isn't actually displayed in the page, such as search keywords and the web page title. These are the only HTML server controls that aren't placed in the <form> section.
HtmlGenericControl	Any other HTML element.	This control can represent a variety of HTML elements that don't have dedicated control classes. For example, if you add the runat="server" attribute to a <div> element, it's provided to your code as an HtmlGenericControl object.

Remember, there are two ways to add any HTML server control. You can add it by hand to the markup in the .aspx file (simply insert the ordinary HTML element, and add the runat="server" attribute). Alternatively, you can drag the control from the HTML tab of the Toolbox, and drop it onto the design surface of a web page in Visual Studio. This approach doesn't work for every HTML server control, because they don't all appear in the HTML tab.

So far, the currency converter defines three controls, which are instances of the HtmlForm, HtmlInputText, and HtmlInputButton classes, respectively. It's useful to know the class names if you want to look up information about these classes in the Visual Studio Help. Table 5-4 gives a quick overview of some of the most important control properties.

Table 5-4. *Important HTML Control Properties*

Control	Most Important Properties
HtmlAnchor	HRef, Name, Target, Title
HtmlImage	Src, Alt, Align, Border, Width, Height
HtmlInputCheckBox and HtmlInputRadioButton	Checked
HtmlInputText	Value
HtmlTextArea	Value
HtmlInputImage	Src, Alt, Align, Border
HtmlSelect	Items (collection)
HtmlGenericControl	InnerText and InnerHtml

Adding the Currency Converter Code

To actually add some functionality to the currency converter, you need to add some ASP.NET code. Web forms are event-driven, which means every piece of code acts in response to a specific event. In the simple currency converter page example, the most useful event occurs when the user clicks the submit button (named Convert). The HtmlInputButton allows you to react to this action by handling the ServerClick event.

Before you continue, it makes sense to add another control that can display the result of the calculation. In this case, you can use a <div> tag named Result. The <div> tag is one way to insert a block of formatted text into a web page. Here's the HTML that you'll need:

```
<div style="font-weight: bold" ID="Result" runat="server"> ... </div>
```

The style attribute applies the CSS properties used to format the text. In this example, it merely applies a bold font.

The example now has the following four server controls:

- A form (HtmlForm object). This is the only control you do not need to access in your code-behind class.
- An input text box named US (HtmlInputText object).
- A submit button named Convert (HtmlInputButton object).
- A <div> tag named Result (HtmlGenericControl object).

Listing 5-1 shows the revised web page (CurrencyConverter.aspx), but leaves out the doctype to save space. Listing 5-2 shows the code-behind class (CurrencyConverter.aspx.vb). The code-behind class includes an event handler that reacts when the convert button is clicked. It calculates the currency conversion and displays the result.

Listing 5-1. *CurrencyConverter.aspx*

```
<%@ Page Language="VB" AutoEventWireup="false"
    CodeFile="CurrencyConverter.aspx.vb" Inherits="CurrencyConverter" %>
<html xmlns="http://www.w3.org/1999/xhtml">
  <head>
    <title>Currency Converter</title>
  </head>
  <body>
    <form runat="server">
      <div>
        Convert:  
        <input type="text" ID="US" runat="server" />
          U.S. dollars to Euros.
        <br /><br />
        <input type="submit" value="OK" ID="Convert" runat="server" />
        <br /><br />
        <div style="font-weight: bold" ID="Result" runat="server"></div>
      </div>
    </form>
  </body>
</html>
```

Listing 5-2. *CurrencyConverter.aspx.vb*

```
Public Partial Class CurrencyConverter
    Inherits System.Web.UI.Page

    Protected Sub Convert_ServerClick(ByVal sender As Object, _
      ByVal e As System.EventArgs) Handles Convert.ServerClick
        Dim USAmount As Double = Val(US.Value)
        Dim EuroAmount As Double = USAmount * 0.85
        Result.InnerText = USAmount.ToString() & " U.S. dollars = "
        Result.InnerText &= EuroAmount.ToString() & " Euros."
    End Sub
End Class
```

The code-behind class is a typical example of an ASP.NET page. You'll notice the following conventions:

- The page class is defined with the Partial keyword. That's because your class code is merged with another code file that you never see. This extra code, which ASP.NET generates automatically, defines all the server controls that are used on the page. This allows you to access them by name in your code.
- The page defines a single event handler. This event handler retrieves the value from the text box, converts it to a numeric value, multiplies it by a preset conversion ratio (which would typically be stored in another file or a database), and sets the text of the <div> tag. You'll notice that the event handler accepts two parameters (sender and e). This is the .NET standard for all control events. It allows your code to identify the control that sent the event (through the sender parameter) and retrieve any other information that may be associated with the event (through the e parameter). You'll see examples of these advanced techniques in the next chapter, but for now, it's important to realize that you won't be allowed to handle an event unless your event handler has the correct, matching signature.
- The event handler is connected to the control event using the Handles keyword in the event handler declaration. Usually, you'll let Visual Studio add this code in automatically, as described in the previous chapter.

■ Note Unlike with web controls, you can't create event handlers for HTML server controls using the Properties window. Instead, you must type the method in by hand, making sure to include the Handles clause at the end. Another option is to use the two drop-down lists at the top of the code window. To take this approach, choose the control in the list on the left (for example, Convert), and then choose the event you want to handle in the list on the right (for example, ServerClick). Visual Studio will create the corresponding event handler.

- The &= operator is used to quickly add information to the end of the label, without replacing the existing text.
- The event handler uses ToString() to convert the numeric value to text. You can perform the conversion without using ToString(), because VB is kind enough to implicitly convert a number to text as needed. However, it's always a good idea to handle these conversions explicitly to prevent unexpected errors. (For example, adding the strings "2" and "1" can produce a result of 3 or 21, depending on whether the conversion is made before or after the addition.)

You can launch this page to test your code. When you enter a value and click the OK button, the page is resubmitted, the event-handling code runs, and the page is returned to you with the conversion details (see Figure 5-3).

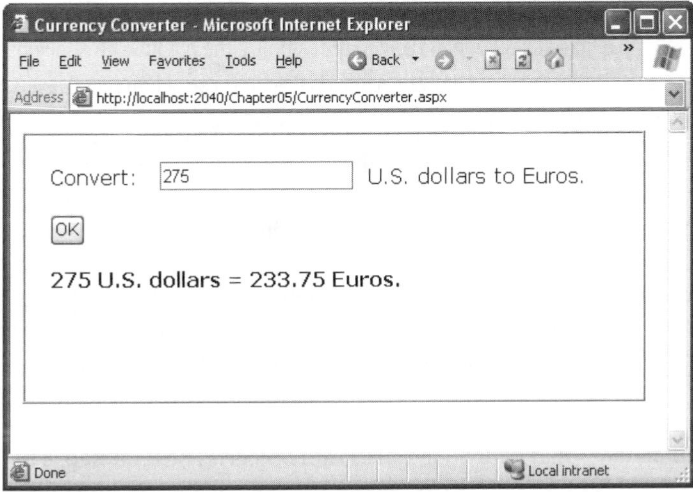

Figure 5-3. *The ASP.NET currency converter*

Behind the Scenes with the Currency Converter

So, what really happens when ASP.NET receives a request for the CurrencyConverter.aspx page? The process actually unfolds over several steps:

1. First, the request for the page is sent to the web server. If you're running a live site, the web server is almost certainly IIS, which you'll learn more about in Chapter 9. If you're running the page in Visual Studio, the request is sent to the built-in test server.
2. The web server determines that the .aspx file extension is registered with ASP.NET and passes it to the ASP.NET worker process. If the file extension belonged to another service (as it would for .asp or .html files), ASP.NET would never get involved.

3. If this is the first time a page in this application has been requested, ASP.NET automatically creates the application domain. It also compiles all the web page code for optimum performance, and caches the compiled files in the directory c:\Windows\Microsoft.NET\Framework\v2.0.50727\Temporary ASP.NET Files. If this task has already been performed, ASP.NET will reuse the compiled version of the page.
4. The compiled CurrencyConverter.aspx page acts like a miniature program. It starts firing events (most notably, the Page.Load event). However, you haven't created an event handler for that event, so no code runs. At this stage, everything is working together as a set of in-memory .NET objects.
5. When the code is finished, ASP.NET asks every control in the web page to render itself into the corresponding HTML markup.

■ **Tip** In fact, ASP.NET performs a little sleight of hand and may customize the output with additional client-side JavaScript or DHTML if it detects that the client browser supports it. In the case of CurrencyConverter.aspx, the output of the page is too simple to require this type of automatic tweaking.

---

6. The final page is sent to the user, and the application ends.

The description is lengthy, but it's important to start with a good understanding of the fundamentals. When you click a button on the page, the entire process repeats itself. However, in step 4 the ServerClick event fires for HtmlInputButton right after the Page.Load event, and your code runs.

Figure 5-4 illustrates the stages in a web page request.

The most important detail is that your code works with objects. The final step is to transform these objects into the appropriate HTML output. A similar conversion from objects to output happens with a Windows program in .NET, but it's so automatic that programmers rarely give it much thought. Also, in those environments, the code always runs locally. In an ASP.NET application, the code runs in a protected environment on the server. The client sees the results only once the web page processing has ended and the web page object has been released from memory.

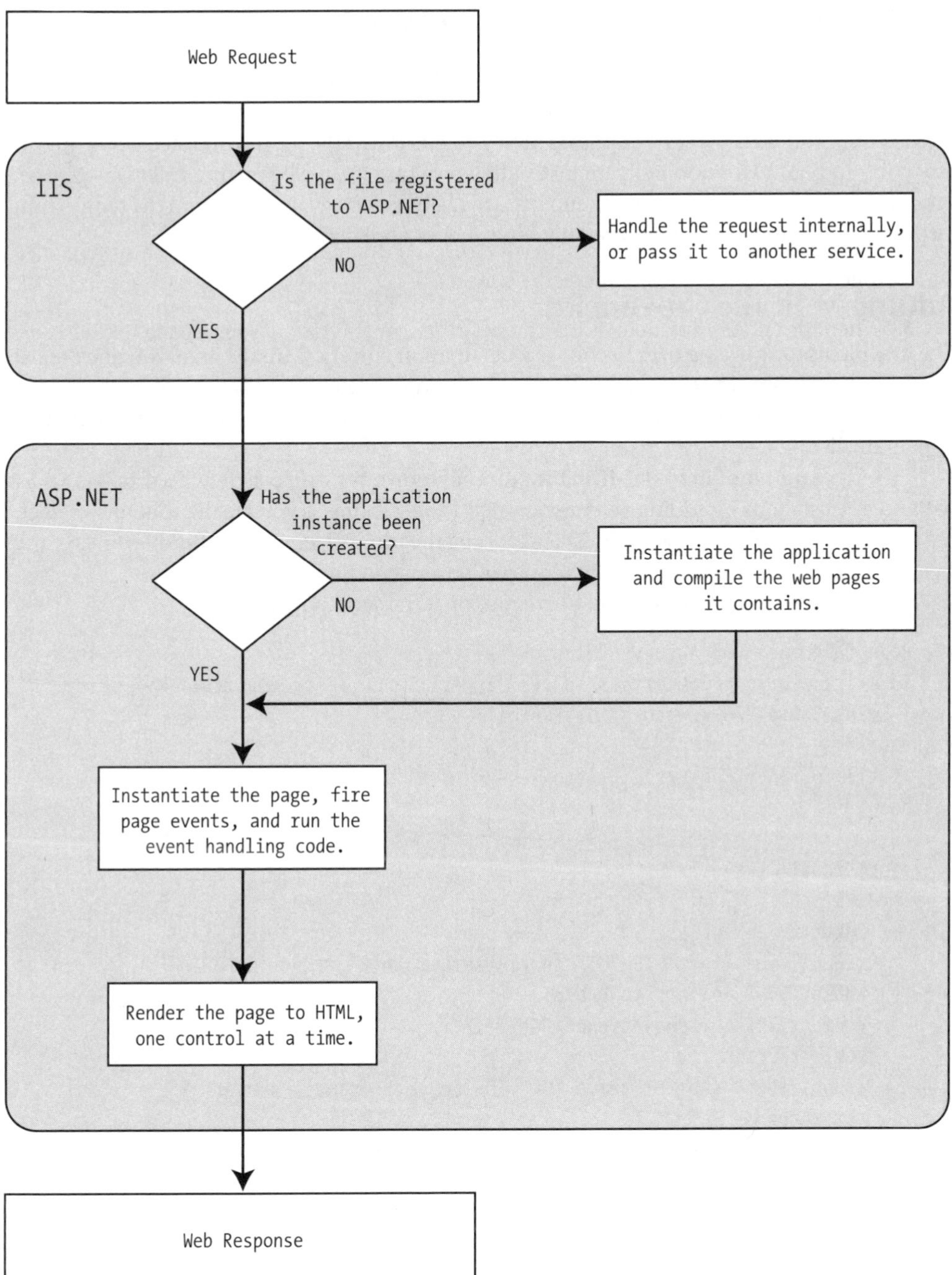

Figure 5-4. *The stages in an ASP.NET request*

Improving the Currency Converter

Now that you've looked at the basic server controls, it might seem that their benefits are fairly minor compared with the cost of learning a whole new system of web programming. In the next section, you'll start to extend the currency converter application. You'll see how you can "snap in" additional functionality to the existing program in an elegant, modular way. As the program grows, ASP.NET handles its complexity easily, steering you away from the tangled and intricate code that would be required in old-style ASP applications.

Adding Multiple Currencies

The first task is to allow the user to choose a destination currency. In this case, you need to use a drop-down list box. In HTML, a drop-down list is represented by a <select> element that contains one or more <option> elements. Each <option> element corresponds to a separate item in the list.

To reduce the amount of HTML in the currency converter, you can define a drop-down list without any list items by adding an empty <select> tag. As long as you ensure that this <select> tag is a server control (by giving it an ID and adding the runat="server" attribute), you'll be able to interact with it in code and add the required items when the page loads.

Here's the revised HTML for the CurrencyConverter.aspx page:

```
<%@ Page Language="VB" AutoEventWireup="false"
    CodeFile="CurrencyConverter.aspx.vb" Inherits="CurrencyConverter" %>
<html xmlns="http://www.w3.org/1999/xhtml">
  <head>
    <title>Currency Converter</title>
  </head>
  <body>
    <form runat="server">
      <div>
        Convert:  
        <input type="text" ID="US" runat="server" />
          U.S. dollars to  
        <select ID="Currency" runat="server" />
        <br /><br />
        <input type="submit" value="OK" ID="Convert" runat="server" />
        <br /><br />
        <div style="font-weight: bold" ID="Result" runat="server"></div>
      </div>
    </form>
  </body>
</html>
```

■ **Note** Up until this point, the samples in this book have included an XHTML doctype. Now that you're familiar with this ingredient, there's no reason to keep repeating it. In the rest of this book, the doctype is left out of the web page markup to save space. Of course, you'll still see it if you download the sample code.

The currency list can now be filled using code at runtime. In this case, the ideal event is the Page.Load event, because this is the first event that occurs when the page is executed. Here's the code you need to add to the CurrencyConverter page class:

```
Protected Sub Page_Load(ByVal sender As Object, ByVal e As System.EventArgs) _
  Handles Me.Load
    If Me.IsPostBack = False Then
        Currency.Items.Add("Euro")
        Currency.Items.Add("Japanese Yen")
        Currency.Items.Add("Canadian Dollar")
    End If
End Sub
```

Dissecting the Code . . .

This example illustrates two important points:

- You can use the Items property to get items in a list control. This allows you to append, insert, and remove <option> elements (which represent the items in the list). Remember, when generating dynamic content with a server control, you set the properties, and the control creates the appropriate HTML tags.
- Before adding any items to this list, you need to make sure this is the first time the page is being served to this particular user. Otherwise, the page will continuously add more items to the list or inadvertently overwrite the user's selection every time the user interacts with the page. To perform this test, you check the IsPostBack property of the current Page. In other words, IsPostback is a property of the CurrencyConverter class, which CurrencyConverter inherits from the generic Page class. If IsPostBack is False, the page is being created for the first time, and it's safe to initialize it.

Storing Information in the List

Of course, if you're a veteran HTML coder, you know that a select list also provides a value attribute that you can use to store a value for each item in the list. Because the currency converter uses a short list of hard-coded currencies, this is an ideal place to store the currency conversion rate.

To set the value tag, you need to create a ListItem object for every item in the list and add that to the HtmlSelect control. The ListItem class provides a constructor that lets you specify the text and value at the same time that you create it, thereby allowing condensed code like this:

```
Protected Sub Page_Load(ByVal sender As Object, ByVal e As System.EventArgs) _
  Handles Me.Load
    If Me.IsPostBack = False Then
        ' The HtmlSelect control accepts text or ListItem objects.
        Currency.Items.Add(New ListItem("Euros", "0.85"))
        Currency.Items.Add(New ListItem("Japanese Yen", "110.33"))
        Currency.Items.Add(New ListItem("Canadian Dollars", "1.2"))
    End If
End Sub
```

To complete the example, you must rewrite the calculation code to take the selected currency into account, as follows:

```
Protected Sub Convert_ServerClick(ByVal sender As Object, _
  ByVal e As System.EventArgs) Handles Convert.ServerClick
    Dim oldAmount As Double = Val(US.Value)

    ' Retrieve the selected ListItem object by its index number.
    Dim item As ListItem = Currency.Items(Currency.SelectedIndex)

    Dim newAmount As Double = oldAmount * Val(item.Value)
    Result.InnerText = oldAmount.ToString() & " U.S. dollars = "
    Result.InnerText &= newAmount.ToString() & " " & item.Text
End Sub
```

Figure 5-5 shows the revamped currency converter.

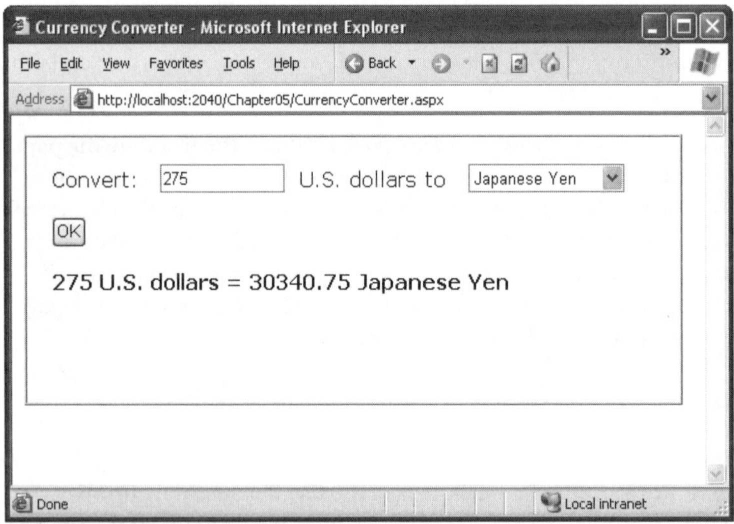

Figure 5-5. *The multicurrency converter*

All in all, this is a good example of how you can store information in HTML tags using the value attribute. However, in a more sophisticated application, you probably wouldn't store the currency rate. Instead, you would just store some sort of unique identifying ID value. Then, when the user submits the page, you would retrieve the corresponding conversion rate from a database or some other storage location (such as an in-memory cache).

Adding Linked Images

Adding other functionality to the currency converter is just as easy as adding a new button. For example, it might be useful for the utility to display a currency conversion rate graph. To provide this feature, the program would need an additional button and image control.

Here's the revised HTML:

```
<%@ Page Language="VB" AutoEventWireup="false"
    CodeFile="CurrencyConverter.aspx.vb" Inherits="CurrencyConverter" %>
<html xmlns="http://www.w3.org/1999/xhtml">
  <head>
    <title>Currency Converter</title>
  </head>
  <body>
    <form runat="server">
      <div>
        Convert:  
        <input type="text" ID="US" runat="server" />
          U.S. dollars to  
        <select ID="Currency" runat="server" />
        <br /><br />
        <input type="submit" value="OK" ID="Convert" runat="server" />
        <input type="submit" value="Show Graph" ID="ShowGraph" runat="server" />
        <br /><br />
        <img ID="Graph" scr="" alt="Currency Graph" runat="server" />
        <br /><br />
        <div style="font-weight: bold" ID="Result" runat="server"></div>
      </div>
    </form>
  </body>
</html>
```

As it's currently declared, the image doesn't refer to a picture. For that reason, it makes sense to hide it when the page is first loaded by using this code:

```
Protected Sub Page_Load(ByVal sender As Object, ByVal e As System.EventArgs) _
  Handles Me.Load
    If Me.IsPostBack = False Then
        Currency.Items.Add(New ListItem("Euros", "0.85"))
        Currency.Items.Add(New ListItem("Japanese Yen", "110.33"))
        Currency.Items.Add(New ListItem("Canadian Dollars", "1.2"))

        Graph.Visible = False
    End If
End Sub
```

Interestingly, when a server control is hidden, ASP.NET omits it from the final HTML page.

Now you can handle the click event of the new button to display the appropriate picture. The currency converter has three possible picture files—pic0.png, pic1.png, and pic2.png—depending on the selected currency:

```
Protected Sub ShowGraph_ServerClick(ByVal sender As Object, _
  ByVal e As System.EventArgs) Handles ShowGraph.ServerClick
    Graph.Src = "Pic" & Currency.SelectedIndex.ToString() & ".png"
    Graph.Visible = True
End Sub
```

Already the currency converter is beginning to look more interesting, as shown in Figure 5-6.

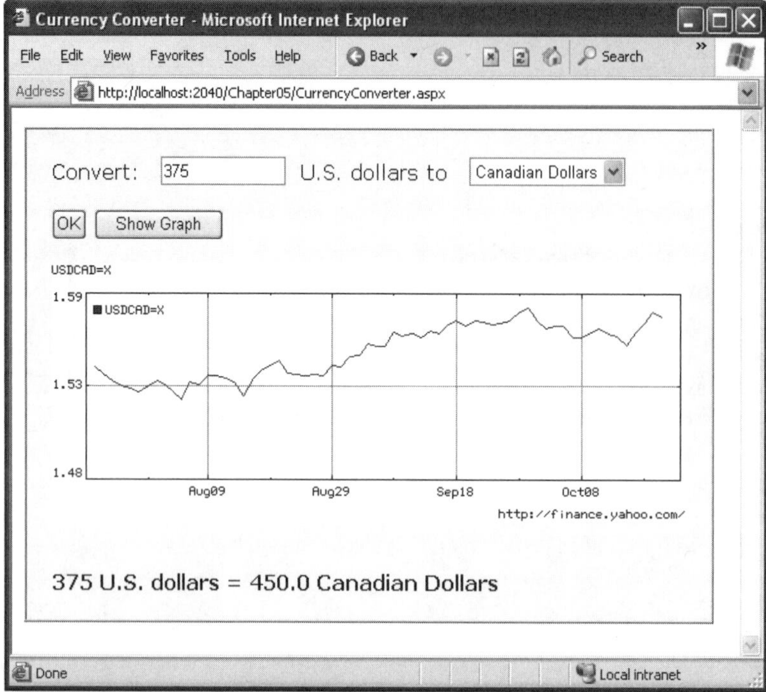

Figure 5-6. *The currency converter with an image control*

Setting Styles

In addition to a limited set of properties, each HTML control also provides access to the CSS attributes through its Style collection. To use this collection, you need to specify the name of the CSS style attribute and the value you want to assign to it. Here's the basic syntax:

```
ControlName.Style("AttributeName") = "AttributeValue"
```

For example, you could use this technique to emphasize an invalid entry in the currency converter with the color red. In this case, you'll also need to reset the color to its original value for valid input, because the control uses view state to remember all its settings, including its style properties:

```
Protected Sub Convert_ServerClick(ByVal sender As Object, _
  ByVal e As System.EventArgs) Handles Convert.ServerClick

    Dim oldAmount As Double = Val(US.Value)

    If oldAmount <= 0 Then
        Result.Style("color") = "Red"
        Result.InnerText = "Specify a positive number"
    Else
```

```
        Result.Style("color") = "Black"

        ' Retrieve the selected ListItem object by its index number.
        Dim item As ListItem = Currency.Items(Currency.SelectedIndex)

        Dim newAmount As Double = oldAmount * Val(item.Value)
        Result.InnerText = oldAmount.ToString() & " U.S. dollars = "
        Result.InnerText &= newAmount.ToString() & " " & item.Text
    End If

End Sub
```

■ **Tip** The Style collection sets the style attribute in the HTML tag with a list of formatting options such as font family, size, and color. You'll learn more in Chapter 13. But if you aren't familiar with CSS styles, you don't need to learn them now. Instead, you could use web controls, which provide higher-level properties that allow you to configure their appearance and automatically create the appropriate style attributes. You'll learn about web controls in the next chapter.

This concludes the simple currency converter application, which now boasts automatic calculation, linked images, and dynamic formatting. In the following sections, you'll look at the building blocks of ASP.NET interfaces more closely.

A Deeper Look at HTML Control Classes

Related classes in the .NET Framework use inheritance to share functionality. For example, every HTML control inherits from the base class HtmlControl. The HtmlControl class provides essential features every HTML server control uses. Figure 5-7 shows the inheritance diagram.

The next few sections dissect the ASP.NET classes that are used for HTML server controls. You can use this material to help understand the common elements that are shared by all HTML controls. For the specific details about each HTML control, you can refer to the class library reference in the Visual Studio Help.

HTML server controls generally provide properties that closely match their tag attributes. For example, the HtmlImage class provides Align, Alt, Border, Src, Height, and Width properties. For this reason, users who are familiar with HTML syntax will find that HTML server controls are the most natural fit. Users who aren't as used to HTML will probably find that web controls (described in the next chapter) have a more intuitive set of properties.

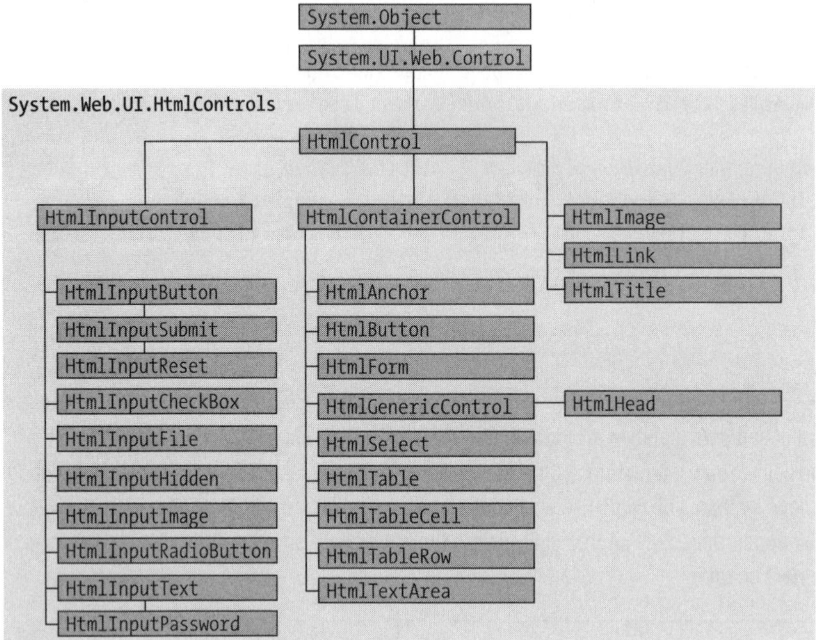

Figure 5-7. *HTML control inheritance*

HTML Control Events

HTML server controls also provide one of two possible events: ServerClick or ServerChange.

The ServerClick is simply a click that's processed on the server side. It's provided by most button controls, and it allows your code to take immediate action. For example, consider the HtmlAnchor control, which is the server control that represents the common HTML hyperlink (the <a> element). There are two ways to use the HtmlAnchor control. One option is to set its HtmlAnchor.HRef property to a URL, in which case the hyperlink will behave exactly like the ordinary HTML <a> element (the only difference being that you can set the URL dynamically in your code). The other option is to handle the HtmlAnchor.ServerClick event. In this case, when the link is clicked it will actually post back the page, allowing your code to run. The user won't be redirected to a new page unless you provide extra code to forward the request.

The ServerChange event responds when a change has been made to a text or selection control. This event isn't as useful as it appears because it doesn't occur until the page is posted back (for example, after the user clicks a submit button). At this point, the ServerChange event occurs for all changed controls, followed by the appropriate ServerClick. The Page.Load event is the first to fire, but you have no way to know the order of events for other controls.

Table 5-5 shows which controls provide a ServerClick event and which ones provide a ServerChange event.

Table 5-5. *HTML Control Events*

Event	Controls That Provide It
ServerClick	HtmlAnchor, HtmlButton, HtmlInputButton, HtmlInputImage, HtmlInputReset
ServerChange	HtmlInputText, HtmlInputCheckBox, HtmlInputRadioButton, HtmlInputHidden, HtmlSelect, HtmlTextArea

Advanced Events with the HtmlInputImage Control

Chapter 4 introduced the .NET event standard, which dictates that every event should pass exactly two pieces of information. The first parameter identifies the object (in this case, the control) that fired the event. The second parameter is a special object that can include additional information about the event.

In the examples you've looked at so far, the second parameter (e) has always been used to pass an empty System.EventArgs object. This object doesn't contain any additional information—it's just a glorified placeholder. Here's one such example:

```
Protected Sub Convert_ServerClick(ByVal sender As Object, _
  ByVal e As EventArgs) Handles Convert.ServerClick
    ...
End Sub
```

In fact, only one HTML server control sends additional information: the HtmlInputImage control. It sends an ImageClickEventArgs object (from the System.Web.UI namespace) that provides X and Y properties representing the location where the image was clicked. You'll notice that the definition for the HtmlInputImage.ServerClick event handler is a little different from the event handlers used with other controls:

```
Protected Sub ImgButton_ServerClick(ByVal sender As Object, _
  ByVal e As ImageClickEventArgs) Handles ImgButton.ServerClick
    ...
End Sub
```

Using this additional information, you can replace multiple button controls and image maps with a single, intelligent HtmlInputImage control.

Here's the markup you need to create the HtmlInputImage control for this example:

```
<input type="image" ID="ImgButton" runat="server" src="button.png" />
```

The sample ImageTest.aspx page shown in Figure 5-8 puts this feature to work with a simple graphical button. Depending on whether the user clicks the button border or the button surface, a different message is displayed.

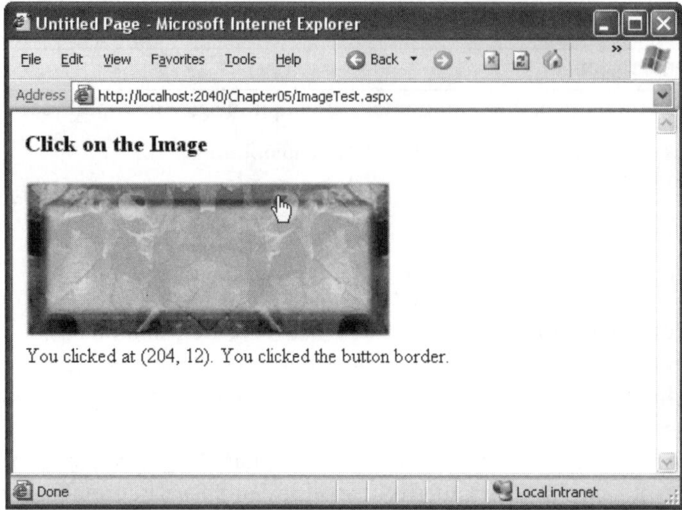

Figure 5-8. *Using an HtmlInputImage control*

The page code examines the click coordinates provided by the ImageClickEventArgs object and displays them in another control. Here's the page code you need:

```
Public Partial Class ImageTest
    Inherits System.Web.UI.Page

    Protected Sub ImgButton_ServerClick(ByVal sender As Object, _
      ByVal e As ImageClickEventArgs) Handles ImgButton.ServerClick

        Result.InnerText = "You clicked at (" & e.X.ToString() & _
          ", " & e.Y.ToString() & "). "

        If e.Y < 100 And e.Y > 20 And e.X > 20 And e.X < 275 Then
            Result.InnerText &= "You clicked on the button surface."
        Else
            Result.InnerText &= "You clicked the button border."
        End If
    End Sub
End Class
```

The HtmlControl Base Class

Every HTML control inherits from the base class HtmlControl. This relationship means that every HTML control will support a basic set of properties and features. Table 5-6 shows these properties.

The HtmlControl class also provides built-in support for data binding, which you'll examine in Chapter 16.

Table 5-6. *HtmlControl Properties*

Property	Description
Attributes	Provides a collection of all the attributes that are set in the control tag, and their values. Rather than reading or setting an attribute through the Attributes, it's better to use the corresponding property in the control class. However, the Attributes collection is useful if you need to add or configure a custom attribute or an attribute that doesn't have a corresponding property.
Controls	Provides a collection of all the controls contained inside the current control. (For example, a <div> server control could contain an <input> server control.) Each object is provided as a generic System.Web.UI.Control object so that you may need to cast the reference to access control-specific properties.
Disabled	Disables the control when set to True, thereby ensuring that the user cannot interact with it, and its events will not be fired.
EnableViewState	Disables the automatic state management for this control when set to False. In this case, the control will be reset to the properties and formatting specified in the control tag every time the page is posted back. If this is set to True (the default), the control uses a hidden input field to store information about its properties, thereby ensuring that any changes you make in code are remembered.
Page	Provides a reference to the web page that contains this control as a System.Web.UI.Page object.
Parent	Provides a reference to the control that contains this control. If the control is placed directly on the page (rather than inside another control), it will return a reference to the page object.
Style	Provides a collection of CSS style properties that can be used to format the control.
TagName	Indicates the name of the underlying HTML element (for example, img or div).
Visible	Hides the control when set to False and will not be rendered to the final HTML page that is sent to the client.

PROPERTIES CAN BE SET IN CODE OR IN THE TAG

To set the initial value of a property, you can configure the control in the Page.Load event handler, or you can adjust the control tag in the .aspx file by adding special attributes. Note that the Page.Load event occurs after the page is initialized with the default values and the tag settings. This means your code can override the properties set in the tag (but not vice versa).

The following HtmlImage control is an example that sets properties through attributes in the control tag. The control is automatically disabled and will not fire any events.

```
<img ID="Graph" runat="server" Visible="false" ... />
```

Remember, if you set control properties in the Properties window, you are using the control tag approach. As you make your changes, Visual Studio updates the control tag in the .aspx file.

The HtmlContainerControl Class

Any HTML control that requires a closing tag inherits from the HtmlContainer class (which in turn inherits from the more basic HtmlControl class). For example, elements such as <a>, <form>, and <div> always use a closing tag, because they can contain other HTML elements. On the other hand, elements such as <img> and <input> are used only as stand-alone tags. Thus, the HtmlAnchor, HtmlForm, and HtmlGenericControl classes inherit from HtmlContainerControl, while HtmlInputImage and HtmlInputButton do not.

The HtmlContainer control adds two properties to those defined in HtmlControl, as described in Table 5-7.

Table 5-7. *HtmlContainerControl Properties*

Property	Description
InnerHtml	The HTML content between the opening and closing tags of the control. Special characters that are set through this property will not be converted to the equivalent HTML entities. This means you can use this property to apply formatting with nested tags such as <b>, <i>, and <h1>.
InnerText	The text content between the opening and closing tags of the control. Special characters will be automatically converted to HTML entities and displayed like text (for example, the less-than character (<) will be converted to `<` and will be displayed as < in the web page). This means you can't use HTML tags to apply additional formatting with this property. The simple currency converter page uses the InnerText property to enter results into a <div> tag.

The HtmlInputControl Class

This control defines some properties (shown in Table 5-8) that are used for the <input> element. As you've already learned, the <input> element can represent different controls, depending on the type attribute. The <input type="text"> element is a text box and <input type="submit"> is a button.

Table 5-8. *HtmlInputControl Properties*

Property	Description
Type	Provides the type of input control. For example, a control based on <input type="file"> would return *file* for the type property.
Value	Returns the contents of the control as a string. In the simple currency converter, this property allowed the code to retrieve the information entered in the text input control.

The Page Class

One control we haven't discussed in detail yet is the Page class. As explained in the previous chapter, every web page is a custom class that inherits from System.Web.UI.Page. By inheriting from this class, your web page class acquires a number of properties and methods that your code can use. These include properties for enabling caching, validation, and tracing, which are discussed throughout this book.

Table 5-9 provides an overview of some of the more fundamental properties, which you'll use throughout this book.

Table 5-9. *Basic Page Properties*

Property	Description
IsPostBack	This Boolean property indicates whether this is the first time the page is being run (False) or whether the page is being resubmitted in response to a control event, typically with stored view state information (True). You'll usually check this property in the Page.Load event handler to ensure that your initial web page initialization is only performed once.
EnableViewState	When set to False, this overrides the EnableViewState property of the contained controls, thereby ensuring that no controls will maintain state information.
Application	This collection holds information that's shared between all users in your website. For example, you can use the Application collection to count the number of times a page has been visited. You'll learn more in Chapter 7.
Session	This collection holds information for a single user, so it can be used in different pages. For example, you can use the Session collection to store the items in the current user's shopping basket on an e-commerce website. You'll learn more in Chapter 7.
Cache	This collection allows you to store objects that are time-consuming to create so they can be reused in other pages or for other clients. This technique, when implemented properly, can improve performance of your web pages. Chapter 24 discusses caching in detail.
Request	This refers to an HttpRequest object that contains information about the current web request. You can use the HttpRequest object to get information about the user's browser, although you'll probably prefer to leave these details to ASP.NET. You'll use the HttpRequest object to transmit information from one page to another with the query string in Chapter 7.
Response	This refers to an HttpResponse object that represents the response ASP.NET will send to the user's browser. You'll use the HttpResponse object to create cookies in Chapter 7, and you'll see how it allows you to redirect the user to a different web page later in this chapter.
Server	This refers to an HttpServerUtility object that allows you to perform a few miscellaneous tasks. For example, it allows you to encode text so that it's safe to place it in a URL or in the HTML markup of your page. You'll learn more about these features in this chapter.
User	If the user has been authenticated, this property will be initialized with user information. Chapter 20 describes this property in more detail.

In the following sections, you'll learn about two tasks that use these properties—redirecting the user to a new page, and encoding text that may contain special characters so it can be inserted into web page HTML.

Sending the User to a New Page

In the currency converter example, everything took place in a single page. In a more typical website, the user will need to surf from one page to another to perform different tasks or complete a single operation.

There are several ways to transfer a user from one page to another. One of the simplest is to use an ordinary <a> anchor element, which turns a portion of text into a hyperlink. In this example, the word *here* is a link to another page:

```
Click <a href="newpage.aspx">here</a> to go to newpage.aspx.
```

Another option is to send the user to a new page using code. This approach is useful if you want to use your code to perform some other work before you redirect the user. It's also handy if you need to use code to decide where to send the user. For example, if you create a sequence of pages for placing an order, you might send existing customers straight to the checkout while new visitors are redirected to a registration page.

To perform redirection in code, you first need a control that causes the page to be posted back. In other words, you need an event handler that reacts to the ServerClick event of a control such as HtmlInputButton or HtmlAnchor. When the page is posted back and your event handler runs, you can use the HttpResponse.Redirect() method to send the user to the new page.

Remember, you can get access to the current HttpResponse object through the Page.Response property. Here's an example that sends the user to a different page in the same website directory:

```
Response.Redirect("newpage.aspx")
```

When you use the Redirect() method, ASP.NET immediately stops processing the page and sends a redirect message back to the browser. Any code that occurs after the Redirect() call won't be executed. When the browser receives the redirect message, it sends a request for the new page.

You can use the Redirect() method to send the user to any type of page. You can even send the user to another website using an absolute URL (a URL that starts with `http://`), as shown here:

```
Response.Redirect("http://www.prosetech.com")
```

ASP.NET gives you one other option for sending the user to a new page. You can use the HttpServerUtility.Transfer() method instead of Response.Redirect(). An HttpServerUtility object is provided through the Page.Server property, so your redirection code would look like this:

```
Server.Transfer("newpage.aspx")
```

The advantage of using the Transfer() method is the fact that it doesn't involve the browser. Instead of sending a redirect message back to the browser, ASP.NET simply starts processing the new page as though the user had originally requested that page. This behavior saves a bit of time, but it also introduces some significant limitations. You can't use Transfer() to send the user to another website or to a non-ASP.NET page (such as an HTML page). The Transfer() method only allows you to jump from one ASP.NET page to another, in the same web application. Furthermore, when you use Transfer() the user won't have any idea that another page has taken over, because the browser will still show the original URL. This can cause a problem if you want to support browser bookmarks. On the whole, it's much more common to use HttpResponse.Redirect() than HttpServerUtility.Transfer().

HTML Encoding

As you already know, there are certain characters that have a special meaning in HTML. For example, the angle brackets (< >) are always used to create tags. This can cause problems if you actually want to use these characters as part of the content of your web page.

For example, imagine you want to display this text on a web page:

```
Enter a word <here>
```

If you try to write this information to a page or place it inside a control, you end up with this instead:

```
Enter a word
```

The problem is that the browser has tried to interpret the <here> as an HTML tag. A similar problem occurs if you actually use valid HTML tags. For example, consider this text:

```
To bold text use the <b> tag.
```

Not only will the text <b> not appear, but the browser will interpret it as an instruction to make the text that follows bold. To circumvent this automatic behavior, you need to convert potential problematic values to their HTML equivalents. For example, < becomes < in your final HTML page, which the browser displays as the < character. Table 5-10 lists some special characters that need to be encoded.

Table 5-10. *Common HTML Special Characters*

Result	Description	Encoded Entity
	Nonbreaking space	
<	Less-than symbol	<
>	Greater-than symbol	>
&	Ampersand	&
"	Quotation mark	"

You can perform this transformation on your own, or you can circumvent the problem by using the InnerText property of an HTML server control. When you set the contents of a control using InnerText, any illegal characters are automatically converted into their HTML equivalents. However, this won't help if you want to set a tag that contains a mix of embedded HTML tags and encoded characters. It also won't be of any use for controls that don't provide an InnerText property, such as the Label web control you'll examine in the next chapter. In these cases, you can use the HttpServerUtility.HtmlEncode() method to replace the special characters. (Remember, an HttpServerUtility object is provided through the Page.Server property.)

Here's an example:

```
' Will output as "Enter a word &lt;here&gt;" in the HTML file, but the
' browser will display it as "Enter a word <here>".
ctrl.InnerHtml = Server.HtmlEncode("Enter a word <here>")
```

Or consider this example, which mingles real HTML tags with text that needs to be encoded:

```
ctrl.InnerHtml = "To <b>bold</b> text use the "
ctrl.InnerHtml &= Server.HtmlEncode("<b>") & " tag."
```

Figure 5-9 shows the results of successfully and incorrectly encoding special HTML characters. You can refer to the HtmlEncodeTest.aspx page included with the examples for this chapter.

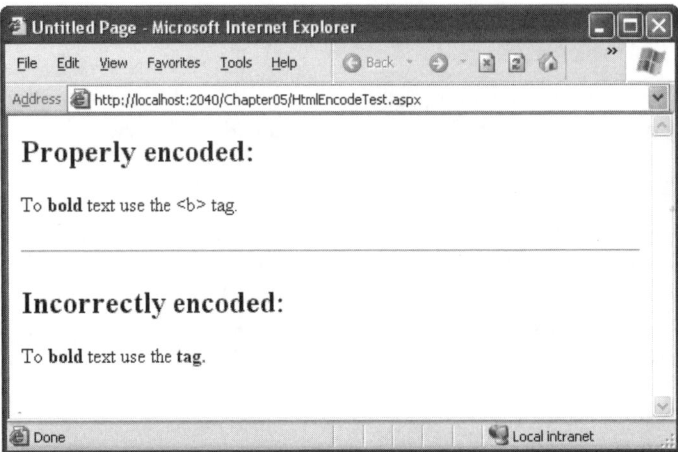

Figure 5-9. *Encoding special HTML characters*

The HtmlEncode() method is particularly useful if you're retrieving values from a database and you aren't sure whether the text is valid HTML. You can use the HtmlDecode() method to revert the text to its normal form if you need to perform additional operations or comparisons with it in your code.

Along with the HtmlEncode() and HtmlDecode() methods, the HttpServerUtility class also includes UrlEncode() and UrlDecode() methods. Much as HtmlEncode() allows you to convert text to valid HTML with no special characters, UrlEncode() allows you to convert text into a form that can be used in a URL. This technique is particularly useful if you want to pass information from one page to another by tacking it onto the end of the URL. You'll see this technique demonstrated in Chapter 7.

Application Events

In this chapter, you've seen how ASP.NET controls fire events that you can handle in your code. Although server controls are the most common source of events, there's another type of event that you'll occasionally encounter: *application events*. Application events aren't nearly as important in an ASP.NET application as the events fired by server controls, but you might use them to perform additional processing tasks. For example, using application events you can write logging code that runs every time a request is received, no matter what page is being requested. Basic ASP.NET features like session state and authentication use application events to plug into the ASP.NET processing pipeline.

You can't handle application events in the code behind for a web form. Instead, you need the help of another ingredient: the Global.asax file.

The Global.asax File

The Global.asax file allows you to write code that responds to global application events. These events fire at various points during the lifetime of a web application, including when the application domain is first created (when the first request is received for a page in your website folder).

To add a Global.asax file to an application in Visual Studio, choose Website ➤ Add New Item, and select the Global Application Class file type. Then, click OK.

The Global.asax file looks similar to a normal .aspx file, except that it can't contain any HTML or ASP.NET tags. Instead, it contains event handlers. For example, the following Global.asax file reacts to the Application.EndRequest event, which happens just before the page is sent to the user:

```
<%@ Application Language="VB" %>

<script runat="server">

    Sub Application_EndRequest(ByVal sender As Object, ByVal e As EventArgs)
        ' Code that runs at the end of every request.
        Response.Write("<hr>This page was served at " & DateTime.Now.ToString())
    End Sub

</script>
```

This event handler uses the Write() method of the built-in Response object to write a footer at the bottom of the page with the date and time that the page was created (see Figure 5-10).

Each ASP.NET application can have one Global.asax file. Once you place it in the appropriate website directory, ASP.NET recognizes it and uses it automatically. For example, if you add the Global.asax file shown previously to a web application, every web page in that application will include a footer.

Note This technique—responding to application events and using the Response.Write() method—isn't the best way to add a footer to the pages in your website. A better approach is to add a user control that creates the footer (Chapter 12) or define a master page template that includes a footer (Chapter 14).

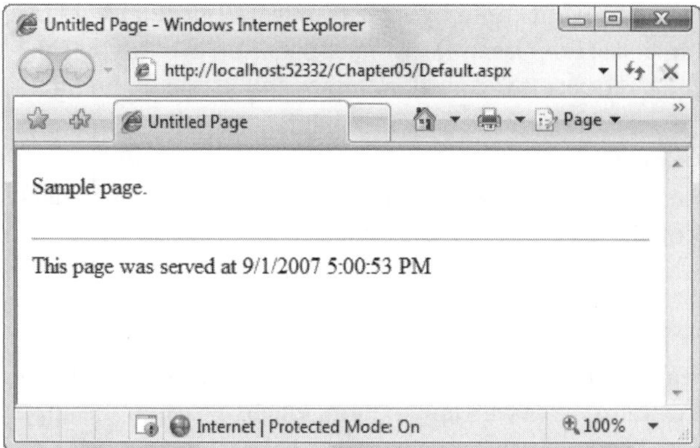

Figure 5-10. *HelloWorld.aspx with an automatic footer*

Additional Application Events

Application.EndRequest is only one of more than a dozen events you can respond to in your code. To create a different event handler, you simply need to create a subroutine with the defined name. Table 5-11 lists some of the most common application events that you'll use.

Table 5-11. *Basic Application Events*

Event-Handling Method	Description
Application_Start()	Occurs when the application starts, which is the first time it receives a request from any user. It doesn't occur on subsequent requests. This event is commonly used to create or cache some initial information that will be reused later.
Application_End()	Occurs when the application is shutting down, generally because the web server is being restarted. You can insert cleanup code here.
Application_BeginRequest()	Occurs with each request the application receives, just before the page code is executed.
Application_EndRequest()	Occurs with each request the application receives, just after the page code is executed.
Session_Start()	Occurs whenever a new user request is received and a session is started. Sessions are discussed in detail in Chapter 7.
Session_End()	Occurs when a session times out or is programmatically ended. This event is only raised if you are using in-process session state storage (the InProc mode, not the StateServer or SQLServer modes).
Application_Error()	Occurs in response to an unhandled error. You can find more information about error handling in Chapter 8.

ASP.NET Configuration

The last topic you'll consider in this chapter is the ASP.NET configuration file system.

Every web application includes a web.config file that configures fundamental settings—everything from the way error messages are shown to the security settings that lock out unwanted visitors. You'll consider the settings in the web.config file throughout this book. (And there are many more settings that you *won't* consider in this book, because they're used much more rarely.)

The ASP.NET configuration files have several key advantages:

They are never locked: You can update web.config settings at any point, even while your application is running. If there are any requests currently under way, they'll continue to use the old settings, while new requests will get the changed settings right away.

They are easily accessed and replicated: Provided you have the appropriate network rights, you can change a web.config file from a remote computer. You can also copy the web.config file and use it to apply identical settings to another application or another web server that runs the same application in a web farm scenario.

The settings are easy to edit and understand: The settings in the web.config file are human-readable, which means they can be edited and understood without needing a special configuration tool.

In the following sections, you'll get a high-level overview of the web.config file and learn how ASP.NET's configuration system works.

The web.config File

The web.config file uses a predefined XML format. The entire content of the file is nested in a root <configuration> element. Inside this element are several more subsections, some of which you'll never change, and others which are more important.

Here's the basic skeletal structure of the web.config file, with the three most important sections highlighted in bold:

```
<?xml version="1.0" ?>
<configuration>
    <configSections>...</configSections>
    <appSettings>...</appSettings>
    <connectionStrings>...</connectionStrings>
    <system.web>...</system.web>
    <system.codedom>...</system.codedom>
    <system.webServer>...</system.webServer>
</configuration>
```

Note that the web.config file is case-sensitive, like all XML documents, and starts every setting with a lowercase letter. This means you cannot write <AppSettings> instead of <appSettings>.

■ **Tip** To learn more about XML, the format used for the web.config file, you can refer to Chapter 19.

As a web developer, there are three sections in the web.config file that you'll work with. The <appSettings> section allows you to add your own miscellaneous pieces of information. You'll learn how to use it in the next section. The <connectionStrings> section allows you to define the connection information for accessing a database. You'll learn about this section in Chapter 15. Finally, the <system.web> section holds every ASP.NET setting you'll need to configure.

Inside the <system.web> element are separate elements for each aspect of website configuration. You can include as few or as many of these as you want. For example, if you need to specify special error settings, you would add the <customErrors> element in the <system.web> section. If you wanted to control how ASP.NET's security works, you'd add the <authentication> and <authorization> sections. You'll consider the different elements that you can add to the <system.web> section throughout this book.

Nested Configuration

ASP.NET uses a multilayered configuration system that allows you to set settings at different levels.

Every web server starts with some basic settings that are defined in two configuration files in the c:\Windows\Microsoft.NET\Framework\v2.0.50727\Config directory. These two files are machine.config and web.config. Generally, you won't edit either of these files manually, because they affect the entire computer. Instead, you'll configure the web.config file in your web application folder. Using that file, you can set additional settings or override the defaults that are configured in the two system files.

More interestingly, you can use different settings for different parts of your application. To use this technique, you need to create additional subdirectories inside your virtual directory. These subdirectories can contain their own web.config files with additional settings.

Subdirectories inherit web.config settings from the parent directory. For example, imagine you create a website in the directory c:\ASP.NET\TestWeb. Inside this directory, you create a folder named Secure. Pages in the c:\ASP.NET\TestWeb\Secure directory can acquire settings from three files, as shown in Figure 5-11.

Any machine.config or web.config settings that aren't explicitly overridden in the c:\ASP.NET\TestWeb\Secure\web.config file will still apply to the SecureHelloWorld.aspx page. In this way, subdirectories can specify just a small set of settings that differ from the rest of the web application. One reason you might want to use multiple directories in an application is to apply different security settings. Files that need to be secured would then be placed in a dedicated directory with a web.config file that defines more stringent security settings.

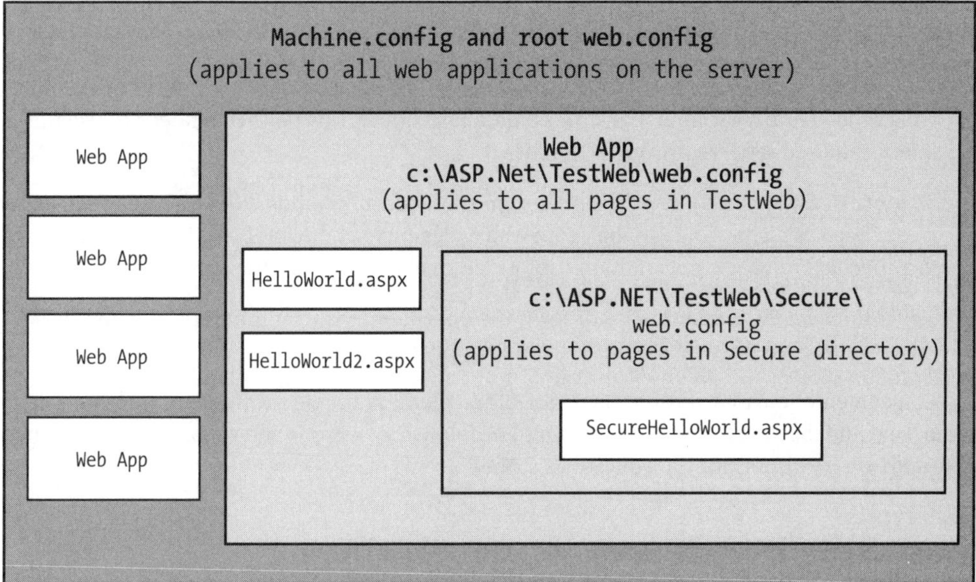

Figure 5-11. *Configuration inheritance*

Storing Custom Settings in the web.config File

ASP.NET also allows you to store your own settings in the web.config file, in an element called <appSettings>. Note that the <appSettings> element is nested in the root <configuration> element. Here's the basic structure:

```
<?xml version="1.0" ?>
<configuration>
    ...
    <appSettings>
        <!-- Custom application settings go here. -->
    </appSettings>
    ...
    <system.web>
        <!-- ASP.NET Configuration sections go here. -->
    </system.web>
    ...
</configuration>
```

■ **Note** This example adds a comment in the place where you'd normally find additional settings. XML comments are bracketed with the <!-- and --> character sequences. You can also use XML comments to temporarily disable a setting in a configuration file.

The custom settings that you add are written as simple string variables. You might want to use a special web.config setting for several reasons:

To centralize an important setting that needs to be used in many different pages: For example, you could create a variable that stores a database query. Any page that needs to use this query can then retrieve this value and use it.

To make it easy to quickly switch between different modes of operation: For example, you might create a special debugging variable. Your web pages could check for this variable and, if it's set to a specified value, output additional information to help you test the application.

To set some initial values: Depending on the operation, the user might be able to modify these values, but the web.config file could supply the defaults.

You can enter custom settings using an <add> element that identifies a unique variable name (key) and the variable contents (value). The following example adds a variable that defines a file path where important information is stored:

```
<appSettings>
    <add key="DataFilePath"
     value="e:\NetworkShare\Documents\WebApp\Shared" />
</appSettings>
```

You can add as many application settings as you want, although this example defines just one.

You can create a simple test page to query this information and display the results, as shown in the following example (which is provided with the sample code as ShowSettings.aspx and ShowSettings.aspx.vb). You retrieve custom application settings from web.config by key name, using the WebConfigurationManager class, which is found in the System.Web.Configuration namespace. This class provides a shared property called AppSettings with a collection of application settings.

```
Imports System.Web.Configuration

Public Partial Class ShowSettings
    Inherits System.Web.UI.Page

    Protected Sub Page_Load(ByVal sender As Object, _
      ByVal e As System.EventArgs) Handles Me.Load
        lblTest.Text = "This app will look for data in the directory:<br /><b>"
        lblTest.Text &= WebConfigurationManager.AppSettings("DataFilePath")
        lblTest.Text &= "</b>"
    End Sub

End Class
```

■ **Tip** Notice that this code formats the text by inserting HTML tags into the label alongside the text content, including bold tags (<b>) to emphasize certain words, and a line break (<br />) to split the output over multiple lines. This is a common technique.

Later, in Chapter 18, you'll learn how to get file and directory information and read and write files. For now, the simple application just displays the custom web.config setting, as shown in Figure 5-12.

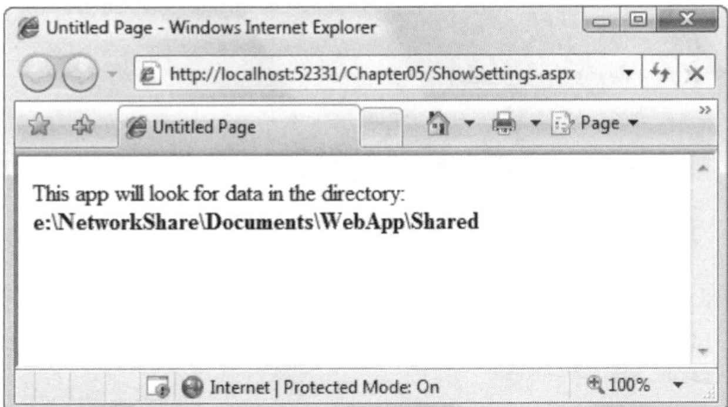

Figure 5-12. *Displaying custom application settings*

ASP.NET is configured, by default, to deny any requests for .config files. This means a remote user will not be able to access the file through IIS. Instead, they'll receive the error message shown in Figure 5-13.

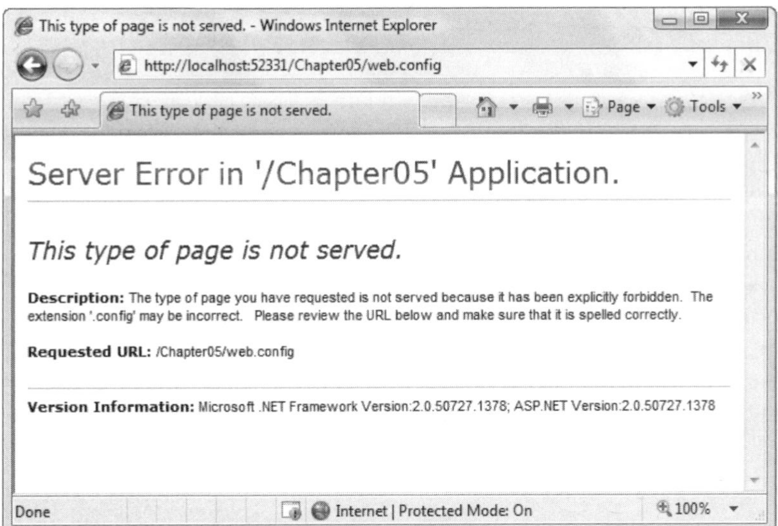

Figure 5-13. *Requests for web.config are denied.*

The Website Administration Tool (WAT)

Editing the web.config file by hand is refreshingly straightforward, but it can be a bit tedious. To help alleviate the drudgery, ASP.NET includes a graphical configuration tool called the Website Administration Tool (WAT), which lets you configure various parts of the web.config file using a web page interface. To run the WAT to configure the current web project in Visual

Studio, select Website ➤ ASP.NET Configuration. A web browser window will appear (see Figure 5-14). Internet Explorer will automatically log you on under the current Windows user account, allowing you to make changes.

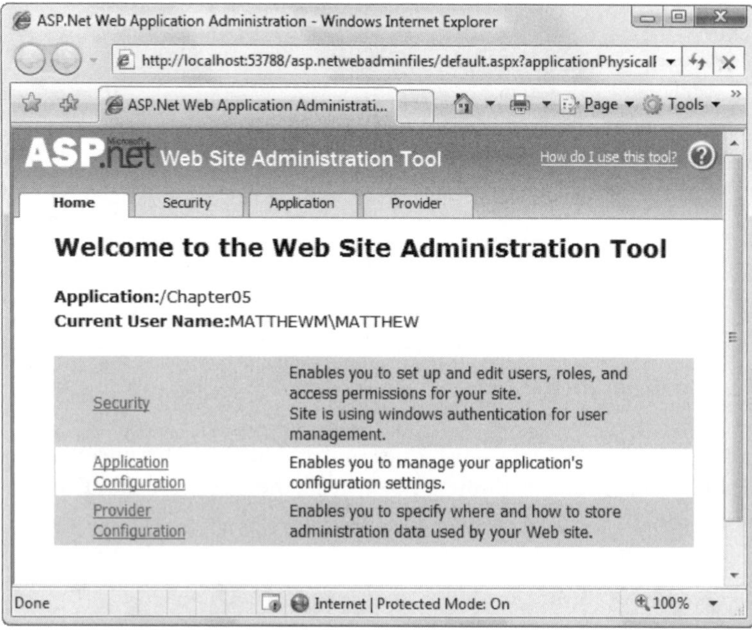

Figure 5-14. *Running the WAT*

You can use the WAT to automate the web.config changes you made in the previous example. To try this, click the Application tab. Using this tab, you can create a new setting (click the Create Application Settings link). If you click Manage Application Settings, you'll see a list with all the applications settings that are defined in your application (Figure 5-15). You can then choose to remove or edit any one of them.

This is the essential idea behind the WAT. You make your changes using a graphical interface (a web page), and the WAT generates the settings you need and adds them to the web.config file for your application behind the scenes. Of course, the WAT has a number of settings for configuring more complex ASP.NET settings, and you'll use it throughout this book.

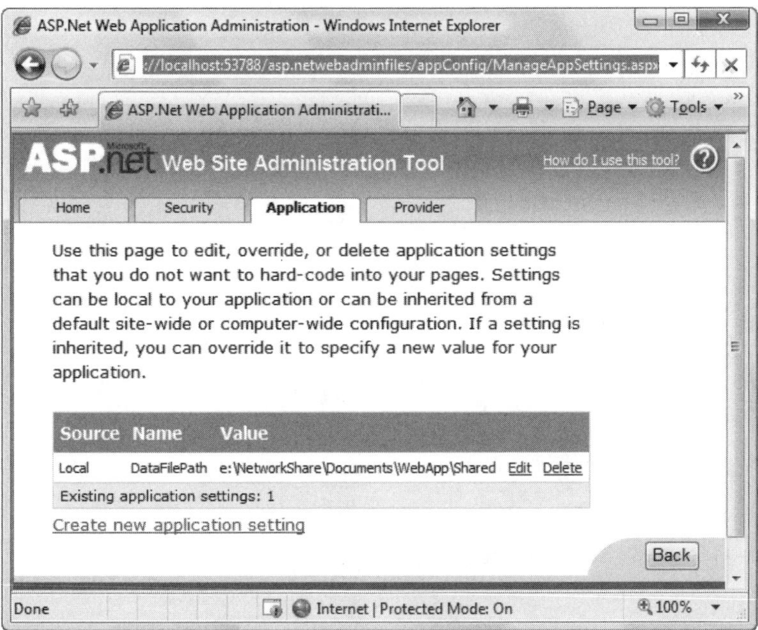

Figure 5-15. *Editing an application setting with the WAT*

The Last Word

This chapter presented you with your first look at web applications, web pages, and configuration. You should now understand how to create an ASP.NET web page and use HTML server controls.

HTML controls are a compromise between web controls and traditional ASP.NET programming. They use the familiar HTML elements but provide a limited object-oriented interface. Essentially, HTML controls are designed to be straightforward, predictable, and automatically compatible with existing programs. With HTML controls, the final HTML page that is sent to the client closely resembles the original .aspx page.

In the next chapter, you'll learn about web controls, which provide a more sophisticated object interface that abstracts away the underlying HTML. If you're starting a new project or need to add some of ASP.NET's most powerful controls, web controls are the best option.

CHAPTER 6

■ ■ ■

Web Controls

The previous chapter introduced the event-driven and control-based programming model of ASP.NET. This model allows you to create programs for the Web using the same object-oriented techniques you would use to write a Windows application.

However, HTML server controls really show only a glimpse of what is possible with ASP.NET's server control model. To see some of the real advantages, you need to dive into the richer and more extensible web controls. In this chapter, you'll explore the basic web controls and their class hierarchy. You'll also delve deeper into ASP.NET's event handling, learn the details of the web page life cycle, and put your knowledge to work by creating a web page that lets the user design a greeting card.

Stepping Up to Web Controls

Now that you've seen the new model of server controls, you might wonder why you need additional web controls. But in fact, HTML controls are much more limited than server controls need to be. For example, every HTML control corresponds directly to an HTML tag, meaning you're bound by the limitations and abilities of HTML. Web controls, on the other hand, have no such restriction. They emphasize the future of web design.

These are some of the reasons you should switch to web controls:

They provide a rich user interface: A web control is programmed as an object but doesn't necessarily correspond to a single element in the final HTML page. For example, you might create a single Calendar or GridView control, which will be rendered as dozens of HTML elements in the final page. When using ASP.NET programs, you don't need to know anything about HTML. The control creates the required HTML tags for you.

They provide a consistent object model: HTML is full of quirks and idiosyncrasies. For example, a simple text box can appear as one of three elements, including <textarea>, <input type="text">, and <input type="password">. With web controls, these three elements are consolidated as a single TextBox control. Depending on the properties you set, the underlying HTML element that ASP.NET renders may differ. Similarly, the names of properties don't follow the HTML attribute names. For example, controls that display text, whether it's a caption or a text box that can be edited by the user, expose a Text property.

They tailor their output automatically: ASP.NET server controls can detect the type of browser and automatically adjust the HTML code they write to take advantage of features such as support for JavaScript. You don't need to know about the client because ASP.NET handles that layer and automatically uses the best possible set of features. This feature is known as *adaptive rendering*.

They provide high-level features: You'll see that web controls allow you to access additional events, properties, and methods that don't correspond directly to typical HTML controls. ASP.NET implements these features by using a combination of tricks.

Throughout this book, you'll see examples that use the full set of web controls. To master ASP.NET development, you need to become comfortable with these user-interface ingredients and understand their abilities. HTML server controls, on the other hand, are less important for web development. You'll only use them if you're migrating an existing HTML page to the ASP.NET world, or if you need to have fine-grained control over the HTML code that will be generated and sent to the client.

Basic Web Control Classes

If you've ever created a Windows application before, you're probably familiar with the basic set of standard controls, including labels, buttons, and text boxes. ASP.NET provides web controls for all these standbys. (And if you've created .NET Windows applications, you'll notice that the class names and properties have many striking similarities, which are designed to make it easy to transfer the experience you acquire in one type of application to another.)

Table 6-1 lists the basic control classes and the HTML elements they generate. Some controls (such as Button and TextBox) can be rendered as different HTML elements. In this case, ASP.NET uses the element that matches the properties you've set. Also, some controls have no real HTML equivalent. For example, the CheckBoxList and RadioButtonList controls output as a <table> that contains multiple HTML check boxes or radio buttons. ASP.NET exposes them as a single object on the server side for convenient programming, thus illustrating one of the primary strengths of web controls.

Table 6-1. *Basic Web Controls*

Control Class	Underlying HTML Element
Label	<span>
Button	<input type="submit"> or <input type="button">
TextBox	<input type="text">, <input type="password">, or <textarea>
CheckBox	<input type="checkbox">
RadioButton	<input type="radio">
Hyperlink	<a>
LinkButton	<a> with a contained <img> tag
ImageButton	<input type="image">
Image	<img>

Table 6-1. *Basic Web Controls*

Control Class	Underlying HTML Element
ListBox	<select size="X"> where X is the number of rows that are visible at once
DropDownList	<select>
CheckBoxList	A list or <table> with multiple <input type="checkbox"> tags
RadioButtonList	A list or <table> with multiple <input type="radio"> tags
BulletedList	An <ol> ordered list (numbered) or <ul> unordered list (bulleted)
Panel	<div>
Table, TableRow, and TableCell	<table>, <tr>, and <td> or <th>

This table omits some of the more specialized controls used for data, navigation, security, and web portals. You'll see these controls as you learn about their features throughout this book.

The Web Control Tags

ASP.NET tags have a special format. They always begin with the prefix `asp:` followed by the class name. If there is no closing tag, the tag must end with `/>`. (This syntax convention is borrowed from XML, which you'll learn about in much more detail in Chapter 19.) Each attribute in the tag corresponds to a control property, except for the runat="server" attribute, which signals that the control should be processed on the server.

The following, for example, is an ASP.NET TextBox:

```
<asp:TextBox ID="txt" runat="server" />
```

When a client requests this .aspx page, the following HTML is returned. The name is a special attribute that ASP.NET uses to track the control.

```
<input type="text" ID="txt" name="txt" />
```

Alternatively, you could place some text in the TextBox, set its size, make it read-only, and change the background color. All these actions have defined properties. For example, the TextBox.TextMode property allows you to specify SingleLine (the default), MultiLine (for a <textarea> type of control), or Password (for an input control that displays bullets to hide the true value). You can adjust the color using the BackColor and ForeColor properties. And you can tweak the size of the TextBox using the Rows property. Here's an example of a customized TextBox:

```
<asp:TextBox ID="txt" BackColor="Yellow" Text="Hello World"
 ReadOnly="True" TextMode="MultiLine" Rows="5" runat="server" />
```

The resulting HTML uses the <textarea> element and sets all the required style attributes. Figure 6-1 shows it in the browser.

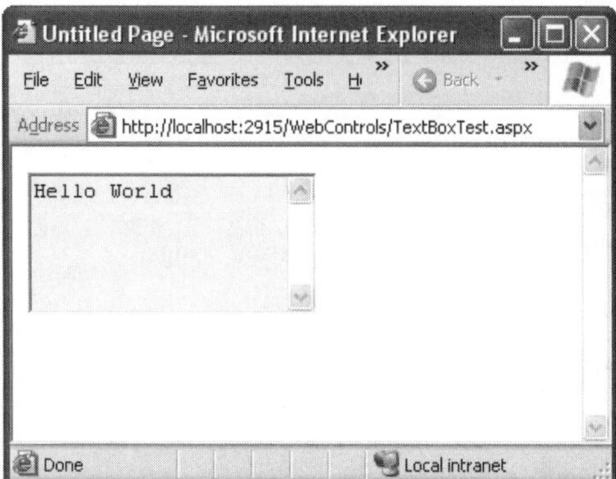

Figure 6-1. *A customized text box*

```
<textarea name="txt" rows="5" cols="20" readonly="readonly" ID="txt"
 style="background-color:Yellow;">Hello World</textarea>
```

Clearly, it's easy to create a web control tag. It doesn't require any understanding of HTML. However, you *will* need to understand the control class and the properties that are available to you.

CASE-SENSITIVITY IN ASP.NET FORMS

The .aspx layout portion of a web page tolerates different capitalization for tag names, property names, and enumeration values. For example, the following two tags are equivalent, and both will be interpreted correctly by the ASP.NET engine, even though their case differs:

```
<asp:Button ID="Button1" runat="server"
  Enabled="False" Text="Button" Font-Size="XX-Small" />
<asp:button ID="Button2" runat="server"
  Enabled="false" tExT="Button" d" />
```

This design was adopted to make .aspx pages behave more like ordinary HTML web pages, which ignore case completely. However, you can't use the same looseness in the tags that apply settings in the web.config file or the machine.config file. Here, case must match *exactly*.

Web Control Classes

Web control classes are defined in the System.Web.UI.WebControls namespace. They follow a slightly more tangled object hierarchy than HTML server controls, as shown in Figure 6-2.

This inheritance diagram includes some controls that you won't study in this chapter, including the data controls, such as the GridView, DetailsView, and FormView, and the validation controls. You'll explore these controls in later chapters.

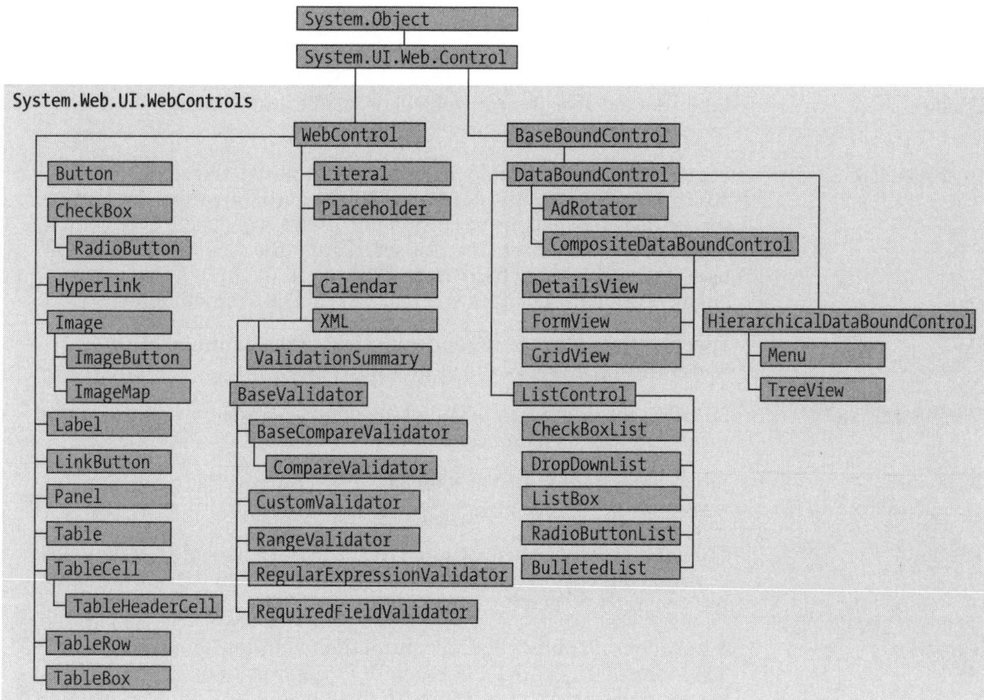

Figure 6-2. *The web control hierarchy*

The WebControl Base Class

Most web controls begin by inheriting from the WebControl base class. This class defines the essential functionality for tasks such as data binding and includes some basic properties that you can use with almost any web control, as described in Table 6-2.

Table 6-2. *WebControl Properties*

Property	Description
AccessKey	Specifies the keyboard shortcut as one letter. For example, if you set this to Y, the Alt+Y keyboard combination will automatically change focus to this web control. This feature is supported only on Internet Explorer 4.0 and higher.
BackColor, ForeColor, and BorderColor	Sets the colors used for the background, foreground, and border of the control. In most controls, the foreground color sets the text color.
BorderWidth	Specifies the size of the control border.
BorderStyle	One of the values from the BorderStyle enumeration, including Dashed, Dotted, Double, Groove, Ridge, Inset, Outset, Solid, and None.
Controls	Provides a collection of all the controls contained inside the current control. Each object is provided as a generic System.Web.UI.Control object, so you will need to cast the reference to access control-specific properties.

Table 6-2. *WebControl Properties (Continued)*

Property	Description
Enabled	When set to False, the control will be visible, but it will not be able to receive user input or focus.
EnableViewState	Set this to False to disable the automatic state management for this control. In this case, the control will be reset to the properties and formatting specified in the control tag (in the .aspx page) every time the page is posted back. If this is set to True (the default), the control uses the hidden input field to store information about its properties, ensuring that any changes you make in code are remembered.
Font	Specifies the font used to render any text in the control as a System.Web.UI.WebControls.FontInfo object.
Height and Width	Specifies the width and height of the control. For some controls, these properties will be ignored when used with older browsers.
Page	Provides a reference to the web page that contains this control as a System.Web.UI.Page object.
Parent	Provides a reference to the control that contains this control. If the control is placed directly on the page (rather than inside another control), it will return a reference to the page object.
TabIndex	A number that allows you to control the tab order. The control with a TabIndex of 0 has the focus when the page first loads. Pressing Tab moves the user to the control with the next lowest TabIndex, provided it is enabled. This property is supported only in Internet Explorer 4.0 and higher.
ToolTip	Displays a text message when the user hovers the mouse above the control. Many older browsers don't support this property.
Visible	When set to False, the control will be hidden and will not be rendered to the final HTML page that is sent to the client.

The next few sections describe some of the common concepts you'll use with almost any web control, including how to set properties that use units and enumerations and how to use colors and fonts.

Units

All the properties that use measurements, including BorderWidth, Height, and Width, require the Unit structure, which combines a numeric value with a type of measurement (pixels, percentage, and so on). This means when you set these properties in a control tag, you must make sure to append px (pixel) or % (for percentage) to the number to indicate the type of unit.

Here's an example with a Panel control that is 300 pixels wide and has a height equal to 50 percent of the current browser window:

```
<asp:Panel Height="300px" Width="50%" ID="pnl" runat="server" />
```

If you're assigning a unit-based property through code, you need to use one of the shared methods of the Unit type. Use Pixel() to supply a value in pixels, and use Percentage() to supply a percentage value:

```
' Convert the number 300 to a Unit object
' representing pixels, and assign it.
pnl.Height = Unit.Pixel(300)

' Convert the number 50 to a Unit object
' representing percent, and assign it.
pnl.Width = Unit.Percentage(50)
```

You could also manually create a Unit object and initialize it using one of the supplied constructors and the UnitType enumeration. This requires a few more steps but allows you to easily assign the same unit to several controls:

```
' Create a Unit object.
Dim myUnit As New Unit(300, UnitType.Pixel)

' Assign the Unit object to several controls or properties.
pnl.Height = myUnit
pnl.Width = myUnit
```

Enumerations

Enumerations are used heavily in the .NET class library to group a set of related constants. For example, when you set a control's BorderStyle property, you can choose one of several predefined values from the BorderStyle enumeration. In code, you set an enumeration using the dot syntax:

```
ctrl.BorderStyle = BorderStyle.Dashed
```

In the .aspx file, you set an enumeration by specifying one of the allowed values as a string. You don't include the name of the enumeration type, which is assumed automatically.

```
<asp:Label BorderStyle="Dashed" Text="Border Test" ID="lbl"
 runat="server" />
```

Figure 6-3 shows the label with the altered border.

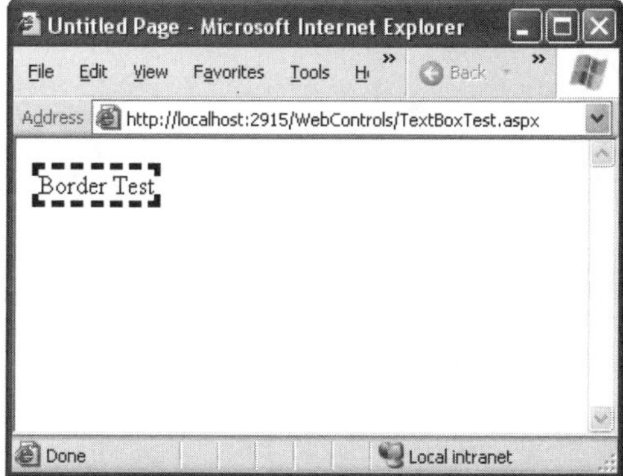

Figure 6-3. *Modifying the border style*

Colors

The Color property refers to a Color object from the System.Drawing namespace. You can create color objects in several ways:

Using an ARGB (alpha, red, green, blue) color value: You specify each value as an integer from 0 to 255. The alpha component represents the transparency of a color, and usually you'll use 255 to make the color completely opaque.

Using a predefined .NET color name: You choose the correspondingly named read-only property from the Color structure. These properties include the 140 HTML color names.

Using an HTML color name: You specify this value as a string using the ColorTranslator class.

To use any of these techniques, you'll probably want to start by importing the System.Drawing namespace, as follows:

```
Imports System.Drawing
```

The following code shows several ways to specify a color in code:

```
' Create a color from an ARGB value
Dim alpha As Integer = 255, red As Integer = 0
Dim green As Integer = 255, blue As Integer = 0
ctrl.ForeColor = Color.FromArgb(alpha, red, green, blue)

' Create a color using a .NET name
ctrl.ForeColor = Color.Crimson

' Create a color from an HTML code
ctrl.ForeColor = ColorTranslator.FromHtml("Blue")
```

When defining a color in the .aspx file, you can use any one of the known color names:

```
<asp:TextBox ForeColor="Red" Text="Test" ID="txt" runat="server" />
```

The HTML color names that you can use are listed in the MSDN Help. Alternatively, you can use a hexadecimal color number (in the format #<red><green><blue>) as shown here:

```
<asp:TextBox ForeColor="#ff50ff" Text="Test"
    ID="txt" runat="server" />
```

Fonts

The Font property actually references a full FontInfo object, which is defined in the System.Web.UI.WebControls namespace. Every FontInfo object has several properties that define its name, size, and style (see Table 6-3).

Table 6-3. *FontInfo Properties*

Property	Description
Name	A string indicating the font name (such as Verdana).
Names	An array of strings with font names, in the order of preference. The browser will use the first matching font that's installed on the user's computer.
Size	The size of the font as a FontUnit object. This can represent an absolute or relative size.
Bold, Italic, Strikeout, Underline, and Overline	Boolean properties that apply the given style attribute.

In code, you can assign a font by setting the various font properties using the familiar dot syntax:

```
ctrl.Font.Name = "Verdana"
ctrl.Font.Bold = True
```

You can also set the size using the FontUnit type:

```
' Specifies a relative size.
ctrl.Font.Size = FontUnit.Small

' Specifies an absolute size of 14 pixels.
ctrl.Font.Size = FontUnit.Point(14)
```

In the .aspx file, you need to use a special "object walker" syntax to specify object properties such as Font. The object walker syntax uses a hyphen (-) to separate properties. For example, you could set a control with a specific font (Tahoma) and font size (40 point) like this:

```
<asp:TextBox Font-Name="Tahoma" Font-Size="40" Text="Size Test" ID="txt"
 runat="server" />
```

Or you could set a relative size like this:

```
<asp:TextBox Font-Name="Tahoma" Font-Size="Large" Text="Size Test"
 ID="txt" runat="server" />
```

Figure 6-4 shows the altered TextBox in this example.

A font setting is really just a recommendation. If the client computer doesn't have the font you request, it reverts to a standard font. To deal with this problem, it's common to specify a list of fonts, in order of preference. To do so, you use the Font.Names property instead of Font.Name, as shown here:

```
<asp:TextBox Font-Names="Verdana,Tahoma,Arial"
 Text="Size Test" ID="txt" runat="server" />
```

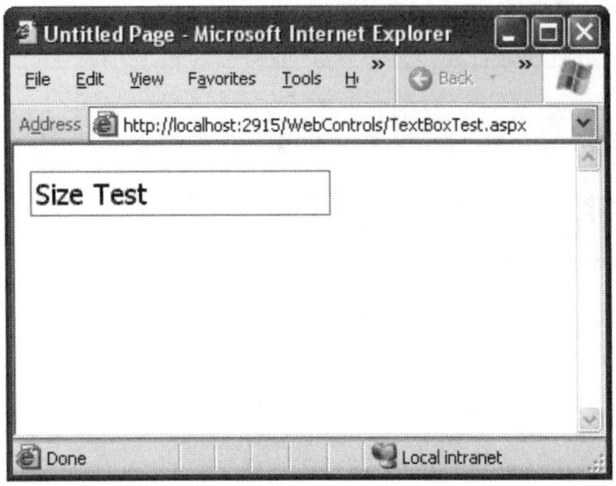

Figure 6-4. *Modifying a control's font*

Here, the browser will use the Verdana font (if it has it). If not, it will fall back on Tahoma or Arial.

When specifying fonts, it's a good idea to end with one of the following fonts, which are supported on all browsers:

- Times
- Arial and Helvetica
- Courier

The following fonts are found on almost all Windows and Mac computers, but not necessarily on other operating systems like Unix:

- Verdana
- Georgia
- Tahoma
- Comic Sans
- Arial Black
- Impact

Focus

Unlike HTML server controls, every web control provides a Focus() method. The Focus() method affects only input controls (controls that can accept keystrokes from the user). When the page is rendered in the client browser, the user starts in the focused control.

For example, if you have a form that allows the user to edit customer information, you might call the Focus() method on the first text box in that form. That way, the cursor appears in this text box immediately when the page first loads in the browser. If the text box is partway down the form, the page even scrolls down to it automatically. The user can then move from control to control using the time-honored Tab key.

If you're a seasoned HTML developer, you know there isn't any built-in way to give focus to an input control. Instead, you need to rely on JavaScript. This is the secret to ASP.NET's implementation. When your code is finished processing and the page is rendered, ASP.NET adds an extra block of JavaScript code to the end of your page. This JavaScript code simply sets the focus to the last control that used the Focus() method. If you haven't called Focus() at all, this code isn't added to the page.

Rather than call the Focus() method programmatically, you can set a control that should always be focused by setting the DefaultFocus property of the <form> tag:

```
<form DefaultFocus="TextBox2" runat="server">
```

You can override the default focus by calling the Focus() method in your code.

Another way to manage focus is using access keys. For example, if you set the AccessKey property of a TextBox to A, pressing Alt+A focus will switch to the TextBox. Labels can also get into the game, even though they can't accept focus. The trick is to set the Label.AssociatedControlID property to specify a linked input control. That way, the label transfers focus to a nearby control.

For example, the following label gives focus to TextBox2 when the keyboard combination Alt+2 is pressed:

```
<asp:Label AccessKey="2" AssociatedControlID="TextBox2" runat="server"
 Text="TextBox2:" />
<asp:TextBox runat="server" ID="TextBox2" />
```

Focusing and access keys are also supported in non-Microsoft browsers, including Firefox.

The Default Button

Along with control focusing, ASP.NET also allows you to designate a default button on a web page. The default button is the button that is "clicked" when the user presses the Enter key. For example, if your web page includes a form, you might want to make the submit button into a default button. That way, if the user hits Enter at any time, the page is posted back and the Button.Click event is fired for that button.

To designate a default button, you must set the HtmlForm.DefaultButton property with the ID of the respective control, as shown here:

```
<form DefaultButton="cmdSubmit" runat="server">
```

The default button must be a control that implements the IButtonControl interface. The interface is implemented by the Button, LinkButton, and ImageButton web controls but not by any of the HTML server controls.

In some cases, it makes sense to have more than one default button. For example, you might create a web page with two groups of input controls. Both groups may need a different default button. You can handle this by placing the groups into separate panels. The Panel control also exposes the DefaultButton property, which works when any input control it contains gets the focus.

CONTROL PREFIXES

When working with web controls, it's often useful to use a three-letter lowercase prefix to identify the type of control. The preceding example (and those in the rest of this book) follows this convention to make user interface code as clear as possible. Some recommended control prefixes are as follows:

- Button: cmd
- CheckBox: chk
- Image: img
- Label: lbl
- List control: lst
- Panel: pnl
- RadioButton: opt
- TextBox: txt

If you're a veteran programmer, you'll also notice that this book doesn't use prefixes to identify data types. This is in keeping with the new philosophy of .NET, which recognizes that data types can often change freely and without consequence and that variables often point to full-featured objects instead of simple data variables.

List Controls

The list controls include the ListBox, DropDownList, CheckBoxList, RadioButtonList, and BulletedList. They all work in essentially the same way but are rendered differently in the browser. The ListBox, for example, is a rectangular list that displays several entries, while the DropDownList shows only the selected item. The CheckBoxList and RadioButtonList are similar to the ListBox, but every item is rendered as a check box or option button, respectively. Finally, the BulletedList is the odd one out—it's the only list control that isn't selectable. Instead, it renders itself as a sequence of numbered or bulleted items.

All the selectable list controls provide a SelectedIndex property that indicates the selected row as a zero-based index (just like the HtmlSelect control you used in the previous chapter). For example, if the first item in the list is selected, the SelectedIndex will be 0. Selectable list controls also provide an additional SelectedItem property, which allows your code to retrieve the ListItem object that represents the selected item. The ListItem object provides three important properties: Text (the displayed content), Value (the hidden value from the HTML markup), and Selected (True or False depending on whether the item is selected).

In the previous chapter, you used code like this to retrieve the selected ListItem object from an HtmlSelect control called Currency, as follows:

```
Dim item As ListItem
item = Currency.Items(Currency.SelectedIndex)
```

If you used the ListBox web control, you can simplify this code with a clearer syntax:

```
Dim item As ListItem
item = Currency.SelectedItem
```

Multiple-Select List Controls

Some list controls can allow multiple selections. This isn't allowed for the DropDownList or RadioButtonList, but it is supported for a ListBox, provided you have set the SelectionMode property to the enumerated value ListSelectionMode.Multiple. The user can then select multiple items by holding down the Ctrl key while clicking the items in the list. With the CheckBoxList, multiple selections are always possible.

If you have a list control that supports multiple selections, you can find all the selected items by iterating through the Items collection of the list control and checking the ListItem.Selected property of each item. Figure 6-5 shows a simple web page example. It provides a list of computer languages and indicates which selections the user made when the OK button is clicked.

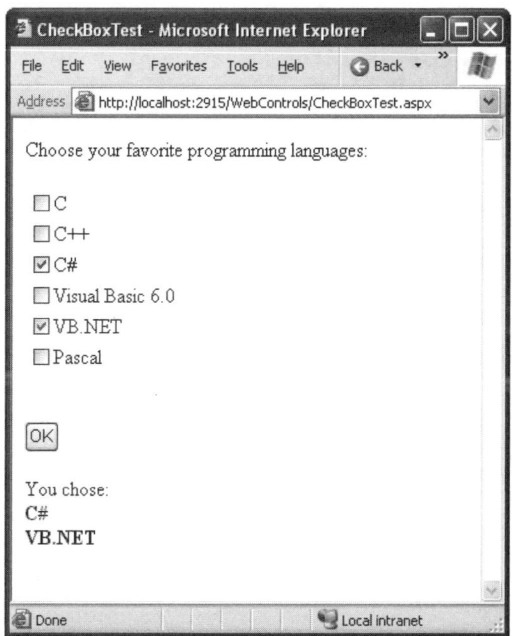

Figure 6-5. *A simple CheckListBox test*

The .aspx file for this page defines CheckListBox, Button, and Label controls, as shown here:

```
<%@ Page Language="VB" AutoEventWireup="false"
    CodeFile="CheckListTest.aspx.vb" Inherits="CheckListTest" %>
<html xmlns="http://www.w3.org/1999/xhtml">
<head runat="server">
  <title>CheckBoxTest</title>
</head>
```

```
<body>
  <form runat="server">
    <div>
      Choose your favorite programming languages:<br /><br />
      <asp:CheckBoxList ID="chklst" runat="server" /><br /><br />
      <asp:Button ID="cmdOK" Text="OK" runat="server" />
      <br /><br />
      <asp:Label ID="lblResult" runat="server" />
    </div>
  </form>
</body>
</html>
```

The code adds items to the CheckListBox at startup and iterates through the collection when the button is clicked:

```
Public Partial Class CheckListTest
  Inherits System.Web.UI.Page

    Protected Sub Page_Load(ByVal sender As Object, _
      ByVal e As EventArgs) Handles Me.Load
        If Me.IsPostBack = False
            chklst.Items.Add("C")
            chklst.Items.Add("C++")
            chklst.Items.Add("C#")
            chklst.Items.Add("Visual Basic 6.0")
            chklst.Items.Add("VB.NET")
            chklst.Items.Add("Pascal")
        End If
    End Sub

    Protected Sub cmdOK_Click(ByVal sender As Object, _
      ByVal e As System.EventArgs) Handles cmdOK.Click
        lblResult.Text = "You chose:<b>"

        Dim lstItem As ListItem
        For Each lstItem In chklst.Items
            If lstItem.Selected = True Then
                ' Add text to label.
                lblResult.Text &= "<br />" & lstItem.Text
            End If
        Next

        lblResult.Text &= "</b>"
    End Sub

End Class
```

The BulletedList Control

The BulletedList control is a server-side equivalent of the <ul> (unordered list) and <ol> (ordered list) elements. As with all list controls, you set the collection of items that should be displayed through the Items property. Additionally, you can use the properties in Table 6-4 to configure how the items are displayed.

Table 6-4. *Added BulletedList Properties*

Property	Description
BulletStyle	Determines the type of list. Choose from Numbered (1, 2, 3, . . .), LowerAlpha (a, b, c, . . .) and UpperAlpha (A, B, C, . . .), LowerRoman (i, ii, iii, . . .) and UpperRoman (I, II, III, . . .), and the bullet symbols Disc, Circle, Square, or CustomImage (in which case you must set the BulletImageUrl property).
BulletImageUrl	If the BulletStyle is set to CustomImage, this points to the image that is placed to the left of each item as a bullet.
FirstBulletNumber	In an ordered list (using the Numbered, LowerAlpha, UpperAlpha, LowerRoman, and UpperRoman styles), this sets the first value. For example, if you set FirstBulletNumber to 3, the list might read 3, 4, 5 (for Numbered) or C, D, E (for UpperAlpha).
DisplayMode	Determines whether the text of each item is rendered as text (use Text, the default) or a hyperlink (use LinkButton or HyperLink). The difference between LinkButton and HyperLink is how they treat clicks. When you use LinkButton, the BulletedList fires a Click event that you can react to on the server to perform the navigation. When you use HyperLink, the BulletedList doesn't fire the Click event—instead, it treats the text of each list item as a relative or absolute URL, and renders them as ordinary HTML hyperlinks. When the user clicks an item, the browser attempts to navigate to that URL.

If you set the DisplayMode to LinkButton, you can react to the Button.Click event to determine which item was clicked. Here's an example:

```
Protected Sub BulletedList1_Click(ByVal sender As Object, _
  ByVal e As BulletedListEventArgs) Handles BulletedList1.Click

    Dim itemText As String = BulletedList1.Items(e.Index).Text
    Label1.Text = "You choose item" & itemText
End Sub
```

Figure 6-6 shows all the BulletStyle values that the BulletList supports. When you click one of the items, the list changes to use that BulletStyle. You can try this example page with the sample WebControls project for this chapter.

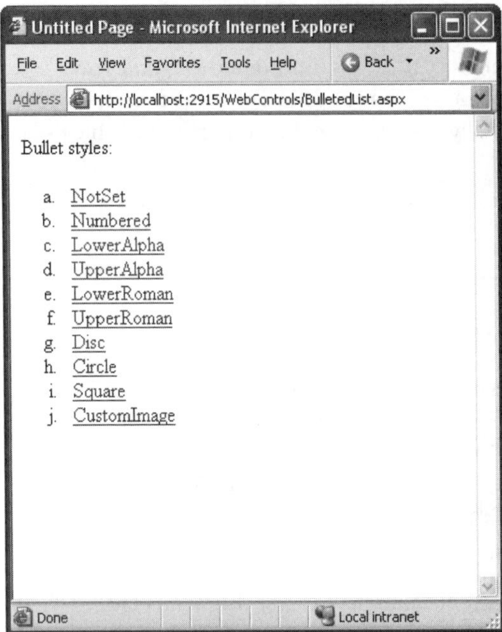

Figure 6-6. *Various BulletedList styles*

Table Controls

Essentially, the Table control is built out of a hierarchy of objects. Each Table object contains one or more TableRow objects. In turn, each TableRow object contains one or more TableCell objects. Each TableCell object contains other ASP.NET controls of HTML content that displays information. If you're familiar with the HTML table tags, this relationship (shown in Figure 6-7) will seem fairly logical.

To create a table dynamically, you follow the same philosophy as you would for any other web control. First, you create and configure the necessary ASP.NET objects. Then, ASP.NET converts these objects to their final HTML representation before the page is sent to the client.

Consider the example shown in Figure 6-8. It allows the user to specify a number of rows and columns as well as whether cells should have borders.

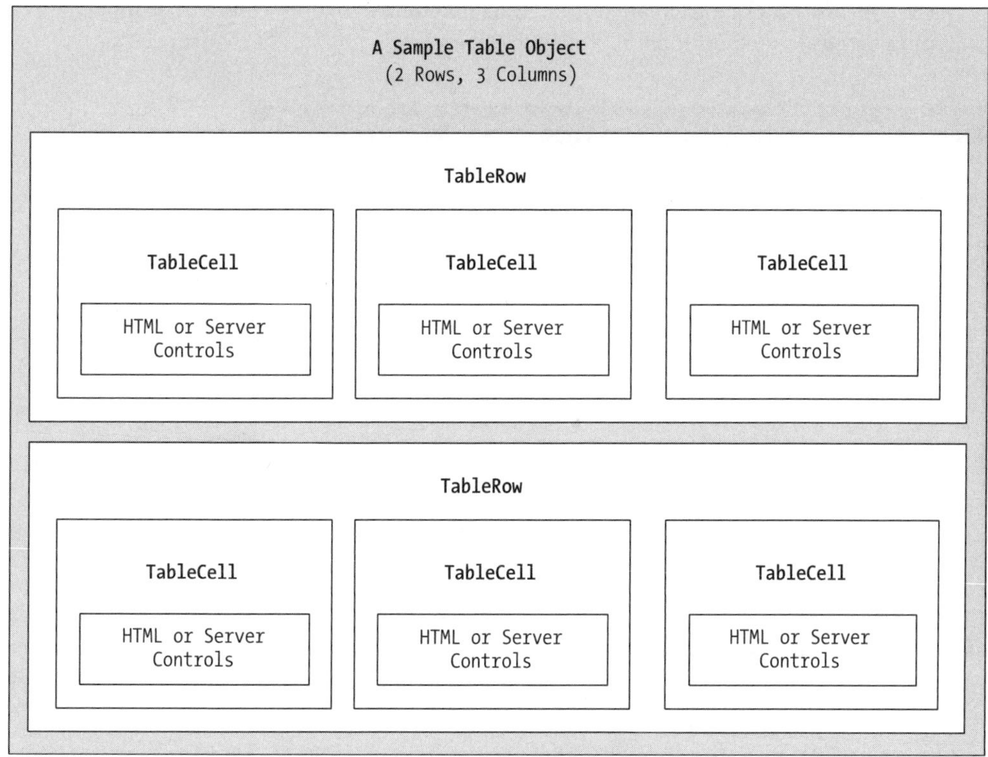

Figure 6-7. *Table control containment*

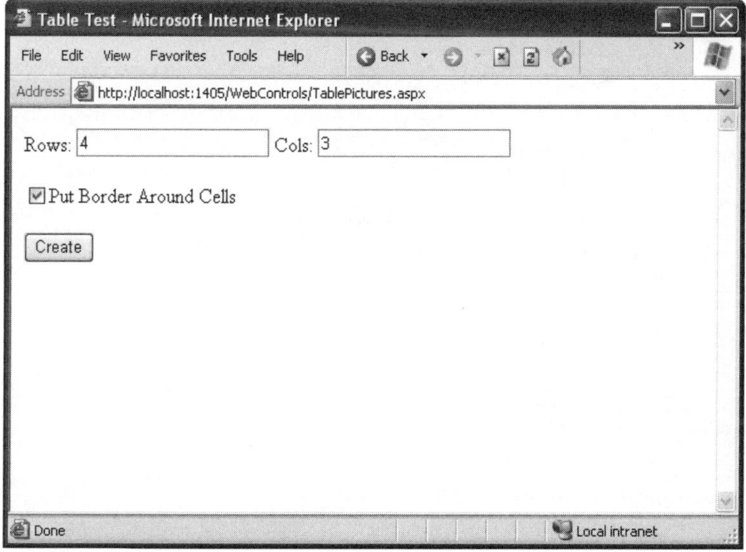

Figure 6-8. *The table test options*

When the user clicks the Create button, the table is filled dynamically with sample data according to the selected options, as shown in Figure 6-9.

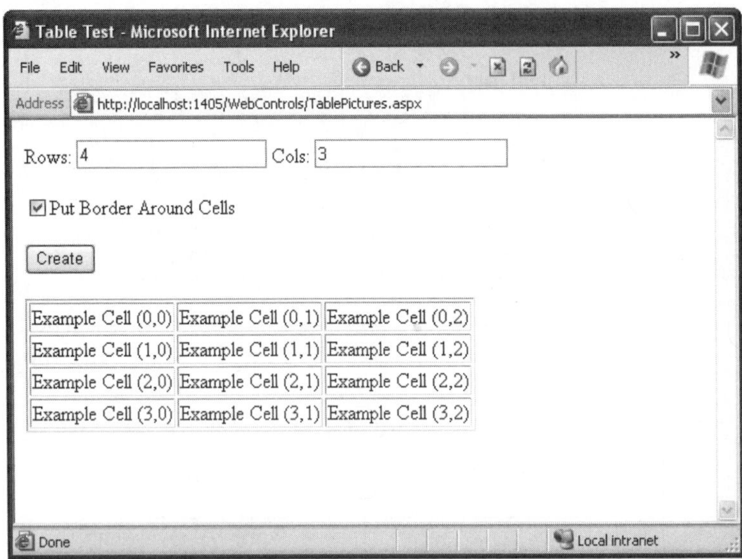

Figure 6-9. *A dynamically generated table*

The .aspx code creates the TextBox, CheckBox, Button, and Table controls:

```
<%@ Page Language="VB" AutoEventWireup="false"
    CodeFile="TableTest.aspx.vb" Inherits="TableTest" %>
<html xmlns="http://www.w3.org/1999/xhtml">
<head runat="server">
  <title>Table Test</title>
</head>
<body>
  <form runat="server">
    <div>
      Rows:
      <asp:TextBox ID="txtRows" runat="server" />
       Cols:
      <asp:TextBox ID="txtCols" runat="server" />
      <br /><br />
      <asp:CheckBox ID="chkBorder" runat="server"
       Text="Put Border Around Cells" />
      <br /><br />
      <asp:Button ID="cmdCreate" runat="server"
       Text="Create" />
      <br /><br />
      <asp:Table ID="tbl" runat="server" />
    </div>
```

```
  </form>
</body>
</html>
```

You'll notice that the Table control doesn't contain any actual rows or cells. To make a valid table, you would need to nest several layers of tags. The following example creates a table with a single cell that contains the text *A Test Row*:

```
<asp:Table ID="tbl" runat="server">
  <asp:TableRow ID="row" runat="server">
    <asp:TableCell ID="cell" runat="server">A Sample Value</asp:TableCell>
  </asp:TableRow>
</asp:Table>
```

The table test web page doesn't have any nested elements. This means the table will be created as a server-side control object, but unless the code adds rows and cells, the table will not be rendered in the final HTML page.

The TableTest class uses two event handlers. When the page is first loaded, it adds a border around the table. When the button is clicked, it dynamically creates the required TableRow and TableCell objects in a loop.

```
Public Partial Class TableTest
    Inherits System.Web.UI.Page

    Protected Sub Page_Load(ByVal sender As Object, _
      ByVal e As EventArgs) Handles Me.Load
        ' Configure the table's appearance.
        ' This could also be performed in the .aspx file,
        ' or in the cmdCreate_Click event handler.
        tbl.BorderStyle = BorderStyle.Inset
        tbl.BorderWidth = Unit.Pixel(1)
    End Sub

    Protected Sub cmdCreate_Click(ByVal sender As Object, _
      ByVal e As EventArgs) Handles cmdCreate.Click

        ' Remove all the current rows and cells.
        ' This would not be necessary if you set EnableViewState = False.
        tbl.Controls.Clear()

        Dim row, col As Integer
        For row = 0 To Val(txtRows.Text - 1)

            ' Create a new TableRow object.
            Dim rowNew As New TableRow()

            ' Put the TableRow in the Table.
            tbl.Controls.Add(rowNew)
```

```
            For col = 0 To Val(txtCols.Text - 1)

                ' Create a new TableCell object.
                Dim cellNew As New TableCell()
                cellNew.Text = "Example Cell (" & row.ToString() & ","
                cellNew.Text &= col.ToString() & ")"

                If chkBorder.Checked = True Then
                    cellNew.BorderStyle = BorderStyle.Inset
                    cellNew.BorderWidth = Unit.Pixel(1)
                End If
                ' Put the TableCell in the TableRow.
                rowNew.Controls.Add(cellNew)

            Next
        Next
    End Sub

End Class
```

This code uses the Controls collection to add child controls. Every container control provides this property. You could also use the TableCell.Controls collection to add web controls to each TableCell. For example, you could place an Image control and a Label control in each cell. In this case, you can't set the TableCell.Text property. The following code snippet uses this technique, and Figure 6-10 displays the results:

```
' Create a new TableCell object.
Dim cellNew As New TableCell()

' Create a new Label object.
Dim lblNew As New Label()
lblNew.Text = "Example Cell (" & row.ToString() & "," & _
  col.ToString() & ")<br />"

Dim imgNew As New System.Web.UI.WebControls.Image()
imgNew.ImageUrl = "cellpic.png"

' Put the label and picture in the cell.
cellNew.Controls.Add(lblNew)
cellNew.Controls.Add(imgNew)

' Put the TableCell in the TableRow.
rowNew.Controls.Add(cellNew)
```

The real flexibility of the table test page is that each Table, TableRow, and TableCell is a full-featured object. If you want, you can give each cell a different border style, border color, and text color by setting the corresponding properties.

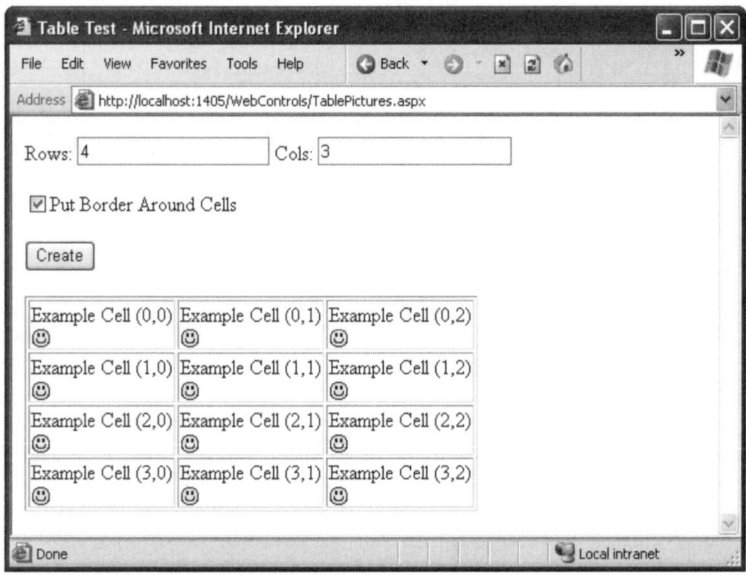

Figure 6-10. *A table with contained controls*

Web Control Events and AutoPostBack

The previous chapter explained that one of the main limitations of HTML server controls is their limited set of useful events—they have exactly two. HTML controls that trigger a postback, such as buttons, raise a ServerClick event. Input controls provide a ServerChange event that doesn't actually fire until the page is posted back.

Server controls are really an ingenious illusion. You'll recall that the code in an ASP.NET page is processed on the server. It's then sent to the user as ordinary HTML. Figure 6-11 illustrates the order of events in page processing.

This is the same in ASP.NET as it was in traditional ASP programming. The question is, how can you write server code that will react *immediately* to an event that occurs on the client?

Some events, such as the Click event of a button, do occur immediately. That's because when clicked, the button posts back the page. This is a basic convention of HTML forms. However, other actions *do* cause events but *don't* trigger a postback. An example is when the user changes the text in a text box (which triggers the TextChanged event) or chooses a new item in a list (the SelectedIndexChanged event). You might want to respond to these events, but without a postback your code has no way to run.

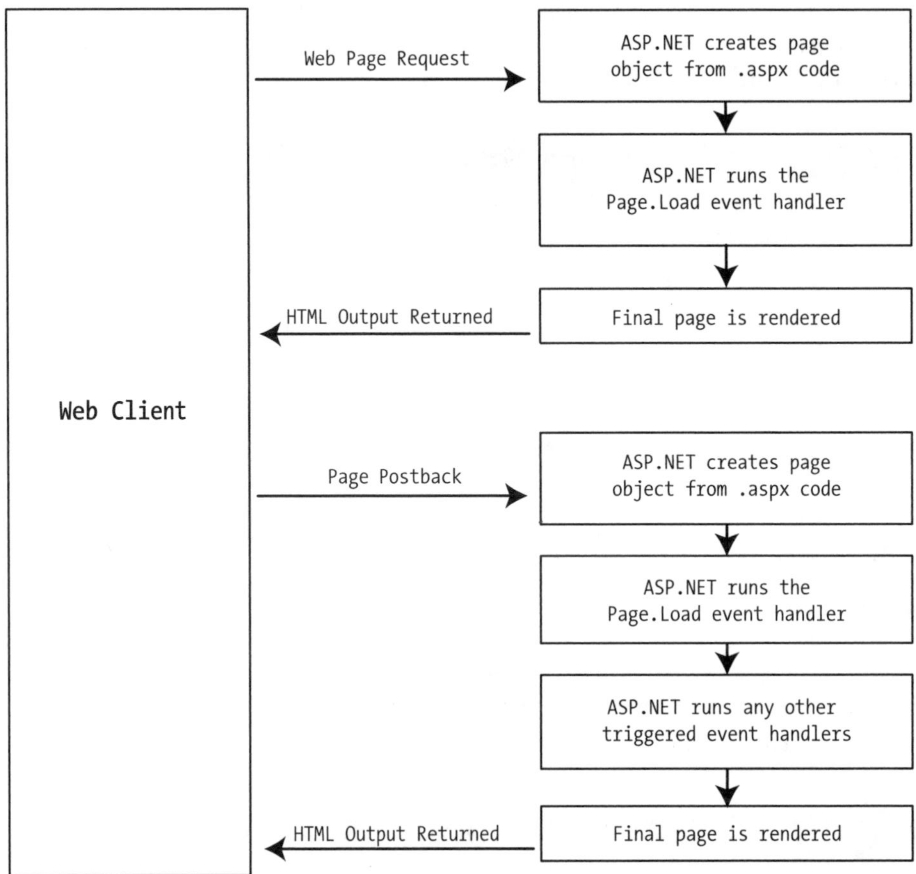

Figure 6-11. *The page processing sequence*

ASP.NET handles this by giving you two options:

- You can wait until the next postback to react to the event. For example, imagine you want to react to the SelectedIndexChanged event in a list. If the user selects an item in a list, nothing happens immediately. However, if the user then clicks a button to post back the page, *two* events fire: Button.Click followed by TextBox.TextChanged. And if you have several controls, it's quite possible for a single postback to result in several change events, which fire one after the other, in an undetermined order.
- You can use the *automatic postback* feature to force a control to post back the page immediately when it detects a specific user action. In this scenario, when the user clicks a new item in the list, the page is posted back, your code executes, and a new version of the page is returned.

The option you choose depends on the result you want. If you need to react immediately (for example, you want to update another control when a specific action takes place), you need to use automatic postbacks. On the other hand, automatic postbacks can sometimes make the page less responsive, because each postback and page refresh adds a short, but noticeable, delay and page refresh. (You'll learn how to create pages that update themselves without a noticeable page refresh when you consider ASP.NET AJAX in Chapter 25.)

All input web controls support automatic postbacks. Table 6-5 provides a basic list of web controls and their events.

Table 6-5. *Web Control Events*

Event	Web Controls That Provide It	Always Posts Back
Click	Button, ImageButton	True
TextChanged	TextBox (fires only after the user changes the focus to another control)	False
CheckedChanged	CheckBox, RadioButton	False
SelectedIndexChanged	DropDownList, ListBox, CheckBoxList, RadioButtonList	False

If you want to capture a change event (such as TextChanged, CheckedChanged, or SelectedIndexChanged) immediately, you need to set the control's AutoPostBack property to True. This way, the page will be submitted automatically when the user interacts with the control (for example, picks a selection in the list, clicks a radio button or a check box, or changes the text in a text box and then tabs away to a new control).

When the page is posted back, ASP.NET will examine the page, load all the current information, and then allow your code to perform some extra processing before returning the page back to the user (see Figure 6-12). Depending on the result you want, you could have a page that has some controls that post back automatically and others that don't.

This postback system isn't ideal for all events. For example, some events that you may be familiar with from Windows programs, such as mouse movement events or key press events, aren't practical in an ASP.NET application. Resubmitting the page every time a key is pressed or the mouse is moved would make the application unbearably slow and unresponsive.

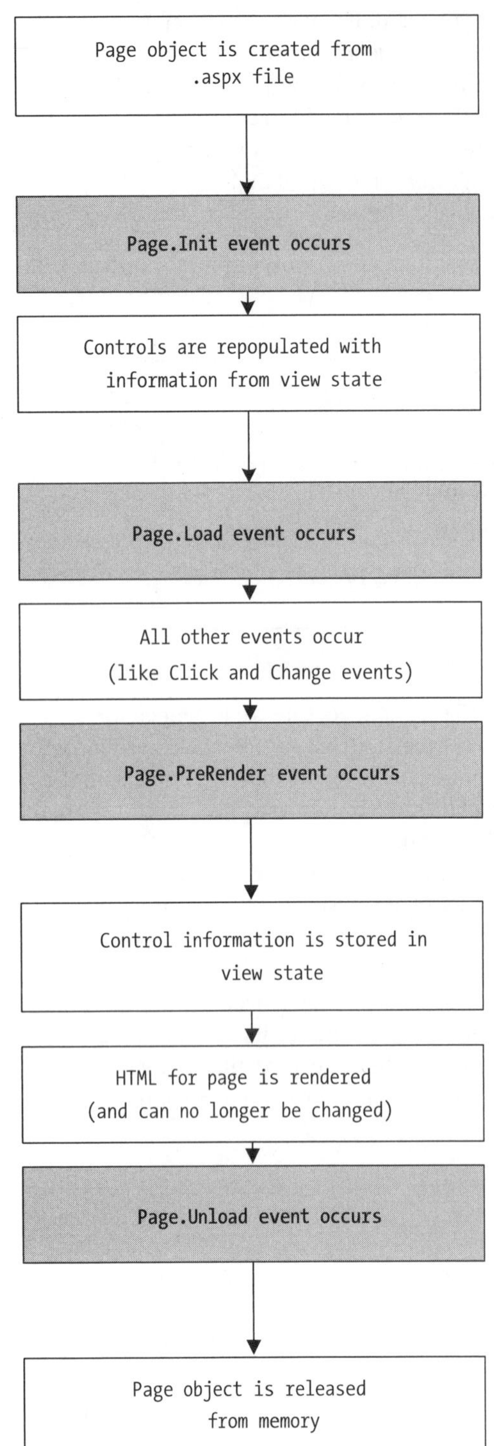

Figure 6-12. *The postback processing sequence*

How Postback Events Work

Chapter 1 explained that not all types of web programming use server-side code like ASP.NET. One common example of client-side web programming is JavaScript, which uses simple code that's limited in scope and is executed by the browser. ASP.NET uses the client-side abilities of JavaScript to bridge the gap between client-side and server-side code. (Another scripting language is VBScript, but JavaScript is the only one that works on all modern browsers, including Internet Explorer, Firefox, Opera, Safari, and Netscape.)

Here's how it works: If you create a web page that includes one or more web controls that are configured to use AutoPostBack, ASP.NET adds a special JavaScript function to the rendered HTML page. This function is named __doPostBack(). When called, it triggers a postback, sending data back to the web server.

ASP.NET also adds two additional hidden input fields that are used to pass information back to the server. This information consists of the ID of the control that raised the event and any additional information that might be relevant. These fields are initially empty, as shown here:

```
<input type="hidden" name="__EVENTTARGET" id="__EVENTTARGET" value="" />
<input type="hidden" name="__EVENTARGUMENT" id="__EVENTARGUMENT" value="" />
```

The __doPostBack() function has the responsibility for setting these values with the appropriate information about the event and then submitting the form. A slightly simplified version of the __doPostBack() function is shown here:

```
<script language="text/javascript">
<!--
    function __doPostBack(eventTarget, eventArgument) {
        var theform = document.Form1;
        theform.__EVENTTARGET.value = eventTarget;
        theform.__EVENTARGUMENT.value = eventArgument;
        theform.submit();
    }
// -->
</script>
```

Remember, ASP.NET generates the __doPostBack() function automatically, provided at least one control on the page uses automatic postbacks.

Finally, any control that has its AutoPostBack property set to True is connected to the __doPostBack() function using the onclick or onchange attributes. These attributes indicate what action the browser should take in response to the client-side JavaScript events onclick and onchange.

The following example shows the tag for a list control named lstBackColor, which posts back automatically. Whenever the user changes the selection in the list, the client-side onchange event fires. The browser then calls the __doPostBack() function, which sends the page back to the server.

```
<select ID="lstBackColor" onchange="__doPostBack('lstBackColor','')"
 language="javascript">
```

In other words, ASP.NET automatically changes a client-side JavaScript event into a server-side ASP.NET event, using the __doPostBack() function as an intermediary. Figure 6-13 shows this process.

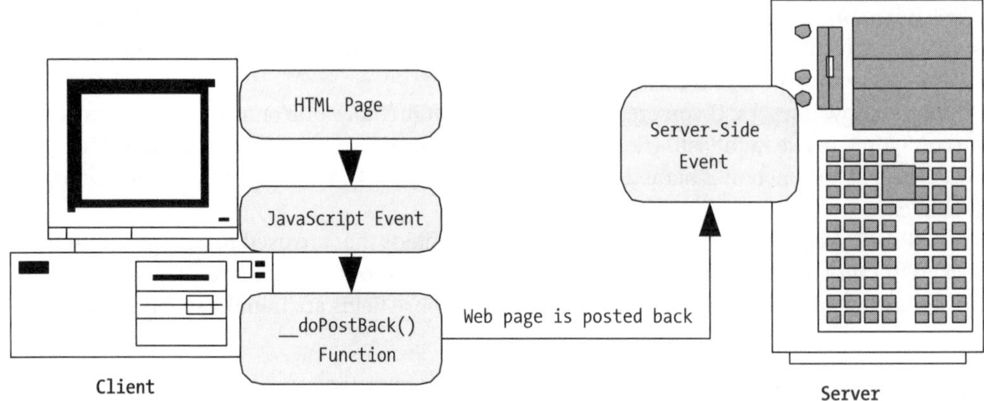

Figure 6-13. *An automatic postback*

The Page Life Cycle

To understand how web control events work, you need to have a solid understanding of the page life cycle. Consider what happens when a user changes a control that has the AutoPostBack property set to True:

1. On the client side, the JavaScript __doPostBack function is invoked, and the page is resubmitted to the server.
2. ASP.NET re-creates the Page object using the .aspx file.
3. ASP.NET retrieves state information from the hidden view state field and updates the controls accordingly.
4. The Page.Load event is fired.
5. The appropriate change event is fired for the control. (If more than one control has been changed, the order of change events is undetermined.)
6. The Page.Unload event fires, and the page is rendered (transformed from a set of objects to an HTML page).
7. The new page is sent to the client.

To watch these events in action, it helps to create a simple event tracker application (see Figure 6-14). All this application does is write a new entry to a list control every time one of the events it is monitoring occurs. This allows you to see the order in which events are triggered.

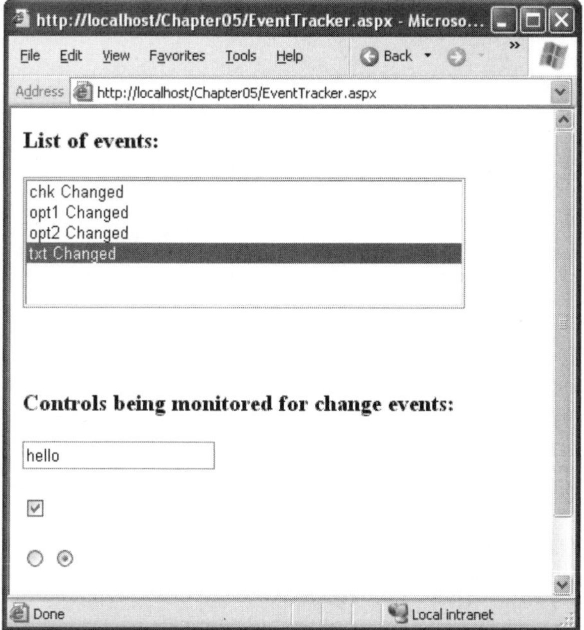

Figure 6-14. *The event tracker*

Listing 6-1 shows the markup code for the event tracker, and Listing 6-2 shows the code-behind class that makes it work.

Listing 6-1. *EventTracker.aspx*

```
<%@ Page Language="VB" AutoEventWireup="false"
    CodeFile="EventTracker.aspx.vb" Inherits="EventTracker" %>
<html xmlns="http://www.w3.org/1999/xhtml">
<head runat="server">
  <title>Event Tracker</title>
</head>
<body>
  <form runat="server">
    <div>
      <h1>List of events:</h1>
      <asp:ListBox ID="lstEvents" runat="server" Width="355px"
       Height="150px" /><br />
      <br /><br /><br />
      <h1>Controls being monitored for change events:</h1>
      <asp:TextBox ID="txt" runat="server" AutoPostBack="True" />
      <br /><br />
      <asp:CheckBox ID="chk" runat="server" AutoPostBack="True" />
      <br /><br />
      <asp:RadioButton ID="opt1" runat="server" GroupName="Sample"
       AutoPostBack="True" />
```

```
      <asp:RadioButton ID="opt2" runat="server" GroupName="Sample"
       AutoPostBack="True" />
    </div>
  </form>
</body>
</html>
```

Listing 6-2. *EventTracker.vb*

```
Public Partial Class EventTracker
    Inherits System.Web.UI.Page

    Protected Sub Page_Load(ByVal sender As Object, _
      ByVal e As EventArgs) Handles Me.Load
        Log("<< Page_Load >>")
    End Sub

    Protected Sub Page_PreRender(ByVal sender As Object, _
      ByVal e As EventArgs) Handles Me.PreRender
        ' When the Page.UnLoad event occurs it is too late
        ' to change the list.
        Log("Page_PreRender")
    End Sub

    ' This control handles an event from all four controls.
    Protected Sub CtrlChanged(ByVal sender As Object, _
      ByVal e As System.EventArgs) _
      Handles chk.CheckedChanged, opt1.CheckedChanged, opt2.CheckedChanged, _
              txt.TextChanged
        ' Find the control ID of the sender.
        ' This requires converting the Object type into a Control class.
        Dim ctrlName As String = CType(sender, Control).ID
        Log(ctrlName & " Changed")
    End Sub

    Private Sub Log(ByVal entry As String)
        lstEvents.Items.Add(entry)

        ' Select the last item to scroll the list so the most recent
        ' entries are visible.
        lstEvents.SelectedIndex = lstEvents.Items.Count - 1
    End Sub

End Class
```

Dissecting the Code . . .

The following points are worth noting about this code:

- The code writes to the ListBox using a private Log() subroutine. The Log() subroutine adds the text and automatically scrolls to the bottom of the list each time a new entry is added, thereby ensuring that the most recent entries remain visible.
- All the change events are handled by the same method, CtrlChanged(). The Handles clause for CtrlChanged() clearly reflects this. The event-handling code in the CtrlChanged() method uses the source parameter to find out what control sent the event, and it incorporates that information in the log string.
- The page includes event handlers for the Page.Load and Page.PreRender events. As with all page events, these event handlers are connected by method name. That means to add the event handler for the Page.PreRender event, you simply need to add a method named Page_PreRender(), like the one shown here.
- The page includes an event handler for the Page.PreRender event. Unlike control events, you can't add the event handler for page events using the Properties window. Instead, you need to use one of two strategies. Your first choice is to type the Page_PreRender() method in by hand, being sure to include the Handles Me.PreRender clause at the end of the method declaration. Your second option is to use the drop-down lists at the top of the code window, which gets Visual Studio to create the method you need. To use the drop-down lists, pick EventTracker Events from the first list (at the top-left) and then pick PreRender from the second list (at the top-right).

A Simple Web Page

Now that you've had a whirlwind tour of the basic web control model, it's time to put it to work with the second single-page utility. In this case, it's a simple example for a dynamic e-card generator. You could extend this sample (for example, allowing users to store e-cards to the database), but even on its own, this example demonstrates basic control manipulation with ASP.NET.

The web page is divided into two regions. On the left is an ordinary <div> tag containing a set of web controls for specifying card options. On the right is a Panel control (named pnlCard), which contains two other controls (lblGreeting and imgDefault) that are used to display user-configurable text and a picture. This text and picture represents the greeting card. When the page first loads, the card hasn't yet been generated, and the right portion is blank (as shown in Figure 6-15).

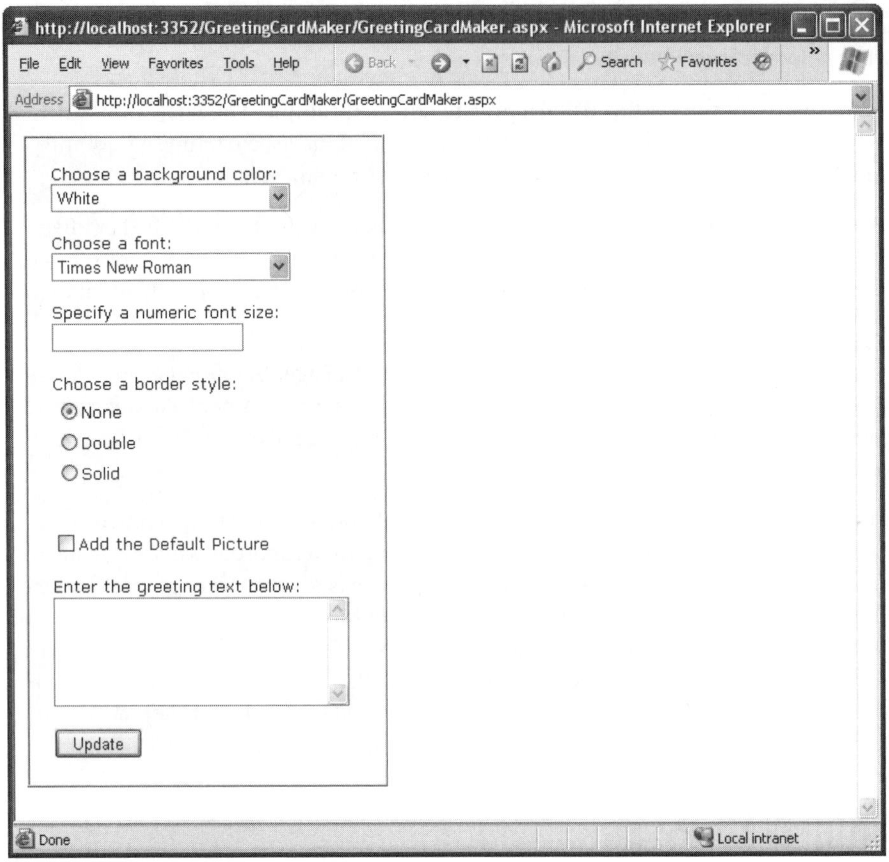

Figure 6-15. *The e-card generator*

■ **Tip** The <div> tag is useful when you want to group text and controls and apply a set of formatting properties (such as a color or font) to all of them. The <div> tag is used in many of the examples in this book, but it can safely be omitted—the only change will be the appearance of the formatted page.

Whenever the user clicks the Update button, the page is posted back and the "card" is updated (see Figure 6-16).

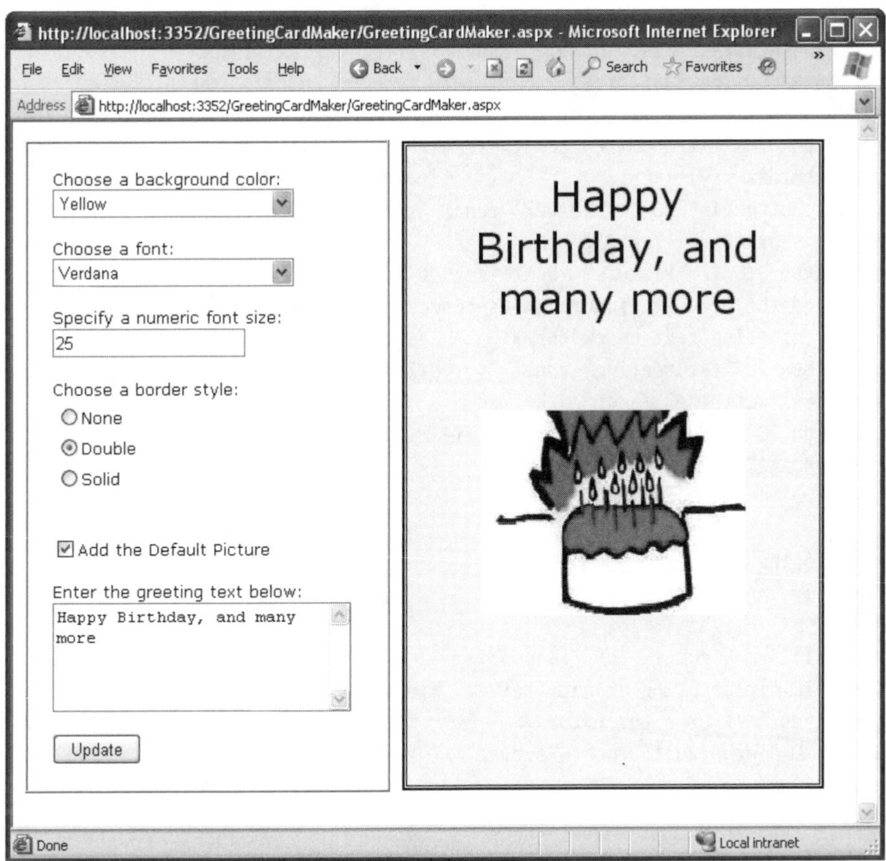

Figure 6-16. *A user-configured greeting card*

The .aspx layout code is straightforward. Of course, the sheer length of it makes it difficult to work with efficiently. Here's the markup, without the formatting details for the <div> element:

```
<%@ Page Language="VB" AutoEventWireup="false"
    CodeFile="GreetingCardMaker.aspx.vb" Inherits="GreetingCardMaker" %>
<html xmlns="http://www.w3.org/1999/xhtml">
<head runat="server">
    <title>Greeting Card Maker</title>
</head>
<body>
  <form runat="server">
    <div>
      <!-- Here are the controls: -->
      Choose a background color:<br />
      <asp:DropDownList ID="lstBackColor" runat="server" Width="194px"
        Height="22px"/><br /><br />
```

```
        Choose a font:<br />
        <asp:DropDownList ID="lstFontName" runat="server" Width="194px"
          Height="22px" /><br /><br />
        Specify a numeric font size:<br />
        <asp:TextBox ID="txtFontSize" runat="server" /><br /><br />
        Choose a border style:<br />
        <asp:RadioButtonList ID="lstBorder" runat="server" Width="177px"
          Height="59px" /><br /><br />
        <asp:CheckBox ID="chkPicture" runat="server"
          Text="Add the Default Picture"></asp:CheckBox><br /><br />
        Enter the greeting text below:<br />
        <asp:TextBox ID="txtGreeting" runat="server" Width="240px" Height="85px"
          TextMode="MultiLine" /><br /><br />
        <asp:Button ID="cmdUpdate" runat="server" Width="71px" Height="24px"
          Text="Update" />
      </div>

      <!-- Here is the card: -->
      <asp:Panel ID="pnlCard" runat="server"
        Width="339px" Height="481px"
        HorizontalAlign="Center"><br /> 
      <asp:Label ID="lblGreeting" runat="server" Width="256px"
        Height="150px" /><br /><br /><br />
      <asp:Image ID="imgDefault" runat="server" Width="212px"
        Height="160px" />
      </asp:Panel>
    </form>
  </body>
</html>
```

The code follows the familiar pattern with an emphasis on two events: the Page.Load event, where initial values are set, and the Button.Click event, where the card is generated.

```
Imports System.Drawing

Public Partial Class GreetingCardMaker
    Inherits System.Web.UI.Page

    Protected Sub Page_Load(ByVal sender As Object, _
      ByVal e As EventArgs) Handles Me.Load
        If Me.IsPostBack = False Then

            ' Set color options.
            lstBackColor.Items.Add("White")
            lstBackColor.Items.Add("Red")
            lstBackColor.Items.Add("Green")
            lstBackColor.Items.Add("Blue")
            lstBackColor.Items.Add("Yellow")
```

```
        ' Set font options.
        lstFontName.Items.Add("Times New Roman")
        lstFontName.Items.Add("Arial")
        lstFontName.Items.Add("Verdana")
        lstFontName.Items.Add("Tahoma")

        ' Set border style options by adding a series of
        ' ListItem objects.
        ' Each item indicates the name of the option, and contains the
        '  corresponding integer in the Value property.
        lstBorder.Items.Add(New _
           ListItem(BorderStyle.None.ToString(), BorderStyle.None))
        lstBorder.Items.Add(New _
           ListItem(BorderStyle.Double.ToString(), BorderStyle.Double))
        lstBorder.Items.Add(New _
           ListItem(BorderStyle.Solid.ToString, BorderStyle.Solid))

        ' Select the first border option.
        lstBorder.SelectedIndex = 0

        ' Set the picture.
        imgDefault.ImageUrl = "defaultpic.png"
    End If
End Sub

Protected Sub cmdUpdate_Click(ByVal sender As Object, _
  ByVal e As EventArgs) Handles cmdUpdate.Click

    ' Update the color.
    pnlCard.BackColor = Color.FromName(lstBackColor.SelectedItem.Text)

    ' Update the font.
    lblGreeting.Font.Name = lstFontName.SelectedItem.Text

    If Val(txtFontSize.Text) > 0 Then
        lblGreeting.Font.Size = FontUnit.Point(Val(txtFontSize.Text))
    End If

    ' Update the border style.
    pnlCard.BorderStyle = Val(lstBorder.SelectedItem.Value)

    ' Update the picture.
    If chkPicture.Checked = True Then
        imgDefault.Visible = True
    Else
        imgDefault.Visible = False
    End If
```

```
        ' Set the text.
        lblGreeting.Text = txtGreeting.Text
    End Sub

End Class
```

As you can see, this example limits the user to a few preset font and color choices. The code for the BorderStyle option is particularly interesting. The lstBorder control has a list that displays the text name of one of the BorderStyle enumerated values. You'll remember from the introductory chapters that every enumerated value is really an integer with a name assigned to it. The lstBorder also secretly stores the corresponding number so that the code can retrieve the number and set the enumeration easily when the user makes a selection and the cmdUpdate_Click event handler fires.

Improving the Greeting Card Generator

ASP.NET pages have access to the full .NET class library. With a little exploration, you'll find classes that might help the greeting-card maker, such as tools that let you retrieve all the known color names and all the fonts installed on the web server.

For example, you can fill the lstFontName control with a list of fonts using the InstalledFontCollection class. To access it, you need to import the System.Drawing.Text namespace. You also need to import the System.Drawing namespace, because it defines the FontFamily class that represents the individual fonts that are installed on the web server:

```
Imports System.Drawing
Imports System.Drawing.Text
```

Here's the code that gets the list of fonts and uses it to fill the list:

```
' Get the list of available fonts, and add them to the font list.
Dim fonts As New InstalledFontCollection()
For Each family As FontFamily In fonts.Families
    lstFontName.Items.Add(family.Name)
Next
```

Figure 6-17 shows the resulting font list.

To get a list of the color names, you need to resort to a more advanced trick. Although you could hard-code a list of common colors, .NET actually provides a long list of color names in the System.Drawing.KnownColor enumeration. However, actually *extracting* the names from this enumeration takes some work.

The trick is to use a basic feature of all enumerations: the shared Enum.GetNames() method, which inspects an enumeration and provides an array of strings, with one string for each value in the enumeration. The web page can then use data binding to automatically fill the list control with the information in the ColorArray. (You'll explore data binding in much more detail in Chapter 16.)

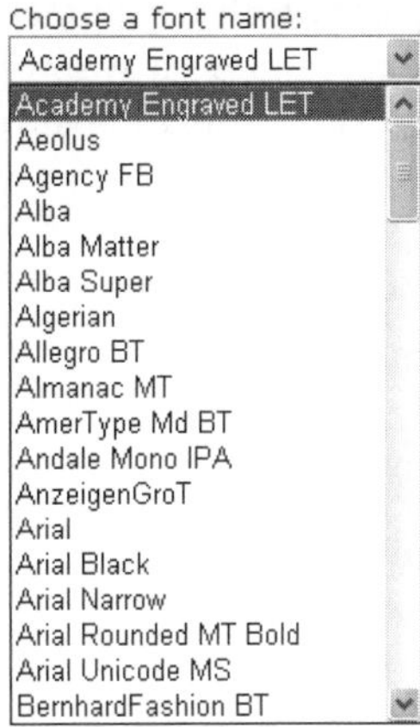

Figure 6-17. *The font list*

■ **Note** Don't worry if this example introduces a few features that look entirely alien! These features are more advanced (and aren't tied specifically to ASP.NET). However, they show you some of the flavor that the full .NET class library can provide for a mature application.

Here's the code that copies all the color names into the list box:

```
' Get the list of colors.
Dim colorArray As String() = System.Enum.GetNames(GetType(KnownColor))
lstBackColor.DataSource = colorArray
lstBackColor.DataBind()
```

A minor problem with this approach is that it includes system environment colors (for example, ActiveBorder) in the list. It may not be obvious to the user what colors these values represent. Still, this approach works well for this simple application. You can use a similar technique to fill in BorderStyle options:

```
' Set border style options.
Dim borderStyleArray As String()
borderStyleArray = System.Enum.GetNames(GetType(BorderStyle))
lstBorder.DataSource = borderStyleArray
lstBorder.DataBind()
```

This code raises a new challenge: how do you convert the value that the user selects into the appropriate constant for the enumeration? When the user chooses a border style from the list, the SelectedItem property will have a text string like "Groove". But to apply this border style to the control, you need a way to determine the enumerated constant that matches this text.

You can handle this problem in a few ways. (Earlier, you saw an example in which the enumeration integer was stored as a value in the list control.) In this case, the most direct approach involves using an advanced feature called a TypeConverter. A TypeConverter is a special class that is able to convert from a specialized type (in this case, the BorderStyle enumeration) to a simpler type (such as a string), and vice versa.

To access this class, you need to import the System.ComponentModel namespace:

```
Imports System.ComponentModel
```

You can then add the following code to the cmdUpdate_Click event handler:

```
' Find the appropriate TypeConverter for the BorderStyle enumeration.
Dim cnvrt As TypeConverter
converter = TypeDescriptor.GetConverter(GetType(BorderStyle))

' Update the border style using the value from the converter.
pnlCard.BorderStyle = converter.ConvertFromString(lstBorder.SelectedItem.Text)
```

This code gets the appropriate TypeConverter (in this case, one that's designed expressly to work with the BorderStyle enumeration). It then converts the text name (such as Solid) to the appropriate value (BorderStyle.Solid).

Generating the Cards Automatically

The last step is to use ASP.NET's automatic postback events to make the card update dynamically every time an option is changed. The Update button could now be used to submit the final, perfected greeting card, which might then be e-mailed to a recipient or stored in a database.

To configure the controls so they automatically trigger a page postback, simply set the AutoPostBack property of each input control to True. An example is shown here:

```
Choose a background color:<br />
<asp:DropDownList ID="lstBackColor" AutoPostBack="True" runat="server"
    Width="194px" Height="22px"/>
```

Next, you need to create an event handler that can handle the change events. To save a few steps, you can use the same event handler for all the input controls. All the event handler needs to do is call the update routine that regenerates the greeting card.

```
Protected Sub ControlChanged(ByVal sender As System.Object, _
  ByVal e As System.EventArgs) _
  Handles lstBackColor.SelectedIndexChanged, chkPicture.CheckedChanged, _
          txtFontSize.TextChanged, lstBorder.SelectedIndexChanged, _
          lstFontName.SelectedIndexChanged, lstForeColor.SelectedIndexChanged, _
          txtGreeting.TextChanged
    ' Refresh the greeting card (because a control was changed).
    UpdateCard()
End Sub
```

```
Protected Sub cmdUpdate_Click(sender As Object, e As EventArgs) _
  Handles cmdUpdate.Click

    ' Refresh the greeting card (because the button was clicked).
    UpdateCard()
End Sub

Private Sub UpdateCard()
    ' (The code that draws the greeting card goes here.)
End Sub
```

With these changes, it's easy to perfect the more extensive card-generating program shown in Figure 6-18. The full code for this application is provided with the online samples.

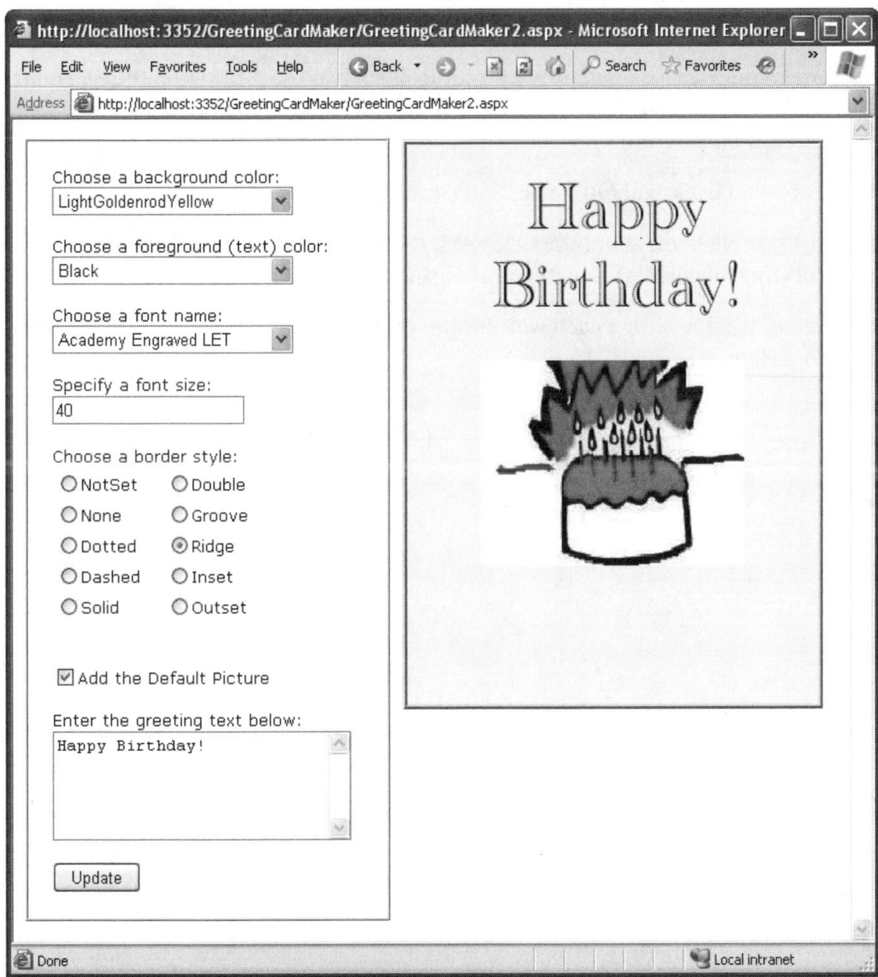

Figure 6-18. *A more extensive card generator*

■ **Tip** Automatic postback isn't always best. Sometimes an automatic postback can annoy a user, especially when the user is working over a slow connection or when the server needs to perform a time-consuming option. For that reason, it's sometimes best to use an explicit submit button and not enable AutoPostBack for most input controls. Alternatively, you might jazz up your web page with the ASP.NET AJAX features described in Chapter 25, which allow you to create user interfaces that feel more responsive, and can update themselves without a distracting full-page refresh.

The Last Word

This chapter introduced you to web controls and their object interface. As you continue through this book, you'll learn about more web controls. The following highlights are still to come:

- In Chapter 11, you'll learn about advanced controls such as the AdRotator, the Calendar, and the validation controls. You'll also learn about specialized container controls, such as the MultiView and Wizard.
- In Chapter 14, you'll learn about navigation controls such as the TreeView and Menu.
- In Chapter 17, you'll learn about the GridView, DetailsView, and FormView—high-level web controls that let you manipulate a complex table of data from any data source.

For a good reference that shows each web control and lists its important properties, refer to the Visual Studio Help.

CHAPTER 7

■ ■ ■

State Management

The most significant difference between programming for the web and programming for the desktop is *state management*—how you store information over the lifetime of your application. This information can be as simple as a user's name, or as complex as a stuffed-full shopping cart for an e-commerce store.

In a traditional Windows application, there's little need to think about state management. Memory is plentiful and always available, and you only need to worry about a single user. In a web application, it's a different story. Thousands of users can simultaneously run the same application on the same computer (the web server), each one communicating over a stateless HTTP connection. These conditions make it impossible to design a web application like a traditional Windows program.

Understanding these state limitations is the key to creating efficient web applications. In this chapter, you'll see how you can use ASP.NET's state management features to store information carefully and consistently. You'll explore different storage options, including view state, session state, and custom cookies. You'll also consider how to transfer information from page to page using cross-page posting and the query string.

The Problem of State

In a traditional Windows program, users interact with a continuously running application. A portion of memory on the desktop computer is allocated to store the current set of working information.

In a web application, the story is quite a bit different. A professional ASP.NET site might look like a continuously running application, but that's really just a clever illusion. In a typical web request, the client connects to the web server and requests a page. When the page is delivered, the connection is severed, and the web server abandons any information it has about the client. By the time the user receives a page, the web page code has already stopped running, and there's no information left in the web server's memory.

This stateless design has one significant advantage. Because clients need to be connected for only a few seconds at most, a web server can handle a huge number of nearly simultaneous requests without a performance hit. However, if you want to retain information for a longer period of time so it can be used over multiple postbacks or on multiple pages, you need to take additional steps.

View State

One of the most common ways to store information is in *view state*. View state uses a hidden field that ASP.NET automatically inserts in the final, rendered HTML of a web page. It's a perfect place to store information that's used for multiple postbacks in a single web page.

In the previous chapters, you learned how web controls use view state to keep track of certain details. For example, if you change the text of a label, the Label control automatically stores its new text in view state. That way, the text remains in place the next time the page is posted back. Web controls store most of their property values in view state, provided the control's EnableViewState property is set to True (which is the default).

However, view state isn't limited to web controls. Your web page code can add bits of information directly to the view state of the containing page and retrieve it later after the page is posted back. The type of information you can store includes simple data types and your own custom objects.

The ViewState Collection

The ViewState property of the page provides the current view state information. This property is an instance of the StateBag collection class. The StateBag is a dictionary collection, which means every item is stored in a separate "slot" using a unique string name.

For example, consider this code:

```
' The Me keyword refers to the current Page object. It's optional.
Me.ViewState("Counter") = 1
```

This places the value 1 (or rather, an integer that contains the value 1) into the ViewState collection and gives it the descriptive name Counter. If currently no item has the name Counter, a new item will be added automatically. If an item is already stored under the name Counter, it will be replaced.

When retrieving a value, you use the key name. You also need to cast the retrieved value to the appropriate data type using the casting syntax you saw in Chapter 2 and Chapter 3. This extra step is required because the ViewState collection stores all items as basic objects, which allows it to handle many different data types.

Here's the code that retrieves the counter from view state and converts it to an integer:

```
Dim counter As Integer
counter = CType(Me.ViewState("Counter"), Integer)
```

■ **Note** ASP.NET provides many collections that use the same dictionary syntax. This includes the collections you'll use for session and application state, as well as those used for caching and cookies. You'll see several of these collections in this chapter.

A View State Example

The following example is a simple counter program that records how many times a button is clicked. Without any kind of state management, the counter will be locked perpetually at 1. With careful use of view state, the counter works as expected.

```
Public Partial Class SimpleCounter
    Inherits System.Web.UI.Page

    Protected Sub cmdIncrement_Click(ByVal sender As Object, _
      ByVal e As EventArgs) Handles cmdIncrement.Click
        Dim Counter As Integer
        If ViewState("Counter") Is Nothing Then
            Counter = 1
        Else
            Counter = CType(ViewState("Counter"), Integer) + 1
        End If

        ViewState("Counter") = Counter
        lblCount.Text = "Counter: " & Counter.ToString()
    End Sub

End Class
```

The code checks to make sure the item exists in view state before it attempts to retrieve it. Otherwise, you could easily run into problems such as the infamous *null reference exception* (which is described in Chapter 8).

Figure 7-1 shows the output for this page.

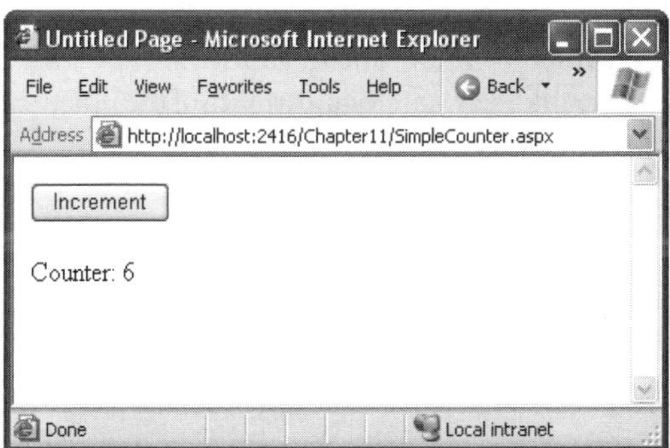

Figure 7-1. *A simple view state counter*

Making View State Secure

You probably remember from Chapter 5 that view state information is stored in a single jumbled string that looks like this:

```
<input type="hidden" name="__VIEWSTATE" id="__VIEWSTATE"
 value="dDw3NDg2NTI5MDg7Oz4=" />
```

As you add more information to view state, this value can become much longer. Because this value isn't formatted as clear text, many ASP.NET programmers assume that their view state data is encrypted. It isn't. Instead, the view state information is simply patched together in memory and converted to a *Base64 string* (which is a special type of string that's always acceptable in an HTML document because it doesn't include any extended characters). A clever hacker could reverse-engineer this string and examine your view state data in a matter of seconds.

Tamperproof View State

If you want to make view state more secure, you have two choices. First, you can make sure the view state information is tamperproof by instructing ASP.NET to use a *hash code*. A hash code is sometimes described as a cryptographically strong checksum. The idea is that ASP.NET examines all the data in view state, just before it renders the final page. It runs this data through a hashing algorithm (with the help of a secret key value). The hashing algorithm creates a short segment of data, which is the hash code. This code is then added at the end of the view state data, in the final HTML that's sent to the browser.

When the page is posted back, ASP.NET examines the view state data and recalculates the hash code using the same process. It then checks whether the checksum it calculated matches the hash code that is stored in the view state for the page. If a malicious user changes part of the view state data, ASP.NET will end up with a new hash code that doesn't match. At this point, it will reject the postback completely. (You might think a really clever user could get around this by generating fake view state information *and* a matching hash code. However, malicious users can't generate the right hash code, because they don't have the same cryptographic key as ASP.NET. This means the hash codes they create won't match.)

Hash codes are actually enabled by default, so if you want this functionality, you don't need to take any extra steps. Occasionally, developers choose to disable this feature to prevent problems in a web farm where different servers have different keys. (The problem occurs if the page is posted back and handled by a new server, which won't be able to verify the view state information.) To disable hash codes, you can use the enableViewStateMac attribute of the <pages> element in the web.config or machine.config file, as shown here:

```
<configuration>
  <system.web>
    <pages enableViewStateMac="false" />
    ...
  </system.web>
</configuration>
```

However, a much better way to solve this problem is to configure multiple servers to use the same key, thereby removing any problem. Chapter 9 describes this technique.

Private View State

Even when you use hash codes, the view state data will still be readable by the user. In many cases, this is completely acceptable—after all, the view state tracks information that's often provided directly through other controls. However, if your view state contains some information you want to keep secret, you can enable view state *encryption*.

You can turn on encryption for an individual page using the ViewStateEncryptionMode property of the Page directive:

```
<%@Page ViewStateEncryptionMode="Always" %>
```

Or you can set the same attribute in a configuration file:

```
<configuration>
  <system.web>
    <pages viewStateEncryptionMode="Always" />
    ...
  </system.web>
</configuration>
```

Either way, this enforces encryption. You have three choices for your view state encryption setting—always encrypt (Always), never encrypt (Never), or encrypt only if a control specifically requests it (Auto). The default is Auto, which means that the page won't encrypt its view state unless a control on that page specifically requests it. (Technically, a control makes this request by calling the Page.RegisterRequiresViewStateEncryption() method.) If no control calls this method to indicate it has sensitive information, the view state is not encrypted, thereby saving the encryption overhead. On the other hand, a control doesn't have absolute power—if it calls Page.RegisterRequiresViewStateEncryption() and the encryption mode is Never, the view state won't be encrypted.

■ **Tip** Don't encrypt view state data if you don't need to do so. The encryption will impose a performance penalty, because the web server needs to perform the encryption and decryption with each postback.

Retaining Member Variables

You have probably noticed that any information you set in a member variable for an ASP.NET page is automatically abandoned when the page processing is finished and the page is sent to the client. Interestingly, you can work around this limitation using view state.

The basic principle is to save all member variables to view state when the Page.PreRender event occurs and retrieve them when the Page.Load event occurs. Remember, the Load event happens every time the page is created. In the case of a postback, the Load event occurs first, followed by any other control events.

The following example uses this technique with a single member variable (named Contents). The page provides a text box and two buttons. The user can choose to save a string of text and then restore it at a later time (see Figure 7-2). The Button.Click event handlers store and retrieve this text using the Contents member variable. These event handlers don't need to save or restore this information using view state, because the PreRender and Load event handlers perform these tasks when page processing starts and finishes.

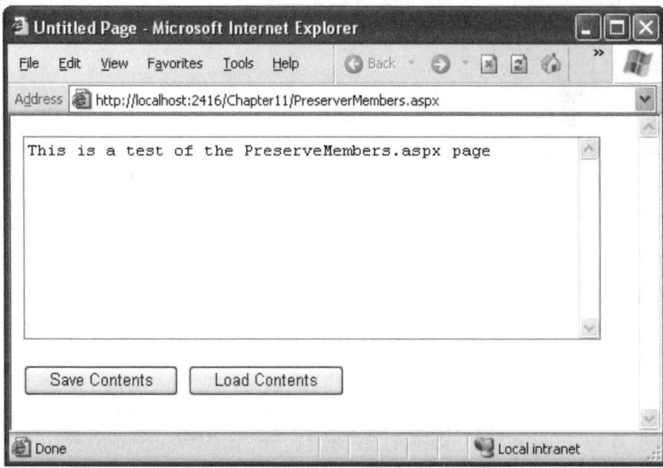

Figure 7-2. *A page with state*

```
Public Partial Class PreserveMembers
    Inherits System.Web.UI.Page

    ' A member variable that will be cleared with every postback.
    Private Contents As String

    Protected Sub Page_Load(ByVal sender As Object, _
      ByVal e As EventArgs) Handles Me.Load
        If Me.IsPostBack Then
            ' Restore variables.
            Contents = CType(ViewState("Text"), String)
        End If
    End Sub

    Protected Sub Page_PreRender(ByVal sender As Object, _
      ByVal e As EventArgs) Handles Me.PreRender
        ' Persist variables.
        ViewState("Text") = Contents
    End Sub

    Protected Sub cmdSave_Click(ByVal sender As Object, _
      ByVal e As EventArgs) Handles cmdSave.Click
        ' Transfer contents of text box to member variable.
        Contents = txtValue.Text
        txtValue.Text = ""
    End Sub
```

```
    Protected Sub cmdLoad_Click(ByVal sender As Object, _
      ByVal e As EventArgs) Handles cmdLoad.Click
        ' Restore contents of member variable to text box.
        txtValue.Text = Contents
    End Sub

End Class
```

The logic in the Load and PreRender event handlers allows the rest of your code to work more or less as it would in a desktop application. However, you must be careful not to store needless amounts of information when using this technique. If you store unnecessary information in view state, it will enlarge the size of the final page output and can thus slow down page transmission times. Another disadvantage with this approach is that it hides the low-level reality that every piece of data must be explicitly saved and restored. When you hide this reality, it's more likely that you'll forget to respect it and design for it.

If you decide to use this approach to save member variables in view state, use it *exclusively*. In other words, refrain from saving some view state variables at the PreRender stage and others in control event handlers, because this is sure to confuse you and any other programmer who looks at your code.

■ **Tip** The previous code example reacts to the Page.PreRender event, which occurs just after page processing is complete and just before the page is rendered in HTML. This is an ideal place to store any leftover information that is required. You cannot store view state information in an event handler for the Page.Unload event. Though your code will not cause an error, the information will not be stored in view state, because the final HTML page output is already rendered.

Storing Custom Objects

You can store your own objects in view state just as easily as you store numeric and string types. However, to store an item in view state, ASP.NET must be able to convert it into a stream of bytes so that it can be added to the hidden input field in the page. This process is called *serialization*. If your objects aren't serializable (and by default they're not), you'll receive an error message when you attempt to place them in view state.

To make your objects serializable, you need to add a Serializable attribute before your class declaration. For example, here's an exceedingly simple Customer class:

```
<Serializable()> _
Public Class Customer

    private _firstName As String
    Public Property FirstName() As String
        Get
            Return _firstName
        End Get
```

```
        Set(ByVal Value As String)
            _firstName = Value
        End Set
    End Property

    private _lastName As String
    Public Property LastName() As String
        Get
            Return _lastName
        End Get
        Set(ByVal Value As String)
            _lastName = Value
        End Set
    End Property

    Public Sub New(ByVal firstName As String, ByVal lastName As String)
        Me.FirstName = firstName
        Me.LastName = lastName
    End Sub
End Class
```

Because the Customer class is marked as serializable, it can be stored in view state:

```
' Store a customer in view state.
Dim cust As New Customer("Marsala", "Simons")
ViewState("CurrentCustomer") = cust
```

Remember, when using custom objects, you'll need to cast your data when you retrieve it from view state.

```
' Retrieve a customer from view state.
Dim cust As Customer
cust = CType(ViewState("CurrentCustomer"), Customer)
```

Once you understand this principle, you'll also be able to determine which .NET objects can be placed in view state. You simply need to find the class information in the Visual Studio Help. The easiest approach is to look the class up in the index. For example, to find out about the FileInfo class (which you'll learn about in Chapter 18), look for the index entry "FileInfo class." In the class documentation, you'll see the declaration for that class, which looks something like this:

```
<Serializable> _
<ComVisible(True)> _
Public NotInheritable Class FileInfo _
    Inherits FileSystemInfo
```

If the class declaration is preceded with the Serializable attribute (as it is here), instances of this class can be placed in view state. If the Serializable attribute isn't present, the class isn't serializable, and you won't be able to place instances in view state.

Transferring Information Between Pages

One of the most significant limitations with view state is that it's tightly bound to a specific page. If the user navigates to another page, this information is lost. This problem has several solutions, and the best approach depends on your requirements.

In the following sections, you'll learn two basic techniques to transfer information between pages: cross-page posting and the query string.

Cross-Page Posting

A cross-page postback is a technique that extends the postback mechanism you've already learned about so that one page can send the user to another page, complete with all the information for that page. This technique sounds conceptually straightforward, but it's a potential minefield. If you're not careful, it can lead you to create pages that are tightly coupled to others and difficult to enhance and debug.

The infrastructure that supports cross-page postbacks is a new property named PostBackUrl, which is defined by the IButtonControl interface and turns up in button controls such as ImageButton, LinkButton, and Button. To use cross-posting, you simply set PostBackUrl to the name of another web form. When the user clicks the button, the page will be posted to that new URL with the values from all the input controls on the current page.

Here's an example—a page named CrossPage1.aspx that defines a form with two text boxes and a button. When the button is clicked, it posts to a page named CrossPage2.aspx.

```
<%@ Page Language="VB" AutoEventWireup="false" CodeFile="CrossPage1.aspx.vb"
    Inherits="CrossPage1" %>
<html xmlns="http://www.w3.org/1999/xhtml">
<head runat="server">
    <title>CrossPage1</title>
</head>
<body>
    <form id="form1" runat="server" >
      <div>
        First Name:
        <asp:TextBox ID="txtFirstName" runat="server"></asp:TextBox>
        <br />
        Last Name:
        <asp:TextBox ID="txtLastName" runat="server"></asp:TextBox>
        <br />
        <br />
        <asp:Button runat="server" ID="cmdPost"
          PostBackUrl="CrossPage2.aspx" Text="Cross-Page Postback" /><br />
      </div>
    </form>
</body>
</html>
```

The CrossPage1 page doesn't include any code. Figure 7-3 shows how it appears in the browser.

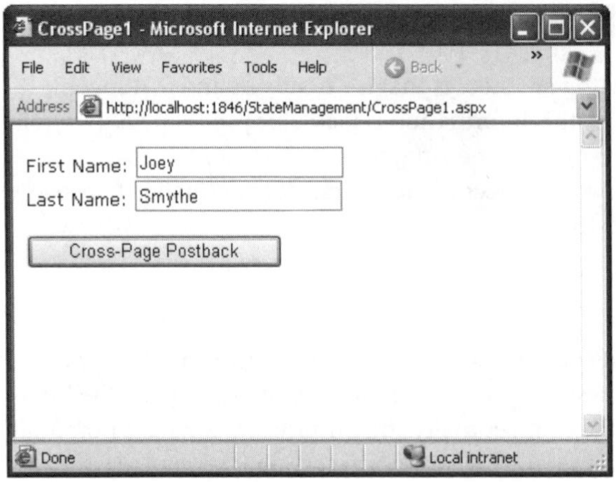

Figure 7-3. *The source of a cross-page postback*

Now if you load this page and click the button, the page will be posted back to CrossPage2.aspx. At this point, the CrossPage2.aspx page can interact with CrossPage1.aspx using the Page.PreviousPage property. Here's an event handler that grabs the title from the previous page and displays it:

```
Public Partial Class CrossPage2
    Inherits System.Web.UI.Page

    Protected Sub Page_Load(ByVal sender As Object, _
      ByVal e As EventArgs) Handles Me.Load

        If PreviousPage IsNot Nothing Then
            lblInfo.Text = "You came from a page titled " & _
              PreviousPage.Title
        End If
    End Sub

End Class
```

Note that this page checks for a null reference before attempting to access the PreviousPage object. If it's a null reference (Nothing), no cross-page postback took place. This means CrossPage2.aspx was requested directly, or CrossPage2.aspx posted back to itself. Either way, no PreviousPage object is available.

Figure 7-4 shows what you'll see when CrossPage1.aspx posts to CrossPage2.aspx.

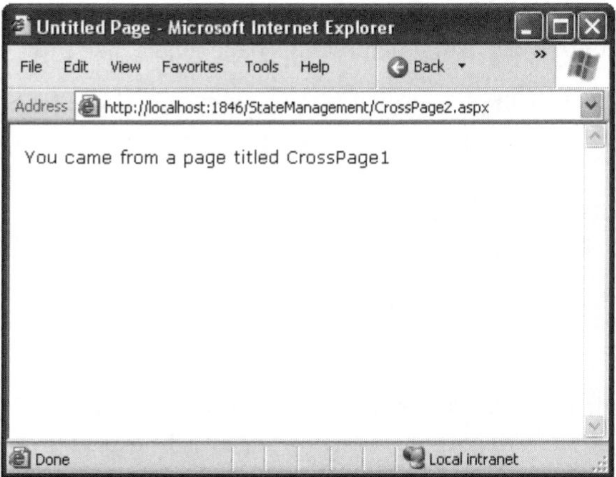

Figure 7-4. *The target of a cross-page postback*

Getting More Information from the Source Page

The previous example shows an interesting initial test, but it doesn't really allow you to transfer any useful information. After all, you're probably interested in retrieving specific details (such as the text in the text boxes of CrossPage1.aspx) from CrossPage2.aspx. The title alone isn't very interesting.

To get more specific details, such as control values, you need to cast the PreviousPage reference to the appropriate page class (in this case it's the CrossPage1 class). Here's an example that handles this situation properly, by checking first whether the PreviousPage object is an instance of the expected class:

```
Protected Sub Page_Load(ByVal sender As Object, _
  ByVal e As EventArgs) Handles Me.Load

    Dim prevPage As CrossPage1
    prevPage = TryCast(PreviousPage, CrossPage1)

    If prevPage IsNot Nothing Then
        ' (Read some information from the previous page.)
    End If

End Sub
```

Rather then checking whether PreviousPage is the correct type of object and then casting it with CType(), this code uses a shortcut with TryCast(). If a conversion can't be made, TryCast() simply returns a null reference.

You can also solve this problem in another way. Rather than casting the reference manually, you can add the PreviousPageType directive to the .aspx page that receives the cross-page postback (in this example, CrossPage2.aspx), right after the Page directive. The PreviousPageType directive indicates the expected type of the page initiating the cross-page postback. Here's an example:

```
<%@ PreviousPageType VirtualPath="~/CrossPage1.aspx" %>
```

Now, the PreviousPage property will automatically use the CrossPage1 type. That allows you to skip the casting code and go straight to work using the previous page object, like this:

```
Protected Sub Page_Load(ByVal sender As Object, _
  ByVal e As EventArgs) Handles Me.Load

    If PreviousPage IsNot Nothing Then
        ' (Read some information from the previous page.)
    End If

End Sub
```

However, this approach is more fragile because it limits you to a single page class. You don't have the flexibility to deal with situations where more than one page might trigger a cross-page postback. For that reason, it's usually more flexible to use the casting approach.

Once you've cast the previous page to the appropriate page type, you still won't be able to directly access the control objects it contains. That's because the controls on the web page are not publicly accessible to other classes. You can work around this by using properties.

For example, if you want to expose the values from two text boxes in the source page, you might add properties that wrap the control variables. Here are two properties you could add to the CrossPage1 class to expose its TextBox controls:

```
Public ReadOnly Property FirstNameTextBox() As TextBox
    Get
        Return txtFirstName
    End Get
End Property

Public ReadOnly Property LastNameTextBox() As TextBox
    Get
        Return txtLastName
    End Get
End Property
```

However, this usually isn't the best approach. The problem is that it exposes too many details, giving the target page the freedom to read everything from the text in the text box to its fonts and colors. If you need to change the page later to use different input controls, it will be difficult to maintain these properties. Instead, you'll probably be forced to rewrite code in both pages.

A better choice is to define specific, limited methods or properties that extract just the information you need. For example, you might decide to add a FullName property that retrieves just the text from the two text boxes. Here's the full page code for CrossPage1.aspx with this property:

```
Partial Class CrossPage1
    Inherits System.Web.UI.Page

    Public ReadOnly Property FullName() As String
        Get
            Return txtFirstName.Text & " " & txtLastName.Text
        End Get
    End Property

End Class
```

This way, the relationship between the two pages is clear, simple, and easy to maintain. You can probably change the controls in the source page (CrossPage1) without needing to change other parts of your application. For example, if you decide to use different controls for name entry in CrossPage1.aspx, you will be forced to revise the code for the FullName property. However, your changes would be confined to CrossPage1.aspx, and you wouldn't need to modify CrossPage2.aspx at all.

Here's how you can rewrite the code in CrossPage2.aspx to display the information from CrossPage1.aspx:

```
Protected Sub Page_Load(ByVal sender As Object, _
  ByVal e As EventArgs) Handles Me.Load

    If PreviousPage IsNot Nothing Then
        lblInfo.Text = "You came from a page titled " & _
          PreviousPage.Title & "<br />"

        Dim prevPage As CrossPage1
        prevPage = TryCast(PreviousPage, CrossPage1)
        If prevPage IsNot Nothing Then
            lblInfo.Text &= "You typed in this: " & prevPage.FullName
        End If
    End If

End Sub
```

Notice that the target page (CrossPage2.aspx) can access the Title property of the previous page (CrossPage1.aspx) without performing any casting. That's because the Title property is defined as part of the base System.Web.UI.Page class, and so every web page includes it. However, to get access to the more specialized FullName property you need to cast the previous page to the right page class (CrossPage1), or use the PreviousPageType directive that was discussed earlier.

Figure 7-5 shows the new result.

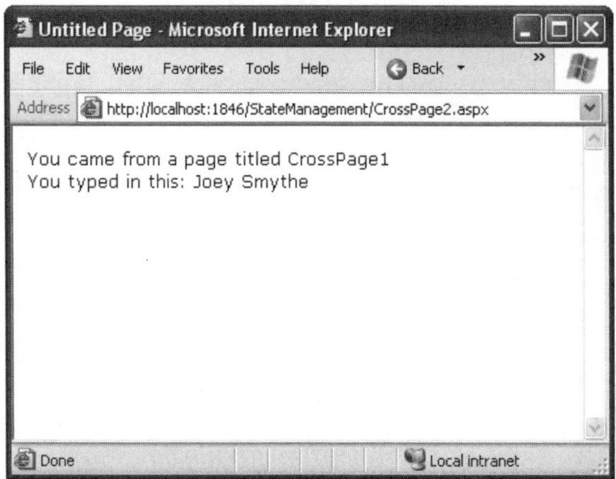

Figure 7-5. *Retrieving specific information from the source page*

Note Cross-page postbacks are genuinely useful, but they can lead the way to more complicated pages. If you allow multiple source pages to post to the same destination page, it's up to you to code the logic that figures out which page the user came from and then act accordingly. To avoid these headaches, it's easiest to perform cross-page postbacks between two specific pages only.

ASP.NET uses some interesting sleight of hand to make cross-page postbacks work. The first time the second page accesses Page.PreviousPage, ASP.NET needs to create the previous page object. To do this, it actually starts the page processing but interrupts it just before the PreRender stage, and it doesn't let the page render any HTML output.

However, this still has some interesting side effects. For example, all the page events of the previous page are fired, including Page.Load and Page.Init, and the Button.Click event also fires for the button that triggered the cross-page postback. ASP.NET fires these events because they might be needed to return the source page to the state it was last in, just before it triggered the cross-page postback.

The Query String

Another common approach is to pass information using a query string in the URL. This approach is commonly found in search engines. For example, if you perform a search on the Google website, you'll be redirected to a new URL that incorporates your search parameters. Here's an example:

```
http://www.google.ca/search?q=organic+gardening
```

The query string is the portion of the URL after the question mark. In this case, it defines a single variable named *q*, which contains the string *organic+gardening*.

The advantage of the query string is that it's lightweight and doesn't exert any kind of burden on the server. However, it also has several limitations:

- Information is limited to simple strings, which must contain URL-legal characters.
- Information is clearly visible to the user and to anyone else who cares to eavesdrop on the Internet.
- The enterprising user might decide to modify the query string and supply new values, which your program won't expect and can't protect against.
- Many browsers impose a limit on the length of a URL (usually from 1KB to 2KB). For that reason, you can't place a large amount of information in the query string and still be assured of compatibility with most browsers.

Adding information to the query string is still a useful technique. It's particularly well suited in database applications where you present the user with a list of items that correspond to records in a database, such as products. The user can then select an item and be forwarded to another page with detailed information about the selected item. One easy way to implement this design is to have the first page send the item ID to the second page. The second page then looks that item up in the database and displays the detailed information. You'll notice this technique in e-commerce sites such as Amazon.

To store information in the query string, you need to place it there yourself. Unfortunately, you have no collection-based way to do this. Typically, this means using a special HyperLink control or a special Response.Redirect() statement such as the one shown here:

```
' Go to newpage.aspx. Submit a single query string argument
' named recordID, and set to 10.
Response.Redirect("newpage.aspx?recordID=10")
```

You can send multiple parameters as long as they're separated with an ampersand (&):

```
' Go to newpage.aspx. Submit two query string arguments:
' recordID (10) and mode (full).
Response.Redirect("newpage.aspx?recordID=10&mode=full")
```

The receiving page has an easier time working with the query string. It can receive the values from the QueryString dictionary collection exposed by the built-in Request object:

```
Dim ID As String = Request.QueryString("recordID")
```

Note that information is always retrieved as a string, which can then be converted to another simple data type. Values in the QueryString collection are indexed by the variable name. If you attempt to retrieve a value that isn't present in the query string, you'll get a null reference (Nothing).

Note Unlike view state, information passed through the query string is clearly visible and unencrypted. Don't use the query string for information that needs to be hidden or made tamperproof.

A Query String Example

The next program presents a list of entries. When the user chooses an item by clicking the appropriate item in the list, the user is forwarded to a new page. This page displays the received ID number. This provides a quick and simple query string test with two pages. In a sophisticated application, you would want to combine some of the data control features that are described later in Part 3 of this book.

The first page provides a list of items, a check box, and a submission button (see Figure 7-6).

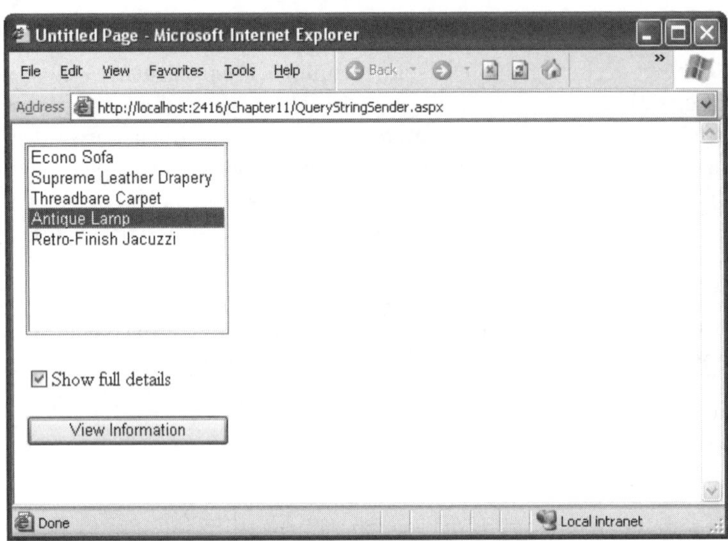

Figure 7-6. *A query string sender*

Here's the code for the first page:

```
Public Partial Class QueryStringSender
    Inherits System.Web.UI.Page

    Protected Sub Page_Load(ByVal sender As Object, _
      ByVal e As EventArgs) Handles Me.Load
        If Not Me.IsPostBack Then
            ' Add sample values.
            lstItems.Items.Add("Econo Sofa")
            lstItems.Items.Add("Supreme Leather Drapery")
            lstItems.Items.Add("Threadbare Carpet")
            lstItems.Items.Add("Antique Lamp")
            lstItems.Items.Add("Retro-Finish Jacuzzi")
        End If
    End Sub
```

```
    Protected Sub cmdGo_Click(ByVal sender As Object, _
      ByVal e As EventArgs) Handles cmdGo.Click
        If lstItems.SelectedIndex = -1 Then
            lblError.Text = "You must select an item."
        Else
            ' Forward the user to the information page,
            ' with the query string data.
            Dim Url As String = "QueryStringRecipient.aspx?"
            Url &= "Item=" & lstItems.SelectedItem.Text & "&"
            Url &= "Mode=" & chkDetails.Checked.ToString()
            Response.Redirect(Url)
        End If
    End Sub

End Class
```

Here's the code for the recipient page (shown in Figure 7-7):

```
Public Partial Class QueryStringRecipient
    Inherits System.Web.UI.Page

    Protected Sub Page_Load(ByVal sender As Object, _
      ByVal e As EventArgs) Handles Me.Load
        lblInfo.Text = "Item: " & Request.QueryString("Item")
        lblInfo.Text &= "<br />Show Full Record: "
        lblInfo.Text &= Request.QueryString("Mode")
    End Sub

End Class
```

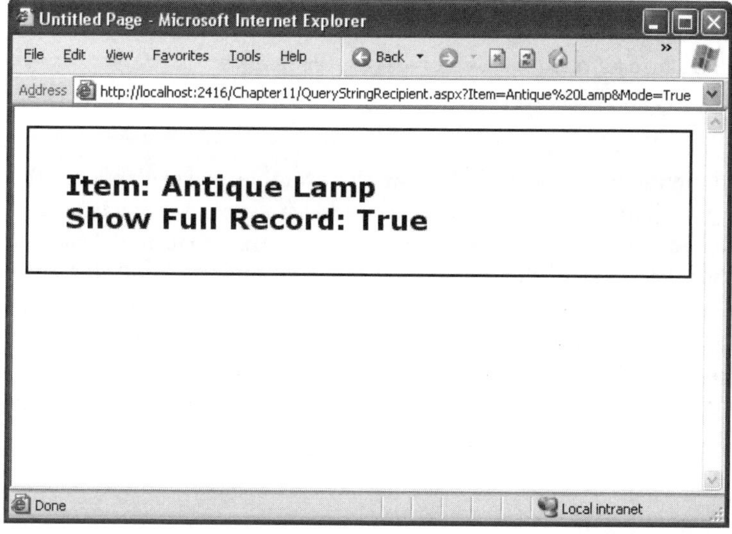

Figure 7-7. *A query string recipient*

One interesting aspect of this example is that it places information in the query string that isn't valid—namely, the space that appears in the item name. When you run the application, you'll notice that ASP.NET encodes the string for you automatically, converting spaces to the valid %20 equivalent escape sequence. The recipient page reads the original values from the QueryString collection without any trouble. This automatic encoding isn't always sufficient. To deal with special characters, you should use the URL-encoding technique described in the next section.

URL Encoding

One potential problem with the query string is that some characters aren't allowed in a URL. In fact, the list of characters that are allowed in a URL is much shorter than the list of allowed characters in an HTML document. All characters must be alphanumeric or one of a small set of special characters (including *$-_.+!*'(),*). Some browsers tolerate certain additional special characters (Internet Explorer is notoriously lax), but many do not. Furthermore, some characters have special meaning. For example, the ampersand (&) is used to separate multiple query string parameters, the plus sign (+) is an alternate way to represent a space, and the number sign (#) is used to point to a specific bookmark in a web page. If you try to send query string values that include any of these characters, you'll lose some of your data. You can test this out with the previous example by adding items with special characters in the list box.

To avoid potential problems, it's a good idea to perform *URL encoding* on text values before you place them in the query string. With URL encoding, special characters are replaced by escaped character sequences starting with the percent sign (%), followed by a two-digit hexadecimal representation. For example, the & character becomes %26. The only exception is the space character, which can be represented as the character sequence %20 or the + sign.

To perform URL encoding, you use the UrlEncode() and UrlDecode() methods of the HttpServerUtility class. As you learned in Chapter 5, an HttpServerUtility object is made available to your code in every web form through the Page.Server property. The following code uses the UrlEncode() method to rewrite the previous example, so it works with product names that contain special characters:

```
Dim Url As String = "QueryStringRecipient.aspx?"
Url &= "Item=" & Server.UrlEncode(lstItems.SelectedItem.Text) & "&"
Url &= "Mode=" & chkDetails.Checked.ToString()
Response.Redirect(Url)
```

Notice that it's important not to encode everything. In this example, you can't encode the & character that joins the two query string values, because it truly *is* a special character.

You can use the UrlDecode() method to return a URL-encoded string to its initial value. However, you don't need to take this step with the query string. That's because ASP.NET automatically decodes your values when you access them through the Request.QueryString collection. (Many people still make the mistake of decoding the query string values a second time. Usually, decoding already decoded data won't cause a problem. The only exception is if you have a value that includes the + sign. In this case, using UrlDecode() will convert the + sign to a space, which isn't what you want.)

Cookies

Cookies provide another way that you can store information for later use. Cookies are small files that are created on the client's hard drive (or, if they're temporary, in the web browser's memory). One advantage of cookies is that they work transparently without the user being aware that information needs to be stored. They also can be easily used by any page in your application and even be retained between visits, which allows for truly long-term storage. They suffer from some of the same drawbacks that affect query strings—namely, they're limited to simple string information, and they're easily accessible and readable if the user finds and opens the corresponding file. These factors make them a poor choice for complex or private information or large amounts of data.

Some users disable cookies on their browsers, which will cause problems for web applications that require them. Also, users might manually delete the cookie files stored on their hard drives. But for the most part, cookies are widely adopted and used extensively on many websites.

Cookies are fairly easy to use. Both the Request and Response objects (which are provided through Page properties) provide a Cookies collection. The important trick to remember is that you retrieve cookies from the Request object, and you set cookies using the Response object.

To set a cookie, just create a new HttpCookie object. You can then fill it with string information (using the familiar dictionary pattern) and attach it to the current web response:

```
' Create the cookie object.
Dim cookie As New HttpCookie("Preferences")

' Set a value in it.
cookie("LanguagePref") = "English"

' Add another value.
cookie("Country") = "US"

' Add it to the current web response.
Response.Cookies.Add(cookie)
```

A cookie added in this way will persist until the user closes the browser and will be sent with every request. To create a longer-lived cookie, you can set an expiration date:

```
' This cookie lives for one year.
cookie.Expires = DateTime.Now.AddYears(1)
```

You retrieve cookies by cookie name using the Request.Cookies collection:

```
Dim cookie As HttpCookie = Request.Cookies("Preferences")

' Check to see whether a cookie was found with this name.
' This is a good precaution to take,
' because the user could disable cookies,
' in which case the cookie will not exist.
```

```
Dim language As String
If cookie IsNot Nothing Then
    language = cookie("LanguagePref")
End If
```

The only way to remove a cookie is by replacing it with a cookie that has an expiration date that has already passed. This code demonstrates the technique:

```
Dim cookie As New HttpCookie("LanguagePref")
cookie.Expires = DateTime.Now.AddDays(-1)
Response.Cookies.Add(cookie)
```

A Cookie Example

The next example shows a typical use of cookies to store a customer name. If the name is found, a welcome message is displayed, as shown in Figure 7-8.

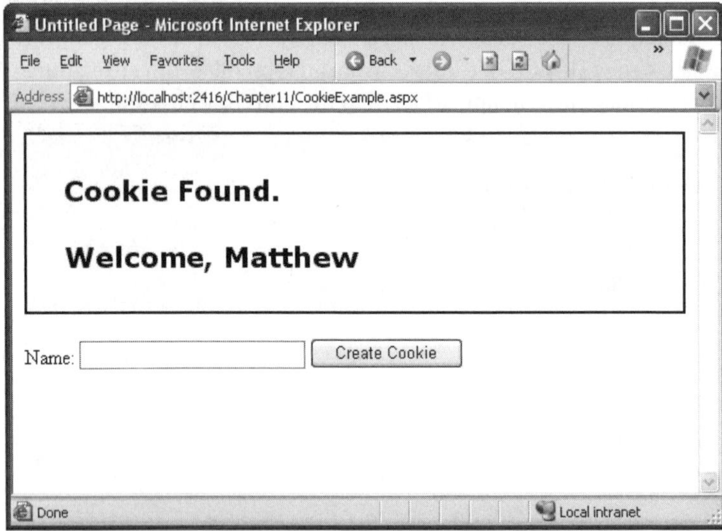

Figure 7-8. *Displaying information from a custom cookie*

Here's the code for this page:

```
Public Partial Class CookieExample
    Inherits System.Web.UI.Page

    Protected Sub Page_Load(ByVal sender As Object, _
      ByVal e As EventArgs) Handles Me.Load
        Dim Cookie As HttpCookie = Request.Cookies("Preferences")
        If Cookie Is Nothing Then
            lblWelcome.Text = "<b>Unknown Customer</b>"
```

```
        Else
            lblWelcome.Text = "<b>Cookie Found.</b><br /><br />"
            lblWelcome.Text &= "Welcome, " & Cookie("Name")
        End If
    End Sub

    Protected Sub cmdStore_Click(ByVal sender As Object, _
      ByVal e As EventArgs) Handles cmdStore.Click
        Dim Cookie As HttpCookie = Request.Cookies("Preferences")
        If Cookie Is Nothing Then
            Cookie = New HttpCookie("Preferences")
        End If

        Cookie("Name") = txtName.Text
        Cookie.Expires = DateTime.Now.AddYears(1)
        Response.Cookies.Add(Cookie)

        lblWelcome.Text = "<b>Cookie Created.</b><br /><br />"
        lblWelcome.Text &= "New Customer: " & Cookie("Name")
    End Sub

End Class
```

Note You'll find that some other ASP.NET features use cookies. Two examples are session state (which allows you to temporarily store user-specific information in server memory) and forms security (which allows you to restrict portions of a website and force users to access it through a login page). Chapter 20 discusses forms security, and the next section of this chapter discusses session state.

Session State

There comes a point in the life of most applications when they begin to have more sophisticated storage requirements. An application might need to store and access complex information such as custom data objects, which can't be easily persisted to a cookie or sent through a query string. Or the application might have stringent security requirements that prevent it from storing information about a client in view state or in a custom cookie. In these situations, you can use ASP.NET's built-in session state facility.

Session state management is one of ASP.NET's premiere features. It allows you to store any type of data in memory on the server. The information is protected, because it is never transmitted to the client, and it's uniquely bound to a specific session. Every client that accesses the application has a different session and a distinct collection of information. Session state is ideal for storing information such as the items in the current user's shopping basket when the user browses from one page to another.

Session Tracking

ASP.NET tracks each session using a unique 120-bit identifier. ASP.NET uses a proprietary algorithm to generate this value, thereby guaranteeing (statistically speaking) that the number is unique and it's random enough that a malicious user can't reverse-engineer or "guess" what session ID a given client will be using. This ID is the only piece of session-related information that is transmitted between the web server and the client.

When the client presents the session ID, ASP.NET looks up the corresponding session, retrieves the objects you stored previously, and places them into a special collection so they can be accessed in your code. This process takes place automatically.

For this system to work, the client must present the appropriate session ID with each request. You can accomplish this in two ways:

Using cookies: In this case, the session ID is transmitted in a special cookie (named ASP.NET_SessionId), which ASP.NET creates automatically when the session collection is used. This is the default, and it's also the same approach that was used in earlier versions of ASP.

Using modified URLs: In this case, the session ID is transmitted in a specially modified (or *munged*) URL. This allows you to create applications that use session state with clients that don't support cookies.

Session state doesn't come for free. Though it solves many of the problems associated with other forms of state management, it forces the server to store additional information in memory. This extra memory requirement, even if it is small, can quickly grow to performance-destroying levels as hundreds or thousands of clients access the site.

In other words, you must think through any use of session state. A careless use of session state is one of the most common reasons that a web application can't scale to serve a large number of clients. Sometimes a better approach is to use caching, as described in Chapter 24.

Using Session State

You can interact with session state using the System.Web.SessionState.HttpSessionState class, which is provided in an ASP.NET web page as the built-in Session object. The syntax for adding items to the collection and retrieving them is basically the same as for adding items to a page's view state.

For example, you might store a DataSet in session memory like this:

```
Session("InfoDataSet") = dsInfo
```

You can then retrieve it with an appropriate conversion operation:

```
dsInfo = CType(Session("InfoDataSet"), DataSet)
```

■ **Note** Chapter 15 explores the DataSet.

Session state is global to your entire application for the current user. However, session state can be lost in several ways:

- If the user closes and restarts the browser.
- If the user accesses the same page through a different browser window, although the session will still exist if a web page is accessed through the original browser window. Browsers differ on how they handle this situation.
- If the session times out due to inactivity. More information about session timeout can be found in the configuration section.
- If your web page code ends the session by calling the Session.Abandon() method.

In the first two cases, the session actually remains in memory on the web server, because ASP.NET has no idea that the client has closed the browser or changed windows. The session will linger in memory, remaining inaccessible, until it eventually expires.

Table 7-1 describes the methods and properties of the HttpSessionState class.

Table 7-1. *HttpSessionState Members*

Member	Description
Count	Provides the number of items in the current session collection.
IsCookieless	Identifies whether the session is tracked with a cookie or modified URLs.
IsNewSession	Identifies whether the session was created only for the current request. If no information is in session state, ASP.NET won't bother to track the session or create a session cookie. Instead, the session will be re-created with every request.
Mode	Provides an enumerated value that explains how ASP.NET stores session state information. This storage mode is determined based on the web.config settings discussed in the "Session State Configuration" section later in this chapter.
SessionID	Provides a string with the unique session identifier for the current client.
Timeout	Determines the number of minutes that will elapse before the current session is abandoned, provided that no more requests are received from the client. This value can be changed programmatically, letting you make the session collection longer when needed.
Abandon()	Cancels the current session immediately and releases all the memory it occupied. This is a useful technique in a logoff page to ensure that server memory is reclaimed as quickly as possible.
Clear()	Removes all the session items but doesn't change the current session identifier.

A Session State Example

The next example uses session state to store several Furniture data objects. The data object combines a few related variables and uses a special constructor so it can be created and initialized in one easy line. Rather than use full property procedures, the class takes a shortcut and uses public member variables so that the code listing remains short and concise. (If you refer to the full code in the downloadable examples, you'll see that it uses property procedures.)

```
Public Class Furniture

    Public Name As String
    Public Description As String
    Public Cost As Double

    Public Sub New(ByVal name As String, _
      ByVal description As String, ByVal cost As Double)
        Me.Name = name
        Me.Description = description
        Me.Cost = cost
    End Sub

End Class
```

Three Furniture objects are created the first time the page is loaded, and they're stored in session state. The user can then choose from a list of furniture piece names. When a selection is made, the corresponding object will be retrieved, and its information will be displayed, as shown in Figure 7-9.

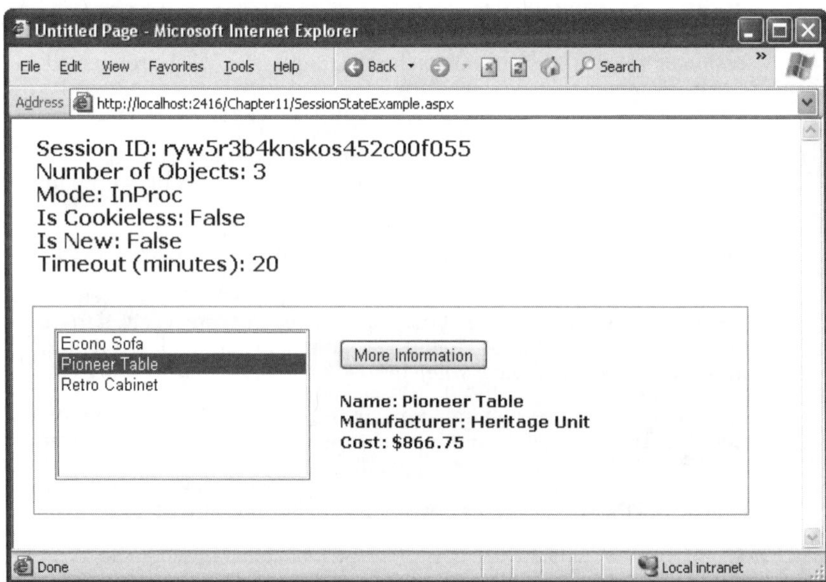

Figure 7-9. *A session state example with data objects*

```
Public Partial Class SessionStateExample
    Inherits System.Web.UI.Page

    Protected Sub Page_Load(ByVal sender As Object, _
      ByVal e As EventArgs) Handles Me.Load

        If Me.IsPostBack = False Then
            ' Create Furniture objects.
            Dim Piece1 As New Furniture("Econo Sofa", _
                                        "Acme Inc.", 74.99)
            Dim Piece2 As New Furniture("Pioneer Table", _
                                        "Heritage Unit", 866.75)
            Dim Piece3 As New Furniture("Retro Cabinet", _
                                        "Sixties Ltd.", 300.11)

            ' Add objects to session state.
            Session("Furniture1") = Piece1
            Session("Furniture2") = Piece2
            Session("Furniture3") = Piece3

            ' Add rows to list control.
            lstItems.Items.Add(Piece1.Name)
            lstItems.Items.Add(Piece2.Name)
            lstItems.Items.Add(Piece3.Name)
        End If

        ' Display some basic information about the session.
        ' This is useful for testing configuration settings.
        lblSession.Text = "Session ID: " & Session.SessionID
        lblSession.Text &= "<br />Number of Objects: "
        lblSession.Text &= Session.Count.ToString()
        lblSession.Text &= "<br />Mode: " & Session.Mode.ToString()
        lblSession.Text &= "<br />Is Cookieless: "
        lblSession.Text &= Session.IsCookieless.ToString()
        lblSession.Text &= "<br />Is New: "
        lblSession.Text &= Session.IsNewSession.ToString()
        lblSession.Text &= "<br />Timeout (minutes): "
        lblSession.Text &= Session.Timeout.ToString()
    End Sub

    Protected Sub cmdMoreInfo_Click(ByVal sender As Object, _
      ByVal e As EventArgs) Handles cmdMoreInfo.Click

        If lstItems.SelectedIndex = -1 Then
            lblRecord.Text = "No item selected."
```

```
        Else
            ' Construct a key name based on the index.
            ' For example, Furniture1, Furniture2, and so on.
            Dim Key As String
            Key = "Furniture" & _
                  (lstItems.SelectedIndex + 1).ToString()

            ' Retrieve the Furniture object from session state.
            Dim Piece As Furniture = CType(Session(Key), Furniture)

            ' Display the information for this object.
            lblRecord.Text = "Name: " & Piece.Name
            lblRecord.Text &= "<br />Manufacturer: "
            lblRecord.Text &= Piece.Description
            lblRecord.Text &= "<br />Cost: " & Piece.Cost.ToString("c")
        End If
    End Sub

End Class
```

It's also a good practice to add a few session-friendly features in your application. For example, you could add a logout button to the page that automatically cancels a session using the Session.Abandon() method. This way, the user will be encouraged to terminate the session rather than just close the browser window, and the server memory will be reclaimed faster.

MAKING SESSION STATE MORE SCALABLE

When web developers need to store a large amount of state information, they face a confounding problem. They can use session state and ensure excellent performance for a small set of users, but they risk poor scalability for large numbers. Alternatively, they can use a database to store temporary session information. This allows them to store a large amount of session information for a long time (potentially weeks or months instead of mere minutes). However, it also slows performance because the database must be queried for almost every page request.

The compromise involves caching. The basic approach is to create a temporary database record with session information and store its unique ID in session state. This ensures that the in-memory session information is always minimal, but your web page code can easily find the corresponding session record. To reduce the number of database queries, you'll also add the session information to the cache (indexed under the session identifier). On subsequent requests, your code can check for the session information in the cache first. If the information is no longer in the cache, your code can retrieve it from the database as a last resort. This process becomes even more transparent if you create a custom component that provides the session information and performs the required cache lookup for you.

For more information, read about custom components in Chapter 23, and caching in Chapter 24.

Session State Configuration

You configure session state through the web.config file for your current application (which is found in the same virtual directory as the .aspx web page files). The configuration file allows you to set advanced options such as the timeout and the session state mode. If you're creating your web application in Visual Studio, your project will include an automatically generated web.config file.

The following listing shows the most important options that you can set for the <sessionState> element. Keep in mind that you won't use all of these details at the same time. Some settings only apply to certain session state *modes*, as you'll see shortly.

```
<?xml version="1.0" encoding="utf-8" ?>
<configuration>
    <system.web>
        <!-- Other settings omitted. -->

        <sessionState
            cookieless="UseCookies" cookieName="ASP.NET_SessionId"
            regenerateExpiredSessionId="false"
            timeout="20"
            mode="InProc"
            stateConnectionString="tcpip=127.0.0.1:42424"
            stateNetworkTimeout="10"
            sqlConnectionString="data source=127.0.0.1;Integrated Security=SSPI"
            sqlCommandTimeout="30"
            allowCustomSqlDatabase="false"
            customProvider=""
        />
    </system.web>
</configuration>
```

The following sections describe the preceding session state settings.

Cookieless

You can set the cookieless setting to one of the values defined by the HttpCookieMode enumeration, as described in Table 7-2.

Table 7-2. *HttpCookieMode Values*

Value	Description
UseCookies	Cookies are always used, even if the browser or device doesn't support cookies or they are disabled. This is the default. If the device does not support cookies, session information will be lost over subsequent requests, because each request will get a new ID.
UseUri	Cookies are never used, regardless of the capabilities of the browser or device. Instead, the session ID is stored in the URL.

Table 7-2. *HttpCookieMode Values (Continued)*

Value	Description
UseDeviceProfile	ASP.NET chooses whether to use cookieless sessions by examining the BrowserCapabilities object. The drawback is that this object indicates what the device should support—it doesn't take into account that the user may have disabled cookies in a browser that supports them.
AutoDetect	ASP.NET attempts to determine whether the browser supports cookies by attempting to set and retrieve a cookie (a technique commonly used on the Web). This technique can correctly determine whether a browser supports cookies but has them disabled, in which case cookieless mode is used instead.

Here's an example that forces cookieless mode (which is useful for testing):

```
<sessionState cookieless="UseUri" ... />
```

In cookieless mode, the session ID will automatically be inserted into the URL. When ASP.NET receives a request, it will remove the ID, retrieve the session collection, and forward the request to the appropriate directory. Figure 7-10 shows a munged URL.

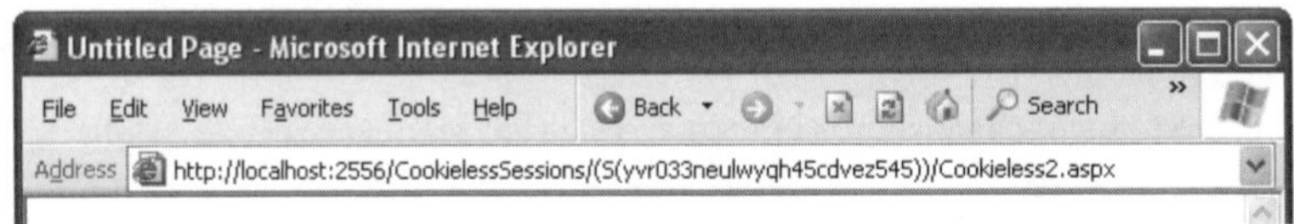

Figure 7-10. *A munged URL with the session ID*

Because the session ID is inserted in the current URL, relative links also automatically gain the session ID. In other words, if the user is currently stationed on Page1.aspx and clicks a relative link to Page2.aspx, the relative link includes the current session ID as part of the URL. The same is true if you call Response.Redirect() with a relative URL, as shown here:

```
Response.Redirect("Page2.aspx")
```

Figure 7-11 shows a sample website (included with the online samples in the CookielessSessions directory) that tests cookieless sessions. It contains two pages and uses cookieless mode. The first page (Cookieless1.aspx) contains a HyperLink control and two buttons, all of which take you to a second page (Cookieless2.aspx). The trick is that these controls have different ways of performing their navigation. Only two of them work with cookieless session—the third loses the current session.

The HyperLink control navigates to the page specified in its NavigateUrl property, which is set to the relative path Cookieless2.aspx. If you click this link, the session ID is retained in the URL, and the new page can retrieve the session information. This demonstrates that cookieless sessions work with relative links.

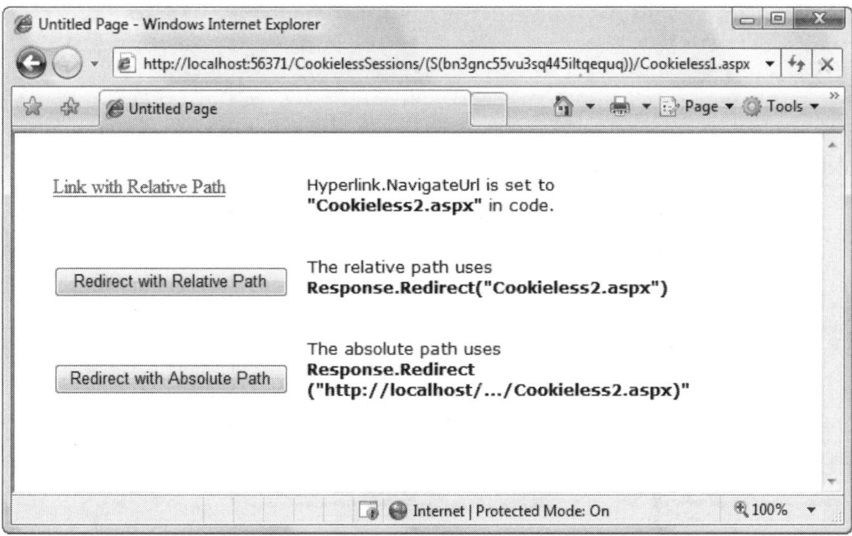

Figure 7-11. *Three tests of cookieless sessions*

The two buttons on this page use programmatic redirection by calling the Response.Redirect() method. The first button uses the relative path Cookieless2.aspx, much like the HyperLink control. This approach works with cookieless session state, and preserves the munged URL with no extra steps required.

```
Protected Sub cmdLink_Click(ByVal sender As Object, _
  ByVal As EventArgs) Handles cmdLink.Click

    Response.Redirect("Cookieless2.aspx")
End Sub
```

The only real limitation of cookieless state is that you cannot use absolute links (links that include the full URL, starting with http://). The second button uses an absolute link to demonstrate this problem. Because ASP.NET cannot insert the session ID into the URL, the session is lost.

```
Protected Sub cmdLinkAbsolute_Click(ByVal sender As Object, _
  ByVal e As EventArgs) Handles cmdLinkAbsolute.Click

    Dim url As String = "http://localhost:56371/CookielessSessions/Cookieless2.aspx"
    Response.Redirect(url)
End Sub
```

Now the target page (Figure 7-12) checks for the session information, but can't find it.

Writing the code to demonstrate this problem in a test environment is a bit tricky. The problem is that Visual Studio's integrated web server chooses a different port for your website every time you start it. As a result, you'll need to edit the code every time you open Visual Studio so that your URL uses the right port number (such as 56371 in the previous example).

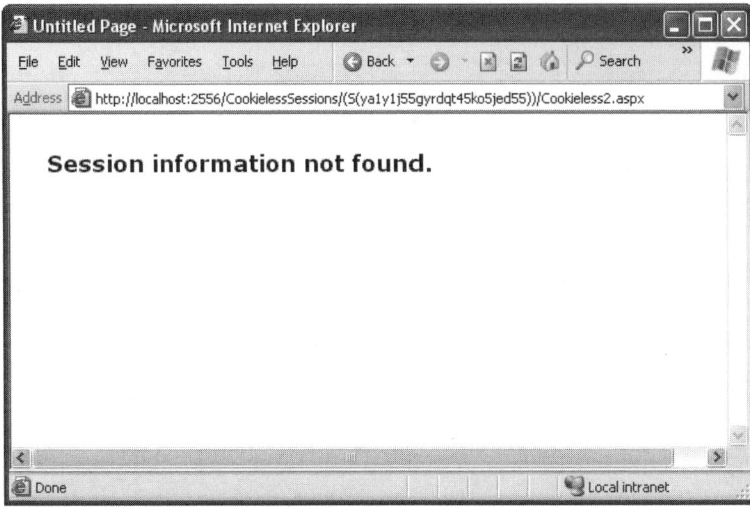

Figure 7-12. *A lost session*

There's another workaround. You can use some crafty code that gets the current URL from the page and just modifies the last part of it (changing the page name from Cookieless1.aspx to Cookieless2.aspx). Here's how:

```
' Create a new URL based on the current URL (but ending with
' the page Cookieless2.aspx instead of Cookieless1.aspx.
Dim url As String = "http://" & Request.Url.Authority & _
  Request.Url.Segments(0) & Request.Url.Segments(1) & _
  "Cookieless2.aspx"

Response.Redirect(url)
```

Of course, if you deploy your website to a real virtual directory that's hosted by IIS, you won't use a randomly chosen port number anymore, and you won't experience this quirk. Chapter 9 has more about virtual directories and website deployment.

DEALING WITH EXPIRED SESSSION IDS

By default, ASP.NET allows you to reuse a session identifier. For example, if you make a request and your query string contains an expired session, ASP.NET creates a new session and uses that session ID. The problem is that a session ID might inadvertently appear in a public place—such as in a results page in a search engine. This could lead to multiple users accessing the server with the same session identifier and then all joining the same session with the same shared data.

To avoid this potential security risk, you should include the optional regenerateExpiredSessionId attribute and set it to true whenever you use cookieless sessions. This way, a new session ID will be issued if a user connects with an expired session ID. The only drawback is that this process also forces the current page to lose all view state and form data, because ASP.NET performs a redirect to make sure the browser has a new session identifier.

Timeout

Another important session state setting in the web.config file is the timeout. This specifies the number of minutes that ASP.NET will wait, without receiving a request, before it abandons the session.

```
<sessionState timeout="20" ... />
```

This setting represents one of the most important compromises of session state. A difference of minutes can have a dramatic effect on the load of your server and the performance of your application. Ideally, you will choose a timeframe that is short enough to allow the server to reclaim valuable memory after a client stops using the application but long enough to allow a client to pause and continue a session without losing it.

You can also programmatically change the session timeout in code. For example, if you know a session contains an unusually large amount of information, you may need to limit the amount of time the session can be stored. You would then warn the user and change the timeout property. Here's a sample line of code that changes the timeout to 10 minutes:

```
Session.Timeout = 10
```

Mode

The remaining session state settings allow you to configure ASP.NET to use different session state services, depending on the mode that you choose. The next few sections describe the modes you can choose from.

■ **Note** If you're hosting ASP.NET using more than one web server (which is affectionately known as a *web farm*), you'll also need to take some extra configuration steps to make sure all the web servers are in sync. Otherwise, one server might encode information in session state differently than another, which will cause a problem if the user is routed from one server to another during a session. The solution is to modify the <machineKey> section of the machine.config file so that it's consistent across all servers. For more information, refer to Chapter 9.

InProc

InProc is the default mode. InProc is similar to how session state was stored in previous versions of ASP. It instructs information to be stored in the same process as the ASP.NET worker threads, which provides the best performance but the least durability. If you restart your server, the state information will be lost.

InProc makes sense for most small websites. In a web farm scenario, though, it won't work. To allow session state to be shared between servers, you must use the out-of-process or SQL Server state service. Another reason you might want to avoid InProc mode is if you find that your users are losing session state information at unpredictable times. In ASP.NET, application domains can be restarted for a variety of reasons, including configuration changes and updated pages, and when certain thresholds are met (regardless of whether an error has occurred). If you find that you're losing sessions *before* the timeout limit, you may want to experiment with a more durable mode.

■ **Note** When using the StateServer and SQLServer modes, the objects you store in session state must be serializable. Otherwise, ASP.NET will not be able to transmit the object to the state service or store it in the database. Earlier in this chapter, you learned how to create a serializable Customer class for storing in view state.

Off

This setting disables session state management for every page in the application. This can provide a slight performance improvement for websites that are not using session state.

StateServer

With this setting, ASP.NET will use a separate Windows service for state management. This service runs on the same web server, but it's outside the main ASP.NET process, which gives it a basic level of protection if the ASP.NET process needs to be restarted. The cost is the increased time delay imposed when state information is transferred between two processes. If you frequently access and change state information, this can make for a fairly unwelcome slowdown.

When using the StateServer setting, you need to specify a value for the stateConnectionString setting. This string identifies the TCP/IP address of the computer that is running the StateServer service and its port number (which is defined by ASP.NET and doesn't usually need to be changed). This allows you to host the StateServer on another computer. If you don't change this setting, the local server will be used (set as address 127.0.0.1).

Of course, before your application can use the service, you need to start it. The easiest way to do this is to use the Microsoft Management Console (MMC). Here's how:

1. Select Start ➤ Settings ➤ Control Panel (or just Start ➤ Control Panel in Windows Vista).
2. Open the Administrative Tools group, and then choose Computer Management.
3. In the Computer Management tool, go to the Services and Applications ➤ Services node.
4. Find the service called ASP.NET State Service in the list, as shown in Figure 7-13.
5. Once you find the service in the list, you can manually start and stop it by right-clicking it. Generally, you'll want to configure Windows to automatically start the service. Right-click it, select Properties, and modify the Startup Type, setting it to Automatic, as shown in Figure 7-14.

■ **Note** When using StateServer mode, you can also set an optional stateNetworkTimeout attribute that specifies the maximum number of seconds to wait for the service to respond before canceling the request. The default value is 10 (seconds).

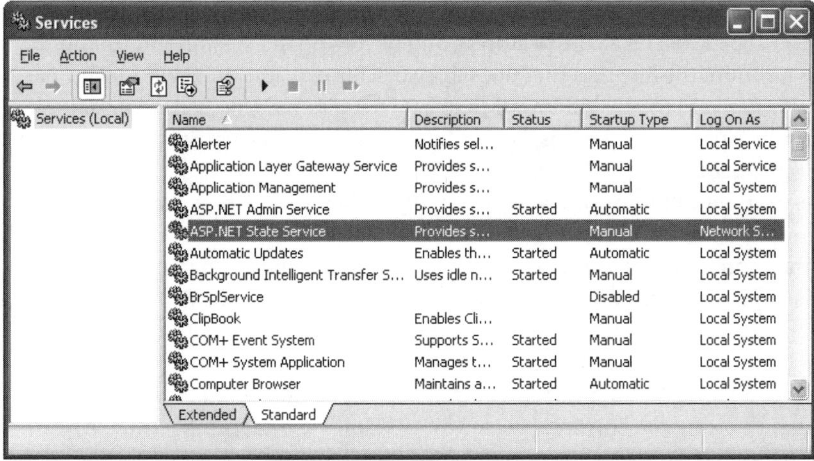

Figure 7-13. *The ASP.NET state service*

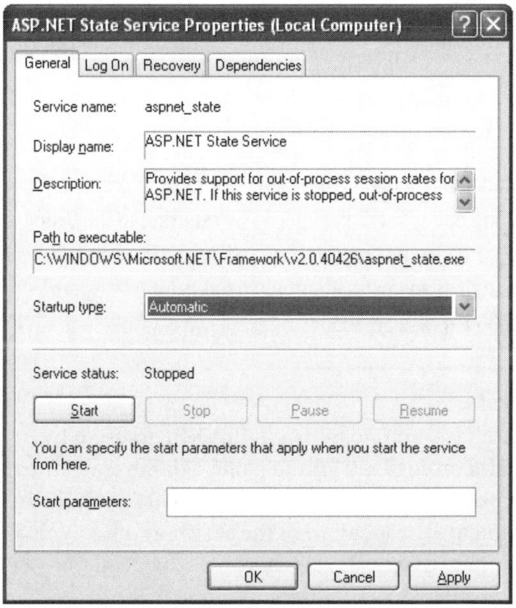

Figure 7-14. *Windows services*

SQLServer

This setting instructs ASP.NET to use an SQL Server database to store session information, as identified by the sqlConnectionString attribute. This is the most resilient state store but also the slowest by far. To use this method of state management, you'll need to have a server with SQL Server installed.

When setting the sqlConnectionString attribute, you follow the same sort of pattern you use with ADO.NET data access. Generally, you'll need to specify a data source (the server address) and a user ID and password, unless you're using SQL integrated security.

In addition, you need to install the special stored procedures and temporary session databases. These stored procedures take care of storing and retrieving the session information. ASP.NET includes a command-line tool that does the work for you automatically, called aspnet_regsql.exe. It's found in the c:\Windows\Microsoft.NET\Framework\v2.0.50727 directory. The easiest way to run aspnet_regsql.exe is to start by launching the Visual Studio command prompt (open the Start menu and choose Programs ➤ Visual Studio 2008 ➤ Visual Studio Tools ➤ Visual Studio 2008 Command Prompt). You can then type in an aspnet_regsql.exe command, no matter what directory you're in.

You can use the aspnet_regsql.exe tool to perform several database-related tasks. As you travel through this book, you'll see how to use aspnet_regsql.exe with ASP.NET features like membership (Chapter 21), profiles (Chapter 22), and caching (Chapter 24). To use aspnet_regsql.exe to create a session storage database, you supply the –ssadd parameter. In addition, you use the –S parameter to indicate the database server name, and the –E parameter to log in to the database using the currently logged-in Windows user account.

Here's a command that creates the session storage database on the current computer, using the default database name ASPState:

```
aspnet_regsql.exe -S localhost -E -ssadd
```

This command uses the alias localhost, which tells aspnet_regsql.exe to connect to the database server on the current computer.

■ **Note** The aspnet_regsql.exe command supports additional options that allow you to store session information in a database with a different name. You can find out about these options by referring to the Visual Studio help (look up aspnet_regsql in the index) or by surfing to `http://msdn2.microsoft.com/en-us/library/ms178586.aspx`. This information also describes the extra steps you need to take to use the database-backed session storage with SQL Server 2005 Express Edition.

Once you've created your session state database, you need to tell ASP.NET to use it by modifying the <sessionState> section of the web.config file. If you're using a database named ASPState to store your session information (which is the default), you don't need to supply the database name. Instead, you simply have to indicate the location of the server and the type of authentication that ASP.NET should use to connect to it, as shown here:

```
<sessionState
 sqlConnectionString="data source=127.0.0.1;Integrated Security=SSPI"
 ... />
```

When using the SQLServer mode, you can also set an optional sqlCommandTimeout attribute that specifies the maximum number of seconds to wait for the database to respond before canceling the request. The default is 30 seconds.

Custom

When using custom mode, you need to indicate which session state store provider to use by supplying the customProvider attribute. The customProvider attribute indicates the name of the class. The class may be part of your web application (in which case the source code is placed in the App_Code subfolder) or it can be in an assembly that your web application is using (in which case the compiled assembly is placed in the Bin subfolder).

Creating a custom state provider is a low-level task that needs to be handled carefully to ensure security, stability, and scalability. Custom state providers are also beyond the scope of this book. However, other vendors may release custom state providers you want to use. For example, Oracle could provide a custom state provider that allows you to store state information in an Oracle database.

Application State

Application state allows you to store global objects that can be accessed by any client. Application state is based on the System.Web.HttpApplicationState class, which is provided in all web pages through the built-in Application object.

Application state is similar to session state. It supports the same type of objects, retains information on the server, and uses the same dictionary-based syntax. A common example with application state is a global counter that tracks how many times an operation has been performed by all the web application's clients.

For example, you could create a Global.asax event handler that tracks how many sessions have been created or how many requests have been received into the application. Or you can use similar logic in the Page.Load event handler to track how many times a given page has been requested by various clients. Here's an example of the latter:

```
Protected Sub Page_Load(ByVal sender As Object, _
  ByVal e As EventArgs) Handles Me.Load

    Dim Count As Integer = CType(Application("HitCounterForOrderPage"), Integer)
    Count += 1
    Application("HitCounterForOrderPage") = Count
    lblCounter.Text = Count.ToString()

End Sub
```

Once again, application state items are stored as objects, so you need to cast them when you retrieve them from the collection. Items in application state never time out. They last until the application or server is restarted, or the application domain refreshes itself (because of automatic process recycling settings or an update to one of the pages or components in the application).

Application state isn't often used, because it's generally inefficient. In the previous example, the counter would probably not keep an accurate count, particularly in times of heavy traffic. For example, if two clients requested the page at the same time, you could have a sequence of events like this:

1. User A retrieves the current count (432).
2. User B retrieves the current count (432).

3. User A sets the current count to 433.

4. User B sets the current count to 433.

In other words, one request isn't counted because two clients access the counter at the same time. To prevent this problem, you need to use the Lock() and Unlock() methods, which explicitly allow only one client to access the Application state collection at a time.

```
Protected Sub Page_Load(ByVal sender As Object, _
  ByVal e As EventArgs) Handles Me.Load

    ' Acquire exclusive access.
    Application.Lock()

    Dim Count As Integer = CType(Application("HitCounterForOrderPage"), Integer)
    Count += 1
    Application("HitCounter") = Count

    ' Release exclusive access.
    Application.Unlock()

    lblCounter.Text = Count.ToString()

End Sub
```

Unfortunately, all other clients requesting the page will be stalled until the Application collection is released. This can drastically reduce performance. Generally, frequently modified values are poor candidates for application state. In fact, application state is rarely used in the .NET world because its two most common uses have been replaced by easier, more efficient methods:

- In the past, application state was used to store application-wide constants, such as a database connection string. As you saw in Chapter 5, this type of constant can be stored in the web.config file, which is generally more flexible because you can change it easily without needing to hunt through web page code or recompile your application.

- Application state can also be used to store frequently used information that is time-consuming to create, such as a full product catalog that requires a database lookup. However, using application state to store this kind of information raises all sorts of problems about how to check whether the data is valid and how to replace it when needed. It can also hamper performance if the product catalog is too large. Chapter 24 introduces a similar but much more sensible approach—storing frequently used information in the ASP.NET cache. Many uses of application state can be replaced more efficiently with caching.

Tip If you decide to use application state, you can initialize its contents when your application first starts. Just add the initialization code to the Global.asax file in a method named Application_OnStart(), as described in Chapter 5.

An Overview of State Management Choices

Each state management choice has a different lifetime, scope, performance overhead, and level of support. Table 7-3 and Table 7-4 show an at-a-glance comparison of your state management options.

Table 7-3. *State Management Options Compared (Part 1)*

	View State	Query String	Custom Cookies
Allowed Data Types	All serializable .NET data types.	A limited amount of string data.	String data.
Storage Location	A hidden field in the current web page.	The browser's URL string.	The client's computer (in memory or a small text file, depending on its lifetime settings).
Lifetime	Retained permanently for postbacks to a single page.	Lost when the user enters a new URL or closes the browser. However, this can be stored in a bookmark.	Set by the programmer. Can be used in multiple pages and can persist between visits.
Scope	Limited to the current page.	Limited to the target page.	The whole ASP.NET application.
Security	Tamperproof by default but easy to read. You can enforce encryption by using the ViewStateEncryptionMode property of the Page directive.	Clearly visible and easy for the user to modify.	Insecure, and can be modified by the user.
Performance Implications	Slow if a large amount of information is stored, but will not affect server performance.	None, because the amount of data is trivial.	None, because the amount of data is trivial.
Typical Use	Page-specific settings.	Sending a product ID from a catalog page to a details page.	Personalization preferences for a website.

Table 7-4. *State Management Options Compared (Part 2)*

	Session State	Application State
Allowed Data Types	All .NET data types for the default in-process storage mode. All serializable .NET data types if you use an out-of-process storage mode.	All .NET data types.
Storage Location	Server memory, state service, or SQL Server, depending on the mode you choose.	Server memory.
Lifetime	Times out after a predefined period (usually 20 minutes, but can be altered globally or programmatically).	The lifetime of the application (typically, until the server is rebooted).
Scope	The whole ASP.NET application.	The whole ASP.NET application. Unlike other methods, application data is global to all users.
Security	Very secure, because data is never transmitted to the client.	Very secure, because data is never transmitted to the client.
Performance Implications	Slow when storing a large amount of information, especially if there are many users at once, because each user will have their own copy of session data.	Slow when storing a large amount of information, because this data will never time out and be removed.
Typical Use	Storing items in a shopping basket.	Storing any type of global data.

■ **Note** ASP.NET has another, more specialized type of state management called *profiles*. Profiles allow you to store and retrieve user-specific information from a database. The only catch is that you need to authenticate the user in order to get the right information. You'll learn about profiles in Chapter 22.

The Last Word

State management is the art of retaining information between requests. Usually, this information is user-specific (such as a list of items in a shopping cart, a user name, or an access level), but sometimes it's global to the whole application (such as usage statistics that track site activity). Because ASP.NET uses a disconnected architecture, you need to explicitly store and retrieve state information with each request. The approach you choose to store this data can dramatically affect the performance, scalability, and security of your application. Remember to consult Table 7-3 and Table 7-4 to help evaluate different types of state management and determine what is best for your needs.

CHAPTER 8

■ ■ ■

Error Handling, Logging, and Tracing

No software can run free from error, and ASP.NET applications are no exception. Sooner or later your code will be interrupted by a programming mistake, invalid data, unexpected circumstances, or even hardware failure. Novice programmers spend sleepless nights worrying about errors. Professional developers recognize that bugs are an inherent part of software applications and code defensively, testing assumptions, logging problems, and writing error-handling code to deal with the unexpected.

In this chapter, you'll learn the error-handling and debugging practices that you can use to defend your ASP.NET applications against common errors, track user problems, and solve mysterious issues. You'll learn how to use structured exception handling, how to use logs to keep a record of unrecoverable errors, and how to set up web pages with custom error messages for common HTTP errors. You'll also learn how to use page tracing to see diagnostic information about ASP.NET pages.

Common Errors

Errors can occur in a variety of situations. Some of the most common causes of errors include attempts to divide by zero (usually caused by invalid input or missing information) and attempts to connect to a limited resource such as a file or a database (which can fail if the file doesn't exist, the database connection times out, or the code has insufficient security credentials).

One infamous type of error is the *null reference exception*, which usually occurs when a program attempts to use an uninitialized object. As a .NET programmer, you'll quickly learn to recognize and resolve this common but annoying mistake. The following code example shows the problem in action, with two SqlConnection objects that represent database connections:

```
' Define a variable named conOne and create the object.
Private conOne As New SqlConnection()

' Define a variable named conTwo, but don't create it.
Private conTwo As SqlConnection

Protected Sub cmdDoSomething_Click(ByVal sender As Object, _
  ByVal e As EventArgs) Handles cmdCompute.Click
```

```
    ' This works, because the object has been created
    ' with the New keyword.
    conOne.ConnectionString = "..."
    ...

    ' The following statement will fail and generate a
    ' null reference exception.
    ' You cannot modify a property (or use a method) of an
    ' object that doesn't exist!
    conTwo.ConnectionString = "..."
    ...
End Sub
```

When an error occurs in your code, .NET checks to see whether any *error handlers* appear in the current scope. If the error occurs inside a method, .NET searches for local error handlers and then checks for any active error handlers in the calling code. If no error handlers are found, the page processing is aborted and an error page is displayed in the browser. Depending on whether the request is from the local computer or a remote client, the error page may show a detailed description (as shown in Figure 8-1) or a generic message. You'll explore this topic a little later in the "Error Pages" section of this chapter.

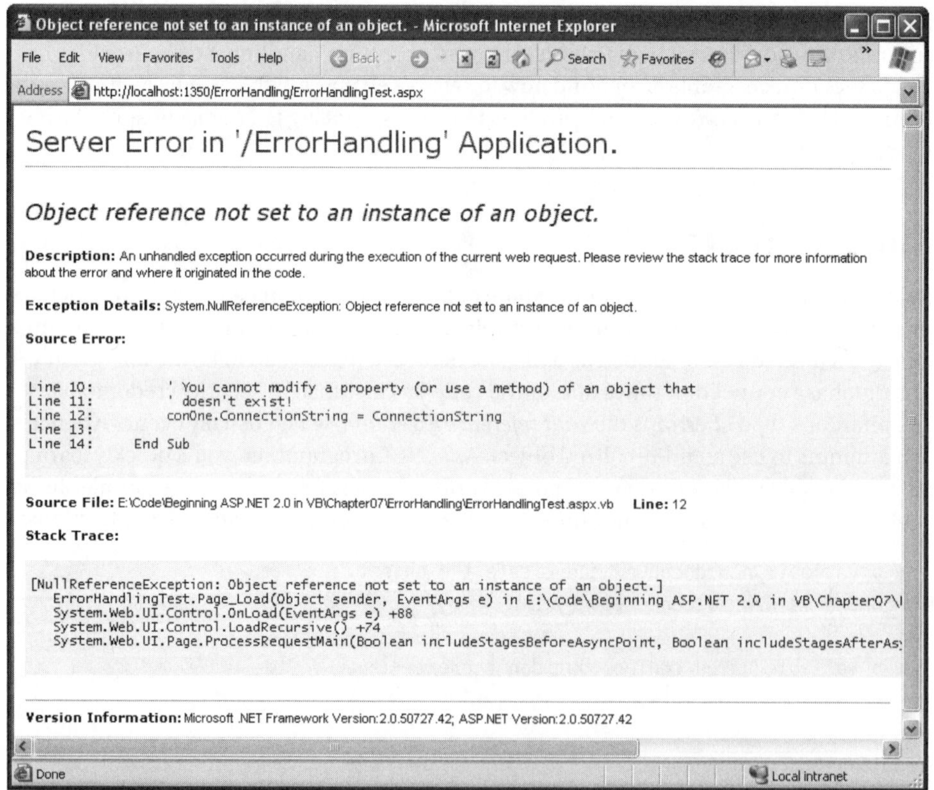

Figure 8-1. *A sample error page*

Even if an error is the result of invalid input or the failure of a third-party component, an error page can shatter the professional appearance of any application. The application users end up with a feeling that the application is unstable, insecure, or of poor quality—and they're at least partially correct.

If an ASP.NET application is carefully designed and constructed, an error page will almost never appear. Errors may still occur because of unforeseen circumstances, but they will be caught in the code and identified. If the error is a critical one that the application cannot solve on its own, it will report a more useful (and user-friendly) page of information that might include a link to a support e-mail or a phone number where the customer can receive additional assistance. You'll look at those techniques in this chapter.

Exception Handling

Most .NET languages support *structured exception handling*. Essentially, when an error occurs in your application, the .NET Framework creates an exception object that represents the problem. You can catch this object using an exception handler. If you fail to use an exception handler, your code will be aborted, and the user will see an error page.

Structured exception handling provides several key features:

Exceptions are object-based: Each exception provides a significant amount of diagnostic information wrapped into a neat object, instead of a simple message and an error code. These exception objects also support an InnerException property that allows you to wrap a generic error over the more specific error that caused it. You can even create and throw your own exception objects.

Exceptions are caught based on their type: This allows you to streamline error-handling code without needing to sift through obscure error codes.

Exception handlers use a modern block structure: This makes it easy to activate and deactivate different error handlers for different sections of code and handle their errors individually.

Exception handlers are multilayered: You can easily layer exception handlers on top of other exception handlers, some of which may check only for a specialized set of errors.

Exceptions are a generic part of the .NET Framework: This means they're completely cross-language compatible. Thus, a .NET component written in C# can throw an exception that you can catch in a web page written in VB.

■ Note Exception handlers are a key programming technique. They allow you to react to problems that occur at runtime due to factors outside your control. However, you obviously shouldn't use exception handlers to hide the bugs that might crop up in your code! Instead, you need to track down these programmer mistakes at development time and correct them. Visual Studio's debugging features (which were described in Chapter 4) can help you in this task.

The Exception Class

Every exception class derives from the base class System.Exception. The .NET Framework is full of predefined exception classes, such as NullReferenceException, IOException, SqlException, and so on. The Exception class includes the essential functionality for identifying any type of error. Table 8-1 lists its most important members.

Table 8-1. *Exception Properties*

Member	Description
HelpLink	A link to a help document, which can be a relative or fully qualified URL (uniform resource locator) or URN (uniform resource name), such as file:///C:/ACME/MyApp/help.html#Err42. The .NET Framework doesn't use this property, but you can set it in your custom exceptions if you want to use it in your web page code.
InnerException	A nested exception. For example, a method might catch a simple file IO (input/output) error and create a higher-level "operation failed" error. The details about the original error could be retained in the InnerException property of the higher-level error.
Message	A text description with a significant amount of information describing the problem.
Source	The name of the application or object where the exception was raised.
StackTrace	A string that contains a list of all the current method calls on the stack, in order of most to least recent. This is useful for determining where the problem occurred.
TargetSite	A reflection object (an instance of the System.Reflection.MethodBase class) that provides some information about the method where the error occurred. This information includes generic method details such as the method name and the data types for its parameter and return values. It doesn't contain any information about the actual parameter values that were used when the problem occurred.
GetBaseException()	A method useful for nested exceptions that may have more than one layer. It retrieves the original (deepest nested) exception by moving to the base of the InnerException chain.

When you catch an exception in an ASP.NET page, it won't be an instance of the generic System.Exception class. Instead, it will be an object that represents a specific type of error. This object will be based on one of the many classes that inherit from System.Exception. These include diverse classes such as DivideByZeroException, ArithmeticException, IOException, SecurityException, and many more. Some of these classes provide additional details about the error in additional properties.

Visual Studio provides a useful tool to browse through the exceptions in the .NET class library. Simply select Debug ➤ Exceptions from the menu (you'll need to have a project open in order for this to work). The Exceptions dialog box will appear. Expand the Common Language Runtime Exceptions group, which shows a hierarchical tree of .NET exceptions arranged by namespace (see Figure 8-2).

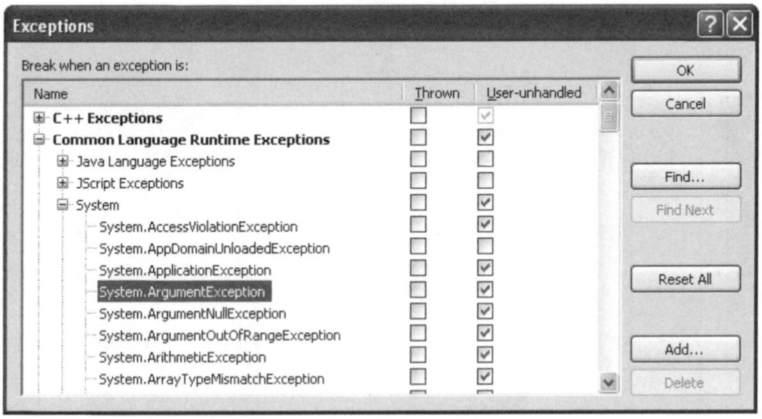

Figure 8-2. *Visual Studio's exception viewer*

The Exceptions dialog box allows you to specify what exceptions should be handled by your code when debugging and what exceptions will cause Visual Studio to enter break mode immediately. That means you don't need to disable your error-handling code to troubleshoot a problem. For example, you could choose to allow your program to handle a common FileNotFoundException (which could be caused by an invalid user selection) but instruct Visual Studio to pause execution if an unexpected DivideByZero exception occurs.

To set this up, add a check mark in the Thrown column next to the entry for the System.DivideByZero exception. This way, you'll be alerted as soon as the problem occurs. If you don't add a check mark to the Thrown column, your code will continue, run any exception handlers it has defined, and try to deal with the problem. You'll be notified only if an error occurs and no suitable exception handler is available.

The Exception Chain

Figure 8-3 shows how the InnerException property works. In the specific scenario shown here, a FileNotFoundException led to a NullReferenceException, which led to a custom UpdateFailedException. Using an exception-handling block, the application can catch the UpdateFailedException. It can then get more information about the source of the problem by following the InnerException property to the NullReferenceException, which in turn references the original FileNotFoundException.

The InnerException property is an extremely useful tool for component-based programming. Generally, it's not much help if a component reports a low-level problem such as a null reference or a divide-by-zero error. Instead, it needs to communicate a more detailed message about which operation failed and what input may have been invalid. The calling code can then often correct the problem and retry the operation.

On the other hand, sometimes you're debugging a bug that lurks deep inside the component itself. In this case, you need to know precisely what caused the error—you don't want to replace it with a higher-level exception that could obscure the root problem. Using an exception chain handles both these scenarios: you receive as many linked exception objects as needed, which can specify information from the least to the most specific error condition.

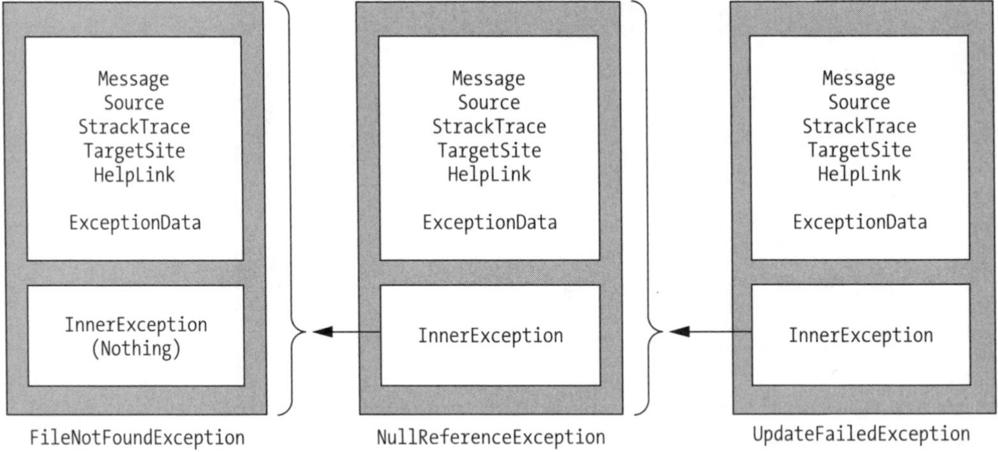

Figure 8-3. *Exceptions can be chained together.*

Handling Exceptions

The first line of defense in an application is to check for potential error conditions before performing an operation. For example, a program can explicitly check whether the divisor is 0 before performing a calculation, or if a file exists before attempting to open it:

```
If Divisor <> 0 Then
    ' Safe to divide some number by Divisor.
End If

If System.IO.File.Exists("myfile.txt") Then
    ' You can now open the myfile.txt file.
    ' However, you should still use exception handling because a variety of
    ' problems can intervene (insufficient rights, hardware failure, etc.).
End If
```

Even if you perform this basic level of "quality assurance," your application is still vulnerable. For example, you have no way to protect against all the possible file access problems that occur, including hardware failures or network problems that could arise spontaneously in the middle of an operation. Similarly, you have no way to validate a user ID and password for a database before attempting to open a connection—and even if you did, that technique would be subject to its own set of potential errors. In some cases, it may not be practical to perform the full range of defensive checks, because they may impose a noticeable performance drag on your application. For all these reasons, you need a way to detect and deal with errors when they occur.

The solution is structured exception handling. To use structured exception handling, you wrap potentially problematic code in the special block structure shown here:

```
Try
    ' Risky code goes here (i.e., opening a file, connecting to a database).
Catch
    ' An error has been detected. You can deal with it here.
Finally
    ' Time to clean up, regardless of whether or not there was an error.
End Try
```

The Try statement enables error handling. Any exceptions that occur in the following lines can be "caught" automatically. The code in the Catch block will be executed when an error is detected. And either way, whether a bug occurs or not, the Finally section of the code will be executed last. This allows you to perform some basic cleanup, such as closing a database connection. The Finally code is important because it will execute even if an error has occurred that will prevent the program from continuing. In other words, if an unrecoverable exception halts your application, you'll still have the chance to release resources.

The act of catching an exception neutralizes it. If all you want to do is render a specific error harmless, you don't even need to add any code in the Catch block of your error handler. Usually, however, this portion of the code will be used to report the error to the user or log it for future reference. In a separate component (such as a business object), this code might handle the exception, perform some cleanup, and then rethrow it to the calling code, which will be in the best position to remedy it or alert the user. Or it might actually create a new exception object with additional information and throw that.

Catching Specific Exceptions

Structured exception handling is particularly flexible because it allows you to catch specific types of exceptions. To do so, you add multiple Catch statements, each one identifying the type of exception (and providing a new variable to catch it in), as follows:

```
Try
    ' Database code goes here.
Catch err As System.Data.SqlClient.SqlException
    ' Catches common database problems like connection errors.
Catch err As System.NullReferenceException
    ' Catches problems resulting from an uninitialized object.
End Try
```

An exception will be caught as long as it's an instance of the indicated class or if it's derived from that class. In other words, if you use this statement:

```
Catch err As Exception
```

you will catch any exception, because every exception object is derived from the System.Exception base class.

Exception blocks work a little like conditional code. As soon as a matching exception handler is found, the appropriate Catch code is invoked. Therefore, you must organize your Catch statements from most specific to least specific:

```
Try
    ' Database code goes here.
Catch err As System.Data.SqlClient.SqlException
    ' Catches common database problems like connection errors.
Catch err As System.NullReferenceException
    ' Catches problems resulting from an uninitialized object.
Catch err As System.Exception
    ' Catches any other errors.
End Try
```

Ending with a Catch statement for the base Exception class is often a good idea to make sure no errors slip through. However, in component-based programming, you should make sure you intercept only those exceptions you can deal with or recover from. Otherwise, it's better to let the calling code catch the original error.

DETERMINING THE EXCEPTIONS YOU NEED TO CATCH

When you're using classes from the .NET Framework, you may not know what exceptions you need to catch. Fortunately, Visual Studio Help can fill you in.

The trick is to look up the method or constructor you're using in the class library reference. One fast way to jump to a specific method is to use the Help index—just type in the class name, followed by a period, followed by the method name, as in File.Open (which is a method you'll use to open files in Chapter 17). If there is more than one overloaded version of the method, you'll see a page that lists them all, and you'll need to click the one that has the parameters you want.

Once you find the right method, scroll through the method documentation until you find a section named Exceptions. This section lists all the possible exceptions that this method can throw. For example, if you look up the File.Open() method, you'll find that possible exceptions include DirectoryNotFoundException, FileNotFoundException, UnauthorizedAccessException, and so on. You probably won't write a Catch block for each possible exception. However, you should still know about all of them so you can decide which exceptions you want to handle separately.

Nested Exception Handlers

When an exception is thrown, .NET tries to find a matching Catch statement in the current method. If the code isn't in a local structured exception block, or if none of the Catch statements match the exception, .NET will move up the call stack one level at a time, searching for active exception handlers.

Consider the example shown here, where the Page.Load event handler calls a private DivideNumbers() method:

```
Protected Sub Page_Load(ByVal sender As Object, _
  ByVal e As EventArgs) Handles Me.Load
    Try
        DivideNumbers(5, 0)
    Catch err As DivideByZeroException
        ' Report error here.
```

```
    End Try
End Sub

Private Function DivideNumbers(ByVal number As Decimal, _
  ByVal divisor As Decimal) As Decimal
    Return number/divisor
End Function
```

In this example, the DivideNumbers() method lacks any sort of exception handler. However, the DivideNumbers() method call is made inside a Try block, which means the problem will be caught further upstream in the calling code. This is a good approach because the DivideNumbers() routine could be used in a variety of circumstances (or if it's part of a component, in a variety of different types of applications). It really has no access to any kind of user interface and can't directly report an error. Only the calling code is in a position to determine whether the problem is a serious one or a minor one, and only the calling code can prompt the user for more information or report error details in the web page.

■ **Note** In this example, great care is taken to use the Decimal data type rather than the more common Double data type. That's because contrary to what you might expect, it *is* acceptable to divide a Double by 0. The result is the special value Double.PositiveInfinity (or Double.NegativeInfinity if you divide a negative number by 0).

You can also overlap exception handlers in such a way that different exception handlers filter out different types of problems. Here's one such example:

```
Protected Sub Page_Load(ByVal sender As Object, _
  ByVal e As EventArgs) Handles Me.Load
    Try
        Dim Average As Integer = GetAverageCost(DateTime.Now)
    Catch err As DivideByZeroException
        ' Report error here.
    End Try
End Sub

Private Function GetAverageCost(saleDate As Date) As Integer
    Try
        ' Use Database access code here to retrieve all the sale records
        ' for this date, and calculate the average.
    Catch err As System.Data.SqlClient.SqlException
        ' Handle a database related problem.
    Finally
        ' Close the database connection.
    End Try
End Function
```

Dissecting the Code . . .

You should be aware of the following points:

- If an SqlException occurs during the database operation, it will be caught in the GetAverageCost() method.
- If a DivideByZeroException occurs (for example, the method receives no records but still attempts to calculate an average), the exception will be caught in the calling Page.Load event handler.
- If another problem occurs (such as a null reference exception), no active exception handler exists to catch it. In this case, .NET will search through the entire call stack without finding a matching Catch statement in an active exception handler and will generate a runtime error, end the program, and return a page with exception information.

Exception Handling in Action

You can use a simple program to test exceptions and see what sort of information is retrieved. This program allows a user to enter two values and attempts to divide them. It then reports all the related exception information in the page (see Figure 8-4).

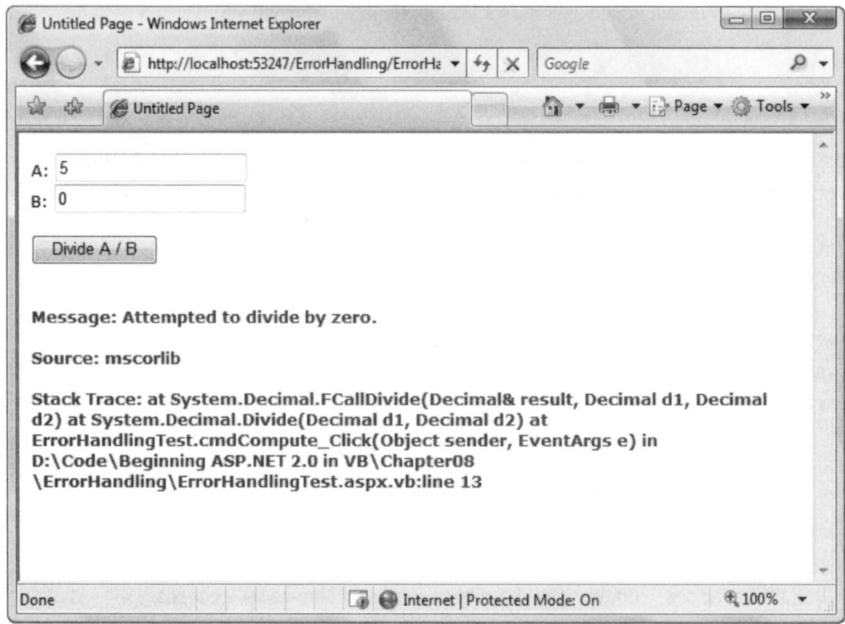

Figure 8-4. *Catching and displaying exception information*

Obviously, you can easily prevent this exception from occurring by using extra code-safety checks, or elegantly resolve it using the validation controls. However, this code provides a good example of how you can deal with the properties of an exception object. It also gives you a good idea about what sort of information will be returned.

Here's the page class code for this example:

```
Public Partial Class ErrorHandlingTest
    Inherits System.Web.UI.Page

    Protected Sub cmdCompute_Click(ByVal sender As Object, _
      ByVal e As EventArgs) Handles cmdCompute.Click

        Try
            Dim A, B, Result As Decimal
            A = Decimal.Parse(txtA.Text)
            B = Decimal.Parse(txtB.Text)
            Result = A / B
            lblResult.Text = Result.ToString()
            lblResult.ForeColor = System.Drawing.Color.Black
        Catch err As Exception
            lblResult.Text = "<b>Message:</b> " & err.Message & "<br /><br />"
            lblResult.Text &= "<b>Source:</b> " & err.Source & "<br /><br />"
            lblResult.Text &= "<b>Stack Trace:</b> " & err.StackTrace
            lblResult.ForeColor = System.Drawing.Color.Red
        End Try
    End Sub

End Class
```

Note that as soon as the error occurs, execution is transferred to an exception handler. The code in the Try block isn't completed. It's for that reason that the result for the label is set in the Try block. These lines will be executed only if the division code runs error-free.

You'll see many more examples of exception handling throughout this book. The data access chapters in Part 4 of this book show the best practices for exception handling when accessing a database.

Mastering Exceptions

Keep in mind these points when working with structured exception handling:

Break down your code into multiple Try/Catch blocks: If you put all your code into one exception handler, you'll have trouble determining where the problem occurred. You have no way to "resume" the code in a Try block. This means that if an error occurs at the beginning of a lengthy Try block, you'll skip a large amount of code. The rule of thumb is to use one exception handler for one related task (such as opening a file and retrieving information).

Report all errors: During debugging, portions of your application's error-handling code may mask easily correctable mistakes in your application. To prevent this from happening, make sure you report all errors, and consider leaving out some error-handling logic in early builds.

Don't use exception handlers for every statement: Simple code statements (assigning a constant value to a variable, interacting with a control, and so on) may cause errors during development testing but will not cause any future problems once perfected. Error handling should be used when you're accessing an outside resource or dealing with supplied data that you have no control over (and thus may be invalid).

Throwing Your Own Exceptions

You can also define your own exception objects to represent custom error conditions. All you need to do is create an instance of the appropriate exception class and then use the Throw statement.

The next example introduces a modified DivideNumbers() method. It explicitly checks whether the specified divisor is 0 and then manually creates and throws an instance of the DivideByZeroException class to indicate the problem, rather than attempt the operation. Depending on the code, this pattern can save time by eliminating some unnecessary steps, or it can prevent a task from being initiated if it can't be completed successfully.

```
Protected Sub Page_Load(ByVal sender As Object, _
  ByVal e As EventArgs) Handles Me.Load
    Try
        DivideNumbers(5, 0)
    Catch err As DivideByZeroException
        ' Report error here.
    End Try
End Sub

Private Function DivideNumbers(ByVal number As Decimal, _
  ByVal divisor As Decimal) As Decimal
    If divisor = 0 Then
        Dim err As New DivideByZeroException()
        Throw err
    Else
        Return number/divisor
    End If
End Function
```

Alternatively, you can create a .NET exception object and specify a custom error message by using a different constructor:

```
Private Function DivideNumbers(ByVal number As Decimal, _
  ByVal divisor As Decimal) As Decimal
    If divisor = 0 Then
        Dim err As New DivideByZeroException( _
           "You supplied 0 for the divisor parameter. You must be stopped.")
        Throw err
    Else
        Return number/divisor
    End If
End Function
```

In this case, any ordinary exception handler will still catch the DivideByZeroException. The only difference is that the error object has a modified Message property that contains the custom string. Figure 8-5 shows the resulting exception.

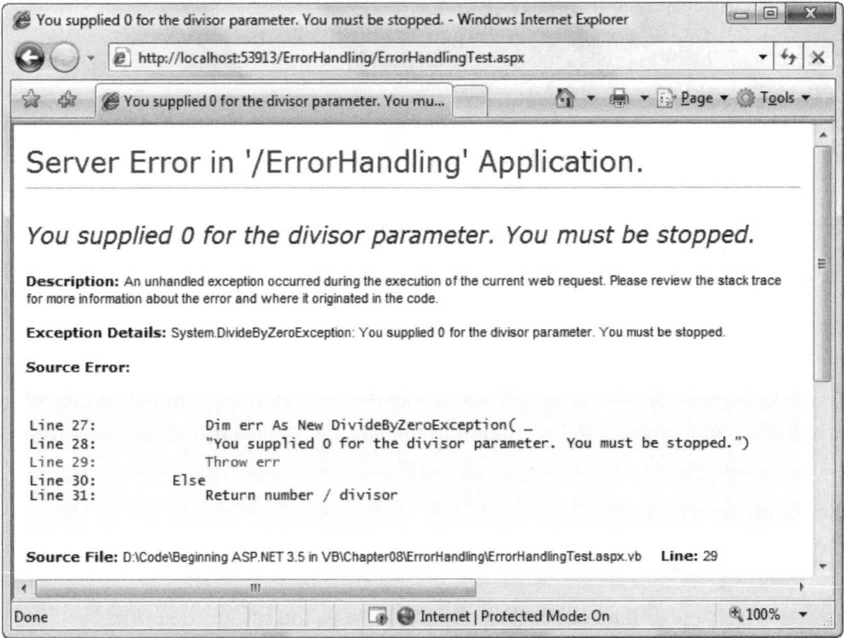

Figure 8-5. *Standard exception, custom message*

Throwing an exception is most useful in component-based programming. In component-based programming, your ASP.NET page is creating objects and calling methods from a class defined in a separately compiled assembly. In this case, the class in the component needs to be able to notify the calling code (the web application) of any errors. The component should handle recoverable errors quietly and not pass them up to the calling code. On the other hand, if an unrecoverable error occurs, it should always be indicated with an exception and never through another mechanism (such as a return code). For more information about component-based programming, refer to Chapter 23.

If you can find an exception in the class library that accurately reflects the problem that has occurred, you should throw it. If you need to return additional or specialized information, you can create your own custom exception class.

Custom exception classes should always inherit from System.ApplicationException, which itself derives from the base Exception class. This allows .NET to distinguish between two broad classes of exceptions—those you create and those that are native to the .NET Framework.

When you create an exception class, you can add properties to record additional information. For example, here is a special class that records information about the failed attempt to divide by zero:

```
Public Class CustomDivideByZeroException
  Inherits ApplicationException

    ' Add a variable to specify the "other" number.
    ' Depending on the circumstance, this might help diagnose the problem.
    Public DividingNumber As Decimal

End Class
```

You can throw this custom exception like this:

```
Private Function DivideNumbers(ByVal number As Decimal, _
  ByVal divisor As Decimal) As Decimal
    If divisor = 0 Then
        Dim err As New CustomDivideByZeroException()
        err.DividingNumber = number
        Throw err
    Else
        Return number/divisor
    End If
End Function
```

To perfect the custom exception, you need to supply it with the three standard constructors. This allows your exception class to be created in the standard ways that every exception supports:

- On its own, with no arguments
- With a custom message
- With a custom message and an exception object to use as the inner exception

These constructors don't actually need to contain any code. All these constructors need to do is forward the parameters to the base class (the constructors in the inherited ApplicationException class) using the MyBase keyword, as shown here:

```
Public Class CustomDivideByZeroException
  Inherits ApplicationException

    ' Add a variable to specify the "other" number.
    ' Depending on the circumstance, this might help diagnose the problem.
    Private _dividingNumber As Decimal
    Public Property DividingNumber() As Decimal
        Get
            Return _dividingNumber
        End Get
        Set(ByVal value As Decimal)
            _dividingNumber = value
        End Set
    End Property

    Public Sub New()
        MyBase.New()
    End Sub

    Public Sub New(ByVal message As String)
        MyBase.New(message)
    End Sub
```

```
    Public Sub New(ByVal message as String, ByVal inner As Exception)
        MyBase.New(message, inner)
    End Sub

End Class
```

The third constructor is particularly useful for component programming. It allows you to set the InnerException property with the exception object that caused the original problem. The next example shows how you could use this constructor with a component class called ArithmeticUtility:

```
Public Class ArithmeticUtilityException
  Inherits ApplicationException
    Public Sub New()
        MyBase.New()
    End Sub

    Public Sub New(ByVal message As String)
        MyBase.New(message)
    End Sub

    Public Sub New(ByVal message as String, ByVal inner As Exception)
        MyBase.New(message, inner)
    End Sub
End Class

Public Class ArithmeticUtility
    Private Function Divide(ByVal number As Decimal, _
      ByVal divisor As Decimal) As Decimal
        Try
            Return number/divisor
        Catch err As Exception
            ' Create an instance of the specialized exception class,
            ' and place the original error in the InnerException property.
            Dim errNew As New ArithmeticUtilityException("Divide by zero", _
              err)

            ' Now throw the new exception.
            Throw errNew
        End Try
    End Function
End Class
```

Remember, custom exception classes are really just a standardized way for one class to communicate an error to a different portion of code. If you aren't using components or your own utility classes, you probably don't need to create custom exception classes.

Logging Exceptions

In many cases, it's best not only to detect and catch exceptions but to log them as well. For example, some problems may occur only when your web server is dealing with a particularly large load. Other problems might recur intermittently, with no obvious causes. To diagnose these errors and build a larger picture of site problems, you need to log exceptions so they can be reviewed later.

The .NET Framework provides a wide range of logging tools. When certain errors occur, you can send an e-mail, add a database record, or create and write to a file. We describe many of these techniques in other parts of this book. However, you should keep your logging code as simple as possible. For example, you'll probably run into trouble if you try to log a database exception using another table in the database.

One of the most fail-safe logging tools is the Windows *event logging* system, which is built into the Windows operating system and available to any application. Using the Windows event logs, your website can write text messages that record errors or unusual events. The Windows event logs store your messages as well as various other details, such as the message type (information, error, and so on) and the time the message was left.

Viewing the Windows Event Logs

To view the Windows event logs, you use the Event Viewer tool that's included with Windows. To launch it, begin by selecting Start ➤ Settings ➤ Control Panel (or just Start ➤ Control Panel in Windows Vista). Open the Administrative Tools group, and then choose Event Viewer.

If you're running Windows XP or Windows Server 2003, you'll see just three logs—Application, Security, and System. If you're running Windows Vista or Windows Server 2008, you'll find these three plus a Setup log, all of which appear under the Windows Logs section (Figure 8-6). Table 8-2 describes these standard Windows logs.

Using the Event Viewer, you can perform a variety of management tasks with the logs. For example, if you right-click one of the logs in the Event Viewer list you'll see options that allow you to clear the events in the log, save the log entries to another file, and import an external log file.

Each event record in an event log identifies the source (generally, the application or service that created the record), the type of notification (error, information, warning), and the time the log entry was inserted. In Windows Vista, you simply need to select a log entry and its information will appear in a display area underneath the list of entries (see Figure 8-6). In Windows XP or Windows Server 2003, you need to double-click a log entry to see the full information.

You can also review event logs in Visual Studio. First, display the Server Explorer window (if it's not already visible) by choosing View ➤ Server Explorer. (The Server Explorer window usually appears at the left side of the Visual Studio window, where it shares space with the Toolbox.) Using the Server Explorer, expand the Servers ➤ [ComputerName] ➤ Event Logs group to see a list of event logs on your computer. This list is a bit longer than what you saw in the Event Viewer, because it includes both the Windows event logs you saw and custom event logs for specific applications (which you'll learn to create later in this chapter).

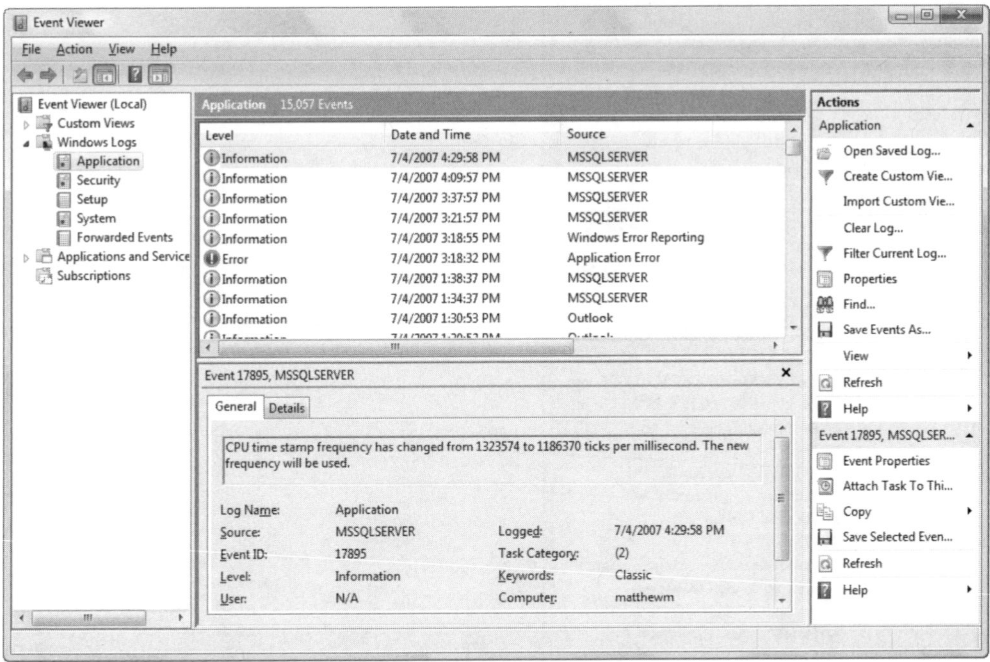

Figure 8-6. *The Event Viewer*

Table 8-2. *Windows Event Logs*

Log Name	Description
Application	Used to track errors or notifications from any application. Generally, you'll use this log when you're performing event logging, or you'll create your own custom log.
Security	Used to track security-related problems but generally used exclusively by the operating system.
System	Used to track operating system events.
Setup	Used to track issues that occur when installing Windows updates or other software. This log only appears in Windows Vista.

If you expand an event log in the Server Explorer window, you'll find all the event log entries, grouped according to the source that made the log entry. Figure 8-7 shows some of the event logs left in the Application log on the current computer by the event source .NET Runtime Optimization Source. Once you select a log entry, you can view its specific details (such as the event log message and the time it was left) in the Properties window.

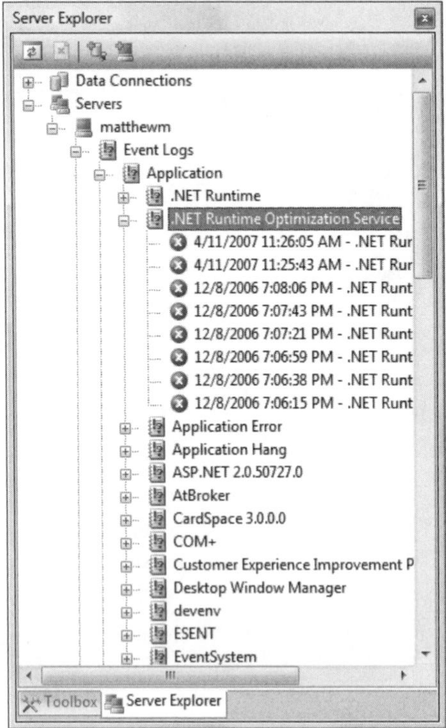

Figure 8-7. *Viewing event log entries in Visual Studio*

One of the potential problems with event logs is that old entries are automatically discarded when the event log reaches a maximum size. In Windows XP, the default log size is a stingy 0.5MB, although log entries are kept for at least 7 days even if they exceed this size limit (unless you specify otherwise). In Windows Vista, logs get a much more reasonable upper limit of 20MB (except for the new Setup log, which gets just 1MB).

No matter which operating system you're using, you'll find that logs grow quickly. That means that unless you're using a custom event log that has lots of space, your log entries might not last for a long period of time. Ideally, you should use event logs to record information that is reviewed and acted on over a relatively short period of time. For example, event logs are a good choice if you plan to log application errors and review them to diagnose strange behavior immediately after it happens. Event logs don't make as much sense if you want to get a detailed picture of application activity six months later, because Windows (or someone else) may delete old log entries. In this scenario, a custom database makes more sense.

If you want to add a little more breathing room to an existing log, you can change its maximum size. This is a particularly worthwhile step if you plan to use the application log in Windows XP. To do so, right-click the log and choose Properties. You'll see the Application Properties window shown in Figure 8-8, where you can change the maximum size.

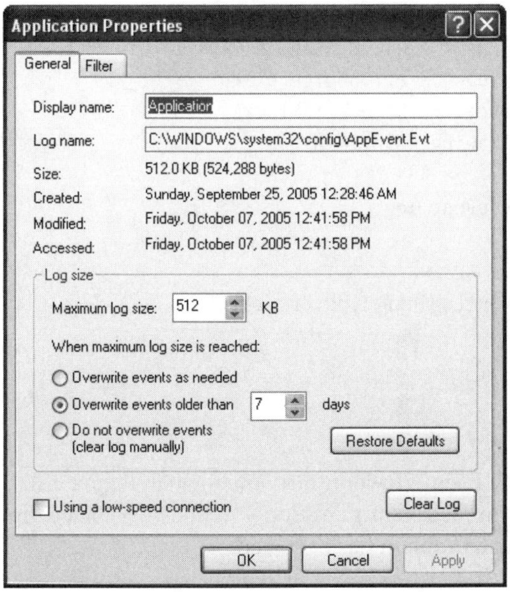

Figure 8-8. *Log properties*

■ **Tip** You can increase the log size, but you really shouldn't disable automatic log deletion altogether, because you could end up consuming a huge amount of space over time if information isn't being regularly removed.

Writing to the Event Log

You can interact with event logs in an ASP.NET page by using the classes in the System.Diagnostics namespace. First, import the namespace at the beginning of your code-behind file:

```
Imports System.Diagnostics
```

The following example rewrites the simple ErrorTest page to use event logging:

```
Public Partial Class ErrorTestLog
    Inherits System.Web.UI.Page

    Protected Sub cmdCompute_Click(ByVal sender As Object, _
      ByVal e As EventArgs) _
      Handles cmdCompute.Click

        Try
            Dim A, B, Result As Decimal
            A = Decimal.Parse(txtA.Text)
            B = Decimal.Parse(txtB.Text)
            Result = A / B
            lblResult.Text = Result.ToString()
            lblResult.ForeColor = System.Drawing.Color.Black
```

```
        Catch err As Exception
            lblResult.Text = "<b>Message:</b> " & err.Message & "<br /><br />"
            lblResult.Text &= "<b>Source:</b> " & err.Source & "<br /><br />"
            lblResult.Text &= "<b>Stack Trace:</b> " & err.StackTrace
            lblResult.ForeColor = System.Drawing.Color.Red

            ' Write the information to the event log.
            Dim Log As New EventLog()
            Log.Source = "DivisionPage"
            Log.WriteEntry(err.Message, EventLogEntryType.Error)
        End Try
    End Sub

End Class
```

The event log record will now appear in the Event Viewer utility, as shown in Figure 8-9. Note that logging is intended for the system administrator or developer. It doesn't replace the code you use to notify the user and explain that a problem has occurred.

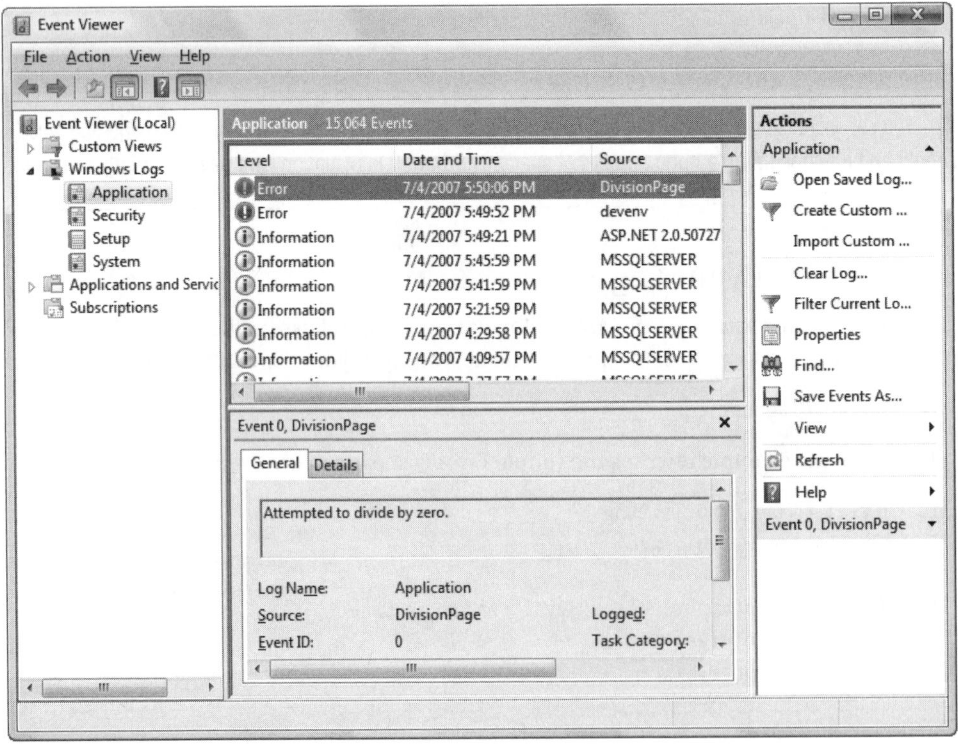

Figure 8-9. *An event record*

EVENT LOG SECURITY

This logging code will run without a hitch when you try it in Visual Studio. However, when you deploy your application to a web server (as described in Chapter 9), you might not be so lucky. The problem is that the ASP.NET service runs under a Windows account that has fewer privileges than an average user. If you're using IIS 5 (the version included with Windows XP), this user is an account named ASPNET. If you're using a later version of IIS (such as the version included with Windows Vista or Windows Server 2003), this is the network service account. Either way, the account that's used to run ASP.NET code ordinarily won't have the permissions to create event log entries.

To remedy this problem, you can use a different account (as explained in Chapter 9), or you can grant the required permissions to the account that ASP.NET is already using (like the ASPNET account). To do the latter, you need to modify the registry as described in these steps:

1. Run regedit.exe, either by using a command-line prompt or by choosing Run from the Start menu.
2. Browse to the HKEY_Local_Machine\SYSTEM\CurrentControlSet\Services\EventLog section of the registry.
3. Select the EventLog folder if you want to give ASP.NET permission to all areas of the event log. Or select a specific folder that corresponds to the event log ASP.NET needs to access.
4. Right-click the folder and choose Permissions.
5. Add the account that ASP.NET is using to the list (or a group that this account belongs to). If you're using IIS 5, this is the ASPNET account. To add it, click the Add button, type in ASPNET, and then click OK. If you're using IIS 6 in Windows Server 2003, you need to add permissions to the IIS_WPG group instead of the ASPNET account. If you're using IIS 7 in Windows Vista or Windows Server 2008, you need to add permissions to the IIS_USRS group.
6. Give the account Full Control for this section of the registry by selecting the Allow check box next to Full Control.

Custom Logs

You can also log errors to a custom log. For example, you could create a log with your company name and add records to it for all your ASP.NET applications. You might even want to create an individual log for a particularly large application and use the Source property of each entry to indicate the page (or web service method) that caused the problem.

Accessing a custom log is easy—you just need to use a different constructor for the EventLog class to specify the custom log name. You also need to register an *event source* for the log. This initial step needs to be performed only once—in fact, you'll receive an error if you try to create the same event source. Typically, you'll use the name of the application as the event source.

Here's an example that uses a custom log named ProseTech and registers the event source DivideByZeroApp:

```
' Register the event source if needed.
If Not EventLog.SourceExists("DivideByZeroApp") Then
    ' This registers the event source and creates the custom log,
    ' if needed.
    EventLog.CreateEventSource("DivideByZeroApp", "ProseTech")
End If

' Open the log. If the log does not exist, it will be created automatically.
Dim Log As New EventLog("ProseTech")
log.Source = "DivideByZeroApp"
log.WriteEntry(err.Message, EventLogEntryType.Error)
```

If you specify the name of a log that doesn't exist when you use the CreateEventSource() method, the system will create a new, custom event log for you the first time you write an entry.

In order to see a newly created event log in the Event Viewer tool, you'll need to exit Event Viewer and restart it. In Windows XP and Windows Server 2003, custom event logs appear alongside the standard Windows event logs. In Windows Vista, they appear in a separate group named Applications and Services Logs, as shown in Figure 8-10.

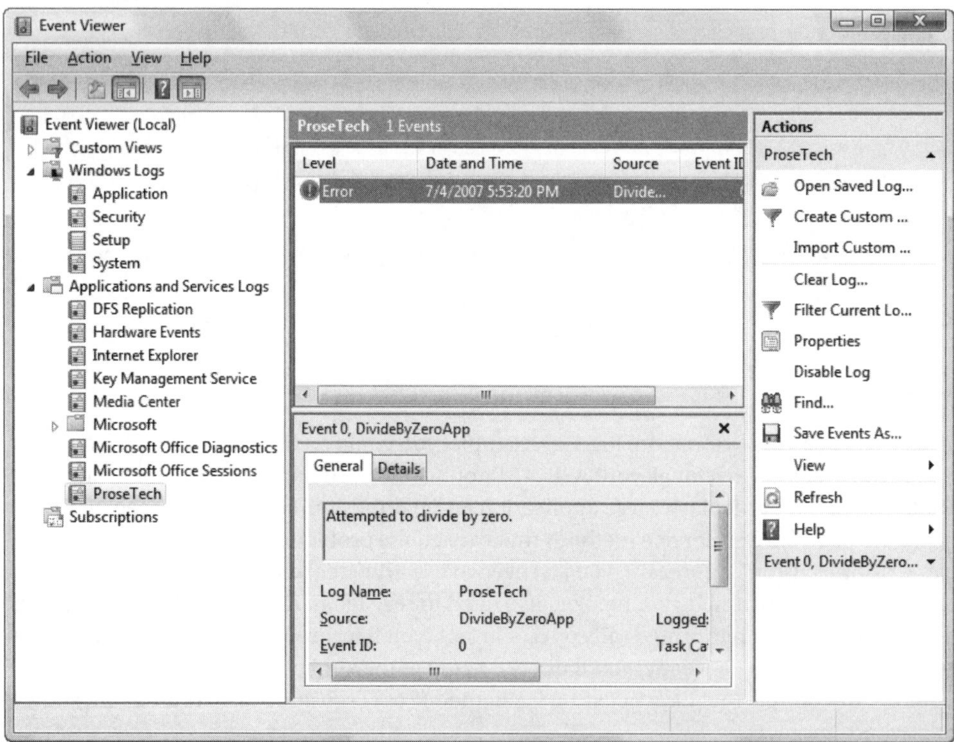

Figure 8-10. *A custom log*

You can use this sort of code anywhere in your application. Usually, you'll use logging code when responding to an exception that might be a symptom of a deeper problem.

A Custom Logging Class

Rather than adding too much logging code in the Catch block, a better approach is to create a separate class that handles the event logging grunt work. You can then use that class from any web page, without duplicating any code.

To use this approach, begin by creating a new code file in the App_Code subfolder of your website. You can do this in Visual Studio by choosing Website ➤ Add New Item. In the Add New Item dialog box, choose Class, pick a suitable file name, and then click Add.

Here's an example of a class named MyLogger that handles the event logging details:

```
Public Class MyLogger
{
    Public Sub LogError(ByVal pageInError As String, By err As Exception)
        RegisterLog()

        Dim log As New EventLog("ProseTech")
        log.Source = pageInError
        log.WriteEntry(err.Message, EventLogEntryType.Error)
    End Sub

    Private Sub RegisterLog()
        ' Register the event source if needed.
        If Not EventLog.SourceExists("ProseTech") Then
           EventLog.CreateEventSource("DivideByZeroApp", "ProseTech")
        End If
    End Sub
End Class
```

Once you have a class in the App_Code folder, it's easy to use it anywhere in your website. Here's how you might use the MyLogger class in a web page to log an exception:

```
Try
    ' Risky code goes here.

Catch err As Exception
    ' Log the error using the logging class.
    Dim logger As New MyLogger()
    logger.LogError(Request.Path, err)

    ' Now handle the error as appropriate for this page.
    lblResult.Text = "Sorry. An error occurred."
Emd Try
```

If you write log entries frequently, you may not want to check if the log exists every time you want to write an entry. Instead, you could create the event source once—when the application first starts up—using an application event handler in the Global.asax file. This technique is described in Chapter 5.

■ **Tip** Event logging uses disk space and takes processor time away from web applications. Don't store unimportant information, large quantities of data, or information that would be better off in another type of storage (such as a relational database). Generally, you should use an event log to log unexpected conditions or errors, not customer actions or performance-tracking information.

Retrieving Log Information

One of the disadvantages of the event logs is that they're tied to the web server. This can make it difficult to review log entries if you don't have a way to access the server (although you can read them from another computer on the same network). This problem has several possible solutions. One interesting technique involves using a special administration page. This ASP.NET page can use the EventLog class to retrieve and display all the information from the event log.

Figure 8-11 shows in a simple web page all the entries that were left by the ErrorTestCustomLog page. The results are shown using a label in a scrollable panel (a Panel control with the Scrollbars property set to Vertical). A more sophisticated approach would use similar code but with one of the data controls discussed in Chapter 17.

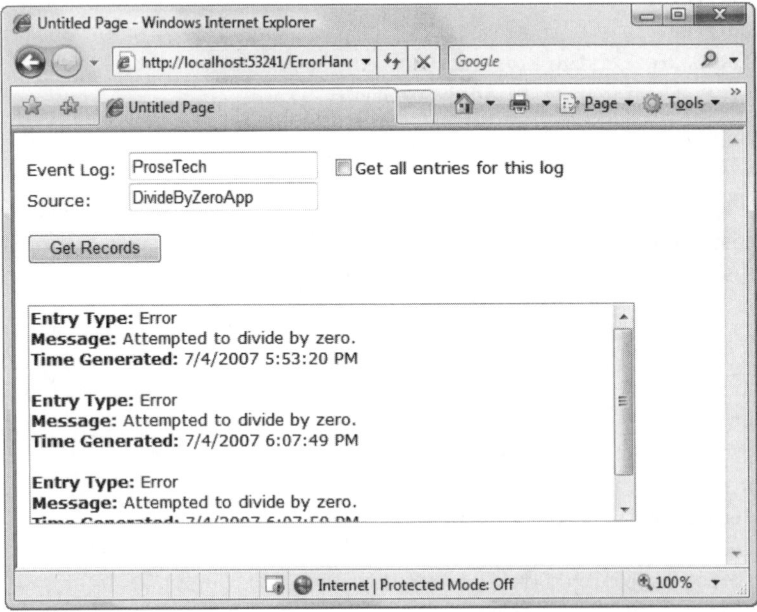

Figure 8-11. *A log viewer page*

Here's the web page code you'll need:

```
Public Partial Class EventReviewPage
    Inherits System.Web.UI.Page

    Protected Sub cmdGet_Click(ByVal sender As Object, _
      ByVal e As EventArgs) Handles cmdGet.Click

        lblResult.Text = ""

        ' Check if the log exists.
        If Not EventLog.Exists(txtLog.Text) Then
            lblResult.Text = "The event log " & txtLog.Text & _
              " does not exist."
        Else
            Dim log As New EventLog(txtLog.Text)

            For Each entry As EventLogEntry In log.Entries
                ' Write the event entries to the page.
                If chkAll.Checked Or entry.Source = txtSource.Text Then
                    lblResult.Text &= "<b>Entry Type:</b> "
                    lblResult.Text &= entry.EntryType.ToString()
                    lblResult.Text &= "<br /><b>Message:</b> " & entry.Message
                    lblResult.Text &= "<br /><b>Time Generated:</b> "
                    lblResult.Text &= entry.TimeGenerated
                    lblResult.Text &= "<br /><br />"
                End If
            Next
        End If
    End Sub

    Protected Sub chkAll_CheckedChanged(ByVal sender As Object, _
      ByVal e As EventArgs) Handles chkAll.CheckedChanged

        ' The chkAll control has AutoPostback = True.
        If chkAll.Checked Then
            txtSource.Text = ""
            txtSource.Enabled = False
        Else
            txtSource.Enabled = True
        End If
    End Sub

End Class
```

If you choose to display all the entries from the application log, the page will perform slowly. Two factors are at work here. First, it takes time to retrieve each event log entry; a typical application log can easily hold several thousand entries. Second, the code used to append text to the Label control is inefficient. Every time you add a new piece of information to the Label.Text property, .NET needs to generate a new String object. A better solution is to use the specialized System.Text.StringBuilder class, which is designed to handle intensive string processing with a lower overhead by managing an internal buffer or memory.

Here's the more efficient way you could write the string processing code:

```
' For maximum performance, join all the event
' information into one large string using the
' StringBuilder.
Dim sb As New System.Text.StringBuilder()

Dim log As New EventLog(txtLog.Text)

For Each entry As EventLogEntry In log.Entries
    ' Write the event entries to the StringBuilder.
    If chkAll.Checked Or entry.Source = txtSource.Text Then
        sb.Append("<b>Entry Type:</b> ")
        sb.Append(entry.EntryType.ToString())
        sb.Append("<br /><b>Message:</b> ")
        sb.Append(entry.Message)
        sb.Append("<br /><b>Time Generated:</b> ")
        sb.Append(entry.TimeGenerated.ToString())
        sb.Append("<br /><br />")
    End If
Next

' Copy the complete text to the web page.
lblResult.Text = sb.ToString()
```

■ **Tip** You can get around some of the limitations of the event log by using your own custom logging system. All the ingredients you need are built into the common class library. For example, you could store error information in a database using the data access techniques described in Chapter 15.

Error Pages

As you create and test an ASP.NET application, you'll become familiar with the rich error pages that are shown to describe unhandled errors. These rich error pages are extremely useful for diagnosing problems during development, because they contain a wealth of information. Some of this information includes the source code where the problem occurred (with the offending line highlighted), the type of error, and a detailed error message describing the problem. Figure 8-12 shows a sample rich error page.

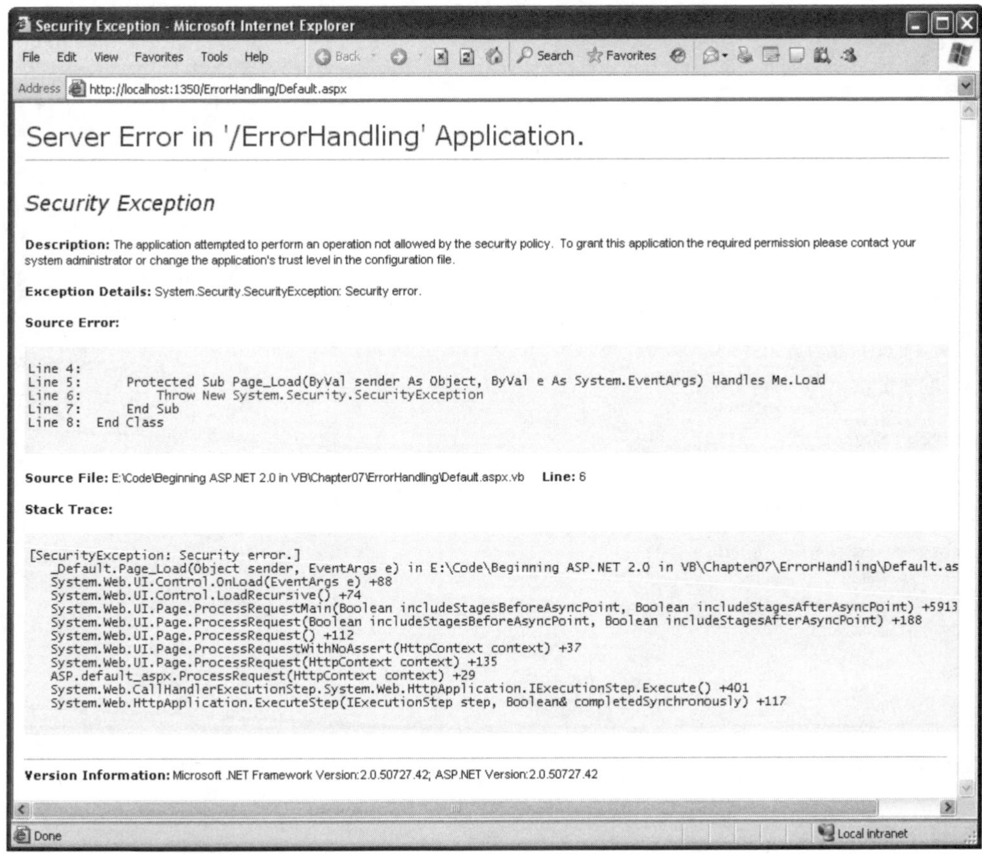

Figure 8-12. *A rich ASP.NET error page*

By default, this error page is shown only for local requests that are sent from the `http://localhost` domain. (This domain always refers to the current computer, regardless of its actual server name or Internet address.) ASP.NET doesn't show rich error pages for requests from other computers; they receive the rather unhelpful generic page shown in Figure 8-13. You can replace these error messages with a friendlier custom error page, as you'll learn a bit later, in the "Custom Error Pages" section.

This generic page lacks any specific details about the type of error or the offending code. Sharing that information with end users would be a security risk (potentially exposing sensitive details about the source code), and it would be completely unhelpful, because clients are never in a position to modify the source code themselves. Instead, the page includes a generic message explaining that an error has occurred and describing how to change the configuration settings (by modifying the web.config file) so that remote users also see the rich error pages. This is the task you'll tackle in the next section.

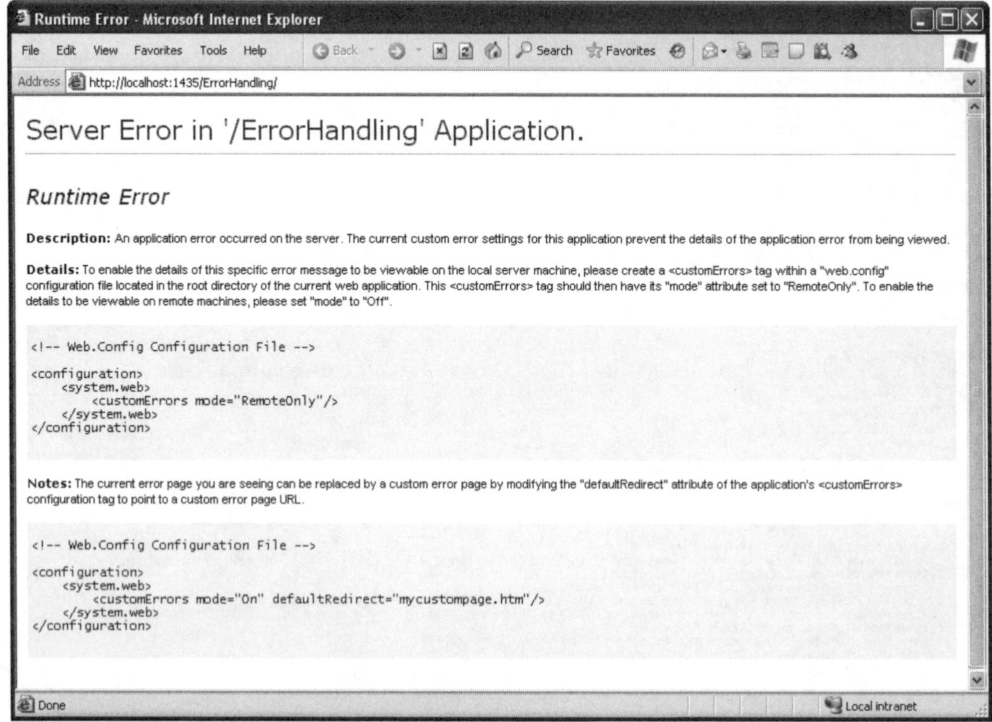

Figure 8-13. *A generic client error page*

Error Modes

You can change the configuration of your web application so that all users see the rich ASP.NET error pages with detailed error information. This option is intended as a testing tool. For example, in the initial rollout of an application beta, you might use field testers. These field testers would need to report specific information about application errors to aid in the debugging process. Similarly, you could use remote error pages if you're working with a team of developers and testing an ASP.NET application from a server on your local network. In both of these situations, the web application is uploaded to a remote computer before you begin testing it.

To change the error mode, you need to add the <customErrors> section to the web.config file. Here it is, with the default setting:

```
<configuration>
  <system.web>
    <customErrors mode="RemoteOnly" />
    ...
  </system.web>
  ...
</configuration>
```

Table 8-3 lists the options for the mode attribute. (Remember, generic error messages are the less-detailed error pages you saw in Figure 8-13, while rich error pages are the detailed error listings that include a portion of the source code and the stack trace, as shown in Figure 8-12.)

Table 8-3. *Error Modes*

Error Mode	Description
RemoteOnly	Generic error pages are shown for remote users. Rich error pages are shown for local requests (requests that are made from the current computer). This is the default setting.
Off	Rich error pages are shown for all users, regardless of the source of the request. This setting is helpful in many development scenarios but should not be used in a deployed application. (Not only will the rich error pages confuse users, but they may reveal sensitive information about your code.)
On	Generic error pages are shown for all users, regardless of the source of the request. This is the most secure option, but it complicates debugging because you'll need logging or tracing code to report error information.

It makes good sense to hide the rich error pages from ordinary users. However, the generic error pages really aren't that much more useful. The message they show has less information and won't reveal any secrets about your code (Figure 8-13), but it's still confusing for mere mortals. ASP.NET allows you to replace the generic error page with a custom error page of your own devising. The next section shows you how.

Custom Error Pages

In a deployed application, you should use the On or RemoteOnly error mode. Any errors in your application should be dealt with through error-handling code, which can then present a helpful and user-oriented message (rather than the developer-oriented code details in ASP.NET's rich error messages).

However, you can't catch every possible error in an ASP.NET application. For example, a hardware failure could occur spontaneously in the middle of an ordinary code statement that could not normally cause an error. More commonly, the user might encounter an HTTP error by requesting a page that doesn't exist. ASP.NET allows you to handle these problems with custom error pages.

You can implement custom error pages in two ways. You can create a single generic error page and configure ASP.NET to use it by modifying the web.config file as shown here:

```
<configuration>
  <system.web>
    <customErrors mode="RemoteOnly" defaultRedirect="DefaultError.aspx" />
  </system.web>
</configuration>
```

ASP.NET will now exhibit the following behavior:

- If ASP.NET encounters an HTTP error while serving the request, it will forward the user to the DefaultError.aspx web page.
- If ASP.NET encounters an unhandled application error and the mode is set to On (see Table 8-3), it will forward the user to the DefaultError.aspx. Remote users will never see the generic ASP.NET error page.

- If ASP.NET encounters an unhandled application error and the mode is set to Off, it will display the ASP.NET error page instead.
- If ASP.NET encounters an unhandled application error and the mode is set to RemoteOnly, the behavior depends on where the request is originating from. If it's a local request being made from the same computer, you'll get the ASP.NET error page with the diagnostic information. Otherwise, you'll see the DefaultError.aspx page.

■ **Note** What happens if an error occurs in the error page itself? In a custom error page (in this case, DefaultError.aspx), ASP.NET will not be able to handle an error. It will not try to reforward the user to the same page. Instead, it will display the normal client error page with the generic message.

You can also create error pages targeted at specific types of HTTP errors (such as the infamous 404 Not Found error or Access Denied). This technique is commonly used with websites to provide friendly equivalents for common problems. Figure 8-14 shows how one site handles this issue.

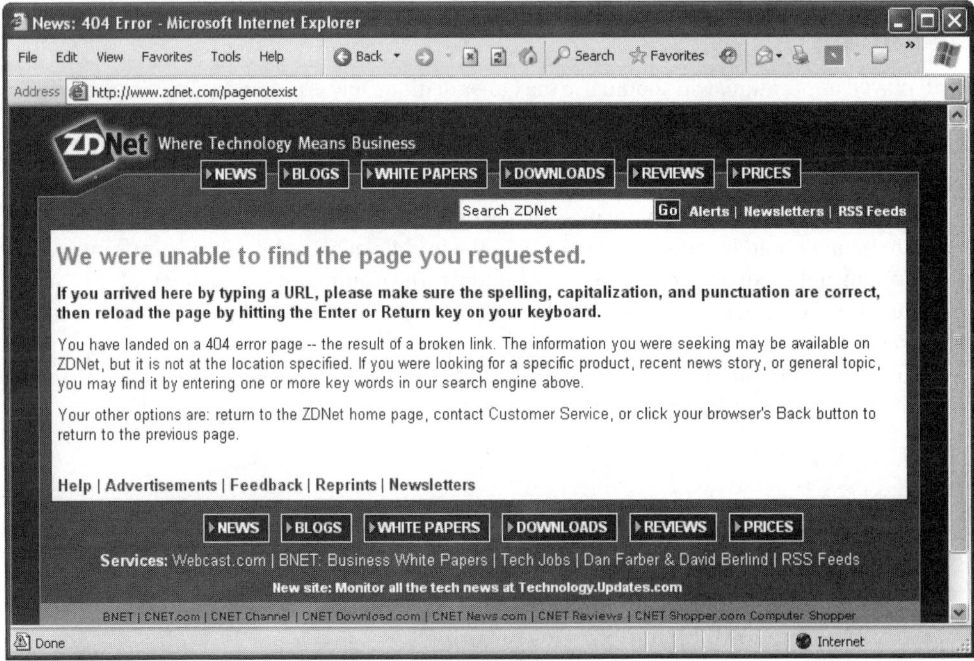

Figure 8-14. *A sample custom error page*

To define an error-specific custom page, you add an <error> element to the <customErrors> element. The <error> element identifies the HTTP error code and the redirect page.

```
<configuration>
  <system.web>
    <customErrors defaultRedirect="DefaultError.aspx">
      <error statusCode="404" redirect="404.aspx" />
    <customErrors>
  </system.web>
</configuration>
```

In this example, the user will be redirected to the 404.aspx page when requesting an ASP.NET page that doesn't exist. This custom error page may not work exactly the way you expect, because it comes into effect only if ASP.NET is handling the request.

For example, if you request the nonexistent page whateverpage.aspx, you'll be redirected to 404.aspx, because the .aspx file extension is registered to the ASP.NET service. However, if you request the nonexistent page whateverpage.html, ASP.NET will not process the request, and the default redirect setting specified in IIS will be used.

When an error occurs that isn't specifically addressed by a custom <error> element, the default error page will be used.

Page Tracing

ASP.NET's detailed error pages are extremely helpful when you're testing and perfecting an application. However, sometimes you need more information to verify that your application is performing properly or to track down logic errors, which may produce invalid data but no obvious exceptions.

You could try to catch these errors by recording diagnostic information in an event log, but this assumes that someone will actually review the log regularly. More aggressively, you could display some information directly in the web page. The problem with this strategy is that you need to remove (or at least comment out) all this extra code before you deploy your web application. Otherwise, your website users could see strange debugging messages when they least expect it.

Fortunately, there's an easier way to solve the problem without resorting to a homegrown solution. ASP.NET provides a feature called *tracing* that gives you a far more convenient and flexible way to report diagnostic information.

Enabling Tracing

To use tracing, you need to explicitly enable it. There are several ways to switch on tracing. One of the easiest ways is by adding an attribute to the Page directive in the .aspx file:

```
<%@ Page Trace="True" ... %>
```

You can also enable tracing using the built-in Trace object (which is an instance of the System.Web.TraceContext class). Here's an example of how you might turn tracing on in the Page.Load event handler:

```
Protected Sub Page_Load(ByVal sender As Object, _
  ByVal e As EventArgs) Handles Me.Load
    Trace.IsEnabled = True
End Sub
```

This technique is useful because it allows you to enable or disable tracing for a page under specific circumstances that you test for in your code.

Note that by default, once you enable tracing it will only apply to local requests. That prevents actual end users from seeing the tracing information. If you need to trace a web page from an offsite location, you should use a technique like the one shown previously (for query string activation). You'll also need to change some web.config settings to enable remote tracing. Information about modifying these settings is found at the end of this chapter, in the "Application-Level Tracing" section.

WHAT ABOUT VISUAL STUDIO?

Visual Studio provides a full complement of debugging tools that allow you to set breakpoints, step through code, and view the contents of variables while your program executes. Though you can use Visual Studio in conjunction with page tracing, you probably won't need to do so. Instead, page tracing will become more useful for debugging problems after you have deployed the application to a web server. Chapter 4 discussed Visual Studio debugging.

Tracing Information

ASP.NET tracing automatically provides a lengthy set of standard, formatted information. Figure 8-15 shows what this information looks like. To build this example, you can start with any basic ASP.NET page. Shown here is a rudimentary ASP.NET page with just a label and a button.

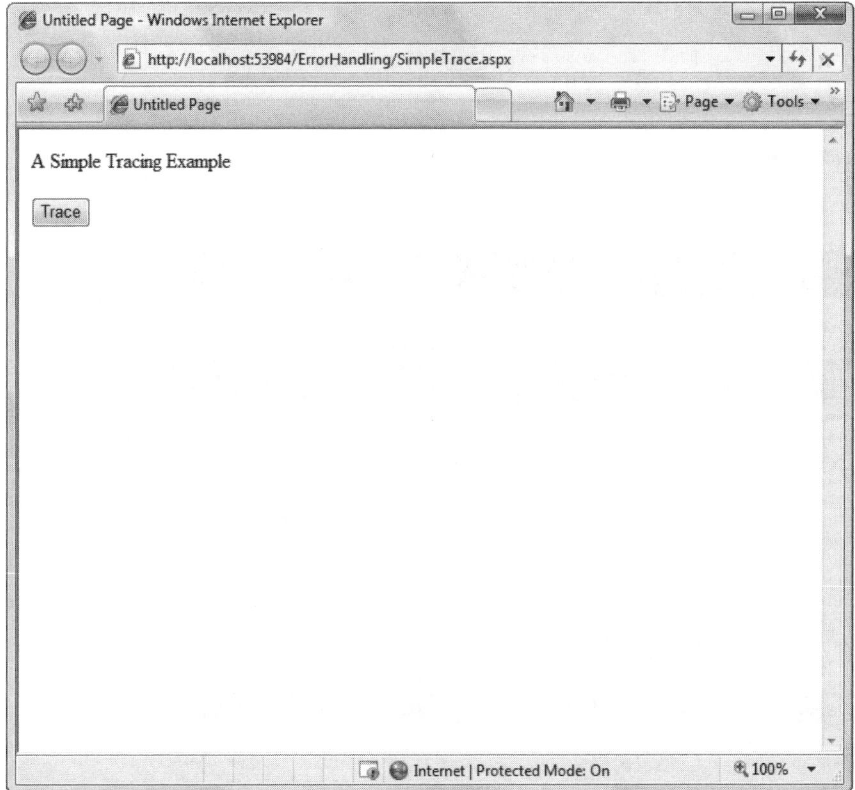

Figure 8-15. *A simple ASP.NET page*

On its own, this page does very little, displaying a single line of text. However, if you click the button, tracing is enabled by setting the Trace.IsEnabled property to True (as shown in the previous code snippet). When the page is rendered, it will include a significant amount of diagnostic information, as shown in Figure 8-16.

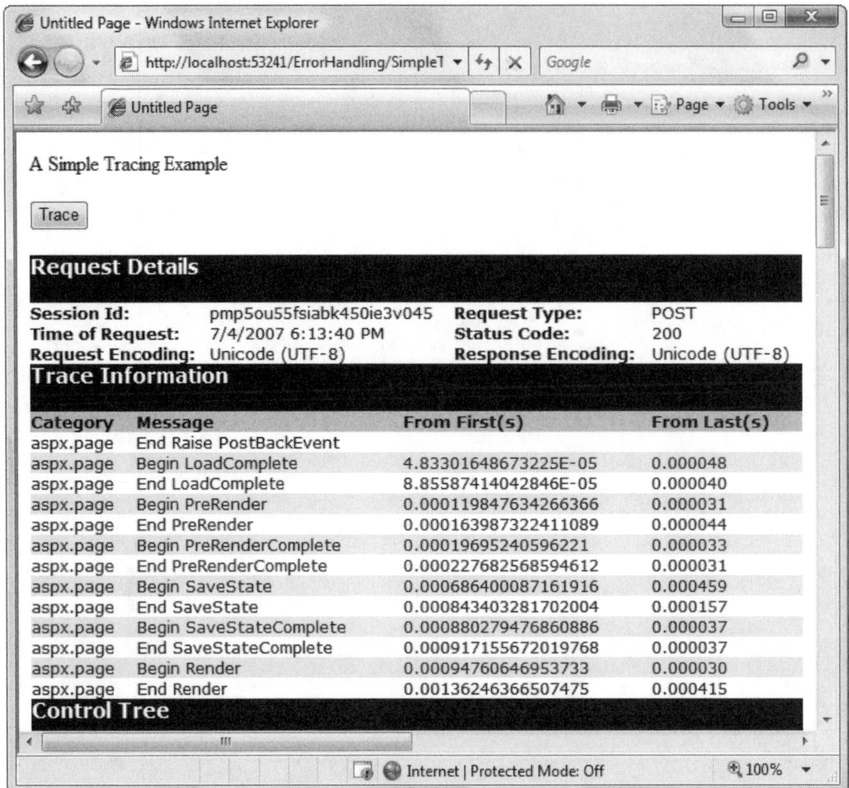

Figure 8-16. *Tracing the simple ASP.NET page*

Tracing information is provided in several different categories, which are described in the following sections. Depending on your page, you may not see all the tracing information. For example, if the page request doesn't supply any query string parameters, you won't see the QueryString collection. Similarly, if there's no data being held in application or session state, you won't see those sections either.

■ **Tip** If you're using style sheets, your rules may affect the formatting and layout of the trace information, potentially making it difficult to read. If this becomes a problem, you can use application-level tracing, as described later in this chapter (see the "Application-Level Tracing" section).

Request Details

This section includes some basic information such as the current session ID, the time the web request was made, and the type of web request and encoding (see Figure 8-17). Most of these details are fairly uninteresting, and you won't spend much time looking at them. The exception is the session ID—it allows you to determine when a new session is created. (Sessions are used to store information for a specific user in between page requests. You learned about them in Chapter 7.)

Request Details

Session Id:	pmp5ou55fsiabk450ie3v045	**Request Type:**	POST
Time of Request:	7/4/2007 6:13:40 PM	**Status Code:**	200
Request Encoding:	Unicode (UTF-8)	**Response Encoding:**	Unicode (UTF-8)

Figure 8-17. *Request details*

Trace Information

Trace information shows the different stages of processing that the page went through before being sent to the client (see Figure 8-18). Each section has additional information about how long it took to complete, as a measure from the start of the first stage (From First) and as a measure from the start of the previous stage (From Last). If you add your own trace messages (a technique described shortly), they will also appear in this section.

Trace Information

Category	Message	From First(s)	From Last(s)
aspx.page	End Raise PostBackEvent		
aspx.page	Begin LoadComplete	4.83301648673225E-05	0.000048
aspx.page	End LoadComplete	8.85587414042846E-05	0.000040
aspx.page	Begin PreRender	0.000119847634266366	0.000031
aspx.page	End PreRender	0.000163987322411089	0.000044
aspx.page	Begin PreRenderComplete	0.00019695240596221	0.000033
aspx.page	End PreRenderComplete	0.000227682568594612	0.000031
aspx.page	Begin SaveState	0.000686400087161916	0.000459
aspx.page	End SaveState	0.000843403281702004	0.000157
aspx.page	Begin SaveStateComplete	0.000880279476860886	0.000037
aspx.page	End SaveStateComplete	0.000917155672019768	0.000037
aspx.page	Begin Render	0.00094760646953733	0.000030
aspx.page	End Render	0.00136246366507475	0.000415

Figure 8-18. *Trace information*

Control Tree

The control tree shows you all the controls on the page, indented to show their hierarchy (which controls are contained inside other controls), as shown in Figure 8-19. In this simple page example, the control tree includes buttons named cmdWrite, cmdWrite_Category, cmdError, and cmdSession, all of which are explicitly defined in the web page markup. ASP.NET also adds literal controls automatically to represent spacing and any other static elements that aren't server controls (such as text or ordinary HTML tags). These controls appear in between the buttons in this example, and have automatically generated names like ctl00, ctl01, ctl02, and so on.

One useful feature of this section is the Viewstate column, which tells you how many bytes of space are required to persist the current information in the control. This can help you gauge whether enabling control state is detracting from performance, particularly when working with data-bound controls such as the GridView.

Control Tree

Control UniqueID	Type	Render Size Bytes (including children)	ViewState Size Bytes (excluding children)	ControlState Size Bytes (excluding children)
__Page	ASP.simpletrace_aspx	775	0	0
ctl02	System.Web.UI.LiteralControl	175	0	0
ctl00	System.Web.UI.HtmlControls.HtmlHead	46	0	0
ctl01	System.Web.UI.HtmlControls.HtmlTitle	33	0	0
ctl03	System.Web.UI.LiteralControl	14	0	0
form1	System.Web.UI.HtmlControls.HtmlForm	520	0	0
ctl04	System.Web.UI.LiteralControl	77	0	0
cmdTrace	System.Web.UI.WebControls.Button	67	0	0
ctl05	System.Web.UI.LiteralControl	12	0	0
ctl06	System.Web.UI.LiteralControl	20	0	0

Figure 8-19. *Control tree*

Session State and Application State

These sections display every item that is in the current session or application state. Each item in the appropriate state collection is listed with its name, type, and value. If you're storing simple pieces of string information, the value is straightforward—it's the actual text in the string. If you're storing an object, .NET calls the object's ToString() method to get an appropriate string representation. For complex objects that don't override ToString() to provide anything useful, the result may just be the class name.

Figure 8-20 shows the session state section after you've added two items to session state (an ordinary string and a DataSet object). Chapter 7 has more about using session state.

Session State

Session Key	Type	Value
TestString	System.String	This is just a string.
MyDataSet	System.Data.DataSet	System.Data.DataSet

Figure 8-20. *Session state*

Request Cookies and Response Cookies

These sections display the cookies that were sent by the web browser with the request for this page, and the cookies that were returned by the web server with the response. ASP.NET shows the content and the size of each cookie in bytes.

Figure 8-21 shows an example with a page that uses a cookie named Preferences that stores a single piece of information: a user name. (You learned to write the code that creates this cookie in Chapter 7.) In addition, the web browser receives a cookie named ASP.NET_SessionId, which ASP.NET creates automatically to store the current session ID.

There's one quirk with the list of cookies in the trace information. If you haven't created at least one custom cookie of your own, you won't see *any* cookies, including the ones that ASP.NET creates automatically (like the session cookie). ASP.NET assumes that if you aren't using cookies yourself, you aren't interested in seeing these details.

Request Cookies Collection		
Name	**Value**	**Size**
ASP.NET_SessionId	lzydtbz0iw5dvoyhne2oevz3	42

Response Cookies Collection		
Name	**Value**	**Size**
Preferences	(Name=Jackson Polenta)	32

Figure 8-21. *Cookies collections*

Headers Collection

This section lists all the HTTP headers (see Figure 8-22). Technically, the headers are bits of information that are sent to the server as part of a request. They include information about the browser making the request, the types of content it supports, and the language it uses. In addition, the Response Headers Collection lists the headers that are sent to the client as part of a response (just before the actual HTML that's shown in the browser). The set of response headers is smaller, and it includes details like the version of ASP.NET and the type of content that's being sent (text/html for web pages).

Generally, you don't need to use the header information directly. Instead, ASP.NET takes this information into account automatically.

Headers Collection	
Name	**Value**
Cache-Control	no-cache
Connection	Keep-Alive
Content-Length	162
Content-Type	application/x-www-form-urlencoded
Accept	image/gif, image/x-xbitmap, image/jpeg, image/pjpeg, application/x-ms-application, application xpsdocument, application/xaml+xml, application/x-ms-xbap, application/vnd.ms-excel, applicati powerpoint, application/msword, application/x-shockwave-flash, application/ag-plugin, */*
Accept-Encoding	gzip, deflate
Accept-Language	en-us
Host	localhost:53241
Referer	http://localhost:53241/ErrorHandling/SimpleTrace.aspx
User-Agent	Mozilla/4.0 (compatible; MSIE 7.0; Windows NT 6.0; SLCC1; .NET CLR 2.0.50727; Media Cente
UA-CPU	x86

Response Headers Collection	
Name	**Value**
X-AspNet-Version	2.0.50727
Cache-Control	private
Content-Type	text/html

Figure 8-22. *Headers collection*

Form Collection

This section lists the posted-back form information. The form information includes all the values that are submitted by web controls, like the text in a text box and the current selection in a list box. The ASP.NET web controls pull the information they need out of the form collection automatically, so you rarely need to worry about it.

Figure 8-23 shows the form values for the simple page shown in Figure 8-15. It includes the hidden view state field, another hidden field that's used for event validation (a low-level ASP.NET feature that helps prevent people from tampering with your web pages before posting them back), and a field for the cmdTrace button, which is the only web control on the page.

Form Collection	
Name	**Value**
__VIEWSTATE	/wEPDwUKMTQ2OTkzNDMyMWRk6PdTEsrgNkgFP9+LyoOOXsjohnM=
cmdTrace	Trace
__EVENTVALIDATION	/wEWAgL9lt3/BQLqhI2yDuBna1E/STtAj+7NCZA4/ezpy4LZ

Figure 8-23. *Form collection*

Query String Collection

This section lists the variables and values submitted in the query string. You can see this information directly in the web page URL (in the address box in the browser). However, if the query string consists of several different values and contains a lot of information, it may be easier to review the individual items in the trace display.

Figure 8-24 shows the information for a page that was requested with two query string values, one named search and the other named style. You can try this out with the SimpleTrace.aspx page by typing in `?search=cat&style=full` at the end of the URL in the address box of your web browser.

Querystring Collection	
Name	Value
search	cat
style	full

Figure 8-24. *Query string collection*

Server Variables

This section lists all the server variables and their contents. You don't generally need to examine this information. Note also that if you want to examine a server variable programmatically, you can do so by name with the built-in Request.ServerVariables collection or by using one of the more useful higher-level properties from the Request object.

Writing Trace Information

The default trace log provides a set of important information that can allow you to monitor some important aspects of your application, such as the current state contents and the time taken to execute portions of code. In addition, you'll often want to generate your own tracing messages. For example, you might want to output the value of a variable at various points in execution so you can compare it with an expected value. Similarly, you might want to output messages when the code reaches certain points in execution so you can verify that various procedures are being used (and are used in the order you expect). Once again, these are tasks you can also achieve using Visual Studio debugging, but tracing is an invaluable technique when you're working with a web application that's been deployed to a test web server.

To write a custom trace message, you use the Write() method or the Warn() method of the built-in Trace object. These methods are equivalent. The only difference is that Warn() displays the message in red lettering, which makes it easier to distinguish from other messages in the list. Here's a code snippet that writes a trace message when the user clicks a button:

```
Protected Sub cmdWrite_Click(ByVal sender As Object, _
  ByVal e As EventArgs) Handles cmdWrite.Click

    Trace.Write("About to place an item in session state.")
    Session("Test") = "Contents"
    Trace.Write("Placed item in session state.")
End Sub
```

These messages appear in the trace information section of the page, along with the default messages that ASP.NET generates automatically (see Figure 8-25).

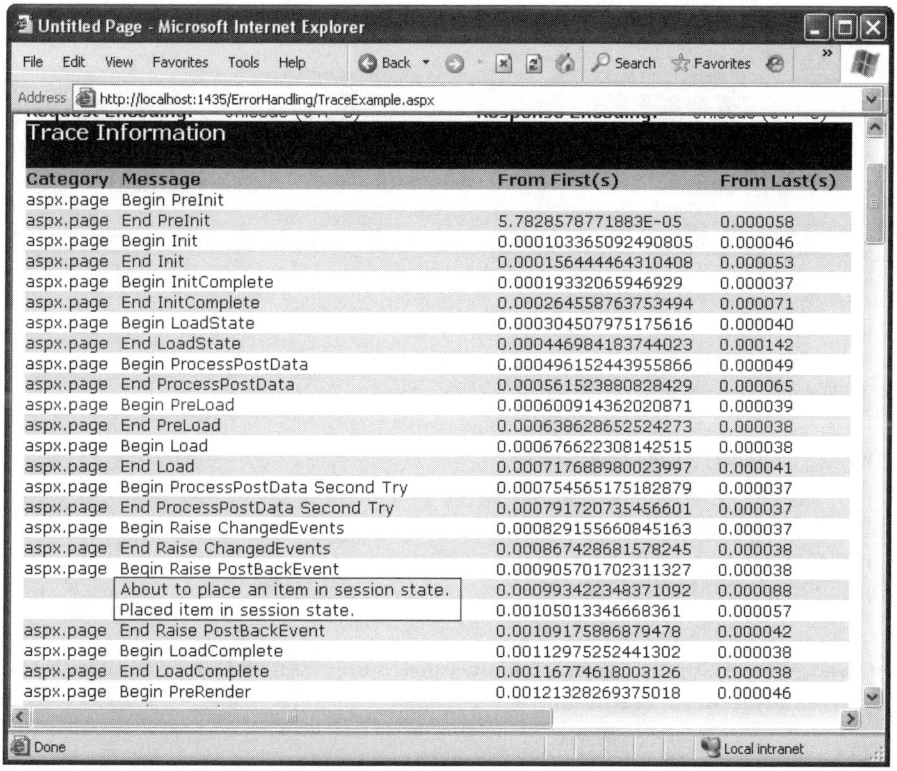
Untitled Page - Microsoft Internet Explorer
File Edit View Favorites Tools Help
Back Search Favorites
Address http://localhost:1435/ErrorHandling/TraceExample.aspx
Trace Information
Category Message From First(s) From Last(s)
aspx.page Begin PreInit
aspx.page End PreInit 5.7828578771883E-05 0.000058
aspx.page Begin Init 0.000103365092490805 0.000046
aspx.page End Init 0.000156444464310408 0.000053
aspx.page Begin InitComplete 0.00019332065946929 0.000037
aspx.page End InitComplete 0.000264558763753494 0.000071
aspx.page Begin LoadState 0.000304507975175616 0.000040
aspx.page End LoadState 0.000446984183744023 0.000142
aspx.page Begin ProcessPostData 0.000496152443955866 0.000049
aspx.page End ProcessPostData 0.000561523880828429 0.000065
aspx.page Begin PreLoad 0.000600914362020871 0.000039
aspx.page End PreLoad 0.000638628652524273 0.000038
aspx.page Begin Load 0.000676622308142515 0.000038
aspx.page End Load 0.000717688980023997 0.000041
aspx.page Begin ProcessPostData Second Try 0.000754565175182879 0.000037
aspx.page End ProcessPostData Second Try 0.000791720735456601 0.000037
aspx.page Begin Raise ChangedEvents 0.000829155660845163 0.000037
aspx.page End Raise ChangedEvents 0.000867428681578245 0.000038
aspx.page Begin Raise PostBackEvent 0.000905701702311327 0.000038
About to place an item in session state. 0.000993422348371092 0.000088
Placed item in session state. 0.00105013346668361 0.000057
aspx.page End Raise PostBackEvent 0.00109175886879478 0.000042
aspx.page Begin LoadComplete 0.00112975252441302 0.000038
aspx.page End LoadComplete 0.00116774618003126 0.000038
aspx.page Begin PreRender 0.00121328269375018 0.000046
Done
Local intranet

Figure 8-25. *Custom trace messages*

You can also use an overloaded method of Write() or Warn() that allows you to specify the category. A common use of this field is to indicate the current method, as shown in Figure 8-26.

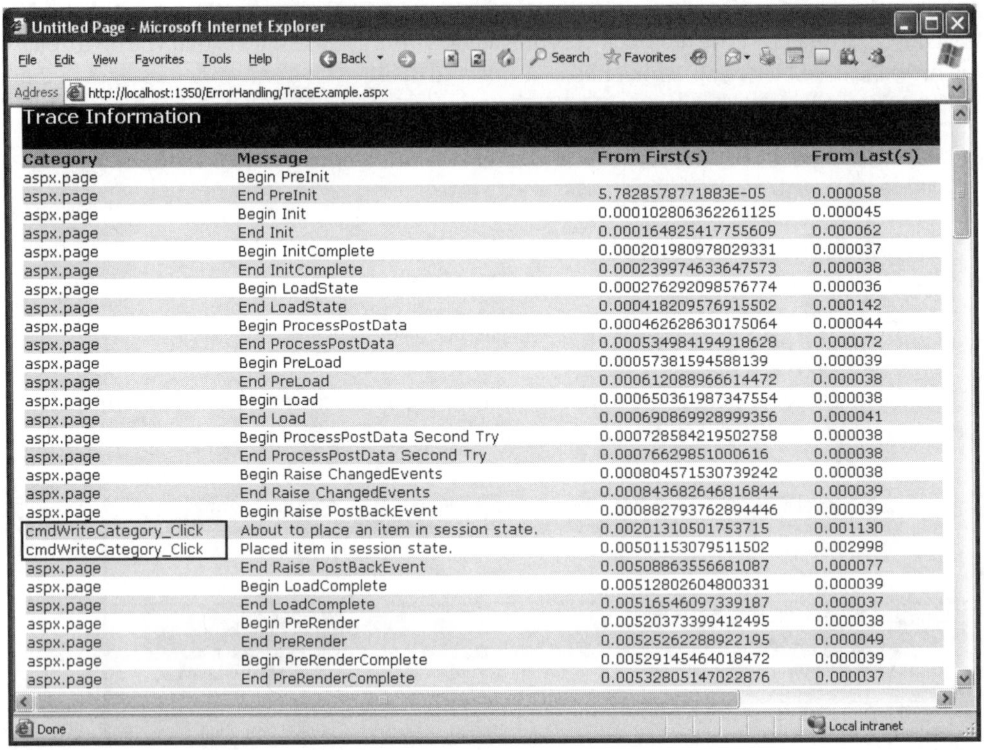

Untitled Page - Microsoft Internet Explorer

http://localhost:1350/ErrorHandling/TraceExample.aspx

Trace Information

Category	Message	From First(s)	From Last(s)
aspx.page	Begin PreInit		
aspx.page	End PreInit	5.7828578771883E-05	0.000058
aspx.page	Begin Init	0.000102806362261125	0.000045
aspx.page	End Init	0.000164825417755609	0.000062
aspx.page	Begin InitComplete	0.000201980978029331	0.000037
aspx.page	End InitComplete	0.000239974633647573	0.000038
aspx.page	Begin LoadState	0.000276292098576774	0.000036
aspx.page	End LoadState	0.000418209576915502	0.000142
aspx.page	Begin ProcessPostData	0.000462628630175064	0.000044
aspx.page	End ProcessPostData	0.000534984194918628	0.000072
aspx.page	Begin PreLoad	0.00057381594588139	0.000039
aspx.page	End PreLoad	0.000612088966614472	0.000038
aspx.page	Begin Load	0.000650361987347554	0.000038
aspx.page	End Load	0.000690869928999356	0.000041
aspx.page	Begin ProcessPostData Second Try	0.000728584219502758	0.000038
aspx.page	End ProcessPostData Second Try	0.00076629851000616	0.000038
aspx.page	Begin Raise ChangedEvents	0.000804571530739242	0.000038
aspx.page	End Raise ChangedEvents	0.000843682646816844	0.000039
aspx.page	Begin Raise PostBackEvent	0.000882793762894446	0.000039
cmdWriteCategory_Click	About to place an item in session state.	0.00201310501753715	0.001130
cmdWriteCategory_Click	Placed item in session state.	0.00501153079511502	0.002998
aspx.page	End Raise PostBackEvent	0.00508863556681087	0.000077
aspx.page	Begin LoadComplete	0.00512802604800331	0.000039
aspx.page	End LoadComplete	0.00516546097339187	0.000037
aspx.page	Begin PreRender	0.00520373399412495	0.000038
aspx.page	End PreRender	0.00525262288922195	0.000049
aspx.page	Begin PreRenderComplete	0.00529145464018472	0.000039
aspx.page	End PreRenderComplete	0.00532805147022876	0.000037

Done Local intranet

Figure 8-26. *A categorized trace message*

```
Protected Sub cmdWriteCategory_Click(ByVal sender As Object, _
  ByVal e As System.EventArgs) Handles cmdWriteCategory.Click

    Trace.Write("cmdWriteCategory_Click", _
      "About to place an item in session state.")
    Session("Test") = "Contents"
    Trace.Write("cmdWriteCategory_Click", _
      "Placed item in session state.")
End Sub
```

Alternatively, you can supply category and message information with an exception object that will automatically be described in the trace log, as shown in Figure 8-27.

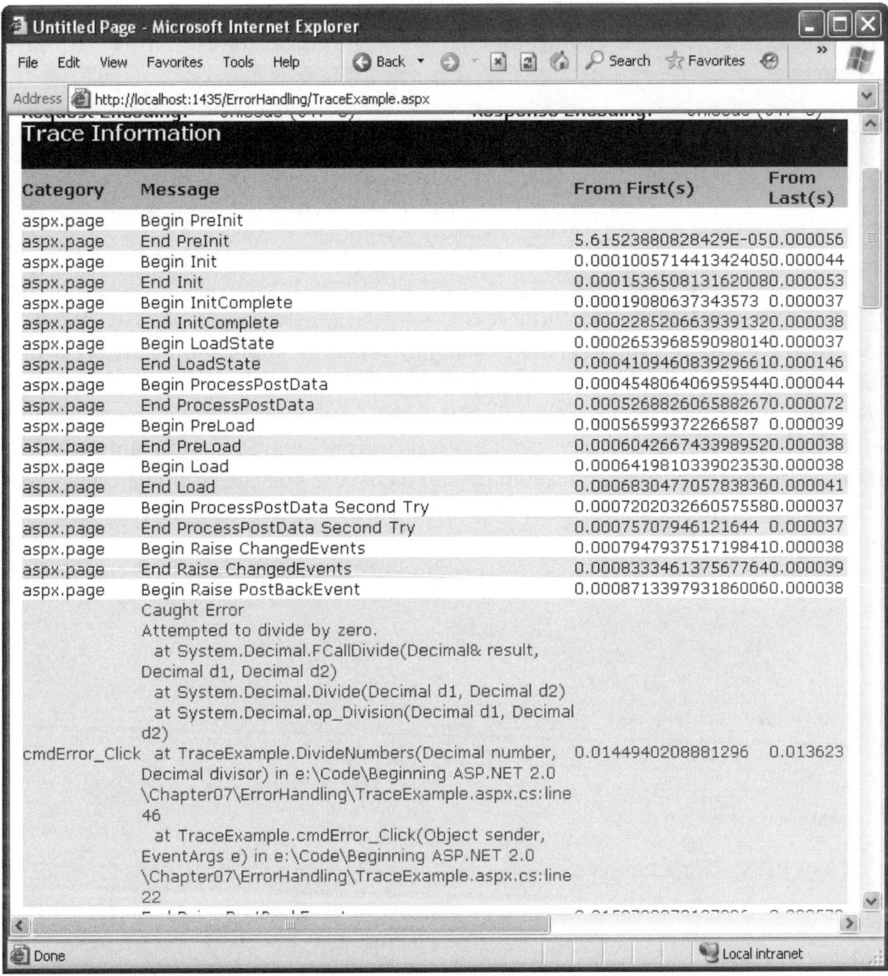

Figure 8-27. *An exception trace message*

```
Protected Sub cmdError_Click(ByVal sender As Object, _
  ByVal e As EventArgs) Handles cmdError.Click

    Try
        DivideNumbers(5, 0)
    Catch err As Exception
        Trace.Warn("cmdError_Click", "Caught Error", err)
    End Try
End Sub

Private Function DivideNumbers(ByVal number As Decimal, _
  ByVal divisor As Decimal) As Decimal
    Return number/divisor
End Sub
```

By default, trace messages are listed in the order they were written by your code. Alternatively, you can specify that messages should be sorted by category using the TraceMode attribute in the Page directive:

```
<%@ Page Trace="True" TraceMode="SortByCategory" %>
```

or the TraceMode property of the Trace object in your code:

```
Trace.TraceMode = TraceMode.SortByCategory
```

Application-Level Tracing

Application-level tracing allows you to enable tracing for an entire application. However, the tracing information won't be displayed in the page. Instead, it will be collected and stored in memory for a short amount of time. You can review the recently traced information by requesting a special URL. Application-level tracing provides several advantages. The tracing information won't be mangled by the formatting and layout in your web page, you can compare trace information from different requests, and you can review the trace information that's recorded for someone else's request.

To enable application-level tracing, you need to modify settings in the web.config file, as shown here:

```
<configuration>
  <system.web>
    <trace enabled="true" requestLimit="10" pageOutput="false"
     traceMode="SortByTime" localOnly="true" />
  </system.web>
</configuration>
```

Table 8-4 lists the tracing options.

Table 8-4. *Tracing Options*

Attribute	Values	Description
enabled	true, false	Turns application-level tracing on or off.
requestLimit	Any integer (for example, 10)	Stores tracing information for a maximum number of HTTP requests. Unlike page-level tracing, this allows you to collect a batch of information from multiple requests. When the maximum is reached, ASP.NET may discard the information from the oldest request (which is the default behavior) or the information from the new request, depending on the mostRecent setting.
pageOutput	true, false	Determines whether tracing information will be displayed on the page (as it is with page-level tracing). If you choose false, you'll still be able to view the collected information by requesting trace.axd from the virtual directory where your application is running.
traceMode	SortByTime, SortByCategory	Determines the sort order of trace messages.

Table 8-4. *Tracing Options*

Attribute	Values	Description
localOnly	true, false	Determines whether tracing information will be shown only to local clients (clients using the same computer) or can be shown to remote clients as well. By default, this is true and remote clients cannot see tracing information.
mostRecent	true, false	Keeps only the most recent trace messages if true. When the requestLimit maximum is reached, the information for the oldest request is abandoned every time a new request is received. If false (the default), ASP.NET stops collecting new trace messages when the limit is reached.

To view tracing information, you request the trace.axd file in the web application's root directory. This file doesn't actually exist; instead, ASP.NET automatically intercepts the request and interprets it as a request for the tracing information. It will then list the most recent collected requests, provided you're making the request from the local machine or have enabled remote tracing (see Figure 8-28).

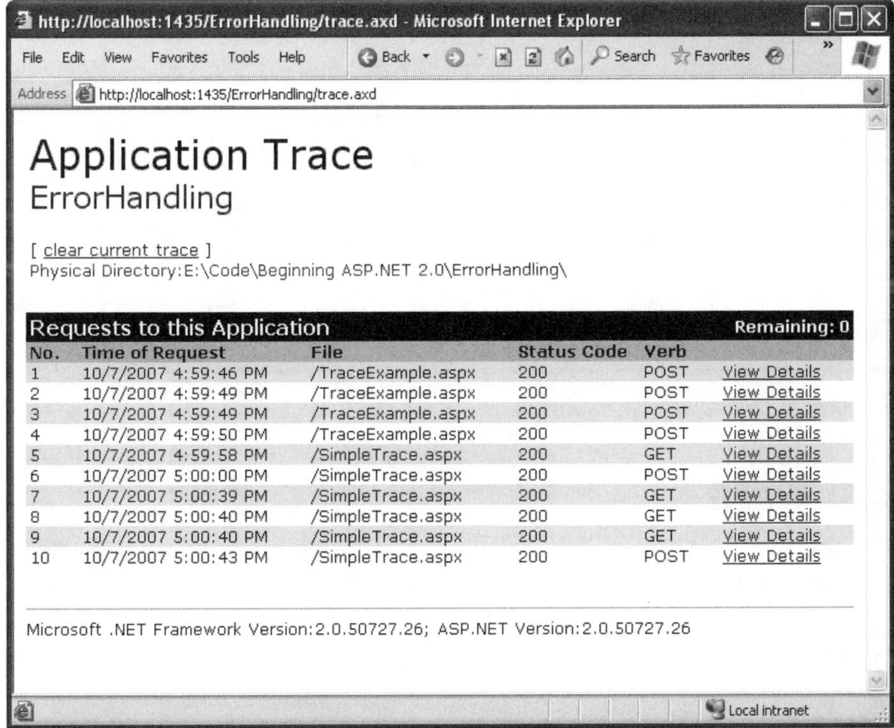

Figure 8-28. *Traced application requests*

You can see the detailed information for any request by clicking the View Details link. This provides a useful way to store tracing information for a short period of time and allows you to review it without needing to see the actual pages (see Figure 8-29).

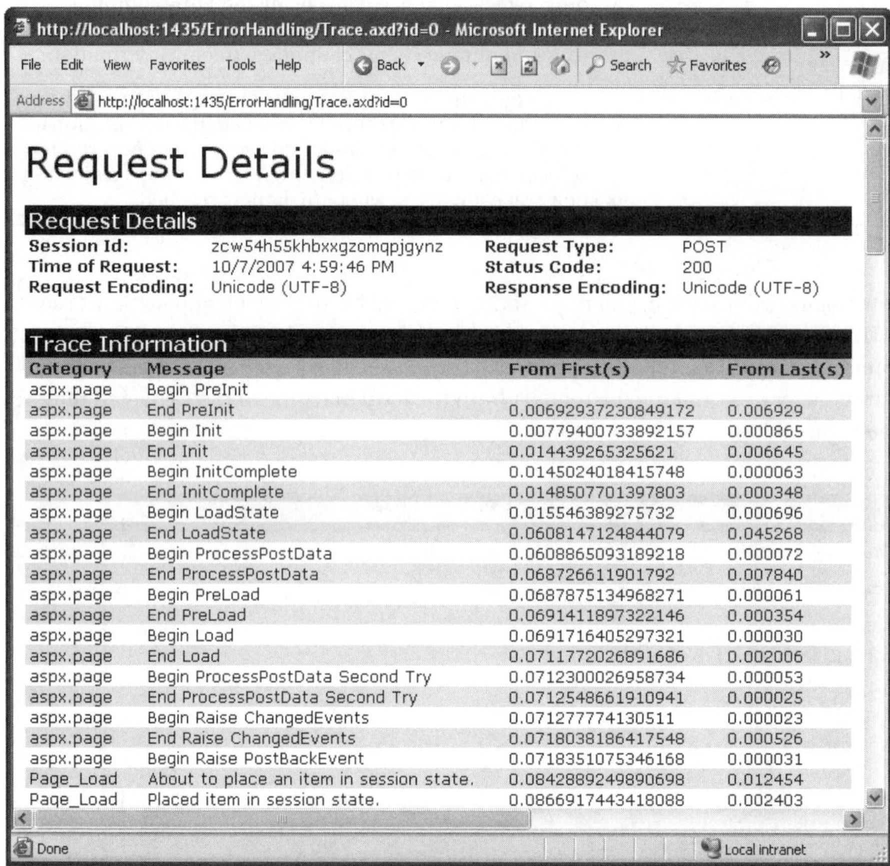

Category	Message	From First(s)	From Last(s)
aspx.page	Begin PreInit		
aspx.page	End PreInit	0.00692937230849172	0.006929
aspx.page	Begin Init	0.00779400733892157	0.000865
aspx.page	End Init	0.014439265325621	0.006645
aspx.page	Begin InitComplete	0.0145024018415748	0.000063
aspx.page	End InitComplete	0.0148507701397803	0.000348
aspx.page	Begin LoadState	0.015546389275732	0.000696
aspx.page	End LoadState	0.0608147124844079	0.045268
aspx.page	Begin ProcessPostData	0.0608865093189218	0.000072
aspx.page	End ProcessPostData	0.068726611901792	0.007840
aspx.page	Begin PreLoad	0.0687875134968271	0.000061
aspx.page	End PreLoad	0.0691411897322146	0.000354
aspx.page	Begin Load	0.0691716405297321	0.000030
aspx.page	End Load	0.0711772026891686	0.002006
aspx.page	Begin ProcessPostData Second Try	0.0712300026958734	0.000053
aspx.page	End ProcessPostData Second Try	0.0712548661910941	0.000025
aspx.page	Begin Raise ChangedEvents	0.071277774130511	0.000023
aspx.page	End Raise ChangedEvents	0.0718038186417548	0.000526
aspx.page	Begin Raise PostBackEvent	0.0718351075346168	0.000031
Page_Load	About to place an item in session state.	0.0842889249890698	0.012454
Page_Load	Placed item in session state.	0.0866917443418088	0.002403

Figure 8-29. *One of the traced application requests*

The Last Word

One of the most significant differences between an ordinary website and a professional web application is often in how it deals with errors. In this chapter, you learned the different lines of defense you can use in .NET, including structured error handling, logging, custom error pages, and tracing.

CHAPTER 9

Deploying ASP.NET Applications

The .NET Framework makes it almost painless to deploy any type of application, including ASP.NET websites. Often, you won't need to do much more than copy your web application directory to the web server and then configure it as a virtual directory. The headaches of the past—registering components and troubleshooting version conflicts—are gone. This simplicity makes it practical to deploy websites by manually copying files, rather than relying on a dedicated setup tool.

In this chapter, you'll begin by learning about IIS (Internet Information Services), the Windows operating system component that acts as a web server. You'll explore how to create virtual directories for your web applications, making them available to other clients on the network or on the Internet. Finally, you'll consider the tools in Visual Studio that simplify website deployment.

ASP.NET Applications and the Web Server

ASP.NET applications always work in conjunction with a web server—a specialized piece of software that accepts requests over HTTP (Hypertext Transport Protocol) and serves content. When you're running your web application in Visual Studio, you use the test web server that's built in. When you deploy your website to a broader audience, you need a real web server, such as IIS.

Web servers run special software to support mail exchange, FTP and HTTP access, and everything else clients need in order to access web content. Before you can go any further, you need to understand a little more about how web servers work.

How Web Servers Work

The easiest job a web server has is to provide ordinary HTML pages. When you request such a file, the web server simply reads it off the hard drive (or retrieves it from an in-memory cache) and sends the complete document to the browser, which displays it. In this case, the web server is just a glorified file server that waits for network requests and dishes out the corresponding documents.

When you use a web server in conjunction with dynamic content such as an ASP.NET page, something more interesting takes place. On its own, the web server has no idea how to process ASP.NET tags or run VB code. However, it's able to enlist the help of the ASP.NET engine to perform all the heavy lifting. Figure 9-1 diagrams how this process works for ASP and ASP.NET pages. For example, when you request the page Default.aspx, the web server sends the request over to the ASP.NET engine (which starts automatically if needed). The ASP.NET engine loads the requested page, runs the code it contains, and then creates the final HTML document, which it passes back to IIS. IIS then sends the HTML document to the client.

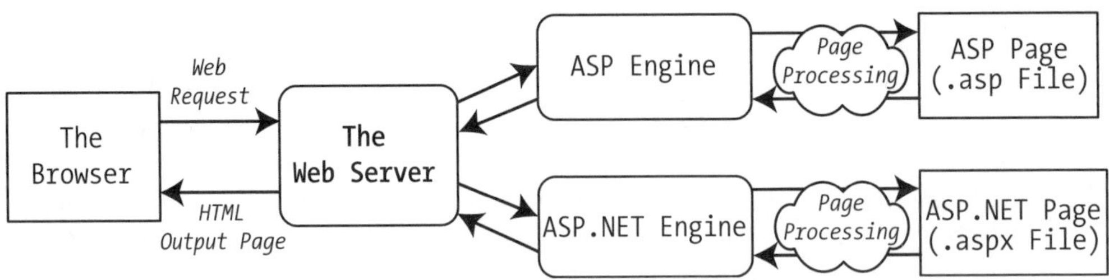

Figure 9-1. *How IIS handles an ASP file request*

At this point, you might be wondering how the web server knows when it needs to get the ASP or ASP.NET engine involved. Essentially, the web server looks at the file extension of the requested page (such as .asp or .aspx) to determine the type of content. The web server compares this extension against a list to determine what program owns this file type. For example, the web server's list indicates that the .aspx extension is owned by the aspnet_isapi.dll component in the c:\Windows\Microsoft.NET\Framework\v2.0.50727 directory. The aspnet_isapi.dll component is known as an *ISAPI extension*, because it uses the ISAPI (Internet Server API) model to plug into the web server.

■ **Note** In theory, you can tweak the file type registrations differently for each application. This way, different websites can use different versions of the ASP.NET engine. You'll see how to do this in the "Registering the ASP.NET File Mappings" section.

All web servers perform the same task as that shown in Figure 9-1. However, when you run an ASP.NET application in Visual Studio, you don't need to worry about deployment and file type registration. That's because Visual Studio includes a built-in web server. It receives the requests for the pages in your web application and then runs the corresponding code. This test web server has a significant limitation—it only accepts requests from the local computer. In other words, there's no way for other people on other computers to access your website.

To run your web application outside the development environment, you need a more powerful web server. The web server software runs continuously on your computer (or, more likely, a dedicated web server computer). This means it's ready to handle HTTP requests at any time and provide your pages to clients who connect from the same network or over the Internet. On Microsoft Windows operating systems, the web server you'll use is IIS.

In most cases, you won't be developing on the same computer you use to host your website. If you do, you will hamper the performance of your web server by tying it up with development work. You will also frustrate clients if a buggy test application crashes the computer and leaves the website unavailable, or if you accidentally overwrite the deployed web application with a work in progress. Generally, you'll perfect your web application on another computer and then copy all the files to the web server.

WEB HOSTING COMPANIES

In this chapter, you'll learn how to do all the deployment work—including installing IIS and configuring your website—by hand. If you're responsible for setting up the web server (for example, your company has a web server on site, or you're using your web application to serve a smaller audience on a local network), you'll need these skills.

However, many developers aren't so intimately involved in the deployment of their web applications. Instead, they use a web hosting company that supports ASP.NET 3.5. If you're in this situation, you simply need to copy your web application files to the web server using an FTP program, or the support that's built into Visual Studio, which you'll explore in this chapter. In this case, you may not be as interested in the specifics of IIS that are covered in this chapter. However, you may still want to review them just to understand more about how web hosting and IIS work.

The Virtual Directory

When you deploy your web application to a web server, it's exposed through something called a *virtual directory*. A virtual directory is simply the public face of your website directory.

For example, your website might exist in a directory on the server named c:\MySite. To allow remote users to access this website through their browsers, you could expose it as a virtual directory. The virtual directory name might match the real directory name (in this case, MySite), or it might be something different. When the user requests a page in a virtual directory (say, http://WebServer/MySite/Checkout.aspx), the web server looks for the corresponding file in the corresponding physical directory (c:\MySite\Checkout.aspx). You'll learn more about this process—how URL requests are processed by the web server—in the next section.

Web Application URLs

You can use ASP.NET applications in a variety of different environments, including LANs (local area networks) and over the Internet. To understand the difference, it helps to review a little about how web servers work with networks and the Internet.

A *network* is defined simply as a group of devices connected by communication links. A traditional LAN connects devices over a limited area, such as within a company site or an individual's house. Multiple LANs are connected into a WAN (wide area network) using a variety of technologies. In fact, the Internet is nothing more than a high-speed backbone that joins millions of LANs.

The cornerstone of the Internet is IP (Internet Protocol). On an IP network, each computer is given a unique 32-bit number called an *IP address*. An IP address is typically written as four numbers from 0 to 255 separated by periods (as in 192.145.0.1). To access another computer over a network, you need to use its IP address.

Of course, IP addresses aren't easy to remember and don't make for great marketing campaigns. To make life easier, web servers on the Internet usually register unique *domain names* such as www.microsoft.com. This domain name is mapped to the IP address by a special catalog, which is maintained by a network of servers on the Internet. This network, called the DNS (Domain Name Service), is a core part of the infrastructure of the Internet. When you type `http://www.microsoft.com` in a web browser, the browser contacts a DNS server, looks up the IP address that's mapped to www.microsoft.com, and contacts it.

So, what effect does all this have on the accessibility of your website? To be easily reached over the Internet, the web server you use needs to be in the DNS registry. To get in the DNS registry, you must have a fixed IP address. Commercial Internet service providers won't give you a fixed IP address unless you're willing to pay a sizable fee. In fact, most will place you behind a firewall or some type of NAT (network address translation), which will hide your computer's IP address. The same is true in most company networks, which are shielded from the outside world.

ASP.NET applications don't *need* to be accessible over the Internet. Many are useful within an internal network. In this case, you don't need to worry about the DNS registry. Other computers can access your website using either the IP address of your machine or, more likely, the network computer name.

For example, imagine you deploy an application to a virtual directory named MyWebApp. On the web server, you can access it like this:

```
http://localhost/MyWebApp
```

■ **Tip** Remember, localhost is a special part of the URL called a *loopback alias*. It always points to the current computer, whatever its name is. Technically, the loopback alias is mapped to something called the *loopback address*, which is the IP address 127.0.0.1. You can use the alias or the numeric address interchangeably.

Assuming the computer is named MyWebServer, here's how you can access the virtual web directory on another computer on the same LAN:

```
http://MyWebServer/MyWebApp
```

■ **Tip** If you don't know the name of your computer, right-click the My Computer icon either on your desktop or in Windows Explorer, and select Properties. Then choose the Computer Name tab. Look for Full Computer Name.

Now, assume that MyWebServer is registered in the DNS as www.MyDomain.com and is exposed to the Internet. You could then use the following URL:

```
http://www.MyDomain.com/MyWebApp
```

Finally, you can always use the computer's IP address, provided the computer is on the same network or visible on the Internet. Assuming the IP address is 123.5.123.4, here's the URL you would use:

```
http://123.5.123.4/MyWebApp
```

Because internal networks often use dynamic IP addresses, and DNS registration changes, using the computer name or domain name to access a website is almost always the best approach.

If you study the URLs that the built-in web server in Visual Studio uses, you'll notice they're a little different than what you usually see when surfing the Internet. Namely, they include a port number. That means instead of requesting a page like this:

```
http://localhost/MyWebApp/Default.aspx
```

you might request a page like this:

```
http://localhost:2040/MyWebApp/Default.aspx
```

That's because the Visual Studio web server watches requests on a dynamically chosen port number. (In this example, the port number is 2040, but you'll see that it changes each time you run Visual Studio.) By using a dynamic port number, Visual Studio makes sure its built-in web server doesn't infringe on any other web server software you have on the computer.

Real web servers are almost always configured to monitor port 80 (and port 443 for encrypted traffic). If you don't type in a port number for a URL, the browser assumes you're using port 80.

Web Farms

Some applications run on *web farms*, a group of server computers that share the responsibility of handling requests. Usually web farms are reserved for high-powered web applications that need to be able to handle heavy loads, because multiple computers can deal with more simultaneous surfers than a single web server. However, web farms are overkill for many small- and midsized websites.

The way a web farm works is deceptively simple. Essentially, instead of placing web application files on a single web server, you place a copy on several separate web servers. When a request is received for your website, it's directed to one of these web servers (based on which one has the lightest load). That web server then deals with the request. Obviously, if you decide to update your application, you need to make sure you update each web server in the web farm with the same version to prevent discrepancies.

Some web hosting companies use web farms to host multiple websites. For example, your website might be running on more than one web server, but each of these web servers might also host multiple websites. This provides a flexible deployment model that lets different web applications share resources.

Web farms pose a few new challenges. For example, if you decide to use session state, it's important you use StateServer or SQLServer mode, as described in Chapter 9. Otherwise, a user's session information might get trapped on one server. If a subsequent request is directed to another server, the information will be lost, and a new session will be created.

Another wrinkle occurs with view state (discussed in Chapter 9) and forms authentication (Chapter 18). The problem in both cases is the same—ASP.NET encodes some information to prevent tampering and verifies the information later. For example, with view state, ASP.NET adds a hash code, which double-checks the next time the page is posted back to make sure the user hasn't changed the hidden view state field (in which case the request is rejected). The problem that can happen with web farms is that the hash code one web server creates might not match the hash code expected by another web server that uses a different secret key. As a result, if a page is posted back to a web farm and a different web server gets involved, an error can occur.

To resolve this problem, you can disable view state hash codes (as described in Chapter 9). This isn't recommended. A better solution is to configure each web server in the web farm to use the same key. With a web hosting provider, this step will already have been performed. If you have your own web farm, it won't be—the default is for each server to create its own random key. So, obviously, these keys won't match.

To configure web servers to use the same key, head to the c:\Windows\Microsoft.NET\Framework\v2.0.50727\Config directory, and crack open the machine.config file in a text editor. In the <system.web> section, add a <machineKey> element, like this:

```
<machineKey validationKey="DE4C0C8F69E34EFC93F2FD3C04484A184A6FF124BFD14504..."
 decryptionKey="0A335689ABD7F3EB3BB79826861359E08..." validation="SHA1" />
```

This explicitly sets a validation key and a decryption key. As long as you set all the servers in the web farm to use the same key, they can share view state (and use other features, such as forms authentication). Of course, you can't create the key string on your own and have it be sufficiently random. So you should use a tool for this (such as the key generator at `http://www.aspnetresources.com/tools/keycreator.aspx`).

Internet Information Services (IIS)

As you've probably guessed by now, deploying a web application is just the process of copying your web application files to a web server. By taking this step, you accomplish three things:

- You ensure your web applications are available even when Visual Studio isn't running.
- You allow users on other computers to run your web applications. (The Visual Studio web server handles only local requests.)
- Your web application URLs will no longer need a port number.

Depending on your organization, you may be in charge of deploying web applications, or a dedicated web administrator may handle the process. Either way, it's worth learning the deployment process, which is quite straightforward.

The Many Faces of IIS

The tricky part about using IIS is the fact that it exists in several different versions. The version of IIS you use depends on the operating system you're using:

- Windows XP Professional includes IIS 5.1. (Other editions of Windows XP don't include any version of IIS.)
- Windows Server 2003 uses IIS 6.
- Windows Vista and Windows Server 2008 use IIS 7.

As a general rule, when you want to publish your website, you should use a server version of Windows to host it. Desktop versions, such as Windows XP and Windows Vista, are fine for development testing, but they implement a connection limit, which makes them less suitable for real-world use. Windows XP Professional and Windows Vista Business, Enterprise, and Ultimate only allow IIS to process ten simultaneous requests. Windows Vista Home Basic and Starter only allow three simultaneous requests.

This chapter provides the basic instructions to get started with IIS, no matter what version you're using. But be prepared for a bit of an adjustment if you need to move from one version to another—and feel free to skip over the instructions that don't apply to your version of IIS.

■ **Tip** As a quick test to find out whether IIS is installed, try firing up a browser and requesting `http://localhost` on the current computer. The exact welcome page you see depends on the version of IIS, but as long as you don't receive an error you'll know that IIS is installed.

Before you can start using IIS, you need to make sure the web server computer has the required IIS software. The following sections provide a high-level overview of the process. They tell you where to go to find IIS and switch it on, depending on the version of Windows that you're using. Once IIS is installed, you'll need to make sure that IIS knows about it, as described in the "Registering the ASP.NET File Mappings" section.

■ **Tip** Remember, if you just want to learn about IIS and practice using its administrative tools and configuring web applications, you can install IIS on your own local computer and use it there.

Installing IIS 5 (in Windows XP)

Installing IIS is easy. Here are the steps you need to follow:

1. Click Start, and choose Settings ➤ Control Panel.
2. Choose Add or Remove Programs.
3. Click Add/Remove Windows Components.
4. If Internet Information Services (IIS) is checked (see Figure 9-2), you already have this component installed. Otherwise, click it, and then click Next to install the required IIS files. You'll probably need to have your Windows setup CD handy.

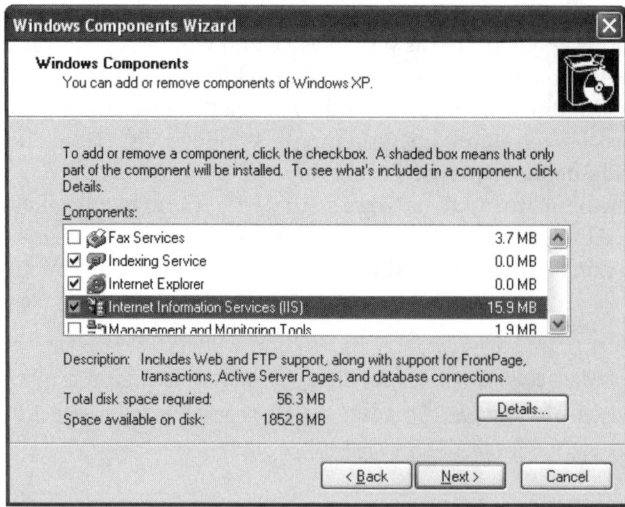

Figure 9-2. *Installing IIS 5*

5. Now you need to install the .NET 3.5 runtime (if you haven't installed it already). There are several ways to install .NET 3.5, but one of the easiest is to choose it from the list of optional downloads available through the Windows Update feature. Just select Windows Update from the Start menu. Another choice is to search for the .NET runtime on the Web.

■ **Note** Best security practices encourage you not to include any development tools (such as Visual Studio) on the web server. You also don't need to have the full .NET Framework on the web server. Instead, install only the .NET runtime, which includes the ASP.NET engine. The .NET runtime is also known as the .NET *redistributable package*.

Installing IIS 6 (in Windows Server 2003)

If you're using Windows Server 2003, you can install IIS through the Add/Remove Windows Components dialog box; but it's more likely you'll use the Manage Your Server Wizard. Here's how it works:

1. Click Start, and then click Manage Your Server.
2. Select Add or Remove a Role from the main Manage Your Server window. This launches the Configure Your Server Wizard.
3. Click Next to continue past the introductory window. The setup wizard will test your available and enabled network connections and then continue to the next step.
4. Now you choose the roles to enable. Select Application Server (IIS, ASP.NET) from the list, as shown in Figure 9-3, and click Next.

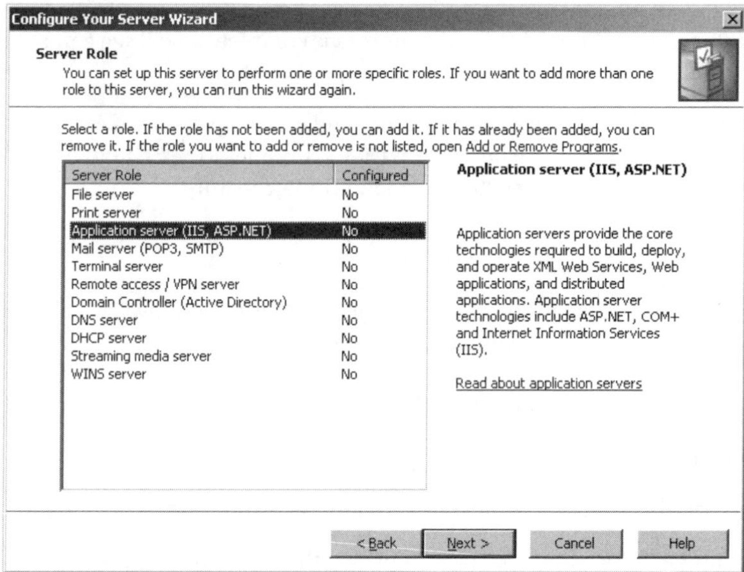

Figure 9-3. *Choosing an application server role*

5. Check the Enable ASP.NET box on the next window (shown in Figure 9-4). If you don't, IIS will be enabled, but it will be able to serve only static content such as ordinary HTML pages. Click Next to continue.

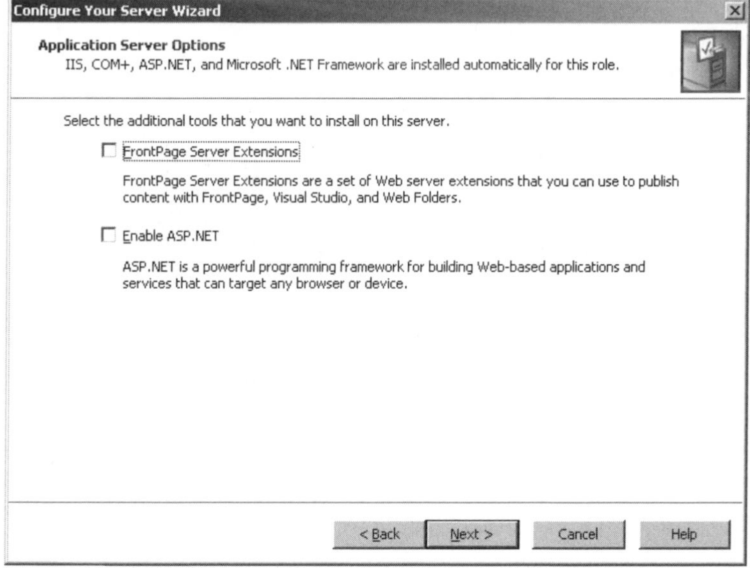

Figure 9-4. *Enabling other services*

6. The next window summarizes the options you've chosen. Click Next to continue by installing IIS 6.0 and ASP.NET. Once the process is complete, you'll see a final confirmation message.

7. At this point, you've successfully installed IIS (and an older version of ASP.NET). To use your ASP.NET 3.5 websites, you need the .NET 3.5 runtime. To get it, hunt it down on the Web or use the Windows Server 2003 Windows Update feature.

Installing IIS 7 (in Windows Vista)

IIS 7 is the next evolutionary step for IIS. As with other versions of Windows, it's included but not initially installed. To switch it on, you need to follow these steps:

1. Click Start, and then click Control Panel.

2. Choose Programs and Features.

3. In the task list (on the left), click the "Turn Windows features on or off" link.

4. Find the Internet Information Services item near the top of the list (see Figure 9-5), and make sure it's checked. Then click OK to complete your configuration change.

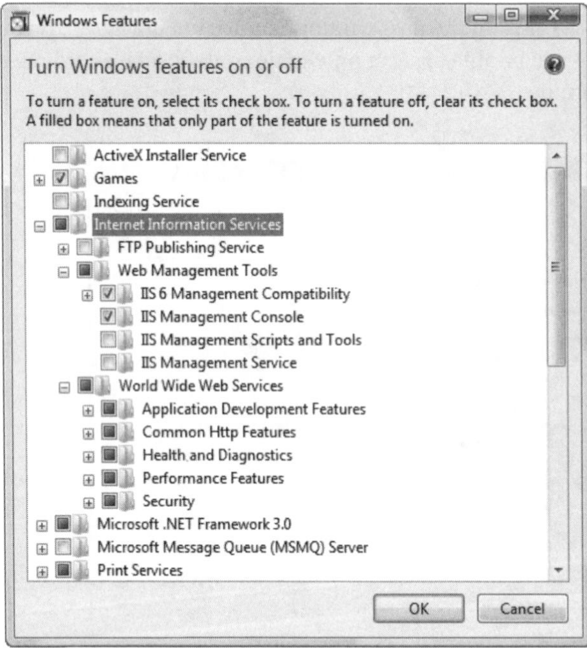

Figure 9-5. *Installing IIS 7*

5. Once IIS is installed, you need to install the .NET 3.5 runtime. You can hunt it down on the Web or use the Windows Update feature.

Note Windows Vista allows you to enable or disable individual features in IIS by choosing the items that appear in the Internet Information Services group. Many of these check boxes correspond to optional IIS features that are outside the scope of this book (although you'll use the security modules in Chapter 20). To learn more about these many settings and IIS administration in general, consult a dedicated book about IIS 7.

Installing IIS 7 (in Windows Server 2008)

Windows Server 2008 uses the same version of IIS as Windows Vista. However, you'll usually use the Server Manager to configure IIS. Here's how:

1. Choose Start Menu, then All Programs, then Administrative Tools ➤ Server Manager.
2. Choose the Roles node in the tree on the left.
3. Click the Add Roles link in the right section of the window. This opens a wizard that allows you to add a new role to your server.
4. Follow the steps within the Wizard until you reach the Select Server Roles step. Check the Web Server role in the list of roles and click Next. You'll probably be prompted to install additional required roles—if so, just accept the operation and continue.
5. After you've installed any additional roles you need, you'll be prompted to configure the Web Server role. As in Windows Vista, you can choose the specific features of IIS 7 that should be enabled (see Figure 9-5).
6. Eventually, you'll end up at a summary page. IIS 7 is now installed with the .NET 3.5 runtime.

Registering the ASP.NET File Mappings

Ideally, you'll install IIS *before* you install the .NET 3.5 runtime (or, if you're using Windows Server 2008, at the same time). That's because when you perform the .NET setup, it configures IIS to recognize all the right file types (such as .aspx). If you install the .NET runtime before IIS, you'll run into a problem because IIS won't recognize your ASP.NET files and won't hand them off to the ASP.NET worker process to execute your code. Instead, it sends the raw text of the page (the .aspx tags) directly to the requesting browser. The next section ("Verifying That ASP.NET Is Correctly Installed") demonstrates this problem.

Fortunately, it's easy to correct this problem by repairing your IIS file mappings. You need to use the aspnet_regiis.exe command-line utility with the -i command-line parameter (for install), as shown here:

```
c:\Windows\Microsoft.NET\Framework\v2.0.50727\aspnet_regiis.exe -i
```

At this point, ASP.NET will check all your virtual directories and register the ASP.NET file types.

If you have more than one version of ASP.NET installed on the computer, make sure you run the correct version of aspnet_regiis. If you use the version of aspnet_regiis included with an older version of ASP.NET, such as 1.1, you'll reset all your web applications to use ASP.NET 1.1.

■ **Tip** The easiest way to make sure you get the right version of aspnet_regiis is to rely on the Visual Studio Command Prompt. The Visual Studio Command Prompt is really just an ordinary Windows command prompt, but it sets the path variable so that the tools you need are at your fingertips. When you type aspnet_regiis.exe in the Visual Studio Command Prompt (without specifying a path), you'll automatically run the correct version. To start the Visual Studio Command Prompt, open the Start menu, choose Programs, and then choose Microsoft Visual Studio 2008 ➤ Visual Studio Tools ➤ Visual Studio 2008 Command Prompt.

This approach could be more drastic than what you really want, because it affects every web application on the web server. What if you want some applications on the web server to execute with ASP.NET 1.1 and others to use ASP.NET 3.5? (This might occur if you're in the process of updating several web applications and the migration isn't yet tested.) In this case, you need to use aspnet_regiis carefully so that it applies its magic to individual applications only.

To change file mappings for a single web application, you use the -s parameter, followed by the full path to your web application. This path always starts with W3SVC/1/ROOT/ followed by the application folder name, as shown here:

```
aspnet_regiis -s W3SVC/1/ROOT/SampleApp1
```

Remember, if you want to register an application to use a different version of ASP.NET, you need to use the version of aspnet_regiis that's included with that version, along with the -s parameter.

Every version of aspnet_regiis is able to give you a list of all the versions of ASP.NET that are installed on the computer (and where they are). Just use the -lv option, as shown here:

```
aspnet_regiis -lv
```

You can get more information about aspnet_regiis.exe from the MSDN Help, and you can see all the parameters by using the -? parameter. Later in this chapter (in the "Managing Websites with IIS Manager" section), you'll learn how you can configure virtual directories using the graphical IIS Manager tool. One of the features it provides is a way to set the ASP.NET version for each web application, without requiring you to run aspnet_regiis.

Verifying That ASP.NET Is Correctly Installed

After installing ASP.NET, it's a good idea to test that it's working. All you need to do is create a simple ASP.NET page, request it in a browser, and make sure it's processed successfully.

To perform this test, create a text file in the c:\Inetpub\wwwroot directory. (This is the directory that IIS creates to represent the root of your web server.) Name this file test.aspx. The file name isn't that important, but the extension is. It's the .aspx extension that tells IIS this file needs to be processed by the ASP.NET engine.

Inside the test.aspx file, paste the following markup:

```
<html>
  <body>
    <h1>The date is <% Response.Write(DateTime.Now.ToLongDateString()) %>
    </h1>
  </body>
</html>
```

When you request this file in a browser, ASP.NET will load the file, execute the embedded code statement (which retrieves the current date and inserts it into the page), and then return the final HTML page. This example isn't a full-fledged ASP.NET web page, because it doesn't use the web control model. However, it's still enough to test that ASP.NET is working properly. When you enter `http://localhost/test.aspx` in the browser, you should see a page that looks like the one shown in Figure 9-6.

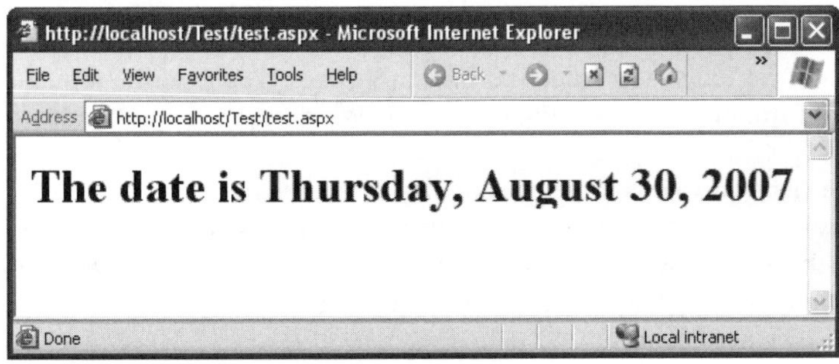

Figure 9-6. *ASP.NET is correctly installed.*

If you see only the plain text, as in Figure 9-7, ASP.NET isn't installed correctly. This problem commonly occurs if ASP.NET is installed but the ASP.NET file types aren't registered in IIS. In this case, ASP.NET won't actually process the request. Instead, the raw page will be sent directly to the user, and the browser will display only the content that isn't inside a tag or a script block.

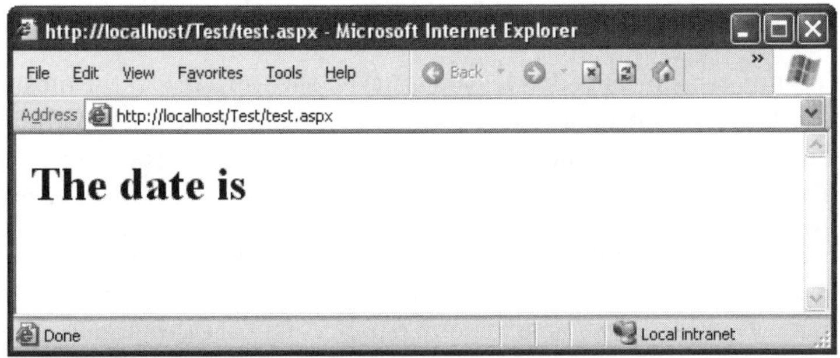

Figure 9-7. *ASP.NET isn't installed or configured correctly.*

To solve this problem, use the aspnet_regiis.exe tool described in the previous section to register the ASP.NET file mappings.

Managing Websites with IIS Manager

When IIS is installed, it automatically creates a directory named c:\Inetpub\wwwroot, which represents your website. Any files in this directory will appear as though they're in the root of your web server.

To add more pages to your web server, you can copy HTML, ASP, or ASP.NET files directly to the c:\Inetpub\wwwroot directory. For example, if you add the file TestFile.html to this directory, you can request it in a browser through the URL `http://localhost/TestFile.html`. You can even create subdirectories to group related resources. For example, you can access the file c:\Inetpub\wwwroot\MySite\MyFile.html through a browser using the URL `http://localhost/MySite/MyFile.html`.

Using the wwwroot directory is straightforward, but it makes for poor organization. To properly use ASP or ASP.NET, you need to make your own virtual directory for each web application you create. With a virtual directory, you can expose any physical directory (on any drive on your computer) on your web server as though it were located in the c:\Inetpub\wwwroot directory.

Before you get started, you need to launch IIS Manager. To do so, open the Start menu and choose Programs ➤ Administrative Tools ➤ Internet Information Services. (You'll see the somewhat longer name Internet Information Services (IIS) Manager in Windows Vista and Windows Server 2008.)

Every version of IIS Manager works a bit differently, but they all allow you to manage virtual directories. And though they also look a bit different, they all include a similar tree structure on the left-hand side. Initially, this tree shows a single item—your computer. You can expand this item to find all the virtual directories that are currently configured on the web server, each of which represents a separate web application.

Figure 9-8 shows the IIS Manager window for IIS 7. It's divided into three parts:

- On the left side is the website tree. In Figure 9-8, there are two web applications in the website tree: EightBall and SampleApp.
- In the middle is a useful set of icons that allow you to perform various configuration tasks with the currently selected item in the tree, which is usually a website folder. These icons are part of Features View. Alternatively, you can switch to Content View by clicking the Content View button at the bottom of the pane. In this case, you'll simply see the contents of the selected folder. Click Features View to switch back.
- On the right side are additional shortcuts that let you quickly perform a few of the most common tasks (again, based on the currently selected item in the tree). This is a standard design that's used in several Windows management tools. However, in IIS Manager these links aren't terribly useful, and you'll be more likely to use the icons in Features View.

The IIS Manager for IIS 5 and IIS 6 is similar, but different (see Figure 9-9). It provides a similar tree on the left, but it doesn't include the Features View in the middle. Instead, it simply shows the contents of the currently selected website folder. To perform most configuration tasks, you'll need to right-click a website in the tree.

Now that you've taken your first look at IIS Manager, you're ready to get started managing your websites. In the next section, you'll learn how to create your first virtual directory.

Figure 9-8. *IIS Manager for IIS 7*

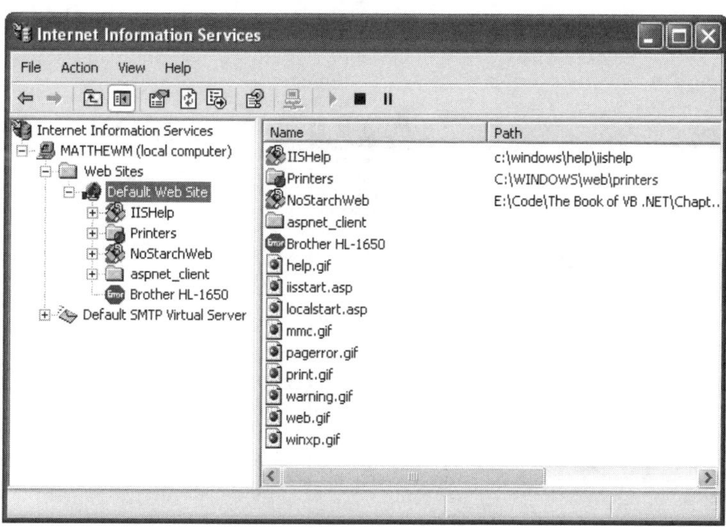

Figure 9-9. *IIS Manager for IIS 5*

Creating a Virtual Directory

When you're ready to deploy a website on a computer that has IIS, the first step you'll usually take is to create the physical directory where the pages will be stored (for example, c:\MySite). The second step is to expose this physical directory as a virtual directory through IIS. This means the website becomes publicly visible to other computers that are connected to your computer. Ordinarily, a remote computer won't be allowed to access your c:\MySite directory. However, if you map c:\MySite to a virtual directory, the remote user will be able to request the files in the directory through IIS.

Before going any further, choose the directory you want to expose as a virtual directory. You can use any directory you want, on any drive, and you can place it as many levels deep as makes sense. You can use a directory that already has your website files, or you can copy these files after you create the virtual directory. Either way, the first step is to register this directory with IIS.

The easiest and most flexible way to create a virtual directory is to use the IIS Manager utility. Here's what you need to do:

1. To create a new virtual directory for an existing physical directory, expand the node for the current computer, expand the Web Sites node underneath, and then right-click the Default Web Site item.

2. If you're using IIS 5 or IIS 6, choose New ➤ Virtual Directory from the context menu. A wizard will start to manage the process (see Figure 9-10). As you step through the wizard, you'll be asked to supply the information IIS needs. If you're using IIS 7, choose Add Application directory. You'll be asked to supply essentially the same information, but in a single window (see Figure 9-11).

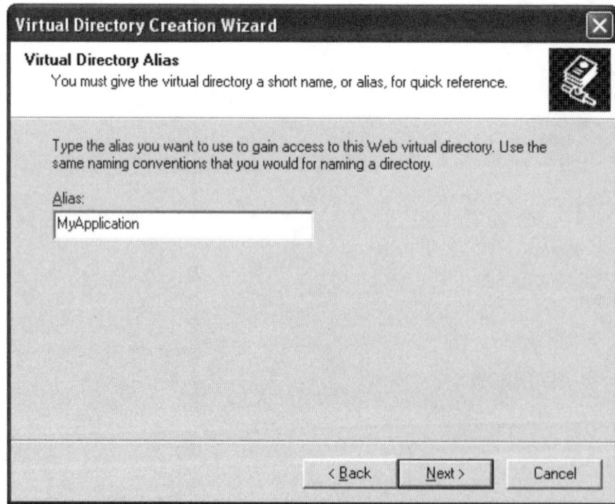

Figure 9-10. *Configuring a web application in IIS 5*

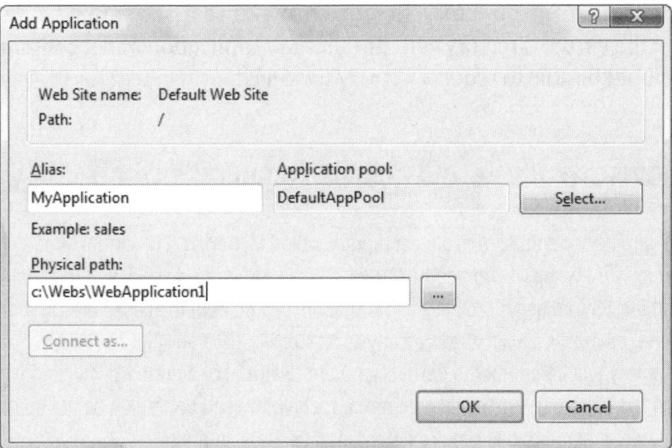

Figure 9-11. *Configuring a web application in IIS 7*

3. The first piece of information you need to supply is the *alias*—the name a remote client will use to access the files in this virtual directory. For example, if your alias is MyApp and your computer is MyServer, you can request pages using URLs such as `http://MyServer/MyApp/MyPage.aspx`.

4. Choose a directory. The directory is the physical directory on your hard drive that will be exposed as a virtual directory. For example, c:\Inetpub\wwwroot is the physical directory that is used for the root virtual directory of your web server. IIS will provide access to all the allowed file types in this directory.

5. If you're using IIS 5 or IIS 6, there's one more step. You need to choose the permissions for your virtual directory. To host an ASP.NET application, you need only to enable the read and execute permissions (the first two check boxes). If you're using a development computer that will never act as a live web server, you can allow additional permissions. (Keep in mind, however, that this could allow other users on a local network to access and modify files in the virtual directory.)

6. If you're using IIS 7, you can also specify the *application pool* by clicking the Select button. An application pool is a group of settings that applies to one or more applications. (Later in this chapter, you'll see how you can create a new application pool to make IIS run under a different Windows account.) For now, just keep the standard DefaultAppPool setting.

7. To finish the process in IIS 5 or IIS 6, advance to the end of the wizard and then click Next. In IIS 7, you simply need to click OK in the Add Virtual Directory dialog box.

When you finish these steps, you'll see your new virtual directory appear in the list in IIS Manager.

You can remove an existing virtual directory by selecting it and pressing the Delete key, or you can change its settings by right-clicking it and choosing Properties (in IIS 5 and IIS 6) or selecting it and using the icons in the Features View on the right (in IIS 7).

Once you've created your virtual directory, fire up a browser to make sure it works. For example, if you've created the virtual directory with the alias MyApplication and it contains the page MyPage.aspx, you should be able to request `http://localhost/MyApplication/MyPage.aspx`.

VIRTUAL DIRECTORIES ALLOW ACCESS TO SUBDIRECTORIES

Imagine you create a virtual directory called MyApp on a computer called MyServer. The virtual directory corresponds to the physical directory c:\MyApp. If you add the subdirectory c:\MyApp\MoreFiles, this directory will automatically be included in the IIS tree as an ordinary folder. Clients will be able to access files in this folder by specifying the folder name, as in `http://MyServer/MyApp/MoreFiles/SomeFile.html`.

By default, the subdirectory will inherit all the permissions of the virtual directory. However, you can change these settings using the IIS Manager. This is a common technique used to break a single application into different parts (for example, if some pages require heightened security settings).

This is also the source of a common mistake in ASP.NET deployment. To understand the problem, imagine you have a website in a folder named c:\Applications\WebApps\Site1. This is the directory you should use when you create your virtual directory. However, if you accidentally create a virtual directory for the parent directory c:\Applications\WebApps, you might not realize the error right away. That's because you'll still be able to access the files in Site1 (because it's a subdirectory of your virtual directory WebApps). However, when you try to request one of the web pages inside Site1, you'll receive an error page informing you that the settings in the web.config file aren't valid. The problem is that certain settings are only valid at the application level, not the subdirectory level. To solve this problem, remove the incorrect virtual directory and create the one you really want.

You can easily solve this problem. In IIS 5 or IIS 6, you need to right-click on the virtual directory, choose Properties, and select the Virtual Directory tab. Finally, click the Create button next to the Application Name box. In IIS 7, the process is even easier—just right-click the virtual directory and choose Convert to Application.

Configuring a Virtual Directory

IIS makes it easy to configure web applications after you've created them. And though there's no way to cover all the options in a single chapter, the following sections cover some of the settings you're most likely to change. For more information, consult a dedicated book about IIS administration.

■ **Note** You won't consider the IIS authentication and security settings in this chapter. Instead, you'll tackle them when you consider the ASP.NET security model in Chapter 20.

Setting a Default Page

Consider the virtual directory `http://localhost/MySite`. A user can request a specific page in this directory using a URL such as `http://localhost/MySite/MyPage1.aspx`. But what happens if the user simply types `http://localhost/MySite` into a web browser?

In this case, IIS will examine the list of *default documents* that are defined for that virtual directory. It will scan the list from top to bottom and return the first matching page. Using the list in Figure 9-12, IIS will check first for a Default.htm file, then for Default.asp, index.htm, iisstart.asp, and Default.aspx, which is the home page that most ASP.NET applications use.

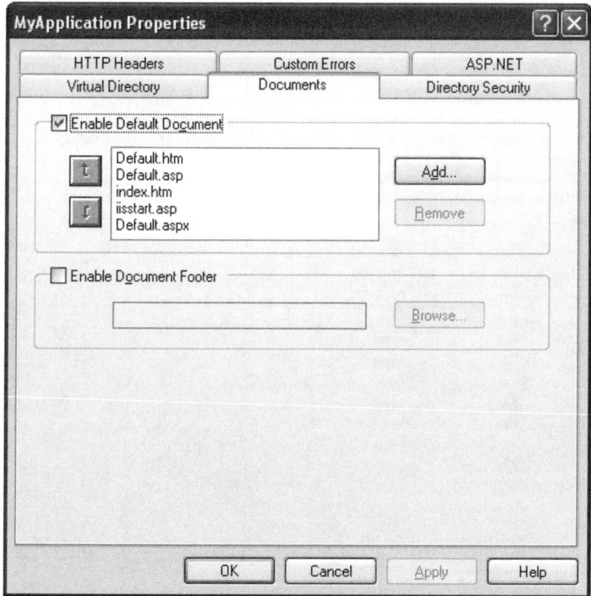

Figure 9-12. *The default document list (in IIS 5)*

If IIS doesn't find any of these pages, it will either return an error message or, if you've enabled the Browse permission (which usually you won't), it will provide a file list.

To configure the default documents in IIS 5 or IIS 6, right-click the virtual directory and choose Properties. The Properties window will appear, with its information divided into several tabs. Then, choose the Documents tab, where you can add, remove, and rearrange the default document list.

To configure the default documents in IIS 7, select the virtual directory. Then double-click the Default Document icon in the Features area on the right. When entering default documents in IIS 7, you place the entire list on one line, with each document separated from the previous one by a comma.

Custom Error Pages

As you learned in Chapter 8, you can use configuration settings to replace application errors with custom error messages. However, this technique won't work if the web request never makes it to the ASP.NET service (for example, if the user requests an HTML file that doesn't exist). In this case, you may want to supplement custom ASP.NET error handling with IIS error pages for other generic error conditions.

To configure custom error pages in IIS 5 or IIS 6, right-click the virtual directory and choose Properties. In the Properties window, pick the Custom Errors tab. You can then specify the error page that will be displayed for specific types of HTTP errors.

To configure custom error pages in IIS 7, start by selecting the virtual directory. Then, double-click the Error Pages icon in the Features area. You'll see a list of HTTP errors that are mapped to specific HTML error pages (as shown in Figure 9-13). You can add or remove items, or double-click an error to choose a different HTML file.

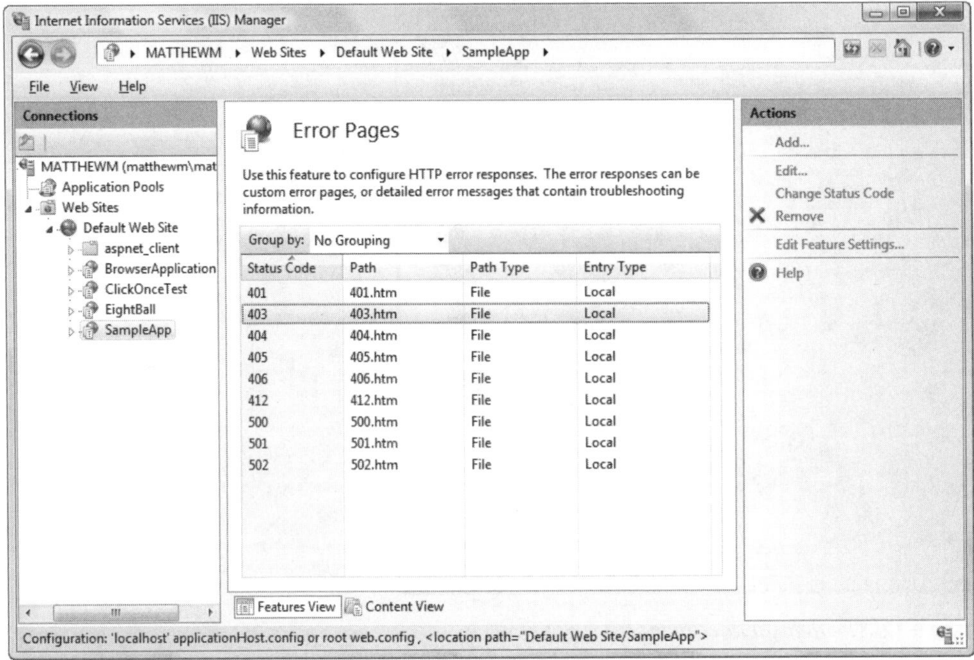

Figure 9-13. *IIS custom errors (in IIS 7)*

ASP.NET Settings

As you learned in Chapter 5, an ASP.NET web application is configured using the settings in the web.config file. You can edit these settings by hand, or you can use the Website Administration Tool to change some of them using a graphical web page interface. Interestingly, you can also tweak some of these settings from directly inside IIS. The actual settings you can adjust depends on the version of IIS you're using. IIS 7 is much more integrated with ASP.NET, and allows you to change far more settings.

To see what you can change in IIS 5 or IIS 6, right-click the virtual directory and choose Properties. Then, pick the ASP.NET tab (shown in Figure 9-14). The ASP.NET tab provides several useful features:

- It gives you at-a-glance information about the current version of ASP.NET you're using for this application.
- It allows you to choose any version of ASP.NET that's installed on the computer just by selecting it from a drop-down list. This is an easy way to configure different applications to use different versions of ASP.NET, without using the aspnet_regiis.exe tool described earlier.

- It provides an Edit Configuration button that, when clicked, launches another set of tabs that you can use to tweak the settings in the web.config file. There's no difference between changing settings through this window and changing them by hand. However, harried website administrators might find this approach makes it easier to monitor and tweak the configuration of different applications without hunting for files.

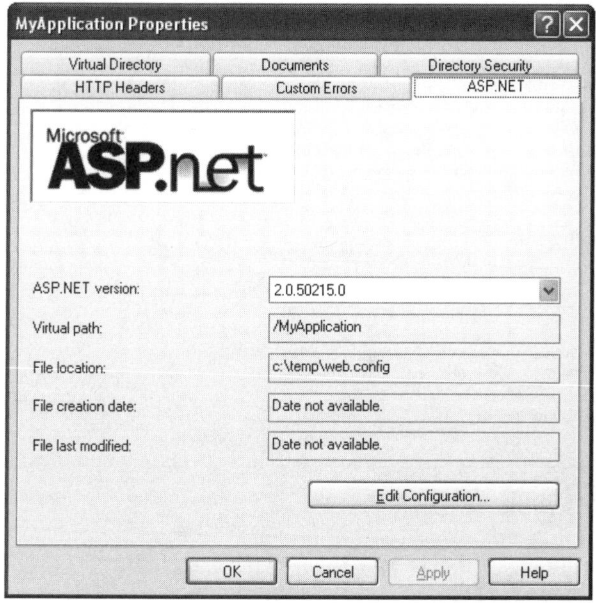

Figure 9-14. *Configuring ASP.NET settings (in IIS 5)*

In IIS 7, select the virtual directory you want to change, and look at the icons in the ASP.NET category of the Features area (as shown in Figure 9-15). There's quite a lot that you can play with. Some of the highlights include

- *Application Settings*: Use this feature to enter custom pieces of information that you want to use in your application (as described in Chapter 5).
- *Connection Strings*: Use this feature to set the connection string used to connect to a database (as described in Chapter 15).
- *Session State*: Use this feature to configure how session state works. You can set the timeout and the way that session state information is stored (in server memory, a separate process, or a custom database). Chapter 7 has more about these options.
- *.NET Users and .NET Roles*: Use these features to define website users and roles (groups of users with different permissions). You'll learn about these features in Chapters 20 and 21.
- *.NET Profile*: Use this feature to define user-specific data that you want ASP.NET to store in a database automatically. You'll learn more about the profiles feature in Chapter 22.

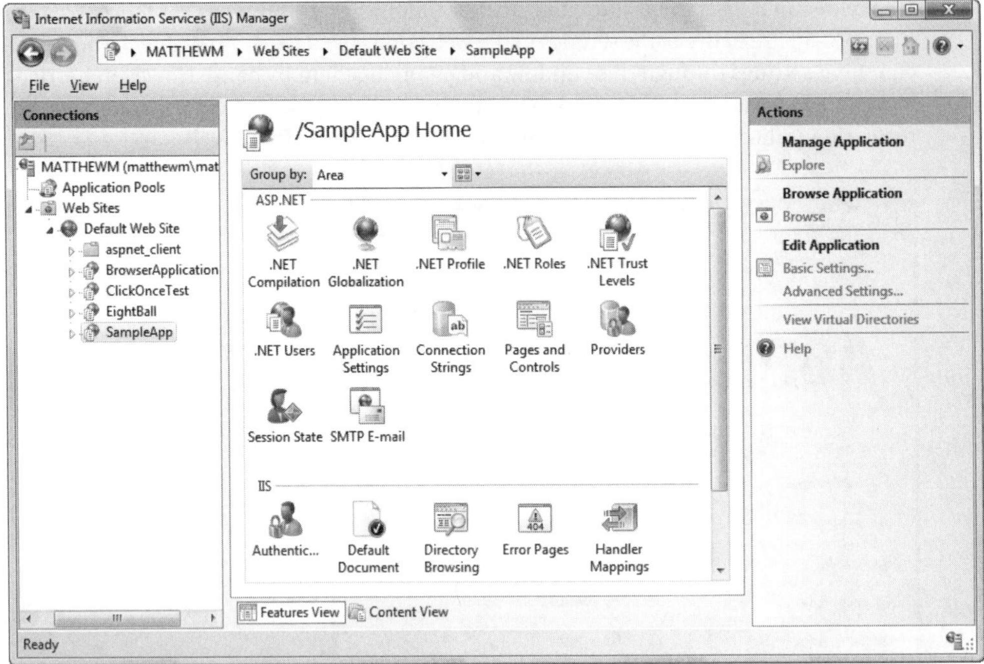

Figure 9-15. *Configuring ASP.NET settings (in IIS 7)*

Deploying a Simple Site

You now know enough to deploy an ordinary ASP.NET website. All you need to do is follow these two simple steps:

1. Create the virtual directory on the web server.
2. Copy the entire site (including subdirectories) to the virtual directory.

How you transfer these files depends on the Internet hosting service you're using. Usually, you'll need to use an FTP program to upload the files to a designated area. However, if both your computer and the web server are on the same internal network, you might just use Windows Explorer or the command prompt to copy files.

If you're using a commercial web host, the virtual directory will already be created for you, and you'll simply need to transfer the files.

Before you transfer your application files, you should make sure debug mode isn't enabled in the deployed version. To do so, find the debug attribute in the compilation tag, if it is present, and set it to false, as shown here:

```
<configuration>
  <system.web>
    <compilation debug="false">
      ...
    </compilation>

    <!-- Other settings omitted. -->
  </system.web>
<configuration>
```

When debugging is enabled, the compiled ASP.NET web page code will be larger and execute more slowly. For that reason, you should use debugging only while testing your web application.

Web Applications and Components

It's just as straightforward to deploy web applications that use other components. That's because any custom components your website uses are copied into the Bin subdirectory when you add a reference in Visual Studio. No additional steps are required to register assemblies or to copy them to a specific system directory.

■Note Private assemblies are quite a boon for web hosting companies that need to host dozens, hundreds, or thousands of web applications on the same computer. Their web servers can't install risky components into a system directory just because one website requires it—especially when the version that one site requires might conflict with the version needed by another site on the same computer.

Of course, this principle doesn't hold true if you're using *shared assemblies*, which are stored in a special system location called the GAC (global assembly cache). Usually, you won't store components in this location, because it complicates development and offers few benefits. The core .NET assemblies are located in the GAC because they're large and likely to be used in almost every .NET application. It doesn't make sense to force you to deploy the .NET assemblies with every website you create. However, this means it's up to the administrator of the web server to install the version of the .NET Framework you require. This detail just isn't in your website's control.

Other Configuration Steps

The simple model of deployment you've seen so far is often called *zero-touch deployment*, because you don't need to manually configure web server resources. (It's also sometimes called *XCopy deployment*, because transferring websites is as easy as copying directories.) However, some applications are more difficult to set up on a web server. Here are some common factors that will require additional configuration steps:

Databases: If your web application uses a database, you'll need to transfer the database to the web server. You can do this by generating a SQL script that will automatically create the database and load it with data. Alternately, you could back up the database and then restore it on the web server. In either case, an administrator needs to use a database management tool.

Alternate machine.config settings: You can control the settings for your web application in the web.config file that you deploy. However, problems can occur if your web application relies on settings in the machine.config file that aren't present on the web server.

Windows account permissions: Usually, a web server will run web page code under a restricted account. This account might not be allowed to perform the tasks you rely on, such as writing to files or the Windows event log, or connecting to a database. In this case, an administrator needs to specifically grant the permissions you need to the account that runs the ASP.NET engine for your website.

IIS security settings: If your website uses SSL encryption or Windows authentication (as described in Chapter 18), the virtual directory settings will need to be tweaked. This also requires the help of an administrator.

To solve these problems in the most effective way, it helps to work with an experienced Windows administrator. That's especially true if the web server is using IIS 6 or IIS 7, which allow every web application on a server to run under a different Windows account. This ensures that your website can be granted the exact permission set it requires, without affecting any other web applications.

Code Compilation

By default, when you deploy an application you've created with Visual Studio, you deploy the uncompiled source files. The first time a page is requested, it is compiled dynamically and cached in a temporary directory for reuse. The advantage of this approach is that it's easy to make last-minute changes directly to your files without needing to go through any compilation steps. However, this approach has some clear disadvantages:

- The first request for a page is slow. After a page has been requested more than once, this problem disappears.
- The web server contains all your source code and is clearly visible to anyone who has access to the server. Even though visitors can't see your code, website administrators can (and they could even change it).

To improve performance and prevent other people from seeing your code, you have another option—you can use ASP.NET's *precompilation* feature. Essentially, you use a command-line tool named aspnet_compiler.exe, which is stored in the familiar c:\Windows\Microsoft.NET\Framework\v2.0.50727 directory. You use this compiler on your development machine before you deploy the application. It compiles the entire website into binary files.

Here's the syntax for the aspnet_compiler tool:

```
aspnet_compiler -m metabasePath targetDirectory
```

Essentially, you need to specify the source (where the web application resides) and the target directory (where the compiled version of the application should be copied).

To specify the source, you use the -m option and specify the metabase path in the form W3SVC/1/ROOT/[VirtualDirectoryName], just as you would with aspnet_regiis. Here's an example:

```
aspnet_compiler -m W3SVC/1/ROOT/MyApp C:\MyAppDeploy
```

You can then copy the files from the target directory to your web server (or if you're really crafty, you can use aspnet_compiler to send the compiled files straight to the target directory as part of your build process).

If you use the command line shown previously, the c:\MyAppDeploy directory will contain all the .aspx files but no .vb files—meaning all the source code is compiled into assemblies in the Bin directory and hidden. Even more interestingly, the information in the .aspx files has also been removed. If you open a web page, you'll find that it doesn't contain any tags. Instead, it just contains the statement "This is a marker file generated by the precompilation tool and should not be deleted!" All the tags have been moved into the compiled files in the Bin directory, along with the source code. The aspnet_compiler just keeps the .aspx files so you can remember what web pages there are.

■ **Note** The aspnet_compiler compiles a web application to prepare it for deployment. However, you can compile a website *after* it's transferred to the web server. This is called *in-place compilation*, and it won't remove your code. Instead, it simply creates and caches the compiled versions of your web pages so there won't be any delay for the first set of requests. In-place compilation is useful when you want to optimize performance but don't want to (or need) to hide the code. To perform an in-place compilation, omit the target directory when you use aspnet_compiler.

The ASP.NET Account

Some of the subtlest issues with ASP.NET deployment involve security. When the web server launches the aspnet_isapi.dll for the first time, it loads under a specific Windows user account. The actual account that's used depends on the version of IIS you're using:

- If you're using IIS 5, the account is ASPNET (which is created automatically when you install the .NET Framework).
- If you're using IIS 6 or IIS 7, it's the *network service* account.
- If you're using the integrated test server in Visual Studio, the server runs under your account. That means it has all your permissions, and as a result you generally won't run into permission problems while you're testing your application. This can be very misleading, because you might not realize that there are potential permission problems waiting for you once you deploy the application.

You can change the account that ASP.NET uses to run code. Under IIS 5, you do this by editing the machine.config file that defines settings for the entire web server. In IIS 6 and IIS 7, you configure this account in IIS Manager, which is a bit easier.

New ASP.NET programmers often ask why ASP.NET code doesn't run under another account—say, the account of the user who is making the request from the browser. However, if you consider this situation, you'll quickly realize the problems. It's almost certain that the end user doesn't have a Windows account defined on the web server. Even if the user has a corresponding user account, that account shouldn't have the same rights as the ASP.NET engine.

The trick is to use an account that's limited enough that it can't be abused by attackers but still has the required permissions to run your code. Both the ASPNET account and the network account achieve that goal, because they have a set of carefully limited privileges.

By default, the ASPNET account won't be allowed to perform tasks such as reading the Windows registry, retrieving information from a database, or writing to most locations on the local hard drive. On the other hand, it will have the permissions that are essential for normal functioning. For example, the ASPNET account *is* allowed to access the c:\Windows\Microsoft.NET\Framework\v2.0.50727\Temporary ASP.NET Files directory so it can compile and cache web pages.

The limited security settings of the ASPNET and network service accounts are designed to prevent attacks on your web server. In most cases, the goal is to prevent any attacks that could exploit flaws in your application and trick it into undertaking actions that it's technically allowed to do (such as deleting a file) but should never perform. Although this is a worthwhile goal, you'll probably find that your applications require some additional permissions beyond those given to the ASPNET and network service accounts. For example, you might need access to a specific file or a database. To make this possible, you grant additional permissions to these accounts in the same way you would grant them to any other Windows user account. However, the process isn't always obvious—so you might want to consult a good handbook about Windows system administration before you take these steps.

Alternatively, you might want to change the account that's used to run the worker process to a different account with the required permissions. The following sections explain how.

■ Note Before changing the account used to run ASP.NET code, make sure you fully understand the effects. If you use an account with more permissions than you need, you open the door to a wide range of potential hacks and attacks. It's always best to use a dedicated account for running ASP.NET code and to restrict what it can do to the bare minimum.

Changing the Account in IIS 5

To change the ASP.NET settings to use a different account, you need to perform the following steps:

1. Open the machine.config file in the c:\Windows\Microsoft.NET\Framework\v2.0.50727\Config directory using Notepad.

2. Search for the setting autoConfig="true". You'll find the processModel setting shown here:

   ```
   <processModel autoConfig="true" />
   ```

3. To specify an account other than ASPNET, you need to add the userName and password attributes. You can use another account that's defined on the system, as shown here:

```
<processModel autoConfig="true"
 userName="MyASPAccount" password="s!pec5%_degrees" />
```

   Alternatively, you can set the userName attribute to System and set the password to AutoGenerate. This tells ASP.NET to use the local system account, which is a local account with wide-ranging permissions.

```
<processModel autoConfig="true"
 userName="System" password="AutoGenerate" />
```

■ **Note** It's tempting to use the local system account, because it has complete power to perform any task on the computer. Although this may make sense for test web server scenarios, it's a dangerous habit. First, using the local system account makes developers less conscious of security while they program, which is never a good approach in the threat-conscious world of modern programming. Second, it also means you are less aware of the minimum permissions the application requires, which can complicate your life when you need to deploy the application to a production server.

---

4. Now you must restart the ASP.NET service. To do this, you can either reboot the computer or you can use Task Manager to manually terminate the ASP.NET service. In the latter case, look for the process named aspnet_wp.exe. Select it, and click End Process. The worker process may restart itself automatically. If not, it will relaunch itself the next time you request an ASP.NET web page.

■ **Note** The ASP.NET account is a global setting that affects all web applications on the computer.

Changing the Account in IIS 6 or IIS 7

In IIS 6 and IIS 7, you change the user account by changing the application pool that's used to run your web application. Editing the machine.config file (as described in the previous section) will have no effect.

Here's what you need to do in IIS 6:

1. In the IIS Manager tree, expand the Application Pools group at the top. Then, find the pool your application is using. By default, this is the DefaultAppPool.
2. If you're using IIS 6, right-click the application pool and select Properties. Then, select the Identity tab. In IIS 7, right-click it and choose Advanced Settings.

3. You have two options when setting the account. You can choose one of the predefined account types from a drop-down list (as shown in Figure 9-16), including Network Service (the default), Local Service (which is essentially the same as ASPNET), or Local System (which runs as an administrator with extensive privileges). Alternatively, you can supply the user name and password for a specific user. If you take this approach, the information you enter is encrypted for the current computer (unlike in IIS 5, where it's stored in ordinary text in the machine.config file).

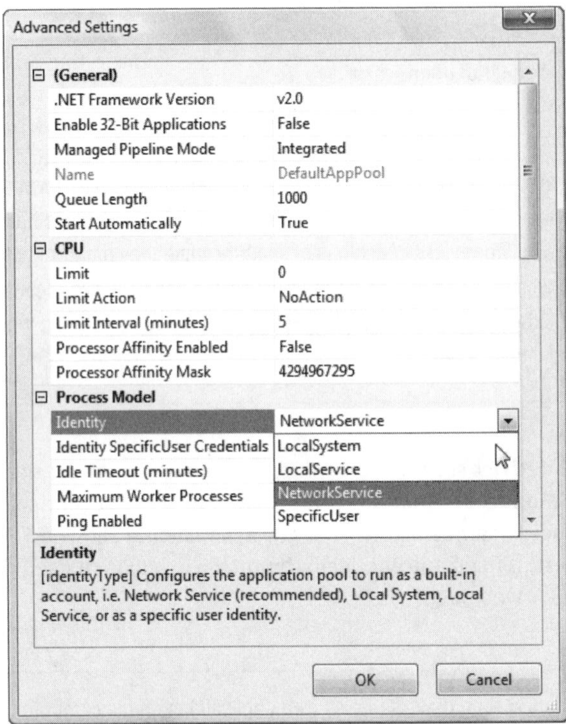

Figure 9-16. *Changing the web application user account (in IIS 7)*

When you make your change in this way, you affect all the web applications that use the DefaultAppPool. Another option is to create a new application pool first. In IIS 6, you simply need to right-click the Application Pools group and choose New ➤ Application Pool. In IIS 7, you right-click the Application Pools group and choose Add Application Pool. You can then configure this application pool to use a specific user account.

Once you've created the application pool, you can modify your web application so that it uses the newly created application. To perform this step in IIS 6, right-click the virtual directory and choose Properties. Look for the Application Pool list, where you can pick from all the application pools that you've created. In IIS 7, right-click the virtual direction and choose Advanced Settings to find the same setting.

Giving the ASP.NET Account More Privileges

Changing the account that ASP.NET uses is a risky step. If you're not careful, you'll end up using an account that has more permissions than it should. It then becomes easier for a malicious user to perform an attack that damages your web server or its data.

For example, imagine you create a web page that allows users to upload files. If you don't design this page carefully, the user might be able to trick your application into uploading a file into a location it shouldn't, such as the c:\Windows directory. If your web application is running with elevated permissions, it might be allowed to overwrite a Windows system file in this directory—which allows the attacker to cause much more damage with this exploit.

For this reason, security experts recommend giving your web applications the smallest set of permissions that still allows them to function properly. One of the easiest ways to implement this design is to start with a strictly limited account (such as ASPNET or the network service account) and then gradually give it the additional permissions it needs (but nothing more).

There's no magic to this approach, but you might need the help of an experienced Windows administrator to figure out how to set permissions for various Windows resources. If you're using IIS 5, you assign these permissions directly to the ASPNET user. If you're using IIS 6 and IIS 7, you don't use the same technique, because the network service account is a special account that's defined by the system. Instead, in IIS 6 you assign permissions to the IIS_WPG group, of which the network service account is a member. In IIS 7, the same principle applies, except the group is named IIS_IUSRS. The IIS_WPG or IIS_IUSRS group is created automatically when you install Windows.

Deploying with Visual Studio

Visual Studio aims to simplify web application deployment in the same way it simplifies the task of designing rich web pages. Although you need to understand how IIS works in order to manage virtual directories effectively (and fix the inevitable configuration problems), Visual Studio includes features that integrate with IIS and allow you to create virtual directories without leaving the comfort of your design-time environment.

Visual Studio has three key deployment-related features:

- You can create a virtual directory when you create a new project.
- You can use the Copy Web Site feature to transfer an existing website to a virtual directory.
- You can use the Publish Web Site feature to compile your website and transfer it to another location.

■ **Note** If your computer is running under Windows Vista, you'll need to take an extra step before you get started. In order for Visual Studio to communicate with IIS, you need to be running Visual Studio as an administrator. To do so, right-click the Visual Studio shortcut and choose Run As Administrator.

Creating a Virtual Directory for a New Project

When you create a website in Visual Studio, you can simultaneously create a virtual directory for that website. If you choose to do so, Visual Studio won't use its built-in web server. Instead, all your requests will flow through IIS. (Happily, you'll still see the same behavior and have access to the same debugging tools.)

To try this, select File ➤ New Web Site. In the New Web Site dialog box, choose HTTP for the location (instead of File System). You can then supply a URL. For example, if you supply `http://localhost/MyWebSite`, Visual Studio will create the virtual directory MyWebSite on the current computer. Figure 9-17 shows an example.

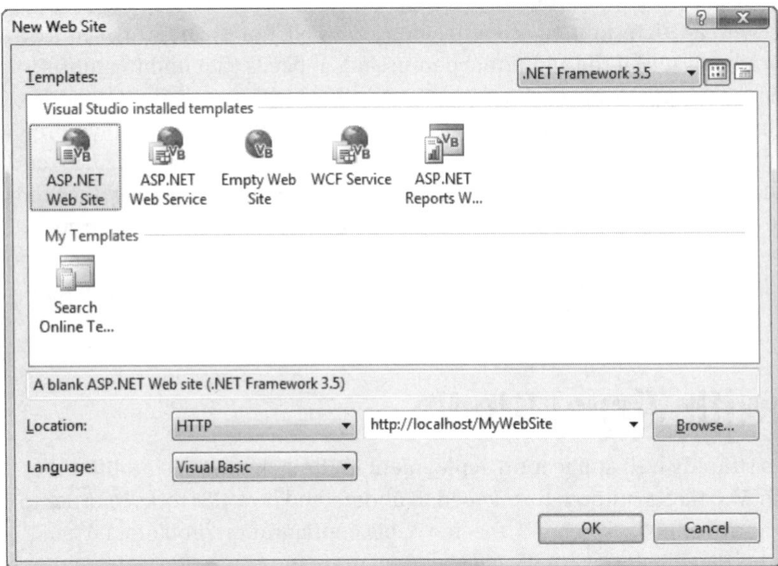

Figure 9-17. *Creating a virtual directory to hold a new project*

■ **Note** If you specify a virtual directory that already exists, Visual Studio won't create it—it will just use the existing directory. This is convenient because it allows you to set up the virtual directory ahead of time with exactly the options you want and then create the website in it. If the virtual directory doesn't already exist, Visual Studio creates the virtual directory in the c:\Inetpub\wwwroot directory.

This approach often isn't the best way to create a virtual directory. It has several limitations:

- It forces you to set up the virtual directory when you first create the application. If you've already created an application, you can't use this approach for creating a virtual directory.
- The virtual directory is always created in the c:\Inetpub\wwwroot directory. This can make it hard to keep track of where your files are. (As you'll discover, you can work around this limitation.)

- You can't configure other settings, such as default pages, custom errors, and virtual directory permissions.
- Any change you make and debugging you perform act on the live version of your application that's running on the web server. If you're using a production web server, this is an unacceptable risk. If you're using a test web server, you may have opened potential security issues, because remote users can request pages in your application from other computers.

For these reasons, it's more common for developers to create their application using the built-in web server in Visual Studio and then create a virtual directory by hand when they're ready to deploy it to a test or production web server.

Visual Studio doesn't give you the full options of IIS Manager, but you can get a little more control. In the New Web Site dialog box, type `http://localhost` (for the current computer), and click the Browse button. You'll see all the virtual directories that are defined in IIS, just as in IIS Manager (see Figure 9-18).

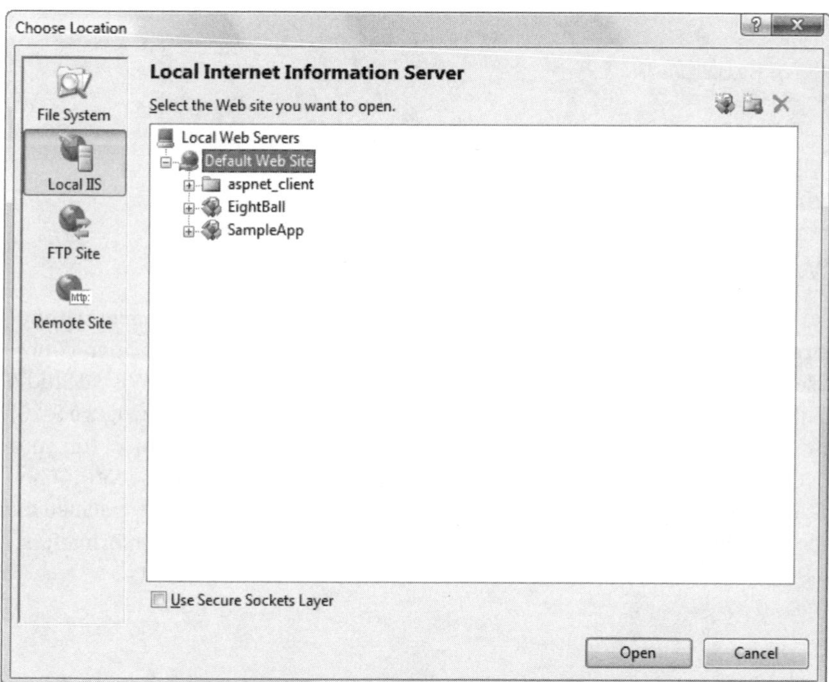

Figure 9-18. *Viewing virtual directories in Visual Studio*

You can't view or change their properties, but you can choose an existing virtual directory where you want to create your application. You can also use the Create New Virtual Directory button in the top-right corner of the window (it appears as a folder icon with a globe). Click this button, and you'll get the chance to supply the virtual directory alias *and* its physical file path (see Figure 9-19).

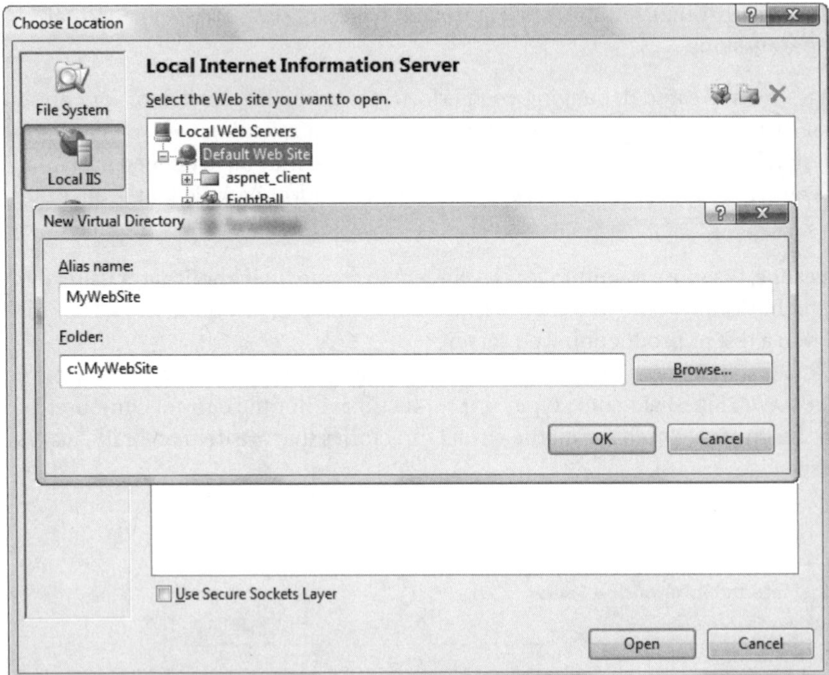

Figure 9-19. *Creating a virtual directory in a specific location*

Copying a Website

Visual Studio also includes a quick and easy way to transfer your web application files without using a separate program or leaving the design environment. You simply need to open your web project and select Website ➤ Copy Web Site from the menu. This opens a new Visual Studio dialog box that will be familiar to anyone who has used Microsoft FrontPage (see Figure 9-20).

This window includes two file lists. On the left are the files in the current project (on your local hard drive). On the right are the files on the target location (the remote web server). When you first open this window, you won't see anything on the right, because you haven't specified the target. You need to click the Connect button at the top of the window to supply this information.

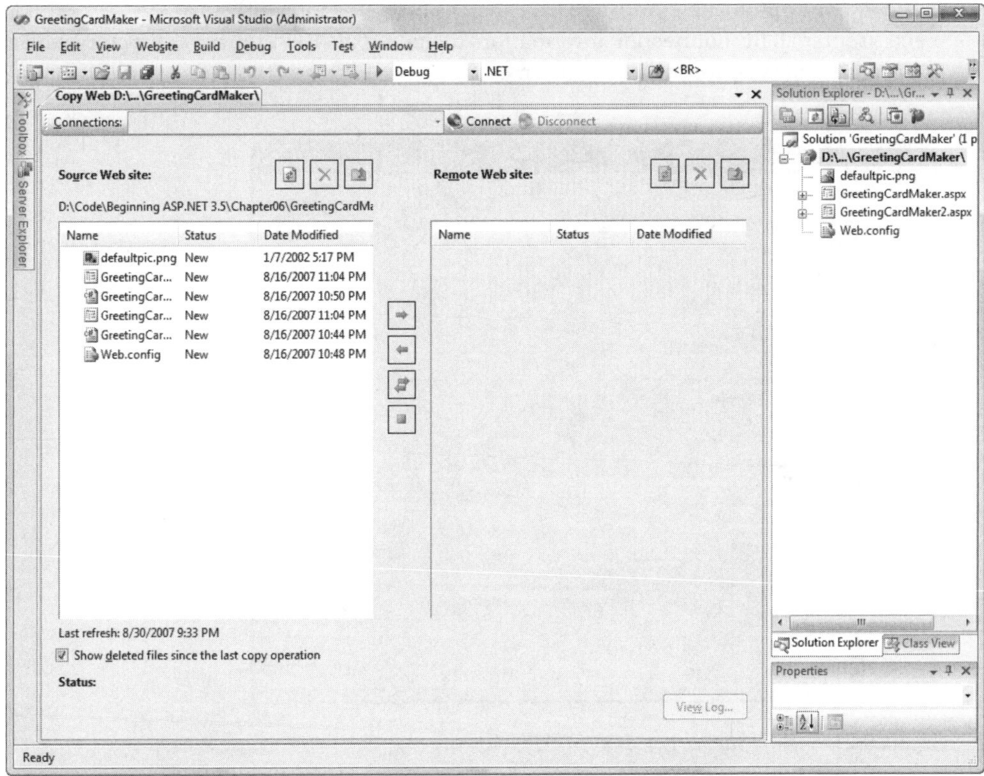

Figure 9-20. *Copying a website*

When you click Connect, Visual Studio shows a familiar dialog box—it looks almost the same as what you see when you create a virtual directory for a new project. Using this window, you can specify one of the following types of locations:

File System: This is the easiest choice—you simply need to browse through a tree of drives and directories or through the shares provided by other computers on the network. If you want to create a new directory for your application, just click the Create New Folder icon above the top-right corner of the directory tree.

Local IIS: This choice allows you to browse the virtual directories made available on the local computer through IIS. To create a new virtual directory for your web application, click the Create New Web Application icon at the top-right corner of the virtual directory tree.

FTP Site: This option isn't quite as convenient as browsing for a directory—instead, you'll need to enter all the connection information, including the FTP site, port, directory, and a user name and password before you can connect (see Figure 9-21).

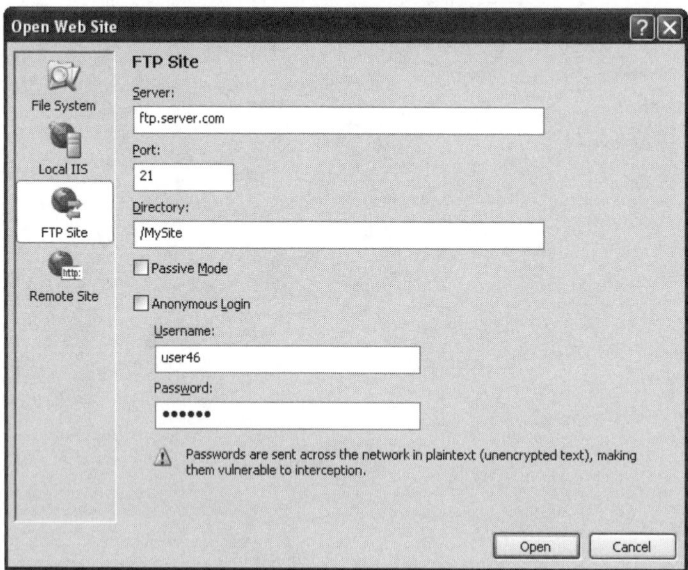

Figure 9-21. *Setting the target site*

Remote Web Server: This option accesses a website at a specified URL using HTTP. For this to work, the web server must have the FrontPage Extensions installed. When you connect, you'll be prompted for a user name and password.

Once you choose the appropriate destination, click Open. Visual Studio will attempt to connect to the remote site and retrieve a list of its files.

The Copy Web Site feature is particularly useful for updating a web server. That's because Visual Studio compares the file list on the local and remote websites, and it flags files that exist in one location only (with the status New) or those that are newer versions (with the status Changed). You can then select the files you want to transfer and click one of the arrow buttons to transfer them from one location to the other (see Figure 9-22).

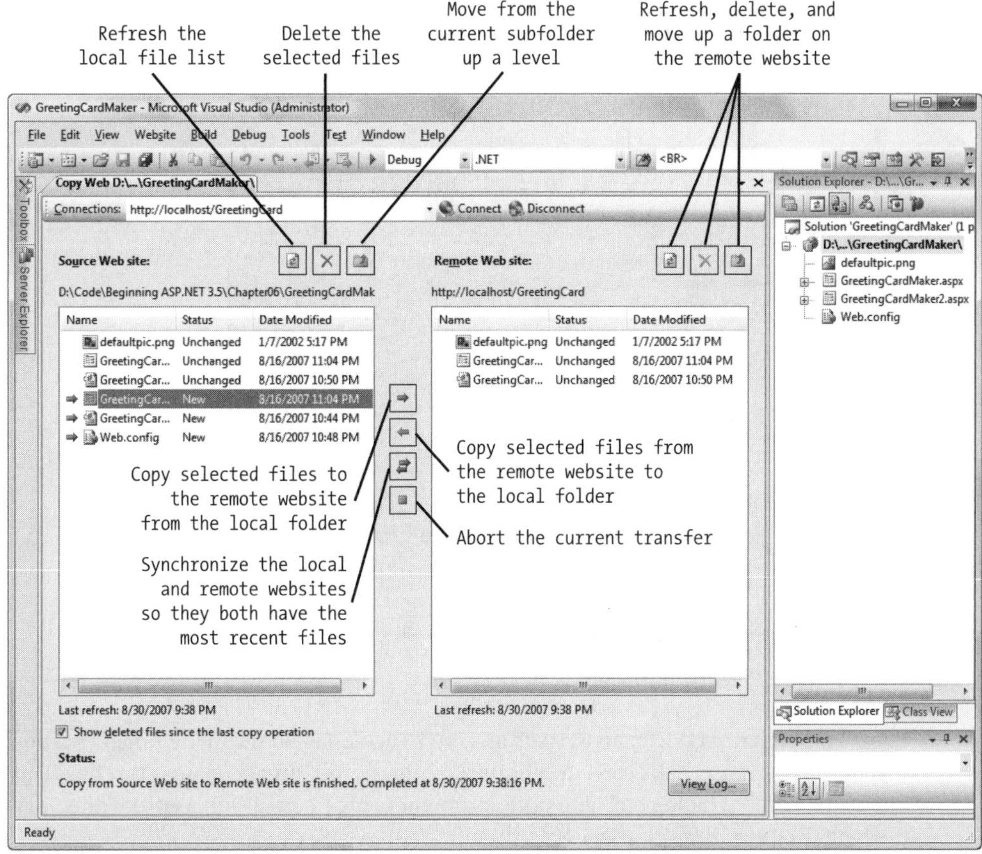

Figure 9-22. *Synchronizing a remote website*

Publishing a Website

The website copying feature is great for transferring files to a test server. However, it doesn't give you the option of precompiling your code. If you're deploying your application to a live web server and you want to keep the source code tightly locked down, you'll want something more.

As described earlier in this chapter, you can use the aspnet_compiler command-line utility to compile ASP.NET applications. This functionality is also available in Visual Studio through the website publishing feature. While the website copying feature is designed to let you update individual files (which is ideal when updating a test server), the publishing feature is intended to transfer your entire website in compiled form with a couple of clicks.

Here's what you need to do:

1. Select Build ➤ Publish Web Site from the menu. The Publish Web Site dialog box will appear (see Figure 9-23).

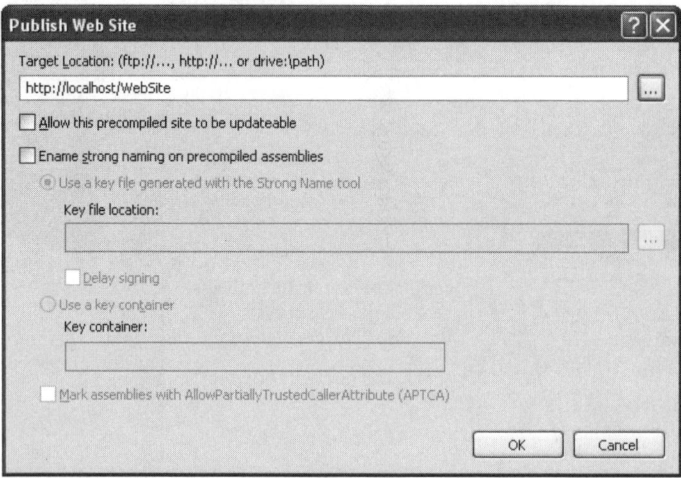

Figure 9-23. *Publishing a website*

2. Enter a file path or a URL for an FTP site or a FrontPage-enabled site in the Target Location text box. To get some help, click the ellipsis (...) next to the Target Location text box. This opens the familiar dialog box with options for choosing (or creating) a virtual directory, file path, FTP site, or remote server.

3. Leave the other check boxes unselected. You can choose to allow updates, in which case the code-behind files are compiled but the .aspx files with the HTML and tags aren't compiled. This option allows you to make only limited changes (and it increases the potential for accidental changes or tampering), so it isn't terribly useful.

4. Click OK. Your website files will be compiled with aspnet_compiler and then transferred to the target location.

The Last Word

This chapter covered IIS (the web server that powers ASP.NET websites) and the deployment model for ASP.NET. You also considered the tools that Visual Studio includes to make deployment easier. This rounds out Part 2 of this book, and you now have all the fundamentals you need to create a basic ASP.NET website. In the next part, you'll refine your web pages with a few new features, like validation and graphics. You'll also learn how to standardize layout and formatting across your website, and build a navigation system that lets users surf from one page to another.

PART 3

Building Better Web Forms

CHAPTER 10

■ ■ ■

Validation

This chapter looks at some of the most useful controls that are included in ASP.NET: the *validation controls.* These controls take a previously time-consuming and complicated task—verifying user input and reporting errors—and automate it with an elegant, easy-to-use collection of validators. Each validator has its own built-in logic. Some check for missing data, others verify that numbers fall in a predefined range, and so on. In many cases, the validation controls allow you to verify user input without writing a line of code.

In this chapter, you'll learn how to use the validation controls in an ASP.NET web page, and how to get the most out of them with sophisticated regular expressions, custom validation functions, and more. And as usual, you'll peer under the hood to see how ASP.NET implements these features.

Understanding Validation

As a seasoned developer, you probably realize users will make mistakes. What's particularly daunting is the range of possible mistakes that users can make. Here are some common examples:

- Users might ignore an important field and leave it blank.
- Users might try to type a short string of nonsense to circumvent a required field check, thereby creating endless headaches on your end. For example, you might get stuck with an invalid e-mail address that causes problems for your automatic e-mailing program.
- Users might make an honest mistake, such as entering a typing error, entering a non-numeric character in a number field, or submitting the wrong type of information. They might even enter several pieces of information that are individually correct but when taken together are inconsistent (for example, entering a MasterCard number after choosing Visa as the payment type).
- Malicious users might try to exploit a weakness in your code by entering carefully structured wrong values. For example, they might attempt to cause a specific error that will reveal sensitive information. A more dramatic example of this technique is the *SQL injection attack,* where user-supplied values change the operation of a dynamically constructed database command. (Of course, validation is no defense for poor coding. When you consider database programming in Chapter 15, you'll learn how to use parameterized commands, which avoid the danger of SQL injection attacks altogether.)

A web application is particularly susceptible to these problems, because it relies on basic HTML input controls that don't have all the features of their Windows counterparts. For example, a common technique in a Windows application is to handle the KeyPress event of a text box, check to see whether the current character is valid, and prevent it from appearing if it isn't. This technique makes it easy to create a text box that accepts only numeric input.

In web applications, however, you don't have that sort of fine-grained control. To handle a KeyPress event, the page would have to be posted back to the server every time the user types a letter, which would slow down the application hopelessly. Instead, you need to perform all your validation at once when a page (which may contain multiple input controls) is submitted. You then need to create the appropriate user interface to report the mistakes. Some websites report only the first incorrect field, while others use a table, list, or window to describe them all. By the time you've perfected your validation strategy, you'll have spent a considerable amount of effort writing tedious code.

ASP.NET aims to save you this trouble and provide you with a reusable framework of validation controls that manages validation details by checking fields and reporting on errors automatically. These controls can even use client-side JavaScript to provide a more dynamic and responsive interface while still providing ordinary validation for older browsers (often referred to as *down-level* browsers).

The Validator Controls

ASP.NET provides five validator controls, which are described in Table 10-1. Four are targeted at specific types of validation, while the fifth allows you to apply custom validation routines. You'll also see a ValidationSummary control in the Toolbox, which gives you another option for showing a list of validation error messages in one place. You'll learn about the ValidationSummary later in this chapter (see the "Other Display Options" section).

Table 10-1. *Validator Controls*

Control Class	Description
RequiredFieldValidator	Validation succeeds as long as the input control doesn't contain an empty string.
RangeValidator	Validation succeeds if the input control contains a value within a specific numeric, alphabetic, or date range.
CompareValidator	Validation succeeds if the input control contains a value that matches the value in another input control, or a fixed value that you specify.
RegularExpressionValidator	Validation succeeds if the value in an input control matches a specified regular expression.
CustomValidator	Validation is performed by a user-defined function.

Each validation control can be bound to a single input control. In addition, you can apply more than one validation control to the same input control to provide multiple types of validation.

If you use the RangeValidator, CompareValidator, or RegularExpressionValidator, validation will automatically succeed if the input control is empty, because there is no value to validate.

If this isn't the behavior you want, you should also add a RequiredFieldValidator and link it to the same input control. This ensures that two types of validation will be performed, effectively restricting blank values.

Server-Side Validation

You can use the validator controls to verify a page automatically when the user submits it or manually in your code. The first approach is the most common.

When using automatic validation, the user receives a normal page and begins to fill in the input controls. When finished, the user clicks a button to submit the page. Every button has a CausesValidation property, which can be set to True or False. What happens when the user clicks the button depends on the value of the CausesValidation property:

- If CausesValidation is False, ASP.NET will ignore the validation controls, the page will be posted back, and your event-handling code will run normally.
- If CausesValidation is True (the default), ASP.NET will automatically validate the page when the user clicks the button. It does this by performing the validation for each control on the page. If any control fails to validate, ASP.NET will return the page with some error information, depending on your settings. Your click event-handling code may or may not be executed—meaning you'll have to specifically check in the event handler whether the page is valid.

Based on this description, you'll realize that validation happens automatically when certain buttons are clicked. It doesn't happen when the page is posted back because of a change event (such as choosing a new value in an AutoPostBack list) or if the user clicks a button that has CausesValidation set to False. However, you can still validate one or more controls manually and then make a decision in your code based on the results. You'll learn about this process in more detail a little later (see the "Manual Validation" section).

Note Many other button-like controls that can be used to submit the page also provide the CausesValidation property. Examples include the LinkButton, ImageButton, and BulletedList.

Client-Side Validation

In most modern browsers (including Internet Explorer 5 or later and any version of Firefox), ASP.NET automatically adds JavaScript code for client-side validation. In this case, when the user clicks a CausesValidation button, the same error messages will appear without the page needing to be submitted and returned from the server. This increases the responsiveness of your web page.

However, even if the page validates successfully on the client side, ASP.NET still revalidates it when it's received at the server. This is because it's easy for an experienced user to circumvent client-side validation. For example, a malicious user might delete the block of JavaScript validation code and continue working with the page. By performing the validation at both ends, ASP.NET makes sure your application can be as responsive as possible while also remaining secure.

The Validation Controls

The validation controls are found in the System.Web.UI.WebControls namespace and inherit from the BaseValidator class. This class defines the basic functionality for a validation control. Table 10-2 describes its key properties.

Table 10-2. *Properties of the BaseValidator Class*

Property	Description
ControlToValidate	Identifies the control that this validator will check. Each validator can verify the value in one input control. However, it's perfectly reasonable to "stack" validators—in other words, attach several validators to one input control to perform more than one type of error checking.
ErrorMessage and ForeColor	If validation fails, the validator control can display a text message (set by the ErrorMessage property). By changing the ForeColor, you can make this message stand out in angry red lettering.
Display	Allows you to configure whether this error message will be inserted into the page dynamically when it's needed (Dynamic) or whether an appropriate space will be reserved for the message (Static). Dynamic is useful when you're placing several validators next to each other. That way, the space will expand to fit the currently active error indicators, and you won't be left with any unseemly whitespace. Static is useful when the validator is in a table and you don't want the width of the cell to collapse when no message is displayed Finally, you can also choose None to hide the error message altogether.
IsValid	After validation is performed, this returns True or False depending on whether it succeeded or failed. Generally, you'll check the state of the entire page by looking at its IsValid property instead to find out if all the validation controls succeeded.
Enabled	When set to False, automatic validation will not be performed for this control when the page is submitted.
EnableClientScript	If set to True, ASP.NET will add JavaScript and DHTML code to allow client-side validation on browsers that support it.

When using a validation control, the only properties you need to implement are ControlToValidate and ErrorMessage. In addition, you may need to implement the properties that are used for your specific validator. Table 10-3 outlines these properties.

Table 10-3. *Validator-Specific Properties*

Validator Control	Added Members
RequiredFieldValidator	None required
RangeValidator	MaximumValue, MinimumValue, Type
CompareValidator	ControlToCompare, Operator, Type, ValueToCompare

Table 10-3. *Validator-Specific Properties*

Validator Control	Added Members
RegularExpressionValidator	ValidationExpression
CustomValidator	ClientValidationFunction, ValidateEmptyText, ServerValidate event

Later in this chapter (in the "A Validated Customer Form" section), you'll see a customer form example that demonstrates each type of validation.

A Simple Validation Example

To understand how validation works, you can create a simple web page. This test uses a single Button web control, two TextBox controls, and a RangeValidator control that validates the first text box. If validation fails, the RangeValidator control displays an error message, so you should place this control immediately next to the TextBox it's validating. The second text box does not use any validation.

Figure 10-1 shows the appearance of the page after a failed validation attempt.

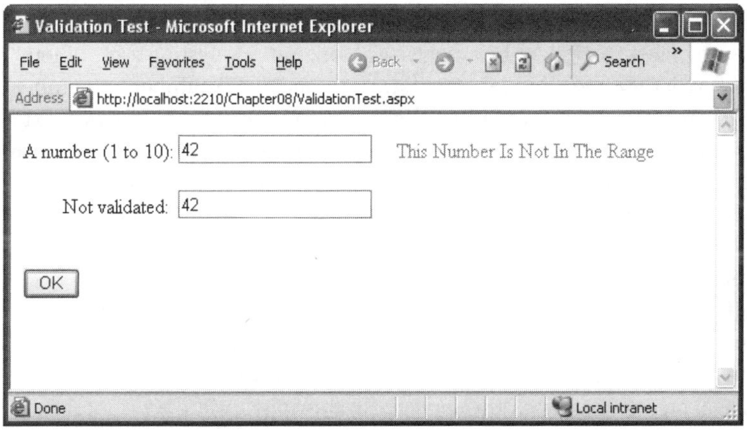

Validation Test - Microsoft Internet Explorer
File Edit View Favorites Tools Help
Address http://localhost:2210/Chapter08/ValidationTest.aspx
A number (1 to 10): 42 This Number Is Not In The Range
Not validated: 42
OK
Done Local intranet

Figure 10-1. *Failed validation*

In addition, place a Label control at the bottom of the form. This label will report when the page has been posted back and the event-handling code has executed. Disable its EnableViewState property to ensure that it will be cleared every time the page is posted back.

The markup for this page defines a RangeValidator control, sets the error message, identifies the control that will be validated, and requires an integer from 1 to 10. These properties are set in the .aspx file, but they could also be configured in the event handler for the Page.Load event. The Button automatically has its CauseValidation property set to True, because this is the default.

```
A number (1 to 10):
<asp:TextBox id="txtValidated" runat="server" />
<asp:RangeValidator id="RangeValidator" runat="server"
  ErrorMessage="This Number Is Not In The Range"
  ControlToValidate="txtValidated"
  MaximumValue="10" MinimumValue="1"
  Type="Integer" />
<br /><br />
Not validated:
<asp:TextBox id="txtNotValidated" runat="server" /><br /><br />
<asp:Button id="cmdOK" runat="server" Text="OK" />
<br /><br />
<asp:Label id="lblMessage" runat="server"
  EnableViewState="False" />
```

Finally, here is the code that responds to the button click:

```
Protected Sub cmdOK_Click(ByVal sender As Object, _
  ByVal e As System.EventArgs) Handles cmdOK.Click

    lblMessage.Text = "cmdOK_Click event handler executed."
End Sub
```

If you're testing this web page in a modern browser, you'll notice an interesting trick. When you first open the page, the error message is hidden. But if you type an invalid number (remember, validation will succeed for an empty value) and press the Tab key to move to the second text box, an error message will appear automatically next to the offending control. This is because ASP.NET adds a special JavaScript function that detects when the focus changes. The actual implementation of this JavaScript code is somewhat complicated, but ASP.NET handles all the details for you automatically. As a result, if you try to click the OK button with an invalid value in txtValidated, your actions will be ignored and the page won't be posted back.

Not all browsers will support client-side validation. To see what will happen on a down-level browser, set the RangeValidator.EnableClientScript property to False, and rerun the page. Now error messages won't appear dynamically as you change focus. However, when you click the OK button, the page will be returned from the server with the appropriate error message displayed next to the invalid control.

The potential problem in this scenario is that the click event-handling code will still execute, even though the page is invalid. To correct this problem and ensure that your page behaves the same on modern and older browsers, you must specifically abort the event code if validation hasn't been performed successfully.

```
Protected Sub cmdOK_Click(ByVal sender As Object, _
  ByVal e As System.EventArgs) Handles cmdOK.Click

    ' Abort the event if the control isn't valid.
    If Not RangeValidator.IsValid Then Return

    lblMessage.Text = "cmdOK_Click event handler executed."
End Sub
```

This code solves the current problem, but it isn't much help if the page contains multiple validation controls. Fortunately, every web form provides its own IsValid property. This property will be False if *any* validation control has failed. It will be True if all the validation controls completed successfully. If validation was not performed (for example, if the validation controls are disabled or if the button has CausesValidation set to False), you'll get an HttpException when you attempt to read the IsValid property.

```
Protected Sub cmdOK_Click(ByVal sender As Object, _
  ByVal e As System.EventArgs) Handles cmdOK.Click

    ' Abort the event if any control on the page is invalid.
    If Not Page.IsValid Then Return

    lblMessage.Text = "cmdOK_Click event handler executed."
End Sub
```

Remember, client-side validation is just nice frosting on top of your application. Server-side validation will always be performed, ensuring that crafty users can't "spoof" pages.

Other Display Options

In some cases, you might have already created a carefully designed form that combines multiple input fields. Perhaps you want to add validation to this page, but you can't reformat the layout to accommodate all the error messages for all the validation controls. In this case, you can save some work by using the ValidationSummary control.

To try this, set the Display property of the RangeValidator control to None. This ensures the error message will never be displayed. However, validation will still be performed and the user will still be prevented from successfully clicking the OK button if some invalid information exists on the page.

Next, add the ValidationSummary in a suitable location (such as the bottom of the page):

```
<asp:ValidationSummary id="Errors" runat="server" />
```

When you run the page, you won't see any dynamic messages as you enter invalid information and tab to a new field. However, when you click the OK button, the ValidationSummary will appear with a list of all error messages, as shown in Figure 10-2. In this case, it retrieves one error message (from the RangeValidator control). However, if you had a dozen validators, it would retrieve all their error messages and create a list.

When the ValidationSummary displays the list of errors, it automatically retrieves the value of the ErrorMessage property from each validator. In some cases, you'll want to display a full message in the summary and some sort of visual indicator next to the offending control. For example, many websites use an error icon or an asterisk to highlight text boxes with invalid input. You can use this technique with the help of the Text property of the validators. Ordinarily, Text is left empty. However, if you set both Text and ErrorMessage, the ErrorMessage value will be used for the summary while the Text value is displayed in the validator. (Of course, you'll need to make sure you aren't also setting the Display property of your validator to None, which hides it completely.)

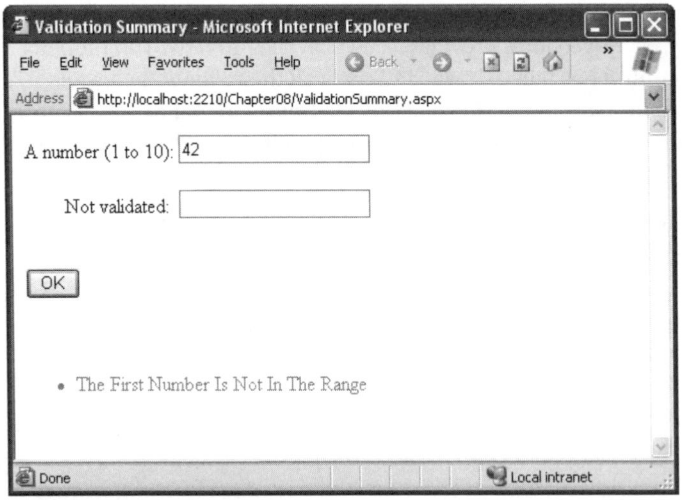

Figure 10-2. *The validation summary*

Here's an example of a validator that includes a detailed error message (which will appear in the ValidationSummary) and an asterisk indicator (which will appear in the validator, next to the control that has the problem):

```
<asp:RangeValidator id="RangeValidator" runat="server"
  Text="*" ErrorMessage="The First Number Is Not In The Range"
  ControlToValidate="txtValidated"
  MaximumValue="10" MinimumValue="1" Type="Integer" />
```

You can even get a bit fancier by replacing the plain asterisk with a snippet of more interesting HTML. Here's an example that uses the <img> tag to add a small error icon image when validation fails:

```
<asp:RangeValidator id="RangeValidator" runat="server"
  Text="<img src='ErrorIcon.gif' />" alt='Error' ... />
```

Figure 10-3 shows this validator in action.

The ValidationSummary control provides some useful properties you can use to fine-tune the error display. You can set the HeaderText property to display a special title at the top of the list (such as *Your page contains the following errors:*). You can also change the ForeColor and choose a DisplayMode. The possible modes are BulletList (the default), List, and SingleParagraph.

Finally, you can choose to have the validation summary displayed in a pop-up dialog box instead of on the page (see Figure 10-3). This approach has the advantage of leaving the user interface of the page untouched, but it also forces the user to dismiss the error messages by closing the window before being able to modify the input controls. If users will need to refer to these messages while they fix the page, the inline display is better.

To show the summary in a dialog box, set the ShowMessageBox property of the ValidationSummary to True. Keep in mind that unless you set the ShowSummary property to False, you'll see both the message box and the in-page summary (as in Figure 10-4).

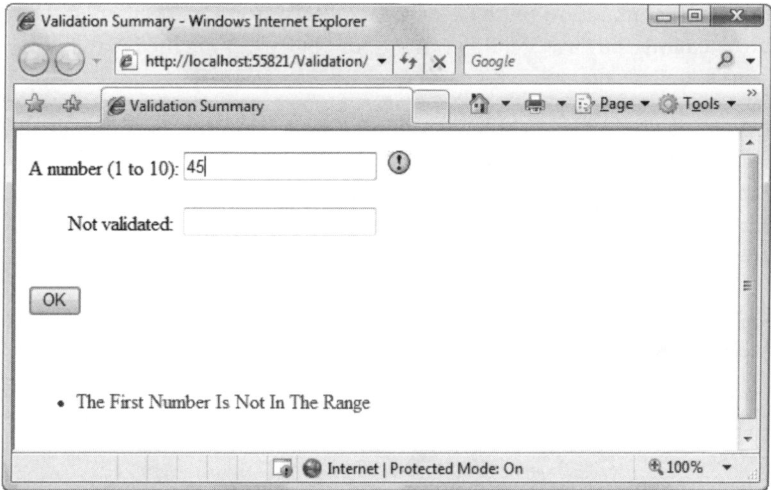

Figure 10-3. *A validation summary and an error indicator*

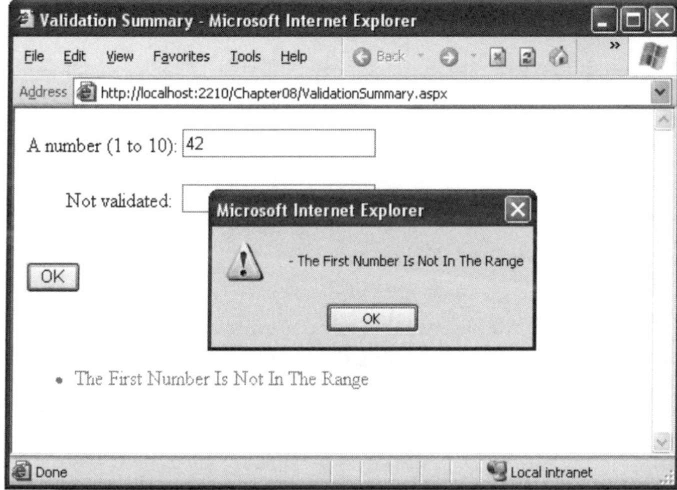

Figure 10-4. *A message box summary*

Manual Validation

Your final option is to disable validation and perform the work on your own, with the help of the validation controls. This allows you to take other information into consideration or create a specialized error message that involves other controls (such as images or buttons).

You can create manual validation in one of three ways:

- Use your own code to verify values. In this case, you won't use any of the ASP.NET validation controls.
- Disable the EnableClientScript property for each validation control. This allows an invalid page to be submitted, after which you can decide what to do with it depending on the problems that may exist.

- Add a button with CausesValidation set to False. When this button is clicked, manually validate the page by calling the Page.Validate() method. Then examine the IsValid property, and decide what to do.

The next example uses the second approach. Once the page is submitted, it examines all the validation controls on the page by looping through the Page.Validators collection. Every time it finds a control that hasn't validated successfully, it retrieves the invalid value from the input control and adds it to a string. At the end of this routine, it displays a message that describes which values were incorrect, as shown in Figure 10-5.

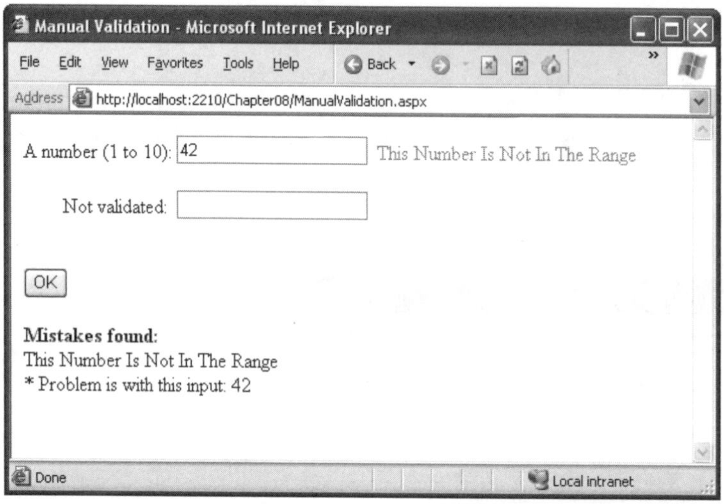

Figure 10-5. *Manual validation*

This technique adds a feature that wouldn't be available with automatic validation, which uses the ErrorMessage property. In that case, it isn't possible to include the actual incorrect values in the message.

Here's the event handler that checks for invalid values:

```
Protected Sub cmdOK_Click(ByVal sender As Object, _
  ByVal e As EventArgs) Handles cmdOK.Click

    Dim ErrorMessage As String = "<b>Mistakes found:</b><br />"

    ' Create a variable to represent the input control.

    ' Search through the validation controls.
    For Each ctrl As BaseValidator In Me.Validators
        If ctrl.IsValid = False Then
            ErrorMessage &= ctrl.ErrorMessage & "<br />"
```

```
            ' Find the corresponding input control, and change the
            ' generic Control variable into a TextBox variable.
            ' This allows access to the Text property.
            Dim ctrlInput As TextBox = CType( _
              Me.FindControl(ctrl.ControlToValidate), TextBox)
            ErrorMessage &= " * Problem is with this input: "
            ErrorMessage &= ctrlInput.Text & "<br />"
        End If
    Next

    lblMessage.Text = ErrorMessage
End Sub
```

This example uses an advanced technique: the Page.FindControl() method. It's required because the ControlToValidate property of each validator simply provides a string with the name of a control, not a reference to the actual control object. To find the control that matches this name (and retrieve its Text property), you need to use the FindControl() method. Once the code has retrieved the matching text box, it can perform other tasks such as clearing the current value, tweaking a property, or even changing the text box color. Note that the FindControl() method returns a generic Control reference, because you might search any type of control. To access all the properties of your control, you need to cast it to the appropriate type (such as TextBox in this example).

Validating with Regular Expressions

One of ASP.NET's most powerful validation controls is the RegularExpressionValidator, which validates text by determining whether or not it matches a specific pattern.

For example, e-mail addresses, phone numbers, and file names are all examples of text that has specific constraints. A phone number must be a set number of digits, an e-mail address must include exactly one @ character (with text on either side), and a file name can't include certain special characters like \ and ?. One way to define patterns like these is with *regular expressions.*

Regular expressions have appeared in countless other languages and gained popularity as an extremely powerful way to work with strings. In fact, Visual Studio even allows programmers to perform a search-and-replace operation in their code using a regular expression (which may represent a new height of computer geekdom). Regular expressions can almost be considered an entire language of their own. How to master all the ways you can use regular expressions—including pattern matching, back references, and named groups—could occupy an entire book (and several books are dedicated to just that subject). Fortunately, you can understand the basics of regular expressions without nearly that much work.

Literals and Metacharacters

All regular expressions consist of two kinds of characters: literals and metacharacters. *Literals* are not unlike the string literals you type in code. They represent a specific defined character. For example, if you search for the string literal "l", you'll find the character *l* and nothing else.

Metacharacters provide the true secret to unlocking the full power of regular expressions. You're probably already familiar with two metacharacters from the DOS world (? and *). Consider the command-line expression shown here:

```
Del *.*
```

The expression *.* contains one literal (the period) and two metacharacters (the asterisks). This translates as "delete every file that starts with any number of characters and ends with an extension of any number of characters (or has no extension at all)." Because all files in DOS implicitly have extensions, this has the well-documented effect of deleting everything in the current directory.

Another DOS metacharacter is the question mark, which means "any single character." For example, the following statement deletes any file named hello that has an extension of exactly one character.

```
Del hello.?
```

The regular expression language provides many flexible metacharacters—far more than the DOS command line. For example, \s represents any whitespace character (such as a space or tab). \d represents any digit. Thus, the following expression would match any string that started with the numbers 333, followed by a single whitespace character and any three numbers. Valid matches would include 333 333 and 333 945 but not 334 333 or 3334 945.

```
333\s\d\d\d
```

One aspect that can make regular expressions less readable is that they use special metacharacters that are more than one character long. In the previous example, \s represents a single character, as does \d, even though they both occupy two characters in the expression.

You can use the plus (+) sign to represent a repeated character. For example, 5+7 means "one or more occurrences of the character 5, followed by a single 7." The number 57 would match, as would 555557. You can also use parentheses to group a subexpression. For example, (52)+7 would match any string that started with a sequence of 52. Matches would include 527, 52527, 5252527, and so on.

You can also delimit a range of characters using square brackets. [a-f] would match any single character from *a* to *f* (lowercase only). The following expression would match any word that starts with a letter from *a* to *f*, contains one or more "word" characters (letters), and ends with *ing*—possible matches include *acting* and *developing*.

```
[a-f]\w+ing
```

The following is a more useful regular expression that can match any e-mail address by verifying that it contains the @ symbol. The dot is a metacharacter used to indicate any character except newline. However, some invalid e-mail addresses would still be allowed, including those that contain spaces and those that don't include a dot (.). You'll see a better example a little later in the customer form example.

```
.+@.+
```

Finding a Regular Expression

Clearly, picking the perfect regular expression may require some testing. In fact, numerous reference materials (on the Internet and in paper form) include useful regular expressions for validating common values such as postal codes. To experiment, you can use the simple RegularExpressionTest page included with the online samples, which is shown in Figure 10-6. It allows you to set a regular expression that will be used to validate a control. Then you can type in some sample values and see whether the regular expression validator succeeds or fails.

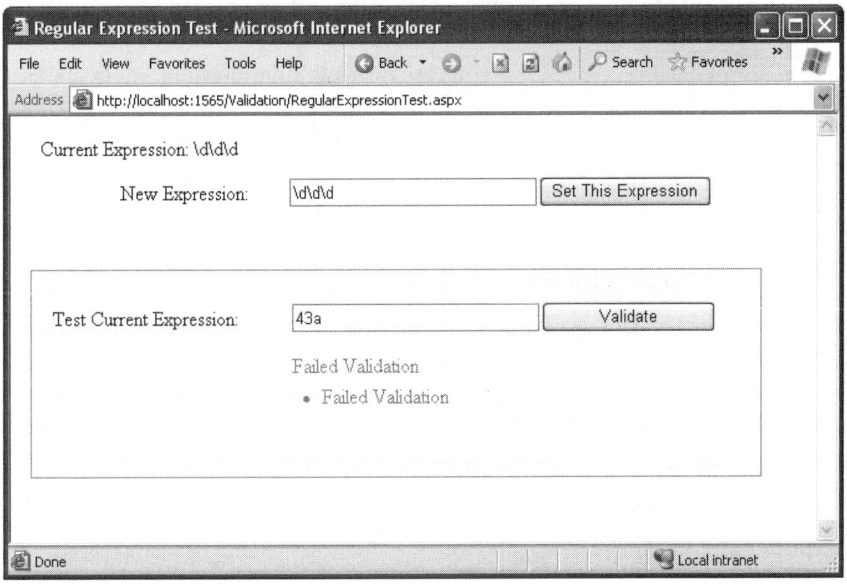

Figure 10-6. *A regular expression test page*

The code is quite simple. The Set This Expression button assigns a new regular expression to the RegularExpressionValidator control (using whatever text you have typed). The Validate button simply triggers a postback, which causes ASP.NET to perform validation automatically. If an error message appears, validation has failed. Otherwise, it's successful.

```
Public Partial Class RegularExpressionTest
    Inherits System.Web.UI.Page

    Protected Sub cmdSetExpression_Click(ByVal sender As Object, _
      ByVal e As EventArgs) Handles cmdSetExpression.Click
        TestValidator.ValidationExpression = txtExpression.Text
        lblExpression.Text = "Current Expression: "
        lblExpression.Text &= txtExpression.Text
    End Sub
End Class
```

Table 10-4 shows some of the fundamental regular expression building blocks. If you need to match a literal character with the same name as a special character, you generally precede it with a \ character. For example, *hello* matches *hello* in a string, because the special asterisk (*) character is preceded by a slash (\).

Table 10-4. *Regular Expression Characters*

Character	Description
*	Zero or more occurrences of the previous character or subexpression. For example, 7*8 matches 7778 or just 8.
+	One or more occurrences of the previous character or subexpression. For example, 7+8 matches 7778 but not 8.
( )	Groups a subexpression that will be treated as a single element. For example, (78)+ matches 78 and 787878.
{m,n}	The previous character (or subexpression) can occur from m to n times. For example, A{1,3} matches A, AA, or AAA.
|	Either of two matches. For example, 8|6 matches 8 or 6.
[ ]	Matches one character in a range of valid characters. For example, [A-C] matches A, B, or C.
[^]	Matches a character that isn't in the given range. For example, [^A-B] matches any character except A and B.
.	Any character except newline. For example, .here matches where and there.
\s	Any whitespace character (such as a tab or space).
\S	Any nonwhitespace character.
\d	Any digit character.
\D	Any character that isn't a digit.
\w	Any "word" character (letter, number, or underscore).
\W	Any character that isn't a "word" character (letter, number, or underscore).

Table 10-5 shows a few common (and useful) regular expressions.

Table 10-5. *Commonly Used Regular Expressions*

Content	Regular Expression	Description
E-mail address*	\S+@\S+\.\S+	Check for an at (@) sign and dot (.) and allow nonwhitespace characters only.
Password	\w+	Any sequence of one or more word characters (letter, space, or underscore).

Table 10-5. *Commonly Used Regular Expressions*

Content	Regular Expression	Description
Specific-length password	\w{4,10}	A password that must be at least four characters long but no longer than ten characters.
Advanced password	[a-zA-Z]\w{3,9}	As with the specific-length password, this regular expression will allow four to ten total characters. The twist is that the first character must fall in the range of a–z or A–Z (that is to say, it must start with a nonaccented ordinary letter).
Another advanced password	[a-zA-Z]\w*\d+\w*	This password starts with a letter character, followed by zero or more word characters, one or more digits, and then zero or more word characters. In short, it forces a password to contain one or more numbers somewhere inside it. You could use a similar pattern to require two numbers or any other special character.
Limited-length field	\S{4,10}	Like the password example, this allows four to ten characters, but it allows special characters (asterisks, ampersands, and so on).
U.S. Social Security number	\d{3}-\d{2}-\d{4}	A sequence of three, two, then four digits, with each group separated by a dash. You could use a similar pattern when requiring a phone number.

* *You have many different ways to validate e-mail addresses with regular expressions of varying complexity. See* `http://www.4guysfromrolla.com/webtech/validateemail.shtml` *for a discussion of the subject and numerous examples.*

Some logic is much more difficult to model in a regular expression. An example is the Luhn algorithm, which verifies credit card numbers by first doubling every second digit, then adding these doubled digits together, and finally dividing the sum by ten. The number is valid (although not necessarily connected to a real account) if there is no remainder after dividing the sum. To use the Luhn algorithm, you need a CustomValidator control that runs this logic on the supplied value. (You can find a detailed description of the Luhn algorithm at `http://en.wikipedia.org/wiki/Luhn_formula`.)

A Validated Customer Form

To bring together these various topics, you'll now see a full-fledged web form that combines a variety of pieces of information that might be needed to add a user record (for example, an e-commerce site shopper or a content site subscriber). Figure 10-7 shows this form.

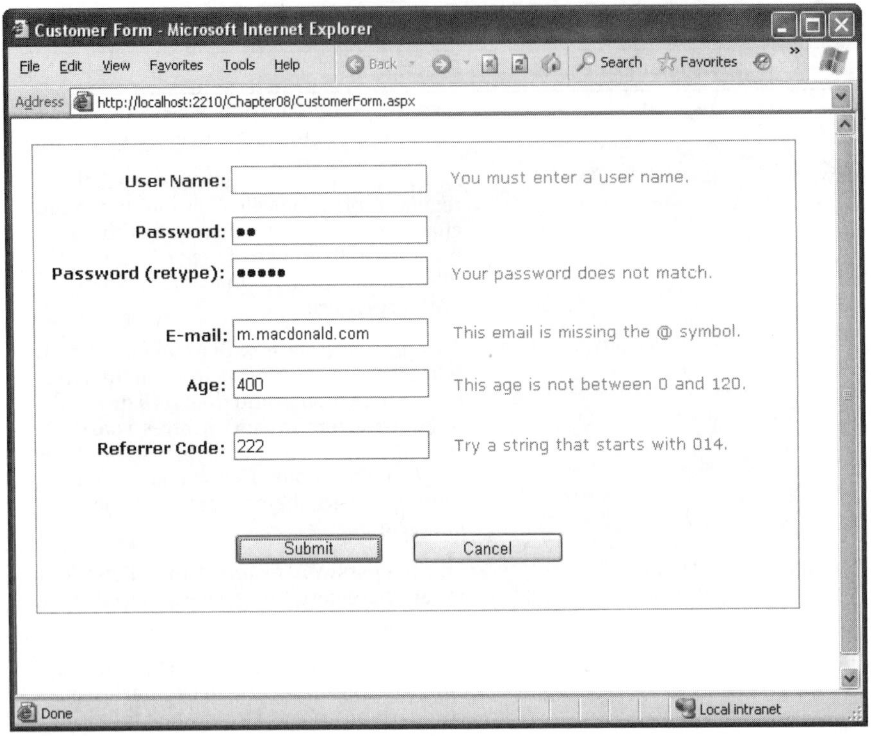

Figure 10-7. *A sample customer form*

Several types of validation are taking place on the customer form:

- Three RequiredFieldValidator controls make sure the user enters a user name, a password, and a password confirmation.
- A CompareValidator ensures that the two versions of the masked password match.
- A RegularExpressionValidator checks that the e-mail address contains an at (@) symbol.
- A RangeValidator ensures the age is a number from 0 to 120.
- A CustomValidator performs a special validation on the server of a "referrer code." This code verifies that the first three characters make up a number that is divisible by 7.

The tags for the validator controls are as follows:

```
<asp:RequiredFieldValidator id="vldUserName" runat="server"
     ErrorMessage="You must enter a user name."
     ControlToValidate="txtUserName" />

<asp:RequiredFieldValidator id="vldPassword" runat="server"
     ErrorMessage="You must enter a password."
     ControlToValidate="txtPassword" />
```

```
<asp:CompareValidator id="vldRetype" runat="server"
     ErrorMessage="Your password does not match."
     ControlToCompare="txtPassword" ControlToValidate="txtRetype" />

<asp:RequiredFieldValidator id="vldRetypeRequired" runat="server"
     ErrorMessage="You must confirm your password."
     ControlToValidate="txtRetype" />

<asp:RegularExpressionValidator id="vldEmail" runat="server"
     ErrorMessage="This email is missing the @ symbol."
     ValidationExpression=".+@.+" ControlToValidate="txtEmail" />

<asp:RangeValidator id="vldAge" runat="server"
     ErrorMessage="This age is not between 0 and 120." Type="Integer"
     MinimumValue="0" MaximumValue="120"
     ControlToValidate="txtAge" />

<asp:CustomValidator id="vldCode" runat="server"
     ErrorMessage="Try a string that starts with 014."
     ValidateEmptyText="False"
     ControlToValidate="txtCode" />
```

The form provides two validation buttons—one that requires validation and one that allows the user to cancel the task gracefully:

```
<asp:Button id="cmdSubmit" runat="server"
  Text="Submit"></asp:Button>
<asp:Button id="cmdCancel" runat="server"
  CausesValidation="False" Text="Cancel">
</asp:Button>
```

Here's the event-handling code for the buttons:

```
Protected Sub cmdSubmit_Click(ByVal sender As Object, _
  ByVal e As EventArgs) Handles cmdSubmit.Click
    If Page.IsValid
        lblMessage.Text = "This is a valid form."
    End If
End Sub

Protected Sub cmdCancel_Click(ByVal sender As Object, _
  ByVal e As EventArgs) Handles cmdCancel.Click
    lblMessage.Text = "No attempt was made to validate this form."
End Sub
```

The only form-level code that is required for validation is the custom validation code. The validation takes place in the event handler for the CustomValidator.ServerValidate event. This method receives the value it needs to validate (e.Value) and sets the result of the validation to True or False (e.IsValid).

```
Protected Sub vldCode_ServerValidate(ByVal sender As Object, _
  ByVal e As ServerValidateEventArgs) Handles vldCode.ServerValidate

    ' Check if the first three digits are divisible by seven.
    If Val(e.Value) <> 0 And Val(e.Value.Substring(0, 3)) Mod 7 = 0 Then
        e.IsValid = True
    Else
        e.IsValid = False
    End If
End Sub
```

■ **Tip** In some cases, you might be able to replace custom validation with a particularly ingenious use of a regular expression. However, you can use custom validation to ensure that validation code is executed only at the server. That prevents users from seeing your regular expression template (in the rendered JavaScript code) and using it to determine how they can outwit your validation routine. For example, a user may not have a valid credit card number, but if they know the algorithm you use to test credit card numbers, they can create a false one more easily.

The CustomValidator has another quirk. You'll notice that your custom server-side validation isn't performed until the page is posted back. This means that if you enable the client script code (the default), dynamic messages will appear informing the user when the other values are incorrect, but they will not indicate any problem with the referral code until the page is posted back to the server.

This isn't really a problem, but if it troubles you, you can use the CustomValidator.ClientValidationFunction property. Add a client-side JavaScript or VBScript validation function to the .aspx portion of the web page. (Ideally, it will be JavaScript for compatibility with browsers other than Internet Explorer.) Remember, you can't use client-side ASP.NET code, because C# and VB aren't recognized by the client browser.

Your JavaScript function will accept two parameters (in true .NET style), which identify the source of the event and the additional validation parameters. In fact, the client-side event is modeled on the .NET ServerValidate event. Just as you did in the ServerValidate event handler, in the client validation function, you retrieve the value to validate from the Value property of the event argument object. You then set the IsValid property to indicate whether validation succeeds or fails.

The following is the client-side equivalent for the code in the ServerValidate event handler. The JavaScript code resembles C# superficially.

```
<script type="text/javascript">
<!--
function MyCustomValidation(objSource, objArgs)
{
    // Get value.
    var number = objArgs.Value;
```

```
        // Check value and return result.
        number = number.substr(0, 3);
        if (number % 7 == 0)
        {
            objArgs.IsValid = true;
        }
        else
        {
            objArgs.IsValid = false;
        }
    }
    // -->
    </script>
```

Once you've added the validation script function, you must set the ClientValidationFunction property of the CustomValidator control to the name of the function. You can edit the CustomValidator tag by hand or use the Properties window in Visual Studio.

```
<asp:CustomValidator id="vldCode" runat="server"
     ErrorMessage="Try a string that starts with 014."
     ControlToValidate="txtCode"
     ClientValidationFunction="MyCustomValidation" />
```

ASP.NET will now call this function on your behalf when it's required.

■ **Tip** Even when you use client-side validation, you must still include the ServerValidate event handler, both to provide server-side validation for clients that don't support the required JavaScript and DHTML features and to prevent clients from circumventing your validation by modifying the HTML page they receive.

By default, custom validation isn't performed on empty values. However, you can change this behavior by setting the CustomValidator.ValidateEmptyText property to True. This is a useful approach if you create a more detailed JavaScript function (for example, one that updates with additional information) and want it to run when the text is cleared.

YOU CAN VALIDATE LIST CONTROLS

The examples in this chapter have concentrated exclusively on validating text entry, which is the most common requirement in a web application. While you can't validate RadioButton or CheckBox controls, you can validate most single-select list controls.

When validating a list control, the value that is being validated is the Value property of the selected ListItem object. Remember, the Value property is the special hidden information attribute that can be added to every list item. If you don't use it, you can't validate the control (validating the text of the selection isn't a supported option).

Validation Groups

In more complex pages, you might have several distinct groups of controls, possibly in separate panels. In these situations, you may want to perform validation separately. For example, you might create a form that includes a box with login controls and a box underneath it with the controls for registering a new user. Each box includes its own submit button, and depending on which button is clicked, you want to perform the validation just for that section of the page.

This scenario is possible thanks to a feature called *validation groups*. To create a validation group, you need to put the input controls, the validators, and the CausesValidation button controls into the same logical group. You do this by setting the ValidationGroup property of every control with the same descriptive string (such as "LoginGroup" or "NewUserGroup"). Every control that provides a CausesValidation property also includes the ValidationGroup property.

For example, the following page defines two validation groups, named Group1 and Group2. The controls for each group are placed into separate Panel controls.

```
<form id="form1" runat="server">
  <asp:Panel ID="Panel1" runat="server">
    <asp:TextBox ID="TextBox1" ValidationGroup="Group1" runat="server" />
    <asp:RequiredFieldValidator ID="RequiredFieldValidator1"
     ErrorMessage="*Required" ValidationGroup="Group1"
     runat="server" ControlToValidate="TextBox1" />
    <asp:Button ID="Button1" Text="Validate Group1"
     ValidationGroup="Group1" runat="server" />
  </asp:Panel> <br />
  <asp:Panel ID="Panel2" runat="server">
    <asp:TextBox ID="TextBox2" ValidationGroup="Group2"
     runat="server" />
    <asp:RequiredFieldValidator ID="RequiredFieldValidator2"
     ErrorMessage="*Required" ValidationGroup="Group2"
     ControlToValidate="TextBox2" runat="server" />
    <asp:Button ID="Button2" Text="Validate Group2"
     ValidationGroup="Group2" runat="server" />
  </asp:Panel>
</form>
```

If you click the button in the topmost Panel, only the first text box is validated. If you click the button in the second Panel, only the second text box is validated (as shown in Figure 10-8).

What happens if you add a new button that doesn't specify any validation group? In this case, the button validates every control that isn't explicitly assigned to a named validation group. In the current example, no controls fit the requirement, so the page is posted back successfully and deemed to be valid.

If you want to make sure a control is always validated, regardless of the validation group of the button that's clicked, you'll need to create multiple validators for the control, one for each group (and one with no validation group).

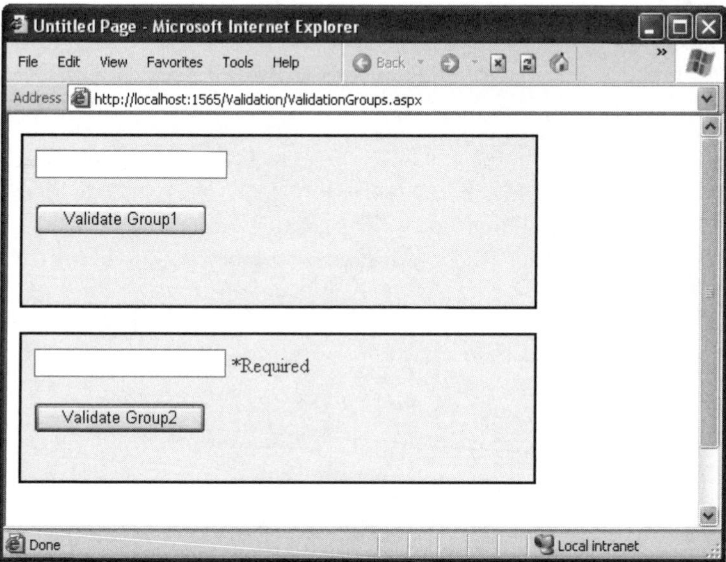

Figure 10-8. *Grouping controls for validation*

The Last Word

In this chapter, you learned how to use one of ASP.NET's most practical features: validation. You saw how ASP.NET combines server-side and client-side validation to ensure bulletproof security without sacrificing the usability of your web pages. You also looked at the types of validation provided by the various validation controls, and even brushed up on the powerful pattern-matching syntax used for regular expressions. Finally, you considered how to customize and extend the validation process to handle a few different scenarios.

CHAPTER 11

■ ■ ■

Rich Controls

Rich controls are web controls that model complex user interface elements. Although no strict definition exists for what is and what isn't a rich control, the term commonly describes a web control that has an object model that's distinctly separate from the HTML it generates. A typical rich control can be programmed as a single object (and added to a web page with a single control tag) but renders itself using a complex sequence of HTML elements. Rich controls can also react to user actions (like a mouse click on a specific region of the control) and raise more meaningful events that your code can respond to on the web server. In other words, rich controls give you a way to create advanced user interfaces in your web pages without writing lines of convoluted HTML.

In this chapter, you'll take a look at several web controls that have no direct equivalent in the world of ordinary HTML. You'll start with the Calendar, which provides slick date-selection functionality. Next, you'll consider the AdRotator, which gives you an easy way to insert a randomly selected image into a web page. Finally, you'll learn how to create sophisticated pages with multiple views using two advanced container controls: the MultiView and the Wizard. These controls allow you to pack a miniature application into a single page. Using them, you can handle a multistep task without redirecting the user from one page to another.

Note ASP.NET includes numerous rich controls that are discussed elsewhere in this book, including rich data controls, security controls, and controls tailored for web portals. In this chapter, you'll focus on a few useful web controls that don't fit neatly into any of these categories. All of these controls appear in the Standard tab of the Visual Studio Toolbox.

The Calendar

The Calendar control presents a miniature calendar that you can place in any web page. Like most rich controls, the Calendar can be programmed as a single object (and defined in a single simple tag), but it renders itself with dozens of lines of HTML output.

```
<asp:Calendar id="MyCalendar" runat="server" />
```

The Calendar control presents a single-month view, as shown in Figure 11-1. The user can navigate from month to month using the navigational arrows, at which point the page is posted back and ASP.NET automatically provides a new page with the correct month values. You don't need to write any additional event-handling code to manage this process. When the user clicks a date, the date becomes highlighted in a gray box (by default). You can retrieve the selected day in your code as a DateTime object from the Calendar.SelectedDate property.

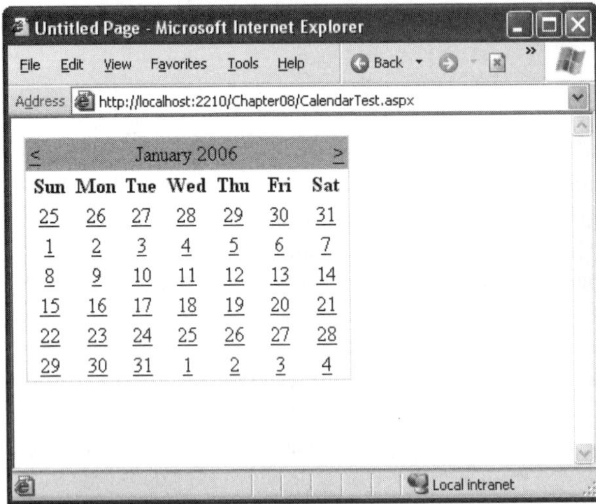

Figure 11-1. *The default Calendar*

This basic set of features may provide everything you need in your application. Alternatively, you can configure different selection modes to allow users to select entire weeks or months or to render the control as a static calendar that doesn't allow selection. The only fact you must remember is that if you allow month selection, the user can also select a single week or a day. Similarly, if you allow week selection, the user can also select a single day.

You set the type of selection through the Calendar.SelectionMode property. You may also need to set the Calendar.FirstDayOfWeek property to configure how a week is selected. (For example, set FirstDayOfWeek to the enumerated value Sunday, and weeks will be selected from Sunday to Saturday.)

When you allow multiple date selection, you need to examine the SelectedDates property, which provides a collection of all the selected dates. You can loop through this collection using the For Each syntax. The following code demonstrates this technique:

```
lblDates.Text = "You selected these dates:<br />"

Dim dt As DateTime
For Each dt In MyCalendar.SelectedDates
    lblDates.Text &= dt.ToLongDateString() & "<br />"
Next
```

Figure 11-2 shows the resulting page after this code has been executed.

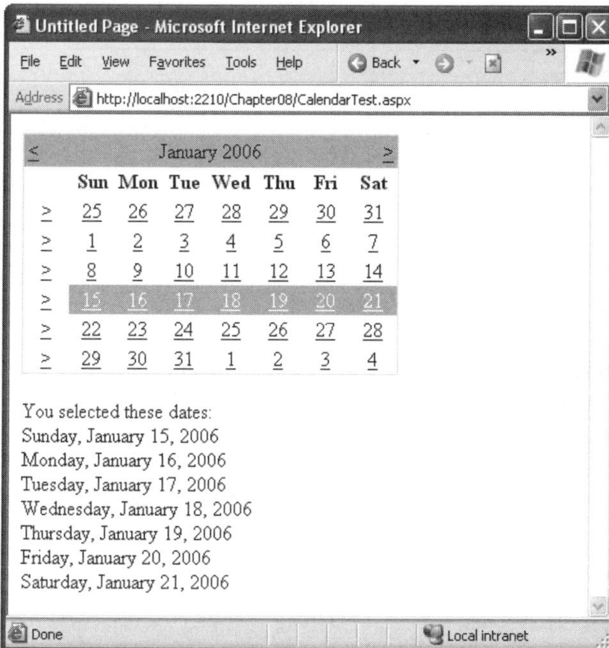

Figure 11-2. *Selecting multiple dates*

Formatting the Calendar

The Calendar control provides a whole host of formatting-related properties. You can set various parts of the calendar, like the header, selector, and various day types, by using one of the style properties (for example, WeekendDayStyle). Each of these style properties references a full-featured TableItemStyle object that provides properties for coloring, border style, font, and alignment. Taken together, they allow you to modify almost any part of the calendar's appearance.

Table 11-1 lists the style properties that the Calendar control provides.

Table 11-1. *Properties for Calendar Styles*

Member	Description
DayHeaderStyle	The style for the section of the Calendar that displays the days of the week (as column headers).
DayStyle	The default style for the dates in the current month.
NextPrevStyle	The style for the navigation controls in the title section that move from month to month.
OtherMonthDayStyle	The style for the dates that aren't in the currently displayed month. These dates are used to "fill in" the calendar grid. For example, the first few cells in the topmost row may display the last few days from the previous month.
SelectedDayStyle	The style for the selected dates on the calendar.

Table 11-1. *Properties for Calendar Styles (Continued)*

Member	Description
SelectorStyle	The style for the week and month date-selection controls.
TitleStyle	The style for the title section.
TodayDayStyle	The style for the date designated as today (represented by the TodaysDate property of the Calendar control).
WeekendDayStyle	The style for dates that fall on the weekend.

You can adjust each style using the Properties window. For a quick shortcut, you can set an entire related color scheme using the Calendar's Auto Format feature. To do so, start by selecting the Calendar on the design surface of a web form. Then, click the arrow icon that appears next to its top-right corner to show the Calendar's smart tag, and click the Auto Format link. You'll be presented with a list of predefined formats that set the style properties, as shown in Figure 11-3.

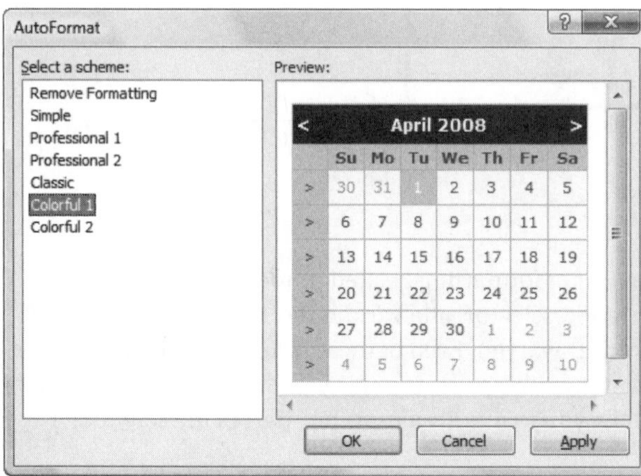

Figure 11-3. *Calendar styles*

You can also use additional properties to hide some elements or configure the text they display. For example, properties that start with "Show" (such as ShowDayHeader, ShowTitle, and ShowGridLines) can be used to hide or show a specific visual element. Properties that end in "Text" (such as PrevMonthText, NextMonthText, and SelectWeekText) allow you to set the text that's shown in part of the calendar.

Restricting Dates

In most situations where you need to use a calendar for selection, you don't want to allow the user to select any date in the calendar. For example, the user might be booking an appointment or choosing a delivery date—two services that are generally provided only on set days. The Calendar control makes it surprisingly easy to implement this logic. In fact, if you've worked with the date and time controls on the Windows platform, you'll quickly recognize that the ASP.NET versions are far superior.

The basic approach to restricting dates is to write an event handler for the Calendar.DayRender event. This event occurs when the Calendar control is about to create a month to display to the user. This event gives you the chance to examine the date that is being added to the current month (through the e.Day property) and decide whether it should be selectable or restricted.

The following code makes it impossible to select any weekend days or days in years greater than 2010:

```
Protected Sub MyCalendar_DayRender(ByVal sender As Object, _
  ByVal e As DayRenderEventArgs) Handles MyCalendar.DayRender

    ' Restrict dates after the year 2010, and those on the weekend.
    If e.Day.IsWeekend Or e.Day.Date.Year > 2010 Then
        e.Day.IsSelectable = False
    End If
End Sub
```

The e.Day object is an instance of the CalendarDay class, which provides various properties. Table 11-2 describes some of the most useful.

Table 11-2. *CalendarDay Properties*

Property	Description
Date	The DateTime object that represents this date.
IsWeekend	True if this date falls on a Saturday or Sunday.
IsToday	True if this value matches the Calendar.TodaysDate property, which is set to the current day by default.
IsOtherMonth	True if this date doesn't belong to the current month but is displayed to fill in the first or last row. For example, this might be the last day of the previous month or the next day of the following month.
IsSelectable	Allows you to configure whether the user can select this day.

The DayRender event is extremely powerful. Besides allowing you to tailor what dates are selectable, it also allows you to configure the cell where the date is located through the e.Cell property. (The calendar is displayed using an HTML table.) For example, you could highlight an important date or even add information. Here's an example that highlights a single day—the fifth of May—by adding a new Label control in the table cell for that day:

```
Protected Sub MyCalendar_DayRender(ByVal sender As Object, _
  ByVal e As DayRenderEventArgs) Handles MyCalendar.DayRender

    ' Check for May 5 in any year, and format it.
    If e.Day.Date.Day = 5 And e.Day.Date.Month = 5 Then
        e.Cell.BackColor = System.Drawing.Color.Yellow
```

```
        ' Add some static text to the cell.
        Dim lbl As New Label()
        lbl.Text = "<br/>My Birthday!"
        e.Cell.Controls.Add(lbl)
    End If
End Sub
```

Figure 11-4 shows the resulting calendar display.

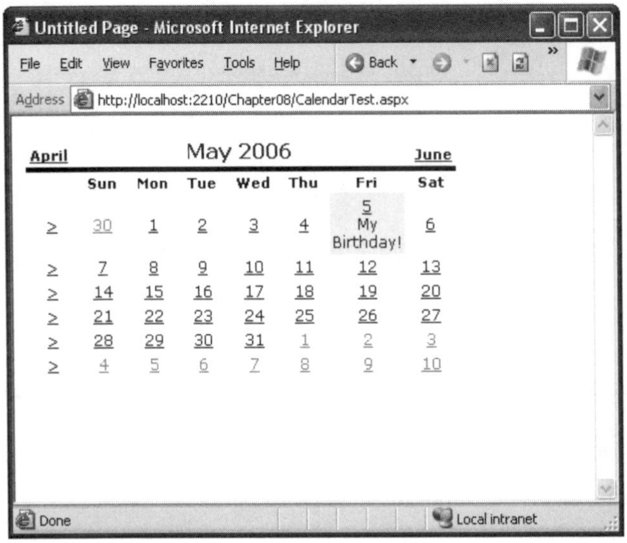

Figure 11-4. *Highlighting a day*

The Calendar control provides two other useful events: SelectionChanged and VisibleMonthChanged. These occur immediately after the user selects a new day or browses to a new month (using the next month and previous month links). You can react to these events and update other portions of the web page to correspond to the current calendar month. For example, you could design a page that lets you schedule a meeting in two steps. First, you choose the appropriate day. Then, you choose one of the available times on that day.

The following code demonstrates this approach, using a different set of time values if a Monday is selected in the calendar than it does for other days:

```
Protected Sub MyCalendar_SelectionChanged(ByVal sender As Object, _
  ByVal e As EventArgs) Handles MyCalendar.SelectionChanged

    lstTimes.Items.Clear()

    Select Case MyCalendar.SelectedDate.DayOfWeek
        Case DayOfWeek.Monday
            ' Apply special Monday schedule.
            lstTimes.Items.Add("10:00")
            lstTimes.Items.Add("10:30")
            lstTimes.Items.Add("11:00")
```

```
        Case Else
            lstTimes.Items.Add("10:00")
            lstTimes.Items.Add("10:30")
            lstTimes.Items.Add("11:00")
            lstTimes.Items.Add("11:30")
            lstTimes.Items.Add("12:00")
            lstTimes.Items.Add("12:30")
    End Select
End Sub
```

To try these features of the Calendar control, run the Appointment.aspx page from the online samples. This page provides a formatted Calendar control that restricts some dates, formats others specially, and updates a corresponding list control when the selection changes.

Table 11-3 gives you an at-a-glance look at almost all the members of the Calendar control class.

Table 11-3. *Calendar Members*

Member	Description
Caption and CaptionAlign	Gives you an easy way to add a title to the calendar. By default, the caption appears at the top of the title area, just above the month heading. However, you can control this to some extent with the CaptionAlign property. Use Left or Right to keep the caption at the top but move it to one side or the other, and use Bottom to place the caption under the calendar.
CellPadding	ASP.NET creates a date in a separate cell of an invisible table. CellPadding is the space, in pixels, between the border of each cell and its contents.
CellSpacing	The space, in pixels, between cells in the same table.
DayNameFormat	Determines how days are displayed in the calendar header. Valid values are Full (as in Sunday), FirstLetter (S), FirstTwoLetters (Su), and Short (Sun), which is the default.
FirstDayOfWeek	Determines which day is displayed in the first column of the calendar. The values are any day name from the FirstDayOfWeek enumeration (such as Sunday).
NextMonthText and PrevMonthText	Sets the text that the user clicks to move to the next or previous month. These navigation links appear at the top of the calendar and are the greater-than (>) and less-than (<) signs by default. This setting is applied only if NextPrevFormat is set to CustomText.
NextPrevFormat	Sets the text that the user clicks to move to the next or previous month. This can be FullMonth (for example, December), ShortMonth (Dec), or CustomText, in which case the NextMonthText and PrevMonthText properties are used. CustomText is the default.

Table 11-3. *Calendar Members (Continued)*

Member	Description
SelectedDate and SelectedDates	Sets or gets the currently selected date as a DateTime object. You can specify this in the control tag in a format like this: "12:00:00 AM, 12/31/2010" (depending on your computer's regional settings). If you allow multiple date selection, the SelectedDates property will return a collection of DateTime objects, one for each selected date. You can use collection methods such as Add, Remove, and Clear to change the selection.
SelectionMode	Determines how many dates can be selected at once. The default is Day, which allows one date to be selected. Other options include DayWeek (a single date or an entire week) or DayWeekMonth (a single date, an entire week, or an entire month). You have no way to allow the user to select multiple noncontiguous dates. You also have no way to allow larger selections without also including smaller selections. (For example, if you allow full months to be selected, you must also allow week selection and individual day selection.)
SelectMonthText and SelectWeekText	The text shown for the link that allows the user to select an entire month or week. These properties don't apply if the SelectionMode is Day.
ShowDayHeader, ShowGridLines, ShowNextPrevMonth, and ShowTitle	These Boolean properties allow you to configure whether various parts of the calendar are shown, including the day titles, gridlines between every day, the previous/next month navigation links, and the title section. Note that hiding the title section also hides the next and previous month navigation controls.
TitleFormat	Configures how the month is displayed in the title area. Valid values include Month and MonthYear (the default).
TodaysDate	Sets which day should be recognized as the current date and formatted with the TodayDayStyle. This defaults to the current day on the web server.
VisibleDate	Gets or sets the date that specifies what month will be displayed in the calendar. This allows you to change the calendar display without modifying the current date selection.
DayRender event	Occurs once for each day that is created and added to the currently visible month before the page is rendered. This event gives you the opportunity to apply special formatting, add content, or restrict selection for an individual date cell. Keep in mind that days can appear in the calendar even when they don't fall in the current month, provided they fall close to the end of the previous month or close to the start of the following month.
SelectionChanged event	Occurs when the user selects a day, a week, or an entire month by clicking the date selector controls.
VisibleMonthChanged event	Occurs when the user clicks the next or previous month navigation controls to move to another month.

The AdRotator

The basic purpose of the AdRotator is to provide a graphic on a page that is chosen randomly from a group of possible images. In other words, every time the page is requested, an image is selected at random and displayed, which is the "rotation" indicated by the name AdRotator. One use of the AdRotator is to show banner-style advertisements on a page, but you can use it any time you want to vary an image randomly.

Using ASP.NET, it wouldn't be too difficult to implement an AdRotator type of design on your own. You could react to the Page.Load event, generate a random number, and then use that number to choose from a list of predetermined image files. You could even store the list in the web.config file so that it can be easily modified separately as part of the application's configuration. Of course, if you wanted to enable several pages with a random image, you would either have to repeat the code or create your own custom control. The AdRotator provides these features for free.

The Advertisement File

The AdRotator stores its list of image files in an XML file. This file uses the format shown here:

```
<Advertisements>
  <Ad>
    <ImageUrl>prosetech.jpg</ImageUrl>
    <NavigateUrl>http://www.prosetech.com</NavigateUrl>
    <AlternateText>ProseTech Site</AlternateText>
    <Impressions>1</Impressions>
    <Keyword>Computer</Keyword>
  </Ad>
</Advertisements>
```

■ **Tip** As you'll see in Chapter 19, an XML file is just a text file with specific tags (as shown previously). You can create an XML file using nothing more than a text editor such as Notepad, but you can also use the Visual Studio text editor. Just select Website ➤ Add New Item from the menu, and choose XML File. It's up to you to fill in the right tags and content. You can place the advertisements file wherever you'd like—either in the main website folder or in a subfolder that you've created.

This example shows a single possible advertisement. To add more advertisements, you would create multiple <Ad> elements and place them all inside the root <Advertisements> element:

```
<Advertisements>
  <Ad>
    <!-- First ad here. -->
  </Ad>
```

```
  <Ad>
    <!-- Second ad here. -->
  </Ad>
</Advertisements>
```

Each <Ad> element has a number of other important properties that configure the link, the image, and the frequency, as described in Table 11-4.

Table 11-4. *Advertisement File Elements*

Element	Description
ImageUrl	The image that will be displayed. This can be a relative link (a file in the current directory) or a fully qualified Internet URL.
NavigateUrl	The link that will be followed if the user clicks the banner.
AlternateText	The text that will be displayed instead of the picture if it cannot be displayed. This text will also be used as a tooltip in some newer browsers.
Impressions	A number that sets how often an advertisement will appear. This number is relative to the numbers specified for other ads. For example, a banner with the value 10 will be shown twice as often (on average) as the banner with the value 5.
Keyword	A keyword that identifies a group of advertisements. You can use this for filtering. For example, you could create ten advertisements and give half of them the keyword Retail and the other half the keyword Computer. The web page can then choose to filter the possible advertisements to include only one of these groups.

The AdRotator Class

The actual AdRotator class provides a limited set of properties. You specify both the appropriate advertisement file in the AdvertisementFile property and the type of window that the link should follow (the Target window). The target can name a specific frame, or it can use one of the values defined in Table 11-5.

Table 11-5. *Special Frame Targets*

Target	Description
_blank	The link opens a new unframed window.
_parent	The link opens in the parent of the current frame.
_self	The link opens in the current frame.
_top	The link opens in the topmost frame of the current window (so the link appears in the full window).

Optionally, you can set the KeywordFilter property so that the banner will be chosen from a specific keyword group. This is a fully configured AdRotator tag:

```
<asp:AdRotator id="Ads" runat="server" AdvertisementFile="MainAds.xml"
     Target="_blank" KeywordFilter="Computer" />
```

■ **Note** The target attribute isn't allowed in XHTML strict. If you decide to use it, make sure you use the XHTML 1.0 transitional doctype, as described in Chapter 4. (This is the default doctype for new web pages that you create in Visual Studio.)

Additionally, you can react to the AdRotator.AdCreated event. This occurs when the page is being created and an image is randomly chosen from the advertisements file. This event provides you with information about the image that you can use to customize the rest of your page. For example, you might display some related content or a link, as shown in Figure 11-5.

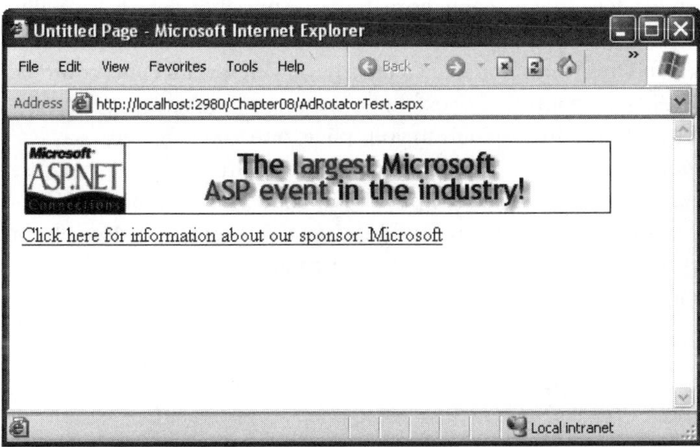

Figure 11-5. *An AdRotator with synchronized content*

The event-handling code for this example simply configures a HyperLink control named lnkBanner based on the randomly selected advertisement:

```
Protected Sub Ads_AdCreated(ByVal sender As Object, _
  ByVal e As AdCreatedEventArgs) Handles Ads.AdCreated

    ' Synchronize the Hyperlink control.
    lnkBanner.NavigateUrl = e.NavigateUrl

    ' Synchronize the text of the link.
    lnkBanner.Text = "Click here for information about our sponsor: "
    lnkBanner.Text &= e.AlternateText
End Sub
```

As you can see, rich controls such as the Calendar and AdRotator don't just add a sophisticated HTML output, they also include an event framework that allows you to take charge of the control's behavior and integrate it into your application.

Pages with Multiple Views

In a typical website, you'll surf through many separate pages. For example, if you want to add an item to your shopping cart and take it to the checkout in an e-commerce site, you'll need to jump from one page to another. This design has its advantages—namely, it lets you carefully separate different tasks into different code files. It also presents some challenges; for example, you need to come up with a way to transfer information from one page to another (a topic that's covered in detail in Chapter 8).

However, in some cases it makes more sense to create a single page that can handle several different tasks. For example, you might want to provide several views of the same data (such as a grid-based view and a chart-based view) and allow the user to switch from one view to the other without leaving the page. Or, you might want to handle a small multistep task in one place (such as supplying user information for an account sign-up process). In these examples, you need a way to create dynamic pages that provide more than one possible view. Essentially, the page hides and shows different controls depending on which view you want to present.

The simplest way to understand this technique is to create a page with several Panel controls. Each panel can hold a group of ASP.NET controls. For example, imagine you're creating a simple three-step wizard. You'll start by adding three panels to your page, one for each step—say, panelStep1, panelStep2, and panelStep3. You can place the panels one after the other, because you'll show only one at a time. Once you've added the panels, you can place the appropriate controls inside each panel. To start, the Visible property of each panel should be False, except for panelStep1, which appears the first time the user requests the page.

Here's an example that shows the way you can arrange your panels:

```
<asp:Panel ID="panelStep1" runat="server">...</asp:Panel>
<asp:Panel ID="panelStep2" Visible="False" runat="server">...</asp:Panel>
<asp:Panel ID="panelStep3" Visible="False" runat="server">...</asp:Panel>
```

■ **Note** When you set the Visible property of a control to False, the control won't appear in the page at runtime. Any controls inside an invisible panel are also hidden from sight, and they won't be present in the rendered HTML for the page. However, these controls will still appear in the Visual Studio design surface so that you can still select them and configure them.

Finally, you'll add one or more navigation buttons outside the panels. For example, the following code handles the click of a Next button, which is placed just after panelStep3 (so it always appears at the bottom of the page). The code checks which step the user is currently on, hides the current panel, and shows the following panel. This way the user is moved to the next step.

```
Protected Sub cmdNext_Click(ByVal sender As Object, _
  ByVal e As System.EventArgs) Handles cmdNext.Click

    If panelStep1.Visible Then
        ' Move to step 2.
        panelStep1.Visible = False
        panelStep2.Visible = True

    ElseIf panelStep2.Visible Then
        ' Move to step 3.
        panelStep2.Visible = False
        panelStep3.Visible = True

        ' Change text of button from Next to Finish.
        cmdNext.Text = "Finish"

    ElseIf panelStep3.Visible Then
        ' The wizard is finished.
        panelStep3.Visible = False

        ' Add code here to perform the appropriate task
        ' with the information you've collected.
    End If

End Sub
```

This approach works relatively well. Even when the panels are hidden, you can still interact with all the controls on each panel and retrieve the information they contain. The problem is that you need to write all the code for controlling which panel is visible. If you make your wizard much more complex—for example, you want to add a button for returning to a previous step—it becomes more difficult to keep track of what's happening. At best, this approach clutters your page with the code for managing the panels. At worst, you'll make a minor mistake and end up with two panels showing at the same time.

Fortunately, ASP.NET gives you a more robust option. You can use two controls that are designed for the job—the MultiView and the Wizard. In the following sections, you'll see how you can use both of these controls with the GreetingCardMaker example developed in Chapter 5.

The MultiView Control

The MultiView is the simpler of the two multiple-view controls. Essentially, the MultiView gives you a way to declare multiple views and show only one at a time. It has no default user interface—you get only whatever HTML and controls you add. The MultiView is equivalent to the custom panel approach explained earlier.

Creating a MultiView is suitably straightforward. You add the <asp:MultiView> tag to your .aspx page file and then add one <asp:View> tag inside it for each separate view:

```
<asp:MultiView ID="MultiView1" runat="server">
  <asp:View ID="View1" runat="server">...</asp:View>
  <asp:View ID="View2" runat="server">...</asp:View>
  <asp:View ID="View3" runat="server">...</asp:View>
</asp:MultiView>
```

In Visual Studio, you create these tags by first dropping a MultiView control onto your form and then using the Toolbox to add as many View controls inside it as you want. This drag-and-drop process can be a bit tricky. When you add the first View control, you must make sure to drop it in the blank area inside the MultiView (not next to the MultiView, or on the MultiView's title bar). When you add more View controls, you must drop each one on one of the gray header bars of one of the existing views. The gray header has the View title (such as "View1" or "View2").

The View control plays the same role as the Panel control in the previous example, and the MultiView takes care of coordinating all the views so that only one is visible at a time.

Inside each view, you can add HTML or web controls. For example, consider the GreetingCardMaker example demonstrated in Chapter 5, which allows the user to create a greeting card by supplying some text and choosing colors, a font, and a background. As the GreetingCardMaker grows more complex, it requires more controls, and it becomes increasingly difficult to fit all those controls on the same page. One possible solution is to divide these controls into logical groups and place each group in a separate view.

Creating Views

Here's the full markup for a MultiView that splits the greeting card controls into three views named View1, View2, and View3:

```
<asp:MultiView id="MultiView1" runat="server" >

  <asp:View ID="View1" runat="server">
    Choose a foreground (text) color:<br />
    <asp:DropDownList ID="lstForeColor" runat="server"
     AutoPostBack="True" />
    <br /><br />
    Choose a background color:<br />
    <asp:DropDownList ID="lstBackColor" runat="server"
     AutoPostBack="True" />
  </asp:View>

  <asp:View ID="View2" runat="server">
    Choose a border style:<br />
    <asp:RadioButtonList ID="lstBorder" runat="server"
     AutoPostBack="True" RepeatColumns="2" />
    <br />
    <asp:CheckBox ID="chkPicture" runat="server"
     AutoPostBack="True" Text="Add the Default Picture"  />
  </asp:View>
```

```
    <asp:View ID="View3" runat="server">
      Choose a font name:<br />
      <asp:DropDownList ID="lstFontName" runat="server"
       AutoPostBack="True" />
      <br /><br />
      Specify a font size:<br />
      <asp:TextBox ID="txtFontSize" runat="server"
       AutoPostBack="True" />
      <br /><br />
      Enter the greeting text below:<br />
      <asp:TextBox ID="txtGreeting" runat="server"
       AutoPostBack="True" TextMode="MultiLine" />
    </asp:View>

</asp:MultiView>
```

Visual Studio shows all your views at design time, one after the other (see Figure 11-6). You can edit these regions in the same way you design any other part of the page.

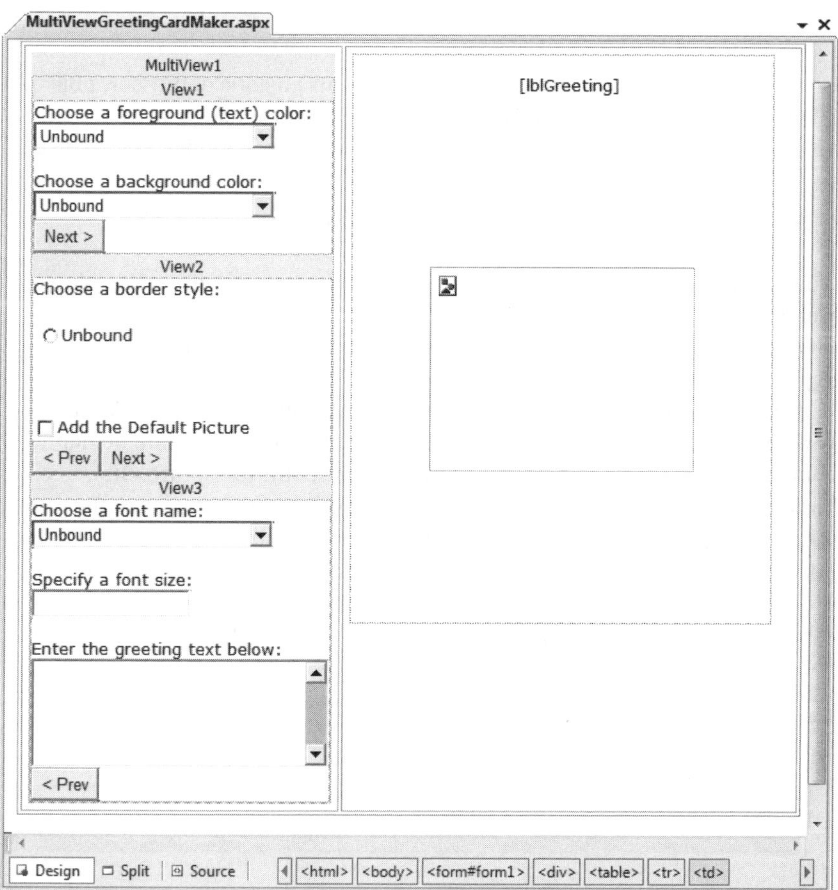

Figure 11-6. *Designing multiple views*

Showing a View

If you run this example, you won't see what you expect. The MultiView will appear empty on the page, and all the controls in all your views will be hidden.

The reason this happens is because the MultiView.ActiveViewIndex property is, by default, set to –1. The ActiveViewIndex property determines which view will be shown. If you set the ActiveViewIndex to 0, however, you'll see the first view. Similarly, you can set it to 1 to show the second view, and so on. You can set this property using the Properties window or using code:

```
' Show the first view.
MultiView1.ActiveViewIndex = 0
```

This example shows the first view (View1) and hides whatever view is currently being displayed, if any.

■ **Tip** To make more readable code, you can create an enumeration that defines a name for each view. That way, you can set the ActiveViewIndex using the descriptive name from the enumeration rather than an ordinary number. Refer to Chapter 3 for a refresher on enumerations.

You can also use the SetActiveView() method, which accepts any one of the view objects you've created. This may result in more readable code (if you've chosen descriptive IDs for your view controls), and it ensures that any errors are caught earlier (at compile time instead of runtime).

```
MultiView1.SetActiveView(View1)
```

This gives you enough functionality that you can create previous and next navigation buttons. However, it's still up to you to write the code that checks which view is visible and changes the view. This code is a little simpler, because you don't need to worry about hiding views any longer, but it's still less than ideal.

Fortunately, the MultiView includes some built-in smarts that can save you a lot of trouble. Here's how it works: the MultiView recognizes button controls with specific command names. (Technically, a button control is any control that implements the IButtonControl interface, including the Button, ImageButton, and LinkButton.) If you add a button control to the view that uses one of these recognized command names, the button gets some automatic functionality. Using this technique, you can create navigation buttons without writing any code.

Table 11-6 lists all the recognized command names. Each command name also has a corresponding shared field in the MultiView class, so you can easily get the right command name if you choose to set it programmatically.

Table 11-6. *Recognized Command Names for the MultiView*

Command Name	MultiView Field	Description
PrevView	PreviousViewCommandName	Moves to the previous view.
NextView	NextViewCommandName	Moves to the next view.
SwitchViewByID	SwitchViewByIDCommandName	Moves to the view with a specific ID (string name). The ID is taken from the CommandArgument property of the button control.
SwitchViewByIndex	SwitchViewByIndexCommandName	Moves to the view with a specific numeric index. The index is taken from the CommandArgument property of the button control.

To try this, add this button to the first view:

```
<asp:Button ID="Button1" runat="server" CommandArgument="View2"
CommandName="SwitchViewByID" Text="Go to View2" />
```

When clicked, this button sets the MultiView to show the view specified by the CommandArgument (View2).

Rather than create buttons that take the user to a specific view, you might want a button that moves forward or backward one view. To do this, you use the PrevView and NextView command names. Here's an example that defines previous and next buttons in the second View:

```
<asp:Button ID="Button1" runat="server" Text="< Prev" CommandName="PrevView" />
<asp:Button ID="Button2" runat="server" Text="Next >" CommandName="NextView" />
```

Once you add these buttons to your view, you can move from view to view easily. Figure 11-7 shows the previous example with the second view currently visible.

■ **Tip** Be careful how many views you cram into a single page. When you use the MultiView control, the entire control model—including the controls from every view—is created on every postback and persisted to view state. In most situations, this won't be a significant factor. However, it increases the overall page size, especially if you're tweaking controls programmatically (which increases the amount of information they need to store in view state).

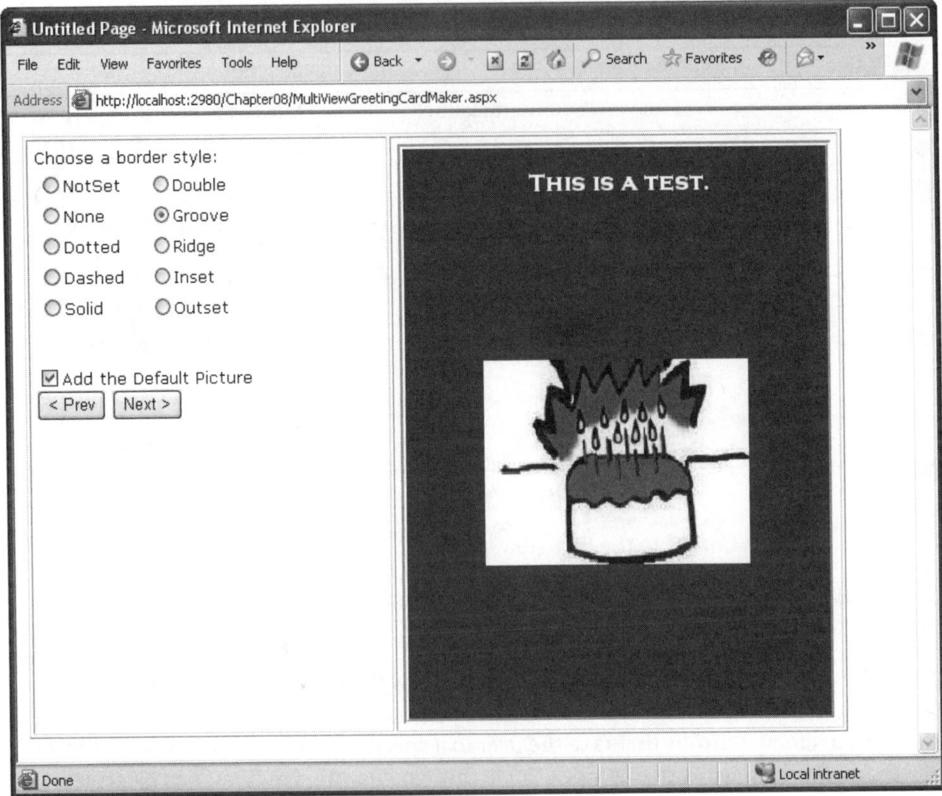

Figure 11-7. *Moving from one view to another*

The Wizard Control

The Wizard control is a more glamorous version of the MultiView control. It also supports showing one of several views at a time, but it includes a fair bit of built-in yet customizable behavior, including navigation buttons, a sidebar with step links, styles, and templates.

Usually, wizards represent a single task, and the user moves linearly through them, moving from the current step to the one immediately following it (or the one immediately preceding it in the case of a correction). The ASP.NET Wizard control also supports nonlinear navigation, which means it allows you to decide to ignore a step based on the information the user supplies.

By default, the Wizard control supplies navigation buttons and a sidebar with links for each step on the left. You can hide the sidebar by setting the Wizard.DisplaySideBar property to False. Usually, you'll take this step if you want to enforce strict step-by-step navigation and prevent the user from jumping out of sequence. You supply the content for each step using any HTML or ASP.NET controls. Figure 11-8 shows the region where you can add content to an out-of-the-box Wizard instance.

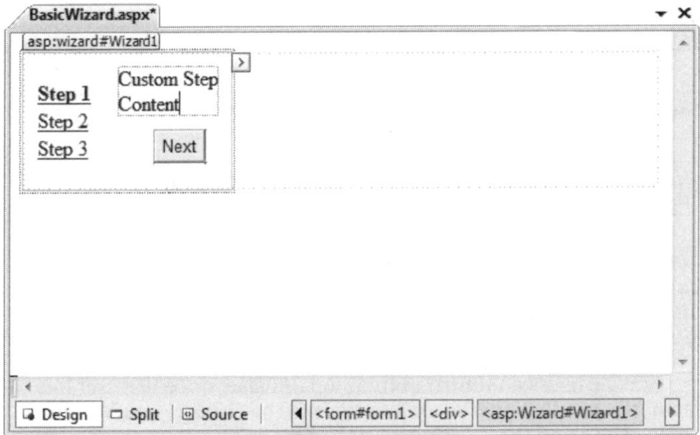

Figure 11-8. *The region for step content*

Wizard Steps

To create a wizard in ASP.NET, you simply define the steps and their content using <asp:WizardStep> tags. Here's the basic structure you'll use:

```
<asp:Wizard ID="Wizard1" runat="server" ... >
  <WizardSteps>

    <asp:WizardStep runat="server" Title="Step 1 ">
      ...
    </asp:WizardStep>

    <asp:WizardStep runat="server" Title="Step 1 ">
      ...
    </asp:WizardStep>

    ...
  <WizardSteps>
</asp:Wizard>
```

You can add as many WizardStep controls inside the Wizard as you want. Conceptually, the WizardStep plays the same role as the View in a MultiView (or the basic Panel in the first example that you considered). You place the content for each step inside the WizardStep control.

Before you start adding the content to your wizard, it's worth reviewing Table 11-7, which shows a few basic pieces of information that you can define for each step.

Table 11-7. *WizardStep Properties*

Property	Description
Title	The descriptive name of the step. This name is used for the text of the links in the sidebar.
StepType	The type of step, as a value from the WizardStepType enumeration. This value determines the type of navigation buttons that will be shown for this step. Choices include Start (shows a Next button), Step (shows Next and Previous buttons), Finish (shows Finish and Previous buttons), Complete (shows no buttons and hides the sidebar, if it's enabled), and Auto (the step type is inferred from the position in the collection). The default is Auto, which means the first step is Start, the last step is Finish, and all other steps are Step.
AllowReturn	Indicates whether the user can return to this step. If False, once the user has passed this step, the user will not be able to return. The sidebar link for this step will have no effect, and the Previous button of the following step will either skip this step or be hidden completely (depending on the AllowReturn value of the preceding steps).

To see how this works, consider a wizard that again uses the GreetingCardMaker example. It guides the user through four steps. The first three steps allow the user to configure the greeting card, and the final step shows the generated card. The entire process is shown in Figure 11-9.

```
<asp:Wizard ID="Wizard1" runat="server" ActiveStepIndex="0"
 BackColor="LemonChiffon" BorderStyle="Groove" BorderWidth="2px" CellPadding="10">

  <WizardSteps>
    <asp:WizardStep runat="server" Title="Step 1 - Colors">
      Choose a foreground (text) color:<br />
      <asp:DropDownList ID="lstForeColor" runat="server" />
      <br />
      Choose a background color:<br />
      <asp:DropDownList ID="lstBackColor" runat="server" />
    </asp:WizardStep>

    <asp:WizardStep runat="server" Title="Step 2 - Background">
      Choose a border style:<br />
      <asp:RadioButtonList ID="lstBorder" runat="server" RepeatColumns="2" />
      <br /><br />
      <asp:CheckBox ID="chkPicture" runat="server"
       Text="Add the Default Picture" />
    </asp:WizardStep>

    <asp:WizardStep runat="server" Title="Step 3 - Text">
      Choose a font name:<br />
      <asp:DropDownList ID="lstFontName" runat="server" />
      <br /><br />
      Specify a font size:<br />
      <asp:TextBox ID="txtFontSize" runat="server" />
      <br /><br />
```

```
      Enter the greeting text below:<br />
      <asp:TextBox ID="txtGreeting" runat="server"
        TextMode="MultiLine" />
    </asp:WizardStep>

    <asp:WizardStep runat="server" StepType="Complete" Title="Greeting Card">
      <asp:Panel ID="pnlCard" runat="server" HorizontalAlign="Center">
        <br />
        <asp:Label ID="lblGreeting" runat="server" />
        <asp:Image ID="imgDefault" runat="server" Visible="False" />
      </asp:Panel>
    </asp:WizardStep>
  </WizardSteps>

</asp:Wizard>
```

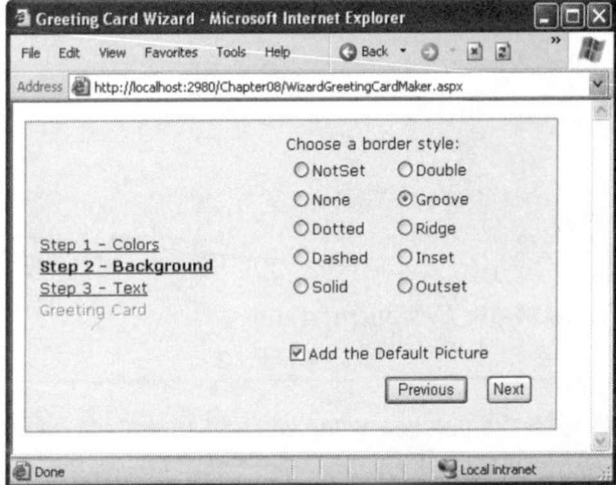

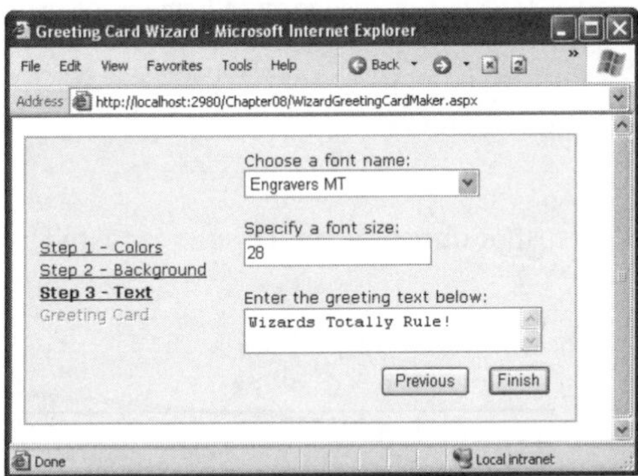

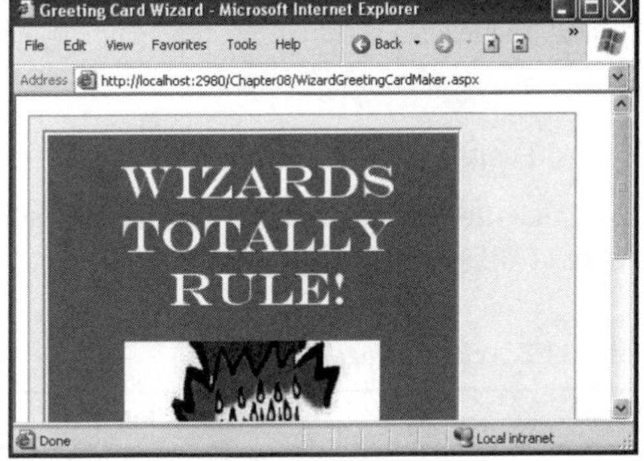

Figure 11-9. *A wizard with four steps*

If you look carefully, you'll find a few differences from the original page and the MultiView-based example. First, the controls aren't set to automatically post back. That's because the greeting card isn't rendered until the final step, at the conclusion of the wizard. (You'll learn more about how to handle this event in the next section.) Another change is that no navigation buttons exist. That's because the wizard adds these details automatically based on the step type. For example, you'll get a Next button for the first two steps, a Previous button for steps 2 and 3, and a Finish button for step 3. The final step, which shows the complete card, doesn't provide any navigation links because the StepType is set to Complete.

Unlike the MultiView control, you can see only one step at a time in Visual Studio. To choose which step you're currently designing, select it from the smart tag, as shown in Figure 11-10. But be warned—every time you do, Visual Studio changes the Wizard.ActiveStepIndex property to the step you choose. Make sure you set this back to 0 before you run your application so it starts at the first step.

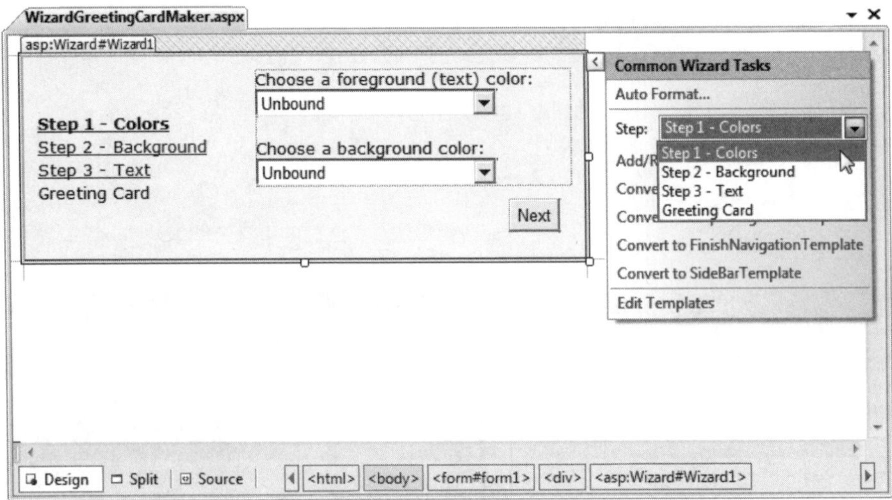

Figure 11-10. *Designing a step*

■Note Remember, when you add controls to separate steps on a wizard, the controls are all instantiated and persisted in view state, regardless of which step is currently shown. If you need to slim down a complex wizard, you'll need to split it into separate pages, use the Server.Transfer() method to move from one page to the next, and tolerate a less elegant programming model.

Wizard Events

You can write the code that underpins your wizard by responding to several events (as listed in Table 11-8).

Table 11-8. *Wizard Events*

Event	Description
ActiveStepChanged	Occurs when the control switches to a new step (either because the user has clicked a navigation button or your code has changed the ActiveStepIndex property).
CancelButtonClick	Occurs when the Cancel button is clicked. The Cancel button is not shown by default, but you can add it to every step by setting the Wizard.DisplayCancelButton property. Usually, a Cancel button exits the wizard. If you don't have any cleanup code to perform, just set the CancelDestinationPageUrl property, and the wizard will take care of the redirection automatically.

Table 11-8. *Wizard Events*

Event	Description
FinishButtonClick	Occurs when the Finish button is clicked.
NextButtonClick and PreviousButtonClick	Occurs when the Next or Previous button is clicked on any step. However, because there is more than one way to move from one step to the next, it's often easier to handle the ActiveStepChanged event.
SideBarButtonClick	Occurs when a button in the sidebar area is clicked.

On the whole, two wizard programming models exist:

Commit-as-you-go: This makes sense if each wizard step wraps an atomic operation that can't be reversed. For example, if you're processing an order that involves a credit card authorization followed by a final purchase, you can't allow the user to step back and edit the credit card number. To support this model, you set the AllowReturn property to False on some or all steps. You may also want to respond to the ActiveStepChanged event to commit changes for each step.

Commit-at-the-end: This makes sense if each wizard step is collecting information for an operation that's performed only at the end. For example, if you're collecting user information and plan to generate a new account once you have all the information, you'll probably allow a user to make changes midway through the process. You execute your code for generating the new account when the wizard ends by reacting to the FinishButtonClick event.

To implement commit-at-the-end with the current example, just respond to the FinishButtonClick event. For example, to implement the greeting card wizard, you simply need to respond to this event and call UpdateCard(), the private method that refreshes the greeting card:

```
Protected Sub Wizard1_FinishButtonClick(ByVal sender As Object, _
  ByVal e As WizardNavigationEventArgs) _
  Handles Wizard1.FinishButtonClick

    UpdateCard()
End Sub
```

For the complete code for the UpdateCard() method, which generates the greeting card, refer to Chapter 5 (or check out the downloadable sample code).

If you decide to use the commit-as-you go model, you would respond to the ActiveStepChanged event and call UpdateCard() at that point to refresh the card every time the user moves from one step to another. This assumes the greeting card is always visible. (In other words, it's not contained in the final step of the wizard.) The commit-as-you-go model is similar to the previous example that used the MultiView.

Formatting the Wizard

Without a doubt, the Wizard control's greatest strength is the way it lets you customize its appearance. This means if you want the basic model (a multistep process with navigation buttons and various events), you aren't locked into the default user interface.

Depending on how radically you want to change the wizard, you have several options. For less dramatic modifications, you can set various top-level properties of the Wizard control. For example, you can control the colors, fonts, spacing, and border style, as you can with any ASP.NET control. You can also tweak the appearance of every button. For example, to change the Next button, you can use the following properties: StepNextButtonType (use a button, link, or clickable image), StepNextButtonText (customize the text for a button or link), StepNextButtonImageUrl (set the image for an image button), and StepNextButtonStyle (use a style from a style sheet). You can also add a header using the HeaderText property.

More control is available through styles. You can use styles to apply formatting options to various portions of the Wizard control just as you can use styles to format parts of rich data controls such as the GridView. Table 11-9 lists all the styles you can use. As with other style-based controls, more specific style settings (such as SideBarStyle) override more general style settings (such as ControlStyle) when they conflict. Similarly, StartNextButtonStyle overrides NavigationButtonStyle on the first step.

Table 11-9. *Wizard Styles*

Style	Description
ControlStyle	Applies to all sections of the Wizard control.
HeaderStyle	Applies to the header section of the wizard, which is visible only if you set some text in the HeaderText property.
BorderStyle	Applies to the border around the Wizard control. You can use it in conjunction with the BorderColor and BorderWidth properties.
SideBarStyle	Applies to the sidebar area of the wizard.
SideBarButtonStyle	Applies to just the buttons in the sidebar.
StepStyle	Applies to the section of the control where you define the step content.
NavigationStyle	Applies to the bottom area of the control where the navigation buttons are displayed.
NavigationButtonStyle	Applies to just the navigation buttons in the navigation area.
StartNextButtonStyle	Applies to the Next navigation button on the first step (when StepType is Start).
StepNextButtonStyle	Applies to the Next navigation button on intermediate steps (when StepType is Step).
StepPreviousButtonStyle	Applies to the Previous navigation button on intermediate steps (when StepType is Step).
FinishPreviousButtonStyle	Applies to the Previous navigation button on the last step (when StepType is Finish).
FinishCompleteButtonStyle	Applies to the Complete navigation button on the last step (when StepType is Finish).
CancelButtonStyle	Applies to the Cancel button, if you have Wizard.DisplayCancelButton set to True.

■ **Note** The Wizard control also supports templates, which give you a more radical approach to formatting. If you can't get the level of customization you want through properties and styles, you can use templates to completely define the appearance of each section of the Wizard control, including the headers and navigation links. Templates require data binding expressions and are discussed in Chapter 16 and Chapter 17.

Validation with the Wizard

The FinishButtonClick, NextButtonClick, PreviousButtonClick, and SideBarButtonClick events are cancellable. That means that you can use code like this to prevent the requested navigation action from taking place:

```
Protected Sub Wizard1_NextButtonClick(ByVal sender As Object, _
  ByVal e As WizardNavigationEventArgs) _
  Handles Wizard1.NextButtonClick

    ' Perform some sort of check.
    If e.NextStepIndex = 1 AndAlso txtName.Text = ""

        ' Cancel navigation and display a message elsewhere on the page.
        e.Cancel = True
        lblInfo.Text = _
          "You cannot move to the next step until you supply your name."
    End If
End Sub
```

Here the code checks if the user is trying to move to step 1 using the NextStepIndex property. (Alternatively, you could examine the current step using the CurrentStepIndex property.) If so, the code then checks a text box and cancels the navigation if it doesn't contain any text, keeping the user on the current step. Writing this sort of logic gets a little tricky, because you need to keep in mind that step-to-step navigation can be performed in several ways. To simplify your life, you can write one event handler that deals with the NextButtonClick, PreviousButtonClick, and SideBarButtonClick events, and performs the same check. You saw this technique in Chapter 5 with the GreetingCardMaker.

■ **Note** You can also use the ASP.NET validation controls in a Wizard without any problem. If the validation controls detect invalid data, they will prevent the user from clicking any of the sidebar links (to jump to another step) and they will prevent the user from continuing by clicking the Next button. However, by default the Previous button has its CausesValidation property set to False, which means the user *will* be allowed to step back to the previous step.

The Last Word

This chapter showed you how the rich Calendar, AdRotator, MultiView, and Wizard controls can go far beyond the limitations of ordinary HTML elements. When you're working with these controls, you don't need to think about HTML at all. Instead, you can focus on the object model that's defined by the control.

Throughout this book, you'll consider some more examples of rich controls and learn how to use them to create rich web applications that are a world apart from HTML basics. Some of the most exciting rich controls that are still ahead include the navigation controls (Chapter 14), the data controls (Chapter 17), and the security controls (Chapter 21).

■ **Tip** You might also be interested in adding third-party controls to your websites. The Internet contains many hubs for control sharing. One such location is Microsoft's own `www.asp.net`, which provides a control gallery where developers can submit their own ASP.NET web controls. Some of these controls are free (at least in a limited version), and others require a purchase.

CHAPTER 12

■ ■ ■

User Controls and Graphics

In this chapter, you'll consider two ways to extend your web pages another notch.

First, you'll tackle user controls, which give you an efficient way to reuse a block of user interface markup—and the code that goes with it. User controls are a key tool for building modular web applications. They can also help you create consistent website designs and reuse your hard work.

Next, you'll explore custom drawing with GDI+. You'll see how you can paint exactly the image you need on request. You'll also learn the best way to incorporate these images into your web pages.

User Controls

A well-built web application divides its work into discrete, independent blocks. The more modular your web application is, the easier it is to maintain your code, troubleshoot problems, and reuse key bits of functionality.

Although it's easy enough to reuse code (you simply need to pull it out of your pages and put it into separate classes), it's not as straightforward to reuse web page markup. You can cut and paste blocks of HTML and ASP.NET control tags, but this causes endless headaches if you want to change your markup later. Instead, you need a way to wrap up web page markup in a reusable package, just as you can wrap up ordinary VB code. The trick is to create a *user control*.

User controls look pretty much the same as ASP.NET web forms. Like web forms, they are composed of a markup portion with HTML and control tags (the .ascx file) and can optionally use a code-behind file with event-handling logic. They can also include the same range of HTML content and ASP.NET controls, and they experience the same events as the Page object (such as Load and PreRender). The only differences between user controls and web pages are as follows:

- User controls use the file extension .ascx instead of .aspx, and their code-behind files inherit from the System.Web.UI.UserControl class. In fact, the UserControl class and the Page class both inherit from the same base classes, which is why they share so many of the same methods and events, as shown in the inheritance diagram in Figure 12-1.
- The .ascx file for a user control begins with a <%@ Control %> directive instead of a <%@ Page %> directive.
- User controls can't be requested directly by a web browser. Instead, they must be embedded inside other web pages.

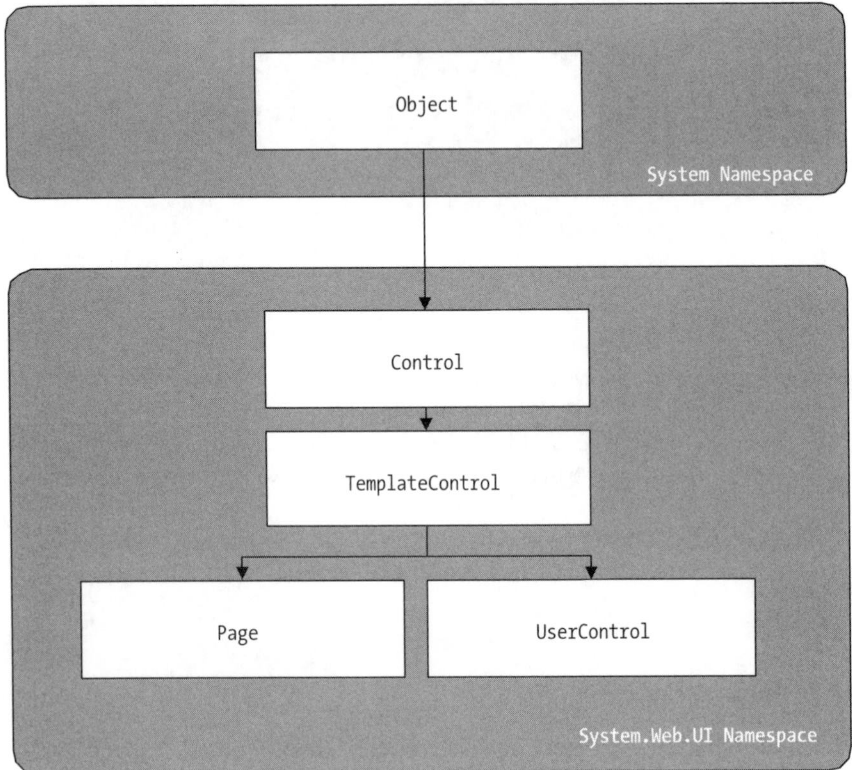

Figure 12-1. *The Page and UserControl inheritance chain*

Creating a Simple User Control

You can create a user control in Visual Studio in much the same way you add a web page. Just select Website ➤ Add New Item, and choose Web User Control from the list.

The following user control contains a single Label control:

```
<%@ Control Language="VB" AutoEventWireup="false"
    CodeFile="Footer.ascx.vb" Inherits="Footer" %>

<asp:Label id="lblFooter" runat="server" />
```

Note that the Control directive uses the same attributes used in the Page directive for a web page, including Language, AutoEventWireup, and Inherits.

The code-behind class for this sample user control is similarly straightforward. It uses the UserControl.Load event to add some text to the label:

```
Public Partial Class Footer
    Inherits System.Web.UI.UserControl

    Protected Sub Page_Load(ByVal sender As Object, _
      ByVal e As System.EventArgs) Handles Me.Load
```

```
        lblFooter.Text = "This page was served at "
        lblFooter.Text &= DateTime.Now.ToString()
    End Sub

End Class
```

To test this user control, you need to insert it into a web page. This is a two-step process. First, you need to add a Register directive to the page that will contain the user control. You place the Register directive immediately after the Page directive. The Register directive identifies the control you want to use and associates it with a unique control prefix, as shown here:

```
<%@ Register TagPrefix="apress" TagName="Footer" Src="Footer.ascx" %>
```

The Register directive specifies a tag prefix and name. Tag prefixes group sets of related controls (for example, all ASP.NET web controls use the tag prefix *asp*). Tag prefixes are usually lowercase—technically, they are case-insensitive—and should be unique for your company or organization. The Src directive identifies the location of the user control template file, not the code-behind file.

Second, you can now add the user control whenever you want (and as many times as you want) in the page by inserting its control tag. Consider this page example:

```
<%@ Page Language="VB" AutoEventWireup="false"
    CodeFile="FooterHost.aspx.vb" Inherits="FooterHost"%>
<%@ Register TagPrefix="apress" TagName="Footer" Src="Footer.ascx" %>

<!DOCTYPE html PUBLIC "-//W3C//DTD XHTML 1.1//EN"
 "http://www.w3.org/TR/xhtml11/DTD/xhtml11.dtd">

<html xmlns="http://www.w3.org/1999/xhtml">
<head runat="server">
    <title>Footer Host</title>
</head>
<body>
    <form id="form1" runat="server">
    <div>
      <h1>A Page With a Footer</h1><hr />
      Static Page Text<br /><br />
      <apress:Footer id="Footer1" runat="server" />
    </div>
    </form>
</body>
</html>
```

This example (shown in Figure 12-2) demonstrates a simple way that you can create a header or footer and reuse it in all the pages in your website just by adding a user control. In the case of your simple footer, you won't save much code. However, this approach will become much more useful for a complex control with extensive formatting or several contained controls.

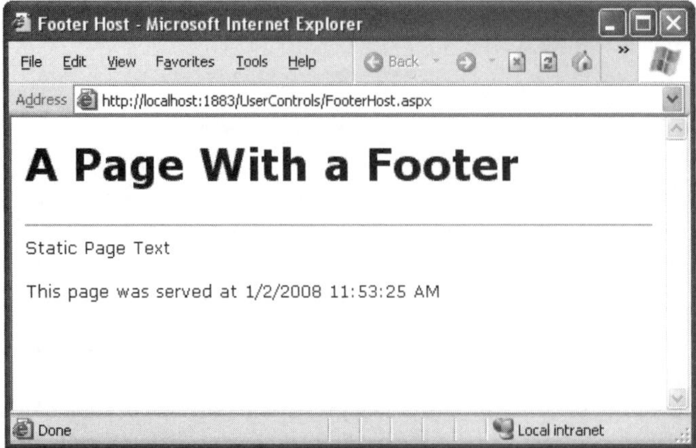

Figure 12-2. *A page with a user control footer*

Of course, this only scratches the surface of what you can do with a user control. In the following sections, you'll learn how to enhance a control with properties, methods, and events—transforming it from a simple "include file" into a full-fledged object.

■ **Note** The Page class provides a special LoadControl() method that allows you to create a user control dynamically at runtime from an .ascx file. The user control is returned to you as a control object, which you can then add to the Controls collection of a container control on the web page (such as PlaceHolder or Panel) to display it on the page. This technique isn't a good substitute for declaratively using a user control, because it's more complex. However, it does have some interesting applications if you want to generate a user interface dynamically.

In Visual Studio, you have a useful shortcut for adding a user control to a page without typing the Register directive by hand. Start by opening the web page you want to use. Then, find the .ascx file for the user control in the Solution Explorer. Drag it from the Solution Explorer and drop it onto the visual design area of your web form (not the source view area). Visual Studio will automatically add the Register directive for the user control, as well as an instance of the user control tag.

Independent User Controls

Conceptually, two types of user controls exist: independent and integrated. *Independent* user controls don't interact with the rest of the code on your form. The Footer user control is one such example. Another example might be a LinkMenu control that contains a list of buttons offering links to other pages. This LinkMenu user control can handle the events for all the buttons and then run the appropriate Response.Redirect() code to move to another web page. Or it can just be an ordinary HyperLink control that doesn't have any associated server-side code. Every page in the website can then include the same LinkMenu user control, enabling painless website navigation with no need to worry about frames.

■ **Note** You can use the more feature-rich navigation controls to provide website navigation. Creating your own custom controls gives you a simple, more flexible, but less powerful approach to providing navigation. You might use custom controls rather than a whole site map for straightforward navigation between a few pages.

The following sample defines a simple control that presents an attractively formatted list of links. Note that the style attribute of the <div> tag (which defines fonts and formatting) has been omitted for clarity.

```
<%@ Control Language="VB" AutoEventWireup="false"
    CodeFile="LinkMenu.ascx.vb" Inherits="LinkMenu" %>
<div>
  Products:<br />
  <asp:HyperLink id="lnkBooks" runat="server"
    NavigateUrl="MenuHost.aspx?product=Books">Books
  </asp:HyperLink><br />
  <asp:HyperLink id="lnkToys" runat="server"
    NavigateUrl="MenuHost.aspx?product=Toys">Toys
  </asp:HyperLink><br />
  <asp:HyperLink id="lnkSports" runat="server"
    NavigateUrl="MenuHost.aspx?product=Sports">Sports
  </asp:HyperLink><br />
  <asp:HyperLink id="lnkFurniture" runat="server"
    NavigateUrl="MenuHost.aspx?product=Furniture">Furniture
  </asp:HyperLink>
</div>
```

The links don't actually trigger any server-side code—instead, they render themselves as ordinary HTML anchor tags with a hard-coded URL.

To test this menu, you can use the following MenuHost.aspx web page. It includes two controls: the Menu control and a Label control that displays the product query string parameter. Both are positioned using a table.

```
<%@ Page Language="VB" AutoEventWireup="false"
    CodeFile="MenuHost.aspx.vb" Inherits="MenuHost"%>
<%@ Register TagPrefix="apress" TagName="LinkMenu" Src="LinkMenu.ascx" %>

<!DOCTYPE html PUBLIC "-//W3C//DTD XHTML 1.1//EN"
 "http://www.w3.org/TR/xhtml11/DTD/xhtml11.dtd">

<html xmlns="http://www.w3.org/1999/xhtml">
<head runat="server">
    <title>Menu Host</title>
</head>
<body>
    <form id="form1" runat="server">
    <div>
```

```
        <table>
          <tr>
            <td><apress:LinkMenu id="Menu1" runat="server" /></td>
            <td><asp:Label id="lblSelection" runat="server" /></td>
          </tr>
        </table>
      </div>
      </form>
</body>
</html>
```

When the MenuHost.aspx page loads, it adds the appropriate information to the lblSelection control:

```
Protected Sub Page_Load(ByVal sender As Object, _
  ByVal e As System.EventArgs) Handles Me.Load

    If Request.Params("product") IsNot Nothing
        lblSelection.Text = "You chose: "
        lblSelection.Text &= Request.Params("product")
    End If
End Sub
```

Figure 12-3 shows the end result. Whenever you click a button, the page is posted back, and the text is updated.

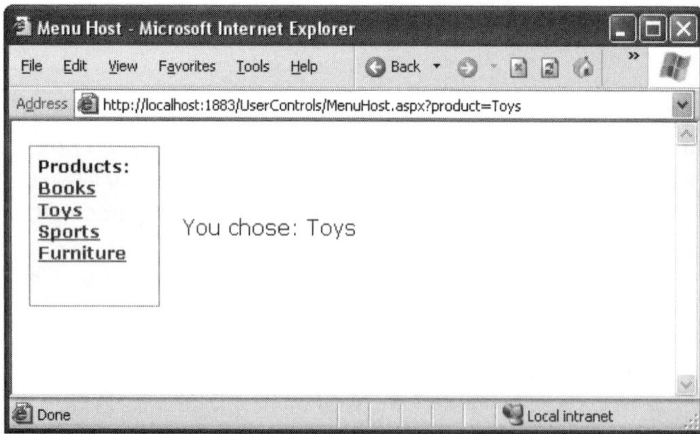

Figure 12-3. *The LinkMenu user control*

You could use the LinkMenu control to repeat the same menu on several pages. This is particularly handy in a situation where you can't use master pages to standardize layout (possibly because the pages are too different).

Integrated User Controls

Integrated user controls interact in one way or another with the web page that hosts them. When you're designing these controls, the class-based design tips you learned in Chapter 4 really become useful.

A typical example is a user control that allows some level of configuration through properties. For instance, you can create a footer that supports two different display formats: long date and short time. To add a further level of refinement, the Footer user control allows the web page to specify the appropriate display format using an enumeration.

The first step is to create an enumeration in the custom Footer class. Remember, an enumeration is simply a type of constant that is internally stored as an integer but is set in code by using one of the allowed names you specify. Variables that use the FooterFormat enumeration can take the value FooterFormat.LongDate or FooterFormat.ShortTime:

```
Public Enum FooterFormat
   LongDate
   ShortTime
End Enum
```

The next step is to add a property to the Footer class that allows the web page to retrieve or set the current format applied to the footer. The actual format is stored in a private variable called _format, which is set to the long date format by default when the control is first created. (You can accomplish the same effect, in a slightly sloppier way, by using a public member variable named Format instead of a full property procedure.) If you're hazy on how property procedures work, feel free to review the explanation in Chapter 3.

```
Private _format As FooterFormat = FooterFormat.LongDate

Public Property Format() As FooterFormat
    Get
        Return _format
    End Get
    Set(ByVal value As FooterFormat)
        _format = value
    End Set
End Property
```

Finally, the UserControl.Load event handler needs to take account of the current footer state and format the output accordingly. The following is the full Footer class code:

```
Public Partial Class Footer
    Inherits System.Web.UI.UserControl

    Public Enum FooterFormat
       LongDate
       ShortTime
    End Enum
```

```
    Private _format As FooterFormat = FooterFormat.LongDate
    Public Property Format() As FooterFormat
        Get
            Return _format
        End Get
        Set(ByVal value As FooterFormat)
            _format = value
        End Set
    End Property

    Protected Sub Page_Load(ByVal sender As Object, _
      ByVal e As System.EventArgs) Handles Me.Load

        lblFooter.Text = "This page was served at "

        If Format = FooterFormat.LongDate Then
            lblFooter.Text &= DateTime.Now.ToLongDateString()
        ElseIf Format = FooterFormat.ShortTime Then
            lblFooter.Text &= DateTime.Now.ToShortTimeString()
        End If
    End Sub

End Class
```

To test this footer, you need to create a page that modifies the Format property of the Footer user control. Figure 12-4 shows an example page, which automatically sets the Format property for the user control to match a radio button selection whenever the page is posted back.

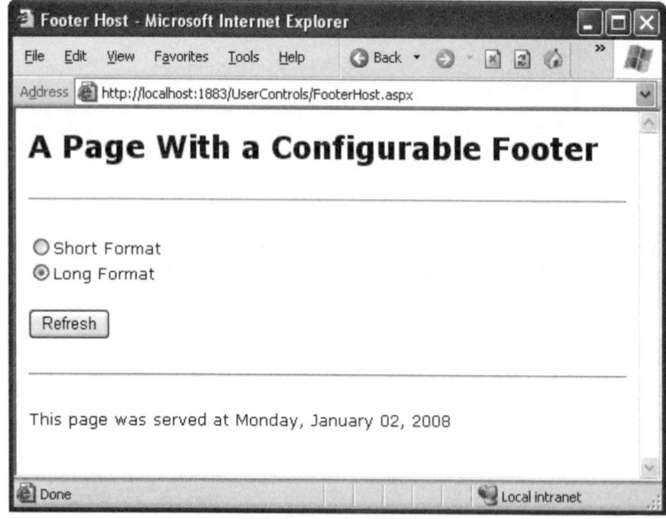

Figure 12-4. *The modified footer*

Note that the user control property is modified in the Page.Load event handler, not the cmdRefresh.Click event handler. The reason is that the Load event occurs before the user control has been rendered each time the page is created. The Click event occurs after the user control has been rendered, and though the property change is visible in your code, it doesn't affect the user control's HTML output, which has already been added to the page.

```
Public Partial Class FooterHost
    Inherits System.Web.UI.Page

    Protected Sub Page_Load(ByVal sender As Object, _
      ByVal e As System.EventArgs) Handles Me.Load

        If optLong.Checked Then
            Footer1.Format = Footer.FooterFormat.LongDate
        ElseIf optShort.Checked Then
            Footer1.Format = Footer.FooterFormat.ShortTime
        Else
            ' The default value in the Footer class will apply.
        End If
    End Sub

End Class
```

You can also set the initial appearance of the footer in the control tag:

```
<apress:Footer Format="ShortTime" id="Footer1" runat="server" />
```

User Control Events

Another way that communication can occur between a user control and a web page is through events. With methods and properties, the user control reacts to a change made by the web page code. With events, the story is reversed: the user control notifies the web page about an action, and the web page code responds.

Creating a web control that uses events is fairly easy. In the following example, you'll see a version of the LinkMenu control that uses events. Instead of navigating directly to the appropriate page when the user clicks a button, the control raises an event, which the web page can choose to handle.

The first step to create this control is to define the events. Remember, to define an event, you must first choose an event signature. The .NET standard for events specifies that every event should use two parameters. The first one provides a reference to the control that sent the event, while the second incorporates any additional information. This additional information is wrapped into a custom EventArgs object, which inherits from the System.EventArgs class. (If your event doesn't require any additional information, you can just use the predefined EventArgs class, which doesn't contain any additional data. Many events in ASP.NET, such as Page.Load or Button.Click, follow this pattern.) You can refer to Chapter 4 for a quick overview of how to use events in .NET.

The LinkMenu2 control uses a single event, which indicates when a link is clicked:

```
Partial Class LinkMenu2
    Inherits System.Web.UI.UserControl

    Public Event LinkClicked As EventHandler( _
      ByVal sender As Object, ByVal e As EventArgs)

    ...
End Class
```

This statement defines an event named LinkClicked, with two parameters—the event sender and the EventArgs class, in true .NET style.

This takes care of defining the event, but what about raising it? This part is easy. To fire the event, the LinkMenu2 control simply uses the RaiseEvent command and passes in the two parameters, like this:

```
' Raise the LinkClicked event, passing a reference to
' the current object (the sender) and an empty EventArgs object.
RaiseEvent LinkClicked(Me, EventArgs.Empty)
```

The LinkMenu2 control actually needs a few more changes. The original version used the HyperLink control. This won't do, because the HyperLink control doesn't fire an event when the link is clicked. Instead, you'll need to use the LinkButton. The LinkButton fires the Click event, which the LinkMenu2 control can intercept, and then raises the LinkClicked event to the web page.

The following is the full user control code:

```
Public Class LinkMenu2
    Inherits System.Web.UI.UserControl

    Public Event LinkClicked(ByVal sender As Object, ByVal e As EventArgs)

    Protected Sub lnk_Click(ByVal sender As Object, _
      ByVal e As System.EventArgs) Handles _
      lnkBooks.Click, lnkToys.Click, lnkSports.Click, lnkFurniture.Click

        ' One of the LinkButton controls has been clicked.
        ' Raise an event to the page.
        RaiseEvent LinkClicked(Me, EventArgs.Empty)
    End Sub

End Class
```

You can create a page that uses the LinkMenu2 control and add an event handler. Here's an example of an event handler that responds to clicks in the web page and displays a message in a label:

```
Protected Sub Menu1_LinkClicked(ByVal sender As Object, _
  ByVal e As System.EventArgs) Handles Menu1.LinkClicked
```

```
    lblClick.Text = "Click detected."
End Sub
```

■ Note You won't be able to create user control event handlers through the Visual Studio Properties window, because the Properties window won't show the custom events the user control provides. However, you can still use the drop-down lists in code view to choose the right event, or you can type in your event handler by hand.

Figure 12-5 shows the result.

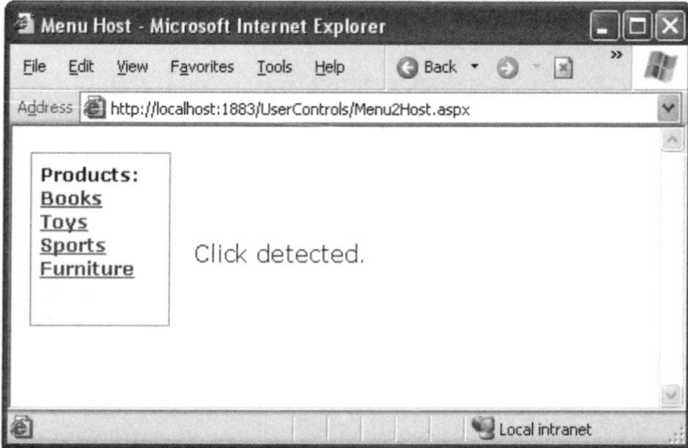

Figure 12-5. *Using the LinkMenu2 user control*

Conceptually, this approach should give your web page more power to customize how the user control works. Unfortunately, that's not the case at the moment, because a key piece of information is missing. When the LinkClicked event occurs, the web page has no way of knowing what link was clicked, which prevents it from taking any kind of reasonable action. The only way to solve this problem is to create a more intelligent event that can transmit some information through event arguments. You'll see how in the next section.

Passing Information with Events

In the current LinkMenu2 example no custom information is passed along with the event. In many cases, however, you want to convey additional information that relates to the event. To do so, you need to create a custom class that derives from EventArgs.

The LinkClickedEventArgs class that follows allows the LinkMenu2 user control to pass the URL that the user selected through a Url property. It also provides a Cancel property. If set to True, the user control will stop its processing immediately. But if Cancel remains False (the default), the user control will send the user to the new page. This way, the user control still handles the task of redirecting the user, but it allows the web page to plug into this process and change it or stop it (for example, if there's unfinished work left on the current page).

```
Public Class LinkClickedEventArgs
    Inherits System.EventArgs

    Private _url As String
    Public Property Url() As String
        Get
            Return _url
        End Get
        Set(ByVal value As String)
            _url = value
        End Set
    End Property

    Private _cancel As Boolean = False
    Public Property Cancel() As Boolean
        Get
            Return _cancel
        End Get
        Set(ByVal value As Boolean)
            _cancel = value
        End Set
    End Property

    Public Sub New(ByVal url As String)
        Me.Url = url
    End Sub

End Class
```

To use this custom EventArgs class, you need to modify the definition of the LinkClicked event so it uses the LinkClickedEventArgs object:

```
Public Event LinkClicked(ByVal sender As Object, ByVal e As LinkClickedEventArgs)
```

Next, your user control code for raising the event needs to submit the required information when calling the event. But how does the user control determine what link was clicked? The trick is to switch from the LinkButton.Click event to the LinkButton.Command event. The Command event automatically gets the CommandArgument that's defined in the tag. So if you define your LinkButton controls like this:

```
<asp:LinkButton ID="lnkBooks" runat="server"
  CommandArgument="Menu2Host.aspx?product=Books">Books
</asp:LinkButton><br />
<asp:LinkButton ID="lnkToys" runat="server"
  CommandArgument="Menu2Host.aspx?product=Toys">Toys
</asp:LinkButton><br />
<asp:LinkButton ID="lnkSports" runat="server"
  CommandArgument="Menu2Host.aspx?product=Sports">Sports
</asp:LinkButton><br />
```

```
<asp:LinkButton ID="lnkFurniture" runat="server"
  CommandArgument="Menu2Host.aspx?product=Furniture">
Furniture</asp:LinkButton>
```

you can pass the link along to the web page like this:

```
Dim args As New LinkClickedEventArgs(e.CommandArgument)
RaiseEvent LinkClicked(Me, args)
```

Here's the complete user control code. It implements one more feature. After the event has been raised and handled by the web page, the LinkMenu2 checks the Cancel property. If it's False, it goes ahead and performs the redirect using Reponse.Redirect().

```
Public Partial Class LinkMenu2
    Inherits System.Web.UI.UserControl

    Public Event LinkClicked(ByVal sender As Object, _
      ByVal e As LinkClickedEventArgs)

    Protected Sub lnk_Click(ByVal sender As Object, _
      ByVal e As System.Web.UI.WebControls.CommandEventArgs) Handles _
      lnkBooks.Click, lnkToys.Click, lnkSports.Click, lnkFurniture.Click

        ' One of the LinkButton controls has been clicked.
        ' Raise an event to the page.

        ' Pass along the link information.
        Dim args As New LinkClickedEventArgs(e.CommandArgument)
        RaiseEvent LinkClicked(Me, args)

        ' Perform the redirect.
        If Not args.Cancel Then
            ' Notice this code uses the Url from the LinkClickedEventArgs
            ' object, not the original link. That means the web page
            ' can change the link if desired before the redirect.
            Response.Redirect(args.Url)
        End If
    End Sub

End Class
```

Finally, you need to update the code in the web page (where the user control is placed) so that its event handler uses the new signature. In the following code, the LinkClicked event handler checks the URL and allows it in all cases except one:

```
Protected Sub Menu1_LinkClicked(ByVal sender As Object, _
  ByVal e As LinkClickedEventArgs) Handles Menu1.LinkClicked
```

```
    If e.Url = "Menu2Host.aspx?product=Furniture" Then
        lblClick.Text = "This link is not allowed."
        e.Cancel = True
    Else
        ' Allow the redirect, and don't make any changes to the URL.
    End If
End Sub
```

If you click the Furniture link, you'll see the message shown in Figure 12-6.

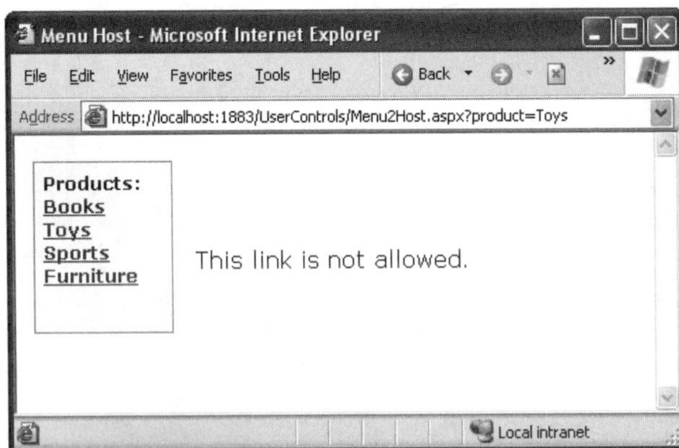

Figure 12-6. *Handling a user control event in the page*

Dynamic Graphics

One of the features of the .NET Framework is GDI+, a set of classes designed for drawing images. You can use GDI+ in a Windows or an ASP.NET application to create dynamic graphics. In a Windows application, the graphics you draw would be copied to a window for display. In ASP.NET, the graphics can be rendered right into the HTML stream and sent directly to the client browser.

In general, using GDI+ code to draw a graphic is slower than using a ready-made image file. However, GDI+ gives you much more freedom. For example, you can tailor your image to suit a particular purpose, incorporating information such as the date or current user name. You can also mingle text, shapes, and other bitmaps to create a complete picture.

Basic Drawing

You need to follow four basic steps when using GDI+. First, you have to create an in-memory bitmap. This is the drawing space where you'll create your masterpiece. To create the bitmap, declare a new instance of the System.Drawing.Bitmap class. You must specify the height and width of the image in pixels. Be careful—don't make the bitmap larger than required, or you'll needlessly waste memory.

```
' Create an in-memory bitmap where you will draw the image.
' The Bitmap is 300 pixels wide and 50 pixels high.
Dim image As New Bitmap(300, 50)
```

The next step is to create a GDI+ graphics context for the image, which is represented by a System.Drawing.Graphics object. This object provides the methods that allow you to render content to the in-memory bitmap. To create a Graphics object from an existing Bitmap object, you just use the shared Graphics.FromImage() method, as shown here:

```
Dim g As Graphics = Graphics.FromImage(image)
```

Note The Graphics.FromImage() method works with any Image object. Classes such as Bitmap derive from Image, so they work fine.

Now comes the interesting part. Using the methods of the Graphics class, you can draw text, shapes, and images on the bitmap. Table 12-1 lists some of the most fundamental methods of the Graphics class. The methods that begin with the word *Draw* draw outlines, while the methods that begin with the word *Fill* draw solid regions. The only exceptions are the DrawString() method, which draws filled-in text using a font you specify, and the methods for copying bitmap images, such as DrawIcon() and DrawImage().

Table 12-1. *Drawing Methods of the Graphics Class*

Method	Description
DrawArc()	Draws an arc representing a portion of an ellipse specified by a pair of coordinates, a width, and a height (or some other combination of information, if you use one of the overloaded versions of this method).
DrawBezier() and DrawBeziers()	Draws the infamous and attractive Bezier curve, which is defined by four control points.
DrawClosedCurve()	Draws a curve and then closes it off by connecting the end points.
DrawCurve()	Draws a curve (technically, a cardinal spline).
DrawEllipse()	Draws an ellipse defined by a bounding rectangle specified by a pair of coordinates, a height, and a width.
DrawIcon() and DrawIconUnstreched()	Draws the icon represented by an Icon object and (optionally) stretches it to fit a given rectangle.
DrawImage() and DrawImageUnscaled()	Draws the image represented by an Image-derived object (such as a Bitmap object) and (optionally) stretches it to fit a given rectangle.
DrawLine() and DrawLines()	Draws one or more lines. Each line connects the two points specified by a coordinate pair.
DrawPie()	Draws a "piece of pie" shape defined by an ellipse specified by a coordinate pair, a width, a height, and two radial lines.
DrawPolygon()	Draws a multisided polygon defined by an array of points.

Table 12-1. *Drawing Methods of the Graphics Class (Continued)*

Method	Description
DrawRectangle() and DrawRectangles()	Draws sone or more ordinary rectangles. Each rectangle is defined by a starting coordinate pair, a width, and a height.
DrawString()	Draws a string of text in a given font.
DrawPath()	Draws a more complex shape that's defined by the Path object.
FillClosedCurve()	Draws a curve, closes it off by connecting the end points, and fills it.
FillEllipse()	Fills the interior of an ellipse.
FillPie()	Fills the interior of a "piece of pie" shape.
FillPolygon()	Fills the interior of a polygon.
FillRectangle() and FillRectangles()	Fills the interior of one or more rectangles.
DrawPath()	Fills the interior of a complex shape that's defined by the Path object.

When calling the Graphics class methods, you need to specify several parameters to indicate the pixel coordinates for what you want to draw. For example, when drawing a rectangle, you need to specify the location of the top-left corner and its width and height. Here's an example of how you might draw a solid rectangle in yellow:

```
' Draw a rectangle starting at location (0, 0)
' that is 300 pixels wide and 50 pixels high.
g.FillRectangle(Brushes.Yellow, 0, 0, 300, 50)
```

When measuring pixels, the point (0, 0) is the top-left corner of your image in (x, y) coordinates. The x coordinate increases as you go farther to the right, and the y coordinate increases as you go farther down. In the current example, the image is 300 pixels wide and 50 pixels high, which means the point (299, 49) is the bottom-right corner.

■ **Note** This code performs its drawing on the in-memory Bitmap object created earlier. Until this image is rendered (a skill you'll pick up shortly), you won't actually see anything on the web page.

You'll also notice that you need to specify either a Brush or a Pen object when you draw most content. (Both of these classes are defined in the System.Drawing namespace, alongside the Graphics class.) Methods that draw shape outlines require a Pen, while methods that draw filled-in shapes require a Brush. You can create your own custom Pen and Brush objects, but .NET provides an easier solution with the Brushes and Pens classes. These classes expose shared properties that provide various Brushes and Pens for different colors. For example, Brushes.Yellow returns a Brush object that fills shapes using a solid yellow color.

Once the image is complete, you can send it to the browser using the Image.Save() method. Conceptually, you "save" the image to the browser's response stream. It then gets sent to the client and displayed in the browser.

```
' Render the image to the HTML output stream.
image.Save(Response.OutputStream, _
  System.Drawing.Imaging.ImageFormat.Gif)
```

■Tip You can save an image to any valid stream, including the FileStream class described in Chapter 18. This technique allows you to save dynamically generated images to disk so you can use them later in other web pages.

Finally, you should explicitly release your image and graphics context when you're finished, because both hold onto some unmanaged resources that might not be released right away if you don't:

```
g.Dispose()
image.Dispose()
```

Using GDI+ is a specialized technique, and its more advanced features are beyond the scope of this book. However, you can learn a lot by considering a couple of straightforward examples.

Drawing a Custom Image

Using the techniques you've learned, it's easy to create a simple web page that uses GDI+. The next example uses GDI+ to render some text in a bordered rectangle with a happy-face graphic next to it.

Here's the code you'll need:

```
Protected Sub Page_Load(ByVal sender As Object, _
  ByVal e As System.EventArgs) Handles Me.Load

    ' Create an in-memory bitmap where you will draw the image.
    ' The Bitmap is 300 pixels wide and 50 pixels high.
    Dim image As New Bitmap(300, 50)

    ' Get the graphics context for the bitmap.
    Dim g As Graphics = Graphics.FromImage(image)

    ' Draw a solid yellow rectangle with a red border.
    g.FillRectangle(Brushes.LightYellow, 0, 0, 300, 50)
    g.DrawRectangle(Pens.Red, 0, 0, 299, 49)
```

```
    ' Draw some text using a fancy font.
    Dim font As New Font("Alba Super", 20, FontStyle.Regular)
    g.DrawString("This is a test.", font, Brushes.Blue, 10, 0)

    ' Copy a smaller gif into the image from a file.
    Dim icon As System.Drawing.Image
    icon = Image.FromFile(Server.MapPath("smiley.gif"))
    g.DrawImageUnscaled(icon, 240, 0)

    ' Render the entire bitmap to the HTML output stream.
    image.Save(Response.OutputStream, _
      System.Drawing.Imaging.ImageFormat.Gif)

    ' Clean up.
    g.Dispose()
    image.Dispose()

End Sub
```

This code is easy to understand. It follows the basic pattern set out earlier—it creates the in-memory Bitmap, gets the corresponding Graphics object, performs the painting, and then saves the image to the response stream. This example uses the FillRectangle(), DrawRectangle(), DrawString(), and DrawImageUnscaled() methods to create the complete drawing shown in Figure 12-7.

■ **Tip** Because this image is generated on the web server, you can use any font that is installed on the server. The client doesn't need to have the same font, because the client receives the text as a rendered image.

Figure 12-7. *Drawing a custom image*

Placing Custom Images Inside Web Pages

The Image.Save() approach demonstrated so far has one problem. When you save an image to the response stream, you overwrite whatever information ASP.NET would otherwise use. If you have a web page that includes other content and controls, this content won't appear at all in the final web page. Instead, the dynamically rendered graphics replace it.

Fortunately, this has a simple solution: you can link to a dynamically generated image using the HTML <img> tag or the Image web control. But instead of linking your image to a fixed image file, link it to the .aspx file that generates the picture.

For example, you could create a file named GraphicalText.aspx that writes a dynamically generated image to the response stream. In another page, you could show the dynamic image by adding an Image web control and setting the ImageUrl property to GraphicalText.aspx. In fact, you'll even see the image appear in Visual Studio's design-time environment before you run the web page!

When you use this technique to embed dynamic graphics in web pages, you also need to think about how the web page can send information to the dynamic graphic. For example, what if you don't want to show a fixed piece of text, but instead you want to generate a dynamic label that incorporates the name of the current user? (In fact, if you do want to show a fixed piece of text, it's probably better to create the graphic ahead of time and store it in a file, rather than generating it using GDI+ code each time the user requests the page.) One solution is to pass the information using the query string, as described in Chapter 7. The page that renders the graphic can then check for the query string information it needs.

Here's how you'd rewrite the dynamic graphic generator with this in mind:

```
' Get the user name.
If Request.QueryString("Name") Is Nothing Then
    ' No name was supplied.
    ' Don't display anything.
Else
    Dim name As String = Request.QueryString("Name")

    ' Create an in-memory bitmap where you will draw the image.
    Dim image As New Bitmap(300, 50)

    ' Get the graphics context for the bitmap.
    Dim g As Graphics = Graphics.FromImage(image)

    g.FillRectangle(Brushes.LightYellow, 0, 0, 300, 50)
    g.DrawRectangle(Pens.Red, 0, 0, 299, 49)

    ' Draw some text based on the query string.
    Dim font As New Font("Alba Super", 20, FontStyle.Regular)
    g.DrawString(name, font, Brushes.Blue, 10, 0)

    ' Render the entire bitmap to the HTML output stream.
    image.Save(Response.OutputStream, _
      System.Drawing.Imaging.ImageFormat.Gif)
```

```
    g.Dispose()
    image.Dispose()
End If
```

Conceptually, this code isn't much different than the examples you've seen before. The only change is that one piece of information—the string that's used with the DrawString() method—is retrieved from the query string.

Figure 12-8 shows a page that uses this dynamic graphic page, along with two Label controls. The page passes the query string argument Joe Brown to the page. The full Image.ImageUrl thus becomes GraphicalText.aspx?Name=Joe%20Brown, as shown here:

```
<asp:Label id="Label1" runat="server">Here is some content.</asp:Label>
<br /><br />
<asp:Image id="Image1" runat="server"
  ImageUrl="GraphicalText2.aspx?Name=Joe%20Brown"></asp:Image>
<br /><br />
<asp:Label id="Label2" runat="server">Here is some more content.</asp:Label>
```

Figure 12-8. *Mingling custom images and controls on the same page*

It's possible that you might need to send more information or more complex information to the page that draws the image. For example, you might want to pass a data object to a page that draws a pie chart. In this case, the query string isn't good enough, and you'll need to use a different type of state management. One option is session state, as described in Chapter 8.

Image Format and Quality

When you render an image, you can also choose the format you want to use. JPEG offers the best color support and graphics, although it uses compression that can lose detail and make text look fuzzy. GIF (the standard used in the examples so far) is often a better choice for graphics containing text, but it doesn't offer good support for color. In .NET, every GIF uses a fixed palette with 256 generic colors. If you use a color that doesn't map to one of these presets, the color will be dithered, leading to a less-than-optimal graphic.

However, the best format choice is PNG. PNG is an all-purpose format that always provides high quality by combining the lossless compression of GIFs with the rich color support of JPEGs. Unfortunately, browsers such as Internet Explorer often don't handle it correctly when you return PNG content directly from a page. Instead of seeing the picture content, you'll receive a message prompting you to download the picture content and open it in another program. To sidestep this problem, you need to use the <img> tag approach shown in the previous example.

You need to be aware of two more quirks when using PNG. First, some older browsers (including Netscape 4.*x*) don't support PNG. Second, you can't use the Bitmap.Save() method shown in earlier examples. If you do, an error will occur. (Technically, the problem is the Save() method requires a *seekable* stream—a stream where the position can be changed at will. That's because .NET needs to be able to move back and forth through the picture content while it's being generated.)

The solution is easy to implement, if a little awkward. Instead of saving directly to Response. OutputStream, you can create a System.IO.MemoryStream object, which represents an in-memory buffer of data. The MemoryStream is always seekable, so you can save the image to this object. Once you've performed this step, you can easily copy the data from the MemoryStream to the Response.OutputStream. The only disadvantage is that this technique requires more memory because the complete rendered content of the graphic needs to be held in memory at once. However, the graphics you use in web pages generally aren't that large, so you probably won't observe any reduction in performance.

To implement this solution, start by importing the System.IO namespace:

```
Imports System.IO
```

Now you can replace the previous example with this modified code that saves the image in PNG format. The changed lines are highlighted.

```
' Get the user name.
If Request.QueryString("Name") Is Nothing Then
    ' No name was supplied.
    ' Don't display anything.
Else
    Dim name As String = Request.QueryString("Name")

    ' Create an in-memory bitmap where you will draw the image.
    Dim image As New Bitmap(300, 50)

    ' Get the graphics context for the bitmap.
    Dim g As Graphics = Graphics.FromImage(image)

    g.FillRectangle(Brushes.LightYellow, 0, 0, 300, 50)
    g.DrawRectangle(Pens.Red, 0, 0, 299, 49)

    ' Draw some text based on the query string.
    Dim font As New Font("Alba Super", 20, FontStyle.Regular)
    g.DrawString(name, font, Brushes.Blue, 10, 0)

    Response.ContentType = "image/png"
```

```
    ' Create the PNG in memory.
    Dim mem As New MemoryStream()
    image.Save(mem, System.Drawing.Imaging.ImageFormat.Png)

    ' Write the MemoryStream data to the output stream.
    mem.WriteTo(Response.OutputStream)

    g.Dispose()
    image.Dispose()
End If
```

■ **Note** You'll learn more about streams when you tackle file access in Chapter 18.

Quality isn't just determined by the image format. It also depends on the way you draw the image content onto the in-memory bitmap. GDI+ allows you to choose between optimizing your drawing code for appearance or speed. When you choose to optimize for the best appearance, .NET uses extra rendering techniques such as antialiasing to improve the drawing.

Antialiasing smooths jagged edges in shapes and text. It works by adding shading at the border of an edge. For example, gray shading might be added to the edge of a black curve to make a corner look smoother. Technically, antialiasing blends a curve with its background. Figure 12-9 shows a close-up of an antialiased ellipse.

Figure 12-9. *Antialiasing with an ellipse*

To use smoothing in your applications, you set the SmoothingMode property of the Graphics object. You can choose between None, HighSpeed (the default), AntiAlias, and HighQuality (which is similar to AntiAlias but uses other, slower optimizations that improve the display on LCD screens). The Graphics.SmoothingMode property is one of the few stateful Graphics class members. This means you set it before you begin drawing, and it applies to any text or shapes you draw in the rest of the paint session (until the Graphics object is released).

```
g.SmoothingMode = Drawing.Drawing2D.SmoothingMode.AntiAlias
```

■ **Tip** Antialiasing makes the most difference when you're displaying curves. That means it will dramatically improve the appearance of ellipses, circles, and arcs, but it won't make any difference with straight lines, squares, and rectangles.

You can also use antialiasing with fonts to soften jagged edges on text. You can set the Graphics.TextRenderingHint property to ensure optimized text. You can choose between SingleBitPerPixelGridFit (fastest performance and lowest quality), AntiAliasGridFit (better quality but slower performance), and ClearTypeGridFit (the best quality on an LCD display). Or you can use the SystemDefault value to apply whatever font-smoothing settings the user has configured. SystemDefault is the default setting, and the default system settings for most computers enable text antialiasing. Even if you don't set this, your dynamically rendered text will probably be drawn in high quality. However, because you can't necessarily control the system settings of the web server, it's a good practice to specify this setting explicitly if you need to draw text in an image.

The Last Word

In this chapter, you put two more tools in your ASP.NET toolkit. First, you saw how user controls allow you to reuse a block of user interface in more than one web page. Next, you considered how custom drawing allows you to create made-to-measure graphics.

In the following chapter, you'll learn about themes and master pages—two features that complement user controls and give you even more ways to standardize the look and feel of your web pages. Themes are more fine-grained than user controls—they group together formatting presets that you can apply to individual controls to ensure a slick, consistent style throughout your application. Master pages are broader than user controls—they allow you to define a standardized page template that you can apply to lock down the appearance and layout of multiple pages, giving you complete consistency. Learning how to mix all these ingredients is part of the fine art of ASP.NET programming.

CHAPTER 13

■ ■ ■

Styles, Themes, and Master Pages

Using the techniques you've learned so far, you can create polished web pages and let users surf from one page to another. However, to integrate your web pages into a unified, consistent website, you need a few more tools. In this chapter, you'll consider three of the most important tools that you can use: styles, themes, and master pages.

Styles are part of the Cascading Style Sheet (CSS) standard. They aren't directly tied to ASP.NET, but they're still a great help in applying consistent formatting across your entire website. With styles, you can define a set of formatting options once, and reuse it to format different elements on multiple pages. You can even create styles that apply their magic automatically—for example, styles that change the font of all the text in your website without requiring you to modify any of the web page code. Best of all, once you've standardized on a specific set of styles and applied them to multiple pages, you can give your entire website a face-lift just by editing your style sheet.

Styles are genuinely useful, but there are some things they just can't do. Because styles are based on the HTML standard, they have no understanding of ASP.NET concepts like control properties. To fill the gap, ASP.NET includes a *themes* feature, which plays a similar role to styles but works exclusively with server controls. Much as you use styles to automatically set the formatting characteristics of HTML elements, you use themes to automatically set the properties of ASP.NET controls.

Another feature for standardizing websites is *master pages*. Essentially, a master page is a blueprint for part of your website. Using a master page, you can define web page layout, complete with all the usual details such as headers, menu bars, and ad banners. Once you've perfected a master page, you can use it to create *content pages*. Each content page automatically acquires the layout and the content of the linked master page.

By using styles, themes, and master pages, you can ensure that all the pages on your website share a standardized look and layout. In many cases, these details are the difference between an average website and one that looks truly professional.

Styles

In the early days of the Internet, website designers used the formatting features of HTML to decorate these pages. These formatting features were limited, inconsistent, and sometimes poorly supported. Worst of all, HTML formatting led to horribly messy markup, with formatting details littered everywhere.

The solution is the CSS standard, which is supported in all modern browsers. Essentially, CSS gives you a wide range of consistent formatting properties that you can apply to any HTML element. Styles allow you to add borders, set font details, change colors, add margin space and padding, and so on. Many of the examples you've seen so far have in this book have used CSS formatting.

In the following sections, you'll learn the basics of the CSS standard. You'll see how web controls use CSS to apply *their* formatting, and you'll learn how you can explicitly use styles in your ASP.NET web pages.

Style Types

Web pages can use styles in three different ways:

- *Inline style*: An inline style is a style that's placed directly inside an HTML tag. This can get messy, but it's a reasonable approach for one-time formatting. You can remove the style and put it in a style sheet later.
- *Internal style sheet*: An internal style sheet is a collection of styles that are placed in the <head> section of your web page markup. You can then use the styles from this style sheet to format the web controls on that page. By using an internal style sheet, you get a clear separation between formatting (your styles) and your content (the rest of your HTML markup). You can also reuse the same style for multiple elements.
- *External style sheet*: An external style sheet is similar to an internal style sheet, except it's placed in a completely separate file. This is the most powerful approach, because it gives you a way to apply the same style rules to many pages.

You can use all types of styles with ASP.NET web pages. You'll see how in the following sections.

Creating a Basic Inline Style

To apply a style to an ordinary HTML element, you set the style attribute. Here's an example that gives a blue background to a paragraph:

```
<p style="background: Blue">This text has a blue background.</p>
```

Every style consists of a list of one or more formatting properties. In the preceding example, the style has a single formatting property, named *background*, which is set to the value Blue. To add multiple style properties, you simply separate them with semicolons, as shown here:

```
<p style="color:White; background:Blue; font-size:x-large; padding:10px">
This text has a blue background.</p>
```

This style creates large white text with a blue background and 10 pixels of spacing between the edge of the element (the blue box) and the text content inside.

■ **Note** The full list of formatting properties is beyond the scope of this book (although you can get all the details at `www.w3schools.com/css`). However, you'll soon see that Visual Studio includes tools that can help you build the styles you want, so you don't need to remember style property names or write styles by hand.

You can use the same approach to apply formatting to a web control using a style. However, you don't need to, because web controls provide formatting properties. For example, if you create a Label control like this:

```
<asp:Label ID="MyLabel" runat="server" ForeColor="White" BackColor="Blue"
 Font-Size="X-Large">Formatted Text</asp:Label>
```

it's actually rendered into this HTML, which uses an inline style:

```
<span id="MyLabel"
 style="color:White; background-color:Blue; font-size:X-Large">
Formatted Text</span>
```

Incidentally, if you specify a theme *and* set formatting properties that overlap with your style, the properties have the final say.

The Style Builder

Visual Studio provides an indispensable style builder that lets you create styles by picking and choosing your style preferences in a dedicated dialog box. To try it out, begin by creating a new page in Visual Studio. Then drop a few controls onto your page (for example, a label, text box, and button).

Every new page starts with an empty <div> element. This <div> is simply a content container—by default, it doesn't have any appearance. However, by applying style settings to the <div>, you can create a bordered content region, and you can change the font and colors of the content inside. In this example, you'll see how to use Visual Studio to build a style for the <div> element.

■ **Note** CSS supports a feature it calls *inheritance*. With inheritance, some formatting properties (such as the font family) are passed down from a parent element to other nested elements. In other words, if you set the font family for a <div> element, all the elements inside will inherit the same font (unless they explicitly specify otherwise). Other properties, like margin and padding settings, don't use inheritance. To learn more about this behavior and the specific properties that use inheritance, you can experiment on your own, consult a dedicated book such as Eric Meyer's *CSS: The Definitive Guide* (O'Reilly, 2006), or use the tutorials at `www.w3schools.com/css`.

Before formatting the page, make sure all your controls are nested inside the <div> element. Your markup should look something like this:

```
<div>
    <asp:Label ID="Label1" runat="server">Type something here:
    </asp:Label>
    <asp:TextBox ID="TextBox1" runat="server">
    </asp:TextBox>
    <br /><br />
    <asp:Button ID="Button1" runat="server" Text="Button">
    </asp:Button>
</div>
```

In the design window, click somewhere inside the <div> (but not on another control). You'll know you're in the right spot when a border appears around your controls, showing you the outline of the <div>, as shown in Figure 13-1.

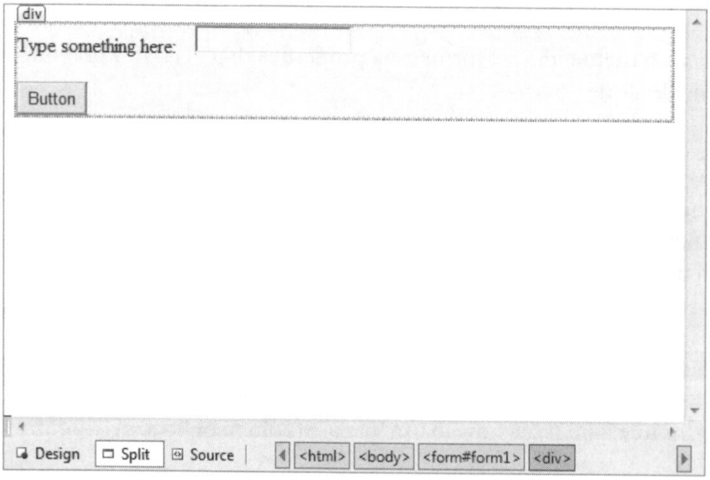

Figure 13-1. *Adding a style to a <div>*

Next, choose Format ➤ New Style from the menu. This opens the New Style dialog box shown in Figure 13-2. In the Selector box at the top of the window, choose Inline Style to specify that you're creating your style directly in the HTML markup.

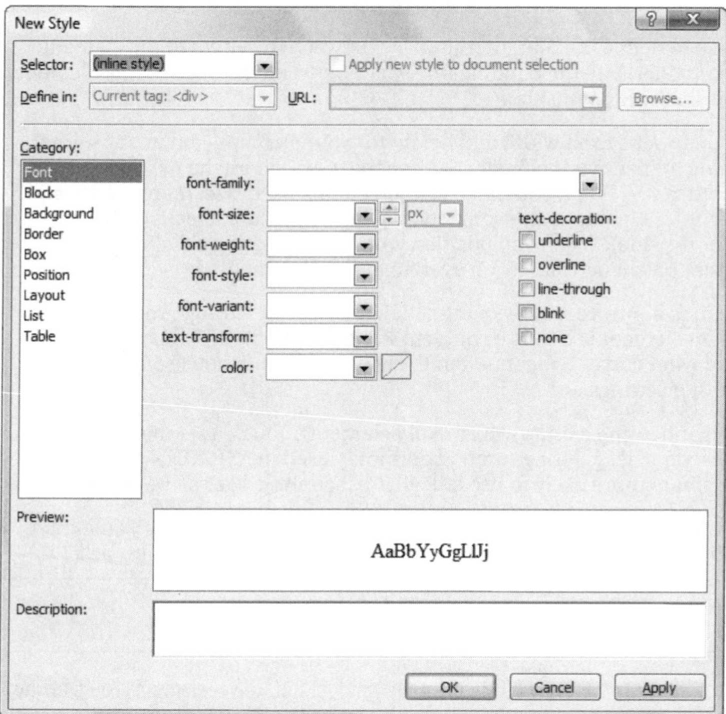

Figure 13-2. *Creating an inline style*

To specify style settings, you first need to choose one of the categories in the Category list. For example, if you choose Font you'll see a list of font-related formatting settings, such as font family, font size, text color, and so on. You can apply settings from as many different categories as you want. Table 13-1 provides a brief explanation for each category.

Table 13-1. *Style Settings in the New Style Dialog Box*

Category	Description
Font	Allows you to choose the font family, font size, and text color, and apply other font characteristics (like italics and bold).
Block	Allows you to fine-tune additional text settings, such as the height of lines in a paragraph, the way text is aligned, the amount of indent in the first list, and the amount of spacing between letters and words.
Background	Allows you to set a background color or image.

Table 13-1. *Style Settings in the New Style Dialog Box (Continued)*

Category	Description
Border	Allows you to define borders on one or more edges of the element. You can specify the border style, thickness, and color of each edge.
Box	Allows you to define the margin (the space between the edges of the element and its container) and the padding (the space between the edges of the element and its nested content inside).
Position	Allows you to set a fixed width and height for your element, and use absolute positioning to place your element at a specific position on the page. Use these settings with care. When you make your element a fixed size, there's a danger that the content inside can become too big (in which case it leaks out the bottom or the side). When you position your element using absolute coordinates, there's a chance that it can overlap another element.
Layout	Allows you to control a variety of miscellaneous layout settings. You can specify whether an element is visible or hidden, whether it floats at the side of the page, and what cursor appears when the user moves the mouse overtop, among other settings.
List	If you're configuring a list (a <ul> or <ol> element), you can set the numbering or bullet style. These settings aren't commonly used in ASP.NET web pages, because you're more likely to use ASP.NET list controls like the BulletedList.
Table	Allows you to set details that only apply to table elements (such as <tr> and <td>). For example, you can control whether borders appear around an empty cell.

■ **Note** Remember, you can build a style for any HTML element, not just the <div> element. You'll always get exactly the same New Style dialog box with the same formatting options.

As you make your selections, Visual Studio shows what your style will look like when applied to some sample text (in the Preview box) and the markup that's needed to define your style (in the Description) box. Figure 13-3 shows the New Style dialog box after formatting the <div> into a nicely shaded and bordered box. In the Category list, all the categories with formatting settings are highlighted in bold.

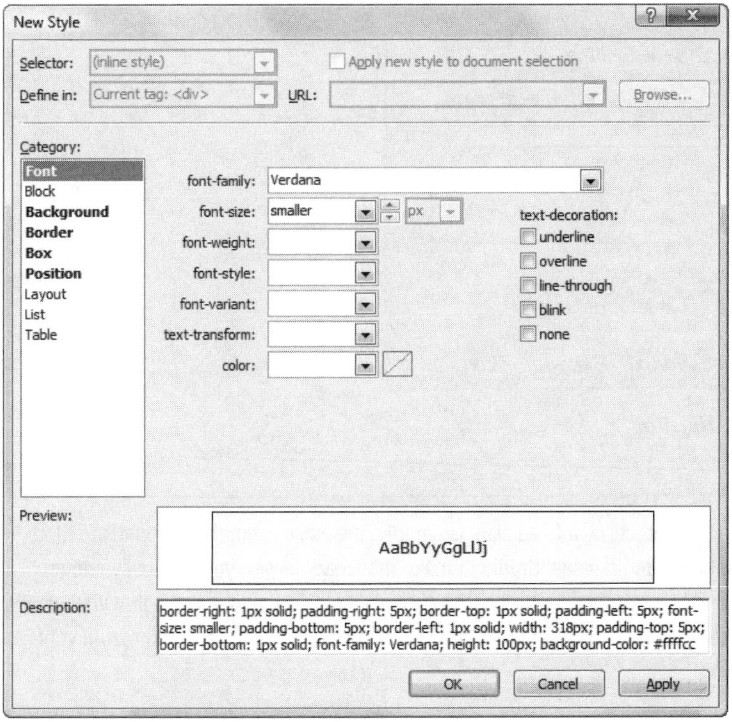

Figure 13-3. *Building a styled division*

When you click OK, Visual Studio will add the style information to your element. Here's the markup for the formatted <div> box:

```
<div style="border-style: solid; border-color: inherit; border-width: 1px;
 padding: 5px; font-size: smaller; font-family: Verdana;
 background-color: #ffffcc">

    <asp:Label ID="Label1" runat="server">Type something here:
    </asp:Label>
    <asp:TextBox ID="TextBox1" runat="server">
    </asp:TextBox>
    <br /><br />
    <asp:Button ID="Button1" runat="server" Text="Button">
    </asp:Button>
</div>
```

Figure 13-4 shows the final result—a shaded yellow box with a bit of padding and a different font.

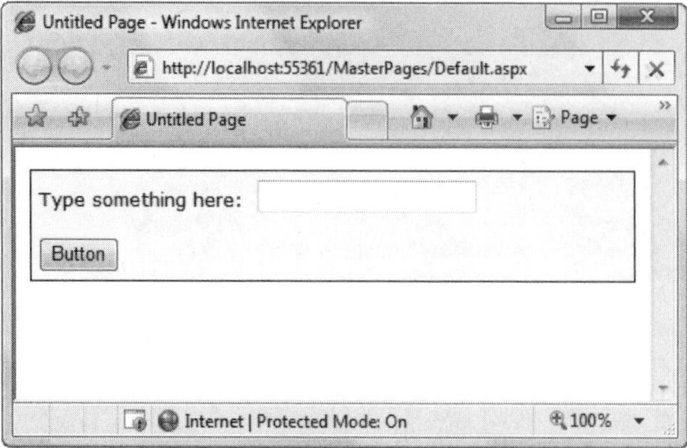

Figure 13-4. *Using a styled division*

■ **Tip** Be careful you don't give your <div> a fixed size. Ordinarily, the <div> container expands to fit its content. However, if you drag its border in Visual Studio to make the <div> larger, you'll actually end up creating a hard-coded width and height, which are set in the style attribute. The end result is that your <div> container can't expand if its content expands or the web browser window changes size. As a result, your content will leak out of the box.

The CSS Properties Window

Once you've created a style, you have two easy options for modifying it in Visual Studio. Both revolve around the CSS Properties window, which allows you to dissect the formatting details of any style.

To show the CSS Properties window, open a web page in Visual Studio and choose View ➤ CSS Properties. The CSS Properties window is usually grouped with the Toolbox and Server Explorer windows at the left of the Visual Studio window.

Now that the CSS Properties window is visible, you can use it to view one of your styles. First, find the element or web control that uses the style attribute. Then, click to select it (in design view) or click somewhere in the element's start tag (in source view). Either way, the style information for that element will appear in the CSS Properties window. For example, Figure 13-5 shows what you'll see for the <div> element that was formatted in the previous section.

The CSS Properties window provides an exhaustive list of all the formatting properties you can use in a style. This list is grouped into categories, and the properties in each category are sorted alphabetically. The ones that are currently set are displayed in bold.

You can use the CSS Properties window to modify existing style properties or set new ones, in the same way that you modify the properties for web controls using the Properties window. For example, in Figure 13-5 the font size is being changed.

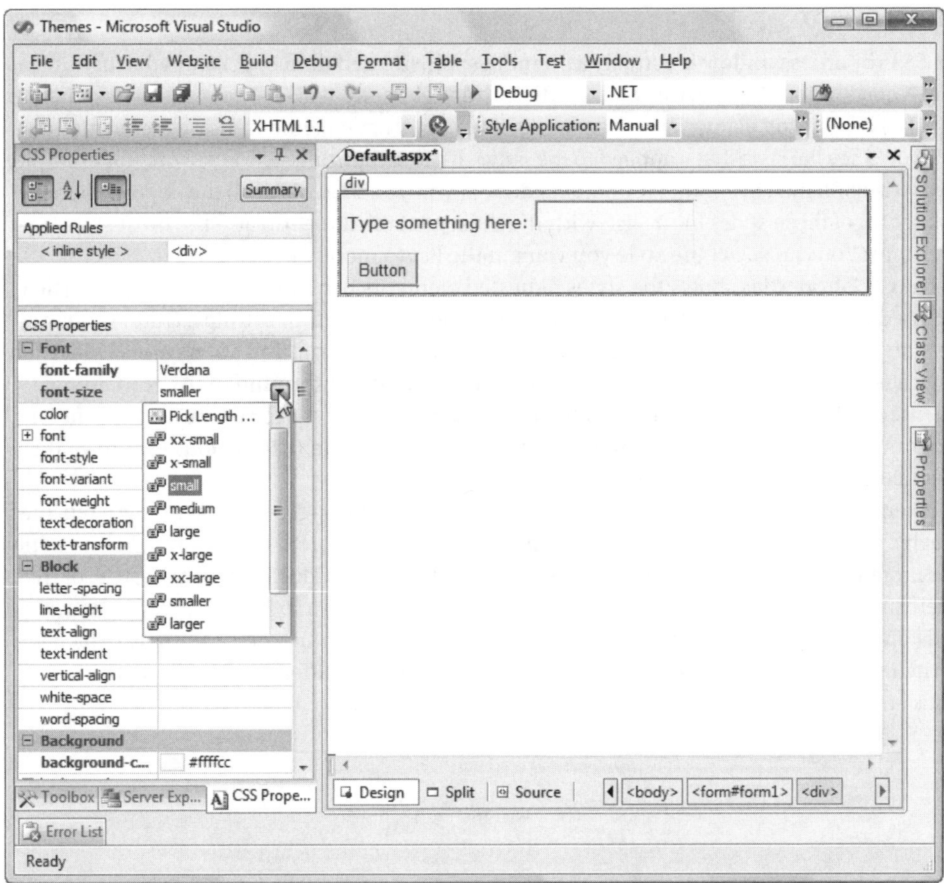

Figure 13-5. *The CSS Properties window (on the left)*

Depending on your personal taste, you may find that the CSS Properties window is more convenient than the style builder because it gives you access to every style property at once. Or, you may prefer the more organized views in the style builder. (Your preference might also depend on how much screen real estate you have to devote to the CSS Properties window.) If you decide that you want to return to the style builder to change a style, the process is fairly straightforward. First, select the element that has the inline style. Next, look at the Applied Rules list at the top of the CSS Properties window, which should show the text < inline style >. Right-click that text and choose Modify Style to open the Modify Style dialog box, which looks identical to the New Style dialog box you considered earlier.

■ Note You can't use the CSS Properties window to create a style. If you select an element that doesn't have a style applied, you won't see anything in the CSS Properties window (unless you select an element that's inside another element, and the containing element uses a style).

Style Inheritance

The CSS Properties window is actually a bit more sophisticated than the current discussion has let on. Not only does it show the style for the current element, it also shows any styles that are applied to containing elements. For example, if you look at an element inside the formatted <div>, you'll see the style that's applied to the <div>. If more than one style is at work (for example, the <div> is contained in another formatted <div>, or you've added a style to the <body> element), you'll see all of these styles in the list, with the most general at the top and the most specific at the bottom. You can select the style you want in the list to modify it.

The CSS Properties shows the styles of nested elements because certain style properties are passed down the element tree through inheritance, such as font settings. Other style properties can indirectly affect a nested element—for example, background colors aren't inherited but because element backgrounds are blank by default, the background of the containing element will show through. It's easy to see this behavior in action—for example, the font and background properties that were applied to the <div> element in the previous example affect the formatting of the elements inside.

When displaying inherited styles, the CSS Properties window will sometimes draw a red line through a property name. It does this if the property is set in the parent element but doesn't apply to the nested element. For example, the nested element may override it with its own style, or the property may not be inherited. Figure 13-6 shows an example with a styled <p> paragraph inside a styled <div>. The style that's inherited from the <div> defines the font-family property (which is inherited), the font-size property (which is inherited but overridden, and is crossed out), and various border properties (which are not inherited, and so are also crossed out).

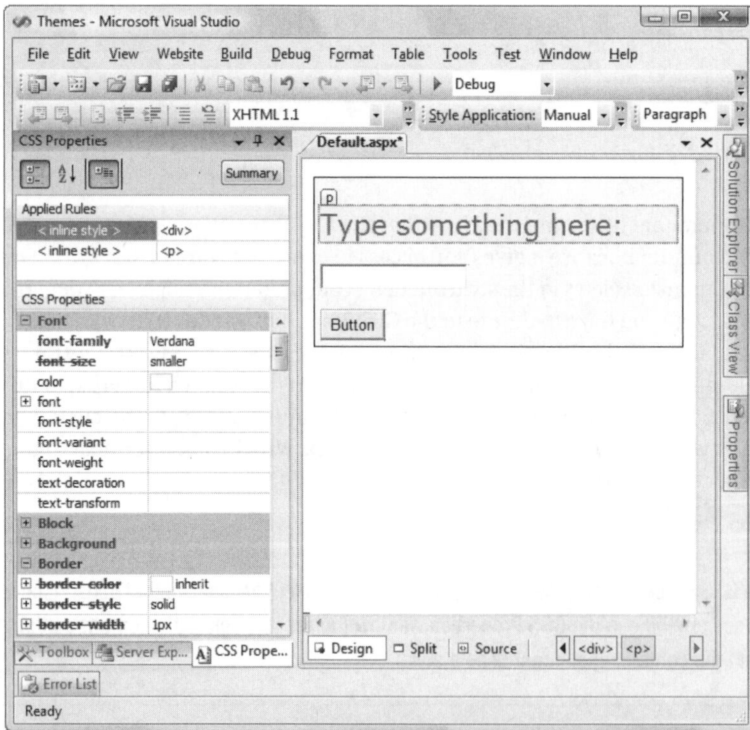

Figure 13-6. *Inherited and overridden style properties*

Creating a Style Sheet

To really get the value out of CSS, you need to create a style sheet. To create a style sheet in Visual Studio, choose Website ➤ Add New Item from the Visual Studio menu. Then, pick the Style Sheet template, specify a file name (like StyleSheet.css), and click Add.

In a style sheet, you define several styles (also known as *rules*). You can then use these rules to format ordinary HTML and ASP.NET controls. Each rule defines a collection of formatting presets that determines how a single ingredient in your web page should be formatted.

For example, if you want to define a rule for formatting headings, you start by defining a rule with a descriptive name, like this:

```
.heading1
{
}
```

Each rule name has two parts. The portion before the period indicates the HTML element to which the rule applies. In this example, nothing appears before the period, which means the rule can apply to any tag. The portion after the period is a unique name (called the CSS *class name*) that you choose to identify your rule. CSS class names are case sensitive.

Once you've defined a rule, you can add the appropriate formatting information. Here's an example the sets the heading1 style to a large sans-serif font with a green foreground color. The font is set to Verdana (if it's available), or Arial (if it's not), or the browser's default sans-serif typeface (if neither Verdana nor Arial is installed).

```
.heading1
{
    font-weight: bold;
    font-size: large;
    color: limegreen;
    font-family: Verdana, Arial, Sans-Serif;
}
```

As you can see, the syntax for defining a style in a style sheet is exactly the same as it is for defining an internal style (not including the rule name and curly braces). By convention, each formatting option in a style is placed on a separate line, but this detail is optional.

You can also create rules that are applied to HTML tags automatically. To do this, specify the tag name for the rule name. Here's a rule that affects all <h2> tags on the page that uses the style sheet:

```
h2
{ ... }
```

If you want to apply formatting that applies to the entire web page, you can create a style sheet rule for the <body> element:

```
body
{ ... }
```

This gives you a good way to set the default font name and font size.

Fortunately, you don't need to hand-write the rules in your style sheet. Visual Studio allows you to build named styles in a style sheet using the same style builder you used to create inline styles earlier. To use this feature, add a blank style with the right rule name, like this:

```
.myStyle
{
}
```

Then, right-click between the two curly braces of an existing style and choose Build Style. You'll see the familiar Modify Style dialog box, where you can point and click your way to custom fonts, borders, backgrounds, and alignment. If you want to create a new style from scratch, simply right-click an empty region of your style sheet and choose Add Style Rule.

A typical style sheet defines a slew of rules. In fact, style sheets are often used to formally define the formatting for every significant piece of a website's user interface. The following style sheet serves this purpose by defining five rules. The first rule sets the font for the <body> element, which ensures that the entire page shares a consistent default font. The rest of the rules are class based, and need to be applied explicitly to the elements that use them. Two rules define size and color formatting for headings, and the final rule configures the formatting that's needed to create a bordered, shaded box of text.

```
body
{
    font-family: Verdana, Arial, Sans-Serif;
    font-size: small;
}

.heading1
{
    font-weight: bold;
    font-size: large;
    color: lime;
}

.heading2
{
    font-weight: bold;
    font-size: medium;
    font-style: italic;
    color: #C0BA72;
}

.blockText
{
    padding: 10px;
    background-color: #FFFFD9;
    border-style: solid;
    border-width: thin;
}
```

The CSS Outline Window

Visual Studio includes a CSS Outline window that shows you an overview of the rules in your style sheet. It appears automatically when editing a style sheet, and is grouped with the Toolbox and Server Explorer window (much like the CSS Properties window you considered earlier). When you're editing a style sheet shown earlier, you'll see the outline shown in Figure 13-7. It clearly indicates that your style sheet includes one element rule (the one that formats the body) and three class rules. You can jump immediately to a specific rule by clicking it in the CSS Outline window.

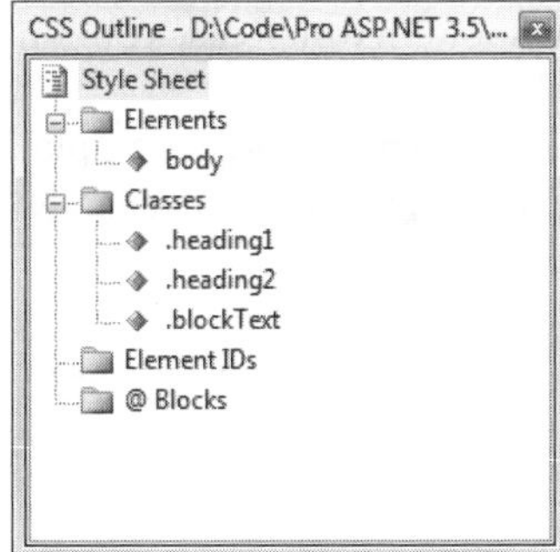

Figure 13-7. *Navigating a style sheet with the CSS Outline window*

Rule names are technically known as *selectors*, because they identify the parts of an HTML document that should be selected for formatting. You've seen how to write selectors that use element types, and selectors that use class names. CSS also supports a few more options for building advanced selectors, which aren't described in this chapter. For example, you can create selectors that only apply to a specific element type *inside* a container (for example, headings in a specific <div> element). Or, you can create selectors that apply formatting to individual elements that have a specific ID value. (These appear in the CSS Outline window under the Element IDs group.) To learn more about CSS, consult a dedicated book such as *CSS: The Definitive Guide.*

Applying Style Sheet Rules

To use a rule in a web page, you first need to link the page to the appropriate style sheet. You do this by adding a <link> element in the <head> section of your page. The <link> element references the file with the styles you want to use. Here's an example that allows the page to use styles defined in the file StyleSheet.css, assuming it's in the same folder as the web page:

```
<html xmlns="http://www.w3.org/1999/xhtml">
  <head runat="server">
    <title>...</title>
    <link href="StyleSheet.css" rel="stylesheet" type="text/css" />
  </head>

  <body>
    ...
  </body>
</html>
```

There's no reason that you need to attach style sheets by hand. An easier option is to drag your style sheet from the Solution Explorer and drop it onto the design surface of your web page (not the source view). Visual Studio will insert the <link> element you need automatically.

Once you've added the <link> element, your style rules are available to use in your web page. You can bind any ordinary HTML element or ASP.NET control to your style rules. For example, if you want an ordinary label to use the heading1 format, set the Label.CssClass property to heading1, as shown here:

```
<asp:Label ID="Label1" runat="server" Text="This Label Uses heading1"
 CssClass="heading1"></asp:Label>
```

You can also set the CssClass property from the Properties window, in which case you can choose from the list of styles that are defined in the linked style sheet.

To apply a style to an ordinary piece of HTML, you set the class attribute. Here's an example that applies a style to a <div> element, which groups together a paragraph of text for easy formatting:

```
<div class="blockText" id="paragraph" runat="server" >
  <p>This paragraph uses the blockText style.</p>
</div>
```

The Apply Styles Window

Once again, you don't need to edit the markup by hand. You can use Visual Studio's Apply Styles window to attach your style to the elements in a web page. To show the Apply Styles window, open your web page and choose View ➤ Apply Styles. The Apply Styles window appears on the left with the Toolbox and Server Explorer, just like the other CSS windows you've seen so far.

The Apply Styles window shows a list of all the styles that are available in the attached style sheets, along with a preview of each one (see Figure 13-8). To apply a style, simply select an element on your web page and then click the appropriate style in the Apply Styles window.

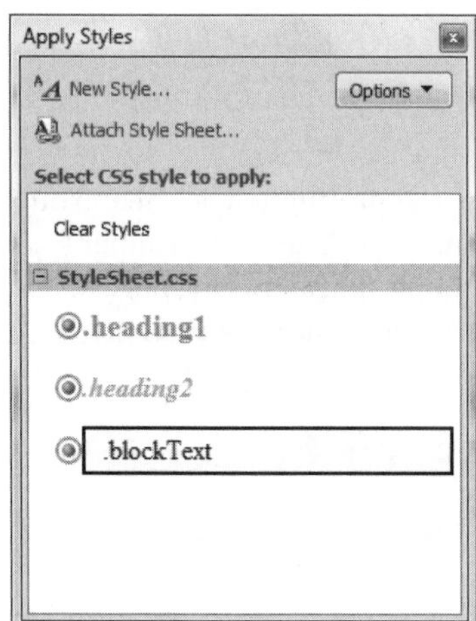

Figure 13-8. *Applying a style with the Apply Styles window*

Visual Studio is intelligent enough to figure out the appropriate way to apply a style based on what you've selected in your web page:

- If you select a web control, it adds or changes the CssClass property.
- If you select an ordinary HTML element, it adds or changes the class attribute.
- If you select a section of HTML content, it adds a <span> or <div> element (depending on the type of content you've selected) and then sets its class attribute.

■ **Tip** Click the Options button in the Apply Styles window to tweak the way it works. For example, you can choose to preview styles in a different order, or include just those styles that are being used in the current page.

Once you've applied a style, you'll see the result of the new formatting in the design window.

Using style sheets accomplishes two things. First, it standardizes your layout so that you can quickly format pages without introducing minor mistakes or idiosyncrasies. Second, it separates the formatting information so that it doesn't appear in your web pages at all, allowing you to modify the format without tracking down each page. And although CSS isn't a .NET-centric standard, Visual Studio still provides rich support for it.

Themes

With the convenience of CSS styles, you might wonder why developers need anything more. The problem is that CSS rules are limited to a fixed set of style attributes. They allow you to reuse specific formatting details (fonts, borders, foreground and background colors, and so on), but they obviously can't control other aspects of ASP.NET controls. For example, the CheckBoxList control includes properties that control how it organizes items into rows and columns. Although these properties affect the visual appearance of the control, they're outside the scope of CSS, so you need to set them by hand. Additionally, you might want to define part of the behavior of the control along with the formatting. For example, you might want to standardize the selection mode of a Calendar control or the wrapping in a TextBox. This obviously isn't possible through CSS.

The themes feature fills this gap. Like CSS, themes allow you to define a set of style details that you can apply to controls in multiple pages. However, with CSS, themes aren't implemented by the browser. Instead, ASP.NET processes your themes when it creates the page.

■ **Note** Themes don't replace styles. Instead, they complement each other. Styles are particularly useful when you want to apply the same formatting to web controls and ordinary HTML elements. Themes are indispensable when you want to configure control properties that can't be tailored with CSS.

How Themes Work

All themes are application specific. To use a theme in a web application, you need to create a folder that defines it. This folder needs to be placed in a folder named App_Themes, which must be placed inside the top-level directory for your web application. In other words, a web application named SuperCommerce might have a theme named FunkyTheme in the folder SuperCommerce\App_Themes\FunkyTheme. An application can contain definitions for multiple themes, as long as each theme is in a separate folder. Only one theme can be active on a given page at a time.

To actually make your theme accomplish anything, you need to create at least one skin file in the theme folder. A *skin file* is a text file with the .skin extension. ASP.NET never serves skin files directly—instead, they're used behind the scenes to define a theme.

A skin file is essentially a list of control tags—with a twist. The control tags in a skin file don't need to completely define the control. Instead, they need to set only the properties that you want to standardize. For example, if you're trying to apply a consistent color scheme, you might be interested in setting only properties such as ForeColor and BackColor. When you add a control tag for the ListBox in the skin file, it might look like this:

```
<asp:ListBox runat="server" ForeColor="White" BackColor="Orange"/>
```

The runat="server" portion is always required. Everything else is optional. You should avoid setting the ID attribute in your skin, because the page that contains the ListBox needs to define a unique name for the control in the actual web page.

It's up to you whether you create multiple skin files or place all your control tags in a single skin file. Both approaches are equivalent, because ASP.NET treats all the skin files in a theme directory as part of the same theme definition. Often, it makes sense to put the control tags for complex controls (such as the data controls) in separate skin files. Figure 13-9 shows the relationship between themes and skins in more detail.

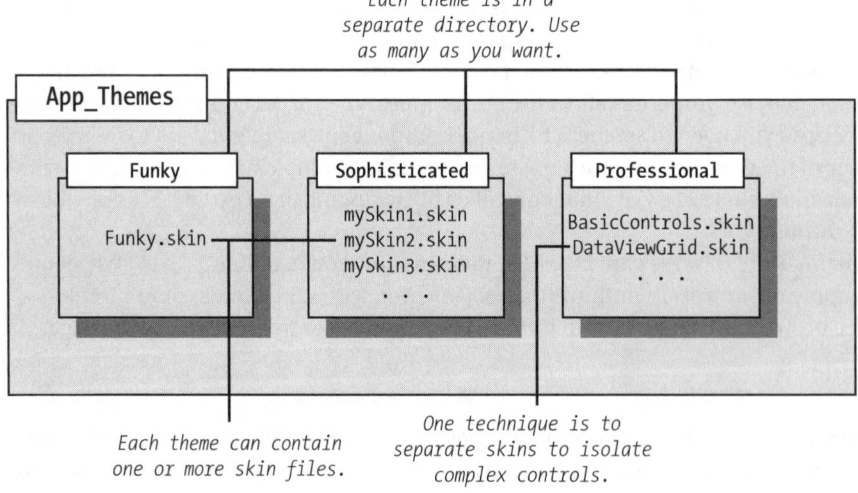

Figure 13-9. *Themes and skins*

ASP.NET also supports global themes. These are themes you place in the c:\Inetpub\wwwroot\aspnet_client\system_web\v2.0.50727\Themes folder. However, it's recommended that you use local themes, even if you want to create more than one website that has the same theme. Using local themes makes it easier to deploy your web application, and it gives you the flexibility to introduce site-specific differences in the future.

If you have a local theme with the same name as a global theme, the local theme takes precedence, and the global theme is ignored. The themes are *not* merged together.

■ **Tip** ASP.NET doesn't ship with any predefined themes. This means you'll need to create your own from scratch or download sample themes from websites such as `www.asp.net`.

Applying a Simple Theme

To add a theme to your project, select Website ➤ Add New Item, and choose Skin File. Visual Studio will warn you that skin files need to be placed in a subfolder of the App_Themes folder and ask you whether that's what you intended. If you choose Yes, Visual Studio will create a folder with the same name as your theme file. You can then rename the folder and the file to whatever you'd like to use. Figure 13-10 shows an example with a theme that contains a single skin file.

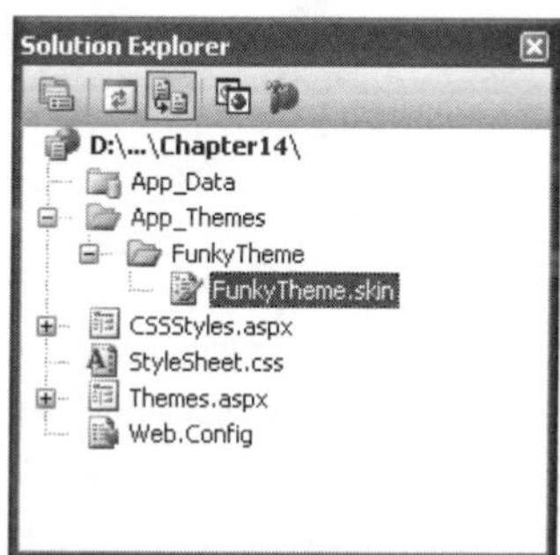

Figure 13-10. *A theme in the Solution Explorer*

Unfortunately, Visual Studio doesn't include any design-time support for creating themes, so it's up to you to copy and paste control tags from other web pages.

Here's a sample skin that sets background and foreground colors for several common controls:

```
<asp:ListBox runat="server" ForeColor="White" BackColor="Orange"/>
<asp:TextBox runat="server" ForeColor="White" BackColor="Orange"/>
<asp:Button runat="server" ForeColor="White" BackColor="Orange"/>
```

To apply the theme in a web page, you need to set the Theme attribute of the Page directive to the folder name for your theme. (ASP.NET will automatically scan all the skin files in that theme.)

```
<%@ Page Language="VB" AutoEventWireup="False" ... Theme="FunkyTheme" %>
```

You can make this change by hand, or you can select the DOCUMENT object in the Properties window at design time and set the Theme property (which provides a handy drop-down list of all your web application's themes). Visual Studio will modify the Page directive accordingly.

When you apply a theme to a page, ASP.NET considers each control on your web page and checks your skin files to see whether they define any properties for that control. If ASP.NET finds a matching tag in the skin file, the information from the skin file overrides the current properties of the control.

Figure 13-11 shows the result of applying the FunkyTheme to a simple page. You'll notice that conflicting settings (such as the existing background for the list box) are overwritten. However, changes that don't conflict (such as the custom font for the buttons) are left in place.

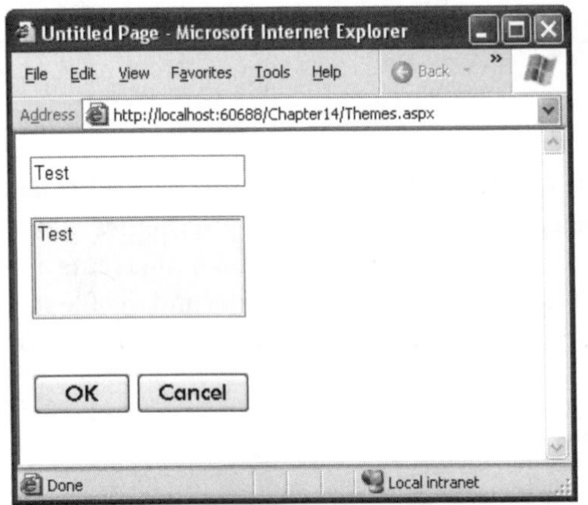

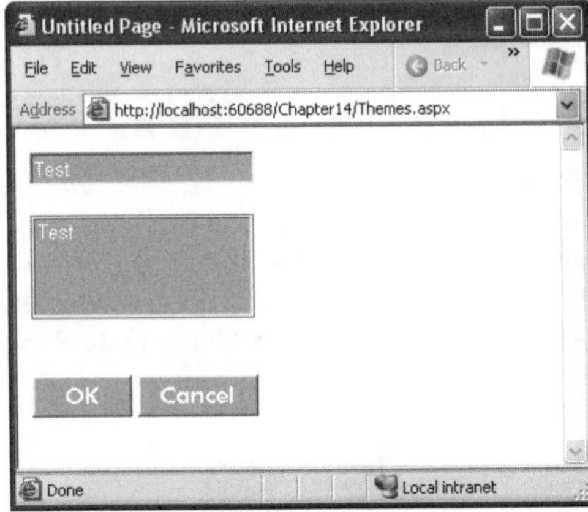

Figure 13-11. *A simple page before and after theming*

■ **Note** This example demonstrates default themes. When you use this approach, your theme settings won't appear in the Visual Studio design environment. That means you won't be able to see the true appearance of your page until you launch it in your browser. If this poses too much of a problem, consider using the SkinID property (described later in the "Creating Multiple Skins for the Same Control" section) to explicitly configure each control. When you use this approach, the themed appearance will appear in Visual Studio.

Handling Theme Conflicts

As you've seen, when properties conflict between your controls and your theme, the theme wins. However, in some cases you might want to change this behavior so that your controls can fine-tune a theme by specifically overriding certain details. ASP.NET gives you this option, but it's an all-or-nothing setting that applies to all the controls on the entire page.

To make this change, just use the StyleSheetTheme attribute instead of the Theme attribute in the Page directive. (The StyleSheet designation indicates that this setting works more like CSS.) Here's an example:

```
<%@ Page Language="VB" AutoEventWireup="False" ... StyleSheetTheme="FunkyTheme" %>
```

Now the custom yellow background of the ListBox control takes precedence over the background color specified by the theme. Figure 13-12 shows the result—and a potential problem. Because the foreground color has been changed to white, the lettering is now difficult to read. Overlapping formatting specifications can cause glitches like this, which is why it's often better to let your themes take complete control by using the Theme attribute.

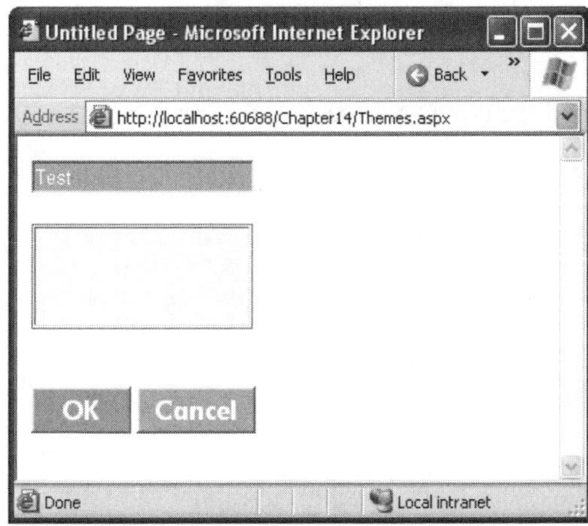

Figure 13-12. *Giving the control tag precedence over the theme*

■ **Note** It's possible to use both the Theme attribute and the StyleSheetTheme attribute at the same time so that some settings are always applied (those in the Theme attribute) and others are applied only if they aren't already specified in the control (those in the StyleSheetTheme attribute). However, in practice, this design is terribly confusing and not recommended.

Another option is to configure specific controls so they opt out of the theming process entirely. To do this, simply set the EnableTheming property of the control on the web page to False. ASP.NET will still apply the theme to other controls on the page, but it will skip over the control you've configured.

```
<asp:Button ID="Button1" runat="server" ... EnableTheming="False" />
```

APPLYING A THEME TO AN ENTIRE WEBSITE

Using the Page directive, you can bind a theme to a single page. However, you might decide that your theme is ready to be rolled out for the entire web application. The cleanest way to apply this theme is by configuring the <pages> element in the web.config file for your application, as shown here:

```
<configuration>
  <system.web>
    <pages theme="FunkyTheme">
      ...
    </pages>
  </system.web>
</configuration>
```

If you want to use the style sheet behavior so that the theme doesn't overwrite conflicting control properties, use the StyleSheetTheme attribute instead of Theme:

```
<configuration>
  <system.web>
    <pages styleSheetTheme="FunkyTheme">
      ...
    </pages>
  </system.web>
</configuration>
```

Either way, when you specify a theme in the web.config file, the theme will be applied throughout all the pages in your website, provided these pages don't have their own theme settings. If a page specifies the Theme attribute, the page setting will take precedence over the web.config setting. If your page specifies the Theme or StyleSheetTheme attribute with a blank string (Theme=""), no theme will be applied at all.

Using this technique, it's just as easy to apply a theme to part of a web application. For example, you can create a separate web.config file for each subfolder and use the <pages> setting to configure different themes.

Creating Multiple Skins for the Same Control

Having each control locked into a single format is great for standardization, but it's probably not flexible enough for a real-world application. For example, you might have several types of text boxes that are distinguished based on where they're used or what type of data they contain. Labels are even more likely to differ, depending on whether they're being used for headings or body text. Fortunately, ASP.NET allows you to create multiple declarations for the same control.

Ordinarily, if you create more than one theme for the same control, ASP.NET will give you a build error stating that you can have only a single default skin for each control. To get around this problem, you need to create a named skin by supplying a SkinID attribute. Here's an example:

```
<asp:ListBox runat="server" ForeColor="White" BackColor="Orange" />
<asp:TextBox runat="server" ForeColor="White" BackColor="Orange" />
<asp:Button runat="server" ForeColor="White" BackColor="Orange" />
<asp:TextBox runat="server" ForeColor="White" BackColor="DarkOrange"
 Font-Bold="True" SkinID="Dramatic"/>
```

```
<asp:Button runat="server" ForeColor="White" BackColor="DarkOrange"
 Font-Bold="True" SkinID="Dramatic"/>
```

The catch is that named skins aren't applied automatically like default skins. To use a named skin, you need to set the SkinID of the control on your web page to match. You can choose this value from a drop-down list that Visual Studio creates based on all your defined skin names, or you can type it in by hand:

```
<asp:Button ID="Button1" runat="server" ... SkinID="Dramatic" />
```

If you don't like the opt-in model for themes, you can make all your skins named. That way, they'll never be applied unless you set the control's SkinID.

ASP.NET is intelligent enough to catch it if you try to use a skin name that doesn't exist, in which case you'll get a build warning. The control will then behave as though you set EnableTheming to False, which means it will ignore the corresponding default skin.

■ **Tip** The SkinID doesn't need to be unique. It just has to be unique for each control. For example, imagine you want to create an alternate set of skinned controls that use a slightly smaller font. These controls match your overall theme, but they're useful on pages that display a large amount of information. In this case, you can create new Button, TextBox, and Label controls, and give each one the same skin name (such as Smaller).

More Advanced Skins

So far, the theming examples have applied relatively simple properties. However, you could create much more detailed control tags in your skin file. Most control properties support theming. If a property can't be declared in a theme, you'll receive a build error when you attempt to launch your application.

For example, many controls support styles that specify a range of formatting information. The data controls are one example, and the Calendar control provides another. Here's how you might define Calendar styles in a skin file to match your theme:

```
<asp:Calendar runat="server" BackColor="White" ForeColor="Black"
 BorderColor="Black" BorderStyle="Solid" CellSpacing="1"
 Font-Names="Verdana" Font-Size="9pt" Height="250px" Width="500px"
 NextPrevFormat="ShortMonth" SelectionMode="Day">
  <SelectedDayStyle BackColor="DarkOrange" ForeColor="White" />
  <DayStyle BackColor="Orange" Font-Bold="True" ForeColor="White" />
  <NextPrevStyle Font-Bold="True" Font-Size="8pt" ForeColor="White" />
  <DayHeaderStyle Font-Bold="True" Font-Size="8pt" ForeColor="#333333"
   Height="8pt" />
  <TitleStyle BackColor="Firebrick" BorderStyle="None" Font-Bold="True"
   Font-Size="12pt" ForeColor="White" Height="12pt" />
  <OtherMonthDayStyle BackColor="NavajoWhite" Font-Bold="False"
   ForeColor="DarkGray" />
</asp:Calendar>
```

This skin defines the font, colors, and styles of the Calendar control. It also sets the selection mode, the formatting of the month navigation links, and the overall size of the calendar. As a result, all you need to use this formatted calendar is the following streamlined tag:

```
<asp:Calendar ID="Calendar1" runat="server" />
```

■ **Caution** When you create skins that specify details such as sizing, be careful. When these settings are applied to a page, they could cause the layout to change with unintended consequences. If you're in doubt, set a SkinID so that the skin is applied only if the control specifically opts in.

Another powerful technique is to reuse images by making them part of your theme. For example, imagine you perfect an image that you want to use for OK buttons throughout your website, and another one for all Cancel buttons. The first step to implement this design is to add the images to your theme folder. For the best organization, it makes sense to create one or more subfolders just for holding images. In this example, the images are stored in a folder named ButtonImages (see Figure 13-13).

Now, you need to create the skins that use these images. In this case, both of these tags should be named skins. That's because you're defining a specific type of standardized button that should be available to the page when needed. You *aren't* defining a default style that should apply to all buttons.

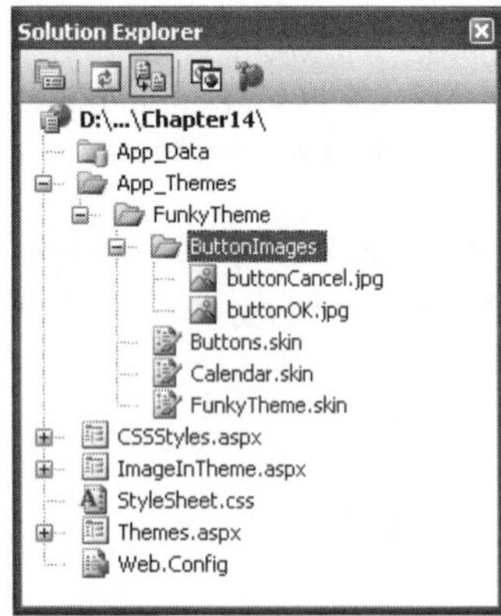

Figure 13-13. *Adding images to a theme*

```
<asp:ImageButton runat="server" SkinID="OKButton"
 ImageUrl="ButtonImages/buttonOK.jpg" />
<asp:ImageButton runat="server" SkinID="CancelButton"
 ImageUrl="ButtonImages/buttonCancel.jpg" />
```

When you add a reference to an image in a skin file, always make sure the image URL is relative to the theme folder, not the folder where the page is stored. When this theme is applied to a control, ASP.NET automatically inserts the App_Themes\ThemeName portion at the beginning of the URL.

Now to apply these images, simply create an ImageButton in your web page that references the corresponding skin name:

```
<asp:ImageButton ID="ImageButton1" runat="server" SkinID="OKButton" />
<asp:ImageButton ID="ImageButton2" runat="server" SkinID="CancelButton" />
```

You can use the same technique to create skins for other controls that use images. For example, you can standardize the node pictures of a TreeView, the bullet image used for the BulletList control, or the icons used in a GridView.

APPLYING THEMES DYNAMICALLY

In some cases, themes aren't used to standardize website appearance but to make that appearance configurable for each user. All you need to do to implement this design is to simply set the Page.Theme or Page.StyleSheetTheme property dynamically in your code. For example, set Page.Theme to the string "FunkyTheme" to apply the theme in the FunkyTheme directory. The only caveat is that you need to complete this step in the Page.Init event stage. After this point, attempting to set the property causes an exception. Similarly, you can also set the SkinID property of a control dynamically to attach it to a different named skin. But be careful—if a theme or skin change leads to a control specifying a skin name that doesn't exist in the current theme, an exception will be thrown.

Master Page Basics

The best websites don't look like a series of web pages—instead, they give the illusion of a continuously running application. For example, try ordering a book on Amazon. While you search, click through the links, and then head to your shopping cart, you'll always see a continuous user interface with a common header at the top and a set of navigation links on the left.

Creating something that polished with ASP.NET is possible, but it isn't as easy as it seems. For example, what if you want a navigation bar on every web page? Not only do you need to copy the same user interface markup to each page, you also need to make sure it ends up in the same place. An offset of a couple of pixels will completely ruin the illusion, making it obvious that the pages aren't really integrated. And even if you copy your markup perfectly, you're still left with an extremely brittle design. If you decide to update your navigation bar later, you'll need to modify every web page to apply the same change.

So how can you deal with the complexity of different pages that need to look and act the same? One option is to subdivide the page into *frames*. Frames are an HTML feature that lets the browser show more than one web page alongside another. Unfortunately, frames have problems of their own, including that each frame is treated as a separate document and requested separately by the browser. This makes it difficult to create code that communicates between frames. A better choice is to use ASP.NET's master pages feature, which allows you to define page templates and reuse them across your website.

■ **Note** Frames are also out of favor because they limit your layout options. That's because each frame occupies a separate, fixed portion of a window. When you scroll one frame, the other frames remain fixed in place. To create frames that work properly, you need to make assumptions about the target device and its screen size. Most popular websites (think Google, Amazon, and eBay) don't use frames.

Master pages are similar to ordinary ASP.NET pages. Like ordinary pages, master pages are text files that can contain HTML, web controls, and code. However, master pages have a different file extension (.master instead of .aspx), and they can't be viewed directly by a browser. Instead, master pages must be used by other pages, which are known as *content pages*. Essentially, the master page defines the page structure and the common ingredients. The content pages adopt this structure and just fill it with the appropriate content.

For example, if a website such as `www.amazon.com` were created using ASP.NET, a single master page might define the layout for the entire site. Every page would use that master page, and as a result, every page would have the same basic organization and the same title, footer, and so on. However, each page would also insert its specific information, such as product descriptions, book reviews, or search results, into this template.

A Simple Master Page and Content Page

To see how this works, it helps to create a simple example. To create a master page in Visual Studio, select Website ➤ Add New Item from the menu. Select Master Page, give it a file name (such as SiteTemplate.master, used in the next example), and click Add.

When you create a new master page in Visual Studio, you start with a blank page that includes a ContentPlaceHolder control (see Figure 13-14). The ContentPlaceHolder is the portion of the master page that a content page can change. Or, to look at it another way, everything else in a master page is unchangeable. If you add a header, that header appears in every content page. If you want to give the content page the opportunity to supply content in a specific section of the page, you need to add a ContentPlaceHolder.

When you first create a master page, you'll start with two ContentPlaceHolder controls. One is defined in the <head> section, which gives content pages the add page metadata, such as search keywords and style sheet links. The second, more important ContentPlaceHolder is defined in the <body> section, and represents the displayed content of the page. It appears on the page as a faintly outlined box. If you click inside it hover over it, the name of ContentPlaceHolder appears in a tooltip, as shown in Figure 13-14.

To make this master page example more practical, try adding a header before the ContentPlaceHolder (using an <img> tag) and a footer after it (using some static text), as shown in Figure 13-15. You'll notice that the content area of the page looks very small, but this appearance is deceptive. The content section will expand to fit the content you place inside.

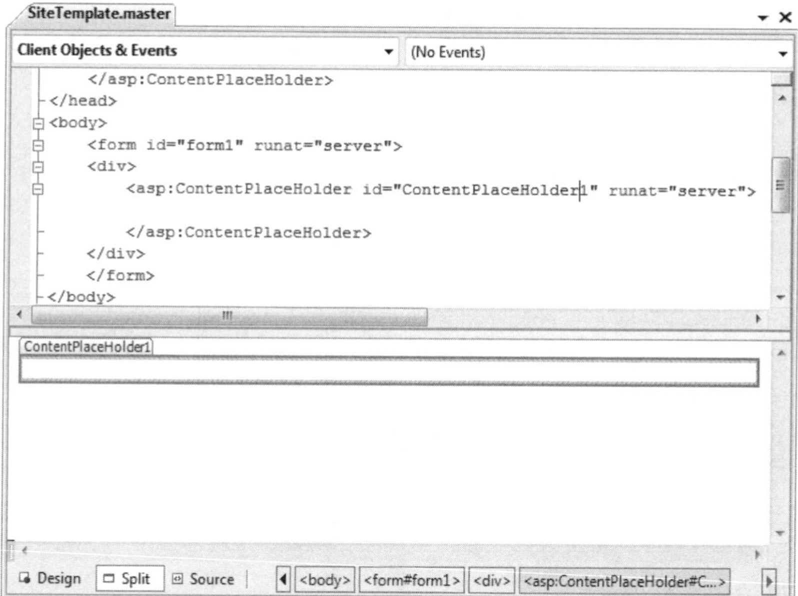

Figure 13-14. *A new master page*

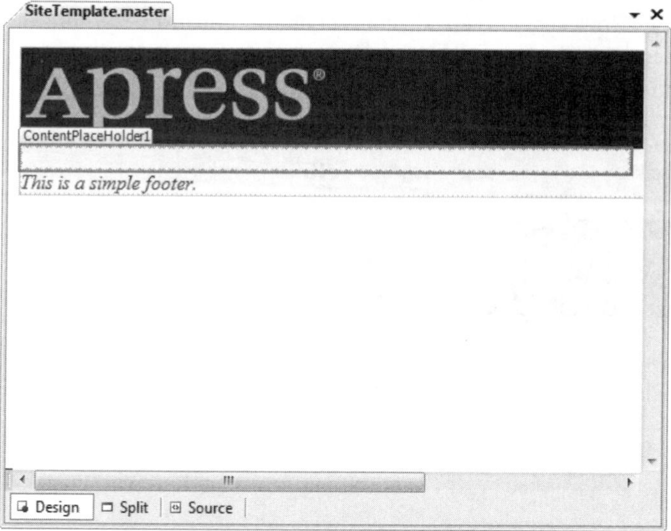

Figure 13-15. *A simple master page with a header and footer*

Now you're ready to create a content page based on this master page. To take this step, select Website ➤ Add New Item from the menu. Select Web Form, and choose to select a master page (see Figure 13-16). Click Add. When you're prompted to choose a master page, use the one you created with the header and footer.

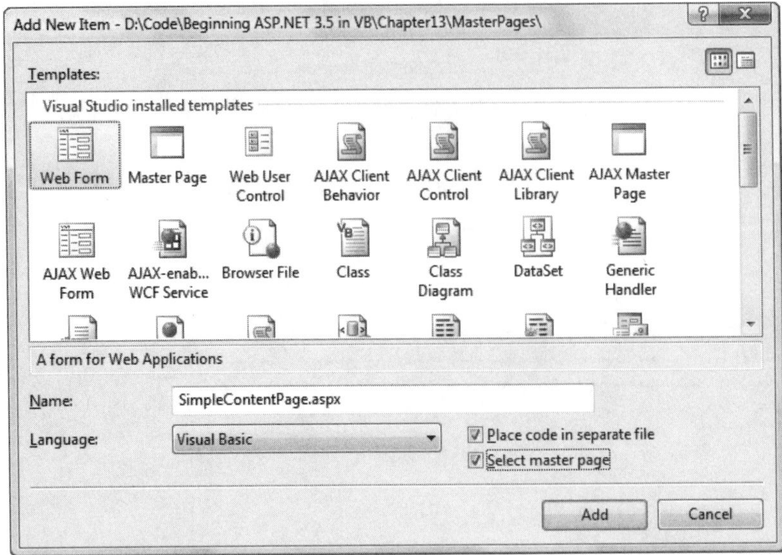

Figure 13-16. *Creating a content page*

Now you'll see something a little more interesting. Your content page will have all the elements of the master page, but the elements will be shaded in gray, indicating that you can't select or change them in any way. However, you can add content or drag and drop new controls into the ContentPlaceHolder region to create a page like the one shown in Figure 13-17. In fact, this is the only editable portion of your page.

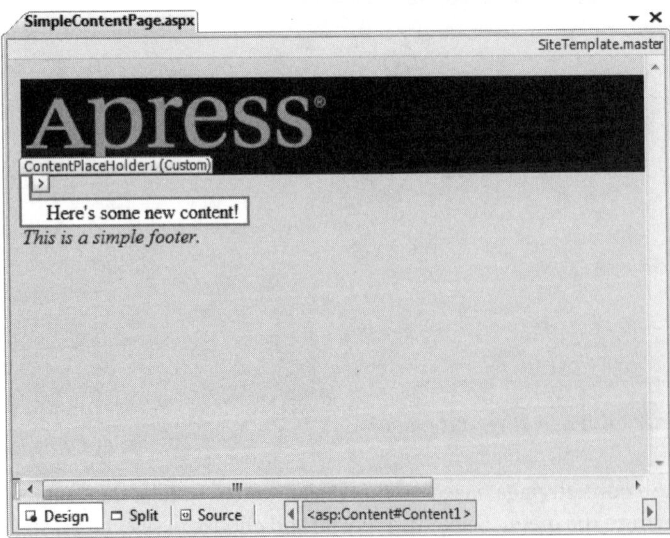

Figure 13-17. *A simple content page at design time*

The ContentPlaceHolder section will expand or collapse to fit the content you place in it. If you've added volumes of text, the footer won't appear until the end. If you've included only a single line of text, you'll see something more compact, as in Figure 13-17. To get a clearer look at your web page, you can run it in the browser. Figure 13-18 shows the content page that's being designed in Figure 13-17.

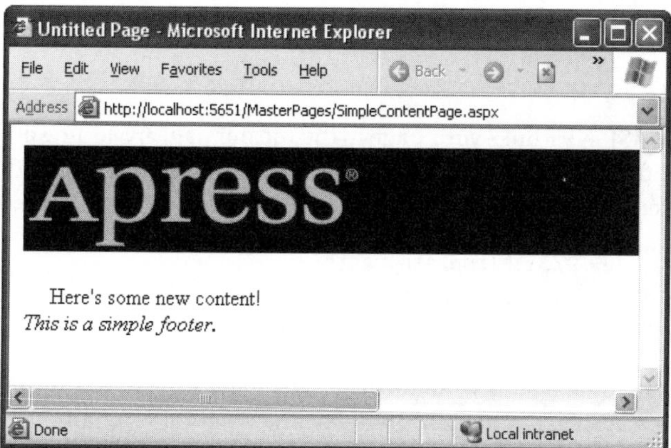

Figure 13-18. *A simple content page at runtime*

The real magic starts when you create multiple pages that use the same master page. Now, each page will have the same header and footer, creating a seamless look across your entire website.

How Master Pages and Content Pages Are Connected

Now that you've seen a master page example, it's worth taking a look behind the scenes to see how you implement the master page.

When you create a master page, you're building something that looks much like an ordinary ASP.NET web form. The key difference is that although web forms start with the Page directive, a master page starts with a Master directive that specifies the same information. Here's the Master directive for the simple master page shown in the previous example:

```
<%@ Master Language="VB" CodeFile="SiteTemplate.master.vb"
    Inherits="SiteTemplate" %>
```

The ContentPlaceHolder is less interesting. You declare it like any ordinary control. Here's the complete code for the simple master page:

```
<%@ Master Language="VB" CodeFile="SiteTemplate.master.vb"
    Inherits="SiteTemplate" %>
<html xmlns="http://www.w3.org/1999/xhtml">
<head runat="server">
    <title>Untitled Page</title>
</head>
```

```
<body>
    <form id="form1" runat="server">
        <img src="apress.jpg" /><br />
        <asp:ContentPlaceHolder id="ContentPlaceHolder1" runat="server">
        </asp:ContentPlaceHolder>
        <i>This is a simple footer.</i>
    </form>
</body>
</html>
```

When you create a content page, ASP.NET links your page to the master page by adding an attribute to the Page directive. This attribute, named MasterPageFile, indicates the associated master page. Here's what it looks like:

```
<%@ Page Language="VB" MasterPageFile="~/SiteTemplate.master"
    AutoEventWireup="False" CodeFile="SimpleContentPage.aspx.vb"
    Inherits="SimpleContentPage" Title="Untitled Page" %>
```

Notice that the MasterPageFile attribute begins with the path ~/ to specify the root website folder. If you specify just the file name, ASP.NET checks a predetermined subfolder (named MasterPages) for your master page. If you haven't created this folder, or your master page isn't there, ASP.NET checks the root of your web folder next. Using the ~/ syntax is better, because it indicates unambiguously where ASP.NET can find your master page.

■ **Note** You can use the ~/ characters to create a *root-relative path*—a path that always starts from the root folder of your web application. This is a special syntax understood by ASP.NET and its server controls. You can't use this syntax with ordinary HTML. For example, this syntax won't work in an ordinary hyperlink that isn't a server control (such as the <a> tag).

The Page directive has another new attribute—Title. That's because the master page, as the outermost shell of the page, always defines the <head> section of the page with a default title. Remember, your content page can't modify anything that's in the master page. However, this is an obvious shortcoming with the title information, so to circumvent it ASP.NET adds the Title attribute, which you can set to override the title specified in the master page with something more appropriate.

The rest of the content page looks a little different from an ordinary web form. That's because the content page can't define anything that's already provided in the master page, including the <head> section, the root <html> element, the <body> element, and so on. In fact, the content page can do only one thing—it can supply a Content tag that corresponds to the ContentPlaceHolder in the master page. This is where you insert the content for this page. As a result, your content pages are a little bit simpler than ordinary web pages.

Here's the complete code for the simple content page, with a single line of text and two line breaks added:

```
<%@ Page Language="VB" MasterPageFile="~/SiteTemplate.master"
    AutoEventWireup="False" CodeFile="SimpleContentPage.aspx.vb"
    Inherits="SimpleContentPage" Title="Content Page" %>
```

```
<asp:Content ID="Content1" ContentPlaceHolderID="ContentPlaceHolder1"
  runat="Server">
    <br />
    Here's some new content!
    <br />
</asp:Content>
```

For ASP.NET to process this page successfully, the ContentPlaceHolderID attribute in the <Content> tag must match the ContentPlaceHolder specified in the master page exactly. This is how ASP.NET knows where it should insert your content in the master page template.

■ **Tip** If a master page defines a ContentPlaceHolder but your content page doesn't define a corresponding Content control, you'll see a black box in its place when you design the page in Visual Studio. To add the required Content control, right-click that section of the page, and choose Create Custom Content.

You should realize one important fact by looking at the content page markup. Namely, the content from the master page (the address bar and the footer) *isn't* inserted into the content file. Instead, ASP.NET grabs these details from the master page when it processes the page. This has an important effect. It means that if you want to change the header or footer that's used in all your content pages, you need to change only one file—the master page. When you make this change, it will appear in all content pages automatically. In other words, master pages don't just let you reuse standard elements; they also make it easy to update these details later.

■ **Tip** Now that you understand how to hook up master pages and child pages, you can easily take an existing page and modify it to use your master page. However, you'll need to remove some of the basic boilerplate tags, such as <html>, <head>, and <body>, and wrap all the content in one or more <Content> tags. Visual Studio won't add the Content control automatically except when you're creating a new content page from scratch.

A Master Page with Multiple Content Regions

Master pages aren't limited to one ContentPlaceHolder. Instead, you can insert as many as you need to give the client the ability to intersperse content in various places. All you need to do is add multiple ContentPlaceHolder controls and arrange them appropriately.

Figure 13-19 shows a master page that needs more careful consideration. It includes an initial ContentPlaceHolder where the user can insert content, and then a shaded box (created by a <div> tag) that contains a heading (*OTHER LINKS*) and a second ContentPlaceHolder. The idea here is that the page is split into two logical sections. In the content page, you won't need to worry about how to format each section or how to position the other links box. Instead, you simply supply content for each portion, and ASP.NET will insert it into the correct location in the master page.

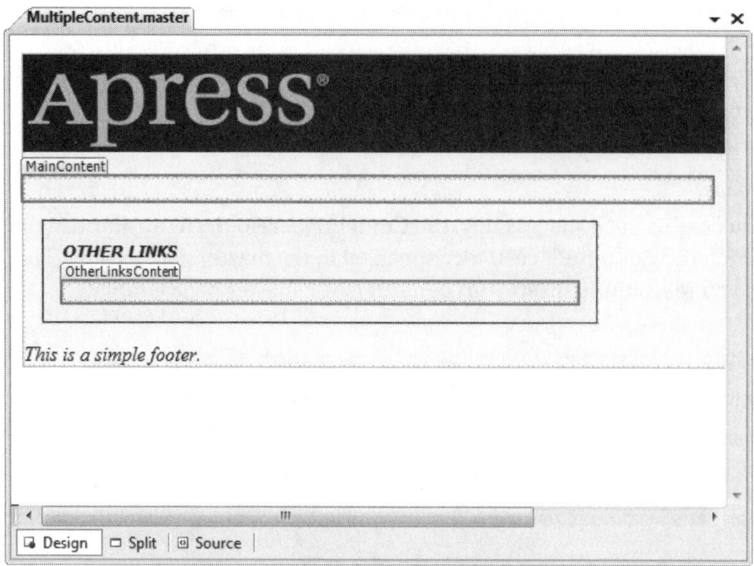

Figure 13-19. *A master page with two content regions*

Here's the code for the master page (with the style portion of the <div> tag omitted to save space):

```
<%@ Master Language="VB" CodeFile="MultipleContent.master.vb"
    Inherits="MultipleContent" %>
<html xmlns="http://www.w3.org/1999/xhtml" >
<head runat="server">
    <title>Untitled Page</title>
</head>
<body>
    <form id="form1" runat="server">
        <img src="apress.jpg" /><br />
        <asp:ContentPlaceHolder id="MainContent" runat="server">
        </asp:ContentPlaceHolder>
        <i>
            <div style="...">
                <b>OTHER LINKS</b>
                <br />
                <asp:ContentPlaceHolder id="OtherLinksContent" runat="server">
                </asp:ContentPlaceHolder>
            </div>
            This is a simple footer.
        </i>
    </form>
</body>
</html>
```

Tip The most underrated part of a master page is the line break, or <br /> tag. If you forget to include it, you can easily end up having child content run into your headings. To avoid this problem, make sure you add the necessary whitespace in your master page. Never rely on adding it in your content pages, because content pages may not insert the correct amount of space (or insert it in the correct place).

When you create a new content page based on this master page, Visual Studio will start you with one Content control for each ContentPlaceHolder in the master page, making your life easy. All you need to do is insert the appropriate information. Here's a slightly shortened example:

```
<%@ Page Language="VB" MasterPageFile="~/MultipleContent.master"
    AutoEventWireup="False" CodeFile="MultipleContentPage.aspx.vb"
    Inherits="MultipleContentPage" Title="Content Page" %>
<asp:Content ID="Content1" ContentPlaceHolderID="MainContent" runat="Server">
    This is the generic content for this page. Here you might provide some site
    specific text ... </asp:Content>
<asp:Content ID="Content2" ContentPlaceHolderID="OtherLinksContent"
  runat="Server">
    Here's a <a href="http://www.prosetech.com">link</a>.<br />
    ...
</asp:Content>
```

Figure 13-20 shows the final result. Notice how the two content sections flow into their designated locations seamlessly.

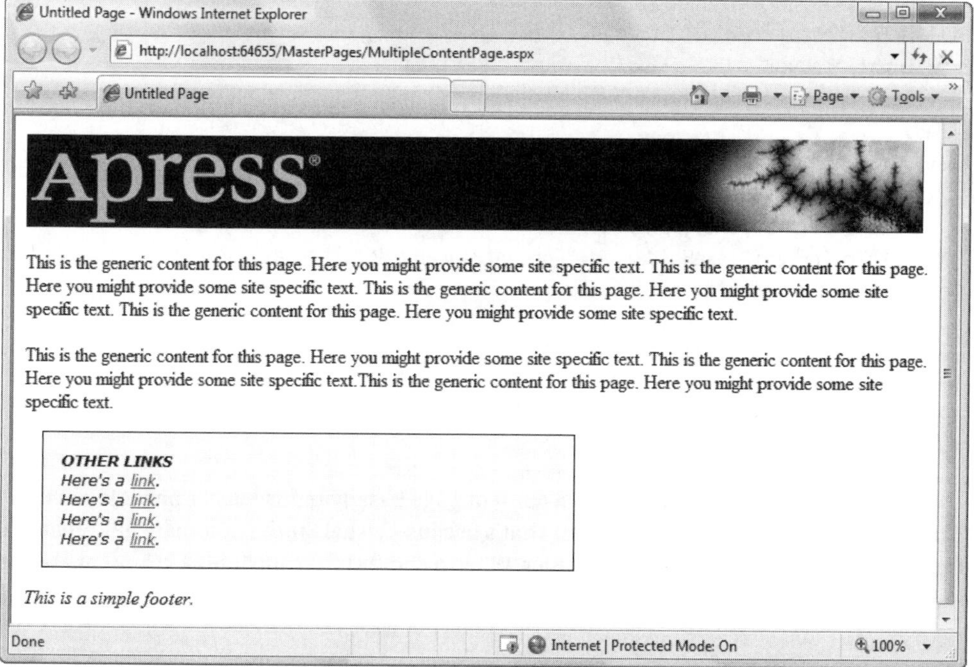

Figure 13-20. *Using the multiple content master page*

Another important trick is at work in this example. The master page doesn't just define the structure of the web page; it also supplies some important style characteristics (such as a default font and background color) through the <div> tag. This is another handy trick to offload the formatting work to the master page, which allows you to maintain it and modify it much more easily.

■ **Caution** If you create a master page without any ContentPlaceHolder controls, content pages won't be able to supply any content at all, and they'll always show an exact copy of the master page.

Default Content

So far, you've seen master page examples with two types of content: fixed content and page-supplied content. However, in some cases your situation might not be as clear-cut. You might have some content that the content page may or may not want to replace. You can deal with this using default content.

Here's how it works: You create a master page and create a ContentPlaceHolder for the content that might change. Inside that tag, you place the appropriate HTML or web controls. (You can do this by hand using the .aspx markup or just by dragging and dropping controls into the ContentPlaceHolder.)

For example, here's a version of the simple header-and-footer master page shown earlier, with default content:

```
<%@ Master Language="VB" CodeFile="SiteTemplate.master.vb"
    Inherits="SiteTemplate" %>
<html xmlns="http://www.w3.org/1999/xhtml" >
<head runat="server">
    <title>Untitled Page</title>
</head>
<body>
    <form id="form1" runat="server">
        <img src="apress.jpg" /><br />
        <asp:ContentPlaceHolder id="ContentPlaceHolder1" runat="server">
         This is default content.<br />
        </asp:ContentPlaceHolder>
        <i>This is a simple footer.</i>
    </form>
</body>
</html>
```

So, what happens when you create a content page based on this master page? If you use Visual Studio, you won't see any change. That's because Visual Studio automatically creates a <Content> tag for each ContentPlaceHolder. When a content page includes a <Content> tag, it automatically overrides the default content.

However, something interesting happens if you delete the <Content> tag from the content page. Now when you run the page, you'll see the default content. In other words, default content appears only when the content page chooses not to specify any content for that placeholder.

You might wonder whether the content pages can use *some* of the default content or just edit it slightly. This isn't possible because the default content is stored only in the master page, not in the content page. As a result, you need to decide between using the default content as is or replacing it completely.

■ **Tip** You don't need to delete the <Content> tag by hand. Instead, you can use the Visual Studio smart tag. First, click to select the content region in design view. Then, click the arrow that appears in the top-right corner of the content region to open the smart tag. Finally, choose Default to Master's Content (to remove the <Content> tag and use the default content) or Create Custom Content (to add the <Content> tag back).

Master Pages and Relative Paths

One quirk that can catch unsuspecting developers is the way that master pages handle relative paths. If all you're using is static text, this issue won't affect you. However, if you add <img> tags or any other HTML tag that points to another resource, problems can occur.

The problem shows up if you place the master page in a different directory from the content page that uses it. This is a recommended best practice for large websites. In fact, Microsoft encourages you to use a dedicated folder for storing all your master pages. However, if you're not suitably careful, this can cause problems when you use relative paths.

For example, imagine you put a master page in a subfolder named MasterPages and add the following <img> tag to the master page:

```
<img src="banner.jpg" />
```

Assuming the file \MasterPages\banner.jpg exists, this appears to work fine. The image will even appear in the Visual Studio design environment. However, if you create a content page in another subfolder, the image path is interpreted relative to that folder. If the file doesn't exist there, you'll get a broken link instead of your graphic. Even worse, you could conceivably get the wrong graphic if another image has the same file name.

This problem occurs because the <img> tag is ordinary HTML. As a result, ASP.NET won't touch it. Unfortunately, when ASP.NET processes your content page, the relative path in this tag is no longer appropriate. The same problem occurs with <a> tags that provide relative links to other pages and with the <link> element that you can use to connect the master page to a style sheet.

To solve your problem, you could try to think ahead and write your URL relative to the content page where you want to use it. But this creates confusion and limits where your master page can be used. A better fix is to turn your <img> tag into a server-side control, in which case ASP.NET will fix the mistake:

```
<img src="banner.jpg" runat="server"/>
```

This works because ASP.NET uses this information to create an HtmlImage server control. This object is created after the Page object for the master page is instantiated. At this point, ASP.NET interprets all the paths relative to the location of the master page.

And as with all server-side controls, you can further clear things up by using the ~/ characters to create a root-relative path. Here's an example that clearly points to a picture in an Images folder in the root web application folder:

```
<img src="~/Images/banner.jpg" runat="server"/>
```

Remember, the ~/ syntax is understood only by ASP.NET controls, so you can't use this trick with an <img> tag that doesn't include the runat="server" attribute.

Advanced Master Pages

Using what you've learned, you can create and reuse master pages across your website. However, still more tricks and techniques can help you take master pages to the next level and make them that much more practical. In the following sections, you'll look at how tables can help you organize your layout and how your content pages can interact with the master page class in code.

Table-Based Layouts

For the most part, HTML uses a flow-based layout. That means as more content is added, the page is reorganized and other content is bumped out of the way. This layout can make it difficult to get the result you want with master pages. For example, what happens if you craft the perfect layout, only to have the structure distorted by a huge block of information that's inserted into a <Content> tag?

Although you can't avoid this problem completely, master pages can use HTML tables to help control the layout. With an HTML table, a portion of your page is broken into columns and rows. You can then add a ContentPlaceHolder in a single cell, ensuring that the other content is aligned more or less the way you want. However, you'll need to type the HTML table tags into the .aspx portion of the master page by hand, as Visual Studio doesn't provide any way to design an HTML table at design time.

For a good example, consider a traditional web application with a header, footer, and navigation bar. Figure 13-21 shows how this structure is broken up into a table.

In HTML, tables are delineated with the <table> tag. Each row is defined with a nested <tr> tag, and inside each row you can place a <td> tag for each cell. You place the content inside the various <td> tags. Content can include any combination of HTML or web controls.

The number of <td> tags you add in a <tr> defines the number of columns in your table. If you aren't consistent (and usually you won't be), the table takes the dimensions of the row with the most cells.

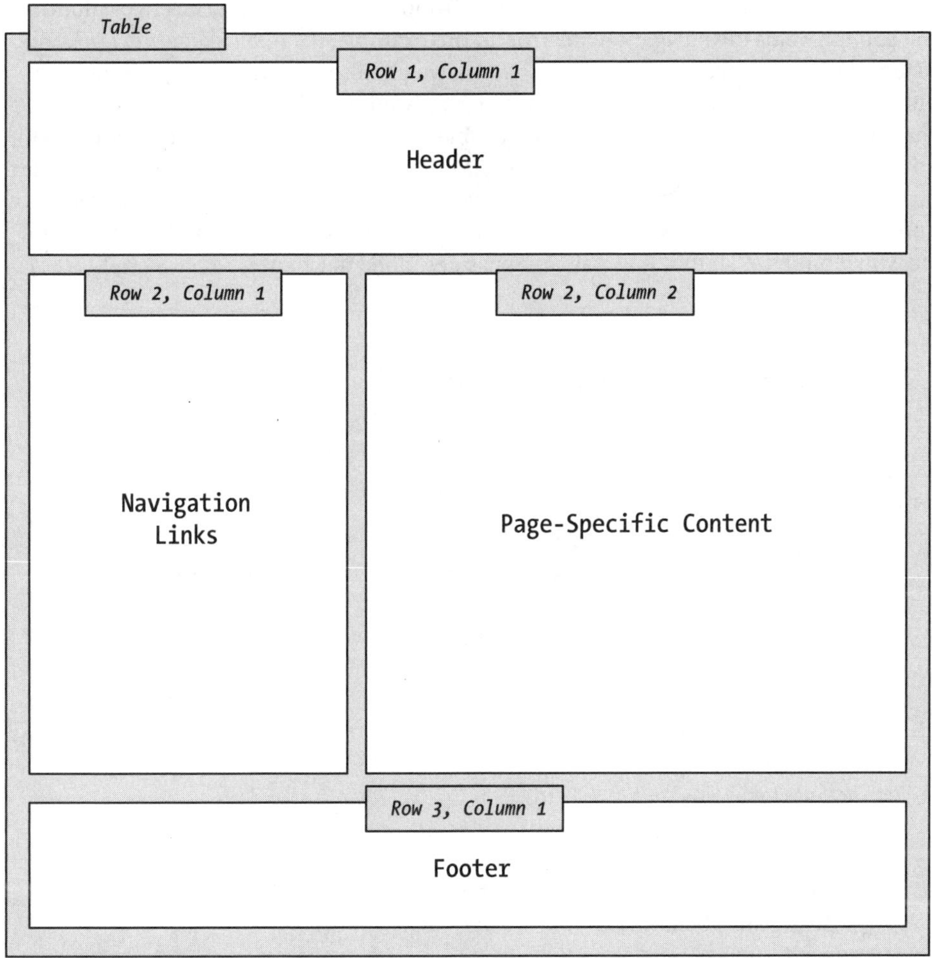

Figure 13-21. *A table-based layout*

To create the table shown in Figure 10-8, start by giving it a width of 100% so it fills the browser window:

```
<table style="width: 100%">
    ...
</table>
```

The next step is to add the first row. You can use a trick here. The complete table actually has two columns, but the first row (with the header) and the last row (with the footer) need to fill the full width of the table. To accomplish this, you add the colspan attribute and set it to 2, indicating that the header spans two columns:

```
<table style="width: 100%">
    <tr><td colspan="2">My Header</td></tr>
    ...
</table>
```

You can fill in the rest of the table in a similar fashion. The second row has two columns. The first column holds the navigation links (or, in this example, the text *Navigation Links*) and has a fixed width of 150 pixels. The second column, which fills the remaining space, holds a ContentPlaceHolder where the content page can supply information.

The following markup shows the complete table, with some added formatting and background colors that make it easier to distinguish the different sections of the table. Also, the text in the navigation controls section has been replaced with a TreeView. (The TreeView also has a few dummy nodes added, just so that it appears in the page. When using this design in a real website, you'd bind the TreeView to a site map, as described in Chapter 14.)

```
<table style="width: 100%">
    <tr>
        <td colspan="2" style="background: #ffccff">
            <h1>My Header</h1>
        </td>
    </tr>
    <tr>
        <td style="width: 150px; background: #ffffcc">
            <asp:TreeView ID="TreeView1" runat="server" Width="150px">
              <Nodes>
                <asp:TreeNode Text="Root" Value="New Node">
                    <asp:TreeNode Text="Page 1" Value="Page 1"></asp:TreeNode>
                    <asp:TreeNode Text="Page 2" Value="Page 2"></asp:TreeNode>
                </asp:TreeNode>
              </Nodes>
            </asp:TreeView>
        </td>
        <td>
            <asp:ContentPlaceHolder id="ContentPlaceHolder1" runat="server">
            </asp:ContentPlaceHolder>
        </td>
    </tr>
    <tr>
        <td colspan="2" style="background: #ccff33">
            <i>My Footer</i>
        </td>
    </tr>
</table>
```

■ **Tip** To learn more about HTML tables and how to specify borders, cell sizes, alignment, and more, refer to the examples at `www.w3schools.com/html/html_tables.asp`.

Figure 13-22 shows the resulting master page and a content page that uses the master page (both in Visual Studio).

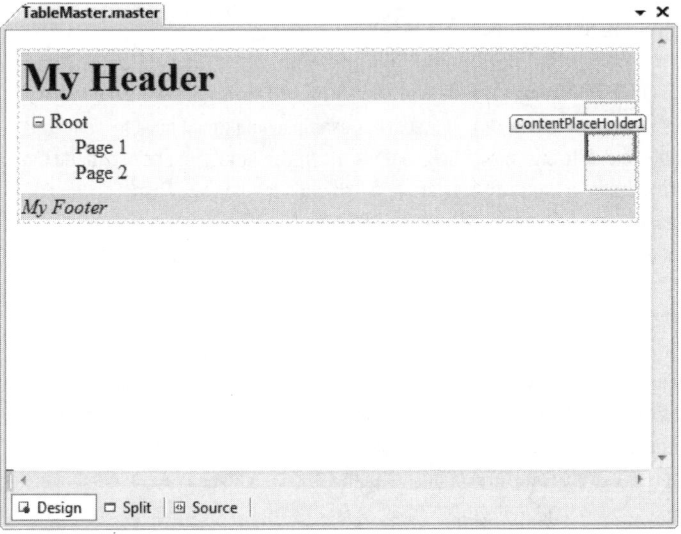

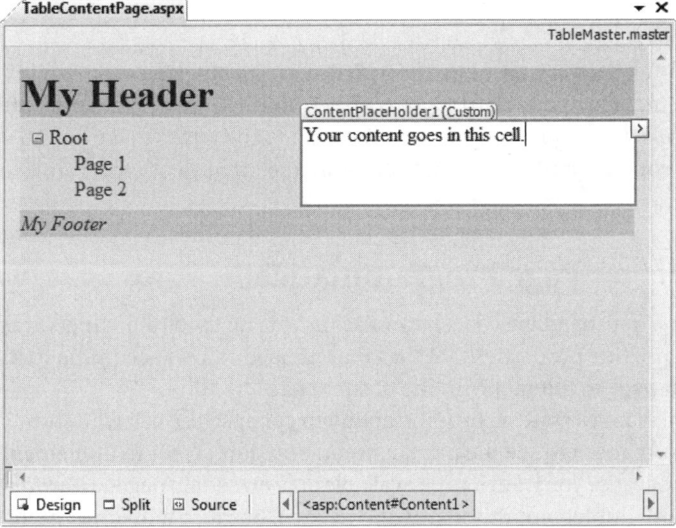

Figure 13-22. *A master page and a content page using a table*

To convert this example into something more practical, just replace the hard-coded text and TreeView nodes in the master page with the actual header, navigation controls, and footer you really want. All the child pages will acquire these features automatically. This is the first step to defining a practical structure for your entire website.

NESTING MASTER PAGES

You can nest master pages so that one master page uses another master page. This is not used too often, but it could allow you to standardize your website to different degrees. For example, you might have two sections of your website. Each section might require its own navigation controls. However, both sections may need the same header. In this case, you could create a top-level master page that adds the header. Then, you would create a second master page that uses the first master page (through the MasterPageFile attribute). This second master page would get the header and could add the navigation controls. You would create two versions of this second master page, one for each section of your website. Finally, your content pages would use one of the two second-level master pages to standardize their layout.

Be careful when implementing this approach—although it sounds like a nifty way to make a modular design, it can tie you down more than you realize. For example, you'll need to rework your master page hierarchy if you decide later that the two website sections need similar but slightly different headers. Another problem is that Visual Studio doesn't support nested master pages, so you'll need to code them by hand (not graphically). For these reasons, it's usually better to use only one level of master pages and copy the few elements that are in common. In most cases, you won't be creating many master pages, so this won't add a significant amount of duplication.

Code in a Master Page

In all the examples in this chapter, master pages have provided static layout. However, just like a web page, master pages also include a code portion that can respond to events in the page life cycle or the constituent controls. For example, you could respond to the Page.Load event to initialize a master page using code, or you could handle clicks in a set of navigation controls to direct a user to the right page.

Interacting with a Master Page Programmatically

A master control isn't limited to event-handling code. It can also provide methods that the content page can trigger as needed or provide properties that the content page can set according to its needs. This allows the content page to interact with the master page.

For example, imagine you want to give the user the ability to collapse the cell with the navigation controls to have more room to see the page content. You don't want to implement this feature in the master page, because you want it to be available only on certain pages. However, the content page obviously can't implement this feature on its own, because it involves modifying a fixed portion of the master page. The solution is to create a way for the content page to interact with the master page so it can politely ask the master page to collapse or hide the navigation controls as needed.

One good way to implement this design is by adding a new property named ShowNavigationControls to the master page class. This property, when set to False, could then automatically hide the navigation controls. Here's the property you need to add to the master page class:

```
Public Property ShowNavigationControls() As Boolean
    Get
        Return TreeView1.Visible
    End Get
    Set (ByVal Value As Boolean)
        TreeView1.Visible = Value
    End Set
End Property
```

You should notice a few important facts about this property. First, it's public so that other classes (and therefore other pages) can access it. Second, it just wraps the Visible property in the TreeView control on the master page. Whatever value is passed to ShowNavigationControls is simply applied to TreeView.Visible. This is useful because ordinarily the TreeView.Visible property isn't directly accessible to the content page.

To access this page, the content page uses the built-in Page.Master property. This page always returns the linked object for the master page. However, you can't access the ShowNavigationControls property directly as Page.Master.ShowNavigationControls, because the Page.Master property uses the base MasterPage class, and doesn't know anything about the properties you've added to your derived master page class. To get access to the custom members you've added (like ShowNavigationControls), you need to cast the Page.Master object to the appropriate type.

Here's the button handling code for a content page that hides or shows the navigation controls depending on whether a Hide or Show button is clicked. In this example, the master page class is named TableMaster.

```
Protected Sub cmdHide_Click(ByVal sender As Object, _
  ByVal e As EventArgs) Handles cmdHide.Click
    Dim master As TableMaster = CType(Me.Master, TableMaster)
    master.ShowNavigationControls = False
End Sub

Protected Sub cmdShow_Click(ByVal sender As Object, _
  ByVal e As EventArgs) Handles cmdShow.Click
    Dim master As TableMaster = CType(Me.Master, TableMaster)
    master.ShowNavigationControls = True
End Sub
```

Figure 13-23 shows this content page in action.

Note that when you navigate from one page to another, all the web page objects are re-created. Even if you move to another content page that uses the same master page, ASP.NET creates a different instance of the master page object. As a result, the TreeView.Visible property of the navigation controls is reset to its default value (True) every time the user navigates to a new page. If this isn't the effect you want, you would need to store the setting somewhere else (such as in a cookie or in session state). Then you could write code in the master page that always checks the last saved value. Chapter 7 has more information about the ways you can store information in an ASP.NET website.

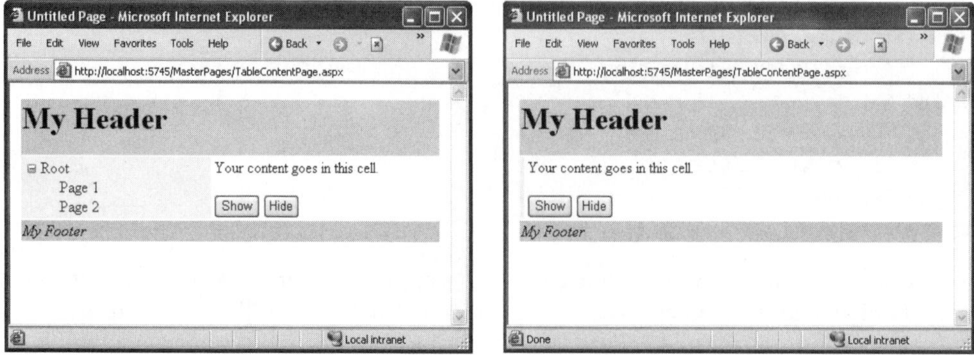

Figure 13-23. *A content page that interacts with its master page*

The Last Word

Building a professional web application involves much more than designing individual web pages. You also need the tools to integrate your web pages in a complete, unified website. In this chapter, you considered three ways to do exactly that. First, you considered CSS, which lets you apply consistent formatting to HTML elements and web controls alike. Then, you considered the ASP.NET themes features, which lets you effortlessly apply a group of property settings to a control. Finally, you learned to use master pages, which allow you to standardize the layout of your website. All these features make it easy to bring your pages together into a well-integrated, consistent web application.

CHAPTER 14

■ ■ ■

Website Navigation

You've already learned simple ways to send a website visitor from one page to another. For example, you can add HTML links (or HyperLink controls) to your page to let users surf through your site. If you want to perform page navigation in response to another action, you can call the Response.Redirect() method or the Server.Transfer() method in your code. But in professional web applications, the navigation requirements are more intensive. These applications need a system that allows users to surf through a hierarchy of pages, without forcing you to write the same tedious navigation code in every page.

Fortunately, ASP.NET includes a navigation model that makes it easy to let users surf through your web applications. Before you can use this model, you need to determine the hierarchy of your website—in other words, how pages are logically organized into groups. You then define that structure in a dedicated file and bind that information to specialized navigation controls. Best of all, these navigation controls include nifty widgets such as the TreeView and Menu.

In this chapter, you'll learn everything you need to know about the new site map model and the navigation controls that work with it.

Site Maps

If your website has more than a handful of pages, you'll probably want some sort of navigation system to let users move from one page to the next. Obviously, you can use the ASP.NET toolkit of controls to implement almost any navigation system, but this requires that *you* perform all the hard work. Fortunately, ASP.NET has a set of navigation features that can simplify the task dramatically.

As with all the best ASP.NET features, ASP.NET navigation is flexible, configurable, and pluggable. It consists of three components:

- A way to define the navigational structure of your website. This part is the XML site map, which is (by default) stored in a file.
- A convenient way to read the information in the site map file and convert it to an object model. The SiteMapDataSource control and the XmlSiteMapProvider perform this part.
- A way to use the site map information to display the user's current position and give the user the ability to easily move from one place to another. This part takes place through the navigation controls you bind to the SiteMapDataSource control, which can include breadcrumb links, lists, menus, and trees.

You can customize or extend each of these ingredients separately. For example, if you want to change the appearance of your navigation controls, you simply need to bind different controls to the SiteMapDataSource. On the other hand, if you want to read site map information from a different type of file or from a different location, you need to change your site map provider.

Figure 14-1 shows how these pieces fit together.

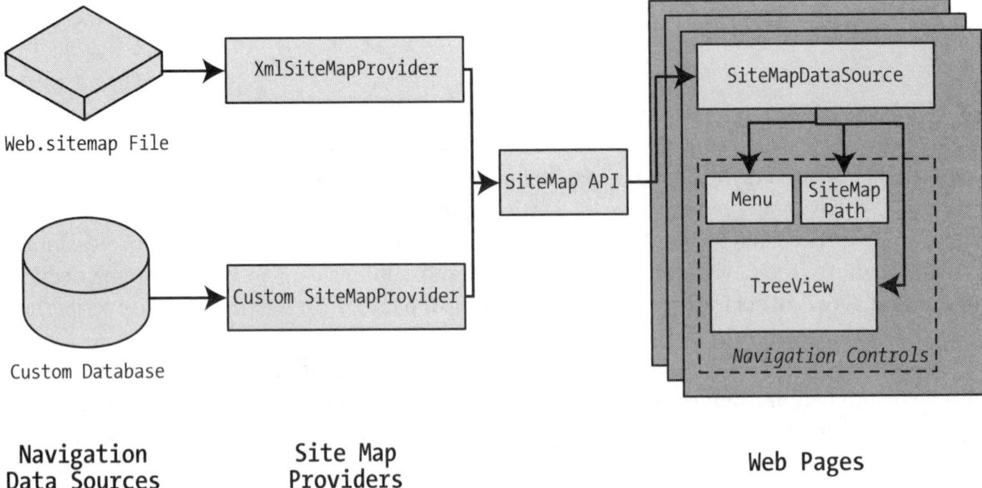

Figure 14-1. *ASP.NET navigation with site maps*

Defining a Site Map

The starting point in site map-based navigation is the site map provider. ASP.NET ships with a single site map provider, named XmlSiteMapProvider, which is able to retrieve site map information from an XML file. If you want to retrieve a site map from another location or in a custom format, you'll need to create your own site map provider or look for a third-party solution on the Web.

The XmlSiteMapProvider looks for a file named Web.sitemap in the root of the virtual directory. Like all site map providers, the task of the XmlSiteMapProvider is to extract the site map data and create the corresponding SiteMap object. This SiteMap object is then made available to the SiteMapDataSource, which you place on every page that uses navigation. The SiteMapDataSource provides the site map information to navigation controls, which are the final link in the chain.

■ Tip To simplify the task of adding navigation to your website, you can use master pages, as described in Chapter 13. That way, you simply need to place the SiteMapDataSource and navigation controls on the master page, rather than on all the individual pages in your website. You'll use this technique in this chapter.

You can create a site map using a text editor such as Notepad, or you can create it in Visual Studio by selecting Website ➤ Add New Item and then choosing the Site Map option. Either way, it's up to you to enter all the site map information by hand. The only difference is that if you create it in Visual Studio, the site map will start with a basic structure that consists of three siteMap nodes.

Before you can fill in the content in your site map file, you need to understand the rules that all ASP.NET site maps must follow. The following sections break these rules down piece by piece.

■ **Note** Before you begin creating site maps, it helps to have a basic understanding of XML, the format that's used for the site map file. You should understand what an element is, how to start and end an element, and why exact capitalization is so important. If you're new to XML, you may find that it helps to refer to Chapter 19 for a quick introduction before you read this chapter.

Rule 1: Site Maps Begin with the <siteMap> Element

Every Web.sitemap file begins by declaring the <siteMap> element and ends by closing that element. You place the actual site map information between the start and end tags (where the three dots are shown here):

```
<siteMap xmlns="http://schemas.microsoft.com/AspNet/SiteMap-File-1.0">
    ...
</siteMap>
```

The xmlns attribute is required, and must be entered exactly as shown here. This tells ASP.NET that the XML file uses the ASP.NET site map standard.

Rule 2: Each Page Is Represented by a <siteMapNode> Element

So, what does the site map content look like? Essentially, every site map defines an organization of web pages. To insert a page into the site map, you add the <siteMapNode> element with some basic information. Namely, you need to supply the title of the page (which appears in the navigation controls), a description (which you may or may not choose to use), and the URL (the link for the page). You add these three pieces of information using three attributes. The attributes are named title, description, and url, as shown here:

```
<siteMapNode title="Home" description="Home" url="~/default.aspx" />
```

Notice that this element ends with the characters />. This indicates it's an *empty element* that represents a start tag and an end tag in one. Empty elements (an XML concept described in Chapter 19) never contain other nodes.

Here's a complete, valid site map file that uses this page to define a website with exactly one page:

```
<siteMap xmlns="http://schemas.microsoft.com/AspNet/SiteMap-File-1.0">
    <siteMapNode title="Home" description="Home" url="~/default.aspx" />
</siteMap>
```

Notice that the URL for each page begins with the ~/ character sequence. This is quite important. The ~/ characters represent the root folder of your web application. In other words, the URL ~/default.aspx points to the default.aspx file in the root folder. This style of URL isn't required, but it's strongly recommended, because it makes sure you always get the right page. If you were to simply enter the URL default.aspx without the ~/ prefix, ASP.NET would look for the default.aspx page in the *current* folder. If you have a web application with pages in more than one folder, you'll run into a problem.

For example, if the user browses into a subfolder and clicks the default.aspx link, ASP.NET will look for the default.aspx page in that subfolder instead of in the root folder. Because the default.aspx page isn't in this folder, the navigation attempt will fail with a 404 Not Found error.

Rule 3: A <siteMapNode> Element Can Contain Other <siteMapNode> Elements

Site maps don't consist of simple lists of pages. Instead, they divide pages into groups. To represent this in a site map file, you place one <siteMapNode> inside another. Instead of using the empty element syntax shown previously, you'll need to split your <siteMapNode> element into a start tag and an end tag:

```
<siteMapNode title="Home" description="Home" url="~/default.aspx">
    ...
</siteMapNode>
```

Now you can slip more nodes inside. Here's an example where a Home group contains two more pages:

```
<siteMapNode title="Home" description="Home" url="~/default.aspx">
    <siteMapNode title="Products" description="Our products"
      url="~/products.aspx" />
    <siteMapNode title="Hardware" description="Hardware choices"
      url="~/hardware.aspx" />
</siteMapNode>
```

Essentially, this represents the hierarchical group of links shown in Figure 14-2.

In this case, all three nodes are links. This means the user could surf to one of three pages. However, when you start to create more complex groups and subgroups, you might want to create nodes that serve only to organize other nodes but aren't links themselves. In this case, just omit the url attribute, as shown here with the Products node:

```
<siteMapNode title="Products" description="Products">
    <siteMapNode title="In Stock" description="Products that are available"
      url="~/inStock.aspx" />
    <siteMapNode title="Not In Stock" description="Products that are on order"
      url="~/outOfStock.aspx" />
</siteMapNode>
```

When you show this part of the site map in a web page, the Products node will appear as ordinary text, not a clickable link.

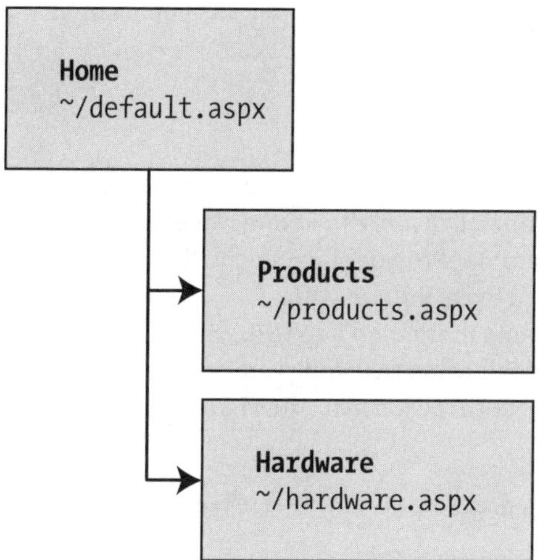

Figure 14-2. *Three nodes in a site map*

No limit exists for how many layers deep you can nest groups and subgroups. However, it's a good rule to go just two or three levels deep; otherwise, it may be difficult for users to grasp the hierarchy when they see it in a navigation control. If you find that you need more than two or three levels, you may need to reconsider how you are organizing your pages into groups.

Rule 4: Every Site Map Begins with a Single <siteMapNode>

Another rule applies to all site maps. A site map must always have a single root node. All the other nodes must be contained inside this root-level node.

That means the following is *not* a valid site map, because it contains two top-level nodes:

```
<siteMap xmlns="http://schemas.microsoft.com/AspNet/SiteMap-File-1.0">
    <siteMapNode title="In Stock" description="Products that are available"
      url="~/inStock.aspx" />
    <siteMapNode title="Not In Stock" description="Products that are on order"
      url="~/outOfStock.aspx" />
</siteMap>
```

The following site map is valid, because it has a single top-level node (Home), which contains two more nodes:

```
<siteMap xmlns="http://schemas.microsoft.com/AspNet/SiteMap-File-1.0">
    <siteMapNode title="Home" description="Home" url="~/default.aspx">
        <siteMapNode title="In Stock"
          description="Products that are available" url="~/inStock.aspx" />
        <siteMapNode title="Not In Stock"
          description="Products that are on order" url="~/outOfStock.aspx" />
    </siteMapNode>
</siteMap>
```

As long as you use only one top-level node, you can nest nodes as deep as you want in groups as large or as small as you want.

Rule 5: Duplicate URLs Are Not Allowed

You cannot create two site map nodes with the same URL. This might seem to present a bit of a problem in cases where you want to have the same link in more than one place—and it does. However, it's a requirement because the default SiteMapProvider included with ASP.NET stores nodes in a collection, with each item indexed by its unique URL.

This limitation doesn't prevent you from creating more than one URL with minor differences pointing to the same page. For example, the following two nodes are acceptable, even though they lead to the same page (products.aspx), because the two URLs have different query string arguments at the end:

```
<siteMapNode title="In Stock" description="Products that are available"
  url="~/products.aspx?stock=1" />
<siteMapNode title="Not In Stock" description="Products that are on order"
  url="~/products.aspx?stock=0" />
```

This approach works well if you have a single page that will display different information, depending on the query string. Using the query string argument, you can add both "versions" of the page to the site map. Chapter 7 describes the query string in more detail.

Seeing a Simple Site Map in Action

A typical site map can be a little overwhelming at first glance. But if you keep the previous five rules in mind, you'll be able to sort out exactly what's taking place.

The following is an example that consists of seven nodes. (Remember, each *node* is either a link to an individual page, or a heading used to organize a group of pages.) The example defines a simple site map for a company named RevoTech.

```
<siteMap xmlns="http://schemas.microsoft.com/AspNet/SiteMap-File-1.0">

  <siteMapNode title="Home" description="Home" url="~/default.aspx">

    <siteMapNode title="Information" description="Learn about our company">
      <siteMapNode title="About Us"
        description="How RevoTech was founded"
        url="~/aboutus.aspx" />
      <siteMapNode title="Investing"
        description="Financial reports and investor analysis"
        url="~/financial.aspx" />
    </siteMapNode>

    <siteMapNode title="Products" description="Learn about our products">
      <siteMapNode title="RevoStock"
        description="Investment software for stock charting"
        url="~/product1.aspx" />
      <siteMapNode title="RevoAnalyze"
```

```
            description="Investment software for yield analysis"
            url="~/product2.aspx" />
      </siteMapNode>

   </siteMapNode>
</siteMap>
```

Note The URL in the site map is not case sensitive.

In the following section, you'll bind this site map to the controls in a page, and you'll see its structure emerge.

Binding an Ordinary Page to a Site Map

Once you've defined the Web.sitemap file, you're ready to use it in a page. First, it's a good idea to make sure you've created all the pages that are listed in the site map file, even if you leave them blank. Otherwise, you'll have trouble testing whether the site map navigation actually works.

The next step is to add the SiteMapDataSource control to your page. You can drag and drop it from the Data tab of the Toolbox. It creates a tag like this:

```
<asp:SiteMapDataSource ID="SiteMapDataSource1" runat="server" />
```

The SiteMapDataSource control appears as a gray box on your page in Visual Studio, but it's invisible when you run the page.

The last step is to add controls that are linked to the SiteMapDataSource. Although you can use any of the data controls described in Part 3, in practice you'll find that you'll get the results you want only with the three controls that are available in the Navigation tab of the Toolbox. That's because these controls support hierarchical data (data with multiple nested levels), and the site map is an example of hierarchical data. In any other control, you'll see only a single level of the site map at a time, which is impractical.

These are the three navigation controls:

TreeView: The TreeView displays a "tree" of grouped links that shows your whole site map at a glance.

Menu: The Menu displays a multilevel menu. By default, you'll see only the first level, but other levels pop up (thanks to some nifty JavaScript) when you move the mouse over the subheadings.

SiteMapPath: The SiteMapPath is the simplest navigation control—it displays the full path you need to take through the site map to get to the current page. For example, it might show Home > Products > RevoStock if you're at the product1.aspx page. Unlike the other navigation controls, the SiteMapPath is useful only for moving up the hierarchy.

To connect a control to the SiteMapDataSource, you simply need to set its DataSourceID property to match the name of the SiteMapDataSource. For example, if you added a TreeView, you should tweak the tag so it looks like this:

```
<asp:TreeView ID="TreeView1" runat="server" DataSourceID="SiteMapDataSource1" />
```

Figure 14-3 shows the result—a tree that displays the structure of the site, as defined in the website. When using the TreeView, the description information doesn't appear immediately. Instead, it's displayed as a tooltip when you hover over an item in the tree.

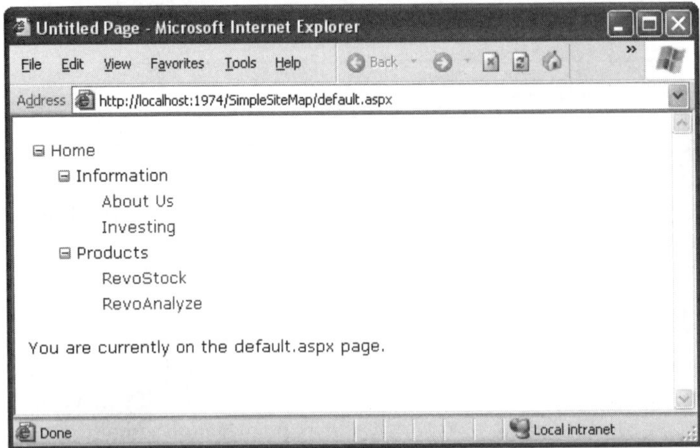

Figure 14-3. *A site map in the TreeView*

Best of all, this tree is created automatically. As long as you link it to the SiteMapDataSource control, you don't need to write any code.

When you click one of the nodes in the tree, you'll automatically be taken to the page you defined in the URL. Of course, unless that page also includes a navigation control such as the TreeView, the site map will disappear from sight. The next section shows a better approach.

Binding a Master Page to a Site Map

Website navigation works best when combined with another ASP.NET feature—master pages. That's because you'll usually want to show the same navigation controls on every page. The easiest way to do this is to create a master page that includes the SiteMapDataSource and the navigation controls. You can then reuse this template for every other page on your site.

Here's how you might define a basic structure in your master page that puts navigation controls on the left:

```
<%@ Master Language="VB" CodeFile="MasterPage.master.vb"
    Inherits="MasterPage" %>
<html>
<head runat="server">
  <title>Navigation Test</title>
</head>
<body>
```

```
<form id="form1" runat="server">
  <table>
    <tr>
      <td style="width: 226px;vertical-align: top;">
        <asp:TreeView ID="TreeView1" runat="server"
         DataSourceID="SiteMapDataSource1" />
      </td>
      <td style="vertical-align: top;">
        <asp:ContentPlaceHolder id="ContentPlaceHolder1" runat="server" />
      </td>
    </tr>
  </table>
  <asp:SiteMapDataSource ID="SiteMapDataSource1" runat="server" />
</form>
</body>
</html>
```

Then, create a child with some simple static content:

```
<%@ Page Language="VB" MasterPageFile="~/MasterPage.master"
  AutoEventWireup="False" CodeFile="default.aspx.vb"
  Inherits="_default" Title="Home Page" %>
<asp:Content ID="Content1" ContentPlaceHolderID="ContentPlaceHolder1"
  runat="Server">
    <br />
    <br />
    You are currently on the default.aspx page (Home).
</asp:Content>
```

In fact, while you're at it, why not create a second page so you can test the navigation between the two pages?

```
<%@ Page Language="VB" MasterPageFile="~/MasterPage.master"
  AutoEventWireup="False" CodeFile="product1.aspx.vb"
  Inherits="product1" Title="RevoStock Page" %>
<asp:Content ID="Content1" ContentPlaceHolderID="ContentPlaceHolder1"
  runat="Server">
    <br />
    <br />
    You are currently on the product1.aspx page (RevoStock).
</asp:Content>
```

Now you can jump from one page to another using the TreeView (see Figure 14-4). The first picture shows the home page as it initially appears, while the second shows the result of clicking the RevoStock link in the TreeView. Because both pages use the same master, and the master page includes the TreeView, the site map always remains visible.

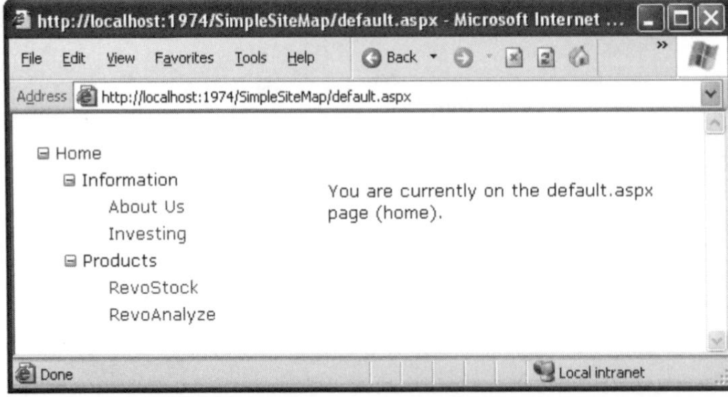

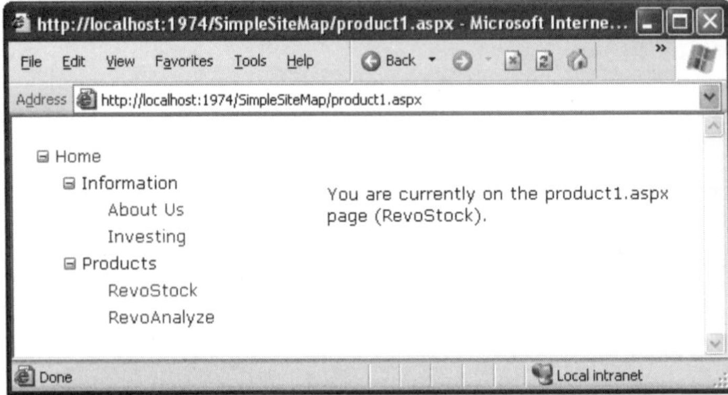

Figure 14-4. *Navigating from page to page with the TreeView*

You can do a lot more to customize the appearance of your pages and navigation controls. You'll consider these topics in the following sections.

Binding Portions of a Site Map

In the previous example, the TreeView shows the structure of the site map file *exactly*. However, this isn't always what you want. For example, you might not like the way the Home node sticks out because of the XmlSiteMapProvider rule that every site map must begin with a single root.

One way to clean this up is to configure the properties of the SiteMapDataSource. For example, you can set the ShowStartingNode property to False to hide the root node:

```
<asp:SiteMapDataSource ID="SiteMapDataSource1" runat="server"
  ShowStartingNode="False" />
```

Figure 14-5 shows the result.

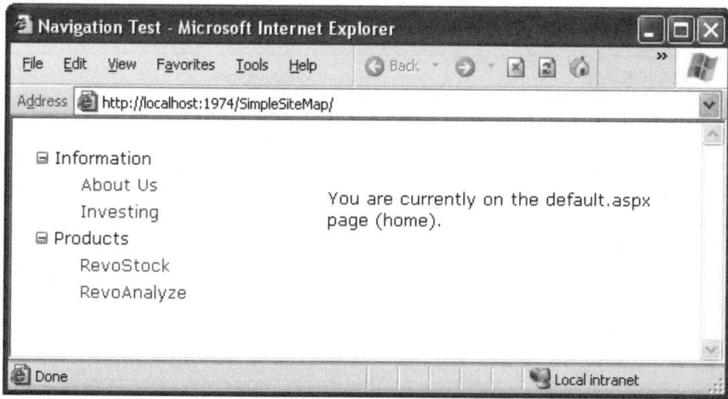

Figure 14-5. *A site map without the root node*

This example shows how you can hide the root node. Another option is to show just a portion of the complete site map, starting from the current node. For example, you might use a control such as the TreeView to show everything in the hierarchy starting from the current node. If the user wants to move up a level, they could use another control (such as the SiteMapPath).

Showing Subtrees

By default, the SiteMapDataSource shows a full tree that starts with the root node. However, the SiteMapDataSource has several properties that can help you configure the navigation tree to limit the display to just a specific branch. Typically, this is useful if you have a deeply nested tree. Table 14-1 describes the full set of properties.

Table 14-1. *SiteMapDataSource Properties*

Property	Description
ShowStartingNode	Set this property to False to hide the first (top-level) node that would otherwise appear in the navigation tree. The default is True.
StartingNodeUrl	Use this property to change the starting node. Set this value to the URL of the node that should be the first node in the navigation tree. This value must match the url attribute in the site map file exactly. For example, if you specify a StartingNodeUrl of "~/home.aspx", then the first node in the tree is the Home node, and you will see nodes only underneath that node.
StartFromCurrentNode	Set this property to True to set the current page as the starting node. The navigation tree will show only pages beneath the current page (which allows the user to move down the hierarchy). If the current page doesn't exist in the site map file, this approach won't work.

Table 14-1. *SiteMapDataSource Properties*

Property	Description
StartingNodeOffset	Use this property to shift the starting node up or down the hierarchy. It takes an integer that instructs the SiteMapDataSource to move from the starting node down the tree (if the number is positive) or up the tree (if the number is negative). The actual effect depends on how you combine this property with other SiteMapDataSource properties. For example, if StartFromCurrentNode is False, you'll use a positive number to move down the tree from the starting node toward the current node. If StartFromCurrentNode is True, you'll use a negative number to move up the tree away from the current node and toward the starting node.

Figuring out these properties can take some work, and you might need to do a bit of experimenting to decide the right combination of SiteMapDataSource settings you want to use. To make matters more interesting, you can use more than one SiteMapDataSource on the same page. This means you could use two navigation controls to show different sections of the site map hierarchy.

Before you can see this in practice, you need to modify the site map file used for the previous few examples into something a little more complex. Currently, the site map has three levels, but only the first level (the Home node) and the third level (the individual pages) have URL links. The second-level groupings (Information and Products) are just used as headings, not links. To get a better feel for how the SiteMapDataSource properties work with multiple navigation levels, modify the Information node as shown here:

```
<siteMapNode title="Information" description="Learn about our company"
  url="~/information.aspx">
```

and change the Products node:

```
<siteMapNode title="Products" description="Learn about our products"
  url="~/products.aspx">
```

Next, create the products.aspx and information.aspx pages.

The interesting feature of the Products node is that not only is it a navigable page, but it's a page that has other pages both above it and below it in the navigation hierarchy. This makes it ideal for testing the SiteMapDataSource properties. For example, you can create a SiteMapDataSource that shows only the current page and the pages below it like this:

```
<asp:SiteMapDataSource ID="SiteMapDataSource1" runat="server"
   StartFromCurrentNode="True" />
```

And you can create one that always shows the Information page and the pages underneath it like this:

```
<asp:SiteMapDataSource ID="SiteMapDataSource2" runat="server"
  StartingNodeUrl="~/information.aspx"  />
```

■ **Note** For this technique to work, ASP.NET must be able to find a page in the Web.sitemap file that matches the current URL. Otherwise, it won't know where the current position is, and it won't provide any navigation information to the bound controls.

Now, just bind two navigation controls. In this case, one TreeView is linked to each SiteMapDataSource:

```
Pages under the current page:
<asp:TreeView ID="TreeView1" runat="server"
  DataSourceID="SiteMapDataSource1" />
<br />
The Information group of pages:<br />
<asp:TreeView ID="TreeView2" runat="server"
  DataSourceID="SiteMapDataSource2" />
```

Figure 14-6 shows the result as you navigate from default.aspx down the tree to products1.aspx. The first TreeView shows the portion of the tree under the current page, and the second TreeView is always fixed on the Information group.

You'll need to get used to the SiteMapDataSource.StartingNodeOffset property. It takes an integer that instructs the SiteMapDataSource to move that many levels down the tree (if the number is positive) or up the tree (if the number is negative). An important detail that's often misunderstood is that when the SiteMapDataSource moves down the tree, it moves *toward* the current node. If it's already at the current node, or your offset takes it beyond the current node, the SiteMapDataSource won't know where to go, and you'll end up with a blank navigation control.

To understand how this works, it helps to consider an example. Imagine you're at this location in a website:

```
Home > Products > Software > Custom > Contact Us
```

If the SiteMapDataSource is starting at the Home node (the default) and you apply a StartingNodeOffset of 2, it will move down the tree two levels and bind to the tree of pages that starts at the Software node.

On the other hand, if you're currently at the Products node, you won't see anything. That's because the starting node is Home, and the offset tries to move it down two levels. However, you're only one level deep in the hierarchy. Or, to look at it another way, no node exists between the top node and the current node that's two levels deep.

Now, what happens if you repeat the same test but set the site map provider to begin on another node? Consider what happens if you set StartFromCurrentNode to True and surf to the Contact Us page. Once again, you won't see any information, because the site map provider attempts to move two levels down from the current node—Contact Us—and it has nowhere to go. On the other hand, if you set StartFromCurrentNode to True and use a StartingNodeOffset of -2, the SiteMapDataSource will move *up* two levels from Contact Us and bind the subtree starting at Software.

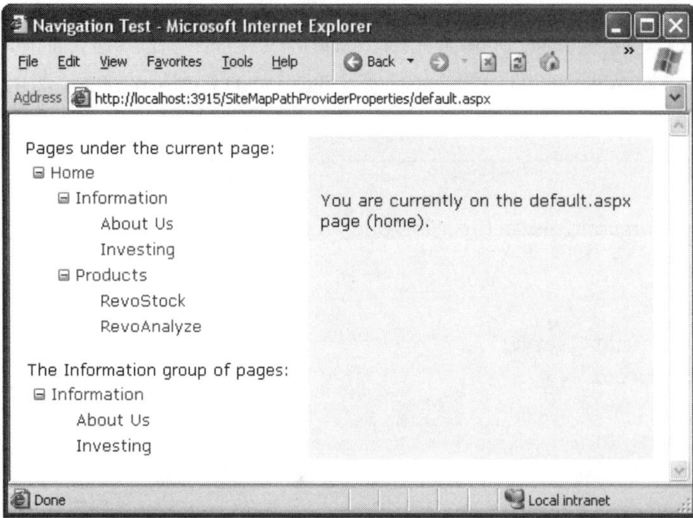

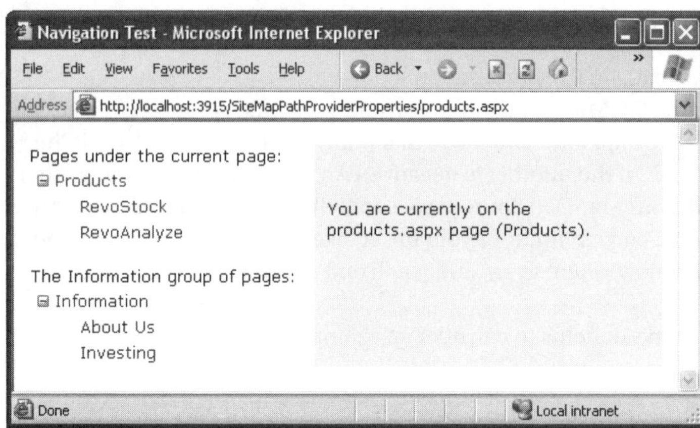

Figure 14-6. *Showing portions of the site map*

Overall, you won't often use the StartingNodeOffset property. However, it can be useful if you have a deeply nested site map and you want to keep the navigation display simple by showing just a few levels up from the current position.

■ **Note** All the examples in this section filtered out higher-level nodes than the starting node. For example, if you're positioned at the Home > Products > RevoStock page, you've seen how to hide the Home and Products levels. You haven't seen how to filter out lower-level nodes. For example, if you're positioned at the Home page, you'll always see the full site map, because you don't have a way to limit the number of levels you see below the starting node. You have no way to change this behavior with the SiteMapDataSource; but later, in "The TreeView Control" section, you'll see that the TreeView.MaxDataBindDepth property serves this purpose.

Using Different Site Maps in the Same File

Imagine you want to have a dealer section and an employee section on your website. You might split this into two structures and define them both under different branches in the same file, like this:

```
<siteMap xmlns="http://schemas.microsoft.com/AspNet/SiteMap-File-1.0" >
  <siteMapNode title="Root" description="Root" url="~/default.aspx">
    <siteMapNode title="Dealer Home" description="Dealer Home"
     url="~/default_dealer.aspx">
      ...
    </siteMapNode>
    <siteMapNode title="Employee Home" description="Employee Home"
      url="~/default_employee.aspx">
      ...
    </siteMapNode>
  </siteMapNode>
</siteMap>
```

To bind the SiteMapDataSource to the dealer view (which starts at the Dealer Home page), you simply set the StartingNodeUrl property to "~/default_dealer.aspx". You can do this programmatically or, more likely, by creating an entirely different master page and implementing it in all your dealer pages. In your employee pages, you set the StartingNodeUrl property to "~/default_employee.aspx". This way, you'll show only the pages under the Employee Home branch of the site map.

You can even make your life easier by breaking a single site map into separate files using the siteMapFile attribute, like this:

```
<siteMap xmlns="http://schemas.microsoft.com/AspNet/SiteMap-File-1.0" >
  <siteMapNode title="Root" description="Root" url="~/default.aspx">
    <siteMapNode siteMapFile="Dealers.sitemap" />
    <siteMapNode siteMapFile="Employees.sitemap" />
  </siteMapNode>
</siteMap>
```

Even with this technique, you're still limited to a single site map tree, and it always starts with the Web.sitemap file. But you can manage your site map more easily because you can factor some of its content into separate files.

However, this seemingly nifty technique is greatly limited because the site map provider doesn't allow duplicate URLs. This means you have no way to reuse the same page in more than one branch of a site map. Although you can try to work around this problem by creating different URLs that are equivalent (for example, by adding query string parameters on the end), this raises more headaches. Sadly, this problem has no solution with the default site map provider that ASP.NET includes.

The SiteMap Class

You aren't limited to no-code data binding in order to display navigation hierarchies. You can interact with the navigation information programmatically. This allows you to retrieve the current node information and use it to configure details such as the page heading and title. All you need to do is interact with the objects that are readily available through the Page class.

The site map API is remarkably straightforward. To use it, you need to work with two classes from the System.Web namespace. The starting point is the SiteMap class, which provides the shared properties CurrentNode (the site map node representing the current page) and RootNode (the root site map node). Both of these properties return a SiteMapNode object. Using the SiteMapNode object, you can retrieve information from the site map, including the title, description, and URL values. You can branch out to consider related nodes using the navigational properties in Table 14-2.

■ **Note** You can also search for nodes using the methods of the current SiteMapProvider object, which is available through the SiteMap.Provider shared property. For example, the SiteMap.Provider.FindSiteMapNode() method allows you to search for a node by its URL.

Table 14-2. *SiteMapNode Navigational Properties*

Property	Description
ParentNode	Returns the node one level up in the navigation hierarchy, which contains the current node. On the root node, this returns a null reference.
ChildNodes	Provides a collection of all the child nodes. You can check the HasChildNodes property to determine whether child nodes exist.
PreviousSibling	Returns the previous node that's at the same level (or a null reference if no such node exists).
NextSibling	Returns the next node that's at the same level (or a null reference if no such node exists).

To see this in action, consider the following code, which configures two labels on a page to show the heading and description information retrieved from the current node:

```
Protected Sub Page_Load(ByVal sender As Object, _
  ByVal e As EventArgs) Handles Me.Load

    lblHead.Text = SiteMap.CurrentNode.Title
    lblDescription.Text = SiteMap.CurrentNode.Description
End Sub
```

If you're using master pages, you could place this code in the code-behind for your master page, so that every page is assigned its title from the site map.

The next example is a little more ambitious. It implements a Previous/Next set of links, allowing the user to traverse an entire set of subnodes. The code checks for the existence of sibling nodes, and if there aren't any in the required position, it simply hides the links:

```
Protected Sub Page_Load(ByVal sender As Object, _
  ByVal e As EventArgs) Handles Me.Load

    If SiteMap.CurrentNode.NextSibling IsNot Nothing Then
        lnkNext.NavigateUrl = SiteMap.CurrentNode.NextSibling.Url
        lnkNext.Visible = True
    Else
        lnkNext.Visible = False
    End If
End Sub
```

Figure 14-7 shows the result. The first picture shows the Next link on the product1.aspx page. The second picture shows how this link disappears when you navigate to product2.aspx (either by clicking the Next link or the RevoAnalyze link in the TreeView).

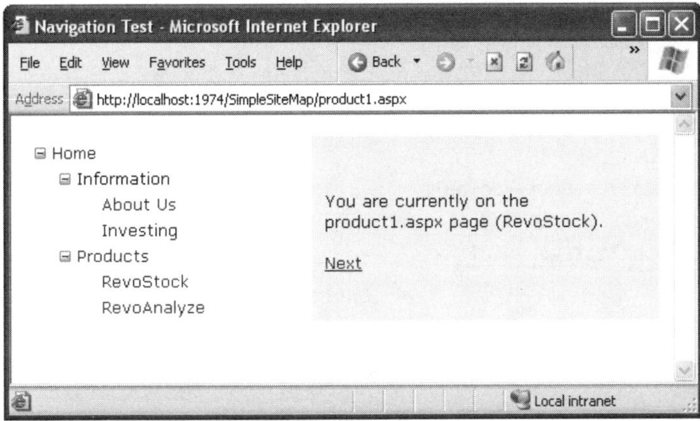

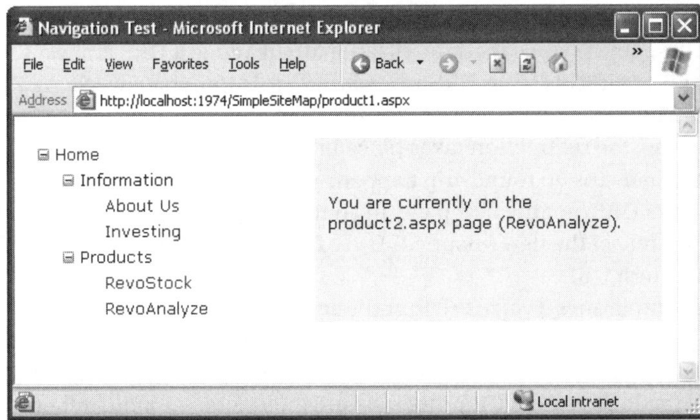

Figure 14-7. *Creating a Next page link*

Mapping URLs

In some situations, you might want to have several URLs lead to the same page. This might be the case for a number of reasons—maybe you want to implement your logic in one page and use query string arguments but still provide shorter and easier-to-remember URLs to your website users (often called *friendly* URLs). Or maybe you have renamed a page, but you want to keep the old URL functional so it doesn't break user bookmarks. Although web servers sometimes provide this type of functionality, ASP.NET includes its own URL mapping feature.

The basic idea behind ASP.NET URL mapping is that you map a request URL to a different URL. The mapping rules are stored in the web.config file, and they're applied before any other processing takes place. Of course, for ASP.NET to apply the remapping, it must be processing the request, which means the request URL must use a file type extension that's mapped to ASP.NET (such as .aspx).

You define URL mapping in the <urlMappings> section of the web.config file. You supply two pieces of information—the request URL (as the attribute url) and the new destination URL (mappedUrl). Here's an example:

```
<configuration>
  <system.web>
    <urlMappings enabled="true">
      <add url="~/category.aspx"
       mappedUrl="~/default.aspx?category=default" />
      <add url="~/software.aspx"
       mappedUrl="~/default.aspx?category=software" />
    </urlMappings>
    ...
  </system.web>
</configuration>
```

In order for ASP.NET to make a match, the URL that the browser submits must match the URL specified in the web.config file almost exactly. However, there are two exceptions. First, the matching algorithm isn't case sensitive, so the capitalization of the request URL is always ignored. Second, any query string arguments in the URL are disregarded. Unfortunately, ASP.NET doesn't support advanced matching rules, such as wildcards or regular expressions.

When you use URL mapping, the redirection takes place in the same way as the Server.Transfer() method, which means no round-trip happens and the URL in the browser will still show the original request URL, not the new page. In your code, the Request.Path and Request.QueryString properties reflect the new (mapped) URL. The Request.RawUrl property returns the original, friendly request URL.

This can introduce some complexities if you use it in conjunction with site maps—namely, does the site map provider try to use the original request URL or the destination URL when looking for the current node in the site map? The answer is both. It begins by trying to match the request URL (provided by the Request.RawUrl property), and if no value is found, it then uses the Request.Path property instead. This is the behavior of the XmlSiteMapProvider, so you could change it in a custom provider if desired.

The SiteMapPath Control

The TreeView shows the available pages, but it doesn't indicate where you're currently positioned. To solve this problem, it's common to use the TreeView in conjunction with the SiteMapPath control. Because the SiteMapPath is always used for displaying navigational information (unlike the TreeView, which can also show other types of data), you don't even need to explicitly link it to the SiteMapDataSource:

```
<asp:SiteMapPath ID="SiteMapPath1" runat="server" />
```

The SiteMapPath provides *breadcrumb navigation*, which means it shows the user's current location and allows the user to navigate up the hierarchy to a higher level using links. Figure 14-8 shows an example with a SiteMapPath control when the user is on the product1.aspx page. Using the SiteMapPath control, the user can return to the default.aspx page. (If a URL were defined for the Products node, you would also be able to click that portion of the path to move to that page.) Once again, the SiteMapPath has been added to the master page, so it appears on all the content pages in your site.

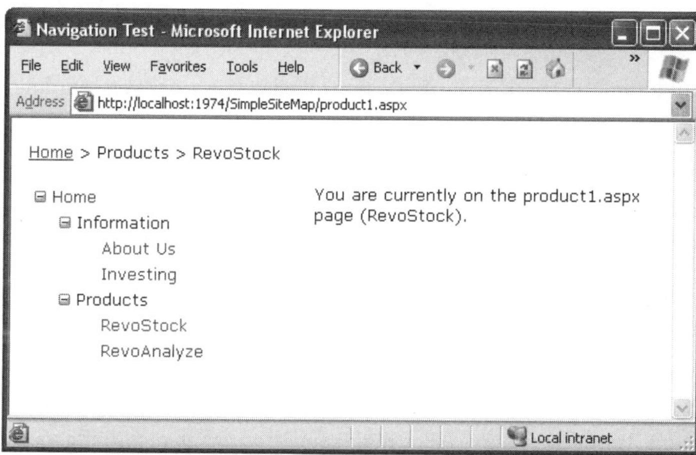

Figure 14-8. *Breadcrumb navigation with SiteMapPath*

The SiteMapPath control is useful because it provides both an at-a-glance view that shows the current position and a way to move up the hierarchy. However, you always need to combine it with other navigation controls that let the user move down the site map hierarchy.

Customizing the SiteMapPath

The SiteMapPath has a subtle but important difference from other navigational controls such as the TreeView and Menu. Unlike these controls, the SiteMapPath works directly with the ASP.NET navigation model—in other words, it doesn't need to get its data through the SiteMapDataSource. As a result, you can use the SiteMapPath on pages that don't have a SiteMapDataSource, and changing the properties of the SiteMapDataSource won't affect the SiteMapPath. However, the SiteMapPath control provides quite a few properties of its own that you can use for customization. Table 14-3 lists some of its most commonly configured properties.

Table 14-3. *SiteMapPath Appearance-Related Properties*

Property	Description
ShowToolTips	Set this to False if you don't want the description text to appear when the user hovers over a part of the site map path.
ParentLevelsDisplayed	This sets the maximum number of levels above the current page that will be shown at once. By default, this setting is -1, which means all levels will be shown.
RenderCurrentNodeAsLink	If True, the portion of the page that indicates the current page is turned into a clickable link. By default, this is False because the user is already at the current page.
PathDirection	You have two choices: RootToCurrent (the default) and CurrentToRoot (which reverses the order of levels in the path).
PathSeparator	This indicates the characters that will be placed between each level in the path. The default is the greater-than symbol (>). Another common path separator is the colon (:).

Using SiteMapPath Styles and Templates

For even more control, you can configure the SiteMapPath control with styles or even redefine the controls and HTML with templates. Table 14-4 lists all the styles and templates that are available in the SiteMapPath control; and you'll see how to use both sets of properties in this section.

Table 14-4. *SiteMapPath Styles and Templates*

Style	Template	Applies To
NodeStyle	NodeTemplate	All parts of the path except the root and current node.
CurrentNodeStyle	CurrentNodeTemplate	The node representing the current page.
RootNodeStyle	RootNodeTemplate	The node representing the root. If the root node is the same as the current node, the current node template or styles are used.
PathSeparatorStyle	PathSeparatorTemplate	The separator in between each node.

Styles are easy enough to grasp—they define formatting settings that apply to one part of the SiteMapPath control. Templates are a little trickier, because they rely on data-binding expressions. Essentially, a *template* is a bit of HTML (that you create) that will be shown for a specific part of the SiteMapPath control. For example, if you want to configure how the root node displays in a site map, you could create a SiteMapPath with <RootNodeTemplate> as follows:

```
<asp:SiteMapPath ID="SiteMapPath1" runat="server">
  <RootNodeTemplate>
    <b>Root</b>
  </RootNodeTemplate>
</asp:SiteMapPath>
```

This simple template does not use the title and URL information in the root node of the sitemap node. Instead, it simply displays the word *Root* in bold. Clicking the text has no effect.

Usually, you'll use a data-binding expression to retrieve some site map information—chiefly, the description, text, or URL that's defined for the current node in the site map file. Chapter 16 covers data-binding expressions in detail, but this section will present a simple example that shows you all you need to know to use them with the SiteMapPath.

Imagine you want to change how the current node is displayed so that it's shown in italics. To get the name of the current node, you need to write a data-binding expression that retrieves the title. This data-binding expression is bracketed between <%# and %> characters and uses a method named Eval() to retrieve information from a SiteMapNode object that represents a page. Here's what the template looks like:

```
<asp:SiteMapPath ID="SiteMapPath1" runat="server">
  <CurrentNodeTemplate>
    <i><%# Eval("Title") %></i>
  </CurrentNodeTemplate>
</asp:SiteMapPath>
```

Data binding also gives you the ability to retrieve other information from the site map node, such as the description. Consider the following example:

```
<asp:SiteMapPath ID="SiteMapPath1" runat="server">
  <PathSeparatorTemplate>
    <asp:Image ID="Image1" ImageUrl="~/arrowright.gif"
     runat="server" />
  </PathSeparatorTemplate>
  <RootNodeTemplate>
    <b>Root</b>
  </RootNodeTemplate>
  <CurrentNodeTemplate>
    <%# Eval("Title") %> <br />
    <small><i><%# Eval("Description") %></i></small>
  </CurrentNodeTemplate>
</asp:SiteMapPath>
```

This SiteMapPath uses several templates. First, it uses the PathSeparatorTemplate to define a custom arrow image that's used between each part of the path. This template uses an Image control instead of an ordinary HTML <img> tag because only the Image control understands the ~/ characters in the image URL, which represent the application's root folder. If you don't include these characters, the image won't be retrieved successfully if you place your page in a subfolder.

Next, the SiteMapPath uses the RootNodeTemplate to supply a fixed string of bold text for the root portion of the site map path. Finally, the CurrentNodeTemplate uses two data-binding expressions to show two pieces of information—both the title of the node and its description (in smaller text, underneath). Figure 14-9 shows the final result.

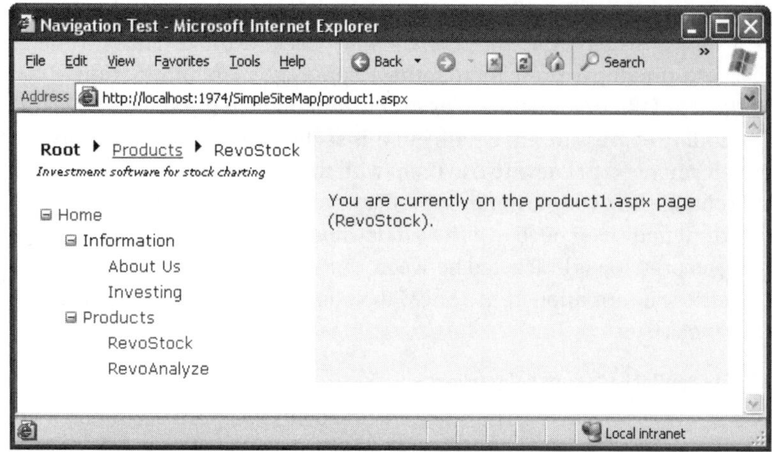

Figure 14-9. *A SiteMapPath with templates*

Keen eyes will notice that the template-based SiteMapPath not only shows more information but is also more interactive. Now you can click any of the page elements that fall between the root item and the current page. In Figure 14-9, that means you can click Products to move up a level to the products.aspx page.

Interestingly, the templates in the SiteMapPath don't contain any elements that provide these links. Instead, the SiteMapPath automatically determines what items should be clickable (by checking if they're linked to a page in the site map). If an item should be clickable, the SiteMapPath wraps the entire CurrentNodeTemplate for that item inside a link.

If you don't want links (or you want to link in a different way, or with a different control), you can change this behavior. The trick is to modify the NodeTemplate. You'll learn how to do this in the next section.

Adding Custom Site Map Information

In the site maps you've seen so far, the only information that's provided for a node is the title, description, and URL. This is the bare minimum of information you'll want to use. However, the schema for the XML site map is open, which means you're free to insert custom attributes with your own data.

You might want to insert additional node data for a number of reasons. This additional information might be descriptive information that you intend to display, or contextual information that describes how the link should work. For example, you could add attributes that specify a target frame or indicate that a link should open in a new window. The only catch is that it's up to you to act on the information later. In other words, you need to configure your user interface so it uses this extra information.

For example, the following code shows a site map that uses a target attribute to indicate the frame where the link should open. This technique is useful if you're using frames-based navigation. In this example, one link is set with a target of _blank so it will open in a new browser window:

```
<siteMapNode title="RevoStock"
  description="Investment software for stock charting"
  url="~/product1.aspx" target="_blank" />
```

Now in your code, you have several options. If you're using a template in your navigation control, you can bind directly to the new attribute. Here's an example with the SiteMapPath from the previous section:

```
<asp:SiteMapPath ID="SiteMapPath1" runat="server" Width="264px" Font-Size="10pt">
    <NodeTemplate>
      <a href='<%# Eval("Url") %>' target='<%# Eval("[target]") %>'>
        <%# Eval("Title") %>
      </a>
    </NodeTemplate>
</asp:SiteMapPath>
```

This creates a link that uses the node URL (as usual) but also uses the target information. There's a slightly unusual detail in this example—the square brackets around the word [target]. You need to use this syntax to look up any custom attribute you add to the Web.sitemap file. That's because this value can't be retrieved directly from a property of the SiteMapNode class—instead, you need to look it up by name using the SiteMapNode indexer.

If your navigation control doesn't support templates, you'll need to find another approach. For example, the TreeView doesn't support templates, but it fires a TreeNodeDataBound event each time an item is bound to the tree. You can react to this event to customize the current item. To apply the new target, use this code:

```
Protected Sub TreeView1_TreeNodeDataBound(ByVal sender As Object, _
  ByVal e As TreeNodeEventArgs) Handles TreeView1.TreeNodeDataBound

    Dim node As SiteMapNode = CType(e.Node.DataItem, SiteMapNode)
    e.Node.Target = node("target")
End Sub
```

As in the template, you can't retrieve the custom attribute from a strongly typed SiteMapNode property. Instead, you retrieve it by name using the SiteMapNode indexer.

The TreeView Control

You've already seen the TreeView at work for displaying navigational information. As you've learned, the TreeView can show a portion of the full site map or the entire site map. Each node becomes a link that, when clicked, takes the user to the new page. If you hover over a link, you'll see the corresponding description information appear in a tooltip.

In the following sections, you'll learn how to change the appearance of the TreeView. In later chapters, you'll learn how to use the TreeView for other tasks, such as displaying data from a database.

■ **Note** The TreeView is one of the most impressive controls in ASP.NET. Not only does it allow you to show site maps, but it also supports showing information from a database and filling portions of the tree on demand (and without refreshing the entire page). But most important, it supports a wide range of styles that can transform its appearance.

TreeView Properties

The TreeView has a slew of properties that let you change how it's displayed on the page. One of the most important properties is ImageSet, which lets you choose a predefined set of node icons. (Each set includes three icons: one for collapsed nodes, one for expanded nodes, and one for nodes that have no children and therefore can't be expanded or collapsed.) The TreeView offers 16 possible ImageSet values, which are represented by the TreeViewImageSet enumeration.

For example, Figure 14-10 shows the same RevoStock navigation page you considered earlier, but this time with an ImageSet value of TreeViewImageSet.Faq. The result is help-style icons that show a question mark (for nodes that have no children) or a question mark superimposed over a folder (for nodes that do contain children).

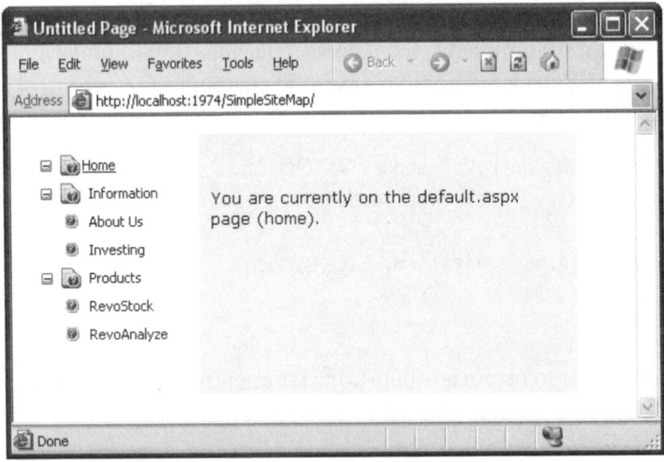

Figure 14-10. *A TreeView with fancy node icons*

You'll notice that this TreeView makes one more change. It removes the indentation between different levels of nodes, so all the sitemap entries fit in the same narrow column, no matter how many levels deep they are. This is accomplished by setting the NodeIndent property of the TreeView to 0.

Here's the complete TreeView markup:

```
<asp:TreeView ID="TreeView1" runat="server"
  DataSourceID="SiteMapDataSource1" ImageSet="Faq" NodeIndent="0" >
</asp:TreeView>
```

The TreeViewImageSet values are useful if you don't have a good set of images handy. Figure 14-11 shows a page with 12 TreeViews, each of which represents one of the options in the Auto Format window.

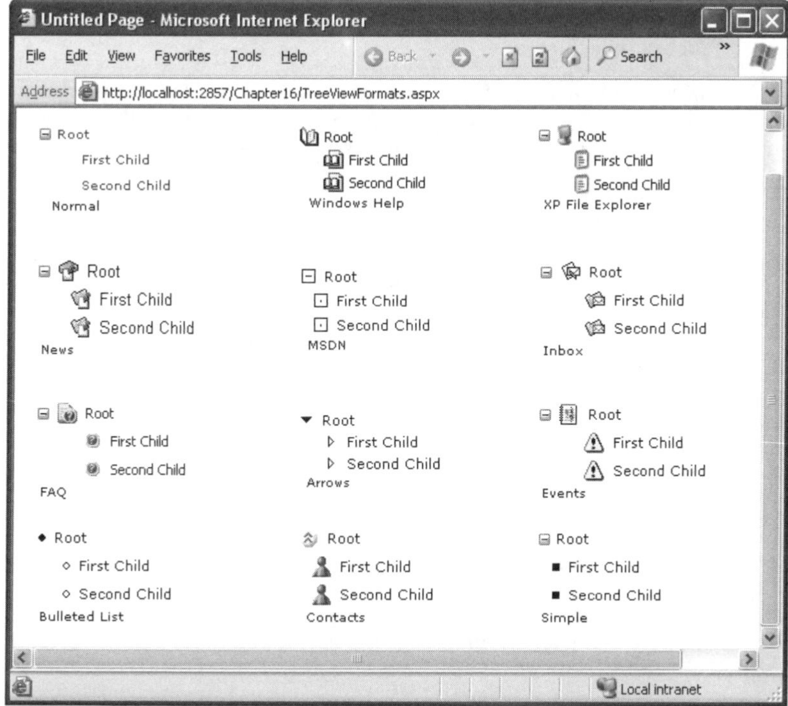

Figure 14-11. *Different looks for a TreeView*

Although the ImageSet and NodeIndent can have a dramatic effect on their own, they aren't the only options when configuring a TreeView. Table 14-5 lists some of the most useful properties of the TreeView.

Table 14-5. *Useful TreeView Properties*

Property	Description
MaxDataBindDepth	Determines how many levels the TreeView will show. By default, MaxDataBindDepth is -1, and you'll see the entire tree. However, if you use a value such as 2, you'll see only two levels under the starting node. This can help you pare down the display of long, multileveled site maps.
ExpandDepth	Lets you specify how many levels of nodes will be visible at first. If you use 0, the TreeView begins completely closed. If you use 1, only the first level is expanded, and so on. By default, ExpandDepth is set to the constant FullyExpand (-1), which means the tree is fully expanded and all the nodes are visible on the page.

Table 14-5. *Useful TreeView Properties (Continued)*

Property	Description
NodeIndent	Sets the number of pixels between each level of nodes in the TreeView. Set this to 0 to create a nonindented TreeView, which saves space. A nonindented TreeView allows you to emulate an in-place menu (see, for example, Figure 14-12).
ImageSet	Lets you use a predefined collection of node images for collapsed, expanded, and nonexpandable nodes. You specify one of the values in the TreeViewImageSet enumeration. You can override any node images you want to change by setting the CollapseImageUrl, ExpandImageUrl, and NoExpandImageUrl properties.
CollapseImageUrl, ExpandImageUrl, and NoExpandImageUrl	Sets the pictures that are shown next to nodes for collapsed nodes (CollapseImageUrl) and expanded nodes (ExpandImageUrl). The NoExpandImageUrl is used if the node doesn't have any children. If you don't want to create your own custom node images, you can use the ImageSet property instead to use one of several built-in image collections.
NodeWrap	Lets a node text wrap over more than one line when set to True.
ShowExpandCollapse	Hides the expand/collapse boxes when set to False. This isn't recommended, because the user won't have a way to expand or collapse a level without clicking it (which causes the browser to navigate to the page).
ShowLines	Adds lines that connect every node when set to True.
ShowCheckBoxes	Shows a check box next to every node when set to True. This isn't terribly useful for site maps, but it is useful with other types of trees.

Properties give you a fair bit of customizing power, but one of the most interesting formatting features comes from TreeView styles, which are described in the next section.

TreeView Styles

Styles are represented by the TreeNodeStyle class, which derives from the more conventional Style class. As with other rich controls, the styles give you options to set background and foreground colors, fonts, and borders. Additionally, the TreeNodeStyle class adds the node-specific style properties shown in Table 14-6. These properties deal with the node image and the spacing around a node.

Table 14-6. *TreeNodeStyle-Added Properties*

Property	Description
ImageUrl	The URL for the image shown next to the node.
NodeSpacing	The space (in pixels) between the current node and the node above and below.
VerticalPadding	The space (in pixels) between the top and bottom of the node text and border around the text.

Table 14-6. *TreeNodeStyle-Added Properties*

Property	Description
HorizontalPadding	The space (in pixels) between the left and right of the node text and border around the text.
ChildNodesPadding	The space (in pixels) between the last child node of an expanded parent node and the following node (for example, between the Investing and Products nodes in Figure 14-10).

Because a TreeView is rendered using an HTML table, you can set the padding of various elements to control the spacing around text, between nodes, and so on. One other property that comes into play is TreeView.NodeIndent, which sets the number of pixels of indentation (from the left) in each subsequent level of the tree hierarchy. Figure 14-12 shows how these settings apply to a single node.

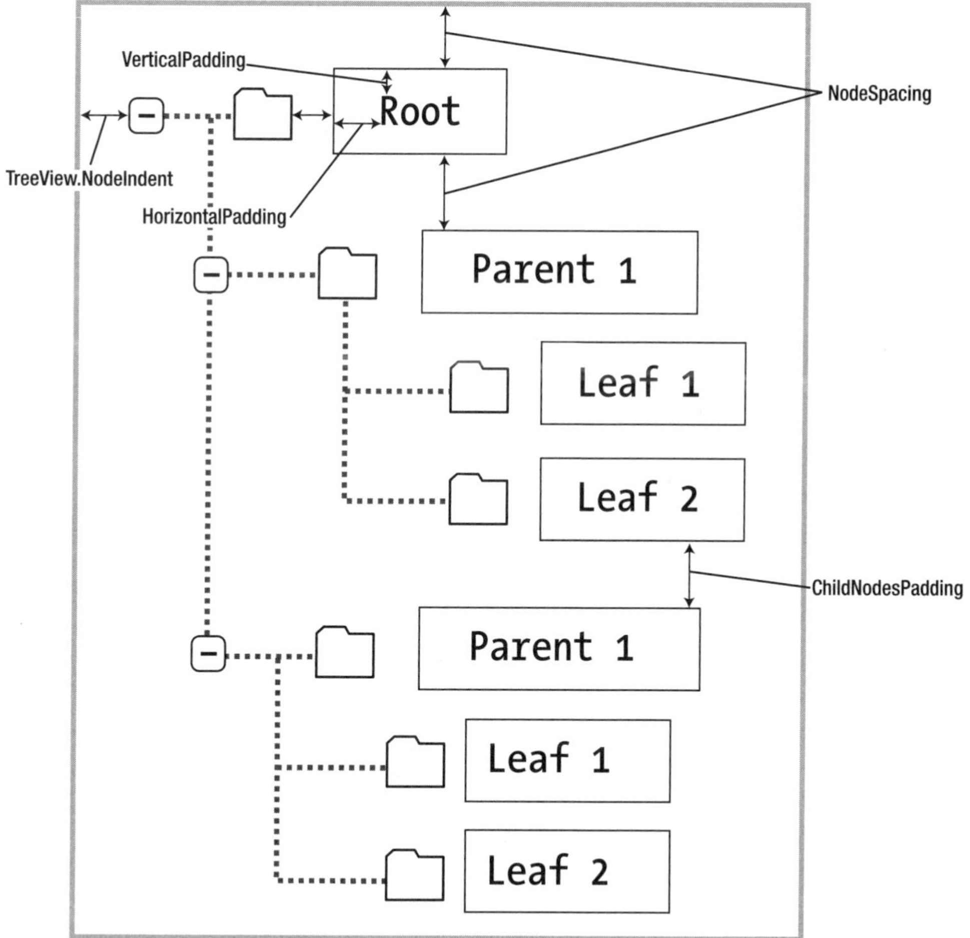

Figure 14-12. *Node spacing*

Clearly, styles give you a lot of control over how different nodes are displayed. To apply a simple TreeView makeover, and to use the same style settings for each node in the TreeView, you apply style settings through the TreeView.NodeStyle property. You can do this directly in the control tag or by using the Properties window.

For example, here's a TreeView that applies a custom font, font size, text color, padding, and spacing:

```
<asp:TreeView ID="TreeView1" runat="server" DataSourceID="SiteMapDataSource1">
    <NodeStyle Font-Names="Tahoma" Font-Size="10pt" ForeColor="Blue"
     HorizontalPadding="5px" NodeSpacing="0px" VerticalPadding="0px" />
</asp:TreeView>
```

Usually, this approach doesn't provide enough fine-tuning. Instead, you'll want to tweak a specific part of the tree. In this case, you need to find the style object that applies to the appropriate part of the tree, as explained in the following two sections.

Applying Styles to Node Types

The TreeView allows you to individually control the styles for types of nodes—for example, root nodes, nodes that contain other nodes, selected nodes, and so on. Table 14-7 lists different TreeView styles and explains what nodes they affect.

Table 14-7. *TreeView Style Properties*

Property	Description
NodeStyle	Applies to all nodes. The other styles may override some or all of the details that are specified in the NodeStyle.
RootNodeStyle	Applies only to the first-level (root) node.
ParentNodeStyle	Applies to any node that contains other nodes, except root nodes.
LeafNodeStyle	Applies to any node that doesn't contain child nodes and isn't a root node.
SelectedNodeStyle	Applies to the currently selected node.
HoverNodeStyle	Applies to the node the user is hovering over with the mouse. These settings are applied only in up-level clients that support the necessary dynamic script.

Here's a sample TreeView that first defines a few standard style characteristics using the NodeStyle property, and then fine-tunes different sections of the tree using the properties from Table 14-7:

```
<asp:TreeView ID="TreeView1" runat="server" DataSourceID="SiteMapDataSource1">
  <NodeStyle Font-Names="Tahoma" Font-Size="10pt" ForeColor="Blue"
   HorizontalPadding="5px" NodeSpacing="0px" VerticalPadding="0px" />
  <ParentNodeStyle Font-Bold="False" />
  <HoverNodeStyle Font-Underline="True" ForeColor="#5555DD" />
  <SelectedNodeStyle Font-Underline="True" ForeColor="#5555DD" />
</asp:TreeView>
```

Styles are listed in Table 14-7 in order of most general to most specific. This means the SelectedNodeStyle settings override any conflicting settings in a RootNodeStyle, for example. (If you don't want a node to be selectable, set the TreeNode.SelectAction to None.) However, the RootNodeStyle, ParentNodeStyle, and LeafNodeStyle settings never conflict, because the definitions for root, parent, and leaf nodes are mutually exclusive. You can't have a node that is simultaneously a parent and a root node, for example—the TreeView simply designates this as a root node.

Applying Styles to Node Levels

Being able to apply styles to different types of nodes is interesting, but often a more useful feature is being able to apply styles based on the node *level*. That's because many trees use a rigid hierarchy. (For example, the first level of nodes represents categories, the second level represents products, the third represents orders, and so on.) In this case, it's not so important to determine whether a node has children. Instead, it's important to determine the node's depth.

The only problem is that a TreeView can have a theoretically unlimited number of node levels. Thus, it doesn't make sense to expose properties such as FirstLevelStyle, SecondLevelStyle, and so on. Instead, the TreeView has a LevelStyles collection that can have as many entries as you want. The level is inferred from the position of the style in the collection, so the first entry is considered the root level, the second entry is the second node level, and so on. For this system to work, you must follow the same order, and you must include an empty style placeholder if you want to skip a level without changing the formatting.

For example, here's a TreeView that differentiates levels by applying different amounts of spacing and different fonts:

```
<asp:TreeView runat="server" HoverNodeStyle-Font-Underline="True"
 ShowExpandCollapse="False" NodeIndent="3" DataSourceID="SiteMapDataSource1">
  <LevelStyles>
    <asp:TreeNodeStyle ChildNodesPadding="10" Font-Bold="True" Font-Size="12pt"
     ForeColor="DarkGreen"/>
    <asp:TreeNodeStyle ChildNodesPadding="5" Font-Bold="True" Font-Size="10pt" />
    <asp:TreeNodeStyle ChildNodesPadding="5" Font-UnderLine="True"
     Font-Size="10pt" />
  </LevelStyles>
</asp:TreeView>
```

If you apply this to the category and product list shown in earlier examples, you'll see a page like the one shown in Figure 14-13.

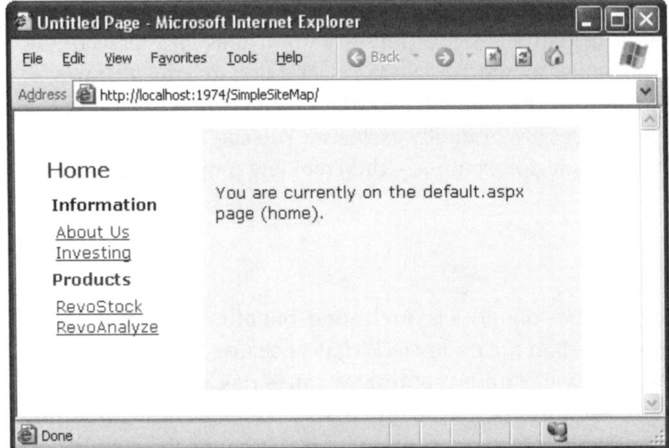

Figure 14-13. *A TreeView with styles*

> **TREEVIEW AUTO FORMAT**
>
> Using the right combination of styles and images can dramatically transform your TreeView. However, for those less artistically inclined, it's comforting to know that Microsoft has made many classic designs available through the TreeView's Auto Format feature. To use it, start by selecting the TreeView on the design surface. Then, click the arrow icon that appears next to the top-right corner of the TreeView to show its smart tag. In the smart tag, click the Auto Format link to show the Auto Format dialog box.
>
> In the Auto Format dialog box, you can pick from a variety of preset formats, each with a small preview. Click Apply to try the format out on your TreeView, Cancel to back out, and OK to make it official and return to Visual Studio.
>
> The different formats correspond loosely to the different TreeViewImageSet values. However, the reality is not quite that simple. When you pick a TreeView format, Visual Studio sets the ImageSet property *and* applies a few matching style settings, to help you get that perfect final look.

The Menu Control

The Menu control is another rich control that supports hierarchical data. Like the TreeView, you can bind the Menu control to a data source, or you can fill it by hand using MenuItem objects.

To try the Menu control, remove the TreeView from your master page, and add the following Menu control tag:

```
<asp:Menu ID="Menu1" runat="server" DataSourceID="SiteMapDataSource1" />
```

Notice that this doesn't configure any properties—it uses the default appearance. The only step you need to perform is setting the DataSourceID property to link the menu to the site map information.

When the Menu first appears, you'll see only the starting node, with an arrow next to it. When you move your mouse over the starting node, the next level of nodes will pop into display. You can continue this process to drill down as many levels as you want, until you find the page you want to click (see Figure 14-14). If you click a menu item, you'll be transported to the corresponding page, just as you are when you click a node in the TreeView.

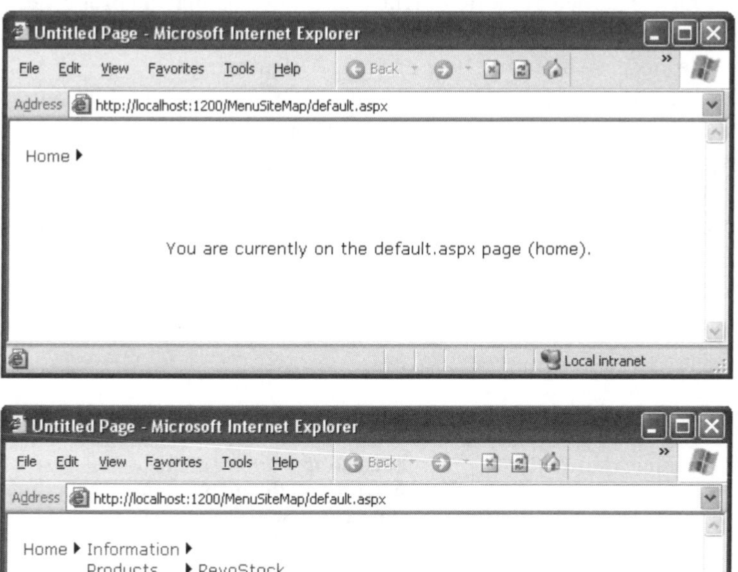

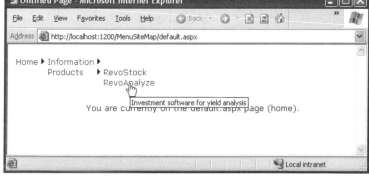

Figure 14-14. *Navigating through the menu*

Overall, the Menu and TreeView controls expose strikingly similar programming models, even though they render themselves quite differently. They also have a similar style-based formatting model. But a few noteworthy differences exist:

- The Menu displays a single submenu. The TreeView can expand an arbitrary number of node branches at a time.
- The Menu displays a root level of links in the page. All other items are displayed using fly-out menus that appear over any other content on the page. The TreeView shows all its items inline in the page.
- The Menu supports templates. The TreeView does not. (Menu templates are discussed later in this section.)
- The TreeView supports check boxes for any node. The Menu does not.
- The Menu supports horizontal and vertical layouts, depending on the Orientation property. The TreeView supports only vertical layout.

Menu Styles

The Menu control provides an overwhelming number of styles. Like the TreeView, the Menu adds a custom style class, which is named MenuItemStyle. This style adds spacing properties such as ItemSpacing, HorizontalPadding, and VerticalPadding. However, you can't set menu item images through the style, because it doesn't have an ImageUrl property.

Much like the TreeView, the Menu supports defining different menu styles for different menu levels. However, the key distinction that the Menu control encourages you to adopt is between *static* items (the root-level items that are displayed in the page when it's first generated) and *dynamic* items (the items in fly-out menus that are added when the user moves the mouse over a portion of the menu). Most websites have a definite difference in the styling of these two elements. To support this, the Menu class defines two parallel sets of styles, one that applies to static items and one that applies to dynamic items, as shown in Table 14-8.

Table 14-8. *Menu Styles*

Static Style	Dynamic Style	Description
StaticMenuStyle	DynamicMenuStyle	Sets the appearance of the overall "box" in which all the menu items appear. In the case of StaticMenuStyle, this box appears on the page, and with DynamicMenuStyle it appears as a pop-up.
StaticMenuItemStyle	DynamicMenuItemStyle	Sets the appearance of individual menu items.
StaticSelectedStyle	DynamicSelectedStyle	Sets the appearance of the selected item. Note that the selected item isn't the item that's currently being hovered over; it's the item that was previously clicked (and that triggered the last postback).
StaticHoverStyle	DynamicHoverStyle	Sets the appearance of the item that the user is hovering over with the mouse.

Along with these styles, you can set level-specific styles so that each level of menu and submenu is different. You do this using three collections: LevelMenuItemStyles, LevelSubMenuStyles, and LevelSelectedStyles. These collections apply to ordinary menus, menus that contain other items, and selected menu items, respectively.

It might seem like you have to do a fair bit of unnecessary work when separating dynamic and static styles. The reason for this model becomes obvious when you consider another remarkable feature of the Menu control—it allows you to choose the number of static levels. By default, only one static level exists, and everything else is displayed as a fly-out menu when the user hovers over the corresponding parent. But you can set the Menu.StaticDisplayLevels property to change all that. If you set it to 2, for example, the first two levels of the menu will be rendered in the page using the static styles. (You can control the indentation of each level using the StaticSubMenuIndent property.)

Figure 14-15 shows the menu with StaticDisplayLevels set to 2 (and some styles applied through the Auto Format link). Each menu item will still be highlighted when you hover over it, as in a nonstatic menu, and selection will also work the same way as it does in the nonstatic menu.

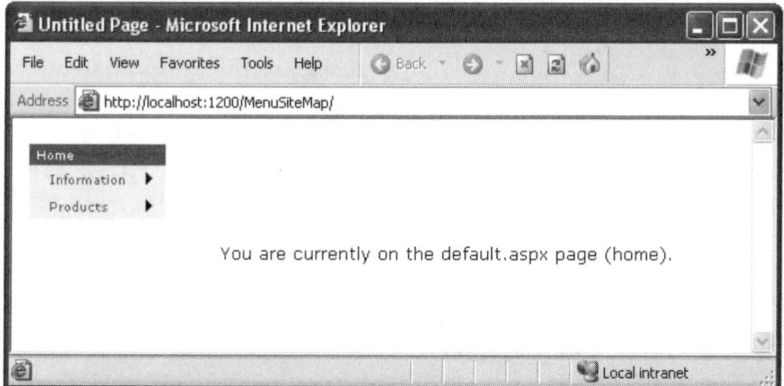

Figure 14-15. *A menu with two static levels*

■ **Tip** The Menu control exposes many more top-level properties for tweaking specific rendering aspects. For example, you can set the delay before a pop-up menu disappears (DisappearAfter), the default images used for expansion icons and separators, the scrolling behavior (which kicks into gear when the browser window is too small to fit a pop-up menu), and much more. Consult MSDN for a full list of properties.

Menu Templates

The Menu control also supports templates through the StaticItemTemplate and DynamicItemTemplate properties. These templates determine the HTML that's rendered for each menu item, giving you complete control.

You've already seen how to create templates for the TreeView, but the process of creating templates for the Menu is a bit different. Whereas each node in the TreeView is bound directly to a SiteMapNode object, the Menu is bound to something else: a dedicated MenuItem object.

This subtle quirk can complicate life. For one thing, you can't rely on properties such as Title, Description, and Url, which are provided by the SiteMapNode object. Instead, you need to use the MenuItem.Text property to get the information you need to display, as shown here:

```
<asp:Menu ID="Menu1" runat="server">
  <StaticItemTemplate>
    <%# Eval("Text") %>
  </StaticItemTemplate>
</asp:Menu>
```

One reason you might want to use the template features of the Menu is to show multiple pieces of information in a menu item. For example, you might want to show both the title *and* the description from the SiteMapNode for this item (rather than just the title). Unfortunately, that's not as easy as it is with the TreeView. Once again, the problem is that the Menu binds directly to MenuItem objects, not the SiteMapNode objects, and MenuItem objects just don't provide the information you need.

If you're really desperate, there is a workaround using an advanced data-binding technique. Rather than binding to a property of the MenuItem object, you can bind to a custom method that you create in your page class. This custom method can then include the code that's needed to get the correct SiteMapNode object (based on the current URL) and provide the extra information you need. In a perfect world, this extra work wouldn't be necessary, but unfortunately it's the simplest workaround in this situation.

For example, consider the following template. It uses two types of data-binding expressions. The first type simply gets the MenuItem text (which is the page title). The second type uses a custom method named GetDescriptionFromTitle(), which you need to create. This method receives the page title as an argument, and then returns the corresponding description:

```
<asp:Menu ID="Menu1" runat="server" DataSourceID="SiteMapDataSource1">
  <StaticItemTemplate>
    <%# Eval("Text") %><br />
    <small>
    <%# GetDescriptionFromTitle(Eval("Text")) %>
    </small>
  </StaticItemTemplate>
  <DynamicItemTemplate>
    <%# Eval("Text") %><br />
    <small>
    <%# GetDescriptionFromTitle(Eval("Text")) %>
    </small>
  </DynamicItemTemplate>
</asp:Menu>
```

This template is designed to create the more descriptive menu items that are shown in Figure 14-16.

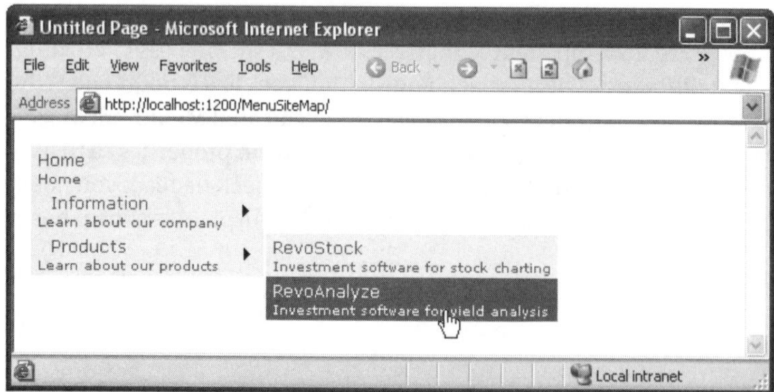

Figure 14-16. *Showing node descriptions in a menu*

In order for this example to work, you need to create a method named GetDescriptionFromTitle() in the code for your page class. It belongs in the page that has the Menu control, which, in this example, is the master page. The GetDescriptionFromTitle() method must also have protected (or public) accessibility, so that ASP.NET can call it during the data-binding process:

```
Protected Function GetDescriptionFromTitle(ByVal title As String) _
  As String
    ...
End Function
```

The tricky part is filling in the code you need. In this example, there are actually two custom methods involved. In order to find the node it needs, GetDescriptionFromTitle() calls another method, named SearchNodes(). The SearchNodes() method calls itself several times to perform a recursive search through the whole hierarchy of nodes. It ends its search only when it finds a matching node, which it returns to GetDescriptionFromTitle(). Finally, GetDescriptionFromTitle() extracts the description information (and anything else you're interested in).

Here's the complete code that makes this example work:

```
Protected Function GetDescriptionFromTitle(ByVal title As String) _
  As String
    Dim startingNode As SiteMapNode = SiteMap.RootNode
    Dim matchNode As SiteMapNode = SearchNodes(startingNode, title)
    If matchNode Is Nothing Then
        ' No match.
        Return ""
    Else
        ' Get the description of the match.
        Return matchNode.Description
    End If
End Function

Private Function SearchNodes(ByVal node As SiteMapNode, ByVal title As String) _
  As SiteMapNode
    If node.Title = title Then
        Return node
    Else
        ' Perform recursive search.
        For Each child As SiteMapNode In node.ChildNodes
            ' Was a match found?
            ' If so, return it.
            Dim match As SiteMapNode = SearchNodes(child, title)
            If match IsNot Nothing Then Return match
        Next
        ' All the nodes were examined, but no match was found.
        Return Nothing
    End If
End Function
```

Once you've finished this heavy lifting, you can use the GetDescriptionFromTitle() method in a template to get the additional information you need.

The Last Word

In this chapter, you explored the new navigation model and learned how to define site maps and bind the navigation data. You then considered three controls that are specifically designed for navigation data: the SiteMapPath, TreeView, and Menu. Using these controls, you can add remarkably rich site maps to your websites with very little coding. But before you begin, make sure you've finalized the structure of your website. Only then will you be able to create the perfect site map and choose the best ways to present the site map information in the navigation controls.

PART 4

Working with Data

CHAPTER 15

ADO.NET Fundamentals

At the beginning of this book, you learned that ASP.NET is just one component in Microsoft's ambitious .NET platform. As you know, .NET also includes new languages, a new philosophy for cross-language integration, an easier way to deploy code, and a toolkit of classes that allows you to do everything from handling errors to analyzing XML documents. In this chapter, you'll explore another one of the many features in the .NET Framework: the ADO.NET data access model.

Quite simply, ADO.NET is the technology that .NET applications use to interact with a database. In this chapter, you'll learn about ADO.NET and the family of objects that provides its functionality. You'll also learn how to put these objects to work by creating simple pages that retrieve and update database records. However, you won't learn about the *easiest* way to use ADO.NET—with the help of ASP.NET data binding. Although data binding is a powerful and practical feature, every ASP.NET developer should start with a solid grasp of ADO.NET fundamentals. That's because you'll need to write your own ADO.NET code to optimize performance-sensitive database routines, to perform data tasks that aren't covered by the data binding model, and to craft database components (as described in Chapter 23). Once you've mastered the basics of ADO.NET in this chapter, you'll be ready to explore the time-saving shortcuts of the data binding model in Chapter 16 and Chapter 17.

Understanding Data Management

Almost every piece of software ever written works with data. In fact, a typical web application is often just a thin user interface shell on top of sophisticated data-driven code that reads and writes information from a database. Often, website users aren't aware (or don't care) that the displayed information originates from a database. They just want to be able to search your product catalog, place an order, or check their payment records.

The Role of the Database

The most common way to manage data is to use a database. Database technology is particularly useful for business software, which typically requires sets of related information. For example, a typical database for a sales program consists of a list of customers, a list of products, and a list of sales that draws on information from the other two tables. This type of information is best described using a *relational model*, which is the philosophy that underlies all modern database products, including SQL Server, Oracle, and even Microsoft Access.

As you probably know, a relational model breaks information down to its smallest and most concise units. For example, a sales record doesn't store all the information about the products that were sold. Instead, it stores just a product ID that refers to a full record in a product table, as shown in Figure 15-1.

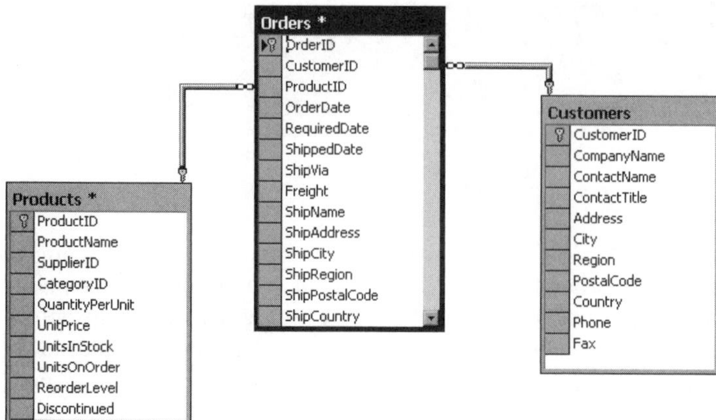

Figure 15-1. *Basic table relationships*

Although it's technically possible to organize data into tables and store it on the hard drive in one or more files (perhaps using a standard like XML), this approach wouldn't be very flexible. Instead, a web application needs a full *relational database management system* (RDBMS), such as SQL Server. The RDBMS handles the data infrastructure, ensuring optimum performance and reliability. For example, the RDBMS takes the responsibility of providing data to multiple users simultaneously, disallowing invalid data, and committing groups of actions at once using transactions.

In most ASP.NET applications, you'll need to use a database for some tasks. Here are some basic examples of data at work in a web application:

- E-commerce sites (like Amazon) use detailed databases to store product catalogs. They also track orders, customers, shipment records, and inventory information in a huge arrangement of related tables.
- Search engines (like Google) use databases to store indexes of page URLs, links, and keywords.
- Knowledge bases (like Microsoft Support) use less structured databases that store vast quantities of information or links to various documents and resources.
- Media sites (like The New York Times) store their articles in databases.

You probably won't have any trouble thinking about where you need to use database technology in an ASP.NET application. What web application couldn't benefit from a guest book that records user comments or a simple e-mail address submission form that uses a back-end database to store a list of potential customers or contacts? This is where ADO.NET comes into the picture. ADO.NET is a technology designed to let an ASP.NET program (or any other .NET program, for that matter) access data.

■ Tip If you're a complete database novice, you can get up to speed on essential database concepts using the video tutorials at `http://msdn.microsoft.com/vstudio/express/sql/learning`. There, you'll find over nine hours of instruction that describes how to use the free SQL Server 2005 Express Edition with Visual Studio. The tutorials move from absolute basics—covering topics such as database data types and table relationships—to more advanced subject matter such as full-text search, reporting services, and network security.

Database Access in the Web World

Accessing a database in a web application is a completely different scenario than accessing a database in a typical client-server desktop application. Most developers hone their database skills in the desktop world and run into serious problems when they try to apply what they have learned with stand-alone applications in the world of the Web. Quite simply, web applications raise two new considerations: problems of scale and problems of state.

Problems of *scale* are the problems that can result from the massively multiuser nature of the Web. A web application has the potential to be used by hundreds or thousands of simultaneous users. This means it can't be casual about using server memory or limited resources such as database connections. If you design an application that acquires a database connection and holds it for even a few extra seconds, other users may notice a definite slowdown. And if you don't carefully consider database concurrency issues (in other words, what happens when the changes from different users overlap), you can run into significant headaches, such as failed updates and inconsistent data.

■ Note Problems of scale can occur when developing traditional client-server desktop applications. The difference is that in most client-server applications they are far less likely to have any negative effect because the typical load (the number of simultaneous users) is dramatically lower. Database practices that might slightly hamper the performance of a client-server application can multiply rapidly and cause significant problems in a web application.

Problems of *state* are problems that can result from the disconnected nature of the Internet. As you already know, HTTP is a stateless protocol. When a user requests a page in an ASP.NET application, the web server processes the code, returns the rendered HTML, and closes the connection immediately. Although users may have the illusion that they are interacting with a continuously running application, they are really just receiving a string of static pages.

Because of the stateless nature of HTTP, web applications need to perform all their work in the space of a single request. The typical approach is to connect to a database, read information, display it, and then close the database connection. This approach runs into difficulties if you want the user to be able to modify the retrieved information. In this scenario, the application requires a certain amount of intelligence in order to be able to identify the original record, build a SQL statement to select it, and update it with the new values.

Fortunately, both ASP.NET and ADO.NET are designed with these challenges in mind. As you work your way through this chapter (and the following two chapters), you'll learn how to deal with databases safely and efficiently.

Configuring Your Database

Before you can run any data access code, you need a database server to take your command. Although there are dozens of good options, all of which work equally well with ADO.NET (and require essentially the same code), a significant majority of ASP.NET applications use Microsoft SQL Server.

This chapter includes code that works with SQL Server 7 or later, although you can easily adapt the code to work with other database products. Ideally you'll use SQL Server 2005 (with Service Pack 2) or SQL Server 2008. Microsoft is phasing out older versions, and they don't have support for Windows Vista and Windows Server 2008.

If you don't have a full version of SQL Server, there's no need to worry—you can simply install the free SQL Server Express Edition (as described in the next section). It includes all the database features you need to develop and test a web application.

■ **Note** This chapter (and the following two chapters) use examples drawn from the pubs and Northwind databases, which are sample databases included with some versions of Microsoft SQL Server. These databases aren't preinstalled in all versions of SQL Server, and they're noticeably absent from SQL Server 2005. However, you can easily install them using the scripts provided with the online samples. See the readme.txt file for full instructions.

SQL Server Express

If you don't have a test database server handy, you may want to use SQL Server 2005 Express Edition, the free data engine included with some versions of Visual Studio and downloadable separately.

SQL Server Express is a scaled-down version of SQL Server 2005 that's free to distribute. SQL Server Express has certain limitations—for example, it can use only one CPU and a maximum of 1GB of RAM; databases can't be larger than 4GB; and graphical tools aren't included. However, it's still remarkably powerful and suitable for many midscale websites. Even better, you can easily upgrade from SQL Server Express to a paid version of SQL Server if you need more features later. For more information about SQL Server 2005 Express or to download it, refer to `http://www.microsoft.com/sql/editions/express`.

Browsing and Modifying Databases in Visual Studio

As an ASP.NET developer, you may have the responsibility of creating the database required for a web application. Alternatively, it may already exist, or it may be the responsibility of a dedicated database administrator. If you're using a full version of SQL Server, you'll probably use a graphical tool such as SQL Server Management Studio to create and manage your databases.

■ **Tip** SQL Server Express doesn't include SQL Server Management Studio in the download that you use to install it. However, you can download it separately. Just search for "SQL Server Management Studio" in your favorite search engine or surf to `http://tinyurl.com/ynl9tv`.

If you don't have a suitable tool for managing your database, or you don't want to leave the comfort of Visual Studio, you can perform many of the same tasks using Visual Studio's Server Explorer window.

Here's how you can get started. First, choose View ➤ Server Explorer from the Visual Studio menu to show the Server Explorer window. Then, using the Data Connections node in the Server Explorer, you can connect to existing databases or create new ones. Assuming you've installed the pubs database (see the readme.txt file for instructions), you can create a connection to it by following these steps:

1. Right-click the Data Connections node, and choose Add Connection. If the Choose Data Source window appears, select Microsoft SQL Server and then click Continue.

2. If you're using a full version of SQL Server, enter **localhost** as your server name. This indicates the database server is the default instance on the local computer. (Replace this with the name of a remote computer if needed.) If you're using SQL Server Express, you'll need to use the server name **localhost\SQLEXPRESS** instead, as shown in Figure 15-2. The SQLEXPRESS part indicates that you're connecting to a *named instance* of SQL Server. By default, this is the way that SQL Server Express configures itself when you first install it.

3. Click Test Connection to verify that this is the location of your database. If you haven't installed a database product yet, this step will fail. Otherwise, you'll know that your database server is installed and running.

4. In the Select or Enter a Database Name list, choose the pubs database. (In order for this to work, the pubs database must already be installed. You can install it using the database script that's included with the sample code, as explained in the following section.) If you want to see more than one database in Visual Studio, you'll need to add more than one data connection.

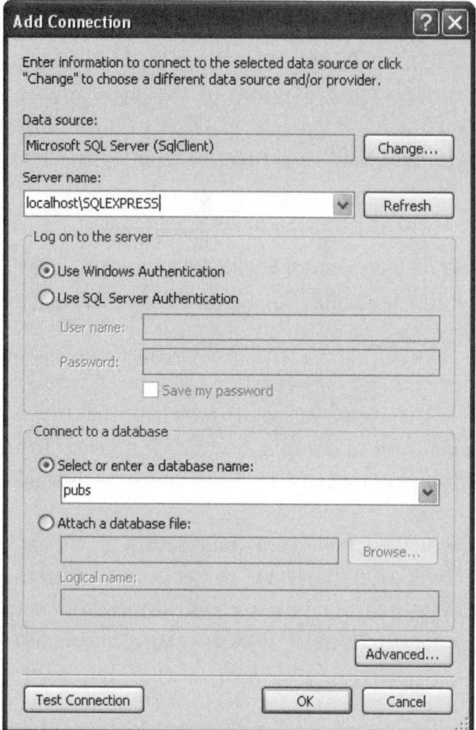

Figure 15-2. *Creating a connection in Visual Studio*

■ **Tip** Alternatively, you can choose to create a new database by right-clicking the Data Connections node and choosing Create New SQL Server Database.

---

5. Click OK. The database connection will appear in the Server Explorer window. You can now explore its groups to see and edit tables, stored procedures, and more. For example, if you right-click a table and choose Show Table Data, you'll see a grid of records that you can browse and edit, as shown in Figure 15-3.

■ **Tip** The Server Explorer window is particularly handy if you're using SQL Server Express Edition, which gives you the ability to place databases directly in the App_Data folder of your web application (instead of placing all your databases in a separate, dedicated location). If Visual Studio finds a database in the App_Data folder, it automatically adds a connection for it to the Data Connections group. To learn more about this feature, check out the "User Instance Connections" section later in this chapter.

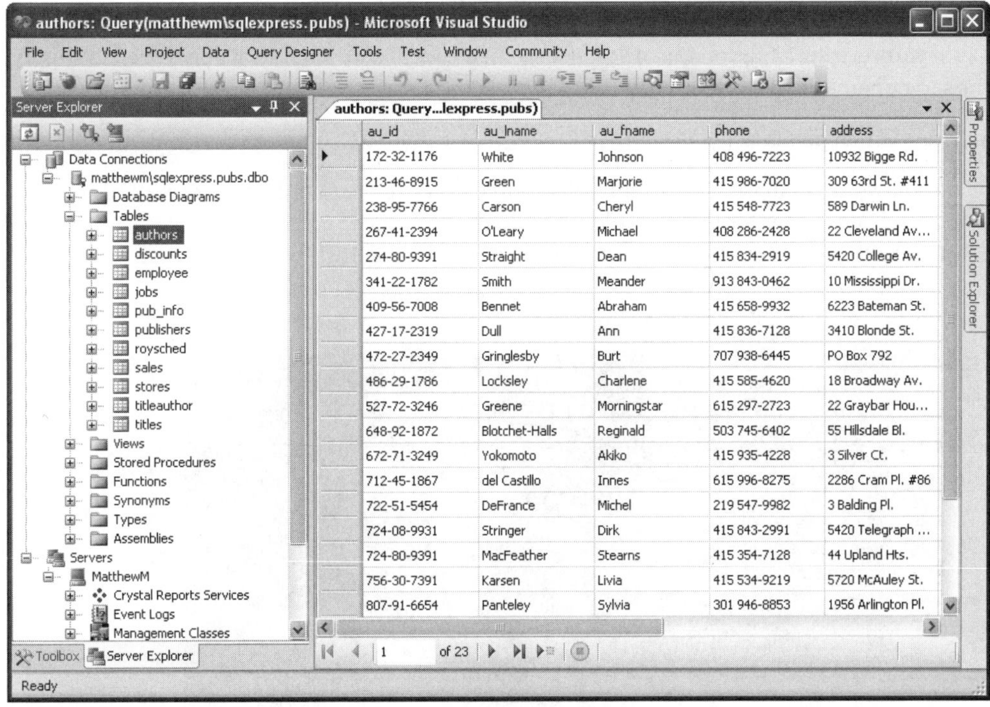

Figure 15-3. *Editing table data in Visual Studio*

The sqlcmd Command-Line Tool

SQL Server 2005 (and 2008) include a handy command-line tool named sqlcmd.exe that you can use to perform database tasks from a Windows command prompt. Compared to a management tool like SQL Server Management Studio, sqlcmd doesn't offer many frills. It's just a quick-and-dirty way to perform a database task. Often, sqlcmd is used in a batch file—for example, to create database tables as part of an automated setup process.

The sqlcmd tool is installed as part of SQL Server 2005 (and 2008), and it's found in a directory like c:\Program Files\Microsoft SQL Server\90\Tools\Binn. The easiest way to run sqlcmd is to launch the Visual Studio command prompt (open the Start menu and choose Programs ➤ Microsoft Visual Studio 2008 ➤ Visual Studio Tools ➤ Visual Studio 2008 Command Prompt). This opens a command window that has the SQL Server directory set in the path variable. As a result, you can use sqlcmd anywhere you want, without typing its full directory path.

When running sqlcmd, it's up to you to supply the right parameters. To see all the possible parameters, type this command:

```
sqlcmd -?
```

Two commonly used sqlcmd parameters are –S (which specifies the location of your database server) and –i (which supplies a script file with SQL commands that you want to run). For example, the downloadable code samples include a file named InstPubs.sql that contains the commands you need to create the pubs database and fill it with sample data. If you're using SQL Server Express, you can run the InstPubs.sql script using this command:

```
sqlcmd -S localhost\SQLEXPRESS -i InstPubs.sql
```

If you're using a full version of SQL Server on the local computer, you don't need to supply the server name at all:

```
sqlcmd -i InstPubs.sql
```

And if your database is on another computer, you need to supply that computer's name with the –S parameter (or just run sqlcmd on that computer).

Figure 15-4 shows the feedback you'll get when you run InstPubs.sql with sqlcmd.

```
Visual Studio 2005 Command Prompt

D:\Code\Beginning ASP.NET 2.0>sqlcmd -i InstPubs.sql
Changed database context to 'master'.
Beginning InstPubs.SQL at 10 Jul 2007 20:55:44:637 ....
Creating pubs database....
Changed database context to 'pubs'.
Now at the create table section ....
Now at the create trigger section ...
Now at the inserts to authors ....
Now at the inserts to publishers ....
Now at the inserts to pub_info ....
Now at the inserts to titles ....
Now at the inserts to titleauthor ....
Now at the inserts to stores ....
Now at the inserts to sales ....
Now at the inserts to roysched ....
Now at the inserts to discounts ....
Now at the inserts to jobs ....
Now at the inserts to employee ....
Now at the create index section ....
Now at the create view section ....
Now at the create procedure section ....
Changed database context to 'master'.
Ending InstPubs.SQL at 10 Jul 2007 20:55:49:463 ....

D:\Code\Beginning ASP.NET 2.0>
```

Figure 15-4. *Running a SQL script with sqlcmd.exe*

In this book, you'll occasionally see instructions about using sqlcmd to perform some sort of database configuration. However, you can usually achieve the same result (with a bit more clicking) using the graphical interface in a tool like SQL Server Management Studio. For example, to install a database by running a SQL script, you simply need to start SQL Server Management Studio, open the SQL file (using the File ➤ Open ➤ File command), and then run it (using the Query ➤ Execute command).

SQL Basics

When you interact with a data source through ADO.NET, you use SQL to retrieve, modify, and update information. In some cases, ADO.NET will hide some of the details for you or even generate required SQL statements automatically. However, to design an efficient database application with a minimal amount of frustration, you need to understand the basic concepts of SQL.

SQL (Structured Query Language) is a standard data access language used to interact with relational databases. Different databases differ in their support of SQL or add other features, but the core commands used to select, add, and modify data are common. In a database product such as SQL Server, it's possible to use SQL to create fairly sophisticated SQL scripts for stored procedures and triggers (although they have little of the power of a full object-oriented programming language). When working with ADO.NET, however, you'll probably use only the following standard types of SQL statements:

- A Select statement retrieves records.
- An Update statement modifies existing records.
- An Insert statement adds a new record.
- A Delete statement deletes existing records.

If you already have a good understanding of SQL, you can skip the next few sections. Otherwise, read on for a quick tour of SQL fundamentals.

■ **Tip** To learn more about SQL, use one of the SQL tutorials available on the Internet, such as the one at `http://www.w3schools.com/sql`. If you're working with SQL Server, you can use its thorough Books Online help to become a database guru.

Running Queries in Visual Studio

If you've never used SQL before, you may want to play around with it and create some sample queries before you start using it in an ASP.NET site. Most database products provide some sort of tool for testing queries. If you're using a full version of SQL Server, you can try SQL Server Management Studio or SQL Query Analyzer. If you don't want to use an extra tool, you can run your queries using the Server Explorer window described earlier. Just follow these steps in Visual Studio:

1. Right-click your connection, and choose New Query.
2. Choose the table (or tables) you want to use in your query from the Add Table dialog box (as shown in Figure 15-5), click Add, and then click Close.

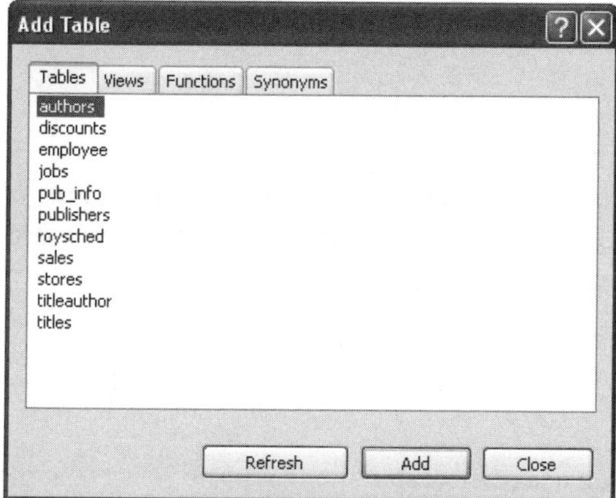

Figure 15-5. *Adding tables to a query*

3. You'll now see a handy query-building window. You can create your query by adding check marks next to the fields you want, or you can edit the SQL by hand in the lower portion of the window. Best of all, if you edit the SQL directly, you can type in anything—you don't need to stick to the tables you selected in step 2, and you don't need to restrict yourself to Select statements.

4. When you're ready to run the query, select Query Designer ➤ Execute SQL from the menu. Assuming your query doesn't have any errors, you'll get one of two results. If you're selecting records, the results will appear at the bottom of the window (see Figure 15-6). If you're deleting or updating records, a message box will appear informing you how many records were affected.

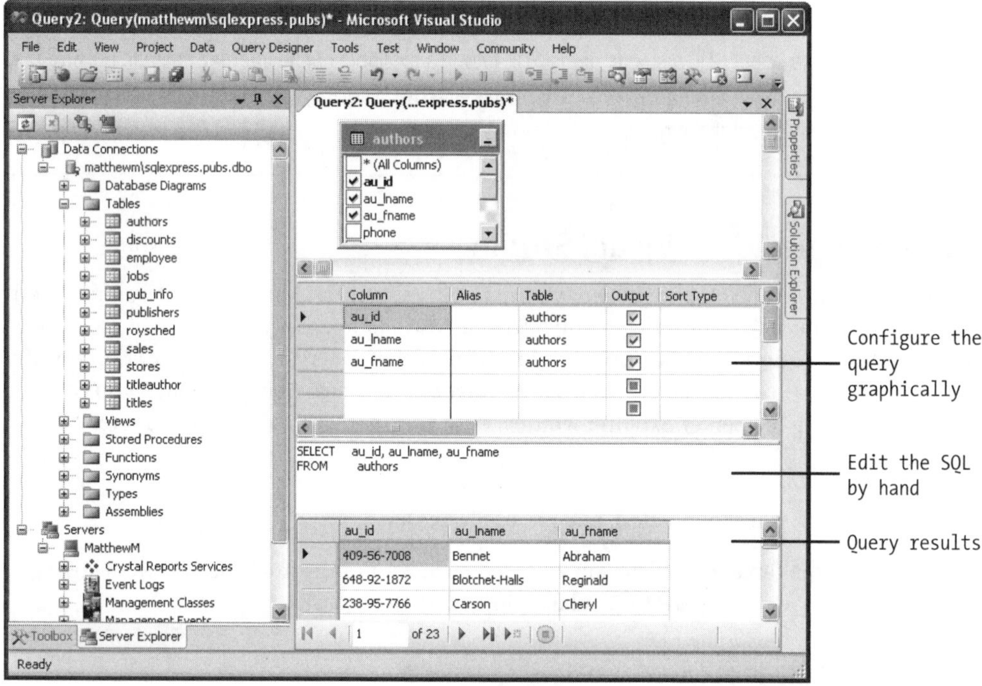

Figure 15-6. *Executing a query*

■ **Tip** When programming with ADO.NET, it always helps to know your database. If you have information on hand about the data types it uses, the stored procedures it provides, and the user account you need to use, you'll be able to work more quickly and with less chance of error.

The Select Statement

To retrieve one or more rows of data, you use a Select statement. A basic Select statement has the following structure:

```
SELECT [columns] FROM [tables] WHERE [search_condition]
       ORDER BY [order_expression ASC | DESC]
```

This format really just scratches the surface of SQL. If you want, you can create more sophisticated queries that use subgrouping, averaging and totaling, and other options (such as setting a maximum number of returned rows). By performing this work in a query (instead of in your application), you can often create far more efficient applications.

The next few sections present sample Select statements. After each example, a series of bulleted points breaks the SQL down to explain how each part of it works.

A Sample Select Statement

The following is a typical (and rather inefficient) Select statement for the pubs database. It works with the Authors table, which contains a list of authors:

```
SELECT * FROM Authors
```

- The asterisk (*) retrieves all the columns in the table. This isn't the best approach for a large table if you don't need all the information. It increases the amount of data that has to be transferred and can slow down your server.
- The From clause identifies that the Authors table is being used for this statement.
- The statement doesn't have a Where clause. This means all the records will be retrieved from the database, regardless of whether it has 10 or 10 million records. This is a poor design practice, because it often leads to applications that appear to work fine when they're first deployed but gradually slow down as the database grows. In general, you should always include a Where clause to limit the possible number of rows (unless you absolutely need them all). Often, queries are limited by a date field (for example, including all orders that were placed in the last three months).
- The statement doesn't have an Order By clause. This is a perfectly acceptable approach, especially if order doesn't matter or you plan to sort the data on your own using the tools provided in ADO.NET.

Improving the Select Statement

Here's another example that retrieves a list of author names:

```
SELECT au_lname, au_fname FROM Authors WHERE State='CA' ORDER BY au_lname ASC
```

- Only two columns are retrieved (au_lname and au_fname). They correspond to the first and last names of the author.
- A Where clause restricts results to those authors who live in the specified state (California). Note that the Where clause requires apostrophes around the value you want to match, because it's a text value.
- An Order By clause sorts the information alphabetically by the author's last name.

An Alternative Select Statement

Here's one last example:

```
SELECT TOP 100 * FROM Sales ORDER BY ord_date DESC
```

This example uses the Top clause instead of a Where statement. The database rows will be sorted by order date, and the first 100 matching results will be retrieved. In this case, it's the 100 most recent orders. You could also use this type of statement to find the most expensive items you sell or the best-performing employees.

The Where Clause

In many respects, the Where clause is the most important part of the Select statement. You can combine multiple conditions with the And keyword, and you can specify greater-than and less-than comparisons by using the greater-than (>) and less-than (<) operators.

The following is an example with a different table and a more sophisticated Where statement:

```
SELECT * FROM Sales WHERE ord_date < '2000/01/01' AND ord_date > '1987/01/01'
```

This example uses the international date format to compare date values. Although SQL Server supports many date formats, yyyy/mm/dd is recommended to prevent ambiguity.

If you were using Microsoft Access, you would need to use the U.S. date format, mm/dd/yyyy, and replace the apostrophes around the date with the number (#) symbol.

String Matching with the Like Operator

The Like operator allows you to perform partial string matching to filter records where a particular field starts with, ends with, or contains a certain set of characters. For example, if you want to see all store names that start with *B*, you could use the following statement:

```
SELECT * FROM Stores WHERE stor_name LIKE 'B%'
```

To see a list of all stores *ending* with *B*, you would put the percent sign *before* the *B*, like this:

```
SELECT * FROM Stores WHERE stor_name LIKE '%B'
```

The third way to use the Like operator is to return any records that contain a certain character or sequence of characters. For example, suppose you want to see all stores that have the word *book* somewhere in the name. In this case, you could use a SQL statement like this:

```
SELECT * FROM Stores WHERE stor_name LIKE '%book%'
```

By default, SQL is not case sensitive, so this syntax finds instances of *BOOK*, *book*, or any variation of mixed case.

Finally, you can indicate one of a set of characters, rather than just any character, by listing the allowed characters within square brackets. Here's an example:

```
SELECT * FROM Stores WHERE stor_name LIKE '[abcd]%'
```

This SQL statement will return stores with names starting with *A*, *B*, *C*, or *D*.

Aggregate Queries

The SQL language also defines special *aggregate functions*. Aggregate functions work with a set of values but return only a single value. For example, you can use an aggregate function to count the number of records in a table or to calculate the average price of a product. Table 15-1 lists the most commonly used aggregate functions.

Table 15-1. *SQL Aggregate Functions*

Function	Description
Avg(fieldname)	Calculates the average of all values in a given numeric field
Sum(fieldname)	Calculates the sum of all values in a given numeric field
Min(fieldname) and Max(fieldname)	Finds the minimum or maximum value in a number field
Count(*)	Returns the number of rows in the result set
Count(DISTINCT fieldname)	Returns the number of unique (and non-null) rows in the result set for the specified field

For example, here's a query that returns a single value—the number of records in the Authors table:

```
SELECT COUNT(*) FROM Authors
```

And here's how you could calculate the total quantity of all sales by adding together the qty field in each record:

```
SELECT SUM(qty) FROM Sales
```

The SQL Update Statement

The SQL Update statement selects all the records that match a specified search expression and then modifies them all according to an update expression. At its simplest, the Update statement has the following format:

```
UPDATE [table] SET [update_expression] WHERE [search_condition]
```

Typically, you'll use an Update statement to modify a single record. The following example adjusts the phone column in a single author record. It uses the unique author ID to find the correct row.

```
UPDATE Authors SET phone='408 496-2222' WHERE au_id='172-32-1176'
```

This statement returns the number of affected rows. (See Figure 15-7 for an example in Visual Studio.) However, it won't display the change. To do that, you need to request the row by performing another Select statement:

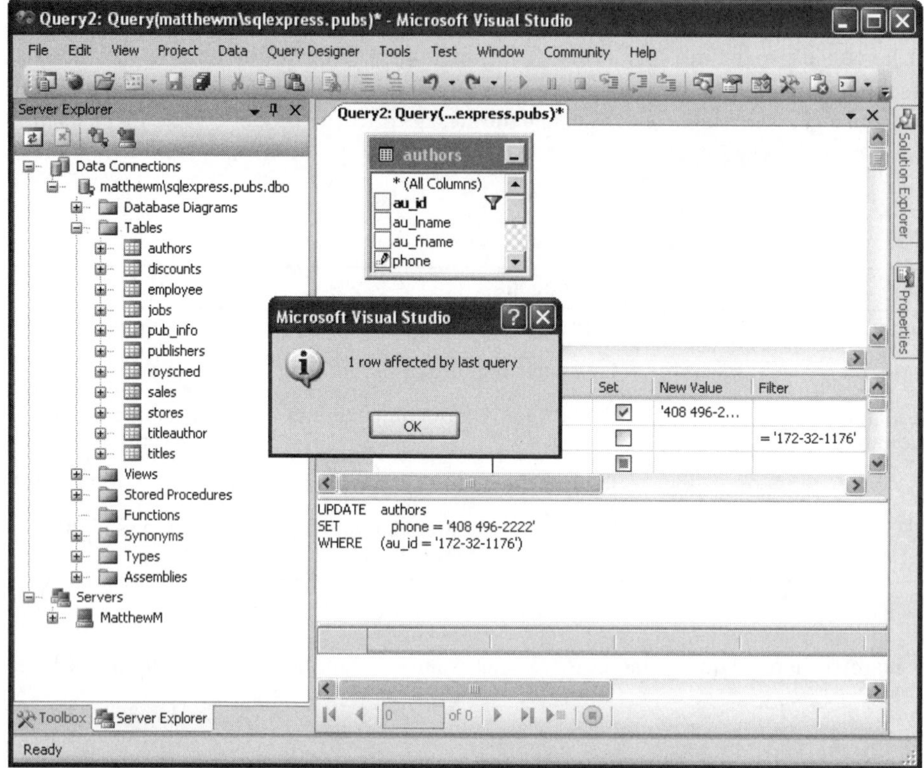

Figure 15-7. *Executing an update query in Visual Studio*

```
SELECT phone FROM Authors WHERE au_id='172-32-1176'
```

As with a Select statement, you can use an Update statement with several criteria:

```
UPDATE Authors SET au_lname='Whiteson', au_fname='John'
    WHERE au_lname='White' AND au_fname='Johnson'
```

You can even use the Update statement to update an entire range of matching records. The following example increases the price of every book in the Titles table that was published in 1991 by one dollar:

```
UPDATE Titles SET price=price+1
    WHERE pubdate >= '1991/01/01' AND pubdate < '1992/01/01'
```

The SQL Insert Statement

The SQL Insert statement adds a new record to a table with the information you specify. It takes the following form:

```
INSERT INTO [table] ([column_list]) VALUES ([value_list])
```

You can provide the information in any order you want, as long as you make sure the list of column names and the list of values correspond exactly:

```
INSERT INTO Authors (au_id, au_lname, au_fname, zip, contract)
      VALUES ('998-72-3566', 'Khan', 'John', 84152, 0)
```

This example leaves out some information, such as the city and address, in order to provide a simple example. However, it provides the minimum information that's required to create a new record in the Authors table.

Remember, database tables often have requirements that can prevent you from adding a record unless you fill in all the fields with valid information. Alternatively, some fields may be configured to use a default value if left blank. In the Authors table, some fields are required, and a special format is defined for the ZIP code and author ID.

One feature the Authors table doesn't use is an automatically incrementing identity field. This feature, which is supported in most relational database products, assigns a unique value to a specified field when you perform an insert operation. When you insert a record into a table that has a unique incrementing ID, you shouldn't specify a value for the ID. Instead, allow the database to choose one automatically.

AUTO-INCREMENT FIELDS ARE INDISPENSABLE

If you're designing a database, make sure you add an auto-incrementing identity field to every table. It's the fastest, easiest, and least error-prone way to assign a unique identification number to every record. Without an automatically generated identity field, you'll need to go to considerable effort to create and maintain your own unique field. Often programmers fall into the trap of using a data field for a unique identifier, such as a Social Security number (SSN) or a name. This almost always leads to trouble at some inconvenient time far in the future, when you need to add a person who doesn't have an SSN (for example, a foreign national) or you need to account for an SSN or a name change (which will cause problems for other related tables, such as a purchase order table that identifies the purchaser by the name or SSN field). A much better approach is to use a unique identifier and have the database engine assign an arbitrary unique number to every row automatically.

If you create a table without a unique identification column, you'll have trouble when you need to select that specific row for deletion or updates. Selecting records based on a text field can also lead to problems if the field contains special embedded characters (such as apostrophes). You'll also find it extremely awkward to create table relationships.

The SQL Delete Statement

The Delete statement is even easier to use. It specifies criteria for one or more rows that you want to remove. Be careful: once you delete a row, it's gone for good!

```
DELETE FROM [table] WHERE [search_condition]
```

The following example removes a single matching row from the Authors table:

```
DELETE FROM Authors WHERE au_id='172-32-1176'
```

■ **Note** If you attempt to run this specific Delete statement, you'll run into a database error. The problem is that this author record is linked to one or more records in the TitleAuthor table. The author record can't be removed unless the linked records are deleted first. (After all, it wouldn't make sense to have a book linked to an author that doesn't exist.)

The Delete and Update commands return a single piece of information: the number of affected records. You can examine this value and use it to determine whether the operation is successful or executed as expected.

The rest of this chapter shows how you can combine SQL with the ADO.NET objects to retrieve and manipulate data in your web applications.

ADO.NET Basics

ADO.NET relies on the functionality in a small set of core classes. You can divide these classes into two groups: those that are used to contain and manage data (such as DataSet, DataTable, DataRow, and DataRelation) and those that are used to connect to a specific data source (such as Connection, Command, and DataReader).

The data container classes are completely generic. No matter what data source you use, once you extract the data, it's stored using the same data container: the specialized DataSet class. Think of the DataSet as playing the same role as a collection or an array—it's a package for data. The difference is that the DataSet is customized for relational data, which means it understands concepts such as rows, columns, and table relationships natively.

The second group of classes exists in several different flavors. Each set of data interaction classes is called an ADO.NET *data provider*. Data providers are customized so that each one uses the best-performing way of interacting with its data source. For example, the SQL Server data provider is designed to work with SQL Server 7 or later. Internally, it uses SQL Server's TDS (tabular data stream) protocol for communicating, thus guaranteeing the best possible performance. If you're using Oracle, you'll need to use the Oracle provider classes instead.

It's important to understand that you can use any data provider in almost the same way, with almost the same code. The provider classes derive from the same base classes, implement the same interfaces, and expose the same set of methods and properties. In some cases, a data provider object will provide custom functionality that's available only with certain data sources, such as SQL Server's ability to perform XML queries. However, the basic members used for retrieving and modifying data are identical.

.NET includes the following four providers:

- *SQL Server provider*: Provides optimized access to a SQL Server database (version 7.0 or later)
- *OLE DB provider*: Provides access to any data source that has an OLE DB driver
- *Oracle provider*: Provides optimized access to an Oracle database (version 8i or later)
- *ODBC provider*: Provides access to any data source that has an ODBC (Open Database Connectivity) driver

In addition, third-party developers and database vendors have released their own ADO.NET providers, which follow the same conventions and can be used in the same way as those that are included with the .NET Framework.

When choosing a provider, you should first try to find one that's customized for your data source. If you can't find a suitable provider, you can use the OLE DB provider, as long as you have an OLE DB driver for your data source. The OLE DB technology has been around for many years as part of ADO, so most data sources provide an OLE DB driver (including SQL Server, Oracle, Access, MySQL, and many more). In the rare situation that you can't find a full provider or an OLE DB driver, you can fall back on the ODBC provider, which works in conjunction with an ODBC driver.

■ **Tip** Microsoft includes the OLE DB provider with ADO.NET so you can use your existing OLE DB drivers. However, if you can find a provider that's customized specifically for your data source, you should use it instead. For example, you can connect to SQL Server database using either the SQL Server provider or the OLE DB provider, but the first approach will perform best.

To help understand the different layers that come into play with ADO.NET, refer to Figure 15-8.

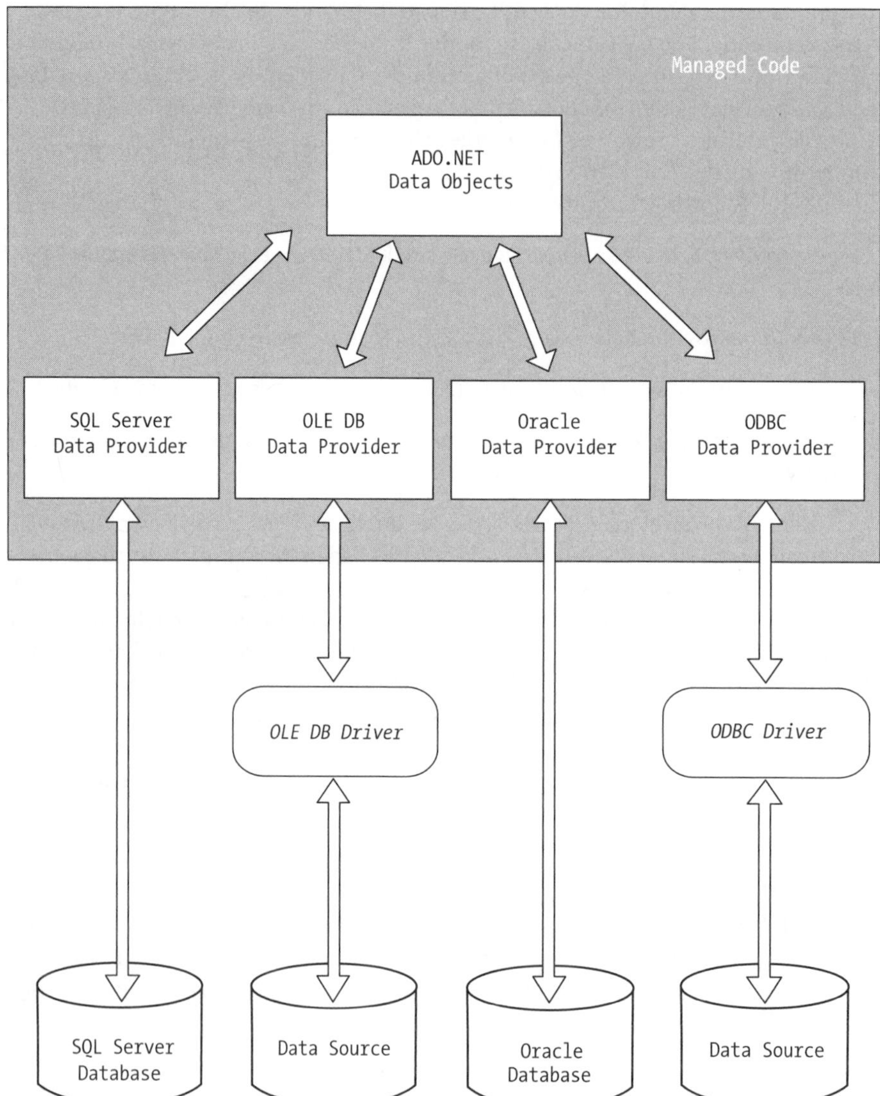

Figure 15-8. *The layers between your code and the data source*

Data Namespaces

The ADO.NET components live in several different namespaces in the .NET class library. Together, these namespaces hold all the functionality of ADO.NET. Table 15-2 describes each data namespace.

Table 15-2. *ADO.NET Namespaces*

Namespace	Purpose
System.Data	Contains fundamental classes with the core ADO.NET functionality. This includes DataSet and DataRelation, which allow you to manipulate structured relational data. These classes are totally independent of any specific type of database or the way you connect to it.
System.Data.Common	Not used directly in your code. These classes are used by other data provider classes that inherit from them and provide versions customized for a specific data source.
System.Data.OleDb	Contains the classes you use to connect to an OLE DB data source and execute commands, including OleDbConnection and OleDbCommand.
System.Data.SqlClient	Contains the classes you use to connect to a Microsoft SQL Server database (version 7.0 or later) and execute commands. These classes, such as SqlCommand and SqlConnection, provide all the same properties and methods as their counterparts in the System.Data.OleDb namespace. The only difference is that they are optimized for SQL Server and provide better performance by eliminating the extra OLE DB layer (and by connecting directly to the optimized TDS interface).
System.Data.SqlTypes	Contains structures for SQL Server–specific data types such as SqlMoney and SqlDateTime. You can use these types to work with SQL Server data types without needing to convert them into the standard .NET equivalents (such as System.Decimal and System.DateTime). These types aren't required, but they do allow you to avoid any potential rounding or conversion problems that could adversely affect data.
System.Data.OracleClient	Contains the classes you use to connect to an Oracle database and execute commands, such as OracleConnection and OracleCommand.
System.Data.Odbc	Contains the classes you use to connect to a data source through an ODBC driver and execute commands. These classes include OdbcConnection and OdbcCommand.

The Data Provider Classes

On their own, the data classes can't accomplish much. Technically, you could create data objects by hand, build tables and rows in your code, and fill them with information. But in most cases, the information you need is located in a data source such as a relational database. To access this information, extract it, and insert it into the appropriate data objects, you need the data provider classes described in this section. Remember, each one of these classes has a database-specific implementation. That means you use a different, but essentially equivalent, object depending on whether you're interacting with SQL Server, Oracle, or any other ADO.NET provider.

Regardless of which provider you use, your code will look almost the same. Often the only differences will be the namespace that's used and the name of the ADO.NET data access classes (as listed in Table 15-3).

Each provider designates its own prefix for naming classes. Thus, the SQL Server provider includes SqlConnection and SqlCommand classes, and the Oracle provider includes OracleConnection and OracleCommand classes. Internally, these classes work quite differently, because they need to connect to different databases using different low-level protocols. Externally, however, these classes look quite similar and provide an identical set of basic methods because they implement the same common interfaces. This means your application is shielded from the complexity of different standards and can use the SQL Server provider in the same way the Oracle provider uses it. In fact, you can often translate a block of code for interacting with a SQL Server database into a block of Oracle-specific code just by editing the class names in your code.

Table 15-3. *The ADO.NET Data Provider Classes*

	SQL Server Data Provider	OLE DB Data Provider	Oracle Data Provider	ODBC Data Provider
Connection	SqlConnection	OleDbConnection	OracleConnection	OdbcConnection
Command	SqlCommand	OleDbCommand	OracleCommand	OdbcCommand
DataReader	SqlDataReader	OleDbDataReader	OracleDataReader	OdbcDataReader
DataAdapter	SqlDataAdapter	OleDbDataAdapter	OracleDataAdapter	OdbcDataAdapter

Remember, though the underlying technical details differ, the classes are almost identical. The only real differences are as follows:

- The names of the Connection, Command, DataReader, and DataAdapter classes are different in order to help you distinguish them.
- The connection string (the information you use to connect to the database) differs depending on what data source you're using, where it's located, and what type of security you're using.
- Occasionally, a provider may choose to add features, such as methods for specific features or classes to represent specific data types. For example, the SQL Server Command class includes a method for executing XML queries that aren't part of the SQL standard. In this chapter, you'll focus on the standard functionality, which is shared by all providers and used for the majority of data access operations.

In the rest of this chapter, you'll consider how to write web page code that uses these objects. First, you'll consider the most straightforward approach—direct data access. Then, you'll consider disconnected data access, which allows you to retrieve data in the DataSet and cache it for longer periods of time. Both approaches complement each other, and in most web applications you'll use a combination of the two.

Direct Data Access

The easiest way to interact with a database is to use direct data access. When you use direct data access, you're in charge of building a SQL command (like the ones you considered earlier in this chapter) and executing it. You use commands to query, insert, update, and delete information.

When you query data with direct data access, you don't keep a copy of the information in memory. Instead, you work with it for a brief period of time while the database connection is open, and then close the connection as soon as possible. This is different than disconnected data access, where you keep a copy of the data in the DataSet object so you can work with it after the database connection has been closed.

The direct data model is well suited to ASP.NET web pages, which don't need to keep a copy of their data in memory for long periods of time. Remember, an ASP.NET web page is loaded when the page is requested and shut down as soon as the response is returned to the user. That means a page typically has a lifetime of only a few seconds (if that).

■ **Note** Although ASP.NET web pages don't need to store data in memory for ordinary data management tasks, they just might use this technique to optimize performance. For example, you could get the product catalog from a database once, and keep that data in memory on the web server so you can reuse it when someone else requests the same page. This technique is called *caching*, and you'll learn to use it in Chapter 24.

To query information with simple data access, follow these steps:

1. Create Connection, Command, and DataReader objects.
2. Use the DataReader to retrieve information from the database, and display it in a control on a web form.
3. Close your connection.
4. Send the page to the user. At this point, the information your user sees and the information in the database no longer have any connection, and all the ADO.NET objects have been destroyed.

To add or update information, follow these steps:

1. Create new Connection and Command objects.
2. Execute the Command (with the appropriate SQL statement).

This chapter demonstrates both of these approaches. Figure 15-9 shows a high-level look at how the ADO.NET objects interact to make direct data access work.

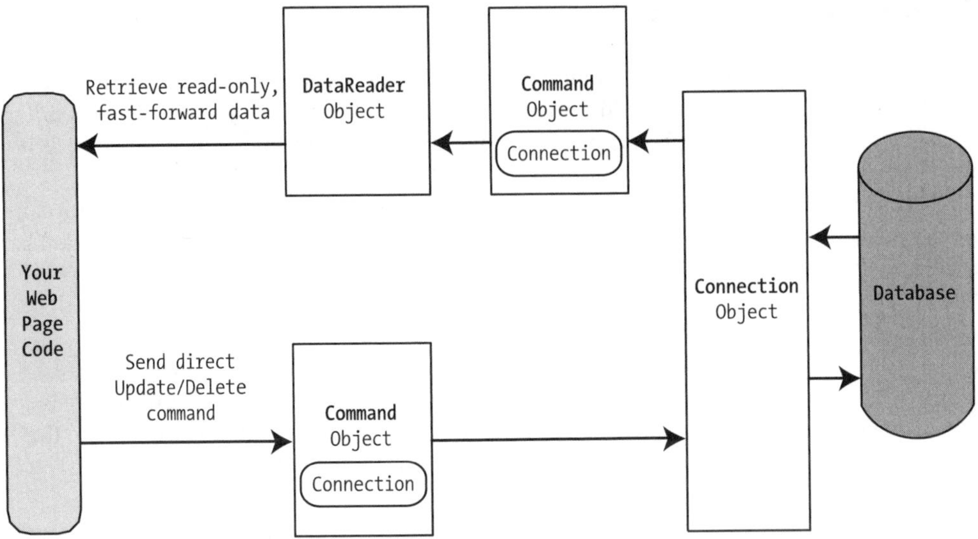

Figure 15-9. *Direct data access with ADO.NET*

Before continuing, make sure you import the ADO.NET namespaces. In this chapter, we assume you're using the SQL Server provider, in which case you need these two namespace imports:

```
Imports System.Data
Imports System.Data.SqlClient
```

Creating a Connection

Before you can retrieve or update data, you need to make a connection to the data source. Generally, connections are limited to some fixed number, and if you exceed that number (either because you run out of licenses or because your database server can't accommodate the user load), attempts to create new connections will fail. For that reason, you should try to hold a connection open for as short a time as possible. You should also write your database code inside a Try/Catch error-handling structure so you can respond if an error does occur, and make sure you close the connection even if you can't perform all your work.

When creating a Connection object, you need to specify a value for its ConnectionString property. This ConnectionString defines all the information the computer needs to find the data source, log in, and choose an initial database. Out of all the details in the examples in this chapter, the ConnectionString is the one value you might have to tweak before it works for the database you want to use. Luckily, it's quite straightforward. Here's an example that uses a connection string to connect to SQL Server through the OLE DB provider:

```
Dim myConnection As New OleDbConnection()
myConnection.ConnectionString = "Provider=SQLOLEDB.1;Data Source=localhost;" & _
  "Initial Catalog=Pubs;Integrated Security=SSPI"
```

For optimum performance, you should use the SqlConnection object from the SQL Server provider instead. The connection string for the SqlConnection object is quite similar and just omits the Provider setting:

```
Dim myConnection As New SqlConnection()
myConnection.ConnectionString = "Data Source=localhost;" & _
 "Initial Catalog=Pubs;Integrated Security=SSPI"
```

If you're using SQL Server 2005 Express Edition, your connection string will include an instance name, as shown here:

```
Dim myConnection As New SqlConnection()
myConnection.ConnectionString = "Data Source=localhost\SQLEXPRESS;" & _
 "Initial Catalog=Pubs;Integrated Security=SSPI"
```

The Connection String

The connection string is actually a series of distinct pieces of information separated by semicolons (;). Each separate piece of information is known as a connection string property.

The following list describes some of the most commonly used connection string properties, including the three properties used in the preceding example:

Data source: This indicates the name of the server where the data source is located. If the server is on the same computer that hosts the ASP.NET site, localhost is sufficient. The only exception is if you're using a named instance of SQL Server. For example, if you've installed SQL Server 2005 Express Edition, you'll need to use the data source localhost\SQLEXPRESS, because the instance name is SQLEXPRESS. You'll also see this written with a period, as .\SQLEXPRESS, which is equivalent.

Initial catalog: This is the name of the database that this connection will be accessing. It's only the "initial" database because you can change it later by using the Connection.ChangeDatabase() method.

Integrated security: This indicates you want to connect to SQL Server using the Windows user account that's running the web page code, provided you supply a value of SSPI (which stands for Security Support Provider Interface). Alternatively, you can supply a user ID and password that's defined in the database for SQL Server authentication, although this method is less secure and generally discouraged.

ConnectionTimeout: This determines how long your code will wait, in seconds, before generating an error if it cannot establish a database connection. Our example connection string doesn't set the ConnectionTimeout, so the default of 15 seconds is used. You can use 0 to specify no limit, but this is a bad idea. This means that, theoretically, the code could be held up indefinitely while it attempts to contact the server.

You can set some other, lesser-used options for a connection string. For more information, refer to the Visual Studio Help. Look under the appropriate Connection class (such as SqlConnection or OleDbConnection) because there are subtle differences in connection string properties for each type of Connection class.

Windows Authentication

The previous example uses *integrated Windows authentication*, which is the default security standard for new SQL Server installations. You can also use *SQL Server authentication*. In this case, you will explicitly place the user ID and password information in the connection string. However, SQL Server authentication is disabled by default in SQL Server 2000 and later versions, because it's not considered to be as secure.

Here's the lowdown on both types of authentication:

- With SQL Server authentication, SQL Server maintains its own user account information in the database. It uses this information to determine whether you are allowed to access specific parts of a database.
- With integrated Windows authentication, SQL Server automatically uses the Windows account information for the currently logged-in process. In the database, it stores information about what database privileges each user should have.

■ **Tip** You can set what type of authentication your SQL Server uses using a tool such as SQL Server Management Studio. Just right-click your server in the tree, and select Properties. Choose the Security tab to change the type of authentication. You can choose either Windows Only (for the tightest security) or SQL Server and Windows, which allows both Windows authentication and SQL Server authentication. This option is also known as *mixed-mode authentication*.

For Windows authentication to work, the currently logged-on Windows user must have the required authorization to access the SQL database. This isn't a problem while you test your websites, because Visual Studio launches your web applications using your user account. However, when you deploy your application to a web server running IIS, you might run into trouble. In this situation, all ASP.NET code is run by a more limited user account that might not have the rights to access the database. By default, that account is an automatically created account named ASPNET (for IIS 5.1), or the network service account (for later versions of IIS). You need to grant database access to this account, or your web pages will receive a security error whenever they try to connect to the database.

■ **Note** If you're running IIS 5.1 (the version that's included with Windows XP), you need to give database access to the ASPNET user. If you're running IIS 6 (the version that's included with Windows Server 2003), you need to give access to the IIS_WPG group. If you're running IIS 7 (the version that's included with Windows Vista and Windows Server 2008), you need to give access to the IIS_USERS group. Chapter 9 has the full details.

User Instance Connections

Every database server stores a master list of all the databases that you've installed on it. This list includes the name of each database and the location of the files that hold the data. When you create a database (for example, by running a script or using a management tool), the information about that database is added to the master list. When you connect to the database, you specify the database name using the Initial Catalog value in the connection string.

■ **Note** If you haven't made any changes to your database configuration, SQL Server will quietly tuck the files for newly created databases into a directory like c:\Program Files\Microsoft SQL Server\MSSQL.1\MSSQL\Data. Each database has at least two files—an .mdf file with the actual data and an .ldf file that stores the database log. Of course, database professionals have a variety of techniques and tricks for managing database storage, and can easily store databases in different locations, create multiple data files, and so on. The important detail to realize is that ordinarily your database files are stored by your database server, and they aren't a part of your web application directory.

Interestingly, SQL Server Express has a feature that lets you bypass the master list and connect directly to any database file, even if it's not in the master list of databases. This feature is called *user instances*. Oddly enough, this feature isn't available in the full edition of SQL Server 2005.

To use this feature, you need to set the User Instances value to True (in the connection string) and supply the file name of the database you want to connect to with the AttachDBFilename value. You don't supply an Initial Catalog value.

Here's an example connection string that uses this approach:

```
myConnection.ConnectionString = "Data Source=localhost\SQLEXPRESS;" & _
  "AttachDBFilename=|DataDirectory|\Northwind.mdf;Integrated Security=True"
```

There's another trick here. The file name starts with |DataDirectory|. This automatically points to the App_Data folder inside your web application directory. This way, you don't need to supply a full file path, which might not remain valid when you move the web application to a web server. Instead, ADO.NET will always look in the App_Data directory for a file named Northwind.mdf.

User instances is a handy feature if you have a web server that hosts many different web applications that use databases and these databases are frequently being added and removed. However, because the database isn't in the master list, you won't see it in any administrative tools (although most administrative tools will still let you connect to it manually, by pointing out the right file location). But remember, this quirky but interesting feature is available in SQL Server Express only—you won't find it in the full version of SQL Server 2005.

VISUAL STUDIO'S SUPPORT FOR USER INSTANCE DATABASES

Visual Studio provides two handy features that make it easier to work with databases in the App_Data folder.

First, Visual Studio gives you a nearly effortless way to create new databases. Simply choose Website ➤ Add New Item. Then, pick SQL Server Database from the list of templates, choose a file name for your database, and click OK. The .mdf and .ldf files for the new database will be placed in the App_Data folder, and you'll see them in the Solution Explorer. Initially, they'll be blank, so you'll need to add the tables you want. (The easiest way to do this is to right-click the Tables group in the Server Explorer, and choose Add Table.)

Visual Studio also simplifies your life with its automatic Server Explorer support. When you open a web application, Visual Studio automatically adds a data connection to the Server Explorer window for each database that it finds in the App_Data folder. To jump to a specific data connection in a hurry, just double-click the .mdf file for the database in the Solution Explorer.

Using the Server Explorer, you can create tables, edit data, and execute commands, all without leaving the comfort of Visual Studio. (For more information about executing commands with the Server Explorer, refer to the "SQL Basics" section earlier in this chapter.)

Storing the Connection String

Typically, all the database code in your application will use the same connection string. For that reason, it usually makes the most sense to store a connection string in a class member variable or, even better, a configuration file.

You can also create a Connection object and supply the connection string in one step by using a dedicated constructor:

```
Dim myConnection As New SqlConnection(connectionString)
' myConnection.ConnectionString is now set to connectionString.
```

You don't need to hard-code a connection string. The <connectionStrings> section of the web.config file is a handy place to store your connection strings. Here's an example:

```
<configuration>
  <connectionStrings>
    <add name="Pubs" connectionString=
"Data Source=localhost;Initial Catalog=Pubs;Integrated Security=SSPI"/>
  </connectionStrings>
  ...
</configuration>
```

You can then retrieve your connection string by name. First, import the System.Web.Configuration namespace. Then, you can use code like this:

```
Dim connectionString As String = _
  WebConfigurationManager.ConnectionStrings("Pubs").ConnectionString
```

This approach helps to ensure all your web pages are using the same connection string. It also makes it easy for you to change the connection string for an application, without needing to edit the code in multiple pages. The examples in this chapter all store their connection strings in the web.config file in this way.

Making the Connection

Once you've created your connection (as described in the previous section), you're ready to use it.

Before you can perform any database operations, you need to explicitly open your connection:

```
myConnection.Open()
```

To verify that you have successfully connected to the database, you can try displaying some basic connection information. The following example writes some basic information to a Label control named lblInfo (see Figure 15-10).

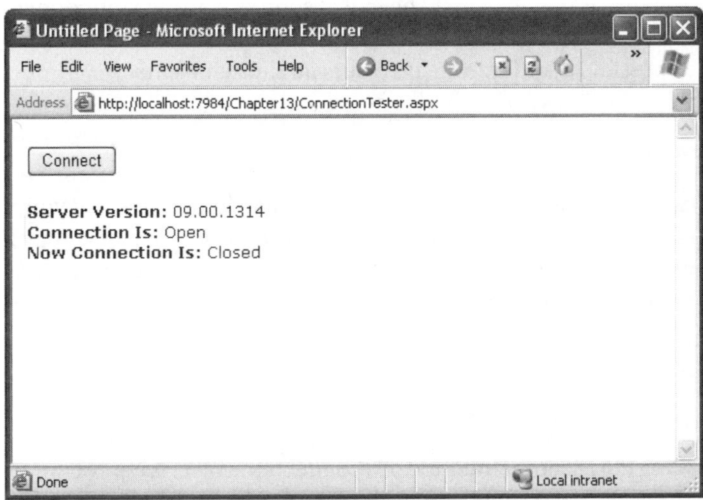

Figure 15-10. *Testing your connection*

Here's the code with basic error handling:

```
' Define the ADO.NET Connection object.
Dim connectionString As String = _
  WebConfigurationManager.ConnectionStrings("Pubs").ConnectionString
Dim myConnection As New SqlConnection(connectionString)

Try
    ' Try to open the connection.
    myConnection.Open()
    lblInfo.Text = "<b>Server Version:</b> " & myConnection.ServerVersion
    lblInfo.Text &= "<br /><b>Connection Is:</b> " & _
      myConnection.State.ToString()
Catch err As Exception
    ' Handle an error by displaying the information.
    lblInfo.Text = "Error reading the database."
    lblInfo.Text &= err.Message
```

```
Finally
    ' Either way, make sure the connection is properly closed.
    ' (Even if the connection wasn't opened successfully,
    '  calling Close() won't cause an error.)
    myConnection.Close()
    lblInfo.Text &= "<br /><b>Now Connection Is:</b> "
    lblInfo.Text &=  myConnection.State.ToString()
End Try
```

Once you use the Open() method, you have a live connection to your database. One of the most fundamental principles of data access code is that you should reduce the amount of time you hold a connection open as much as possible. Imagine that as soon as you open the connection, you have a live, ticking time bomb. You need to get in, retrieve your data, and throw the connection away as quickly as possible in order to ensure your site runs efficiently.

Closing a connection is just as easy, as shown here:

```
myConnection.Close()
```

Another approach is to use the Using statement. The Using statement declares that you are using a disposable object for a short period of time. As soon as you finish using that object and the Using block ends, the common language runtime will release it immediately by calling the Dispose() method. Here's the basic structure of the Using block:

```
Using object
    ...
End Using
```

It just so happens that calling the Dispose() method of a connection object is equivalent to calling Close(). That means you can shorten your database code with the help of a Using block. The best part is that you don't need to write a Finally block—the Using statement releases the object you're using even if you exit the block as the result of an unhandled exception.

Here's how you could rewrite the earlier example with a Using block:

```
Dim myConnection As New SqlConnection(connectionString)

Try
    Using myConnection
        ' Try to open the connection.
        myConnection.Open()
        lblInfo.Text = "<b>Server Version:</b> " & myConnection.ServerVersion
        lblInfo.Text &= "<br /><b>Connection Is:</b> " & _
          myConnection.State.ToString()
    End Using
Catch err As Exception
    ' Handle an error by displaying the information.
    lblInfo.Text = "Error reading the database."
    lblInfo.Text &= err.Message
End Try
```

```
lblInfo.Text &= "<br /><b>Now Connection Is:</b> "
lblInfo.Text &= myConnection.State.ToString()
```

There's one difference in the way this code is implemented as compared to the previous example. The error-handling code wraps the Using block. As a result, if an error occurs the database connection is closed first, and *then* the exception-handling code is triggered. In the first example, the error-handling code responded first, and then the Finally block closed the connection afterward. Obviously, this rewrite is a bit better, as it's always good to close database connections as soon as possible.

The Select Command

The Connection object provides a few basic properties that supply information about the connection, but that's about all. To actually retrieve data, you need a few more ingredients:

- A SQL statement that selects the information you want
- A Command object that executes the SQL statement
- A DataReader or DataSet object to access the retrieved records

Command objects represent SQL statements. To use a Command, you define it, specify the SQL statement you want to use, specify an available connection, and execute the command.

You can use one of the earlier SQL statements, as shown here:

```
Dim myCommand As New SqlCommand()
myCommand.Connection = myConnection
myCommand.CommandText = "SELECT * FROM Authors ORDER BY au_lname"
```

Or you can use the constructor as a shortcut:

```
Dim myCommand As New SqlCommand(_
  "SELECT * FROM Authors ORDER BY au_lname ", myConnection)
```

■ **Note** It's also a good idea to dispose of the Command object when you're finished, although it isn't as critical as closing the Connection object.

The DataReader

Once you've defined your command, you need to decide how you want to use it. The simplest approach is to use a DataReader, which allows you to quickly retrieve all your results. The DataReader uses a live connection and should be used quickly and then closed. The DataReader is also extremely simple. It supports fast-forward-only read-only access to your results, which is generally all you need when retrieving information. Because of the DataReader's optimized nature, it provides better performance than the DataSet. It should always be your first choice for direct data access.

Before you can use a DataReader, make sure you've opened the connection:

```
myConnection.Open()
```

To create a DataReader, you use the ExecuteReader() method of the command object, as shown here:

```
' You don't need the new keyword, as the Command will create the DataReader.
Dim myReader As SqlDataReader
myReader = myCommand.ExecuteReader()
```

These two lines of code define a variable for a DataReader and then create it by executing the command. Once you have the reader, you retrieve a single row at a time using the Read() method:

```
myReader.Read()    ' The first row in the result set is now available.
```

You can then access the values in the current row using the corresponding field names. The following example adds an item to a list box with the first name and last name for the current row:

```
lstNames.Items.Add(myReader("au_lname") & ", " & myReader("au_fname"))
```

To move to the next row, use the Read() method again. If this method returns True, a row of information has been successfully retrieved. If it returns False, you've attempted to read past the end of your result set. There is no way to move backward to a previous row.

As soon as you've finished reading all the results you need, close the DataReader and Connection:

```
myReader.Close()
myConnection.Close()
```

Putting It All Together

The next example demonstrates how you can use all the ADO.NET ingredients together to create a simple application that retrieves information from the Authors table. You can select an author record by last name using a drop-down list box, as shown in Figure 15-11.

The full record is then retrieved and displayed in a simple label, as shown in Figure 15-12.

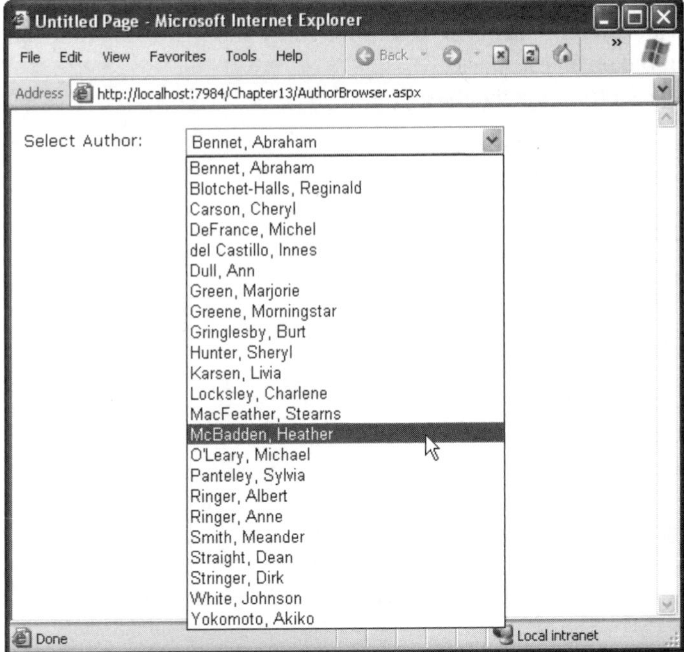

Figure 15-11. *Selecting an author*

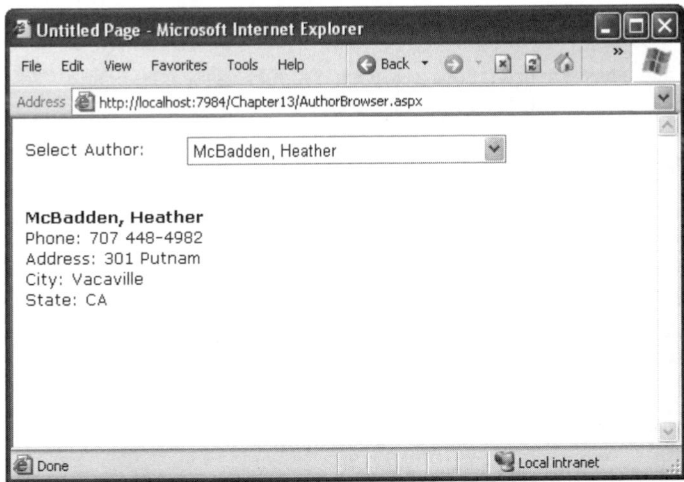

Figure 15-12. *Author information*

Filling the List Box

To start, the connection string is defined as a private variable for the page class and retrieved from the connection string:

```
Private connectionString As String = _
  WebConfigurationManager.ConnectionStrings("Pubs").ConnectionString
```

The list box is filled when the Page.Load event occurs. Because the list box is set to persist its view state information, this information needs to be retrieved only once—the first time the page is displayed. It will be ignored on all postbacks.

Here's the code that fills the list from the database:

```
Protected Sub Page_Load(ByVal sender As Object, _
  ByVal e As EventArgs) Handles Me.Load

    If Not Page.IsPostBack Then
        FillAuthorList()
    End If
End Sub

Private Sub FillAuthorList()
    lstAuthor.Items.Clear()

    ' Define the Select statement.
    ' Three pieces of information are needed: the unique id
    ' and the first and last name.
    Dim selectSQL As String = "SELECT au_lname, au_fname, au_id FROM Authors"

    ' Define the ADO.NET objects.
    Dim con As New SqlConnection(connectionString)
    Dim cmd As New SqlCommand(selectSQL, con)
    Dim reader As SqlDataReader

    ' Try to open database and read information.
    Try
        con.Open()
        reader = cmd.ExecuteReader()

        ' For each item, add the author name to the displayed
        ' list box text, and store the unique ID in the Value property.
        Do While reader.Read()
            Dim newItem As New ListItem()
            newItem.Text = reader("au_lname") & ", " & reader("au_fname")
            newItem.Value = reader("au_id").ToString()
            lstAuthor.Items.Add(newItem)
        Loop
        reader.Close()

    Catch err As Exception
        lblResults.Text = "Error reading list of names."
        lblResults.Text &= err.Message
    Finally
        con.Close()
    End Try
End Sub
```

This example looks more sophisticated than the previous bite-sized snippets in this chapter, but it really doesn't introduce anything new. It uses the standard Connection, Command, and DataReader objects. The Connection is opened inside an error-handling block so your page can handle any unexpected errors and provide information. A Finally block makes sure the connection is properly closed, even if an error occurs.

The actual code for reading the data uses a loop. With each pass, the Read() method is called to get another row of information. When the reader has read all the available information, this method will return False, the loop condition will evaluate to False, and the loop will end gracefully.

The unique ID (the value in the au_id field) is stored in the Value property of the list box for reference later. This is a crucial ingredient that is needed to allow the corresponding record to be queried again. If you tried to build a query using the author's name, you would need to worry about authors with the same name. You would also have the additional headache of invalid characters (such as the apostrophe in O'Leary) that would invalidate your SQL statement.

Retrieving the Record

The record is retrieved as soon as the user changes the selection in the list box. To make this possible, the AutoPostBack property of the list box is set to True so that its change events are detected automatically.

```
Protected Sub lstAuthor_SelectedIndexChanged(ByVal sender As Object, _
  ByVal e As EventArgs) Handles lstAuthor.SelectedIndexChanged

    ' Create a Select statement that searches for a record
    ' matching the specific author ID from the Value property.
    Dim selectSQL As String
    selectSQL = "SELECT * FROM Authors "
    selectSQL &= "WHERE au_id='" & lstAuthor.SelectedItem.Value & "'"

    ' Define the ADO.NET objects.
    Dim con As New SqlConnection(connectionString)
    Dim cmd As New SqlCommand(selectSQL, con)
    Dim reader As SqlDataReader

    ' Try to open database and read information.
    Try
        con.Open()
        reader = cmd.ExecuteReader()
        reader.Read()

        ' Build a string with the record information,
        ' and display that in a label.
        Dim sb As New StringBuilder()
        sb.Append("<b>")
        sb.Append(reader("au_lname"))
        sb.Append(", ")
        sb.Append(reader("au_fname"))
```

```
        sb.Append("</b><br />")
        sb.Append("Phone: ")
        sb.Append(reader("phone"))
        sb.Append("<br />")
        sb.Append("Address: ")
        sb.Append(reader("address"))
        sb.Append("<br />")
        sb.Append("City: ")
        sb.Append(reader("city"))
        sb.Append("<br />")
        sb.Append("State: ")
        sb.Append(reader("state"))
        sb.Append("<br />")
        lblResults.Text = sb.ToString()

        reader.Close()

    Catch err As Exception
        lblResults.Text = "Error getting author. "
        lblResults.Text &= err.Message
    Finally
        con.Close()
    End Try
End Sub
```

The process is similar to the procedure used to retrieve the last names. There are only a couple of differences:

- The code dynamically creates a SQL statement based on the selected item in the drop-down list box. It uses the Value property of the selected item, which stores the unique identifier. This is a common (and useful) technique.
- Only one record is read. The code assumes that only one author has the matching au_id, which is reasonable since this field is unique.

■ **Note** This example shows how ADO.NET works to retrieve a simple result set. Of course, ADO.NET also provides handy controls that go beyond this generic level and let you provide full-featured grids with sorting and editing. These controls are described in Chapter 16 and Chapter 17. For now, you should concentrate on understanding the fundamentals about ADO.NET and how it works with data.

Updating Data

Now that you understand how to retrieve data, it isn't much more complicated to perform simple delete and update operations. Once again, you use the Command object, but this time you don't need a DataReader because no results will be retrieved. You also don't use a SQL Select command. Instead, you use one of three new SQL commands: Update, Insert, or Delete.

To execute an Update, an Insert, or a Delete statement, you need to create a Command object. You can then execute the command with the ExecuteNonQuery() method. This method returns the number of rows that were affected, which allows you to check your assumptions. For example, if you attempt to update or delete a record and are informed that no records were affected, you probably have an error in your Where clause that is preventing any records from being selected. (If, on the other hand, your SQL command has a syntax error or attempts to retrieve information from a nonexistent table, an exception will occur.)

Displaying Values in Text Boxes

Before you can update and insert records, you need to make a change to the previous example. Instead of displaying the field values in a single, fixed label, you need to show each detail in a separate text box. Figure 15-13 shows the revamped page. It includes two new buttons that allow you to update the record (Update) or delete it (Delete), and two more that allow you to begin creating a new record (Create New) and then insert it (Insert New).

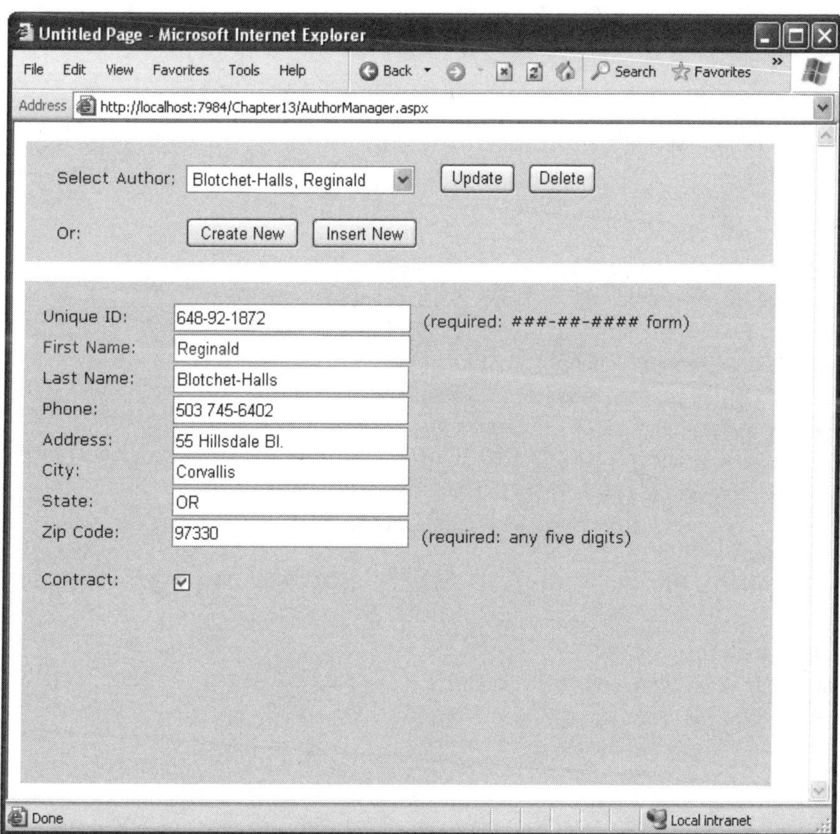

Figure 15-13. *A more advanced author manager*

The record selection code is identical from an ADO.NET perspective, but it now uses the individual text boxes:

```
Protected Sub lstAuthor_SelectedIndexChanged(ByVal sender As Object, _
  ByVal e As EventArgs) Handles lstAuthor.SelectedIndexChanged

    ' Create a Select statement that searches for a record
    ' matching the specific author ID from the Value property.
    Dim selectSQL As String
    selectSQL = "SELECT * FROM Authors "
    selectSQL &= "WHERE au_id='" & lstAuthor.SelectedItem.Value & "'"

    ' Define the ADO.NET objects.
    Dim con As New SqlConnection(connectionString)
    Dim cmd As New SqlCommand(selectSQL, con)
    Dim reader As SqlDataReader

    ' Try to open database and read information.
    Try
        con.Open()
        reader = cmd.ExecuteReader()
        reader.Read()

        ' Fill the controls.
        txtID.Text = reader("au_id").ToString()
        txtFirstName.Text = reader("au_fname").ToString()
        txtLastName.Text = reader("au_lname").ToString()
        txtPhone.Text = reader("phone").ToString()
        txtAddress.Text = reader("address").ToString()
        txtCity.Text = reader("city").ToString()
        txtState.Text = reader("state").ToString()
        txtZip.Text = reader("zip").ToString()
        chkContract.Checked = CType(reader("contract"), Boolean)
        reader.Close()
        lblResults.Text = ""

    Catch err As Exception
        lblResults.Text = "Error getting author. "
        lblResults.Text &= err.Message
    Finally
        con.Close()
    End Try
End Sub
```

To see the full code, refer to the online samples for this chapter. If you play with the example at length, you'll notice that it lacks a few niceties that would be needed in a professional website. For example, when creating a new record, the name of the last selected user is still visible, and the Update and Delete buttons are still active, which can lead to confusion or errors. A more sophisticated user interface could prevent these problems by disabling inapplicable controls (perhaps by grouping them in a Panel control) or by using separate pages. In this case, however, the page is useful as a quick way to test some basic data access code.

Adding a Record

To start adding a new record, click Create New to clear all the text boxes. Technically this step isn't required, but it simplifies the user's life:

```
Protected Sub cmdNew_Click(ByVal sender As Object, _
  ByVal e As EventArgs) Handles cmdNew.Click

    txtID.Text = ""
    txtFirstName.Text = ""
    txtLastName.Text = ""
    txtPhone.Text = ""
    txtAddress.Text = ""
    txtCity.Text = ""
    txtState.Text = ""
    txtZip.Text = ""
    chkContract.Checked = False

    lblResults.Text = "Click Insert New to add the completed record."
End Sub
```

The Insert New button triggers the ADO.NET code that inserts the finished record using a dynamically generated Insert statement:

```
Protected Sub cmdInsert_Click(ByVal sender As Object, _
  ByVal e As EventArgs) Handles cmdInsert.Click

    ' Perform user-defined checks.
    ' Alternatively, you could use RequiredFieldValidator controls.
    If txtID.Text = "" Or txtFirstName.Text = "" Or txtLastName.Text = "" Then
        lblResults.Text = "Records require an ID, first name, and last name."
        Return
    End If
```

```
    ' Define ADO.NET objects.
    Dim insertSQL As String
    insertSQL = "INSERT INTO Authors ("
    insertSQL &= "au_id, au_fname, au_lname, "
    insertSQL &= "phone, address, city, state, zip, contract) "
    insertSQL &= "VALUES ('"
    insertSQL &= txtID.Text & "', '"
    insertSQL &= txtFirstName.Text & "', '"
    insertSQL &= txtLastName.Text & "', '"
    insertSQL &= txtPhone.Text & "', '"
    insertSQL &= txtAddress.Text & "', '"
    insertSQL &= txtCity.Text & "', '"
    insertSQL &= txtState.Text & "', '"
    insertSQL &= txtZip.Text & "', '"
    insertSQL &= Val(chkContract.Checked) & "')"

    Dim con As New SqlConnection(connectionString)
    Dim cmd As New SqlCommand(insertSQL, con)

    ' Try to open the database and execute the update.
    Dim added As Integer = 0
    Try
        con.Open()
        added = cmd.ExecuteNonQuery()
        lblResults.Text = added.ToString() & " records inserted."
    Catch err As Exception
        lblResults.Text = "Error inserting record. "
        lblResults.Text &= err.Message
    Finally
        con.Close()
    End Try

    ' If the insert succeeded, refresh the author list.
    If added > 0 Then
        FillAuthorList()
    End If
End Sub
```

If the insert fails, the problem will be reported to the user in a rather unfriendly way (see Figure 15-14). This is typically the result of not specifying valid values. If the insert operation is successful, the page is updated with the new author list.

■ **Note** In a more polished application, you would use validators (as shown in Chapter 8) and provide more useful error messages. You should never display the detailed database error information shown in Figure 15-14, because it could give valuable information to malicious users.

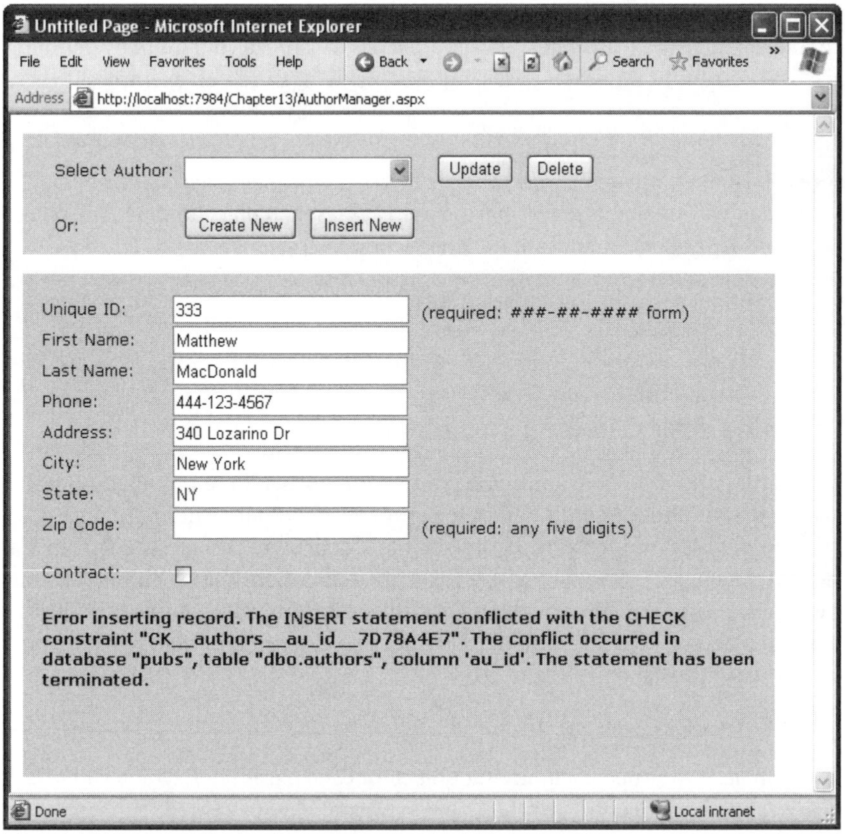

Figure 15-14. *A failed insertion*

Creating More Robust Commands

The previous example performed its database work using a dynamically pasted-together SQL string. This off-the-cuff approach is great for quickly coding database logic, and it's easy to understand. However, it has two potentially serious drawbacks:

- Users may accidentally enter characters that will affect your SQL statement. For example, if a value contains an apostrophe ('), the pasted-together SQL string will no longer be valid.
- Users might *deliberately* enter characters that will affect your SQL statement. Examples include using the single apostrophe to close a value prematurely and then following the value with additional SQL code.

The second of these is known as *SQL injection attack*, and it facilitates an amazingly wide range of exploits. Crafty users can use SQL injection attacks to do anything from returning additional results (such as the orders placed by other customers) or even executing additional SQL statements (such as deleting every record in another table in the same database). In fact, SQL Server includes a special system stored procedure that allows users to execute arbitrary programs on the computer, so this vulnerability can be extremely serious.

You could address these problems by carefully validating the supplied input and checking for dangerous characters such as apostrophes. One approach is to sanitize your input by doubling all apostrophes in the user input (in other words, replace ' with "). Here's an example:

```
Dim authorID As String = txtID.Text.Replace("'", "''")
```

A much more robust and convenient approach is to use a *parameterized command*. A parameterized command is one that replaces hard-coded values with placeholders. The placeholders are then added separately and automatically encoded.

For example, this SQL statement:

```
SELECT * FROM Customers WHERE CustomerID = 'ALFKI'
```

would become this:

```
SELECT * FROM Customers WHERE CustomerID = @CustomerID
```

The syntax used for parameterized commands differs from provider to provider. For the SQL Server provider, parameterized commands use named placeholders with unique names. You can use any name you want, as long as it begins with the @ character. Usually, you'll choose a parameter name that matches the field name (such as @CustomerID for the CustomerID value in the previous example). The OLE DB provider uses a different syntax. It requires that each hard-coded value is replaced with a question mark. Parameters aren't identified by name but by their position in the SQL string.

```
SELECT * FROM Customers WHERE CustomerID = ?
```

In either case, you need to supply a Parameter object for each parameter, which you insert in the Command.Parameters collection. In OLE DB, you must make sure you add the parameters in the same order they appear in the SQL string. In SQL Server this isn't a requirement, because the parameters are matched to the placeholders based on their name.

The following example rewrites the insert code of the author manager example with a parameterized command:

```
Protected Sub cmdInsert_Click(ByVal sender As Object, _
  ByVal e As EventArgs) Handles cmdInsert.Click

    ' Perform user-defined checks.
    If txtID.Text = "" Or txtFirstName.Text = "" Or txtLastName.Text = "" Then
        lblResults.Text = "Records require an ID, first name, and last name."
        Return
    End If

    ' Define ADO.NET objects.
    Dim insertSQL As String
    insertSQL = "INSERT INTO Authors ("
    insertSQL &= "au_id, au_fname, au_lname, "
    insertSQL &= "phone, address, city, state, zip, contract) "
    insertSQL &= "VALUES ("
    insertSQL &= "@au_id, @au_fname, @au_lname, "
    insertSQL &= "@phone, @address, @city, @state, @zip, @contract)"
```

```
    Dim con As New SqlConnection(connectionString)
    Dim cmd As New SqlCommand(insertSQL, con)

    ' Add the parameters.
    cmd.Parameters.AddWithValue("@au_id", txtID.Text)
    cmd.Parameters.AddWithValue("@au_fname", txtFirstName.Text)
    cmd.Parameters.AddWithValue("@au_lname", txtLastName.Text)
    cmd.Parameters.AddWithValue("@phone", txtPhone.Text)
    cmd.Parameters.AddWithValue("@address", txtAddress.Text)
    cmd.Parameters.AddWithValue("@city", txtCity.Text)
    cmd.Parameters.AddWithValue("@state", txtState.Text)
    cmd.Parameters.AddWithValue("@zip", txtZip.Text)
    cmd.Parameters.AddWithValue("@contract", Val(chkContract.Checked))

    ' Try to open the database and execute the update.
    Dim added As Integer = 0
    Try
        con.Open()
        added = cmd.ExecuteNonQuery()
        lblResults.Text = added.ToString() & " record inserted."
    Catch err As Exception
        lblResults.Text = "Error inserting record. "
        lblResults.Text &= err.Message
    Finally
        con.Close()
    End Try

    ' If the insert succeeded, refresh the author list.
    If added > 0 Then
        FillAuthorList()
    End If
End Sub
```

Now that the values have been moved out of the SQL command and to the Parameters collection, there's no way that a misplaced apostrophe or scrap of SQL can cause a problem.

■ **Caution** For basic security, *always* use parameterized commands. Many of the most infamous attacks on e-commerce websites weren't fueled by hard-core hacker knowledge but were made using simple SQL injection by modifying values in web pages or query strings.

Updating a Record

When the user clicks the Update button, the information in the text boxes is applied to the database as follows:

```
Protected Sub cmdUpdate_Click(ByVal sender As Object, _
  ByVal e As EventArgs) Handles cmdUpdate.Click

    ' Define ADO.NET objects.
    Dim updateSQL As String
    updateSQL = "UPDATE Authors SET "
    updateSQL &= "au_fname=@au_fname, au_lname=@au_lname, "
    updateSQL &= "phone=@phone, address=@address, city=@city, state=@state, "
    updateSQL &= "zip=@zip, contract=@contract "
    updateSQL &= "WHERE au_id=@au_id_original"

    Dim con As New SqlConnection(connectionString)
    Dim cmd As New SqlCommand(updateSQL, con)

    ' Add the parameters.
    cmd.Parameters.AddWithValue("@au_fname", txtFirstName.Text)
    cmd.Parameters.AddWithValue("@au_lname", txtLastName.Text)
    cmd.Parameters.AddWithValue("@phone", txtPhone.Text)
    cmd.Parameters.AddWithValue("@address", txtAddress.Text)
    cmd.Parameters.AddWithValue("@city", txtCity.Text)
    cmd.Parameters.AddWithValue("@state", txtState.Text)
    cmd.Parameters.AddWithValue("@zip", txtZip.Text)
    cmd.Parameters.AddWithValue("@contract", Val(chkContract.Checked))
    cmd.Parameters.AddWithValue("@au_id_original", lstAuthor.SelectedItem.Value)

    ' Try to open database and execute the update.
    Dim updated As Integer = 0
    Try
        con.Open()
        updated = cmd.ExecuteNonQuery()
        lblResults.Text = updated.ToString() & " record updated."
    Catch err As Exception
        lblResults.Text = "Error updating author. "
        lblResults.Text &= err.Message
    Finally
        con.Close()
    End Try

    ' If the update succeeded, refresh the author list.
    If deleted > 0 Then
        FillAuthorList()
    End If
End Sub
```

The update code is similar to the code for inserting a record. The main differences are as follows:

- No DataReader is used, because no results are returned.
- A dynamically generated Update command is used for the Command object. This command finds the current author record in the database and changes all the fields to correspond to the values entered in the text boxes.
- This example doesn't attempt to update the ID, because that detail can't be changed in the database.
- The ExecuteNonQuery() method returns the number of affected records. This information is displayed in a label to confirm to the user that the operation was successful. The FillAuthorList() method is then called to update the list, just in case the author's name information was changed.

Deleting a Record

When the user clicks the Delete button, the author information is removed from the database. The number of affected records is examined, and if the delete operation was successful, the FillAuthorList() function is called to refresh the page.

```
Protected Sub cmdDelete_Click(ByVal sender As Object, _
  ByVal e As EventArgs) Handles cmdDelete.Click

    ' Define ADO.NET objects.
    Dim deleteSQL As String
    deleteSQL = "DELETE FROM Authors "
    deleteSQL &= "WHERE au_id=@au_id"

    Dim con As New SqlConnection(connectionString)
    Dim cmd As New SqlCommand(deleteSQL, con)
    cmd.Parameters.AddWithValue("@au_id ", lstAuthor.SelectedItem.Value)

    ' Try to open the database and delete the record.
    Dim deleted As Integer = 0
    Try
        con.Open()
        deleted = cmd.ExecuteNonQuery()
        lblResults.Text &= "Record deleted."
    Catch err As Exception
        lblResults.Text = "Error deleting author. "
        lblResults.Text &= err.Message
    Finally
        con.Close()
    End Try

    ' If the delete succeeded, refresh the author list.
    If deleted > 0 Then
        FillAuthorList()
    End If
End Sub
```

Interestingly, delete operations rarely succeed with the records in the pubs database, because they have corresponding child records linked in another table of the pubs database. Specifically, each author can have one or more related book titles. Unless the author's records are removed from the TitleAuthor table first, the author cannot be deleted. Because of the careful error handling used in the previous example, this problem is faithfully reported in your application (see Figure 15-15) and doesn't cause any real problems.

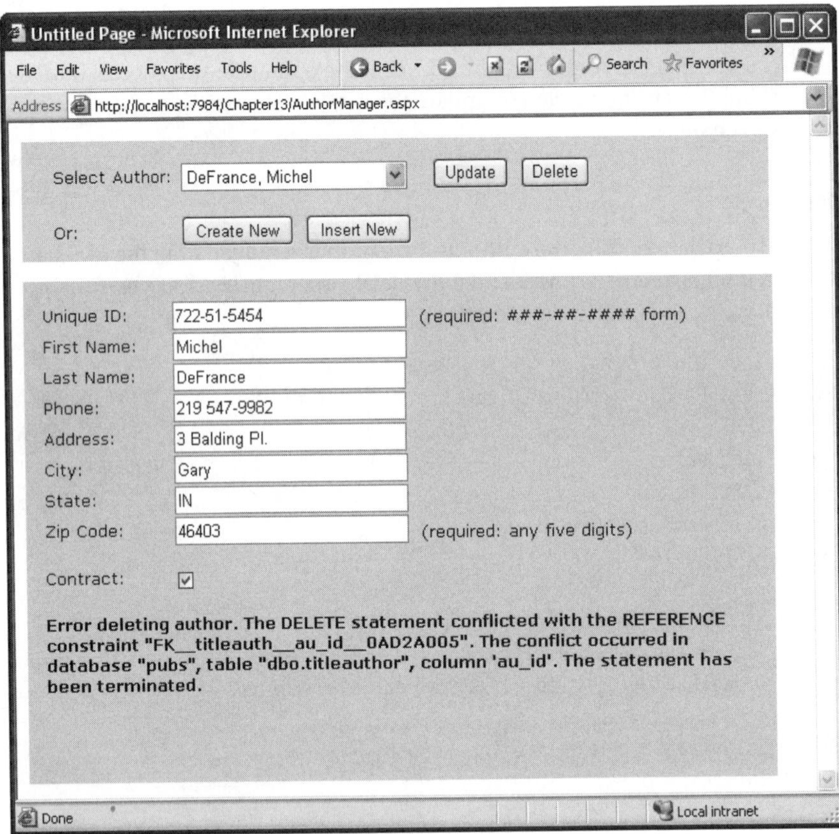

Figure 15-15. *A failed delete attempt*

To get around this limitation, you can use the Create New and Insert New buttons to add a new record and then delete this record. Because this new record won't be linked to any other records, its deletion will be allowed.

Disconnected Data Access

When you use disconnected data access, you keep a copy of your data in memory using the DataSet. You connect to the database just long enough to fetch your data and dump it into the DataSet, and then you disconnect immediately.

There are a variety of good reasons to use the DataSet to hold onto data in memory. Here are a few:

- You need to do something time-consuming with the data. By dumping it into a DataSet first, you ensure that the database connection is kept open for as little time as possible.
- You want to use ASP.NET data binding to fill a web control (like a grid) with your data. Although you can use the DataReader, it won't work in all scenarios. The DataSet approach is more straightforward.
- You want to navigate backward and forward through your data while you're processing it. This isn't possible with the DataReader, which goes in one direction only—forward.
- You want to navigate from one table to another. Using the DataSet, you can store several tables of information. You can even define relationships that allow you to browse through them more efficiently.
- You want to save the data to a file for later use. In Chapter 19 you'll learn how any DataSet object can be saved in XML format in an ordinary file.
- You need a convenient package to send data from one component to another. For example, in Chapter 23 you'll learn to build a database component that provides its data to a web page using the DataSet. A DataReader wouldn't work in this scenario, because the database component would need to leave the database connection open, which is a dangerous design.
- You want to store some data so it can be used for future requests. Chapter 24 demonstrates how you can use caching with the DataSet to achieve this result.

UPDATING DISCONNECTED DATA

The DataSet tracks the changes you make to the records inside. This allows you to use the DataSet to update records. The basic principle is simple. You fill a DataSet in the normal way, modify one or more records, and then apply your update using a DataAdapter.

However, ADO.NET's disconnected update feature makes far more sense in a desktop application than in a web application. Desktop applications run for a long time, so they can efficiently store a batch of changes and perform them all at once. But in a web application, you need to commit your changes the moment they happen. Furthermore, the point at which you retrieve the data (when a page is first requested) and the point at which it's changed (during a postback) are different, which makes it very difficult to use the same DataSet object, and maintain the change tracking information for the whole process.

For these reasons, the great majority of ASP.NET web applications use the DataSet to store data but not to make updates. Instead, they use direct commands to commit changes. This is the model you'll see in this book.

Selecting Disconnected Data

With disconnected data access, a copy of the data is retained in memory while your code is running. Figure 15-16 shows a model of the DataSet.

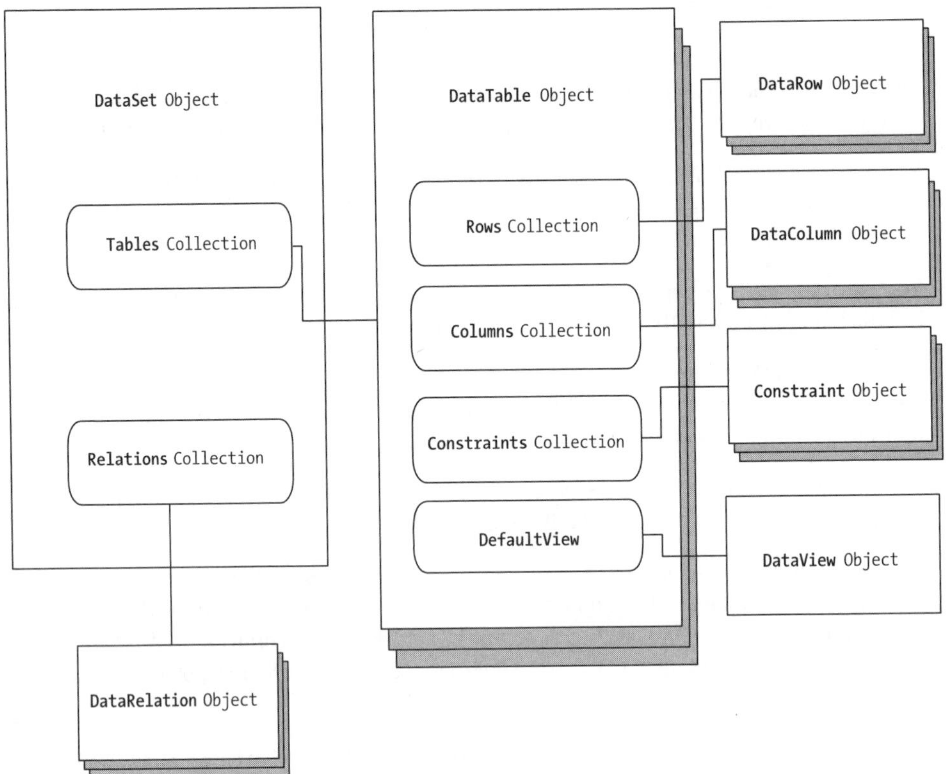

Figure 15-16. *The DataSet family of objects*

You fill the DataSet in much the same way that you connect a DataReader. However, although the DataReader holds a live connection, information in the DataSet is always disconnected.

The following example shows how you could rewrite the FillAuthorList() method from the earlier example to use a DataSet instead of a DataReader. The changes are highlighted in bold.

```
Private Sub FillAuthorList()

    lstAuthor.Items.Clear()

    ' Define ADO.NET objects.
    Dim selectSQL As String
    selectSQL = "SELECT au_lname, au_fname, au_id FROM Authors"
    Dim con As New SqlConnection(connectionString)
    Dim cmd As New SqlCommand(selectSQL, con)
    Dim adapter As New SqlDataAdapter(cmd)
    Dim dsPubs As New DataSet()
```

```
    ' Try to open database and read information.
    Try
        con.Open()

        ' All the information in transferred with one command.
        ' This command creates a new DataTable (named Authors)
        ' inside the DataSet.
        adapter.Fill(dsPubs, "Authors")

    Catch err As Exception
        lblResults.Text = "Error reading list of names. "
        lblResults.Text &= err.Message
    Finally
        con.Close()
    End Try

    For Each row As DataRow In dsPubs.Tables("Authors").Rows
        Dim newItem As New ListItem()
        newItem.Text = row("au_lname") & ", " & _
          row("au_fname")
        newItem.Value = row("au_id").ToString()
        lstAuthor.Items.Add(newItem)
    Next
End Sub
```

If you want to extract records from a database and place them in a DataSet, you need to use a DataAdapter. Every DataAdapter can hold four commands: SelectCommand, InsertCommand, UpdateCommand, and DeleteCommand. This allows you to use a single DataAdapter object for multiple tasks. The Command object supplied in the constructor is automatically assigned to the DataAdapter.SelectCommand property. Figure 15-17 shows how the DataAdapter interacts with your web application.

The DataAdapter.Fill() method takes a DataSet and inserts one table of information. In this case, the table is named Authors, but any name could be used. That name is used later to access the appropriate table in the DataSet.

To access the individual DataRows, you can loop through the Rows collection of the appropriate table. Each piece of information is accessed using the field name, as it was with the DataReader.

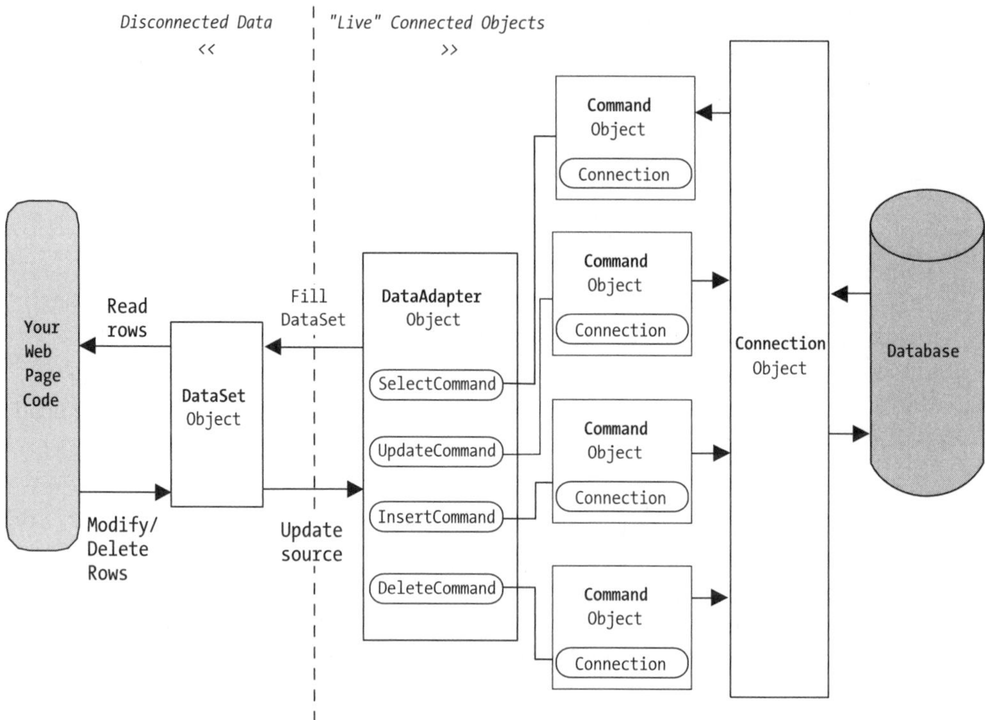

Figure 15-17. *Using a DataSet with ADO.NET*

Selecting Multiple Tables

A DataSet can contain as many tables as you need, and you can even add relationships between the tables to better emulate the underlying relational data source. Unfortunately, you have no way to connect tables together automatically based on relationships in the underlying data source. However, you can add relations with a few extra lines of code, as shown in the next example.

In the pubs database, authors are linked to titles using three tables. This arrangement (called a *many-to-many* relationship, shown in Figure 15-18) allows several authors to be related to one title and several titles to be related to one author. Without the intermediate TitleAuthor table, the database would be restricted to a one-to-many relationship, which would allow only a single author for each title.

In an application, you would rarely need to access these tables individually. Instead, you would need to combine information from them in some way (for example, to find out what author wrote a given book). On its own, the Titles table indicates only the author ID. It doesn't provide additional information such as the author's name and address. To link this information together, you can use a special SQL Select statement called a *Join query*. Alternatively, you can use the features built into ADO.NET, as demonstrated in this section.

The next example provides a simple page that lists authors and the titles they have written. The interesting thing about this page is that it's generated using ADO.NET table linking.

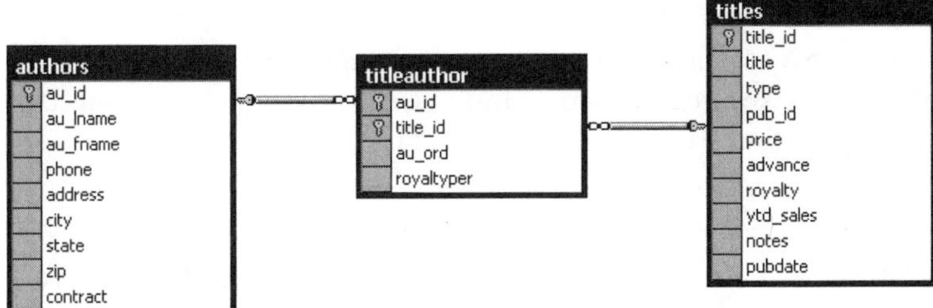

Figure 15-18. *A many-to-many relationship*

To start, the standard ADO.NET data access objects are created, including a DataSet. All these steps are performed in a custom CreateList() method, which is called from the Page.Load event handler so that the output is created when the page is first generated:

```
' Define ADO.NET objects.
Dim selectSQL As String = "SELECT au_lname, au_fname, au_id FROM Authors"
Dim con As New SqlConnection(connectionString)
Dim cmd As New SqlCommand(selectSQL, con)
Dim adapter As New SqlDataAdapter(cmd)
Dim dsPubs As New DataSet()
```

Next, the information for all three tables is pulled from the database and placed in the DataSet. This task could be accomplished with three separate Command objects, but to make the code a little leaner, this example uses only one and modifies the CommandText property as needed.

```
Try
    con.Open()
    adapter.Fill(dsPubs, "Authors")

    ' This command is still linked to the data adapter.
    cmd.CommandText = "SELECT au_id, title_id FROM TitleAuthor"
    adapter.Fill(dsPubs, "TitleAuthor")

    ' This command is still linked to the data adapter.
    cmd.CommandText = "SELECT title_id, title FROM Titles"
    adapter.Fill(dsPubs, "Titles")

Catch err As Exception
    lblList.Text = "Error reading list of names. "
    lblList.Text &= err.Message
Finally
    con.Close()
End Try
```

Defining Relationships

Now that all the information is in the DataSet, you can create two DataRelation objects to make it easier to navigate through the linked information. In this case, these DataRelation objects match the foreign key restrictions that are defined in the database.

■ **Note** A foreign key is a constraint that you can set up in your database to link one table to another. For example, the TitleAuthor table is linked to the Titles and the Authors tables by two foreign keys. The title_id field in the TitleAuthor table has a foreign key that binds it to the title_id field in the Titles table. Similarly, the au_id field in the TitleAuthor table has a foreign key that binds it to the au_id field in the Authors table. Once these links are established, certain rules come into play. For example, you can't create a TitleAuthor record that specifies author or title records that don't exist.

To create a DataRelation, you need to specify the linked fields from two different tables, and you need to give your DataRelation a unique name. The order of the linked fields is important. The first field is the parent, and the second field is the child. (The idea here is that one parent can have many children, but each child can have only one parent. In other words, the *parent-to-child* relationship is another way of saying a *one-to-many* relationship.) In this example, each book title can have more than one entry in the TitleAuthor table. Each author can also have more than one entry in the TitleAuthor table:

```
Dim Titles_TitleAuthor As New DataRelation("Titles_TitleAuthor", _
  dsPubs.Tables("Titles").Columns("title_id"), _
  dsPubs.Tables("TitleAuthor").Columns("title_id"))

Dim Authors_TitleAuthor As New DataRelation("Authors_TitleAuthor", _
  dsPubs.Tables("Authors").Columns("au_id"), _
  dsPubs.Tables("TitleAuthor").Columns("au_id"))
```

Once you've create these DataRelation objects, you must add them to the DataSet:

```
dsPubs.Relations.Add(Titles_TitleAuthor)
dsPubs.Relations.Add(Authors_TitleAuthor)
```

The remaining code loops through the DataSet. However, unlike the previous example, which moved through one table, this example uses the DataRelation objects to branch to the other linked tables. It works like this:

1. Select the first record from the Author table.

2. Using the Authors_TitleAuthor relationship, find the child records that correspond to this author. This step uses the GetChildRows method of the DataRow.

3. For each matching record in TitleAuthor, look up the corresponding Title record to get the full text title. This step uses the GetParentRows method of the DataRow.

4. Move to the next Author record, and repeat the process.

The code is lean and economical:

```
For Each rowAuthor As DataRow In dsPubs.Tables("Authors").Rows

    lblList.Text &= "<br /><b>" & rowAuthor("au_fname")
    lblList.Text &= " " & rowAuthor("au_lname") & "</b><br />"

    For Each rowTitleAuthor As DataRow In _
     rowAuthor.GetChildRows(Authors_TitleAuthor)

        For Each rowTitle As DataRow In _
         rowTitleAuthor.GetParentRows(Titles_TitleAuthor)

            lblList.Text &= "  "
            lblList.Text &= rowTitle("title") & "<br />"
        Next
    Next
Next
```

Figure 15-19 shows the final result.

If authors and titles have a simple one-to-many relationship, you could leave out the inner For Each statement and use simpler code, as follows:

```
For Each rowAuthor As DataRow In dsPubs.Tables("Authors").Rows
    ' Display author.

    For Each rowTitle As DataRow In rowAuthor.GetChildRows(Authors_Titles)
        ' Display title.
    Next
Next
```

Having seen the more complicated example, you're ready to create and manage multiple DataRelation objects on your own.

■ **Note** Using a DataRelation implies certain restrictions. For example, if you try to create a child row that refers to a nonexistent parent, ADO.NET will generate an error. Similarly, you can't delete a parent that has linked children records. These restrictions are already enforced by the data source, but by adding them to the DataSet, you ensure that they will be enforced by ADO.NET as well. This technique can allow you to catch errors as soon as they occur rather than waiting until you attempt to commit changes to the data source.

If this isn't the behavior you want, there's an easy solution. When you create the DataRelation, pass an extra parameter to the constructor with the value False:

```
Dim Titles_TitleAuthor As New DataRelation("Titles_TitleAuthor", _
  dsPubs.Tables("Titles").Columns("title_id"), _
  dsPubs.Tables("TitleAuthor").Columns("title_id"), False)
```

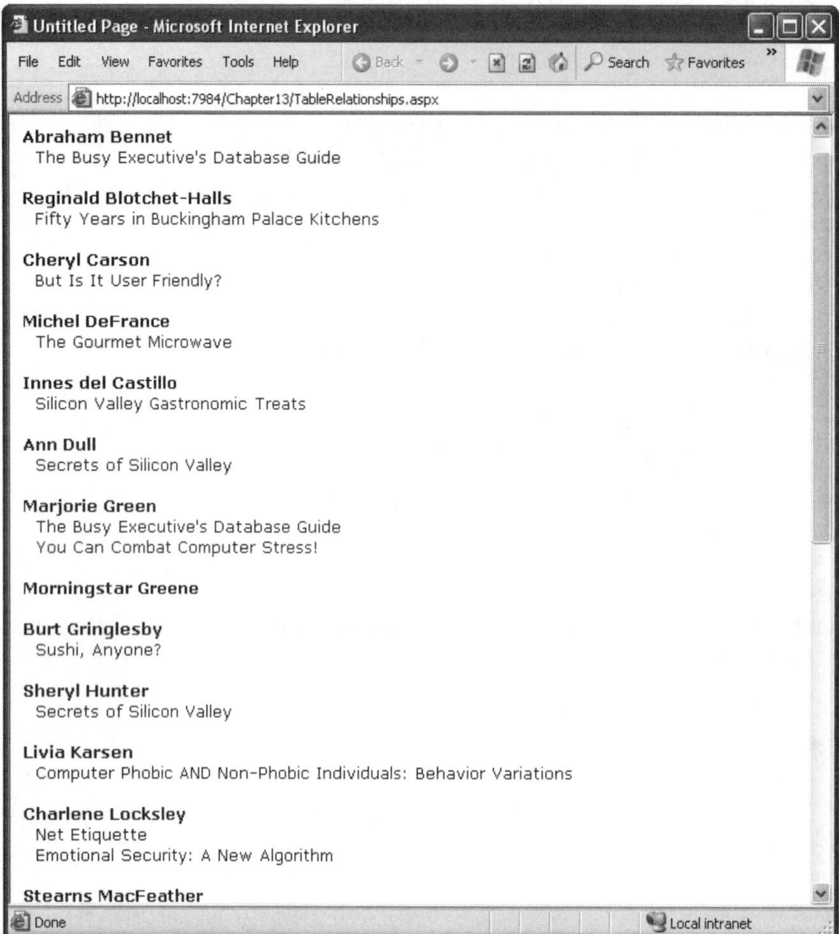

Figure 15-19. *Hierarchical information from two tables*

This tells the DataRelation not to create any constraints in the DataSet. In other words, you end up with a DataRelation that you can use to navigate between related records, but won't impose extra rules. This technique is useful if you're retrieving only some of the records in a table. For example, if you've retrieved the entire Titles and TitleAuthor tables but only some of the Authors table, you might have a book that refers to an author that's not in your DataSet. This isn't an error—it's just a reflection of the fact that you don't have all the information on hand.

The Last Word

This chapter gave you a solid introduction to ADO.NET. You know now how to connect to a database in your web pages, retrieve the information you need, and execute commands to update, insert, and delete data.

Although you've seen all the core concepts behind ADO.NET, there's still much more to learn. For a comprehensive book that focuses exclusively on ADO.NET, you may be interested in a book such as *Microsoft ADO.NET 2.0: Core Reference* (Microsoft Press, 2005), which investigates some of the techniques you can use to optimize ADO.NET data access code, and demonstrates how to perform batch updates with the DataSet.

In the next two chapters, you'll learn about ASP.NET's data-binding features and see how you can use them to write more practical data-driven web pages.

CHAPTER 16

■ ■ ■

Data Binding

In the previous chapter, you learned how to use ADO.NET to retrieve information from a database, how to store it in the DataSet, and how to apply changes using direct commands. These techniques are flexible and powerful, but they aren't always convenient.

For example, you can use the DataSet or the DataReader to retrieve rows of information, format them individually, and add them to an HTML table on a web page. Conceptually, this isn't too difficult. However, it still requires a lot of repetitive code to move through the data, format columns, and display it in the correct order. Repetitive code may be easy, but it's also error-prone, difficult to enhance, and unpleasant to read. Fortunately, ASP.NET adds a feature that allows you to skip this process and pop data directly into HTML elements and fully formatted controls. It's called *data binding*. In this chapter, you'll learn how to use data binding to display data more efficiently. You'll also learn how you can use the ASP.NET *data source controls* to retrieve your data from a database without writing a line of ADO.NET code.

Introducing Data Binding

The basic principle of data binding is this: you tell a control where to find your data and how you want it displayed, and the control handles the rest of the details. Data binding in ASP.NET is superficially similar to data binding in the world of desktop or client/server applications, but in truth, it's fundamentally different. In those environments, data binding involves creating a direct connection between a data source and a control in an application window. If the user changes a value in the on-screen control, the data in the linked database is modified automatically. Similarly, if the database changes while the user is working with it (for example, another user commits a change), the display can be refreshed automatically.

This type of data binding isn't practical in the ASP.NET world, because you can't effectively maintain a database connection over the Internet. This "direct" data binding also severely limits scalability and reduces flexibility. In fact, data binding has acquired a bad reputation for exactly these reasons.

ASP.NET data binding, on the other hand, has little in common with direct data binding. ASP.NET data binding works in one direction only. Information moves *from* a data object *into* a control. Then the data objects are thrown away, and the page is sent to the client. If the user modifies the data in a data-bound control, your program can update the corresponding record in the database, but nothing happens automatically.

ASP.NET data binding is much more flexible than old-style data binding. Many of the most powerful data binding controls, such as the GridView and DetailsView, give you unprecedented control over the presentation of your data, allowing you to format it, change its layout, embed it in other ASP.NET controls, and so on. You'll learn about these features and ASP.NET's rich data controls in Chapter 17.

Types of ASP.NET Data Binding

Two types of ASP.NET data binding exist: single-value binding and repeated-value binding. Single-value data binding is by far the simpler of the two, whereas repeated-value binding provides the foundation for the most advanced ASP.NET data controls.

Single-Value, or "Simple," Data Binding

You can use *single-value data binding* to add information anywhere on an ASP.NET page. You can even place information into a control property or as plain text inside an HTML tag. Single-value data binding doesn't necessarily have anything to do with ADO.NET. Instead, single-value data binding allows you to take a variable, a property, or an expression and insert it dynamically into a page. Single-value binding also helps you create templates for the rich data controls you'll study in Chapter 17.

Repeated-Value, or "List," Binding

Repeated-value data binding allows you to display an entire table (or just a single field from a table). Unlike single-value data binding, this type of data binding requires a special control that supports it. Typically, this will be a list control such as CheckBoxList or ListBox, but it can also be a much more sophisticated control such as the GridView (which is described in Chapter 17). You'll know that a control supports repeated-value data binding if it provides a DataSource property. As with single-value binding, repeated-value binding doesn't necessarily need to use data from a database, and it doesn't have to use the ADO.NET objects. For example, you can use repeated-value binding to bind data from a collection or an array.

How Data Binding Works

Data binding works a little differently depending on whether you're using single-value or repeated-value binding. To use single-value binding, you must insert a data binding expression into the markup in the .aspx file (not the code-behind file). To use repeated-value binding, you must set one or more properties of a data control. Typically, you'll perform this initialization when the Page.Load event fires. You'll see examples of both these techniques later in this chapter.

Once you specify data binding, you need to activate it. You accomplish this task by calling the DataBind() method. The DataBind() method is a basic piece of functionality supplied in the Control class. It automatically binds a control and any child controls that it contains. With repeated-value binding, you can use the DataBind() method of the specific list control you're using. Alternatively, you can bind the whole page at once by calling the DataBind() method of the current Page object. Once you call this method, all the data binding expressions in the page are evaluated and replaced with the specified value.

Typically, you call the DataBind() method in the Page.Load event handler. If you forget to use it, ASP.NET will ignore your data binding expressions, and the client will receive a page that contains empty values.

This is a general description of the whole process. To really understand what's happening, you need to work with some specific examples.

Single-Value Data Binding

Single-value data binding is really just a different approach to dynamic text. To use it, you add special data binding expressions into your .aspx files. These expressions have the following format:

```
<%# expression_goes_here %>
```

This may look like a script block, but it isn't. If you try to write any code inside this tag, you will receive an error. The only thing you can add is a valid data binding expression. For example, if you have a public or protected variable named Country in your page, you could write the following:

```
<%# Country %>
```

When you call the DataBind() method for the page, this text will be replaced with the value for Country (for example, Spain). Similarly, you could use a property or a built-in ASP.NET object as follows:

```
<%# Request.Browser.Browser %>
```

This would substitute a string with the current browser name (for example, IE). In fact, you can even call a function defined on your page, or execute a simple expression, provided it returns a result that can be converted to text and displayed on the page. Thus, the following data binding expressions are all valid:

```
<%# GetUserName(ID) %>
<%# 1 + (2 * 20) %>
<%# "John " & "Smith" %>
```

Remember, you place these data binding expressions in the markup portion of your .aspx file, not your code-behind file.

A Simple Data Binding Example

This section shows a simple example of single-value data binding. The example has been stripped to the bare minimum amount of detail needed to illustrate the concept.

You start with a variable defined in your Page class, which is called TransactionCount:

```
Public Partial Class SimpleDataBinding
    Inherits System.Web.UI.Page

    Protected TransactionCount As Integer

    ' (Additional code omitted.)
End Class
```

Note that this variable must be designated as public, protected, or internal, but not private. If you make the variable private, ASP.NET will not be able to access it when it's evaluating the data binding expression.

Now, assume that this value is set in the Page.Load event handler using some database lookup code. For testing purposes, the example skips this step and hard-codes a value:

```
Protected Sub Page_Load(ByVal sender As Object, _
  ByVal e As EventArgs) Handles Me.Load

    ' (You could use database code here
    ' to look up a value for TransactionCount.)
    TransactionCount = 10

    ' Now convert all the data binding expressions on the page.
    Me.DataBind()
End Sub
```

Two actions actually take place in this event handler: the TransactionCount variable is set to 10, and all the data binding expressions on the page are bound. Currently, no data binding expressions exist, so this method has no effect. Notice that this example uses the Me keyword to refer to the current page. You could just write DataBind() without the Me keyword, because the default object is the current Page object. However, using the Me keyword makes it a bit clearer what object is being used.

To make this data binding accomplish something, you need to add a data binding expression. Usually, it's easiest to add this value directly to the markup in the .aspx file. To do so, click the Source button at the bottom of the web page designer window. Figure 16-1 shows an example with a Label control.

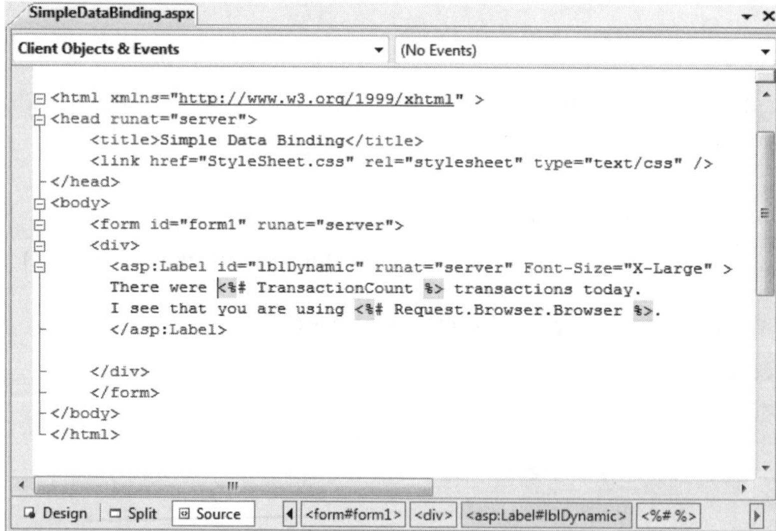

Figure 16-1. *Source view in the web page designer*

To add your expression, find the tag for the Label control. Modify the text inside the label as shown here:

```
<asp:Label id="lblDynamic" runat="server" Font-Size="X-Large">
There were <%# TransactionCount %> transactions today.
I see that you are using <%# Request.Browser.Browser %>.
</asp:Label>
```

This example uses two separate data binding expressions, which are inserted along with the normal static text. The first data binding expression references the TransactionCount variable, and the second uses the built-in Request object to determine some information about the user's browser. When you run this page, the output looks like Figure 16-2.

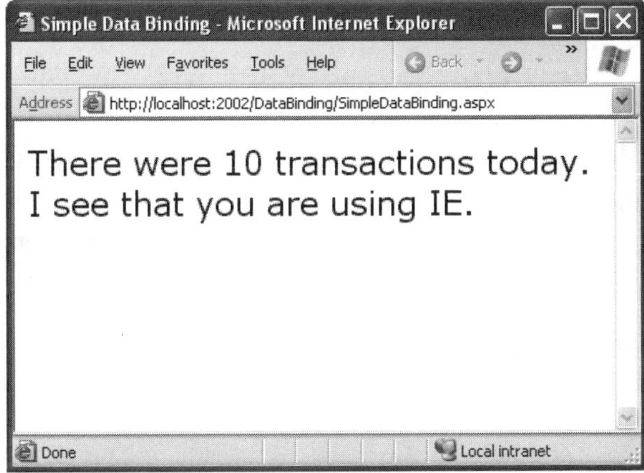

Figure 16-2. *The result of data binding*

The data binding expressions have been automatically replaced with the appropriate values. If the page is posted back, you could use additional code to modify TransactionCount, and as long as you call the DataBind() method, that information will be popped into the page in the data binding expression you've defined.

If, however, you forget to call the DataBind() method, the data binding expressions will be ignored, and the user will see a somewhat confusing window that looks like Figure 16-3.

■ **Note** When using single-value data binding, you need to consider when you should call the DataBind() method. For example, if you made the mistake of calling it before you set the TransactionCount variable, the corresponding expression would just be converted to 0. Remember, data binding is a one-way street. This means changing the TransactionCount variable after you've used the DataBind() method won't produce any visible effect. Unless you call the DataBind() method again, the displayed value won't be updated.

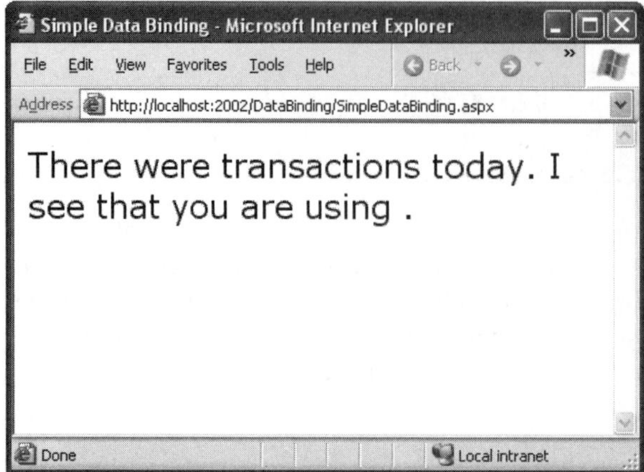

Figure 16-3. *The non-data-bound page*

Simple Data Binding with Properties

The previous example uses a data binding expression to set static text information inside a label tag. However, you can also use single-value data binding to set other types of information on your page, including control properties. To do this, you simply have to know where to put the data binding expression in the web page markup.

For example, consider the following page, which defines a variable named URL and uses it to point to a picture in the application directory:

```
Public Partial Class DataBindingUrl
    Inherits System.Web.UI.Page

    Protected URL As String

    Protected Sub Page_Load(ByVal sender As Object, _
      ByVal e As EventArgs) Handles Me.Load
        URL = "Images/picture.jpg"
        Me.DataBind()
    End Sub
End Class
```

You can now use this URL to create a label, as shown here:

```
<asp:Label id="lblDynamic" runat="server"><%# URL %></asp:Label>
```

You can also use it for a check box caption:

```
<asp:CheckBox id="chkDynamic" Text="<%# URL %>" runat="server" />
```

or you can use it for a target for a hyperlink:

```
<asp:Hyperlink id="lnkDynamic" Text="Click here!" NavigateUrl="<%# URL %>"
 runat="server" />
```

You can even use it for a picture:

```
<asp:Image id="imgDynamic" ImageUrl="<%# URL %>" runat="server" />
```

The only trick is that you need to edit these control tags manually. Figure 16-4 shows what a page that uses all these elements would look like.

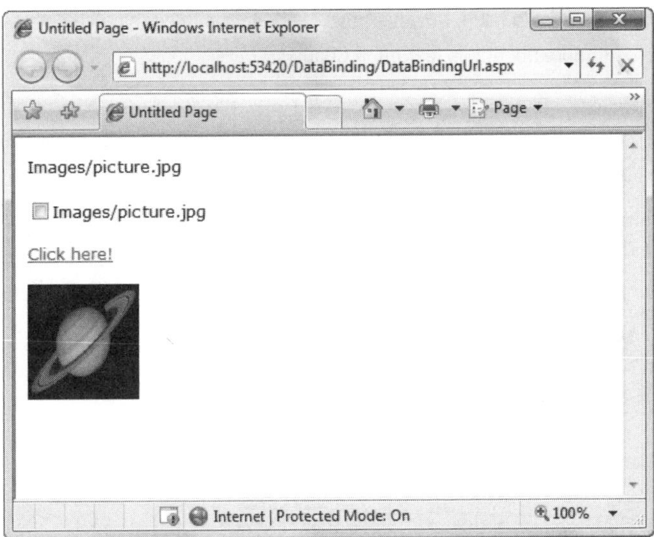

Figure 16-4. *Multiple ways to bind the same data*

To examine this example in more detail, try the sample code for this chapter.

Problems with Single-Value Data Binding

Before you start using single-value data binding techniques in every aspect of your ASP.NET programs, you should consider some of the serious drawbacks this approach can present:

Putting code into a page's user interface: One of ASP.NET's great advantages is that it allows developers to separate the user interface code (the HTML and control tags in the .aspx file) from the actual code used for data access and all other tasks (in the code-behind file). However, overenthusiastic use of single-value data binding can encourage you to disregard that distinction and start coding function calls and even operations into your page. If not carefully managed, this can lead to complete disorder.

Fragmenting code: When using data binding expressions, it may not be obvious where the functionality resides for different operations. This is particularly a problem if you blend both approaches—for example, if you use data binding to fill a control and also modify that control directly in code. Even worse, the data binding code may have certain dependencies that aren't immediately obvious. If the page code changes, or a variable or function is removed or renamed, the corresponding data binding expression could stop providing valid information without any explanation or even an obvious error. All of these details make it more difficult to maintain your code, and make it more difficult for multiple developers to work together on the same project.

Of course, some developers love the flexibility of single-value data binding and use it to great effect, making the rest of their code more economical and streamlined. It's up to you to be aware of (and avoid) the potential drawbacks.

■ **Note** In one case, single-value data binding is quite useful—when building *templates*. Templates declare a block of markup that's reused for each record in a table. However, they work only with certain rich data controls, such as the GridView. You'll learn more about this feature in Chapter 17.

Using Code Instead of Simple Data Binding

If you decide not to use single-value data binding, you can accomplish the same thing using code. For example, you could use the following event handler to display the same output as the first label example:

```
Protected Sub Page_Load(ByVal sender As Object, _
  ByVal e As EventArgs) Handles Me.Load

    TransactionCount = 10
    lblDynamic.Text = "There were " & TransactionCount.ToString()
    lblDynamic.Text &= " transactions today. "
    lblDynamic.Text &= "I see that you are using " & Request.Browser.Browser
End Sub
```

This code dynamically fills in the label without using data binding. The trade-off is more code.

When you use data binding expressions, you end up complicating your markup with additional details about your code (such as the names of the variables in your code-behind class). When you use the code-only approach, you end up doing the reverse—complicating your code with additional details about the page markup (like the text you want to display). In many cases, the best approach depends on your specific scenario. Data binding expressions are great for injecting small bits of information into an otherwise detailed page. The dynamic code approach gives you more flexibility, and works well when you need to perform more extensive work to shape the page (for example, interacting with multiple controls, changing content and formatting, retrieving the information you want to display from different sources, and so on).

Repeated-Value Data Binding

Although using simple data binding is optional, repeated-value binding is so useful that almost every ASP.NET application will want to use it somewhere.

Repeated-value data binding works with the ASP.NET list controls (and the rich data controls described in the next chapter). To use repeated-value binding, you link one of these controls to a data source (such as a field in a data table). When you call DataBind(), the control automatically creates a full list using all the corresponding values. This saves you from writing code that loops through the array or data table and manually adds elements to a control. Repeated-value binding can also simplify your life by supporting advanced formatting and template options that automatically configure how the data should look when it's placed in the control.

To create a data expression for list binding, you need to use a list control that explicitly supports data binding. Luckily, ASP.NET provides a number of list controls, many of which you've probably already used in other applications or examples:

ListBox, DropDownList, CheckBoxList, and RadioButtonList: These web controls provide a list for a single field of information.

HtmlSelect: This server-side HTML control represents the HTML <select> element and works essentially the same way as the ListBox web control. Generally, you'll use this control only for backward compatibility.

GridView, DetailsView, FormView, and ListView: These rich web controls allow you to provide repeating lists or grids that can display more than one field of information at a time. For example, if you bind one of these controls to a full-fledged table in a DataSet, you can display the values from multiple fields. These controls offer the most powerful and flexible options for data binding.

With repeated-value data binding, you can write a data binding expression in your .aspx file, or you can apply the data binding by setting control properties. In the case of the simpler list controls, you'll usually just set properties. Of course, you can set properties in many ways, such as by using code in a code-behind file or by modifying the control tag in the .aspx file, possibly with the help of Visual Studio's Properties window. The approach you take doesn't matter. The important detail is that you don't use any <%# expression %> data binding expressions.

To continue any further with data binding, it will help to divide the subject into a few basic categories. You'll start by looking at data binding with the list controls.

Data Binding with Simple List Controls

In some ways, data binding to a list control is the simplest kind of data binding. You need to follow only three steps:

1. Create and fill some kind of data object. You have numerous options, including an array, the basic ArrayList and Hashtable collections, the strongly typed List and Dictionary collections, and the ADO.NET DataTable and DataSet objects. Essentially, you can use any type of collection that supports the IEnumerable interface, although you'll discover each class has specific advantages and disadvantages.

2. Link the object to the appropriate control. To do this, you need to set only a couple of properties, including DataSource. If you're binding to a full DataSet, you'll also need to set the DataMember property to identify the appropriate table you want to use.

3. Activate the binding. As with single-value binding, you activate data binding by using the DataBind() method, either for the specific control or for all contained controls at once by using the DataBind() method for the current page.

This process is the same whether you're using the ListBox, the DropDownList, the CheckBoxList, the RadioButtonList, or even the HtmlSelect control. All these controls provide the same properties and work the same way. The only difference is in the way they appear on the final web page.

A Simple List Binding Example

To try this type of data binding, add a ListBox control to a new web page. Next, import the System.Collections namespace in your code. Finally, use the Page.Load event handler to create an ArrayList collection to use as a data source as follows:

```
Dim fruit As New ArrayList()
fruit.Add("Kiwi")
fruit.Add("Pear")
fruit.Add("Mango")
fruit.Add("Blueberry")
fruit.Add("Apricot")
fruit.Add("Banana")
fruit.Add("Peach")
fruit.Add("Plum")
```

Now, you can link this collection to the ListBox control:

```
lstItems.DataSource = fruit
```

Because an ArrayList is a straightforward, unstructured type of object, this is all the information you need to set. If you were using a DataTable (which has more than one field) or a DataSet (which has more than one DataTable), you would have to specify additional information.

To activate the binding, use the DataBind() method:

```
Me.DataBind()
```

You could also use lstItems.DataBind() to bind just the ListBox control. Figure 16-5 shows the resulting web page.

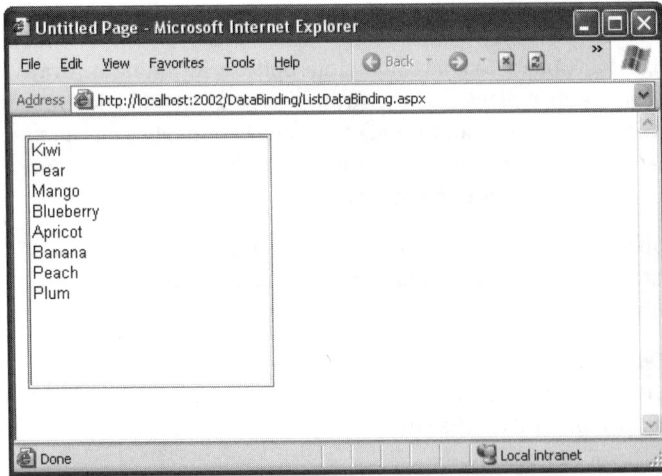

Figure 16-5. *A data-bound list*

This technique can save quite a few lines of code. This example doesn't offer a lot of savings because the collection is created just before it's displayed. In a more realistic application, however, you might be using a function that returns a ready-made collection to you:

```
Dim fruit As ArrayList
fruit = GetFruitsInSeason("Summer")
```

In this case, it's extremely simple to add the extra two lines needed to bind and display the collection in the window:

```
lstItems.DataSource = fruit
Me.DataBind()
```

or you could even change it to the following, even more compact, code:

```
lstItems.DataSource = GetFruitsInSeason("Summer")
Me.DataBind()
```

On the other hand, consider the extra trouble you would have to go through if you didn't use data binding. This type of savings compounds rapidly, especially when you start combining data binding with multiple controls, advanced objects such as DataSets, or advanced controls that apply formatting through templates.

Strongly Typed Collections

You can use data binding with the Hashtable and ArrayList, two of the more useful collection classes in the System.Collections namespace. However, as you learned in Chapter 3, .NET includes a more stringent set of collections in another namespace: System.Collections.Generic. These collections are ideal in cases where you want your collection to hold just a single type of object (for example, just strings). When you use the generic collections, you choose the item type you want to use, and the collection object is "locked in" to your choice (which is similar to how an array works). This means if you try to add another type of object that doesn't belong in the collection, you'll get a compile-time error. Similarly, when you pull an item out of the collection, you don't need to write casting code to convert it to the right type, because the compiler already knows what type of objects you're using. This behavior is safer and more convenient, and it's what you'll want most of the time.

To use a generic collection, you must import the right namespace:

```
Imports System.Collections.Generic
```

The generic version of the ArrayList class is named List. Here's how you create a List collection object that can only store strings:

```
Dim fruit As New List(Of String)()
fruit.Add("Kiwi")
fruit.Add("Pear")
```

The only real difference is that you need to specify the type of data you want to use when you declare the List object.

Multiple Binding

You can bind the same data list object to multiple different controls. Consider the following example, which compares all the types of list controls at your disposal by loading them with the same information:

```
Protected Sub Page_Load(ByVal sender As Object, _
  ByVal e As EventArgs) Handles Me.Load

    ' Create and fill the collection.
    Dim fruit As New List(Of String)()
    fruit.Add("Kiwi")
    fruit.Add("Pear")
    fruit.Add("Mango")
    fruit.Add("Blueberry")
    fruit.Add("Apricot")
    fruit.Add("Banana")
    fruit.Add("Peach")
    fruit.Add("Plum")

    ' Define the binding for the list controls.
    MyListBox.DataSource = fruit
    MyDropDownListBox.DataSource = fruit
    MyHtmlSelect.DataSource = fruit
    MyCheckBoxList.DataSource = fruit
    MyRadioButtonList.DataSource = fruit

    ' Activate the binding.
    Me.DataBind()
End Sub
```

Figure 16-6 shows the rendered page.

This is another area where ASP.NET data binding may differ from what you have experienced in a desktop application. In traditional data binding, all the different controls are sometimes treated like “views” on the same data source, and you can work with only one record from the data source at a time. In this type of data binding, when you select Pear in one list control, the other list controls automatically refresh so that they too have Pear selected (or the corresponding information from the same row). This isn’t how ASP.NET uses data binding. If you want this sort of effect, you need to write custom code to pull it off.

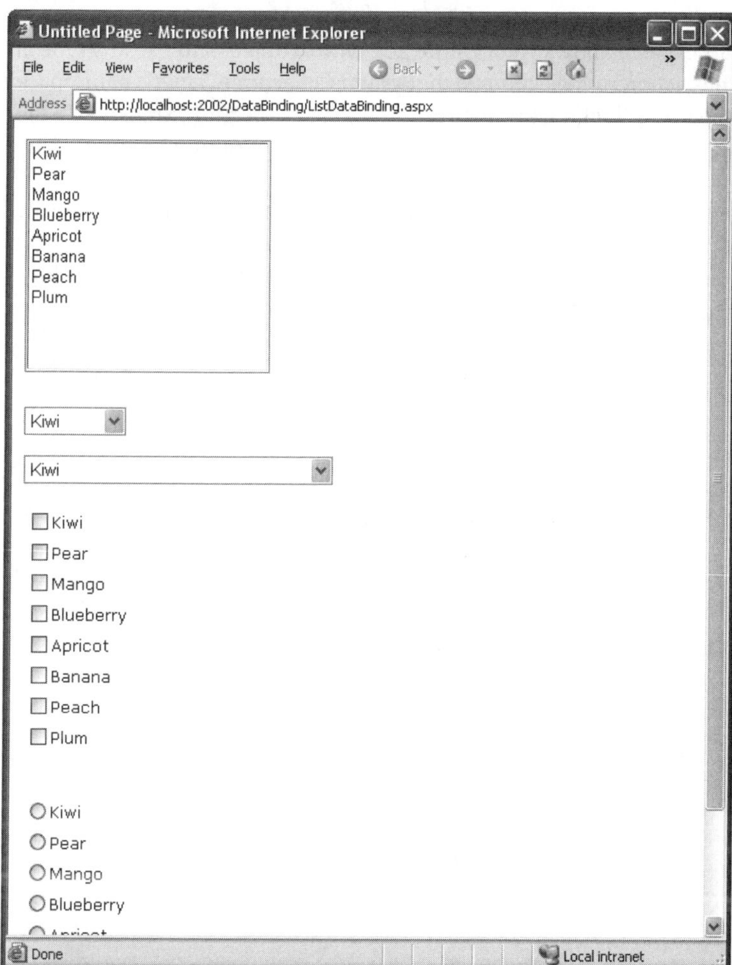

Figure 16-6. *Multiple bound lists*

Data Binding with a Dictionary Collection

A *dictionary collection* is a special kind of collection in which every item (or *definition*, to use the dictionary analogy) is indexed with a specific key (or dictionary *word*). This is similar to the way that built-in ASP.NET collections such as Session, Application, and Cache work.

Dictionary collections always need keys. This makes it easier to retrieve the item you want. In ordinary collections, like the ArrayList or List, you need to find the item you want by its index number position, or—more often—by traveling through the whole collection until you come across the right item. With a dictionary collection, you retrieve the item you want using its key. Generally, ordinary collections make sense when you need to work with all the items at once, while dictionary collections make sense when you frequently retrieve a single specific item.

You can use two basic dictionary-style collections in .NET. The Hashtable collection (in the System.Collections namespace) allows you to store any type of object and use any type of object for the key values. The Dictionary collection (in the System.Collections.Generic namespace) uses generics to provide the same "locking in" behavior as the List collection. You choose the item type and the key type upfront to prevent errors and reduce the amount of casting code you need to write.

The following example uses the Dictionary collection class, which it creates once—the first time the page is requested. You create a Dictionary object in much the same way you create an ArrayList or a List collection. The only difference is that you need to supply a unique key for every item. This example uses the lazy practice of assigning a sequential number for each key:

```
Protected Sub Page_Load(ByVal sender As Object, _
  ByVal e As EventArgs) Handles Me.Load

    If Not Me.IsPostBack
        ' Use integers to index each item. Each item is a string.
        Dim fruit As New Dictionary(Of Integer, String)()

        fruit.Add(1, "Kiwi")
        fruit.Add(2, "Pear")
        fruit.Add(3, "Mango")
        fruit.Add(4, "Blueberry")
        fruit.Add(5, "Apricot")
        fruit.Add(6, "Banana")
        fruit.Add(7, "Peach")
        fruit.Add(8, "Plum")

        ' Define the binding for the list controls.
        MyListBox.DataSource = fruit

        ' Choose what you want to display in the list.
        MyListBox.DataTextField = "Value"

        ' Activate the binding.
        Me.DataBind()
    End If
End Sub
```

There's one new detail here. It's this line:

```
MyListBox.DataTextField = "Value"
```

Each item in a dictionary-style collection has both a key and a value associated with it. If you don't specify which property you want to display, ASP.NET simply calls the ToString() method on each collection item. This may or may not produce the result you want. However, by inserting this line of code, you control exactly what appears in the list. The page will now appear as expected, with all the fruit names.

■ **Note** Notice that you need to enclose the property name in quotation marks. ASP.NET uses reflection to inspect your object and find the property that has the name Value at runtime.

You might want to experiment with what other types of collections you can bind to a list control. One interesting option is to use a built-in ASP.NET control such as the Session object. An item in the list will be created for every currently defined Session variable, making this trick a nice little debugging tool to quickly check current session information.

Using the DataValueField Property

Along with the DataTextField property, all list controls that support data binding also provide a DataValueField property, which adds the corresponding information to the value attribute in the control element. This allows you to store extra (undisplayed) information that you can access later. For example, you could use these two lines to define your data binding with the previous example:

```
MyListBox.DataTextField = "Value"
MyListBox.DataValueField = "Key"
```

The control will appear the same, with a list of all the fruit names in the collection. However, if you look at the rendered HTML that's sent to the client browser, you'll see that value attributes have been set with the corresponding numeric key for each item:

```
<select name="MyListBox" id="MyListBox" >
    <option value="1">Kiwi</option>
    <option value="2">Pear</option>
    <option value="3">Mango</option>
    <option value="4">Blueberry</option>
    <option value="5">Apricot</option>
    <option value="6">Banana</option>
    <option value="7">Peach</option>
    <option value="8">Plum</option>
</select>
```

You can retrieve this value later using the SelectedItem property to get additional information. For example, you could set the AutoPostBack property of the list control to True, and add the following code:

```
Protected Sub MyListBox_SelectedIndexChanged(ByVal sender As Object, _
  ByVal e As EventArgs) Handles MyListBox.SelectedIndexChanged

    lblMessage.Text = "You picked: " & MyListBox.SelectedItem.Text
    lblMessage.Text &= " which has the key: " & MyListBox.SelectedItem.Value
End Sub
```

Figure 16-7 demonstrates the result. This technique is particularly useful with a database. You could embed a unique ID into the value property and be able to quickly look up a corresponding record depending on the user's selection by examining the value of the SelectedItem object.

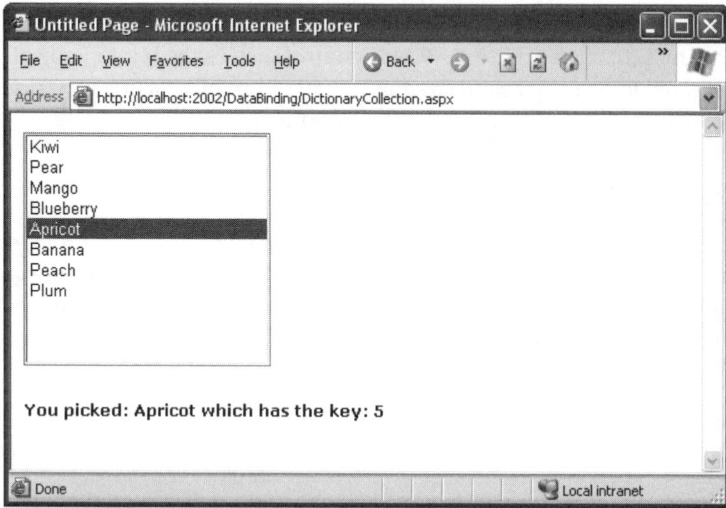

Figure 16-7. *Binding to the key and value properties*

Note that for this to work, you can't regenerate the list after every postback. If you do, the selected item information will be lost and an error will occur. The preceding example handles this by checking the Page.IsPostBack property. If it's False (which indicates that the page is being requested for the first time), the page builds the list. When the page is rendered, the current list of items is stored in view state. When the page is posted back, the list of items already exists and doesn't need to be re-created.

Data Binding with ADO.NET

So far, the examples in this chapter have dealt with data binding that doesn't involve databases or any part of ADO.NET. Although this is an easy way to familiarize yourself with the concepts, and a useful approach in its own right, you get the greatest advantage of data binding when you use it in conjunction with a database.

When you're using data binding with the information drawn from a database, the data binding process takes place in the same three steps. First you create your data source, which will be a DataReader or DataSet object. A DataReader generally offers the best performance, but it limits your data binding to a single control because it is a forward-only reader. As it fills a control, it traverses the results from beginning to end. Once it's finished, it can't go back to the beginning; so it can't be used in another data binding operation. For this reason, a DataSet is a more common choice.

The next example creates a DataSet and binds it to a list. In this example, the DataSet is filled by hand, but it could just as easily be filled using a DataAdapter object, as you saw in the previous chapter.

To fill a DataSet by hand, you need to follow several steps:

1. First, create the DataSet.
2. Next, create a new DataTable, and add it to the DataSet.Tables collection.
3. Next, define the structure of the table by adding DataColumn objects (one for each field) to the DataTable.Colums collection.
4. Finally, supply the data. You can get a new, blank row that has the same structure as your DataTable by calling the DataTable.NewRow() method. You must then set the data in all its fields, and add the DataRow to the DataTable.Rows collection.

Here's how the code unfolds:

```
' Define a DataSet with a single DataTable.
Dim dsInternal As New DataSet()
dsInternal.Tables.Add("Users")

' Define two columns for this table.
dsInternal.Tables("Users").Columns.Add("Name")
dsInternal.Tables("Users").Columns.Add("Country")

' Add some actual information into the table.
Dim rowNew As DataRow = dsInternal.Tables("Users").NewRow()
rowNew("Name") = "John"
rowNew("Country") = "Uganda"
dsInternal.Tables("Users").Rows.Add(rowNew)

rowNew = dsInternal.Tables("Users").NewRow()
rowNew("Name") = "Samantha"
rowNew("Country") = "Belgium"
dsInternal.Tables("Users").Rows.Add(rowNew)

rowNew = dsInternal.Tables("Users").NewRow()
rowNew("Name") = "Rico"
rowNew("Country") = "Japan"
dsInternal.Tables("Users").Rows.Add(rowNew)
```

Next, you bind the DataTable from the DataSet to the appropriate control. Because list controls can only show a single column at a time, you also need to choose the field you want to display for each item by setting the DataTextField property:

```
' Define the binding.
lstUser.DataSource = dsInternal.Tables("Users")
lstUser.DataTextField = "Name"
```

Alternatively, you could use the entire DataSet for the data source, instead of just the appropriate table. In that case, you would have to select a table by setting the control's DataMember property. This is an equivalent approach, but the code is slightly different:

```
' Define the binding.
lstUser.DataSource = dsInternal
lstUser.DataMember = "Users"
lstUser.DataTextField = "Name"
```

As always, the last step is to activate the binding:

```
Me.DataBind()
```

The final result is a list with the information from the specified database field, as shown in Figure 16-8. The list box will have an entry for every single record in the table, even if it appears more than once, from the first row to the last.

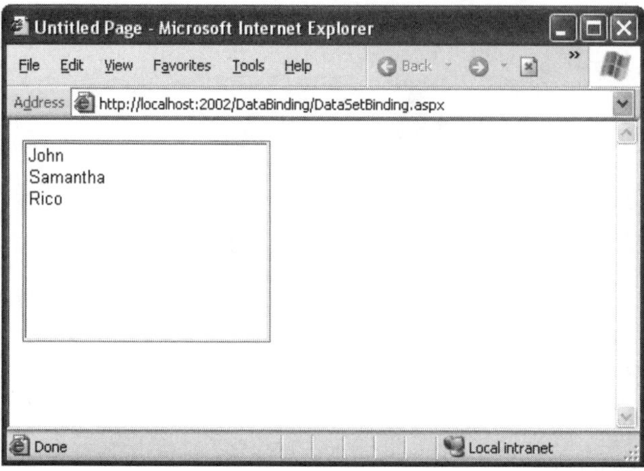

Figure 16-8. *DataSet binding*

■ **Tip** The simple list controls require you to bind their Text or Value property to a single data field in the data source object. However, much more flexibility is provided by the more advanced data binding controls examined in the next chapter. They allow fields to be combined in just about any way you can imagine.

Creating a Record Editor

The next example is more practical. It's a good example of how you might use data binding in a full ASP.NET application. This example allows the user to select a record and update one piece of information by using data-bound list controls.

The first step is to add the connection string to your web.config file. This example uses the Products table from the Northwind database included with many versions of SQL Server. Here's how you can define the connection string for SQL Server Express:

```
<configuration>
  <connectionStrings>
    <add name="Northwind" connectionString=
```

```
"Data Source=localhost\SQLEXPRESS;Initial Catalog=Northwind;Integrated Security=SSPI" />
  </connectionStrings>
  ...
</configuration>
```

To use the full version of SQL Server, remove the \SQLEXPRESS portion. To use a database server on another computer, supply the computer name for the Data Source connection string property. (For more details about connection strings, refer to Chapter 15.)

The next step is to retrieve the connection string and store it in a private variable in the Page class so that every part of your page code can access it easily. Once you've imported the System.Web.Configuration namespace, you can create a member variable in your code-behind class that's defined like this:

```
Private connectionString As String = _
  WebConfigurationManager.ConnectionStrings("Northwind").ConnectionString
```

The next step is to create a drop-down list that allows the user to choose a product for editing. The Page.Load event handler takes care of this task—retrieving the data, binding it to the drop-down list control, and then activating the binding. Before you go any further, make sure you've imported the System.Data.SqlClient namespace, which allows you to use the SQL Server provider to retrieve data.

```
Protected Sub Page_Load(ByVal sender As Object, _
  ByVal e As EventArgs) Handles Me.Load

    If Not Me.IsPostBack
        ' Define the ADO.NET objects for selecting products from the database.
        Dim selectSQL As String = "SELECT ProductName, ProductID FROM Products"
        Dim con As New SqlConnection(connectionString)
        Dim cmd As New SqlCommand(selectSQL, con)

        ' Open the connection.
        con.Open()

        ' Define the binding.
        lstProduct.DataSource = cmd.ExecuteReader()
        lstProduct.DataTextField = "ProductName"
        lstProduct.DataValueField = "ProductID"

        ' Activate the binding.
        Me.DataBind()

        con.Close()

        ' Make sure nothing is currently selected in the list box.
        lstProduct.SelectedIndex = -1
    End If
End Sub
```

Once again, the list is only filled the first time the page is requested (and stored in view state automatically). If the page is posted back, the list keeps its current entries. This reduces the amount of database work, and keeps the page working quickly and efficiently. You should also note that this page doesn't attempt to deal with errors. If you were using it in a real application, you'd need to use the exception-handling approach demonstrated in Chapter 15.

The actual database code is similar to what was used in the previous chapter. The example uses a Select statement but carefully limits the returned information to just the ProductName and ProductID fields, which are the only pieces of information it will use. The resulting window lists all the products defined in the database, as shown in Figure 16-9.

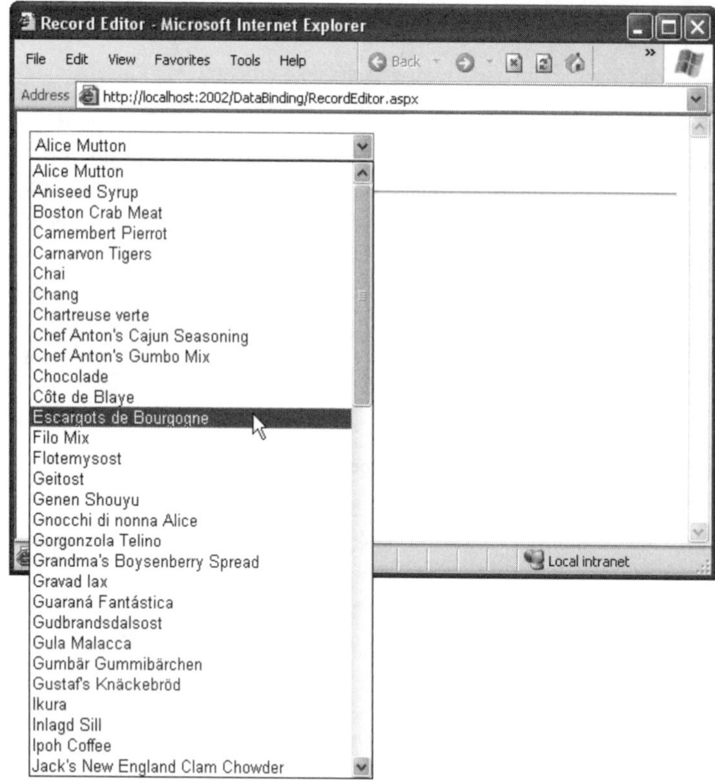

Figure 16-9. *Product choices*

The drop-down list enables AutoPostBack, so as soon as the user makes a selection, a lstProduct.SelectedItemChanged event fires. At this point, your code performs the following tasks:

- It reads the corresponding record from the Products table and displays additional information about it in a label. In this case, a Join query links information from the Products and Categories tables. The code also determines what the category is for the current product. This is the piece of information it will allow the user to change.
- It reads the full list of CategoryNames from the Categories table and binds this information to a different list control. Initially, this list is hidden in a panel with its Visible property set to False. The code reveals the content of this panel by setting Visible to True.

- It highlights the row in the category list that corresponds to the current product. For example, if the current product is a Seafood category, the Seafood entry in the list box will be selected.

This logic appears fairly involved, but it's really just an application of what you've learned over the past two chapters. The full listing is as follows:

```
Protected Sub lstProduct_SelectedIndexChanged(ByVal sender As Object, _
  ByVal e As EventArgs) Handles lstProduct.SelectedIndexChanged

    ' Create a command for selecting the matching product record.
    Dim selectProduct As String = "SELECT ProductName, QuantityPerUnit, " & _
     "CategoryName FROM Products INNER JOIN Categories ON " & _
     "Categories.CategoryID=Products.CategoryID " & _
     "WHERE ProductID=@ProductID"

    ' Create the Connection and Command objects.
    Dim con As New SqlConnection(connectionString)
    Dim cmdProducts As New SqlCommand(selectProduct, con)
    cmdProducts.Parameters.AddWithValue("@ProductID", _
      lstProduct.SelectedItem.Value)

    ' Retrieve the information for the selected product.
    Using con
        con.Open()
        Dim reader As SqlDataReader = cmdProducts.ExecuteReader()
        reader.Read()

        ' Update the display.
        lblRecordInfo.Text = "<b>Product:</b> " & _
          reader("ProductName") & "<br />"
        lblRecordInfo.Text &= "<b>Quantity:</b> " & _
          reader("QuantityPerUnit") & "<br />"
        lblRecordInfo.Text &= "<b>Category:</b> " & reader("CategoryName")

        ' Store the corresponding CategoryName for future reference.
        Dim matchCategory As String = reader("CategoryName")

        ' Close the reader.
        reader.Close()

        ' Create a new Command for selecting categories.
        Dim selectCategory As String = "SELECT CategoryName, " & _
          "CategoryID FROM Categories"
        Dim cmdCategories As New SqlCommand(selectCategory, con)
```

```
        ' Retrieve the category information, and bind it.
        lstCategory.DataSource = cmdCategories.ExecuteReader()
        lstCategory.DataTextField = "CategoryName"
        lstCategory.DataValueField = "CategoryID"
        lstCategory.DataBind()

        ' Highlight the matching category in the list.
        lstCategory.Items.FindByText(matchCategory).Selected = True
    End Using

    pnlCategory.Visible = True
End Sub
```

You could improve this code in several ways. It probably makes the most sense to remove these data access routines from this event handler and put them into more generic functions. For example, you could use a function that accepts a ProductName and returns a single DataRow with the associated product information. Another improvement would be to use a stored procedure to retrieve this information.

The end result is a window that updates itself dynamically whenever a new product is selected, as shown in Figure 16-10.

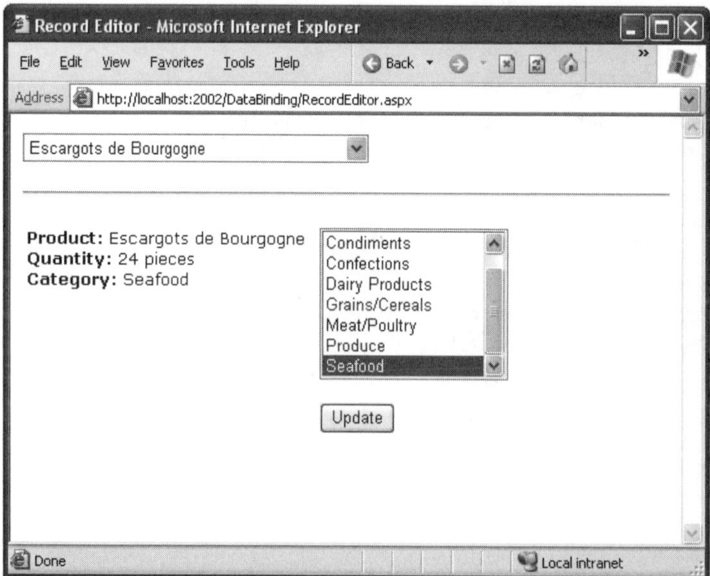

Figure 16-10. *Product information*

This example still has one more trick in store. If the user selects a different category and clicks Update, the change is made in the database. Of course, this means creating new Connection and Command objects, as follows:

```
Protected Sub cmdUpdate_Click(ByVal sender As Object, _
  ByVal e As EventArgs) Handles cmdUpdate.Click

    ' Define the Command.
    Dim updateCommand As String = "UPDATE Products " & _
     "SET CategoryID=@CategoryID WHERE ProductID=@ProductID"

    Dim con As New SqlConnection(connectionString)
    Dim cmd As New SqlCommand(updateCommand, con)

    cmd.Parameters.AddWithValue("@CategoryID", lstCategory.SelectedItem.Value)
    cmd.Parameters.AddWithValue("@ProductID", lstProduct.SelectedItem.Value)

    ' Perform the update.
    Using con
        con.Open()
        cmd.ExecuteNonQuery()
    End Using
End Sub
```

You could easily extend this example so that it allows you to edit all the properties in a product record. But before you try that, you might want to experiment with the rich data controls that are shown in the next chapter. Using these controls, you can create sophisticated lists and grids that provide automatic features for selecting, editing, and deleting records.

Data Source Controls

In Chapter 15, you saw how to directly connect to a database, execute a query, loop through the records in the result set, and display them on a page. In this chapter, you've already seen a simpler option—with data binding, you can write your data access logic and then show the results in the page with no looping or control manipulation required. Now, it's time to introduce *another* convenience: data source controls. Amazingly enough, data source controls allow you to create data-bound pages without writing any data access code at all.

■ **Note** As you'll soon see, often a gap exists between what you *can* do and what you *should* do. In most professional applications, you'll need to write and fine-tune your data access code for optimum performance or access to specific features. That's why you've spent so much time learning how ADO.NET works, rather than jumping straight to the data source controls.

The data source controls include any control that implements the IDataSource interface. The .NET Framework includes the following data source controls:

- *SqlDataSource*: This data source allows you to connect to any data source that has an ADO.NET data provider. This includes SQL Server, Oracle, and OLE DB or ODBC data sources. When using this data source, you don't need to write the data access code.
- *AccessDataSource:* This data source allows you to read and write the data in an Access database file (.mdb).

■Note Access databases do not have a dedicated server engine (like SQL Server) that coordinates the actions of multiple people and ensures that data won't be lost or corrupted. For that reason, Access databases are best suited for very small websites, where few people need to manipulate data at the same time. A much better small-scale data solution is SQL Server Express, which is described in Chapter 15.

- *ObjectDataSource*: This data source allows you to connect to a custom data access class. This is the preferred approach for large-scale professional web applications, but it forces you to write much more code. You'll tackle the ObjectDataSource in Chapter 23.
- *XmlDataSource*: This data source allows you to connect to an XML file. You'll learn more in Chapter 19.
- *SiteMapDataSource*: This data source allows you to connect to a .sitemap file that describes the navigational structure of your website. You saw this data source in Chapter 14.

You can find all the data source controls in the Data tab of the Toolbox in Visual Studio.

When you drop a data source control onto your web page, it shows up as a gray box in Visual Studio. However, this box won't appear when you run your web application and request the page (see Figure 16-11).

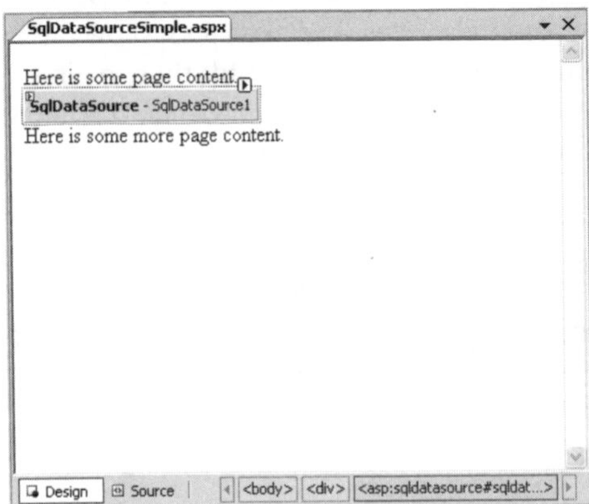

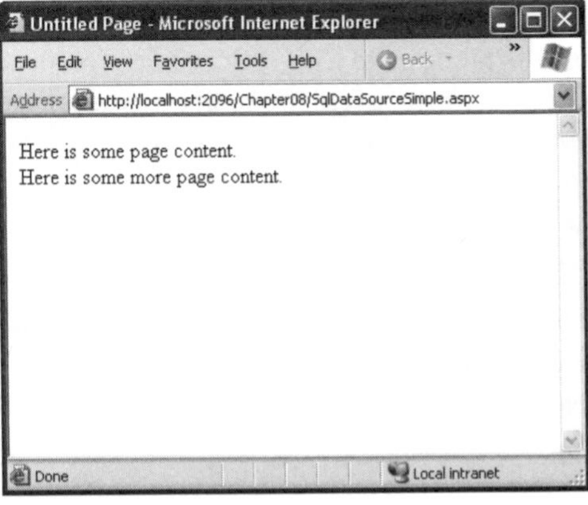

Figure 16-11. *A data source control at design time and runtime*

If you perform more than one data access task in the same page (for example, if you need to be able to query two different tables), you'll need more than one data access control.

The Page Life Cycle with Data Binding

Data source controls can perform two key tasks:

- They can retrieve data from a data source and supply it to bound controls. When you use this feature, your bound controls are automatically filled with data. You don't even need to call DataBind().
- They can update the data source when edits take place. In order to use this feature, you must use one of ASP.NET's rich data controls, like the GridView or DetailsView. For example, if you make an edit in the GridView and click Update, the GridView will trigger the update in the data source control, and the data source control will then update the database.

Before you can use the data source controls, you need to understand the page life cycle. The following steps explain the sequence of stages your page goes through in its lifetime. The two steps in bold (4 and 6) are the steps where the data source controls will spring into action:

1. The page object is created (based on the .aspx file).
2. The page life cycle begins, and the Page.Init and Page.Load events fire.
3. All other control events fire.
4. **If the user is applying a change, the data source controls perform their update operations now. If a row is being updated, the Updating and Updated events fire. If a row is being inserted, the Inserting and Inserted events fire. If a row is being deleted, the Deleting and Deleted events fire.**
5. The Page.PreRender event fires.
6. **The data source controls perform their queries and insert the data they retrieve into the bound controls. This step happens the first time your page is requested and every time the page is posted back, ensuring you always have the most up-to-date data. The Selecting and Selected events fire at this point.**
7. The page is rendered and disposed.

In the rest of this chapter, you'll take a closer look at the SqlDataSource control, and you'll use it to build the record editor example demonstrated earlier—with a lot less code.

The SqlDataSource

Data source controls turn up in the .aspx markup portion of your web page like ordinary controls. Here's an example:

```
<asp:SqlDataSource ID="SqlDataSource1" runat="server" ... />
```

The SqlDataSource represents a database connection that uses an ADO.NET provider. However, this has a catch. The SqlDataSource needs a generic way to create the Connection, Command, and DataReader objects it requires. The only way this is possible is if your data provider includes something called a *data provider factory*. The factory has the responsibility of creating the provider-specific objects that the SqlDataSource needs to access the data source. Fortunately, .NET includes a data provider factory for each of its four data providers:

- System.Data.SqlClient
- System.Data.OracleClient
- System.Data.OleDb
- System.Data.Odbc

You can use all of these providers with the SqlDataSource. You choose your data source by setting the provider name. Here's a SqlDataSource that connects to a SQL Server database using the SQL Server provider:

```
<asp:SqlDataSource ProviderName="System.Data.SqlClient" ... />
```

■ Tip Technically, you can omit this piece of information, because the System.Data.SqlClient provider factory is the default.

The next step is to supply the required connection string—without it, you cannot make any connections. Although you can hard-code the connection string directly in the SqlDataSource tag, it's always better to keep it in the <connectionStrings> section of the web.config file to guarantee greater flexibility and ensure you won't inadvertently change the connection string.

To refer to a connection string in your .aspx markup, you use a special syntax in this format:

```
<%$ ConnectionStrings:[NameOfConnectionString] %>
```

This looks like a data binding expression, but it's slightly different. (For one thing, it begins with the character sequence <%$ instead of <%#.)

For example, if you have a connection string named Northwind in your web.config file that looks like this:

```
<configuration>
  <connectionStrings>
    <add name="Northwind" connectionString=
"Data Source=localhost\SQLEXPRESS;Initial Catalog=Northwind;Integrated Security=SS-
PI" />
  </connectionStrings>
  ...
</configuration>
```

you would specify it in the SqlDataSource using this syntax:

```
<asp:SqlDataSource ConnectionString="<%$ ConnectionStrings:Northwind %>" ... />
```

Once you've specified the provider name and connection string, the next step is to add the query logic that the SqlDataSource will use when it connects to the database.

■ **Tip** If you want some help creating your connection string, select the SqlDataSource, open the Properties window, and select the ConnectionString property. A drop-down arrow will appear at the right side of the value. If you click that drop-down arrow, you'll see a list of all the connection strings in your web.config file. You can pick one of these connections, or you can choose New Connection (at the bottom of the list) to open the Add Connection dialog box, where you can pick the database you want. Best of all, if you create a new connection Visual Studio copies the connection string into your web.config file, so you can reuse it with other SqlDataSource objects.

Selecting Records

You can use each SqlDataSource control you create to retrieve a single query. Optionally, you can also add corresponding commands for deleting, inserting, and updating rows. For example, one SqlDataSource is enough to query and update the Customers table in the Northwind database. However, if you need to independently retrieve or update Customers and Orders information, you'll need two SqlDataSource controls.

The SqlDataSource command logic is supplied through four properties—SelectCommand, InsertCommand, UpdateCommand, and DeleteCommand—each of which takes a string. The string you supply can be inline SQL (in which case the corresponding SelectCommandType, InsertCommandType, UpdateCommandType, or DeleteCommandType property should be Text, the default) or the name of a stored procedure (in which case the command type is StoredProcedure). You need to define commands only for the types of actions you want to perform. In other words, if you're using a data source for read-only access to a set of records, you need to define only the SelectCommand property.

■ **Note** If you configure a command in the Properties window, you'll see a property named SelectQuery instead of SelectCommand. The SelectQuery is actually a virtual property that's displayed as a design-time convenience. When you edit the SelectQuery (by clicking the ellipsis next to the property name), you can use a special designer to write the command text (the SelectCommand) and add the command parameters (the SelectParameters) at the same time. However, this tool works best once you've reviewed the examples in this section, and you understand the way the SelectCommand and SelectParameters properties really work.

Here's a complete SqlDataSource that defines a Select command for retrieving product information from the Products table:

```
<asp:SqlDataSource ID="sourceProducts" runat="server"
  ProviderName="System.Data.SqlClient"
  ConnectionString="<%$ ConnectionStrings:Northwind %>"
  SelectCommand="SELECT ProductName, ProductID FROM Products"
/>
```

■ **Tip** You can write the data source logic by hand or by using a design-time wizard that lets you create a connection and create the command logic in a graphical query builder. To launch this tool, select the data source control, and choose Configure Data Source from the smart tag.

This is enough to build the first stage of the record editor example shown earlier—namely, the drop-down list box that shows all the products. All you need to do is set the DataSourceID property to point to the SqlDataSource you've created. The easiest way to do this is using the Properties window, which provides a drop-down list of all the data sources on your current web page. At the same time, make sure you set the DataTextField and DataValueField properties. Once you make these changes, you'll wind up with a control tag like this:

```
<asp:DropDownList ID="lstProduct" runat="server" AutoPostBack="True"
  DataSourceID="sourceProducts" DataTextField="ProductName"
  DataValueField="ProductID" />
```

The best part about this example is that you don't need to write any code. When you run the page, the DropDownList control asks the SqlDataSource for the data it needs. At this point, the SqlDataSource executes the query you defined, fetches the information, and binds it to the DropDownList. The whole process unfolds automatically.

How the Data Source Controls Work

As you learned earlier in this chapter, you can bind to a DataReader or a DataSet. So it's worth asking—which approach does the SqlDataSource control use? It's actually your choice, depending on whether you set the DataSourceMode to SqlDataSourceMode.DataSet (the default) or to SqlDataSourceMode.DataReader. The DataSet mode is almost always better, because it supports advanced sorting, filtering, and caching settings that depend on the DataSet. All these features are disabled in DataReader mode. However, you can use the DataReader mode with extremely large grids, because it's more memory-efficient. That's because the DataReader holds only one record in memory at a time—just long enough to copy the record's information to the linked control.

Another important fact to understand about the data source controls is that when you bind more than one control to the same data source, you cause the query to be executed multiple times. For example, if two controls are bound to the same data source, the data source control performs its query twice—once for each control. This is somewhat inefficient—after all, if you wrote the data binding code yourself by hand, you'd probably choose to perform the query once and then bind the returned DataSet twice. Fortunately, this design isn't quite as bad as it might seem. First, you can avoid this multiple-query overhead using caching, which allows you to store the retrieved data in a temporary memory location where it will be reused automatically. The SqlDataSource supports automatic caching if you set EnableCaching to True. Chapter 26 provides a full discussion of how caching works and how you can use it with the SqlDataSource.

Second, contrary to what you might expect, most of the time you *won't* be binding more than one control to a data source. That's because the rich data controls you'll learn about in Chapter 17—the GridView, DetailsView, and FormsView—have the ability to present multiple pieces of data in a flexible layout. If you use these controls, you'll need to bind only one control, which allows you to steer clear of this limitation.

It's also important to remember that data binding is performed at the end of your web page processing, just before the page is rendered. This means the Page.Load event will fire, followed by any control events, followed by the Page.PreRender event, and only then will the data binding take place. Data binding is performed on every postback (unless you redirect to another page).

Parameterized Commands

In the previous example (which used the SqlDataSource to retrieve a list of products), the complete query was hard-coded. Often, you won't have this flexibility. Instead, you'll want to retrieve a subset of data, such as all the products in a given category or all the employees in a specific city.

The record editor that you considered earlier offers an ideal example. Once you select a product, you want to execute another command to get the full details for that product. (You might just as easily execute another command to get records that are related to this product.) To make this work, you need two data sources. You've already created the first SqlDataSource, which fetches limited information about every product. Here's the second SqlDataSource, which gets more extensive information about a single product (the following query is split over several lines to fit the printed page):

```
<asp:SqlDataSource ID="sourceProductDetails" runat="server"
  ProviderName="System.Data.SqlClient"
  ConnectionString="<%$ ConnectionStrings:Northwind %>"
  SelectCommand="SELECT * FROM Products WHERE ProductID=@ProductID"
/>
```

But this example has a problem. It defines a parameter (@ProductID) that identifies the ID of the product you want to retrieve. How do you fill in this piece of information? It turns out you need to add a <SelectParameters> section to the SqlDataSource tag. Inside this section, you must define each parameter that's referenced by your SelectCommand and tell the SqlDataSource where to find the value it should use. You do that by *mapping* the parameter to a value in a control.

Here's the corrected command:

```
<asp:SqlDataSource ID="sourceProductDetails" runat="server"
  ProviderName="System.Data.SqlClient"
  ConnectionString="<%$ ConnectionStrings:Northwind %>"
  SelectCommand="SELECT * FROM Products WHERE ProductID=@ProductID">
  <SelectParameters>
    <asp:ControlParameter ControlID="lstProduct" Name="ProductID"
     PropertyName="SelectedValue" />
  </SelectParameters>
</asp:SqlDataSource>
```

You always indicate parameters with an @ symbol, as in @City. You can define as many symbols as you want, but you must map each provider to another value. In this example, the value for the @ProductID parameter comes from the lstProduct.SelectedValue property. In other words, you are binding a value that's currently in a control to place it into a database command. (You could also use the SelectedText property to get the currently displayed text, which is the ProductName in this example.)

Now all you need to do is bind the SqlDataSource to the remaining controls where you want to display information. This is where the example takes a slightly different turn. In the previous version of the record editor, you took the information and used a combination of values to fill in details in a label and a list control. This type of approach doesn't work well with data source controls. First, you can bind only a single data field to most simple controls such as lists. Second, each bound control makes a separate request to the SqlDataSource, triggering a separate database query. This means if you bind a dozen controls, you'll perform the same query a dozen times, with terrible performance. You can alleviate this problem with data source caching (see Chapter 26), but it indicates you aren't designing your application in a way that lends itself well to the data source control model.

The solution is to use one of the rich data controls, such as the GridView, DetailsView, or FormView. These controls have the smarts to show multiple fields at once, in a highly flexible layout. You'll learn about these three controls in detail in the next chapter, but the following example shows a simple demonstration of how to use the DetailsView.

The DetailsView is a rich data control that's designed to show multiple fields in a data source. As long as its AutoGenerateRows is True (the default), it creates a separate row for each field, with the field caption and value. Figure 16-12 shows the result.

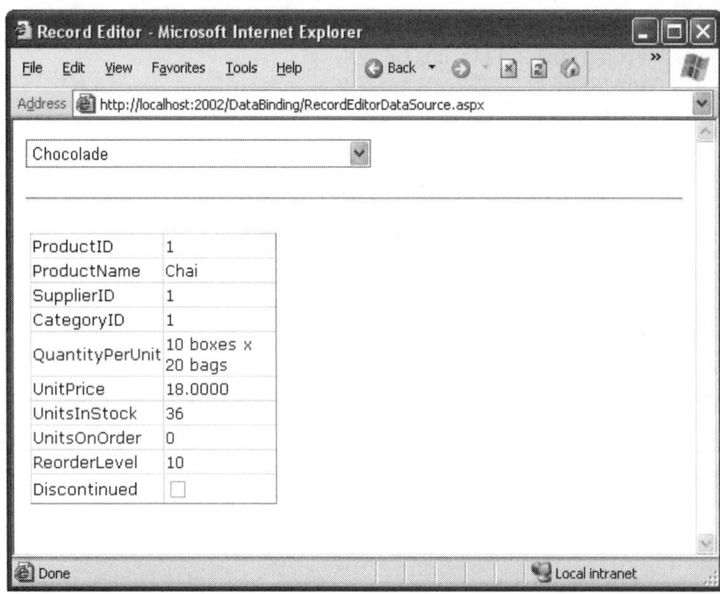

Figure 16-12. *Displaying full product information in a DetailsView*

Here's the basic DetailsView tag that makes this possible:

```
<asp:DetailsView ID="detailsProduct" runat="server"
  DataSourceID="sourceProductDetails" />
```

As you can see, the only property you need to set is DataSourceID. That binds the DetailsView to the SqlDataSource you created earlier. This SqlDataSource gets the full product information for a single row, based on the selection in the list control. Best of all, this whole example still hasn't required a line of code.

Other Types of Parameters

In the previous example, the @ProductID parameter in the second SqlDataSource is configured based on the selection in a drop-down list. This type of parameter, which links to a property in another control, is called a *control parameter*. But parameter values aren't necessarily drawn from other controls. You can map a parameter to any of the parameter types defined in Table 16-1.

Table 16-1. *Parameter Types*

Source	Control Tag	Description
Control property	<asp:ControlParameter>	A property from another control on the page.
Query string value	<asp:QueryStringParameter>	A value from the current query string.
Session state value	<asp:SessionParameter>	A value stored in the current user's session.
Cookie value	<asp:CookieParameter>	A value from any cookie attached to the current request.
Profile value	<asp:ProfileParameter>	A value from the current user's profile (see Chapter 20 for more about profiles).
A form variable	<asp:FormParameter>	A value posted to the page from an input control. Usually, you'll use a control property instead, but you might need to grab a value straight from the Forms collection if you've disabled view state for the corresponding control.

For example, you could split the earlier example into two pages. In the first page, define a list control that shows all the available products:

```
<asp:SqlDataSource ID="sourceProducts" runat="server"
  ProviderName="System.Data.SqlClient"
  ConnectionString="<%$ ConnectionStrings:Northwind %>"
  SelectCommand="SELECT ProductName, ProductID FROM Products"
/>
<asp:DropDownList ID="lstProduct" runat="server" AutoPostBack="True"
  DataSourceID="sourceProducts" DataTextField="ProductName"
  DataValueField="ProductID" />
```

Now, you'll need a little extra code to copy the selected city to the query string and redirect the page. Here's a button that does just that:

```
Protected Sub cmdGo_Click(ByVal sender As Object, _
  ByVal e As EventArgs) Handles cmdGo.Click

    If lstProduct.SelectedIndex <> -1 Then
        Response.Redirect( _
          "QueryParameter2.aspx?prodID=" & lstProduct.SelectedValue)
    End If
End Sub
```

Finally, the second page can bind the DetailsView according to the ProductID value that's supplied in the query string:

```
<asp:SqlDataSource ID="sourceProductDetails" runat="server"
  ProviderName="System.Data.SqlClient"
  ConnectionString="<%$ ConnectionStrings:Northwind %>"
  SelectCommand="SELECT * FROM Products WHERE ProductID=@ProductID">

  <SelectParameters>
    <asp:QueryStringParameter Name="ProductID" QueryStringField="prodID" />
  </SelectParameters>
</asp:SqlDataSource>

<asp:DetailsView ID="detailsProduct" runat="server"
  DataSourceID="sourceProductDetails" />
```

Setting Parameter Values in Code

Sometimes you'll need to set a parameter with a value that isn't represented by any of the parameter classes in Table 16-1. Or, you might want to manually modify a parameter value before using it. In both of these scenarios, you need to use code to set the parameter value just before the database operation takes place.

For example, consider the page shown in Figure 16-13. It includes two data-bound controls. The first is a list of all the customers in the database. Here's the markup that defines the list and its data source:

```
<asp:SqlDataSource ID="sourceCustomers" runat="server"
  ProviderName="System.Data.SqlClient"
  ConnectionString="<%$ ConnectionStrings:Northwind %>"
  SelectCommand="SELECT CustomerID, ContactName FROM Customers"
/>
  <asp:DropDownList ID="lstCustomers" runat="server"
  DataSourceID="sourceCustomers" DataTextField="ContactName"
  DataValueField="CustomerID" AutoPostBack="True">
</asp:DropDownList>
```

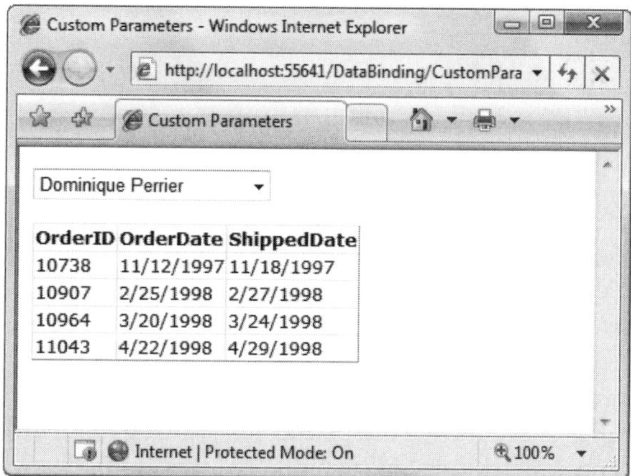

Figure 16-13. *Using parameters in a master-details page*

When the user picks a customer from the list, the page is posted back (because AutoPostBack is set to True) and the matching orders are shown in a GridView underneath, using a second data source. This data source pulls the CustomerID for the currently selected customer from the drop-down list using a ControlParameter:

```
<asp:SqlDataSource ID="sourceOrders" runat="server"
 ProviderName="System.Data.SqlClient"
 ConnectionString="<%$ ConnectionStrings:Northwind %>"
 SelectCommand="SELECT OrderID,OrderDate,ShippedDate FROM Orders WHERE
CustomerID=@CustomerID">
  <SelectParameters>
    <asp:ControlParameter Name="CustomerID"
     ControlID="lstCustomers" PropertyName="SelectedValue" />
  </SelectParameters>
</asp:SqlDataSource>

<asp:GridView ID="gridOrders" runat="server" DataSourceID="sourceOrders">
</asp:GridView>
```

Now, imagine you want to limit the order list so it only shows orders made in the last week. This is easy enough to accomplish with a Where clause that examines the OrderDate field. But there's a catch. It doesn't make sense to hard-code the OrderDate value in the query itself, because the range is set based on the current date. And there's no parameter that provides exactly the information you need. The easiest way to solve this problem is to add a new parameter—one that you'll be responsible for setting yourself:

```
<asp:SqlDataSource ID="sourceOrders" runat="server"
 ProviderName="System.Data.SqlClient"
 ConnectionString="<%$ ConnectionStrings:Northwind %>"
 SelectCommand="SELECT OrderID,OrderDate,ShippedDate FROM Orders WHERE Customer-
ID=@CustomerID AND OrderDate>=@EarliestOrderDate"
 OnSelecting="sourceOrders_Selecting">
```

```
  <SelectParameters>
    <asp:ControlParameter Name="CustomerID"
     ControlID="lstCustomers" PropertyName="SelectedValue" />
    <asp:Parameter Name="EarliestOrderDate" DefaultValue="1900/01/01" />
  </SelectParameters>
</asp:SqlDataSource>
```

Although you can modify the value of any parameter, if you aren't planning to pull the value out of any of the places listed in Table 16-1, it makes sense to use an ordinary Parameter object, as represented by the <asp:Parameter> element. You can set the data type (if required) and the default value (as demonstrated in this example).

Now that you've created the parameter, you need to set its value before the command takes place. The SqlDataSource has a number of events that are perfect for setting parameter values. You can fill in parameters for a select operation by reacting to the Selecting event. Similarly, you can use the Updating, Deleting, and Inserting events when updating, deleting, or inserting a record. In these event handlers, you can access the command that's about to be executed through the SqlDataSourceSelectingEventArgs.Command property, and modify its parameter values by hand. (The SqlCommand also provides similarly named Selected, Updated, Deleted, and Inserted events, but these take place after the operation has been completed, so it's too late to change the parameter value.)

Here's the code that's needed to set the parameter value to a date that's seven days in the past, ensuring you see one week's worth of records:

```
Protected Sub sourceOrders_Selecting(ByVal sender As Object, _
  ByVal e As SqlDataSourceSelectingEventArgs) Handles sourceOrders.Selecting

    e.Command.Parameters("@EarliestOrderDate").Value = _
      DateTime.Today.AddDays(-7)
End Sub
```

■ **Note** You'll have to tweak this code slightly if you're using it with the standard Northwind database. The data in the Northwind database is historical, and most orders bear dates around 1997. As a result, the previous code won't actually retrieve any records. But if you use the AddYears() method instead of AddDays(), you can easily move back ten years to the place you need to be.

Handling Errors

When you deal with an outside resource such as a database, you need to protect your code with a basic amount of error-handling logic. Even if you've avoided every possible coding mistake, you still need to defend against factors outside your control—for example, if the database server isn't running or the network connection is broken.

You can count on the SqlDataSource to properly release any resources (such as connections) if an error occurs. However, the underlying exception won't be handled. Instead, it will bubble up to the page and derail your processing. As with any other unhandled exception, the user will receive a cryptic error message or an error page. This design is unavoidable—if the SqlDataSource suppressed exceptions, it could hide potential problems and make debugging extremely difficult. However, it's a good idea to handle the problem in your web page and show a more suitable error message.

To do this, you need to handle the data source event that occurs immediately *after* the error. If you're performing a query, that's the Selected event. If you're performing an update, a delete, or an insert operation, you would handle the Updated, Deleted, or Inserted event instead. (If you don't want to offer customized error messages, you could handle all these events with the same event handler.)

In the event handler, you can access the exception object through the SqlDataSourceStatusEventArgs.Exception property. If you want to prevent the error from spreading any further, simply set the SqlDataSourceStatusEventArgs.ExceptionHandled property to True. Then, make sure you show an appropriate error message on your web page to inform the user that the command was not completed.

Here's an example:

```
Protected Sub sourceProducts_Selected(ByVal sender As Object, _
 ByVal e As SqlDataSourceStatusEventArgs) Handles sourceProducts.Selected

    If e.Exception IsNot Nothing Then
        lblError.Text = "An exception occurred performing the query."

        ' Consider the error handled.
        e.ExceptionHandled = True
    End If
End Sub
```

Updating Records

Selecting data is only half the equation. The SqlDataSource can also apply changes. The only catch is that not all controls support updating. For example, the humble ListBox doesn't provide any way for the user to edit values, delete existing items, or insert new ones. Fortunately, ASP.NET's rich data controls—including the GridView, DetailsView, and FormView—all have editing features you can switch on.

Before you can switch on the editing features in a given control, you need to define suitable commands for the operations you want to perform in your data source. That means supplying commands for inserting (InsertCommand), deleting (DeleteCommand), and updating (UpdateCommand). If you know you will allow the user to perform only certain operations (such as updates) but not others (such as insertions and deletions), you can safely omit the commands you don't need.

You define the InsertCommand, DeleteCommand, and UpdateCommand in the same way you define the command for the SelectCommand property—by using a parameterized query. For example, here's a revised version of the SqlDataSource for product information that defines a basic update command to update every field:

```
<asp:SqlDataSource ID="sourceProductDetails" runat="server"
  ProviderName="System.Data.SqlClient"
  ConnectionString="<%$ ConnectionStrings:Northwind %>"
  SelectCommand="SELECT ProductID, ProductName, UnitPrice, UnitsInStock,
UnitsOnOrder, ReorderLevel, Discontinued FROM Products WHERE ProductID=@ProductID"
  UpdateCommand="UPDATE Products SET ProductName=@ProductName, UnitPrice=@UnitPrice,
UnitsInStock=@UnitsInStock, UnitsOnOrder=@UnitsOnOrder, ReorderLevel=@ReorderLevel,
Discontinued=@Discontinued WHERE ProductID=@ProductID">
  <SelectParameters>
    <asp:ControlParameter ControlID="lstProduct" Name="ProductID"
     PropertyName="SelectedValue" />
  </SelectParameters>
</asp:SqlDataSource>
```

In this example, the parameter names aren't chosen arbitrarily. As long as you give each parameter the same name as the field it affects, and preface it with the @ symbol (so ProductName becomes @ProductName), you don't need to define the parameter. That's because the ASP.NET data controls automatically submit a collection of parameters with the new values before triggering the update. Each parameter in the collection uses this naming convention, which is a major time-saver.

You also need to give the user a way to enter the new values. Most rich data controls make this fairly easy—with the DetailsView, it's simply a matter of setting the AutoGenerateEditButton property to True, as shown here:

```
<asp:DetailsView ID="DetailsView1" runat="server"
  DataSourceID="sourceProductDetails" AutoGenerateEditButton="True" />
```

Now when you run the page, you'll see an edit link. When clicked, this link switches the DetailsView into edit mode. All fields are changed to edit controls (typically text boxes), and the Edit link is replaced with an Update link and a Cancel link (see Figure 16-14).

Clicking the Cancel link returns the row to its initial state. Clicking the Update link triggers an update. The DetailsView extracts the field values, uses them to set the parameters in the SqlDataSource.UpdateParameters collection, and then triggers the SqlDataSource.UpdateCommand to apply the change to the database. Once again, you don't have to write any code.

You can create similar parameterized commands for the DeleteCommand and InsertCommand. To enable deleting and inserting, you need to set the AutoGenerateDeleteButton and AutoGenerateInsertButton properties of the DetailsView to True. To see a sample page that allows updating, deleting, and inserting, refer to the UpdateDeleteInsert.aspx page that's included with the downloadable samples for this chapter.

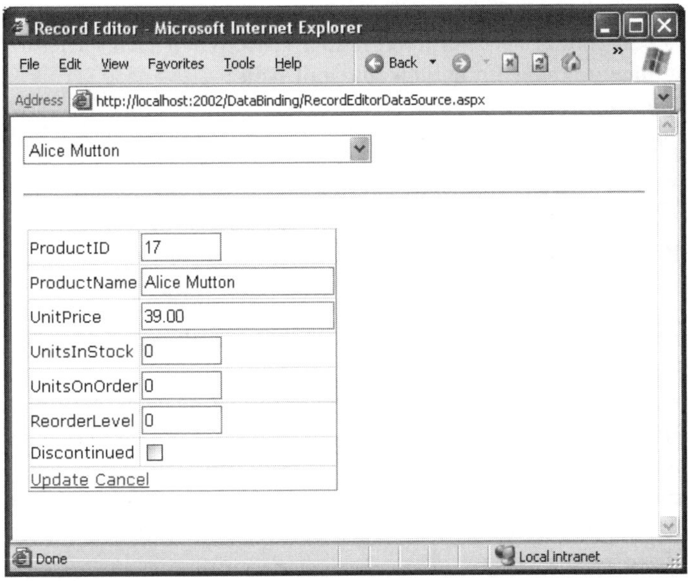

Figure 16-14. *Editing with the DetailsView*

Strict Concurrency Checking

The update command in the previous example matches the record based on its ID. You can tell this by examining the Where clause:

```
UpdateCommand="UPDATE Products SET ProductName=@ProductName, UnitPrice=@UnitPrice,
 UnitsInStock=@UnitsInStock, UnitsOnOrder=@UnitsOnOrder, ReorderLevel=@ReorderLevel,
 Discontinued=@Discontinued WHERE ProductID=@ProductID"
```

The problem with this approach is that it opens the door to an update that overwrites the changes of another user, if these changes are made between the time your page is requested and the time your page commits its update.

For example, imagine Chen and Lucy are viewing the same table of product records. Lucy commits a change to the price of a product. A few seconds later, Chen commits a name change to the same product record. Chen's update command not only applies the new name but it also overwrites all the other fields with the values from Chen's page—replacing the price Lucy entered with the price from the original page.

This is the same sort of concurrency problem you considered in Chapter 13 with the DataSet. The difference is that the DataSet uses automatically generated updating commands created with the CommandBuilder. The CommandBuilder uses a different approach. It always attempts to match every field. As a result, if the original is changed, the update command won't find it and the update won't be performed at all. So in the scenario described previously, using the CommandBuilder, Chen would receive an error when he attempts to apply the new product name, and he would need to edit the record and apply the change again.

You can use the same approach that the CommandBuilder uses with the SqlDataSource. All you need to do is write your commands a little differently so that the Where clause tries to match every field. Here's what the modified command would look like:

```
UpdateCommand="UPDATE Products SET ProductName=@ProductName, UnitPrice=@UnitPrice,
 UnitsInStock=@UnitsInStock, UnitsOnOrder=@UnitsOnOrder, ReorderLevel=@ReorderLevel,
 Discontinued=@Discontinued WHERE ProductID=@ProductID AND
 ProductName=@original_ProductName AND UnitPrice=@original_UnitPrice AND
 UnitsInStock=@original_UnitsInStock AND UnitsOnOrder=@original_UnitsOnOrder AND
 ReorderLevel=@original_ReorderLevel AND Discontinued=@original_Discontinued"
```

Although this makes sense conceptually, you're not finished yet. Before this command can work, you need to tell the SqlDataSource to maintain the old values from the data source and to give them parameter names that start with original_. You do this by setting two properties. First, set the SqlDataSource.ConflictDetection property to ConflictOptions.CompareAllValues instead of ConflictOptions.OverwriteChanges (the default). Next, set the long-winded OldValuesParameterFormatString property to the text "original_{0}". This tells the SqlDataSource to insert the text original_ before the field name to create the parameter that stores the old value. Now your command will work as written.

The SqlDataSource doesn't raise an exception to notify you if no update is performed. So, if you use the command shown in this example, you need to handle the SqlDataSource.Updated event and check the SqlDataSourceStatusEventArgs.AffectedRows property. If it's 0, no records have been updated, and you should notify the user about the concurrency problem so the update can be attempted again, as shown here:

```
Protected Sub sourceProductDetails_Updated(ByVal sender As Object, _
  ByVal e As SqlDataSourceStatusEventArgs) Handles sourceProductDetails.Updated

    If e.AffectedRows = 0 Then
        lblInfo.Text = "No update was performed. " & _
          "A concurrency error is likely, or the command is incorrectly written."
    Else
        lblInfo.Text = "Record successfully updated."
    End If
End Sub
```

Figure 16-15 shows the result you'll get if you run two copies of this page in two separate browser windows, begin editing in both of them, and then try to commit both updates.

Matching every field is an acceptable approach for small records, but it isn't the most efficient strategy if you have tables with huge amounts of data. In this situation, you have two possible solutions: you can match some of the fields (leaving out the ones with really big values) or you can add a timestamp field to your database table, and use that for concurrency checking.

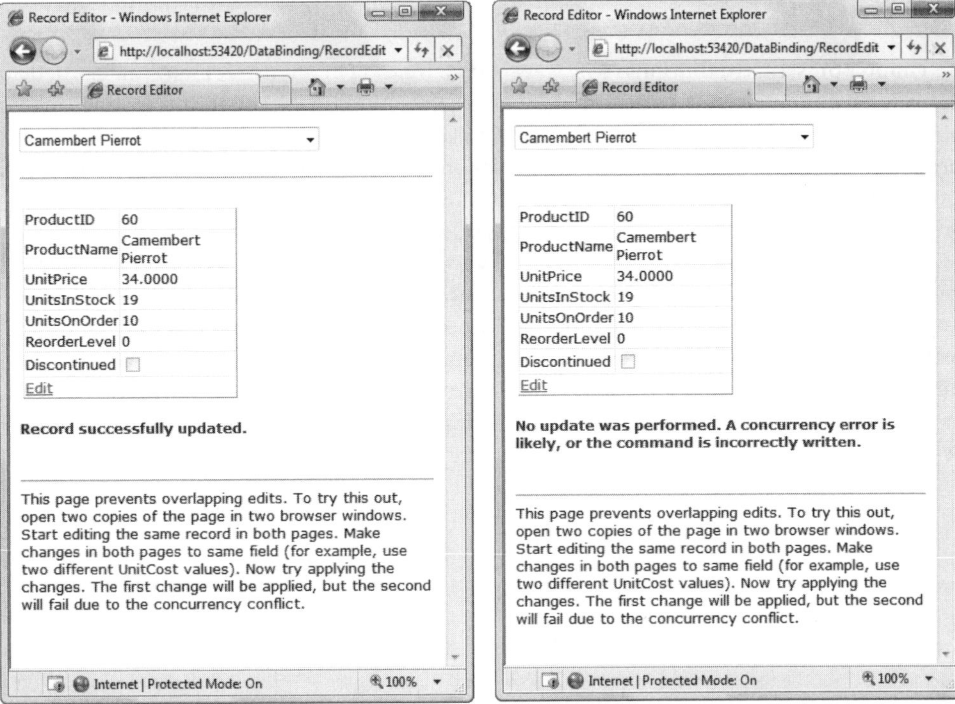

Figure 16-15. *A concurrency error in action*

Timestamps are special fields that the database uses to keep track of the state of a record. Whenever any change is made to a record, the database engine updates the timestamp field, giving it a new, automatically generated value. The purpose of a timestamp field is to make strict concurrency checking easier. When you attempt to perform an update to a table that includes a timestamp field, you use a Where clause that matches the appropriate unique ID value (like ProductID) and the timestamp field:

```
UpdateCommand="UPDATE Products SET ProductName=@ProductName, UnitPrice=@UnitPrice,
 UnitsInStock=@UnitsInStock, UnitsOnOrder=@UnitsOnOrder,
 ReorderLevel=@ReorderLevel, Discontinued=@Discontinued
 WHERE ProductID=@ProductID AND RowTimestamp=@RowTimestamp"
```

The database engine uses the ProductID to look up the matching record. Then, it attempts to match the timestamp in order to update the record. If the timestamp matches, you know the record hasn't been changed. The actual *value* of the timestamp isn't important, because that's controlled by the database. You just need to know whether it's changed.

Creating a timestamp is easy. In SQL Server, you create a timestamp field using the timestamp data type. In other database products, timestamps are sometimes called row versions.

The Last Word

This chapter presented a thorough overview of data binding in ASP.NET. First, you learned an interesting way to create dynamic text with simple data binding. Although this is a reasonable approach to get information into your page, it doesn't surpass what you can already do with pure code. You also learned how ASP.NET builds on this infrastructure with much more useful features, including repeated-value binding for quick-and-easy data display in a list control, and data source controls, which let you create code-free bound pages.

Using the techniques in this chapter, you can create a wide range of data-bound pages. However, if you want to create a page that incorporates record editing, sorting, and other more advanced tricks, the data binding features you've learned about so far are just the first step. You'll also need to turn to specialized controls, such as the DetailsView and the GridView, which build upon these data binding features. You'll learn how to master these controls in the next chapter. In Chapter 23 you'll learn how to extend your data binding skills to work with data access components.

CHAPTER 17

■ ■ ■

The Data Controls

When it comes to data binding, not all ASP.NET controls are created equal. In the previous chapter, you saw how data binding could help you automatically insert single values and lists into all kinds of common controls. In this chapter, you'll concentrate on three more advanced controls—GridView, DetailsView, and FormView—that allow you to bind entire tables of data.

The rich data controls are quite a bit different from the simple list controls—for one thing, they are designed exclusively for data binding. They also have the ability to display more than one field at a time, often in a table-based layout, or according to what you've defined. They also support higher-level features such as selecting, editing, and sorting.

The rich data controls include the following:

- *GridView*: The GridView is an all-purpose grid control for showing large tables of information. The GridView is the heavyweight of ASP.NET data controls.
- *DetailsView*: The DetailsView is ideal for showing a single record at a time, in a table that has one row per field. The DetailsView also supports editing.
- *FormView*: Like the DetailsView, the FormView shows a single record at a time and supports editing. The difference is that the FormView is based on templates, which allow you to combine fields in a flexible layout that doesn't need to be table-based.
- *ListView*: The ListView plays the same role as the GridView—it allows you to show multiple records. The difference is that the ListView is based on templates. As a result, using the ListView requires a bit more work and gives you slightly more layout flexibility. The ListView isn't described in this book, although you can learn more about it in the Visual Studio Help, or in the book *Pro ASP.NET 3.5 in VB* (Apress, 2008).

In this chapter, you'll explore the rich data controls in detail.

The GridView

The GridView is an extremely flexible grid control that displays a multicolumn table. Each record in your data source becomes a separate row in the grid. Each field in the record becomes a separate column in the grid.

The GridView is the most powerful of the three rich data controls you'll learn about in this chapter, because it comes equipped with the most ready-made functionality. This functionality includes features for automatic paging, sorting, selecting, and editing. The GridView is also the only data control you'll consider in this chapter that can show more than one record at a time.

Automatically Generating Columns

The GridView provides a DataSource property for the data object you want to display, much like the list controls you saw in Chapter 16. Once you've set the DataSource property, you call the DataBind() method to perform the data binding and display each record in the GridView. However, the GridView doesn't provide properties, such as DataTextField and DataValueField, that allow you to choose what column you want to display. That's because the GridView automatically generates a column for *every* field, as long as the AutoGenerateColumns property is True (which is the default).

Here's all you need to create a basic grid with one column for each field:

```
<asp:GridView ID="GridView1" runat="server" />
```

Once you've added this GridView tag to your page, you can fill it with data. Here's an example that performs a query using the ADO.NET objects and binds the retrieved DataSet:

```
Protected Sub Page_Load(ByVal sender As Object, _
  ByVal e As EventArgs) Handles Me.Load

    ' Define the ADO.NET objects.
    Dim connectionString As String = _
      WebConfigurationManager.ConnectionStrings("Northwind").ConnectionString
    Dim selectSQL As String = _
      "SELECT ProductID, ProductName, UnitPrice FROM Products"
    Dim con As New SqlConnection(connectionString)
    Dim cmd As New SqlCommand(selectSQL, con)
    Dim adapter As New SqlDataAdapter(cmd)

    ' Fill the DataSet.
    Dim ds As New DataSet()
    adapter.Fill(ds, "Products")

    ' Perform the binding.
    GridView1.DataSource = ds
    GridView1.DataBind()
End Sub
```

Remember, in order for this code to work you must have a connection string named Northwind in the web.config file (just as you did for the examples in the previous two chapters).

Figure 17-1 shows the GridView this code creates.

Of course, you don't need to write this data access code by hand. As you learned in the previous chapter, you can use the SqlDataSource control to define your query. You can then link that query directly to your data control, and ASP.NET will take care of the entire data binding process.

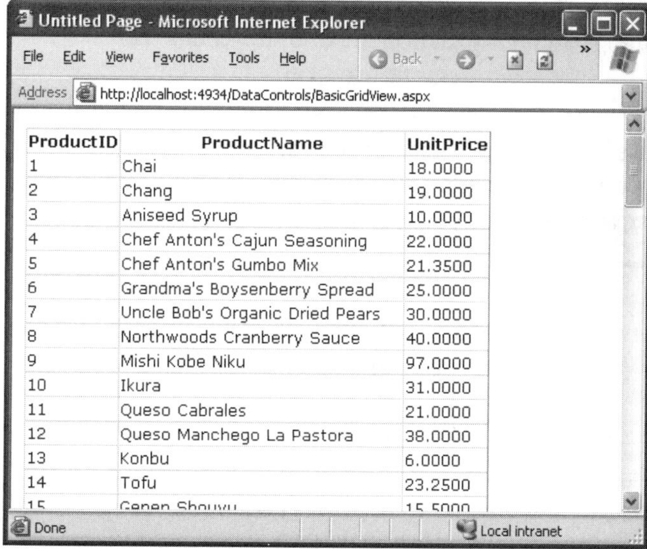

ProductID	ProductName	UnitPrice
1	Chai	18.0000
2	Chang	19.0000
3	Aniseed Syrup	10.0000
4	Chef Anton's Cajun Seasoning	22.0000
5	Chef Anton's Gumbo Mix	21.3500
6	Grandma's Boysenberry Spread	25.0000
7	Uncle Bob's Organic Dried Pears	30.0000
8	Northwoods Cranberry Sauce	40.0000
9	Mishi Kobe Niku	97.0000
10	Ikura	31.0000
11	Queso Cabrales	21.0000
12	Queso Manchego La Pastora	38.0000
13	Konbu	6.0000
14	Tofu	23.2500
15	Genen Shouyu	15.5000

Figure 17-1. *The bare-bones GridView*

Here's how you would define a SqlDataSource to perform the query shown in the previous example:

```
<asp:SqlDataSource ID="sourceProducts" runat="server"
  ConnectionString="<%$ ConnectionStrings:Northwind %>"
  SelectCommand="SELECT ProductID, ProductName, UnitPrice FROM Products" />
```

Next, set the GridView.DataSourceID property to link the data source to your grid:

```
<asp:GridView ID="GridView1" runat="server"
DataSourceID="sourceProducts" />
```

These two tags duplicate the example in Figure 17-1 but with significantly less effort. Now you don't have to write any code to execute the query and bind the DataSet.

Using the SqlDataSource has positive and negative sides. Although it gives you less control, it streamlines your code quite a bit, and it allows you to remove all the database details from your code-behind class. In this chapter, we'll focus on the data source approach, because it's much simpler when creating complex data-bound pages that support features such as editing. In Chapter 23, you'll learn how to adapt these examples to use the ObjectDataSource instead of the SqlDataSource. The ObjectDataSource is a great compromise—it allows you to write customized data access code in a database component without giving up the convenient design-time features of the data source controls.

Defining Columns

By default, the GridView.AutoGenerateColumns property is True, and the GridView creates a column for each field in the bound DataTable. This automatic column generation is good for creating quick test pages, but it doesn't give you the flexibility you'll usually want. For example, what if you want to hide columns, change their order, or configure some aspect of their display, such as the formatting or heading text? In all these cases, you need to set AutoGenerateColumns to False and define the columns in the <Columns> section of the GridView control tag.

■ **Tip** It's possible to have AutoGenerateColumns set to True and define columns in the <Columns> section. In this case, the columns you explicitly define are added before the autogenerated columns. However, for the most flexibility, you'll usually want to explicitly define every column.

Each column can be any of several column types, as described in Table 17-1. The order of your column tags determines the left-to-right order of columns in the GridView.

Table 17-1. *Column Types*

Class	Description
BoundField	This column displays text from a field in the data source.
ButtonField	This column displays a button in this grid column.
CheckBoxField	This column displays a check box in this grid column. It's used automatically for true/false fields (in SQL Server, these are fields that use the bit data type).
CommandField	This column provides selection or editing buttons.
HyperLinkField	This column displays its contents (a field from the data source or static text) as a hyperlink.
ImageField	This column displays image data from a binary field (providing it can be successfully interpreted as a supported image format).
TemplateField	This column allows you to specify multiple fields, custom controls, and arbitrary HTML using a custom template. It gives you the highest degree of control but requires the most work.

The most basic column type is BoundField, which binds to one field in the data object. For example, here's the definition for a single data-bound column that displays the ProductID field:

```
<asp:BoundField DataField="ProductID" HeaderText="ID" />
```

This tag demonstrates how you can change the header text at the top of a column from ProductID to just ID.

Here's a complete GridView declaration with explicit columns:

```
<asp:GridView ID="GridView1" runat="server" DataSourceID="sourceProducts"
 AutoGenerateColumns="False">
  <Columns>
    <asp:BoundField DataField="ProductID" HeaderText="ID" />
    <asp:BoundField DataField="ProductName" HeaderText="Product Name" />
    <asp:BoundField DataField="UnitPrice" HeaderText="Price" />
  </Columns>
</asp:GridView>
```

Explicitly defining columns has several advantages:

- You can easily fine-tune your column order, column headings, and other details by tweaking the properties of your column object.
- You can hide columns you don't want to show by removing the column tag. (Don't overuse this technique, because it's better to reduce the amount of data you're retrieving if you don't intend to display it.)
- You'll see your columns in the design environment (in Visual Studio). With automatically generated columns, the GridView simply shows a few generic placeholder columns.
- You can add extra columns to the mix for selecting, editing, and more.

This example shows how you can use this approach to change the header text. However, the HeaderText property isn't the only column property you can change in a column. In the next section, you'll learn about a few more.

Configuring Columns

When you explicitly declare a bound field, you have the opportunity to set other properties. Table 17-2 lists these properties.

Table 17-2. *BoundField Properties*

Property	Description
DataField	Identifies the field (by name) that you want to display in this column.
DataFormatString	Formats the field. This is useful for getting the right representation of numbers and dates.
ApplyFormatInEditMode	If True, the DataFormat string is used to format the value even when the value appears in a text box in edit mode. The default is False, which means the underlying value will be used (such as 1143.02 instead of $1,143.02).
FooterText, HeaderText, and HeaderImageUrl	Sets the text in the header and footer region of the grid if this grid has a header (GridView.ShowHeader is True) and footer (GridView.ShowFooter is True). The header is most commonly used for a descriptive label such as the field name; the footer can contain a dynamically calculated value such as a summary. To show an image in the header *instead* of text, set the HeaderImageUrl property.
ReadOnly	If True, it prevents the value for this column from being changed in edit mode. No edit control will be provided. Primary key fields are often read-only.
InsertVisible	If True, it prevents the value for this column from being set in insert mode. If you want a column value to be set programmatically or based on a default value defined in the database, you can use this feature.

Table 17-2. *BoundField Properties (Continued)*

Property	Description
Visible	If False, the column won't be visible in the page (and no HTML will be rendered for it). This gives you a convenient way to programmatically hide or show specific columns, changing the overall view of the data.
SortExpression	Sorts your results based on one or more columns. You'll learn about sorting later in the "Sorting and Paging the GridView" section of this chapter.
HtmlEncode	If True (the default), all text will be HTML encoded to prevent special characters from mangling the page. You could disable HTML encoding if you want to embed a working HTML tag (such as a hyperlink), but this approach isn't safe. It's always a better idea to use HTML encoding on all values and provide other functionality by reacting to GridView selection events.
NullDisplayText	Displays the text that will be shown for a null value. The default is an empty string, although you could change this to a hard-coded value, such as "(not specified)."
ConvertEmptyStringToNull	If True, converts all empty strings to null values (and uses the NullDisplayText to display them).
ControlStyle, HeaderStyle, FooterStyle, and ItemStyle	Configures the appearance for just this column, overriding the styles for the row. You'll learn more about styles throughout this chapter.

Generating Columns with Visual Studio

As you've already learned, you can create a GridView that shows all your fields by setting the AutoGenerateColumns property to True. Unfortunately, when you use this approach you lose the ability to control any of the details over your columns, including their order, formatting, sorting, and so on. To configure these details, you need to set AutoGenerateColumns to False and define your columns explicitly. This requires more work, and it's a bit tedious.

However, there is a nifty trick that solves this problem. You can use explicit columns but get Visual Studio to create the column tags for you automatically. Here's how it works: select the GridView control, and click Refresh Schema in the smart tag. At this point, Visual Studio will retrieve the basic schema information from your data source (for example, the names and data type of each column) and then add one <BoundField> element for each field.

■ **Tip** If you modify the data source so it returns a different set of columns, you can regenerate the GridView columns. Just select the GridView, and click the Refresh Schema link in the smart tag. This step will wipe out any custom columns you've added (such as editing controls).

Once you've created your columns, you can also use some helpful design-time support to configure the properties of each column (rather than editing the column tag by hand). To do this, select the GridView, and click the ellipsis (. . .) next to the Columns property in the Properties window. You'll see a Fields dialog box that lets you add, remove, and refine your columns (see Figure 17-2).

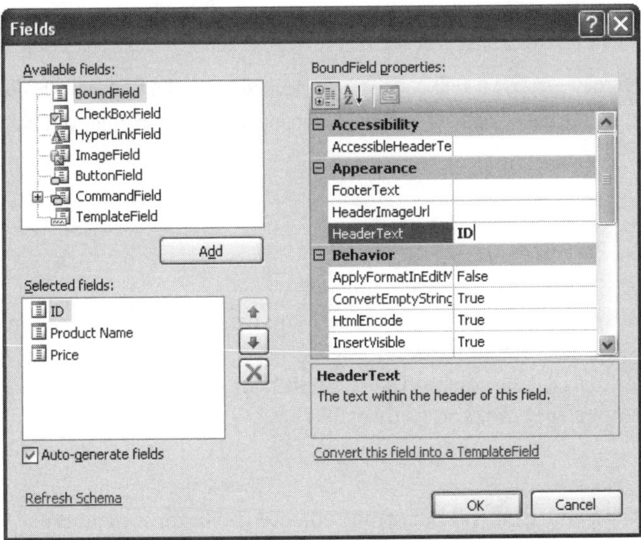

Figure 17-2. *Configuring columns in Visual Studio*

Now that you understand the underpinnings of the GridView, you've still only started to explore its higher-level features. In the following sections, you'll tackle these topics:

Formatting: How to format rows and data values

Selecting: How to let users select a row in the GridView and respond accordingly

Editing: How to let users commit record updates, inserts, and deletes

Sorting: How to dynamically reorder the GridView in response to clicks on a column header

Paging: How to divide a large result set into multiple pages of data

Templates: How to take complete control of designing, formatting, and editing by defining templates

Formatting the GridView

Formatting consists of several related tasks. First, you want to ensure that dates, currencies, and other number values are presented in the appropriate way. You handle this job with the DataFormatString property. Next, you'll want to apply the perfect mix of colors, fonts, borders, and alignment options to each aspect of the grid, from headers to data items. The GridView supports these features through styles. Finally, you can intercept events, examine row data, and apply formatting to specific values programmatically. In the following sections, you'll consider each of these techniques.

The GridView also exposes several self-explanatory formatting properties that aren't covered here. These include GridLines (for adding or hiding table borders), CellPadding and CellSpacing (for controlling the overall spacing between cells), and Caption and CaptionAlign (for adding a title to the top of the grid).

■ **Tip** Want to create a GridView that scrolls—inside a web page? It's easy. Just place the GridView inside a Panel control, set the appropriate size for the panel, and set the Panel.Scrollbars property to Auto, Vertical, or Both.

Formatting Fields

Each BoundField column provides a DataFormatString property you can use to configure the appearance of numbers and dates using a *format string*.

Format strings generally consist of a placeholder and a format indicator, which are wrapped inside curly brackets. A typical format string looks something like this:

```
{0:C}
```

In this case, the 0 represents the value that will be formatted, and the letter indicates a predetermined format style. Here, C means currency format, which formats a number as an amount of money (so 3400.34 becomes $3,400.34). Here's a column that uses this format string:

```
<asp:BoundField DataField="UnitPrice" HeaderText="Price"
  DataFormatString="{0:C}" />
```

Table 17-3 shows some of the other formatting options for numeric values.

Table 17-3. *Numeric Format Strings*

Type	Format String	Example
Currency	{0:C}	$1,234.50. Brackets indicate negative values: ($1,234.50). The currency sign is locale-specific.
Scientific (Exponential)	{0:E}	1.234.50E+004
Percentage	{0:P}	45.6%
Fixed Decimal	{0:F?}	Depends on the number of decimal places you set. {0:F3} would be 123.400. {0:F0} would be 123.

You can find other examples in the MSDN Help. For date or time values, you'll find an extensive list. For example, if you want to write the BirthDate value in the format month/day/year (as in 12/30/08), you use the following column:

```
<asp:BoundField DataField="BirthDate" HeaderText="Birth Date"
 DataFormatString="{0:MM/dd/yy}" />
```

Table 17-4 shows some more examples.

Table 17-4. *Time and Date Format Strings*

Type	Format String	Syntax	Example
Short Date	{0:d}	M/d/yyyy	10/30/2008
Long Date	{0:D}	dddd, MMMM dd, yyyy	Monday, January 30, 2008
Long Date and Short Time	{0:f}	dddd, MMMM dd, yyyy HH:mm aa	Monday, January 30, 2008 10:00 AM
Long Date and Long Time	{0:F}	dddd, MMMM dd, yyyy HH:mm:ss aa	Monday, January 30 2008 10:00:23 AM
ISO Sortable Standard	{0:s}	yyyy-MM-ddTHH:mm:ss	2008-01-30T10:00:23
Month and Day	{0:M}	MMMM dd	January 30
General	{0:G}	M/d/yyyy HH:mm:ss aa (depends on locale-specific settings)	10/30/2008 10:00:23 AM

The format characters are not specific to the GridView. You can use them with other controls, with data-bound expressions in templates (as you'll see later in the "Using GridView Templates" section), and as parameters for many methods. For example, the Decimal and DateTime types expose their own ToString() methods that accept a format string, allowing you to format values manually.

Using Styles

The GridView exposes a rich formatting model that's based on *styles*. Altogether, you can set eight GridView styles, as described in Table 17-5.

Table 17-5. *GridView Styles*

Style	Description
HeaderStyle	Configures the appearance of the header row that contains column titles, if you've chosen to show it (if ShowHeader is True).
RowStyle	Configures the appearance of every data row.
AlternatingRowStyle	If set, applies additional formatting to every other row. This formatting acts in addition to the RowStyle formatting. For example, if you set a font using RowStyle, it is also applied to alternating rows, unless you explicitly set a different font through AlternatingRowStyle.
SelectedRowStyle	Configures the appearance of the row that's currently selected. This formatting acts in addition to the RowStyle formatting.

Table 17-5. *GridView Styles (Continued)*

Style	Description
EditRowStyle	Configures the appearance of the row that's in edit mode. This formatting acts in addition to the RowStyle formatting.
EmptyDataRowStyle	Configures the style that's used for the single empty row in the special case where the bound data object contains no rows.
FooterStyle	Configures the appearance of the footer row at the bottom of the GridView, if you've chosen to show it (if ShowFooter is True).
PagerStyle	Configures the appearance of the row with the page links, if you've enabled paging (set AllowPaging to True).

Styles are not simple single-value properties. Instead, each style exposes a Style object that includes properties for choosing colors (ForeColor and BackColor), adding borders (BorderColor, BorderStyle, and BorderWidth), sizing the row (Height and Width), aligning the row (HorizontalAlign and VerticalAlign), and configuring the appearance of text (Font and Wrap). These style properties allow you to refine almost every aspect of an item's appearance.

Here's an example that changes the style of rows and headers in a GridView:

```
<asp:GridView ID="GridView1" runat="server" DataSourceID="sourceProducts"
  AutoGenerateColumns="False">
    <RowStyle BackColor="#E7E7FF" ForeColor="#4A3C8C" />
    <HeaderStyle BackColor="#4A3C8C" Font-Bold="True" ForeColor="#F7F7F7" />
    <Columns>
      <asp:BoundField DataField="ProductID" HeaderText="ID" />
      <asp:BoundField DataField="ProductName" HeaderText="Product Name" />
      <asp:BoundField DataField="UnitPrice" HeaderText="Price" />
    </Columns>
</asp:GridView>
```

In this example, every column is affected by the formatting changes. However, you can also define column-specific styles. To create a column-specific style, you simply need to rearrange the control tag so that the formatting tag becomes a nested tag *inside* the appropriate column tag. Here's an example that formats just the ProductName column:

```
<asp:GridView ID="GridView2" runat="server" DataSourceID="sourceProducts"
  AutoGenerateColumns="False" >
    <Columns>
      <asp:BoundField DataField="ProductID" HeaderText="ID" />
      <asp:BoundField DataField="ProductName" HeaderText="Product Name">
        <ItemStyle BackColor="#E7E7FF" ForeColor="#4A3C8C" />
        <HeaderStyle BackColor="#4A3C8C" Font-Bold="True" ForeColor="#F7F7F7" />
      </asp:BoundField>
```

```
        <asp:BoundField DataField="UnitPrice" HeaderText="Price" />
    </Columns>
</asp:GridView>
```

Figure 17-3 compares these two examples. You can use a combination of ordinary style settings and column-specific style settings (which override ordinary style settings if they conflict).

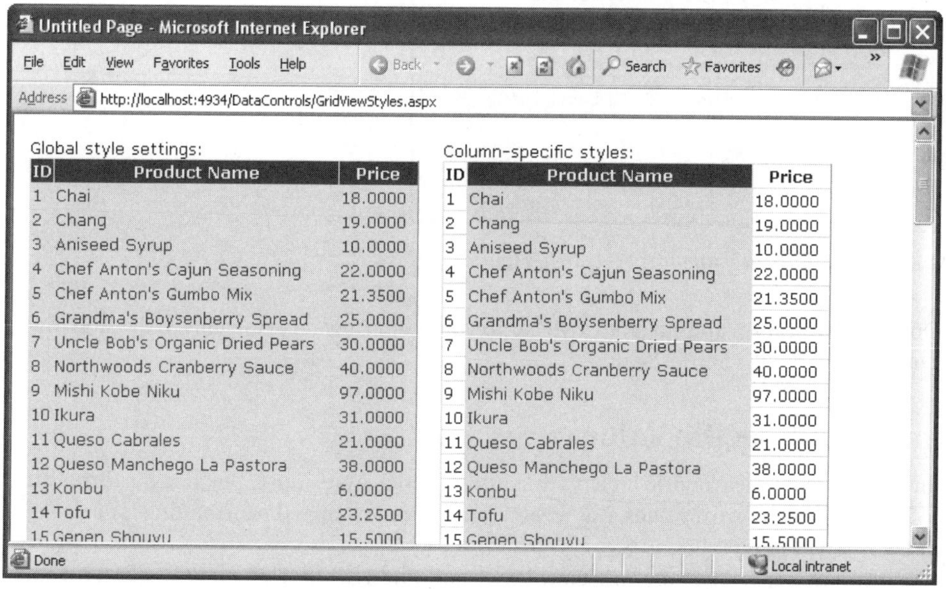

Figure 17-3. *Formatting the GridView*

One reason you might use column-specific formatting is to define specific column widths. If you don't define a specific column width, ASP.NET makes each column just wide enough to fit the data it contains (or, if wrapping is enabled, to fit the text without splitting a word over a line break). If values range in size, the width is determined by the largest value or the width of the column header, whichever is larger. However, if the grid is wide enough, you might want to expand a column so it doesn't appear to be crowded against the adjacent columns. In this case, you need to explicitly define a larger width.

Configuring Styles with Visual Studio

There's no reason to code style properties by hand in the GridView control tag, because the GridView provides rich design-time support. To set style properties, you can use the Properties window to modify the style properties. For example, to configure the font of the header, expand the HeaderStyle property to show the nested Font property, and set that. The only limitation of this approach is that it doesn't allow you to set the style for individual columns—if you need that trick, you must first call up the Fields dialog box (shown in Figure 17-2) by editing the Columns property. Then, select the appropriate column, and set the style properties accordingly.

You can even set a combination of styles using a preset theme by clicking the Auto Format link in the GridView smart tag. Figure 17-4 shows the Auto Format dialog box with some of the preset styles you can choose. Select Remove Formatting to clear all the style settings.

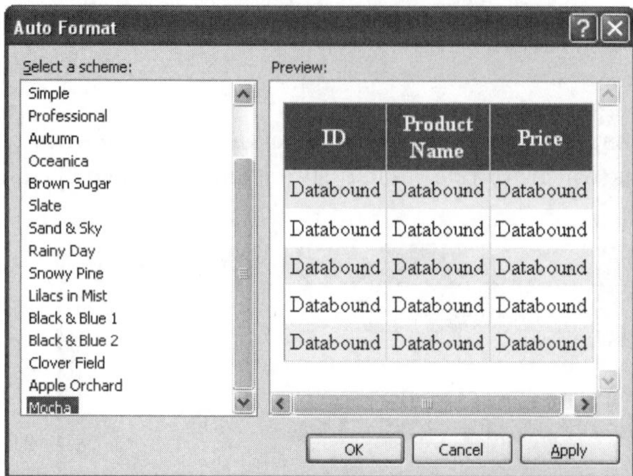

Figure 17-4. *Automatically formatting a GridView*

Once you've chosen and inserted styles into your GridView tag, you can tweak them by hand or by using the Properties window.

Formatting-Specific Values

The formatting you've learned so far isn't that fine-grained. At its most specific, this formatting applies to a single column of values. But what if you want to change the formatting for a specific row or even just a single cell?

The solution is to react to the GridView.RowDataBound event. This event is raised for each row, just after it's filled with data. At this point, you can access the current row as a GridViewRow object. The GridViewRow.DataItem property provides the data object for the given row, and the GridViewRow.Cells collection allows you to retrieve the row content. You can use the GridViewRow to change colors and alignment, add or remove child controls, and so on.

The following example handles the RowDataBound event and changes the background color to highlight high prices (those more expensive than $50):

```
Protected Sub grid_RowDataBound(ByVal sender As Object, _
  ByVal e As System.Web.UI.WebControls.GridViewRowEventArgs) _
  Handles grid.RowDataBound

    If e.Row.RowType = DataControlRowType.DataRow Then
        ' Get the price for this row.
        Dim price As Decimal
        price = CType(DataBinder.Eval(e.Row.DataItem, "UnitPrice"), Decimal)

        If price > 50 Then
            e.Row.BackColor = System.Drawing.Color.Maroon
            e.Row.ForeColor = System.Drawing.Color.White
            e.Row.Font.Bold = True
        End If
    End If
End Sub
```

First, the code checks whether the item being created is an item or an alternate item. If neither, it means the item is another interface element, such as the pager, footer, or header, and the procedure does nothing. If the item is the right type, the code extracts the UnitPrice field from the data-bound item.

To get a value from the bound data object (provided through the GridViewRowEventArgs.Row.DataItem property), you need to cast the data object to the correct type. The trick is that the type depends on the way you're performing your data binding. In this example, you're binding to the SqlDataSource in DataSet mode, which means each data item will be a DataRowView object. (If you were to bind in DataReader mode, a DbDataRecord represents each item instead.) To avoid coding these details, which can make it more difficult to change your data access code, you can rely on the DataBinder.Eval() helper method, which understands all these types of data objects. That's the technique used in this example.

Figure 17-5 shows the resulting page.

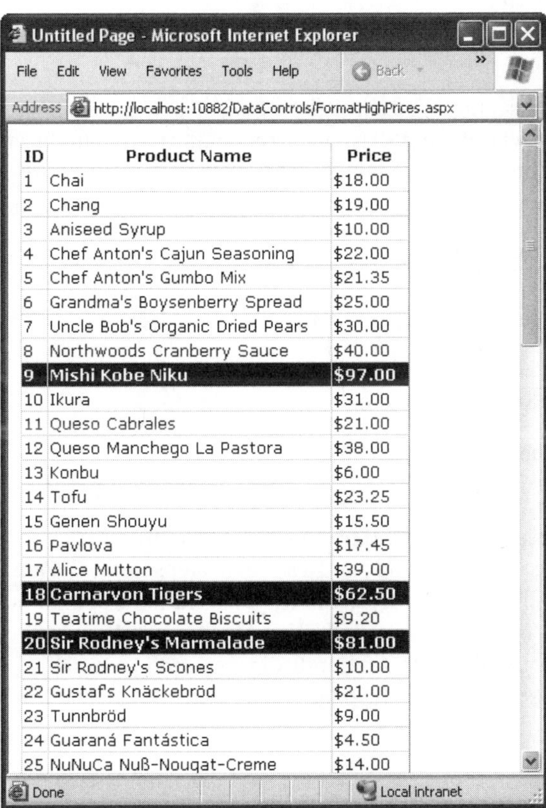

Figure 17-5. *Formatting individual rows based on values*

Selecting a GridView Row

Selecting an item refers to the ability to click a row and have it change color (or become highlighted) to indicate that the user is currently working with this record. At the same time, you might want to display additional information about the record in another control. With the GridView, selection happens almost automatically once you set up a few basics.

Before you can use item selection, you must define a different style for selected items. The SelectedRowStyle determines how the selected row or cell will appear. If you don't set this style, it will default to the same value as RowStyle, which means the user won't be able to tell which row is currently selected. Usually, selected rows will have a different BackColor property.

To find out what item is currently selected (or to change the selection), you can use the GridView.SelectedIndex property. It will be -1 if no item is currently selected. Also, you can react to the SelectedIndexChanged event to handle any additional related tasks. For example, you might want to update another control with additional information about the selected record.

Adding a Select Button

The GridView provides built-in support for selection. You simply need to add a CommandField column with the ShowSelectButton property set to True. ASP.NET can render the CommandField as a hyperlink, a button, or a fixed image. You choose the type using the ButtonType property. You can then specify the text through the SelectText property or specify the link to the image through the SelectImageUrl property.

Here's an example that displays a select button:

```
<asp:CommandField ShowSelectButton="True" ButtonType="Button"
 SelectText="Select" />
```

And here's an example that shows a small clickable icon:

```
<asp:CommandField ShowSelectButton="True" ButtonType="Image"
 SelectImageUrl="select.gif" />
```

Figure 17-6 shows a page with a text select button (and product 14 selected).

When you click a select button, the page is posted back, and a series of steps unfolds. First, the GridView.SelectedIndexChanging event fires, which you can intercept to cancel the operation. Next, the GridView.SelectedIndex property is adjusted to point to the selected row. Finally, the GridView.SelectedIndexChanged event fires, which you can handle if you want to manually update other controls to reflect the new selection. When the page is rendered, the selected row is given the selected row style.

■ **Tip** Rather than add the select button yourself, you can choose Enable Selection from the GridView's smart tag, which adds a basic select button for you.

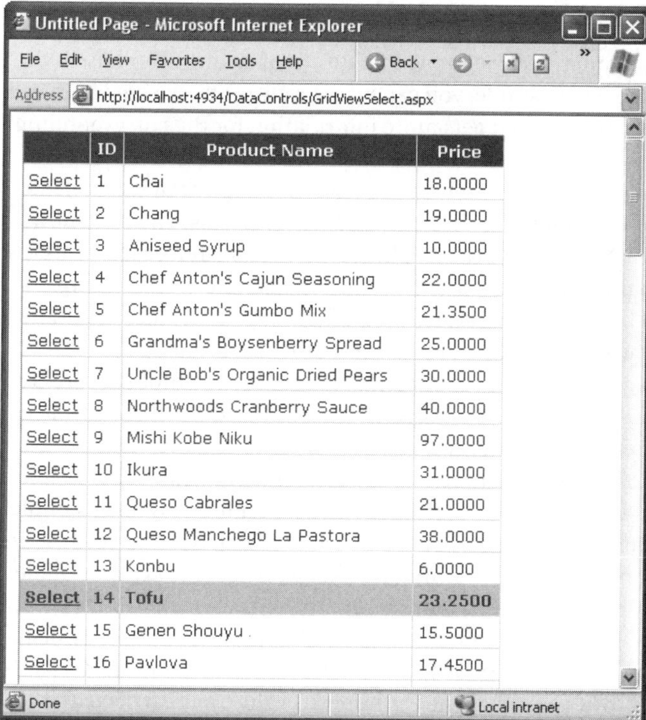

	ID	Product Name	Price
Select	1	Chai	18.0000
Select	2	Chang	19.0000
Select	3	Aniseed Syrup	10.0000
Select	4	Chef Anton's Cajun Seasoning	22.0000
Select	5	Chef Anton's Gumbo Mix	21.3500
Select	6	Grandma's Boysenberry Spread	25.0000
Select	7	Uncle Bob's Organic Dried Pears	30.0000
Select	8	Northwoods Cranberry Sauce	40.0000
Select	9	Mishi Kobe Niku	97.0000
Select	10	Ikura	31.0000
Select	11	Queso Cabrales	21.0000
Select	12	Queso Manchego La Pastora	38.0000
Select	13	Konbu	6.0000
Select	**14**	**Tofu**	**23.2500**
Select	15	Genen Shouyu	15.5000
Select	16	Pavlova	17.4500

Figure 17-6. *GridView selection*

Using a Data Field As a Select Button

You don't need to create a new column to support row selection. Instead, you can turn an existing column into a link. This technique is commonly implemented to allow users to select rows in a table by the unique ID value.

To use this technique, remove the CommandField column, and add a ButtonField column instead. Then, set the DataTextField to the name of the field you want to use.

```
<asp:ButtonField ButtonType="Button" DataTextField="ProductID" />
```

This field will be underlined and turned into a button that, when clicked, will post back the page and trigger the GridView.RowCommand event. You could handle this event, determine which row has been clicked, and programmatically set the SelectedIndex property of the GridView. However, you can use an easier method. Instead, just configure the link to raise the SelectedIndexChanged event by specifying a CommandName with the text *Select*, as shown here:

```
<asp:ButtonField CommandName="Select" ButtonType="Button"
 DataTextField="ProductID" />
```

Now clicking the data field automatically selects the record.

Using Selection to Create Master-Details Pages

As demonstrated in the previous chapter, you can draw a value out of a control and use it to perform a query in your data source. For example, you can take the currently selected item in a list, and feed that value to a SqlDataSource that gets more information for the corresponding record.

This trick is a great way to build *master-details pages*—pages that let you navigate relationships in a database. A typical master-details page has two GridView controls. The first shows the master (or parent) table. When a user selects an item in the first GridView, the second GridView is filled with related records from the details (or parent) table. For example, a typical implementation of this technique might have a customers table in the first GridView. Select a customer, and the second GridView is filled with the list of orders made by that customer.

To create a master-details page, you need to extract the SelectedIndex property from the first GridView and use that to craft a query for the second GridView. However, this approach has one problem. SelectedIndex returns a zero-based index number that represents where the row occurs in the grid. This isn't the information you need to insert into the query that gets the related records. Instead, you need a unique key field from the corresponding row. For example, if you have a table of products, you need to be able to get the ProductID for the selected row. In order to get this information, you need to tell the GridView to keep track of the key field values.

The way you do this is by setting the DataKeyNames property for the GridView. This property requires a comma-separated list of one or more key fields. Each name you supply must match one of the fields in the bound data source. Usually, you'll have only one key field. Here's an example that tells the GridView to keep track of the CustomerID values in a list of customers:

```
<asp:GridView ID="gridCustomers" runat="server"
DataKeyNames="CustomerID" ... >
```

Once you've established this link, the GridView is nice enough to keep track of the key fields for the selected record. It allows you to retrieve this information at any time through the SelectedDataKey property.

The following example puts it all together. It defines two GridView controls. The first shows a list of categories. The second shows the products that fall into the currently selected category (or, if no category has been selected, this GridView doesn't appear at all).

Here's the page markup for this example:

```
Categories:<br />
<asp:GridView ID="gridCategories" runat="server" DataSourceID="sourceCategories"
  DataKeyNames="CategoryID">
    <Columns>
      <asp:CommandField ShowSelectButton="True" />
    </Columns>
    <SelectedRowStyle BackColor="#FFCC66" Font-Bold="True"
     ForeColor="#663399" />
</asp:GridView>
<asp:SqlDataSource ID="sourceCategories" runat="server"
  ConnectionString="<%$ ConnectionStrings:Northwind %>"
  SelectCommand="SELECT * FROM Categories"></asp:SqlDataSource>
<br />
```

```
Products in this category:<br />
<asp:GridView ID="gridProducts" runat="server" DataSourceID="sourceProducts">
  <SelectedRowStyle BackColor="#FFCC66" Font-Bold="True" ForeColor="#663399" />
</asp:GridView>
<asp:SqlDataSource ID="sourceProducts" runat="server"
  ConnectionString="<%$ ConnectionStrings:Northwind %>"
  SelectCommand="SELECT ProductID, ProductName, UnitPrice FROM Products WHERE
CategoryID=@CategoryID">
    <SelectParameters>
      <asp:ControlParameter Name="CategoryID" ControlID="gridCategories"
        PropertyName="SelectedDataKey.Value" />
    </SelectParameters>
</asp:SqlDataSource>
```

As you can see, you need two data sources, one for each GridView. The second data source uses a ControlParameter that links it to the SelectedDataKey property of the first GridView. Best of all, you still don't need to write any code or handle the SelectedIndexChanged event on your own.

Figure 17-7 shows this example in action.

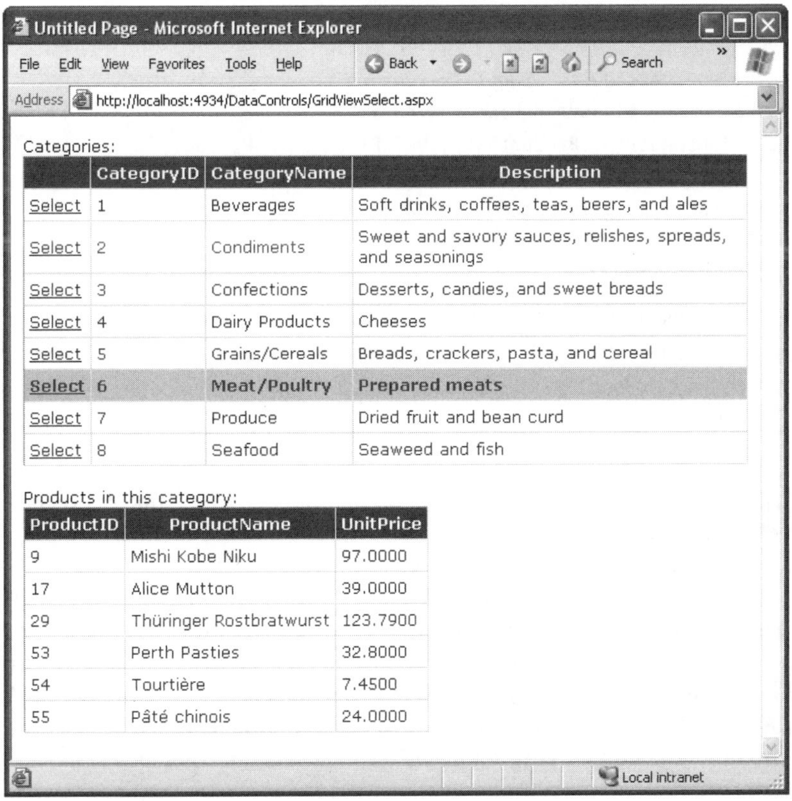

Untitled Page - Microsoft Internet Explorer

http://localhost:4934/DataControls/GridViewSelect.aspx

Categories:

	CategoryID	CategoryName	Description
Select	1	Beverages	Soft drinks, coffees, teas, beers, and ales
Select	2	Condiments	Sweet and savory sauces, relishes, spreads, and seasonings
Select	3	Confections	Desserts, candies, and sweet breads
Select	4	Dairy Products	Cheeses
Select	5	Grains/Cereals	Breads, crackers, pasta, and cereal
Select	**6**	**Meat/Poultry**	**Prepared meats**
Select	7	Produce	Dried fruit and bean curd
Select	8	Seafood	Seaweed and fish

Products in this category:

ProductID	ProductName	UnitPrice
9	Mishi Kobe Niku	97.0000
17	Alice Mutton	39.0000
29	Thüringer Rostbratwurst	123.7900
53	Perth Pasties	32.8000
54	Tourtière	7.4500
55	Pâté chinois	24.0000

Local intranet

Figure 17-7. *A master-details page*

Editing with the GridView

The GridView provides support for editing that's almost as convenient as its support for selection. To switch a row into select mode, you simply set the SelectedIndex property to the corresponding row number. To switch a row into edit mode, you set the EditIndex property in the same way.

Of course, both of these tasks can take place automatically if you use specialized button types. For selection, you use a CommandField column with the ShowSelectButton property set to True. To add edit controls, you follow almost the same step—once again, you use the CommandField column, but now you set ShowEditButton to True.

Here's an example of a GridView that supports editing:

```
<asp:GridView ID="gridProducts" runat="server" DataSourceID="sourceProducts"
  AutoGenerateColumns="False" DataKeyNames="ProductID" >
    <Columns>
      <asp:BoundField DataField="ProductID" HeaderText="ID" ReadOnly="True" />
      <asp:BoundField DataField="ProductName" HeaderText="Product Name"/>
      <asp:BoundField DataField="UnitPrice" HeaderText="Price" />
      <asp:CommandField ShowEditButton="True" />
    </Columns>
</asp:GridView>
```

And here's a revised data source control that can commit your changes:

```
<asp:SqlDataSource id="sourceProducts" runat="server"
  ConnectionString="<%$ ConnectionStrings:Northwind %>"
  SelectCommand="SELECT ProductID, ProductName, UnitPrice FROM Products"
  UpdateCommand="UPDATE Products SET ProductName=@ProductName,
UnitPrice=@UnitPrice WHERE ProductID=@ProductID" />
```

■ **Note** If you receive a SqlException that says "Must declare the scalar variable @ProductID," the most likely problem is that you haven't set the GridView.DataKeyNames property. Because the ProductID field can't be modified, the GridView won't pass the ProductID value to the SqlDataSource unless it's designated a key field.

Remember, you don't need to define the update parameters, as long as you make sure they match the field names (with an *at* sign [@] at the beginning). Chapter 16 has more information about using update commands with the SqlDataSource control.

When you add a CommandField with the ShowEditButton property set to True, the GridView editing controls appear in an additional column. When you run the page and the GridView is bound and displayed, the edit column shows an Edit link next to every record (see Figure 17-8).

When clicked, this link switches the corresponding row into edit mode. All fields are changed to text boxes, with the exception of read-only fields (which are not editable) and true/false bit fields (which are shown as check boxes). The Edit link is replaced with an Update link and a Cancel link (see Figure 17-9).

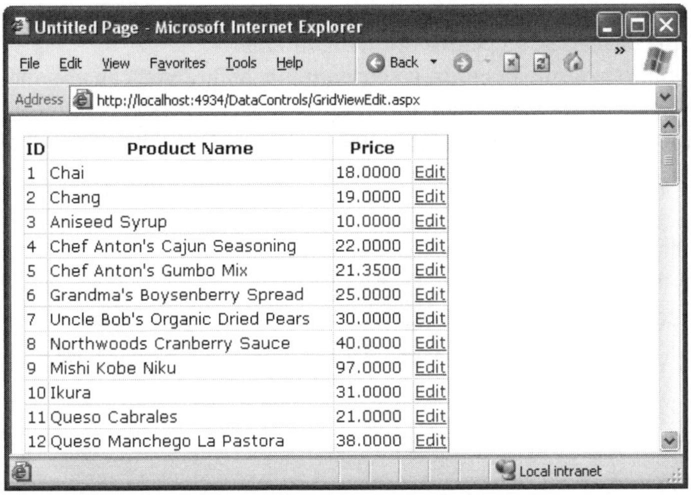

Figure 17-8. *The editing controls*

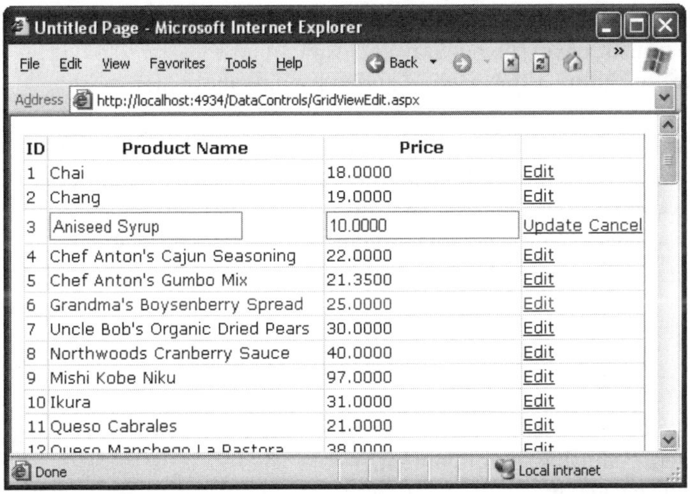

Figure 17-9. *Editing a record*

The Cancel link returns the row to its initial state. The Update link passes the values to the SqlDataSource.UpdateParameters collection (using the field names) and then triggers the SqlDataSource.Update() method to apply the change to the database. Once again, you don't have to write any code, provided you've filled in the UpdateCommand for the linked data source control.

You can use a similar approach to add support for record deleting. To enable deleting, you need to add a column to the GridView that has the ShowDeleteButton property set to True. As long as your linked SqlDataSource has the DeleteCommand property filled in, these operations will work automatically. If you want to write your own code that plugs into this process (for example, updating a label to inform the user the update has been made), consider reacting to the GridView event that fires after an update operation is committed, such as RowDeleted and RowUpdated. You can also prevent changes you don't like by reacting to the RowDeleting and RowUpdating events and setting the cancel flag in the event arguments.

The GridView does not support inserting records. If you want that ability, you can use one of the single-record display controls described later in this chapter, such as the DetailsView or FormView. For example, a typical ASP.NET page for data entry might show a list of records in a GridView, and provide a DetailsView that allows the user to add new records.

■ **Note** The basic built-in updating features of the GridView don't give you a lot of flexibility. You can't change the types of controls that are used for editing, format these controls, or add validation. However, you can add all these features by building your own editing templates, a topic you'll consider later in the "Using GridView Templates" section.

Sorting and Paging the GridView

The GridView is a great all-in-one solution for displaying all kinds of data, but it becomes a little unwieldy as the number of fields and rows in your data source grows. Dense grids contribute to large pages that are slow to transmit over the network and difficult for the user to navigate. The GridView has two features that address these issues and make data more manageable: sorting and paging.

Both sorting and paging can be performed by the database server, provided you craft the right SQL using the Order By and Where clauses. In fact, sometimes this is the best approach for performance. However, the sorting and paging provided by the GridView and SqlDataSource is easy to implement and thoroughly flexible. These techniques are particularly useful if you need to show the same data in several ways and you want to let the user decide how the data should be ordered.

Sorting

The GridView sorting features allow the user to reorder the results in the GridView by clicking a column header. It's convenient—and easy to implement.

Although you may not realize it, when you bind to a DataTable, you actually use another object called the DataView. The DataView sits between the ASP.NET web page binding and your DataTable. Usually it does little aside from providing the information from the associated DataTable. However, you can customize the DataView so it applies its own sort order. That way, you can customize the data that appears in the web page, without needing to actually modify your data.

You can create a new DataView object by hand and bind the DataView directly to a data control such as the GridView. However, the GridView and SqlDataSource controls make it even easier. They provide several properties you can set to control sorting. Once you've configured these properties, the sorting is automatic, and you still won't need to write any code in your page class.

To enable sorting, you must set the GridView.AllowSorting property to True. Next, you need to define a SortExpression for each column that can be sorted. In theory, a sort expression can use any syntax that's understood by the data source control. In practice, a sort expression almost always takes the form used in the ORDER BY clause of a SQL query. This means the sort expression can include a single field or a list of comma-separated fields, optionally with the word *ASC* or *DESC* added after the column name to sort in ascending or descending order.

Here's how you could define the ProductName column so it sorts by alphabetically ordering rows:

```
<asp:BoundField DataField="ProductName" HeaderText="Product Name"
 SortExpression="ProductName" />
```

Note that if you don't want a column to be sort-enabled, you simply don't set its SortExpression property. Figure 17-10 shows an example with a grid that has sort expressions for all three columns, and is currently sorted by product name.

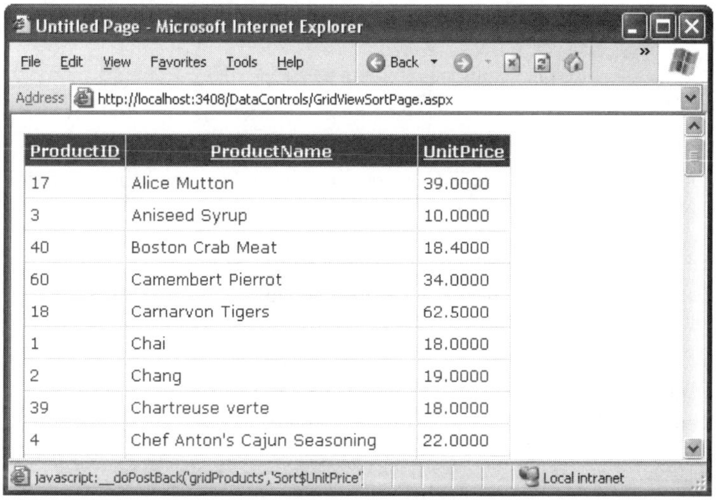

Figure 17-10. *Sorting the GridView*

Once you've associated a sort expression with the column and set the AllowSorting property to True, the GridView will render the headers with clickable links, as shown in Figure 17-10. However, it's up to the data source control to implement the actual sorting logic. How the sorting is implemented depends on the data source you're using.

Not all data sources support sorting, but the SqlDataSource does, provided the DataSourceMode property is set to DataSet (the default), not DataReader. In DataReader mode, the records are retrieved one at a time, and each record is stuffed into the bound control (such as a GridView) before the SqlDataSource moves to the next one. In DataSet mode, the entire results are placed in a DataSet and then the records are copied from the DataSet into the bound control. If the data needs to be sorted, the sorting happens between these two steps—after the records are retrieved but before they're bound in the web page.

■ **Note** The sort is according to the data type of the column. Numeric and date columns are ordered from smallest to largest. String columns are sorted alphanumerically without regard to case. Columns that contain binary data cannot be sorted.

Sorting and Selecting

If you use sorting and selection at the same time, you'll discover another issue. To see this problem in action, select a row, and then sort the data by any column. You'll see that the selection will remain, but it will shift to a new item that has the same index as the previous item. In other words, if you select the second row and perform a sort, the second row will still be selected in the new page, even though this isn't the record you selected. The only way to solve this problem is to programmatically change the selection every time a header link is clicked.

The simplest option is to react to the GridView.Sorted event to clear the selection, as shown here:

```
Protected Sub GridView1_Sorted(ByVal sender As Object, _
  ByVal e As GridViewSortEventArgs) Handles GridView1.Sorted

    ' Clear selected index.
    GridView1.SelectedIndex = -1
End Sub
```

In some cases you'll want to go even further and make sure a selected row remains selected when the sorting changes. The trick here is to store the selected value of the key field in view state each time the selected index changes:

```
Protected Sub GridView1_SelectedIndexChanged(ByVal sender As Object, _
  ByVal e As EventArgs) Handles GridView1.SelectedIndexChanged

    ' Save the selected value.
    If GridView1.SelectedIndex <> -1 Then
        ViewState("SelectedValue") = GridView1.SelectedValue.ToString()
    End If
End Sub
```

Now, when the grid is bound to the data source (for example, after a sort operation), you can reapply the last selected index:

```
Protected Sub GridView1_DataBound(ByVal sender As Object, _
  ByVal e As EventArgs) Handles GridView1.DataBound

    If ViewState("SelectedValue") IsNot Nothing Then
        Dim selectedValue As String = CType(ViewState("SelectedValue"), String)

        ' Reselect the last selected row.
        For Each row As GridViewRow In GridView1.Rows

            Dim keyValue As String
            keyValue = GridView1.DataKeys(row.RowIndex).Value.ToString()

            If keyValue = selectedValue Then
                GridView1.SelectedIndex = row.RowIndex
                Return
            End If
```

```
        Next
    End If
End Sub
```

Keep in mind that this approach can be confusing if you also have enabled paging (which is described in the next section). This is because a sorting operation might move the current row to another page, rendering it not visible but keeping it selected. This makes sense but is quite confusing in practice.

Paging

Often, a database search will return too many rows to be realistically displayed in a single page. If the client is using a slow connection, an extremely large GridView can take a frustrating amount of time to arrive. Once the data is retrieved, the user may find out it doesn't contain the right content anyway or that the search was too broad and they can't easily wade through all the results to find the important information.

The GridView handles this scenario with an automatic paging feature. When you use automatic paging, the full results are retrieved from the data source and placed into a DataSet. Once the DataSet is bound to the GridView, however, the data is subdivided into smaller groupings (for example, with 20 rows each), and only a single batch is sent to the user. The other groups are abandoned when the page finishes processing. When the user moves to the next page, the same process is repeated—in other words, the full query is performed once again. The GridView extracts just one group of rows, and the page is rendered.

To allow the user to skip from one page to another, the GridView displays a group of pager controls at the bottom of the grid. These pager controls could be previous/next links (often displayed as < and >) or number links (1, 2, 3, 4, 5, . . .) that lead to specific pages. If you've ever used a search engine, you've seen paging at work.

By setting a few properties, you can make the GridView control manage the paging for you. Table 17-6 describes the key properties.

Table 17-6. *Paging Members of the GridView*

Property	Description
AllowPaging	Enables or disables the paging of the bound records. It is False by default.
PageSize	Gets or sets the number of items to display on a single page of the grid. The default value is 10.
PageIndex	Gets or sets the zero-based index of the currently displayed page, if paging is enabled.
PagerSettings	Provides a PagerSettings object that wraps a variety of formatting options for the pager controls. These options determine where the paging controls are shown and what text or images they contain. You can set these properties to fine-tune the appearance of the pager controls, or you can use the defaults.

Table 17-6. *Paging Members of the GridView (Continued)*

Property	Description
PagerStyle	Provides a style object you can use to configure fonts, colors, and text alignment for the paging controls.
PageIndexChanging and PageIndexChanged events	Occur when one of the page selection elements is clicked, just before the PageIndex is changed (PageIndexChanging) and just after (PageIndexChanged).

To use automatic paging, you need to set AllowPaging to True (which shows the page controls), and you need to set PageSize to determine how many rows are allowed on each page.

Here's an example of a GridView control declaration that sets these properties:

```
<asp:GridView ID="GridView1" runat="server" DataSourceID="sourceProducts"
 PageSize="10" AllowPaging="True" ...>
  ...
</asp:GridView>
```

This is enough to start using paging. Figure 17-11 shows an example with ten records per page (for a total of eight pages).

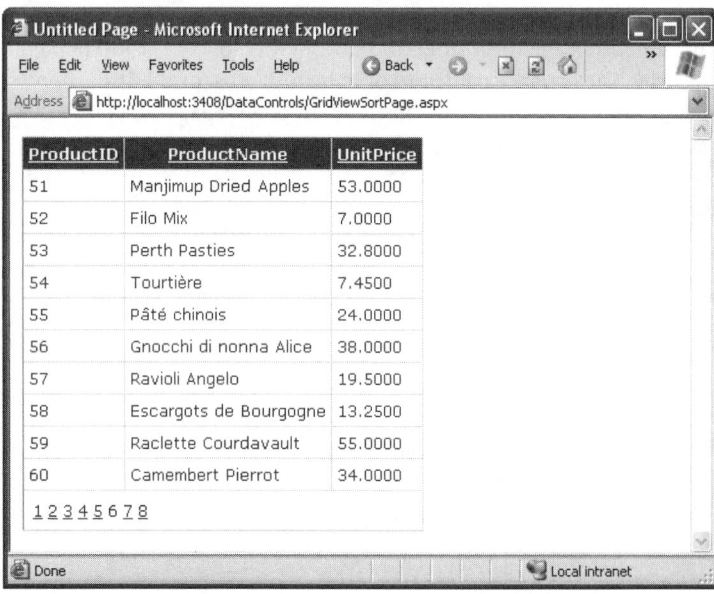

Figure 17-11. *Paging the GridView*

PAGING AND PERFORMANCE

When you use paging, every time a new page is requested, the full DataSet is queried from the database. This means paging does not reduce the amount of time required to query the database. In fact, because the information is split into multiple pages and you need to repeat the query every time the user moves to a new page, the database load actually *increases*. However, because any given page contains only a subset of the total data, the page size is smaller and will be transmitted faster, reducing the client's wait. The end result is a more responsive and manageable page.

You can use paging in certain ways without increasing the amount of work the database needs to perform. One option is to cache the entire DataSet in server memory. That way, every time the user moves to a different page, you simply need to retrieve the data from memory and rebind it, avoiding the database altogether. You'll learn how to use this technique in Chapter 24.

Using GridView Templates

So far, the examples have used the GridView control to show data using separate bound columns for each field. If you want to place multiple values in the same cell, or you have the unlimited ability to customize the content in a cell by adding HTML tags and server controls, you need to use a TemplateField.

The TemplateField allows you to define a completely customized *template* for a column. Inside the template you can add control tags, arbitrary HTML elements, and data binding expressions. You have complete freedom to arrange everything the way you want.

For example, imagine you want to create a column that combines the in stock, on order, and reorder level information for a product. To accomplish this trick, you can construct an ItemTemplate like this:

```
<asp:TemplateField HeaderText="Status">
  <ItemTemplate>
    <b>In Stock:</b>
    <%# Eval("UnitsInStock") %><br />
    <b>On Order:</b>
    <%# Eval("UnitsOnOrder") %><br />
    <b>Reorder:</b>
    <%# Eval("ReorderLevel") %>
  </ItemTemplate>
</asp:TemplateField>
```

■ **Note** Your template only has access to the fields that are in the bound data object. So if you want to show the UnitsInStock, UnitsOnOrder, and ReorderLevel fields, you need to make sure the SqlDataSource query returns this information.

To create the data binding expressions, the template uses the Eval() method, which is a shared method of the System.Web.UI.DataBinder class. Eval() is an indispensable convenience—it automatically retrieves the data item that's bound to the current row, uses reflection to find the matching field, and retrieves the value.

■ **Tip** The Eval() method also adds the extremely useful ability to format data fields on the fly. To use this feature, you must call the overloaded version of the Eval() method that accepts an additional format string parameter. Here's an example:

```
<%# Eval("BirthDate", "{0:MM/dd/yy}") %>
```

You can use any of the format strings defined in Table 17-3 and Table 17-4 with the Eval() method.

You'll notice that this example template includes three data binding expressions. These expressions get the actual information from the current row. The rest of the content in the template defines static text, tags, and controls.

You also need to make sure the data source provides these three pieces of information. If you attempt to bind a field that isn't present in your result set, you'll receive a runtime error. If you retrieve additional fields that are never bound to any template, no problem will occur.

Here's the revised data source with these fields:

```
<asp:SqlDataSource ID="sourceProducts" runat="server"
  ConnectionString="<%$ ConnectionStrings:Northwind %>"
  SelectCommand="SELECT ProductID, ProductName, UnitPrice, UnitsInStock,
UnitsOnOrder,ReorderLevel FROM Products"
  UpdateCommand="UPDATE Products SET ProductName=@ProductName,
UnitPrice=@UnitPrice WHERE ProductID=@ProductID">
</asp:SqlDataSource>
```

When you bind the GridView, it fetches the data from the data source and walks through the collection of items. It processes the ItemTemplate for each item, evaluates the data binding expressions, and adds the rendered HTML to the table. You're free to mix template columns with other column types. Figure 17-12 shows an example with several normal columns and the template column at the end.

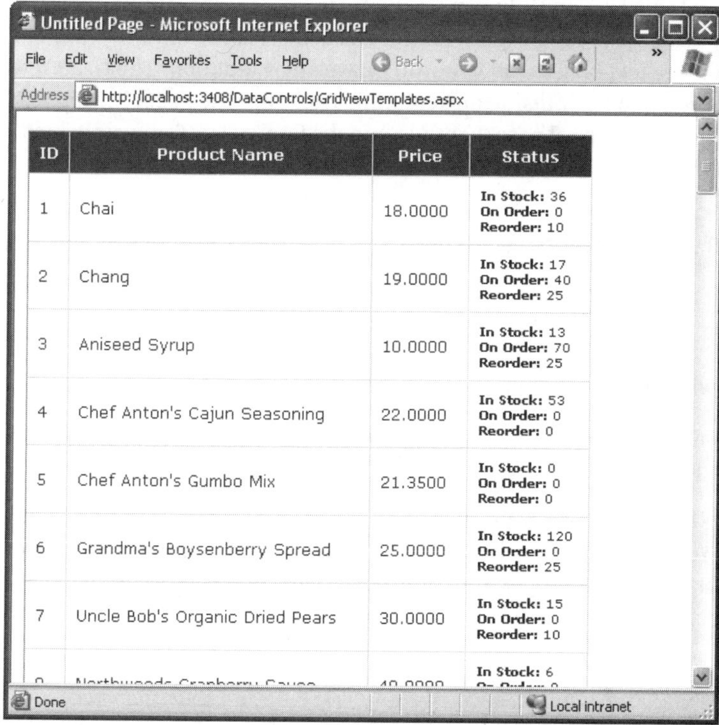

Figure 17-12. *A GridView with a template column*

Using Multiple Templates

The previous example uses a single template to configure the appearance of data items. However, the ItemTemplate isn't the only template that the TemplateField provides. In fact, the TemplateField allows you to configure various aspects of its appearance with a number of templates. Inside every template column, you can use the templates listed in Table 17-7.

Table 17-7. *TemplateField Templates*

Mode	Description
HeaderTemplate	Determines the appearance and content of the header cell.
FooterTemplate	Determines the appearance and content of the footer cell (if you set ShowFooter to True).
ItemTemplate	Determines the appearance and content of each data cell.
AlternatingItemTemplate	Determines the appearance of even-numbered rows. For example, if you set the AlternatingItemTemplate to have a shaded background color, the GridView applies this shading to every second row.
EditItemTemplate	Determines the appearance and controls used in edit mode.
InsertItemTemplate	Determines the appearance and controls used in edit mode. The GridView doesn't support this template, but the DetailsView and FormView controls (which are described later in this chapter) do.

Of the templates listed in Table 17-7, the EditItemTemplate is one of the most useful, because it gives you the ability to control the editing experience for the field. If you don't use template fields, you're limited to ordinary text boxes, and you won't have any validation. The GridView also defines two templates you can use outside any column. These are the PagerTemplate, which lets you customize the appearance of pager controls, and the EmptyDataTemplate, which lets you set the content that should appear if the GridView is bound to an empty data object.

Editing Templates in Visual Studio

Visual Studio 2008 includes solid support for editing templates in the web page designer. To try this, follow these steps:

1. Create a GridView with at least one template column.
2. Select the GridView, and click Edit Templates in the smart tag. This switches the GridView into template edit mode.
3. In the smart tag, use the Display drop-down list to choose the template you want to edit (see Figure 17-13). You can choose either of the two templates that apply to the whole GridView (EmptyDataTemplate or PagerTemplate), or you can choose a specific template for one of the template columns.

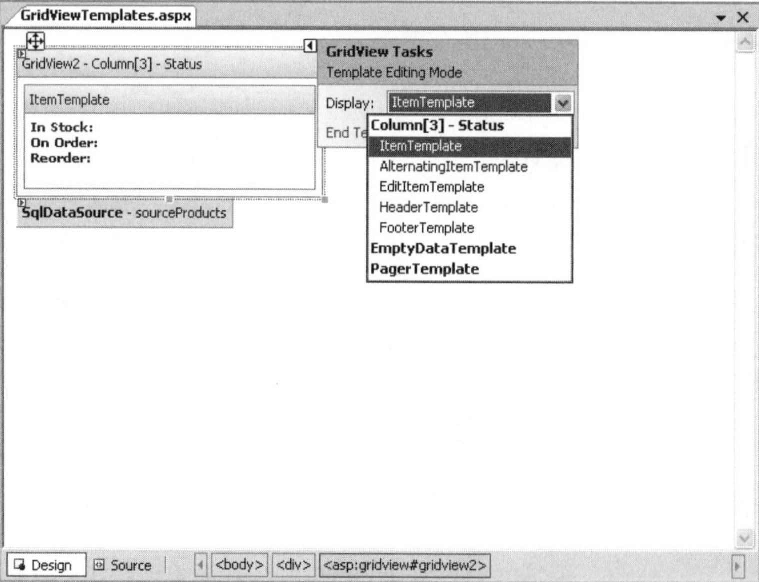

Figure 17-13. *Editing a template in Visual Studio*

4. Enter your content in the control. You can enter static content, drag and drop controls, and so on.
5. When you're finished, choose End Template Editing from the smart tag.

Handling Events in a Template

In some cases, you might need to handle events that are raised by the controls you add to a template column. For example, imagine you want to add a clickable image link by adding an ImageButton control. This is easy enough to accomplish:

```
<asp:TemplateField HeaderText="Status">
  <ItemTemplate>
    <asp:ImageButton ID="ImageButton1" runat="server"
     ImageUrl="statuspic.gif" />
  </ItemTemplate>
</asp:TemplateField>
```

The problem is that if you add a control to a template, the GridView creates multiple copies of that control, one for each data item. When the ImageButton is clicked, you need a way to determine which image was clicked and to which row it belongs.

The way to resolve this problem is to use an event from the GridView, *not* the contained button. The GridView.RowCommand event serves this purpose, because it fires whenever any button is clicked in any template. This process, where a control event in a template is turned into an event in the containing control, is called *event bubbling*.

Of course, you still need a way to pass information to the RowCommand event to identify the row where the action took place. The secret lies in two string properties that all button controls provide: CommandName and CommandArgument. CommandName sets a descriptive name you can use to distinguish clicks on your ImageButton from clicks on other button controls in the GridView. The CommandArgument supplies a piece of row-specific data you can use to identify the row that was clicked. You can supply this information using a data binding expression.

Here's a template field that contains the revised ImageButton tag:

```
<asp:TemplateField HeaderText="Status">
  <ItemTemplate>
    <asp:ImageButton ID="ImageButton1" runat="server"
     ImageUrl="statuspic.gif"
     CommandName="StatusClick" CommandArgument='<%# Eval("ProductID") %>' />
  </ItemTemplate>
</asp:TemplateField>
```

And here's the code you need in order to respond when an ImageButton is clicked:

```
Protected Sub GridView1_RowCommand(ByVal sender As Object, _
  ByVal e As GridViewCommandEventArgs) Handles GridView1.RowCommand

    If e.CommandName = "StatusClick" Then
      lblInfo.Text = "You clicked product #" & e.CommandArgument.ToString()
    End If
End Sub
```

This example simply displays the ProductID in a label.

Editing with a Template

One of the best reasons to use a template is to provide a better editing experience. In the previous chapter, you saw how the GridView provides automatic editing capabilities—all you need to do is switch a row into edit mode by setting the GridView.EditIndex property. The easiest way to make this possible is to add a CommandField column with the ShowEditButton set to True. Then, the user simply needs to click a link in the appropriate row to begin editing it. At this point, every label in every column is replaced by a text box (unless the field is read-only).

The standard editing support has several limitations:

It's not always appropriate to edit values using a text box: Certain types of data are best handled with other controls (such as drop-down lists). Large fields need multiline text boxes, and so on.

You get no validation: It would be nice to restrict the editing possibilities so that currency figures can't be entered as negative numbers, for example. You can do that by adding validator controls to an EditItemTemplate.

The visual appearance is often ugly: A row of text boxes across a grid takes up too much space and rarely seems professional.

In a template column, you don't have these issues. Instead, you explicitly define the edit controls and their layout using the EditItemTemplate. This can be a somewhat laborious process.

Here's the template column used earlier for stock information with an editing template:

```
<asp:TemplateField HeaderText="Status">
  <ItemStyle Width="100px" />
    <ItemTemplate>
      <b>In Stock:</b> <%# Eval("UnitsInStock") %><br />
      <b>On Order:</b> <%# Eval("UnitsOnOrder") %><br />
      <b>Reorder:</b> <%# Eval("ReorderLevel") %>
    </ItemTemplate>
  <EditItemTemplate>
    <b>In Stock:</b> <%# Eval("UnitsInStock") %><br />
    <b>On Order:</b> <%# Eval("UnitsOnOrder") %><br /><br />
    <b>Reorder:</b>
    <asp:TextBox Text='<%# Bind("ReorderLevel") %>' Width="25px"
     runat="server" id="txtReorder" />
  </EditItemTemplate>
</asp:TemplateField>
```

Figure 17-14 shows the row in edit mode.

When binding an editable value to a control, you must use the Bind() method in your data binding expression instead of the ordinary Eval() method. Only the Bind() method creates the two-way link, ensuring that updated values will be returned to the server.

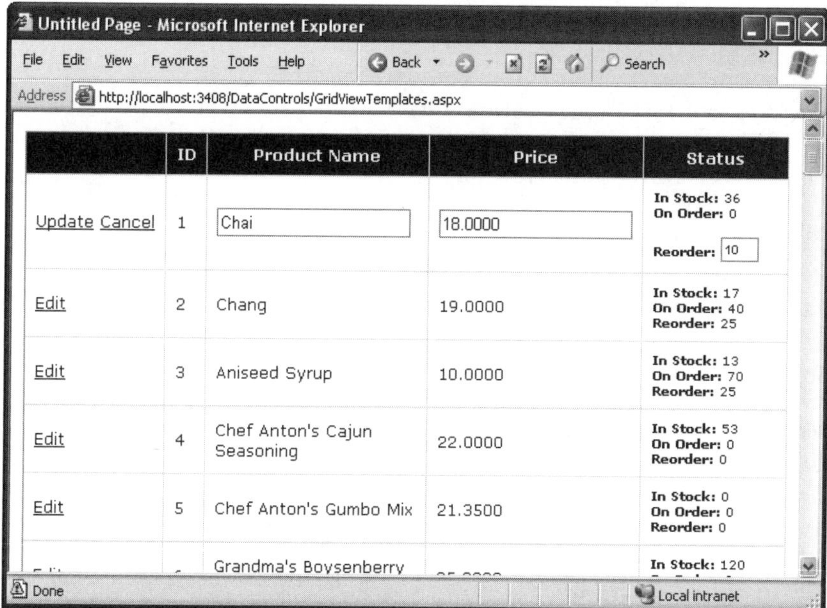

Figure 17-14. *Using an edit template*

One interesting detail here is that even though the item template shows three fields, the editing template allows only one of these to be changed. When the GridView commits an update, it will submit only the bound, editable parameters. In the previous example, this means the GridView will pass back a @ReorderLevel parameter but *not* a @UnitsInStock or @UnitsOnOrder parameter. This is important, because when you write your parameterized update command, it must use only the parameters you have available. Here's the modified SqlDataSource control with the correct command:

```
<asp:SqlDataSource ID="sourceProducts" runat="server"
  ConnectionString="<%$ ConnectionStrings:Northwind %>"
  SelectCommand="SELECT ProductID, ProductName, UnitPrice, UnitsInStock,
UnitsOnOrder,ReorderLevel FROM Products"
  UpdateCommand="UPDATE Products SET ProductName=@ProductName, UnitPrice=@UnitPrice,
ReorderLevel=@ReorderLevel WHERE ProductID=@ProductID">
</asp:SqlDataSource>
```

Editing with Validation

Now that you have your template ready, why not add an extra frill, such as a validator, to catch editing mistakes? In the following example, a RangeValidator prevents changes that put the ReorderLevel at less than 0 or more than 100:

```
<asp:TemplateField HeaderText="Status">
  <ItemStyle Width="100px" />
    <ItemTemplate>
      <b>In Stock:</b> <%# Eval("UnitsInStock") %><br />
      <b>On Order:</b> <%# Eval("UnitsOnOrder") %><br />
      <b>Reorder:</b> <%# Eval("ReorderLevel") %>
    </ItemTemplate>
  <EditItemTemplate>
    <b>In Stock:</b> <%# Eval("UnitsInStock") %><br />
    <b>On Order:</b> <%# Eval("UnitsOnOrder") %><br /><br />
    <b>Reorder:</b>
    <asp:TextBox Text='<%# Bind("ReorderLevel") %>' Width="25px"
     runat="server" id="txtReorder" />
    <asp:RangeValidator id="rngValidator" MinimumValue="0" MaximumValue="100"
     ControlToValidate="txtReorder" runat="server"
     ErrorMessage="Value out of range." Type="Integer"/>
  </EditItemTemplate>
</asp:TemplateField>
```

Figure 17-15 shows the validation at work. If the value isn't valid, the browser doesn't allow the page to be posted back, and no database code runs.

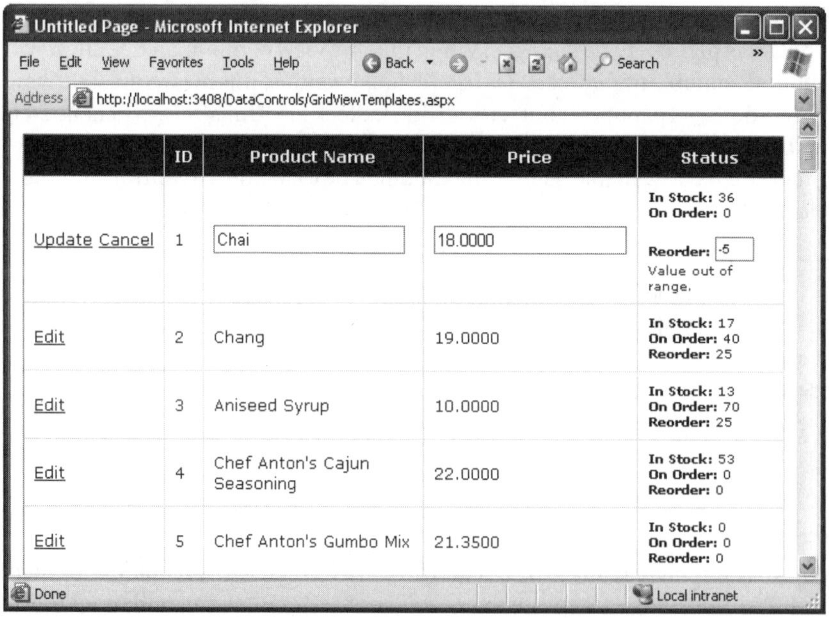

Figure 17-15. *Creating an edit template with validation*

■ Note The SqlDataSource is intelligent enough to handle validation properly even if you disabled client-side validation (or the browser doesn't support it). In this situation, the page is posted back, but the SqlDataSource notices that it contains invalid data and doesn't attempt to perform its update. For more information about client-side and server-side validation, refer to Chapter 10.

Editing Without a Command Column

So far, all the examples you've seen have used a CommandField that automatically generates edit controls. However, now that you've made the transition over to a template-based approach, it's worth considering how you can add your own edit controls.

It's actually quite easy. All you need to do is add a button control to the item template and set the CommandName to Edit. This automatically triggers the editing process, which fires the appropriate events and switches the row into edit mode.

```
<ItemTemplate>
  <b>In Stock:</b> <%# Eval("UnitsInStock") %><br />
  <b>On Order:</b> <%# Eval("UnitsOnOrder") %><br />
  <b>Reorder:</b> <%# Eval("ReorderLevel") %>
  <br /><br />
  <asp:LinkButton runat="server" Text="Edit"
   CommandName="Edit" ID="Linkbutton1" />
</ItemTemplate>
```

In the edit item template, you need two more buttons with CommandName values of Update and Cancel:

```
<EditItemTemplate>
  <b>In Stock:</b> <%# Eval("UnitsInStock") %><br />
  <b>On Order:</b> <%# Eval("UnitsOnOrder") %><br /><br />
  <b>Reorder:</b>
  <asp:TextBox Text='<%# Bind("ReorderLevel") %>' Width="25px"
   runat="server" id="txtReorder" />
  <br /><br />
  <asp:LinkButton runat="server" Text="Update"
   CommandName="Update" ID="Linkbutton1" />
  <asp:LinkButton runat="server" Text="Cancel"
   CommandName="Cancel" ID="Linkbutton2" CausesValidation="False" />
</EditItemTemplate>
```

Notice that the Cancel button must have its CausesValidation property set to False to bypass validation. That way, you can cancel the edit even if the current data isn't valid.

As long as you use these names, the GridView editing events will fire and the data source controls will react in the same way as if you were using the automatically generated editing controls. Figure 17-16 shows the custom edit buttons.

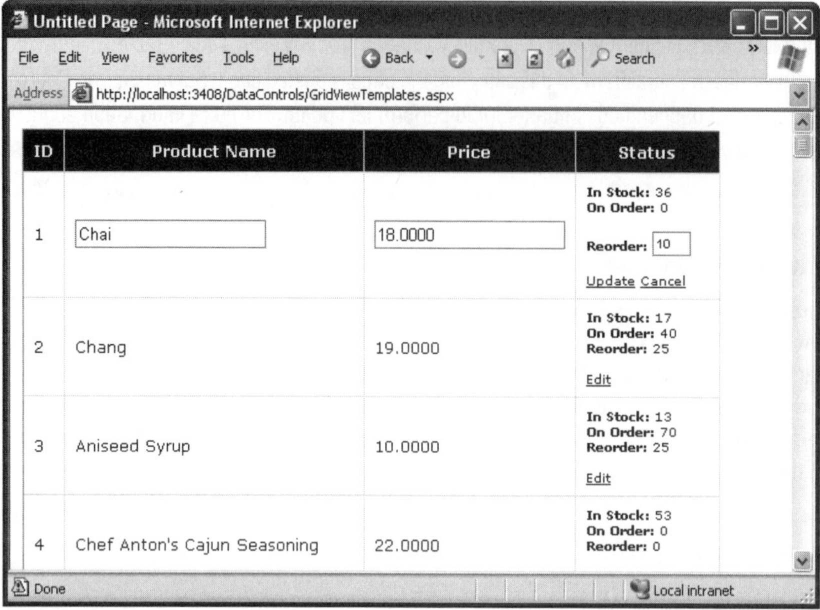

Figure 17-16. *Custom edit controls*

The DetailsView and FormView

The GridView excels at showing a dense table with multiple rows of information. However, sometimes you want to provide a detailed look at a single record. You could work out a solution using a template column in a GridView, but ASP.NET includes two controls that are tailored for this purpose: the DetailsView and the FormView. Both show a single record at a time but can include optional pager buttons that let you step through a series of records (showing one per page). Both give you an easy way to insert a new record, which the GridView doesn't allow. And both support templates, but the FormView *requires* them. This is the key distinction between the two controls.

One other difference is the fact that the DetailsView renders its content inside a table, while the FormView gives you the flexibility to display your content without a table. Thus, if you're planning to use templates, the FormView gives you the most flexibility. But if you want to avoid the complexity of templates, the DetailsView gives you a simpler model that lets you build a multirow data display out of field objects, in much the same way that the GridView is built out of column objects.

Now that you understand the features of the GridView, you can get up to speed with the DetailsView and the FormView quite quickly. That's because both borrow a portion of the GridView model.

The DetailsView

The DetailsView displays a single record at a time. It places each field in a separate row of a table.

You saw in Chapter 16 how to create a basic DetailsView to show the currently selected record. The DetailsView also allows you to move from one record to the next using paging controls, if you've set the AllowPaging property to True. You can configure the paging controls using the PagerStyle and PagerSettings properties in the same way as you tweak the pager for the GridView.

Figure 17-17 shows the DetailsView when it's bound to a set of product records, with full product information.

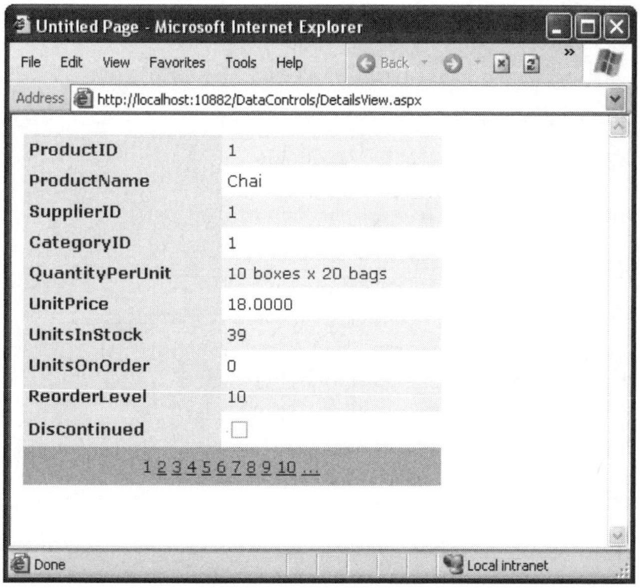

Figure 17-17. *The DetailsView with paging*

It's tempting to use the DetailsView pager controls to make a handy record browser. Unfortunately, this approach can be quite inefficient. One problem is that a separate postback is required each time the user moves from one record to another (whereas a grid control can show multiple records on the same page). But the real drawback is that each time the page is posted back, the full set of records is retrieved, even though only a single record is shown. This results in needless extra work for the database server. If you choose to implement a record browser page with the DetailsView, at a bare minimum you must enable caching to reduce the database work (see Chapter 24).

■ **Tip** It's almost always a better idea to use another control to let the user choose a specific record (for example, by choosing an ID from a list box), and then show the full record in the DetailsView using a parameterized command that matches just the selected record. Chapter 16 demonstrates this technique.

Defining Fields

The DetailsView uses reflection to generate the fields it shows. This means it examines the data object and creates a separate row for each field it finds, just like the GridView. You can disable this automatic row generation by setting AutoGenerateRows to False. It's then up to you to declare information you want to display.

Interestingly, you use the same field tags to build a DetailsView as you use to design a GridView. For example, fields from the data item are represented with the BoundField tag, buttons can be created with the ButtonField, and so on. For the full list, refer to the earlier Table 17-1.

The following code defines a DetailsView that shows product information. This tag creates the same grid of information shown in Figure 17-17, when AutoGenerateRows was set to True.

```
<asp:DetailsView ID="DetailsView1" runat="server" AutoGenerateRows="False"
 DataSourceID="sourceProducts">
  <Fields>
    <asp:BoundField DataField="ProductID" HeaderText="ProductID"
     ReadOnly="True" />
    <asp:BoundField DataField="ProductName" HeaderText="ProductName" />
    <asp:BoundField DataField="SupplierID" HeaderText="SupplierID" />
    <asp:BoundField DataField="CategoryID" HeaderText="CategoryID" />
    <asp:BoundField DataField="QuantityPerUnit" HeaderText="QuantityPerUnit" />
    <asp:BoundField DataField="UnitPrice" HeaderText="UnitPrice" />
    <asp:BoundField DataField="UnitsInStock" HeaderText="UnitsInStock" />
    <asp:BoundField DataField="UnitsOnOrder" HeaderText="UnitsOnOrder" />
    <asp:BoundField DataField="ReorderLevel" HeaderText="ReorderLevel" />
    <asp:CheckBoxField DataField="Discontinued" HeaderText="Discontinued" />
  </Fields>
  ...
</asp:DetailsView>
```

You can use the BoundField tag to set properties such as header text, formatting string, editing behavior, and so on (refer to Table 17-2). In addition, you can use the ShowHeader property. When it's False, the header text is left out of the row, and the field data takes up both cells.

■ Tip Rather than coding each field by hand, you can use the same shortcut you used with the GridView. Simply select the control at design time, and select Refresh Schema from the smart tag.

The field model isn't the only part of the GridView that the DetailsView control adopts. It also uses a similar set of styles, a similar set of events, and a similar editing model. The only difference is that instead of creating a dedicated column for editing controls, you simply set one of the Boolean properties of the DetailsView, such as AutoGenerateDeleteButton, AutoGenerateEditButton, and AutoGenerateInsertButton. The links for these tasks are added to the bottom of the DetailsView. When you add or edit a record, the DetailsView always uses standard text box controls (see Figure 17-18), just like the GridView does. For more editing flexibility, you'll want to use the FormView control.

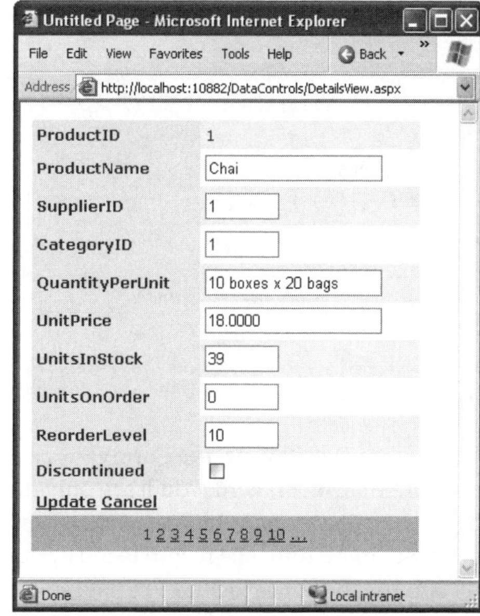

Figure 17-18. *Editing in the DetailsView*

The FormView

If you need the ultimate flexibility of templates, the FormView provides a template-only control for displaying and editing a single record.

The beauty of the FormView template model is that it matches the model of the TemplateField in the GridView quite closely. This means you can work with the following templates:

- ItemTemplate
- EditItemTemplate
- InsertItemTemplate
- FooterTemplate
- HeaderTemplate
- EmptyDataTemplate
- PagerTemplate

You can use the same template content you use with a TemplateField in a GridView in the FormView. Earlier in this chapter, you saw how you can use a template field to combine the stock information of a product into one column (as shown in Figure 17-12). Here's how you can use the same template in the FormView:

```
<asp:FormView ID="FormView1" runat="server" DataSourceID="sourceProducts">
  <ItemTemplate>
    <b>In Stock:</b>
    <%# Eval("UnitsInStock") %>
    <br />
    <b>On Order:</b>
    <%# Eval("UnitsOnOrder") %>
    <br />
    <b>Reorder:</b>
    <%# Eval("ReorderLevel") %>
    <br />
  </ItemTemplate>
</asp:FormView>
```

Like the DetailsView, the FormView can show a single record at a time. (If the data source has more than one record, you'll see only the first one.) You can deal with this issue by setting the AllowPaging property to True so that paging links are automatically created. These links allow the user to move from one record to the next, as in the previous example with the DetailsView.

Another option is to bind to a data source that returns just one record. Figure 17-19 shows an example where a drop-down list control lets you choose a product, and a second data source shows the matching record in the FormView control.

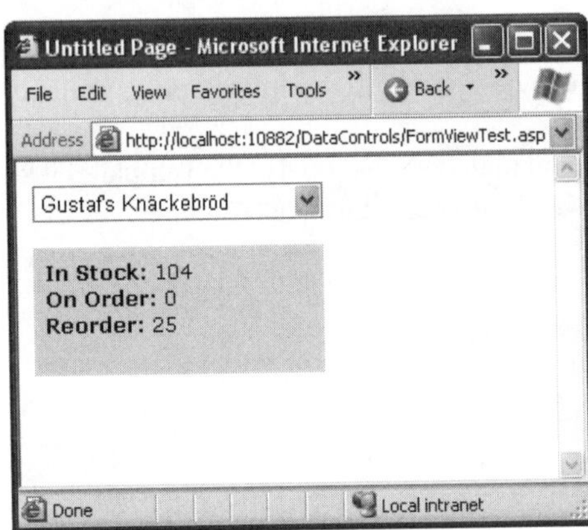

Figure 17-19. *A FormView that shows a single record*

Here's the markup you need to define the drop-down list and its data source:

```
<asp:SqlDataSource ID="sourceProducts" runat="server"
  ConnectionString="<%$ ConnectionStrings:Northwind %>"
  SelectCommand="SELECT * FROM Products">
</asp:SqlDataSource>
```

```
<asp:DropDownList ID="lstProducts" runat="server"
  AutoPostBack="True" DataSourceID="sourceProducts"
  DataTextField="ProductName" DataValueField="ProductID" Width="184px">
</asp:DropDownList>
```

The FormView uses the template from the previous example (it's the shaded region on the page). Here's the markup for the FormView (not including the template) and the data source that gets the full details for the selected product.

```
<asp:SqlDataSource ID="sourceProductFull" runat="server"
  ConnectionString="<%$ ConnectionStrings:Northwind %>"
  SelectCommand="SELECT * FROM Products WHERE ProductID=@ProductID">
    <SelectParameters>
        <asp:ControlParameter Name="ProductID"
         ControlID="lstProducts" PropertyName="SelectedValue" />
    </SelectParameters>
</asp:SqlDataSource>

<asp:FormView ID="formProductDetails" runat="server"
  DataSourceID="sourceProductFull"
  BackColor="#FFE0C0" CellPadding="5">
    <ItemTemplate>
        ...
    </ItemTemplate>
</asp:FormView>
```

■ **Note** If you want to support editing with the FormView, you need to add button controls that trigger the edit and update processes, as described in the "Editing with a Template" section.

The Last Word

In this chapter, you considered everything you need to build rich data-bound pages. You took a detailed tour of the GridView and considered its support for formatting, selecting, sorting, paging, using templates, and editing. You also considered the DetailsView and the FormView, which allow you to display and edit individual records. Using these three controls, you can build all-in-one pages that display and edit data, without needing to write pages of ADO.NET code. Best of all, every data control is thoroughly configurable, which means you can tailor it to fit just about any web application.

CHAPTER 18

Files and Streams

There's a good reason that this book covered ADO.NET before dealing with simpler data access techniques, such as writing and reading ordinary files. Traditional file access is generally much less useful in a web application than it is in a desktop program. Databases, on the other hand, are designed from the ground up to support a large number of simultaneous users with speed, safety, and efficiency. Most web applications will rely on a database for some features, but many won't have any reason to use direct file access.

Of course, enterprising ASP.NET developers can find a use for almost any technology. If this book didn't cover file access, no doubt many developers would be frustrated when designing web applications with legitimate (and innovative) uses for ordinary files. In fact, file access is so easy and straightforward in .NET that it may be perfect for simple, small-scale solutions that don't need a full-fledged database product like SQL Server.

This chapter explains how you can use the classes in .NET to read and change file system information and even build a simple file browser. You'll also learn how to create simple text and binary files of your own. Finally, you'll consider how you can allow users to upload their own files to your web server.

Files and Web Applications

Why is it that most web applications don't use files? There are several limitations to files:

File-naming limitations: When you create a new file, it obviously can't have the same name as an existing file in the same directory. That means you'll probably need to fall back on some system for randomly generating files names. For example, you might create a file name based on a random number combined with the current date and time, or create a file name that incorporates a GUID (globally unique identifier). With both of these approaches, file names would be statistically unique, which means duplicates would be extremely unlikely. However, the file names wouldn't be very meaningful. In databases, this problem is solved more neatly with the auto-increment data type, which automatically fills a specific field with a unique number when you create a record.

Multiuser limitations: Relational databases provide features like locking and transactions to prevent inconsistencies and make sure multiple people can use the same data at the same time. Comparatively, the web server's file system is woefully backward. Although you can allow multiple users to read a file at once, it's almost impossible to let multiple users update the same file at the same time without catastrophe.

Scalability problems: File operations suffer from some overhead. In a simple scenario, file access may be faster than connecting to a database and performing a query. But the cumulative effect in a large web application is very different. When multiple users are working with files at the same time, your web server may slow down dramatically.

Security risks: If you allow the user to specify a file or path name, the user could devise a way to trick your application into accessing or overwriting a protected system file. Even without this ability, a malicious or careless user might use an ASP.NET page that creates or uploads files to fill up your web server hard drive and cause it to stop working. All of these problems are preventable, but they require a bit more work than a database-backed solution.

Of course, file access does have its uses. Maybe you need to access information that another application has stored in a file. Or maybe you need to store *your* information in a file so that other applications can access it. For example, you might be creating an intranet application that allows a small set of trusted employees to upload and manage documents. You could store their documents in a binary field in a database table, but that would make it more difficult to browse and open those files without using your web front end.

In these situations, you'll be happy to know that ASP.NET can use all the file access features of the .NET Framework. That means your web applications can freely explore the file system, manage files, and create new files with custom content.

File System Information

The simplest level of file access just involves retrieving information about existing files and directories and performing typical file system operations such as copying files and creating directories.

.NET provides five basic classes for retrieving this sort of information. They are all located in the System.IO namespace (and, incidentally, can be used in desktop applications in exactly the same way they are used in web applications). They include the following:

- The Directory and File classes, which provide shared methods that allow you to retrieve information about any files and directories visible from your server
- The DirectoryInfo and FileInfo classes, which use similar instance methods and properties to retrieve the same sort of information
- The DriveInfo class, which provides shared methods that allow you to retrieve information about a drive and the amount of free space it provides

In Chapter 3, you saw how a class can provide two types of members. Shared members are always available—you just use the name of the class. But instance members are only available if you have a live object.

With the file access classes, shared methods are more convenient to use because they don't require you to create an instance of the class. That means you can use a quick one-line code statement to perform a simple task like checking whether a file exists. On the other hand, if you need to retrieve several pieces of information from the same file or directory, it's easier to use the instance members. That way, you don't need to keep specifying the name of the directory or file each time you call a method. The instance approach is also a bit faster in this situation. That's because the FileInfo and DirectoryInfo classes perform their security checks once—when you create the object instance. The Directory and File classes perform a security check every time you invoke a method, which adds more overhead.

You'll learn about all of these classes in this chapter. But first, it's worth taking a detour to look at another class that can simplify code that deals with the file system: the Path class.

The Path Class

Along with the five classes outlined in the previous section, .NET also includes a helper class named Path in the same System.IO namespace. The Path class doesn't include any real file management functionality. It simply provides a few shared methods that are useful when manipulating strings that contain file and directory paths.

For example, the Path class includes a GetFileName() method that pulls the file name out of a full string. Here's an example:

```
Dim file As String = Path.GetFileName( _
  "c:\Documents\Upload\Users\JamesX\resume.doc")
' file now contains "resume.doc"
```

The Path class also includes a Combine() method that can tack a relative path on the end of an absolute path. Here it is at work, fusing two strings together:

```
Dim absolutePath As String = "c:\Users\MyDocuments"
Dim subPath As String = "Sarah\worksheet.xls"
Dim combined As String = Path.Combine(absolutePath, subPath)
' combined now contains "c:\Users\MyDocuments\Sarah\worksheet.xls"
```

You could perform all of these tasks on your own, but the Path class is a great way to avoid errors. Table 18-1 lists the methods of the Path class.

Table 18-1. *Path Methods*

Methods	Description
Combine()	Combines a path with a file name or a subdirectory.
ChangeExtension()	Returns a copy of the string with a modified extension. If you don't specify an extension, the current extension is removed.
GetDirectoryName()	Returns all the directory information, which is the text between the first and last directory separators (\).
GetFileName()	Returns just the file name portion of a path, which is the portion after the last directory separator.
GetFileNameWithoutExtension()	Returns just the file name portion of a path, but omits the file extension at the end.
GetFullPath()	Changes a relative path into an absolute path using the current directory. For example, if c:\Temp\ is the current directory, calling GetFullPath() on a file name such as test.txt returns c:\Temp\test.txt. This method has no effect on an absolute path.

Table 18-1. *Path Methods (Continued)*

Methods	Description
GetPathRoot()	Retrieves a string with the root drive (for example, "c:\"), provided that information is in the string. For a relative path, it returns a null reference.
HasExtension()	Returns True if the path ends with an extension.
IsPathRooted()	Returns True if the path is an absolute path and False if it's a relative path.

The Directory and File Classes

The Directory and File classes provide a number of useful shared methods. Table 18-2 and Table 18-3 show an overview of the most important methods. Most of these methods take the same parameter: a fully qualified path name identifying the directory or file you want the operation to act on. A few methods, such as Delete() and Move(), take additional parameters.

Table 18-2. *Directory Class Members*

Method	Description
CreateDirectory()	Creates a new directory. If you specify a directory inside another nonexistent directory, ASP.NET will thoughtfully create *all* the required directories.
Delete()	Deletes the corresponding empty directory. To delete a directory along with its contents (subdirectories and files), add the optional second parameter of True.
Exists()	Returns True or False to indicate whether the specified directory exists.
GetCreationTime(), GetLastAccessTime(), and GetLastWriteTime()	Returns a DateTime object that represents the time the directory was created, accessed, or written to. Each Get*Xxx*() method has a corresponding Set*Xxx*() method, which isn't shown in this table.
GetDirectories() and GetFiles()	Returns an array of strings, one for each subdirectory or file (depending on the method you're using) in the specified directory. These methods can accept a second parameter that specifies a search expression (such as ASP*.*).
GetLogicalDrives()	Returns an array of strings, one for each drive that's defined on the current computer. Drive letters are in this format: "c:\".
GetParent()	Parses the supplied directory string and tells you what the parent directory is. You could do this on your own by searching for the \ character (or, more generically, the Path.DirectorySeparatorChar), but this function makes life a little easier.

Table 18-2. *Directory Class Members*

Method	Description
GetCurrentDirectory() and SetCurrentDirectory()	Allows you to set or retrieve the current directory, which is useful if you need to use relative paths instead of full paths. Generally, these functions aren't necessary.
Move()	Accepts two parameters: the source path and the destination path. The directory and all its contents can be moved to any path, as long as it's located on the same drive.

Table 18-3. *File Class Members*

Method	Description
Copy()	Accepts two parameters: the fully qualified source file name and the fully qualified destination file name. To allow overwriting, use the version that takes a Boolean third parameter and set it to True.
Delete()	Deletes the specified file but doesn't throw an exception if the file can't be found.
Exists()	Indicates True or False in regard to whether a specified file exists.
GetAttributes() and SetAttributes()	Retrieves or sets an enumerated value that can include any combination of the values from the FileAttributes enumeration.
GetCreationTime(), GetLastAccessTime(), and GetLastWriteTime()	Returns a DateTime object that represents the time the file was created, accessed, or last written to. Each Get method has a corresponding Set method, which isn't shown in this table.
Move()	Accepts two parameters: the fully qualified source file name and the fully qualified destination file name. You can move a file across drives and even rename it while you move it (or rename it without moving it).

The File class also includes some methods that allow you to create and open files as streams. You'll explore these features in the "Reading and Writing with Streams" section of this chapter. The only feature the File class lacks (and the FileInfo class provides) is the ability to retrieve the size of a specified file.

The File and Directory methods are quite intuitive. For example, consider the code for a simple page that displays some information about the files in a specific directory. You might use this code to create a simple admin page that allows you to review the contents of an FTP directory (see Figure 18-1). Clients could use this page to review their documents and remove suspicious files.

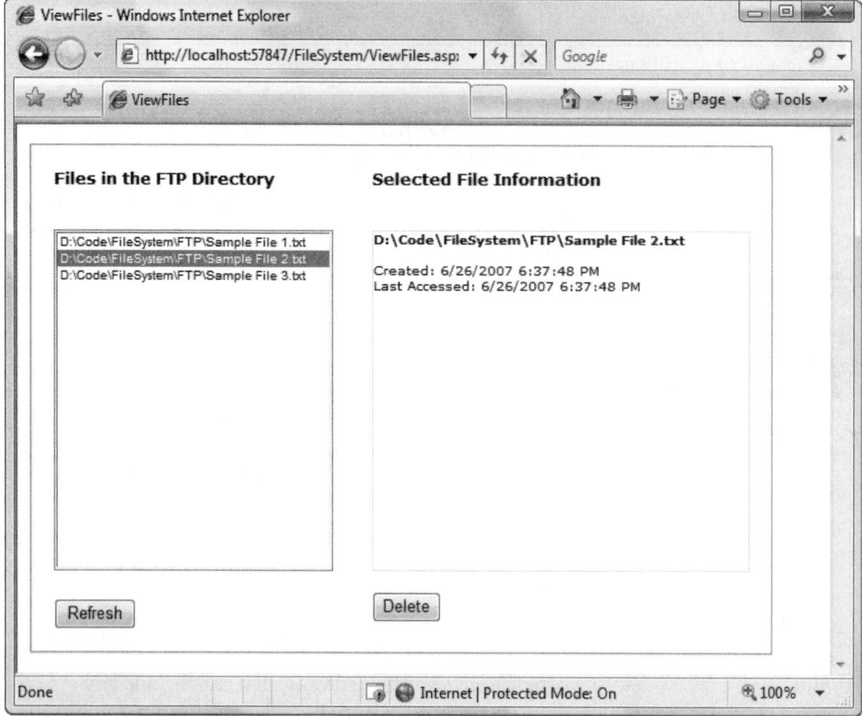

Figure 18-1. *An admin page with file information*

You should begin by importing the namespace that has the IO classes:

```
Imports System.IO
```

The code for this page is as follows:

```
Public Partial Class ViewFiles
    Inherits System.Web.UI.Page

    Private ftpDirectory As String

    Protected Sub Page_Load(ByVal sender As Object, _
      ByVal e As EventArgs) Handles Me.Load
        ftpDirectory = Path.Combine(Request.PhysicalApplicationPath, "FTP")
        If Not Me.IsPostBack Then
            CreateFileList()
        End If
    End Sub
```

```
Private Sub CreateFileList()
    ' Retrieve the list of files, and display it in the page.
    ' This code also disables the delete button, ensuring the
    ' user must view the file information before deleting it.
    Dim fileList() As String = Directory.GetFiles(ftpDirectory)
    lstFiles.DataSource = fileList
    lstFiles.DataBind()
    lblFileInfo.Text = ""
    cmdDelete.Enabled = False
End Sub

Protected Sub cmdRefresh_Click(ByVal sender As Object, _
  ByVal e As EventArgs) Handles cmdRefresh.Click
    CreateFileList()
End Sub

Protected Sub lstFiles_SelectedIndexChanged(ByVal sender As Object, _
  ByVal e As EventArgs) Handles lstFiles.SelectedIndexChanged

    ' Display the selected file information.
    ' Use the StringBuilder for the fastest way to build the string.
    Dim fileName As String = lstFiles.SelectedItem.Text
    Dim sb As New System.Text.StringBuilder
    sb.Append("<b>")
    sb.Append(fileName)
    sb.Append("</b><br /><br />")
    sb.Append("Created: ")
    sb.Append(File.GetCreationTime(fileName).ToString())
    sb.Append("<br />Last Accessed: ")
    sb.Append(File.GetLastAccessTime(fileName).ToString())
    sb.Append("<br />")

    ' Show attribute information. GetAttributes can return a combination
    ' of enumerated values, so you need to evaluate it with the
    ' And keyword.
    Dim Attr As FileAttributes = File.GetAttributes(fileName)
    If (Attr And FileAttributes.Hidden) = FileAttributes.Hidden Then
        sb.Append("This is a hidden file.<br />")
    End If
    If (Attr And FileAttributes.ReadOnly) = FileAttributes.ReadOnly Then
        sb.Append("This is a read-only file.<br />")
    End If
```

```
        ' Allow the file to be deleted.
        If (Attr And FileAttributes.ReadOnly) <> _
         FileAttributes.ReadOnly Then
            cmdDelete.Enabled = True
        End If

        ' Display the information.
        lblFileInfo.Text = sb.ToString()
    End Sub

    Protected Sub cmdDelete_Click(ByVal sender As Object, _
      ByVal e As EventArgs) Handles cmdDelete.Click
        File.Delete(lstFiles.SelectedItem.Text)
        CreateFileList()
    End Sub

End Class
```

Dissecting the Code . . .

- Every time the page loads, it sets the ftpDirectory string. The path is set to the FTP subfolder in the current web application directory (which is provided by the Request.PhysicalApplicationPath property). These two details (the current web application directory and the FTP subfolder) are fused together into one path string using the Combine() method of the Path class.
- The CreateFileList() procedure is easy to code, because it uses the data-binding feature of the ListBox. The array returned from the GetFiles() method can be placed in the list with just a couple of lines of code.
- The AutoPostBack property of the ListBox is set to True. That way, when the user chooses an item in the list, the ListBox posts the page back immediately so the code can read the file information and refresh the file details on the page.
- When evaluating the FileAttributes enumeration, you need to use the And operator to perform *bitwise arithmetic*. This is because the value returned from GetAttributes() can actually contain a combination of more than one attribute. Using bitwise arithmetic, you can pull out just the attribute that you're interested in, and then determine whether it's set.
- The code that gets the file information builds a long string of text, which is then displayed in a label. For optimum performance, this code uses the System.Text.StringBuilder class. Without the StringBuilder, you'd need to use string concatenation to join the string together. This is much slower, because every time the code adds a piece of text to the string, .NET creates an entirely new string object behind the scenes.

- The code that displays file information could benefit by switching to the FileInfo class (as shown in the next section). As it is, every method needs to specify the same file name. This is a bit tedious, and it's a bit slower because each method requires a separate security check.

One ingredient this code lacks is error handling. When using any external resource, including files, it's essential that you defend yourself with a Try/Catch block. This way you can deal with unpredictable occurrences that are beyond your control—for example, if the file isn't accessible because it's already open in another program, or the account running the code doesn't have the required permissions. The code in this example is easy to correct—simply wrap all the file operations into a Try/Catch block. (You'll need three—one for the code that reads the files in the current directory, one for the code that retrieves the information from the selected file, and one for the code that deletes the file.) To see the code with the added error-handling logic, refer to the downloadable samples for this chapter.

FILE PERMISSIONS

When you're testing your application in Visual Studio, you're unlikely to run into file permission errors. However, when you deploy your application, life gets more complicated. As you learned in Chapter 9, in a deployed website ASP.NET runs under an account with carefully limited privileges. If you're using IIS 5.1, this is the ASPNET account. Otherwise, it's the network service account, which is a member of the IIS_WPG group (in IIS 6) or the IIS_USERS group (in IIS 7).

If you attempt to access a file using an account that doesn't have the required permissions, you'll receive a SecurityException. To solve problems like these, you can modify the permissions for a file or an entire directory. To do so, right-click the file or directory, select Properties, and choose the Security tab. Here you can add or remove users and groups and configure what operations they're allowed to do. Alternatively, you might find it easier to modify the account ASP.NET uses or change its group membership. For more information, refer to Chapter 9.

The DirectoryInfo and FileInfo Classes

The DirectoryInfo and FileInfo classes mirror the functionality in the Directory and File classes. In addition, they make it easy to walk through directory and file relationships. For example, you can easily retrieve the FileInfo objects for the files in a directory represented by a DirectoryInfo object.

Note that while the Directory and File classes expose only methods, DirectoryInfo and FileInfo provide a combination of properties and methods. For example, while the File class had separate GetAttributes() and SetAttributes() methods, the FileInfo class includes an Attributes property.

Another nice thing about the DirectoryInfo and FileInfo classes is that they share a common set of properties and methods because they derive from the common FileSystemInfo base class. Table 18-4 describes the members they have in common.

Table 18-4. *DirectoryInfo and FileInfo Members*

Member	Description
Attributes	Allows you to retrieve or set attributes using a combination of values from the FileAttributes enumeration.
CreationTime, LastAccessTime, and LastWriteTime	Allows you to set or retrieve the creation time, last-access time, and last-write time using a DateTime object.
CreationTime, LastAccessTime, and LastWriteTime	Allows you to set or retrieve the creation time, last-access time, and last-write time using a DateTime object.
Exists	Returns True or False depending on whether the file or directory exists. In other words, you can create FileInfo and DirectoryInfo objects that don't actually correspond to current physical directories, although you obviously won't be able to use properties such as CreationTime and methods such as MoveTo().
FullName, Name, and Extension	Returns a string that represents the fully qualified name, the directory or file name (with extension), or the extension on its own, depending on which property you use.
Delete()	Removes the file or directory, if it exists. When deleting a directory, it must be empty, or you must specify an optional parameter set to True.
Refresh()	Updates the object so it's synchronized with any file system changes that have happened in the meantime (for example, if an attribute was changed manually using Windows Explorer).
Create()	Creates the specified directory or file.
MoveTo()	Copies the directory and its contents or the file. For a DirectoryInfo object, you need to specify the new path; for a FileInfo object, you specify a path and file name.

In addition, the FileInfo and DirectoryInfo classes have a few unique members, as indicated in Table 18-5 and Table 18-6.

Table 18-5. *Unique DirectoryInfo Members*

Member	Description
Parent and Root	Returns a DirectoryInfo object that represents the parent or root directory.
CreateSubdirectory()	Creates a directory with the specified name in the directory represented by the DirectoryInfo object. It also returns a new DirectoryInfo object that represents the subdirectory.

Table 18-5. *Unique DirectoryInfo Members*

Member	Description
GetDirectories()	Returns an array of DirectoryInfo objects that represent all the subdirectories contained in this directory.
GetFiles()	Returns an array of FileInfo objects that represent all the files contained in this directory.

Table 18-6. *Unique FileInfo Members*

Member	Description
Directory	Returns a DirectoryInfo object that represents the parent directory.
DirectoryName	Returns a string that identifies the name of the parent directory.
Length	Returns a Long (64-bit integer) with the file size in bytes.
CopyTo()	Copies a file to the new path and file name specified as a parameter. It also returns a new FileInfo object that represents the new (copied) file. You can supply an optional additional parameter of True to allow overwriting.

When you create a DirectoryInfo or FileInfo object, you specify the full path in the constructor:

```
Dim myDirectory As New DirectoryInfo("c:\Temp")
Dim myFile As New FileInfo("c:\Temp\readme.txt")
```

This path may or may not correspond to a real physical file or directory. If it doesn't, you can always use the Create() method to create the corresponding file or directory:

```
' Define the new directory and file.
Dim myDirectory As New DirectoryInfo("c:\Temp\Test")
Dim myFile As New FileInfo("c:\Temp\Test\readme.txt")

' Now create them. Order here is important.
' You can't create a file in a directory that doesn't exist yet.
myDirectory.Create()
myFile.Create()
```

The DriveInfo Class

The DriveInfo class allows you to retrieve information about a drive on your computer. Just a few pieces of information will interest you. Typically, the DriveInfo class is merely used to retrieve the total amount of used and free space.

Table 18-7 shows the DriveInfo members. Unlike the FileInfo and DriveInfo classes, there's no Drive class with instance versions of these methods.

Table 18-7. *DriveInfo Members*

Member	Description
TotalSize	Gets the total size of the drive, in bytes. This includes allocated and free space.
TotalFreeSpace	Gets the total amount of free space, in bytes.
AvailableFreeSpace	Gets the total amount of available free space, in bytes. Available space may be less than the total free space if you've applied disk quotas limiting the space the ASP.NET process can use.
DriveFormat	Returns the name of the file system used on the drive (such as NTFS or FAT32).
DriveType	Returns a value from the DriveType enumeration, which indicates whether the drive is a Fixed, Network, CDRom, Ram, or Removable drive (or Unknown if the drive's type cannot be determined).
IsReady	Returns whether the drive is ready for reading or writing operations. Removable drives are considered "not ready" if they don't have any media. For example, if there's no CD in a CD drive, IsReady will return False. In this situation, it's not safe to query the other DriveInfo properties. Fixed drives are always readable.
Name	Returns the drive letter name of the drive (such as c: or e:).
VolumeLabel	Gets or sets the descriptive volume label for the drive. In an NTFS-formatted drive, the volume label can be up to 32 characters. If not set, this property returns a null reference (Nothing).
RootDirectory	Returns a DirectoryInfo object for the root directory in this drive.
GetDrives()	Retrieves an array of DriveInfo objects, representing all the logical drives on the current computer.

■ **Tip** Attempting to read from a drive that's not ready (for example, a CD drive that doesn't have a CD in it) will throw an exception. To avoid this problem, check the DriveInfo.IsReady property, and attempt to read other properties only if it returns True.

A Sample File Browser

You can use methods such as DirectoryInfo.GetFiles() and DirectoryInfo.GetDirectories() to create a simple file browser. The following example shows you how. Be warned that, although this code is a good example of how to use the DirectoryInfo and FileInfo classes, it isn't a good example of security. Generally, you wouldn't want a user to be able to find out so much information about the files on your web server.

The sample file browser program allows the user to see information about any file in any directory in the current drive, as shown in Figure 18-2.

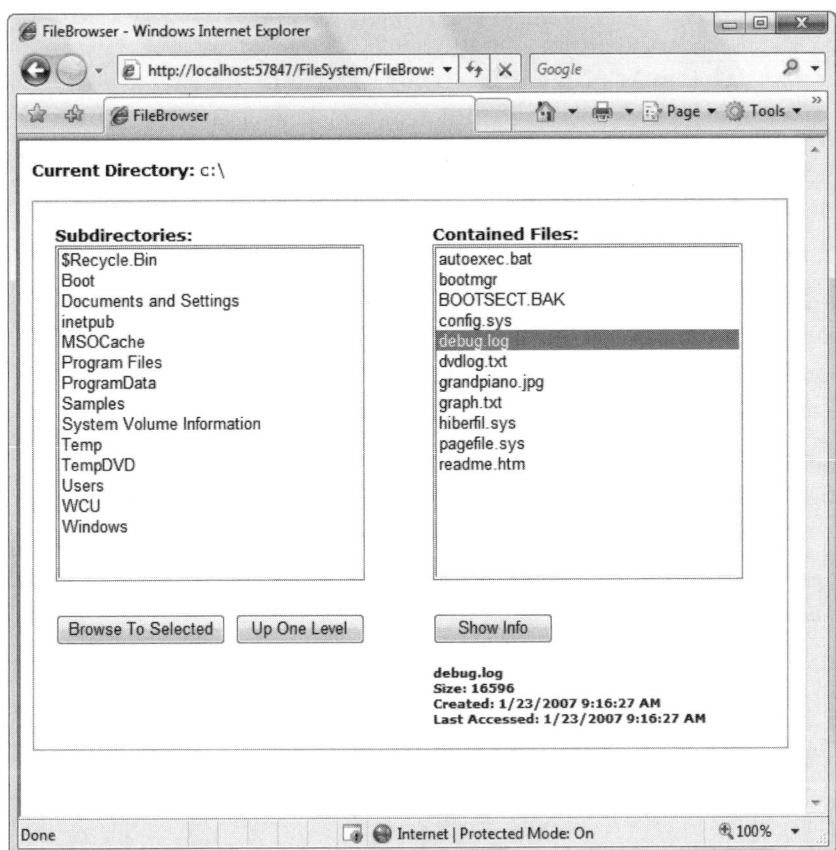

Figure 18-2. *A web server file browser*

The code for the file browser page is as follows:

```
Public Partial Class FileBrowser
    Inherits System.Web.UI.Page

    Protected Sub Page_Load(ByVal sender As Object, _
      ByVal e As EventArgs) Handles Me.Load
        If Not Me.IsPostBack Then
            Dim startingDir As String = "c:\"
            lblCurrentDir.Text = startingDir
            ShowFilesIn(startingDir)
            ShowDirectoriesIn(startingDir)
        End If
    End Sub
```

```
Private Sub ShowFilesIn(ByVal dir As String)
    lstFiles.Items.Clear()

    Try
        Dim dirInfo As New DirectoryInfo(dir)
        For Each fileItem As FileInfo In dirInfo.GetFiles()
            lstFiles.Items.Add(fileItem.Name)
        Next
    Catch err As Exception
        ' Ignore the error and leave the list box empty.
    End Try
End Sub

Private Sub ShowDirectoriesIn(ByVal dir As String)
    lstDirs.Items.Clear()

    Try
        Dim dirInfo As New DirectoryInfo(dir)
        For Each dirItem As DirectoryInfo In dirInfo.GetDirectories()
            lstDirs.Items.Add(dirItem.Name)
        Next
    Catch err As Exception
        ' Ignore the error and leave the list box empty.
    End Try
End Sub

Protected Sub cmdBrowse_Click(ByVal sender As Object, _
  ByVal e As EventArgs) Handles cmdBrowse.Click
    ' Browse to the currently selected subdirectory.
    If lstDirs.SelectedIndex <> -1 Then
        Dim newDir As String = Path.Combine(lblCurrentDir.Text, _
          lstDirs.SelectedItem.Text)
        lblCurrentDir.Text = newDir
        ShowFilesIn(newDir)
        ShowDirectoriesIn(newDir)
    End If
End Sub
```

```
    Protected Sub cmdParent_Click(ByVal sender As Object, _
      ByVal e As EventArgs) Handles cmdParent.Click
        ' Browse up to the current directory's parent.
        ' The Directory.GetParent method helps us out.
        Dim newDir As String
        If Directory.GetParent(lblCurrentDir.Text) Is Nothing Then
            ' This is the root directory; there are no more levels.
            Exit Sub
        Else
            newDir = Directory.GetParent(lblCurrentDir.Text).FullName
        End If

        lblCurrentDir.Text = newDir
        ShowFilesIn(newDir)
        ShowDirectoriesIn(newDir)
    End Sub

    Protected Sub cmdShowInfo_Click(ByVal sender As Object, _
      ByVal e As EventArgs) Handles cmdShowInfo.Click
        ' Show information for the currently selected file.
        If lstFiles.SelectedIndex <> -1 Then
            Dim fileName As String = Path.Combine(lblCurrentDir.Text, _
              lstFiles.SelectedItem.Text)

            Dim displayText As New StringBuilder()
            Try
                Dim selectedFile As New FileInfo(fileName)
                displayText.Append("<b>")
                displayText.Append(selectedFile.Name)
                displayText.Append("</b><br />Size: ")
                displayText.Append(selectedFile.Length)
                displayText.Append("<br />")
                displayText.Append("Created: ")
                displayText.Append(selectedFile.CreationTime.ToString())
                displayText.Append("<br />Last Accessed: ")
                displayText.Append(selectedFile.LastAccessTime.ToString())
            Catch err As Exception
                displayText.Append(err.Message)
            End Try

            lblFileInfo.Text = displayText.ToString()
        End If
    End Sub

End Class
```

Dissecting the Code . . .

- The list controls in this example don't post back immediately. Instead, the web page relies on the Browse to Selected, Up One Level, and Show Info buttons.
- By default, directory names don't end with a trailing backslash (\) character (for example, c:\Temp is used instead of c:\Temp\). However, when referring to the root drive, a slash is required. This is because of an interesting inconsistency that dates back to the days of DOS. When using directory names, c:\ refers to the root drive, but c: refers to the current directory, whatever it may be. This quirk can cause problems when you're manipulating strings that contain file names, because you don't want to add an extra trailing slash to a path (as in the invalid path c:\\myfile.txt). To solve this problem, the page uses the Combine() method of the Path class. This method correctly joins any file and path name together, adding the \ when required.
- The code includes all the necessary error-handling code. If you attempt to read the information for a file that you aren't permitted to examine, the error message is displayed instead of the file details section. If an error occurs when calling DirectoryInfo.GetFiles() or DirectoryInfo.GetDirectories(), the error is simply ignored and the files or subdirectories aren't shown. This error occurs if the account that's running your code doesn't have permission to read the contents of the directory. For example, this occurs if you try to access the c:\System Volume Information directory in Windows.
- The ShowFilesIn() and ShowDirectoriesIn() methods loop through the file and directory collections to build the lists. Another approach is to use data binding instead, as shown in the following code sample:

  ```
  ' Another way to fill lstFiles.
  Dim dirInfo As New DirectoryInfo(dir)

  lstFiles.DataSource = dirInfo.GetFiles()
  lstFiles.DataMember = "Name"
  lstFiles.DataBind()
  ```

  Just remember that when you bind a collection of objects, you need to specify which property will be used for the list. In this case, it's the DirectoryInfo.Name or FileInfo.Name property.

Reading and Writing with Streams

The .NET Framework makes it easy to create simple "flat" files in text or binary format. Unlike a database, these files don't have any internal structure (that's why they're called flat). Instead, these files are really just a list of whatever information you want to store.

Text Files

You can write to a file and read from a file using a StreamWriter and a StreamReader—dedicated classes that abstract away the process of file interaction. There really isn't much to it. You can create the StreamWriter and StreamReader classes on your own, or you can use one of the helpful shared methods included in the File class, such as CreateText() or OpenText().

Here's an example that gets a StreamWriter for writing data to the file c:\myfile.txt:

```
' Define a StreamWriter (which is designed for writing text files).
Dim w As StreamWriter

' Create the file, and get a StreamWriter for it.
w = File.CreateText("c:\myfile.txt")
```

When you call the CreateText() method, you create the file and receive the StreamWriter object. At this point, the file is open and ready to receive your content. You need to write your data to the file, and then close it as soon as possible.

Using the StreamWriter, you can call the WriteLine() method to add information to the file. The WriteLine() method is overloaded so it can write many simple data types, including strings, integers, and other numbers. These values are essentially all converted into strings when they're written to a file and must be converted back into the appropriate types manually when you read the file.

```
w.WriteLine("This file generated by ASP.NET")   ' Write a string.
w.WriteLine(42)                                 ' Write a number.
```

When you finish with the file, you must make sure to close it. Otherwise, the changes may not be properly written to disk, and the file could be locked open. At any time, you can also call the Flush() method to make sure all data is written to disk, as the StreamWriter will perform some in-memory caching to optimize performance.

```
' Tidy up.
w.Flush()
w.Close()
```

Finally, when you're debugging an application that writes to files it's always a good idea to look at what you wrote using a text editor like Notepad. Figure 18-3 shows the contents that are created in c:\myfile.txt with the simple code you've considered.

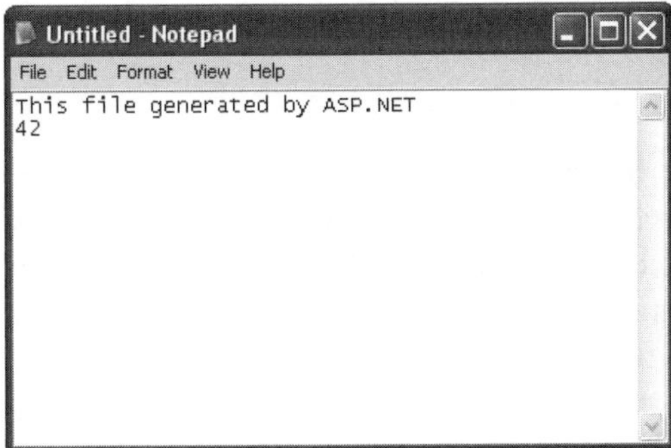

Figure 18-3. *A sample text file*

To read the information, you use the corresponding StreamReader class. It provides a ReadLine() method that gets the next available value and returns it as a string. ReadLine() starts at the first line and advances the position to the end of the file, one line at a time.

```
Dim r As StreamReader = File.OpenText("c:\myfile.txt")
Dim inputString As String
inputString = r.ReadLine()     ' = "This file generated by ASP.NET"
inputString = r.ReadLine()     ' = "42"
```

ReadLine() returns a null reference when there is no more data in the file. This means you can read all the data in a file using code like this:

```
' Read and display the lines from the file until the end
' of the file is reached.
Dim line As String
Do
    line = r.ReadLine()
    If line IsNot Nothing Then
        ' (Process the line here.)
    End If
Loop Until line Is Nothing
```

As when writing to a file, you must close the file once you're finished:

```
r.Close()
```

The code you've seen so far opens a file in single-user mode. If a second user tries to access the same file at the same time, an exception will occur. You can reduce this problem when opening files using the more generic four-parameter version of the File.Open() method instead of File.OpenText(). You must specify FileShare.Read for the final parameter. Unlike the OpenText() method, the Open() method returns a FileStream object, and you must manually create a StreamReader that wraps it.

Here's the code you need to create a multiuser-friendly StreamReader:

```
Dim fs As FileStream
fs = File.Open("c:\myfile.txt", FileMode.Open, _
  FileAccess.Read, FileShare.Read)
Dim r As New StreamReader(fs)
```

■ **Tip** In Chapter 7, you saw how you can create a cookie for the current user, which can be persisted to disk as a simple text file. This is a common technique for storing information in a web application, but it's quite a bit different from the file access code you've seen in this chapter. Cookies are created on the client side rather than on the server. This means your ASP.NET code may be able to use them on subsequent requests from the same user, but they aren't suitable when storing information you need to review later, information that's more permanent, or information that affects more than one user.

Binary Files

You can also read and write to binary files. Binary data uses space more efficiently but also creates files that aren't human-readable. If you open a file in Notepad, you'll see a lot of extended ASCII characters (politely known as *gibberish*).

To open a file for binary writing, you need to create a new BinaryWriter object. The constructor accepts a stream, which you can retrieve using the File.OpenWrite() method. Here's the code to open the file c:\binaryfile.bin for binary writing:

```
Dim w As New BinaryWriter(File.OpenWrite("c:\binaryfile.bin"))
```

.NET concentrates on stream objects, rather than the source or destination for the data. This means you can write binary data to any type of stream, whether it represents a file or some other type of storage location, using the same code. In addition, writing to a binary file is almost the same as writing to a text file.

```
Dim str As String = "ASP.NET Binary File Test"
Dim int As Integer = 42
w.Write(str)
w.Write(int)

w.Flush()
w.Close()
```

Reading data from a binary file is easy, but not quite as easy as reading data from a text file. The problem is that you need to know the data type of the data you want to retrieve. To retrieve a string, you use the ReadString() method. To retrieve an integer, you must use ReadInt32(). That's why the preceding code example writes variables instead of literal values. If the value 42 were hard-coded as the parameter for the Write() method, it wouldn't be clear if the value would be written as a 16-bit integer, 32-bit integer, decimal, or something else. Unfortunately, you may need to micromanage binary files in this way to prevent errors.

```
Dim r As New BinaryReader(File.OpenRead("c:\binaryfile.bin"))
Dim str As string
Dim int As Integer
str = r.ReadString()
int = r.ReadInt32()

r.Close()
```

Once again, if you want to use file sharing, you need to use File.Open() instead of File.OpenRead(). You can then create a BinaryReader by hand, as shown here:

```
Dim fs As FileStream
fs = File.Open("c:\binaryfile.bin", FileMode.Open, _
  FileAccess.Read, FileShare.Read)
Dim r As New BinaryReader(fs)
```

■ **Note** You have no easy way to jump to a location in a text or binary file without reading through all the information in order. Although you can use methods such as Seek() on the underlying stream, you need to specify an offset in bytes, which involves some fairly involved calculations based on data type sizes. If you need to store a large amount of information and move through it quickly, you need a dedicated database, not a binary file.

Shortcuts for Reading and Writing Files

.NET includes functionality for turbo-charging your file writing and reading. This functionality comes from several shared methods in the File class that let you read or write an entire file in a single line of code.

For example, here's a quick code snippet that writes a three-line file and then retrieves it into a single string:

```
Dim lines() As String = {"This is the first line of the file.", _
  "This is the second line of the file.", _
  "This is the third line of the file."}

' Write the file in one shot.
File.WriteAllLines("c:\testfile.txt", lines)

' Read the file in one shot (into a variable named content).
Dim content As String = File.ReadAllText("c:\testfile.txt")
```

Table 18-8 describes the full set of quick file access methods. All of these are shared methods.

Table 18-8. *File Methods for Quick Input/Output*

Method	Description
ReadAllText()	Reads the entire contents of a file and returns it as a single string.
ReadAllLines()	Reads the entire contents of a file and returns it as an array of strings, one for each line.
ReadAllBytes()	Reads the entire file and returns its contents as an array of bytes.
WriteAllText()	Creates a file, writes a supplied string to the file, and closes it. If the file already exists, it is overwritten.
WriteAllLines()	Creates a file, writes a supplied array of strings to the file (separating each line with a hard return), and closes the file. If the file already exists, it is overwritten.
WriteAllBytes()	Creates a file, writes a supplied byte array to the file, and closes it. If the file already exists, it is overwritten.

The quick file access methods are certainly convenient for creating small files. They also ensure a file is kept only for as short a time as possible, which is always the best approach to minimize concurrency problems. But are they really practical? It all depends on the size of the file. If you have a large file (say, one that's several megabytes), reading the entire content into memory at once is a terrible idea. It's much better to read one piece of data at a time and process the information bit by bit. Even if you're dealing with medium-sized files (say, several hundreds of kilobytes), you might want to steer clear of the quick file access methods. That's because in a popular website you might have multiple requests dealing with files at the same time, and the combined overhead of keeping every user's file data in memory might reduce the performance of your application.

A Simple Guest Book

The next example demonstrates the file access techniques described in the previous sections to create a simple guest book. The page actually has two parts. If there are no current guest entries, the client will see only the controls for adding a new entry, as shown in Figure 18-4.

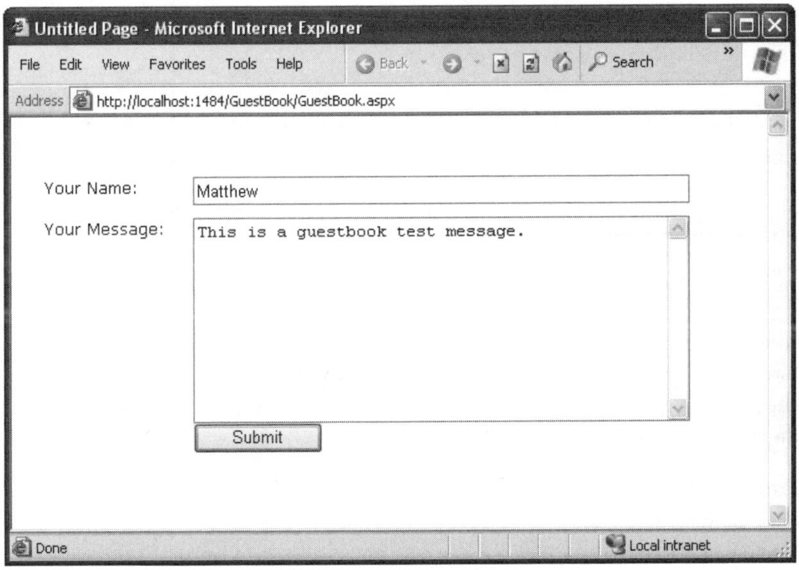

Figure 18-4. *The initial guest book page*

When the user clicks Submit, a file will be created for the new guest book entry. As long as at least one guest book entry exists, a GridView control will appear at the top of the page, as shown in Figure 18-5.

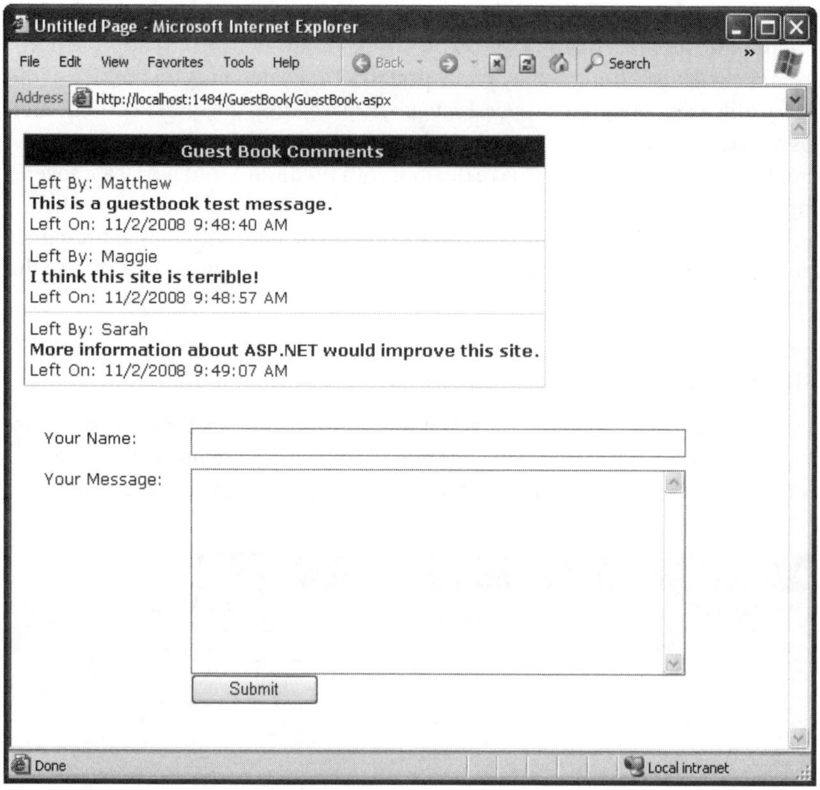

Figure 18-5. *The full guest book page*

The GridView that represents the guest book is constructed using data binding, which you explored in Chapters 16 and 17. Technically speaking, the GridView is bound to a collection that contains instances of the BookEntry class. The BookEntry class definition is included in the code-behind file for the web page and looks like this:

```
Public Class BookEntry
    Private _author As String
    Private _submitted As Date
    Private _message As String

    Public Property Author() As String
        Get
            Return _author
        End Get
        Set(ByVal Value As String)
            _author = Value
        End Set
    End Property
```

```
    Public Property Submitted() As Date
        Get
            Return _submitted
        End Get
        Set(ByVal Value As Date)
            _submitted = Value
        End Set
    End Property

    Public Property Message() As String
        Get
            Return _message
        End Get
        Set(ByVal Value As String)
            _message = Value
        End Set
    End Property
End Class
```

The GridView uses a single template column, which fishes out the values it needs to display. Here's what it looks like (without the style details):

```
<asp:GridView ID="GuestBookList" runat="server" AutoGenerateColumns="False">
  <Columns>
      <asp:TemplateField HeaderText="Guest Book Comments">
        <ItemTemplate>
          Left By:
          <%# Eval("Author") %>
          <br />
          <b><%# Eval("Message") %></b>
          <br />
          Left On:
          <%# Eval("Submitted") %>
      </ItemTemplate>
    </asp:TemplateField>
  </Columns>
</asp:GridView>
```

It also adds some style information that isn't included here (because it isn't necessary to understand the logic of the program). In fact, these styles were applied in Visual Studio using the GridView's Auto Format feature.

As for the entries, the guest book page uses a special directory (GuestBook) to store a collection of files. Each file represents a separate entry in the guest book. A better approach would usually be to create a GuestBook table in a database and make each entry a separate record.

The code for the web page is as follows:

```
Public Partial Class GuestBook
    Inherits System.Web.UI.Page

    Private guestBookName As String

    Protected Sub Page_Load(ByVal sender As Object, _
      ByVal e As EventArgs) Handles MyBase.Load
        guestBookName = Server.MapPath("GuestBook")

        If Not Me.IsPostBack Then
            GuestBookList.DataSource = GetAllEntries()
            GuestBookList.DataBind()
        End If
    End Sub

    Protected Sub cmdSubmit_Click(ByVal sender As Object, _
      ByVal e As EventArgs) Handles cmdSubmit.Click
        ' Create a new BookEntry object.
        Dim newEntry As New BookEntry()
        newEntry.Author = txtName.Text
        newEntry.Submitted = DateTime.Now
        newEntry.Message = txtMessage.Text

        ' Let the SaveEntry procedure create the corresponding file.
        Try
            SaveEntry(newEntry)
        Catch err As Exception
            ' An error occurred. Notify the user and don't clear the
            ' display.
            lblError.Text = err.Message & " File not saved."
            Exit Sub
        End Try

        ' Refresh the display.
        GuestBookList.DataSource = GetAllEntries()
        GuestBookList.DataBind()

        txtName.Text = ""
        txtMessage.Text = ""
    End Sub
```

```
Private Function GetAllEntries() As List(Of BookEntry)
    ' Return a collection that contains BookEntry objects
    ' for each file in the GuestBook directory.
    ' This method relies on the GetEntryFromFile method.
    Dim entries As New List(Of BookEntry)()

    Try
        Dim guestBookDir As New DirectoryInfo(guestBookName)

        For Each fileItem As FileInfo In guestBookDir.GetFiles()
            Try
                entries.Add(GetEntryFromFile(fileItem))
            Catch
                ' An error occurred when calling GetEntryFromFile().
                ' Ignore this file because it can't be read.
            End Try
        Next
    Catch err As Exception
        ' An error occurred when calling GetFiles().
        ' Ignore this error and leave the entries collection empty.
    End Try

    Return entries
End Function

Private Function GetEntryFromFile(ByVal entryFile As FileInfo) _
  As BookEntry
    ' Turn the file information into a BookEntry object.
    Dim newEntry As New BookEntry()
    Dim r As StreamReader = entryFile.OpenText()
    newEntry.Author = r.ReadLine()
    newEntry.Submitted = DateTime.Parse(r.ReadLine())
    newEntry.Message = r.ReadLine()
    r.Close()

    return newEntry
End Function

Private Sub SaveEntry(ByVal entry As BookEntry)
    ' Create a new file for this entry, with a file name that should
    ' be statistically unique.
    Dim random As New Random()
    Dim fileName As String = guestBookName & "\"
    fileName &= DateTime.Now.Ticks.ToString() & random.Next(100).ToString()
    Dim newFile As New FileInfo(fileName)
    Dim w As StreamWriter = newFile.CreateText()
```

```
        ' Write the information to the file.
        w.WriteLine(entry.Author)
        w.WriteLine(entry.Submitted.ToString())
        w.WriteLine(entry.Message)
        w.Flush()
        w.Close()
    End Sub

End Class
```

Dissecting the Code . . .

- The code uses text files so you can easily review the information on your own with Notepad. You could use binary files just as easily, which would save a small amount of space.
- The file name for each entry is generated using a combination of the current date and time (in ticks) and a random number. Practically speaking, this makes it impossible for a file to be generated with a duplicate file name.
- This program uses error handling to defend against possible problems. However, errors are handled in a different way depending on when they occur. If an error occurs when saving a new entry in the cmdSubmit_Click() method, the user is alerted to the problem, but the display is not updated. Instead, the user-supplied information is left in the controls so the save operation can be reattempted. When reading the existing files in the cmdGetAllEntries_Click() method, two problems can occur, and they're dealt with using separate exception blocks. A problem can happen when the code calls GetFiles() to retrieve the file list. In this situation, the problem is ignored but no files are found, and so no guest book entries are shown. If this step succeeds, a problem can still occur when reading each file in the GetEntryFromFile() method. In this situation, the file that caused the problem is ignored, but the code continues and attempts to read the remaining files.

■ **Note** The error-handling code in this example does a good job of recovering from the brink of disaster and allowing the user to keep working, when it's possible. However, the error-handling code might not do enough to alert you that there's a problem. If the problem is a freak occurrence, this behavior is fine. But if the problem is a symptom of a deeper issue in your web application, you should know about it.

To make sure that problems aren't overlooked, you might choose to show an error message on the page when an exception occurs. Even better, your code could quietly create an entry in the event log that records the problem (as explained in Chapter 8). That way, you can find out about the problems that have occurred and correct them later.

- Careful design makes sure this program isolates file writing and reading code in separate functions, such as SaveEntry(), GetAllEntries(), and GetEntryFromFile(). For even better organization, you could move these routines in a separate class or even a separate component. This would allow you to use the ObjectDataSource to reduce your data binding code. For more information, read Chapter 23.

Allowing File Uploads

Although you've seen detailed examples of how to work with files and directories on the web server, you haven't yet considered the question of how to allow file uploads. The problem with file uploading is that you need some way to retrieve information from the client—and as you already know, all ASP.NET code executes on the server.

The FileUpload Control

Fortunately, ASP.NET includes a control that allows website users to upload files to the web server. Once the web server receives the posted file data, it's up to your application to examine it, ignore it, or save it to a back-end database or a file on the web server. The FileUpload control does this work, and it represents the <input type="file"> HTML tag.

Declaring the FileUpload control is easy. It doesn't expose any new properties or events you can use through the control tag:

```
<asp:FileUpload ID="Uploader" runat="server" />
```

The <input type="file"> tag doesn't give you much choice as far as user interface is concerned (it's limited to a text box that contains a file name and a Browse button). When the user clicks Browse, the browser presents an Open dialog box and allows the user to choose a file. This part is hard-wired into the browser, and you can't change this behavior. Once the user selects a file, the file name is filled into the corresponding text box. However, the file isn't uploaded yet—that happens later, when the page is posted back. At this point, all the data from all input controls (including the file data) is sent to the server. For that reason, it's common to add a button to post back the page.

To get information about the posted file content, you can access the FileUpload.PostedFile object. You can save the content by calling the PostedFile.SaveAs() method:

```
Uploader.PostedFile.SaveAs("c:\Uploads\newfile")
```

Figure 18-6 shows a complete web page that demonstrates how to upload a user-specified file. This example introduces a twist—it allows the upload of only those files with the extensions .bmp, .gif, and .jpg.

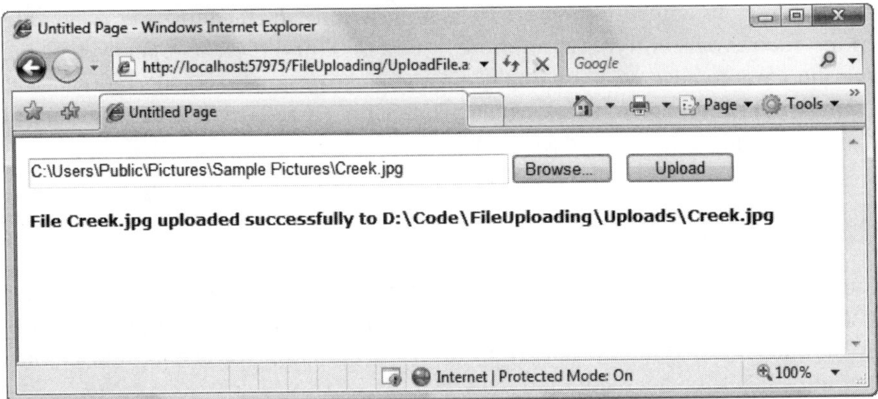

Figure 18-6. *A simple file uploader*

Here's the code for the upload page:

```
Public Partial Class UploadFile
    Inherits System.Web.UI.Page

    Private uploadDirectory As String

    Protected Sub Page_Load(ByVal sender As Object, _
      ByVal e As EventArgs)  Handles Me.Load

        ' Place files in a website subfolder named Uploads.
        uploadDirectory = Path.Combine( _
          Request.PhysicalApplicationPath, "Uploads")
    End Sub

    Protected Sub cmdUpload_Click(ByVal sender As Object, _
      ByVal e As System.EventArgs) Handles cmdUpload.Click

        ' Check that a file is actually being submitted.
        If Uploader.PostedFile.FileName = "" Then
            lblInfo.Text = "No file specified."
        Else
            ' Check the extension.
            Dim extension As String = _
              Path.GetExtension(Uploader.PostedFile.FileName)
```

```
        Select Case extension.ToLower()
            Case ".bmp", ".gif", ".jpg"
                ' This is an allowed file type.
            Case Else
                lblInfo.Text = "This file type is not allowed."
                Return
        End Select

        ' Using this code, the saved file will retain its original
        ' file name when it's placed on the server.
        Dim serverFileName As String = _
          Path.GetFileName(Uploader.PostedFile.FileName)
        Dim fullUploadPath As String = _
          Path.Combine(uploadDirectory, serverFileName)

        Try
            Uploader.PostedFile.SaveAs(fullUploadPath)

            lblInfo.Text = "File " & serverFileName
            lblInfo.Text &= " uploaded successfully to "
            lblInfo.Text &= fullUploadPath
        Catch Err As Exception
            lblInfo.Text = err.Message
        End Try
    End If

End Sub

End Class
```

Dissecting the Code . . .

- The saved file keeps its original (client-side) name. The code uses the Path.GetFileName() shared method to transform the fully qualified name provided by FileUpload.PostedFile.FileName and retrieve just the file, without the path.
- The FileUpload.PostedFile object contains only a few properties. One interesting property is ContentLength, which returns the size of the file in bytes. You could examine this setting and use it to prevent a user from uploading excessively large files.

THE MAXIMUM SIZE OF A FILE UPLOAD

By default, ASP.NET will reject a request that's larger than 4MB. However, you can alter this maximum by modifying the maxRequestLength setting in the web.config file. This sets the largest allowed file in kilobytes. The web server will refuse to process larger requests.

The following sample setting configures the server to accept files up to 8MB:

```
<?xml version="1.0" encoding="utf-8" ?>
<configuration>
  <system.web>
    <!-- Other settings omitted for clarity. -->
    <httpRuntime maxRequestLength="8192"
    />
  </system.web>
</configuration>
```

Be careful, though. When you allow an 8MB upload, your code won't run until that full request has been received. This means a malicious server could cripple your server by sending large request messages to your application. Even if your application ultimately rejects these messages, the ASP.NET worker process threads will still be tied up waiting for the requests to complete. This type of attack is called a *denial-of-service attack*, and the larger your allowed request size is, the more susceptible your website becomes.

The Last Word

Although databases and websites make a perfect fit, nothing is preventing you from using the classes in the .NET Framework to access other types of data, including files. In fact, the code you use to interact with the file system is the same as what you would use in a desktop application or any .NET program. Thanks to the .NET Framework, you can finally solve common programming problems in the same way, regardless of the type of application you're creating.

CHAPTER 19

XML

XML is woven right into the fabric of .NET, and it powers key parts of ASP.NET. In this chapter, you'll learn why XML comes into play in every ASP.NET web application—whether you realize it or not.

You'll also learn how you can create and read XML documents on your own by using the classes of the .NET library. Along the way, you'll sort through some of the near-hysteric XML hype and consider what practical role XML can play in a web application. You may find that ASP.NET's built-in XML support is all you need and decide you don't want to manually create and manipulate XML data. On the other hand, you might want to use the XML classes to read data created by other applications, or just as a convenient replacement for simple text files. But before you can get into the details of XML processing, you need to know the ground rules of the XML standard. This chapter starts with a whirlwind introduction to XML that explains how it works and why it exists.

XML's Hidden Role in .NET

The most useful place for XML isn't in your web applications but in the infrastructure that supports them. Microsoft has taken this philosophy to heart with ASP.NET. ASP.NET uses XML quietly behind the scenes to accomplish a wide range of tasks. If you don't know much about XML yet, the first thing you should realize is that you're already using it.

Configuration Files

ASP.NET stores settings in a human-readable XML format using configuration files such as machine.config and web.config, which were first introduced in Chapter 6. Arguably, a plain-text file could be just as efficient. However, that would force the designers of the ASP.NET platform to create their own proprietary format, which developers would then need to learn. XML provides an all-purpose syntax for storing any data in a customized yet consistent and standardized way using tags. Anyone who understands XML will immediately understand how the ASP.NET configuration files are organized.

XHTML

As you learned in Chapter 4, ASP.NET web controls use XHTML rendering. XHTML is a stricter version of HTML that's based on the XML standard. Thus, when you craft the markup for a web page, you're actually using XML.

ADO.NET Data Access

The ADO.NET DataSet can represent any data as an XML document, without requiring an error-prone conversion step. This has a number of interesting consequences. For example, it allows you to easily save the information you've retrieved from the database in an XML file so you can retrieve it for later use. This feature is particularly useful for client applications that aren't always connected to the network, but you may choose to use it occasionally in a web application.

Anywhere Miscellaneous Data Is Stored

Just when you think you've identified everywhere XML markup is used, you'll find it appearing somewhere new. You'll find XML when you write an advertisement file that defines the content for the AdRotator control, when you create an ASP.NET site map, or when you use .NET serialization to write an object to a file. That these formats use XML probably won't change the way they work, but it does open up other possibilities for integrating the data with other applications and tools. It's also one more example that the developers of the .NET Framework have embraced XML in unprecedented ways, abandoning Microsoft's traditional philosophy of closed standards and proprietary technologies.

XML Explained

The basic premise of XML is fairly simple, although the possible implementations of it (and the numerous extensions to it) can get quite complex. XML is designed as an all-purpose format for organizing data. In many cases, when you decide to use XML, you're deciding to store data in a standardized way, rather than creating your own new (and to other developers, unfamiliar) format conventions. The actual location of this data—in memory, in a file, in a network stream—is irrelevant.

The best way to understand the role XML plays is to consider the evolution of a simple file format *without* XML. For example, consider a simple program that stores product items as a list in a file. Say when you first create this program, you decide it will store three pieces of product information (ID, name, and price), and you'll use a simple text file format for easy debugging and testing. The file format you use looks like this:

```
1
Chair
49.33
2
Car
43399.55
3
Fresh Fruit Basket
49.99
```

This is the sort of format you might create by using .NET classes such as the StreamWriter. It's easy to work with—you just write all the information, in order, from top to bottom. Of course, it's a fairly fragile format. If you decide to store an extra piece of information in the file (such as a flag that indicates whether an item is available), your old code won't work. Instead, you might need to resort to adding a header that indicates the version of the file:

```
SuperProProductList
Version 2.0
1
Chair
49.33
True
2
Car
43399.55
True
3
Fresh Fruit Basket
49.99
False
```

Now, you could check the file version when you open it and use different file-reading code appropriately. Unfortunately, as you add more and more possible versions, the file-reading code will become incredibly tangled, and you may accidentally break compatibility with one of the earlier file formats without realizing it. A better approach would be to create a file format that indicates where every product record starts and stops. Your code would then just set some appropriate defaults if it finds missing information in an older file format.

Here's a relatively crude solution that improves the SuperProProductList by adding a special sequence of characters (##Start##) to show where each new record begins:

```
SuperProProductList
Version 3.0
##Start##
1
Chair
49.33
True
##Start##
2
Car
43399.55
True
##Start##
3
Fresh Fruit Basket
49.99
False
```

All in all, this isn't a bad effort. Unfortunately, you may as well use the binary file format at this point—the text file is becoming hard to read, and it's even harder to guess what piece of information each value represents. On the code side, you'll also need some basic error checking abilities of your own. For example, you should make your code able to skip over accidentally entered blank lines, detect a missing ##Start## tag, and so on, just to provide a basic level of protection.

The central problem with this homegrown solution is that you're reinventing the wheel. While you're trying to write basic file access code and create a reasonably flexible file format for a simple task, other programmers around the world are creating their own private, ad hoc solutions. Even if your program works fine and you can understand it, other programmers will definitely not find it easy.

Improving the List with XML

This is where XML comes into the picture. XML is an all-purpose way to identify any type of data using *elements*. These elements use the same sort of format found in an HTML file, but while HTML elements indicate formatting, XML elements indicate content. (Because an XML file is just about data, there is no standardized way to display it in a browser, although Internet Explorer shows a collapsible view that lets you show and hide different portions of the document.)

The SuperProProductList could use the following, clearer XML syntax:

```
<?xml version="1.0"?>
<SuperProProductList>
    <Product>
        <ID>1</ID>
        <Name>Chair</Name>
        <Price>49.33</Price>
        <Available>True</Available>
        <Status>3</Status>
    </Product>
    <Product>
        <ID>2</ID>
        <Name>Car</Name>
        <Price>43399.55</Price>
        <Available>True</Available>
        <Status>3</Status>
    </Product>
    <Product>
        <ID>3</ID>
        <Name>Fresh Fruit Basket</Name>
        <Price>49.99</Price>
        <Available>False</Available>
        <Status>4</Status>
    </Product>
</SuperProProductList>
```

This format is clearly understandable. Every product item is enclosed in a <Product> element, and every piece of information has its own element with an appropriate name. Elements are nested several layers deep to show relationships. Essentially, XML provides the basic element syntax, and you (the programmer) define the elements you want to use. That's why XML is often described as a *metalanguage*—it's a language you use to create your own language. In the SuperProProductList example, this custom XML language defines elements such as <Product>, <ID>, <Name>, and so on.

Best of all, when you read this XML document in most programming languages (including those in the .NET Framework), you can use XML parsers to make your life easier. In other words, you don't need to worry about detecting where an element starts and stops, collapsing whitespace, and so on (although you do need to worry about capitalization, because XML is case sensitive). Instead, you can just read the file into some helpful XML data objects that make navigating the entire document much easier.

XML FILES VS. DATABASES

You can perform many tasks with XML—perhaps including some things it was never designed to do. This book is not intended to teach you XML programming but good ASP.NET application design. For most ASP.NET programmers, XML file processing is an ideal replacement for custom file access routines and works best in situations where you need to store a small amount of data for relatively simple tasks.

XML files aren't a good substitute for a database, because they have the same limitations as any other type of file access. In a web application, only a single user can update a file at a time without causing serious headaches, regardless of whether the file contains an XML document or binary content. Database products provide a far richer set of features for managing multiuser concurrency and providing optimized performance. Of course, nothing is stopping you from storing XML data *in* a database, which many database products actively encourage. In fact, the newest versions of leading database products such as SQL Server and Oracle even include extended XML features that support some of the standards you'll see in this chapter.

XML Basics

Part of XML's popularity is a result of its simplicity. When creating your own XML document, you need to remember only a few rules:

- XML elements are composed of a start tag (like <Name>) and an end tag (like </Name>). Content is placed between the start and end tags. If you include a start tag, you *must* also include a corresponding end tag. The only other option is to combine the two by creating an empty element, which includes a forward slash at the end and has no content (like <Name />). This is similar to the syntax for ASP.NET controls.
- Whitespace between elements is ignored. That means you can freely use tabs and hard returns to properly align your information.
- You can use only valid characters in the content for an element. You can't enter special characters, such as the angle brackets (< >) and the ampersand (&), as content. Instead, you'll have to use the entity equivalents (such as < and > for angle brackets, and & for the ampersand). These equivalents will be automatically converted to the original characters when you read them into your program with the appropriate .NET classes.
- XML elements are case sensitive, so <ID> and <id> are completely different elements.

- All elements must be nested in a root element. In the SuperProProductList example, the root element is <SuperProProductList>. As soon as the root element is closed, the document is finished, and you cannot add anything else after it. In other words, if you omit the <SuperProProductList> element and start with a <Product> element, you'll be able to enter information for only one product; this is because as soon as you add the closing </Product>, the document is complete. (HTML has a similar rule and requires that all page content be nested in a root <html> element, but most browsers let you get away without following this rule.)
- Every element must be fully enclosed. In other words, when you open a subelement, you need to close it before you can close the parent. <Product><ID></ID></Product> is valid, but <Product><ID></Product></ID> isn't. As a general rule, indent when you open a new element, because this will allow you to see the document's structure and notice if you accidentally close the wrong element first.
- XML documents must start with an XML declaration like <?xml version="1.0"?>. This signals that the document contains XML and indicates any special text encoding. However, many XML parsers work fine even if this detail is omitted.

These requirements should sound familiar—they're the same rules you learned for XHTML in Chapter 4. After all, XHTML is just another specialized language that's built using the standardized rules of XML.

As long as you meet these requirements, your XML document can be parsed and displayed as a basic tree. This means your document is well formed, but it doesn't mean it is valid. For example, you may still have your elements in the wrong order (for example, <ID><Product></Product></ID>), or you may have the wrong type of data in a given field (for example, <ID>Chair</ID><Name>2</Name>). You can impose these additional rules on your XML documents, as you'll see later in this chapter when you consider XML schemas.

Elements are the primary units for organizing information in XML (as demonstrated with the SuperProProductList example), but they aren't the only option. You can also use *attributes.*

Attributes

Attributes add extra information to an element. Instead of putting information into a subelement, you can use an attribute. In the XML community, deciding whether to use subelements or attributes—and what information should go into an attribute—is a matter of great debate, with no clear consensus.

Here's the SuperProProductList example with ID and Name attributes instead of ID and Name subelements:

```
<?xml version="1.0"?>
<SuperProProductList>
    <Product ID="1" Name="Chair">
        <Price>49.33</Price>
        <Available>True</Available>
        <Status>3</Status>
    </Product>
```

```
    <Product ID="2" Name="Car">
        <Price>43399.55</Price>
        <Available>True</Available>
        <Status>3</Status>
    </Product>
    <Product ID="3" Name="Fresh Fruit Basket">
        <Price>49.99</Price>
        <Available>False</Available>
        <Status>4</Status>
    </Product>
</SuperProProductList>
```

Of course, you've already seen this sort of syntax with HTML elements and ASP.NET server controls:

```
<asp:DropDownList id="lstBackColor" AutoPostBack="True"
  Width="194px" Height="22px" runat="server" />
```

Attributes are also common in the configuration file:

```
<sessionState mode="Inproc" cookieless="false" timeout="20" />
```

Using attributes in XML is more stringent than in HTML. In XML, attributes must always have values, and these values must use quotation marks. For example, <Product Name="Chair" /> is acceptable, but <Product Name=Chair /> or <Product Name /> isn't. However, you do have one bit of flexibility—you can use single or double quotes around any attribute value. It's convenient to use single quotes if you know the text value inside will contain a double quote (as in <Product Name='Red "Sizzle" Chair' />). If your text value has both single and double quotes, use double quotes around the value and replace the double quotes inside the value with the " entity equivalent.

■ **Tip** Order is not important when dealing with attributes. XML parsers treat attributes as a collection of unordered information relating to an element. On the other hand, the order of elements often *is* important. Thus, if you need a way of arranging information and preserving its order, or if you have repeated items with the same name, then use elements, not attributes.

Comments

You can also add comments to an XML document. Comments go just about anywhere and are ignored for data-processing purposes. Comments are bracketed by the <!-- and --> character sequences. The following listing includes three valid comments:

```
<?xml version="1.0"?>
<SuperProProductList>
<!-- This is a test file. -->
    <Product ID="1" Name="Chair">
        <Price>49.33<!-- Why so expensive? --></Price>
        <Available>True</Available>
        <Status>3</Status>
    </Product>
    <!-- Other products omitted for clarity. -->
</SuperProProductList>
```

The only place you can't put a comment is embedded within a start or an end tag (as in <myData <!-- A comment should not go here --></myData>).

The XML Classes

.NET provides a rich set of classes for XML manipulation in several namespaces that start with System.Xml. One of the most confusing aspects of using XML with .NET is deciding which combination of classes you should use. Many of them provide similar functionality in a slightly different way, optimized for specific scenarios or for compatibility with specific standards.

The majority of the examples you'll explore use the types in the core System.Xml namespace. The classes here allow you to read and write XML files, manipulate XML data in memory, and even validate XML documents.

In this chapter, you'll look at the following options for dealing with XML data:

- Reading and writing XML directly, just like you read and write text files using XmlTextWriter and XmlTextReader
- Dealing with XML as a collection of in-memory objects, such as XmlDocument and XmlNode
- Binding to the XmlDataSource to display XML information with minimum fuss

In addition, you'll get a preview of three *more* ways to manipulate XML in the "Still More Ways to Read XML" sidebar at the end of this chapter.

The XML TextWriter

One of the simplest ways to create or read any XML document is to use the basic XmlTextWriter and XmlTextReader classes. These classes work like their StreamWriter and StreamReader relatives, except that they write and read XML documents instead of ordinary text files. This means you follow the same process you saw in Chapter 18 for creating a file. First, you create or open the file. Then, you write to it or read from it, moving from top to bottom. Finally, you close it and get to work using the retrieved data in whatever way you'd like.

Before beginning this example, you'll need to import the namespaces for file handling and XML processing:

```
Imports System.IO
Imports System.Xml
```

Here's an example that creates a simple version of the SuperProProductList document:

```
' Place the file in the App_Data subfolder of the current website.
' The System.IO.Path class makes it easy to build the full file name.
Dim file As String = Path.Combine(Request.PhysicalApplicationPath, _
  "App_Data\SuperProProductList.xml")

Dim fs As New FileStream(file, FileMode.Create)
Dim w As New XmlTextWriter(fs, Nothing)

w.WriteStartDocument()
w.WriteStartElement("SuperProProductList")
w.WriteComment("This file generated by the XmlTextWriter class.")

' Write the first product.
w.WriteStartElement("Product")
w.WriteAttributeString("ID", "", "1")
w.WriteAttributeString("Name", "", "Chair")

w.WriteStartElement("Price")
w.WriteString("49.33")
w.WriteEndElement()

w.WriteEndElement()

' Write the second product.
w.WriteStartElement("Product")
w.WriteAttributeString("ID", "2")
w.WriteAttributeString("Name", "Car")

w.WriteStartElement("Price")
w.WriteString("43399.55")

w.WriteEndElement()

w.WriteEndElement()

' Write the third product.
w.WriteStartElement("Product")
w.WriteAttributeString("ID", "3")
w.WriteAttributeString("Name", "Fresh Fruit Basket")

w.WriteStartElement("Price")
w.WriteString("49.99")
w.WriteEndElement()

w.WriteEndElement()
```

```
' Close the root element.
w.WriteEndElement()
w.WriteEndDocument()
w.Close()
```

This code is similar to the code used for writing a basic text file. It does have a few advantages, however. You can close elements quickly and accurately, the angle brackets (< >) are included for you automatically, and some errors (such as closing the root element too soon) are caught automatically, thereby ensuring a well-formed XML document as the final result.

To check that your code worked, open the file in Internet Explorer, which automatically provides a collapsible view for XML documents (see Figure 19-1).

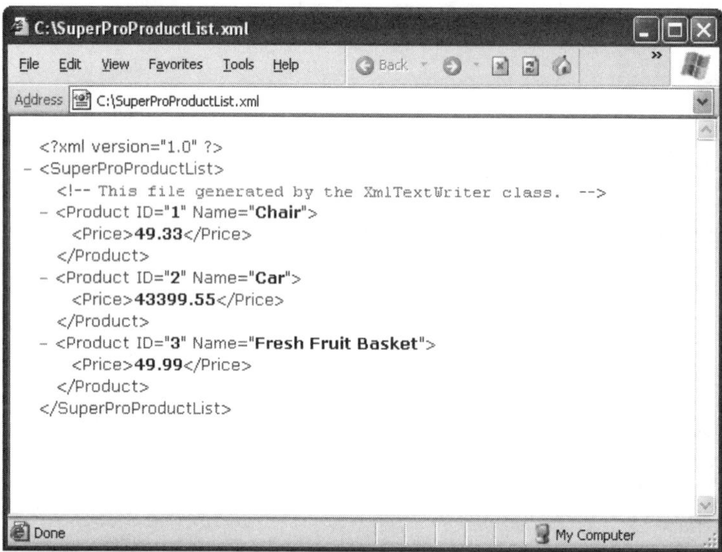

Figure 19-1. *SuperProProductList.xml*

FORMATTING YOUR XML

By default, the XmlTextWriter will create an XML file that has all its elements lumped together in a single line without any helpful carriage returns or indentation. You don't see this limitation in Figure 19-1, because Internet Explorer uses a style sheet to give the XML a more readable (and more colorful) appearance. However, if you open the XML document in Notepad, you'll see the difference.

Although additional formatting isn't required (and doesn't change how the data will be processed), it can make a significant difference if you want to read your XML files in Notepad or another text editor. Fortunately, the XmlTextWriter supports formatting; you just need to enable it, as follows:

```
' Set it to indent output.
w.Formatting = Formatting.Indented

' Set the number of indent spaces.
w.Indentation = 5
```

The XML Text Reader

Reading the XML document in your code is just as easy with the corresponding XmlTextReader class. The XmlTextReader moves through your document from top to bottom, one node at a time. You call the Read() method to move to the next node. This method returns True if there are more nodes to read or False once it has read the final node. The current node is provided through the properties of the XmlTextReader class, such as NodeType and Name.

A node is a designation that includes comments, whitespace, opening tags, closing tags, content, and even the XML declaration at the top of your file. To get a quick understanding of nodes, you can use the XmlTextReader to run through your entire document from start to finish and display every node it encounters. The code for this task is as follows:

```
Dim fs As New FileStream(file, FileMode.Open)
Dim r As New XmlTextReader(fs)

' Use a StringWriter to build up a string of HTML that
' describes the information read from the XML document.
Dim writer As New StringWriter()

' Parse the file, and read each node.
Do While r.Read()
    writer.Write("<b>Type:</b> ")
    writer.Write(r.NodeType.ToString())
    writer.Write("<br />")

    ' The name is available when reading the opening and closing tags
    ' for an element. It's not available when reading the inner content.
    If r.Name <> "" Then
        writer.Write("<b>Name:</b> ")
        writer.Write(r.Name)
        writer.Write("<br />")
    End If

    ' The value is when reading the inner content.
    If r.Value <> "" Then
        writer.Write("<b>Value:</b> ")
        writer.Write(r.Value)
        writer.Write("<br />")
    End If

    If r.AttributeCount > 0 Then
        writer.Write("<b>Attributes:</b> ")
        For i As Integer = 0 To r.AttributeCount - 1
            writer.Write("  ")
            writer.Write(r.GetAttribute(i))
            writer.Write("  ")
```

```
        Next
        writer.Write("<br />")
    End If

    writer.Write("<br />")
Loop
fs.Close()

' Copy the string content into a label to display it.
lblXml.Text = writer.ToString()
```

To test this, try the XmlText.aspx page included with the online samples. It produces the result shown in Figure 19-2.

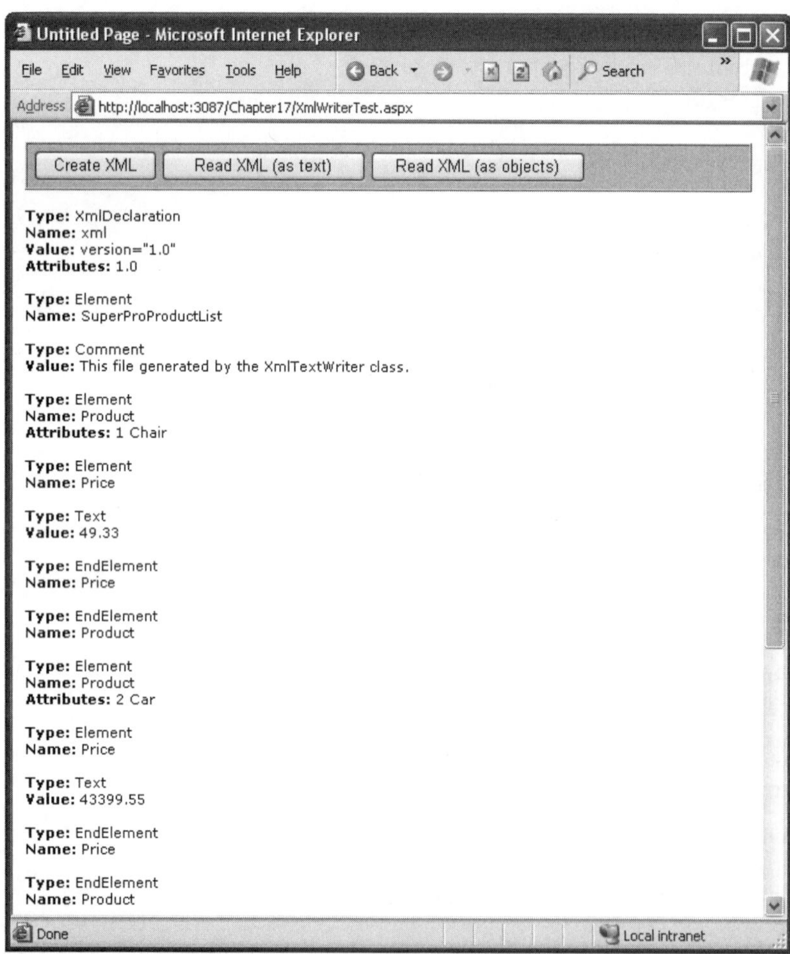

Figure 19-2. *Reading XML structure*

The following is a list of all the nodes that are found, shortened to include only one product:

```
Type: XmlDeclaration
Name: xml
Value: version="1.0"
Attributes: 1.0

Type: Element
Name: SuperProProductList

Type: Comment
Value: This file generated by the XmlTextWriter class.

Type: Element
Name: Product
Attributes: 1, Chair

Type: Element
Name: Price

Type: Text
Value: 49.33

Type: EndElement
Name: Price

Type: EndElement
Name: Product

Type: EndElement
Name: SuperProProductList
```

If you use the indentation trick described earlier (in the "Formatting Your XML" sidebar), you'll see additional nodes that represent the bits of whitespace between elements.

In a typical application, you would need to go fishing for the elements that interest you. For example, you might read information from an XML file such as SuperProProductList.xml and use it to create Product objects based on the Product class shown here:

```
Public Class Product
    Private _id As Integer
    Private _name As String
    Private _price As Decimal

    Public Property ID() As Integer
        Get
            Return _id
        End Get
```

```
        Set(ByVal Value As Integer)
            _id = Value
        End Set
    End Property

    Public Property Name() As String
        Get
            Return _name
        End Get
        Set(ByVal Value As String)
            _name = Value
        End Set
    End Property

    Public Property Price() As Decimal
        Get
            Return _price
        End Get
        Set(ByVal Value As Decimal)
            _price = Value
        End Set
    End Property

End Class
```

Nothing is particularly special about this class—all it does is allow you to store three related pieces of information (price, name, and ID). Note that this class uses properties rather than public member variables, so its information can be displayed in a web page with ASP.NET data binding.

A typical application might read data from an XML file and place it directly into the corresponding objects. The next example (also a part of the XmlWriterTest.aspx page) shows how you can easily create a group of Product objects based on the SuperProProductList.xml file. This example uses the generic List collection, so you'll need to import the System.Collections.Generic namespace.

```
' Open a stream to the file.
Dim fs As New FileStream(file, FileMode.Open)
Dim r As New XmlTextReader(fs)

' Create the collection of products.
Dim Products As New List(Of Product)()

' Loop through the products.
Do While r.Read()
```

```
    If r.NodeType = XmlNodeType.Element And r.Name = "Product" Then
        Dim NewProduct As New Product()
        NewProduct.ID = Int32.Parse(r.GetAttribute(0))
        NewProduct.Name = r.GetAttribute(1)

        ' Get the rest of the subelements for this product.
        Do Until r.NodeType = XmlNodeType.EndElement
            r.Read()

            ' Look for Price subelement.
            If r.Name = "Price" Then
                Do Until (r.NodeType = XmlNodeType.EndElement)
                    r.Read()
                    If r.NodeType = XmlNodeType.Text Then
                        NewProduct.Price = Val(r.Value)
                    End If
                Loop
            End If

            ' We could check for other Product nodes
            ' (like Available, Status, etc.) here.
        Loop

        ' Add the product to the list.
        Products.Add(NewProduct)
    End If
Loop

fs.Close()

' Display the retrieved document.
gridResults.DataSource = Products
gridResults.DataBind()
```

Dissecting the Code . . .

- This code uses a nested looping structure. The outside loop iterates over all the products, and the inner loop searches through all the child elements of <Product> (in this case, there is only a possible <Price> element). This keeps the code well organized. The EndElement node alerts you when a node is complete and the loop can end. Once all the information is read for a product, the corresponding object is added into the collection.
- All the information is retrieved from the XML file as a string. Thus, you need to use methods like Int32.Parse() to convert it to the right data type.
- Data binding is used to display the contents of the collection. A GridView set to generate columns automatically creates the table shown in Figure 19-3.

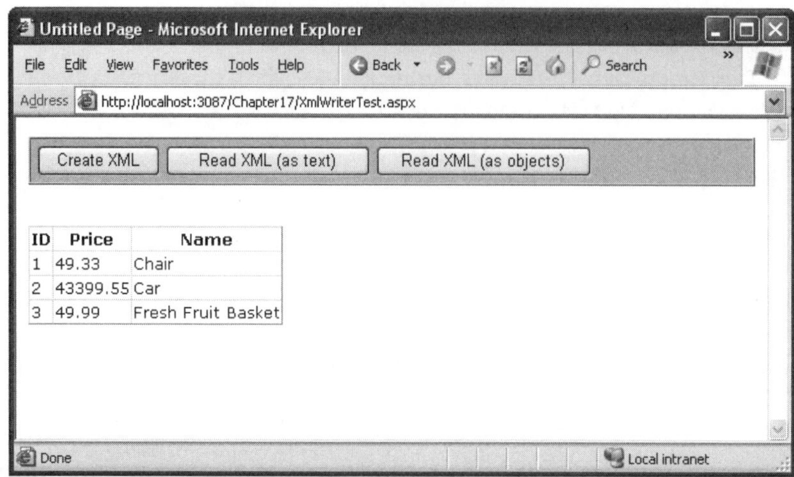

Figure 19-3. *Reading XML content*

Note The XmlTextReader provides many more properties and methods. These additional members don't add functionality; they allow for increased flexibility. For example, you can read a portion of an XML document into a string using methods such as ReadString(), ReadInnerXml(), and ReadOuterXml(). These members are all documented in the class library reference in the Visual Studio Help.

Working with XML Documents in Memory

The XmlTextReader and XmlTextWriter use XML as a *backing store.* These classes are streamlined for quickly getting XML data into and out of a file (or some other source). When using these classes, you open your XML file, retrieve the data you need, and use that data to create the appropriate objects or fill the appropriate controls. Your goal is to *translate* the XML into something more practical and usable. The rest of your code has no way of knowing that the data was initially extracted from an XML document—and it doesn't care.

■ Note Remember, the terms XML document and XML file are different. An XML *document* is a collection of elements structured according to the rules of XML. An XML document can be stored in virtually any way you want—it can be placed in a file, in a field, or in a database, or it can simply exist in memory.

This approach is ideal for storing simple blocks of data. For example, you could modify the guest book page in the previous chapter to store guest book entries in an XML format, which would provide greater standardization but wouldn't change how the application works. Your code for serializing and deserializing the XML data would change, but the rest of the application would remain untouched.

The XmlDocument class provides a different approach to XML data. It provides an in-memory model of an entire XML document. You can then browse through the entire document, reading, inserting, or removing nodes at any location.

When using this approach, you begin by loading XML content from a file (or some other source) into an XmlDocument object. The XmlDocument holds the entire document at once, so it isn't a practical approach if your XML content is several megabytes in size. (If you have a huge XML document, the XmlTextReader and XmlTextWriter classes offer the best approach.) However, the XmlDocument really excels with the editing capabilities that it gives you. Using the XmlDocument object, you can manipulate the content or structure of any part of the XML document. When you're finished, you can save the content back to a file. Unlike the XmlTextReader and XmlTextWriter, the XmlDocument class doesn't maintain a direct connection to the file.

■ Note In this respect, the XmlDocument is analogous to the DataSet in ADO.NET programming: it's always disconnected. The XmlTextWriter and XmlTextReader, on the other hand, are always connected to a stream, which is usually a file.

When you use the XmlDocument class, your XML document is created as a series of linked .NET objects in memory. Figure 19-4 shows the object model. (The diagram is slightly simplified from what you'll find when you start using the XmlDocument class—namely, it doesn't show the attributes, each of which is represented by an XmlAttribute object.)

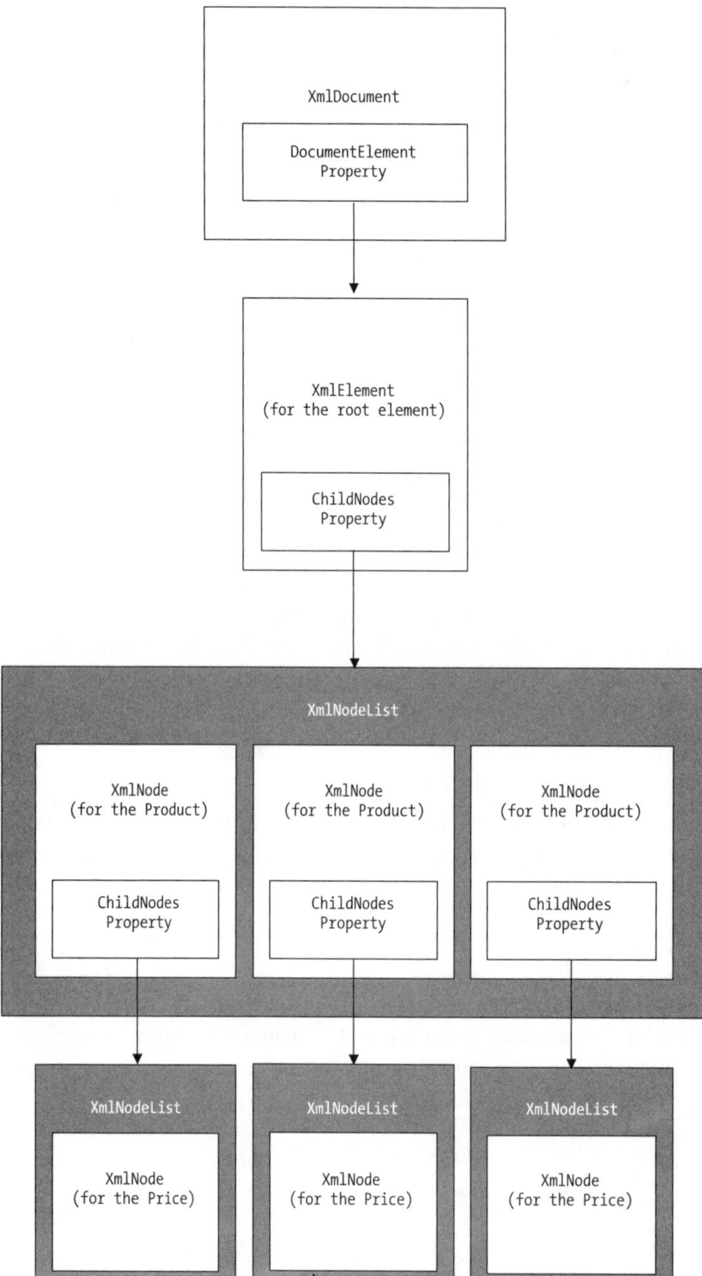

Figure 19-4. *An XML document in memory*

The following is an example that creates the SuperProProductList document in memory, using an XmlDocument class. When the document is completely built, the code saves it to a file using the XmlDocument.Save() method.

```
' Start with a blank in memory document.
Dim doc As New XmlDocument()

' Create some variables that will be useful for
' manipulating XML data.
Dim RootElement, ProductElement, PriceElement As XmlElement
Dim ProductAttribute As XmlAttribute
Dim Comment As XmlComment

' Create the declaration.
Dim Declaration As XmlDeclaration
Declaration = doc.CreateXmlDeclaration("1.0", Nothing, "yes")

' Insert the declaration as the first node.
doc.InsertBefore(Declaration, doc.DocumentElement)

' Add a comment.
Comment = doc.CreateComment("Created with the XmlDocument class.")
doc.InsertAfter(Comment, Declaration)

' Add the root element.
RootElement = doc.CreateElement("SuperProProductList")
doc.InsertAfter(RootElement, Comment)

' Add the first product.
ProductElement = doc.CreateElement("Product")
RootElement.AppendChild(ProductElement)

' Set and add the product attributes.
ProductAttribute = doc.CreateAttribute("ID")
ProductAttribute.Value = "1"
ProductElement.SetAttributeNode(ProductAttribute)
ProductAttribute = doc.CreateAttribute("Name")
ProductAttribute.Value = "Chair"
ProductElement.SetAttributeNode(ProductAttribute)

' Add the price element.
PriceElement = doc.CreateElement("Price")
PriceElement.InnerText = "49.33"
ProductElement.AppendChild(PriceElement)

' (Code to add two more products omitted.)

' Save the document.
Dim file As String = Path.Combine(Request.PhysicalApplicationPath, _
  "App_Data\SuperProProductList.xml")
doc.Save(file)
```

One of the best features of the XmlDocument class is that it doesn't rely on any underlying file. When you use the Save() method, the file is created, a stream is opened, the information is written, and the file is closed, all in one line of code. This means this is probably the only line you need to put inside a Try/Catch error-handling block.

While you're manipulating data with the XML objects, your text file isn't being changed. Once again, this is conceptually similar to the ADO.NET DataSet.

Dissecting the Code . . .

- Every separate part of the XML document is created as an object. Elements are created as XmlElement objects, comments are created as XmlComment objects, and attributes are represented as XmlAttribute objects.

■ **Tip** For leaner code, you can call the SetAttribute() and GetAttribute() methods on an XmlElement object. This technique allows you to bypass the XmlAttribute objects, and manipulate your attribute values directly.

- To create a new element, comment, or attribute for your XML document, you need to use one of the methods of the XmlDocument class, such as CreateComment(), CreateAttribute(), or CreateElement(). This ensures the XML is generated correctly for your document, but it doesn't actually place any information into the XmlDocument.
- Once you have created the appropriate object and entered any additional inner information (such as text content), you need to add it to the in-memory XmlDocument. You can do so by adding the new XmlElement object next to an existing XmlElement, using methods such as InsertBefore() or InsertAfter(). To add a child element (such as the <Product> element inside the <SuperProProductList> element), you need to find the appropriate parent object and use a method such as AppendChild(). You can't write a child element directly to the document in the same way you could with the XmlTextWriter.
- You can insert nodes anywhere. While the XmlTextWriter and XmlTextReader forced you to read every node, from start to finish, the XmlDocument is a much more flexible collection of objects.

Figure 19-5 shows the file written by this code (as displayed by Internet Explorer).

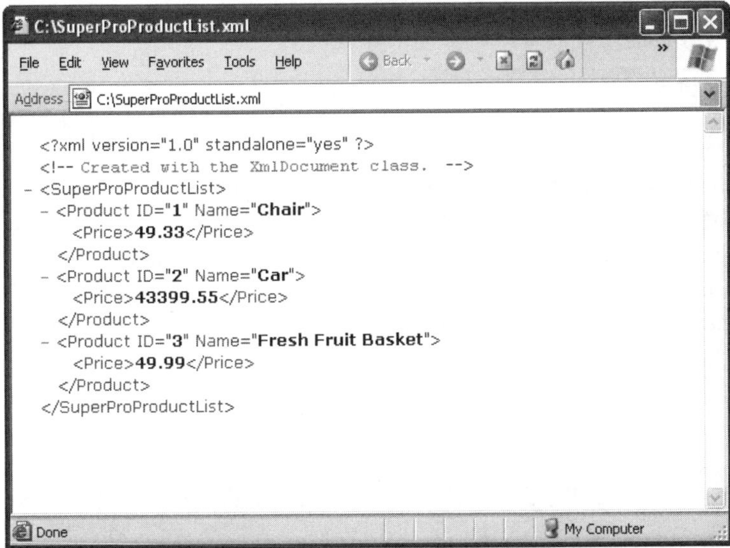

Figure 19-5. *The XML file*

Reading an XML Document

To read information from your XML file, all you need to do is create an XmlDocument object and use its Load() method. Once you have the XmlDocument in memory, you can extract content by looping through the collection of linked XmlNode objects. This process is similar to the XmlTextReader example, but the code is noticeably cleaner.

```
' Create the document.
Dim doc As New XmlDocument()
doc.Load(file)

' Loop through all the nodes, and create the list of Product objects.
Dim products As New List(Of Product)()

For Each element As XmlElement In doc.DocumentElement.ChildNodes
    Dim newProduct As New Product()
    newProduct.ID = Int32.Parse(element.GetAttribute("ID"))
    newProduct.Name = element.GetAttribute("Name")

    ' If there were more than one child node, you would probably use
    ' another For Each loop here, and move through the
    ' element.ChildNodes collection.
    newProduct.Price = Val(element.ChildNodes(0).InnerText())

    Products.Add(newProduct)
Next
```

```
' Display the results.
gridResults.DataSource = products
gridResults.DataBind()
```

■ **Tip** Whether you use the XmlDocument or the XmlTextReader class depends on a number of factors. Generally, you use XmlDocument when you want to deal directly with XML, rather than just use XML as a way to persist some information. It also gives you the ability to modify the structure of an XML document, and it allows you to browse XML information in a more flexible way (not just from start to finish). On the other hand, the XmlTextReader is best when dealing with large XML files, because it won't attempt to load the entire document into memory at once.

THE DIFFERENCE BETWEEN XMLNODE AND XMLELEMENT

You may have noticed that the XmlDocument is created with specific objects such as XmlComment and XmlElement but read back as a collection of XmlNode objects. The reason is that XmlComment and XmlElement are customized classes that inherit their basic functionality from XmlNode.

The ChildNodes collection allows you to retrieve all the content contained inside any portion of an XML document. Because this content could include comments, elements, and any other types of node, the ChildNodes collection uses the lowest common denominator. Thus, it provides child nodes as a collection of standard XmlNode objects. Each XmlNode has basic properties similar to what you saw with the XmlTextReader, including NodeType, Name, Value, and Attributes. You'll find that you can do all your XML processing with XmlNode objects.

You have a variety of other options for manipulating your XmlDocument and extracting or changing pieces of data. Table 19-1 provides an overview.

Table 19-1. *XmlNode Manipulation*

Technique	Description	Example
Finding a node's relative	Every XmlNode leads to other XmlNode objects. You can use properties such as FirstChild, LastChild, PreviousSibling, NextSibling, and ParentNode to return a reference to a related node.	`myParentNode = myNode.ParentNode`
Cloning a portion of an XmlDocument	You can use the CloneNode() method with any XmlNode to create a duplicate copy. You need to specify True or False to indicate whether you want to clone all children (True) or just the single node (False).	`newNode = myNode.Clone(True)`

Table 19-1. *XmlNode Manipulation*

Technique	Description	Example
Removing or adding nodes	Find the parent node, and then use one of its node-adding methods. You can use AppendChild() to add the child to the end of the child list and PrependChild() to add the node to the start of the child list. You can also remove nodes with RemoveChild(), ReplaceChild(), and RemoveAll(), which delete all the children and all the attributes for the current node.	`myNode.RemoveChild(nodeToDelete)`
Adding inner content	Find the node, and add a XmlNodeType.Text child node. One possible shortcut is just to set the InnerText property of your node, but that will erase any existing child nodes.	`myNode.InnerText = "190.99"`
Manipulating attributes	Every node provides an XmlAttributeCollection of all its attributes through the XmlNode.Attributes property. You can add new XmlAttribute objects to this collection using methods such as Append(), Prepend(), InsertBefore(), or InsertAfter(). However, a simpler approach is to call the SetAttribute(), RemoveAttribute(), and GetAttribute() methods of the XmlElement that contains the attribute.	`myNode.SetAttribute("Price", "43.99")`
Working with content as string data	You can retrieve or set the content inside a node using properties such as InnerText, InnerXml, and OuterXml. Be warned that the inner content of a node includes all child nodes. Thus, setting this property carelessly could wipe out other information, such as subelements.	

The XmlDocument class provides a rich set of events that fire before and after nodes are inserted, removed, and changed. The likelihood of using these events in an ordinary ASP.NET application is fairly slim, but it represents an interesting example of the features .NET puts at your fingertips.

Searching an XML Document

One of the nicest features of the XmlDocument is its support of searching, which allows you to find nodes when you know they are there—somewhere—but you aren't sure how many matches exist or where the elements are.

To search an XmlDocument, all you need to do is use the GetElementById() or GetElementsByTagName() method. The following code example puts the GetElementsByTagName() method to work and creates the output shown in Figure 19-6:

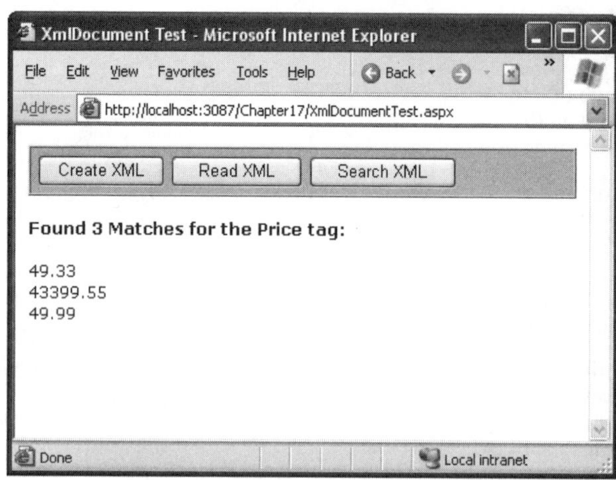

Figure 19-6. *Searching an XML document*

```
Dim doc As New XmlDocument()
doc.Load(file)
Dim Results As XmlNodeList

' Find the matches.
Results = doc.GetElementsByTagName("Price")

' Display the results.
lblXml.Text = "<b>Found " & Results.Count.ToString() & " Matches "
lblXml.Text &= " for the Price tag: </b><br /><br />"
For Each Result As XmlNode In Results
    lblXml.Text &= Result.FirstChild.Value & "<br />"
Next
```

This technique works well if you want to find an element based on its name. If you want to use more sophisticated searching, match only part of a name, or examine only part of a document, you'll have to fall back on the traditional standard: looping through all the nodes in the XmlDocument.

■Tip The search method provided by the XmlDocument class is relatively primitive. For a more advanced tool, you might want to learn the XPath language, which is a W3C recommendation (defined at `http://www.w3.org/TR/xpath`) designed for performing queries on XML data. NET provides XPath support through the classes in the System.Xml.XPath namespace, which include an XPath parser and evaluation engine. Of course, these aren't much use unless you learn the syntax of the XPath language. Another option is to use LINQ to XML, which is described in the "Still More Ways to Read XML" sidebar at the end of this chapter.

XML Validation

XML has a rich set of supporting standards, many of which are far beyond the scope of this book. One of the most useful in this family of standards is XSD (XML Schema Definition). XSD defines the rules to which a specific XML document should conform, such as the allowable elements and attributes, the order of elements, and the data type of each element.

When you're creating an XML file on your own, you don't need to create a corresponding XSD file—instead, you might just rely on the ability of your code to behave properly. While this is sufficient for tightly controlled environments, if you want to open your application to other programmers or allow it to interoperate with other applications, you should create an XSD document. Think of it this way: XML allows you to create a custom language for storing data, and XSD allows you to define the syntax of the language you create.

XML Namespaces

Before you can create an XSD document, you'll need to understand one other XML standard, called XML namespaces.

The core idea behind XML namespaces is that every XML markup language has its own namespace, which is used to uniquely identify all related elements. Technically, namespaces *disambiguate* elements, by making it clear what markup language they belong to. For example, you could tell the difference between your SuperProProductList standard and another organization's product catalog because the two XML languages would use different namespaces.

Namespaces are particularly useful in compound documents, which contain separate sections, each with a different type of XML. In this scenario, namespaces ensure that an element in one namespace can't be confused with an element in another namespace, even if it has the same element name. Namespaces are also useful for applications that support different types of XML documents. By examining the namespace, your code can determine what type of XML document it's working with, and can then process it accordingly.

■Note XML namespaces aren't related to .NET namespaces. XML namespaces identify different XML languages. NET namespaces are a code construct used to organize types.

Before you can place your XML elements in a namespace, you need to choose an identifying name for that namespace. Most XML namespaces use URIs (Universal Resource Identifiers). Typically, these URIs look like a web page URL. For example, `http://www.mycompany.com/mystandard` is a typical name for a namespace. Though the namespace looks like it points to a valid location on the Web, this isn't required (and shouldn't be assumed).

The reason that URIs are used for XML namespaces is because they are more likely to be unique. Typically, if you create a new XML markup, you'll use a URI that points to a domain or website you control. That way, you can be sure that no one else is likely to use that URI. For example, the namespace `http://www.SuperProProducts.com/SuperProProductList` is much more likely to be unique than just SuperProProductList if you own the domain `www.SuperProProducts.com`.

■ **Tip** Namespace names must match exactly. If you change the capitalization in part of a namespace, add a trailing / character, or modify any other detail, it will be interpreted as a different namespace by the XML parser.

To specify that an element belongs to a specific namespace, you simply need to add the xmlns attribute to the start tag, and indicate the namespace. For example, the <Price> element shown here is part of the `http://www.SuperProProducts.com/SuperProProductList` namespace:

```
<Price xmlns="http://www.SuperProProducts.com/SuperProProductList">
49.33
</Price>
```

If you don't take this step, the element will not be a part of any namespace.

It would be cumbersome if you needed to type in the full namespace URI every time you wrote an element in an XML document. Fortunately, when you assign a namespace in this fashion, it becomes the *default namespace* for all child elements. For example, in the XML document shown here, the <SuperProProductList> element and all the elements it contains are placed in the `http://www.SuperProProducts.com/SuperProProductList` namespace:

```
<?xml version="1.0"?>
<SuperProProductList
 xmlns="http://www.SuperProProducts.com/SuperProProductList">
    <Product>
        <ID>1</ID>
        <Name>Chair</Name>
        <Price>49.33</Price>
        <Available>True</Available>
        <Status>3</Status>
    </Product>

    <!-- Other products omitted. -->
</SuperProProductList>
```

In compound documents, you'll have markup from more than one XML language, and you'll need to place different sections into different namespaces. In this situation, you can use *namespace prefixes* to sort out the different namespaces.

Namespace prefixes are short character sequences that you can insert in front of a tag name to indicate its namespace. You define the prefix in the xmlns attribute by inserting a colon (:) followed by the characters you want to use for the prefix. Here's the SuperProProductList document rewritten to use the prefix *super*:

```
<?xml version="1.0"?>
<super:SuperProProductList
 xmlns:super="http://www.SuperProProducts.com/SuperProProductList">
    <super:Product>
        <super:ID>1</super:ID>
        <super:Name>Chair</super:Name>
        <super:Price>49.33</super:Price>
        <super:Available>True</super:Available>
        <super:Status>3</super:Status>
    </super:Product>

    <!-- Other products omitted. -->
</super:SuperProProductList>
```

Namespace prefixes are simply used to map an element to a namespace. The actual prefix you use isn't important as long as it remains consistent throughout the document. By convention, the attributes that define XML namespace prefixes are usually added to the root element of an XML document.

Although the xmlns attribute looks like an ordinary XML attribute, it isn't. The XML parser interprets it as a namespace declaration. (The reason XML namespaces use XML attributes is a historical one. This design ensured that old XML parsers that didn't understand namespaces could still read newer XML documents that use them.)

■ **Note** Attributes act a little differently than elements when it comes to namespaces. You can use namespace prefixes with both elements and attributes. However, attributes don't pay any attention to the default namespace of a document. That means if you don't add a namespace prefix to an attribute, the attribute will *not* be placed in the default namespace. Instead, it will have no namespace.

XML Schema Definition

An XSD document, or *schema*, defines what elements and attributes a document should contain and the way these nodes are organized (the structure). It can also identify the appropriate data types for all the content. XSD documents are written using an XML syntax with specific element names. All the XSD elements are placed in the `http://www.w3.org/2001/XMLSchema` namespace. Often, this namespace uses the prefix xsd: or xs:, as in the following example.

The full XSD specification is out of the scope of this chapter, but you can learn a lot from a simple example. The following is a slightly abbreviated SuperProProductList.xsd file that defines the rules for SuperProProductList documents:

```
<?xml version="1.0"?>
<xs:schema
    targetNamespace="http://www.SuperProProducts.com/SuperProProductList"
    xmlns:xs="http://www.w3.org/2001/XMLSchema" elementFormDefault="qualified" >
  <xs:element name="SuperProProductList">
    <xs:complexType>
      <xs:sequence maxOccurs="unbounded">
        <xs:element name="Product">
          <xs:complexType>
            <xs:sequence>
              <xs:element name="Price" type="xs:double" />
            </xs:sequence>
            <xs:attribute name="ID" use="required" type="xs:int" />
            <xs:attribute name="Name" use="required" type="xs:string" />
          </xs:complexType>
        </xs:element>
      </xs:sequence>
    </xs:complexType>
  </xs:element>
</xs:schema>
```

At first glance, this markup looks a bit intimidating. However, it's actually not as complicated as it looks. Essentially, this schema indicates that a SuperProProductList document consists of a list of <Product> elements. Each <Product> element is a complex type made up of a string (Name), a decimal value (Price), and an integer (ID). This example uses the second version of the SuperProProductList document to demonstrate how to use attributes in a schema file.

Dissecting the Code . . .

By examining the SuperProProductList.xsd schema, you can learn a few important points:

- Schema documents use their own form of XML markup. In the previous example, you'll quickly see that all the elements are placed in the `http://www.w3.org/2001/XMLSchema` namespace using the *xs:* namespace prefix.
- Every schema document starts with a root <schema> element.
- The schema document must specify the namespace of the documents it can validate. It specifies this detail with the targetNamespace attribute on the root <schema> element.
- The elements inside the <schema> element describe the structure of the target document. The <element> element represents an element, while the <attribute> element represents an attribute. To find out what the name of an element or attribute is, look at the name attribute. For example, you can tell quite easily that the first <element> has the name SuperProProductList. This indicates that the first element in the validated document must be <SuperProProductList>.

- If an element can contain other elements or has attributes, it's considered a *complex type*. Complex types are represented in a schema by the <complexType> element. The simplest complex type is a *sequence*, which requires that elements are always in the exact same order (the order that's set out in the schema document).
- When defining elements, you can define the maximum number of times an element can appear (using the maxOccurs attribute) and the minimum number of times it *must* occur (using the minOccurs attribute). If you leave out these details, the default value of both is 1, which means that every element must appear exactly once in the target document. Use a maxOccurs value of *unbounded* if you want to allow an unlimited list. For example, this allows there to be an unlimited number of <Product> elements in the SuperProProductList catalog. However, the <Price> element must occur exactly once in each <Product>.
- When defining an attribute, you can use the *use* attribute with a value of *required* to make that attribute mandatory.
- When defining elements and attributes, you can specify the data type using the type attribute. The XSD standard defines 44 data types that map closely to the basic data types in .NET, including the double, int, and string data types used in this example.

Validating an XML Document

To validate an XML document against a schema, you need to create an XmlReader that has validation features built in.

The first step when performing validation is to import the System.Xml.Schema namespace, which contains types such as XmlSchema and XmlSchemaCollection:

```
Imports System.Xml.Schema
```

You must perform two steps to create the validating reader. First, you create an XmlReaderSettings object that specifically indicates you want to perform validation. You do this by setting the ValidationType property and loading your XSD schema file into the Schemas collection, as shown here:

```
' Configure the reader to use validation.
Dim settings As New XmlReaderSettings()
settings.ValidationType = ValidationType.Schema

' Create the path for the schema file.
Dim schemaFile As String = Path.Combine(Request.PhysicalApplicationPath, _
  "App_Data\SuperProProductList.xsd")

' Indicate that elements in the namespace
' http://www.SuperProProducts.com/SuperProProductList should be
' validated using the schema file.
settings.Schemas.Add("http://www.SuperProProducts.com/SuperProProductList", _
  schemaFile)
```

Second, you need to create the validating reader using the shared XmlReader.Create() method. This method has several overloads, but the version used here requires a FileStream (with the XML document) and the XmlReaderSettings object that has your validation settings:

```
' Open the XML file.
Dim fs As New FileStream(file, FileMode.Open)

' Create the validating reader.
Dim r As XmlReader = XmlReader.Create(fs, settings)
```

The XmlReader in this example works in the same way as the XmlTextReader you've been using up until now, but it adds the ability to verify that the XML document follows the schema rules. This reader throws an exception (or raises an event) to indicate errors as you move through the XML file.

The following example shows how you can create a validating reader that uses the SuperProProductList.xsd file to verify that the XML in SuperProProductList.xml is valid:

```
' Set the validation settings.
Dim settings As New XmlReaderSettings()
settings.Schemas.Add("http://www.SuperProProducts.com/SuperProProductList", _
  schemaFile)
settings.ValidationType = ValidationType.Schema

' Open the XML file.
Dim fs As New FileStream(filePath, FileMode.Open)

' Create the validating reader.
Dim r As XmlReader = XmlReader.Create(fs, settings)

' Read through the document.
Do While r.Read()
    ' Process document here.
    ' If an error is found, an exception will be thrown.
Loop
fs.Close()
```

Using the current file, this code will succeed, and you'll be able to access each node in the document. However, consider what happens if you make the minor modification shown here:

```
<Product ID="A" Name="Chair">
```

Now when you try to validate the document, an XmlSchemaException (from the System.Xml.Schema namespace) will be thrown, alerting you to the invalid data type, as shown in Figure 19-7.

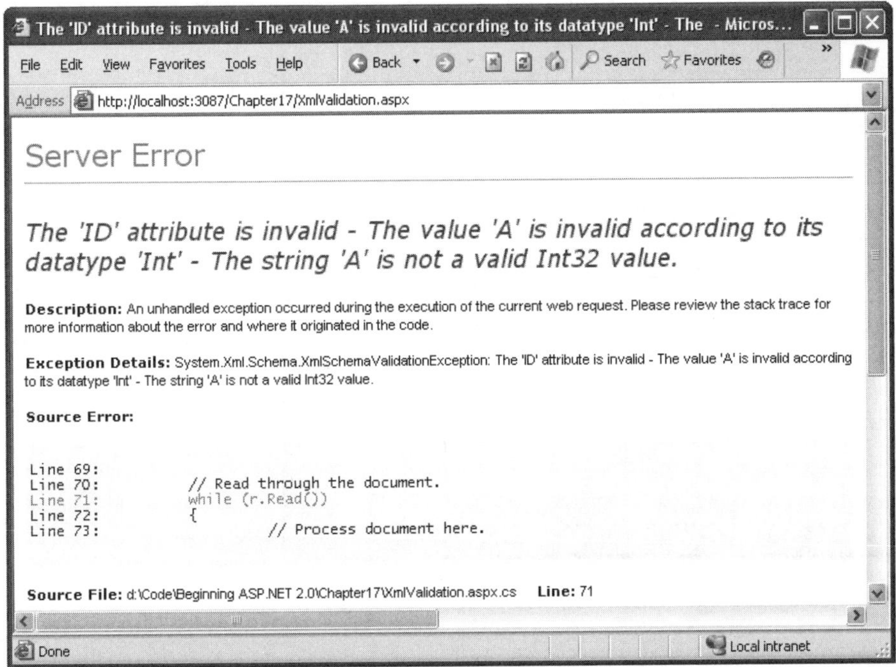

Figure 19-7. *An XmlSchemaException*

Instead of catching errors, you can react to the XmlReaderSettings.ValidationEventHandler event. If you react to this event, you'll be provided with information about the error, but no exception will be thrown. To connect an event handler to this event, you can attach an event handler before you create the XmlReader:

```
AddHandler settings.ValidationEventHandler, AddressOf ValidateHandler
```

The event handler receives a ValidationEventArgs object as a parameter, which contains the exception, a message, and a number representing the severity:

```
Private Sub ValidateHandler(ByVal sender As Object, _
  ByVal e As ValidationEventArgs)
    lblStatus.Text &= "Error: " & e.Message & "<br />"
End Sub
```

To test the validation, you can use the XmlValidation.aspx page in the online samples. It allows you to validate a valid SuperProProductList, as well as two other versions, one with incorrect data and one with an incorrect element (see Figure 19-8).

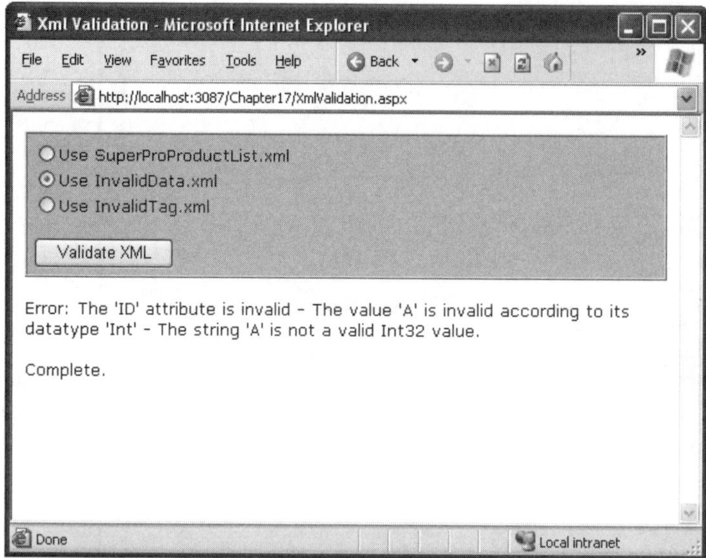

Figure 19-8. *The validation test page*

XML Display and Transforms

Another standard associated with XML is XSLT (XSL Transformations). XSLT allows you to create style sheets that can extract a portion of a large XML document or transform an XML document into another type of XML document. An even more popular use of XSLT is to convert an XML document into an HTML document that can be displayed in a browser.

■ **Note** XSL (eXtensible Stylesheet Language) is a family of standards for searching, formatting, and transforming XML documents. XSLT is the specific standard that deals with the transformation step.

XSLT is easy to use from the point of view of the .NET class library. All you need to understand is how to create an XslCompiledTransform object (found in the System.Xml.Xsl namespace). You use its Load() method to specify a style sheet and its Transform() method to output the result to a file or stream:

```
' Define the file paths this code uses. The XSLT file and the
' XML source file already exist, but the XML result file
' will be created by this code.
Dim xsltFile As String = Path.Combine(Request.PhysicalApplicationPath, _
  "App_Data\SuperProProductList.xml")
Dim xmlSourceFile As String = Path.Combine(Request.PhysicalApplicationPath, _
  "App_Data\SuperProProductList.xsl")
```

```
Dim xmlResultFile As String = Path.Combine(Request.PhysicalApplicationPath, _
  "App_Data\TransformedFile.xml")

' Load the XSLT stylesheet.
Dim transformer As New XslCompiledTransform()
transformer.Load(xsltFile)

' Create a transformed XML file.
' SuperProProductList.xml is the starting point.
transformer.Transform(xmlSourceFile, xmlResultFile)
```

However, this doesn't spare you from needing to learn the XSLT syntax. Once again, the intricacies of XSLT aren't directly related to core ASP.NET programming, so they're outside the scope of this book. To get started with XSLT, however, it helps to review a simple style sheet example. The following example shows an XSLT style sheet that transforms the no-namespace version of the SuperProProductList document into a formatted HTML table:

```
<?xml version="1.0" encoding="UTF-8" ?>
<xsl:stylesheet xmlns:xsl="http://www.w3.org/1999/XSL/Transform"
    version="1.0" >

  <xsl:template match="SuperProProductList">
    <html>
      <body>
        <table border="1">
          <xsl:apply-templates select="Product"/>
        </table>
      </body>
    </html>
  </xsl:template>

  <xsl:template match="Product">
    <tr>
      <td><xsl:value-of select="@ID"/></td>
      <td><xsl:value-of select="@Name"/></td>
      <td><xsl:value-of select="Price"/></td>
    </tr>
  </xsl:template>

</xsl:stylesheet>
```

Every XSLT document has a root xsl:stylesheet element. The style sheet can contain one or more templates (the sample file SuperProProductList.xslt has two). In this example, the first template searches for the root SuperProProductList element. When it finds it, it outputs the tags necessary to start an HTML table and then uses the xsl:apply-templates command to branch off and perform processing for any contained Product elements.

```
<xsl:template match="SuperProProductList">
  <html>
    <body>
      <table border="1">
        <xsl:apply-templates select="Product"/>
```

When that process is complete, the HTML tags for the end of the table will be written:

```
      </table>
    </body>
  </html>
</xsl:template>
```

When processing each <Product> element, the value from the nested ID attribute, Name attribute, and <Price> element is extracted and written to the output using the xsl:value-of command. The at sign (@) indicates that the value is being extracted from an attribute, not a subelement. Every piece of information is written inside a table row.

```
<xsl:template match="Product">
  <tr>
    <td><xsl:value-of select="@ID"/></td>
    <td><xsl:value-of select="@Name"/></td>
    <td><xsl:value-of select="Price"/></td>
  </tr>
</xsl:template>
```

For more advanced formatting, you could use additional HTML elements to format some text in bold or italics.

The final result of this process is the HTML file shown here:

```
<html>
  <body>
    <table border="1">
      <tr>
        <td>1</td>
        <td>Chair</td>
        <td>49.33</td>
      </tr>
      <tr>
        <td>2</td>
        <td>Car</td>
        <td>43398.55</td>
      </tr>
      <tr>
        <td>3</td>
        <td>Fresh Fruit Basket</td>
        <td>49.99</td>
      </tr>
    </table>
  </body>
</html>
```

In the next section, you'll look at how this output appears in an Internet browser.

Generally speaking, if you aren't sure you need XSLT, you probably don't. The .NET Framework provides a rich set of tools for searching and manipulating XML files using objects and code, which is the best approach for small-scale XML use.

■ **Tip** To learn more about XSLT, consider Jeni Tennison's excellent book *Beginning XSLT 2.0: From Novice to Professional* (Apress, 2005).

The Xml Web Control

If you use an XLST style sheet such as the one demonstrated in the previous example, you might wonder what your code should do with the generated HTML. You could try to write it directly to the browser or save it to the hard drive, but these approaches are awkward, especially if you want to display the generated HTML inside a normal ASP.NET web page that contains other controls. The XslCompiledTransform object just converts XML files—it doesn't provide any way to insert the output into your web page.

ASP.NET includes an Xml web control that fills the gap and can display XML content. You can specify the XML content for this control in several ways: by assigning an XmlDocument object to the Document property, by assigning a string containing the XML content to the DocumentContent property, or by specifying a string that refers to an XML file using the DocumentSource property.

```
' Display the information from an XML file in the Xml control.
XmlProducts.DocumentSource = Path.Combine(Request.PhysicalApplicationPath, _
  "App_Data\SuperProProductList.xml")
```

If you assign the SuperProProductList.xml file to the Xml control, you're likely to be disappointed. The result is just a string of the inner text (the price for each product), bunched together without a space (see Figure 19-9).

However, you can also apply an XSLT style sheet, either by assigning an XslCompiledTransform object to the Transform property or by using a string that refers to the XSLT file with the TransformSource property:

```
' Specify a XSLT file.
XmlProducts.TransformSource = Path.Combine(Request.PhysicalApplicationPath, _
  "App_Data\SuperProProductList.xslt")
```

Now the output is automatically formatted according to your style sheet (see Figure 19-10).

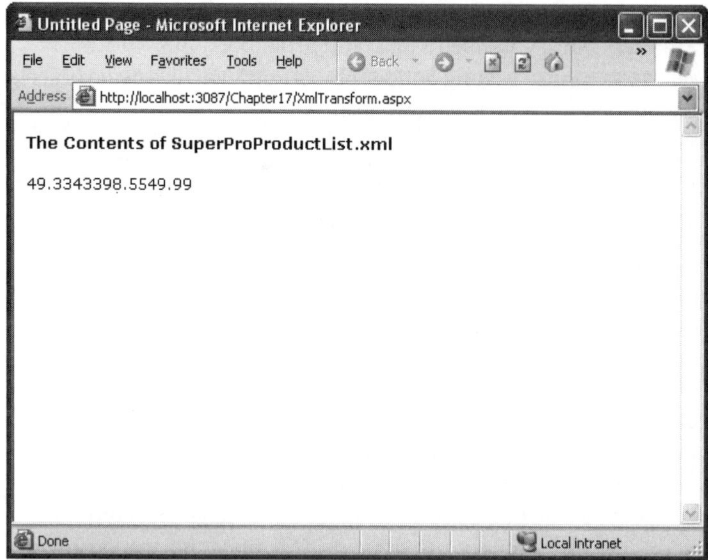

Figure 19-9. *Unformatted XML content*

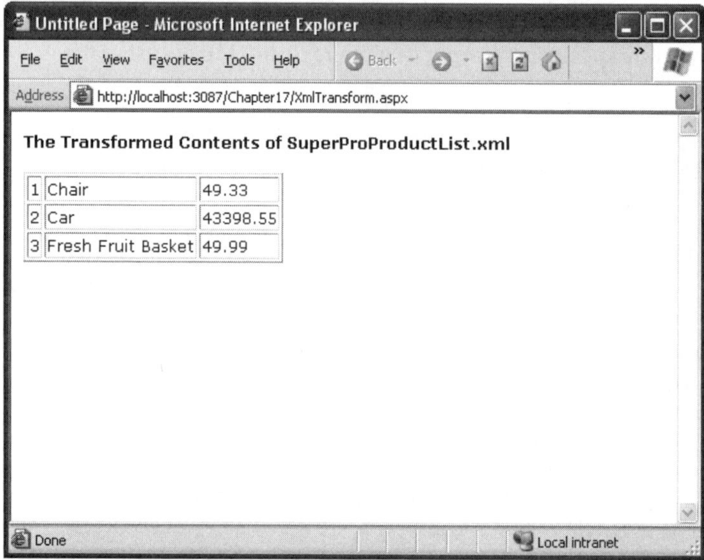

Figure 19-10. *Transformed XML content*

XML Data Binding

The Xml control is a great way to display XML data in a web page by converting it to HTML. But what if you want to display data in another type of control, such as a GridView? You could use the XML classes you learned about earlier, which is definitely the most flexible approach. However, if you don't need that much control, you may be interested in the XmlDataSource control, which allows you to take XML from a file and feed it right into another control.

The XmlDataSource control works much like the SqlDataSource control you learned about in Chapter 16. However, it has two key differences:

- The XmlDataSource extracts information from an XML file, rather than a database or data access class. It provides other controls with an XmlDocument object for data binding.
- XML content is hierarchical and can have an unlimited number of levels. By contrast, the SqlDataSource returns a flat table of data.

The XmlDataSource also provides a few features in common with the other data source controls, including caching.

■ **Note** The XmlDataSource is a more limited approach than the XML classes you've learned about so far. The XmlDataSource assumes you're using files, doesn't give you as much flexibility for processing your data, and doesn't support updateable binding (saving the changes you make in a control to the original XML file). However, it also makes some scenarios much simpler.

Nonhierarchical Binding

The simplest way to deal with the hierarchical nature of XML data is to ignore it. In other words, you can bind the XML data source directly to an ordinary grid control such as the GridView.

The first step is to define the XML data source and point it to the file with the content you want to implement using the DataFile property:

```
<asp:XmlDataSource ID="sourceXml" runat="server"
 DataFile="App_Data\SuperProProductList.xml" />
```

Now you can bind the GridView with automatically generated columns, in the same way you bind it to any other data source:

```
<asp:GridView ID="GridView1" runat="server" AutoGenerateColumns="True"
 DataSourceID="sourceXml" />
```

■ **Note** Remember, you don't need to use automatically generated columns. If you refresh the schema at design time, Visual Studio will read the linked XML file, determine its structure, and define the corresponding GridView columns explicitly.

Now, when you run the page, the XmlDataSource will extract the data from the SuperProProductList.xml file, provide it to the GridView as an XmlDocument object, and call DataBind(). However, this approach has a catch. As explained earlier, the XmlDocument.Nodes collection contains only the first level of nodes. Each node can contain nested nodes through its own XmlNode.Nodes collection. However, the XmlDataSource doesn't take this into account. It walks over the upper level of XmlNode objects, and as a result you'll see only the top level of elements. In this example, that means you'll see a row for each <Product> element, complete with all the attribute information, as shown in Figure 19-11. You won't see inner text content or nested elements, such as the <Price> element.

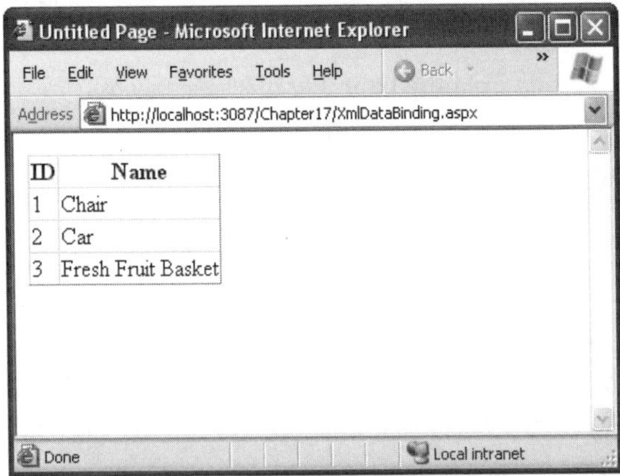

Figure 19-11. *XML data binding (attributes only)*

The problem is even more glaring if you have an XML document with a more deeply nested structure. For example, imagine you use the following XML that divides its products into categories:

```
<?xml version="1.0" standalone="yes"?>
<SuperProProductList xmlns="SuperProProductList" >
  <Category Name="Hardware">
    <Product ID="1" Name="Chair">
      <Price>49.33</Price>
    </Product>
    <Product ID="2" Name="Car">
      <Price>43398.55</Price>
    </Product>
  </Category>
  <Category Name="Produce">
    <Product ID="3" Name="Fresh Fruit Basket">
      <Price>49.99</Price>
    </Product>
  </Category>
</SuperProProductList>
```

Now all you'll see is the list of categories, because these make up the first level of nodes (see Figure 19-12).

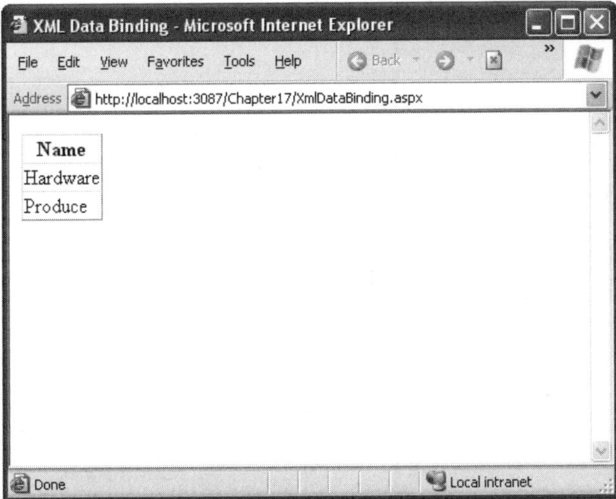

Figure 19-12. *XML data binding (top-level nodes only)*

Clearly, the XmlDataSource has two significant limitations. First, it displays only attribute values, not the text inside elements (in this case, the product price). Second, it shows only the top level of nodes, which may not be what you want. To solve these problems, you need to return to the XML classes, or you need to use one of the following approaches:

- You can use XPath to filter out the important elements, even if they're several layers deep.
- You can use an XSLT style sheet to flatten the XML into exactly the structure you want. Just make sure all the information is in the top level of nodes and in attributes only.
- You can nest one data control inside another (however, this can get quite complex).
- You can use a control that supports hierarchical data. The only ready-made .NET controls that fit are the TreeView and Menu.

All of these options require considerably more work. In the next section, you'll see how to use the TreeView.

Hierarchical Binding with the TreeView

Some controls have the built-in smarts to show hierarchical data. In .NET, the principal example is the TreeView. When you bind the TreeView to an XmlDataSource, it uses the XmlDataSource.GetHierarchcialView() method and displays the full structure of the XML document (see Figure 19-13).

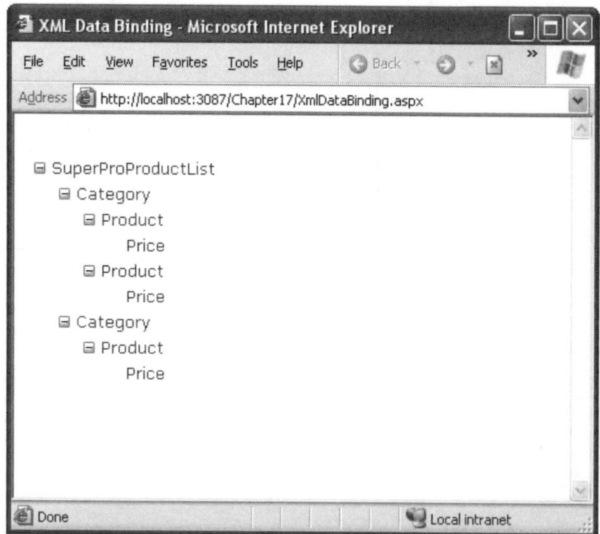

Figure 19-13. *Automatically generated TreeView bindings*

The TreeView's default XML representation still leaves a lot to be desired. It shows only the document structure (the element names), not the document content (the element text). It also ignores attributes. To improve this situation, you need to set the TreeView.AutomaticallyGenerateDataBindings property to False, and you then need to explicitly map different parts of the XML document to TreeView nodes.

```
<asp:TreeView ID="TreeView1" runat="server" DataSourceID="sourceXml"
 AutoGenerateDataBindings="False">
  ...
</asp:TreeView>
```

To create a TreeView mapping, you need to add <TreeNodeDataBinding> elements to the <DataBindings> section. You must start with the root element in the XML document and then add a binding for each level you want to show. You cannot skip any levels.

Each <TreeNodeBinding> must name the node it binds to (through the DataMember property), the text it should display (TextField), and the hidden value for the node (ValueField). Unfortunately, both TextField and ValueField are designed to bind to attributes. If you want to bind to element content, you can use an ugly hack and specify the #InnerText code. However, this shows *all* the inner text, including text inside other, more deeply nested nodes.

The next example defines a basic set of nodes to show the product information:

```
<asp:TreeView ID="TreeView1" runat="server" DataSourceID="sourceXml"
 AutoGenerateDataBindings="False">
  <DataBindings>
    <asp:TreeNodeBinding DataMember="SuperProProductList" Text="Product List" />
    <asp:TreeNodeBinding DataMember="Category" TextField="Name" />
    <asp:TreeNodeBinding DataMember="Product" TextField="Name" />
    <asp:TreeNodeBinding DataMember="Price" TextField="#InnerText" />
  </DataBindings>
</asp:TreeView>
```

Figure 19-14 shows the result.

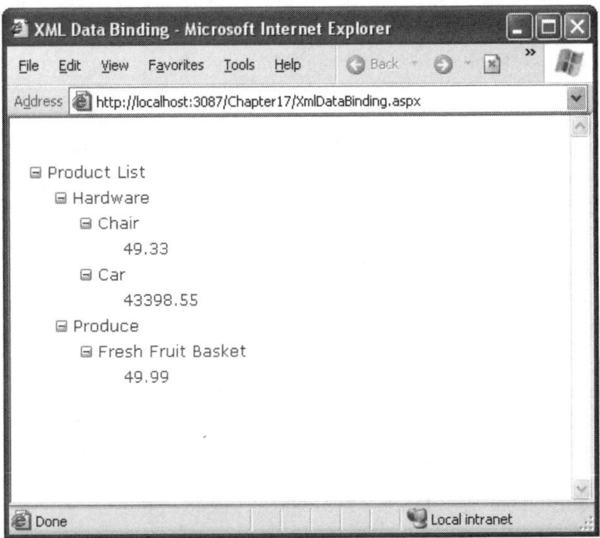

Figure 19-14. *Binding to specific content*

Tip To learn how to format the TreeView, including how to tweak gridlines and node pictures, refer to Chapter 14.

Binding to XML Content from Other Sources

So far, all the XML data-binding examples you've seen have bound to XML content in a file. This is the standard scenario for the XmlDataSource control, but it's not your only possibility. The other option is to supply the XML as text through the XmlDataSource.Data property.

You can set the Data property at any point before the binding takes place. One convenient time is during the Page.Load event:

```
Protected Sub Page_Load(ByVal sender As Object, _
  ByVal e As System.EventArgs) Handles Me.Load

    Dim xmlContent As String
    ' (Retrieve XML content from another location.)
    sourceXml.Data = xmlContent
End Sub
```

This allows you to read XML content from another source (such as a database) and still work with the bound data controls.

STILL MORE WAYS TO READ XML

Microsoft has been a bit overenthusiastic in the XML world. In this chapter, you've learned about a vast number of options for reading and writing XML data. However, this isn't the whole story. There are at least three more specialized alternatives for dealing with XML in .NET:

- **XML serialization:** Using this feature, you can pull information out of an XML file and pop it into a custom class that you've created. Best of all, it happens almost automatically, without you needing to write the code that moves through all the nodes. You can use a similar technique to pull the live information out of your objects and convert it back to XML. The only disadvantage is flexibility, as the structure of your class needs to match the structure of your XML document.
- **LINQ to XML:** LINQ is a set of language extensions that allows you to write query expressions that can pull information out of various data sources. For example, you can use LINQ to filter the objects in a collection, to extract data from a SQL Server database, or to pull interesting information out of an XML file. The advantage is that you only need to learn the LINQ syntax once, and it applies to a wide range of different types of data and scenarios. (The disadvantage is that you have one more standard to master.)
- **The XmlDataDocument:** The XmlDataDocument fuses together two different classes: the XmlDocument that you learned about in this chapter and the ADO.NET DataSet. By doing so, it allows you to see your data in two different ways at once—as a DataSet with tables and rows, and as an XML document that holds a collection of elements. For example, you can fill a DataSet using a database query, use the DataSet to create an XmlDataDocument, and then use the XmlDataDocument to perform XML-specific tasks on that data (such as applying an XSLT style sheet). It's definitely a nifty trick, but one that isn't used very often.

To learn more about XML serialization, look up "XML serialization" in the index of the Visual Studio Help. To get started with LINQ, you can surf to Microsoft's LINQ developer center at `http://msdn.microsoft.com/data/ref/linq`. And to try out the XmlDataDocument, check out the downloadable code for this chapter, which includes an example that uses it.

The Last Word

Now that your tour of XML and ASP.NET is drawing to a close, you should have a basic understanding of what XML is, how it looks, and why you might use it in a web page. XML represents a new tool for breaking down the barriers between businesses and platforms—it's nothing less than a universal model for storing and communicating all types of information.

XML on its own is a remarkable innovation. However, to get the most out of XML, you need to embrace other standards that allow you to validate XML, transform it, and search it for specific information. The .NET Framework provides classes for all these tasks in the namespaces under the System.Xml branch. To continue your exploration, start with a comprehensive review of XML standards (such as the one provided at `http://www.w3schools.com/xml`) and then dive into the class library.

PART 5

Website Security

CHAPTER 20

Security Fundamentals

Ordinarily, your ASP.NET website is available to anyone who connects to your web server, whether over a local network or the Internet. Although this is ideal for many web applications (and it suits the original spirit of the Internet), it isn't always an appropriate design choice. For example, an e-commerce site needs to provide a secure shopping experience to attract customers. A subscription-based site needs to limit content to extract a fee. And even a wide-open public site may provide some resources or features that shouldn't be available to all users.

ASP.NET provides an extensive security model that makes it easy to protect your web applications. Although this security model is powerful and profoundly flexible, it can appear confusing because of the many different layers that it includes. Much of the work in securing your application isn't writing code, but determining the appropriate places to implement your security strategy.

In this chapter, you'll sort out the tangled ASP.NET security model. You'll learn two ways to authenticate users—first, using forms authentication (which is ideal for a public website that uses a custom database) and then using Windows authentication (which is ideal for an intranet application on a company network). You'll also take a brief look at SSL (Secure Sockets Layer), the standard for secure web communication.

Determining Security Requirements

The first step in securing your applications is deciding where you need security and what it needs to protect. For example, you may need to block access in order to protect private information. Or, maybe you just need to enforce a pay-for-content system. Perhaps you don't need any sort of security at all, but you want an optional login feature to provide personalization for frequent visitors. These requirements will determine the approach you use.

Security doesn't need to be complex, but it does need to be wide-ranging and multilayered. For example, consider an e-commerce website that allows users to view reports of their recently placed orders. You probably already know the first line of defense that this website should use—a login page that forces users to identify themselves before they can see any personal information. In this chapter, you'll learn how to use this sort of authentication system. However, it's important to realize that, on its own, this layer of protection is not enough to truly secure your system. You also need to protect the back-end database with a strong password, and you might even choose to encrypt sensitive information before you store it (scrambling so that it's unreadable without the right key to decrypt it). Steps like these protect your website from other attacks that get beyond your authentication system. For example, they can deter a disgruntled employee with an account on the local network, a hacker who has gained access to your network through the company firewall, or a careless technician who discards a hard drive used for data storage without erasing it first.

Furthermore, you'll need to hunt carefully for weaknesses in the code you've written. A surprising number of websites fall prey to relatively simple attacks in which a malicious user simply tampers with a query string argument or a bit of HTML in the rendered page. For example, in the e-commerce example you need to make sure that a user who successfully logs in can't view another user's recent orders. Imagine you've created a ViewOrders.aspx page that takes a query string argument named userID, like this:

```
http://localhost/InsecureStore/ViewOrders.aspx?userID=4191
```

This example is a security nightmare, because any user can easily modify the userID parameter by editing the URL to see another user's information. A better solution would be to design the ViewOrders.aspx page so that it gets the user ID from the currently logged-on user identity (a trick you'll learn in this chapter), and then uses that to construct the right database command.

■ **Note** Another example of a security vulnerability introduced by poor coding is the ever-common SQL injection attack. You learned to prevent this attack by using parameterized database commands in Chapter 15.

When designing with security in mind, it's important to consider the different avenues for attack. However, you can't always anticipate potential problems. For that reason, it makes great sense to layer your security. The mantra of security architects can be summed up like this: "Don't force an attacker to do one impossible thing to break into your system—force them to do several."

The ASP.NET Security Model

As you've seen in previous chapters, web requests are fielded first by the IIS web server, which examines the file type. If the file type is registered to ASP.NET, the web server passes the request to ASP.NET. Figure 20-1 shows how these levels interact.

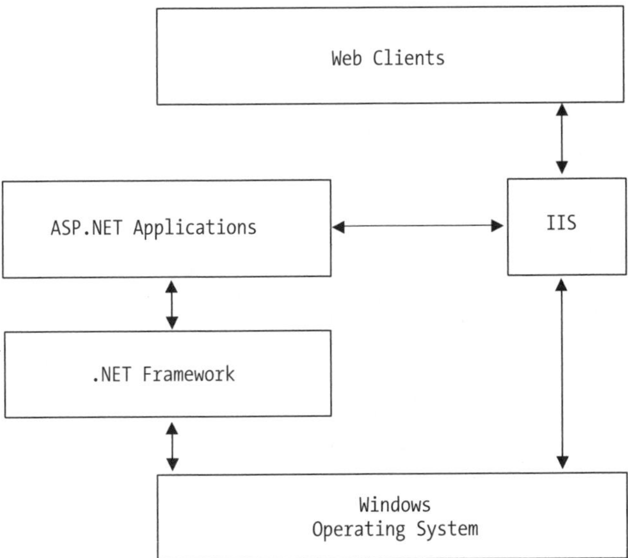

Figure 20-1. *IIS and ASP.NET interaction*

You can apply security at several places in this chain. First, consider the process for an ordinary (non-ASP.NET) web page request:

1. IIS attempts to authenticate the user. Generally, IIS allows requests from all anonymous users and automatically logs them in under the IUSR_[ComputerName] account. IIS security settings are configured on a per-directory basis. (On Windows Vista, this account is simply named IUSR.)

2. If IIS authenticates the user successfully, it attempts to send the user the appropriate HTML file. The operating system performs its own security checks to verify that the authenticated user (typically IUSR) is allowed access to the specified file and directory.

An ASP.NET request requires several additional steps (as shown in Figure 20-2). The first and last steps are similar, but the process has intermediary layers:

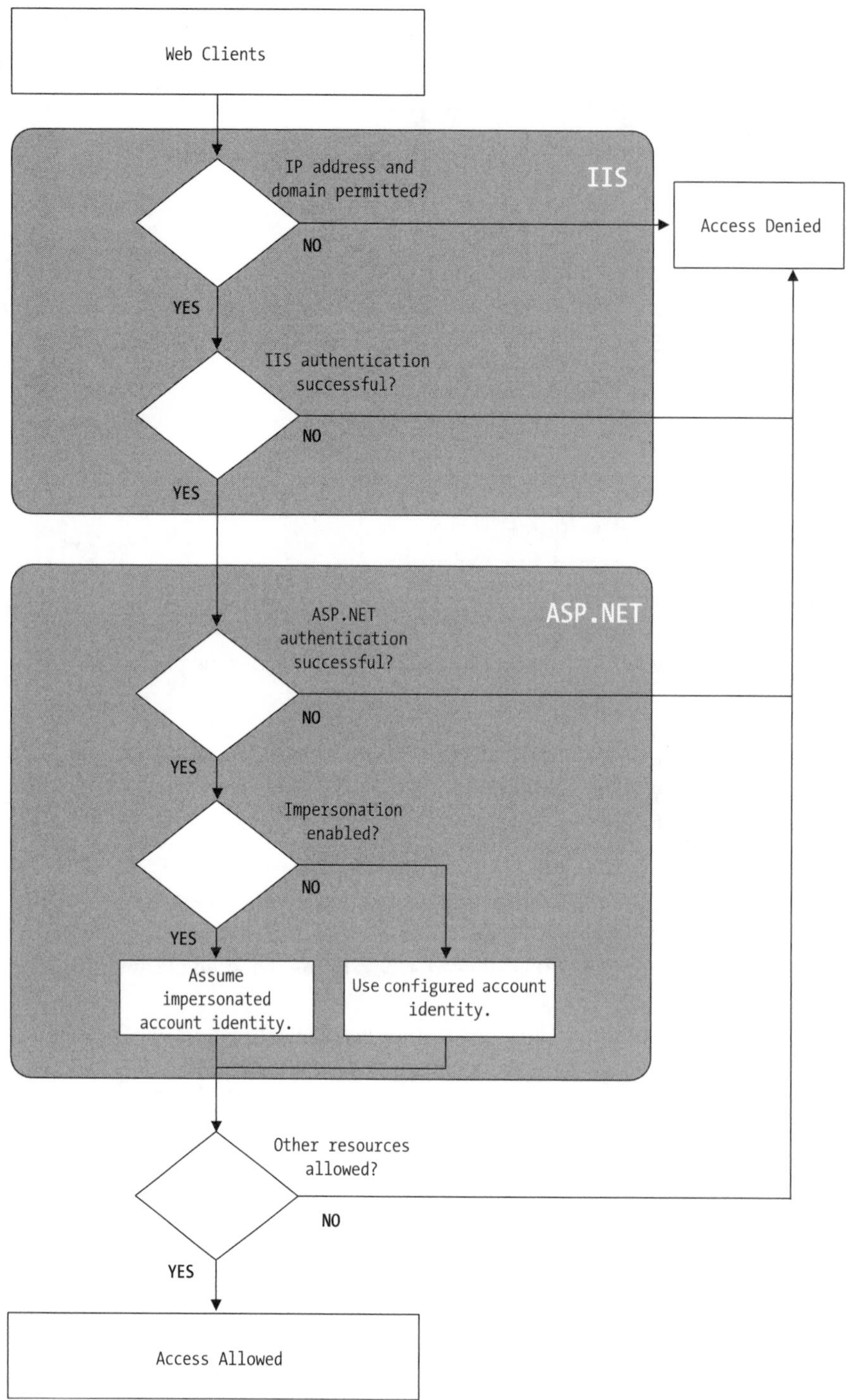

Figure 20-2. *Authenticating a request*

1. IIS attempts to authenticate the user. Generally, IIS allows requests from all anonymous users and automatically logs them in under the IUSR account.
2. If IIS authenticates the user successfully, it passes the request to ASP.NET with additional information about the authenticated user. ASP.NET can then use its own security services, depending on the settings in the web.config file and the page that was requested.
3. If ASP.NET authenticates the user, it allows requests to the .aspx page or .asmx web service. Your code can perform additional custom security checks (for example, manually asking for another password before allowing a specific operation).
4. When the ASP.NET code requests resources (for example, tries to open a file or connect to a database), the operating system performs its own security checks. In a live website, ASP.NET code runs under a fixed account. This account is defined in the machine.config file (if you're running IIS 5) or in IIS Manager (if you're running IIS 6 or IIS 7). As your code performs various actions, Windows checks to make sure the account has the required permissions.

One important and easily missed concept is that the ASP.NET code doesn't run under the IUSR account, even if you're using anonymous user access. The reason is the IUSR account doesn't have sufficient privileges for ASP.NET code, which needs to be able to create and delete temporary files in order to manage the compilation process. Instead, the ASP.NET account is set through the machine.config file (if you're using IIS 5) or the application pool identity (under IIS 6 and IIS 7), as described in Chapter 9. When designing ASP.NET pages, you must keep this in mind and ensure your program can't be used to make dangerous modifications or delete important files.

■ **Note** There is one exception to the rules set out in this section. If you enable impersonation (which is described at the end of this chapter), ASP.NET runs all code under the account of an authenticated user. Impersonation is rarely used, because it forces you to grant additional permissions to all users so that ASP.NET can run properly and compile code.

The Visual Studio Web Server

So far, this discussion assumes you're using IIS, which is what all live ASP.NET websites use. However, IIS isn't involved when you test a web application using the integrated web server in Visual Studio. Instead, the Visual Studio web server plays the same role.

Conceptually, the Visual Studio web server works in the same way as the IIS web server. For example, it handles requests for different types of files (such as HTML pages and ASP.NET web forms) and passes requests on to ASP.NET when required. However, the security model is simplified. Because the Visual Studio web server is designed to be used by one person at a time—the current user of the local computer—it doesn't support anonymous access. Instead, every time you run the Visual Studio web server it logs you on automatically, using your current Windows identity. As a result, your web page code runs with the permissions of your Windows user account. Typically, this gives your web application code more privileges than it would have in a deployed website, where it's forced to run under a more limited account.

RESTRICTED FILE TYPES

ASP.NET automatically provides a basic level of security by blocking requests for certain file types (such as configuration and source code files). To accomplish this, ASP.NET registers the file types with IIS but specifically assigns them to the HttpForbiddenHandler class. This class has a single role in life—it denies every request it receives.

ASP.NET uses this technique to block access to source code files, Visual Studio project files, and other resources. Some of the restricted file types include the following:

```
.asax
.ascx
.config
.vb
.vbproj
.cs
.csproj
.resx
.resources
```

To see the full list, refer to the web.config.default file in the c:\Windows\Microsoft.NET\Framework\v2.0.50727\Config folder, and search for the text *System.Web.HttpForbiddenHandler*.

Authentication and Authorization

Two concepts form the basis of any discussion about security:

Authentication: This is the process of determining a user's identity and forcing users to prove they are who they claim to be. Usually, this involves entering credentials (typically a user name and password) into some sort of login page or window. These credentials are then authenticated against the Windows user accounts on a computer, a list of users in a file, or a back-end database.

Authorization: Once a user is authenticated, authorization is the process of determining whether that user has sufficient permissions to perform a given action (such as viewing a page or retrieving information from a database). Windows imposes some authorization checks (for example, when you open a file), but your code will probably want to impose its own checks (for example, when a user performs a task in your web application such as submitting an order, assigning a project, or giving a promotion).

Authentication and authorization are the two cornerstones of creating a secure user-based site. The Windows operating system provides a good analogy. When you first boot up your computer, you supply a user ID and password, thereby authenticating yourself to the system. After that point, every time you interact with a restricted resource (such as a file, database, registry key, and so on), Windows quietly performs authorization checks to ensure your user account has the necessary rights.

You can use two types of authentication to secure an ASP.NET website:

Forms authentication: With forms authentication, IIS is configured to allow anonymous users (which is its default setting). However, you use ASP.NET's forms authentication model to secure parts of your site. This allows you to create a subscription site or e-commerce store. You can manage the login process easily, and write your own login code for authenticating users against a database or simple user account list.

Windows authentication: With Windows authentication, IIS forces every user to log in as a Windows user. (Depending on the specific configuration you use, this login process may take place automatically, as it does in the Visual Studio test web server, or it may require that the user type a name and password into a Login dialog box.) This system requires that all users have Windows user accounts on the server (although users could share accounts). This scenario is poorly suited for a public web application but is often ideal with an intranet or company-specific site designed to provide resources for a limited set of users.

You'll concentrate on these two approaches in this chapter. First, you'll explore the forms authentication model, which is perfect for publicly accessible websites. Then, you'll consider Windows authentication, which makes sense in smaller network environments where you have a group of known users.

Forms Authentication

In traditional ASP programming developers often had to create their own security systems. A common approach was to insert a little snippet of code at the beginning of every secure page. This code would check for the existence of a custom cookie. If the cookie didn't exist, the user would be redirected to a login page, where the cookie would be created after a successful login.

ASP.NET uses the same approach in its forms authentication model. You are still responsible for creating the login page (although you can use a set of specially designed controls to help you, as described in Chapter 21). However, you don't need to create the security cookie manually, or check for it in secure pages, because ASP.NET handles these tasks automatically. You also benefit from ASP.NET's support for sophisticated validation algorithms, which make it all but impossible for users to spoof their own cookies or try other hacking tricks to fool your application into giving them access.

Figure 20-3 shows a simplified security diagram of the forms authentication model in ASP.NET.

To implement forms-based security, you need to follow three steps:

1. Set the authentication mode to forms authentication in the web.config file (or use the WAT).

2. Restrict anonymous users from a specific page or directory in your application.

3. Create the login page.

You'll walk through these steps in the following sections.

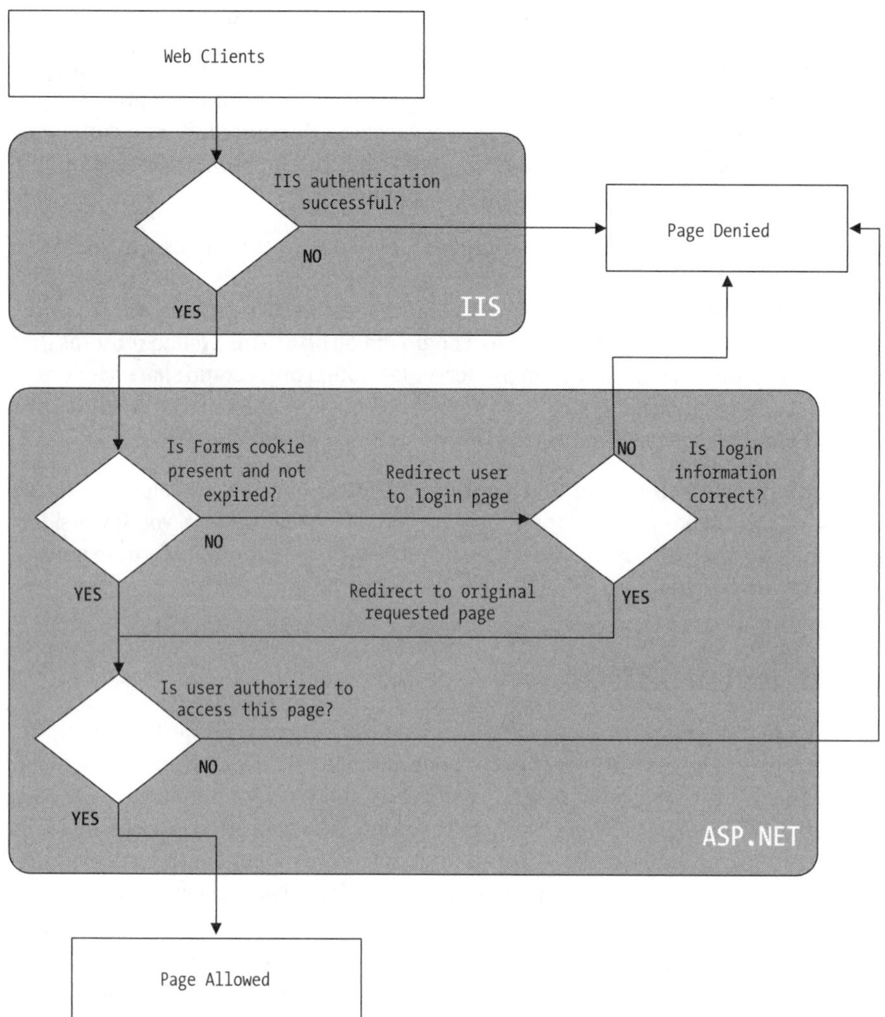

Figure 20-3. *ASP.NET forms authentication*

Web.config Settings

You define the type of security in the web.config file by using the <authentication> tag.

The following example configures the application to use forms authentication by using the <authentication> tag. It also sets several of the most important settings using a nested <forms> tag. Namely, it sets the name of the security cookie, the length of time it will be considered valid (in minutes), and the page that allows the user to log in.

```
<configuration>
    <system.web>
        ...
        <authentication mode="Forms">
            <forms name="MyAppCookie"
                   loginUrl="~/Login.aspx"
                   protection="All"
                   timeout="30" path="/" />
        </authentication>
    </system.web>
    ...
</configuration>
```

Table 20-1 describes these settings. They all supply default values, so you don't need to set them explicitly. For a complete list of supported attributes, consult the Visual Studio Help.

Table 20-1. *Forms Authentication Settings*

Attribute	Description
name	The name of the HTTP cookie to use for authentication (defaults to .ASPXAUTH). If multiple applications are running on the same web server, you should give each application's security cookie a unique name.
loginUrl	Your custom login page, where the user is redirected if no valid authentication cookie is found. The default value is Login.aspx.
protection	The type of encryption and validation used for the security cookie (can be All, None, Encryption, or Validation). Validation ensures the cookie isn't changed during transit, and encryption (typically Triple-DES) is used to encode its contents. The default value is All.
timeout	The number of minutes before the cookie expires. ASP.NET will refresh the cookie when it receives a request, as long as half of the cookie's lifetime has expired. The default value is 30.
path	The path for cookies issued by the application. The default value (/) is recommended, because case mismatches can prevent the cookie from being sent with a request.

Authorization Rules

If you make these changes to an application's web.config file and request a page, you'll notice that nothing unusual happens, and the web page is served in the normal way. This is because even though you have enabled forms authentication for your application, you have not restricted anonymous users. In other words, you've chosen the system you want to use for authentication, but at the moment none of your pages needs authentication.

To control who can and can't access your website, you need to add access control rules to the <authorization> section of your web.config file. Here's an example that duplicates the default behavior:

```
<configuration>
    <system.web>
        ...
        <authentication mode="Forms">
            <forms loginUrl="~/Login.aspx" />
        </authentication>

        <authorization>
            <allow users="*" />
        </authorization>
    </system.web>
    ...
</configuration>
```

The asterisk (*) is a wildcard character that explicitly permits all users to use the application, even those who haven't been authenticated. Even if you don't include this line in your application's web.config file, this is still the behavior you'll see, because the default settings inherited from the machine.config file allow all users. To change this behavior, you need to explicitly add a more restrictive rule, as shown here:

```
<authorization>
    <deny users="?" />
</authorization>
```

The question mark (?) is a wildcard character that matches all anonymous users. By including this rule in your web.config file, you specify that anonymous users are not allowed. Every user must be authenticated, and every user request will require the security cookie. If you request a page in the application directory now, ASP.NET will detect that the request isn't authenticated and attempt to redirect the request to the login page (which will probably cause an error, unless you've already created this file).

Now consider what happens if you add more than one rule to the authorization section:

```
<authorization>
    <allow users="*" />
    <deny users="?" />
</authorization>
```

When evaluating rules, ASP.NET scans through the list from top to bottom and then continues with the settings in any .config file inherited from a parent directory, ending with the settings in the base machine.config file. As soon as it finds an applicable rule, it stops its search. Thus, in the previous case, it will determine that the rule <allow users="*"> applies to the current request and will not evaluate the second line. This means these rules will allow all users, including anonymous users.

But consider what happens if these two lines are reversed:

```
<authorization>
    <deny users="?" />
    <allow users="*" />
</authorization>
```

Now these rules will deny anonymous users (by matching the first rule) and allow all other users (by matching the second rule).

Controlling Access to Specific Directories

A common application design is to place files that require authentication in a separate directory. With ASP.NET configuration files, this approach is easy. Just leave the default <authorization> settings in the normal parent directory, and add a web.config file that specifies stricter settings in the secured directory. This web.config simply needs to deny anonymous users (all other settings and configuration sections can be omitted).

```
<!-- This web.config file is in a subfolder. -->
<configuration>
    <system.web>
        <authorization>
            <deny users="?" />
        </authorization>
    </system.web>
</configuration>
```

■Note You cannot change the <authentication> tag settings in the web.config file of a subdirectory in your application. Instead, all the directories in the application must use the same authentication system. However, each directory can have its own authorization rules.

Controlling Access to Specific Files

Generally, setting file access permissions by directory is the cleanest and easiest approach. However, you also have the option of restricting specific files by adding <location> tags to your web.config file.

The location tags sit outside the main <system.web> tag and are nested directly in the base <configuration> tag, as shown here:

```
<configuration>
    <system.web>
        ...
        <authentication mode="Forms">
            <forms loginUrl="~/Login.aspx" />
        </authentication>

        <authorization>
            <allow users="*" />
        </authorization>
    </system.web>
    ...
```

```
    <location path="SecuredPage.aspx">
        <system.web>
            <authorization>
                <deny users="?" />
            </authorization>
        </system.web>
    </location>

    <location path="AnotherSecuredPage.aspx">
        <system.web>
            <authorization>
                <deny users="?" />
            </authorization>
        </system.web>
    </location>
</configuration>
```

In this example, all files in the application are allowed, except SecuredPage.aspx and AnotherSecuredPage.aspx, which have an additional access rule denying anonymous users. Notice that even when you use multiple <location> sections to supply different sets of authorization rules, you still only include one <authentication> section. That's because a web application can use only one type of authentication.

■ **Tip** You can also use the location tags to set rules for a specific subdirectory. It's up to you whether you want to use this approach or you prefer to create separate web.config files for each subdirectory, as described in the previous section.

Controlling Access for Specific Users

The <allow> and <deny> rules don't need to use the asterisk or question mark wildcards. Instead, they can specifically identify a user name or a list of comma-separated user names. For example, the following list specifically restricts access from three users. These users will not be able to access the pages in this directory. All other authenticated users will be allowed.

```
<authorization>
    <deny users="?" />
    <deny users="matthew,sarah" />
    <deny users="john" />
    <allow users="*" />
</authorization>
```

You'll notice that the first rule in this example denies all anonymous users. Otherwise, the following rules won't have any effect, because users won't be forced to authenticate themselves.

The following rules explicitly allow two users. All other user requests will be denied access, even if they are authenticated.

```
<authorization>
    <deny users="?" />
    <allow users="matthew,sarah" />
    <deny users="*" />
</authorization>
```

Don't confuse these user names with the Windows user account names that are configured on your web server. When you use forms authentication, your application's security model is separate from the Windows user account system. Your application assigns the user name when a user logs in through the login page. Often, you'll choose user names that correspond to IDs in a database. The only requirement is that your user names need to be unique.

The WAT

You have another way to set up your authentication and authorization rules. Rather than edit the web.config file by hand, you can use the WAT (website administration tool) from inside Visual Studio. The WAT guides you through the process, although you'll find it's still important to understand what changes are actually being made to your web.config file. It's also often quicker to enter a list of authorization rules by hand than to use the WAT.

To use the WAT for this type of configuration, select Website ➤ ASP.NET Configuration from the menu. Next, click the Security tab. You'll see the window shown in Figure 20-4, which gives you links to set the authentication type, define authorization rules (using the Access Rules section), and enable role-based security. (Role-based security is an optional higher-level feature you can use with forms authentication. You'll learn more about how it works and how to enable it in the next chapter.)

To set an application to use forms authentication, follow these steps:

1. Click Select Authentication Type.
2. Choose the From the Internet option. (If you chose From a Local Network instead, you'd wind up using the built-in Windows authentication approach described later in the "Windows Authentication" section.)
3. Click Done. The appropriate <authorization> tag will be created in the web.config file.

■ **Tip** The Select Authentication options are worded in a slightly misleading way. It's true that applications that have users connecting from all over the Internet are sure to use forms authentication. However, applications that run on a local network might also use forms authentication—it all depends on how they connect and whether you want to use the information in existing accounts. In other words, a local intranet gives you the *option* to use Windows authentication but doesn't require it.

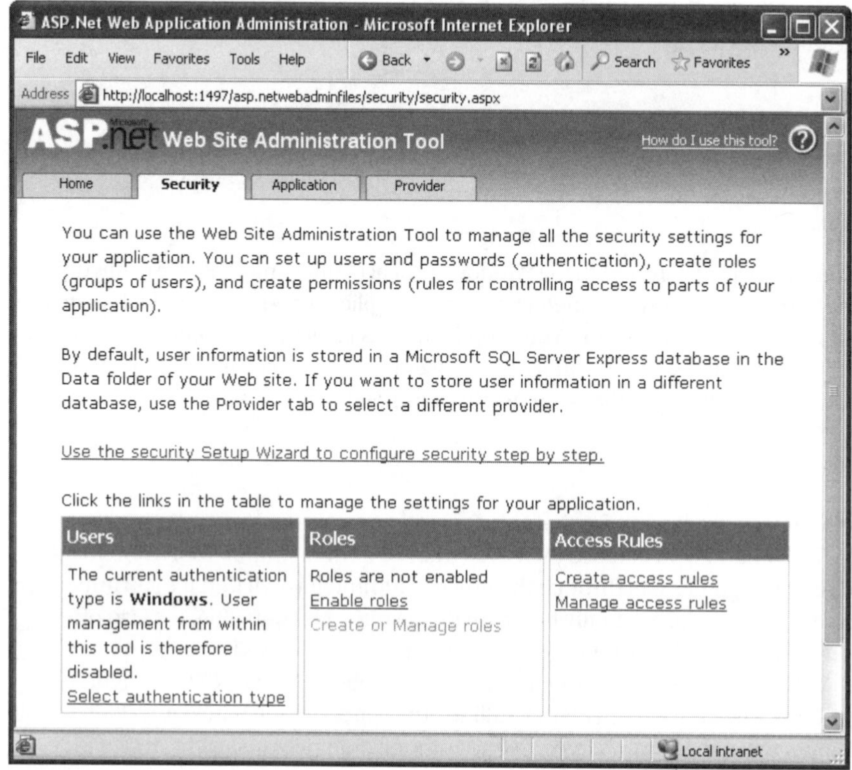

Figure 20-4. *The Security tab in the WAT*

Next, it's time to define the authorization rules. To do so, click the Create Access Rules link. (You can also change existing rules by clicking the Manage Access Rules link.) Using the slightly convoluted page shown in Figure 20-5, you have the ability to create a rule allowing or restricting specific users to the entire site or a specific page or subfolder. For example, the rule in Figure 20-5 will deny the user jenny from the entire site once you click OK to add it.

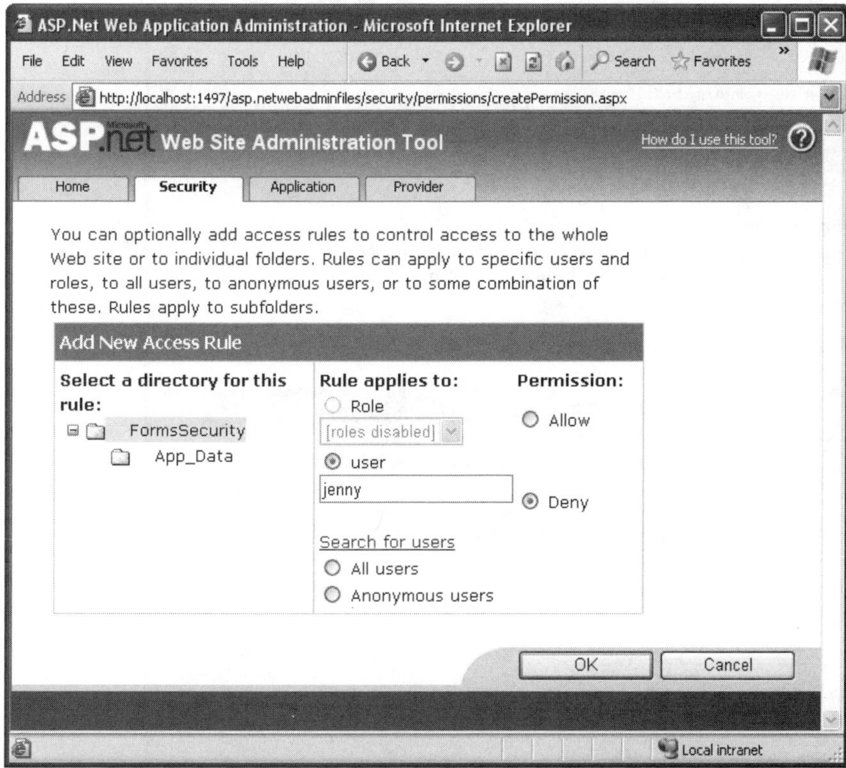

Figure 20-5. *Adding an authorization rule*

To manage multiple rules, you'll need to click the Manage Access Rules link. Now you'll have the chance to change the order of rules (and hence the priority, as described earlier), as shown in Figure 20-6. If you have a large number of rules to create, you may find it's easier to edit the web.config file by hand. You might just want to create one initial rule to make sure it's in the right place and then copy and paste your way to success.

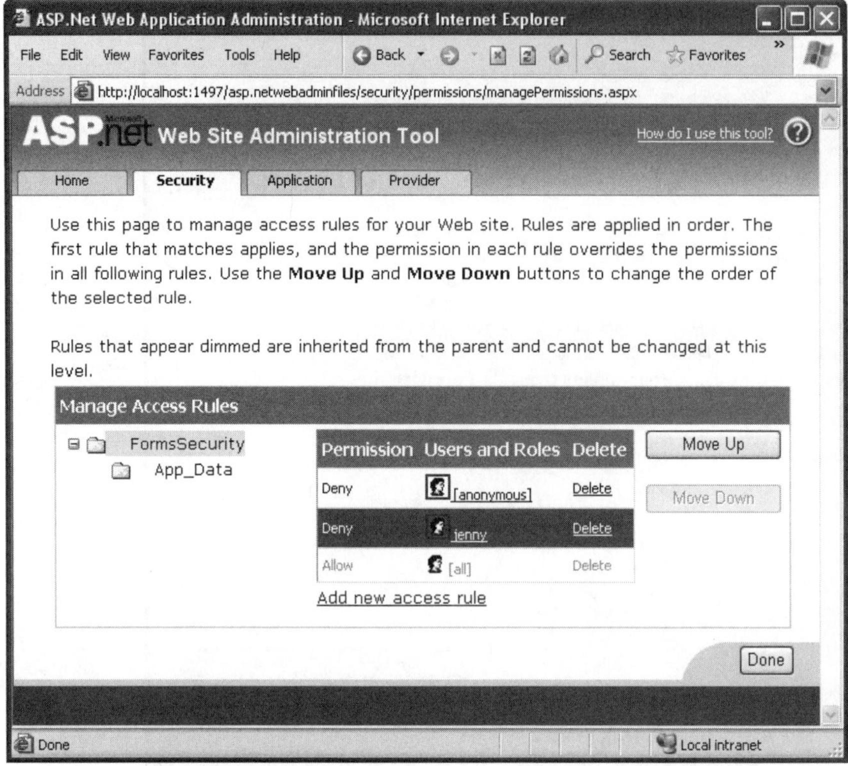

Figure 20-6. *Ordering authorization rules*

The Security tab is a little overwhelming at first glance because it includes a few features you haven't been introduced to yet. For example, the Security tab also allows you to create and manage user records and roles, as long as you're willing to use the prebuilt database structure that ASP.NET requires. You'll learn more about these details, which are a part of a broad feature called *membership*, in the next chapter. For now, you'll concentrate on the authentication and authorization process.

The Login Page

Once you've specified the authentication mode and the authorization rules, you need to build the actual login page, which is an ordinary .aspx page that requests information from the user and decides whether the user should be authenticated.

ASP.NET provides a special FormsAuthentication class in the System.Web.Security namespace, which provides shared methods that help manage the process. Table 20-2 describes the most important methods of this class.

Table 20-2. *Members of the FormsAuthentication Class*

Member	Description
FormsCookieName	A read-only property that provides the name of the forms authentication cookie.
FormsCookiePath	A read-only property that provides the path set for the forms authentication cookie.
Authenticate()	Checks a user name and password against a list of accounts that can be entered in the web.config file.
RedirectFromLoginPage()t	Logs the user into an ASP.NET application by creating the cookie, attaching it to the current response, and redirecting the user to the page originally requested.
SignOut()	Logs the user out of the ASP.NET application by removing the current encrypted cookie.
SetAuthCookie()	Logs the user into an ASP.NET application by creating and attaching the forms authentication cookie. Unlike the RedirectFromLoginPage() method, it doesn't forward the user back to the initially requested page.
GetRedirectUrl()	Provides the URL of the originally requested page. You could use this with SetAuthCookie() to log a user into an application and make a decision in your code whether to redirect to the requested page or use a more suitable default page.
GetAuthCookie()	Creates the authentication cookie but doesn't attach it to the current response. You can perform additional cookie customization and then add it manually to the response, as described in Chapter 7.
HashPasswordForStoringInConfigFile()	Encrypts a string of text using the specified algorithm (SHA1 or MD5). This hashed value provides a secure way to store an encrypted password in a file or database.

A simple login page can put these methods to work with little code. To try it out, begin by enabling forms authentication and denying anonymous users in the web.config, as described earlier:

```
<configuration>
    <system.web>
        ...
        <authentication mode="Forms">
            <forms loginUrl="~/Login.aspx" />
        </authentication>
```

```
        <authorization>
            <deny users="?" />
            <allow users="*" />
        </authorization>
    </system.web>
    ...
</configuration>
```

Now, users will be redirected to a login page named Login.aspx that you need to create. Figure 20-7 shows an example of the simple login page that you might build.

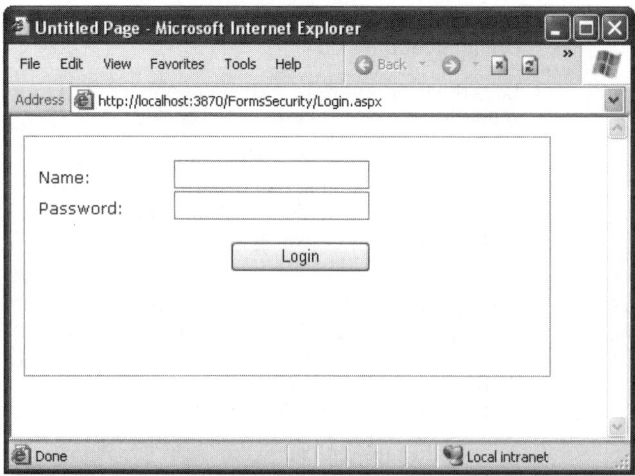

Figure 20-7. *A typical login page*

When the user clicks the Login button, the page checks whether the user has typed in the password *Secret* and then uses the RedirectFromLoginPage() method to log the user in. Here's the complete page code:

```
Public Partial Class Login
    Inherits System.Web.UI.Page

    Protected Sub cmdLogin_Click(ByVal sender As Object, _
      ByVal e As System.EventArgs) Handles cmdLogin.Click
        If txtPassword.Text.ToLower() = "secret" Then
            FormsAuthentication.RedirectFromLoginPage(txtName.Text, False)
        Else
            lblStatus.Text = "Try again."
        End If
    End Sub

End Class
```

The RedirectFromLoginPage() method requires two parameters. The first sets the name of the user. The second is a Boolean variable that creates a persistent forms authentication cookie when set to True or an ordinary forms authentication cookie when set to False. A persistent cookie will be stored on the user's hard drive with an expiration date set to 50 years in the future. This is a convenience that's sometimes useful when you're using the forms authentication login for personalization instead of security. It's also a security risk because another user could conceivably log in from the same computer, acquiring the cookie and the access to the secured pages. If you want to allow the user to create a persistent cookie, you should make it optional, because the user may want to access your site from a public or shared computer. Generally, sites that use this technique include a check box with text such as *Persist Cookie* or *Keep Me Logged In.*

```
FormsAuthentication.RedirectFromLoginPage(txtName.Text, chkPersist.Checked)
```

Obviously, the approach used in the login page isn't terribly secure—it simply checks that the user supplies a hard-coded password. In a real application, you'd probably check the user name and password against the information in a database and sign the user in only if the information matches exactly. You could write this code easily using the ADO.NET programming you learned in Part 4, although it requires a bit of tedious code. You'll consider more practical ways to accomplish this task in the next chapter.

You can test this example with the FormsSecurity sample included with the online code. If you request the SecuredPage.aspx file, you'll be redirected to Login.aspx. After entering the correct password, you'll return to SecuredPage.aspx.

Retrieving the User's Identity

Once the user is logged in, you can retrieve the identity through the built-in User property, as shown here:

```
Protected Sub Page_Load(ByVal sender As Object, _
  ByVal e As System.EventArgs) Handles Me.Load

    lblMessage.Text = "You have reached the secured page, "
    lblMessage.Text &= User.Identity.Name + "."
End Sub
```

You don't need to place the code in the login page. Instead, you can use the User object to examine the current user's identity anytime you need to.

Figure 20-8 shows the result of running this code.

You can access the User object in your code because it's a property of the current Page object. The User object provides information about the currently logged-in user. It's fairly simple—in fact, User provides only one property and one method:

- The Identity property lets you retrieve the name of the logged-in user and the type of authentication that was used.
- The IsInRole() method lets you determine whether a user is a member of a given role (and thus should be given certain privileges). You'll use IsInRole() later in this chapter.

Figure 20-8. *Accessing a secured page*

> **UNDERSTANDING IDENTITIES**
>
> The User object is standardized so that it can work with any type of authentication system. One consequence of this design is that the User.Identity property returns a different type of object depending on the type of authentication you're using.
>
> For example, when using forms authentication, the identity object is an instance of the FormsIdentity class. When using Windows authentication, you get a WindowsIdentity object instead. (Either way, the object implements the IIdentity interface, which standardizes it.)
>
> Most of the time, you don't need to worry about this sleight of hand. But occasionally you might want to cast the User.Identity property to the more specific type to get access to an extra piece of information. For example, the FormsIdentity object provides the security ticket (in a property named Ticket), which isn't available through the standard IIdentity interface. This ticket is an instance of the FormsAuthenticationTicket class, and it provides a few miscellaneous details, like the time the user logged in and when the ticket will expire. Similarly, the WindowsIdentity object provides additional information that relates to Windows accounts (such as whether the current user is using a guest account or a system account). You'll see an example of this technique later in this chapter in the "Impersonation" section.

Signing Out

Any web application that uses forms authentication should also feature a prominent logout button that destroys the forms authentication cookie:

```
Protected Sub cmdSignOut_Click(ByVal sender As Object, _
  ByVal e As System.EventArgs) Handles cmdSignOut.Click

    FormsAuthentication.SignOut()
    Response.Redirect("~/Login.aspx")
End Sub
```

■Tip In the next chapter, you'll learn how to simplify life with the login controls. These controls allow you to build login pages (and other types of security-related user interfaces) with no code. However, they require another feature—membership—in order to work.

Windows Authentication

With Windows authentication, the web server takes care of the authentication process. ASP.NET simply uses the authenticated IIS user and makes this identity available to your code for your security checks.

If your virtual directory uses the default settings, users will be authenticated under the anonymous IUSR account. But when you use Windows authentication, you'll force users to log into IIS before they're allowed to access secure content in your website. The user login information can be transmitted in several ways, but the end result is that the user is authenticated using a local Windows account. Typically, this makes Windows authentication best suited to intranet scenarios, in which a limited set of known users is already registered on a network server.

The advantages of Windows authentication are that it can be performed transparently with no browser prompts (depending on the client's operating system and browser) and your ASP.NET code can examine all the account information. For example, you can use the User.IsInRole() method to check which groups a user belongs to.

To implement Windows-based security with known users, you need to follow three steps:

1. Set the authentication mode to Windows authentication in the web.config file (or use the WAT).
2. Disable anonymous access for a directory by using an authorization rule (or by disabling access in IIS Manager). You can also choose the protocol that will be used to transmit the user name and password information with IIS Manager.
3. Configure the Windows user accounts on your web server (if they aren't already present).

You'll walk through these steps in the following sections.

■Note Most of the discussion in this chapter describes how IIS behaves with Windows authentication. However, when you're testing a web application, you're probably not using IIS. Instead, you're using the built-in web server that's included with Visual Studio. For the most part, this web server works the same as IIS but has one important distinction—it doesn't support anonymous use. This means Visual Studio always logs you into the web server using your Windows account. In IIS, you need to force the user to log in by explicitly denying anonymous access to a page or subdirectory with authorization rules. To see the difference, you may want to test your application with IIS by creating a virtual directory (as explained in Chapter 9).

Web.config Settings

To use Windows authentication, you need to make sure the <authentication> element is set accordingly in your web.config file. Here's how:

```
<configuration>
    <system.web>
        ...
        <authentication mode="Windows" />

        <authorization>
          <deny users="?" />
        </authorization>
    </system.web>
    ...
</configuration>
```

At the moment, there's only one authorization rule, which uses the question mark to refuse all anonymous users. This step is critical for Windows authentication (as it is for forms authentication). Without this step, the user will never be forced to log in.

Ideally, you won't even see the login process take place. Instead, Internet Explorer will pass along the credentials of the current Windows user, which IIS uses automatically. The Visual Studio integrated web server always works this way. IIS also works this way, provided you've set up integrated Windows authentication (which is described in the next section). In order for integrated Windows authentication to work, your clients must be using Internet Explorer, and must already be logged on to a computer or domain on the same network.

You can also add <allow> and <deny> elements to specifically allow or restrict users from specific files or directories. Unlike with forms authentication, you need to specify the name of the server or domain where the account exists. For example, this rule allows the user account matthew, which is defined on the computer named WebServer:

```
<allow users="WebServer\matthew" />
```

For a shortcut, you can use localhost (or just a period) to refer to an account on the current computer, as shown here:

```
<allow users=".\matthew" />
```

You can also restrict certain types of users, provided their accounts are members of the same Windows group, by using the roles attribute:

```
<authorization>
    <deny users="?" />
    <allow roles=".\SalesAdministrator,.\SalesStaff" />
    <deny users=".\matthew" />
</authorization>
```

In this example, all users who are members of the SalesAdministrator or SalesStaff groups will be automatically authorized to access ASP.NET pages in this directory. Requests from the user matthew will be denied, unless he is a member of the SalesAdministrator or SalesStaff group. Remember, ASP.NET examines rules in the order they appear and stops when it finds a match. Reversing these two authorization lines would ensure that the user matthew was always denied, regardless of group membership.

You can also examine a user's group membership programmatically in your code, as shown here.

```
Protected Sub Page_Load(ByVal sender As Object, _
  ByVal e As System.EventArgs) Handles Me.Load

    If User.IsInRole("MyDomainName\SalesAdministrators") Then
        ' Do nothing; the page should be accessed as normal because
        ' the user has administrator privileges.
    Else
        ' Don't allow this page. Instead, redirect to the home page.
        Response.Redirect("Default.aspx")
    End If
End Sub
```

In this example, the code checks for membership in a custom Windows group called SalesAdministrators. If you want to check whether a user is a member of one of the built-in groups, you don't need to specify a computer or domain name. Instead, you use this syntax:

```
If User.IsInRole("BUILTIN\Administrators") Then
    ' (Code goes here.)
End If
```

For more information about the <allow> and <deny> rules and configuring individual files and directories, refer to the discussion in the "Authorization Rules" section earlier in this chapter.

Note that you have no way to retrieve a list of available groups on the web server (that would violate security), but you can find out the names of the default built-in Windows roles using the System.Security.Principal.WindowsBuiltInRole enumeration. Table 20-3 describes these roles. Not all will apply to ASP.NET use, although Administrator, Guest, and User probably will.

Table 20-3. *Default Windows Roles*

Role	Description
AccountOperator	Users with the special responsibility of managing the user accounts on a computer or domain.
Administrator	Users with complete and unrestricted access to the computer or domain.
BackupOperator	Users who can override certain security restrictions only as part of backing up or restore operations.
Guest	Like the User role but even more restrictive.
PowerUser	Similar to Administrator but with some restrictions.
PrintOperator	Like User but with additional privileges for taking control of a printer.
Replicator	Like User but with additional privileges to support file replication in a domain.

Table 20-3. *Default Windows Roles (Continued)*

Role	Description
SystemOperator	Similar to Administrator with some restrictions. Generally, system operators manage a computer.
User	Users are prevented from making systemwide changes and can run only *certified applications* (see `http://www.microsoft.com/windows2000/server/evaluation/business/certified.asp` for more information).

IIS Settings

When you deploy a web application that uses Windows authentication to a real, live web server, you need to configure IIS. That's because IIS supports several different protocols that it can use when authenticating a user with Windows authentication. Depending on your network and the level of security you want, you need to choose the right one. Table 20-4 describes your options.

Table 20-4. *Windows Authentication Methods*

Mode	Description
Anonymous	Anonymous authentication is technically not a true authentication method, because the client isn't required to submit any information. Instead, users are given free access to the website under a special user account, IUSR. Anonymous authentication is the default.
Basic	Basic authentication is a part of the HTTP 1.0 standard, and almost all browsers and web servers support it. When using Basic authentication, the browser presents the user with a login box with a user name and password field. This information is then transmitted to IIS, where it's matched with a local Windows user account. The disadvantage of Basic authentication is that the password is transmitted in clear text and is visible over the Internet (unless you combine it with SSL technology).
Digest	Digest authentication remedies the primary weakness of Basic authentication: sending passwords in plain text. Digest authentication sends a digest (also known as a *hash*) instead of a password over the network. The primary disadvantage is that Digest authentication is supported only by Internet Explorer 5.0 and later. Your web server also needs to use Active Directory or have access to an Active Directory server.
Integrated	Integrated Windows authentication is the best choice for most intranet scenarios. When using Integrated authentication, Internet Explorer can send the required information automatically using the currently logged-in Windows account on the client, provided it's on a trusted domain. Integrated authentication is supported only on Internet Explorer 2.0 and later and won't work across proxy servers. In Windows Vista and Windows Server 2008, this is simply called Windows authentication.

The IIS documentation has more about these different authentication methods. However, choosing the one that's right for your network environment may involve a long discussion with your friendly neighborhood network administrator.

To choose your authentication method in IIS 5 (the version included with Windows XP) or IIS 6 (the version included with Windows Server 2003), follow these steps:

1. Start IIS Manager (select Settings ➤ Control Panel ➤ Administrative Tools ➤ Internet Information Services).
2. Expand your computer, then the Web Sites group, and then expand the Default Web Site item to see all the virtual directories on your web server.
3. Right-click the virtual directory you want to configure, and choose Properties.
4. Select the Directory Security tab and click Edit. You'll see all the options listed in Table 20-4. Figure 20-9 shows the IIS 5 version of the window. IIS 6 has the same options, but in a slightly different arrangement.

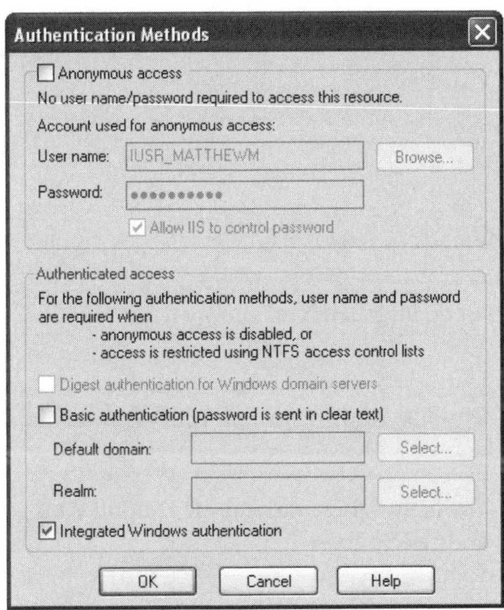

Figure 20-9. *Configuring Windows authentication (in IIS 5)*

In IIS 7 (the version included with Windows Vista and Windows Server 2008), the process is a bit different. If you're using Windows Vista, you need to make sure you're using a version that supports the type of Windows authentication you need. Unfortunately, only the Business and Ultimate editions support the most useful authentication methods (digest authentication and Windows integrated authentication). Next, you need to make sure that the support for that type of authentication is installed. To do so, open Control Panel, choose Programs and Features, and then click the link "Turn Windows features on or off." Head to the Internet Information Services ➤ World Wide Web Services ➤ Security group, which is shown in Figure 20-10. You'll find settings named Basic Authentication, Digest Authentication, and Windows Authentication (which is what earlier IIS versions call integrated Windows authentication).

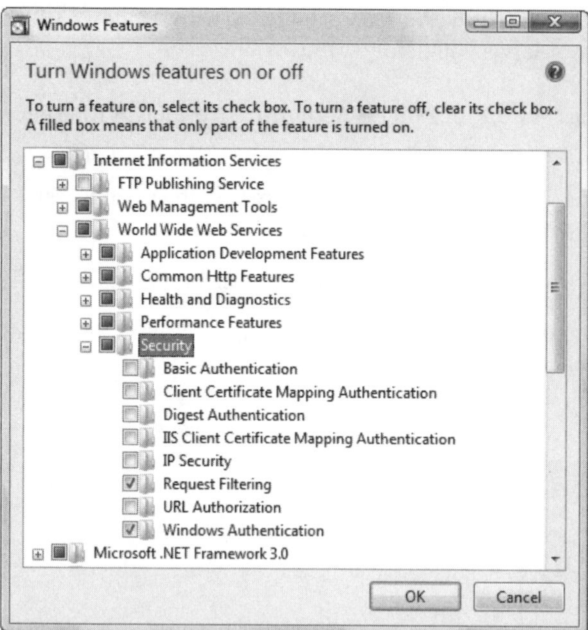

Figure 20-10. *Installing support for authentication methods (IIS 7)*

Once you have the authentication features you need installed, you simply need to follow these steps:

1. Start IIS Manager (select Settings ➤ Control Panel ➤ Administrative Tools ➤ Internet Information Services (IIS) Manager).

2. Expand your computer, then the Web Sites group, and then expand the Default Web Site item to see all the virtual directories on your web server.

3. Select the virtual directory you want to configure.

4. Double-click the Authentication icon in the Features area on the right. Now you'll see whatever authentication options you've installed. Figure 20-11 shows an example on a web server that supports integrated Windows authentication.

You can enable more than one authentication method. In this case, the client will use the strongest authentication method it supports, as long as anonymous access is *not* enabled. If anonymous access is enabled, the client will automatically access the website anonymously, unless the web application explicitly denies anonymous users with this rule in the web.config file:

```
<deny users="?" />
```

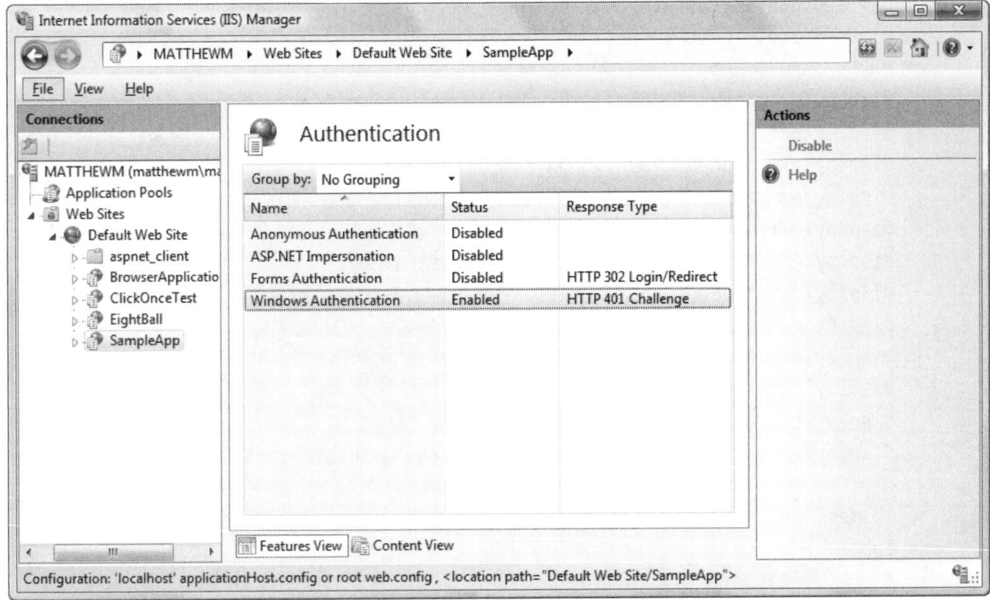

Figure 20-11. *Configuring Windows authentication (in IIS 7)*

A Windows Authentication Test

One of the nice features of Windows authentication is that no login page is required. Once you enable it in IIS and deny anonymous users in your web.config file, IIS springs into action. Depending on the authentication protocol you're using, the login process may take place automatically or the browser may show a login dialog box. Either way, you don't need to perform any additional work.

You can retrieve information about the currently logged-on user from the User object. As you learned earlier, the User object provides identity information through the User.Identity property. Depending on the type of authentication, a different identity object is used, and each identity object can provide customized information. To get some additional information about the identity of the user who has logged in with Windows authentication, you can convert the generic IIdentity object to a WindowsIdentity object (which is defined in the System.Security.Principal namespace).

The following is a sample test page that uses Windows authentication (see Figure 20-12). To use this code as written, you need to import the System.Security.Principal namespace (where the WindowsIdentity class is defined).

```
Public Partial Class SecuredPage
    Inherits System.Web.UI.Page

    Protected Sub Page_Load(ByVal sender As Object, _
      ByVal e As System.EventArgs) Handles Me.Load
        Dim displayText As New StringBuilder()
        displayText.Append("You have reached the secured page, ")
        displayText.Append(User.Identity.Name)
```

```
        Dim winIdentity As WindowsIdentity
        winIdentity = CType(User.Identity, WindowsIdentity)

        displayText.Append(".<br /><br />Authentication Type: ")
        displayText.Append(winIdentity.AuthenticationType)
        displayText.Append("<br />Anonymous: ")
        displayText.Append(winIdentity.IsAnonymous)
        displayText.Append("<br />Authenticated: ")
        displayText.Append(winIdentity.IsAuthenticated)
        displayText.Append("<br />Guest: ")
        displayText.Append(winIdentity.IsGuest)
        displayText.Append("<br />System: ")
        displayText.Append(winIdentity.IsSystem)
        displayText.Append("<br />Administrator: ")
        displayText.Append(User.IsInRole("BUILTIN\Administrators"))

        lblMessage.Text = displayText.ToString()
    End Sub

End Class
```

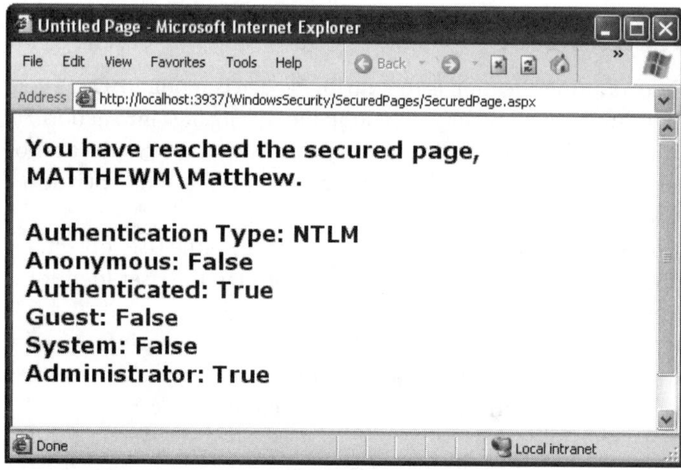

Figure 20-12. *Retrieving Windows authentication information*

Impersonation

In ASP.NET, all code runs under a carefully limited account. In Windows XP, this is typically an account that ASP.NET creates automatically, which is named ASPNET. In Windows Server 2003, Windows Vista, and Windows Server 2008, ASP.NET uses the network service account instead.

The account that ASP.NET uses determines what Windows will allow your application to do. As you've already learned earlier in this book, this account needs to be able to access the databases you want to use, the files you want to change, and so on. From a security standpoint, this design makes sense, because it limits what your application can do if it's tricked into performing the wrong action or compromised in some way.

Obviously, the permissions that are given to the ASP.NET account do not match the permissions that you want your users to have. For example, the ASP.NET account is allowed to perform tasks that the application users are not, like compile code. Furthermore, the ASP.NET account usually has the free run of any databases and files you use, whereas individual users are only allowed to see some of the information inside. Because of this mismatch of permissions, you need to write security checks in your code. For example, if the user goes to the current account page, your code makes sure the user only sees the information for their account, and only sees that if they're properly logged in.

In some cases, you might want your ASP.NET application to temporarily assume the permissions of the ASP.NET user. This process, whereby a portion of your code runs under a different Windows account, with a different set of Windows permissions, is called *impersonation.*

Understanding Impersonation

With impersonation, your ASP.NET code interacts with the system under the identity of the authenticated user—not the normal ASP.NET account. This changes the equation of what your website code is allowed to do. For example, if you try to perform a database operation, Windows will now evaluate whether that specific Windows user is allowed to access the database.

Impersonation is useful when you don't want to worry about authorization details in your code. For example, imagine you have a simple application that lets users upload, view, and manage some personal files on the web server. Each user has a separate folder to store files, and each folder has a different set of Windows permissions that allow the appropriate user and restrict everyone else.

Now, imagine you build an ASP.NET web page that lets users browse and view these files. You want the permissions to remain in effect—in other words, users should only be allowed to view the files they own. But ordinarily, your ASP.NET web pages are executed by an account that has permission to view *all* the files (or even worse, none of them). If you want to make sure users are only allowed to see their files, you need to write the tedious security checks into your code by hand.

In this situation, impersonation can save a lot of work. You simply need to use impersonation to assume the current user's account. Then, you can attempt to view the file the user has requested. Now, the code will only succeed if the user has the right permissions—in other words, if they're trying to view one of the files they own. Of course, this means your application will encounter an error when you try to read the file—so you'll need to use exception handling code to deal with the situation gracefully.

Programmatic Impersonation

The most useful way to use impersonation is programmatically, using the WindowsIdentity.Impersonate() method. This allows you to execute some code in the identity of a specific user (such as your file access routine) but allows the rest of your code to run under the local system account, guaranteeing it won't encounter any problems.

To use programmatic impersonation, you need to use Windows authentication and disable anonymous access for the website virtual directory. This way, IIS will authenticate the user, and that user identity will be available for you to use when you need it.

The following code shows how your code can use the Impersonate() method to switch identities:

```
If TypeOf User Is WindowsPrincipal Then
    Dim ID As WindowsIdentity
    ID = CType(User.Identity, WindowsIdentity)
    Dim ImpersonateContext As WindowsImpersonationContext

    ImpersonateContext = ID.Impersonate()
    ' Now perform tasks under the impersonated ID.
    ' This code will not be able to access perform any task
    ' (like reading a file) that the user would not be allowed to do.

    ' Revert to the original ID as shown below.
    ImpersonateContext.Undo()
Else
    ' User is not Windows authenticated.
    ' Throw an error to or take other steps.
End If
```

Confidentiality with SSL

One topic this chapter doesn't treat in detail is SSL (Secure Sockets Layer) connections. These technologies are supported by IIS and are really independent from ASP.NET programming. However, they are an important ingredient in creating a secure website.

Essentially, certificates allow you to demonstrate that your site and your organization information are registered and verified with a certificate authority. This generally encourages customer confidence, although it doesn't guarantee the company or organization acts responsibly or fairly. A certificate is a little like a driver's license—it doesn't prove you can drive, but it demonstrates that a third party (in this case, a department of the government) is willing to attest to your identity and your qualifications. Your web server requires a certificate in order to use SSL, which automatically encrypts all the information sent between the client and server.

To add a certificate to your site, you first need to purchase one from a certificate authority. These are some well-known certificate authorities:

- VeriSign (`http://www.verisign.com`)
- GeoTrust (`http://www.geotrust.com`)
- GlobalSign (`http://www.globalsign.com`)
- Thawte (`http://www.thawte.com`)

Creating a Certificate Request

The first step in the process of getting a certificate is to e-mail a certificate request for your web server. IIS Manager allows you to create a certificate request automatically.

The exact process depends on the version of IIS that you have installed. In IIS 5 (the version included with Windows XP) or IIS 6 (the version included with Windows Server 2003), follow these steps:

1. Launch IIS Manager by opening the Start menu and choosing Settings ➤ Control Panel ➤ Administrative Tools ➤ Internet Information Services.
2. Expand your computer, then the Web Sites group, and then expand the Default Web Site item to see all the virtual directories on your web server.
3. Right-click the virtual directory for your website and choose Properties.
4. Under the Directory Security tab, you'll find a Server Certificate button. Click this button to start the Web Server Certificate wizard.

In IIS 7 (the version included with Windows Vista and Windows Server 2008), follow these steps:

1. Launch IIS Manager by opening the Start menu and choosing Settings ➤ Control Panel ➤ Administrative Tools ➤ Internet Information Services (IIS) Manager.
2. Select the first item in the tree in IIS Manager, which is your computer. In the Features area on the right, double-click the Server Certificates icon.
3. In the Actions pane, click Create Certificate Request to start the Request Certificate wizard (shown in Figure 20-13).

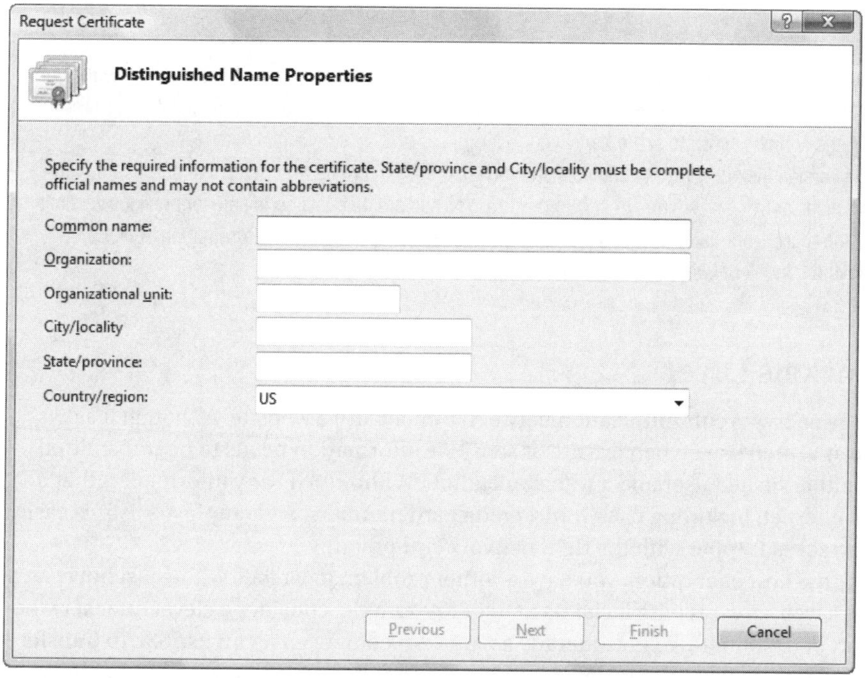

Figure 20-13. *Requesting a certificate*

The Web Server Certificate wizard and the Request Certificate wizard serve the same purpose. They collect some basic information, such as your address, the strength of encryption key you would like (the higher the bit length, the stronger the key), and so on.

At the end of the process, you'll create a key request. You can save the generated file as a text file, but you must ultimately e-mail it to a certificate authority. The following is a sample (slightly abbreviated) request file:

```
Webmaster: administrator@certificatecompany.com
Phone: (555) 555-5555
Server: Microsoft Key Manager for IIS Version 4.0

Common-name: www.yourcompany.com
Organization: YourOrganization

-----BEGIN NEW CERTIFICATE REQUEST-----
MIIB1DCCAToCAQAwgZMxCzAJBgNVBAYTAlVTMREwDwYDVQQIEwhOZXcgWW9yazEQ
MA4GA1UEBxMHQnVmZmFsbzEeMBwGA1UEChMVVW5pdmVyc2l0eSBhdCBCdWZmYWxv
MRwwGgYDVQQLExNSZXNlYXJjaCBGb3VuZGF0aW9uMSEwHwYDVQQDExh3d3cucmVz
ZWFyY2guYnVmZmFsby5lZHUwgZ8wDQYJKoZIhvcNAQEBBQADgYOAMIGJAoGBALJO
hbsCagHN4KMbl7uzOGwvcjJeWH8JqIUFVFi352tnoA15PZfCxW18KNtFeBtrbOpf
-----END NEW CERTIFICATE REQUEST-----
```

The certificate authority will return a certificate that you can install according to its instructions.

> **TEST CERTIFICATES**
>
> If you don't want to go to the trouble of buying a certificate, you can create a test certificate to use with your application. However, test certificates aren't suitable for real, live websites, because they lead to lots of browser security warnings (which is sure to scare away your users).
>
> IIS 7 (the version included with Windows Vista) makes it easy to create and use a test certificate. You can find instructions at `http://tinyurl.com/2hndyq`. You can create a test certificate for previous versions of IIS with a little more work using the makecert.exe command line tool. For more information, look up makecert.exe in the index of Visual Studio Help.

Secure Sockets Layer

SSL technology encrypts communication between a client and a website. Although it slows performance, it's often used when private or sensitive information needs to be transmitted between an authenticated user and a web application. Without SSL, any information that's sent over the Internet, including passwords, credit card numbers, and employee lists, is easily viewable to an eavesdropper with the right network equipment.

Even with the best encryption, you have another problem to wrestle with—just how can a client be sure a web server is who it claims to be? For example, consider a clever attacker who uses some sort of IP spoofing to masquerade as Amazon.com. Even if you use SSL to transfer your credit card information, the malicious web server on the other end will still be able to decrypt all your information seamlessly. To prevent this type of deception, SSL uses certificates. The certificate establishes the identity, and SSL protects the communication. If a malicious user abuses a certificate, the certificate authority can revoke it.

To use SSL, you need to install a valid certificate. You can then set IIS directory settings specifying that individual folders require an SSL connection. To access this page over SSL, the client simply types the URL with a preceding *https* instead of *http* at the beginning of the request.

In your ASP.NET code, you can check whether a user is connecting over a secure connection using code like this:

```
Protected Sub Page_Load(ByVal sender As Object, _
  ByVal e As System.EventArgs) Handles Me.Load

    If Request.IsSecureConnection Then
        lblStatus.Text = "This page is running under SSL."
    Else
        lblStatus.Text = "This page isn't secure.<br />"
        lblStatus.Text &= "Please request it with the "
        lblStatus.Text &= "prefix https:// instead of http://"
    End If
End Sub
```

HOW DOES SSL WORK?

With SSL, the client and web server start a secure session before they communicate any information. This secure session uses a randomly generated encryption key.

Here's how the process works:

1. The client requests an SSL connection.
2. The server signs its digital certificate and sends it to the client.
3. The client verifies the certificate was issued by a certificate authority it trusts, matches the web server it wants to communicate with, and has not expired or been revoked. If the certificate is valid, the client continues to the next step.
4. The client tells the server what encryption key sizes it supports.
5. The server chooses the strongest key length that is supported by both the client and server. It then informs the client what size this is.
6. The client generates a session key (a random string of bytes). It encrypts this session key using the server's public key (which was provided through the server's digital certificate). It then sends this encrypted package to the server.
7. The server decrypts the session key using its private key. Both the client and server now have the same random session key, which they can use to encrypt communication for the duration of the session.

The Last Word

In this chapter, you learned about the multilayered security architecture in ASP.NET and IIS and how you can safeguard your web pages and web services by using a custom login page or Windows authentication. You also learned the basics about certificates and SSL.

In the next chapter, you'll continue to build on your knowledge by considering some add-on features that can simplify your life and enhance your security. You'll learn how to get ASP.NET to create a basic user database for your site (complete with password encryption), saving you from creating it yourself or writing any ADO.NET code. You'll also extend your authorization rules by learning how you can group forms-authenticated users into logical groups, each of which can be assigned its own permissions.

CHAPTER 21

Membership

In the previous chapter, you learned how you can use ASP.NET forms authentication as the cornerstone of your website security. With forms authentication, you can identify users and restrict them from pages they shouldn't access. Best of all, ASP.NET manages the whole process for you by creating and checking the forms authentication cookie.

As convenient as forms authentication is, it isn't a complete solution. It's still up to you to take care of a variety of related tasks. For example, you need to maintain a user list and check it during the authentication process. You also need to create the login page, decide how to separate public from private content, and decide what each user should be allowed to do. These tasks aren't insurmountable, but they can be tedious. That's why Microsoft adds another layer of features to its forms authentication framework. This extra layer is known as *membership*.

The membership features fall into three broad categories:

User record management: Rather than create your own user database, if you use the membership features, ASP.NET can create and maintain this catalog of user information. It can even implement advanced rules (such as requiring e-mail addresses, asking security questions, and implementing strong passwords).

Security controls: Every secure website needs a login page. With ASP.NET's security controls, you don't need to design your own—instead, you can use a ready-made version straight from the Login section of the Toolbox. And along with the basic Login control are other controls for displaying secure content, creating new users, and changing passwords. Best of all, you can customize how every security control works by setting properties and reacting to events.

Role-based security: In many websites, you need to give different permissions to different users. Of course, life would be far too complex if you had to maintain a different set of settings for each user, so instead it's useful to assemble users into groups that define certain permissions. These groups are called *roles*, and ASP.NET's membership features include tools for automatically creating a database with role information.

In this chapter, you'll explore all three of these feature areas and see how you can create secure sites with surprisingly little code.

The Membership Data Store

The key membership feature is the ability of ASP.NET to store user credentials in a database. The idea is that you make a few choices about the information that will be stored and the security policy that will be used. From that point on, ASP.NET manages the user database for you—adding new user information, checking credentials when users try to log in, and so on.

Clearly, the membership data store has the ability to greatly reduce the amount of code you need to write. You can create a secure website with much less code and, hence, much less work. You also don't need to worry about inevitable bugs, because the ASP.NET membership module is a well-known, carefully tested component.

So, why *wouldn't* you want to use the membership data store? A few possible reasons exist:

You don't want to store your data in a database: In theory, you can store your user list in any type of data store, from an XML file to an Oracle database. Technically, each data store requires a different membership provider. However, ASP.NET includes only two providers—the SQL Server provider you'll use in this chapter and a provider for Active Directory. If you want to use another data store, such as a different relational database, you'll need to find a corresponding membership, or you'll need to forgo membership altogether.

You need backward compatibility: If you've already created a table to store user information, it may be too much trouble to switch over to the membership data store. That's because the SQL Server membership provider expects a specific table structure. It won't work with existing tables, because they'll have a subtly different combination of fields and data types. And even if you don't need to keep the current table structure, you might find it's just too much work to re-create all your user records in the membership data store.

You want to manage user information in non-ASP.NET applications: As you'll see in this chapter, ASP.NET gives you a powerful set of objects for interacting with membership data. For example, you can update user records, delete user records, retrieve user records based on certain criteria, and so on. However, if you're creating another application outside ASP.NET that needs to perform these tasks, you might find it's not as easy, because you'll need to understand the membership table structure. In this case, you may find that it's easier to manage users with straight SQL statements that work with your own user table.

If you decide not to use the membership data store, it's up to you to write ADO.NET code to retrieve user records and check user credentials. Using these techniques, you can create your own login pages the hard way, as explained in Chapter 20.

Before continuing any further, you should set up your website to use forms authentication by adding the <forms> tag. Here's what you need to add:

```
<configuration>
    <system.web>
        ...
        <authentication mode="Forms" />
    </system.web>
    ...
</configuration>
```

Optionally, you can define additional details such as the location of the login page and the time before the security cookie times out, as described in Chapter 20. You may also want to add an authorization rule that prevents anonymous users from accessing a specific page or subfolder so you can better test your website security.

Membership with SQL Server 2005 Express

Assuming you do decide to use membership, you need to create the membership database. If you're using SQL Server 2005 Express Edition, the task is a lot easier than you might expect. In fact, it all happens automatically.

By default, membership is enabled for every new website you create. The default membership provider makes the following assumptions:

- You want to store your membership database using SQL Server 2005 Express.
- SQL Server 2005 Express is installed on the current computer, with the instance name SQLEXPRESS.
- Your membership data store will be a file named aspnetdb.mdf, which will be stored in the App_Data subfolder in your web application directory.

These assumptions make a lot of sense. They allow you to create as many web applications as you want while still keeping the user databases separate. That's because each website will have its own aspnetdb.mdf file. These files are never registered in SQL Server, which means when you open a connection in another application, you won't see dozens of user databases. Instead, the only way to connect to them is to specify the file path in the connection string, which ASP.NET does.

Another advantage of this setup is that it's potentially easier to deploy your website. Assuming the web server where you'll deploy your application has SQL Server 2005 Express, you won't need to change the connection string. You also don't need to perform any extra steps to install the database—you simply copy the aspnetdb.mdf file with your website. If the target server is using the full version of SQL Server 2005, your application will still work, provided the default connection string in the machine.config file has been adjusted accordingly. You still won't need to worry about installing the database manually. This is clearly a great advantage for large web hosting companies, because it's otherwise quite complex to support multiple websites, each with its own custom database that needs to be installed and maintained.

To see how this works, it helps to create a new web project with a simple test page. Drag the CreateUserWizard control onto your page from the Login section of the Toolbox. Now run the page (shown in Figure 21-1), without adding any code or configuring the control.

Fill in all the text boxes with user information. Note that by default you need to supply a password that includes at least one character that isn't a number or a letter (such as an underscore or an asterisk) and is at least seven characters long. Once you've filled in all the information, click Create User.

At this point, the CreateUserWizard control uses the ASP.NET Membership class behind the scenes to create a new user. The default membership provider creates the aspnetdb.mdf file (if it doesn't exist already) and then adds the new user record. Once this process is complete, the CreateUserWizard control shows a message informing you that the user was created. Miraculously, all of this takes place automatically even though you haven't configured anything in the web.config file and you didn't create the database file in advance.

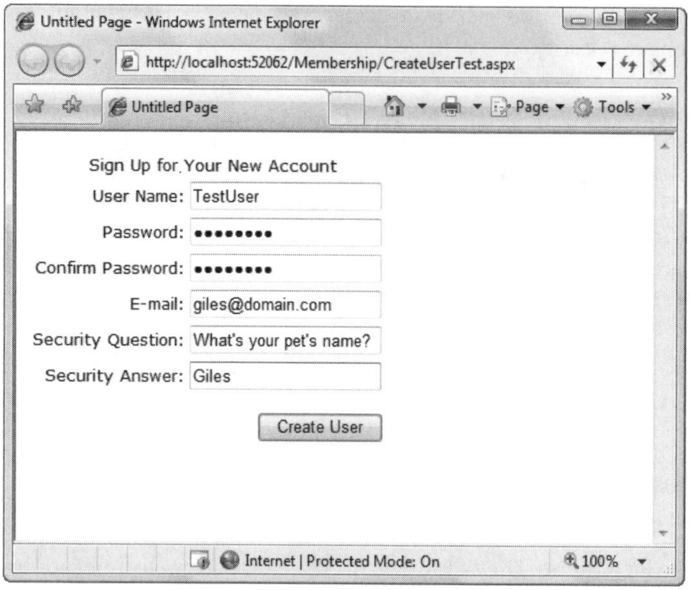

Figure 21-1. *The CreateUserWizard control*

To reassure yourself that the user really was created, you can check for the aspnetdb.mdf file. In the Solution Explorer, right-click the App_Data folder, and select Refresh Folder. You'll see the aspnetdb.mdf file appear immediately. Using Visual Studio, you can even dig into the contents of the aspnetdb.mdf file. To do so, double-click the file in the Solution Explorer. Visual Studio will configure a new connection and add it to the Server Explorer on the left. Using the Server Explorer, you can roam freely through the database, examining its tables and stored procedures.

Check the aspnet_Users table to find the user record you created. Just right-click the table name, and choose Show Table Data. You'll see something like the record shown in Figure 21-2. Among other details, you'll find a randomly generated GUID that uniquely identifies the user and the date the user last used your web application. You won't see the password and password question—that's stored in a linked record in the aspnet_Membership table, and it's encrypted to prevent casual snooping.

■ **Note** At first glance, you'll find the membership database includes a dizzying number of tables. Some of these tables are for other related features you may or may not use, such as role-based security (discussed later in the "Role-Based Security" section) and profiles (discussed in Chapter 21).

Before diving into the rest of ASP.NET's membership features in detail, it's important to consider what you should do if you don't want the default membership data store. For example, you might decide to store your membership tables in a different database, or you might want to configure one of the many options for the membership provider. You'll learn how to do so in the next two sections.

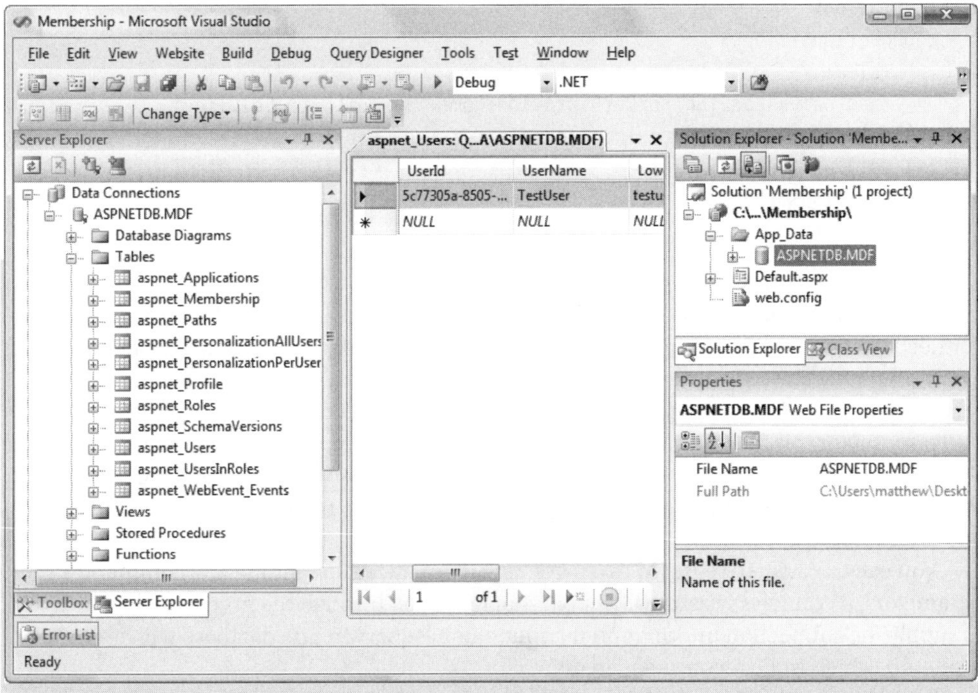

Figure 21-2. *A user record in the aspnetdb.mdf database*

Using the Full Version of SQL Server

If you're using the automatically generated database for SQL Server 2005 Express, you don't need to touch the web.config file. In any other case, you'll need to do a bit of configuration tweaking.

The simplest case is if you're using the full version of SQL Server 2005 (or another supported version, such as SQL Server 2000 or SQL Server 2008). In this case, you can still use the default membership settings. However, you need to change the connection string.

■ **Tip** The default membership settings and local connection string are set in the machine.config file. You can take a look at this file (and even edit it to update the settings for all web applications on your computer). Look in the c:\Windows\Microsoft.NET\Framework\v2.0.50727\Config directory.

The default connection string that's used with membership is named LocalSqlServer. You can edit this setting directly in the machine.config. However, if you just need to tweak it for a single application, it's better to adjust the web.config file for your web application. First, you need to remove all the existing connection strings using the <clear> element. Then, add the LocalSqlServer connection string—but this time with the right value:

```
<configuration>
    <connectionStrings>
        <clear />
        <add name="LocalSqlServer" providerName="System.Data.SqlClient"
connectionString="Data Source=localhost;Integrated Security=SSPI;
Initial Catalog=aspnetdb" />
    </connectionStrings>
    ...
</configuration>
```

This <connectionStrings> section removes all connection strings and then creates a new connection string. This new connection string connects to a database named aspnetdb on the local computer. The only catch is that the aspnetdb database won't be created automatically. Instead, you'll need to generate it with the aspnet_regsql.exe command-line tool. Rather than hunt around for this file, the easiest way to launch it is to fire up the Visual Studio command prompt (open the Start menu and choose Programs ➤ Microsoft Visual Studio 2008 ➤ Visual Studio Tools ➤ Visual Studio 2008 Command Prompt). You can then type in commands that use aspnet_regsql.

You can use aspnet_regsql in two ways. If you use it without adding any command-line parameters, a Windows wizard will appear that leads you through the process. You'll be asked to supply the connection information for your database server. The database will be named aspnetdb, which is the recommended default.

Your other option is to specify exactly what you want to happen using command-line switches. This is particularly useful when deploying your application—you can use aspnet_regsql as part of a setup batch file, which will then create the membership data store automatically. This is the option you'll use if you want to choose the database name or if you want to install only some of the database tables. By default, the aspnet_regsql tool installs tables that can be used for user authentication, role-based authorization, profiles, and Web Parts personalization. This gives you maximum flexibility, but you may feel it's overkill if you aren't planning to use some of these features.

Table 21-1 describes the most important command-line options. Here's an example command line that connects to an unnamed SQL Server instance on the current computer (using the -S parameter), connects with the current Windows account (using the -E parameter), installs all tables (using the -A *all* parameter), and places them all in a database named aspnetdb (which is the default):

```
aspnet_regsql -S (local) -E -A all
```

If you want to use a different database, you must specify the database name using the -d parameter.

■ **Tip** It's a good idea to install all the tables at once (using the –A *all* option). This way, your database will be ready for the profile feature discussed in the next chapter. Once you've finished testing your application and you're ready to create the final database, you can create a database that only has the options you've decided to use. (For example, use –A *mr* to use membership and role management but nothing else.)

Table 21-1. *Command-Line Switches for aspnet_regsql.exe*

Switch	Description
-S ServerName	Specify the location of the SQL Server instance where you want to install the database.
-E	Connects to the server through Windows authentication, using the currently logged-in Windows account.
-U UserName and -P Password	Specify the user name and password you need to connect to the SQL Server database. Usually, you'll use -E instead.
-A	Specifies the features you want to use (and determines the database tables that are created). Valid options for this switch are all, m (membership), r (role-based security), p (profiles), c (Web Part personalization), and w (for database cache dependencies with SQL Server 2000).
-R	Removes the databases that support the features specified by the -A switch.
-d DatabaseName	Allows you to specify the name of the database in which the tables will be created. If you don't specify this parameter, a database named aspnetdb is created automatically.
-sqlexportonly	Creates SQL scripts for adding or removing the specified features to the database, but doesn't actually create the tables in the database. Instead, you can run the script afterward. This can be a useful technique when deploying your application.

■ **Note** If you're deploying your website to a web hosting company, you probably won't be allowed to run aspnet_regsql on the web server. Instead, you'll probably need to use SQL Server Express. In this case, your database will be deployed in the App_Data folder as part of your web application, and no extra configuration steps will be required. If your web host doesn't support SQL Server Express, you'll need to use a tool like SQL Server Management Studio to prepare a .sql script file that installs your database. The administrators at the web hosting company can then run your script file to create the database you need.

Configuring the Membership Provider

Configuring the connection string is the simplest change you can make when setting up the membership data store. However, you may also want to tweak other membership settings. For example, you can change the default password policy.

■ **Note** As with the connection string, the default membership provider is defined in the machine.config file. You can edit the machine.config file to change these defaults for all applications on the computer, but you shouldn't, because it will complicate your life when you deploy the application. Instead, you should make the changes by configuring a new membership provider in your application's web.config file.

To configure your membership provider, you need to add the <membership> element to your web application. Inside the <membership> element, you define a new membership provider with your custom settings. Then, you set the defaultProvider attribute of the <membership> element so it refers to your membership provider by name.

Here's the basic structure you need to follow:

```
<configuration>
    <system.web>
        <membership defaultProvider="MyMembershipProvider">
            <providers>
                <!-- Clear any existing providers. -->
                <clear />

                <!-- Define your provider, with custom settings. -->
                <add name="MyMembershipProvider" ... />
            </providers>
        </membership>
        ...
    </system.web>
    ...
</configuration>
```

Of course, the interesting part is the attributes you use in the <add> tag to configure your membership provider. Here's an example that defines a membership provider with relaxed password settings. The first three attributes supply required settings (the name, type, and connection string for the membership provider). The remaining settings remove the requirement for a security question and allow a password to be as short as one character and contain only letters:

```
<membership defaultProvider="MyMembershipProvider">
    <providers>
        <clear/>
        <add
          name="MyMembershipProvider"
          type="System.Web.Security.SqlMembershipProvider"
          connectionStringName="LocalSqlServer"
          requiresQuestionAndAnswer="false"
          minRequiredPasswordLength="1"
          minRequiredNonalphanumericCharacters="0" />
      </providers>
</membership>
```

Table 21-2 describes the most commonly used membership settings.

Table 21-2. *Attributes for Configuring a Membership Provider*

Attribute	Description
name*	Specifies a name for the membership provider. You can choose any name you want. This is the name you use later to reference the provider (for example, when you set the defaultProvider attribute). You can also use it to get provider information programmatically.
type*	Specifies the type of membership provider. In this chapter, you will always be using the System.Web.Security.SqlMembershipProvider. ASP.NET also includes an ActiveDirectoryMembershipProvider, which allows you to use the membership features with Windows authentication through an Active Directory server. (For more information on this topic, consult the Visual Studio Help.) Finally, you can use a custom membership provider that you or a third-party developer creates.
applicationName	Specifies the name of the web application. This setting is primarily useful if you have several web applications using the same membership database. If you give each one a separate application name, all the information (including user, profiles, and so on) is completely separated so it's usable only in the appropriate application.
connectionStringName*	Specifies the name of the connection string setting. This must correspond to a connection string defined in the <connectionStrings> section of web.config or machine.config.
description	Allows an optional description for the membership provider.
passwordFormat	Sets the way passwords are stored in the database. You can use Clear (passwords are stored as is, with no encryption), Encrypted (passwords are encrypted using a computer-specific key), or Hashed (passwords are hashed, and the hash value is stored in the database). Hashing passwords offers similar protection to encrypting them (namely, if you look at the hash you'll have a difficult time reverse-engineering the password). However, when passwords are hashed, they can never be retrieved—only reset. If you decide to use encryption, you'll need to create a unique encryption key for your web application. You do this by adding the <machineKey> element to the <system.web> section of your web.config file. To help you out, you can use an online tool (like the one at `http://www.developmentnow.com/articles/machinekey_generator.aspx`), which can create a suitable <machineKey> element complete with randomly generated keys.

Table 21-2. *Attributes for Configuring a Membership Provider (Continued)*

Attribute	Description
minRequiredPasswordLength	Specifies the minimum length of a password. If the user enters fewer characters when creating an account, the attempt will be rejected with an error message.
minRequiredNonalphanumericCharacters	Specifies the number of nonalphanumeric characters (characters other than numbers and letters) the password needs to have. If the user enters fewer of these characters when creating an account, the attempt will be rejected with an error message. Although requiring nonalphanumeric characters makes for stronger (less guessable) passwords, it also can confuse users, causing them to forget their passwords more often or (worse) write them down in a conspicuous place, where they might be stolen.
maxInvalidPasswordAttempts	Specifies the number of times a user is allowed to enter an invalid password for their login before the user account is locked and made inaccessible. The default is five attempts.
passwordAttemptWindow	Sets the internal time in which maxInvalidPasswordAttempts is measured. For example, if you set a window of 30 minutes, after 30 minutes the number of invalid password attempts is reset. If the user surpasses the maxInvalidPasswordAttempts within passwordAttemptWindow, the account is locked.
enablePasswordReset	Determines whether a password can be reset, which is useful if a password is forgotten.
enablePasswordRetrieval	Determines whether a password can be requested (and e-mailed to the user), which is useful if a user forgets a password. This feature is never supported if passwordFormat is set to Hashed, because the password isn't stored in that case.
requiresQuestionAndAnswer	Determines whether the membership security answer will be required when you request or reset a user password.
requiresUniqueEmail	If false, allows more than one user to have the same e-mail address. The e-mail address information is always optional.

* *This setting is required.*

Now that you've seen the settings you can tweak, it's worth asking what the defaults are. If you look at the <membership> section in the machine.config file, here's what you'll find:

```
<membership>
    <providers>
        <add name="AspNetSqlMembershipProvider"
            type="System.Web.Security.SqlMembershipProvider ..."
            connectionStringName="LocalSqlServer"
            enablePasswordRetrieval="false"
            enablePasswordReset="true"
            requiresQuestionAndAnswer="true"
            applicationName="/"
            requiresUniqueEmail="false"
            passwordFormat="Hashed"
            minRequiredPasswordLength="7"
            minRequiredNonalphanumericCharacters="1"
            passwordAttemptWindow="10"
            maxInvalidPasswordAttempts="5" />
    </providers>
</membership>
```

As you can see, the default membership provider is AspNetSqlMembershipProvider. It connects using the LocalSqlServer connection string and supports password resets but not password retrieval. Accounts require a security question but not a unique e-mail. The passwords themselves are hashed in the database for security, so they can't be retrieved. Passwords must be at least seven characters long with at least one nonalphanumeric character. Finally, if a user makes five invalid password attempts in 10 minutes, the account is disabled.

Creating Users with the WAT

Once you've created the membership data store and (optionally) configured the membership provider, you're ready to use membership-backed security in your web application. As you've already seen, you can create new users with the CreateUserWizard control. You'll consider the CreateUserWizard control and the other security controls later in this chapter. First, it's worth considering your other options for setting up your user list.

One option is to use the WAT. Choose Website ➤ ASP.NET Configuration to launch this tool. Next, click the Security tab. In the bottom-left corner, a box indicates how many users are currently in the database (see Figure 21-3). This box also provides links that allow you to examine the existing user records or add new ones.

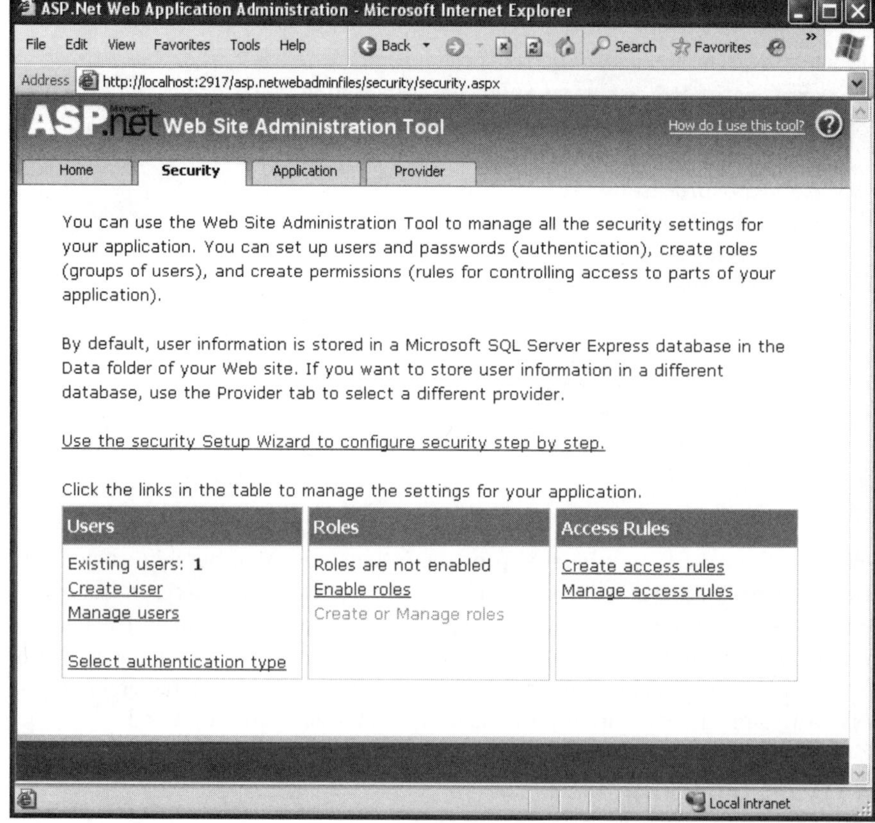

Figure 21-3. *Managing website security with the WAT*

If you want to browse the current user list or update an existing user record, click the Manage Users link. To add new users, click Create User. You'll see a set of controls that are similar to the CreateUserWizard control used in the test page earlier (see Figure 21-4). After you've created a few users, you may want to take another look at the aspnet_Users and aspnet_Membership tables in your database to see what the user records look like.

Although the WAT is a perfectly sensible way to add user records, you might find the web interface is a little sluggish if you have a large number of users to create. Another option is to use the Membership class, as shown here:

```
' Create a user record based with user name, password, and e-mail information.
Membership.CreateUser(userName, password, email)
```

Here's an example with hard-coded values:

```
Membership.CreateUser("joes", "ignreto12__", "joes@domains.com")
```

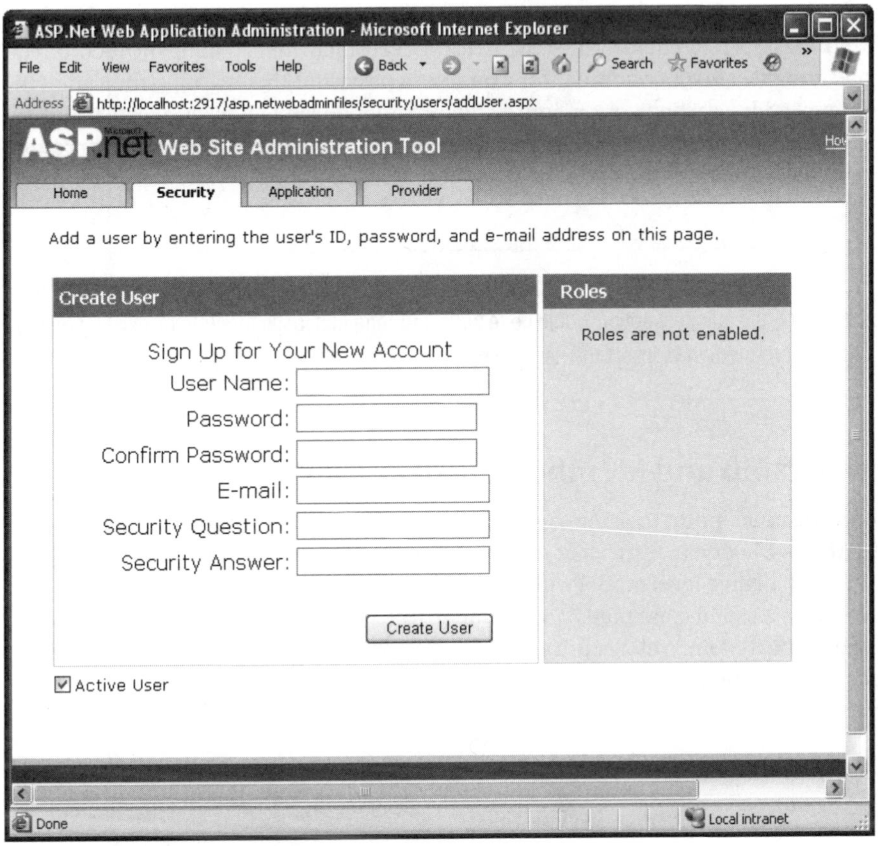

Figure 21-4. *Creating a new user*

This creates a new user with just a single line of code. Of course, the CreateUser() method has multiple overloads, which you can use to supply details such as the password question and answer. If you haven't changed the default membership settings, you won't be able to create an account unless you provide these details. Instead, you'll need to use this more complex overload:

```
Dim createStatus As MembershipCreateStatus
Membership.CreateUser("joes", "ignreto12__", "joes@domains.com", _
  "What is your favorite restaurant?", "Saigon", True, createStatus)
```

The first few parameters are self-explanatory—they take the user name, password, e-mail address, password question, and password answer. The second-to-last parameter takes a Boolean value that determines whether the account is given the IsApproved flag. If you supply False, the account won't be approved, and so it won't be active (and usable) until you modify it using the Membership.UpdateUser() method. In the simpler overload that doesn't include this parameter, accounts are always marked as approved.

The last parameter *returns* a value from the MembershipCreateStatus enumeration. If this value isn't MembershipCreateStatus.Success, an error occurred when creating the record. The value indicates the exact error condition (for example, a password that wasn't strong enough, a duplicate e-mail address when your membership provider doesn't allow duplicates, and so on). In the simpler overload that doesn't include the MembershipCreateStatus, any error results in an exception object being thrown that has the same information.

■ **Tip** Clearly, if you needed to transfer a large number of user accounts from a custom database into the membership data store, the quickest option would be to write a routine that loops through the existing records and use the CreateUser() method to insert the new ones.

The Membership and MembershipUser Classes

There wouldn't be much point to using the membership data store if you still needed to write handcrafted ADO.NET code to retrieve or modify user information. That's why ASP.NET offers a more convenient, higher-level model with the Membership class.

Membership is a useful class that's full of practical shared methods such as CreateUser(). You can find it in the System.Web.Security namespace. Table 21-3 provides a snapshot of its most useful shared methods.

Table 21-3. *Membership Methods*

Method	Description
CreateUser()	Adds a new user to the database.
DeleteUser()	Deletes an existing user from the database. You specify the user by the user name. You can also choose whether you want to delete all related data in other tables (the default is to remove it).
GetUser()	Gets a specific user from the database, by user name.
GetUserNameByEmail()	Retrieves a user name for the user that matches a given e-mail address. Keep in mind that duplicate e-mail addresses are allowed by default, in which case this method will find only the first match.
FindUsersByName()	Gets users from the membership database that match a given user name. This supports partial matches, so User will match TestUser, User001, and so on.
FindUsersByEmail()	Gets users from the membership database that match a specific e-mail address. You can also supply part of an e-mail address (such as the domain name), in which case you'll get every user who has an e-mail address that contains this text.
GetAllUsers()	Gets a collection that represents all the users in the database. An overloaded version of this method allows you to get just a portion of the full user list (a single page of users, based on a starting index and length).

Table 21-3. *Membership Methods*

Method	Description
GetNumberOfUsersOnline()	Gets the number of logged-in users currently accessing an application. This calculation assumes a user is online if that user's last activity time stamp falls within a set time limit (such as 20 minutes).
GeneratePassword()	Generates a random password of the specified length. This is useful when programmatically creating new user records.
UpdateUser()	Updates the database with new information for a specific user.
ValidateUser()	Tests whether the supplied user name and password are valid.

The Membership class also provides shared read-only properties that let you retrieve information about the configuration of your membership provider, as set in the configuration file. For example, you can retrieve the required password length, the maximum number of password attempts, and all the other details described in Table 21-2.

Many of these methods use the MembershipUser class, which represents a user record. For example, when you call GetUser(), you receive the information as a MembershipUser object. If you want to update that user, you can change its properties and then call Membership.UpdateUser() with the modified MembershipUser object.

■ **Note** The MembershipUser object combines the details from the aspnet_Users table and the linked aspnet_Membership table. For example, it includes the password question. However, the password answer and the password itself aren't available.

The MembershipUser class also provides its own smaller set of instance methods. The most important ones are detailed in Table 21-4.

Table 21-4. *Membership User Methods*

Method	Description
UnlockUser()	Reactivates a user account that was locked out for too many invalid login attempts.
GetPassword()	Retrieves a user password. If requiresQuestionAndAnswer is true in the membership configuration (which is the default), you must supply the answer to the password question in order to retrieve a password. Note that this method won't work at all if the passwordFormat setting is Hashed, which is also the default.

Table 21-4. *Membership User Methods (Continued)*

Method	Description
ResetPassword()	Resets a user password using a new, randomly generated password, which this method returns. If requiresQuestionAndAnswer is true in the membership configuration (which is the default), you must supply the answer to the password question in order to reset a password. You can display the new password for the user or send it in an e-mail.
ChangePassword()	Changes a user password. You must supply the current password in order to apply a new one.
ChangePasswordQuestionAndAnswer()	Changes a user password question and answer. You must supply the current password in order to change the security question.

To get a sense of how the Membership class works, you can create a simple test page that displays a list of all the users in the membership database. Figure 21-5 shows this page.

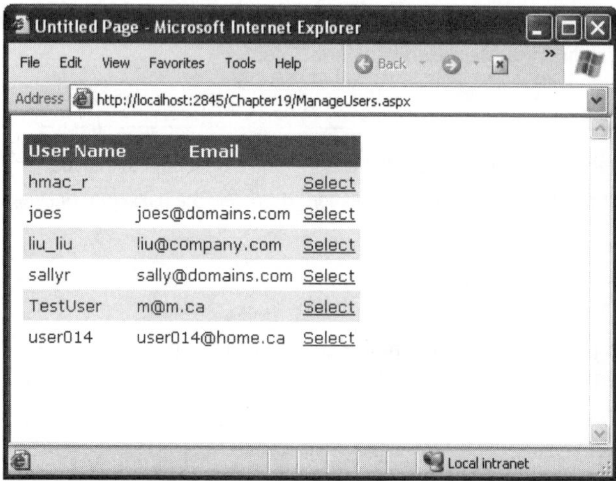

Figure 21-5. *Getting a list of users*

To create this page, you simply need to begin by defining the GridView. The GridView will show a list of MembershipUser objects. For each user, it shows the values from the UserName and Email properties, along with a Select link. Here's the markup that creates the GridView (without the formatting details):

```
<asp:GridView ID="gridUsers" runat="server"

  AutoGenerateColumns="False" DataKeyNames="UserName" >
        <Columns>
        <asp:BoundField DataField="UserName" HeaderText="User Name" />
        <asp:BoundField DataField="Email" HeaderText="Email" />
        <asp:CommandField ShowSelectButton="True" />
    </Columns>
</asp:GridView>
```

When the page is first loaded, it calls the Membership.GetAllUsers() method and binds the results to the GridView, as shown here:

```
Protected Sub Page_Load(ByVal sender As Object, _
  ByVal e As System.EventArgs) Handles Me.Load

    gridUsers.DataSource = Membership.GetAllUsers()
    gridUsers.DataBind()
End Sub
```

To make the example more interesting, when a record is selected, the corresponding MembershipUser object is retrieved. This object is then added to a collection so it can be bound to the DetailsView for automatic display:

```
Protected Sub gridUsers_SelectedIndexChanged(ByVal sender As Object, _
  ByVal e As System.EventArgs) Handles gridUsers.SelectedIndexChanged

    Dim list As New List(Of MembershipUser)()
    list.Add(Membership.GetUser(gridUsers.SelectedValue.ToString()))
    detailsUser.DataSource = list
    detailsUser.DataBind()
End Sub
```

Here's the DetailsView that does the work (again, without the formatting details):

```
<asp:DetailsView ID="detailsUser" runat="server"></asp:DetailsView>
```

This DetailsView uses automatic row creation (because AutoGenerateRows defaults to True). As a result, the DetailsView shows all the MembershipUser properties.

Figure 21-6 shows the information that's available in a single record. Among other details, you can use the MembershipUser object to check whether a user is online, when they last accessed the system, and what their e-mail address is.

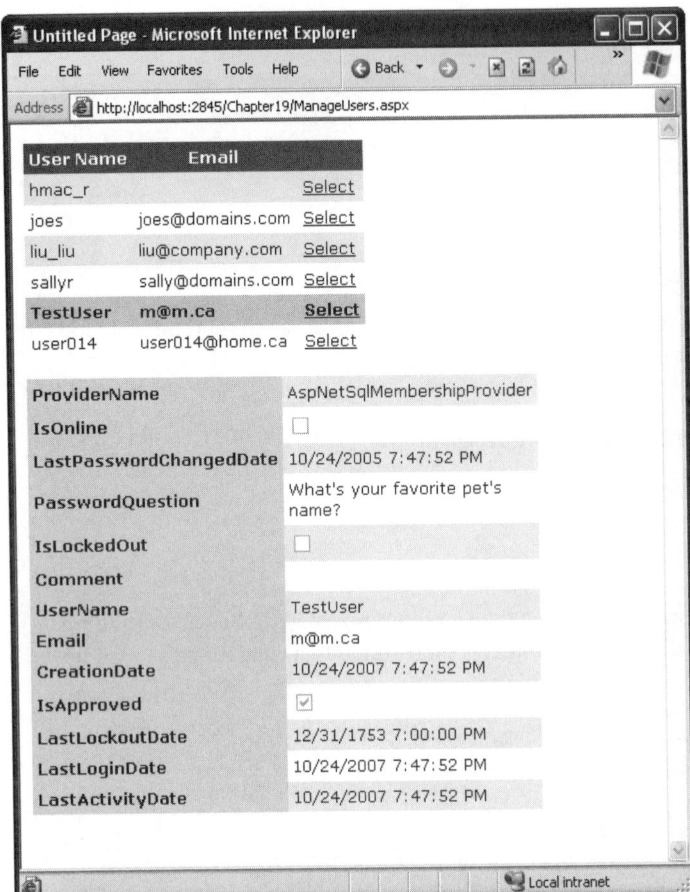

Figure 21-6. *The information in a MembershipUser object*

Authentication with Membership

Now that you've switched to membership, and all your users are stored in the membership data store, you need to change the way your login page works. Life now gets a lot simpler—rather than create ADO.NET objects to query a database and see whether a matching user record exists, you can let the Membership class perform all the work for you. The method you need is Membership.ValidateUser(). It takes a user name and password and returns True if there's a valid match in the database.

Here's the new code you need in your login page:

```
Protected Sub cmdLogin_Click(ByVal sender As Object, _
  ByVal e As EventArgs) Handles cmdLogin.Click

    If Membership.ValidateUser(txtName.Text, txtPassword.Text) Then
        FormsAuthentication.RedirectFromLoginPage(txtName.Text, False)
```

```
    Else
        lblStatus.Text = "Invalid username or password."
    End If
End Sub
```

Actually, a fair bit of work is taking place behind the scenes. If you're using the default membership provider settings, passwords are hashed. That means when you call ValidateUser(), ASP.NET hashes the newly supplied password using the same hashing algorithm and then compares it to the hashed password that's stored in the database.

Disabled Accounts

An account can become disabled in the membership database in two ways:

The account isn't approved: This occurs if you create an account programmatically and supply False for the isApproved parameter. You might take this step if you want to create an account automatically but allow an administrator to review it before it becomes live. To make this account active, you need to get a MembershipUser object for the corresponding user record, set MembershipUser.IsApproved to True, and call Membership.UpdateUser().

The account is locked out: This occurs if the user makes multiple attempts to access a user account with an invalid password. In this case, you need to get a MembershipUser object for the user, and call MembershipUser.UnlockUser(). You may also want to call MembershipUser.ResetPassword() to prevent another lockout.

To help you with these tasks, you might want to create an administrative page like the one shown in Figure 21-6. For example, you can allow a user to review all accounts that aren't yet approved and approve them by clicking a button.

Similarly, if you want to disable an account at any time, you can retrieve a MembershipUser object for that user and set the IsApproved property to False. However, you have no way to programmatically lock a user account.

You're probably already thinking of a wide range of pages you can create using the Membership and MembershipUser classes. For example, you can build pages that allow users to request a password reset or check whether they are locked out. However, you might not need to create all these pages, because ASP.NET includes a rich set of security controls that automate many common tasks. You'll learn more about the security controls in the next section.

The Security Controls

The basic membership features are a remarkable time-saver. They allow you to concentrate on programming your web application, without worrying about managing security and crafting the perfect database or user information. Instead, you can use the higher-level Membership and MembershipUser classes to do everything you need.

However, the ASP.NET membership feature doesn't stop there. Not only does the Membership class simplify common security tasks, it also standardizes them. As a result, other components and controls can use the Membership class to integrate themselves with the ASP.NET security model, without worrying about the specifics of each web application. You can find the best example of this new flexibility in ASP.NET's security controls. These controls interact with the membership provider using the methods of the Membership and MembershipUser classes to implement common bits of user interfaces such as a login page, a set of user creation controls, and a password recovery wizard.

Table 21-5 lists all the ASP.NET security controls that work with membership. In Visual Studio, you can find these controls in the Login section of the Toolbox.

Table 21-5. *Security Controls*

Control	Description
Login	Displays the familiar user name and password text boxes, with a login button.
LoginStatus	Shows a login button, if the user isn't already logged in, that redirects the user to the configured login page. Otherwise, it displays a sign-out button. You can choose the test used for the login and sign-out buttons, but that's about it.
LoginName	Displays the user name of the logged-in user.
LoginView	Displays different content depending on whether the user is logged in. You can even use this control to show different content for different groups of users, or *roles*.
PasswordRecovery	Allows the user to request a password via e-mail or reset it. Typically, the user must supply the answer to the security question to get the password.
ChangePassword	Allows the user to set a new password (as long as the user can supply the current password).
CreateUserWizard	Allows a user to create a new record, complete with e-mail address and a password question and answer.

There is a simple way and a complex way to use most of these controls. At their simplest, you merely drop the control on a page, without writing a line of code. (You saw this approach with the CreateUserWizard control at the beginning of this chapter.) You can also modify properties, handle events, and even create templates to customize these controls.

In the following sections, you'll take a closer look at the Login, PasswordRecovery, and CreateUserWizard controls. And later, in the "Role-Based Security" section, you'll put the LoginView control to work to show different content to users in different roles.

The Login Control

So far, the secure websites you've seen have used handmade login pages. In many websites this is what you'll want—after all, it gives you complete control to adjust the user interface exactly the way you want it. However, a login page is standard, so it makes sense for ASP.NET to give developers some extra shortcuts that can save them work.

Along these lines, ASP.NET includes a Login control that pairs a user name and a password text box with a login button. The Login control also adds a few features:

- It includes validator controls that prevent the page from being posted back until a user name and password have been entered. These validators use client-side validation if it's supported by the browser (with the help of a bit of JavaScript) and server-side validation, as described in Chapter 10.
- It automatically handles the signing in and redirection process when the user logs in successfully. If invalid login credentials are entered, it shows an error message.
- It provides a Remember Me check box that, if selected, stores a persistent cookie that remains indefinitely on the user's computer; therefore, the user doesn't need to log back in at the beginning of each visit.

In other words, if the basic Login control is right for your needs (it gives the user interface you want), you won't need to write a line of code.

To try this, drop the Login control onto a new page. Make sure this page is named Login.aspx so it's used as the default login page for forms authentication (or edit the <forms> tag to choose a different login page, as explained in the previous chapter). Then, run the page. You'll see the basic interface shown in Figure 21-7.

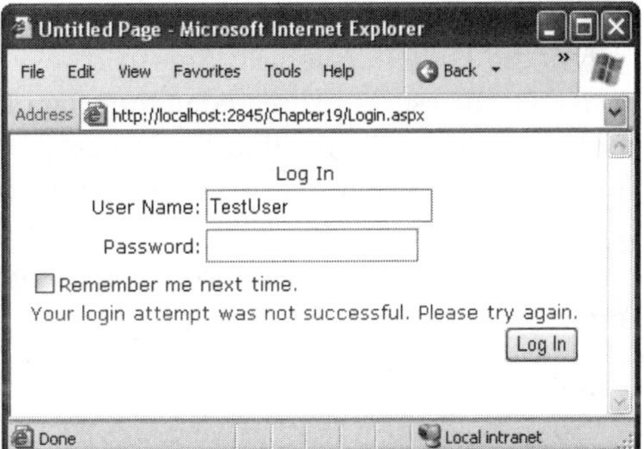

Figure 21-7. *The Login control and a failed login attempt*

Although the Login control takes care of the login process for you automatically, you can step in with your own custom code. To do so, you must react to one of the Login control events, as listed in Table 21-6.

Table 21-6. *Events of the Login Control*

Event	Description
LoggingIn	Raised before the user is authenticated.
LoggedIn	Raised after the user has been authenticated by the control.
LoginError	Raised when the login attempt fails (for example, if the user enters the wrong password).
Authenticate	Raised to authenticate the user. If you handle this event, it's up to you to supply the login code—the Login control won't perform any action.

The LoggingIn, LoggedIn, and LoginError events are primarily useful if you want to update other controls to display certain information based on the login process. For example, after the first login failure, you might choose to show a link that redirects the user to a password retrieval page:

```
Protected Sub Login1_LoginError(ByVal sender As Object, _
  ByVal e As EventArgs) Handles Login1.LoginError

    lblStatus.Text = "Have you forgotten your password?"
    lnkRedirectToPasswordRetrieval.Visible = True
End Sub
```

The Authenticate event is the most important event. It allows you to write your own authentication logic, as you did in the previous chapter. This is typically useful in two situations. First, you might want to supplement the default checking in the Login control with other requirements (for example, prevent any users from logging in at specific times of day, allow users to log in only if they've entered information in another control, and so on). The other reason you might handle the Authenticate event is if you aren't using the membership provider at all. In this case, you can still use the Login control, as long as you provide the authentication logic.

In the Authenticate event handler, you can check the user name and password using the UserName and Password properties of the Login control. You then set the Authenticated property of the AuthenticateEventArgs to True or False. If True, the LoggedIn event is raised next, and then the user is redirected to the Login.DestinationPageUrl (or the original page the user came from if the DestinationPageUrl property is not set). If you set Authenticated to False, the LoginError event is raised next, and the control displays the error message defined by the Login.FailureText property.

Here's an event handler for the Authenticated event that uses the membership classes directly:

```
Protected Sub Login1_Authenticate(ByVal sender As Object, _
  ByVal e As AuthenticateEventArgs) Handles Login1.Authenticate

    If Membership.ValidateUser(Login1.UserName, Login1.Password) Then
        e.Authenticated = True
    Else
        e.Authenticated = False
    End If
End Sub
```

That covers everything you need to know about interacting with the Login control, but you can tweak many properties to configure the appearance of the Login control. There's even an Auto Format link you can choose from the Properties window (or the smart tag) to give the Login control a face-lift with a single click.

The most powerful formatting properties for the Login control are style properties, which allow you to tweak fonts, coloring, and alignment for individual parts of the control. You've already seen styles at work with several other controls, including the Calendar (Chapter 11) and the GridView (Chapter 17), and they work in the same way with the security controls. Table 21-7 details the style properties of the Login control.

Table 21-7. *Style Properties of the Login Control*

Style	Description
TitleTextStyle	Defines a style for the title text of the Login control.
LabelStyle	Defines the style for the Username and Password labels.
TextBoxStyle	Defines the style for the user name and password text boxes.
LoginButtonStyle	Defines the style for the login button.
FailureTextStyle	Defines the style for the text displayed if the login attempt fails.
CheckBoxStyle	Defines the style properties for the Remember Me check box.
ValidatorTextStyle	Defines styles for RequiredFieldValidator controls that validate the user name and password information. These style properties tweak how the error text looks. (By default, the error text is simply an asterisk that appears next to the empty text box.)
HyperLinkStyle	Configures all the links that the Login control shows. This includes the links that let you create a new user record, retrieve a password, and so on. These links appear only if you've set the CreateUserUrl and PasswordRecoveryUrl properties.
InstructionTextStyle	Formats the Login.InstructionText, which is help instruction text you can add under the Login control. By default, the Login control has no instruction text.

Of course, styles aren't the only feature you can change in the Login control. You can adjust several properties to change the text it uses and to add links. For example, the following tag for the Login control adjusts the formatting and uses the CreateUserUrl and PasswordRecoveryUrl properties to add links to a page for registering a new user and another for recovering a lost password. (Obviously, you'll need to create both of these pages in order for the links to work.)

```
<asp:Login ID="Login1" runat="server" BackColor="#EFF3FB" BorderColor="#B5C7DE"
  BorderPadding="4" BorderStyle="Solid" BorderWidth="1px" Font-Names="Verdana"
  ForeColor="#333333" Height="256px" Width="368px"
  CreateUserText="Register for the first time"
  CreateUserUrl="Register.aspx"
  PasswordRecoveryText="Forgot your password?"
  PasswordRecoveryUrl="PasswordRecovery.aspx"
  InstructionText=
   "Please enter your username and password for logging into the system.">

    <TitleTextStyle BackColor="#507CD1" Font-Bold="True" Font-Size="Large"
      ForeColor="White" Height="35px" />
    <InstructionTextStyle Font-Italic="True" ForeColor="Black"  />
    <LoginButtonStyle BackColor="White" BorderColor="#507CD1"
      BorderStyle="Solid" BorderWidth="1px" Font-Names="Verdana"
      ForeColor="#284E98" />

</asp:Login>
```

Figure 21-8 shows the revamped Login control. Table 21-8 explains the other properties of the Login control.

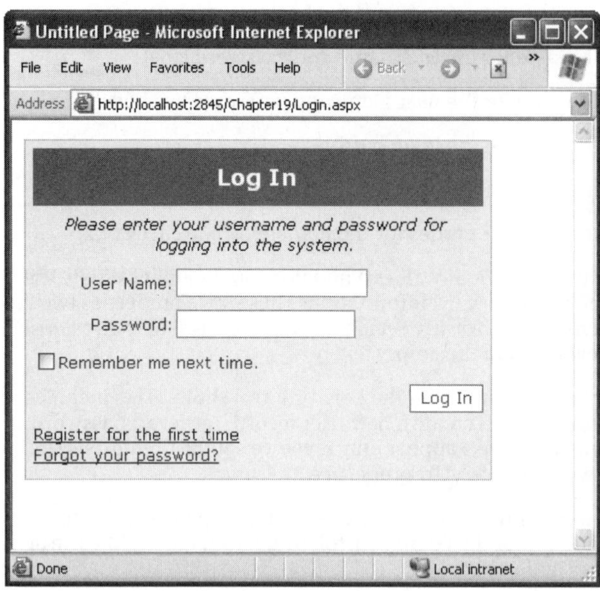

Figure 21-8. *A formatted Login control*

Table 21-8. *Useful Properties of the Login Control*

Property	Description
TitleText	The text that's displayed in the heading of the control.
InstructionText	The text that's displayed just below the heading but above the login controls. By default, the Login control has no instruction text.
FailureText	The text that's displayed when a login attempt fails.
UserNameLabelText	The text that's displayed before the user name text box.
PasswordLabelText	The text that's displayed before the password text box.
UsernameRequiredErrorMessage	The error message that's shown by the RequiredFieldValidator if the user doesn't type in a user name. By default, this is simply an asterisk (*).
PasswordRequiredErrorMessage	The error message that's shown by the RequiredFieldValidator if the user doesn't type in a password. By default, this is simply an asterisk (*).
LoginButtonText	The text displayed for the login button.
LoginButtonType	The type of button control that's used as the login button. It can be displayed as Link, Button, or Image.

Table 21-8. *Useful Properties of the Login Control*

Property	Description
LoginButtonImageUrl	The URL that points to the image you want to display for the login button. You must set the LoginButtonStyle property to Image to use this property.
DestinationPageUrl	The page to which the user is redirected if the login attempt is successful. This property is blank by default, which means the Login control uses the forms infrastructure and redirects the user to the originally requested page (or to the defaultUrl configured in web.config file).
DisplayRememberMe	Determines whether the Remember Me check box will be shown. You may want to remove this option to ensure stricter security, so malicious users can't gain access to your website through another user's computer.
RememberMeSet	Sets the default value for the Remember Me check box. By default, this option is set to False, which means the check box is not checked initially.
VisibleWhenLoggedIn	If set to False, the Login control automatically hides itself if the user is already logged in. If set to True (the default), the Login control is displayed even if the user is already logged in.
CreateUserUrl	Supplies a URL to a user registration page. This property is used in conjunction with the CreateUserText.
CreateUserText	Sets the text for a link to the user registration page. If this text is not supplied, this link is not displayed in the Login control.
CreateUserIconUrl	Supplies a URL to an image that will be displayed alongside the CreateUserText for the user registration link.
HelpPageUrl	Supplies a URL to a page with help information.
HelpPageText	Sets the text for the link to the help page. If this text is not supplied, this link is not displayed in the Login control.
HelpPageIconUrl	Supplies a URL to an image that will be displayed alongside the HelpPageText for the help page link.
PasswordRecoveryUrl	Supplies a URL to a password recovery page.
PasswordRecoveryText	Sets the text for the link to the password recovery page. If this text is not supplied, this link is not displayed in the Login control.
PasswordRecoveryIconUrl	Supplies a URL to an image that will be displayed alongside the PasswordRecoveryText for the password recovery page link.

To round out the example in Figure 21-8, you must create the Register.aspx and PasswordRecovery.aspx pages. In the next sections, you'll learn how you can do this easily using two more of the ASP.NET security controls.

The CreateUserWizard Control

You already used the CreateUserWizard control to create a basic user record at the beginning of this chapter. Now that you've seen the flexibility of the Login control, it should come as no surprise to learn that you have just as many options for tweaking the appearance and behavior of the CreateUserWizard control.

The CreateUserWizard control operates in two steps. The first step collects the user information that's needed to generate the user record. The second step displays a confirmation message once the account is created.

Overall, the CreateUserWizard provides a dizzying number of properties you can adjust. However, it helps to understand that really only three types of properties exist:

Style properties that format just a section of the control: For example, TitleTextStyle configures how the text heading is formatted.

Properties that set the text for the control: For example, you can configure each label, the success text, and the messages shown under different error conditions. You can also retrieve or set the values in each text box.

Properties that hide or show a part of the control: For example, you can use DisplaySideBar, DisplayCancelButton, and RequireEmail to show or hide the sidebar, cancel button, and e-mail text box, respectively.

The CreateUserWizard control also provides a familiar set of events, including CreatingUser, CreatedUser, and CreateUserError. Once again, these events are handy for synchronizing other controls on the page or for overriding the user creation process if you decide not to use the membership features.

■ **Tip** By default, newly created users are automatically logged in. You can change this behavior by setting the CreateUserWizard.LoginCreatedUser property to False. You can also set the ContinueDestinationPageUrl property to set the URL where the user should be redirected once the new record is created.

Interestingly enough, the CreateUserWizard control inherits from the Wizard control you explored in Chapter 11. As a result, you can add as many extra steps as you want, just as you can with the Wizard control. These steps might perform other tasks, such as signing the user up to receive a regular newsletter. However, the actual user creation process must always take place in a single step.

For example, consider the markup for the basic CreateUserWizard (with style tags omitted):

```
<asp:CreateUserWizard ID="CreateUserWizard1" runat="server" ... >
    <WizardSteps>
        <asp:CreateUserWizardStep runat="server" Title="Create User">
        </asp:CreateUserWizardStep>
        <asp:CompleteWizardStep runat="server">
        </asp:CompleteWizardStep>
    </WizardSteps>
</asp:CreateUserWizard>
```

Essentially, the CreateUserWizard is a Wizard control that supports two specialized step types: a CreateUserWizardStep where the user information is collected and the user record is created, and a CompleteWizardStep where the confirmation message is shown.

The following example shows how you can add an ordinary WizardStep into this sequence. In this case, the extra step simply provides some additional options for the newly created user (namely, the choice to subscribe to automatic e-mail newsletters).

```
<asp:CreateUserWizard ID="CreateUserWizard1" runat="server"
 DisplaySideBar="True" ... >
    <WizardSteps>
        <asp:CreateUserWizardStep runat="server" Title="Create User">
        </asp:CreateUserWizardStep>

        <asp:WizardStep runat="server" Title="Subscribe">
            Would you like to sign up for the following newsletters?<br />
            <br />
            <asp:CheckBoxList ID="chkSubscription" runat="server">
                <asp:ListItem>MSN Today</asp:ListItem>
                <asp:ListItem>VB Planet</asp:ListItem>
                <asp:ListItem>The High-Tech Herald</asp:ListItem>
            </asp:CheckBoxList>
        </asp:WizardStep>

        <asp:CompleteWizardStep runat="server">
        </asp:CompleteWizardStep>
    </WizardSteps>
</asp:CreateUserWizard>
```

Figure 21-9 shows the first two steps. Notice that the sidebar appears (because the CreateUserWizard.DisplaySidebar property is set to True) to show the order of steps.

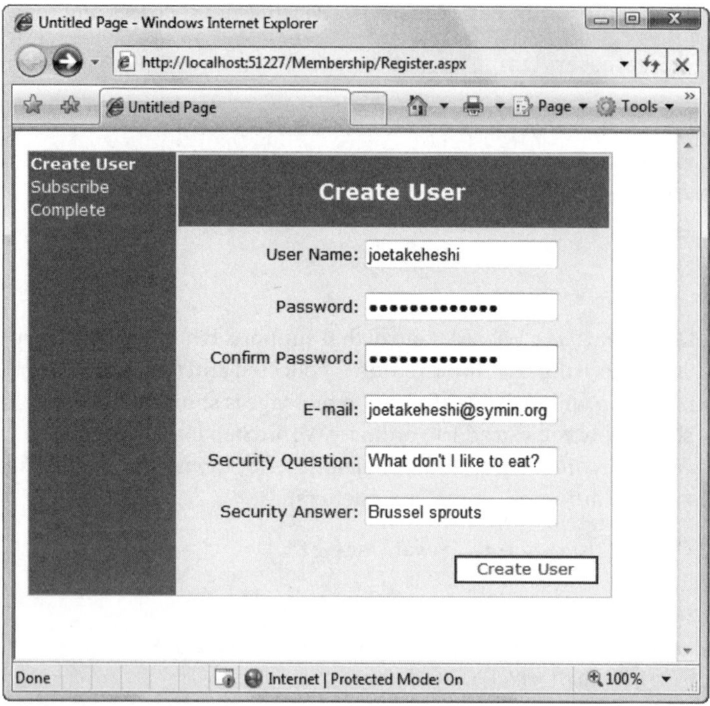

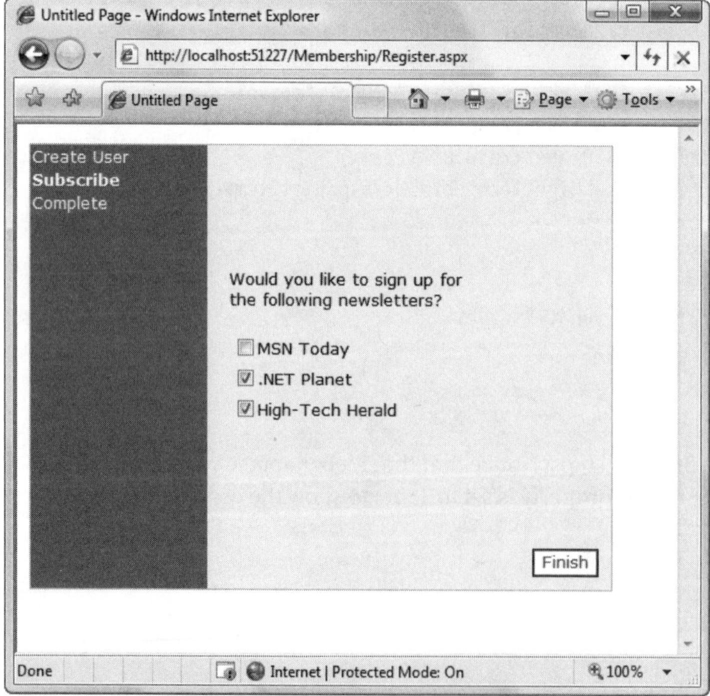

Figure 21-9. *A CreateUserWizard with a custom step*

It's still up to you to take the appropriate action in your code by reacting to one of the CreateUserWizard events. In this case, you use the FinishButtonClick event, because it occurs on the last step before the completion message. If you place your step earlier in the sequence, you'll need to react to NextButtonClick. In the current example, you might want to add this information to the user's profile table. You'll learn how to use profiles in the next chapter.

For complete layout and formatting power, you can convert one of the CreateUserWizard steps into a template. You're then free to rearrange the existing content and add new controls and HTML content. However, be careful not to remove any of the required elements. The CreateUserWizard will throw an exception if you try to use it but you're missing one of the required text boxes for account information.

The easiest way to convert a step into a template is to use the smart tag links. First, select the CreateUserControl on the design surface of your web page in Visual Studio. Next, click the arrow icon that appears next to the top-right corner to show the smart tag. Then, select the Customize Create User Step link or the Customize Complete Step link, depending on which step you want to modify. ASP.NET will then insert the controls into a template in the CreateUserWizard control tag.

For example, imagine you want to show the options the user selected in your custom step in the final summary. In this case, you might want to add a new Label control, as shown here:

```
<asp:CompleteWizardStep ID="CompleteWizardStep1" runat="server">
    <ContentTemplate>
        <table border="0" style="...">
            <tr>
                <td align="center" colspan="2" style="...">
                    Complete
                </td>
            </tr>
            <tr>
                <td>
                    Your account has been successfully created.<br /><br />
                    You subscribed to:
                    <asp:Label ID="lblSubscriptionList" runat="server">
                    </asp:Label>
                </td>
            </tr>
            <tr>
                <td align="right" colspan="2">
                    <asp:Button ID="ContinueButton" runat="server"
                     BackColor="White" BorderColor="#507CD1"
                     BorderStyle="Solid" BorderWidth="1px"
                     CausesValidation="False" CommandName="Continue"
                     Font-Names="Verdana" ForeColor="#284E98" Text="Continue"
                     ValidationGroup="CreateUserWizard1" />
                </td>
            </tr>
        </table>
    </ContentTemplate>
</asp:CompleteWizardStep>
```

Now, when the user moves to the last step, you can fill in the label with the information from the CheckBoxList control. However, because the Label and CheckBoxList controls are placed inside a template, you can't access them directly by name. Instead, you need to extract them from the CreateUserWizard control. To get the label, you need to access the complete step, grab the first control it contains (which is the content template), and then use the FindControl() method to search for the label. To get the CheckBoxList, you perform a similar operation, except you can use the FindControl() method of the CreateWizardControl itself, which searches all ordinary steps.

Here's the code that performs this task:

```
Protected Sub CreateUserWizard1_FinishButtonClick(ByVal sender As Object, _
  ByVal e As System.Web.UI.WebControls.WizardNavigationEventArgs) _
  Handles CreateUserWizard1.FinishButtonClick

    Dim lbl, chk As Control
    lbl = CreateUserWizard1.CompleteStep.Controls(0).FindControl( _
        "lblSubscriptionList")
    chk = CreateUserWizard1.FindControl("chkSubscription")

    Dim selection As String = ""
    For Each item As ListItem in CType(chk, CheckBoxList).Items
        If item.Selected Then
            selection &= "<br />" & item.Text
        End If
    Next
    CType(lbl, Label).Text = selection
End Sub
```

Figure 21-10 shows the final step.

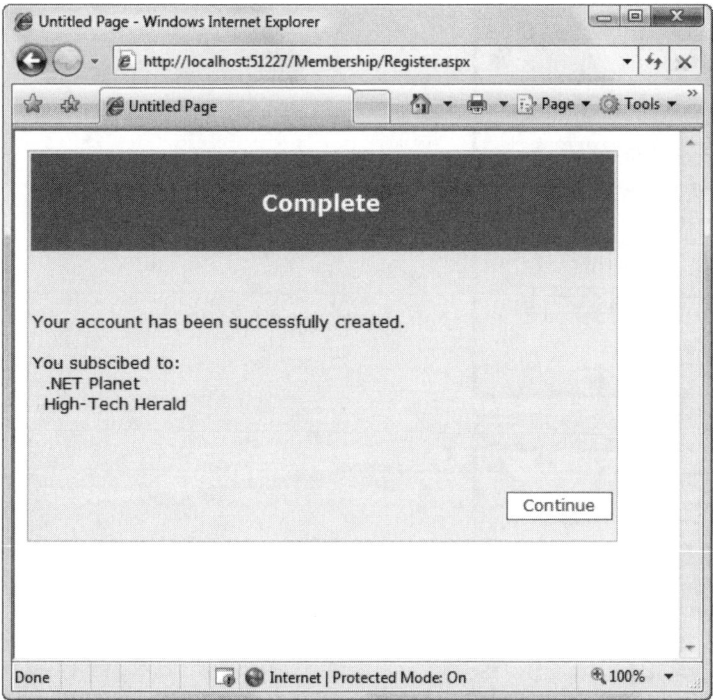

Figure 21-10. *Enhancing the complete step with extra content*

The PasswordRecovery Control

The PasswordRecovery control comes in handy when users forget their passwords. It allows them to retrieve their password using a short wizard.

The PasswordRecovery control leads the user through three steps. First, it requests the user name. Next, it shows the security questions and requests the answer. Finally, if the correct answer is provided, the PasswordRecovery sends an e-mail to the user's e-mail address. If you use a password format of Encrypted or Clear (refer to Table 21-2), the e-mail contains the original password. If you are using the default password format Hashed, a new random password is generated, and that password is sent in the e-mail. Either way, the last step shows a confirmation message informing you that the e-mail was sent. Figure 21-11 shows the PasswordRecovery control in action.

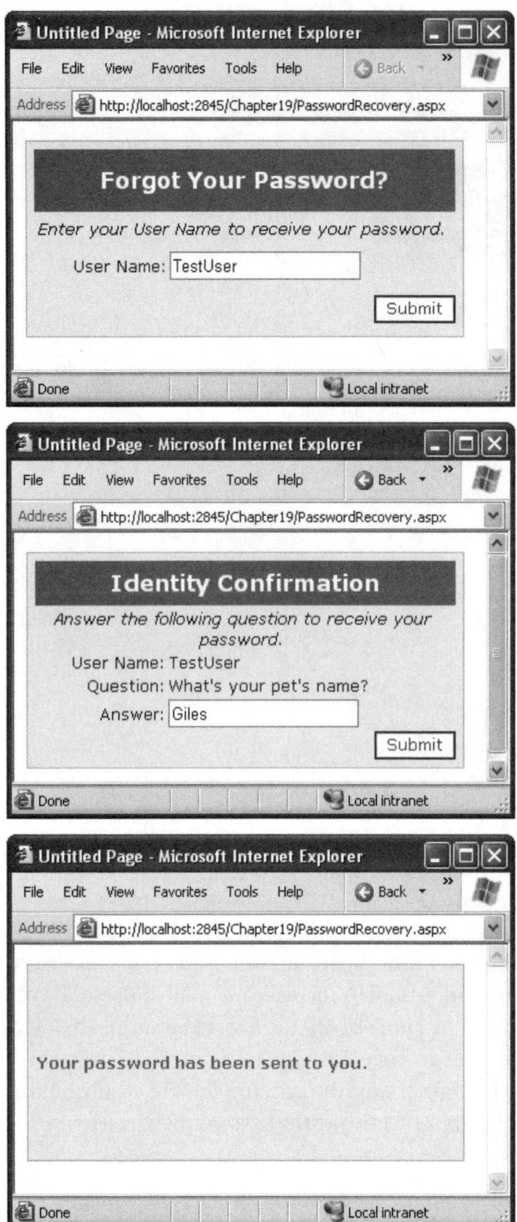

Figure 21-11. *Requesting a password*

For the PasswordRecovery control to do its work, your computer must have a correctly configured SMTP server, and the user must have an e-mail address in the user record.

■Note You can configure your SMTP server by selecting the PasswordRecovery control and choosing Administer Website from the smart tag. Then, choose the Application tab, and click the Configure SMTP E-mail Settings link.

If your application doesn't meet these two requirements—you can't send e-mail messages, or users aren't guaranteed to have an e-mail address—you can display the new password directly in the page. The easiest approach is to handle the PasswordRecovery.SendingMail event. First, set the MailMessageEventArgs.Cancel property to True to prevent the message from being sent. Next, you can retrieve the message content from the MailMessageEventArgs.Message object and display it on the page. Here's an example:

```
Protected Sub PasswordRecovery1_SendingMail(ByVal sender As Object, _
  ByVal e As System.Web.UI.WebControls.MailMessageEventArgs) _
  Handles PasswordRecovery1.SendingMail

    e.Cancel = True
    PasswordRecovery1.SuccessText = e.Message.Body
End Sub
```

When you use this event handler, you'll see a final step like the one shown in Figure 21-12.

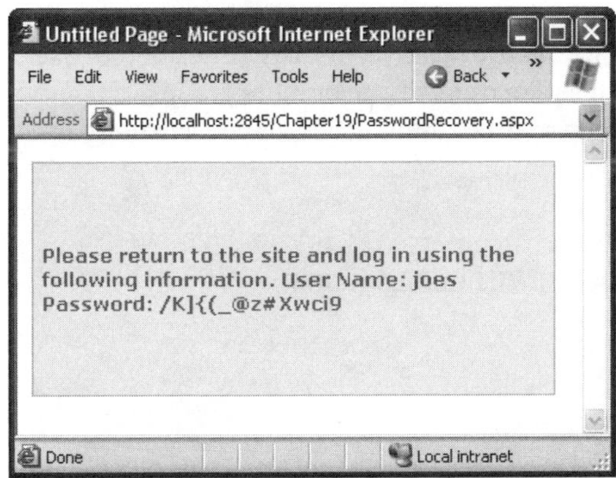

Figure 21-12. *Displaying the retrieved or regenerated password*

Of course, for complete flexibility you can create your own page that resets passwords. You just need to use the methods of the Membership and MembershipUser classes described earlier.

Role-Based Security

The authentication examples you've examined so far provide an all-or-nothing approach that either forbids or allows a user. In many cases, however, an application needs to recognize different levels of users. Some users will be provided with a limited set of capabilities, and other users might be allowed to perform potentially dangerous changes or use the administrative portions of a website.

To allow this type of multitiered access, you need ASP.NET's role-based authorization feature. As with membership, ASP.NET takes care of storing the role information and making it available to your code. All you need to do is create the roles, assign users to each role, and then test for role membership in your code.

Before you can use role-based authorization, you need to enable it. Although you can perform this step using the WAT (just click the Enable Roles link in the Security tab), it's easy enough just to add the required line to your web.config file directly:

```
<configuration>
    <system.web>
        <roleManager enabled="true" />
        ...
    </system.web>
    ...
</configuration>
```

As with the membership data store, ASP.NET will automatically create the role information in the aspnetdb.mdf file using SQL Server 2005 Express. If you want to use a different database, you need to follow the steps discussed earlier in this chapter to create the database using aspnet_regsql.exe and modify the connection string.

Creating and Assigning Roles

Once you enable role management, you need to create a basic set of roles (for example, User, Administrator, Guest, and so on). You can then assign users to one or more groups.

You can create roles in two ways. You can do so programmatically, or you can do so by hand, using the WAT.

To use the WAT, follow these steps:

1. Launch the WAT by selecting Website ➤ ASP.NET Configuration.
2. Click the Security tab.
3. Click the Create or Manage Roles link.
4. To add a new role, type it into the provided text box, and click Add Role (see Figure 21-13). Or use the Manage and Delete links in the role list to modify or delete an existing role record.

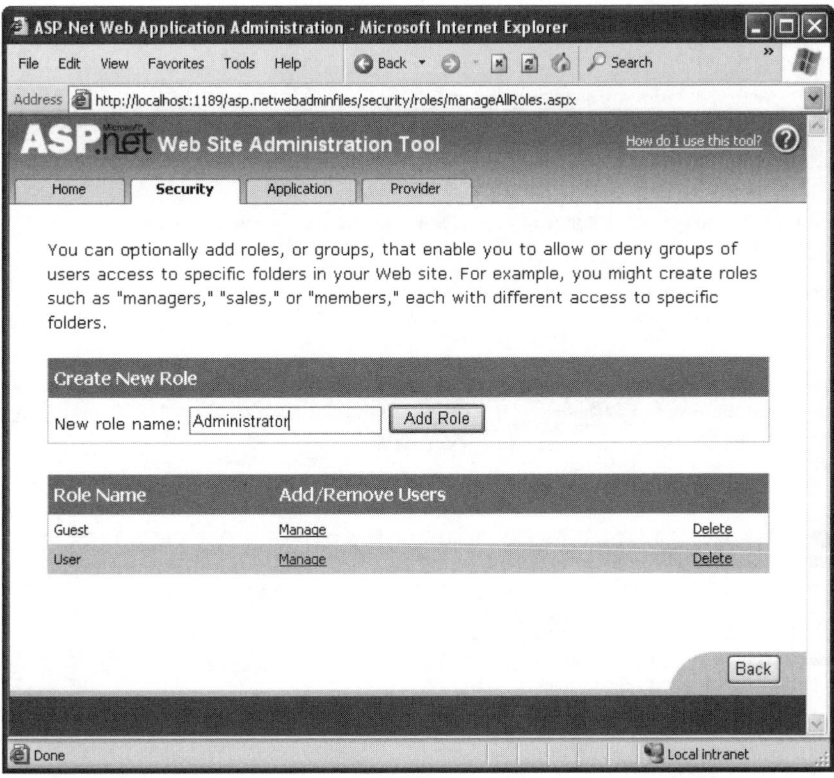

Figure 21-13. *Creating roles*

To place a user into a role, you'll need to head back to the main security page (click the Back button in the role management page). Then follow these steps:

1. Select Manage Users from the Security tab. You'll see the full list of users for your website (subdivided into pages).
2. Find the user you want to change, and click the Edit Roles link next to that user.
3. Fill in the check box for each role you want to assign to that user.

Figure 21-14 shows an example where the user joes is being given the User role.

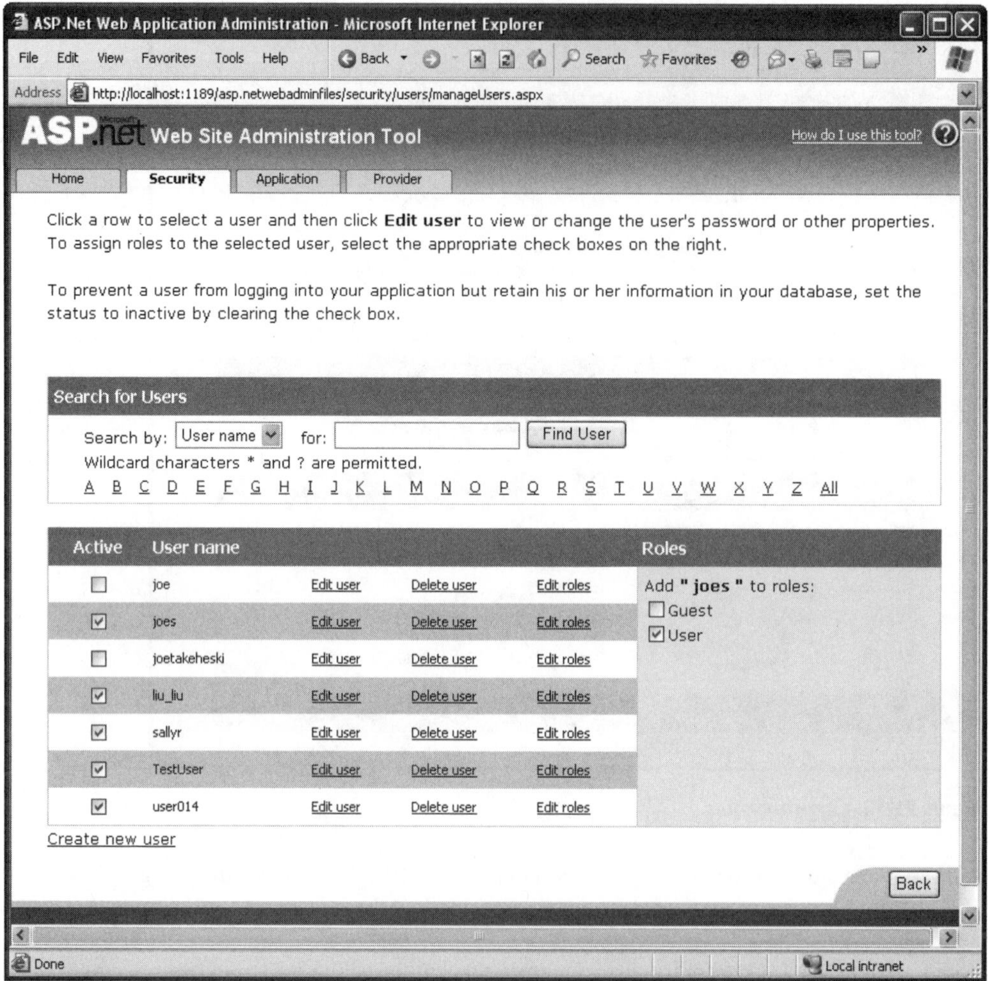

Figure 21-14. *Applying roles*

Of course, you don't need to use the WAT. You can also use the Roles class. The Roles class serves the same purpose for role management as the Membership class does for membership—it provides a number of shared utility methods that let you modify role information. Table 21-9 lists the methods you can use.

Table 21-9. *Methods of the Roles Class*

Method	Description
CreateRole()	Adds a new role to the database.
DeleteRole()	Deletes an existing role from the database.
RoleExists()	Checks whether a specific role name exists in the database.

Table 21-9. *Methods of the Roles Class*

Method	Description
GetAllRoles()	Retrieves a list of all the roles for this application.
AddUserToRole(), AddUserToRoles(), AddUsersToRole(), and AddUsersToRoles()	Assigns a role to a user, assigns several roles to a user at once, assigns a role to several users, or assigns several roles to several users. If you want to assign a role to a large number of users, the quickest approach is to use the Membership class to retrieve the corresponding user names (if needed), and then use the AddUsersToRole() or AddUsersToRoles() method of the Roles class to apply the change to everyone at once.
RemoveUserFromRole(), RemoveUserFromRoles(), RemoveUsersFromRole(),and RemoveUsersFromRoles()	Allow you to remove a user from a role. You can perform this operation on multiple users at once or remove a user from multiple roles at once, depending on which method you use.
IsUserInRole()	Checks whether a user is part of a specific role.
GetRolesForUser()	Retrieves all the roles for a specific user.
GetUsersInRole()	Retrieves all the users who are part of a specific role.
FindUsersInRole()	Retrieves all the users who are part of a specific role (much like GetUsersInRole()). However, it allows you to limit the results to users who have a specific piece of text in their user names.

For example, you could use the following event handler with the CreateUserWizard control to assign a newly created user into a specific role:

```
Protected Sub CreateUserWizard1_CreatedUser(ByVal sender As Object, _
  ByVal e As System.EventArgs) Handles CreateUserWizard1.CreatedUser

    Roles.AddUserToRole(CreateUserWizard1.UserName, "User")
End Sub
```

Restricting Access Based on Roles

Once you've created and assigned your roles, you need to adjust your application to take the role information into account. You can use several techniques:

- You can write authorization rules that specifically deny certain roles from specific pages or subfolders. You can write these rules by hand by adding the <authorization> section to your web.config file, or you can define them with the help of the WAT by clicking the Manage Access Rules link.
- You can use the User.IsInRole() method in your code to test whether the user belongs to a specific role and then decide whether to allow an action or show certain content accordingly.
- You can use the LoginView control to set different content for different roles.

You already learned how to use the first two techniques in the previous chapter. For example, you already know how to write web.config rules that restrict a specific group, like this:

```
<authorization>
    <deny users="?" />
    <deny roles="Guest" />
    <allow users="*" />

</authorization>
```

These rules deny all anonymous users and any users in the Guest role. Remember, a user may be part of more than one role, so the order of the <deny> tags matters. The first rule that matches determines whether the user is allowed or denied.

Similarly, you know how to use the User.IsInRole() method to make a programmatic authorization decision:

```
Protected Sub Page_Load(ByVal sender As Object, _
  ByVal e As System.EventArgs) Handles Me.Load

    lblMessage.Text = "You have reached the secured page, "
    lblMessage.Text &= User.Identity.Name & "."

    If User.IsInRole("Administrator") Then
        lblMessage.Text &= "<br /><br />Congratulations:"
        lblMessage.Text &= "you are an administrator."
    End If
End Sub
```

The only remaining technique to consider is the LoginView control.

The LoginView Control

The LoginView is a view control like the Panel or MultiView control you learned about in Chapter 11. The difference is that the user doesn't choose which view is used. Instead, the view is set based on the authentication status of the user.

The simplest way to use the LoginView is to show separate content for authenticated and anonymous users. To use this design, you simply fill some content in the <AnonymousTemplate> and <LoggedInTemplate> sections of the control. Here's an example:

```
<asp:LoginView ID="LoginView1" runat="server">
    <AnonymousTemplate>
        <h1>You are anonymous</h1>
         Why don't you <a href="Login.aspx">log in</a>?
    </AnonymousTemplate>
    <LoggedInTemplate>
        <h1>You are logged in</h1>
        <p>You are now ready to see this super-secret content.</p>
    </LoggedInTemplate>
</asp:LoginView>
```

Figure 21-15 shows the two ways this control can appear, depending on whether the user is currently logged in.

Figure 21-15. *Showing different content with the LoginView*

■ **Tip** You can also react to the ViewChanging and ViewChanged events of the LoginView control to initialize your controls just before they become visible in the current view. This approach is faster than initializing all the controls every time the page is served.

The LoginView also supports one other tag—the RoleGroups tag. Inside the RoleGroups tag, you add one or more RoleGroup controls. Each role group is specifically mapped to one or more roles. In other words, when you use the RoleGroups template, you can show different content for authenticated users, depending to which role they belong.

Here's an example:

```
<asp:LoginView ID="LoginView1" runat="server">
    <AnonymousTemplate>
        <h1>You are anonymous</h1>
         Why don't you <a href="Login.aspx">log in</a>?
    </AnonymousTemplate>
    <RoleGroups>
        <asp:RoleGroup Roles="User, Guest">
            <ContentTemplate>
                <p>If you can see this, you are a member of the
                   User or Guest roles.</p>
            </ContentTemplate>
        </asp:RoleGroup>
        <asp:RoleGroup Roles="Administrator">
            <ContentTemplate>
                <p>Congratulations, you are an administrator.</p>
            </ContentTemplate>
        </asp:RoleGroup>
    </RoleGroups>
</asp:LoginView>
```

Remember, a user can belong to more than one role. However, only one template can display at a time. When matching the role to a RoleGroup, the LoginView control goes through the RoleGroup tags in order and uses the first match. If it can't find a match, it uses the ordinary <LoggedInTemplate>, if provided.

The LoginView is a fairly powerful control. It gives you an effective way to separate secure content from ordinary content declaratively—that is, without writing custom code to hide and show labels. This approach is clearer, more concise, and less error prone.

The Last Word

ASP.NET's membership features give you several high-level services that work with the basic form authentication and Windows authentication systems you learned about in Chapter 20.

In this chapter, you saw how to use membership to maintain a database of users, either with the free SQL Server 2005 Express Edition or with another version of SQL Server. You also learned how to use the prebuilt security controls, which give you a convenient and flexible way to add user management features and organize secure content. Finally, you considered how you can use role management in conjunction with membership to determine exactly what actions a user should—and shouldn't—be allowed to perform in your applications.

CHAPTER 22

■ ■ ■

Profiles

You can store information for the users of your website in a variety of ways. In Chapter 7, you learned how to use techniques such as view state, session state, and cookies to keep track of information for a short period of time. But if you need to store information between visits, the only realistic option is a server-side database. Using the ADO.NET skills you've learned so far, it's fairly easy to save information such as customer addresses and user preferences in a database and retrieve it later.

The only problem with the database approach is that it's up to you to write all the code for retrieving information and updating records. This code isn't terribly complex—Chapter 15 covers everything you need to know—but it can be tedious. ASP.NET includes a feature that allows you to avoid this tedium, if you're able to work within certain limitations. This feature is called *profiles*, and it's designed to keep track of user-specific information automatically.

When you use profiles, ASP.NET handles the unglamorous work of retrieving the information you need and updating the database when it changes. You don't need to write any ADO.NET code, or even design the appropriate database tables, because ASP.NET takes care of all the details. Best of all, the profiles feature integrates with ASP.NET authentication so the information for the currently logged-in user (referred to as that user's *profile*) is always available to your web page code.

The only drawback to the profiles feature is that it forces you to use a preset database structure. This prevents you from using tables you've already created to store user-specific details, and it poses a new challenge if you want to use the same information in other applications or reporting tools. If the locked-in structure is too restricting, your only choice is to create a custom profile provider that extends the profiles feature (which is a more challenging task outside the scope of this book) or forego profiles altogether and write your own ADO.NET code by hand.

In this chapter, you'll learn how to use profiles, how the profile system works, and when profiles make the most sense.

Understanding Profiles

One of the most significant differences between profiles and other types of state management is that profiles are designed to store information permanently, using a back-end data source such as a database. Most other types of state management are designed to maintain information for a series of requests occurring in a relatively short space of time (such as session state) or in the current browser session (such as view state and nonpersistent cookies) or to transfer information from one page to another (such as the query string and cross-page posting). If you need to store information for the longer term in a database, profiles simply provide a convenient model that manages the retrieval and persistence of this information for you.

Before you begin using profiles, you need to assess them carefully. In the following sections, you'll learn how they stack up.

Profile Performance

The goal of ASP.NET's profiles feature is to provide a transparent way to manage user-specific information, without forcing you to write custom data access code using the ADO.NET data classes. Unfortunately, many features that seem convenient suffer from poor performance or scalability. This is particularly a concern with profiles, because they involve database access, and database access can easily become a scalability bottleneck for any web application.

So, do profiles suffer from scalability problems? This question has no simple answer. It all depends on how much data you need to store and how often you plan to access it. To make an informed decision, you need to know a little more about how profiles work.

Profiles plug into the page life cycle in two ways:

- The first time you access the Profile object in your code, ASP.NET retrieves the complete profile data for the current user from the database. If you read the profile information more than once in the same request, ASP.NET reads it once and then reuses it, saving your database from unnecessary extra work.
- If you change any profile data, the update is deferred until the page processing is complete. At that point (after the PreRender, PreRenderComplete, and Unload events have fired for the page), the profile is written back to the database. This way, multiple changes are batched into one operation. If you don't change the profile data, no extra database work is incurred.

Overall, the profiles feature could result in two extra database trips for each request (in a read-write scenario) or one extra database trip (if you are simply reading profile data). The profiles feature doesn't integrate with caching, so every request that uses profile data requires a database connection.

From a performance standpoint, profiles work best when the following is true:

- You have a relatively small number of pages accessing the profile data.
- You are storing small amounts of data.

They tend to work less well when the following is true:

- You have a large number of pages needing to use profile information.
- You are storing large amounts of data. This is particularly inefficient if you need to use only some of that data in a given request (because the profile model always retrieves the full block of profile data).

Of course, you can combine profiles with another type of state management. For example, imagine your website includes an order wizard that walks the user through several steps. At the beginning of this process, you could retrieve the profile information and store it in session state. You could then use the Session collection for the remainder of the process. Assuming you're using the in-process or out-of-process state server to maintain session data, this approach is more efficient because it saves you from needing to connect to the database repeatedly.

How Profiles Store Data

The most significant limitation with profiles doesn't have anything to do with performance—instead, it's a limitation of how the profiles are serialized. The default profile provider included with ASP.NET serializes profile information into a block of data that's inserted into a single field in a database record. For example, if you serialize address information, you'll end up with something like this:

```
Marty Soren315 Southpart DriveLompocCalifornia93436U.S.A.
```

Another field indicates where each value starts and stops, using a format like this:

```
Name:S:0:11:Street:S:11:19:City:S:30:6:State:S:36:10:ZipCode:S:46:5:Country:S:51:6
```

Essentially, this string identifies the value (Name, Street, City, and so on), the way it's stored (S for string), the starting position, and the length. So the first part of this string

```
Name:S:0:11
```

indicates that the first profile property is Name, which is stored as a string, starts at position 0, and is 11 characters long.

Although this approach gives you the flexibility to store just about any combination of data, it makes it more difficult to use this data in other applications. You can write custom code to parse the profile data to find the information you want, but depending on the amount of data and the data types you're using, this can be an extremely tedious process. And even if you do this, you're still limited in the ways you can reuse this information. For example, imagine you use profiles to store customer address information. Because of the proprietary format, it's no longer possible to generate customer lists in an application such as Microsoft Word or perform queries that filter or sort records using this profile data. (For example, you can't easily perform a query to find all the customers living in a specific city.)

This problem has two solutions:

- Use your own custom ADO.NET code instead of profiles.
- Create a custom profile provider that's designed to store information using your database schema.

Of the two options, creating a custom data access component is easier, and it gives you more flexibility. You can design your data component to have any interface you want, and you can then reuse that component with other .NET applications. Currently, ASP.NET developers are more likely to use this approach because it has been around since .NET 1.0 and is well understood.

The second option is interesting because it allows your page to keep using the profile model. In fact, you could create an application that uses the standard profile serialization with the SqlProfileProvider and then switch it later to use a custom provider. To make this switch, you don't need to change any code. Instead, you simply modify the profile settings in the web.config file. As it becomes more common for websites to use the profiles features, custom profile providers will become more attractive.

■Note It's also important to consider the type of data that works best in a profile. As with many other types of state management, you can store any serializable types into a profile, including simple types and custom classes.

One significant difference between profiles and other types of state management is that profiles are stored as individual records, each of which is uniquely identified by user name. This means profiles require you to use some sort of authentication system. It makes no difference what type of authentication system you use (Windows, forms, or a custom authentication system)—the only requirement is that authenticated users are assigned a unique user name. That user name is used to find the matching profile record in the database.

■Note Later in this chapter (in the section "Anonymous Profiles"), you'll learn how the anonymous identification feature lets you temporarily store profile information for users who haven't logged in.

When deciding whether to use profiles, it's natural to compare the profiles feature with the kind of custom data access code you wrote in Chapter 15 (and the database components you'll learn to build in Chapter 23). Clearly, writing your own ADO.NET code is far more flexible. It allows you to store other types of information and perform more complex business tasks. For example, an e-commerce website could realistically use profiles to maintain customer address information (with the limitations discussed in the previous section). However, you wouldn't use a profile to store information about previous orders. Not only is it far too much information to store efficiently, it's also awkward to manipulate.

Using the SqlProfileProvider

The SqlProfileProvider allows you to store profile information in a SQL Server 7.0 (or later) database (including SQL Server 2005 Express Edition). You can choose to create the profile tables in any database. However, you can't change any of the other database schema details, which means you're locked into specific table names, column names, and serialization format.

From start to finish, you need to perform the following steps to use profiles:

1. Enable authentication for a portion of your website.
2. Configure the profile provider. (This step is optional if you're using SQL Server 2005 Express. Profiles are enabled by default.)
3. Create the profile tables. (This step isn't required if you're using SQL Server 2005 Express.)
4. Define some profile properties.
5. Use the profile properties in your web page code.

You'll tackle these steps in the following sections.

Enabling Authentication

Because profiles are stored in a user-specific record, you need to authenticate the current user before you can read or write profile information. You can use any type of authentication system, including Windows-based authentication and forms-based authentication. The profile system doesn't care—it simply stores the user-specific information in a record that's identified based on the user ID. Seeing as every authentication system identifies users uniquely by user ID, any authentication system will work.

The following web.config file uses Windows authentication:

```
<configuration>
  ...
  <system.web>
    <authentication mode="Windows"/>
    <authorization>
      <deny users="?"/>
    </authorization>
    ...
  </system.web>
</configuration>
```

Because this example uses Windows authentication, you don't need to create a record for each user. Instead, you'll use the existing Windows user accounts that are defined on the web server. This approach also saves you from creating a login page, because the browser handles the login process. (For more information about Windows authentication, refer to Chapter 20.)

If you decide to use forms authentication instead, you'll need to decide whether you want to perform the authentication using your own custom user list (Chapter 20) or in combination with the membership features (Chapter 21). In most cases, the membership and profiles features are used in conjunction—after all, if you're using the profiles feature to store user-specific information automatically, why not also store the list of user credentials (user names and passwords) automatically in the same database?

■ **Tip** The downloadable examples for this chapter show profiles in action in one site that uses forms authentication, and in another site that uses Windows authentication.

Once you've chosen your authentication system (and taken care of any other chores that may be necessary, such as creating a user list and generating your login page), you're ready to use profiles. Remember, profiles store user-specific information, so the user needs to be authenticated before their profile is available. In the web.config file shown previously, an authorization rule ensures this by denying all anonymous users.

Using the Full Version of SQL Server

In the previous chapter, you learned that no special steps are required to configure a web application to use membership with SQL Server 2005 Express. The same is true of profiles.

As with the membership details, profile information is stored in the automatically generated aspnetdb.mdf file. If this file doesn't exist, it's created the first time you use any membership or profiles features, and it's placed in the App_Data subdirectory of your web application. This automatic creation feature relies on SQL Server 2005 Express. If you're using a non-Express version of SQL Server, you'll need to modify the profile configuration and create the database you need manually.

By default, the connection string that is used with profiles is named LocalSqlServer. You can edit this connection string directly in the machine.config file. However, if you just need to tweak a single application, it's better to adjust the web.config file for your web application.

To do so, you need to remove all the existing connection strings using the <clear> element in your web application's web.config file. Then, add the LocalSqlServer connection string again—but this time with the right value:

```
<configuration>
    <connectionStrings>
        <clear />
        <add name="LocalSqlServer" providerName="System.Data.SqlClient"
connectionString="Data Source=localhost;Integrated Security=SSPI;
Initial Catalog=aspnetdb" />
    </connectionStrings>
    ...
</configuration>
```

This is the same process you used in Chapter 20, because both the membership feature and the profiles feature use the LocalSqlServer connection string. In this example, the new connection string is for the full version of SQL Server 2005. It uses a database named aspnetdb on the local computer.

You'll then need to create the aspnetdb database using the aspnet_regsql.exe command-line utility. This is the same tool that allows you to generate databases for other ASP.NET features, such as SQL Server–based session state, membership, roles, database cache dependencies, and Web Parts personalization. You can find the aspnet_regsql.exe tool in the c:\Windows\Microsoft.NET\Framework\v2.0.50727 folder.

To create the tables, views, and stored procedures required for profiles, you use the -A p command-line option. The other details you may need to supply include the server location (-S), database name (-d), and authentication information for connecting to the database (use -U and -P to supply a password and user name, or use -E to use the current Windows account). If you leave out the server location and database name, aspnet_regsql.exe uses the default instance on the current computer and creates a database named aspnetdb.

The easiest way to use aspnet_regsql is to open the Visual Studio command prompt. To do so, open the Start menu and choose Programs ➤ Microsoft Visual Studio 2008 ➤ Visual Studio Tools ➤ Visual Studio 2008 Command Prompt. The following example creates a database named aspnetdb in the SQL Server database server on the current computer:

```
aspnet_regsql.exe -S (local) -E -A all
```

If you want to use a different database, you must specify the database name using the -d parameter. Either way, you should use a new, blank database that doesn't include any other custom tables. That's because aspnet_regsql.exe creates several tables for profiles (see Table 22-1 in the next section), and you shouldn't risk confusing them with business data.

■ Note This command line uses the -A *all* option to create tables for all of ASP.NET's database features, including profiles and membership. You can also choose to add tables for just one feature at a time. For more information about -A and the other command-line parameters you can use with aspnet_regsql, refer to Table 21-2 in Chapter 21.

The Profile Databases

Whether you use aspnet_regsql to create the profile databases on your own or you use SQL Server 2005 and let ASP.NET create them automatically, you'll wind up with the same tables. Table 22-1 briefly describes them. (The rather unexciting views aren't included.)

If you want to look at the data in these tables, you can peer into this database in the same way that you peered into the membership database in Chapter 21. However, the contents aren't of much interest, because ASP.NET manages them automatically. All the information you store in a profile is combined into one record and quietly placed in a field named PropertyValuesString in a table named aspnet_Profile.

Table 22-1. *Database Tables Used for Profiles*

Table Name	Description
aspnet_Applications	Lists all the web applications that have records in this database. It's possible for several ASP.NET applications to use the same aspnetdb database. In this case, you have the option of separating the profile information so it's distinct for each application (by giving each application a different application name when you register the profile provider) or sharing it (by giving each application the same application name).
aspnet_Profile	Stores the user-specific profile information. Each record contains the complete profile information for a single user. The PropertyNames field lists the property names, and the PropertyValuesString and PropertyValuesBinary fields list all the property data, although you'll need to do some work if you want to parse this information for use in other non-ASP.NET programs. Each record also includes the last update date and time (LastUpdatedDate).
aspnet_SchemaVersions	Lists the supported schemas for storing profile information. In the future, this could allow new versions of ASP.NET to provide new ways of storing profile information without breaking support for old profile databases that are still in use.
aspnet_Users	Lists user names and maps them to one of the applications in aspnet_Applications. Also records the last request date and time (LastActivityDate) and whether the record was generated automatically for an anonymous user (IsAnonymous). You'll learn more about anonymous user support later in this chapter (in the section "Anonymous Profiles").

Figure 22-1 shows the relationships between the most important profile tables.

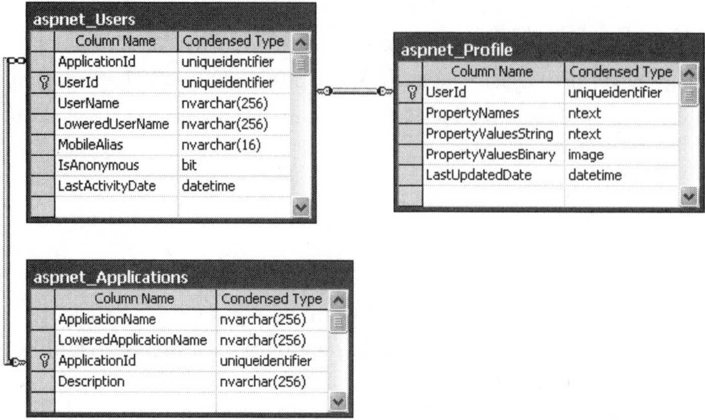

Figure 22-1. *The profile tables*

Defining Profile Properties

Before you can store any profile information, you need to specifically define what you want to store. You do this by adding the <properties> element inside the <profile> section of the web.config file. Inside the <properties> element, you place one <add> tag for each user-specific piece of information you want to store. At a minimum, the <add> element supplies the name for the property, like this:

```
<configuration>
  <system.web>
  ...
    <profile>
      <properties>
        <add name="FirstName"/>
        <add name="LastName"/>
      </properties>
    </profile>
  </system.web>
  ...
</configuration>
```

Usually, you'll also supply the data type. (If you don't, the property is treated as a string.) You can specify any serializable .NET data type, as shown here:

```
<add name="FirstName" type="System.String"/>
<add name="LastName" type="System.String"/>
<add name="DateOfBirth" type="System.DateTime"/>
```

You can set a few more property attributes to create the more advanced properties shown in Table 22-2.

Table 22-2. *Profile Property Attributes*

Attribute (for the <add> Element)	Description
name	The name of the property.
type	The fully qualified class name that represents the data type for this property. By default, this is System.String.
serializeAs	The format to use when serializing this value (String, Binary, Xml, or ProviderSpecific). You'll look more closely at the serialization model in the section "Profile Serialization."
readOnly	A Boolean value that determines whether a value is changeable. If true, the property can be read but not changed. (Attempting to change the property will cause a compile-time error.) By default, this is false.
defaultValue	A default value that will be used if the profile doesn't exist or doesn't include this particular piece of information. The default value has no effect on serialization—if you set a profile property, ASP.NET will commit the current values to the database, even if they match the default values.
allowAnonymous	A Boolean value that indicates whether this property can be used with the anonymous profiles feature discussed later in this chapter. By default, this is false.
provider	The profile provider that should be used to manage just this property. By default, all properties are managed using the provider specified in the <profile> element, but you can assign different properties to different providers.

Using Profile Properties

With these details in place, you're ready to access the profile information using the Profile property of the current page. When you run your application, ASP.NET creates a new class to represent the profile by deriving from System.Web.Profile.ProfileBase, which wraps a collection of profile settings. ASP.NET adds a strongly typed property to this class for each profile property you've defined in the web.config file. These strongly typed properties simply call the GetPropertyValue() and SetPropertyValue() methods of the ProfileBase base class to retrieve and set the corresponding profile values.

For example, if you've defined a string property named FirstName, you can set it in your page like this:

```
Profile.FirstName = "Henry"
```

Figure 22-2 presents a complete test page that allows the user to display the profile information for the current user or set new profile information.

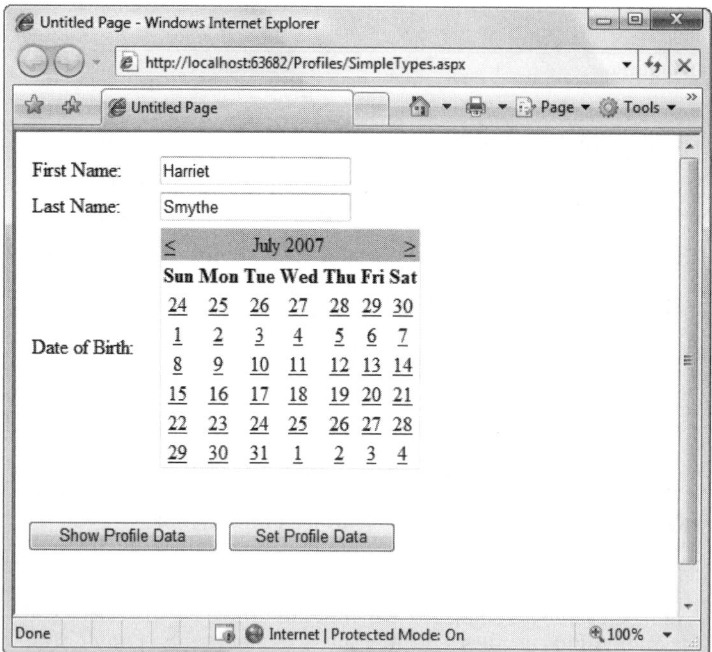

Figure 22-2. *Testing profile*

The first time this page runs, no profile information is retrieved, and no database connection is used. However, if you click the Show Profile Data button, the profile information is retrieved and displayed on the page:

```
Protected Sub cmdShow_Click(ByVal sender As Object, _
  ByVal e As System.EventArgs) Handles cmdShow.Click

    lbl.Text = "First Name: " & Profile.FirstName & "<br />" & _
      "Last Name: " & Profile.LastName & "<br />" & _
      "Date of Birth: " & Profile.DateOfBirth.ToString("D")
End Sub
```

At this point, an error will occur if the profile database is missing or the connection can't be opened. Otherwise, your page will run without a hitch, and you'll see the newly retrieved profile information. Technically, the complete profile is retrieved when your code accesses the Profile.FirstName property in the first line and is used for the subsequent code statements.

■ **Note** Profile properties behave like any other class member variable. This means if you read a profile value that hasn't been set, you'll get a default initialized value (such as an empty string or 0).

If you click the Set Profile Data button, the profile information is set based on the current control values:

```
Protected Sub cmdSet_Click(ByVal sender As Object, _
  ByVal e As System.EventArgs) Handles cmdSet.Click

    Profile.FirstName = txtFirst.Text
    Profile.LastName = txtLast.Text
    Profile.DateOfBirth = Calendar1.SelectedDate
End Sub
```

Now the profile information is committed to the database when the page request finishes. If you want to commit some or all of the information earlier (and possibly incur multiple database trips), just call the Profile.Save() method. As you can see, the profiles feature is unmatched for simplicity.

■ **Tip** The Profile object doesn't just include the properties you've defined. It also provides LastActivityDate and LastUpdatedDate properties with information drawn from the database.

Profile Serialization

Earlier, you learned how properties are serialized into a single string. For example, if you save a FirstName of Harriet and a LastName of Smythe, both values are crowded together in the PropertyValuesString field of the aspnet_Profile table in the database, like so:

```
HarrietSmythe
```

The PropertyNames field (also in the aspnet_Profile table) gives the information you need to parse each value from the PropertyValuesString field. Here's what you'll see in the PropertyNames field in this example:

```
FirstName:S:0:7:LastName:S:7:6:
```

The colons (:) are used as delimiters. The basic format is as follows:

```
PropertyName:StringOrBinarySerialization:StartingCharacterIndex:Length:
```

Something interesting happens if you create a profile with a DateTime data type. When you look at the PropertyValuesString field, you'll see something like this:

```
<?xml version="1.0" encoding="utf-16"?><dateTime>2007-07-12T00:00:00-04:00
</dateTime>HarrietSmythe
```

Initially, it looks like the profile data is serialized as XML, but the PropertyValuesString clearly doesn't contain a valid XML document (because of the text at the end). What has actually happened is that the first piece of information, the DateTime, is serialized (by default) as XML. The following two profile properties are serialized as ordinary strings.

The PropertyNames field makes it slightly clearer:

```
DateOfBirth:S:0:81:FirstName:S:87:7:LastName:S:94:6:
```

Interestingly, you have the ability to change the serialization format of any profile property by adding the serializeAs attribute to its declaration in the web.config file. Table 22-3 lists your choices.

Table 22-3. *Serialization Options*

SerializeAs	Description
String	Converts the type to a string representation. Requires a type converter that can handle the job.
Xml	Converts the type to an XML representation, which is stored in a string, using the System.Xml.XmlSerialization.XmlSerializer (the same class that's used with web services).
Binary	Converts the type to a proprietary binary representation that only .NET understands using the System.Runtime.Serialization.Formatters.Binary.Binary-Formatter. This is the most compact option but the least flexible. Binary data is stored in the PropertyValuesBinary field instead of the PropertyValues.
ProviderSpecific	Performs customized serialization that's implemented in a custom provider.

For example, here's how you can change the serialization for the profile settings:

```
<add name="FirstName" type="System.String" serializeAs="Xml"/>
<add name="LastName" type="System.String" serializeAs="Xml"/>
<add name="DateOfBirth" type="System.DateTime" serializeAs="String"/>
```

Now the next time you set the profile, the serialized representation in the PropertyValuesString field will store information for FirstName and LastName. It takes this form:

```
2007-06-27<?xml version="1.0" encoding="utf-16"?><string>Harriet</string>
<?xml version="1.0" encoding="utf-16"?><string>Smythe</string>
```

If you use the binary serialization mode, the property value will be placed in the PropertyValuesBinary field instead of the PropertyValuesString field. The only indication of this shift is the use of the letter *B* instead of *S* in the PropertyNames field. Here's an example where the FirstName property is serialized in the PropertyValuesBinary field:

```
DateOfBirth:S:0:9:FirstName:B:0:31:LastName:S:9:64:
```

All of these serialization details raise an important question—what happens when you change profile properties or the way they are serialized? Profile properties don't have any support for versioning. However, you can add or remove properties with relatively minor consequences. For example, ASP.NET will ignore properties that are present in the aspnet_Profile table but not defined in the web.config file. The next time you modify part of the profile, these properties will be replaced with the new profile information. Similarly, if you define a profile in the web.config file that doesn't exist in the serialized profile information, ASP.NET will just use the default value. However, more dramatic changes—such as renaming a property, changing its data type, and so on, are likely to cause an exception when you attempt to read the profile information.

Even worse, because the serialized format of the profile information is proprietary, you have no easy way to migrate existing profile data to a new profile structure.

■ **Tip** Not all types are serializable in all ways. For example, classes that don't provide a parameterless constructor can't be serialized in Xml mode. Classes that don't have the Serializable attribute can't be serialized in Binary mode. You'll consider this distinction when you contemplate how to use custom types with profiles (see the "Profiles and Custom Data Types" section), but for now just keep in mind that you may run across types that can be serialized only if you choose a different serialization mode.

Profile Groups

If you have a large number of profile settings, and some settings are logically related to each other, you may want to use profile groups to achieve better organization.

For example, you may have some properties that deal with user preferences and others that deal with shipping information. Here's how you could organize these profile properties using the <group> element:

```
<profile>
  <properties>
    <group name="Preferences">
      <add name="LongDisplayMode" defaultValue="true" type="Boolean" />
      <add name="ShowSummary" defaultValue="true" type="Boolean" />
    </group>
    <group name="Address">
      <add name="Name" type="String" />
      <add name="Street" type="String" />
      <add name="City" type="String" />
      <add name="ZipCode" type="String" />
      <add name="State" type="String" />
      <add name="Country" type="String" />
    </group>
  </properties>
</profile>
```

Now you can access the properties through the group name in your code. For example, here's how you retrieve the country information:

```
lblCountry.Text = Profile.Address.Country
```

Groups are really just a poor man's substitute for a full-fledged custom structure or class. For instance, you could achieve the same effect as in the previous example by declaring a custom Address class. You'd also have the ability to add other features (such as validation in the property procedures). The next section shows how.

Profiles and Custom Data Types

Using a custom class with profiles is easy. You need to begin by creating the class that wraps the information you need. In your class, you can use public member variables or full-fledged property procedures. The latter choice, though longer, is the preferred option because it ensures your class will support data binding, and it gives you the flexibility to add property procedure code later.

Here's a slightly abbreviated Address class that ties together the same information you saw in the previous example:

```
<Serializable()> _
Public Class Address

    Private _name As String
    Public Property Name() As String
        ...
    End Property

    Private _street As String
    Public Property Street() As String
        ...
    End Property

    Private _city As String
    Public Property City() As String
        ...
    End Property

    Private _zipCode As String
    Public Property ZipCode() As String
        ...
    End Property

    Private _state As String
    Public Property State() As String
        ...
    End Property

    Private _country As String
    Public Property Country() As String
        ...
    End Property
```

```
    Public Sub New(ByVal name As String, ByVal street As String, _
      ByVal city As String, ByVal zipCode As String, _
      ByVal state As String, ByVal country As String)

        Me.Name = name
        Me.Street = street
        Me.City = city
        Me.ZipCode = zipCode
        Me.State = state
        Me.Country = country
    End Sub

    Public Sub New()
    End Sub

End Class
```

You can place this class in the App_Code directory. The final step is to add a property that uses it:

```
<properties>
  <add name="Address" type="Address" />
</properties>
```

Now you can create a test page that uses the Address class. Figure 22-3 shows an example that simply allows you to load, change, and save the address information in a profile.

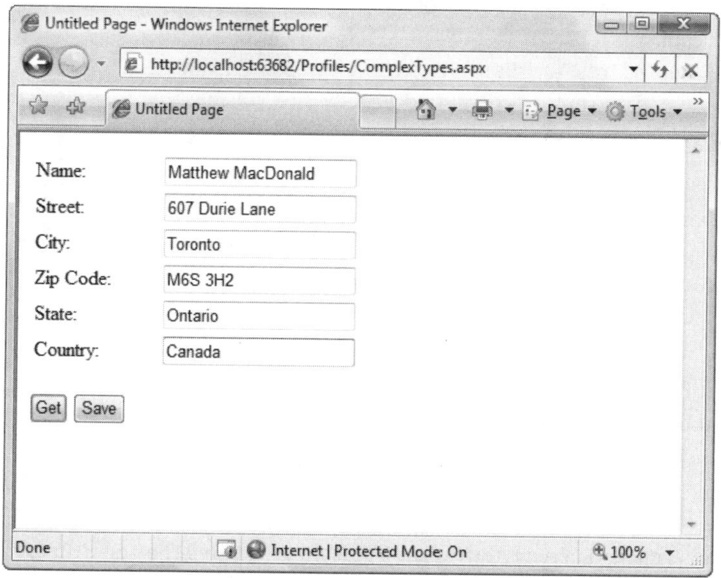

Figure 22-3. *Editing complex information in a profile*

Here's the page class that makes this possible:

```
Public Partial Class ComplexTypes
    Inherits System.Web.UI.Page

    Protected Sub Page_Load(ByVal sender As Object, _
      ByVal e As System.EventArgs) Handles Me.Load
        If Not Page.IsPostBack Then
            LoadProfile()
        End If
    End Sub

    Protected Sub cmdGet_Click(ByVal sender As Object, _
      ByVal e As System.EventArgs) Handles cmdGet.Click
        LoadProfile()
    End Sub

    Private Sub LoadProfile()
        txtName.Text = Profile.Address.Name
        txtStreet.Text = Profile.Address.Street
        txtCity.Text = Profile.Address.City
        txtZip.Text = Profile.Address.ZipCode
        txtState.Text = Profile.Address.State
        txtCountry.Text = Profile.Address.Country
    End Sub

    Protected Sub cmdSave_Click(ByVal sender As Object, _
      ByVal e As System.EventArgs) Handles cmdSave.Click
        Profile.Address = new Address(txtName.Text, _
          txtStreet.Text, txtCity.Text, txtZip.Text, _
          txtState.Text, txtCountry.Text)
    End Sub

End Class
```

Dissecting the Code . . .

- When the page loads (and when the user clicks the Get button), the profile information is copied from the Profile.Address object into the various text boxes. A private LoadProfile() method handles this task.
- The user can make changes to the address values in the text boxes. However, the change isn't committed until the user clicks the Save button.
- When the Save button is clicked, a new Address object is created using the constructor that accepts name, street, city, zip code, state, and country information. This object is then assigned to the Profile.Address property. Instead of using this approach, you could modify each property of the current Profile.Address object to match the text values.

- The content of the Profile object is saved to the database automatically when the request ends. No extra work is required.

Custom Type Serialization

You need to keep in mind a few points, depending on how you decide to serialize your custom class. By default, all custom data types use XML serialization with the XmlSerializer. This class is relatively limited in its serialization ability. It simply copies the value from every public property or member variable into a straightforward XML format like this:

```
<Address>
  <Name>...</Name>
  <Street>...</Street>
  <City>...</City>
  <ZipCode>...</ZipCode>
  <State>...</State>
  <Country>...</Country>
</Address>
```

When deserializing your class, the XmlSerializer needs to be able to find a parameterless public constructor. In addition, none of your properties can be read-only. If you violate either of these rules, the deserialization process will fail.

If you decide to use binary serialization instead of XmlSerialization, .NET uses a completely different approach:

```
<add name="Address" type="Address" serializeAs="Binary"/>
```

In this case, ASP.NET enlists the help of the BinaryFormatter. The BinaryFormatter can serialize the full public and private contents of any class, provided the class is decorated with the <Serializable()> attribute. Additionally, any class it derives from or references must also be serializable.

Automatic Saves

The profiles feature isn't able to detect changes in complex data types (anything other than strings, simple numeric types, Boolean values, and so on). This means if your profile includes complex data types, ASP.NET saves the complete profile information at the end of every request that accesses the Profile object.

This behavior obviously adds unnecessary overhead. To optimize performance when working with complex types, you have several choices. One option is to set the corresponding profile property to be read-only (if you know it never changes). Another approach is to disable the autosave behavior completely by adding the automaticSaveEnabled attribute on the <profile> element and setting it to false, as shown here:

```
<profile defaultProvider="SqlProvider" automaticSaveEnabled="false">...</profile>
```

If you choose this approach, it's up to you to call Profile.Save() to explicitly commit changes. Generally, this approach is the most convenient, because it's easy to spot the places in your code where you modify the profile. Just add the Profile.Save() call at the end:

```
Profile.Address = New Address(txtName.Text, txtStreet.Text, _
  txtCity.Text, txtZip.Text, txtState.Text, txtCountry.Text)
Profile.Save()
```

For instance, you could modify the earlier example (shown in Figure 22-3) to save address information only when it changes. The easiest way to do this is to disable automatic saves, but call Profile.Save() when the Save button is clicked. You could also handle the TextBox.TextChanged event to determine when changes are made, and save the profile immediately at this point.

The Profile API

Although your page automatically gets the profile information for the current user, this doesn't prevent you from retrieving and modifying the profiles of other users. In fact, you have two tools to help you—the ProfileBase class and the ProfileManager class.

The Profile object (provided by the Page.Profile property) includes a useful GetProfile() method that retrieves the profile information for a specific user by user name. Figure 22-4 shows an example with a Windows-authenticated user.

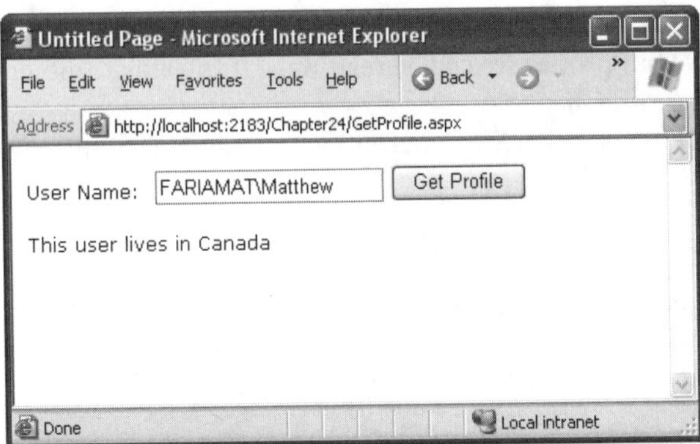

Figure 22-4. *Retrieving a profile manually*

Here's the code that gets the profile:

```
Protected Sub cmdGet_Click(ByVal sender As Object, _
  ByVal e As System.EventArgs) Handles cmdGet.Click

    Dim currentProfile As ProfileCommon
    currentProfile = Profile.GetProfile(txtUserName.Text)
    lbl.Text = "This user lives in " & currentProfile.Address.Country
End Sub
```

GetProfile() returns a ProfileCommon object. However, you won't find ProfileCommon in the .NET class library. That's because ProfileCommon is a dynamically generated class that ASP.NET creates to hold the profile information for your web application. In this example, the profile defines a property named Address, so that you can retrieve this information using the ProfileCommon.Address property.

Notice that once you have a ProfileCommon object, you can interact with it in the same way you interact with the profile for the current user. You can even make changes. The only difference is that changes aren't saved automatically. If you want to save a change, you need to call the Save() method of the ProfileCommon object. ProfileCommon also adds the LastActivityDate and LastUpdatedDate properties, which you can use to determine the last time a specific profile was accessed and modified.

If you try to retrieve a profile that doesn't exist, you won't get an error. Instead, you'll simply end up with blank data (for example, empty strings). If you change and save the profile, a new profile record will be created.

You can test for this condition by examining the ProfileCommon.LastUpdatedDate property. If the profile hasn't been created yet, this value will be a zero-date value (in other words, day 0 on month 0 in year 0000). Here's the code you'd use:

```
Protected Sub cmdGet_Click(ByVal sender As Object, _
  ByVal e As System.EventArgs) Handles cmdGet.Click

    Dim currentProfile As ProfileCommon
    currentProfile = Profile.GetProfile(txtUserName.Text)
    If profile.LastUpdatedDate = DateTime.MinValue Then
        lbl.Text = "No user match found."
    Else
        lbl.Text = "This user lives in " & currentProfile.Address.Country
    End If
End Sub
```

If you need to perform other tasks with profiles, you can use the ProfileManager class in the System.Web.Profile namespace, which exposes the useful shared methods described in Table 22-4. Many of these methods work with a ProfileInfo class, which provides information about a profile. The ProfileInfo includes the user name (UserName), last update and last activity dates (LastUpdatedDate and LastActivityDate), the size of the profile in bytes (Size), and whether the profile is for an anonymous user (IsAnonymous). It doesn't provide the actual profile values.

Table 22-4. *ProfileManager Methods*

Method	Description
DeleteProfile()	Deletes the profile for the user you specify.
DeleteProfiles()	Deletes multiple profiles at once. You supply a collection of user names.
DeleteInactiveProfiles()	Deletes profiles that haven't been used since a time you specify. You also must supply a value from the ProfileAuthenticationOption enumeration to indicate what type of profiles you want to remove (All, Anonymous, or Authenticated).
GetNumberOfProfiles()	Returns the number of profile records in the data source.
GetNumberOfInactiveProfiles()	Returns the number of profiles that haven't been used since the time you specify.

Table 22-4. *ProfileManager Methods (Continued)*

Method	Description
GetAllInactiveProfiles()	Retrieves profile information for profiles that haven't been used since the time you specify. The profiles are returned as ProfileInfo objects.
GetAllProfiles()	Retrieves all the profile data from the data source as a collection of ProfileInfo objects. You can choose what type of profiles you want to retrieve (All, Anonymous, or Authenticated). You can also use an overloaded version of this method that uses paging and retrieves only a portion of the full set of records based on the starting index and page size you request.
FindProfilesByUserName()	Retrieves a collection of ProfileInfo objects matching a specific user name. The SqlProfileProvider uses a LIKE clause when it attempts to match user names, which means you can use wildcards such as the % symbol. For example, if you search for the user name user%, you'll return values such as user1, user2, user_guest, and so on. You can use an overloaded version of this method that uses paging.
FindInactiveProfilesByUserName()	Retrieves profile information for profiles that haven't been used since the time you specify. You can also filter out certain types of profiles (All, Anonymous, or Authenticated) or look for a specific user name (with wildcard matching). The return value is a collection of ProfileInfo objects.

For example, if you want to remove the profile for the current user, you need only a single line of code:

```
ProfileManager.DeleteProfile(User.Identity.Name)
```

And if you want to display the full list of users in a web page (not including anonymous users), just add a GridView with AutoGenerateColumns set to True and use this code:

```
Protected Sub Page_Load(ByVal sender As Object, _
  ByVal e As System.EventArgs) Handles Me.Load

    gridProfiles.DataSource = ProfileManager.GetAllProfiles( _
      ProfileAuthenticationOption.Authenticated)
    gridProfiles.DataBind()
End Sub
```

Figure 22-5 shows the result.

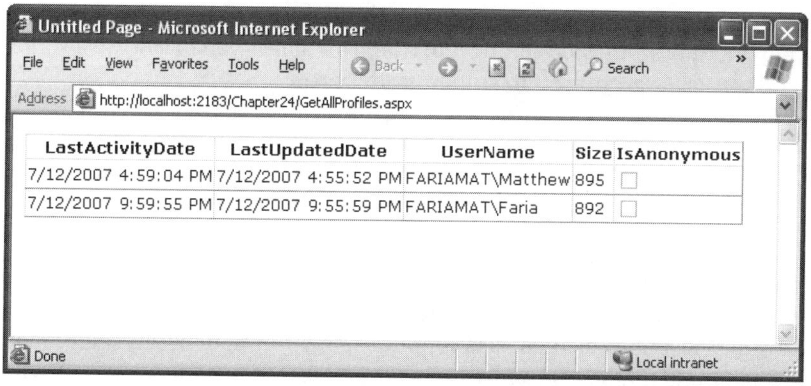
Untitled Page - Microsoft Internet Explorer
File Edit View Favorites Tools Help
Back Search
Address http://localhost:2183/Chapter24/GetAllProfiles.aspx
LastActivityDate LastUpdatedDate UserName Size IsAnonymous
7/12/2007 4:59:04 PM 7/12/2007 4:55:52 PM FARIAMAT\Matthew 895
7/12/2007 9:59:55 PM 7/12/2007 9:55:59 PM FARIAMAT\Faria 892
Done
Local intranet

Figure 22-5. *Retrieving information about all the profiles in the data source*

Anonymous Profiles

So far, all the examples have assumed that the user is authenticated before any profile information is accessed or stored. Usually, this is the case. However, sometimes it's useful to create a temporary profile for a new, unknown user. For example, most e-commerce websites allow new users to begin adding items to a shopping cart before registering. If you want to provide this type of behavior and you choose to store shopping cart items in a profile, you'll need some way to uniquely identify anonymous users.

■ **Note** It's worth asking whether it makes sense to store a shopping cart in a profile. It's a reasonable, workable design, but many developers find it easier to explicitly control how this type of information is stored in their database using custom ADO.NET code instead of the profile feature.

ASP.NET provides an anonymous identification feature that fills this gap. The basic idea is that the anonymous identification feature automatically generates a random identifier for any anonymous user. This random identifier stores the profile information in the database, even though no user ID is available. The user ID is tracked on the client side using a cookie (or in the URL, if you've enabled cookieless mode). Once this cookie disappears (for example, if the anonymous user closes and reopens the browser), the anonymous session is lost and a new anonymous session is created.

Anonymous identification has the potential to leave a lot of abandoned profiles, which wastes space in the database. For that reason, anonymous identification is disabled by default. However, you can enable it using the <anonymousIdentification> element in the web.config file, as shown here:

```
<configuration>
  ...
  <system.web>
    <anonymousIdentification enabled="true" />
    ...
  </system.web>
</configuration>
```

You also need to flag each profile property that will be retained for anonymous users by adding the allowAnonymous attribute and setting it to true. This allows you to store just some basic information and restrict larger objects to authenticated users.

```
<properties>
  <add name="Address" type="Address" allowAnonymous="true" />
  ...
</properties>
```

If you're using a complex type, the allowAnonymous attribute is an all-or-nothing setting. You configure the entire object to support anonymous storage or not support it.

The <anonymousIdentification> element also supports numerous optional attributes that let you set the cookie name and timeout, specify whether the cookie will be issued only over an SSL connection, control whether cookie protection (validation and encryption) is used to prevent tampering and eavesdropping, and configure support for cookieless ID tracking. Here's an example:

```
<anonymousIdentification enabled="true" cookieName=".ASPXANONYMOUS"
  cookieTimeout="43200" cookiePath="/" cookieRequireSSL="false"
  cookieSlidingExpiration="true" cookieProtection="All"
  cookieless="UseCookies"/>
```

For more information, refer to the Visual Studio Help.

■ **Tip** If you use anonymous identification, it's a good idea to delete old anonymous sessions regularly using the aspnet_Profile_DeleteInactiveProfiles stored procedure, which you can run at scheduled intervals using the SQL Server Agent. You can also delete old profiles using the ProfileManager class, as described in the previous section.

Migrating Anonymous Profiles

One challenge that occurs with anonymous profiles is what to do with the profile information when a previously anonymous user logs in. For example, in an e-commerce website a user might select several items and then register or log in to complete the transaction. At this point, you need to make sure the shopping cart information is copied from the anonymous user's profile to the appropriate authenticated (user) profile.

Fortunately, ASP.NET provides a solution through the ProfileModule.MigrateAnonymous event. This event fires whenever an anonymous identifier is available (either as a cookie or in the URL if you're using cookieless mode) *and* the current user is authenticated. To handle the MigrateAnonymous event, you need to add an event handler to the file that handles all application events—the Global.asax file, which you learned about in Chapter 7.

The basic technique when handling the MigrateAnonymous event is to load the profile for the anonymous user by calling Profile.GetProfile() and passing in the anonymous ID, which is provided to your event handler through the ProfileMigrateEventArgs.

Once you've loaded this data, you can then transfer the settings to the new profile manually. You can choose to transfer as few or as many settings as you want, and you can perform any other processing that's required. Finally, your code should remove the anonymous profile data from the database and clear the anonymous identifier so the MigrateAnonymous event won't fire again. For example:

```
Public Sub Profile_OnMigrateAnonymous(sender As Object, _
 e As ProfileMigrateEventArgs)

    ' Get the anonymous profile.
    Dim anonProfile As ProfileCommon = Profile.GetProfile(e.AnonymousID)

    ' Copy information to the authenticated profile
    ' (but only if there's information there).
    If Not anonProfile.IsNullOfEmpty() Then
        If anonProfile.Address.Name <> "" Then
            Profile.Address = anonProfile.Address
        End If
    End If

    ' Delete the anonymous profile from the database.
    ' (You could decide to skip this step to increase performance
    '  if you have a dedicated job scheduled on the database server
    '  to remove old anonymous profiles.)
    System.Web.Profile.ProfileManager.DeleteProfile(e.AnonymousID)

    ' Remove the anonymous identifier.
    AnonymousIdentificationModule.ClearAnonymousIdentifier()
End Sub
```

You need to handle this task with some caution. If you've enabled anonymous identification, the MigrateAnonymous event fires every time a user logs in, even if the user hasn't entered any information into the anonymous profile. That's a problem—if you're not careful, you could easily overwrite the real (saved) profile for the user with the blank anonymous profile. The problem is further complicated by the fact that complex types (such as the Address object) are created automatically by ASP.NET, so you can't just check for a null reference to determine whether the user has anonymous address information.

In the previous example, the code tests for a missing Name property in the Address object. If this information isn't part of the anonymous profile, no information is migrated. A more sophisticated example might test for individual properties separately or might migrate an anonymous profile only if the information in the user profile is missing or outdated.

The Last Word

In this chapter, you learned how to use profiles and how they store information in the database. Many ASP.NET developers will prefer to write their own ADO.NET code for retrieving and storing user-specific information. Not only does this allow you to use your own database structure, it allows you to add your own features, such as caching, logging, validation, and encryption. But profiles are handy for quickly building modest applications that don't store a lot of user-specific information and don't have special requirements for how this information is stored.

PART 6

Advanced ASP.NET

CHAPTER 23

Component-Based Programming

Component-based programming is a simple, elegant idea. When used properly, it allows your code to be more organized, consistent, and reusable. It's also incredibly easy to implement in a .NET application, because you never need to use the Windows registry or perform any special configuration.

A component, at its simplest, is one or more classes that are compiled into a separate DLL assembly file. These classes provide some unit of logically related functionality. You can access a component in a single application, or you can share the component between multiple applications. Your web pages (or any other .NET application) can use the classes in your components in the same way they use any other .NET class. Best of all, your component is *encapsulated*, which means it provides exactly the features your code requires and hides all the other messy details.

When combined with careful organization, component-based programming is the basis of good ASP.NET application design. In this chapter, you'll examine how you can create components (and why you should) and consider examples that show you how to encapsulate database functionality with a well-written business object. You'll also learn how to bind your database component to the web controls on a page using the ObjectDataSource.

Why Use Components?

To master ASP.NET development you need to become a skilled user of the .NET class library. So far, you've learned how to use .NET components designed for reading files, communicating with databases, calling web services, and storing information about the user. Though these class library ingredients are powerful, they aren't customizable, which is both an advantage and a weakness.

For example, if you want to retrieve data from a SQL Server database, you need to weave database details (such as SQL queries) directly into your code-behind class or (if you're using the SqlDataSource) into the .aspx markup portion of your web page file. Either way if the structure of the database changes even slightly, you could be left with dozens of pages to update and retest. To solve these problems, you need to create an extra layer between your web page code and the database. This extra layer takes the form of a custom component.

This database scenario is only one of the reasons you might want to create your own components. Component-based programming is really just a logical extension of good code-organizing principles, and it offers a long list of advantages:

Safety: Because the source code isn't contained in your web page, you can't modify it. Instead, you're limited to the functionality your component provides. For example, you could configure a database component to allow only certain operations with specific tables, fields, or rows. This is often easier than setting up complex permissions in the database. Because the application has to go through the component, it needs to play by its rules.

Better organization: Components move the clutter out of your web page code. It also becomes easier for other programmers to understand your application's logic when it's broken down into separate components. Without components, commonly used code has to be copied and pasted throughout an application, making it extremely difficult to change and synchronize.

Easier troubleshooting: It's impossible to oversell the advantage of components when testing and debugging an application. Component-based programs are broken down into smaller, tighter blocks of code, making it easier to isolate exactly where a problem is occurring. It's also easier to test individual components separate from the rest of your web application.

More manageability: Component-based programs are much easier to enhance and modify because the component and web application code can be modified separately. Taken to its extreme, this approach allows you to have one development team working on the component and another team coding the website that uses the component.

Code reuse: Components can be shared with any ASP.NET application that needs the component's functionality. Even better, any .NET application can use a component, meaning you could create a common "backbone" of logic that's used by a web application and an ordinary Windows application.

Simplicity: Components can provide multiple related tasks for a single client request (writing several records to a database, opening and reading a file in one step, or even starting and managing a database transaction). Similarly, components hide details—an application programmer can use a database component without worrying about the database name, the location of the server, or the user account needed to connect. Even better, you can perform a search using certain criteria, and the component itself can decide whether to use a dynamically generated SQL statement or stored procedure.

Component Jargon

Component-based programming is sometimes shrouded in a fog of specialized jargon. Understanding these terms helps sort out exactly what a component is supposed to do, and it also allows you to understand MSDN articles about application design. If you're already familiar with the fundamentals of components, feel free to skip ahead.

Three-Tier Design

The idea of *three-tier* design is that the functionality of most complete applications can be divided into three main levels (see Figure 23-1). The first level is the user interface (or presentation tier), which displays controls and receives and validates user input. All the event handlers in your web page are in this first level. The second level is the business tier, where the application-specific logic takes place. For an e-commerce site, application-specific logic includes rules such as how shipping charges are applied to an order, when certain promotions are valid, and what customer actions should be logged. It doesn't involve generic .NET details such as how to open a file or connect to a database. The third level is the data tier, where you place the logic that stores your information in files, a database, or some other data store. The third level contains logic about how to retrieve and update data, such as SQL queries or stored procedures.

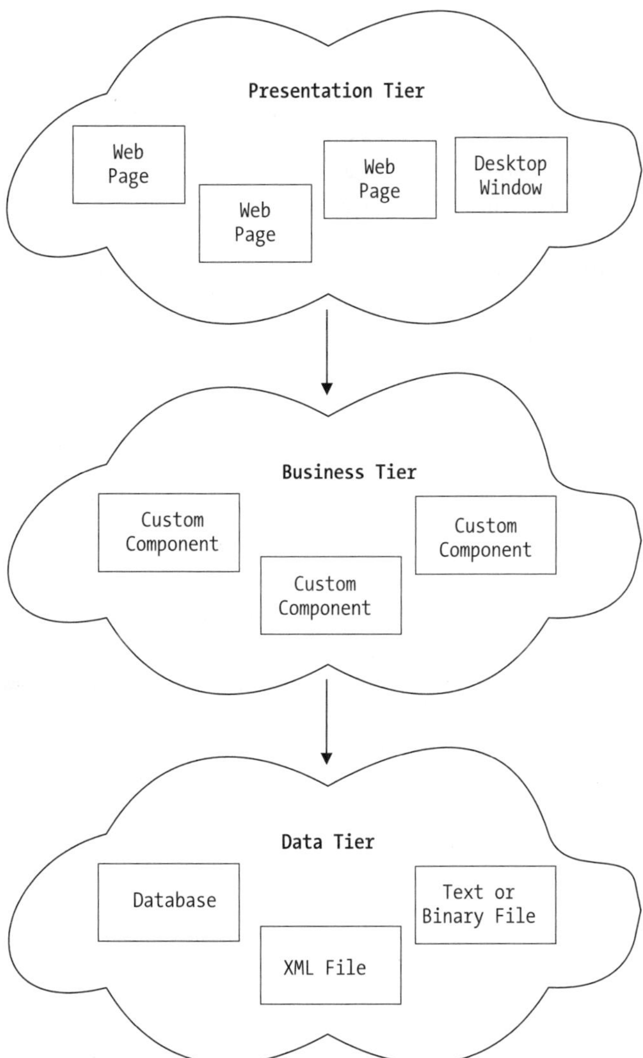

Figure 23-1. *Three-tier design*

The important detail about three-tier design is that information travels from only one level to an adjacent level. In other words, your web page code shouldn't connect directly to the database to retrieve information. Instead, it should go through a component in the business tier that connects to the database and returns the data.

This basic organization principle can't always be adhered to, but it's a good model to follow. When you create a component it's almost always used in the second level to bridge the gap between the data and the user interface. In other words, if you want to fill a list of product categories in a list box, your user interface code calls a component, which gets the list from the database and then returns it to your code. Your web page code is isolated from the database—and if the database structure changes, you need to change one concise component instead of every page on your site.

Encapsulation

If three-tier design is the overall goal of component-based programming, *encapsulation* is the best rule of thumb. Encapsulation is the principle that you should create your application out of "black boxes" that hide information. So, if you have a component that logs a purchase on an e-commerce site, that component handles all the details and allows only the essential variables to be specified.

For example, this component might accept a user ID and an order item ID and then handle all the other details. The calling code doesn't need to worry about how the component works or where the data is coming from—it just needs to understand how to use the component. (This principle is described in a lot of picturesque ways. For example, you know how to drive a car because you understand its component interface—the steering wheel and pedals—not because you understand the low-level details about internal combustion and the engine. As a result, you're able to transfer your knowledge to many different types of automobiles, even if they have dramatically different internal workings.)

Business Objects

The term *business object* often means different things to different people. Generally, business objects are the components in the second level of your application that provide the extra layer between your code and the data source. They are called business objects because they enforce *business rules*. For example, if you try to submit a purchase order without any items, the appropriate business object will throw an exception and refuse to continue. In this case, no .NET error has occurred—instead, you've detected the presence of a condition that shouldn't be allowed according to your application's logic.

In this chapter's examples, business objects are also going to contain data access code. In an extremely complicated, large, and changeable system, you might want to further subdivide components and actually have your user interface code talking to a business object, which in turn talks to another set of objects that interact with the data source. However, for most programmers, this extra step is overkill, especially with the increased level of sophistication ADO.NET provides.

Data Objects

The term *data object* is also used in a variety of ways. In this book, data objects are simply packages of data that you use to send information between your web page and your business objects. For example, you might create a data class named Employee that represents the information from one record in an Employees table, complete with properties like FirstName, LastName, and DateOfBirth. A typical data object is filled with properties, but provides no methods.

Components and Classes

Technically, a component is just a collection of one or more classes (and possibly other .NET types, such as structures and enumerations) that are compiled together as a unit. For example, Microsoft's System.Web.dll is a single (but very large) component that provides the types found in many of the namespaces that start with System.Web.

So far, the code examples in this book have used only a few kinds of classes—mainly custom web page classes that inherit from System.Web.UI.Page and contain mostly event-handling procedures. Component classes, on the other hand, usually won't include any user interface logic (which would limit their use unnecessarily) and don't need to inherit from an existing class. They are more similar to the custom web service classes described in Part 4 of this book, which collect related features together in a series of utility methods.

Creating a Component

To create a component, you create a new class library project in Visual Studio. Just select File ➤ New ➤ Project, and choose the Class Library project template in the New Project dialog box (see Figure 23-2). You'll need to choose a file location and a project name.

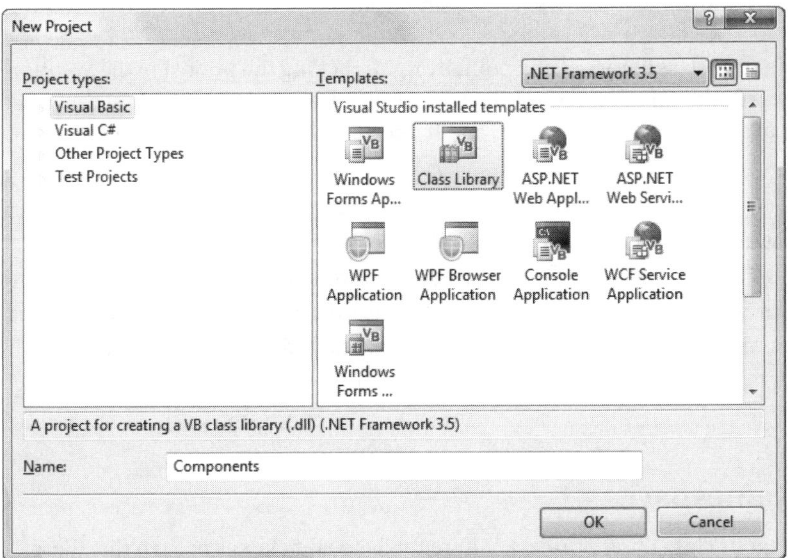

Figure 23-2. *Creating a component in Visual Studio*

Rather than just choosing File ➤ New Project to create the class library, you can add it to the same solution as your website. This makes it easy to debug the code in your component while you're testing it with a web page. (On its own, there's no way to run a component, so there's no way to test it.) To create a new class library in an existing web solution, start by opening your website, and then choose File ➤ Add ➤ New Project. Specify the directory and project name in the Add New Project dialog box.

Figure 23-3 shows a solution with both a website and a class library named Components. The website is in bold in the Solution Explorer to indicate that it runs on start-up (when you click the Start button).

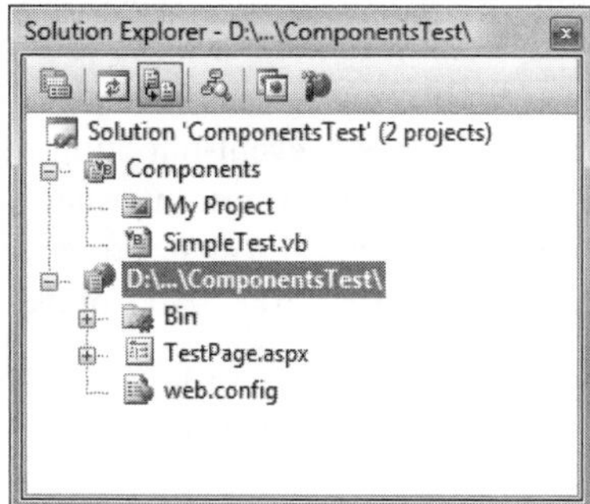

Figure 23-3. *A solution with a website and class library project*

To make it easy to open this solution, you might want to take a moment to save it. Click the solution name (which is "Components" in Figure 23-3) in the Solution Explorer. Then choose File ➤ Save [SolutionName] As. You can open this .sln file later to load both the website and class library project.

You can compile your class library at any point by right-clicking the project in the Solution Explorer and choosing Build. This creates a DLL assembly file (Components.dll). You can't run this file directly, because it isn't an application, and it doesn't provide any user interface.

■ **Note** Unlike web pages and web services, you must compile a component before you can use it. Components aren't hosted by the ASP.NET service and IIS; thus, they can't be compiled automatically when they are needed. However, you can easily recompile your component in Visual Studio (and depending on the references and project settings you use, Visual Studio may perform this step automatically when you launch your web application in the design environment).

Classes and Namespaces

Once you've created your class library project, you're ready to add classes in a .vb file. Class library projects begin with one file named Class1.vb, which you can use, delete, or rename. You can also add more class files simply by right-clicking on the project in the Solution Explorer and choosing Add ➤ Class. The only difference between class library projects and web applications is that your class files won't be placed in an App_Code subdirectory.

Here's an example that creates a class named SimpleTest:

```
Public Class SimpleTest
    ' (Code goes here, inside one or more methods.)
End Class
```

Remember, a component can contain more than one class. You can create these other classes in the same file, or you can use separate files for better organization. In either case, all the classes and source code files are compiled together into one assembly:

```
Public Class SimpleTest
    ...
End Class

Public Class SimpleTest2
    ...
End Class
```

The classes in your component are automatically organized into a namespace that's named after your project. This namespace is known as the *root namespace*. For example, if you've created a project named Components, the SimpleTest and SimpleTest2 classes will be in the Components namespace, and their fully qualified names will be Components.SimpleTest and Components.SimpleTest2. You need to know the fully qualified name in order to use your classes in another application, because other applications won't share the same namespace.

If you decide that you want to change the root namespace, you can change it quite easily. First, right-click the project in the Solution Explorer and choose Properties. You'll see a multi-tabbed display of application settings. Choose the Application tab and then edit the namespace in the Root Namespace text box. You can also use the Assembly Name text box in this window to configure the name that is given to the compiled assembly file.

If you have a complex component, you might choose to subdivide it into nested namespaces. For example, you might have a namespace named Components.Database and another named Components.Validation. To create a nested namespace inside the default project namespace, you use a Namespace block like this:

```
Namespace Database

    Public Class SimpleDatabaseTest
        ' (Class code omitted.)
    End Class

End Namespace
```

Now this class has the fully qualified name Components.Database.SimpleDatabaseTest.

■ **Tip** The general rule for naming namespaces is to use the company name followed by the technology name and optionally followed by a feature-specific division, as in CompanyName.TechnologyName.Feature. Example namespaces that follow this syntax include Microsoft.Media and Microsoft.Media.Audio. These namespace conventions dramatically reduce the possibility that more than one company might release components in the same namespaces, which would lead to naming conflicts. The only exception to the naming guidelines is in the base assemblies that are part of .NET. They use namespaces that begin with System.

Class Members

To add functionality to your class, add public methods or properties. The web page code can then call these members to retrieve information or perform a task.

The following example shows one of the simplest possible components, which does nothing more than return a string to the calling code:

```
Public Class SimpleTest

    Public Function GetInfo(ByVal param As String) As String
        Return "You invoked SimpleTest.GetInfo() with '" & _
          param & "'"
    End Function

End Class

Public Class SimpleTest2

    Public Function GetInfo(ByVal param As String) As String
        Return "You invoked SimpleTest2.GetInfo() with '" & _
          param & "'"
    End Function

End Class
```

In the following sections, you'll learn how to use this component in a web application. A little later, you'll graduate to a more complex, practical component.

Adding a Reference to the Component

Using the component in an actual ASP.NET page is easy. Essentially, your website needs a copy of your component in its Bin directory. ASP.NET automatically monitors this directory and makes all of its classes available to any web page in the application. To create this copy, you use a Visual Studio feature called *references*.

Here's how it works: First, select your website in the Solution Explorer. Then, select Website ➤ Add Reference from the menu. This brings you to the Add Reference dialog box. (Don't choose Add Web Reference, which is used to connect an application to a web service, and has little in common with the similarly named Add Reference command.)

You can take one of two approaches in the Add Reference dialog box:

Add a project reference: If your class library project is in the same solution, use the Projects tab. This shows you a list of all the class library projects in your current solution (see Figure 23-4). Select the class library, and click OK.

Add an assembly reference: If your class library is in a different solution, or you have the compiled DLL file only (perhaps the component was created by another developer), use the Browse tab (see Figure 23-5). Browse through your directories until you find the DLL file, select it, and click OK.

■ **Note** If you're using an assembly reference, you need to compile your component first (choose Build ➤ Build Solution from the Visual Studio menu) before you can add the reference.

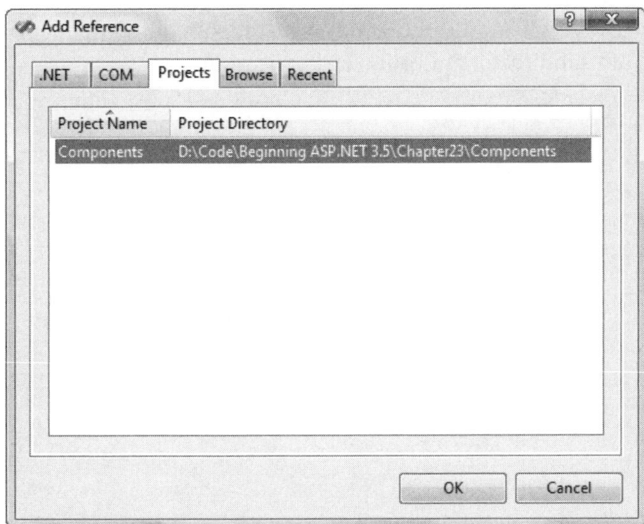

Figure 23-4. *Adding a project reference*

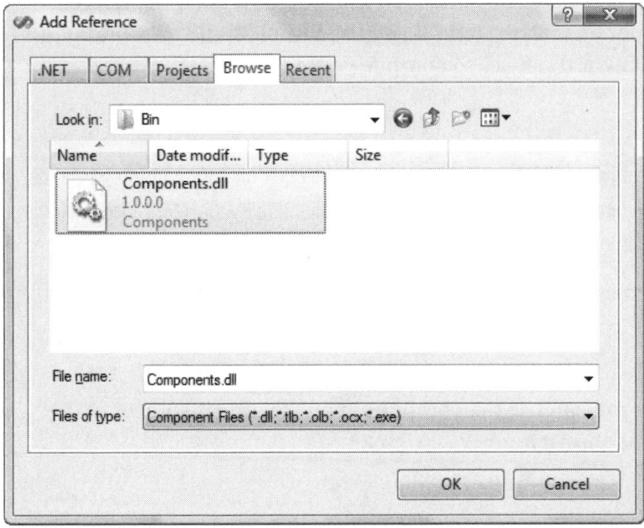

Figure 23-5. *Adding an assembly reference*

Either way, .NET copies the compiled DLL file to the Bin subdirectory of your web application (see Figure 23-6).

Visual Studio also takes extra care to make sure that you keep using the most up-to-date version of the component. If you change the component and recompile it, Visual Studio will notice the change. The next time you run your web application, Visual Studio will automatically copy the new component to the Bin subdirectory.

If you're using a project reference, Visual Studio goes one step further. Every time you run the website project, Visual Studio checks for any changes in your component's source code files. If any of these files have been changed, Visual Studio automatically recompiles the component and copies the new version to the Bin subdirectory in your web application.

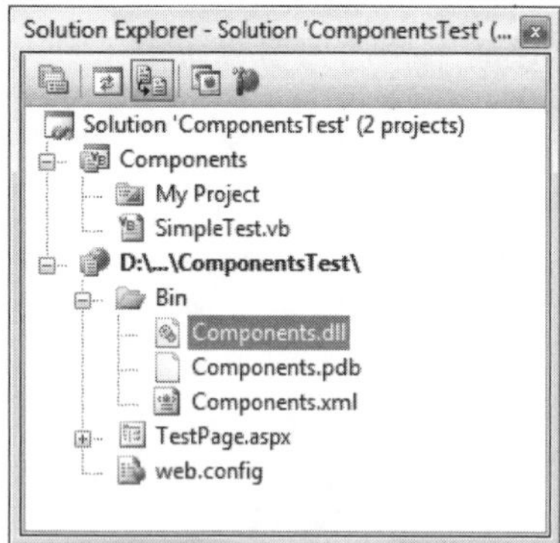

Figure 23-6. *A component in the Bin directory*

When you add a reference to a component, Visual Studio also allows you to use its classes in your code with the usual syntax checking and IntelliSense. If you don't add the reference, you won't be able to use the component classes (and if you try, Visual Studio interprets your attempts to use the class as mistakes and refuses to compile your code).

■ **Note** Removing a reference is a bit trickier. The easiest way is to right-click on your web project and choose Property Pages. Then, choose References from the list. You'll see a list of all your references (including assembly and project references). To remove one, select it and click Remove.

Using the Component

Once you've added the reference, you can use the component by creating instances of the SimpleTest or SimpleTest2 class, as shown here:

```
Imports Components

Public Partial Class TestPage
    Inherits System.Web.UI.Page

    Protected Sub Page_Load(ByVal sender As Object, _
      ByVal e As System.EventArgs) Handles Me.Load
```

```
        Dim testComponent As New SimpleTest()
        Dim testComponent2 As New SimpleTest2()
        lblResult.Text = testComponent.GetInfo("Hello") & "<br /><br />"
        lblResult.Text &= testComponent2.GetInfo("Bye")
    End Sub
End Class
```

The output for this page, shown in Figure 23-7, combines the return value from both GetInfo() methods.

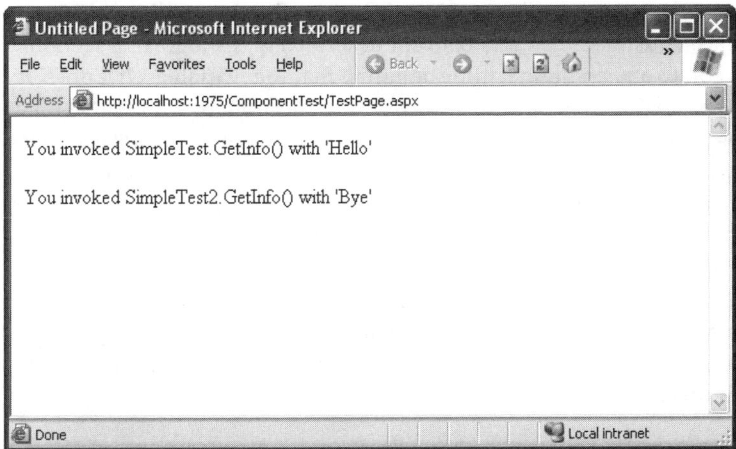

Figure 23-7. *The SimpleTest component output*

To make this code slightly simpler, you can choose to use shared methods in the component class, so that you don't need to create an instance before using the methods. A shared GetInfo() method looks like this:

```
Public Class SimpleTest

    Public Shared Function GetInfo(param As String) As String
        Return "You invoked SimpleTest.GetInfo() with '" & _
          param & "'"
    End Function

End Class
```

In this case, the web page accesses the shared GetInfo() method through the class name and doesn't need to create an object:

```
Protected Sub Page_Load(ByVal sender As Object, _
  ByVal e As System.EventArgs) Handles Me.Load

    lblResult.Text = SimpleTest.GetInfo("Hello")
End Sub
```

■ **Tip** Remember, if you're using assembly references and your component and web application *aren't* in the same solution, you won't see the effect of your changes right away. Instead, you need to recompile your component assembly (choose Build ➤ Build Solution) and then relaunch your web application. If you're using project references, this isn't necessary—Visual Studio notices every change you make and recompiles your component automatically.

Deciding when to use instance methods and when to use shared methods is part of the art of object-oriented design, and it takes experience. Shared methods impose additional considerations—namely, your class must be *stateless* (a concept described in the following section), which means it can't hold on to any additional information in member variables. If it does, it risks a potential conflict if more than one piece of code uses the component at the same time.

As a rule of thumb, use instance methods if you need to be able to create several instances of your class at the same time. For example, instance methods make sense for the SqlConnection class, because you might choose to open a connection to several different databases for one operation. Instance methods are also the best choice if you want to configure an object once and use it several times. For example, the SqlConnection class lets you set the connection string and then open and close the connection as much as needed. On the other hand, consider shared methods if your methods perform a single, discrete task that doesn't require any initialization. Examples include the calculations in the Math class, and the business tasks (such as registering a new customer) in a high-level business component.

Properties and State

The SimpleTest classes provide functionality through public methods. If you're familiar with class-based programming (as described in Chapter 3), you'll remember that classes can also store information in private member variables and provide property procedures that allow the calling code to modify this information. For example, a Person class might have a FirstName property.

When you use properties and store information in member variables, you're using *stateful design*. In stateful design, the class has the responsibility of maintaining certain pieces of information. In stateless design, no information is retained between method calls. Compare the earlier SimpleTest class, which uses stateless design, to the stateful SimpleTest class shown here:

```
Public Class SimpleTest
    Private _data As String

    Public Property Data() As String
        Get
            Return _data
        End Get
        Set(ByVal value As String)
            _data = value
        End Set
    End Property
```

```
    Public Function GetInfo() As String
        Return "You invoked SimpleTest.GetInfo()," & _
          "and data is '" & Data & "'"
    End Function
End Class
```

Programmers who design large-scale applications (such as web applications) sometimes debate whether stateful or stateless programming is best. Stateful programming is the most natural, object-oriented approach, but it also has a few disadvantages. To accomplish a common task, you might need to set several properties before calling a method. Each of these steps adds a little bit of unneeded overhead. A stateless design, on the other hand, often performs all its work in a single method call. However, because no information is retained in state, you may need to specify several parameters, which can make for tedious programming. A good example of stateful versus stateless objects is shown by the FileInfo and File classes, which are described in Chapter 18.

There is no short answer about whether stateful or stateless design is best, and it often depends on the task at hand. Components that are high-performance, components that use transactions, components that use limited resources such as a database connection, or components that need to be invoked remotely (such as web services) usually use stateless design, which is the simplest and most reliable approach. Because no information is retained in memory, fewer server resources are used, and no danger exists of losing valuable data if a software or hardware failure occurs. The next example illustrates the difference with two ways to design an Account class.

A Stateful Account Class

Consider a stateful account class that represents a single customer account. Information is read from the database when it's first created in the constructor method, and this information can be updated using the Update() method.

```
Public Class CustomerAccount
    Private _accountNumber As Integer
    Private _balance As Decimal

    Public Property Balance() As Decimal
        Get
            Return _balance
        End Get
        Set(ByVal value As Decimal)
            _balance = value
        End Set
    End Property

    Public Sub New(ByVal accountNumber As Integer)
        ' (Code to read account record from database goes here.)
    End Sub

    Public Sub Update()
        ' (Code to update database record goes here.)
    End Sub
End Class
```

If you have two CustomerAccount objects that expose a Balance property, you need to perform two separate steps to transfer money from one account to another. Conceptually, the process works like this:

```
' Create an account object for each account,
' using the account number.
Dim accountOne As New CustomerAccount(122415)
Dim accountTwo As New CustomerAccount(123447)
Dim amount As Decimal = 1000

' Withdraw money from one account.
accountOne.Balance -= amount

' Deposit money in the other account.
accountTwo.Balance += amount

' Update the underlying database records using the Update() method.
accountOne.Update()
accountTwo.Update()
```

The problem here is that if this task is interrupted halfway through by an error, you'll end up with at least one unhappy customer.

A Stateless AccountUtility Class

A stateless object might expose only a shared method named FundTransfer(), which performs all its work in one method:

```
Public Class AccountUtility
    Public Shared Sub FundTransfer(ByVal accountOne As Integer, _
      ByVal accountTwo As Integer, ByVal amount As Decimal)
        ' (The code here retrieves the two database records,
        '  changes them, and updates them.)
    End Sub
End Class
```

The calling code can't use the same elegant CustomerAccount objects, but it can be assured that account transfers are protected from error. Because all the database operations are performed at once, they can use a database stored procedure for greater performance and can use a transaction to ensure that the withdrawal and deposit either succeed or fail as a whole.

```
' Set the account and transfer details.
Dim amount As Decimal = 1000
Dim accountIDOne As Integer = 122415
Dim accountIDTwo As Integer = 123447

AccountUtility.FundTransfer(accountIDOne, accountIDTwo, _
  amount)
```

In a mission-critical system, transactions are often required. For that reason, classes that retain little state information are often the best design approach, even though they aren't quite as satisfying from an object-oriented perspective.

■ **Tip** There is one potential compromise. You can create stateful classes to represent common items such as accounts, customers, and so on, without adding any functionality. Then, you can use these classes as data packages to send information to and from a stateless utility class. (These are the data objects that were described in the beginning of this chapter.)

Data-Access Components

Clearly, components are extremely useful. But if you're starting a large programming project, you may not be sure what features are the best candidates for being made into separate components. Learning how to break an application into components and classes is one of the great arts of programming, and it takes a good deal of practice and fine-tuning.

One of the most common types of components is a data-access component. Data-access components are an ideal application of component-based programming for several reasons:

Databases require extraneous details: These details include connection strings, field names, and so on, all of which can distract from the application logic and can easily be encapsulated by a well-written component.

Databases evolve over time: Even if the underlying table structure remains constant and additional information is never required (which is far from certain), queries may be replaced by stored procedures, and stored procedures may be redesigned.

Databases have special connection requirements: You may even need to change the database access code for reasons unrelated to the application. For example, after profiling and testing a database, you might discover that you can replace a single query with two queries or a more efficient stored procedure. In either case, the returned data remains constant, but the data access code is dramatically different.

Databases are used repetitively in a finite set of ways: In other words, a common database routine should be written once and is certain to be used many times.

A Simple Data-Access Component

To examine the best way to create a data-access component, you'll consider a simple application that provides a classifieds page that lists items that various individuals have for sale. The database uses two tables: one is an Items table that lists the description and price of a specific sale item, and the other is a Categories table that lists the different groups you can use to categorize an item. Figure 23-8 shows the relationship.

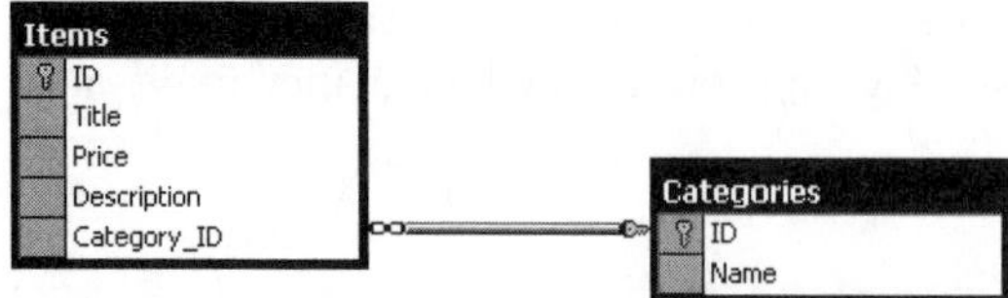

Figure 23-8. *The AdBoard database relationships*

In this example, you're connecting to a SQL Server database using ADO.NET. You can create this database yourself, or you can refer to the online samples, which include a SQL script that generates it automatically. To start, the Categories table is preloaded with a standard set of allowed categories.

The data-access component is simple. It's a single class (named DBUtil), which is placed in a namespace named DatabaseComponent (which is the root namespace for the project). The DBUtil class uses instance methods, and retains some basic information (such as the connection string to use), but it doesn't allow the client to change this information. Therefore, it doesn't need any property procedures. Instead, it performs most of its work in methods such as GetCategories() and GetItems(). These methods return DataSets with the appropriate database records. This type of design creates a fairly thin layer over the database—it handles some details, but the client is still responsible for working with familiar ADO.NET classes such as the DataSet.

■ **Note** To use this example as written, you need to add a reference to the System.Configuration.dll and System.Web.dll assemblies in the class library. Otherwise, you can't use the WebConfigurationManager to dig up the connection string you need. To add these references, select Project ➤ Add Reference, and look in the .NET tab.

```
Imports System
Imports System.Data
Imports System.Data.SqlClient
Imports System.Web.Configuration

Public Class DBUtil

    Private connectionString As String

    Public Sub New()
        connectionString = _
          WebConfigurationManager.ConnectionStrings( _
          "AdBoard").ConnectionString
    End Sub
```

```
Public Function GetCategories() As DataSet
    Dim query As String = "SELECT * FROM Categories"
    Dim cmd As New SqlCommand(query)
    Return FillDataSet(cmd, "Categories")
End Function

Public Function GetItems() As DataSet
    Dim query As String = "SELECT * FROM Items"
    Dim cmd As New SqlCommand(query)
    Return FillDataSet(cmd, "Items")
End Function

Public Function GetItems(ByVal categoryID As Integer) As DataSet
    ' Create the Command.
    Dim query As String = "SELECT * FROM Items WHERE Category_ID=@CategoryID"
    Dim cmd As New SqlCommand(query)
    cmd.Parameters.AddWithValue("@CategoryID", categoryID)

    ' Fill the DataSet.
    Return FillDataSet(cmd, "Items")
End Function

Public Sub AddCategory(ByVal name As String)
    Dim con As New SqlConnection(connectionString)

    ' Create the Command.
    Dim insertSQL As String = "INSERT INTO Categories "
    insertSQL &= "(Name) VALUES @Name"
    Dim cmd As New SqlCommand(insertSQL, con)
    cmd.Parameters.AddWithValue("@Name", name)

    Try
        con.Open()
        cmd.ExecuteNonQuery()
    Finally
        con.Close()
    End Try
End Sub

Public Sub AddItem(ByVal title As String, ByVal description As String, _
  ByVal price As Decimal, ByVal categoryID As Integer)
    Dim con As New SqlConnection(connectionString)
```

```
        ' Create the Command.
        Dim insertSQL As String = "INSERT INTO Items "
        insertSQL &= "(Title, Description, Price, Category_ID)"
        insertSQL &= "VALUES (@Title, @Description, @Price, @CategoryID)"
        Dim cmd As New SqlCommand(insertSQL, con)
        cmd.Parameters.AddWithValue("@Title", title)
        cmd.Parameters.AddWithValue("@Description", description)
        cmd.Parameters.AddWithValue("@Price", price)
        cmd.Parameters.AddWithValue("@CategoryID", categoryID)

        Try
            con.Open()
            cmd.ExecuteNonQuery()
        Finally
            con.Close()
        End Try
    End Sub

    Private Function FillDataSet(ByVal cmd As SqlCommand, ByVal tableName As String) _
      As DataSet
        Dim con As New SqlConnection(connectionString)
        cmd.Connection = con
        Dim adapter As New SqlDataAdapter(cmd)

        Dim ds As New DataSet()
        Try
            con.Open()
            adapter.Fill(ds, tableName)
        Finally
            con.Close()
        End Try
        return ds
    End Function

End Class
```

Dissecting the Code . . .

- When a DBUtil object is created, the constructor automatically retrieves the connection string from the web.config file, using the technique described in Chapter 5. However, it's important to note that this is the web.config file of the web application (as the component doesn't have a configuration file). This is a good design, because it allows a website to use the database component with any database server. However, if the client web application doesn't have the appropriate configuration setting, the database component won't work.

- The code includes methods for retrieving data (those methods that start with Get) and methods for updating data (those methods that start with Add).
- This class includes an overloaded method named GetItems(). This means the client can call GetItems() with no parameters to return the full list or with a parameter indicating the appropriate category. (Chapter 2 provides an introduction to overloaded methods.)
- Each method that accesses the database opens and closes the connection. This is a far better approach than trying to hold a connection open over the lifetime of the class, which is sure to result in performance degradation in multiuser scenarios.

■ **Tip** Your web server can open and close connections frequently without causing any slowdown. That's because ADO.NET uses connection pooling to keep a small set of open connections ready to use. As long as you don't change the connection string, every time you call SqlConnection.Open() you receive one of these already-open connections, thereby avoiding the overhead of setting up a new connection.

- The code uses its own private FillDataSet() function to make the code more concise. This isn't made available to clients. Instead, the GetItems() and GetCategories() methods use the FillDataSet() function.

Using the Data-Access Component

To use this component in a web application, you first have to make sure the appropriate connection string is configured in the web.config file, as shown here:

```
<configuration>

  <connectionStrings>
    <add name="AdBoard" connectionString=
"Data Source=localhost\SQLEXPRESS;Initial Catalog=AdBoard;Integrated Security=SSPI"
/>
  </connectionStrings>
  ...
</configuration>
```

Next, compile and copy the component DLL file, or add a reference to it if you're using Visual Studio. The only remaining task is to add the user interface for the web page that uses the component.

To test this component, you can create a simple test page. In the example shown in Figure 23-9, this page allows users to browse the current listing by category and add new items. When the user first visits the page, it prompts the user to select a category.

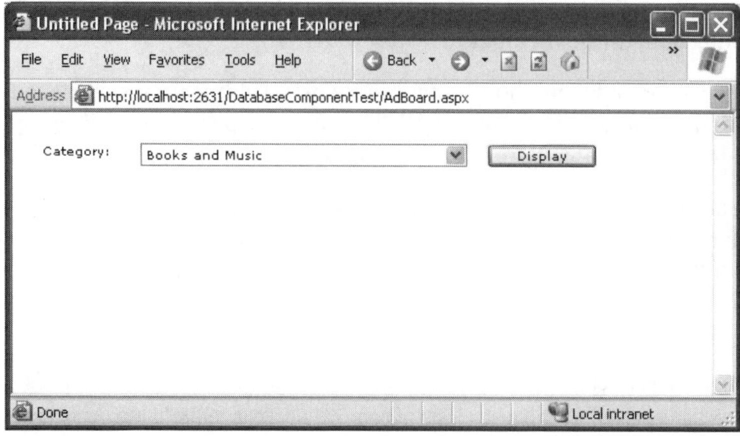

Figure 23-9. *The AdBoard listing*

Once a category is chosen, the matching items display, and a panel of controls appears, which allows the user to add a new entry to the AdBoard under the current category, as shown in Figure 23-10.

Untitled Page - Microsoft Internet Explorer

File Edit View Favorites Tools Help Back

Address http://localhost:2631/DatabaseComponentTest/AdBoard.aspx

Category: Books and Music Display

Add Item To Current Category

Title:

Price:

Description:

Add

ID	Title	Price	Description	Category_ID
1	Learning Thermodynamics	7.9900	A great place to start learning about entropy.	6
2	ASP.NET: The Complete Reference	17.9900	A steal at this price!	6
3	The Sound And the Fury	2.9900	Mild wear and coffee stains throughout. Still readable.	6

Done Local intranet

Figure 23-10. *The AdBoard listing*

In order to access the component more easily, the web page imports its namespace:

```
Imports DatabaseComponent
```

The page code creates the component to retrieve information from the database and displays it by binding the DataSet to the drop-down list or GridView control:

```
Public Partial Class AdBoard
    Inherits System.Web.UI.Page

    Protected Sub Page_Load(ByVal sender As Object, _
      ByVal e As System.EventArgs) Handles Me.Load

        If Not Page.IsPostBack
            Dim DB As New DBUtil()

            lstCategories.DataSource = DB.GetCategories()
            lstCategories.DataTextField = "Name"
            lstCategories.DataValueField = "ID"
            lstCategories.DataBind()
            pnlNew.Visible = False
        End If
    End Sub

    Protected Sub cmdDisplay_Click(ByVal sender As Object, _
      ByVal e As System.EventArgs) Handles cmdDisplay.Click

        Dim DB As New DBUtil()

        gridItems.DataSource = DB.GetItems( _
          Val(lstCategories.SelectedItem.Value))
        gridItems.DataBind()
        pnlNew.Visible = True
    End Sub

    Protected Sub cmdAdd_Click(ByVal sender As Object, _
      ByVal e As System.EventArgs) Handles cmdAdd.Click

        Dim DB As New DBUtil()

        Try
            DB.AddItem(txtTitle.Text, txtDescription.Text, _
              Val(txtPrice.Text), Val(lstCategories.SelectedItem.Value))

            gridItems.DataSource = DB.GetItems( _
              Val(lstCategories.SelectedItem.Value))
            gridItems.DataBind()
```

```
        Catch err As FormatException
            ' An error occurs if the user has entered an
            ' invalid price (non-numeric characters).
            ' In this case, take no action.
            ' Another option is to add a validator control
            ' for the price text box to prevent invalid input.
        End Try
    End Sub
End Class
```

Dissecting the Code . . .

- Not all the functionality of the component is used in this page. For example, the page doesn't use the AddCategory() method or the version of GetItems() that doesn't require a category number. This is completely normal. Other pages may use different features from the component.
- The code for the web page is free of data access code. It does, however, need to understand how to use a DataSet, and it needs to know specific field names to create a more attractive GridView with custom templates for layout (instead of automatically generated columns).
- The page could be improved with error handling code or validation controls. As it is, no validation is performed to ensure that the price is numeric or even to ensure that the required values are supplied.

■ **Tip** If you're debugging your code in Visual Studio, you'll find you can single-step from your web page code right into the code for the component, even if it isn't a part of the same solution. The appropriate source code file is loaded into your editor automatically, as long as it's available (and you've compiled the component in debug mode).

Enhancing the Component with Error Handling

One way you could enhance the component is with better support for error reporting. As it is, any database errors that occur are immediately returned to the calling code. In some cases (for example, if there is a legitimate database problem), this is a reasonable approach, because the component can't handle the problem.

However, the component fails to handle one common problem properly. This problem occurs if the connection string isn't found in the web.config file. Though the component tries to read the connection string as soon as it's created, the calling code doesn't realize a problem exists until it tries to use a database method.

A better approach is to notify the client as soon as the problem is detected, as shown in the following code example:

```
Public Class DBUtil
    Private connectionString As String

    Public Sub New()
        If WebConfigurationManager.ConnectionStrings("AdBoard") _
          Is Nothing Then
            Throw New ApplicationException( _
              "Missing ConnectionString variable in web.config.")
        Else
            connectionString = _
              WebConfigurationManager.ConnectionStrings( _
              "AdBoard").ConnectionString
        End If
    End Sub

    ' (Other class code omitted.)
End Class
```

This code throws an ApplicationException with a custom error message that indicates the problem. To provide even better reporting, you could create your own exception class that inherits from ApplicationException, as described in Chapter 8.

■ **Tip** Components often catch the exceptions that occur during low-level tasks (like reading a file or interacting with a database) and then throw less detailed exceptions like ApplicationException to notify the web page. That way, there's no chance that the user will see the technical error information. This is important, because detailed error messages can give hackers clues to how your code works—and how to subvert it.

Enhancing the Component with Aggregate Information

The component doesn't have to limit the type of information it provides to DataSets. Other information is also useful. For example, you might provide a read-only property called ItemFields that returns an array of strings representing the names for fields in the Items table. Or you might add another method that retrieves aggregate information about the entire table, such as the average cost of items in the database or the total number of currently listed items, as shown here:

```
Public Class DBUtil
    ' (Other class code omitted.)

    Public Function GetAveragePrice() As Decimal
        Dim query As String = "SELECT AVG(Price) FROM Items"

        Dim con As New SqlConnection(connectionString)
        Dim cmd As New SqlCommand(query, con)
```

```
        con.Open()
        Dim average As Decimal = CType(cmd.ExecuteScalar(), Decimal)
        con.Close()

        Return average
    End Function

    Public Function GetTotalItems() As Integer
        Dim query As String = "SELECT COUNT(*) FROM Items"

        Dim con As New SqlConnection(connectionString)
        Dim cmd As New SqlCommand(query, con)

        con.Open()
        Dim count As Integer = CType(cmd.ExecuteScalar(), Integer)
        con.Close()

        Return count
    End Function
End Class
```

These queries use some SQL that may be new to you (namely, the COUNT and AVG aggregate functions). However, these methods are just as easy to use from the client's perspective as GetItems() and GetCategories():

```
Dim DB As New DBUtil()
Dim averagePrice As Decimal = DB.GetAveragePrice()
Dim totalItems As Integer = DB.GetTotalItems()
```

It may have occurred to you that you can return information such as the total number of items through a read-only property procedure (such as TotalItems) instead of a method (in this case, GetTotalItems). Though this does work, property procedures are better left to information that is maintained with the class (in a private variable) or is easy to reconstruct. In this case, it takes a database operation to count the number of rows, and this database operation can cause an unusual problem or slow down performance if used frequently. To help reinforce that fact, a method is used instead of a property.

The ObjectDataSource

Using a dedicated database component is a great way to keep your code efficient and well-organized. It also makes it easy for you to apply changes later. However, this has a drawback—namely, you need to write quite a bit of code to create a web page *and* a separate data-access component. In Chapter 16, you saw that you could simplify your life by using components such as the SqlDataSource to encapsulate all your data access details. Unfortunately, that code-free approach won't work if you're using a separate component—or will it?

It turns out there is a way to get the best of both worlds and use a separate data-access component and easier web page data binding. Instead of using the SqlDataSource, you use the ObjectDataSource, which defines a link between your web page and your component. This won't save you from writing the actual data access code in your component, but it will save you from writing the tedious code in your web page to call the methods in your component, extract the data, format it, and display it in the page.

■ **Note** The ObjectDataSource allows you to create code-free web pages, but you still need to write the code in your component. You shouldn't view this as a drawback—after all, you need to write this code to get fine-grained control over exactly what's taking place and thereby optimize the performance of your data access strategy.

In the following sections, you'll learn how to take the existing DBUtil class presented earlier and use it in a data-bound web page. You'll learn how to replicate the example shown in Figure 23-9 and Figure 23-10 without writing any web page code.

Making Classes the ObjectDataSource Can Understand

Essentially, the ObjectDataSource allows you to create a declarative link between your web page controls and a data access component that queries and updates data. Although the ObjectDataSource is remarkably flexible, it can't support every conceivable component you could create. In fact, for your data component to be usable with the ObjectDataSource, you need to conform to a few rules:

- Your class must be stateless. That's because the ObjectDataSource will create an instance only when needed and destroy it at the end of every request.
- Your class must have a default, no-argument constructor.
- All the logic must be contained in a single class. (If you want to use different classes for selecting and updating your data, you'll need to wrap them in another higher-level class.)
- The query results must be provided as a DataSet, DataTable, or some sort of collection of objects. (If you decide to use a collection of objects, each data object needs to expose all the data fields as public properties.)

Fortunately, many of these rules are best practices that you should already be following. Even though the DBUtil class wasn't expressly designed for the ObjectDataSource, it meets all these criteria.

Selecting Records

You can learn a lot about the ObjectDataSource by building the page shown in Figure 23-10. In the following sections, you'll tackle this challenge.

The first step is to create the list box with the list of categories. For this list, you need an ObjectDataSource that links to the DBUtil class and calls the GetCategories() method to retrieve the full list of category records.

Next, define the ObjectDataSource and indicate the name of the class that contains the data access methods. You do this by specifying the fully qualified class name with the TypeName property, as shown here:

```
<asp:ObjectDataSource ID="sourceCategories" runat="server"
 TypeName="DatabaseComponent.DBUtil" ... />
```

Once you've attached the ObjectDataSource to a class, the next step is to point it to the methods it can use to select and update records.

The ObjectDataSource defines SelectMethod, DeleteMethod, UpdateMethod, and InsertMethod properties that you use to link your data access class to various tasks. Each property takes the name of the method in the data access class. In this example, you simply need to enable querying, so you need to set the SelectMethod property so it calls the GetCategories() method:

```
<asp:ObjectDataSource ID="sourceCategories" runat="server"
 TypeName="DatabaseComponent.DBUtil" SelectMethod="GetCategories" />
```

Once you've set up the ObjectDataSource, you can bind your web page controls in the same way you do with the SqlDataSource. Here's the tag you need for the list box:

```
<asp:DropDownList ID="lstCategories" runat="server"
  DataSourceID="sourceCategories" DataTextField="Name" DataValueField="ID">
</asp:DropDownList>
```

This tag shows a list of category names (thanks to the DataTextField property) and also keeps track of the category ID (using the DataValueField property).

This example works fine so far. You can run the test web page and see the list of categories in the list (as shown in Figure 23-9).

Using Method Parameters

The next step is to show the list of items in the current category in the GridView underneath. As with the SqlDataSource, the ObjectDataSource can be used only for a single query. That means you'll need to create a second ObjectDataSource that's able to retrieve the list of items by calling GetItems().

The trick here is that the GetItems() method requires a single parameter (named categoryID). That means you need to create an ObjectDataSource that includes a single parameter. You can use all the same types of parameters used with the SqlDataSource to get values from the query string, other controls, and so on. In this case, the category ID is provided by the SelectedValue property of the list box, so you can use a control parameter that points to this property.

Here's the ObjectDataSource definition you need:

```
<asp:ObjectDataSource ID="sourceItems" runat="server" SelectMethod="GetItems"
 TypeName="DatabaseComponent.DBUtil" >
  <SelectParameters>
      <asp:ControlParameter ControlID="lstCategories" Name="categoryID"
        PropertyName="SelectedValue" Type="Int32" />
  </SelectParameters>
</asp:ObjectDataSource>
```

Again, you use the DBUtil class, but this time it's the GetItems() method you need. Even though there are two overloaded versions of the GetItems() method (one that takes a categoryID parameter and one that doesn't), you don't need to worry. The ObjectDataSource automatically uses the correct overload by looking at the parameters you've defined.

In this case, you use a single parameter that extracts the selected category ID from the list box and passes it to the GetItems() method. Notice that the name defined in the ControlParameter tag matches the parameter name of the GetItems() method. This is an absolute requirement. The ObjectDataSource searches for the GetItems() method using reflection, and it verifies that any potential match has the number of parameters, parameter names, and data types that you've indicated. This searching process allows the ObjectDataSource to distinguish between different overloaded versions of the same method. If the ObjectDataSource can't find the method you've specified, an exception is raised at this point.

■ **Tip** If you're ever in doubt what method is being called in your data-access component, place a breakpoint on the possible methods, and use Visual Studio's debugging features (as described in Chapter 4).

The final step is to link the GridView to the new ObjectDataSource using the DataSourceID. Here's the tag that does it:

```
<asp:GridView ID="GridView1" runat="server" DataSourceID="sourceItems"/>
```

This is all you need. You should keep the Display button, because it triggers a page post-back and allows the ObjectDataSource to get to work. (If you don't want to use this button, set the AutoPostback property on the list box to True so it posts back whenever you change the selection.) You don't need to write any event-handling code to react when the button is clicked. The queries are executed automatically, and the controls are bound automatically.

Updating Records

The final step is to provide a way for the user to add new items. The easiest way to make this possible is to use a rich data control that deals with individual records—either the DetailsView or the FormsView. The DetailsView is the simpler of the two, because it doesn't require a template. It's the one used in the following example.

Ideally, you'd define the DetailsView using a tag like this and let it generate all the fields it needs based on the bound data source:

```
<asp:DetailsView ID="DetailsView1" runat="server" DataSourceID="sourceItems"/>
```

Unfortunately, this won't work in this example. The problem is that this approach creates too many fields. In this example, you don't want the user to specify the item ID (that's set by the database automatically) or the category ID (that's based on the currently selected category). So neither of these details should appear. The only way to make sure this is the case is to turn off automatic field generation and define each field you want explicitly, as shown here:

```
<asp:DetailsView ID="DetailsView1" runat="server"
  DataSourceID="sourceItems" AutoGenerateRows="False">
  <Fields>
    <asp:BoundField DataField="Title" HeaderText="Title" />
    <asp:BoundField DataField="Price" HeaderText="Price"/>
    <asp:BoundField DataField="Description" HeaderText="Description" />
  </Fields>
</asp:DetailsView>
```

You need to make a couple of other changes. To allow inserting, you need to set the AutoGenerateInsertButton to True. This way, the DetailsView creates the links that allow you to start entering a new record and then insert it. At the same time, you can set the DefaultMode property to Insert. This way, the DetailsView is always in insert mode and is used exclusively for adding records (not displaying them), much like the non-data-bound page shown earlier.

```
<asp:DetailsView ID="DetailsView1" runat="server"
  DefaultMode="Insert" AutoGenerateInsertButton="True"
  DataSourceID="sourceItems" AutoGenerateRows="False">
  ...
</asp:DetailsView>
```

The ObjectDataSource provides the same type of support for updatable data binding as the SqlDataSource. The first step is to specify the InsertMethod, which needs to be a public method in the same class:

```
<asp:ObjectDataSource ID="sourceItems" runat="server"
 TypeName="DatabaseComponent.DBUtil"
 SelectMethod="GetItems" InsertMethod="AddItem" >
</asp:ObjectDataSource>
```

The challenge is in making sure the InsertMethod has the right signature. As with the SqlDataSource, updates, inserts, and deletes automatically receive a collection of parameters from the linked data control. These parameters have the same names as the corresponding field names. So in this case, the fields are Title, Price, and Description, which exactly match the parameter names in the AddItem() method. (The capitalization is not the same, but the ObjectDataSource is not case-sensitive, so this isn't a problem.)

This still has a problem, however. When the user commits an edit, the DetailsView submits the three parameters you expect (Title, Price, and Description). However, the AddItem() method needs a *fourth* parameter—CategoryID. We've left that parameter out of the DetailsView fields, because you don't want the user to be able to set the category ID. However, you still need to supply it to the method.

So where can you get the current category ID from? The easiest choice is to extract it from the list box, just as you did for the GetItems() method. All you need to do is add a ControlParameter tag that defines a parameter named CategoryID and binds it to the SelectedValue property of the list box. Here's the revised tag for the ObjectDataSource:

```
<asp:ObjectDataSource ID="sourceItems" runat="server" SelectMethod="GetItems"
 TypeName="DatabaseComponent.DBUtil" InsertMethod="AddItem" >
  <SelectParameters>
    ...
  </SelectParameters>
  <InsertParameters>
    <asp:ControlParameter ControlID="lstCategories" Name="categoryID"
     PropertyName="SelectedValue" Type="Int32" />
  </InsertParameters>
</asp:ObjectDataSource>
```

Now you have all the parameters you need—the three from the DetailsView and the one extra from the list box. When the user attempts to insert a new record, the ObjectDataSource collects these four parameters, makes sure they match the signature for the AddItem() method, puts them in order, and then calls the method.

Figure 23-11 shows an insert in progress.

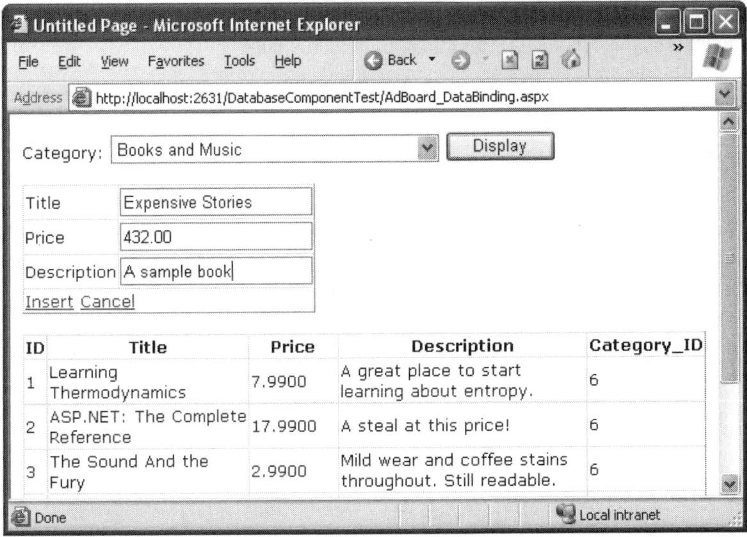

Figure 23-11. *Inserting with the DetailsView*

When you click the Insert button, quite a bit takes place behind the scenes. Here's a breakdown of what actually happens:

1. The DetailsView gathers all the new values, and passes them to the ObjectDataSource.
2. The ObjectDataSource calls the DBUtil.AddItem() method, passing all the values it received from the DetailsView in the right positions (by matching the field names with the parameter names) and the selected value from the lstCategories list box.
3. The DBUtil.AddItem() method builds a parameterized SQL command. It then opens a database connection and executes the command to insert the new record. (At this point, the ASP.NET data binding system takes a break and lets other events occur, such as Page.Load.)
4. Just before the page is rendered, the data binding process begins. The DropDownList asks the first ObjectDataSource for the list of categories (which triggers a call to the DBUtil.GetCategories() method), and the GridView requests the list of items from the second ObjectDataSource (which triggers the DBUtil.GetItems() method).

Because the page is always re-bound *after* any insert and update operations are finished, you'll always see the latest information in your web controls. For example, if you add a new item, you'll see it appear immediately, complete with the unique ID value that the database server generates automatically.

■ **Note** In some cases, you might need to supply an extra parameter that needs to be set programmatically. In this case, you need to define a plain-vanilla Parameter tag (instead of a ControlParameter tag), with a name and data type but no value. Then you can respond to the ObjectDataSource.Updating event to fill in the value you need just in time. It's a little messy (and it forces you to write code in your web page), but it's sometimes a necessity. Chapter 16 demonstrates this technique with the SqlDataSource control.

The Last Word

The examples in this chapter demonstrate safe, solid ways to create components and integrate them into your website. As you can see, these objects respect the rules of encapsulation, which means they do a specific business task, but they don't get involved in generating the user interface for the application. For example, the DBUtil class uses ADO.NET code to retrieve records or update a database. It's up to other controls, such as the GridView and DetailsView, to provide the presentation.

CHAPTER 24

■ ■ ■

Caching

ASP.NET applications are a bit of a contradiction. On the one hand, because they're hosted over the Internet, they have unique requirements—namely, they need to be able to serve hundreds of clients as easily and quickly as they deal with a single user. On the other hand, ASP.NET includes some remarkable tricks that let you design and code a web application in the same way you program a desktop application. These tricks are useful, but they can lead developers into trouble. The problem is that ASP.NET makes it easy to forget you're creating a web application—so easy, that you might introduce programming practices that will slow or cripple your application when it's used by a large number of users in the real world.

Fortunately, a middle ground exists. You can use the incredible timesaving features such as view state, web controls, and session state that you've spent the last 20-odd chapters learning about and still create a robust web application. But to finish the job properly, you'll need to invest a little extra time to profile and optimize your website's performance. One of the easiest ways to improve perform is to use *caching*, a technique that temporarily stores valuable information in server memory so it can be reused. Unlike the other types of state management you learned about in Chapter 7, caching includes some built-in features that ensure good performance.

Understanding Caching

ASP.NET has taken some dramatic steps forward with caching. Many developers who first learn about caching see it as a bit of a frill, but nothing could be further from the truth. Used intelligently, caching can provide a twofold, threefold, or even tenfold performance improvement by retaining important data for just a short period of time.

Caching is often used to store information that's retrieved from a database. This makes sense—after all, retrieving information from a database takes time. With careful optimization, you can reduce the time and lessen the burden imposed on the database to a certain extent, but you can never eliminate it. But with a system that uses caching, some data requests won't require a database connection and a query. Instead, they'll retrieve the information directly from server memory, which is a much faster proposition.

Of course, storing information in memory isn't always a good idea. Server memory is a limited resource; if you try to store too much, some of that information will be paged to disk, potentially slowing down the entire system. That's why ASP.NET caching is *self-limiting*. When you store information in a cache, you can expect to find it there on a future request, most of the time. However, the lifetime of that information is at the discretion of the server. If the cache becomes full or other applications consume a large amount of memory, data will be selectively evicted from the cache, ensuring that the application continues to perform well. It's this self-sufficiency that makes caching so powerful (and would make it extremely complicated to implement on your own).

When to Use Caching

The secret to getting the most out of caching is choosing the right time to use it. A good caching strategy identifies the most frequently used pieces of data that are the most time-consuming to create, and stores them. If you store too much information, you risk filling up the cache with relatively unimportant data, and forcing out the content you really want to keep.

Here are two caching guidelines to keep you on the right track:

Cache data (or web pages) that are expensive: In other words, cache information that's time-consuming to create. The results of a database query or contents of a file are good examples. Not only does it take time to open a database connection or a file, but it can also delay or lock out other users who are trying to do the same thing at the same time.

Cache data (or web pages) that are used frequently: There's no point setting aside memory for information that's never going to be needed again. For example, you might choose not to cache product detail pages, because there are hundreds of different products, each with its own page. But it makes more sense to cache the list of product categories, because that information will be reused to serve many different requests.

If you keep these two rules in mind, you can get two benefits from caching at once—you can improve both performance and scalability.

Performance is a measure of how quickly a web page works for a single user. Caching improves performance, because it bypasses bottlenecks like the database. As a result, web pages are processed and sent back to the client more quickly.

Scalability measures how the performance of your web application degrades as more and more people use it at the same time. Caching improves scalability, because it allows you to reuse the same information for requests that happen in quick succession. With caching, more and more people can use your website, but the number of trips to the database won't change very much. Therefore, the overall burden on the system will stay relatively constant, as shown in Figure 24-1.

Many optimization techniques enhance scalability at the cost of performance, or vice versa. Caching is remarkable because it gives you the best of both worlds.

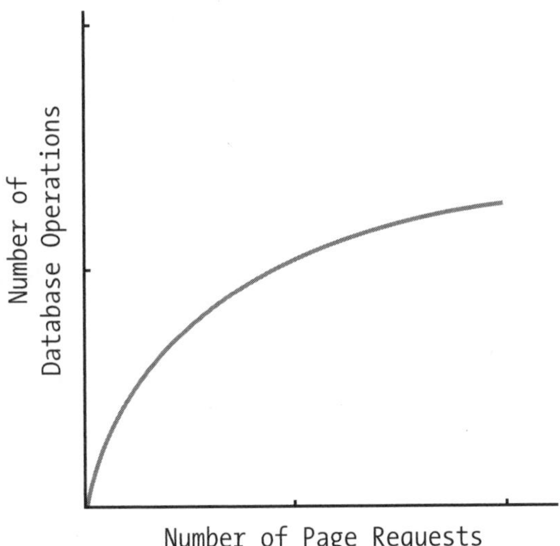

Figure 24-1. *The effect of good caching*

Caching in ASP.NET

ASP.NET really has two types of caching. Your applications can and should use both types, because they complement each other:

- *Output caching*: This is the simplest type of caching. It stores a copy of the final rendered HTML page that is sent to the client. The next client that submits a request for this page doesn't actually run the page. Instead, the final HTML output is sent automatically. The time that would have been required to run the page and its code is completely reclaimed.

- *Data caching*: This is carried out manually in your code. To use data caching, you store important pieces of information that are time-consuming to reconstruct (such as a DataSet retrieved from a database) in the cache. Other pages can check for the existence of this information and use it, thereby bypassing the steps ordinarily required to retrieve it. Data caching is conceptually the same as using application state, but it's much more server-friendly because items will be removed from the cache automatically when it grows too large and performance could be affected. Items can also be set to expire automatically.

Also, two specialized types of caching build on these models:

- *Fragment caching*: This is a specialized type of output caching—instead of caching the HTML for the whole page, it allows you to cache the HTML for a portion of it. Fragment caching works by storing the rendered HTML output of a user control on a page. The next time the page is executed, the same page events fire (and so your page code will still run), but the code for the appropriate user control isn't executed.

- *Data source caching*: This is the caching that's built into the data source controls, including the SqlDataSource, ObjectDataSource, and XmlDataSource. Technically, data source caching uses data caching. The difference is that you don't need to handle the process explicitly. Instead, you simply configure the appropriate properties, and the data source control manages the caching storage and retrieval.

In this chapter, you'll learn about all these types of caching. You'll begin by learning the basics of output caching and data caching. Next, you'll examine the caching in the data source controls. Finally, you'll explore one of ASP.NET's hottest new features—linking cached items to tables in a database with SQL cache dependencies.

Output Caching

With output caching, the final rendered HTML of the page is cached. When the same page is requested again, the control objects are not created, the page life cycle doesn't start, and none of your code executes. Instead, the cached HTML is served. Clearly, output caching gets the theoretical maximum performance increase, because all the overhead of your code is sidestepped.

To see output caching in action, you can create a simple page that displays the current time of day. Figure 24-2 shows this page.

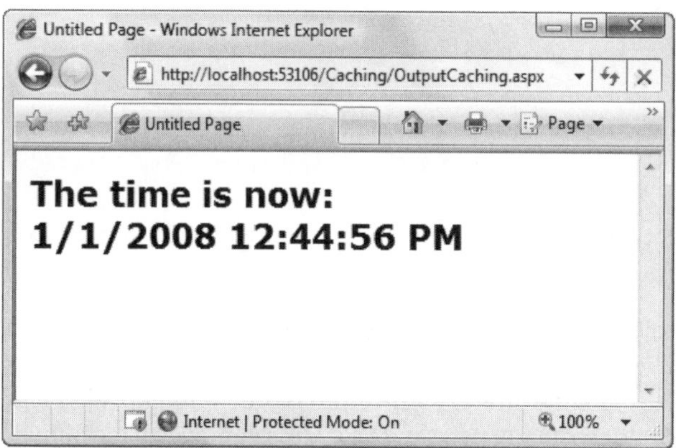

Figure 24-2. *Displaying the time a page is served*

The code for this task is elementary:

```
Public Partial Class OutputCaching
    Inherits System.Web.UI.Page

    Protected Sub Page_Load(ByVal sender As Object, _
      ByVal e As System.EventArgs) Handles Me.Load
        lblDate.Text = "The time is now:<br />"
        lblDate.Text &= DateTime.Now.ToString()
    End Sub

End Class
```

You can cache an ASP.NET page in two ways. The most common approach is to insert the OutputCache directive at the top of your .aspx file, just below the Page directive, as shown here:

```
<%@ OutputCache Duration="20" VaryByParam="None" %>
```

The Duration attribute instructs ASP.NET to cache the page for 20 seconds. The VaryByParam attribute is also required—but you'll learn about its effect later on in the "Caching and the Query String" section.

When you run the test page, you'll discover some interesting behavior. The first time you access the page, you will see the current time displayed. If you refresh the page a short time later, however, the page will not be updated. Instead, ASP.NET will automatically send the cached HTML output to you, until it expires in 20 seconds. If ASP.NET receives a request after the cached page has expired, ASP.NET will run the page code again, generate a new cached copy of the HTML output, and use that for the next 20 seconds.

Twenty seconds may seem like a trivial amount of time, but in a high-volume site, it can make a dramatic difference. For example, you might cache a page that provides a list of products from a catalog. By caching the page for 20 seconds, you limit database access for this page to three operations per minute. Without caching, the page will try to connect to the database once for each client and could easily make dozens of requests in the course of 20 seconds.

Of course, just because you request that a page should be stored for 20 seconds doesn't mean that it actually will be. The page could be evicted from the cache early if the system finds that memory is becoming scarce. This allows you to use caching freely, without worrying too much about hampering your application by using up vital memory.

■ **Tip** When you recompile a cached page, ASP.NET will automatically remove the page from the cache. This prevents problems where a page isn't properly updated, because the older, cached version is being used. However, you might still want to disable caching while testing your application. Otherwise, you may have trouble using variable watches, breakpoints, and other debugging techniques, because your code will not be executed if a cached copy of the page is available.

Caching on the Client Side

Another option is to cache the page exclusively on the client side. In this case, the browser stores a copy and will automatically use this page if the client browses back to the page or retypes the page's URL. However, if the user clicks the Refresh button, the cached copy will be abandoned, and the page will be rerequested from the server, which will run the appropriate page code once again. You can cache a page on the client side using the Location attribute in the OutputCache directive, which specifies a value from the System.Web.UI.OutputCacheLocation enumeration, as shown here:

```
<%@ OutputCache Duration="20" VaryByParam="None" Location="Client" %>
```

Client-side caching is less common than server-side caching. Because the page is still re-created for every separate user, it won't reduce code execution or database access nearly as dramatically as server-side caching (which shares a single cached copy among all users). However, client-side caching can be a useful technique if your cached page uses some sort of personalized data. Even though each user is in a separate session, the page will be created only once and reused for all clients, ensuring that most will receive the wrong greeting. Instead, you can either use fragment caching to cache the generic portion of the page or use client-side caching to store a user-specific version on each client's computer.

Caching and the Query String

One of the main considerations in caching is deciding when a page can be reused and when information must be accurate up to the latest second. Developers, with their love of instant gratification (and lack of patience), generally tend to overemphasize the importance of real-time information. You can usually use caching to efficiently reuse slightly stale data without a problem and with a considerable performance improvement.

Of course, sometimes information needs to be dynamic. One example is if the page uses information from the current user's session to tailor the user interface. In this case, full page caching just isn't appropriate, because the same page can't be reused for requests from different users (although fragment caching may help). Another example is if the page is receiving information from another page through the query string. In this case, the page is too dynamic to cache—or is it?

The current example sets the VaryByParam attribute on the OutputCache directive to None, which effectively tells ASP.NET that you need to store only one copy of the cached page, which is suitable for all scenarios. If the request for this page adds query string arguments to the URL, it makes no difference—ASP.NET will always reuse the same output until it expires. You can test this by adding a query string parameter manually in the browser window. For example, try tacking ?a=b on to the end of your URL. The cached output is still used.

Based on this experiment, you might assume that output caching isn't suitable for pages that use query string arguments. But ASP.NET actually provides another option. You can set the VaryByParam attribute to * to indicate that the page uses the query string and to instruct ASP.NET to cache separate copies of the page for different query string arguments:

```
<%@ OutputCache Duration="20" VaryByParam="*" %>
```

Now when you request the page with additional query string information, ASP.NET will examine the query string. If the string matches a previous request and a cached copy of that page exists, it will be reused. Otherwise, a new copy of the page will be created and cached separately.

To get a better idea of how this process works, consider the following series of requests:

1. You request a page without any query string parameter and receive page copy A.
2. You request the page with the parameter ProductID=1. You receive page copy B.
3. Another user requests the page with the parameter ProductID=2. That user receives copy C.
4. Another user requests the page with ProductID=1. If the cached output B has not expired, it's sent to the user.
5. The user then requests the page with no query string parameters. If copy A has not expired, it's sent from the cache.

You can try this on your own, although you might want to lengthen the amount of time that the cached page is retained to make it easier to test.

■ **Note** Output caching works well if the pages depend only on server-side data (for example, the data in a database) and the data in the query string. However, output caching doesn't work if the page output depends on user-specific information such as session data or cookies, because there's no way to vary caching based on these criteria. Output caching also won't work with dynamic pages that change their content in response to control events. In these situations, use fragment caching instead to cache a portion of the page, or use data caching to cache specific information. Both techniques are discussed later in this chapter.

Caching with Specific Query String Parameters

Setting VaryByParam to the wildcard asterisk (*) is unnecessarily vague. It's usually better to specifically identify an important query string variable by name. Here's an example:

```
<%@ OutputCache Duration="20" VaryByParam="ProductID" %>
```

In this case, ASP.NET will examine the query string, looking for the ProductID parameter. Requests with different ProductID parameters will be cached separately, but all other parameters will be ignored. This is particularly useful if the page may be passed additional query string information that it doesn't use. ASP.NET has no way to distinguish the "important" query string parameters without your help.

You can specify several parameters as long as you separate them with semicolons:

```
<%@ OutputCache Duration="20" VaryByParam="ProductID;CurrencyType" %>
```

In this case, ASP.NET will cache separate versions, provided the query string differs by ProductID or CurrencyType.

A Multiple Caching Example

The following example uses two web pages to demonstrate how multiple versions of a web page can be cached separately. The first page, QueryStringSender.aspx, isn't cached. It provides three buttons, as shown in Figure 24-3.

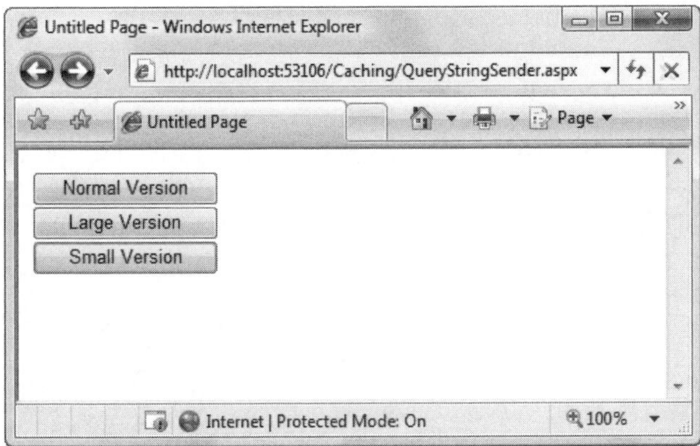

Figure 24-3. *Three page options*

A single event handler handles the Click event for all three buttons. The event handler navigates to the QueryStringRecipient.aspx page and adds a Version parameter to the query string to indicate which button was clicked—cmdNormal, cmdLarge, or cmdSmall.

```
Protected Sub cmdVersion_Click(ByVal sender As Object, _
  ByVal e As System.EventArgs) _
  Handles cmdNormal.Click, cmdLarge.Click, cmdSmall.Click

    Response.Redirect("QueryStringRecipient.aspx" & _
      "?Version=" & CType(sender, Control).ID)
End Sub
```

The QueryStringRecipient.aspx destination page displays the familiar date message. The page uses an OutputCache directive that looks for a single query string parameter (named Version):

```
<%@ OutputCache Duration="60" VaryByParam="Version" %>
```

In other words, this has three separately maintained HTML outputs: one where Version equals cmdSmall, one where Version equals cmdLarge, and one where Version equals cmdNormal.

Although it isn't necessary for this example, the Page.Load event handler in QueryRecipient.aspx tailors the page by changing the font size of the label accordingly. This makes it easy to distinguish the three versions of the page and verify that the caching is working as expected.

```
Protected Sub Page_Load(ByVal sender As Object, _
  ByVal e As System.EventArgs) Handles Me.Load

    lblDate.Text = "The time is now:<br />" & DateTime.Now.ToString()

    Select Case Request.QueryString("Version")
        Case "cmdLarge"
            lblDate.Font.Size = FontUnit.XLarge
        Case "cmdNormal"
            lblDate.Font.Size = FontUnit.Large
        Case "cmdSmall"
            lblDate.Font.Size = FontUnit.Small
    End Select
End Sub
```

Figure 24-4 shows one of the cached outputs for this page.

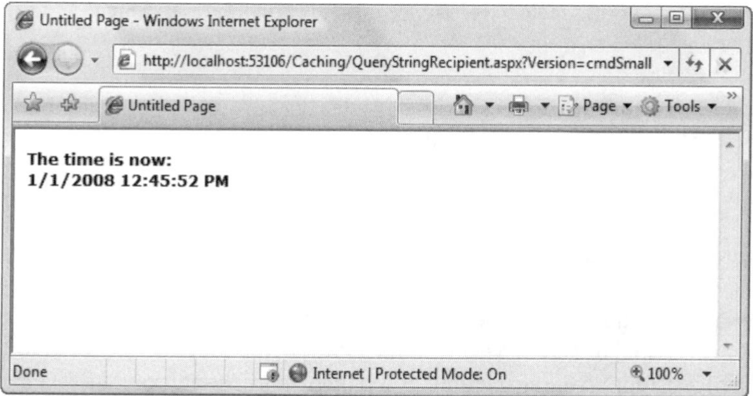

Figure 24-4. *One page with three cached outputs*

Custom Caching Control

Varying by query string parameters isn't the only option when storing multiple cached versions of a page. ASP.NET also allows you to create your own procedure that decides whether to cache a new page version or reuse an existing one. This code examines whatever information is appropriate and then returns a string. ASP.NET uses this string to implement caching. If your code generates the same string for different requests, ASP.NET will reuse the cached page. If your code generates a new string value, ASP.NET will generate a new cached version and store it separately.

One way you could use custom caching is to cache different versions of a page based on the browser type. That way, Firefox browsers will always receive Firefox-optimized pages, and Internet Explorer users will receive IE-optimized HTML. To set up this sort of logic, you start by adding the OutputCache directive to the pages that will be cached. Use the VaryByCustom attribute to specify a name that represents the type of custom caching you're creating. (You can pick any name you like.) The following example uses the name Browser because pages will be cached based on the client browser:

```
<%@ OutputCache Duration="10" VaryByParam="None" VaryByCustom="Browser" %>
```

Next, you need to create the procedure that will generate the custom caching string. This procedure must be coded in the Global.asax application file (or its code-behind file) and must use the following syntax:

```
Public Overrides Function GetVaryByCustomString( _
  ByVal context As HttpContext, ByVal arg As String) As String

    ' Check for the requested type of caching.
    If arg = "Browser"
        ' Determine the current browser.
        Dim BrowserName As String
        BrowserName = Context.Request.Browser.Browser
```

```
        ' Indicate that this string should be used to vary caching.
        Return BrowserName
    Else
        ' For any other type of caching, use the default logic.
        Return MyBase.GetVaryByCustomString(context, arg)
    End If
End Function
```

The GetVaryByCustomString() function passes a string with a value of "VaryByCustom" in the arg parameter. This allows you to create an application that implements several types of custom caching in the same function. Each type would use a different VaryByCustom name (such as Browser, BrowserVersion, or DayOfWeek). Your GetVaryByCustomString() function would see the value "VaryByCustom" in the arg parameter and then return the appropriate caching string. If the caching strings for different requests match, ASP.NET will reuse the cached copy of the page. Or to look at it another way, ASP.NET will create and store a separate cached version of the page for each caching string it encounters.

Interestingly, the base implementation of the GetVaryByCustomString() method already includes the logic for browser-based caching. That means you don't need to code the method shown previously. The base implementation of GetVaryByCustomString() creates the cached string based on the browser name *and* major version number, which makes it a bit more selective than the version shown here. If you want to change how this logic works (for example, to vary based on name, major version, and minor version), you could override the GetVaryByCustomString() method, as in the previous example.

The OutputCache directive has a third attribute that you can use to define caching. This attribute, VaryByHeader, allows you to store separate versions of a page based on the value of an HTTP header received with the request. You can specify a single header or a list of headers separated by semicolons. Multilingual sites could use this technique to cache different versions of a page based on the client browser language.

```
<%@ OutputCache Duration="20" VaryByParam="None"
    VaryByHeader="Accept-Language" %>
```

Fragment Caching

In some cases, you may find that you can't cache an entire page, but you would still like to cache a portion that is expensive to create and doesn't vary frequently (like a list of categories in a product catalog). One way to implement this sort of scenario is to use data caching to store just the underlying information used for the page. You'll examine this technique in the next section. Another option is to use fragment caching.

To implement fragment caching, you need to create a user control for the portion of the page you want to cache. You can then add the OutputCache directive to the user control. The result is that the page will not be cached, but the user control will.

Fragment caching is conceptually the same as page caching. It has only one catch—if your page retrieves a cached version of a user control, it cannot interact with it in code. For example, if your user control provides properties, your web page code cannot modify or access these properties. When the cached version of the user control is used, a block of HTML is simply inserted into the page. The corresponding user control object is not available.

Cache Profiles

One problem with output caching is that you need to embed the instruction into the page—either in the .aspx markup portion or in the code of the class. Although the first option (using the OutputCache directive) is relatively clean, it still produces management problems if you create dozens of cached pages. If you want to change the caching for all these pages (for example, moving the caching duration from 30 to 60 seconds), you need to modify every page. ASP.NET also needs to recompile these pages.

ASP.NET includes a feature called *cache profiles* that makes it easy to apply the same caching settings to a group of pages. With cache profiles, you define a group of caching settings in the web.config file, associate a name with these settings, and then apply these settings to multiple pages using the name. That way, you have the freedom to modify all the linked pages at once simply by changing the caching profile in the web.config file.

To define a cache profile, you use the <add> tag in the <outputCacheProfiles> section, as follows. You assign a name and a duration.

```
<configuration>
  <system.web>
    <caching>
      <outputCacheSettings>
        <outputCacheProfiles>
          <add name="ProductItemCacheProfile" duration="60" />
        </outputCacheProfiles>
      </outputCacheSettings>
    </caching>
  ...
  </system.web>
</configuration>
```

You can now use this profile in a page through the CacheProfile attribute:

```
<%@ OutputCache CacheProfile="ProductItemCacheProfile" VaryByParam="None" %>
```

Interestingly, if you want to apply other caching details, such as the VaryByParam behavior, you can set it either as an attribute in the OutputCache directive or as an attribute of the <add> tag for the profile. Just make sure you start with a lowercase letter if you use the <add> tag, because the property names are camel case, as are all configuration settings, and case is important in XML.

Data Caching

Data caching is the most flexible type of caching, but it also forces you to take specific additional steps in your code to implement it. The basic principle of data caching is that you add items that are expensive to create to a built-in collection object called Cache. Cache is a property of the Page class, and it returns an instance of the System.Web.Caching.Cache class. This object works much like the Application object you saw in Chapter 7. It's globally available to all requests from all clients in the application. But it has three key differences:

The Cache object is thread-safe: This means you don't need to explicitly lock or unlock the Cache object before adding or removing an item. However, the objects in the Cache object will still need to be thread-safe themselves. For example, if you create a custom business object, more than one client could try to use that object at once, which could lead to invalid data. You can code around this limitation in various ways—one easy approach that you'll see in this chapter is to just make a duplicate copy of the object if you need to work with it in a web page.

Items in the Cache object are removed automatically: ASP.NET will remove an item if it expires, if one of the objects or files it depends on changes, or if the server becomes low on memory. This means you can freely use the cache without worrying about wasting valuable server memory, because ASP.NET will remove items as needed. But because items in the cache can be removed, you always need to check whether a cache object exists before you attempt to use it. Otherwise, you could generate a null reference exception.

Items in the cache support dependencies: You can link a cached object to a file, a database table, or another type of resource. If this resource changes, your cached object is automatically deemed invalid and released.

Adding Items to the Cache

You can insert an object into the cache in several ways. You can simply assign it to a new key name (as you would with the Session or Application collection):

```
Cache("KeyName") = objectToCache
```

However, this approach is generally discouraged because it doesn't give you any control over the amount of time the object will be retained in the cache. A better approach is to use the Insert() method.

The Insert() method has four overloaded versions. The most useful one requires five parameters:

```
Cache.Insert(key, item, dependencies, absoluteExpiration, slidingExpiration)
```

Table 24-1 describes these parameters.

Table 24-1. *Cache.Insert() Parameters*

Parameter	Description
key	A string that assigns a name to this cached item in the collection and allows you to look it up later.
item	The actual object you want to cache.
dependencies	A CacheDependency object that allows you to create a dependency for this item in the cache. If you don't want to create a dependent item, just specify a null reference (Nothing) for this parameter.
absoluteExpiration	A DateTime object representing the date and time at which the item will be removed from the cache.
slidingExpiration	A TimeSpan object representing how long ASP.NET will wait between requests before removing a cached item. For example, if this value is 20 minutes, ASP.NET will evict the item if it isn't used by any code for a 20-minute period.

Typically, you won't use all of these parameters at once. Cache dependencies, for example, are a special tool you'll consider a little later in the "Caching with Dependencies" section. Also, you cannot set both a sliding expiration and an absolute expiration policy at the same time. If you want to use an absolute expiration, set the slidingExpiration parameter to TimeSpan.Zero:

```
Cache.Insert("MyItem", obj, Nothing, _
  DateTime.Now.AddMinutes(60), TimeSpan.Zero)
```

Absolute expirations are best when you know the information in a given item can be considered valid only for a specific amount of time (such as a stock chart or a weather report). Sliding expiration, on the other hand, is more useful when you know that a cached item will always remain valid (such as with historical data or a product catalog) but should still be allowed to expire if it isn't being used. To set a sliding expiration policy, set the absoluteExpiration parameter to DateTime.MaxValue, as shown here:

```
Cache.Insert("MyItem", obj, Nothing, _
  DateTime.MaxValue, TimeSpan.FromMinutes(10))
```

Tip Don't be afraid to cache for a long time. For example, Microsoft's case studies often store cached data for 100 minutes or more.

A Simple Cache Test

The following page presents a simple caching test. An item is cached for 30 seconds and reused for requests in that time. The page code always runs (because the page itself isn't cached), checks the cache, and retrieves or constructs the item as needed. It also reports whether the item was found in the cache.

```
Public Partial Class SimpleDataCache
    Inherits System.Web.UI.Page

     Protected Sub Page_Load(ByVal sender As Object, _
       ByVal e As System.EventArgs) Handles Me.Load

        If Me.IsPostBack Then
            lblInfo.Text &= "Page posted back.<br />"
        Else
            lblInfo.Text &= "Page created.<br />"
        End If

        If Cache("TestItem") Is Nothing Then
            lblInfo.Text &= "Creating TestItem...<br />"
            Dim testItem As DateTime = DateTime.Now
```

```
            lblInfo.Text &= "Storing TestItem in cache "
            lblInfo.Text &= "for 30 seconds.<br />"
            Cache.Insert("TestItem", testItem, Nothing, _
              DateTime.Now.AddSeconds(30), TimeSpan.Zero)
        Else
            lblInfo.Text &= "Retrieving TestItem...<br />"
            Dim testItem As DateTime = CType(Cache("TestItem"), DateTime)
            lblInfo.Text &= "TestItem is '" & testItem.ToString()
            lblInfo.Text &= "'<br />"
        End If

        lblInfo.Text &= "<br />"
    End Sub

End Class
```

Figure 24-5 shows the result after the page has been loaded and posted back several times in the 30-second period.

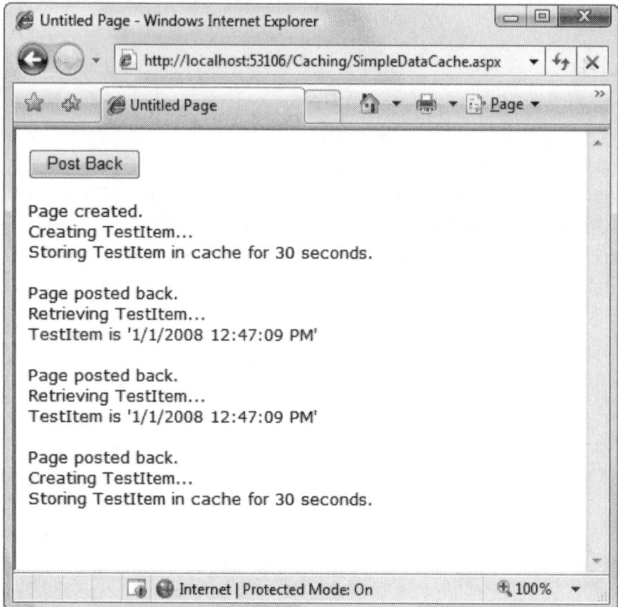

Figure 24-5. *A simple cache test*

Caching to Provide Multiple Views

The next example shows a more interesting demonstration of caching, which includes retrieving information from a database and storing it in a DataSet. This information is then displayed in a GridView. However, the output for the web page can't be efficiently cached because the user is given the chance to customize the display by hiding any combination of columns. Note that even with just ten columns, you can construct more than a thousand different possible views by hiding and showing various columns. These are far too many columns for successful output caching!

Figure 24-6 shows the page.

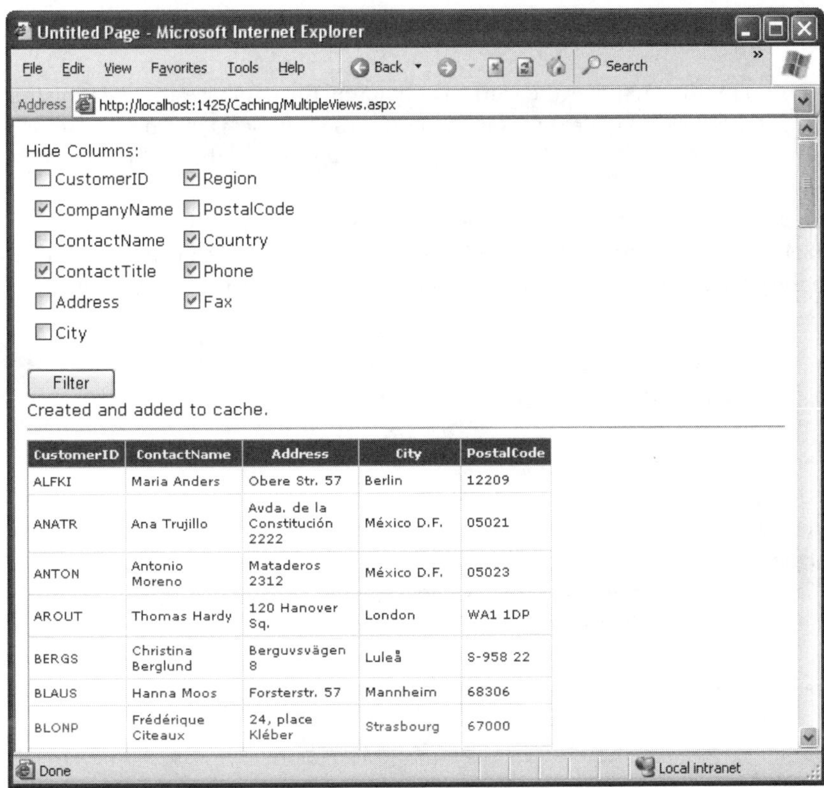

Figure 24-6. *Filtering information from a cached DataSet*

The DataSet is constructed in the dedicated RetrieveData() function shown here. In order to use this code as written, you must import the System.Data, System.Data.SqlClient, and System.Web.Configuration namespaces in the web page.

```
Private Function RetrieveData() As DataSet
    Dim connectionString As String = _
      WebConfigurationManager.ConnectionStrings("Northwind").ConnectionString
    Dim SQLSelect As String = "SELECT * FROM Customers"
    Dim con As New SqlConnection(connectionString)
    Dim cmd As New SqlCommand(SQLSelect, con)
    Dim adapter As New SqlDataAdapter(cmd)
    Dim ds As New DataSet()

    Try
        con.Open()
        adapter.Fill(ds, "Customers")
```

```
    Finally
        con.Close()
    End Try

    Return ds
End Function
```

The RetrieveData() method handles the work of contacting the database and creating the DataSet. You need another level of code that checks to see if the DataSet is in the cache and adds it when needed. The best way to write this code is to add another method. This method is called GetDataSet().

The GetDataSet() method attempts to retrieve the DataSet from the cache. If it cannot retrieve the DataSet, it calls the RetrieveData() method and then adds the DataSet to the cache. It also reports on the page whether the DataSet was retrieved from the cache or generated manually.

```
Private Function GetDataSet() As DataSet
    Dim ds As DataSet = CType(Cache("Customers"), DataSet)

    ' Contact the database if necessary.
    If ds Is Nothing Then
        ds = RetrieveData()
        Cache.Insert("Customers", ds, Nothing, _
          DateTime.MaxValue, TimeSpan.FromMinutes(2))
        lblCacheStatus.Text = "Created and added to cache."
    Else
        lblCacheStatus.Text = "Retrieved from cache."
    End If

    Return ds
End Function
```

The advantage of this approach is that you can call GetDataSet() in any event handler in your web page code to get the DataSet when you need it. You don't need to worry about checking the cache first and calling RetrieveDataSet() when needed—instead, GetDataSet() handles the whole process transparently.

■ **Tip** This two-step approach (with one method that creates the data object you need and another that manages cache) is a common, time-tested design. It's always a good strategy to ensure that you deal with the cache consistently. If you want to use the same cached object in multiple web pages, you can take this design one step further by moving the GetDataSet() and RetrieveDataSet() methods into a separate class. In this case, you'd probably make the RetrieveDataSet() method private and the GetDataSet() method public—that way, web pages can request the DataSet whenever they need it but don't determine when to contact the database.

When the page is first loaded, it calls GetDataSet() to retrieve the DataSet. It then gets the DataTable with the customer records, and binds the DataTable.Columns collection to a CheckBoxList control named chkColumns:

```
Protected Sub Page_Load(ByVal sender As Object, ByVal e As EventArgs) _
  Handles Me.Load
    If Not Me.IsPostBack Then
        Dim ds As DataSet = GetDataSet()
        chkColumns.DataSource = ds.Tables("Customers").Columns
        chkColumns.DataTextField = "ColumnName"
        chkColumns.DataBind()
    End If
End Sub
```

As you learned in Chapter 15, the DataTable.Columns collection holds one DataColumn object for each column in the DataTable. Each DataColumn specifies details such as data type and column name. In this example, the DataColumn.ColumnName property is used to display the name of each column (as configured by the DataTextField property of the CheckBoxList control).

Every time the Filter button is clicked, the page calls GetDataSet() to retrieve the DataSet. To provide the configurable grid, the code loops through the DataTable, removing all the columns that the user has selected to hide. The code then binds the data by calling GridView.DataBind().

The full code for the Filter button is as follows:

```
Protected Sub cmdFilter_Click(ByVal sender As Object, _
  ByVal e As System.EventArgs) Handles cmdFilter.Click

    Dim ds As DataSet = GetDataSet()

    ' Copy the DataSet so you can remove columns without
    ' changing the cached item.
    ds = ds.Copy()

    For Each item As ListItem in chkColumns.Items
        If item.Selected Then
            ds.Tables(0).Columns.Remove(item.Text)
        End If
    Next

    gridCustomers.DataSource = ds.Tables(0)
    gridCustomers.DataBind()

End Sub
```

This example demonstrates an important fact about the cache. When you retrieve an item, you actually retrieve a reference to the cached object. If you modify that object, you're actually modifying the cached item as well. For the page to be able to delete columns without affecting the cached copy of the DataSet, the code needs to create a duplicate copy before performing the operations using the DataSet.Copy() method.

Caching with the Data Source Controls

The SqlDataSource (Chapter 16), ObjectDataSource (Chapter 23), and XmlDataSource (Chapter 19) all support built-in data caching. Using caching with these controls is highly recommended, because unlike your own custom data code, the data source controls always requery the data source in every postback. They also query the data source once for every bound control, so if you have three controls bound to the same data source, three separate queries are executed against the database just before the page is rendered. Even a little caching can reduce this overhead dramatically.

■ **Note** Although many data source controls support caching, it's not a required data source control feature, and you'll run into data source controls that don't support it or for which it may not make sense (such as the SiteMapDataSource).

To support caching, the SqlDataSource, ObjectDataSource, and XmlDataSource controls all use the same properties, which are listed in Table 24-2.

Table 24-2. *Caching Properties of the Data Source Controls*

Property	Description
EnableCaching	If True, switches caching on. It's False by default.
CacheExpirationPolicy	Uses a value from the DataSourceCacheExpiry enumeration—Absolute for absolute expiration (which times out after a fixed interval of time), or Sliding for sliding expiration (which resets the time window every time the data object is retrieved from the cache).
CacheDuration	Determines the number of seconds to cache the data object. If you are using sliding expiration, the time limit is reset every time the object is retrieved from the cache. The default value, 0, keeps cached items perpetually.
CacheKeyDependency and SqlCacheDependency	Allow you to make a cached item dependent on another item in the data cache (CacheKeyDependency) or on a table in your database (SqlCacheDependency). Dependencies are discussed in the "Cache Dependencies" section.

Caching with SqlDataSource

When you enable caching for the SqlDataSource control, you cache the results of the SelectCommand. However, if you create a select query that takes parameters, the SqlDataSource will cache a separate result for every set of parameter values.

For example, imagine you create a page that allows you to view employees by city. The user selects the desired city from a list box, and you use a SqlDataSource control to fill in the matching employee records in a grid (see Figure 24-7).

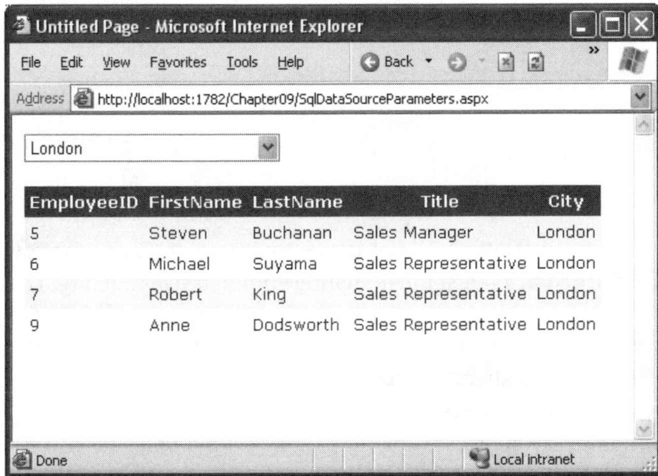

Figure 24-7. *Retrieving data from the cache*

There are two SqlDataSource controls at work in this example. The first SqlDataSource gets the list of cities for the drop-down list. These results don't change often, and so they are cached for one hour (3600 seconds):

```
<asp:SqlDataSource ID="sourceEmployeeCities" runat="server"
 ProviderName="System.Data.SqlClient"
 EnableCaching="True" CacheDuration="3600"
 ConnectionString="<%$ ConnectionStrings:Northwind %>"
 SelectCommand="SELECT DISTINCT City FROM Employees">
</asp:SqlDataSource>

<asp:DropDownList ID="lstCities" runat="server"
 DataSourceID="sourceEmployeeCities"
 DataTextField="City" AutoPostBack="True">
</asp:DropDownList>
```

The second SqlDataSource gets the employees in the currently selected city. These results are cached for 600 seconds and bound to a GridView:

```
<asp:SqlDataSource ID="sourceEmployees" runat="server"
 ProviderName="System.Data.SqlClient"
 EnableCaching="True" CacheDuration="600"
 ConnectionString="<%$ ConnectionStrings:Northwind %>"
 SelectCommand="SELECT EmployeeID, FirstName, LastName, Title, City
```

```
FROM Employees WHERE City=@City">
  <SelectParameters>
    <asp:ControlParameter ControlID="lstCities" Name="City"
     PropertyName="SelectedValue" />
  </SelectParameters>
</asp:SqlDataSource>

<asp:GridView ID="GridView1" runat="server"
 DataSourceID="sourceEmployees" ... >
  ...
</asp:GridView>
```

This SqlDataSource is a bit more sophisticated because it uses a parameter. Each time you select a city, a separate query is performed to get just the matching employees in that city. The query is used to fill a DataSet, which is then cached for up to ten minutes (600 seconds). If you select a different city, the process repeats, and the new DataSet is cached separately. However, if you pick a city that you or another user has already requested, the appropriate DataSet is fetched from the cache (provided it hasn't yet expired).

Thus, this single SqlDataSource can result in a surprisingly large number of cache entries. If there are 20 different cities in your list (and therefore 20 different possible parameter values), you can end up with as many as 20 different DataSet objects in the cache at once.

■ **Note** SqlDataSource caching works only when the DataSourceMode property is set to DataSet (the default). It doesn't work when the mode is set to DataReader, because the DataReader object maintains a live connection to the database and can't be efficiently cached.

On the other hand, if the parameter values are all used with similar frequency, this approach isn't as suitable. One of the problems it imposes is that when the items in the cache expire, you'll need multiple database queries to repopulate the cache (one for each combination of parameter values), which isn't as efficient as getting the combined results with a single query.

If you fall into the second situation, you can change the SqlDataSource so it retrieves a DataSet with all the employee records and caches that. The SqlDataSource can then extract just the records it needs to satisfy each request from the DataSet. This way, a single DataSet with all the records is cached, which can satisfy any parameter value.

To use this technique, you need to rewrite your SqlDataSource to use *filtering*. First, the select query should return all the rows and not use any SelectParameters:

```
<asp:SqlDataSource ID="sourceEmployees" runat="server"
 SelectCommand=
"SELECT EmployeeID, FirstName, LastName, Title, City FROM Employees"
 ...>
</asp:SqlDataSource>
```

Second, you need to define the filter expression. This is the portion that goes in the WHERE clause of a typical SQL query. However, this has a catch—if you're supplying the filter value from another source (such as a control), you need to define one or more placeholders, using the syntax {0} for the first placeholder, {1} for the second, and so on. You then supply the filter values using the <FilterParameters> section, in much the same way you supplied the select parameters in the first version.

Here's the completed SqlDataSource tag:

```
<asp:SqlDataSource ID="sourceEmployees" runat="server"
 ProviderName="System.Data.SqlClient"
 ConnectionString="<%$ ConnectionStrings:Northwind %>"
 SelectCommand=
"SELECT EmployeeID, FirstName, LastName, Title, City FROM Employees"
 FilterExpression="City='{0}'" EnableCaching="True">
  <FilterParameters>
    <asp:ControlParameter ControlID="lstCities" Name="City"
     PropertyName="SelectedValue" />
  </FilterParameters>
</asp:SqlDataSource>
```

■ **Tip** Don't use filtering unless you are using caching. If you use filtering without caching, you are essentially retrieving the full result set each time and then extracting a portion of its records. This combines the worst of both worlds—you have to repeat the query with each postback, and you fetch far more data than you need each time.

Caching with ObjectDataSource

The ObjectDataSource caching works on the data object returned from the SelectMethod. If you are using a parameterized query, the ObjectDataSource distinguishes between requests with different parameter values and caches them separately. Unfortunately, the ObjectDataSource caching has a significant limitation—it works only when the select method returns a DataSet or a DataTable. If you return any other type of object, you'll receive a NotSupportedException.

This limitation is unfortunate, because there's no technical reason you can't cache custom objects in the data cache. If you want this feature, you'll need to implement data caching inside your method by manually inserting your objects into the data cache and retrieving them later. In fact, caching inside your method can be more effective, because you have the ability to share the same cached object in multiple methods. For example, you could cache a DataTable with a list of products and categories and use that cached item in both the GetProductCategories() and GetProductsByCategory() methods.

■ **Tip** The only consideration you should keep in mind is to make sure you use unique cache key names that aren't likely to collide with the names of cached items that the page might use. This isn't a problem when using the built-in data source caching, because it always stores its information in a hidden slot in the cache.

If your custom class returns a DataSet or DataTable, and you do decide to use the built-in ObjectDataSource caching, you can also use filtering as discussed with the SqlDataSource control. Just instruct your ObjectDataSource to call a method that gets the full set of data, and set the FilterExpression to retrieve just those items that match the current view.

Caching with Dependencies

As time passes, the information in your data source may change. If your code uses caching, you may remain unaware of the changes and continue using out-of-date information from the cache. To help mitigate this problem, ASP.NET supports *cache dependencies*. Cache dependencies allow you to make a cached item dependent on another resource, so that when that resource changes, the cached item is removed automatically.

ASP.NET includes three types of dependencies:

- Dependencies on other cached items
- Dependencies on files or folders
- Dependencies on a database query

You'll see all these types of dependencies in the following section.

File Dependencies

To use a cache dependency, you need to create a CacheDependency object. You then need to supply the CacheDependency object when you add the dependent cached item.

For example, the following code creates a CacheDependency that depends on an XML file named ProductList.xml. When the XML file is changed, the CacheDependency will be invalidated and the dependent cached item will be evicted from the cache immediately.

```
' Create a dependency for the ProductList.xml file.
Dim prodDependency As New CacheDependency( _
  Server.MapPath("ProductList.xml"))

' Add a cache item that will be dependent on this file.
Cache.Insert("ProductInfo", prodInfo, prodDependency)
```

Monitoring begins as soon as the CacheDependency object is created. If the XML file changes before you have added the dependent item to the cache, the item will expire immediately as soon as it's added.

Figure 24-8 shows a simple test page that is included with the samples for this chapter. It sets up a dependency, modifies the file, and allows you to verify that the cached item has been dropped from the cache.

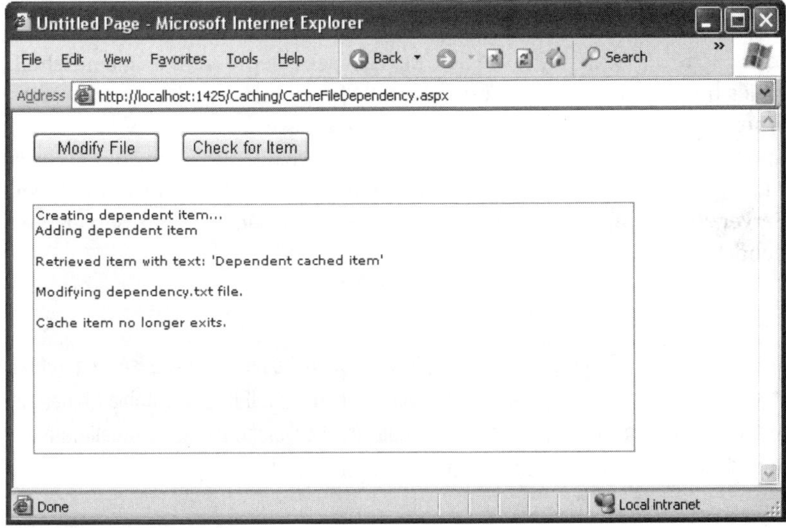

Figure 24-8. *Testing cache dependencies*

The CacheDependency object provides several constructors. You've already seen how it can make a dependency based on a file by using the file name constructor. You can also specify a directory that needs to be monitored for changes, or you can use a constructor that accepts an array of strings that represent multiple files and directories.

Cache Item Dependencies

The CacheDependency class provides another constructor that accepts an array of file names *and* an array of cache keys. Using the array of cache keys, you can create a cached item that's dependent on another item in the cache. (If you don't want to use file dependencies at all, you simply supply a null reference (Nothing) for the first parameter.)

Here's an example that makes one item dependent on another cached item, without using file dependencies:

```
Cache("Key1") = "Cache Item 1"

' Make Cache("Key2") dependent on Cache("Key1").
Dim dependencyKey(0) As String
dependencyKey(0) = "Key1"
Dim dependency As New CacheDependency(Nothing, dependencyKey)

Cache.Insert("Key2", "Cache Item 2", dependency)
```

Now, when the first cached item changes or is removed from the cache, the second cached item will automatically be dropped from the cache as well.

SQL Server 2000 Cache Dependencies

A more complex kind of cache dependency is the SQL Server cache dependency. In a nutshell, SQL cache dependencies provide the ability to automatically invalidate a cached data object (such as a DataSet) when the related data is modified in the database.

This feature is supported in most versions of SQL Server, although the underlying plumbing is quite a bit different. If you're using SQL Server 2000, keep reading this section for the lowdown. If you're using SQL Server 2005 or SQL Server 2008, skip ahead to the section "SQL Server 2005 and 2008 Cache Dependencies."

■ Tip Using SQL cache dependencies still entails more complexity than just using a time-based expiration policy. It's more difficult to set up, and it can be more of a headache to maintain. If it's acceptable for certain information to be used without reflecting all the most recent changes (and developers often overestimate the importance of up-to-the-millisecond live information), you may not need it at all.

ASP.NET uses a polling model for SQL Server 2000. With the polling model, ASP.NET keeps a connection open to the database and checks periodically whether a table has been updated. The effect of tying up one connection in this way isn't terribly significant, but the extra database work involved with polling does add some database overhead. For the polling model to be effective, the polling process needs to be quicker and lighter than the original query that extracts the data.

You must take several steps to enable notification with SQL Server 2000. Here's an overview of the process:

1. The first step is to determine which tables need notification support.
2. Next, use the aspnet_regsql.exe command-line utility to create the notification tables for your database.
3. Then, you need to register each table that requires notification support. You also use the aspnet_regsql.exe command for this step.
4. Finally, you enable ASP.NET polling through a web.config file. You're now ready to create SqlCacheDependency objects.

The following sections describe these steps.

Enabling Notifications

Before you can use SQL Server cache invalidation, you need to enable notifications for the database. This task is performed with the aspnet_regsql.exe command-line utility, which is located in the c:\Windows\Microsoft.NET\Framework\v2.0.50727 directory. To enable notifications, you need to use the -ed command-line switch. You also need to identify the server (use -E for a trusted connection, and -S to choose a server other than the current computer) and the database (use -d). Here's an example that enables notifications for the Northwind database on the current server:

```
aspnet_regsql -ed -E -d Northwind
```

When you take this step, a new table named SqlCacheTablesForChangeNotification is added to the database named Northwind (which must already exist). The SqlCacheTablesForChangeNotification table has three columns: tableName, notificationCreated, and changeId. This table is used to track changes. Essentially, when a change takes place, SQL Server writes a record to this table. ASP.NET's polling service queries this table.

This design achieves a number of benefits:

- Because the change notification table is much smaller than the table with the cached data, it's much faster to query.
- Because the change notification table isn't used for other tasks, reading these records won't risk locking and concurrency issues.
- Because multiple tables in the same database will use the same notification table, you can monitor several tables at once without increasing the polling overhead.

Figure 24-9 shows an overview of how SQL Server 2000 cache invalidation works.

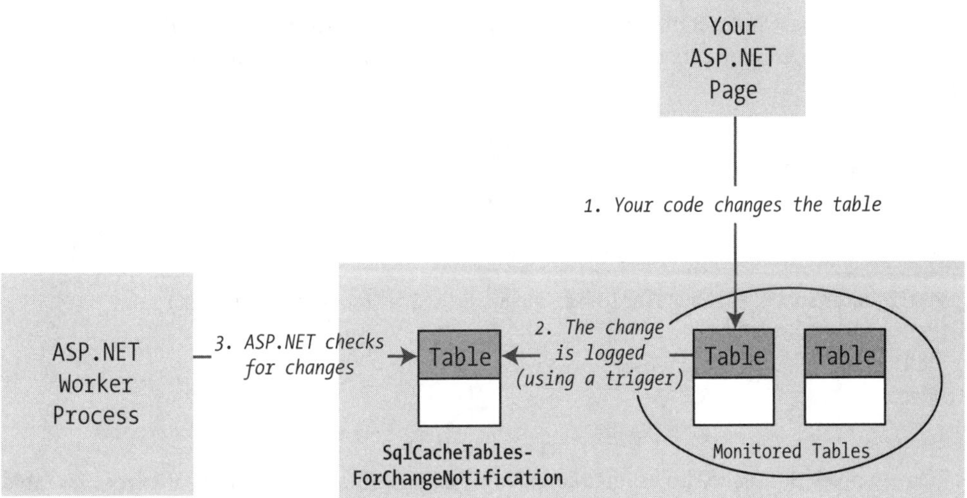

Figure 24-9. *Monitoring a database for changes in SQL Server 2000*

Even once you've created the SqlCacheTablesForChangeNotification table, you still need to enable notification support for each table. You can do this manually using the SqlCacheRegisterTableStoredProcedure, or you can rely on aspnet_regsql by using the -et parameter to turn on the notifications and the -t parameter to name the table. Here's an example that enables notifications for the Employees table in the Northwind database:

```
aspnet_regsql -et -E -d Northwind -t Employees
```

This step generates the notification trigger for the Employees table.

How Notifications Work

Now you have all the ingredients in place to use the notification system. For example, imagine you cache the results of a query like this:

```
SELECT * FROM Employees
```

This query retrieves records from the Employees table. To check for changes that might invalidate your cached object, you need to know whether any record in the Employees table is inserted, deleted, or updated. You can watch for these operations using triggers. For example, here's the trigger on the Employees table that aspnet_regsql creates:

```
CREATE TRIGGER dbo.[Employees_AspNet_SqlCacheNotification_Trigger]
  ON [Employees]
  FOR INSERT, UPDATE, DELETE AS BEGIN

  SET NOCOUNT ON
  EXEC dbo.AspNet_SqlCacheUpdateChangeIdStoredProcedure N'Employees'
END
```

In other words, when a change takes place on the table that's being monitored, that change triggers the AspNet_SqlCacheUpdateChangeIdStoredProcedure stored procedure. This stored procedure simply increments the changeId of the corresponding row in the change notification table:

```
CREATE PROCEDURE dbo.AspNet_SqlCacheUpdateChangeIdStoredProcedure
  @tableName NVARCHAR(450)
AS

  BEGIN
  UPDATE dbo.AspNet_SqlCacheTablesForChangeNotification WITH (ROWLOCK)
    SET changeId = changeId + 1
    WHERE tableName = @tableName
  END
GO
```

The AspNet_SqlCacheTablesForChangeNotification contains a single record for every table you're monitoring. As you can see, when you make a change in the table (such as inserting a record), the changeId column is incremented by 1. ASP.NET queries this table repeatedly and keeps track of the most recent changeId values for every table. When this value changes in a subsequent read, ASP.NET knows that the table has changed.

This hints at one of the major limitations of cache invalidation as implemented in SQL Server 2000 and SQL Server 7. *Any* change to the table is deemed to invalidate *any* query for that table. In other words, if you use this query

```
SELECT * FROM Employees WHERE City='London'
```

the caching still works in the same way. That means if any employee record is touched, even if the employee resides in another city (and therefore isn't one of the cached records), the notification is still sent and the cached item is considered invalid. Keeping track of which changes do and do not invalidate a cached data object is simply too much work for SQL Server 2000 (although it is possible when using cache dependencies with SQL Server 2005 or 2008).

■ **Tip** The implementation of cache invalidation with SQL Server 2000 isn't as fine-grained as the implementation with SQL Server 2005 and SQL Server 2008. As a result, it doesn't make sense for tables that change frequently, or for narrowly defined queries that retrieve only a small subset of records from a table.

Enabling ASP.NET Polling

The next step is to instruct ASP.NET to poll the database. You do this on a per-application basis. In other words, every application that uses cache invalidation will hold a separate connection and poll the notification table on its own.

To enable the polling service, you use the <sqlCacheDependency> element in the web.config file. You set the enabled attribute to true to turn it on, and you set the pollTime attribute to the number of milliseconds between each poll. (The higher the poll time, the longer the potential delay before a change is detected.) You also need to supply the connection string information.

For example, this web.config file checks for updated notification information every 15 seconds:

```
<configuration>
  <connectionStrings>
    <add name="Northwind" connectionString=
"Data Source=localhost;Initial Catalog=Northwind;Integrated Security=SSPI"/>
  </connectionStrings>

  <system.web>
    <caching>
      <sqlCacheDependency enabled="true" pollTime="15000" >
        <databases>
          <add name="Northwind" connectionStringName="Northwind" />
        </databases>
      </sqlCacheDependency>
    </caching>
    ...
  </system.web>
</configuration>
```

Creating the Cache Dependency

Now that you've seen how to set up your database to support SQL Server notifications, the only remaining detail is the code, which is quite straightforward. You can use your cache dependency with programmatic data caching, a data source control, and output caching.

For programmatic data caching, you need to create a new SqlCacheDependency and supply that to the Cache.Insert() method, much as you did with file dependencies. In the SqlCacheDependency constructor, you supply two strings. The first is the name of the database you defined in the <add> element in the <sqlCacheDependency> section of the web.config file. The second is the name of the linked table.

Here's an example:

```
' Create a dependency for the Employees table.
Dim empDependency As New SqlCacheDependency("Northwind", "Employees")

' Add a cache item that will be invalidated if this table changes.
Cache.Insert("Employees", dsEmployees, empDependency)
```

To perform the same trick with output caching, you simply need to set the SqlCacheDependency property of the OutputCache directive. Use the database dependency name and the table name, separated by a colon:

```
<%@ OutputCache Duration="600" SqlDependency="Northwind:Employees"
    VaryByParam="none" %>
```

The same technique works with the SqlDataSource and ObjectDataSource controls:

```
<asp:SqlDataSource EnableCaching="True"
 SqlCacheDependency="Northwind:Employees" ... />
```

To try a complete example, you can use the downloadable code for this chapter.

SQL Server 2005 and 2008 Cache Dependencies

SQL Server 2005 and SQL Server 2008 get closest to the ideal notification solution, because the notification infrastructure is built into the database with a messaging system called the *Service Broker*. The Service Broker manages *queues*, which are database objects that have the same standing as tables, stored procedures, or views.

■ **Note** SQL Server 2005 and SQL Server 2008 share the same Service Broker model. Although SQL Server 2008 wasn't yet released at the time of this writing, it's expected to support the ASP.NET cache dependency feature in exactly the same way as SQL Server 2005.

Essentially, you can instruct SQL Server to send notifications for specific events using the CREATE EVENT NOTIFICATION command. ASP.NET offers a higher-level model—you register a query, and ASP.NET automatically instructs SQL Server to send notifications for any operations that would affect the results of that query. Every time you perform an operation, SQL Server determines whether your operation affects a registered command. If it does, SQL Server sends a notification message and stops the notification process. Figure 24-10 shows an overview of how cache invalidation works with SQL Server 2005 and SQL Server 2008.

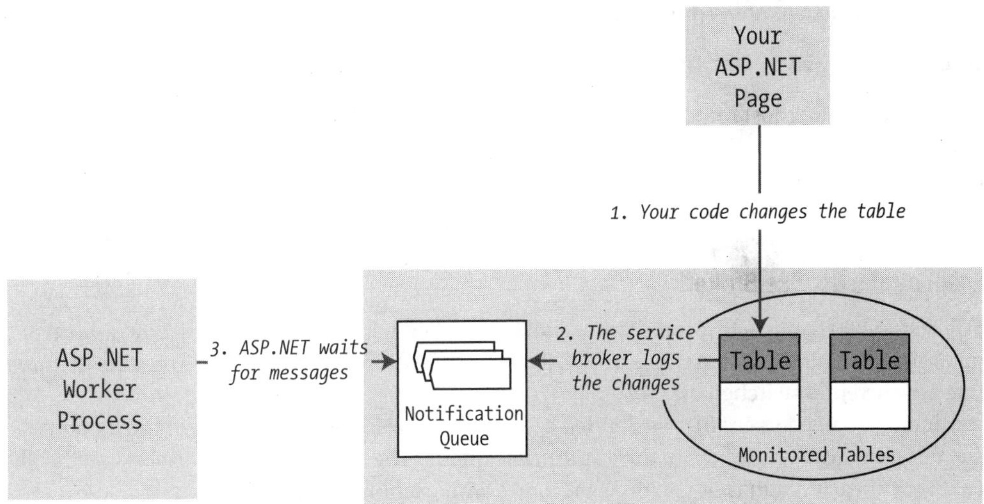

Figure 24-10. *Monitoring a database for changes in SQL Server 2005 or 2008*

When using notification with SQL Server 2005 or SQL Server 2008, you get the following benefits over SQL Server 2000:

Notification is much more fine-grained: Instead of invalidating your cached object when the table changes, SQL Server invalidates your object only when a row that affects your query is inserted, updated, or deleted.

Notification is more intelligent: A notification message is sent the first time the data is changed but not if the data is changed again (unless you reregister for notification messages by adding an item back to the cache).

No special steps are required to set up notification: You do not run aspnet_regsql or add polling settings to the web.config file. However, you do need to call the shared SqlDependency.Start() method somewhere in your code to start the polling service.

Notifications work with SELECT queries and stored procedures. However, some restrictions exist for the SELECT syntax you can use. To properly support notifications, your command must adhere to the following rules:

- You must fully qualify table names in the form [Owner].table, as in dbo.Employees (not just Employees).
- Your query cannot use an aggregate function, such as COUNT(), MAX(), MIN(), or AVERAGE().
- You cannot select all columns with the wildcard * (as in SELECT * FROM Employees). Instead, you must specifically name each column so that SQL Server can properly track changes that do and do not affect the results of your query.

Here's an acceptable command:

```
SELECT EmployeeID, FirstName, LastName, City FROM dbo.Employees
```

These are the most important rules, but the SQL Server Books Online has a lengthy list of caveats and exceptions. If you break one of these rules, you won't receive an error. However, the notification message will be sent as soon as you register the command, and the cached item will be invalidated immediately.

Enabling the Service Broker

SQL Server 2005 and SQL Server 2008 are often installed with carefully locked-down settings for optimum security. In order to use SQL Server notifications, you may have to enable features that are currently switched off.

First, you need to enable the Service Broker, which watches for changes in the database and delivers the notifications to the appropriate queue. The Service Broker must be specifically enabled for each database that you want to use with cache dependencies.

If the Service Broker isn't currently enabled for your database (or if you're just not sure), there's an easy solution. First, launch the Visual Studio 2008 Command Prompt window (click the Start button and choose Programs ➤ Microsoft Visual Studio 2008 ➤ Visual Studio Tools ➤ Visual Studio 2008 Command Prompt). Then, run the SqlCmd.exe command-line utility, specifying the –S parameter and the name of your server. Here's an example:

```
SqlCmd -S localhost\SQLEXPRESS
```

This connects to SQL Server Express on the current computer. If you're using the full version of SQL Server, you won't need to supply the instance name (you can use just localhost instead of localhost\SQLEXPRESS). If your database is installed on another server, use its computer name instead of localhost.

The SqlCmd.exe utility provides a command prompt where you can enter SQL commands. Use it to enter the following SQL statements:

```
USE Northwind
ALTER DATABASE Northwind SET ENABLE_BROKER
GO
```

Of course, if you want to enable the Service Broker for a different database (other than Northwind), you can modify this SQL accordingly. You can enable the Service Broker for as many databases as you'd like.

Once you're finished, type quit to exit the SqlCmd tool.

Initializing the Caching Service

Before you can use SQL cache dependencies with SQL Server 2005 or SQL Server 2008, you need to call the shared SqlDependency.Start() method. This initializes the listening service on the web server.

```
Dim connectionString As String = _
  WebConfigurationManager.ConnectionStrings("Northwind").ConnectionString
SqlDependency.Start(connectionString)
```

You need to call the Start() method only once over the lifetime of your web application, so it often makes sense to place the call in the Application_Start() method of the Global.asax file so it's triggered automatically. It's safe to call the Start() method even if the listener is already started, as this won't cause an error. You can also use the Stop() method to halt the listener.

Creating the Cache Dependency

When you create the dependency object you need to supply the command that you're using to retrieve your data. That way, SQL Server knows what range of records you want to monitor.

To specify the command, you create the SqlCacheDependency using the constructor that accepts a SqlCommand object. Here's an example:

```
' Create the ADO.NET objects.
Dim con As New SqlConnection(connectionString)
Dim query As String = _
 "SELECT EmployeeID, FirstName, LastName, City FROM dbo.Employees"
Dim cmd As New SqlCommand(query, con)
Dim adapter As New SqlDataAdapter(cmd)

' Fill the DataSet.
Dim ds As New DataSet()
adapter.Fill(ds, "Employees")

' Create the dependency.
Dim empDependency As New SqlCacheDependency(cmd)

' Add a cache item that will be invalidated if one of its records changes
' (or a new record is added in the same range).
Cache.Insert("Employees", ds, empDependency)
```

Now, when you change the data in the table the notification will be delivered and the item will be removed from the cache. The next time you create the DataSet, you'll need to add it back to the cache with a new SqlCacheDependency. To try a page that uses this technique, check out the sample code for this chapter.

FAILED NOTIFICATIONS

If your cached item never expires, the ASP.NET polling service is not receiving the invalidation message. This has several possible causes. The most common is that your database server doesn't have the common language runtime enabled. The procedure that sends notification messages is a .NET procedure, so it requires this support.

To enable CLR support, fire up the Visual Studio 2008 Command Prompt window, and run the SqlCmd.exe command-line utility. Here's how to do it for SQL Server Express:

```
SqlCmd -S localhost\SQLEXPRESS
```

Now enter the following SQL statements:

```
EXEC sp_configure 'show advanced options', '1'
GO
RECONFIGURE
GO
EXEC sp_configure 'clr enabled', 1
GO
RECONFIGURE
GO
```

Then type quit to exit the SqlCmd tool.

On the other hand, if your cached item expires *immediately*, the most likely problem is that you've broken one of the rules for writing commands that work with notifications, as described earlier.

The Last Word

The most performance-critical area in most web applications is the data layer. But many ASP.NET developers don't realize that you can dramatically reduce the burden on your database and increase the scalability of all your web applications with just a little caching code.

However, with any performance-optimization strategy, the best way to gauge the value of a change is to perform stress testing and profiling. Without this step, you might spend a great deal of time perfecting code that will achieve only a minor improvement in performance or scalability, at the expense of more effective changes.

CHAPTER 25

■ ■ ■

ASP.NET AJAX

So far, you've learned to build web pages that use the *postback* model. With the postback model, pages are perpetually being sent back to the web server and regenerated.

For example, consider the greeting card maker you first saw in Chapter 6. When the user picks a font, enters some text, or chooses new colors, the page is posted back to the web server, allowing your code to run. The web page code makes the necessary adjustments, ASP.NET renders the page to HTML all over again, and the browser receives (and displays) the new version of the page.

This process seems somewhat labor intensive, but it's actually not that bad. The time required to complete the whole process (transmitting the posted-back page, running the code, rendering the page, and returning the final HTML) is surprisingly short. However, the process isn't seamless. When the greeting card is updated in the greeting card maker, the entire page is refreshed, including the parts that haven't changed. This produces a distracting flicker. This browser refresh is also a bit intrusive—for example, this process might interrupt users while they're in the middle of entering information in another control, or it might scroll them back to the beginning of the page even though they were previously looking at the end. The overall experience of using the greeting card maker is quite different than the experience of using a rich Windows application, which has no noticeable flicker and feels much more responsive.

Recently, a new generation of web applications has begun to appear that behave more like Windows applications than traditional web pages. These applications refresh themselves quickly and flicker-free, and sometimes include slick new features like animation and drag and drop. Notable examples include web-based email applications like Gmail and mapping tools like Google Maps.

This new breed of web applications uses a set of design practices and technologies known as *Ajax*. Ajax is programming shorthand for a set of techniques that create more responsive, dynamic pages. One of the hallmarks of Ajax is the ability to refresh part of the page while leaving the rest untouched.

In this chapter, you'll learn how Ajax works and you'll see how you can use it to create rich, responsive web pages. You won't delve into the intricate details of do-it-yourself Ajax (which requires an extensive understanding of JavaScript), but you will explore the Ajax features of ASP.NET. These features allow you to use the familiar ASP.NET model—.NET objects and server-side controls—to get Ajax effects with surprisingly little effort.

Understanding Ajax

Before you really get started with Ajax, it's important to understand its capabilities and limitations. Only then will you know how to fit it into your web applications.

Ajax: The Good

The key benefit of Ajax is responsiveness. An Ajax application, when done properly, provides a better experience for the user. Even if the user can't do anything new (or do anything faster), this improved experience can make your web application seem more modern and sophisticated. If you're creating a website that's competing against other similar sites, you just might find that Ajax allows you to distinguish your work from the rest of the pack.

Ajax can also provide genuinely new features that aren't possible in traditional web pages. For example, Ajax pages often use JavaScript code that reacts to client-side events like mouse movements and key presses. These events occur frequently, so it's not practical to deal with them using the postback model. For example, imagine you want to highlight a TextBox when the user moves the mouse over it. With the postback approach, you'd need to send the entire page back to the web server, regenerate it, and refresh it in the browser—by which point the mouse might be somewhere completely different. This approach is clearly impractical. However, an Ajax page can deal with this scenario because it can react immediately, updating the page if needed or requesting additional information from the web server in the background. While this request is under way, the user is free to keep working with the page. In fact, the user won't even realize that the request is taking place.

■ **Note** Ajax isn't really a whole new technology. More accurately, it's a set of techniques, some of which extend existing practices. For example, you've already seen quite a few ASP.NET controls that use client-side JavaScript to provide a richer experience, such as the validation controls (Chapter 10) and the Menu control (Chapter 14). However, Ajax pages use much more JavaScript than normal, they often require interactions between controls, and they often request additional information from the web server using a special browser object called XMLHttpRequest, which is available to client-side JavaScript code.

Ajax: The Bad

There are two key challenges to using Ajax. The first is complexity. Writing the JavaScript code needed to implement an Ajax application is a major feat. Fortunately, you'll sidestep this problem in this chapter, because you'll use ASP.NET's Ajax-enabled features. That means you'll let Microsoft manage the complexity instead of worrying about it yourself.

The other challenge to using Ajax is browser support. The technology that supports Ajax has existed for several years, but it's only now found consistently in all major browsers. If you use the Ajax features that ASP.NET provides, they'll work in Internet Explorer 5 and newer, Netscape 7 and newer, Opera 7.6 and newer, Safari 1.2 and newer, and Firefox 1.0 and newer. This captures the overwhelming majority of web users. (The actual percentage depends on your audience, but over 90 percent is a good initial assumption.)

But what about the minority of users who *are* using old browsers or have JavaScript switched off? It all depends on the feature you're using and the way it's implemented. If you're using the partial rendering support that's provided by ASP.NET's UpdatePanel control (which you'll learn about in this chapter), your page will continue to work with non-Ajax-enabled browsers—it will simply use full postbacks instead of more streamlined partial updates. On the other hand, if you're using a more advanced Ajax-enabled web control, you may find that it doesn't work properly or at all. The only way to know is to switch JavaScript off in your browser and try it out. Either way, there's a price to be paid for slick Ajax features, and that price is increased web browser requirements.

Finally, Ajax applications introduce a few quirks that might not be to your liking. Web pages that use Ajax often do a lot of work on a single page. This is different than traditional web pages, which often move the user from one page to another to complete a task. Although the multiple-page approach is a little more roundabout, it allows the user to place bookmarks along the way and use the browser's Back and Forward buttons to step through the sequence. These techniques usually don't work with Ajax applications, because there's only a single page to bookmark or navigate to, and the URL for that page doesn't capture the user's current state. This isn't a showstopper of an issue, but it might cause you to consider the design of your web application a little more closely.

The ASP.NET AJAX Toolkit

There are a variety of ways to implement Ajax in any web application, including ASP.NET. To implement it on your own, you need to have a thorough understanding of JavaScript, because it's JavaScript code that runs in the browser, requesting the new information from the web server when needed and updating the page accordingly. Although JavaScript isn't terribly complex, it's remarkably difficult to program correctly, for two reasons:

- The implementation of key JavaScript details varies from browser to browser, which means you need a tremendous amount of experience to write a solid web page that runs equally well on all browsers.
- JavaScript is a notoriously loose language that tolerates many minor typos and mistakes. Catching these mistakes and removing them is a tedious process. Even worse, the mistakes might be fatal on some browsers and harmless in others, which complicates debugging.

In this chapter, you won't use JavaScript directly. Instead, you'll use a higher-level model called ASP.NET AJAX. ASP.NET AJAX gives you a set of server-side components and controls that you can use when designing your web page. These components automatically render all the JavaScript you need to get the effect you want. The result is that you can create a page with Ajax effects while programming with a familiar (and much more productive) model of server-side objects. Of course, you won't get quite as much control to customize every last detail about the way your web pages work, but you will get some great functionality with minimal effort.

■ **Note** It's generally accepted that Ajax isn't written in all capitals, because the word isn't an acronym. (Technically, it's a short form for *Asynchronous JavaScript and XML*, although this technique is now considered to be just one of several possible characteristics of an Ajax web application.) However, Microsoft chose to write the term in uppercase when it named ASP.NET AJAX. For that reason, you'll see two capitalizations of Ajax in this chapter—*Ajax* when talking in general terms about the technology and philosophy of Ajax, and *AJAX* when talking about ASP.NET AJAX, which is Microsoft's specific implementation of these concepts.

The ScriptManager

In order to use ASP.NET AJAX, you need to place a new web control on your page. This control is the ScriptManager, and it's the brains of ASP.NET AJAX.

Like all ASP.NET AJAX controls, the ScriptManager is placed on a Toolbox tab named AJAX Extensions. When you can drag the ScriptManager onto your page, you'll end up with this declaration:

```
<asp:ScriptManager ID="ScriptManager1" runat="server"></asp:ScriptManager>
```

At design time, the ScriptManager appears as a blank gray box. But when you request a page that uses the ScriptManager you won't see anything, because the ScriptManager doesn't generate any HTML tags. Instead, the ScriptManager performs a different task—it adds the links to the ASP.NET AJAX JavaScript libraries. It does that by inserting a script block that looks something like this:

```
<script src="/YourWebSite/ScriptResource.axd?d=RUSU1mI ..."
 type="text/javascript">
</script>
```

This script block doesn't contain any code. Instead, it uses the src attribute to pull the JavaScript code out of a separate file.

However, the ScriptManager is a bit craftier than you might expect. Rather than use a separate file to get its JavaScript (which would then need to be deployed along with your application), the src attribute uses a long, strange-looking URL that points to ScriptResource.axd. ScriptResource.axd isn't an actual file—instead, it's a resource that tells ASP.NET to find a JavaScript file that's embedded in one of the compiled .NET 3.5 assemblies. The long query string argument at the end of the URL tells the ScriptResource.axd extension which file to send to the browser.

■ **Note** The JavaScript files that ASP.NET AJAX uses contain hundreds of lines of highly complex, concise code that forms the basis for all the Ajax features you'll see in this chapter. However, these files are quite compact, requiring the client to download less than 200 KB of script code (depending on the features that you're using). When you're visiting an ASP.NET AJAX-powered site, the script code is only downloaded once, and then cached by the browser so it can be used in various ways by various pages in the website. (In addition, ASP.NET sends a compressed version of the script document, if the browser supports it. Currently, ASP.NET uses compression when receiving requests from Internet Explorer 7 or later.) The bottom line is pages that use ASP.NET AJAX features don't require significantly longer download times.

Each page that uses ASP.NET AJAX features requires an instance of the ScriptManager. However, you can only use one ScriptManager on a page. ASP.NET AJAX-enabled controls can interact with the ScriptManager, asking it to render links to additional JavaScript resources.

■ **Tip** If you're using ASP.NET AJAX features throughout your website, you might choose to place the ScriptManager in a master page. However, this can occasionally cause problems, because different content pages may want to configure the properties of the ScriptManager differently. In this scenario, the solution is to use the ScriptManager in the master page and the ScriptManagerProxy in your content page. (You can find the ScriptManagerProxy on the same AJAX Extensions tab of the Toolbox.) Each content page can configure the ScriptManagerProxy control in the same way it would configure the ScriptManager.

Now that you've taken a brief overview of Ajax, it's time to start building Ajax-enabled pages. In this chapter, you'll consider the following topics:

- Using partial refreshes to avoid full-page postbacks and page flicker
- Using progress notifications to deal with slower updates
- Using timed refreshes to automatically update a portion of your page
- Using the ASP.NET AJAX Control Toolkit to get a range of slick new controls with Ajax features

Partial Refreshes

The key technique in an Ajax web application is *partial refreshes*. With partial refreshes, the entire page doesn't need to be posted back and refreshed in the browser. Instead, when something happens the web page asks the web server for more information. The request takes place in the background, so the web page remains responsive. (It's up to you whether you use some sort of progress indicator if you think the request might take a noticeable amount of time.) When the web page receives the response, it updates just the changed portion of the page, as shown in Figure 25-1.

ASP.NET includes a handy control that lets you take an ordinary page with server-side logic and make sure it refreshes itself in flicker-free Ajax style using partial updates. This control is the UpdatePanel.

The basic idea is that you divide your web page into one or more distinct regions, each of which is wrapped inside an invisible UpdatePanel. When an event occurs in a control that's located inside an UpdatePanel, and this event would normally trigger a full-page postback, the UpdatePanel intercepts the event and performs an asynchronous callback instead. Here's an example of how it happens:

1. The user clicks a button inside an UpdatePanel.
2. The UpdatePanel intercepts the client-side click. Now, ASP.NET AJAX performs a callback to the server instead of a full-page postback.
3. On the server, your normal page life cycle executes, with all the usual events. Finally, the page is rendered to HTML and returned to the browser.
4. ASP.NET AJAX receives the full HTML and updates every UpdatePanel on the page by replacing its current HTML with the new content. (If a change has occurred to content that's not inside an UpdatePanel, it's ignored.)

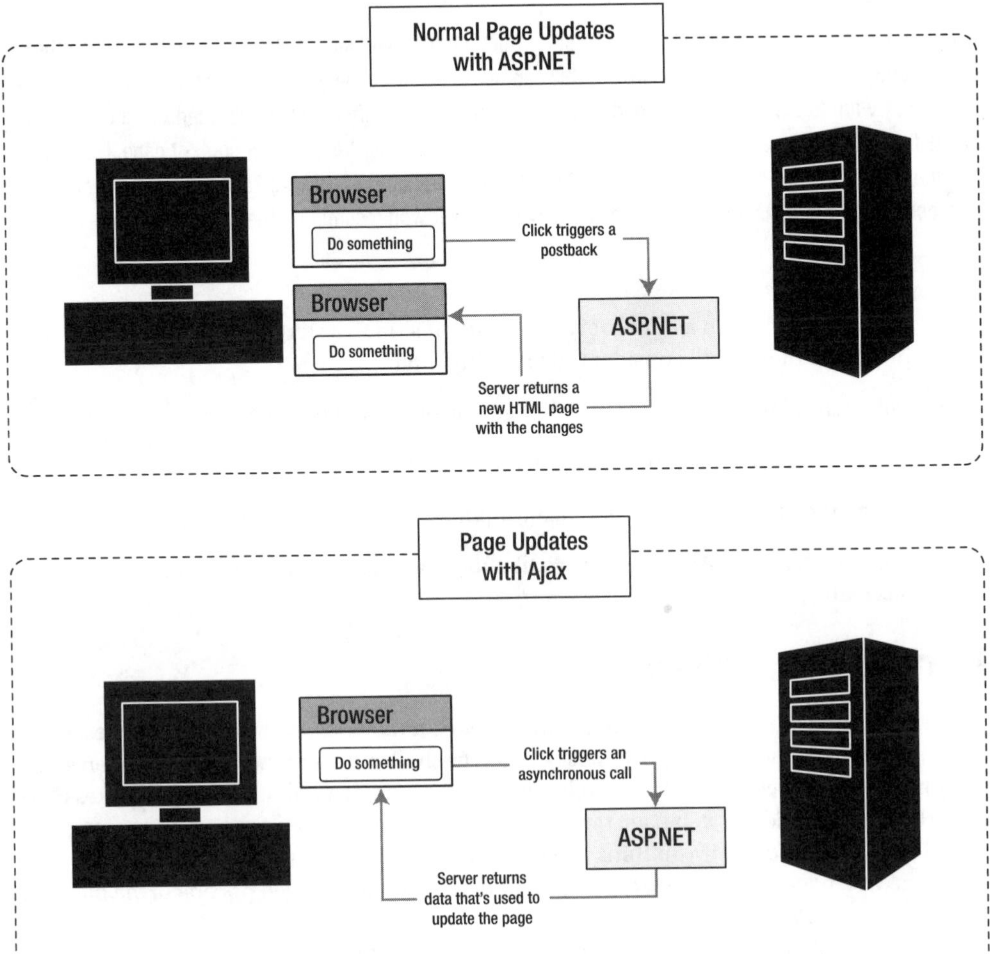

Figure 25-1. *Ordinary server-side pages versus Ajax*

■ **Note** If you access a page that uses the UpdatePanel with a browser that doesn't support Ajax or doesn't have JavaScript switched on, it uses normal postbacks instead of partial updates. However, everything else still works correctly.

A Simple UpdatePanel Test

To try out the UpdatePanel, it makes sense to build a simple test page.

The following example (Figure 25-2) uses a simple page that includes two ingredients: an animated GIF image, and a shaded box that shows the current time and includes a Refresh

Time button. When you click the Refresh Time button, the page grabs the current time from the web server and updates the label. However, the refresh process uses a partial update. As a result, the page won't flicker when it takes place. The animated GIF helps illustrate the point—even as you click the button to refresh the label, the lamp continues bubbling without a pause or hiccup.

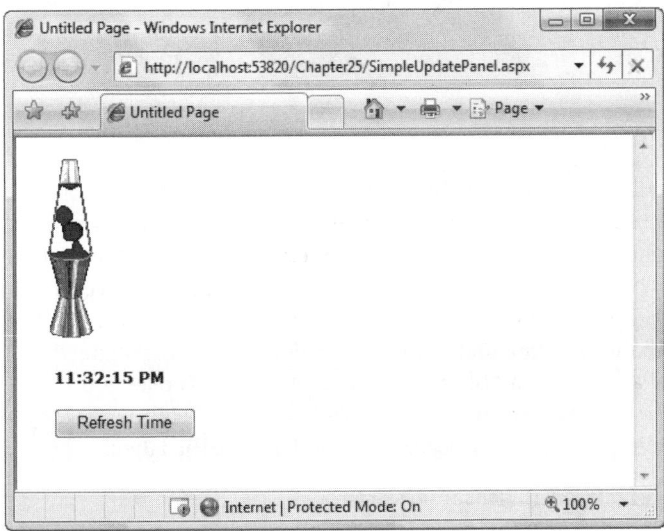

Figure 25-2. *Refreshing a label with a partial update*

Building this page is easy. First, you need to add the ScriptManager control to the page. Like all controls that use ASP.NET AJAX, the UpdatePanel works in conjunction with the ScriptManager. If you don't have it in your page, the UpdatePanel won't work. Furthermore, the ScriptManager needs to appear before the UpdatePanel, because the rendered page must have the JavaScript script block in place before the UpdatePanel can use it. It's a good idea to always place the ScriptManager at the top of the page.

Next, you need to add the content to the page. The animated GIF is fairly straightforward—you can use an ordinary <img> element to show it. However, the label and button require a bit more effort. To refresh the label using a partial refresh, you need to wrap it in an UpdatePanel. So start by adding an UpdatePanel to your page, and then drag and drop the button and label inside.

The UpdatePanel has one role in life—to serve as a container for content that you want to refresh asynchronously. Interestingly enough, the UpdatePanel doesn't derive from Panel. Instead, it derives directly from Control. This design causes a few quirks that you should take into account.

First, the UpdatePanel is invisible. Unlike the standard ASP.NET Panel, an UpdatePanel doesn't support style settings. If you want to display a border around your UpdatePanel or change the background color, you'll need to place an ordinary Panel (or just a plain <div> tag) in your UpdatePanel. Here's how it's done in the example shown in Figure 25-2:

```
<asp:UpdatePanel ID="UpdatePanel1" runat="server" UpdateMode="Conditional">
  <ContentTemplate>
    <div style="background-color:LightYellow;padding: 20px">
      <asp:Label ID="lblTime" runat="server" Font-Bold="True"></asp:Label>
      <br />
      <br />
      <asp:Button ID="cmdRefreshTime" runat="server"
        Text="Refresh Time" />
    </div>
  </ContentTemplate>
</asp:UpdatePanel>
```

This markup reveals another difference between the UpdatePanel and an ordinary Panel—the UpdatePanel uses a template. All the controls you add to an UpdatePanel are placed in an element named <ContentTemplate>. When the UpdatePanel renders itself, it copies the content from the ContentTemplate into the page. This seems like a fairly unimportant low-level detail, but it does have one important side effect. If you want to use code to dynamically add controls to an UpdatePanel, you can't use the UpdatePanel.Controls collection. Instead, you need to add new controls to the UpdatePanels.ContentTemplateContainer.Controls collection.

Now that you have the controls you need, you're ready to add the code. This part is easy—when the button is clicked, you simply react to the Click event and update the label:

```
Protected Sub cmdRefreshTime_Click(ByVal sender As Object, _
  ByVal e As EventArgs) Handles cmdRefreshTime.Click

    lblTime.Text = DateTime.Now.ToLongTimeString()
End Sub
```

Remarkably, that's all you need to do to complete this example. Now, when you click the Refresh Time button, the label will refresh without a full postback and without any flicker.

So how does it all work? Here's a blow-by-blow analysis of what's taking place:

1. When rendering the HTML, the UpdatePanel looks at its contents. It notices that it contains one control that's able to trigger a postback—the button. It adds some JavaScript code that will intercept the button's click event on the client and use a JavaScript routine to handle it.

2. When you click the Refresh Time button, you trigger the JavaScript routine.

3. The JavaScript routine doesn't perform a full-page postback. Instead, it sends a background request to the web server. This request is asynchronous, which means your page remains responsive while the request is under way.

■ **Note** Because the UpdatePanel uses asynchronous requests, it's possible to click the Refresh Time button several times before the result is returned and the time is updated. In this case, the response from the first few requests is ignored, and the response from the last request is used. (It's similar to what happens if you refresh a posted-back page several times before it's finished being processed on the server.)

---

4. The background request is processed in *exactly* the same way as a normal postback. All the data from all the web controls is sent back to the web server, along with the view state information and any cookies. On the web server, the page life cycle is the same—first the Page.Load event fires, followed by the event that triggered the postback (in this case, Button.Click). If you're using data source controls like SqlDataSource, all the normal querying and data binding takes place. The final page is then rendered to HTML and sent back to the page.

5. When the browser receives the rendered HTML for the page, it updates the current view state and grabs any cookies that were returned.

6. The JavaScript routine then replaces a portion of the HTML on the page—just the portion that you wrapped in the UpdatePanel. The rest of the HTML for the page is simply discarded. In the current example, that means the HTML with the animated GIF is tossed out. (This really has no effect, because this part of the HTML is exactly the same in the new response as it was originally. However, it's important to understand that if you modify this part of your page on the web server, you won't see the results of your change in the web browser, because that area of the page isn't being updated.)

The most impressive aspect of the UpdatePanel control is that it allows your web page to behave in the same way it would if you weren't using any Ajax techniques. There is a bit of a price to pay for this convenience—namely, the request might take a little longer than necessary because of all the extra work that's taking place. In a more streamlined do-it-yourself approach, you'd simply ask the web server for exactly what you need. In this example, that means you'd simply ask for the current time, rather than an entire HTML document.

However, in most scenarios the UpdatePanel's more long-winded approach doesn't introduce any noticeable delay. Even better, it gives you the ability to deal with much more complex scenarios—for example, when you're modifying a section of a web page much more dramatically. You'll see an example later in this chapter, when you use the UpdatePanel to improve the greeting card maker.

■ **Note** When you use the UpdatePanel, you don't reduce the amount of bandwidth being used or the time taken to receive the response from the server, because the entire page is still sent. The only difference is that the page is updated without a distracting flicker. Small as that advantage seems, it can make a major difference in how your web page "feels" to the person using it.

Handling Errors

As you've seen, when the UpdatePanel performs its callback, the web page code runs in exactly the same way as if the page had been posted back. The only difference is the means of communication (the page uses an asynchronous call to get the new data) and the way the received data is dealt with (the UpdatePanel refreshes its inner content, but the remainder of the page is not changed). For that reason, you don't need to make significant changes to your server-side code or deal with new error conditions.

That said, problems can occur when performing an asynchronous postback just as they do when performing a synchronous postback. To find out what happens, you can add code like this to the event handler for the Page.Load event, which causes an unhandled exception to occur when an asynchronous callback takes place:

```
If Me.IsPostBack Then
    Throw New ApplicationException("This operation failed.")
End If
```

When the web page throws an unhandled exception, the error is caught by the ScriptManager and passed back to the client. The client-side JavaScript then throws a JavaScript error. What happens next depends on your browser settings, but usually browsers are configured to quietly suppress JavaScript errors. In Internet Explorer, an “Error on page” message appears in the status bar that indicates the problem. If you double-click this notification, a dialog box appears with the full details, as shown in Figure 25-3.

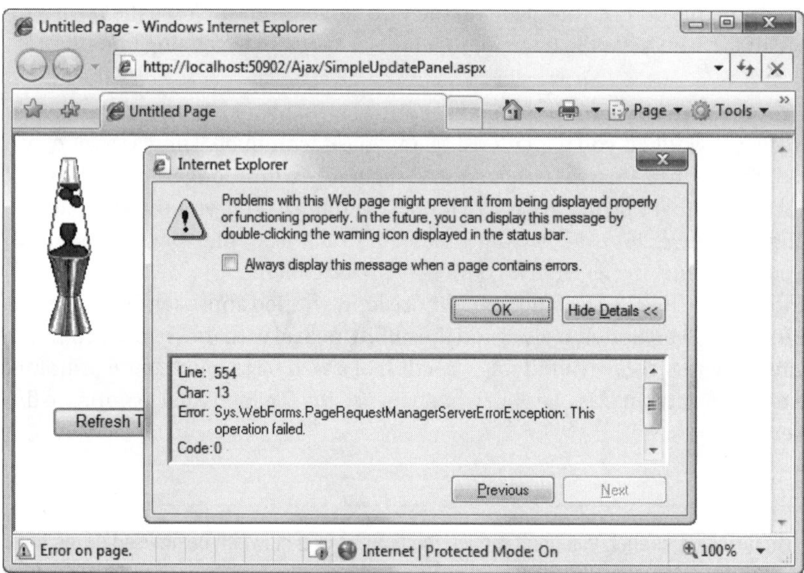

Figure 25-3. *Displaying a client-side message about a server-side error*

There’s another option for dealing with the errors that occur during an asynchronous postback. You can use custom error pages, just as you do with ordinary web pages. All you need to do is add the <customErrors> element to the web.config file, as you did in Chapter 8.

For example, here’s a <customErrors> element that redirects all errors to the page named ErrorPage.aspx:

```
<customErrors defaultRedirect="ErrorPage.aspx" mode="On"></customErrors>
```

Now, when the PageRequestManager is informed of an error it will redirect the browser to ErrorPage.aspx. It also adds an aspxerrorpath query string argument to the URL that indicates the URL of the page where the problem originated, as shown here:

```
http://localhost/Ajax/ErrorPage.aspx?aspxerrorpath=/Ajax/UpdatePanels.aspx
```

You can write code in ErrorPage.aspx that reads the aspxerrorpath information. For example, you might include a button that redirects the user to the original requested page, like this:

```
Dim url As String = Request.QueryString("aspxerrorpath")
If url <> "" Then Response.Redirect(url)
```

If your website uses custom error pages but you don't want them to apply to asynchronous postbacks, you must set the ScriptManager.AllowCustomErrorsRedirect property to false.

■ **Note** ASP.NET 3.5 includes two controls that can't be used in an UpdatePanel: the FileInput control and HtmlInputFile the control. However, these controls *can* be used on a page that contains an UpdatePanel, so long as they aren't actually in the UpdatePanel.

Conditional Updates

In complex pages, you might have more than one UpdatePanel. In this case, when one UpdatePanel triggers an update, all the UpdatePanel regions will be refreshed.

If you have more than one UpdatePanel and each one is completely self-contained, this isn't necessary. In this situation, you can configure the panels to update themselves independently. Simply change the UpdatePanel.UpdateMode property from Always to Conditional. Now, the UpdatePanel will refresh itself only if an event occurs in one of the controls in that UpdatePanel.

To try this out, create a page that has several UpdatePanel controls, each with its own time display and button. Then, add code that places the current time in the label of all three controls:

```
Protected Sub Page_Load(ByVal sender As Object, ByVal e As EventArgs) _
  Handles Me.Load
    lblTime1.Text = DateTime.Now.ToLongTimeString()
    lblTime2.Text = DateTime.Now.ToLongTimeString()
    lblTime3.Text = DateTime.Now.ToLongTimeString()
End Sub
```

Now, when you click one of the Refresh Time buttons, only the label in that panel will be updated. The other panels will remain untouched.

■ **Note** There's an interesting quirk here. Technically, when you click the button all the labels are updated, but only part of the page is refreshed to show that fact. The next time the page is posted back, the most recent values are pulled out of view state and applied to all the labels, including the ones that weren't refreshed on the client.

Most of the time, this distinction isn't important. But if this isn't the behavior you want in this example, you could use a separate event handler for each button. Each event handler would update just one label—the label that's in the appropriate UpdatePanel. That way, when the page is posted back just one label is changed, and you don't waste time changing parts of the page that won't be updated in the browser.

There's one caveat with this approach. If you perform an update that takes a long time, it could be interrupted by another update. As you know, ASP.NET AJAX posts the page back asynchronously, so the user is free to click other buttons while the postback is under way. ASP.NET AJAX doesn't allow concurrent updates, because it needs to ensure that other information—such as the page view state information, the session cookie, and so on—remains consistent. Instead, when a new asynchronous postback is started, the previous asynchronous postback is abandoned. For the most part, this is the behavior you want. If you want to prevent the user from interrupting an asynchronous postback, you can add JavaScript code that disables controls while the asynchronous postback is under way, but this takes significantly more work. Another option is to use the UpdateProgress control discussed later in this chapter.

■ **Tip** There's one other way to update a conditional UpdatePanel—you can call the UpdatePanel.Update() method from your server-side code. This allows you to decide on the fly whether a certain panel should be refreshed. However, you must be careful not to call Update() on a panel that uses an UpdateMode of Always, and you must not call Update() after the page has been rendered. If you make either of these mistakes, you'll cause an exception.

Triggers

So far, the examples you've seen have used the built-in behavior of the UpdatePanel. In the next example, you'll use the UpdatePanel in a slightly more sophisticated page, and you'll learn to control its refreshes with triggers.

Earlier in this book, you learned how to build a web page that allows the user to dynamically build a greeting card. This page lets the user specify several details—such as text, font, colors, border options, and so on—and then updates a portion of the page to show the greeting card.

Chapter 6 demonstrated two versions of the greeting card maker. The first version allowed the user to specify a number of options at once, and then click a button to update the greeting card. The second version used automatic postback events, so that the greeting card was updated after every change. This second approach gave a more immediate result, but the cost was a less responsive user interface with distracting flicker. If this version of the greeting card maker was running on a slow web server (or over a slow network), the problems get even worse. That's because after every postback the user is forced to wait for the page update before making another change.

The UpdatePanel gives you the ability to get the best of both versions. You can create a greeting card page that updates its display automatically but feels more responsive and doesn't lock the user out.

The simplest approach is to add a ScriptManager and wrap the entire web page—including the controls and the greeting card—in one giant UpdatePanel. Here's the markup you'd use:

```
<asp:ScriptManager ID="ScriptManager1" runat="server"></asp:ScriptManager>

<asp:UpdatePanel ID="UpdatePanel1" runat="server">
  <ContentTemplate>

    <!-- These are the controls for creating the greeting card. -->
    <div style="...">
      Choose a background color:<br />
      <asp:DropDownList id="lstBackColor" runat="server"
       Width="194px" AutoPostBack="True">
      </asp:DropDownList>
      <br /><br />
      Choose a foreground (text) color:<br />
      <asp:DropDownList id="lstForeColor" runat="server"
       Height="22px" Width="194px" AutoPostBack="True" >
      </asp:DropDownList>
      <br /><br />
      Choose a font name:<br />
      <asp:DropDownList id="lstFontName" runat="server"
       Height="22px" Width="194px" AutoPostBack="True">
      </asp:DropDownList>
      <br /><br />
      Specify a font size:<br />
      <asp:TextBox id="txtFontSize" runat="server"
       AutoPostBack="True">
      </asp:TextBox>
      <br /><br />
      Choose a border style:<br />
      <asp:RadioButtonList id="lstBorder" runat="server"
       Height="59px" Width="177px" Font-Size="X-Small"
       AutoPostBack="True" RepeatColumns="2">
      </asp:RadioButtonList>
      <br /><br />
      <asp:CheckBox id="chkPicture" runat="server"
       Text="Add the Default Picture" AutoPostBack="True">
      </asp:CheckBox>
      <br /><br />
      Enter the greeting text below:<br />
      <asp:TextBox id="txtGreeting" runat="server"
       Height="85px" Width="240px" TextMode="MultiLine"
       AutoPostBack="True">
      </asp:TextBox>
    </div>
```

```
    <!-- This is the panel that shows the greeting card. -->
    <asp:Panel ID="pnlCard" runat="server" ... >
      <asp:Label id="lblGreeting" runat="server" Width="272px"
        Height="150px"></asp:Label>
      <br />
      <asp:Image id="imgDefault" runat="server" Width="212px" Height="160px"
        Visible="False"></asp:Image>
    </asp:Panel>

  </ContentTemplate>
</asp:UpdatePanel>
```

The greeting card is then generated when the Page.Load event fires:

```
Protected Sub Page_Load(ByVal sender As Object, ByVal e As EventArgs) _
  Handles Me.Load

    If Not Me.IsPostBack Then
        ' (Initialize all the controls here.)
    Else
        ' Refresh the greeting card.
        UpdateCard()
    End If
End Sub
```

The UpdatePanel watches its child controls and intercepts any events that could trigger a postback. The Button.Click is an obvious example, but in this example the TextBox.TextChanged and ListBox.SelectedItemChanged events also trigger a postback, because these controls set the AutoPostBack property to True. Thus, these events are also intercepted by the UpdatePanel. If these controls didn't use the AutoPostBack property, they wouldn't trigger a postback, the UpdatePanel wouldn't get involved, and the greeting card won't be updated until another control causes a postback.

This solution achieves the desired result. Although the greeting card page looks essentially the same (see Figure 25-4), when you interact with the controls on the left, the card on the right is updated without a postback. If you make several changes in quick succession, you'll trigger several postbacks, and the result from the last postback (with the completely updated card) will be used.

Although this example works perfectly well, it's doing more work than necessary. Because the entire page is wrapped in the UpdatePanel, the HTML for the entire page is refreshed. A better option is to wrap just the label and image that represents the greeting card in the UpdatePanel. Unfortunately, this won't work. Once you move the other controls out of the UpdatePanel, their events won't be intercepted any longer, and they'll trigger full-page postbacks with the familiar flicker.

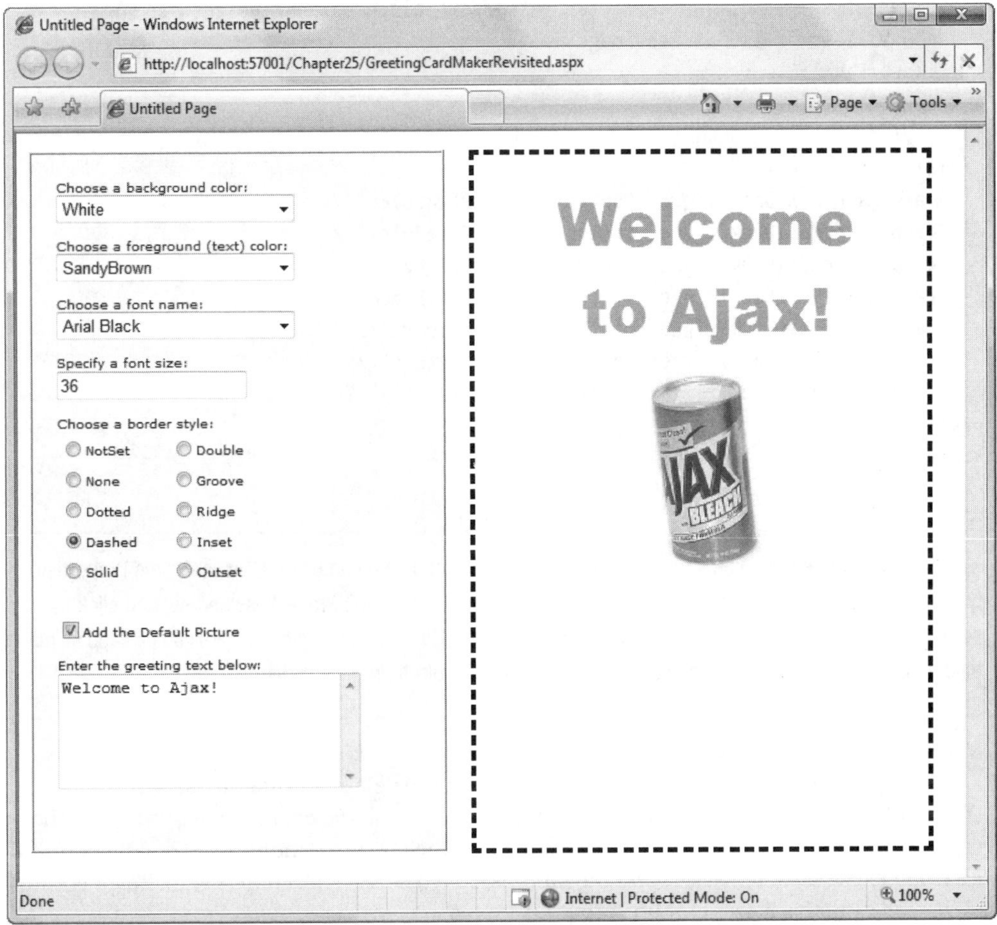

Figure 25-4. *The greeting card maker, Ajax style*

The solution is to explicitly tell the UpdatePanel to monitor those controls, even though they aren't inside the UpdatePanel. You can do this by adding triggers to the UpdatePanel. You add one trigger for each button.

Here's the markup you need:

```
<asp:ScriptManager ID="ScriptManager1" runat="server"></asp:ScriptManager>

<!-- The controls for creating the greeting card go here. -->

<asp:UpdatePanel ID="UpdatePanel1" runat="server">
  <ContentTemplate>
    <!-- This is the panel that shows the greeting card. -->
    <asp:Panel ID="pnlCard" runat="server" ... >
      <asp:Label id="lblGreeting" runat="server" Width="272px"
        Height="150px"></asp:Label>
```

```
      <asp:Image id="imgDefault" runat="server" Width="212px" Height="160px"
        Visible="False"></asp:Image>
    </asp:Panel>
  </ContentTemplate>

  <Triggers>
    <asp:AsyncPostBackTrigger ControlID="lstBackColor" />
    <asp:AsyncPostBackTrigger ControlID="lstForeColor" />
    <asp:AsyncPostBackTrigger ControlID="lstFontName" />
    <asp:AsyncPostBackTrigger ControlID="txtFontSize" />
    <asp:AsyncPostBackTrigger ControlID="lstBorder" />
    <asp:AsyncPostBackTrigger ControlID="chkPicture" />
    <asp:AsyncPostBackTrigger ControlID="txtGreeting" />
  </Triggers>
</asp:UpdatePanel>
```

■ **Tip** You don't need to type your triggers in by hand. Instead, you can use the Visual Studio Properties window. Just select the UpdatePanel, click the Triggers property in the Properties window, and click the ellipsis (. . .) that appears in the Triggers box. Visual Studio will open a dialog box where you can add as many triggers as you want, and pick the control for each trigger from a drop-down list.

These triggers tell the UpdatePanel to intercept the default event in these seven controls. (You could specify the event you want to monitor by setting the EventName property of the trigger, but you don't need to, because you're using the most commonly used default event for each one.) As a result, the page works the same as it did before—it just refreshes a smaller portion of the page after each asynchronous request.

Technically, the UpdatePanel always uses triggers. All the controls inside an UpdatePanel automatically become the triggers for the UpdatePanel. However, you need to add the triggers if the controls are placed elsewhere in the page.

■ **Note** You can add the same trigger to several different conditional UpdatePanel controls, in which case that event will update them all.

You can use triggers in one other way. Instead of using them to monitor more controls, you can use them to tell the UpdatePanel to ignore certain controls. For example, imagine you have a button in your UpdatePanel. Ordinarily, clicking that button will trigger an asynchronous request and partial update. If you want it to trigger a full-page postback instead, you simply need to add a PostBackTrigger (instead of an AsynchronousPostBackTrigger).

For example, here's an UpdatePanel that contains a nested button that triggers a full post-back rather than an asynchronous postback:

```
<asp:UpdatePanel ID="UpdatePanel1" runat="server" UpdateMode="Conditional">
  <ContentTemplate>
    <asp:Label ID="Label1" runat="server" Font-Bold="True"></asp:Label>
    <br />
    <br />
    <asp:Button ID="cmdPostback" runat="server" Text="Refresh Full Page" />
  </ContentTemplate>
  <Triggers>
    <asp:PostBackTrigger ControlID="cmdPostback" />
  </Triggers>
</asp:UpdatePanel>
```

This technique isn't as common, but it can be useful if you have several controls in an UpdatePanel that perform limited updates (and so use asynchronous request) and one that performs more significant changes to the whole page (and so uses a full-page postback).

Progress Notification

As you've learned, the UpdatePanel performs its work asynchronously in the background. As a result, the user can keep working with the page. This is generally the behavior you want, but there's one catch. While the asynchronous request is under way, the user won't necessarily realize that anything's happening. If the asynchronous request takes some time, this could be a bit of a problem. At worst, the user will assume the page is broken or click the same button multiple times, creating needless extra work for your web application and slowing down the process further.

ASP.NET includes another control that can help—the UpdateProgress control. The UpdateProgress control works in conjunction with the UpdatePanel. Essentially, the UpdateProgress control allows you to show a message while a time-consuming update is under way.

■ **Note** The UpdateProgress control is slightly misnamed. It doesn't actually indicate progress; instead, it provides a wait message that reassures the user that the page is still working and the last request is still being processed.

Showing a Simulated Progress Bar

When you add the UpdateProgress control to a page, you get the ability to specify some content that will appear as soon as an asynchronous request is started and disappear as soon as the request is finished. This content can include a fixed message, but many people prefer to use an animated GIF, because it more clearly suggests that the page is still at work. Often, this animated GIF simulates a progress bar.

Figure 25-5 shows a page that uses the UpdateProgress control at three different points in its life cycle. The top figure shows the page as it first appears, with a straightforward UpdatePanel control containing a button. When the button is clicked, the asynchronous callback process begins. At this point, the contents of the UpdateProgress control appear underneath (as shown in the middle figure). In this example, the UpdateProgress includes a text message and an animated GIF that appears as a progress bar, with green blocks that perpetually fill it from left to right, and then start over. When the callback is complete, the UpdateProgress disappears and the UpdatePanel is updated, as shown in the bottom figure.

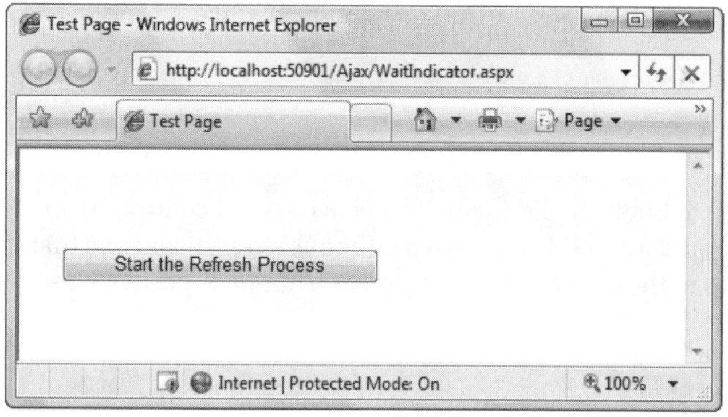

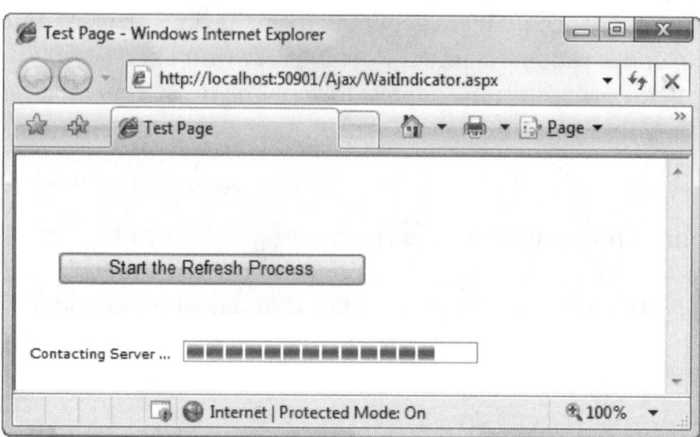

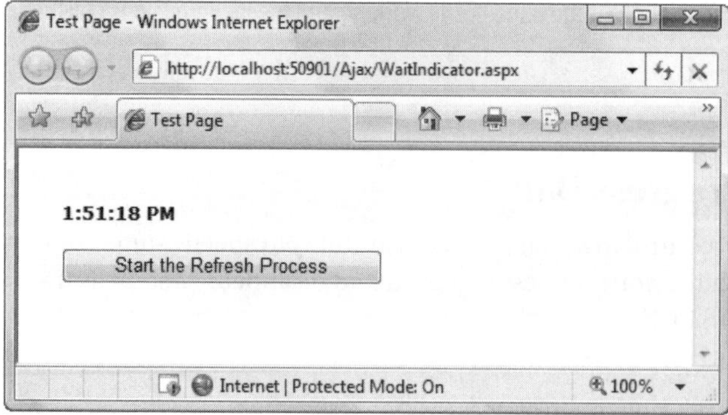

Figure 25-5. *A wait indicator*

The markup for this page defines an UpdatePanel followed by an UpdateProgress:

```
<asp:UpdatePanel ID="UpdatePanel1" runat="server">
  <ContentTemplate>
    <div style="background-color:#FFFFE0;padding: 20px">
      <asp:Label ID="lblTime" runat="server" Font-Bold="True"></asp:Label>
      <br /><br />
      <asp:Button ID="cmdRefreshTime" runat="server"
       Text="Start the Refresh Process" />
    </div>
  </ContentTemplate>
</asp:UpdatePanel>
<br />

<asp:UpdateProgress runat="server" id="updateProgress1">
  <ProgressTemplate>
    <div style="font-size: xx-small">
      Contacting Server ... <img src="wait.gif" />
    </div>
  </ProgressTemplate>
</asp:UpdateProgress>
```

This isn't the only possible arrangement. Depending on the layout you want, you can place your UpdateProgress control somewhere inside your UpdatePanel control.

The code for this page has a slight modification from the earlier examples. Because the UpdateProgress control only shows its content while the asynchronous callback is under way, it only makes sense to use it with an operation that takes time. Otherwise, the UpdateProgress will only show its ProgressTemplate for a few fractions of a second. To simulate a slow process, you can add a line to delay your code 10 seconds, as shown here:

```
Protected Sub cmdRefreshTime_Click(ByVal sender As Object, _
  ByVal e As EventArgs) Handles cmdRefreshTime.Click
    System.Threading.Thread.Sleep(TimeSpan.FromSeconds(10))
    lblTime.Text = DateTime.Now.ToLongTimeString()
End Sub
```

There's no need to explicitly link the UpdateProgress control to your UpdatePanel control. The UpdateProgress automatically shows its ProgressTemplate whenever *any* UpdatePanel begins a callback. However, if you have a complex page with more than one UpdatePanel, you can choose to limit your UpdateProgress to pay attention to just one of them. To do so, simply set the UpdateProgress.AssociatedUpdatePanelID property with the ID of the appropriate UpdatePanel. You can even add multiple UpdateProgress controls to the same page, and link each one to a different UpdatePanel.

Cancellation

The UpdateProgress control supports one other detail: a cancel button. When the user clicks a cancel button, the asynchronous callback will be cancelled immediately, the UpdateProgress content will disappear, and the page will revert to its original state.

Adding a cancel button is a two-step process. First you need to add a fairly intimidating block of JavaScript code, which you can copy verbatim. You should place this code at the end of your page, after all your content but just before the </body> end tag. Here's the code you need, in its rightful place:

```
<%@ Page Language="VB" AutoEventWireup="false" CodeFile="WaitIndicator.aspx.vb"
 Inherits="WaitIndicator" %>
<html xmlns="http://www.w3.org/1999/xhtml">
<head runat="server">
    ...
</head>
<body>
  <form id="form1" runat="server">
    ...
  </form>

  <script type="text/javascript">
    var prm = Sys.WebForms.PageRequestManager.getInstance();
    prm.add_initializeRequest(InitializeRequest);

    function InitializeRequest(sender, args)
    {
        if (prm.get_isInAsyncPostBack())
        {
            args.set_cancel(true);
        }
    }

    function AbortPostBack()
    {
        if (prm.get_isInAsyncPostBack()) {
         prm.abortPostBack();
        }
    }
    </script>
</body>
</html>
```

■ **Tip** You can cut and paste this code from the WaitIndicator.aspx page (which is included with the samples for this chapter) into your own pages.

Once you've added this code, you can use JavaScript code to call its AbortPostBack() function at any time and cancel the callback. The easiest way to do to this is to connect a JavaScript event to the AbortPostBack() function using a JavaScript event attribute. You can add a JavaScript event attribute to virtually any HTML element. For example, you can deal with client-side clicks using the onclick attribute. Here's a basic HTML button (not a server control) that uses this technique to connect itself to the AbortPostBack() function:

```
<input id="cmdCancel" onclick="AbortPostBack()" type="button" value="Cancel" />
```

If you click this Cancel button, the client-side AbortPostBack() function will be triggered and the callback will be cancelled immediately. Typically, you'll place this button (or an element like this) in the ProgressTemplate of the UpdateProgress control, as shown in Figure 25-6.

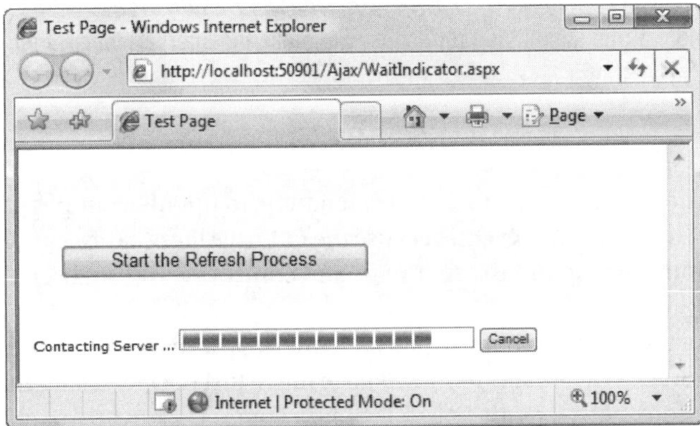

Figure 25-6. *An UpdateProgress control with a cancel button*

Don't confuse this approach with server-side event handling—the client-side onclick attribute allows you to intercept an event in the browser and process it using JavaScript code. The server doesn't get involved at all. In fact, when you cancel an operation, the server continues to process the request, but the browser simply closes the connection and stops listening for the response.

■ **Tip** It makes sense to use an abort button for tasks that can be safely canceled because they don't change external state. For example, users should be able to cancel an operation that retrieves information from a database. However, it's not a good idea to add cancellation to an operation that updates a database, because the server will continue until it finishes the update, even if the client has stopped listening for the response.

Timed Refreshes

Using the two controls you've seen so far—the UpdatePanel and UpdateProgress controls—you can create self-contained regions on your page that refresh themselves when certain actions take place. Of course, in order for this technique to work, the user needs to initiate an action that would ordinarily cause a postback, such as clicking a button, selecting an item in an AutoPostBack list, checking an AutoBostBack check box, and so on.

In some situations, you might want to force a full or partial page refresh without waiting for a user action. For example, you might create a page that includes a stock ticker, and you might want to refresh this ticker periodically (say, every 5 minutes) to ensure it doesn't become drastically outdated. ASP.NET includes a Timer control that allows you to implement this design easily.

The Timer control is refreshingly straightforward. You simply add it to a page and set its Interval property to the maximum number of milliseconds that should elapse before an update. For example, if you set Interval to 60000, the timer will force a postback after one minute elapses.

```
<asp:Timer ID="Timer1" runat="server" Interval="60000" />
```

■ **Note** Obviously, the timer has the potential to greatly increase the overhead of your web application and reduce its scalability. Think carefully before introducing timed refreshes, and make the intervals long rather than short.

The timer also raises a server-side Tick event, which you can handle to update your page. However, you don't necessarily need to use the Tick event, because the full-page life cycle executes when the timer fires. This means you can respond to other page and control events, such as Page.Load.

The timer is particularly well suited to pages that use partial rendering, as discussed in the previous section. That's because a refresh in a partially rendered page might just need to change a single portion of the page. Furthermore, partial rendering makes sure your refreshes are much less intrusive. Unlike a full postback, a callback with partial rendering won't cause flicker and won't interrupt the user in the middle of a task.

To use the timer with partial rendering, wrap the updateable portions of the page in UpdatePanel controls with the UpdateMode property set to Conditional. Then, add a trigger that forces the UpdatePanel to update itself whenever the Timer.Tick event occurs. Here's the markup you need:

```
<asp:UpdatePanel ID="UpdatePanel1" runat="server" UpdateMode="Conditional">
  <ContentTemplate>
    ...
  </ContentTemplate>
  <Triggers>
    <asp:AsyncPostBackTrigger ControlID="Timer1" EventName="Tick" />
  </Triggers>
</asp:UpdatePanel>
```

All the other portions of the page can be left as is, or you can wrap them in conditional UpdatePanel controls with different triggers if you need to update them in response to other actions.

■ **Note** You must use triggers with the Timer control. You can't simply place the timer inside an UpdatePanel and expect it to work without a trigger (unlike other controls). If you don't use a trigger, the timer will force a full postback, with flicker.

To stop the timer, you simply need to set the Enabled property to False in server-side code. For example, here's how you could disable the timer after ten updates:

```
Protected Sub Timer1_Tick(ByVal sender As Object, ByVal e As EventArgs) _
  Handles Timer1.Tick

    ' Update the tick count and store it in view state.
    Dim tickCount As Integer = 0
    If ViewState("TickCount") IsNot Nothing Then
        tickCount = CType(ViewState("TickCount"), Integer)
    End If

    tickCount += 1
    ViewState("TickCount") = tickCount

    ' Decide whether to disable the timer.
    If tickCount > 10 Then
        Timer1.Enabled = False
    End If
End Sub
```

The ASP.NET AJAX Control Toolkit

The UpdatePanel, UpdateProgress, and Timer controls are fairly useful. However, they're the only ASP.NET AJAX-enabled controls you'll find in ASP.NET. Despite their value, developers who have heard the Ajax hype and used advanced Ajax websites like Gmail might expect a bit more.

In fact, ASP.NET's support for Ajax is a bit deceptive. Although there are only three controls that use ASP.NET AJAX features, ASP.NET actually includes a sophisticated library of JavaScript functions that can be used to create all sorts of advanced effects. Business application developers aren't likely to use these libraries (because they're quite complex and require a significant time investment), but third-party component developers will use them enthusiastically.

The first and best example of what ASP.NET AJAX can really do is the ASP.NET AJAX Control Toolkit. The ASP.NET AJAX Control Toolkit is a joint project between Microsoft and the ASP.NET community. It consists of dozens of controls that use the ASP.NET AJAX libraries to create sophisticated effects.

The ASP.NET AJAX Control Toolkit has a lot going for it:

- It's completely free.
- It includes full source code, which is helpful if you're ambitious enough to want to create your own custom controls that use ASP.NET AJAX features.
- It uses extenders that enhance the standard ASP.NET web controls. That way, you don't have to replace all the controls on your web pages—instead, you simply plug in the new bits of functionality that you need.

These advantages have generated a great deal of excitement around the ASP.NET AJAX Control Toolkit. It's currently being used in cutting-edge web development with ASP.NET 2.0 and ASP.NET 3.5.

Installing the ASP.NET AJAX Control Toolkit

To get the ASP.NET AJAX Control Toolkit, surf to `http://ajax.asp.net/ajaxtoolkit` and follow the links. Eventually, you'll find your way to a download page. (At the time of this writing, the download page is `http://www.codeplex.com/AtlasControlToolkit/Release/ProjectReleases.aspx`.)

On the download page, you'll see several download options, depending on the version of .NET that you're using and whether you want the source code. As of this writing, the simplest download option is a 2 MB ZIP file named AjaxControlToolkit-Framework3.5-NoSource.zip, which is designed for .NET 3.5 and doesn't include the source code. Once you've downloaded this ZIP file, you can extract the files it contains to a more permanent location on your hard drive.

Inside the ZIP file, you'll find a folder named SampleWebSite, which contains a huge sample website that demonstrates all the ASP.NET AJAX Control Toolkit ingredients. Inside the SampleWebSite\Bin subfolder are the key support files you need to use ASP.NET AJAX, including a central assembly named AjaxControlToolkit.dll and a host of smaller satellite assemblies that support localization for different cultures.

To get started developing with ASP.NET AJAX Control Toolkit, you could simply copy the contents of the SampleWebSite\Bin folder to the Bin folder of your own web application. However, life is much easier if you get Visual Studio to help you out by adding the new components to the Toolbox. Here's how:

1. Make sure the SampleWebSite folder is in a reasonably permanent location on your hard drive. If you move the SampleWebSite folder after you complete this process, Visual Studio won't be able to find the AjaxControlToolkit.dll assembly. As a result, it won't be able to add the necessary assembly reference when you drag the controls onto a web page. (The only way to fix this problem is to remove the controls from the Toolbox and then repeat the process to add them from their new location.)

2. First, you need to create a new Toolbox tab for the controls. Right-click the Toolbox and choose Add Tab. Then, enter a name (like AJAX Toolkit) and hit Enter.

3. Now, you need to add the controls to the new tab. Right-click the blank tab you've created and select Choose Items.

4. In the Choose Toolbox Items dialog box, click Browse. Find the AjaxControlToolkit.dll (which is in the SampleWebSite\Bin folder) and click OK.

5. Now, all the components from AjaxControlToolkit.dll will appear in the list, selected and with check marks next to each one. To add all the controls to the Toolbox in one step, just click OK.

Figure 25-7 shows some of the controls that will appear in the new Toolbox tab.

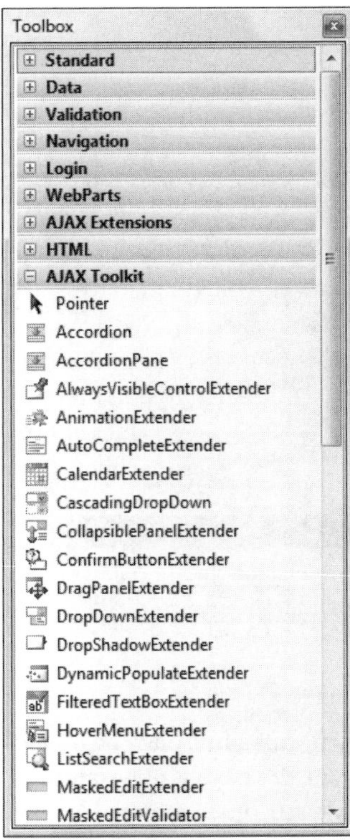

Figure 25-7. *Adding the ASP.NET AJAX Control Toolkit to the Toolbox*

Now you can use the components from the ASP.NET AJAX Control Toolkit in any web page in any website. First, begin by adding the ScriptManager control to the web page. Then, head to the new Toolbox tab you created and drag the ASP.NET AJAX control you want onto your page. The first time you do add a component from the ASP.NET AJAX Control Toolkit, Visual Studio will copy the AjaxControlToolkit.dll assembly to the Bin folder of your web application, along with the localization assemblies.

The ASP.NET AJAX Control Toolkit is stuffed full of useful components. In the following sections, you'll get your feet wet by considering just two of the controls you'll find—the Accordion and the AutoCompleteExtender.

The Accordion

The Accordion is a container that stacks several panels on top of one another, and allows you to view one at a time. Each panel has a header (which usually displays a section title) and some content. When you click the header of one of the panels, that panel is expanded and the other panels are collapsed, leaving just their headers visible. Figure 25-8 demonstrates the effect you'll see as you click different headers.

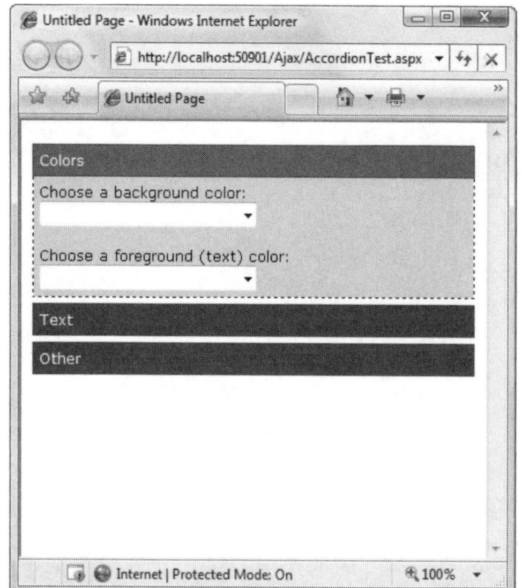

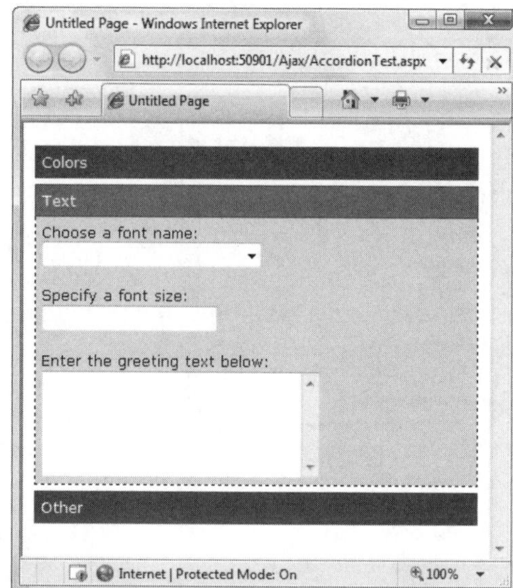

Figure 25-8. *Choosing a panel in the Accordion*

It goes without saying that the collapsing behavior happens without a full-page postback. In fact, there's no need to contact the web server at all. The first time the page is generated, all the panels are rendered to HTML, but they're hidden using CSS style attributes. When you click a header, a JavaScript routine runs and changes these style attributes. (In truth, the Accordion control is a bit more sophisticated than that.) When you choose a new panel, it gradually *expands* into view, which is much more impressive than simply popping into existence in one step. Furthermore, you can set the FadeTransitions property to True if you want panels to fade into and out of sight when you change from one panel to another.

Using the Accordion control is a bit like using the MultiView control you learned about in Chapter 11. The Accordion control contains a collection of AccordionPane controls. Each AccordionPane represents a separate panel in the Accordion.

Here's an example that illustrates this structure by putting two AccordionPane objects inside the Accordion:

```
<ajaxToolkit:Accordion ID="Accordion1" runat="server">
  <Panes>
    <ajaxToolkit:AccordionPane runat="server">
      ...
    </ajaxToolkit:AccordionPane>

    <ajaxToolkit:AccordionPane runat="server">
      ...
    </ajaxToolkit:AccordionPane>
  </Panes>
</ajaxToolkit:Accordion>
```

Tip To determine what AccordionPane is currently visible (or to set it), you use the Accordion.SelectedIndex property. If RequiredOpenedPane is True, there will always be at least one expanded panel. If it's False, you can collapse all the panels—just click the header of the currently expanded section (or set the SelectedIndex property to -1 in your code).

Each AccordionPane consists of two sections. The Header section is used for the clickable header of the panel, while the Content holds the details inside. Here's the markup you need to create the example shown in Figure 25-6:

```
<ajaxToolkit:Accordion ID="Accordion1" runat="server"
  HeaderCssClass="accordionHeader"
  HeaderSelectedCssClass="accordionHeaderSelected"
  ContentCssClass="accordionContent">

  <Panes>
    <ajaxToolkit:AccordionPane runat="server">
      <Header>Colors</Header>
      <Content>
        Choose a background color:<br />
        <asp:DropDownList id="lstBackColor" runat="server"
         Width="194px" AutoPostBack="True">
        </asp:DropDownList>
        <br /><br />
        Choose a foreground (text) color:<br />
        <asp:DropDownList id="lstForeColor" runat="server"
         Height="22px" Width="194px" AutoPostBack="True" >
        </asp:DropDownList>
      </Content>
    </ajaxToolkit:AccordionPane>

    <ajaxToolkit:AccordionPane runat="server">
      <Header>Text</Header>
      <Content>
        Choose a font name:<br />
        <asp:DropDownList id="lstFontName" runat="server"
         Height="22px" Width="194px" AutoPostBack="True">
        </asp:DropDownList>
        <br /><br />
        Specify a font size:<br />
        <asp:TextBox id="txtFontSize" runat="server"
         AutoPostBack="True">
        </asp:TextBox>
        <br /><br />
        Enter the greeting text below:<br />
        <asp:TextBox id="txtGreeting" runat="server"
```

```
          Height="85px" Width="240px" TextMode="MultiLine"
          AutoPostBack="True">
        </asp:TextBox>
      </Content>
    </ajaxToolkit:AccordionPane>

    <ajaxToolkit:AccordionPane runat="server">
      <Header>Other</Header>
      <Content>
        Choose a border style:<br />
        <asp:RadioButtonList id="lstBorder" runat="server"
          Height="59px" Width="177px" Font-Size="X-Small"
          AutoPostBack="True" RepeatColumns="2">
        </asp:RadioButtonList>
        <br /><br />
        <asp:CheckBox id="chkPicture" runat="server"
          Text="Add the Default Picture" AutoPostBack="True">
        </asp:CheckBox>
        </Content>
    </ajaxToolkit:AccordionPane>
  </Panes>
</ajaxToolkit:Accordion>
```

Along with the content, this example adds three properties: HeaderCssClass, HeaderSelectedCssClass, and ContentCssClass. These properties take the names of CSS styles that the Accordion uses to format the appropriate region. The styles are defined in a separate style sheet, and look like this:

```
.accordionHeader
{
    border: 1px solid #2F4F4F;
    color: white;
    background-color: #2E4d7B;
    padding: 5px;
    margin-top: 5px;
    cursor: pointer;
}

.accordionHeaderSelected
{
    border: 1px solid #2F4F4F;
    color: white;
    background-color: #5078B3;
    padding: 5px;
    margin-top: 5px;
    cursor: pointer;
}
```

```
.accordionContent
{
    background-color: #D3DEEF;
    border: 1px dashed;
    border-top: none;
    padding: 5px;
}
```

Chapter 13 has more about styles. You don't need to use them with the Accordion—after all, you could just set the formatting properties of your controls, or wrap each separate section in a formatted Panel or <div> element—but the style approach is pretty convenient once you get used to it.

You can really fine-tune the display that the Accordion uses by setting a few more properties. TransitionDuration sets the number of milliseconds that the collapsing and expanding animation lasts. FramesPerSecond controls how smooth the transition animation is—a higher value produces better quality, but requires more work from the browser. Finally, AutoSize lets you control how the Accordion expands when you show a panel with a large amount of content. Use a value of None to let the Accordion grow as large as it needs (in which case other content underneath the Accordion is simply bumped out of the way). Use Limit or Fill to restrict the Accordion to whatever you've set in the Height property (the difference is the Limit allows the Accordion to shrink smaller, while Fill keeps it at the maximum height by leaving any unused space blank). With Limit or Fill, the Accordion panels will use scrolling if they can't fit all their content into the available space.

Clearly, the Accordion is a simple-to-use, yet impressive way to deal with dense displays of data and groups of information. If you want to have a similar collapsing and expanding effect with a single panel, you might want to try another one of the components in the ASP.NET AJAX Control Toolkit—the CollapsiblePanelExtender.

The AutoCompleteExtender

The Accordion is an example of a completely new control that has ASP.NET AJAX features baked in. Although this is a perfectly reasonable approach to integrating Ajax techniques with the web control model, it's not the most common solution that you'll see used in ASP.NET AJAX Control Toolkit. In fact, the ASP.NET AJAX Control Toolkit includes just a few new controls, and a much larger set of control extenders.

A *control extender* is a .NET component that adds features to an existing ASP.NET control. Control extenders allow you to use the same Ajax effects with countless different controls. This is useful when you're dealing with multipurpose features such as automatic completion, drag-and-drop, animation, resizing, collapsing, masked editing, and so on.

One of the many control extenders in the ASP.NET AJAX Control Toolkit is the AutoCompleteExtender, which allows you to show a list of suggestions while a user types in another control (such as a text box). Figure 25-9 shows the AutoCompleteExtender at work on an ordinary TextBox control. As the user types, the drop-down list offers suggestions. If the user clicks one of these items in the list, the corresponding text is copied to the text box.

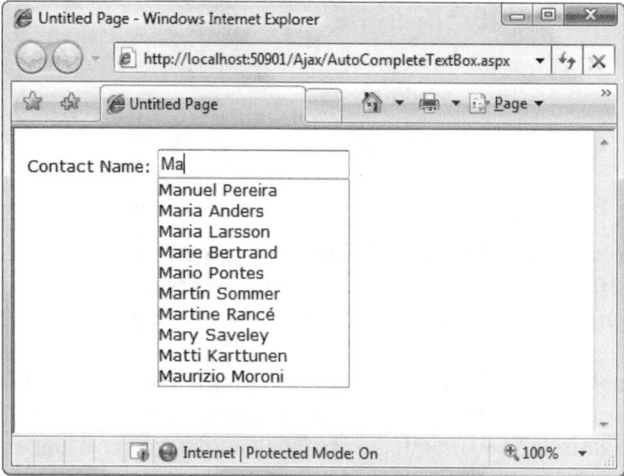

Figure 25-9. *Providing an autocomplete list of names*

To create this example, you need an ordinary text box, like this:

```
Contact Name:<asp:TextBox ID="txtName" runat="server"></asp:TextBox>
```

Next, you need to add the ScriptManager and an AutoCompleteExtender control that extends the text box with the autocomplete feature. The trick is that the list of suggestions needs to be retrieved from a specialized code routine called a web method, which you need to create in your page.

■ **Note** You may have heard about web methods and web services, which are remotely callable code routines that can share data between different organizations, programming platforms, and operating systems. The web method you'll use with ASP.NET AJAX isn't quite as ambitious. Although it uses some of the same plumbing, it has a much simpler goal. It's really just a way for the text box to get a list of word suggestions without going through the whole page life cycle.

Here's an example of how you might define the AutoCompleteExtender. It uses the TargetControlID property to bind itself to the txtName text box, and it sets the MinimumPrefixLength property to 2, which means autocomplete suggestions won't be provided until the user has entered at least two characters of text. Finally, the ServiceMethod property indicates the web method you're going to use is named GetNames(). Before you can run this page, you need to create that method.

```
<ajaxToolkit:AutoCompleteExtender ID="autoComplete1" runat="server"
  TargetControlID="txtName" ServiceMethod="GetNames" MinimumPrefixLength="2">
</ajaxToolkit:AutoCompleteExtender>
```

The next step is to create the GetNames() web method. Here's the basic method you need to add to the code-behind class of your web page:

```
<System.Web.Services.WebMethod> _
<System.Web.Script.Services.ScriptMethod> _
Public Shared Function GetNames(ByVal prefixText As String, _
  ByVal count As Integer) As List(Of String)
    ...
End Function
```

The web method accepts two parameters, which indicate the text the user has typed so far and the desired number of matches (which is ten by default). It returns the list of suggestions. The two attributes that precede the GetNames() method indicate that it's a web method (meaning the client should be allowed to call it directly with HTTP requests) and that it supports JavaScript calls (which is what the AutoCompleteExtender uses).

Actually writing the code that retrieves or generates the suggestion list can be quite tedious. In this example, the code retrieves the list of name suggestions from the Northwind database. To ensure that this step is performed just once (rather than every single time the user hits a key in the text box), the name list is cached using the techniques you learned about in Chapter 24:

```
Dim names As List(Of String)

' Check if the list is in the cache.
If HttpContext.Current.Cache("NameList") Is Nothing Then
    ' If not, regenerate the list. The ADO.NET code for this part
    ' isn't shown (but you can see it in the downloadable examples
    ' for this chapter.
    names = GetNameListFromDB()

    ' Store the name list in the cache for sixty minutes.
    HttpContext.Current.Cache.Insert("NameList", names, Nothing, _
      DateTime.Now.AddMinutes(60), TimeSpan.Zero)
Else
    ' Get the name list out of the cache.
    names = CType(HttpContext.Current.Cache("NameList"), List(Of String))
End If
...
```

With the list in hand, the next step is to cut down the list so it provides only the ten closest suggestions. In this example, the list is already sorted. This means you simply need to find the starting position—the first match that starts with the same letters as the prefix text. Here's the code that finds the first match:

```
...
Dim index As Integer = -1
For i As Integer = 0 To names.Count - 1
    ' Check if this is a suitable match.
    If names(i).StartsWith(prefixText) Then
        index = i
        Exit For
    End If
Next
```

```
' Give up if there isn't a match.
If index = -1 Then Return New List(Of String)()
...
```

The search code then begins at the index number position and moves through the list in an attempt to get ten matches. However, if it reaches the end of the list or finds a value that doesn't match the prefix, the search stops.

```
...
Dim wordList As New List(Of String)()
For i As Integer = index To (index + count - 1)
    ' Stop if the end of the list is reached.
    If i >= names.Count Then Exit For

    ' Stop if the names stop matching.
    If Not names(i).StartsWith(prefixText) Then Exit For

    wordList.Add(names(i))
Next
...
```

Finally, all the matches that were found are returned:

```
...
Return wordList
```

You now have all the code you need to create the effect shown in Figure 25-9.

Getting More Controls

The Accordion and AutoCompleteExtender only scratch the surface of the ASP.NET AJAX ControlToolkit, which currently includes over 30 components. The easiest way to start experimenting with other controls is to surf to `http://ajax.asp.net/ajaxtoolkit`, where you'll find a reference that describes each control and lets you try it out online. Table 25-1 highlights a few of the more interesting ingredients you'll find.

Table 25-1. *Components in the ASP.NET AJAX Control Toolkit*

Name	Description
AlwaysVisibleControlExtender	This extender keeps a control fixed in a specific position (such as the top-left corner of the web page) even as you scroll through the content in a page.
AnimationExtender	This powerful and remarkably flexible extender allows you to add animated effects such as resizing, moving, fading, color changing, and many more, on their own or in combination.
CalendarExtender	This extender shows a pop-up calendar that can be attached to a text box for easier entry of dates. When the user chooses a date, it's inserted in the linked control.

Table 25-1. *Components in the ASP.NET AJAX Control Toolkit (Continued)*

Name	Description
DragPanelExtender	This extender allows you to drag a panel around the page.
DynamicPopulateExtender	This simple extender replaces the contents of a control with the result of a web service method call.
FilteredTextBoxExtender	This extender allows you to restrict certain characters from being entered in a text box (such as letters in a text box that contains numeric data). This is meant to supplement validation, not replace it, as malicious users could circumvent the filtering by tampering with the rendered page or disabling JavaScript in the browser.
HoverMenuExtender	This extender allows content to pop up next to a control when the user hovers over it.
ListSearchExtender	This extender allows the user to search for items in a ListBox or DropDownList by typing the first few letters of the item text. The control searches the items and jumps to the first match as the user types.
ModalPopupExtender	This extender allows you to create the illusion of a modal dialog box by darkening the page, disabling controls, and showing a superimposed panel over the top of the page.
MutuallyExclusiveCheckboxExtender	This extender allows you to associate a "key" with multiple CheckBox controls. When the user clicks a check box that's extended in this way, any other check box with the same key will be unchecked automatically.
NumericUpDownExtender	This extender attaches to a text box to provide configurable up and down arrow buttons (at the right side). These buttons increment the numeric or date value in the text box.
PagingBulletedListExtender	This extender attaches to a BulletedList and gives it client-side paging capabilities, so that it can split a long list into smaller sections.
PasswordStrengthExtender	This extender attaches to a text box. As you type, it ranks the cryptographic strength of the text box value (the higher the ranking, the more difficult the password is to crack). It's meant to be used as a guideline for a password-creation box.
PopupControlExtender	This extender provides pop-up content that can be displayed next to any control.
Rating	This control allows users to set a rating by moving the mouse over a series of stars until the desired number of stars are highlighted.
ResizableControlExtender	This extender allows the user to resize a control with a configurable handle that appears in the bottom-right corner.

Table 25-1. *Components in the ASP.NET AJAX Control Toolkit (Continued)*

Name	Description
SlideShowExtender	This extender attaches to an image and causes it to display a sequence of images. The images are supplied using a web service method, and the slide show can loop endlessly or use play, pause, previous, and next buttons that you create.
TabContainer	This control resembles the tabs you'll find in Windows applications. Each tab has a header, and the user can move from one tab to another by clicking the header.
TextBoxWatermark	This extender allows you to automatically change the background color and supply specific text when a TextBox control is empty. For example, your text box might include the text *Enter Value* in light gray writing on a pale blue background. This text disappears while the cursor is positioned in the text box or once you've entered a value.

To use any of these controls or control extenders, you simply need to drop it onto a form, set the appropriate properties, and run your page.

The Last Word

Ajax techniques and the ASP.NET's Ajax integration are evolving rapidly. In future versions of ASP.NET, you'll see a broader set of controls and features that use Ajax. However, the Ajax support that you'll find in ASP.NET AJAX is already surprisingly powerful—and practical. As you saw in this chapter, the UpdatePanel, UpdateProgress, and Timer controls give you a surprisingly painless way to take a traditional postback-heavy web form and give it a more responsive Ajax-powered user interface, often without requiring new code. And if you want to step further into the world of Ajax frills and get collapsible panels, autocompleting text boxes, and a wide range of animated effects, you need to look no further than the ASP.NET AJAX Control Toolkit, which provides a lot more to play with.

To learn more about ASP.NET AJAX, check out the Microsoft ASP.NET AJAX site at `http://asp.net/ajax` and the ASP.NET AJAX Control Toolkit at `http://asp.net/ajaxtoolkit`.

Index

B

Find it faster at http://superindex.apress.com

F

I

K

L

N

O

P

Q

S

U

X

Y

Z